Problems in Health Care Law: Challenges for the 21st Century

Tenth Edition

Edited by

John E. Steiner, Jr., Esq., CHC
Chief Compliance Officer and Privacy Official
Cancer Treatment Centers of America

JONES & BARTLETT
LEARNING

World Headquarters
Jones & Bartlett Learning
5 Wall Street
Burlington, MA 01803
978-443-5000
info@jblearning.com
www.jblearning.com

Jones & Bartlett Learning books and products are available through most bookstores and online booksellers. To contact Jones & Bartlett Learning directly, call 800-832-0034, fax 978-443-8000, or visit our website, www.jblearning.com.

Substantial discounts on bulk quantities of Jones & Bartlett Learning publications are available to corporations, professional associations, and other qualified organizations. For details and specific discount information, contact the special sales department at Jones & Bartlett Learning via the above contact information or send an email to specialsales@jblearning.com.

Production Credits
Publisher: Michael Brown
Editorial Assistant: Chloe Falivene
Production Manager: Tracey McCrea
Senior Marketing Manager: Sophie Fleck Teague
Manufacturing and Inventory Control Supervisor: Amy Bacus
Composition: Lapiz, Inc.
Cover Design: Michael O'Donnell
Cover Image: © Andreas Guskos/ShutterStock, Inc.
Printing and Binding: Edwards Brothers Malloy
Cover Printing: Edwards Brothers Malloy

To order this product, use ISBN: 978-1-4496-8552-2

Library of Congress Cataloging-in-Publication Data
Steiner, John (John E.)
Problems in health care law: challenges for the 21st century / John E. Steiner. — 10th ed.
    p. cm.
  Rev. ed. of: Problems in health care law / Robert D. Miller. 9th ed. c2006.
  Includes bibliographical references and index.
  ISBN 978-1-4496-0462-2 (pbk.)
  1. Hospitals—Law and legislation—United States. 2. Medical care—Law and legislation—United States. I. Miller, Robert D. (Robert Desle), 1947- Problems in health care law. II. Title.
KF3825.M53 2013
344.7303'21—dc23
                    2012020954

6048
Printed in the United States of America
17 16 15 14 13   10 9 8 7 6 5 4 3 2 1

Brief Contents

Table of Contents

CHAPTER 3

CHAPTER 4

APPENDIX 4-1

CHAPTER 5

CHAPTER 6

CHAPTER **7**   **Decision Making Concerning
                  Individuals 209**

Donna Page

CHAPTER 8   Healthcare Information 263

Joan M. Lebow, JD, Joseph L. Ternullo, JD,
MPH, Cavan K. Doyle, JD, LLM, Cheryl A. Miller,
JD, and Kelly L. Gawne, JD

CHAPTER 12 Criminal and Civil Penalties................. 397

Lawrence Vernaglia, Lisa Noller,
Joseph Van Leer, Katie Miller

CHAPTER 13 Reproductive Issues............................. 417

Nicole Huberfeld

CHAPTER 14 Antitrust... 433

John E. Steiner, Jr., Esq.

**CHAPTER 18   Intellectual Property Issues in
Health Care 509**

Alicia M. Passerin, PhD, Esq., and Christine W.
Trebilcock, Esq.

Preface

We are excited to present the 10th edition of *Problems in Health Care Law*. This substantially updated edition includes many new features designed to enhance the reader's learning experience, including:

- Concise, key learning objectives at the beginning of each chapter and instructor-led questions at the end of each chapter;

- Strategically placed *flag* icons that emphasize important concepts, court decisions, and terminology;

- Numerous sidebars that complement the text and reinforce key themes or specific points in each chapter;

- Checklists, spreadsheets, diagrams, and other useful reference tools; and

- Lists of key terms and definitions in each chapter, as well as a comprehensive glossary for the entire textbook.

The 10th edition is a contributed work including content from some of the country's leading healthcare lawyers and consultants. Their combined expertise and practical insights are presented in each of the 10th edition chapters.

Overview of Chapters

Chapter 1 introduces our legal system, the roles of each branch of the federal government, and contract law principles.

Chapters 2 through 4 cover the major organizational models, facility, staffing, and operational issues associated with healthcare delivery.

Chapters 5 through 7 address the various relationships between patients, physicians, and healthcare organizations, as well as the numerous issues that arise in medical decision making that involves those parties.

Chapter 8 is a thoroughly updated chapter on healthcare information, including "e-health" and the methods and techniques for creating, handling, and protecting health information.

Chapters 9 and 10 address methods of financing healthcare services, including coverage for patient care and limitations on payment to providers and suppliers for their services. There is also new content that explains important business processes (commonly referred to as the "revenue cycle").

Chapter 11 covers the basic principles of both negligence and intentional torts.

Chapter 12 deals with theories of legal liability and their application in civil and criminal matters, including antitrust liability.

Chapter 13 is an updated and expanded chapter on reproductive issues.

Chapter 14 addresses antitrust law principles and agency enforcement theories and actions.

Chapter 15 is a new chapter dedicated to bioethics.

Chapter 16 introduces the topic of clinical research and the many legal, ethical, and practical issues associated with research involving human beings.

Chapter 17 is a new chapter on behavioral health.

Chapter 18 provides a comprehensive explanation of intellectual property law principles.

The overarching goal for the 10th edition of *Problems in Health Care Law* is to make it an engaging, expansive, and practical textbook, building upon the solid work of previous authors and editors since 1968.

Acknowledgments

This is the 10th edition of *Problems in Health Care Law*. This textbook has been in print since 1968. In its truest sense, this is a "contributed work" involving many authors. I relied on the solid foundation laid by Robert Miller, Esq. and the editors who preceded him to develop this edition. I did not do it alone. In the chapters contained within this 10th edition you will benefit from the combined experience, wisdom, and expertise of numerous authors. Their credentials and affiliations are presented in the contributor section of this book. The authors were selected to help update and expand the topics in the 10th edition, based on their specialized knowledge and clear, compelling communication style. All of the authors deserve high praise for their individual and collective contributions to a significant textbook in the healthcare field. I trust that this edition will be useful to a wide range of readers, both those in training and those who are active participants in our excellent and complex, healthcare delivery system.

I am also indebted to the fine staff at Jones & Bartlett Learning who went above and beyond the call of duty to ensure that the 10th edition not only meets, but exceeds, your expectations. I also wish to acknowledge the support and encouragement of my wife, Ilene, my daughters, Meagan and Emily, my parents, John and Louise, and my father-in-law, Charles. Collectively, they provided insight, wisdom, attention to detail, and their professional expertise in the healthcare field. In particular, my family patiently tolerated the many weekends and evenings spent to bring the 10th edition to fruition.

Contributors

Heidi R. Carroll, JD
Clinical Research Regulatory Specialist II
University Hospitals
Cleveland, OH

Cavan K. Doyle, JD, LLM
Associate Attorney
Lebow, Malecki & Tasch, LLC
Oak Brook, IL

Jon Englander, CPA
Vice President
MedCom Solutions
Pittsburgh, PA

Donna F. Flynn, JD, LLM, CHC
Glencoe, IL

Erin Dougherty Foley, Esq.
Seyfarth Shaw LLP
Chicago, IL

Michele M. Garvey, Esq.
Associate Attorney
Ungaretti + Harris LLP
Chicago, IL

Kelly L. Gawne, JD
Counsel
Ulmer & Berne, LLP
Chicago, IL

Nicole Huberfeld
Gallion & Baker Professor of Law
University of Kentucky College of Law
Bioethics Associate
University of Kentucky College of Medicine
Lexington, KY

William A. Hunt
President
MedCom Solutions
Pittsburgh, PA

MaryRose Jeffry, MS, MA
Manhattan Beach, CA

Russell A. Kolsrud, Esq.
Co-Chair
Clark Hill PLC Health Care Practice Group
Scottsdale, AZ

Isabel Lazar, Esq.
Seyfarth Shaw LLP
Chicago, IL

Joan M. Lebow, JD
Counsel
Ulmer & Berne, LLP
Chicago, IL

Amy S. Leopard, JD
Partner
Bradley Arant Boult Cummings LLP
Nashville, TN

Ryan J. Lorenz, Esq.
Senior Attorney
Clark Hill PLC Health Care Practice Group
Scottsdale, AZ

Michael W. Matthews, JD
Vice President
Holland Hospital Medical Groups
Holland, MI

Ryan D. Meade
Partner
Meade & Roach, LLP
Chicago, IL

Cheryl A. Miller, JD
Associate Attorney
Lebow, Malecki & Tasch, LLC
Oak Brook, IL

Katie J. Miller, Esq.
Hall, Render, Killian, Heath & Lyman, P.C.
Indianapolis, IN

Gregory W. Moore, Esq.
Co-Chair
Clark Hill PLC Health Care Practice Group
Birmingham, MI

Daniel E. Nickelson
Consultant
Independent Healthcare Financing and Organization
Spotsylvania, VA

Lisa M. Noller
Partner
Foley & Lardner LLP
Chicago, IL

Alicia M. Passerin, PhD, Esq.
Attorney
Pietragallo, Gordon, Alfano, Bosick & Raspanti LLP
Pittsburgh, PA

Joseph L. Ternullo, JD, MPH
Associate Director
Center for Connected Health
Partners HealthCare
Adjunct Faculty
HealthCare Informatics Program
Northeastern University
Boston, MA

Christine W. Trebilcock
Senior Counsel
PPG Industries, Inc.
Pittsburgh, PA

Joseph Van Leer, JD
Associate
Polsinelli Shughart PC
Chicago, IL

Lawrence W. Vernaglia, JD, MPH
Partner
Foley & Lardner LLP
Chicago, IL

Paul J. Voss, JD
Adjunct Professor of Law
School of Law and Graduate School of Business
Loyola University Chicago
Chicago, IL

Chapter 1

Introduction to the American Legal System

John E. Steiner, Jr., Esq.

Key Learning Objectives

By the end of this chapter, the reader will be able to:

- Understand the framework of the legal system.

- Understand how government entities interact to create and change the law, how the court system functions and how private contracts are created and enforced in the American legal system.

- Understand the workings of the legal system, especially as applied to our healthcare system.

- Understand the nature of legal advice and how to use it.

- Appreciate that interpretation of laws and decisions to enforce the laws are not consistent and are sometimes unpredictable.

- The special role of the U.S. Supreme Court.

Chapter Outline

Introduction

The objective of this chapter is to provide an overview of the framework of the legal system. The remainder of the book fits into this framework. That framework should help the reader assess which laws need to be followed, which laws are likely to change, and how laws are changed. The reader will learn about the nature of legal advice and how to use it.

Healthcare services are essential and highly regulated. Those services include clinical care and drugs, devices, other products, and the sites for providing those services. Those who provide, receive, pay for, and regulate healthcare services make decisions that often are based on legal principles with specific legal consequences. Legal advice cannot be obtained before each decision, so it is useful to have a general understanding of the law to help identify when a decision or situation may require legal counsel.

◤ An important feature of civilized societies is the "rule of law" (as opposed to a supreme individual or group of individuals). The rule of law provides a degree of predictability and stability for human interaction and greatly

> American society is governed by the "rule of law," not the rules of a single individual.

facilitates contracting between private parties. In turn, there is a wide variety of contracts in force or in litigation at all times. Those contracts apply to many activities, including the purchase of goods and services, exchange of patient information, construction of healthcare facilities, protection of the results of creative work (such as inventions, new drugs, or published works on scientific advances, etc.). An overview of contracts is provided in section 1-5.

The special role of the U.S. Supreme Court (often referred to simply as the "Supreme Court") in healthcare policy and legislation is an important element of this chapter and our legal system. For example, shortly after passage of the Patient Protection and Affordability Care Act ("PPACA" – sometimes referred to as "Obama Care") several state attorney generals filed a lawsuit that challenged PPACA based on constitutional arguments. Section 1-6 summarizes the legal issues related to that challenge. At the time of the writing of this chapter, the Supreme Court had not yet ruled on the legal arguments presented in this landmark case.

1-1 The Nature of the Law

The law combines a variety of social norms, processes, and an overall system to guide and govern human conduct, facilitate cooperative enterprise, minimize the use of force to resolve conflicts, and punish those who break the law. A major benefit of laws that are respected by those who are subject to those laws is a sustainable structure for cooperative enterprise. The law also serves to reduce and, as needed, address conflict between individuals and between government and individuals. Since conflicting interests are inevitable, the law also provides ways to resolve disputes.

Like medicine, law is not an exact science. Lawyers often cannot provide a precise answer to a legal question or predict with certainty the outcome of a legal disagreement. ◤ Much of the law is subject to interpretation, which creates uncertainty. Many questions have never been precisely addressed by the legal system. Even when questions are answered by the courts or legislature, those answers may change by acts of a "higher court" (i.e., one with greater authority) or by passage of a new law. The ability of the law to adjust to individual situations is one of its strengths. Legal uncertainty is similar to the uncertainty encountered in making medical and nursing diagnostic and treatment decisions. When dealing with

> Law and medicine are similar fields; both are "practiced," and changes are common.

systems as complicated as the human body or human society, uncertainty is inevitable. A lawyer's advice is always valuable, just as a physician's advice is valuable, because an attorney can use knowledge of how the law has addressed similar questions in the past to predict the most probable answer in the present. After a dispute arises, a lawyer plays the role of an advocate and represents his or her client's interests as strongly as possible, and within the bounds of the code of professional responsibility and ethics for lawyers.

In daily life, the law helps guide our behaviors. Most disputes or controversies between persons or organizations are resolved without lawyers or courts. In many situations, the existence of the legal system is a stimulus to address and settle private disputes in an orderly fashion. Legal principles reinforce those settlements. The likelihood of success in court affects the willingness of parties to negotiate private settlements. So, it is advantageous to have a basic knowledge of legalities when faced with a dispute.

Laws govern the relationships of private individuals and entities with each other and with government. Laws are divided into civil law and criminal law. Civil law can be divided further into contract law, tort law, and other governmental statutes and regulations. Contract law concerns enforcement of agreements and payment of compensation for failure to fulfill those agreements. In a few situations, courts can order parties to a contract to perform the duties described in the contract, instead of paying compensation for failure to perform the duties. This is a contract remedy called "specific performance." Tort law defines duties that are not based on contractual agreement and provides remedies for injuries that are caused by breaches of those duties. Within the area of tort law, there are two general categories: intentional torts and unintentional torts. One often hears or reads the word "negligence" to describe an error or bad result in healthcare delivery. One also hears the work "malpractice" to describe the same situation. Both words generally apply to unintentional torts. As described later in this book, there also are situations where physicians, nurses, or other healthcare providers have intentionally harmed patients, which would be considered an "intentional tort."

A third area of civil law includes governmental statutes and regulations that require individuals and organizations to act in specified ways. There is a special area of law called "administrative law," which applies in many areas of healthcare regulation and oversight. Examples of the areas addressed by such statutes and regulations include healthcare quality, medical device safety, hazardous waste disposal, labor relations, business arrangements between physicians and healthcare facilities, employment policies, facility safety, and other important topics. The primary goal of most of these regulations is to attain compliance, not to punish offenders.

 Criminal law describes and punishes certain conduct that may or does injure people and property. The basic difference between civil and criminal law is the concept of "intent" on the part of someone charged with a crime. Over the past twenty years, criminal law has become a more significant concern for healthcare providers (including individuals and organizations). Both federal and state enforcement authorities have expanded the use of criminal laws to address perceived and actual fraud and abuse in the healthcare system. Some conduct in the healthcare system has been defined or redefined as criminal. In addition, criminal penalties have been expanded or increased in more recent federal legislation. For example, federal privacy laws designed to protect an individual's health information include criminal penalties. If someone

> The key difference between "civil" and criminal" violations is the concept of "intent," i.e., did the person intend the result that he or she achieved?

improperly takes your healthcare information and tries to make a personal profit with that information and are caught, that person might be sentenced to jail.

1-2 Governmental Organization and Functions

Government is divided into three branches: legislative, executive, and judicial. Each branch of government has a primary function. The legislature makes laws, the executive enforces laws, and the judiciary interprets laws. There are many court decisions, including those of the Supreme Court, that address how the three branches are supposed to share power, according to our Constitution. In practice, the separation of these three branches is not always precise, and there is some overlap.

Separation of Powers. Separation of powers means that none of the branches is clearly dominant over the other two; each branch can affect and limit the functions of the others. Thus, the process for enacting legislation is a system of checks and balances. On the federal level, "Bills" are introduced and become statutes (or "Acts") in Congress. However, a Bill usually does not become a law until signed by the President. When the President refuses to approve the law, it is called a veto. Congress has the option to override the President's veto by a two-thirds vote. In addition, if the President fails to veto or approve within a given time

> The separation of powers between our three branches of government is not crystal clear. That lack of clarity creates an important "dynamic tension" in our system of government.

limit, a Bill can become law. A Bill that has become law can ultimately be overturned by the Supreme Court or by another court in the judicial branch if it is decided that the law violates the Constitution.

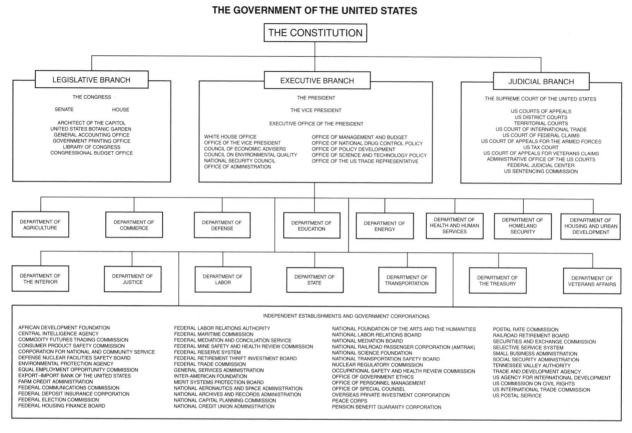

Figure 1-1 The Government of the United States

The executive and legislative branches affect the composition of the judicial branch. The President's nominees for federal judges, including Supreme Court justices, must be approved by the Senate. The Supreme Court's decision is final unless Congress and the President enact or revise legislation that changes a decision by the Supreme Court. That is, a Supreme Court decision is considered the "law of the land," unless the legislature (Congress) and the executive branch (President) pass a law that differs from a Supreme Court decision. Another method of overriding a Supreme Court decision, described later in this chapter, is to amend the Constitution. This takes time and is a complex process.

⚑ Here is an explanation of the primary functions of each branch:

LEGISLATIVE. The legislative branch enacts new laws and amends existing laws. It determines the need for new laws and for changes in existing laws, primarily through public hearings and committee meetings. Legislatures typically assign legislative proposals to specific committees with members who have or gain expertise in the areas addressed by the proposals. The committees investigate and hold hearings at which interested persons may present their views. These hearings provide information to assist the committees in considering the Bills. Hearings help publicize issues and develop public support for action. Some Bills are released from the committees and reach the full legislative body, where after consideration and debate, the Bills can be either approved or rejected. Congress and every state legislature, with the exception of Nebraska, consist of two houses. (Nebraska has only one house.) Both houses must pass identical versions of a Bill before it can be presented to the chief executive. Differences in the versions passed by the two houses are sometimes resolved by a joint conference committee. That committee is composed of leaders from both houses, and their compromise is then voted on by both houses.

EXECUTIVE. The primary function of the executive branch is to enforce and administer laws. The chief executive, state governor, or President of the United States also has a role in law creation through the power to approve or veto Bills passed by legislatures. If the chief executive approves a passed Bill, it becomes law. If the chief executive vetoes the Bill, it can become law if the legislature overrides the veto.

The executive branch is organized into departments. Each department is assigned responsibility for specific areas of public affairs and enforces the law that applies to its assigned areas. Most federal laws that directly affect hospitals are administered by the Department of Health and Human Services. In most states, a department is responsible for health and welfare matters, including the administration and enforcement of most laws affecting hospitals. Other departments and governmental agencies also affect hospital affairs. On the federal level, for example, laws concerning wages and hours of employment are enforced by the Department of Labor.

JUDICIAL. The function of the judicial branch is adjudication – deciding disputes in accordance with the law. For example, courts decide suits brought against hospitals by patients seeking compensation for harm they feel was caused by the wrongful conduct of hospital personnel. News of malpractice suits and suits by the government against hospitals frequently receives the greatest attention. However, a less well-known fact is that hospitals also sue to enforce rights or to protect legally protected interests. For example, hospitals initiate suits to challenge acts by governmental agencies; to have legislation concerning hospitals declared invalid; to collect unpaid hospital bills; and to enforce contracts.

Many disputes are resolved by negotiation or arbitration without resort to the courts. However, sometimes a controversy cannot be resolved without going to court. When a dispute is brought before a court, the judge (and, sometimes, juries) decides the meaning of agreements and laws, confirms the facts, and decides which facts are relevant to the dispute at hand. Application of law to the facts is the essence of the judicial process. There are many steps, some more complex than others, to follow before a "fact" is allowed to be considered part of the evidence in a dispute. That is one reason why litigation may take a long time and become expensive.

1-3 Sources of Law

The four primary sources of law are:

- Constitutions (1-3.1)
- Statutes (1-3.2)

- Decisions and rules of administrative agencies (1-3.3)
- Court decisions (1-3.4)

International law embodied in treaties (1-3.5) is a fifth source of law, but it rarely has a direct effect on healthcare providers.

Private agreements can be viewed as a sixth source of law. In many situations, legal requirements in private contracts have a more direct effect on day-to-day decision-making than do government sources of law.

1-3.1 Constitutions

The Constitution of the United States is the supreme law of the land. It establishes the general organization of the federal

> The U.S. Constitution is the supreme law in America.

government, grants powers to the federal government, and places limits on what federal and state governments can do. The Constitution establishes and grants power to the three branches of federal government.

The Constitution is a grant of power from the states to the federal government. The federal government has only the powers that the Constitution grants expressly or by implication. Express powers include, for example, the power to collect taxes, declare war, and regulate interstate commerce. The federal government is also granted broad implied powers to enact laws "necessary and proper" for exercising its other powers. However, federal courts do enforce limits on how expansively Congress can define its powers by sometimes declaring laws to be outside the authorized powers.[1] When the federal government establishes law within the scope of its powers, that law is supreme. All conflicting state and local laws are invalid.

▶ The Constitution also limits what federal and state governments can do. Many limits on federal power appear in the first ten amendments to the Constitution, called the Bill of Rights. The Bill of Rights protections include the right to free speech; free exercise of religion; freedom from unreasonable searches and seizures; trial by jury; and no deprivation of life, liberty, or property without due process of law. Some of the most frequently applied limits on state power are stated in the Fourteenth Amendment: "...nor shall any State deprive any person of life, liberty, or property, without due process of law; nor deny to any person within its jurisdiction the equal protection of the laws." These clauses are frequently referred to as the "due process" clause and the "equal protection" clause.

> The "due process" and "equal protection" clauses in the Constitution provide a basis for many interesting and important Supreme Court decisions.

DUE PROCESS OF LAW. The due process clause restricts state action, not private action. Actions by state and local governmental agencies, including public hospitals, are state actions and must comply with due process requirements. Actions by private individuals at the direction of the state can also be subject to these requirements. In the past, private hospitals were sometimes considered to be engaged in state action when they were regulated or partially funded by governmental agencies. As discussed elsewhere in this book, it is now rare for private hospitals to be engaged in state action.

The due process clause applies to state actions that deprive a person of "life, liberty, or property." Liberty and property interests can include a physician's appointment to the medical staff of a public hospital and a hospital's institutional license. Thus, in some situations public hospitals must provide due process, and in other situations, hospitals are entitled to due process. The process that is due varies depending on the situation.

The two primary elements of due process are (1) rules must be reasonable and not vague and (2) fair procedures must be followed in enforcing rules. Rules that are too arbitrary or vague violate the due process clause and are not enforceable. The primary elements of a fair procedure are notice of the proposed action and an opportunity to present information as to why the action should not be taken. The phrase "due process" in the Fourteenth Amendment has been interpreted by the Supreme Court to include nearly all of the rights in the Bill of Rights. Thus, state governments cannot infringe on those rights.

EQUAL PROTECTION OF THE LAWS. The equal protection clause also restricts state action, not private action. Equal protection means that like persons must be dealt with in a like fashion. The equal protection clause addresses categories or classifications used to distinguish persons for various legal purposes. When a classification is challenged, the court must determine whether a different classification between persons justifies a difference in application of rules or procedures. Courts generally require governmental agencies to justify

such different treatment with a "rational reason." A major exception to this standard is the "strict scrutiny" standard applied by courts to distinctions based on "suspect classifications," such as race. Another exception is the "intermediate level" of scrutiny applied to sex-based classifications.

Courts have ruled that the equal protection clause imposes a constitutional right of interstate travel that has been applied to strike down state limitations on welfare benefits for new residents.[2]

The equal protection clause of the Fourteenth Amendment includes an express grant of enforcement powers to the Congress. That grant of power supersedes the Eleventh Amendment to the Constitution. The Eleventh Amendment bars most lawsuits that seek money from being brought against a state, unless the state consents. Congress can authorize suits against states to enforce equal protection.[3] Other federal powers, such as the Commerce Power, generally do not permit Congress to violate a state's Eleventh Amendment immunity from lawsuits that seek money.[4]

STATE CONSTITUTIONS. Each state has a constitution. The state constitution establishes the organization of state government; grants powers to state government; and places limits on what state government can do. Many of these documents contain rights similar to the rights in the U.S. Constitution, and some provide additional rights.

1-3.2 Statutes

Another major source of law is statutory law, enacted by a legislature. Legislative bodies include the U.S. Congress, state legislatures, and local legislative bodies, such as city councils and county boards of supervisors. Congress has only the powers delegated by the Constitution, but those powers have been broadly interpreted. A state legislature has all powers not denied by the U.S. Constitution, valid federal laws, or the state constitution. A local legislative body has only those powers granted by the state. Some states have granted local governments broad powers through either statutes or constitutional amendments authorizing the "home rule."

▶ PREEMPTION. When state or local law conflicts with federal law, valid federal law controls, and this is referred to as the "preemption doctrine." In addition, certain Federal laws preempt some areas of law. In those areas, state law is superseded by federal law even when it is not in direct conflict with the federal law. Some laws, such as bankruptcy laws and the Employee Retirement and Income Security Act

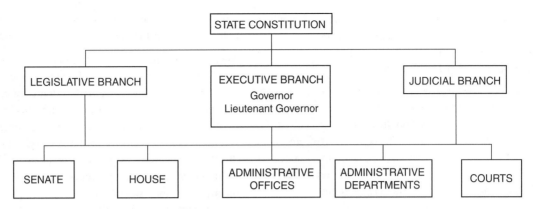

Figure 1-2 State Government Organizations

(ERISA),[5] clearly prohibit state regulation of those subjects. In other laws, where such a clear prohibition is not stated, the courts have concluded that federal law controls (that is,

> The "preemption" doctrine is important to understand. It also can be complex to apply and helps shape how courts make decisions that affect our daily lives.

it "pre-empts" state law) based on the aim and scope of the federal law. In these situations, the courts also point out the need for uniformity, and the likelihood that state regulation would obstruct the goals of the federal law.

Courts tend not to find implied preemption of state law by a federal law when the state is exercising its police power to protect public health. For example, in 1960 the Supreme Court ruled that the extensive federal regulation of shipping did not preempt a city ordinance concerning smoke emissions. In that case, a federally licensed vessel could be prosecuted for violating the pollution ordinance.[6] In 1985, the Supreme Court ruled that county ordinances regulating blood plasma collection were not preempted by federal regulation of drugs.[7] Some federal laws preempt only some aspects of an area, leaving others to state regulation. For example, the Minnesota Supreme Court ruled in 1986 that federal law preempted state licensure of air ambulances, but that the state could enforce staffing, equipment, and sanitary requirements.[8]

When local laws conflict with state laws, valid state laws supersede. State law can preempt an entire area of law, so local law is superseded even when it is not in direct conflict with state law.[9]

PRIVATE RIGHT OF ACTION. When a statute does not specifically authorize private individuals to bring a lawsuit to enforce the statute, the courts have to determine whether a private right of action is implied.[10] If there is no private right of action, then only the government can enforce the statute. For example, the Health Insurance Portability and Accountability Act (HIPAA) does not create a private right of action for violations of the privacy rights established for individuals and their protected health information.

1-3.3 Decisions and Rules of Administrative Agencies

The decisions and rules of administrative agencies are another source of law. Legislatures delegate to administrative agencies the responsibility and power to implement various laws. The agencies do so by writing regulations that further the purposes of the legislation. In addition, agencies exercise quasi-judicial power when they decide how the statutes and regulations apply to individual situations. These powers are delegated because the legislature does not have the time or expertise to address the complex issues concerning many regulated areas. Examples of federal administrative agencies include the Centers for Medicare and Medicaid Services (CMS); Food and Drug Administration (FDA); National Labor Relations Board (NLRB); and Internal Revenue Service (IRS). CMS administers the Medicare program and the federal aspects of the Medicaid program. The FDA publishes regulations and applies them in decisions related to manufacturing, marketing, and advertising foods, drugs, cosmetics, and medical

> Many areas of conduct are regulated by federal agencies. Thus, a basic understanding of "administrative law" and its application are essential for a well-rounded understanding of the American legal system.

devices. The NLRB decides how national labor laws apply to individual disputes. The IRS publishes regulations and applies them to a variety of situations involving personal, corporate, partnership, and other taxable entities.

Many administrative agencies seek to achieve some consistency in their decisions by following the position they adopted in previous cases involving similar matters.[11] This is similar to the way courts develop "common law," discussed later in this chapter. When dealing with these agencies, previous decisions, as well as rules, should be reviewed. Also, federal agencies must follow policies and procedures that are designed to be fair and comply with the Administrative Procedure Act (APA), passed by Congress in 1946.

Administrative regulations are valid only to the extent they are within the authority validly granted to the agency by legislation. Delegation can be invalid when it violates the constitutional requirement of separation of powers. That can happen when the legislation does not sufficiently specify what regulations the administrative body can make. Delegations by Congress usually are found to be valid by the courts. Broad delegation, specifying the general area of law, is permitted.[12] In the past, state courts often declared delegations unconstitutional unless there was considerable specificity. Today, state courts often permit much broader delegation.

As mentioned above, Congress and many state legislatures have passed administrative procedure acts. These laws specify the procedure for administrative agencies to adopt rules and to reach decisions in individual cases when no other law specifies different procedures for the agency. Generally, these laws require proposed rules to be published so that individuals have an opportunity to comment before a rule is considered final. Many federal agencies must publish both proposed and final rules in the Federal Register. Some changes do not have to be published.[13] Many states have similar publications that include proposed and final rules of state agencies. Healthcare providers usually monitor proposed and final rules in these publications and trade association publications. Those publications are used by lobbyists to advocate for or against certain agency positions. Despite their expertise, administrative agencies do not know all the implications of their proposals. They rely on the public and those regulated to alert them to potential problems through the public comment and rule-making processes.

Some administrative agencies use "negotiated rule-making," giving those regulated and other interested parties more input in the development of regulations.[14] This technique typically is used when a regulated activity may involve more than one agency; for example, CMS and the FDA.

Agency enforcement of statutes and regulations may be constrained by agency resources. Sometimes, when legislators are opposed to a law or regulation that they cannot change or repeal directly (for political or procedural reasons), they may curtail or eliminate funding for enforcement.[15] Even when an agency is not the subject of selective funding in this manner, its funding generally is subject to budget limits. Enforcement funds and practices often define the practical meaning of the regulations. When approvals from the government are required, delays in approvals can slow down actual enforcement of regulations.[16]

1-3.4 Court Decisions

Judicial decisions are a fourth source of law. The role of courts is to resolve disputes. In deciding individual cases, courts interpret statutes and regulations; determine whether specific statutes and regulations are permitted by the state or federal constitution; and create the common law when deciding cases not controlled by statutes, regulations, or a constitution. ⚑ "Common law" is sometimes referred to as "judge made law." Briefly, "common law" is a set of principles and rules of action reflected in court decisions rather than legislation. The common law applies to the protection of persons and property and is based on customs and traditions, as interpreted over time by judges.

INTERPRETING STATUTES AND RULES. There is frequent disagreement over the application of statutes or regulations to specific situations. Often an administrative agency has the initial authority to decide how to apply its rules. ⚑ Under the doctrine of primary jurisdiction, courts generally will refuse to accept a lawsuit until the appropriate administrative processes have been used.[17] This is sometimes referred to as the doctrine of "exhaustion of administrative remedies." The final administrative decision usually can be appealed to the courts. The courts, in turn, generally defer to decisions of administrative agencies in certain areas, for example, when the administrative agency's experts are shown to be well qualified to set certain administrative standards that are required to be established under the law. While there is some deference to the agency interpretation of the law concerning the agency, there is no presumption that agency conclusions of law are correct.[18] Courts review whether the delegation to the agency was constitutional. In addition, courts look to see whether the agency acted within its delegated authority, followed proper procedures, had a

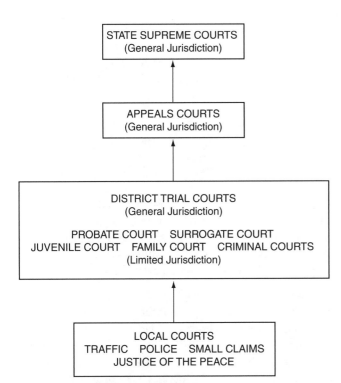

STATE SUPREME COURTS
(General Jurisdiction)

APPEALS COURTS
(General Jurisdiction)

DISTRICT TRIAL COURTS
(General Jurisdiction)

PROBATE COURT   SURROGATE COURT
JUVENILE COURT   FAMILY COURT   CRIMINAL COURTS
(Limited Jurisdiction)

LOCAL COURTS
TRAFFIC   POLICE   SMALL CLAIMS
JUSTICE OF THE PEACE

Figure 1-3 State Court System

substantial basis for its decision, and did not discriminate or act arbitrarily in making its decision. The court might have to interpret a statute or regulation or decide which of several

> Since agencies touch many areas of our daily activities, the courts often are asked to determine whether an agency is exceeding the authority delegated to it by the legislature.

conflicting statutes or regulations applies. Courts have developed rules for interpreting statutes. Some states also have a statute specifying interpretation rules. These rules or statutes are designed to help determine the intent of the legislature.

CONSTITUTIONALITY OF STATUTES AND RULES. Courts also determine whether statutes or regulations violate Constitutional principles, some of those were discussed earlier in this chapter. Courts can declare a law invalid when it is unconstitutional.[19] Laws can be declared unconstitutional because of their content or how they are enacted. For example, in Florida and other states, an appropriation bill (sometimes called a "funding" bill) cannot change the law that says how the money will be spent. Thus, in 1995, the Florida Supreme Court ruled as unconstitutional a provision of the Medicaid appropriation bill that attempted to reinstate pharmacy copayments.[20] The legislature had to make the change in a nonappropriation bill.

COMMON LAW. Many legal principles and rules applied by courts are the product of the common law developed in England and the United States. The term "common law" refers to principles that evolve from court decisions. Common law is continually being adapted and expanded. During the colonial period in North America, English common law applied. After the American Revolution, each state adopted part or all of the existing common law. Subsequent common law has been developed by each state, and so common law differs from state to state. The federal courts have also developed a federal common law. Statutory laws have been enacted to restate many legal principles that initially were established by courts as part of the common law. Many cases, especially disputes among private entities, are decided according to the common law. The common law can be changed by statutes that modify the principles or by court decisions that establish different common law principles.

1-3.5 International Law

International law expressed in the treaties between the United States and other nations is a fifth source of law. International law has rarely had an impact on healthcare providers except when they enter business transactions with businesses in other countries. There may be increased relevance of international law to health care as "medical tourism," global innovations, financing, and research continues to grow and expand beyond borders.

International law can have an impact on domestic policy and practices. For example, the European Union adopted strict requirements for privacy of medical information, which some American businesses had to address in order to engage in business involving European medical information.[21] This has been less of a problem because U.S. standards were strengthened under the federal Health Insurance Portability and Accountability Act (HIPAA) in 2003. Another example is the use of the North American Free Trade Agreement (NAFTA) to challenge a large liability award by an American court.[22]

1-4 Organization of the Court System

The structure of the court system determines which court decisions serve as precedents in a geographic area. There are over fifty court systems in the United States, including the federal system, each state's system, the District of Columbia's system, and the systems of Puerto Rico and the territories. These courts do not all reach the same decisions concerning specific issues. Frequently, a majority approach and several minority approaches exist on an issue. Careful review is necessary to find the court decisions applicable to an individual hospital and, if there are no such court decisions, to predict which approach courts are likely to adopt.

Some of the variation in outcome is due to different approaches to the law. In some cases, courts consider subsequent social developments when interpreting constitutional and statutory language and common law principles. Also, some judges may take a more active role in the development of the law; these are sometimes referred to as "activist judges" because they

> Judges who seek to actively shape societal norms through their court decisions are sometimes called "activist judges."

bring a certain, relevant perspective to a decision that may not have been raised by the parties. In some cases, courts seek to interpret constitutional and statutory law more strictly, leaving development of the law to other branches of government.

The federal court system and many state court systems have three levels of courts: trial courts, intermediate courts of appeal, and a supreme court. Some states do not have intermediate courts of appeal.

This section is divided into discussions of:

- Trial courts (1-4.1)
- State court system (1-4.2)
- Federal court system (1-4.3)

This is followed by discussions of key legal principles that determine the effect of court decisions: stare decisis (1-4.4) and res judicata (1-4.5). Finally, there is an explanation of how and when matters may be heard by a court: standing (1-4.6).

1-4.1 Trial Courts

In both state and federal trial courts, the applicable law is determined, and the evidence is assessed to determine what the "facts" are. The applicable law is then applied to those facts. The judge determines what the law is. If there is a jury, the judge instructs the jury as to what the law is, and the jury determines the facts and applies the law. If there is no jury, the judge also determines the facts. In some cases,

everyone agrees on the facts, and the court is asked only to determine what the law is. In other cases, everyone agrees what the law is, but there is disagreement over the facts. Many cases involve both questions of law and questions of fact.

> In a court setting, establishing the "facts" is a critical first step. In a court of law, the "facts" may not always be what actually happened.

The determination of facts must be based on evidence properly admitted during trial, so "facts" are not necessarily what actually happened. To determine facts for purposes of deciding a case, the credibility of witnesses and the weight to be given to other evidence must be determined.

The judge has significant control over the trial even when a jury is involved. If the judge finds that insufficient evidence has been presented to establish a factual issue for the jury to resolve, the judge can dismiss the case. Or, in civil cases, the judge can direct the jury to decide the case in a specific way. In civil cases, after the jury has come to a decision, the judge can decide in favor of the other side.

DEFAULT OUTCOME AND BURDEN OF PROOF. When analyzing any statute or legal principle, it is helpful to identify the default outcome. That is, what happens if no one can prove that something else should happen. If that default outcome is not desired, the next step is to identify what must be done to convince the judge or jury to determine that the default outcome should not occur. The person who wants a different outcome has the burden of proof. Much of legal planning is to make the default outcome favorable or at least to design documentation to meet the burden of proof for the desired outcome.

Generally, in a trial the plaintiff who brings the suit has the initial burden of proof. When that initial burden is met, the burden usually shifts to the defendant to prove that an exception or specific defense applies to what the plaintiff has alleged.

An example of this analysis is a Florida case in which a hospital sought to collect the balance of a bill from a guarantor where the balance had not been paid by insurance. The trial court placed the burden of proof on the hospital to demonstrate that the services beyond those paid by insurance were medically necessary. In this case, the default position was no payment due from the guarantor. The hospital lost at the trial court level. The appellate court ruled that the burden of proof should have been on the guarantor to prove lack of medical necessity, so the default position was payment by the guarantor. A new trial was ordered to give the guarantor an opportunity to meet the burden of proof.[23]

Courts often distinguish three aspects of the burden of roof:

- First, the plaintiff generally has to demonstrate a prima facie case before the defendant is obligated to do anything. A prima facie case is demonstrated by providing some evidence that all of the elements necessary for the claim are present. Failure to submit a prima facie case can lead to dismissal.

- Second, when a prima facie case is presented, there is the burden of going forward, frequently called a burden of production. In some types of cases, the burden of production requires the defendant to explain why some defenses apply. For example, after a prima facie case of employment disability discrimination is made, the employer has the burden of production to articulate a legitimate, nondiscriminatory reason for the adverse action against the plaintiff.

- Third, there is the ultimate burden of persuasion. This is the burden to convince the court that, based on the evidence, the court should rule in a particular way. If the burden of persuasion is not met, then the court should rule for the default position. The burden of persuasion generally remains with the plaintiff.[24]

1-4.2 State Court System

The trial courts in some states are divided into separate courts for specific issues, such as family courts, juvenile courts, probate courts, courts limited to lesser crimes, or courts limited to civil cases involving limited amounts of money. Some states have created specific courts with new functions.[25] Each state has trial courts of general jurisdiction that can decide all disputes that are not assigned to other courts or that are barred by valid federal or state law.

Most state court systems have intermediate appellate courts. Usually, these courts decide only appeals from trial court decisions. Some states permit a few issues to be taken directly to an intermediate appellate court. When an appellate court is deciding an appeal, additional evidence is not accepted. Only evidence in the trial court record is used. An appellate court almost always accepts determinations of fact from the trial court because the jury and judge see witnesses and can better judge their credibility. Usually, the appellate court bases its decision on whether proper procedures were followed in the trial court and whether the trial court properly interpreted the law. However, an appellate court will occasionally find that a jury or trial judge verdict is so clearly contrary to the evidence that it will either reverse the decision or order a new trial.

Each state has a single highest court, usually called the Supreme Court. In some states, the name is different. For example, in New York the highest court is called the Court of Appeals, while trial courts are called supreme courts. The highest court decides appeals from intermediate appellate courts and some direct appeals from trial courts. The highest court usually also has other duties, including adopting procedural rules for the state court system, determining who can practice law in the state, and disciplining lawyers and other judges for improper conduct.

In most states, there is no right to review by the highest state court. The highest court has discretion whether or not to grant review. Thus, the intermediate appellate court decision is the final decision in many cases.

1-4.3 Federal Court System

The federal court system has a structure similar to that of state court systems. The trial courts are the U.S. District Courts and special purpose courts such as the Court of Claims, which determines certain claims against the United States.

LIMITED JURISDICTION. Federal trial courts are fundamentally different from a state trial court because they all have limited jurisdiction. Proper "jurisdiction" for a federal trial court lawsuit must either present a federal question or be between citizens of different states. In many types of cases, the controversy must involve at least $75,000. Federal question cases include those involving applications of federal statutes and regulations and those involving possible violations of rights under the U.S. Constitution. When a federal trial court decides a controversy between citizens of different states that does not involve a federal question, it is acting under what is called its diversity jurisdiction. In diversity cases, federal

> To bring a case in federal court, there must be proper "jurisdiction." There are two types of proper jurisdiction and each has specific requirements.

court procedures are used, but the law of the applicable state is used, rather than federal law.

ABSTENTION. Sometimes federal trial courts will decline to decide state law questions until they have been decided by a state court. This is called abstention.[26] It is designed to leave state issues for state courts and minimize the federal court workload. Federal courts generally do not abstain when important federal questions are affected by the state law question. Some states have procedures by which federal courts can ask the highest state court to decide a question of state law.

FEDERAL CIRCUIT COURTS OF APPEALS. An appeal from a federal trial court goes to a U.S. Circuit Court of Appeals. The United States is divided into twelve circuits, geographic areas numbered one through eleven plus the District of Columbia Circuit and a nongeographic Federal Circuit.

U.S. SUPREME COURT. The highest court is the U.S. Supreme Court. It decides appeals from courts of appeals. Decisions of the highest state courts can also be appealed to the Supreme Court if they involve federal laws or the U.S. Constitution. Sometimes when the court of appeals or the highest state court declines to review a lower court decision, a lower court decision can be reviewed by the Supreme Court.

The Supreme Court has the authority to decline to review most cases. With few exceptions, a request for review is made by filing a petition for a writ of certiorari. If the Court grants the writ, the lower court record is transmitted to the Supreme Court for review. In most cases, the Court denies the writ, which is indicated by "cert denied, [vol.] U.S. [page] [year]" at the end of the case citation. Denial of a writ of certiorari does not indicate approval of the lower court decision; it merely means the Supreme Court declined to review the decision.

1-4.4 Stare Decisis

Courts generally adhere to the doctrine of stare decisis, which is frequently described as "following precedent." By applying principles developed in previous, similar cases, the court arrives at the same ruling in the current case as it did in the preceding one. Slight differences in circumstances can provide a reason for the court not to apply the previous rule to the current case. Even when such differences are absent, a court may conclude that a common law principle is no longer appropriate and may depart from precedent. An example of this overruling of precedent is the reconsideration and elimination of the common law principle of charitable immunity,

which for many decades provided nonprofit hospitals with virtual freedom from liability for harm to patients.[27] Courts in nearly every state overruled precedent that had provided

> Courts adhere to an important doctrine in American law, which is following decisions made by courts with higher authority. The Latin term "stare decisis" is used to refer to this doctrine; it is also referred to as "following precedent."

immunity, so now nonprofit hospitals can generally be sued,[28] except in the few states that have reestablished charitable immunity by statute.[29]

When a court is presented with an issue, it is bound by the doctrine of stare decisis to follow the precedents of higher courts in the same court system that have jurisdiction over the geographic area where the court is located. Each appellate court, including the highest court, is also generally bound to follow the precedents of its own decisions unless it decides to overrule such precedent due to changing conditions. However, many courts issue some opinions that are not published and cannot be used as precedent.[30] Another reason that a court can change its prior position is that controlling statutes or regulations have changed. Most decisions by a federal circuit court of appeals are made by a panel of three judges. There is a special procedure, called en banc review, by which all the active judges in the circuit can review the decision of a panel and overrule the decision.[31]

Decisions from equal or lower courts do not have to be followed. Federal circuit courts consider but do not defer to decisions of other circuits.[32] Usually, decisions from courts in other court systems do not have to be followed. One exception is when a federal court is deciding a controversy between citizens of different states and must follow state law as determined by the highest court of that state. Another exception is when a state court is deciding a controversy involving a federal law or constitutional question and must follow the decisions of the U.S. Supreme Court.

A third exception occurs when a court determines that the law of another jurisdiction governs some aspect of the case. The court must then follow the decisions of the highest court in the state or country whose law governs. With the growth of interstate and international transactions and travel, courts are frequently confronted with issues of choice of law, having to decide what law governs. It is not unusual for the law of another state or country to govern some or all aspects of a case, especially in contract disputes, where the contract will often specify that the law of another jurisdiction governs. Many courts will not research foreign law. They place the burden of proof on the person who is relying on the foreign law to prove what that law is and adopt the default outcome of assuming that the other law is no different than the forum state's laws.

When a court is presented with a question that is not answered by statutes or regulations and that has not been addressed by the applicable court system, the court will often examine judicial decisions in other systems to help decide the new issue. Judicial decisions from other systems are also examined when a court reexamines an issue to decide whether to overrule precedent. Most court systems tend toward some consistency. However, a court is not bound by decisions from other systems, and it may reach a different conclusion.

There can be a majority approach to an issue that many state court systems follow and one or more minority approaches that other state courts follow. State courts show more consistency on some issues than others. For example, nearly all state courts have completely eliminated charitable immunity. However, while nearly all states require informed consent to medical procedures, some states determine the information that must be provided to patients by reference to what a patient needs to know, while other states make the determination by reference to what other physicians would disclose. Thus, there are the "reasonable patient" and the "reasonable physician" standards as to this element of informed consent.

Courts can reach different conclusions because state statutes and regulations differ. For example, Georgia had a statute that specified that a physician need only disclose "in general terms the treatment or course of treatment" to obtain informed consent.[33] In 1975, a Georgia court interpreted that statute to eliminate the requirement that risks be disclosed to obtain informed consent.[34] As a result, Georgia courts stopped basing liability on failure to disclose risks[35] until 1989, when a state statute again required risk disclosure for most surgery and some other procedures.[36] Courts in other states are unlikely to consider Georgia court decisions concerning this issue because these decisions are based on Georgia statutes, not on Georgia common law.

In summary, while it is important to be aware of trends in court decisions across the country, legal advice should be sought before taking actions based on decisions from court systems that do not have jurisdiction over the geographic area in which the hospital is located.

1-4.5 Res Judicata

Another doctrine that courts follow to avoid duplicative litigation and conflicting decisions is res judicata, which means "a thing or matter settled by judgment." When a legal controversy has been decided by a court and no more

> "Res judicata" is an important legal doctrine used in our court system. It means "a thing or matter settled by judgment."

appeals are available, those involved in the suit cannot take the same matters to court again.[37] This is different from stare decisis in that res judicata applies only to the parties involved in the prior suit and to issues decided in that suit. The application of res judicata can be complicated by disagreements over whether specific matters were actually decided in the prior case.

1-4.6 Standing

Another important requirement is that the person bringing the suit must have standing. Courts can only decide actual controversies, and the person bringing the suit must have an actual stake in the controversy. Persons with such a stake are said to have standing. Sometimes parties with a stake do not have standing for other reasons. For example, in some states governmental entities do not have standing to challenge the constitutionality of state statutes and regulations.[38]

1-5 Contracts

A contract is a legally enforceable agreement. Healthcare providers have many contracts involving all areas of operations, including employment contracts; contracts to purchase supplies and equipment; construction contracts; sales contracts; contracts to purchase services; and contracts involving leases, loans, and other matters. The primary purpose of a written contract is to set forth the elements of a legally binding agreement and to facilitate compliance, not to prepare for litigation. All elements of contracts should be carefully thought through and clearly articulated. This section outlines some of the legal problems associated with contracts. ▰ The law of contracts is complex, and there are exceptions to these general rules. Contracts should be reviewed with the assistance of legal counsel. Healthcare administrators are expected to be sophisticated in business matters and will find themselves bound by contracts, even if a properly created contract is not in the organization's best interest.

WHEN IS THERE A CONTRACT? Usually, agreements to agree in the future are not enforceable. Generally, there is no contract until the agreement itself is reached. However, sometimes courts find that a contract exists before the formal contract is signed, so administrators should be circumspect with promises, negotiations, correspondence, and letters of intent.

Agreement can sometimes be inferred from conduct. Thus, it is prudent to state the parties' intent clearly and in writing. For example, when a contract between a Pennsylvania hospital and a managed care company expired, the hospital sent the company a written rejection of the company's offer to extend the contract. Yet, the hospital continued to submit claims and accept payments from the managed care company. The company asserted that the hospital had accepted the offer of extension by its conduct. A Pennsylvania court rejected this assertion, ruling that the hospital's express written rejection barred implied assent by conduct.[39]

CONSIDERATION. Courts usually require all participants, often called parties, to pay a price in order for a binding contract to exist. This price, called the consideration for the contract, can be an act, forbearance to do or request something, change of legal relationship, or promise. When one party has not provided any consideration, the courts usually will not let that party enforce the contract. One exception is that most written sales contracts are enforceable against merchants without consideration because of the Uniform Commercial Code (UCC), which has been adopted by the states.

UNENFORCEABLE CONTRACTS. Courts will not enforce many other contracts, such as illegal contracts,[40] contracts that are viewed by the court as against public policy,[41] oral contracts of the type the law requires to be written, and unconscionable contracts. The public policy rule was applied by a federal appellate court to declare that a contract with an unlicensed nursing agency was unenforceable.[42] The agency could not sue to enforce the contract because it did not have the license required by state law. The statute of frauds requires contracts of certain types (e.g., conveyances of land, leases for over a year, and certain employment contracts) be in writing to be enforceable, unless an exception applies.[43] Unconscionable contracts are contracts that shock the conscience of the court, usually by being extortionate. Because courts usually apply the unconscionability doctrine only to consumer contracts, healthcare providers are seldom protected by the doctrine in dealings with other businesses. However, some contracts

with patients, such as exculpatory contracts purporting to limit the patient's right to sue, could be found to be unconscionable and thus unenforceable.

Courts occasionally refuse to enforce part of an agreement. For example, courts will generally not enforce penalty provisions. Another example is that in many circumstances courts will not enforce agreements not to compete.[44] Many contracts specify that if the agreement is found partly invalid that the remainder is still enforceable. This provision can create problems when the invalid portion was of central importance, but it can also save advantageous arrangements when the invalid portion is less significant.

PAROLE EVIDENCE RULE. Courts tend to review only the words in the written contract by applying the parole evidence rule. Under that rule, oral promises made during negotiations that are not included in the final written agreement are assumed to have been negotiated away.[45] Healthcare providers must be diligent to include in a written contract any oral statements important to them and made before signing the contract. If these statements are important to the agreement, they should be in the written contract.

COURT-ADDED TERMS. In some circumstances, a court will add terms to contracts.

Ambiguous or missing elements. When a written contract is ambiguous or does not have critical elements, the court will sometimes consider testimony concerning oral understandings. The court will try to avoid this, but sometimes oral understandings must be considered. The court then must sift through the usually conflicting recollections of the parties and decide what to believe.

> The "parole evidence" rule is important in many contract negotiations, especially for healthcare services to be provided by medical professionals.

Lack of agreement. Sometimes it is clear that no agreement, written or oral, was reached concerning critical elements, such as the delivery date. The court will sometimes fill these gaps with a provision the court considers to be reasonable. However, courts will not always fill the gaps, thus forcing the parties to solve the problem on their own.

Implied elements. The law routinely implies some elements in contracts if the element is not otherwise addressed. For example, the UCC specifies that certain sales contracts will be interpreted as having certain provisions unless the contract provides otherwise. One such provision specified by the UCC is an implied warranty of merchantability. This means that the merchant is making a strong representation to the purchaser that the goods are fit for the ordinary purposes for which such goods are normally used. In addition, another provision is an implied warranty of fitness for a particular purpose. This means that the goods are fit for the specific purpose the seller has reason to know the buyer intends for the goods. There are many exceptions to these warranties. One of the clearest is when the contract explicitly disclaims warranties.

Some states recognize an implied covenant of good faith and fair dealing in every contract.[46] However, some of these states restrict the scope of this covenant. In those states, this implied covenant cannot be used to override the express terms of the agreement and can only be used when an express term of the contract has been breached.[47] Where the covenant is restricted in this manner, it cannot be used to add a term that the parties did not address in the agreement.

Courts will sometimes imply additional elements, for example, that the person signing the contract has the authority to do so. Administrators should be cautious about making promises or concessions, especially in writing. Other employees should be instructed not to sign documents without proper authority and review.

BREACH OF CONTRACT. The purpose of the contract is to document plans for completing the agreement and for dealing with contingencies that preclude completion. As a last resort, litigation can be required to deal with breach of contract. The courts will compel performance of some contracts, such as contracts to transfer land or unique goods. Courts will also sometimes issue an injunction prohibiting another party from violating a restrictive covenant. Examples of restrictive covenants include an agreement not to compete or not to disclose a trade secret. However, in most situations the only remedy the court will award is money, called damages. When it is difficult to calculate the damages from breach of a contract, the parties sometimes agree in advance what the amount of damages will be. This agreed amount is called liquidated damages and is stated in the contract. Although courts usually do not enforce contract provisions that are considered penalties, courts frequently enforce liquidated damages provisions when the amounts are reasonable. Or, stated another way, an amount stated in a contract that a court considers excessive (in light of the breach) usually

is treated as an unenforceable penalty. But, a reasonably negotiated amount intended to address the harm caused by a breach of the contract to the nonbreaching party is considered an enforceable "liquidated damages" clause.

DISPUTE RESOLUTION. Contracts can address other issues concerning dispute resolution. They can specify which state's law governs the contract and where lawsuits may be filed.[48] Some contracts specify that disputes will be resolved by arbitration, rather than by court litigation.

DEFENSES TO CONTRACT LAWSUITS. There are several defenses to contract lawsuits, including waiver and default. Sometimes courts interpret conduct of the parties, such as regular acceptance of late delivery without complaint, as implying a modification to the agreement. In this example, one party waives its contract right of timely delivery.

The defense of default is based on the logic that some promises are dependent on others and that some events must occur in a sequence. A party that fails to perform an earlier step in the sequence can be found to be in default, excusing the other parties from carrying out subsequent steps. Vendors sometimes claim that their delay is due to failure of the hospital to provide needed data or material. Sequences should be carefully structured so that this defense is available only when it is appropriate.

THIRD-PARTY BENEFICIARIES. Sometimes courts will permit persons, called third-party beneficiaries, who are not parties to contracts to enforce the part of the contract that is intended to benefit them.[49] Sometimes this contracting structure is intended by the parties to the contract. For example, a contract between a hospital and a health maintenance organization (HMO) may state that the hospital will not bill the patient even if the HMO does not pay. In this example, the patient generally can use that contract statement to oppose billing efforts by the hospital. Generally, a third-party beneficiary must take the limitations in the contract along with the benefits. In a Colorado case, a physician claimed to be a third-party beneficiary to a hospital purchase contract. The court ruled that the claim had to be arbitrated under the arbitration clause in the contract because third-party beneficiaries have to take the contract burdens with the benefits.[50]

CONTRACTS WITH GOVERNMENT AGENCIES. One ambiguous area of the law is the extent to which relationships with governmental agencies are governed by generally accepted contract law principles. In some areas, contract law principles are applied. In other areas, the government retains the power to make unilateral changes which a party to a private contract could not do. In some areas, the government claims that contract principles do not apply. For example, a federal appellate court ruled that the relationship between the federal government and a physician in the National Health Service Corps is a statutory relationship, not a contractual relationship, so no contractual defenses were available.[51]

MALPRACTICE SUITS BASED ON CONTRACT. Most malpractice suits against physicians, hospitals, and other healthcare providers are based on tort law, not on contract law. One type of malpractice case based on contract law is the claim that the physician promised a certain outcome that was not achieved. Absent a specific promise to cure, a physician is not an insurer of a particular outcome. However, if the physician is imprudent enough to make a promise, the law will sometimes enforce it. One of the most publicized cases was *Guilmet v. Campbell*,[52] in which the Michigan Supreme Court upheld a jury finding that a physician had promised to cure a bleeding ulcer. On that basis, the court imposed liability for the unsuccessful outcome, even though the physician was not negligent in providing the care. The Michigan legislature later passed a law[53] making promises to cure unenforceable unless they are in writing, in effect overruling *Guilmet*. In states that do not have these laws, a consent form that disavows any assurance of results can provide protection from such claims.[54]

A breach of contract suit can also arise from failure to use a promised procedure. In a Michigan case, the patient had been promised that her child would be delivered by a cesarean operation.[55] The physician failed to arrange for the operation, and the baby was stillborn. The physician was found liable for breaking his promise to arrange for the operation. A New York appellate court ruled that when a physician orally agreed to deliver a baby for a Jehovah's Witness mother without using transfusions, obtaining a court order and giving a transfusion could constitute a breach of contract.[56]

Cases based on oral promises are unusual, but they demonstrate that physicians and other healthcare providers should be careful in what they say to patients so that their efforts to reassure do not become promises they cannot fulfill.

1-6 Role of the Supreme Court in the 2010 Health Care Reform Legislation

The Patient Protection and Affordable Care Act ("PPACA") was challenged the day after President Obama signed it into law. The challenges were brought by a number of state attorney generals and, at the time this chapter was written, PPACA challenges were heard by the Supreme Court decision of June 2012 addressed several legal arguments,

> The "Commerce Clause" in the U.S. Constitution is the basis for one of the Constitutional challenges to the "Patient Protection and Affordable Care Act."

including the "Commerce Clause" argument. In its decision, the Court found that the Commerce Clause is brief and states that Congress has authority "[t]o regulate Commerce with foreign Nations, and among the several States, and with the Indian Tribes."[57]

PPACA, as currently written, imposes a penalty on those who fail to purchase health insurance by the beginning of 2014. This part of PPACA is referred to as the "minimum essential coverage" requirement. As written, PPACA imposes a tax penalty for each month an individual does not have minimum essential coverage. In brief, it is accepted that Congress can, and does, regulate activity that affects interstate commerce, such as transportation and many other basic, economic activities. However, it is highly unusual to attempt, through legislation, to impose a penalty (i.e., a fine or tax) on someone who fails to engage in a certain type of economic activity, such as buying health insurance coverage.

Thus, the requirement that individuals purchase a minimum amount of health insurance, or pay a penalty, is at the heart of the constitutional challenge to PPACA. The plaintiffs argue that such a requirement exceeds the intended scope of the Commerce Clause.

Chapter Summary

The overview of our legal system in this chapter serves as a framework for the remainder of this book. Subsequent chapters will address a variety of specific legal problems and issues in healthcare law. The main points and themes in this chapter are applied daily in our healthcare system. It is helpful and important to be aware of many of those points and their interplay with planning and decisions by healthcare persons, including executives, business planners, physicians, and other caregivers. Both the law and medicine are "arts," as opposed to firmly established, little changing "science." This is partly due to the fact that there are multiple sources of law. In addition, our legal system balances federal and state powers in a unique way that is based primarily on the Constitution of the United States of America. Also, our judicial system is structured both to allow for a reasonably ordered way to resolve disputes and to recognize geographic and cultural differences.

Given the ambiguity and subjectivity inherent in human efforts to legislate, interpret, apply, and enforce laws, the reader should appreciate why and how court decisions change the law.

Key Terms and Definitions

Administrative Law - The collection of rules, regulations, guidance, and decisions created by administrative agencies of the government.

Breach - Failure to keep a promise or a violation of a legal obligation, such as a contract or a law.

Commerce Clause - One of the "enumerated powers" listed in the U.S. Constitution (Article I, Section 8, Clause 3). The Commerce Clause states that the Congress shall have power "To regulate Commerce with foreign nations and among the several States, and with the Indian Tribes." The clause is one of the most fundamental powers delegated to Congress by the framers of the U.S. Constitution.

Common Law - Principles and rules of action, reflected in court decisions, rather than in legislation. The common law applies to the protection of persons and property and is based on community customs and traditions, as interpreted over time by judges.

Exhaustion of Administrative Remedies - This principle is important in administrative law. Many disputes are first handled by administrative agencies. The applicable agency typically has primary responsibility for disputes (or cases) that involve the rules or regulations that are administered by the agency. "Exhaustion of administrative remedies" requires a person to first seek a resolution of a matter by following agency hearing and appeals processes. Once those steps are completed, a party who is dissatisfied with the agency decision may file a complaint in court.

Jurisdiction - Authority given by law to a court to determine the outcome of disputes and rule of legal matters in a specific geographic area or over specific types of legal disputes.

Res Judicata - In Latin it means "the thing has been judged." In the law, the term refers to a thing or matter decided by the judgment of a court that involves the same parties.

Standing - The right of a party to file a lawsuit under the circumstances in a particular court or other body with authority to make decisions that bind the party.

Instructor-Led Questions

1. What are some of the reasons that legal advisers cannot give precise answers?

2. What are the roles of the branches of government? How does the system of checks and balances function so that each limits the powers of the others?

3. What are the primary sources of law?

4. How do the Due Process Clause and Equal Protection Clause of the U.S. Constitution restrict the scope of permissible laws?

5. Which law should be followed when there are conflicts among laws?

6. On what grounds can the enforceability of laws be challenged? How does this differ when the law being challenged is a statute, regulation, or court decision?

7. How does the role of the courts as a source of law differ when they are interpreting statutes and regulations, determining the constitutionality of laws, or creating the common law?

8. What are the "facts" for the purpose of a trial?

9. Discuss the effect of the designation of the default outcome and the assignment of burden of proof in communicating priorities and determining the outcome of disputes.

10. What are some of the limits that are placed on who may take cases to court and the types of cases courts will consider? How does this differ between federal and state courts?

11. Discuss the extent to which precedent binds other courts.

12. When do private parties have a binding contract? What is necessary to create a contract? What types of contracts are unenforceable?

13. When will courts add terms to private contracts?

14. When does a contract create rights for persons who are not parties to the contract?

Endnotes

1   E.g., *Brzonkala v. Virginia Polytechnic Inst.*, 169 F.3d 820 (4th Cir. 1999) (en banc) [law making rape a federal crime exceeds interstate commerce power]; Civil rights law on rape victims is unconstitutional, court says, N.Y. Times, Mar. 6, 1999, A8.

2   *Shapiro v. Thompson*, 394 U.S. 618 (1960) [state cannot require year residency for welfare benefits]; *Memorial Hosp. v. Maricopa County*, 415 U.S. 250 (1974); *Bethesda Lutheran Homes & Servs. v. Leean*, 122 F.3d 443 (7th Cir. 1997) [state Medicaid residency rule for coverage of intermediate care struck down]; *Maldonado v. Houstoun*, 157 F.3d 179 (3d Cir. 1998) [striking down state law limiting welfare benefits to new residents for one year to lesser of state's benefits or prior state's benefits]; but see *Jones v. Helms*, 452 U.S. 412 (1981) [state may impose additional penalty for leaving state after abandoning child]; *McCarthy v. Philadelphia Civil Serv. Comm'n*, 424 U.S. 645 (1976) [city may require city employees to be residents of city].

3   *Fitzpatrick v. Bitzer*, 427 U.S. 445 (1976).

4   *Seminole Tribe of Fla. v. Florida*, 517 U.S. 44 (1996); *Abril v. Virginia*, 145 F.3d 182 (4th Cir. 1998) [cannot authorize private suits against states under Fair Labor Standards Act].

5   29 U.S.C. § 1144 [ERISA preemption].

6   *Huron Portland Cement Co. v. Detroit*, 362 U.S. 440 (1960).

7   *Hillsborough County v. Automated Med. Labs.*, 471 U.S. 707 (1985).

8   *Hiawatha Aviation of Rochester, Inc. v. Minnesota Dep't of Health*, 389 N.W. 2d 507 (Minn. 1986).

9   E.g., *Robin v. Incorporated Village of Hempstead*, 30 N.Y.2d 347, 285 N.E.2d 285 (1972).

10 E.g., *Suter v. Artist M.*, 503 U.S. 347 (1992) [child beneficiaries of Adoption Act cannot enforce requirement of reasonable state efforts to keep children in their homes]; *Gentry v. Department of Pub. Health*, 190 Mich. App. 102, 475 N.W.2d 849 (1991) [no private right of action to enforce nursing home patient bill of rights]; *Evelyn V. v. Kings County Hosp. Ctr.*, 819 F. Supp. 183 (E.D.N.Y. 1993) [Medicaid recipients have no statutory right to enforce Medicaid regulations against provider]; but see *Wilder v. Virginia Hosp. Ass'n*, 496 U.S. 498 (1990) [providers can enforce Medicaid "reasonable rates" requirement]; *Fulkerson v. Comm'r, Maine Dep't of Human Servs.*, 802 F. Supp. 529 (D. Me. 1992) [Medicaid recipients may enforce equal access to care provision].

11 E.g., *Citrosuco Paulista, S.A. v. United States*, 704 F. Supp. 1075, 1088 (Ct. Int'l Trade 1988).

12 *Yakus v. United States*, 321 U.S. 414 (1994) [broad price control delegation during World War II upheld].

13 E.g., *National Med. Enterprises v. Shalala*, 43 F.3d 691 (D.C. Cir. 1995) [reclassification of labor costs to different cost center for Medicare payment purposes was not substantive rule requiring notice and comment]; *Association of Am. R.R. v. Dep't of Transportation*, 309 U.S. App. D.C. 7, 38 F.3d 582 (D.C. Cir. 1994) [when final rule differs from proposed rule, agency not required to give separate notice if final rule is "logical outgrowth" of rule-making proceeding].

14 E.g., Negotiated rulemaking panel reaches consensus; sends outline of rule to HCFA, 7 Health L. Rptr. (BNA) 425 (1998) [hereinafter Health L. Rptr. (BNA) will be cited as H.L.R.]; Advisory group gives seal of approval to managed care anti-kickback safe harbor, 7 H.L.R. 155 (1998); S. Martin, Reinventing rule-making, Am. Med. News, Feb. 23, 1998, 7.

15 See House GOP hopes to cut funding used to enforce dozens of U.S. regulations, Wall St. J., June 1, 1995, at A16.

16 E.g., Lack of funds forces HCFA to revise survey priorities, 4 H.L.R. 407 (1995) [HCFA could not complete survey and certification of home health agencies (HHAs), which threatened moratorium on new HHAs].

17 E.g., *Johnson v. Nyack Hosp.*, 964 F.2d 116 (2d Cir. 1992) [physician must first pursue N.Y. state administrative remedies before suit challenging privilege termination].

18 E.g., *Keeton v. D.H.H.S.*, 21 F.3d 1064 (11th Cir. 1994).

19 *Marbury v. Madison*, 5 U.S. (1 Cranch) 137 (1803).

20 *Moreau v. Lewis*, 648 So. 2d 124 (Fla. 1995).

21 European Union directive may not impact health care, other business operations, 7 H.L.R. 1705 (1998).

22 T. Carlisle, Loewen seeks $725 million from U.S., Wall St. J., Jan. 13, 1999, B11 [notice of claim filed with U.S. Dep't of State under North American Free Trade Agreement, claiming bias and seeking damages for state jury verdict].

23 *Public Health Trust v. Holmes*, 646 So. 2d 266 (Fla. 3d DCA 1994).

24 E.g., *Brenneman v. Medcentral Health Sys.*, 366 F.3d 412 (6th Cir. 2004); *St. Mary's Honor Ctr. v. Hicks*, 509 U.S. 502 (1993).

25 L. Eaton & L. Kaufman, In problem-solving court, judges turn therapist, N.Y. Times, Apr. 26, 2005, A1.

26 E.g., *Trent v. Dial Med. of Fla., Inc.*, 33 F.3d 217 (3d Cir. 1994).

27 E.g., *Mikota v. Sisters of Mercy*, 183 Iowa 1378, 168 N.W. 219 (1918) [established charitable immunity].

28 E.g., *Haynes v. Presbyterian Hosp. Ass'n*, 241 Iowa 1269, 45 N.W.2d 151 (1950) [overruled charitable immunity].

29 E.g., *Marsella v. Monmouth Med. Ctr.*, 224 N.J. Super. 336, 540 A.2d 865 (1988).

30 See *Hart v. Massanari*, 266 F.3d 1155 (9th Cir. 2001) [constitutional to forbid use of unpublished decisions].

31 E.g., *Atchison, Topeka and Santa Fe Ry. Co. v. Pena*, 44 F.3d 437 (7th Cir. 1994) (en banc), aff'd, 516 U.S. 152 (1996).

32 Id.

33 Ga. Code Ann. § 31-9-6(d) (1985).

34 *Young v. Yarn*, 136 Ga. App. 737, 222 S.E.2d 113 (1975).

35 E.g., *Padgett v. Ferrier*, 172 Ga. App. 335, 323 S.E.2d 166 (1984). The Georgia Supreme Court has interpreted a similar statute concerning consent to sterilization as limiting the applicability of the informed consent doctrine, *Robinson v. Parrish*, 251 Ga. 496, 306 S.E.2d 922 (1983).

36 Ga. Code Ann. § 31-9-6.1 (1988 Supp.).

37 E.g., *Lim v. Central DuPage Hosp.*, 972 F.2d 758 (7th Cir. 1992), cert. denied, 507 U.S. 987 (1993) [physician's second antitrust suit barred by res judicata].

38 E.g., *Trustees of Worcester State Hosp. v. Governor*, 395 Mass. 377, 480 N.E.2d 291 (1985) [statutes]; *Palomar Pomerado Health System v. Belsh*, 180 F.3d 1104 (9th Cir. 1999) [regulations].

39 *Temple Univ. Hosp., Inc. v. Healthcare Management Alternatives, Inc.*, 764 A.2d 587 (Pa. Super. 2000).

40 E.g., *Nursing Home Consultants Inc. v. Quantum Health Srvcs.*, 112 F.3d 514 (without op.). 1997 U.S. App. LEXIS 10544 (8th Cir. 1997) [contract violating anti-kickback provisions is void].

41 E.g., *Swafford v. Harris*, 967 S.W.2d 319 (Tenn. 1998) [contingency fee contract with physician expert witness void as against public policy].

42 *United States Nursing Corp. v. Saint Joseph Med. Ctr.*, 39 F.3d 790 (7th Cir. 1994).

43 E.g., *Preventive Med. Inst. v. Weill Med. College* (N.Y. Sup. Ct.), N.Y.L.J., July 19, 2002, 17 [alleged oral agreement concerning name on clinic sign barred by statute of frauds]; *Americare Health Alliance of Ga. LLC v. America's Health Plan Inc.*, (N.D. Ga. Mar. 3, 1998) as discussed in 7 H.L.R. 473 (1998) [alleged contract between health plan, provider group unenforceable under statute of frauds which requires such contracts to be in writing].

44 E.g., *Meadox Meds., Inc. v. Life Sys., Inc.*, 3 F. Supp. 2d 549 (D. N.J. 1998) [medical products manufacturer granted two-year exclusive distribution agreement that included a noncompetition covenant for term plus one year, court refused to enforce one year noncompetition after non-renewal, lack of proprietary relationship in information manufacturer sought to protect].

45 E.g., *Coram Healthcare Corp. v. Aetna U.S. Healthcare Inc.*, 94 F. Supp. 2d 589 (E.D. Pa. 1999); *International Business Mach. Corp. v. Medlantic Healthcare Group*, 708 F. Supp. 417 (D. D.C. 1989).

46 E.g., *Maglione v. Aegis Family Health Ctrs.*, 607 S.E.2d 286 (N.C. App. 2005); *County of Brevard v. Miorelli Eng'g, Inc.*, 703 So. 2d 1049 (Fla. 1997).

47 E.g., *Insurance Concepts & Design, Inc. v. HealthPlan Servs., Inc.*, 785 So. 2d 1232 (Fla. 4th DCA 2001).

48 See *Hyland Lakes Spuds, Inc. v. Schmieding Produce Co., Inc.*, 25 F. Supp. 2d 941 (E.D. Wis. 1998) [contract construed to be consent to jurisdiction, not exclusive forum selection].

49 *Smith v. Chattanooga Med. Investors, Inc.*, 62 S.W.3d 178 (Tenn. App. 2001) [Medicaid-eligible person was third-party beneficiary of Medicaid contract between nursing and state which was breached by refusal to readmit after hospitalization]; but see *Kirkpatrick v. Merit Behavioral Care Corp.*, 99 F. Supp. 2d 458 (D. Vt. 2000) [beneficiaries of health plan not third-party beneficiaries of plan contract with utilization review provider].

50 *Lee v. Gandcor Med. Sys., Inc.*, 702 F. Supp. 252 (D. Colo. 1988).

51 *United States v. Vanhorn*, 20 F.3d 104 (4th Cir. 1994).

52 *Guilmet v. Campbell*, 385 Mich. 57, 188 N.W.2d 601 (1971); see also *Bobrick v. Bravstein*, 116 A.D.2d 682, 497 N.Y.S.2d 749 (2d Dept. 1986) [contract suit allowed against physician].

53 MICH. COMP. LAWS § 566.132. Some states have similar laws, e.g., FLA. STAT. § 725.01; *Flora v. Moses*, 727 A.2d 596 (Pa. Super. 1999).

54 E.g., *Moore v. Averi*, 534 So. 2d 250 (Ala. 1988).

55 *Stewart v. Rudner & Bunyan*, 349 Mich. 459, 84 N.W.2d 816 (1957).

56 *Nicoleau v. Brookhaven Mem. Hosp.*, 201 A.D.2d 544, 607 N.Y.S.2d 703 (2d Dept. 1994).

57 U.S. Const. art.I, Section 8, cl.3.

Additional Resources:

Free dictionary of Law Terms and Legal Definitions: http://www.nolo.com/dictionary

Glossary of Legal Terms: http://www.nycourts.gov/lawlibraries/glossary.shtml

Relating to the Feds: The Do's and Don'ts of Interacting with Your Federal Government

Daniel E. Nickelson

Overview

Once you have completed your analysis and review of the point in controversy in federal law, regulation or policy, it would be reasonable to assume that the major heavy lifting is done and the rest will be easy. Not so! In fact, in many ways the hardest part of resolving your issue is just beginning. Considering and enacting legislation are long and complex processes and a history is developed through that process to support the final product. Then there is the overlay of partisan politics. The Executive Branch, which has responsibility for administering the laws passed by Congress, has its own long and complex process where a detailed history is developed to defend the decisions the regulators have made in their interpretation of the underlying statute. How one relates to either body is quite distinct because the cultural differences are major.

So, before jumping one way or another in seeking resolution to your issue, it is important to determine whether the matter is subject to differing interpretations of the law, or with the law itself. If it is the latter, then your primary focus will be Congress. If the former, it will be the Executive Branch. You also need to consider whether your particular issue is relevant to other entities and a coalition approach would be helpful, and whether the national trade associations could also provide leadership. If that is the case, time needs to be taken to organize prior to marching to Capitol Hill or taking on the federal bureaucracy.

A cautionary note – Before venturing into actual advocacy, you need to do homework on your employer/client and determine whether the entity already has a government relations capacity. There may be a government relations office as part of the CEO's office, marketing, public affairs, office of general counsel, or as a stand-alone. In many instances, the entity may already have on retainer consultants to advocate the organization's views to the government. The individuals in these offices are responsible for ongoing relationships with legislators and regulators, and it is the bane of their existence to discover that someone else is in their environment without first having brought the matter to their attention. Assuming you find such an office, a conversation is needed to ascertain whether this particular issue fits within the framework of already existing advocacy priorities for the organization and how it will be addressed within this overall framework.

Dealing with Congress

In general – It is always important to engage the local House of Representative and U.S. Senators from the State in the initial stage of interaction. Start with their staff. Only once you have clarity and consensus with the staff, perhaps see the member. It may be that the staff will be able to assist in a way that a visit with the member is not necessary; this is the case in the majority of instances.

Congress is ruled by its committee structure, so it will be important for you to also interact with the authorizing and/or appropriating committees for the issue in question. The committees have full-time staff expert in specific areas under the committee/subcommittee jurisdiction. The staff of your representative or senator can be a facilitator for this contact. Here again, the focus is to work the issue through with the relevant staff expert prior to going to the actual member, if at all. If you have a representative or senator on the committee of jurisdiction you are in a relatively strong position to be heard. If not, it is more difficult. In these cases, it is prudent to see if you can find a sister organization in the state or district of a committee member, and then work with that organization to see if they share your concern and will participate with you in the issue advocacy.

Congress has a major responsibility to pass, repeal, and amend legislation. Additionally, Congress is responsible for oversight of the Executive Branch administration of existing law. This oversight may be exercised in a number of different ways, ranging from requests to the administering agency for information, requiring studies, conducting formal hearings, and arranging meetings for constituents with executive branch staff. These methods can be useful as a way to gain attention for the issue, but there is no guarantee of any particular result.

Framing the issue – It is crucial to go in prepared, but not with a ton of paper and documentation. Frame your issue as directly as you can, keep the write-up as short as possible, and eliminate jargon. Limit the length of the write-up to a few pages at most. The following is a brief outline of how to organize your information:

- Issue: A statement of the problem.
- Underlying basis: Relevant sections of law or regulation, identify sections, summarize.
- Discussion: Your rationale about the problem and why it needs fixing.
- Recommendation: Identify and justify what you think needs to be fixed. Do not attempt to write actual legislative or regulatory language unless asked. They have staff to do this.
- Impact: It is important to provide an assessment of potential impact, be it on beneficiaries, providers, or the government.

The Senate

While the Senate and House have many similar functions, they differ considerably in process. Senators are elected for six years, and are elected statewide, which tends to create a more open environment between parties. Additionally, the filibuster, which is available for most legislation, requires a sixty-vote majority and that also tends to slow things and force compromise. Last, when a bill is brought to the floor senators have opportunity to offer amendments germane only to that bill, and many changes to legislation in the Senate occur in this manner.

Still, the committees remain as the originators of legislation brought to the floor and so it is important to know which committee/subcommittee to target with your concern. The following is an overview of the committees most relevant to health law.

- *Senate Finance Committee* – This committee is one of the most powerful in the Senate and has jurisdiction over all aspects of Medicare and Medicaid. Additionally, it has jurisdiction over taxes and the Internal Revenue Service, and pensions and social security.
- *Health, Education, Labor, and Pensions (HELP) Committee* – This committee has jurisdiction over public health, general health, aging, biomedical research, and private pension plans. In essence, it covers the health areas not addressed in Senate Finance.
- *Senate Committee on the Judiciary* – An important committee because of its antitrust jurisdiction. With

the push for more integration in the health provider community, issues of antitrust will be increasing.

- *Senate Select Committee on Aging* – This committee offers a unique opportunity to bring an issue to public attention through the hearing process.
- *Appropriations Subcommittees* – These committees are important because they deal with real money. For health issues outside Medicare and Medicaid as entitlements, appropriations are central. Expenditures may be authorized by the originating committees, such as the HELP committee, and passed into law, but if there is no appropriation, there is no money. There are two particularly relevant subcommittees – the Subcommittee on Agriculture, Rural Development, Food and Drug Administration, and Related Agencies, and the Subcommittee on Labor, Health and Human Services, Education, and Related Agencies.

The appropriations committees are supposed to deal primarily with levels of funding and not policy, but as you might imagine, there are times when the two are mixed.

The U.S. House of Representatives

Compared to the Senate, the House runs in a highly disciplined manner and daily operations tend to be more partisan. House rules allow the majority party to exercise control. The majority party can limit the time of debate and the number of amendments that may be offered, so legislation strictly along party lines can be passed. The minority party's ability to slow or change legislation moving through the House is quite limited. As in the Senate, the committee structure is very important, but the House committee structure is quite different from the Senate. The following is an overview of the committees most relevant to health law.

- *Committee on Ways and Means, Health Subcommittee* – This very powerful committee and its subcommittees is one of the most powerful in Congress, especially on health issues. It has jurisdiction over Medicare, Medicaid, the Internal Revenue Service, tax policy, and the employer deduction for health insurance.
- *Committee on Energy and Commerce, Health Subcommittee* – This important committee has jurisdiction over public health, biomedical research, public and private health insurance, and the FDA.

- *Committee on the Judiciary* – There are two relevant subcommittees – the Subcommittee on the Constitution, which has jurisdiction over tort reform, and the Subcommittee on Intellectual Property, Competition and the Internet, which includes in its portfolio jurisdiction over antitrust matters.

- *Committee on Education and the Workforce* – Workforce training programs sometimes fall under this committee's jurisdiction as does employment related retirement and security.

- *Appropriations Subcommittees* – There are two subcommittees of relevance and their jurisdiction parallels those in the Senate. They are the Subcommittee on Agriculture, Rural Development, Food and Drug Administration, and Related Agencies, and the Subcommittee on Labor, Health and Human Services, Education, and Related Agencies.

Dealing with the Executive Branch

Dealing with the Executive Branch tends to be far more complex than Congress. The administering agencies tend to be more specialized and detailed than Congress. It is not unusual for several pages of law to translate into hundreds of pages of regulation. It is also challenging to find the particular individual or office you may need to contact. Then there is always the matter of whether to start at the top or the bottom. If your issue is not highly political, it is best to take the time to find the area of expertise within the agency and start your dialogue there. It all ends up there anyway.

You will be expected to bring to bear far more content to this environment. Whenever possible, set up these meetings on your own. Agency staff tend to be suspect of meetings dictated by congressional pressure. Data to support your argument are particularly important; otherwise, it is just your opinion versus theirs. Understand that the analyst you may be engaging in the agency is likely to be familiar in depth with both the legal basis for the agency stance and the agency's history with the issue, going back many years. Rhetorical approaches in this setting tend to be ineffective.

The Administrative Procedures Act governs how agencies go about implementing law through detailed requirements called regulations. These regulations, proposed and final, are published in a document called the Federal Register. It is issued daily. Comment periods may vary, but typically are between forty-five and sixty days. Once a comment period closes, one is prohibited from contacting the agency directly about a proposed rule. (This prohibition, however, does not apply to Congress.) If there is no major controversy that stalls finalizing the proposed rule, a final rule is normally published sixty to ninety days later.

Before the Rule-Making Process Has Started

As you approach dealing with the particular agency in question, it is crucial for you to know the status of any governing regulation. If you are in a situation where a law has recently been enacted, but the implementing rule has not been published, then your approach with the agency can be one of general discussion of the implications of the law and how you think it should best be administered. Convenience isn't a good recommendation. Frame your thoughts positively and in terms of how they reasonably support the law's intent. Most regulators have little experience in healthcare administration at the local level, and are open to learn about practical implications. Think of circumstances such as this as an "educational" opportunity.

Once the Rule-Making Process Is Under Way

A more common circumstance is the period after a proposed rule has been published and the agency is requesting comment. The proposed rule will typically offer a particular course and there may be several options. Here, detailed responses, both legal and programmatic, are important. Many other organizations and associations also comment on these proposed rules, and you can improve your effectiveness if you liaison with those entities to see if you can find additional support for your particular concerns and in turn, offer support to those groups for positions they deem important.

Once a Rule Has Been Finalized

It is not unusual to be unaware of a problem until it happens. Unfortunately, issues in this situation tend to be the most difficult to resolve. The rule is already set and the inertia to maintain the status quo is very powerful. Further, agencies rarely do fixes for individual providers; they write rules for general administration.

A tactic commonly used by many is to go right to your congressman and have him or her bring it to the agency's attention and ask for relief. As a first step, don't do it! The nice letter sent from Congress to the head of the agency trickles down to the analyst's desk who is responsible for this particular area, and now he or she has to drop ongoing work to answer congressional mail. The easiest thing for an analyst to do in this situation that will move through the system without controversy is to reiterate existing policy. Thus, the letter you got your senator or representative to send to get you relief ends up locking the agency even tighter into its position.

A preferred course, once again, is to find the particular analyst within the bureaucracy that is in charge of the area in concern, and talk or meet with him or her directly. He or she is accessible by email as well. Be respectful. Honey works far better than confrontation. Expect it to take a while. If a change is needed, it can take anywhere from sixty days to three or four years before a resolution is finalized. The time frame is long because to change a final rule takes one back through the whole process of a proposed rule again and for ongoing activities, these rules come out annually, so one may have to wait for the next cycle to start.

If You're Unable to Work It Out

Let's say you've done all the right things, but still were unable to achieve satisfaction and still believe you have a strong case. Now is the time to escalate, and there are a variety of options. The more outside support you can generate for your position, the better. Without widespread support from like entities who also have the same grievance, and from the relevant trade associations, the odds of overturning existing policy are remote. Even if you obtain all that support, it still remains a difficult fight to win and it takes a significant investment of resources to carry the fight. Agency leadership and congressional intervention become the places one will need to invest the effort. Professional assistance from Washington lobby firms can be a helpful ingredient.

In Summary

This brief tutorial provides you with a sense of the landscape you will face as you move from analysis to advocacy. While some approaches tend to be more effective than others, there is no one simple answer. Welcome to the magic of our political system.

Chapter 2

Organization of the Healthcare Delivery System

John E. Steiner, Jr., Esq

Key Learning Objectives

By the end of this chapter, the reader will be able to

- Provide an overview of the organization of the healthcare delivery system.

- Explain the most common legal structures of healthcare entities and how those structures affect the organization and operation of the entities.

- Understand the selection and roles of leadership positions in an organization.

- Address licensing and accreditation requirements for organizations.

- Describe several ways that organizations can be reorganized, changed, or closed.

Chapter Outline

Introduction

Most health care is delivered within an organized system. Given the clinical and regulatory complexity associated with our system, a well-ordered business or corporate structure is essential for safe and effective delivery of healthcare services. A hospital, practitioner office, or other healthcare organization is a legal entity that derives both its powers and limitations on those powers from its legal structure. Thus, it is essential to understand both the choice of legal entities and related powers of each entity. ▶ A hospital or other healthcare entity can be one of six types of organizations: governmental entity, nonprofit corporation, for-profit corporation, partnership (limited or general), limited liability company ("LLC"), or sole proprietorship. There are also special organizations that combine features of more than one of these types. In some cases, the hospital or healthcare organization is not a distinct entity, but is a whollyowned component or division of an entity that is one of these types.

The organization of most healthcare entities, regardless of their type, includes a governing body and a chief executive officer (CEO). Most hospitals also include an organized medical staff. The governing body ("board") has the ultimate responsibility and authority to establish goals and policies, select the CEO, and appoint medical staff members. The board delegates responsibility and authority to the CEO to manage day-to-day business. This delegation provides the CEO some discretion in exercising authority. However, for the most part, the CEO manages the organization in accordance with policies approved by the board. The organized medical staff is delegated responsibility and authority to maintain the quality of medical services, subject to ultimate board responsibility. The duties, authority, liability, selection, and rights of the board, CEO, and medical staff are discussed in more detail in this chapter and in Chapter 5 "Medical Staff."

A typical, community hospital is a unique organization because many decisions concerning use of its staff, equipment, and supplies are made by physicians who may be employees or agents of the hospital. ▶ Physicians are often legally independent of the hospital and accountable primarily through the organized medical staff. Some physicians are employees of hospitals, medical groups, or other entities. Changes in the relationships between physicians and hospitals occur periodically, depending on an organization's strategic plans, marketplace business dynamics, and regulatory issues.

Changing utilization, payment rules, market conditions, and changing government requirements often drive organizations to voluntarily or involuntarily change their legal structures. Such changes are accomplished through conversions, mergers, consolidations, sales, and other restructurings. In some cases, changes occur through dissolution, closure, relocation, and bankruptcy.

This chapter focuses predominantly on hospitals, but the same principles generally apply to other healthcare organizations.

2-1 What Are the Key Characteristics of the Six Types of Organizations?

The powers and governance structure of a healthcare organization are derived from its legal basis, which also imposes limitations on those powers. Some states do not permit certain forms of ownership. The Rhode Island Supreme Court ruled that the state could ban ownership of healthcare facilities by corporations with publicly traded stock.[1] The Arkansas Supreme Court ruled that ownership of retail pharmacies by nonprofit hospitals could be banned.[2]

A healthcare organization's powers usually cannot be expanded without changing the underlying legal basis. Moreover, many additional limitations are imposed by government regulations or by private actions, such as restrictions imposed by accepting gifts and bequests, or in the contracts entered into by the organization.

As mentioned previously, the six, basic types of organizations are:

- Governmental entity (2-1.1)
- Nonprofit corporation (2-1.2)
- For-profit corporation (2-1.2)
- Partnership (2-1.3)
- Limited liability company (2-1.4)
- Sole proprietorship (2-1.5)

2-1.1 Governmental Entity

The legal basis of governmental hospitals is found in state and federal statutes and in local ordinances. Many governmental hospitals are not corporations. They are created by a special statute for the specific hospital or by a governmental unit, pursuant to a statute authorizing such units to create hospitals. For example, some counties and cities create hospitals under laws authorizing counties to establish hospitals. However, some governmental hospitals, such as some public hospital authorities, are considered corporations.

These statutes often include specific duties or limitations. In some states, county hospitals are required to care for indigent residents. In 1997, a Colorado court ruled that hospital service districts in Colorado can only provide care directly; they cannot contract with other facilities to provide the services.[3] Some county hospital statutes prohibit purchases from board members and restrict how and to whom hospital property can be sold or leased. Illinois law gives county commissioners the power to establish a limit on expenditures by county hospitals regardless of the source of funds.[4] Asset transfers, facility leases, and joint ventures of public hospitals with private corporations have been challenged. In 2000, the Tennessee Supreme Court ruled that a county hospital was a quasi-governmental entity and the state constitutional restrictions on lending credit were not applicable to quasi-governmental facilities. Therefore, the hospital could enter a joint venture and guaranty financing for a building project without voter approval.[5]

When a governmental entity acts outside its authority, its actions are usually void. For example, a Missouri court ruled that a hospital district created for certain counties could not operate a home health agency outside those counties.[6] The North Carolina Supreme Court ruled that a three-year contract with a public hospital administrator was unenforceable. The board's authority to enter long-term contracts had been revoked by implication when it adopted a resolution of intent to transfer control to a nonprofit corporation.[7] The Missouri Supreme Court ruled that a bank could not collect on certain debts that a public hospital had endorsed because the hospital did not have authority to endorse them.[8]

In some states, governmental hospitals are subject to open meetings and open records laws. For example, a Minnesota appellate court ruled that a county hospital board could not give the CEO a private performance evaluation because of the state open meetings law.[9] States vary as to whether open meetings and records laws apply to governmental hospitals that are leased to or operated by private entities.[10]

2-1.2 Corporations

A corporation is a separate, legal entity distinct from the individuals who own and control it. In the past, each corporation was created by an individual act of the state legislature, granting articles of incorporation. In some states, nonprofit corporations were created under judicial petitions filed by citizens. Today, states have general corporation laws that authorize a state official to create a corporation by issuing articles of incorporation. Legislatures in most states can still create some corporations, especially public corporations. So some corporations do not have articles of incorporation; their legal authority is the statute creating them.

One legal benefit of incorporation is that each owner's liability is generally limited to that owner's investment in the corporation. Usually, an owner is not individually liable beyond this investment, except when the owner causes the injury by personal acts or omissions; fails to observe the corporate formalities; personally guarantees the corporation's debts; or is involved in situations where special statutory liabilities apply, such as environmental and pension laws. The corporation itself is liable to the extent of its resources, which include the owners' investments in that corporation.

To maintain corporate status and the attendant immunity from personal liability, there must be compliance with corporate formalities, such as filing required reports with the state, holding required meetings, and maintaining required records.

Another benefit of incorporation is corporate perpetual life. Death of an owner does not terminate the corporation; only the ownership is changed.

Unless the corporation is tax-exempt or elects another special tax status, the corporation must pay taxes on its earnings. But, in most situations, the owners do not have to pay personal income tax on corporate earnings until the earnings are distributed to them.

Corporations can be nonprofit or for-profit.

NONPROFIT CORPORATIONS. The earnings of a nonprofit corporation cannot be distributed for the benefit of private individuals.

Governmental hospitals often are subject to the requirements of a state "Open Records Act," which creates governance and operating challenges in many respects. On the other hand, there is greater transparency to the public of many aspects of the hospital's activities.

Many healthcare corporations in the United States were created as nonprofit corporations. In addition, most of those corporations also are exempt from federal income taxation. Therefore, it is important to understand basic principles and rules that apply to nonprofit, tax-exempt corporations.

Many nonprofit healthcare institutions are also charitable organizations, and many are exempt from some taxes. However, these characteristics are not always linked. The corporation must engage in charitable activities as defined by state law in order to be considered a charity. Some tax exemption usually results from charitable status, but the two are not always linked. In some states, charities are subject to an implied charitable trust to carry out their purposes and protect charitable assets. The charitable trust doctrine is a basis for state challenges to certain actions by a charity.

Nonprofit corporations are held to various standards of public accountability. In most states, the state attorney general or other officials can take steps to compel nonprofit corporations to meet those standards.[11] This issue arises most frequently when a nonprofit corporation seeks to sell or otherwise convert some or all of its assets to a for-profit organization. Examples of challenges to these transactions are discussed later in this chapter. Some states require state approval before nonprofit corporations may engage in certain transactions.[12] In other cases, nonprofit corporations voluntarily seek prior approval to avoid the risk and delay involved with such challenges. For example, in 2002, under state charity laws, the Massachusetts Attorney General approved a complex deal that was designed to continue the operation of a hospital through a sale-leaseback arrangement.[13]

There are limits to a state's control over entities incorporated in other states. For example, in 2003, a Kansas judge ruled that the Kansas Attorney General could not challenge how a Missouri nonprofit corporation compensated its CEO in the sale of the corporation to a for-profit hospital.[14] However, when an out-of-state nonprofit corporation plans to sell assets located in a state, some states where the assets are located will exercise oversight of whether such sales can occur and how the proceeds are used. In 2003, the South Dakota Supreme Court ruled under the Implied Charitable Trust Doctrine that the state could restrict the transfer of out-of-state of proceeds from the sale of a hospital in South Dakota.[15] In 2004, a settlement was reached in which a $1.8 million payment was divided among five communities.[16]

FOR-PROFIT CORPORATIONS. A for-profit corporation is operated with the intention of earning a profit that can be distributed to its owners. A for-profit hospital is sometimes called an investor-owned, or proprietary hospital.

For-profit hospitals can be owned in various ways. Some are closely held by a small number of investors. Some are wholly owned by a multihospital system or other parent corporation. The parent can then have publicly traded stock that can be purchased through the equity markets. The stock of some hospitals has been owned by their employees' pension plans through an Employee Stock Ownership Plan (ESOP). In some cases, the parent owns only part of the stock in the hospital, and other local investors, sometimes physicians, own the remainder. Sometimes, the ownership of a hospital is structured as a partnership, which will be discussed later in this chapter.

Securities laws and shareholder rights. There is extensive federal and state regulation of the offering and sale of stock and partnership interests. The details of securities laws, shareholders rights, and other restrictions on for-profit corporate behavior are beyond the scope of this book. Shareholders have various rights, including access to corporate books and records[17] and the right to challenge the failure of a corporation to disclose important information that could affect the value of the shares.[18] Corporate officers and other insiders can be held personally liable when they purchase or sell shares based on important information that only they know, but have yet to disclose to other shareholders and the public.[19] Securities laws require that a formal filing be made before certain transactions.[20]

Sarbanes-Oxley Act. The degree of public scrutiny and regulation of corporations increased substantially in 2002. After a series of corporate scandals, Congress enacted the Sarbanes-Oxley Act (SOA).[21] This law directly applies only to companies with publicly traded stock. Full compliance is very costly; as such some smaller publicly traded companies elected to become private.[22] However, some companies (both nonprofit and private for-profit) are not subject to the law, and have voluntarily elected to comply with some of the Act's provisions to achieve confidence of the public, lenders, bondholders, donors, and others relying on the integrity of the governance and financial status of the institution.[23] A few states have passed laws extending to nonprofit corporations certain requirements that are similar to some of the Sarbanes-Oxley requirements.[24]

Recurring corporate finance scandals, involving publicly traded companies, prompted Congress to pass the Sarbanes-Oxley Act.

Section 101[25] of SOA establishes a Public Company Accounting Oversight Board to register, regulate, and inspect accounting firms. Section 107[26] provides that the Board functions under the oversight and authority of the Securities Exchange Commission (SEC). Section 103[27] establishes auditing, quality control, and independence standards for auditing firms. Section 104[28] requires inspections of auditing firms. Section 105[29] provides investigation and disciplinary procedures for auditing firms. Section 108[30] specifies when the SEC is authorized to recognize accounting standards.

Section 201[31] prohibits auditing firms from providing many nonauditing services contemporaneously with an audit, unless they are preapproved by the company's audit committee. Section 203[32] requires that the lead auditor must change at least every five years. Section 204[33] specifies certain items that auditors must report to the audit committee. Section 206[34] precludes the use of any auditing firm that employed individuals in the prior year and who then become key officers of the audited company.

Section 301[35] specifies the composition of the company's audit committee and requires that the committee members be independent, which means that they cannot be paid fees by the company other than a fee for being on the board. Moreover, they cannot be an affiliated person of the company or any subsidiary. The audit committee must be responsible for the appointment, compensation, and oversight of the auditing firm. The audit committee must also have authority to engage independent advisers. ⚑ Section 906[36] requires the CEO and the CFO of the company to certify that financial statements comply with requirements and that each periodic report "fairly presents, in all material aspects, the financial condition and results of operations" of the company. A knowing and intentional violation gives rise to liability. Section 303[37] makes it a crime to fraudulently influence, coerce, manipulate, or mislead an auditor in an effort to make the financial statements materially misleading. Sections 304 and 305[38] impose various penalties for violations, including barring a violator from serving as an officer or director of any publicly traded company.

Section 401[39] specifies additional disclosures that must be made in financial reports, including off-balance sheet transactions and other relationships with consolidated entities that might have a material effect on the financial condition of the company. Section 402[40] prohibits nearly all personal loans to executives and directors. Section 403[41] requires reporting of certain transactions with officers, directors, or 10 percent owners. Section 404[42] requires each annual report to include an internal control report by the management and an attestation by the auditing firm. Companies are required to disclose their codes of ethics and any change or waiver of that code. Section 409[43] requires prompt public disclosure of information on material changes in the financial condition or operations of the company.

Title VIII extends whistle-blower protections to employees who lawfully disclose information.[44]

The details of the SOA and its implementing regulations are beyond the scope of this book.

Taxation. In standard for-profit corporations, there is so-called double taxation of income through the tax on the corporation and the tax on the individual shareholder when dividends are distributed to the shareholders. This double taxation does not apply to corporations that qualify as Subchapter S corporations; they are taxed similar to partnerships with their income being taxed to the individual owners and not at the company level.

MULTIHOSPITAL SYSTEMS. Many hospitals, both for-profit and nonprofit, are part of multihospital systems. For financial and liability reasons, each hospital is usually owned by a distinct entity, and those entities are owned or controlled by a parent corporation. The parent corporation generally retains control over many aspects of the hospital to take advantage of size efficiencies and to achieve other organizational goals. Nonetheless, the parent usually leaves some business decisions to local control by the individual hospital. Various structures are used to ensure that the parent corporation retains control over other entities within the health system.

An example of this control is illustrated when a parent company's board of directors ousted the board at one of its hospitals and substituted itself as the board for the local hospital. The local board had been opposing a merger that the parent favored.[45]

⚑ ARTICLES OF INCORPORATION. The powers of a corporation include only those powers expressed or implied in the articles of incorporation. Some corporations have articles that limit the type of business the corporation can conduct. When a hospital corporation plans to start a new line of business or abandon a present activity, the articles must be examined. Many modern corporations have articles that do not limit the scope of their activities; the articles authorize any business that a corporation can lawfully conduct. Other corporations might find it necessary to amend their articles before substantially changing their scope of business.

Some hospital corporations have articles of incorporation that limit them to hospital-related activities. Activities that provide services for patients, their families, and other visitors, (e.g., gift shops and parking lots) usually are considered hospital-related. The scope of hospital-related activities has tended to expand.

EXPRESS CORPORATE AUTHORITY. Any corporation derives authority to act from the state that creates it. The articles of incorporation state the corporation's purposes and create its express powers to carry out those purposes. State corporation laws also grant some express authority. Acts performed within the scope of this express authority are proper, while expressly prohibited acts are improper.

IMPLIED CORPORATE AUTHORITY. In addition to express authority, implied powers are inferred from corporate existence. Examples of implied authority include the power to have a corporate seal and perpetual existence; to enact corporate bylaws; and to purchase and hold property. For some corporations, these powers can be enumerated as an express authority.

Corporations have implied authority to do any acts necessary to exercise their express authority and to accomplish corporate purposes. While the act need not be indispensably necessary, the act must tend to accomplish the corporate purpose in a manner not otherwise prohibited by law. Benefit or profit to the corporation alone is usually not sufficient.

CONSEQUENCES OF ULTRA VIRES ACTS. When a corporation acts outside its authority, the act is said to be ultra vires. In some states, an ultra vires contract cannot be enforced. Therefore, courts will not require the parties to perform acts specified in the contract. Courts will not order payments for injuries that result from nonperformance of acts that are "ultra vires" of the corporation's authority.

In other states, the defense that an action was ultra vires has been abolished, so these contracts can be enforced, unless a corporate member or the state obtains an injunction to prevent performance of ultra vires acts. For example, the South Dakota Supreme Court ruled, in 2003, in the case of *Banner Health System v. Long*, that the not-for-profit corporation was not allowed to transfer its own proceeds in the form of charitable assets across state lines. The court ruled against Banner Health, after it had sold 27 of its healthcare facilities for the purposes of reinvesting assets in other nonprofit organizations in Colorado and Arizona. That sale met with strong opposition from attorney generals in New Mexico, South Dakota, and North Dakota that argued those charitable assets should remain within the community. Although Banner Health strongly believed that it had authority for the sale and transfer of proceeds, the Supreme Court ruled otherwise, and concluded that the actions were "ultra vires."

In another example, a California appellate court ruled that the articles of incorporation required a nonprofit corporation to continue to operate a hospital, so the board was barred from leasing the hospital and using the rent to operate clinics.[46] Ultra vires acts can also justify revocation of the articles of incorporation by the state, thus dissolving the corporation.

If an ultra vires act is already completed, courts will normally permit the act to stand, unless the state intervenes. The state may obtain an order for the corporation to reverse the ultra vires act by disposing of property, discontinuing services, or taking other steps.

Some courts have imposed a stricter standard on nonprofit corporations because of the public interest in their charitable activities. For example, in New York, a nonprofit hospital is required to obtain judicial approval before selling the bulk of its assets. A New York City hospital entered a contract to sell its assets and agreed to pay the purchaser its out-of-pocket expenses of $800,000 if the court did not approve the sale. In 1999, the court found that the sale did not meet the statutory tests and denied approval.[47] When the purchaser sought to collect its out-of-pocket expenses, the hospital refused to pay, and the purchaser sued. The lower courts ruled that the court's disapproval of the transaction had rendered the entire agreement void, so no money was owed. The highest court reversed this decision and returned the case to the lower court to determine whether the agreement to pay the purchaser was fair, reasonable, and in furtherance of the not-for-profit's purpose.[48] If the lower court found this to be the case, then that provision of the agreement would be valid and the money would be owed. If the court found otherwise, the provision to pay the out-of-pocket expenses would be beyond the hospital's authority and invalid.

CHANGING CORPORATE DOCUMENTS. Articles of incorporation and bylaws are changed for many reasons, including:

1. authorizing expansion into new activities;

2. reorganizing the corporation; and

3. adapting to other environmental changes.[49]

Corporate document changes can be made if proper legal procedures are followed and if other corporate members are treated fairly.

Articles of Incorporation. When changing basic corporate documents, there is a duty to deal fairly with other members of the corporation. If this duty is violated, changes can be declared void. An Arizona court ruled that an amendment to the articles of incorporation was void because of the unfair way it was adopted.[50] A few hours before the vote on the amendment, the board designated 159 new corporate members from among their associates so that, together, they would have more votes than the sixty physicians who were the other corporate members. Although the board had the authority to appoint new members, the court found the appointment of the new members, plus the way their proxy votes were used, to be unfair.

In some states, the legislature that creates the corporation reserves the power to amend the articles of incorporation. The highest court of New York upheld a legislative amendment to the articles of a hospital requiring outgoing board members to be replaced by persons selected by the remaining board members, rather than by a vote of the corporation's membership.[51]

Bylaws. Corporations adopt bylaws to define certain elements of their internal operations. Bylaws cannot expand

> The corporate bylaws describe how corporate authority will be exercised and by whom.

the authority of the corporation. Bylaws can describe how corporate authority will be exercised. Corporations have broad powers to change their bylaws if they comply with the procedures and restrictions in their articles and in state corporation law. In an Illinois case, the Illinois Supreme Court ruled that, because the corporate articles did not forbid the change, a board could amend its bylaws to change the election process for board members and, instead, provide for the selection of replacement board members by present board members.[52]

Agreements not to change corporate documents. In some circumstances, hospitals can enter enforceable agreements not to change their corporate documents. In 1998, at the request of the state attorney general, a Rhode Island court issued a temporary restraining order prohibiting a hospital from changing its corporate bylaws, allegedly contrary to promises made when the attorney general approved a prior hospital merger.[53]

2-1.3 Partnership

A business can be organized as a partnership of several individuals or organizations.

One benefit of a partnership is that income tax is paid only by the partners; no separate income tax is paid by the partnership, avoiding the double taxation effect that applies to income of most for-profit corporations. A limited liability company (LLC) also avoids double taxation. (See **Section 2-1.4**.)

It may be more difficult to arrange partnership affairs to survive the death or withdrawal of a partner, when compared to the transfer of shares in a corporation. Often, partnerships are structured so that one or more partners have an option to buy out others or to require others to buy them out.[54]

One disadvantage of the partnership is that there is no limit on the potential liability of general partners.[55] However, the potential liability of some partners can be limited by creating a "limited partnership." Limited partners are only liable to the extent of their investment, provided they do not participate in the management or operation of the business or interfere with control of the partnership business.[56] Physicians and others who invest as limited partners in hospitals need to limit their involvement in control of the business, unless they are willing to accept the risk of unlimited liability, beyond any insurance coverage that may be in place. There must be at least one general partner whose liability is not limited. Usually, the general partner is a corporation. In multihospital systems, the general partner is usually controlled by the parent corporation.

Liability of general partners can include criminal liability. A New York court ruled that, without any showing of individual culpability, the forty-two partners in a hospital could be charged in an indictment alleging that the hospital permitted an unauthorized person to participate in a surgical procedure and falsified records to conceal the crime.[57]

Partners owe duties to each other. For example, a Texas court ruled that a general partner had a fiduciary duty to notify a limited partner before selling partnership assets.[58]

Some states permit limited liability partnerships (LLPs) that permit partners to fully participate in management and operations, while limiting their individual liability for their partners' acts to their investment in the partnership.

2-1.4 Limited Liability Company ("LLC")

> LLCs are increasingly common in business.

Some states have authorized the formation of LLCs that function like partnerships, without personal liability of the participants for the acts of the company.[59] Similar to

S corporations, LLCs "flow-through" income to the owners and avoid double taxation at the company level. Unlike corporations, LLCs are more flexible and offer different types of ownership structures. Also, LLCs usually are less complicated than corporations in terms of formation and administration. Some courts will intervene to require fair dealing among LLC participants. For example, in 2005, at the request of a participant, a Delaware court ordered the dissolution of an LLC when the corporate documents did not provide a fair exit mechanism.[60]

2-1.5 Sole Proprietorship

A business can also be organized as a sole proprietorship, which means it is owned by one individual who has not incorporated the business. All income of the business is taxed as personal income of the owner, and there is no limitation on the owner's potential, personal liability. Hospitals are seldom operated as sole proprietorships. However, it is not unusual for small professional practices or consulting businesses to be sole proprietorships.

2-2 How Are Governing Bodies Selected and What Are Their Roles and Responsibilities?

Most healthcare entities have a governing board, which has the ultimate governance responsibility. The CEO and the organized medical staff also have roles in governance.

> The board has ultimate, legal responsibility for a legal entity's key activities.

Active involvement of board members is essential, as communities, governmental agencies, and courts hold the board accountable for the entity's activities.

Similar duties of supervision and management apply to boards of for-profit and nonprofit entities. Most governmental boards have similar duties. Each member has a duty to act as a reasonably prudent person would act under similar circumstances, when faced with a similar problem.

In some multihospital systems, a local, hospital board may only have some of the powers and responsibilities of the board of an independent hospital. Likewise, certain powers and responsibilities may be centralized in the board of the parent company. For example, it is common for the bylaws of the parent corporation in a health system to provide for "recommending powers" and "approval powers" for each hospital in the system. In this situation, for example, a hospital's annual capital budget may be "recommended" by the local hospital board for approval by the parent board of the health system. Similar bylaw controls are expressed for other major, corporate decisions that are important for the parent board to be able to control.

This section addresses the following questions:

2-2.1. What are the duties of board members?

2-2.2. When can board members be personally liable for their actions related to the healthcare organization?

2-2.3. How are board members selected and removed?

2-2.1 What Are the Duties of Board Members?

The duties of board members generally include the duty of care and the duty of loyalty. Board members have a duty to exercise reasonable care and skill in the management of the entity's affairs and to act at all times in good faith and with complete loyalty to the entity.

> The most important duties of a board member are the "duty of care" and the "duty of loyalty."

DUTY OF CARE. The duty of care generally requires that board members be informed and make good faith decisions intended to further the organization's purposes. Board members must exercise the degree of diligence, care, and skill that an ordinarily prudent person would in similar circumstances. The details of the standard vary among the states and can also differ somewhat between governmental, nonprofit, and for-profit boards.

While board members are sometimes called trustees, they are usually not held to the strict standards of a trustee of a trust. Instead, they are judged by the standard applicable to directors of other business corporations.[61] Trustees of trusts are generally liable for simple negligence. Directors of business corporations are generally not liable for mere negligence in exercising their judgment concerning corporate business; they are only liable for gross or willful negligence. 🚩 This "business judgment" rule offers board members wide latitude for actions taken in good faith.[62] In 1985, the Delaware Supreme Court ruled that there was a presumption that directors acted with due care.[63]

In some settings, the business judgment rule might not apply. For example, in 2003, the Maryland Insurance Administration Commissioner reviewed the proposed conversion of the nonprofit CareFirst health plan to a for-profit entity, followed by acquisition by another for-profit network. The Commissioner ruled that the business judgment rule did not apply in the regulatory review, so he did not have to show any deference to the board's judgment concerning the public interest. The board was vested with a public trust to address the economic value of the enterprise as a public asset. The Commissioner found that the valuation process used by the board was deficient, and therefore, the board had not used the requisite due diligence.[64] The reorganization was not approved, and the state adopted legislation exerting more control over CareFirst. When the national Blue Cross organization sought to withdraw use of the Blue Cross trademark, the state reached a settlement modifying some of the state control.[65]

The duty of due care requires each board member to fulfill membership functions personally. The board member must attend meetings and participate in the consideration of matters before the board. All board members assume responsibility for board decisions that they do not oppose.

Board members cannot bargain away their duties, nor can they act in ways that would indicate direct, reckless disregard of their fiduciary duty of care. A Minnesota court declared void an agreement by two individuals not to take part in hospital management if elected to the board.[66] A District of Columbia court found that delegation of investment decisions to a committee of board members without any supervision by the board was a failure to use due diligence.[67]

Board members can rely on information and data provided by others, as long as the reliance is reasonable and prudent under the circumstances.[68] When directors know that those presenting the information are not disclosing all relevant information or know that they have a conflict of interest, they have a duty to challenge the information.

The Sarbanes-Oxley Act, discussed earlier in this chapter, places more focus on board responsibility for assuring appropriate financial controls. The law places this responsibility directly upon directors of publicly traded companies.

Preservation of assets. The general duty to act with due care requires reasonable steps to preserve assets from injury, destruction, and loss. Prudent judgment must be exercised to decide and plan how to protect property. That duty can extend to maintenance, adequate insurance, and other protections. The duty applies beyond land, buildings, equipment, and investments to include rights under contracts, wills, and other legal claims and protection against liability losses. In some circumstances, it may be prudent to sell the organization's assets. Such sales are discussed later in this chapter.

🚩 Some healthcare organizations have complete or partial immunity from liability based on their governmental or charitable nature. In some states, liability insurance might not be necessary, but purchasing liability insurance is seldom considered beyond the board's authority. Sometimes, purchasing insurance waives immunity from liability, to the extent of the insurance coverage.

The board has a duty to ensure that taxes are paid. The board should treat tax exemption status as a corporate asset, to be preserved and protected like other corporate assets. There are circumstances where it may be prudent for the board to decide to relinquish tax-exempt status, as it might another corporate asset, if that decision is likely to further the purposes of the corporation.

The board should ensure that the organization's rights are being enforced. This includes collection of bills for services and authorizing appropriate legal suits when justified. The board has a corollary duty to defend the organization from claims. The board must act reasonably under the circumstances. Some claims are not worth pursuing, or should be settled out of court. The board's duty generally will be satisfied if the board conforms to sound business practices.

Basic management duties. The board has general authority to manage the organization's business. This authority is absolute when the board acts within the law. Courts generally leave questions of policy and internal management to board discretion. When departure from board duties is clear, courts will intervene.

🚩 Some of the basic management functions of the board include:

1. selection of corporate officers and other agents;
2. general control of compensation of such agents;
3. delegation of authority to the CEO and subordinates;
4. establishment of policies;

5. exercise of businesslike control of expenditures;

6. providing for planning; and

7. supervision of and vigilance over the welfare of the whole corporation.

Authority to manage the business can be delegated to the CEO or to committees. In practice, much authority is expressly or implicitly delegated. If authority is not delegated or is not conferred on officers by statute or by the articles or bylaws, the board is generally the only body authorized to exercise that authority and to represent the organization. The board has no obligation to delegate any management functions. Any delegation of policy-making functions is subject to revocation by the board at any time. If revocation breaches a contract, the organization might have to pay for injuries caused by the revocation.

The board cannot delegate its responsibility as a board. The power to delegate authority is implied from the business necessities of managing corporations. To avoid abdicating its responsibility, the board should have some procedure to oversee the use of delegated authority.

The board has inherent authority to establish organizational policies. The board can directly exercise this authority by adopting rules, or it can delegate the authority. An example of this policy-making power is a Georgia Supreme Court decision upholding a hospital rule requiring all computerized tomography (CT) scans of hospital patients to be performed with the internal hospital equipment, not with external equipment.[69] Similarly, the Arkansas Supreme Court upheld a hospital rule prohibiting mega-dose vitamin therapy for allergies.[70] A Florida appellate court upheld a board rule that the surgeon, not the anesthesiologist, makes the final decision on whether to attempt emergency surgery.[71] Hospital CEOs, their subordinates, or hospital committees are often permitted to make policies or formulate rules and regulations.

The duty to provide satisfactory patient care is an essential element of the board's duty to operate the healthcare organization with due care, applying equally to for-profit and nonprofit organizations. Through fulfillment of this duty, the basic purpose of the organization is accomplished. Actions required by this duty extend from the purchase of suitable equipment for patient treatment (subject to the organization's financial ability) to the hiring of competent employees. Two important required actions are:

1. selection and review of the performance of medical staff, and

2. selection and supervision of a competent chief executive officer.

The board has the duty to select medical staff members as part of its duty to manage the organization and maintain a satisfactory standard of patient care. The board, while cognizant of the importance of medical staff membership to physicians, must meet its obligation to maintain standards of good medical practice in dealing with matters of staff appointment and discipline.

> The Darling Hospital case established an important precedent for the duties of a hospital board.

In 1965, the Illinois Supreme Court ruled in the famous Darling case that a hospital board has a duty to establish procedures for the medical staff to evaluate, provide advice, and, where necessary, take action when an unreasonable risk of harm to a patient arises from the treatment being provided.[72]

In 1981, a Wisconsin hospital was found liable for failing to exercise due care in evaluating and checking the claimed credentials of an applicant for medical staff membership.[73] This has evolved into the corporate liability doctrine discussed in Chapter 11 "Civil and Criminal Penalties." Hospitals should have appropriate procedures for evaluating the competency of candidates for staff appointments and for determining privileges to be given to physicians. Hospital responsibilities and physician rights concerning medical staff matters are discussed further in Chapter 5 "Medical Staff."

DUTY OF LOYALTY. The board's duty of loyalty requires directors to act in good faith and in a way that they reasonably believe is in accordance with the best interests of the corporation. Good faith is generally a subjective requirement that looks at the person's motivation. Reasonable belief in the best interests of the corporation is both a subjective and objective test. The director must honestly have the belief (subjective), and it must be a belief that a reasonable person could have in the circumstances (objective). Some of the ways that the duty of loyalty can be violated include seizing corporate opportunities, self-dealing, and not disclosing conflicts of interest.

Duty of obedience. Part of the duty of loyalty for nonprofit healthcare organizations is the duty of obedience to the purposes stated in the hospital's charter. It is not always sufficient that the assets continue to be used for any charitable purpose. They generally need to be used for the stated charitable purpose.[74]

Corporate opportunities. A board member who becomes aware of an opportunity for the corporation has a duty not to seize that opportunity for private gain unless the corporation elects not to pursue the opportunity. On November 12, 1993, the Boston Children's Heart Foundation charged

Dr. Bernardo Nadal-Ginard on the misappropriation of corporate funds in excess of $6.562M. Dr. Nadal-Ginard had been President of the board to BCHF and Chairman for the Department of Cardiology. One of many charges involved him setting his BCHF salary without disclosure to the Board. Ultimately, the court decided in favor of BCHF, and also awarded BCHF two-thirds of the costs of the litigation. Another example of inappropriate seizure of a corporate opportunity involved a professional service corporation that contracted to provide services to a hospital in Illinois.[75] While the corporation was negotiating with the hospital to continue the contract, one of the two board members of the corporation created a competing corporation that contracted with the hospital to provide the services. The court found the new contract was an improper seizure of a corporate opportunity, violating the duty of loyalty to the first corporation.

Not all opportunities are subject to this rule. In 1996, the Delaware Supreme Court ruled that there was no duty to present an opportunity to a corporation when the corporation could not afford the opportunity.[76]

As healthcare organizations become involved in corporate ventures with competitors and place their officers on the boards of those corporations, they should structure the relationship so those corporations cannot claim a right to corporate opportunities that the healthcare organization identifies.

Self-dealing. Self-dealing is a contract between the corporation and an entity in which a board member has a financial interest. Statutes in some states specifically forbid some types of self-dealing transactions. One state makes it a crime for trustees or officers of a public hospital to own stock in any company that does business with the hospital.[77] Forbidding all self-dealing can be disadvantageous to the hospital because sometimes the most advantageous contract is with a board member or with a company in which a board member has an interest.[78] Unless there is a statutory prohibition, most healthcare organizations permit contracts between the corporation and a board member if (1) the contract is fair; (2) the interested board member does not speak or vote in favor of the contract; and (3) the board member makes full disclosure of all important facts concerning the interest, including both favorable and unfavorable facts. Courts generally believe the disinterested remainder of the board is able to protect corporate interests.

Courts have the power to declare any self-dealing contract void. On June 25, 2010 Culver Hospital Holdings had a preliminary injunction against defendants, Prospect Medical Holdings, Inc. and Prospect Hospital Advisory Services, Inc. In the beginning all companies had engaged as shareholders with Brotman Medical Company who issued promissory notes. However, Culver, being the minority shareholder, claimed that the majority shareholders were in breach of their fiduciary duties. Most allegations involved Culver claiming that the majority shareholders manipulated Brotman Medical Companies to let them have an unfair involvement with the representation, interests, and control of promissory notes given to all shareholders. For example, there were allegations of self-dealing amongst the majority shareholders related to the promissory notes and the contract terms of certain service agreements. In the end, the court found that no such claims could stand up in court and the injunction was reversed with appeal costs going back to the majority shareholders, Prospect Medical Holdings, Inc. and Prospect Hospital Advisory Services, Inc.

In a South Carolina case, two board members challenged the sale of hospital land to another board member.[79] Although the purchaser did not participate in the final vote on the sale, a board member who was his business associate actively participated. The court declared the sale void because the board members did not meet the standard of loyalty. If the fairness of the contract is questioned, the burden of proving fairness falls upon the board member with the financial interest. For example, the North Carolina Supreme Court required those involved to prove the fairness of a lease of an entire hospital to one board member.[80]

Courts sometimes adopt a strict view of the responsibility of board members of governmental entities. An Arkansas court held that a laundry service contract between a board member and a governmental hospital was improper, even though the board member's bid was the lowest bid.[81] The court allowed the hospital to pay the fair value of services already performed.

Membership on the board of a governmental hospital is a public office. Many courts consider the danger of conflicts of interest of public officers to justify holding all contracts between board members and governmental hospitals improper and invalid even when otherwise advantageous to the hospital. However, the Mississippi Supreme Court ruled that it was not a violation of ethics or the prohibition of contracts with state officers for a public hospital to grant a physician board member medical staff membership and clinical privileges.[82]

Conflict of interest. Conflict of interest is closely akin to self-dealing. There might be a case where no actual self-dealing is involved; however, nondisclosure of conflicting interests can result in statutory penalties or breach of common law fiduciary duties. Boards should require periodic disclosure of all potential conflict of interests.

One of the most extensive judicial discussions of duties of hospital board members concerning self-dealing and conflicts of interest arose out of Sibley Hospital, a nonprofit hospital in the District of Columbia.[83] The board had routinely approved financial arrangements made by two members, the treasurer and the CEO. When the CEO died, the other trustees discovered that substantial hospital assets were in bank accounts drawing inadequate or no interest and the banks were associated with several board members.

The court ruled that board members have a general financial responsibility and breach their duty to the hospital if they (1) fail to supervise actions of persons to whom responsibility for making those decisions has been delegated; (2) allow the hospital to conduct a transaction with a business in which they have a substantial interest or hold a significant position, without disclosing their interest and any facts that would indicate such a transaction would not be in the hospital's best interest; (3) vote in favor of or actively participate in decisions concerning transactions with any business in which they have a substantial interest or hold a significant position; or (4) fail to perform their duties honestly, in good faith, and with a reasonable amount of care and diligence. Although the court found that the board members had breached their duty, it did not remove the members from their positions. Written financial procedures and policies were required, and board members were required to disclose their interests in financial institutions with which the hospital dealt. Written financial statements were to be issued to the board before each meeting. In addition, the court required newly elected board members to read the court's directions.

In 1999, a Delaware court ruled that the board of a health company could be sued for failing to disclose the motives behind an asset sale that favored the majority shareholder. This breach of the duty of loyalty placed the action outside the immunity granted to the directors by the company charter.[84]

Board membership on healthcare entities can be an important service to the community and a rewarding experience, but the days are past when board membership can simply be an honor or a reward for past contributions to the organization. It is increasingly important for board members to be attentive to their duties.

In the healthcare industry, there are several, joint publications by the Office of Inspector General of the Department of Health and Human Services and the American Health Lawyers Association that address the responsibilities of boards and directors. Those titles include:

- Corporate Responsibility and Corporate Compliance (2003)
- An Integrated Approach to Corporate Compliance: A Resource for Health Care Boards of Directors (2004)
- Corporate Responsibility and Health Care Quality (2007)
- The Health Care Director's Compliance Duties: A Continued Focus of Attention and Enforcement (2010)

Those publications are intended to help educate board members of healthcare organizations in carrying out their duties and compliance program oversight obligations. The documents emphasize many points, including an increasing focus on quality of care. For example, the 2007 document referenced above states that a director's obligation to monitor organizational quality of care arises from the following bases:

- Basic duty of care and the director's obligation to oversee day-to-day corporate obligations. Imbedded in the duty of care is the concept of reasonable inquiry. In short, directors should make inquiries of management to obtain information necessary to satisfy their duty of care.
- The related duty to oversee the compliance program.
- The duty of obedience to corporate purpose/mission.

2-2.2 When Can Board Members Be Personally Liable for Their Actions Related to the Healthcare Organization?

CRIMINAL LIABILITY. Board members may be found individually liable for crimes. A federal court affirmed criminal convictions of several members of a county council that served as the county hospital board. They were found culpable for soliciting and receiving kickbacks from architects in return for awarding contracts for a hospital project financed with federal funds. Each board member was sentenced to one year in prison.[85] Board members of for-profit corporations have been convicted of violations of securities laws.[86] A Texas hospital board member was indicted for violating the state open meetings act, but charges were dropped when she agreed to probation.[87]

CIVIL LIABILITY. As discussed earlier, under the "business judgment" rule, board members usually are not liable for simple negligence in exercising their judgment concerning corporate business. Instead, liability is imposed for "gross or willful negligence." The "business judgment" rule offers board members wide latitude for actions taken in good faith.

The business judgment rule was applied to hospital board members in the Sibley Hospital case.[88] In that case, board members were not personally liable for the money lost while hospital funds were earning inadequate interest.

Board members sometimes are named as individual defendants in malpractice suits involving hospitals. A board member is generally not personally liable for medical malpractice, unless the member participated in or directed the wrongful act that caused the injury. A South Carolina court ruled that board members could not be sued for a patient's death during an operation due to erroneous installation of a medical gas system in which the oxygen and nitrous oxide lines were crossed.[89] The court stated that board members would not be personally liable, even if the plaintiff's claims were true. Those assertions included that board members failed to hold meetings, oversee hospital management, and confirm inspection of the medical gas unit. While the hospital could be found liable for the consequences of the crossed lines, the individual board members could not be found liable. However, when a corporate officer or director knows that the corporation is violating a standard of care and fails to take any action, the officer or director can be personally liable. A District of Columbia court ruled that a corporate officer of a clinic could be personally liable to a patient harmed by overnight treatment. The treatment was prohibited by local law, and the officer knew of the practice and did nothing to stop it.[90]

Some federal laws impose personal liability on directors. Directors can be personally responsible for the costs of environmental cleanup of lands owned by the corporation.[91] Board members have been sued under federal law for alleged misuses of pension funds.[92] Sometimes, shareholders bring suits against board members of for-profit corporations.[93]

LIABILITY LIMITS, INDEMNITY, AND INSURANCE. State laws may limit liability exposure of directors of nonprofit corporations for their actions as directors. For example, Illinois forbids suits against uncompensated directors unless their actions are willful or wanton.[94] Even though the liability exposure of board members is limited, defense of these suits can be costly. It is not reasonable to expect board members to serve unless the corporation protects them from defense costs and from liability for good faith actions. Corporations generally can indemnify directors for defense costs, judgments, fines, and other expenses resulting from civil or criminal actions. To do so, the directors must act in good faith and reasonably believe their actions to be lawful and in the corporation's best interests. Many hospitals purchase insurance to protect board members from these costs. This insurance is generally called directors and officers (D&O) liability insurance. However, some D&O insurance policies might not provide the protection they appear to provide. A federal district court ruled that one officer's misrepresentations in the insurance application invalidated the coverage for all directors and officers.[95]

If litigation occurs, selection of defense counsel is very important. The person being defended wants a good defense, and the entity wants the fees to be reasonable. In 1999, a Delaware court dealt with a case where the entity paying the defense counsel misused its authority to select defense counsel. The entity coerced the executive, who was charged with wrongdoing, to accept a weak defense. The Delaware Supreme Court found this to be a violation of the indemnity agreement.[96]

2-2.3 How Are Board Members Selected and Removed?

SELECTION OF BOARD MEMBERS. Board members are selected in several ways. Many boards are self-perpetuating. Vacancies are filled by replacement members selected by the remaining board members. Some boards are elected by stockholders or corporate members. Board members for governmental hospitals are frequently elected by a vote of the people in a governmental subdivision or appointed by elected officials.[97] Usually, terms of office are staggered so that all members are not replaced at the same time. Experienced members can provide continuity of governance.

If board members are not selected in accordance with applicable laws, articles of incorporation and bylaws, courts can declare board actions void. In a Tennessee case, board members were not selected as specified in the articles, and several members did not satisfy membership qualifications.[98] As a result, the court declared a board vote to transfer ownership of the hospital to the county to be void. In 1997, a New York court ordered a new board not to act. That board was elected by a committee established by the CEO. The court authorized the existing board to act until the next annual meeting.[99]

Composition of the board is one of the factors that the Internal Revenue Service (IRS) uses in determining whether a nonprofit corporation is eligible for tax exemption. Therefore, nonprofit hospitals need to consider IRS guidelines in selecting board members.

At least one legislature has controlled the composition of boards. West Virginia requires 40 percent of the board of each nonprofit or local governmental hospital to be consumer representatives selected in equal proportions from small businesses, organized labor, elderly persons, and lower-income persons. Special consideration must also be given to women, racial minorities, and the disabled. Failure to comply can result in loss of the hospital's license, a fine, or imprisonment.[100] Federal courts have ruled that the statute is constitutional.[101]

Sometimes, board composition becomes an issue in litigation or in state challenges to mergers or other corporate transactions.[102] In 1997, a settlement of a California challenge to alleged self-dealing by directors included an agreement that four directors would resign, the board size would be expanded, and more persons would be made eligible to participate in selection of new directors.[103] In 2003, the hospital chain, HCA, Inc., entered a settlement with state pension funds that included an agreement that at least two-thirds of its board would be independent directors.[104]

REMOVAL OF BOARD MEMBERS. Sometimes a board tries to remove a member. The procedure specified in the articles and bylaws must be followed. In New Jersey, a private hospital board member must be provided with notice of the reason for the action and an opportunity to be heard even if the articles and bylaws do not require these steps.[105] In an Oregon case, the court affirmed the removal of a public hospital board member by the board of county commissioners after he was provided with notice and opportunity to be heard.[106] The court ruled that substantial evidence supported the commissioners' decision that the member's lack of candor caused a lack of trust, which diminished his effectiveness as a board member. That was sufficient reason to remove him from the board.

Some board members are removed by public vote. In 2001, it was reported that the behavior of one board member of a California public hospital led to the hiring of a security guard for meetings, installation of a microphone cutoff system, and restrictions on her entering the hospital. In the 2002 election, she was voted out of office.[107]

There are many reasons why boards might want to remove members. Board members who do not attend meetings generally can be removed.[108] Sometimes medical staffs seek to remove board members.[109] In 1997, a California hospital removed two physicians from the board after the physicians filed suit to have the board dissolved.[110]

Sometimes the state attorney general or regulatory agencies seek to change board composition. For example, in 2003, the Minnesota attorney general sought to install additional members on the board of a health system. The system opposed the effort. A compromise was reached where the board agreed to accept an additional person as an adviser, rather than as a board member.[111]

Sometimes, competing groups seek to be recognized as the board of directors. Unless the matters can be settled, courts have to resolve the matter.[112] For example, in 2002, an Alabama judge had to determine who constituted the board of a health services company and appointed an overseer during the transition.[113] In 2003, a New York appellate court affirmed the appointment of a receiver by the court to run the hospital while the courts sorted out a power struggle over control.[114]

2-3 How Are CEOs Selected and What Is Their Role and Responsibility?

The CEO of the hospital is concerned with all the topics covered in this book. The CEO's personal intervention probably will be required when certain legal problems arise. In this section, the CEO's duties, authority, qualifications, and personal liability will be covered.

DUTIES. The CEO is directly in charge of the organization and is generally responsible only to the governing board, but can be responsible to systems officers when the organization is part of a larger system. The CEO is the general supervisor of all operations, and the board delegates to the CEO the authority to fulfill this responsibility. Although areas of responsibility are usually delegated to subordinates, the CEO is primarily responsible for management. The CEO is the agent and usually the employee of the governing board and is subject to its superior authority. Even when the CEO is also a board member or a part owner, the CEO is a board agent and has a duty to carry out board policies.

Many healthcare facilities are part of a larger organization. Both for-profit and nonprofit organizations apply system-wide policies concerning many aspects of management. To promote efficiency, the organization often uses shared services, uniform accounting procedures, centralized support services, and other management methods made possible by the umbrella structure. A CEO in a larger system might or might not be an employee of the larger organization, but will be subject to its policies.

CEOs of governmental organizations are usually appointed public officials. Whether they are public officials or hired supervisors, they are held directly responsible to the governmental body that controls the organization. Their conditions of employment can fall within civil service laws or other statutory requirements.

The CEO has duties imposed by law, delegated expressly or by implication by the board. The CEO is usually charged with certain general management duties. By resolution, bylaw, order, or contract, the board can assign the CEO additional duties.

Chief executive officers sometimes have dual roles in which they also serve as board members.[115] When CEOs are nonvoting members, their positions do not present legal difficulties. When CEOs serve as voting members of a nonprofit hospital board, caution is required; CEOs cannot vote on any question concerning their personal status or compensation.

When a new CEO is appointed, there usually is a duty to abide by the contractual and other commitments of the predecessor until he or she is legally terminated. For example, at one hospital, a new president committed an unfair labor practice by refusing to bargain with a union that the predecessor had voluntarily recognized.[116]

In addition to delegated duties, duties are imposed on CEOs by statutes and regulations.

⚑ As discussed in Section 2-2 on the board of directors, there is increasing focus on the personal responsibilities of the CEO for financial controls. The Sarbanes-Oxley Act requires the CEO to personally certify financial statements of publicly traded companies. CEOs of all corporations are increasingly expected to focus attention on these areas and to make sure that there are appropriate financial controls in place. CEOs are expected to avoid conflicts of interest.

In addition, CEOs are expected to assure that their institutions maintain an environment that is committed to compliance with legal requirements. An effective compliance program can be one part of this effort.

AUTHORITY. The CEO's primary source of authority is the governing board. The board delegates to the CEO the duty, authority and responsibility to manage the hospital. Board resolutions or policies usually specify the CEO's authority or grant special authority to deal with certain problems. Authority can be granted in legal documents governing the hospital, such as hospital articles or bylaws, while some aspects of the

CEO's authority can be covered in an employment contract. State statutes or regulations can provide for certain administrative powers of the office of the CEO.

Authority can be either express or implied. Express authority is a written or oral grant giving the CEO power to accomplish certain objectives. The scope of the CEO's express authority can be as broad or as limited as the board desires. Implied authority consists of those powers that are conveyed, along with express authority, so that desired objectives may be accomplished. The CEO possesses powers and duties that may be properly delegated. The board cannot delegate authority that it does not possess, and it cannot delegate certain responsibilities that are nondelegable. For example, in most states, the board usually cannot delegate the power to grant appointments to the medical staff, except on a temporary basis.

The CEO can do many things that are not challenged, either because people are unaware of the actions or because people with the right to challenge or forbid them do not do so. A CEO acting beyond authority is subject to several possible legal consequences, including being dismissed by the board in accordance with its established rules; being sued by the hospital for breach of an employment contract and for any resultant financial damage to the hospital; being held liable by employees or other persons for damages resulting from negligence or intentional wrongdoing; and being subject to prosecution for violating criminal laws.

SELECTION, EVALUATION, AND TERMINATION. Governing boards are responsible for selecting CEOs to act as their agents in hospital management. Boards that try to run hospitals without CEOs are subject to extensive criticism and risk legal liability.[117] Some boards use interim CEOs while searching for permanent CEOs.[118] The board must select a competent CEO who will set and maintain satisfactory patient care standards. Minimum standards for CEOs are contained in some hospital licensing statutes and regulations and in some statutes creating governmental hospitals. Where legal requirements exist, the CEO must satisfy those requirements.

After appointing a CEO, the board must periodically evaluate the CEO's performance. The board may be liable if it fails to exercise proper oversight of the CEO's performance. When not satisfied with performance, the board should take appropriate action.

When the board is considering replacement of the CEO, it should follow the procedures under applicable state law, the articles of incorporation, and the bylaws.

However, some courts have declined to intervene when bylaws were not followed. For example, in a Louisiana case, a public hospital CEO was terminated without the warning and opportunity to correct deficiencies required by the bylaws. The Louisiana Supreme Court refused to order reinstatement because the CEO could not show that he had been harmed by the deviation from the bylaws.[119] Similarly, the Minnesota Supreme Court refused to intervene when a CEO was discharged.[120] The applicable law provided that the CEO served "at the pleasure of the county board," and he was not entitled to a hearing. In some circumstances, CEOs of public hospitals may be entitled to due process.[121]

Generally, courts will not order reinstatement of removed CEOs, but the hospital will generally be liable to pay damages when the removal breaches a contract[122] or is done in an improper manner.[123] On the other hand, in certain circumstances, some severance packages can be unenforceable.[124]

Under some state laws, it is possible for someone other than the board or a court to order removal of a CEO. A New York court ruled that the state's Department of Health had authority to order removal of a CEO for not being sufficiently qualified by education or experience.[125] In 2002, the board removed the four top administrators of an Arizona hospital when it received a petition signed by 138 hospital shareholders demanding the removal of the executives and threatening recall of the board if it did not act.[126] Nursing home administrators are another example because they are licensed under state law. This license can be revoked by the state for patient abuse or other violations of the licensing law.[127]

LIABILITY. CEOs can be criminally or civilly liable for certain actions related to their employment.

Criminal liability. CEOs involved in fraudulent and other illegal schemes can be held criminally liable, similar to those in other industries.[128] For example, a Florida CEO caused a hospital to issue twenty-one checks, fraudulently endorsed them, and appropriated the proceeds which exceeded $850,000. He was sentenced to twenty-five years in prison.[129] Embezzlement or bribery also is a federal crime when committed by an agent of an organization that received over $10,000 under a federal program in a one-year period.[130] A hospital CEO was convicted under this law.[131] In 2002, a federal appellate court upheld the conviction of a former West Virginia hospital administrator for misusing hospital funds on a shopping center and other ventures.[132]

Fraudulent schemes can also result in forfeiture of benefits. An Ohio court ruled that a CEO who had embezzled funds forfeited all compensation, including deferred compensation, during the period of culpable conduct.[133]

Some prosecutors pursue criminal charges against CEOs for treatment of patients. The Wisconsin Supreme Court upheld the conviction of a nursing home CEO for abuse of residents, but reversed a conviction for reckless conduct causing death.[134] One resident had died of exposure after walking away from the facility. Other residents lost weight and developed bed sores. The state claimed this was due to understaffing by the CEO. Several other nursing home administrators have been convicted of patient abuse or neglect.[135]

Civil liability. CEOs, like other members of society, can be individually liable for their own wrongful actions that injure others.

A CEO can be liable for injuries caused by a subordinate when the CEO negligently supervises or carelessly hires the subordinate. If not personally at fault, the CEO is not liable for injuries caused by subordinates.[136] Employers are liable for the injuries wrongfully caused by their employees since the organization is the employer, not the CEO. Likewise, because CEOs are employees of the organization, the organization can be liable for wrongful acts of CEOs. If the organization pays money to an injured person as the result of a lawsuit, it usually has the right of repayment from the employee who caused the injury. Healthcare organizations seldom exercise this right of indemnification beyond the employee's individual insurance coverage. Liability issues are discussed in Chapter 11 "Criminal and Civil Penalties."

CEOs are not personally liable for contracts they make on behalf of the organization when acting within their authority to contract. When CEOs engage the organization in contracts that exceed the CEO's authority to do so, the organization is not always bound by the contract. CEOs can be personally liable to the other party to the contract for loss resulting from the failure to bind the organization. CEOs are not liable if the organization ratifies the contract and adopts it as its own. CEOs generally are not liable for unauthorized acts if: (1) they innocently believe they have authority to make the contract and (2) the organization presents the CEO's position with such apparent authority that the other contracting parties reasonably believe the CEO has said authority. If the organization creates this apparent authority and innocent third parties are misled, the law imposes liability on the organization. If the other contracting parties should have suspected the CEO lacked authority, they are required to make appropriate inquiries. If the inquiries would have disclosed the lack of authority, no recovery is allowed against the organization.

The CEO can be liable to the other contracting parties, even when the CEO has apparent authority, but makes the contract with intent to defraud. In a Mississippi case, an insurance company sought to recover excessive amounts it had paid to a hospital because the CEO had padded bills.[137] The court found both the CEO and the hospital liable to repay overcharges.

CEOs can be liable civilly or criminally for breach of duties imposed on them by statute. For example, when a license or permit is required before the hospital performs certain acts, often the CEO is required to obtain the license or permit. Failure to obtain it can lead to fine or imprisonment. CEOs can also be required to submit certain reports to the state. While hospital CEOs are seldom fined personally for failure to discharge such a statutory duty, the possibility does exist. In a Mississippi Supreme Court case involving the same CEO and hospital as the case discussed here, a state auditor sought to force the CEO and the hospital board to repay county hospital funds that had been spent without authority.[138] The court analyzed each type of expenditure the state auditor claimed to be unauthorized. The court agreed with the auditor's findings. The CEO and board members were required to make repayment.

Some laws impose personal liability on CEOs. For example, the CEO can be personally liable for unpaid wages under the Fair Labor Standards Act.[139] A New York federal court ruled that a new CEO could be personally sued for sex discrimination for excluding the vice president/chief nursing officer from vice presidential meetings, refusing to meet with her, and firing her.[140]

The federal government and some states have provided some official immunity from personal civil liability for some public officials when following a legal mandate (i.e., performing a "ministerial duty") or when exercising administrative judgment (i.e., performing a "discretionary duty"). Rules vary considerably, and courts tend to restrict the application of immunity doctrines.

MANAGEMENT CONTRACTS. Some hospital boards have entered into contracts with other corporations to manage their hospitals. The CEO often is provided by the management corporation. The board retains ultimate authority, so no change is required in the hospital's license in most states. The authority of the board and the contractor should be carefully defined. The board should preserve authority to terminate the contract without significant, financial penalties.

Management contracts may be difficult to terminate. A Mississippi board tried to terminate a management contract after the management company increased hospital rates and revised the hospital budget without the board approval required in the contract. The court ruled that termination was not justified because the board had authority to nullify the action, without terminating the contract.[141]

Hospitals that have or plan to issue tax-exempt bonds need to consider the IRS requirements limiting the length and other features of such contracts.[142]

Often hospitals enter management contracts because of confidence in individuals who own or manage the management corporation. However, they do not want to transfer management oversight to a third party, so they restrict assignment of the contract. Restrictions on assignment of contracts with corporations can easily be avoided by sale of the management corporation's stock. Unless provided in the contract, the hospital will not be able to terminate the contract if a stock sale occurs. An Alabama hospital sued when all the stock of a management company was sold to another company, despite a prohibition of assignment of the management contract. The court upheld a temporary injunction of transfer of hospital funds, conversion of the hospital into a substance abuse facility, and movement of property out of the hospital.[143] Hospitals should not rely on courts to provide these protections. It is prudent to require the management corporation to inform the hospital of all substantial changes in stock ownership and to give the hospital the option to terminate the contract after such a change.

2-4 What Are the Licensing and Accreditation Requirements for Healthcare Organizations?

Hospitals and other healthcare entities are among the most extensively regulated institutions. They are regulated by all levels of government and by numerous agencies within each level. They occasionally are confronted with conflicting mandates. Such conflicts are often a reflection of underlying conflicts in societal goals. There also are private entities that develop standards and accredit institutions that meet applicable standards.

LICENSURE. Licensure differs from accreditation in that a license presumes the presence of a governmental authority. Thus, licensure also implies some degree of governmental regulation. For example, the state legislature grants an administrative agency authority to adopt standards hospitals must meet, grant licenses to complying institutions, and enforce continuing compliance. Hospitals are not permitted to operate without a license. Persons who operate hospitals that violate the standards can lose their licenses or be fined or penalized. Numerous other healthcare entities must obtain state and local licenses and comply with licensing standards. Some of the entities that are licensed include health maintenance organizations, nursing homes, ambulatory surgery centers, hospices, home health agencies, and clinical laboratories.

The discussion of licensure of institutions is divided into:

- Authority to license (2-4.1)
- Scope of regulations (2-4.2)
- Inspections (2-4.3)
- Violations and sanctions (2-4.4)

ACCREDITATION. In contrast, accreditation is granted by nongovernmental organizations and usually is not legally mandated. Accreditation is discussed in section 2-4.5.

> Medicare's Conditions of Participation have an important influence on how healthcare institutions structure administrative and clinical functions and delegate authority within the institution.

MEDICARE CONDITIONS OF PARTICIPATION. Medicare also has standards called Conditions of Participation[144] that apply to healthcare organizations including hospitals; immediate care facilities for the mentally handicapped; home health agencies; comprehensive outpatient rehabilitation facilities; organ procurement organizations; rural primary care hospitals; and providers of outpatient physical therapy and speech-language pathology services. The Conditions of Participation frequently are referred to verbally as the "COPs" (with each letter pronounced individually). These are not licensing standards, per se, but healthcare organizations must meet the COPs to qualify for receipt of Medicare payments. The Medicare law provides

that hospitals accredited by The Joint Commission (TJC) or American Osteopathic Association (AOA) are deemed to meet most COPs, unless a special Medicare inspection finds noncompliance.[145] Institutions have mixed results in their efforts to use the courts to stop termination of Medicare participation.[146]

OTHER PRIVATE STANDARDS. Some institutions are subject to other private standards that they have voluntarily accepted. For example, hospitals operated by the Roman Catholic Church are subject to the rules of the Church, including canon law. Canon law has played an important role in many of the decisions of these institutions.[147]

2-4.1 Authority to License

State governments have "police power" that grants them authority to regulate healthcare institutions.

LEGISLATION. All states have enacted hospital and nursing home licensing statutes, and many have statutes that license other healthcare entities.

AGENCY ACTIONS. Licensing statutes usually grant an agency authority to adopt standards, grant licenses, and revoke licenses or impose other penalties when standards are violated. Licensing statutes and regulations must be a reasonable exercise of the police power and must not deny due process or equal protection of the laws.

Authority to adopt rules. To be enforceable, agency rules must be within authority properly delegated to the agency by statute. Rules must be adopted using the state procedure for administrative rule-making. This procedure usually includes public notice of proposed rules and an opportunity for public comment before they become final. In some circumstances, emergency rules are exempt from some requirements, but rules can be declared unenforceable when rules are not eligible for the emergency rule process.[148] Some states require additional steps, such as an economic impact statement, before a rule becomes enforceable.[149]

Rules are difficult to challenge if they are within the statutory authority of the agency, do not violate due process by being vague or arbitrary and are adopted through proper procedures. For example, detailed hospital licensing rules were contested in Pennsylvania on the grounds that they were an attempt by the Department of Health to take away "management prerogatives" of hospital boards and administrators. The Pennsylvania Supreme Court decided that the department had statutory authority and upheld the rules, even though they might supplant part of traditional management authority.[150]

When rules conflict with statutory law or exceed the rule-making authority granted to the agency, courts will invalidate the rules. For example, in 2004, a Florida appellate court struck down a rule that required supervision of nurse anesthetists in outpatient facilities because the agency had exceeded its delegated authority.[151]

Not a taking of private property. Most actions that states take under licensing laws have been interpreted not to constitute a taking of private property, so the constitutional requirement of just compensation for takings generally does not apply.[152]

2-4.2 Scope of Regulations

The scope of licensing regulations varies depending on the entity being regulated.

HOSPITALS. Hospital licensing regulations usually address hospital organization, requiring an organized governing body or some equivalent, an organized medical staff, and an administrator. Regulations can require general hospitals to provide certain basic services, including laboratory, radiology, pharmacy, and some emergency services. Regulations generally require use of adequate nursing personnel. They also can establish standards for facilities, equipment, and personnel for specific services, such as obstetrics, pediatrics, and surgery. Regulations can also address safety, sanitation, infection control, record preparation and retention, and other matters.

Objective versus subjective rules. All standards do not have to be in objective numerical terms to satisfy due process requirements, but some courts are reluctant to uphold overly subjective rules. A New York court found that several nursing home rules violated due process requirements because they were so subjective that they did not provide adequate notice of the conduct required.[153] The invalidated rules required sewage facilities, nursing staff, and linen laundering to meet the "approval" and "satisfaction" of the Commissioner of the Department of Health. No objective standard was included in the rules. The court upheld another rule that required nursing staffing be based on "needs of the patients." The court considered this to be an objective standard because it believed the needs would be "reasonably well identifiable by all competent observers." Courts recognize that in some areas objective standards either are impossible to develop or, if developed, would be too arbitrary. Thus, courts have upheld enforcement of some subjective standards if fairly applied. This is illustrated by another New York nursing home case in which somewhat vague standards were upheld because the actual violations clearly deviated from the rules' objective and the agency had provided written explanations of violations to the owners.[154]

Building integrity. Another focus of hospital licensure is the integrity of hospital buildings. This topic is addressed in Chapter 3 "Regulation of Healthcare Facilities, Equipment, Devices, and Drugs."

Exceptions and waivers. Administrative agencies usually have authority to permit exceptions to their rules by granting a waiver or variance. Undue hardship can result from unbending application of the rules, and the public's best interest might not be served by inflexibility. For example, one state required all hospital rooms to have showers for patients. When the rules were written, apparently no one thought of intensive care units where patients could not use showers, so it was necessary for hospitals to obtain waivers until the rule could be changed. Waivers are sometimes needed because some rules, especially building and fire codes, are so complex that individual rules contradict each other when applied to unusual situations. It might be necessary to obtain an official determination of which rule to follow and a waiver for conflicting rules. Waivers also may be necessary to implement innovative practices. Waivers are generally granted only when:

(1) there is a substantial need for relief from the rule;

(2) the public purpose will be better served by the exception; and

(3) the exception will not create a hazard to the health and well-being of patients or others that is excessive in light of the public purpose being served.

Bed count. Hospital licenses usually specify the number of beds the institution is permitted to operate. The license can specify that certain numbers of beds be approved for a specified use. In 1992, a Washington court ruled that a lessee/operator of a nursing home facility did not breach its lease or other agreements by entering into an agreement with the state agency to reduce its number of licensed beds.[155] States usually look to the licensed operator for issues related to licenses. Thus, owners and lenders need to clearly specify in their contracts with operators any limits on their authority to modify the license.

Have regulations gone too far? Sometimes questions are voiced concerning whether the state has gone too far in its regulation. Occasionally, courts will ask an agency to reconsider the scope of its regulations. In 1999, a California appellate court ordered a state agency to reconsider regulations that would have required friends of a paralyzed woman to obtain a state license before she could live with them.[156] The regulation required any nonrelative to obtain a license before caring for a disabled person.

When regulatory agencies act contrary to or beyond the scope of their statutory authority, courts may strike down the regulations. See section 2-4.1 for examples.

2-4.3 Inspections

Generally, licensing agencies have a right to make unannounced inspections of certain licensed entities, including hospitals. Applying for the license is viewed as consent to reasonable inspections, within the scope of the agency's authority. However, some inspections, even with search warrants, can be conducted in such a manner as to violate the rights of those searched. For example, with a search warrant, an agency searched a birthing clinic at 2 a.m., rousting newborns and parents and photographing them. The basis for the search was suspected practice of medicine without a license. A federal appellate court ruled that those involved in the search could be sued for violating the civil rights of the newborns and parents.[157]

In most jurisdictions, licensing agencies have discretion as to whether and how to inspect. They cannot be held liable for either failure to inspect or failing to discover or correct deficiencies through inspections.[158]

> The two basic elements of "due process" are: i. notice and ii. the opportunity to be heard.

2-4.4 Violations and Sanctions

DUE PROCESS. Two fundamental elements of due process are "notice" and "an opportunity to be heard." Unless deficiencies immediately threaten life or health, the state can close a licensed institution or impose other penalties for licensing law violations only after giving adequate notice of violations and an opportunity to be heard. For example, a New York court ordered the hospital-licensing agency to provide a hearing before deciding not to renew a hospital's license; even though the hospital lacked many basic services.[159]

OPPORTUNITY TO CORRECT DEFICIENCIES. Some state statutes and regulations require licensing agencies to give the licensed entity an opportunity to correct deficiencies before imposing sanctions. Although this opportunity is not constitutionally required, it must be provided when guaranteed by state law. Otherwise, sanctions that are imposed will be invalid, unless immediate action by the licensing agency was justified by deficiencies that threatened life or health.

DEGREE OF VIOLATION AND LESSER PENALTIES. Some licensing statutes recognize that it might not be in the public's interest to revoke a healthcare institution's license for minor violations. These statutes provide a range of lesser penalties, such as monetary penalties, and reserve license suspension or revocation for "substantial" violations. Definitions of substantial violation vary from state to state. However, in every state sufficiently serious violations lead to license revocation.[160]

AGENCY ENFORCEMENT DISCRETION. Generally, agencies have discretion whether to impose penalties authorized by law. Private individuals cannot compel licensing agencies to take action.[161] However, agencies cannot exercise this discretion on discriminatory grounds, such as religion. A federal appellate court permitted the orthodox Jewish operators of a nursing home to sue state officials for allegedly citing their facility for reasons the nursing home viewed as discrimination against their religion.[162]

⚑ SCOPE OF JUDICIAL REVIEW. When a licensing agency makes an adverse decision, the institution can generally seek judicial review. In most states, courts will only review the administrative hearing record and generally will not accept additional evidence. Courts will only overrule the agency if the decision was beyond the agency's authority, the agency did not follow proper procedures, or the evidence was insufficient to justify the decision.

CRIMINAL PENALTIES. In addition to fines and license suspension or revocation, some licensing statutes provide criminal penalties for violations. For example, the operation of a hospital without a license can lead to criminal prosecution.

PROTECTION OF THOSE WHO REPORT VIOLATIONS. The law protects persons who report violations to appropriate government agencies. For example, after visiting a nursing home in which they were planning to place a relative, family members reported what they believed to be violations to federal and state officials. The home lost its Medicare and Medicaid eligibility and was not allowed to admit new patients during a state investigation. The nursing home sued the family members, claiming that they had conspired and tortiously interfered with its business relationships. A federal appellate court upheld a summary judgment in the family members' favor because any interference was justified by the greater public interest in the proper operation of such facilities.[163]

USE OF LICENSING VIOLATIONS IN OTHER CONTEXTS. Private individuals sometimes use licensing requirements in disputes with hospitals and other healthcare entities. A hospital avoided honoring a contract with a nurse staffing agency because the agency did not have a license required by state law.[164] Employee groups and others sometimes use regulatory violations to try to apply pressure.[165] Violations of regulations can sometimes be used to help establish liability in malpractice suits.

2-4.5 Accreditation

Accreditation is a private function that is not legally mandated. Private accrediting bodies assess whether participating institutions and programs meet their standards and issue accreditation to those that do meet the standards. ⚑ The primary focus of most of the accreditation standards is the quality and safety of services, but many also include additional documentation and other requirements.

Some states accept accreditation by some organizations, such as The Joint Commission (TJC) – formerly called the Joint Commission on Accreditation of Healthcare Organizations (JCAHO) – as the basis for full or partial licensing of some providers without further state inspection. Other states coordinate accreditation and state compliance surveys to reduce the burden of multiple inspections. In most states, there is no link between accreditation and institutional licensure.

Accreditation can be helpful with federal compliance. Hospitals that are accredited by TJC and other accrediting organizations are "deemed" to meet Medicare's COPs. Thus, they can continue to participate in Medicare, unless a Medicare validation survey finds noncompliance with the COPs. On the other hand, Medicare will sometimes approve hospitals that have lost accreditation.[166]

Another incentive for accreditation is that some healthcare payers will only contract with providers that are accredited.

TJC includes representatives from the American College of Physicians; American College of Surgeons; American Dental Association; American Hospital Association; American Medical Association; and American Nurses Association; plus representatives of the public. Healthcare organizations seeking accreditation apply to TJC, pay a fee, and submit to a survey to determine whether they satisfy TJC standards. TJC publishes accreditation manuals, such as the Comprehensive Accreditation Manual for Hospitals.[167] TJC also accredits long-term care facilities; mental health, chemical dependency, and mental retardation/developmental disabilities services; home care; and pathology and clinical laboratory services. When an organization ceases to meet the standards, it can lose its accreditation.[168]

TJC continues to experiment with new approaches to assess and improve quality of services from the patient's perspective. For example, surveys use a "tracer methodology" that tracks many aspects of the care of individual patients through their entire stay in the facility.[169]

The American Osteopathic Association (AOA) accredits osteopathic hospitals and functions similarly to TJC. There are accrediting bodies for other healthcare entities. For example, the National Committee for Quality Assurance (NCQA) and TJC accredit managed care entities.

2-5 What Are the Issues When an Organization Is Converted from One Type into Another?

Healthcare organizations sometimes change their legal basis and operations. This section discusses some of the legal issues related to conversions between organizational structures. Conversions may be between:

- Private nonprofit and for-profit (2-5.1)
- Public and private (2-5.2)
- Certain types of public organizations (2-5.3)
- Secular and religious organizations (2-5.4)

Many of these conversions stir up controversy and have led to judicial, legislative, and political challenges.

2-5.1 Conversion Between Private Nonprofit and For-Profit

Generally, it is not possible to convert a nonprofit legal entity into a for-profit legal entity. Conversions to for-profit status are accomplished by sale of the business or sale of the assets of the nonprofit entity to a for-profit entity. Likewise, a for-profit entity can sell its business or assets to a nonprofit entity. In the alternative, a for-profit entity can generally be converted into a nonprofit entity if its owners all agree or the contrary minority owners are bought out; in essence, the assets are donated to the charity.

Most of the controversy arises when a for-profit entity takes over a nonprofit facility. The public has contributed to the facility over the years directly through donations and indirectly through tax exemptions. In most cases, the focus is on whether the price is fair and the public interest will continue to be served. Legal battles have been fought over whether technical legal requirements had been met. Many states have enacted laws that require review and approval of such transactions by state officials, usually the attorney general. For the most part, the focus in such challenges is on fairness of price and ongoing public interest in services.[170]

Often, after such transactions the nonprofit entity continues and makes grants or supports services with the proceeds from the sale.[171] These arrangements have generally been upheld.[172] In 1998, the Kansas Supreme Court upheld such an arrangement.[173] A church organization founded a hospital and later made the hospital independent to avoid church liability for hospital operations. The church sought to dissolve the hospital corporation after the hospital sold its assets to a for-profit entity. The church wanted a portion of the assets distributed to the church, rather than using the assets for other, local healthcare purposes. The court rejected the challenge.

Nonprofit Blue Cross and Blue Shield plans in many states have been sold to for-profit entities. In some states, this has been controversial. Several states have ultimately permitted the sales to occur.[174] Some states have barred the proposed sales. For example, in 2003, the Kansas Supreme Court blocked a proposed sale, and it was dropped.[175]

2-5.2 Conversion Between Public and Private

The legality of the sale, lease, or other transaction that places public healthcare organizations under the control of private entities generally is determined by the scope of the laws that create the public entities. Occasionally, state constitutional principles are invoked to challenge these transactions. For example, a North Carolina court ruled that a county hospital could not be leased to a for-profit management company because (1) there was no statutory authority for the lease and (2) the lease violated a restriction in the deed to the property that would have caused the loss of the property.[176] A Michigan appellate court upheld the leasing of a county hospital because the patient care management system in the contract fulfilled the county's duties.[177] The Kansas Supreme Court upheld the transfer of assets of a county hospital to a nonprofit corporation

because the transfer was authorized by statute.[178] In 1997, the Oklahoma Supreme Court approved a fifty-year lease of the university hospital to a for-profit entity.[179]

Sometimes the legal analysis focuses on public interest more than on technical statutory issues. For example, the Georgia Supreme Court upheld the restructuring of a county hospital in which the hospital was leased to a nonprofit corporation governed by a board controlled by members of the county hospital authority.[180] The court found that public hospitals needed to be more competitive and that the lease would enable the hospital to better serve the public health needs of the community.

EMINENT DOMAIN. Federal and state governments have the power to take property for public uses. This is called the power of eminent domain. States can authorize local governmental entities to exercise eminent domain. This power can be used in some circumstances to involuntarily convert a private healthcare facility into a public facility. The Fifth Amendment to the Constitution requires the payment of just compensation in exchange for the property. When there is no agreement on compensation, generally courts set the compensation. Eminent domain can be used to take ongoing businesses as well as land.[181]

Hospitals are usually confronted with eminent domain only when highway authorities take a strip of land to widen a bordering road or when a public hospital authority takes neighboring land for expansion. There have been a few cases where the taking of whole hospitals has been proposed and even completed. In 1981, the Michigan Supreme Court approved the taking of a neighborhood to build an automobile manufacturing plant. A hospital was taken as part of the project and was demolished.[182] In 1985, the city and county of St. Louis, Missouri decided that they needed to replace their inner-city public hospitals. Instead of building a new hospital, they proposed to use eminent domain to take a hospital from a for-profit chain and convert it to a public hospital. Faced with the takeover, the chain sold the hospital to a new nonprofit corporation organized by the city and the county to operate the hospital.[183] In 1991, there was a proposal in Miami, Florida to use eminent domain to take a hospital for public use, but the proposal was abandoned.[184] In 2002, in California, the newly formed North Sonoma County Hospital District acquired the Healdsburg General Hospital through eminent domain.[185]

In 1998, a Missouri appellate court ruled that a city could not use eminent domain to take over a nonprofit private hospital after it reduced services and entered a lease to another operator. The court found the property already committed to a public use and ruled that eminent domain could not be used to convert such property to another public use without specific statutory authority.[186]

2-5.3 Conversion Between Types of Public Organizations

Some states have converted hospitals that were state agencies into separate public entities, frequently called hospital authorities.[187] The hospitals remain public, but are governed by a separate public board rather than by the state administrative structure. These reorganizations are usually done to give the institutions more flexibility to deal with market forces than is generally permitted for state agencies.

2-5.4 Conversion Between Secular and Religious Organizations

Conversions from secular to religious and from religious to secular organizations have led to controversies. Some controversies have arisen over control and distribution of proceeds from the transaction.[188] The controversy has often arisen from the desire of religious organizations to prohibit the use of their facilities for certain procedures that violate their beliefs.[189] Religious organizations have had difficulty entering into transactions that result in the loss of that control.[190] However, some sales of religious hospitals have occurred with loss of control.[191] Mergers present more difficulties because religious organizations generally will not participate in the ongoing operations of facilities that violate their beliefs. This has led to community concerns about the loss of the availability of services, especially when alternate providers are not available.[192] In some cases, it has been possible to offer alternate providers.

2-6 What Are the Issues When an Organization Is Merged, Consolidated, Sold, or Dissolved?

MERGER OR CONSOLIDATION. Merger occurs when two or more organizations combine and one organization is the survivor. Consolidation (sometimes, referred to as a merger in a nonlegal sense) occurs when two or more organizations combine and the result is an entirely new organization.[193] In a merger or consolidation, the resulting organization assumes the assets and liabilities of the former organizations.

SALE. As distinguished from a merger or consolidation, an organization or facility can be sold to an entirely new owner. Sometimes the new owner is a large organization,[194] and sometimes it is another local organization. Usually, the organization or facility is sold as an ongoing enterprise, with the buyer assuming the assets and liabilities. Sometimes only the assets are sold, and the liabilities are not assumed.[195] This is often not feasible, if the intention is to continue to operate the facility, due to requirements for new licenses, other regulatory approvals, and Medicare, Medicaid, and other payer contracts.

When the owner of a facility is excluded from Medicare and Medicaid participation, one way for the facility to restore Medicare and Medicaid participation is to change the ownership of the facility to an owner that is not excluded. Sometimes, the Center for Medicare and Medicaid Services (CMS) will permit a facility to participate during a transition period while the sale is arranged, provided the facility is operated by independent management that is acceptable to CMS.[196]

PROCEDURES. Proper procedures must be followed in a merger, consolidation, or sale, including procedures required by statutes applicable to constituent organizations, by their articles of incorporation, and by their bylaws. Some governmental organizations have special requirements that can include a vote of the residents of the governmental unit, such as a county. When one or more of the organizations is dissolved in the process, the applicable procedures for dissolution must be followed.

The selection of the proper approach requires a careful analysis that is beyond the scope of this book.[197] Combination or sale of organizations is often difficult in practice[198] due to (1) philosophical differences, especially religious orientations; (2) reduction in the number of leadership positions; (3) necessary changes in established relationships with physicians, employees, suppliers, the community, and others; and (4) the technical complexity of developing an acceptable approach and obtaining necessary approvals.

Some of the legal considerations in developing the proper approach are restrictions in state statutes, articles of incorporation, bylaws, deeds, grants, gifts, loans, collective bargaining agreements,[199] and other legal documents. For example, if certain changes are made, Hill-Burton hospital construction grants must be repaid to the government,[200] some loans can require accelerated repayment,[201] and some depreciation can be recaptured by governmental payers.[202] There are also complex tax and reimbursement implications. One hospital had to take its case to the California Supreme Court to establish that it did not have to pay sales tax on the sale of its furnishings and equipment as part of the sale of all the assets of the hospital.[203] Proper notification must be given to licensure, certificate-of-need, and other regulatory authorities, and in some cases licenses, certificates, or permits must be obtained. Some types of changes may even involve federal securities law.

In 1950, the Attorney General of Missouri challenged a proposed affiliation of Barnard Free Skin and Cancer Hospital with Washington University Medical Center that involved relocation of Barnard Hospital.[204] The Attorney General asserted that the proposal violated several provisions of the gifts and will of Mr. Barnard that established and supported Barnard Hospital. The Missouri Supreme Court found the affiliation contract to be a reasonable exercise of board powers that did not violate any conditions imposed by gifts and bequests of Mr. Barnard.

In any merger, consolidation, or sale, consideration must be given to antitrust implications.

DISSOLUTION. An organization can dissolve as part of a closure or a reorganization, merger, or consolidation. The facility might continue to operate under another organization, or the services of the facility might be relocated or discontinued. Proper procedures must be followed in any dissolution, including the procedures in applicable statutes, articles of incorporation, and bylaws. The procedures usually include (1) an approval mechanism, which can involve a state administrative official, a court, or a vote of a specified percentage of the stockholders, members of the corporation, or others; (2) a notification of creditors and others; and (3) clearance by governmental tax departments. Some governmental hospitals have special requirements, including a vote of the residents of the district, city, or county that supports the organization.

Usually, authority to dissolve a corporation is clear, but it is sometimes questioned. In one case, a Missouri nonprofit hospital association was chartered to provide hospital services to employees of a railroad company. The association sold the hospital and distributed some of the assets to members. Several members challenged the dissolution of the association.[205] The court found the dissolution to be beyond the authority of the board under Missouri law because it was not: (1) expressly authorized by the articles of incorporation; (2) approved by a sufficient percentage of the membership; and (3) of imperative necessity because

there was a reasonable prospect of successfully continuing the business.

Dissolution can be voluntarily initiated by the organization. In appropriate circumstances, dissolution of a corporation can be involuntarily initiated by outside parties, such as the state attorney general, shareholders, directors, and creditors.[206] A person called a receiver can be appointed to operate the organization during the process of involuntary dissolution. Appointment of a receiver is not limited to dissolutions. For example, as mentioned earlier in this chapter, receivers can be appointed on a temporary basis while a court sorts out who should control the organization.

The corporation continues for a period of time after it ceases to operate the facility so that the affairs of the organization can be concluded. After satisfying any debts and liabilities that have not been assumed by other organizations, the assets of the corporation must be distributed. Some assets might have to be returned to those who gave them to the organization or to others designated by the donor because of restrictions imposed on the grants or gifts. All other assets are distributed under a plan of distribution that might have to be approved by an administrative agency or court. Assets of for-profit corporations are distributed to their shareholders. Assets designated for charitable purposes usually are distributed to a corporation or organization engaged in activities that are substantially similar to those of the dissolving corporation.

Some nonprofit corporations choose not to dissolve after selling their assets. They continue as independent foundations and use the proceeds of the sale of the business for other charitable purposes, such as paying for indigent patient care.[207]

2-7 What Are the Issues When an Organization Closes or Relocates a Hospital or Other Delivery Location?

A hospital building or other healthcare facility can close:

1. as part of relocation of functions, or

2. without transfer or replacement of the functions because they are viewed as excess capacity or are otherwise not viable.

Some communities have challenged planned closures, causing costly delays. Although courts have seldom found the plans illegal, some of the challenges have resulted in modifications of the plans. It is important to determine community concerns when planning relocations and closures and to consider reasonable accommodations to avoid protracted challenges.[208]

One example that illustrates the extent of such opposition to closure is the Wilmington Medical Center cases. Two private hospitals in Wilmington, Delaware planned to replace a large portion of their inner-city facilities with one suburban hospital. Various opponents conducted an extensive legal challenge. The plaintiffs claimed that the Medicare law had been violated,[209] that the relocation discriminated against minorities in violation of Title VI of the Civil Rights Act[210] and against the handicapped in violation of section 504 of the Rehabilitation Act of 1973,[211] and that an environmental impact statement was required under the National Environmental Policy Act of 1969.[212] A court required the Secretary of the Department of Health, Education, and Welfare (HEW) [now known as the Department of Health and Human Services] to determine whether there had been any violation and report to the court.[213] The court ruled that an environmental impact statement was not required because no major federal action was involved.[214] The court also ruled that it was constitutional to provide different administrative appeal procedures for recipients and complainants under Title VI and section 504.[215] The court ruled that the approval of the project by HEW was not subject to judicial review and that it was constitutional not to provide an appeal mechanism for opponents.[216] In the fifth reported decision, the court ruled that there was a private right of action to challenge discrimination that violated Title VI or section 504 and ordered a trial.[217] After the trial, the court ruled that the evidence was adequate to justify the reorganization and relocation plans, so they did not violate Title VI or section 504.[218]

In 1998, a federal appellate court rejected a challenge to a municipal hospital's relocation of services for disabled children, finding that neither the Rehabilitation Act of 1973 nor the Americans with Disabilities Act guaranteed a level of medical care for the disabled.[219]

In June 2001, the inpatient services at D.C. General Hospital were closed. The closure was challenged in court by two city council members and a union representing medical residents. In 2001, a federal court rejected the challenge finding that the union did not have standing and the city council members did not state a legal claim because the closure was properly authorized.[220]

Some courts find that neither patients nor citizens have a right to challenge decisions to close public hospitals.[221] However, when a court ordered consultation with a community board, failure to do so was contempt of court.[222]

In the 1960s, a New Jersey city sought to enjoin a hospital from relocating outside city limits.[223] The court denied the injunction because the hospital had legally amended its articles of incorporation to give the board authority to relocate and the board had found relocation to be in the hospital's best interests.

Sometimes, a hospital is forced to close. In 2001, Edgewater Medical Center in Chicago closed. Medicare had stopped making payments after a grand jury indicted three doctors, an administrator, and a hospital management firm for an alleged kickback scheme. When a federal judge refused to order reinstatement of Medicare payments, all patients were discharged or transferred and the hospital closed.[224]

Frequently, public hospitals must obtain voter approval before closing. Some consumer groups have attempted to use these requirements to preclude the hospital from changing its services. For example, a group in Texas sought to bar the closure of an emergency room of a public hospital. The group asserted that closing the emergency room was equivalent to closing the hospital, so the requirement of a vote before the hospital could be closed should apply. In 1984, a Texas appellate court ruled that they were not equivalent, so no vote was required.[225]

Some states impose a duty on local government to provide certain healthcare services. In 2004, a federal appellate court affirmed a preliminary injunction stopping Los Angeles County from closing a county rehabilitation center or reducing the number of beds at the USC Medical Center. The court said that the proposed closures could violate the state law duty of California counties to provide healthcare services.[226]

Contractual barriers to closure can also arise. An Arkansas court ordered a corporation to continue to operate a nursing home on a certain property because it had promised to do so in the lease to the property.[227] In many circumstances, federal law requires that employees be given sixty days' notice of closings or large layoffs.[228] Employee challenges to closure have generally been unsuccessful.[229] However, a federal appellate court ruled that a union was entitled to obtain copies of some transactional documents from a hospital that was closing so that the union could determine worker rights and union responsibilities.[230]

Care must be taken in carrying out the closure. In 1994, all the patients were discharged from a small Florida hospital, but the hospital did not relinquish its license or its Certificate of Need while it pursued sale or consolidation. The city sued to stop the closure. After the hospital refused to treat an emergency patient, the state initiated proceedings to revoke the hospital license. The owner settled with the state, agreeing to transfer ownership by a specified date or lose the license.[231]

2-8 What Is the Impact of Bankruptcy Law?

When healthcare entities and those with whom they do business become insolvent, it is important to understand the impact of bankruptcy law. Even large hospital systems can become insolvent and enter the bankruptcy process. In 1998, a multihospital system, the Allegheny Health, Education & Research Foundation, entered bankruptcy.[232]

There is a specific definition of "bankruptcy" under the law that is important to understand.

For bankruptcy purposes, the Federal Bankruptcy Reform Act of 1978 (called the Bankruptcy Code) defines an entity as being "insolvent"

...when the sum of such entity's debts is greater than all of such entity's property, at fair evaluation, exclusive of (i) property transferred, concealed, or removed with intent to hinder, delay, or defraud such entity's creditors, and (ii) property that may be exempted.[233]

When a healthcare organization discovers that it is insolvent and cannot work out other arrangements with creditors, it might need to consider bankruptcy to settle its accounts and obligations on an equitable and final basis. Because bankruptcy proceedings are entirely a matter of federal law, they are conducted in the federal district courts under the provisions of the Bankruptcy Code. A petition for bankruptcy can be voluntary (by the debtor) or involuntary (by creditors).

Nonprofit corporations, including charitable hospitals, are not subject to involuntary bankruptcy, so they cannot be forced into bankruptcy by creditors. Domestic insurance companies are not subject to bankruptcy. This restriction has led to numerous cases addressing whether health maintenance organizations and life care facilities are insurance companies and, thus, not subject to federal bankruptcy. The answer depends on how they are treated under state law.[234] The only remedy available to creditors of a nonprofit organization or insurance company is through applicable state law proceedings.[235] Nonprofit corporations, but not insurance companies, can voluntarily petition to be adjudicated bankrupt. Petitions can be filed with the federal court even after state insolvency proceedings have been instituted.

Bankruptcy does not necessarily require the corporation to dissolve. While bankruptcy under Chapter 7 of the Bankruptcy Code does include dissolution, bankruptcy under Chapter 11 permits the corporation to continue to operate through modification of its operations and debt structure.

Most lawsuits and other actions against a debtor must stop when the petition for bankruptcy is filed. This is called the automatic stay.[236] There are some exceptions,[237] and there are procedures creditors can follow to seek permission from the bankruptcy court to pursue their suits, which is generally called "relief from stay."[238] There are also restrictions on others changing their relationships with the debtor. For example, a federal appellate court ruled that a malpractice insurance company could not cancel insurance without notice to the court and creditors.[239] Clauses in contracts that purport to permit termination of the contract if a party becomes bankrupt are not enforceable in most situations.

When the healthcare organization is a creditor, it is important to file in the bankruptcy court most claims against the debtor, or the claims might be lost.

In bankruptcy proceedings, the debtor or bankruptcy trustee has an opportunity to either assume or reject most ongoing contracts.[240] This has been most controversial when debtors have sought to reject collective bargaining agreements, so the Bankruptcy Code was amended to permit rejections of collective bargaining agreements only after a court finds that certain conditions exist and approves the rejection or modification.[241] Limits have also been placed on the modification of insurance benefits to retired employees.[242]

The bankruptcy court has broad powers to undo many transactions that occurred before the filing if they are considered to be preferences that favor one creditor improperly or fraudulent transfers that tried to place assets improperly beyond the reach of creditors.[243]

When a provider continues to operate after filing for bankruptcy, the state Medicaid agency can recoup prior overpayments by reducing current payments. Even though this would be forbidden if done by a private payer,[244] in 1989, the U.S. Supreme Court ruled that a state agency can do so. This is because the Eleventh Amendment to the

Constitution grants states immunity from money judgments, even those handed down by bankruptcy courts. The bankruptcy court cannot order the state to make full payment unless the state waives its immunity by filing a claim against the provider.[245] The U.S. Department of Health and Human Services (HHS) is also permitted to recoup Medicare overpayments.[246] While bankruptcy courts have broad powers to extend contractual deadlines in some circumstances, they generally cannot extend Medicare deadlines.[247]

While a debtor is in the bankruptcy process, it must obtain court approval for some major business transactions.[248] In some cases, the bankruptcy court appoints a trustee to operate the business.[249]

For the debtor to successfully leave Chapter 11 bankruptcy, the bankruptcy court must approve a plan for its reorganization.[250] The debtor has the first opportunity to propose a plan. If the plan is not approved, the creditors can develop a plan.

In a Chapter 7 bankruptcy, the assets of the debtor are sold, and the proceeds are distributed to the creditors in a priority order specified by the Bankruptcy Code.

An important aspect of either Chapter 7 or Chapter 11 is that the court can discharge some debts so that the debtor is protected from personal liability on those debts.[251] Liability for willful and malicious injuries is not discharged in bankruptcy. But in 1998, the U.S. Supreme Court ruled that medical malpractice judgments generally do not fit in this exception, so they are discharged in bankruptcy.[252]

In 2005, the bankruptcy law was extensively amended to reduce the opportunity for the discharge of debts and to make other changes.[253]

Another extraordinary power of the bankruptcy court is that it can authorize the sale of property free and clear of prior interests in the property. Thus, it can extinguish liens, mortgages, judgment, writs of garnishment, and the like. The applicability of bias claims and settlement obligations to the property can also be extinguished. In 2003, a federal appellate court upheld a bankruptcy court ruling that the purchaser of the assets of a bankrupt airline company would be free and clear of twenty-nine bias claims against the bankrupt company. Those claims were pending before the Equal Employment Opportunity Commission for ongoing obligations arising out of settlement of prior claims.[254]

The bankruptcy court has broad latitude in the sales arrangements that can be approved. In 2003, a federal bankruptcy court authorized an auction to sell a hospital in the District of Columbia.[255]

Healthcare organizations facing insolvency need to evaluate their options in order to avoid personal liability for directors and to use the available bankruptcy proceedings to optimize the outcome. Directors can be personally liable for voting to authorize improper distribution of corporate assets when the corporation is insolvent.[256] Bankruptcy proceedings can often be used to implement changes that permit the institution to survive.

Chapter Summary

This chapter covered many topics that are essential for a basic understanding of legal and business principles that form the foundation for the organization of healthcare resources in America. The topics interrelate to a certain degree. That is because health care is both an essential industry that involves many parties and interests and is also heavily regulated. Therefore, it is important to understand sources of legal authority, such as licensure laws and federal oversight activities, and responsibilities assumed by individuals (e.g.,

officers and directors) who manage and govern healthcare organizations. The content in this chapter did not require extensive updating, in part, because many of the principles, including those established by certain court decisions, are fundamental to the organization of healthcare organizations. However, it is important to bear in mind how the law changes over time and places specific responsibilities on those who dedicate their working lives to serving patients and overseeing healthcare organizations.

Key Terms and Definitions

Articles of Incorporation - A document required to be filed with a government agency, usually the Secretary of State, if the owners of a business want it to be recognized as a corporation. The "articles" (sometimes called a Certificate of Incorporation) must contain certain information, as required by state law.

Bankruptcy - A federally authorized procedure that allows a debtor (e.g., person, corporation, or municipality) to discharge all liability for debts in return for making court-approved arrangements for partial repayment. In general, one is "bankrupt" when one is unable to pay debts as they are due (referred to as "cash flow insolvency") and a court issues a legal order intended to remedy the bankruptcy.

Board of Directors - A body of individuals, elected or appointed, who jointly oversee the activities of a company or organization. The board's activities are determined by the powers, duties, and responsibilities typically delegated to the board by the bylaws of the company or organization. In short, the board "governs" the company, but does not "manage" it.

Duty of Care - As used in corporate law, this is part of the fiduciary duty owed to a corporation by its directors. It means that a director owes a duty to exercise good business judgment and to use ordinary care and prudence in the operation of the business.

Duty of Loyalty - As used in corporate law, this duty requires fiduciaries of the company (principally, its directors) to put the corporation's interests ahead of their own.

Police Power - This is the basic authority of governments to make laws and regulations for the benefit of their communities. The police power is granted to the states through the Tenth Amendment to the U.S. Constitution.

Subchapter S - A choice, under the Internal Revenue Code, that allows a small corporation to be treated like a partnership for taxation purposes.

Ultra Vires Doctrine - In the law of corporations, if a corporation enters into a contract that is beyond the scope of its corporate powers, the contract is illegal.

Instructor-Led Questions

1. What are six types of organizations, and what are their major differences?

2. How do government organizations differ from other organizations?

3. How does government control nonprofit corporations?

4. What rights do shareholders have in for-profit corporations?

5. Discuss the impact of Sarbanes-Oxley on for-profit corporations and nonprofit corporations.

6. What is the source of corporate authority, and what happens when a corporation acts outside that authority?

7. What are the duties of board members? Discuss the "business judgment" rule. When can board members be held personally liable?

8. What are some of the potential self-dealing and conflicts of interest of board members, and how should they be addressed?

9. What are the duties of CEOs, and what is the source of their authority? When can CEOs be held personally liable?

10. What is the difference between licensure and accreditation? What is the role of the Medicare Conditions of Participation?

11. When can licensing rules be successfully challenged?

12. What are the consequences for violating licensing rules?

13. Discuss the issues involved in converting an organization from one type to another. What approvals are usually required?

14. Discuss the issues involved when an organization ceases to exist due to merger, consolidation, sale, or closure. What approvals are usually required?

15. Discuss the issues involved when a service delivery site is closed or relocated. What are the grounds for challenging such changes?

16. What is the effect on the provider and others when a healthcare provider seeks protection under the bankruptcy law?

Endnotes

1 In re *Advisory Opinion to House of Representatives*, 519 A.2d 578 (R.I. 1987).

2 *Arkansas Hosp. Ass'n v. Arkansas State Bd. of Pharmacy*, 297 Ark. 454, 763 S.W.2d 73 (1989).

3 *Haggerty v. Pudre Health Servs. Dist.*, 940 P.2d 1105 (Colo. Ct. App. 1997).

4 *County of Cook v. Ayala*, 76 Ill. 2d 219, 390 N.E.2d 877 (1979).

5 *Cleveland Surgery Ctr. v. Bradley County Mem. Hosp.*, 30 S.W.3d 278 (Tenn. 2000).

6 *Professional Home Health & Hospice, Inc. v. Jackson-Madison County Gen. Hosp. Dist.*, 759 S.W.2d 416 (Tenn. Ct. App. 1988).

7 *Rowe v. Franklin County*, 318 N.C. 344, 349 S.E.2d 65 (1986).

8 *Fulton Nat'l Bank v. Callaway Mem. Hosp.*, 465 S.W.2d 549 (Mo. 1971); accord *Board of Trustees v. Peoples Bank*, 538 So. 2d 361 (Miss. 1989) [copier lease void because not approved by purchasing department].

9 *Itasca County Bd. of Comm'rs v. Olson*, 372 N.W.2d 804 (Minn. Ct. App. 1985).

10 E.g., *Memorial Hosp. Ass'n, Inc. v. Knutson*, 239 Kan. 663, 722 P.2d 1093 (1986) [private lessee not subject to Kansas open meetings law]; *State* ex rel. *Fostoria Daily Review Co. v. Fostoria Hosp. Ass'n*, 40 Ohio St. 3d 10, 531 N.E.2d 313 (1988) [private lessee subject to Ohio open records law]; *Memorial Hosp. - West Volusia Inc. v. News-Journal Corp.*, 729 So. 2d 373 (Fla. 1999) [operator of public hospital subject to open meeting requirements].

11 E.g., *Tauber v. Commonwealth*, 255 Va. 445, 499 S.E.2d 839 (Va. 1998) ["This Court long ago recognized the common law authority of the Attorney General to act on behalf of the public in matters involving charitable assets."]; *Hatch v. Allina Health Sys.*, No. MC 01-004160 (Minn. Dist. Ct. Aug. 14, 2004), as discussed in HEALTH L. RTPR. [BNA] Aug. 21, 2004, 1303 [confirming authority of attorney general to oversee "corporate rehabilitation" of health plan].

12 E.g., WIS. STAT. § 165.40 [certain hospital acquisitions].

13 J. Chesto, AG approves Waltham Hospital deal, BOSTON HERALD, May 25, 2002, 20. Unfortunately, the plan did not succeed, and the hospital was closed about a year later. E. Sweeney, Hospital draws last breath: The sad end of an era for patients and employees, BOSTON GLOBE, July 27, 2003, 1.

14 Judge rules Kansas can't sue over Health Midwest CEO pay, AP, Jan. 17, 2003.

15 *Banner Health System v. Long*, 2003 SD 60, 2003 S.D. LEXIS 86.

16 State settles lawsuit with Banner Health, AP, Mar. 18, 2004.

17 E.g., *Estate of Purnell v. LH Radiologists*, 90 N.Y.2d 524, 664 N.Y.S.2d 238, 686 N.E.2d 1332 (1997).

18 E.g., J. Jacob, Shareholders file class-action lawsuit against United, AM. MED. NEWS, Sept. 7, 1998, 18 [alleged withholding of information about Medicare HMO losses].

19 E.g., Oxford Health faces NY AG probe on top of shareholder class actions, 6 HEALTH L. RPTR. [BNA] 1758 (1997) [alleged insider trading; alleged officers sold stock before announcing loss] [hereinafter HEALTH L. RPTR. [BNA] cited as H.L.R.].

20 E.g., Columbia/HCA plan to spin off hospitals is outlined in filing, WALL ST. J., Dec. 15, 1998, B8 [filing with Securities Exchange Commission discussed].

21 Pub. L. No. 107-204, 116 Stat. 745 [codified at 15 U.S.C. §§ 7201 et seq. & scattered sections of the U.S.C.]

22 A.R. Sorkin, Kissing the public goodbye, N.Y. TIMES, Aug. 8, 2004, 4BU [first year of Sarbanes-Oxley – 99 public companies became private; second year – 59].

23 See A. Field, Some private companies embrace tougher rules, N.Y. TIMES, July 15, 2004, C6; Nonprofits pressured to stay "ahead of the curve" in governance, H.L.R., Aug. 5, 2004, 1149; M.W. Peregrine, J.R. Schwartz & W.W. Horton, Advising the nonprofit audit committee, H.L.R., May 26, 2005, 726.

24 E.g., Uniform Supervision of Trustees for Charitable Purposes Act, CAL. GOV. CODE §§ 12581 et. seq.

25 15 U.S.C. § 7202.

26 15 U.S.C. § 7217.

27 15 U.S.C. § 7213.

28 15 U.S.C. § 7214.

29 15 U.S.C. § 7215.

30 15 U.S.C. § 7218.

31 15 U.S.C. § 78j-1(g)-(i).

32 15 U.S.C. § 78j-1(j).

33 15 U.S.C. § 78j-1(k).

34 15 U.S.C. § 78j-1(l).

35 15 U.S.C. § 78j-1(m).

36 18 U.S.C. § 1350.

37 15 U.S.C. § 7242.

38 15 U.S.C. §§ 77t, 78u, & 7243.

39 15 U.S.C. § 78m(j).

40 15 U.S.C. § 78m(k).

41 15 U.S.C. § 78p.

42 15 U.S.C. § 7262.

43 15 U.S.C. § 78m(l).

44 18 U.S.C. § 1514A.

45 P.A. McKay, Health system trustees oust hospital's board, WASHINGTON POST, Apr. 10, 1999, V3.

46 *Queen of Angels Hosp. v. Younger*, 66 Cal. App. 3d 359, 136 Cal. Rptr. 36 (2d Dist. 1977); *Banner Health System v. Lawrence E. Long*, 663 N.W.2d 242 (2003).

47 In re *Manhattan Eye, Ear & Throat Hosp.*, 186 Misc. 2d 126, 715 N.Y.S.2d 575 (Sup Ct. 1999).

48 *64th Assocs., L.L.C. v. Manhattan Eye, Ear & Throat Hosp.*, 2 N.Y.3d 585, 813 N.E.2d 887, 780 N.Y.S.2d 746 (2004).

49 E.g., Queen of Angels board amends bylaws to eliminate need for bishop's approval, 7 H.L.R. 493 (1998); B. Japsen, Baylor system blocked sale by bylaw change, 27 MOD. HEALTHCARE, June 23, 1997, 3 [5 of 13 hospitals changed articles, barring university from appointing their boards].

50 *Hatch v. Emery, I Ariz. App.* 142, 400 P.2d 349 (1965); contra *Harris v. Board of Directors*, 55 Ill. App. 3d 392, 370 N.E.2d 1121 (1st Dist. 1977) [board could unilaterally amend bylaws to become self-perpetuating despite desire of members to remove board].

51 In re *Mt. Sinai Hosp.*, 250 N.Y. 103, 164 N.E. 871 (1928).

52 *Westlake Hosp. Ass'n v. Blix*, 13 Ill. 2d 183, 148 N.E.2d 471, appeal dismissed, 358 U.S. 43 (1958). *Muhammad v. Muhammad-Rahmah*, 844 N.E.2d 49 (2006), 363 Ill. App. 3d 407.

53 *Rhode Island v. Lifespan*, No. 98-2801 (R.I. Super. Ct. June 16, 1998), as discussed in 7 H.L.R. 1103 (1998).

54 E.g., P. Limbacher, Optioned in Fargo, 27 MOD. HEALTHCARE, Sept. 1, 1997, 12 [one partner required to buy out another pursuant to option].

55 See, e.g., S. Harris, Don't get stuck picking up your business partner's tab, AM. MED. NEWS, Feb. 23, 1998, 16.

56 See Annotation, Liability of limited partner arising from taking part in control of business under Uniform Limited Partnership Act, 79 A.L.R. 4TH 427.

57 *People v. Smithtown Gen. Hosp.*, 92 Misc. 2d 144, 399 N.Y.S.2d 993 (Sup. Ct. 1977); *State of Kansas, Appellee, v. L. Stan Naramore, D.O., Appellant No. 77,069 Court of Appeals of Kansas* 25 Kan. App. 2d 302; 965 P.2d 211; (1998 Kan. App. Lexis 79).

58 *Hughes v. St. David's Support Corp.*, No. 03-00197-CV (Tex. Ct. App. Mar. 6, 1997), as discussed in 6 H.L.R. 549 (1997).

59 E.g., WIS. STAT. ch. 183; IOWA CODE ch. 490A; e.g., *Jana L. v. West 129th Street Realty Co., LLC*, 2005 NY Slip Op.50199U, 6 Misc. 3d 1026A (Sup. Ct. Feb. 22, 2005) (unpub.).

60 *Haley v. Talcott* (Del. Ch. Dec. 16, 2004), 8 DEL. L. WEEKLY 4 (Jan. 26, 2005).

61 E.g., *Stern v. Lucy Webb Hayes Nat'l Training School*, 381 F. Supp. 10003 (D. D.C. 1974); but see *People v. Larkin*, 413 F. Supp. 978 (N.D. Cal. 1976) [trust principles applied]. *Lucy Thomas, Individually and as Personal Representative of the Estate of Mildred Thomas, Deceased Appellant, v. The HOSPITAL BOARD OF DIRECTORS OF LEE COUNTY, d/b/a Lee Memorial Health Systems, Inc.*; Kenneth W. Backstrand, M.D.; Kenneth W. Backstrand & Associates, M.D., P.A.; Clara Hughes, R.N.; Jeanie Smith, R.N.; Robert Arnall, M.D.; and Robert McCurdy, P.A., Appellees. No. 2D08-1671. District Court of Appeal of Florida, Second District. May 7, 2010. Rehearing denied August 17, 2010.

62 For discussion of cases concerning business judgment rule, see K. Christophe, Recent developments in the law affecting professionals, officers, and directors, 33 TORT & INS. L. J. 629, 644-47 (Wint. 1998).

63 *Aronson v. Lewis*, 473 A.2d 805 (Del. 1985).

64 T.K. Hyatt & E.S. Kornreich, Legal ethics: Governance reforms for nonprofit organizations: Sarbanes-Oxley and beyond, presented at Am. Health Lawyers Ass'n 2004 Annual Meeting; the text of the Commissioner's report is posted at http://www.mdinsurance.state.md.us/jsp/availPubInfo/Reports.jsp10?divisionName=Reports&pageName=/jsp/availPubInfo/Reports.jsp10 [accessed Sept. 11, 2004].

65 P. Dickens, Gov. Ehrlich signs CareFirst reform legislation, triggers lawsuit, DAILY RECORD (Baltimore, Md.), May 23, 2003; MD. INS. CODE §§ 14-102 et seq.; T. Stuckey, Settlement reached in state dispute with Blue Cross, AP, June 6, 2003.

66 *Ray v. Homewood Hosp.*, 223 Minn. 440, 27 N.W.2d 409 (1947).

67 *Stern v. Lucy Webb Hayes Nat'l Training School*, 381 F. Supp. 1003 (D. D.C. 1974); *McCall v. Scott* 239 F.3d 808 (2001) United States Court of Appeals, Sixth Circuit. Argued: December 7, 2000.

68 E.g., N.Y. NOT-FOR-PROFIT CORP. LAW § 717(b).

69 *Cobb County-Kennestone Hosp. v. Prince*, 242 Ga. 139, 249 S.E.2d 581 (1978); *Conrad v. Medical Bd. Of California* 48 Cal. App.4th 1038 (1996) Court of Appeals of California, Fourth District, Division One August 19, 1996.

70 *Brandt v. St. Vincent Infirmary*, 287 Ark. 431, 701 S.W.2d 103 (1985).

71 *Martin Mem. Hosp. Ass'n, Inc. v. Noble*, 496 So. 2d 222 (Fla. 4th DCA 1986).

72 *Darling v. Charleston Comm. Mem. Hosp.*, 33 Ill. 2d 326, 211 N.E.2d 253 (1965), cert. denied, 383 U.S. 946 (1966).

73 *Johnson v. Misericordia Comm. Hosp.*, 99 Wis. 2d 708, 301 N.W.2d 156 (1981).

74 See M.G. Tebo, A matter of trust: Art and chocolate mix over the issue of who should benefit from an endowment, 89 A.B.A.J. 24 (Jan. 2003); *Commonwealth v. Barnes Found.*, 398 Pa. 158, 159 A.2d 500 (1960); in re *Milton Hershey School Trust*, 807 A.2d 324 (Pa. Commw. 2002).

75 *Patient Care Servs., S.C. v. Segal*, 32 Ill. App. 3d 1021, 337 N.E.2d 471 (1st Dist. 1975); *Boston Children's Heart v. Nadal-Ginard* 73 F.3d 429 (1996) United States Court of Appeals, First Circuit. Heard August 4, 1995.

76 *Broz v. Cellular Info. Sys., Inc.*, 673 A.2d 148 (Del. 1996); see also *Robinson Leatham & Nelson, Inc. v. Nelson*, 109 F.3d 1388 (9th Cir. 1997) [restructuring transaction not a corporate opportunity, so no violation for former director to relinquish interest in entity related to restructuring].

77 N.C. GEN. STAT. § 14-234 (1986 Supp.); N.C. Att'y Gen. Op. Dec. 6, 1982.

78 See V. Rouch, Proposed policy change at Wilmington, N.C., hospital questioned by trustees, MORNING STAR (Wilmington, N.C.), Mar. 22, 2003 [local debate over proposal to ban all business with companies owned in part by directors or senior staff].

79 *Gilbert v. McLeod Infirmary*, 219 S.C. 174, 64 S.E.2d 524 (1951).

80 *Fowle Mem. Hosp. v. Nicholson*, 189 N.C. 44, 126 S.E. 94 (1925).

81 *Warren v. Reed*, 231 Ark. 714, 331 S.W.2d 847 (1960); *Culver Hospital Holdings v. Prospect Medical Holdings, Inc. Culver Hospital Holdings, Plaintiff and Respondent, v. Prospect Medical Holdings, Inc. et al.*, Defendants and Appellants. No. B226382. Court of Appeals of California, Second District, Division Five. Filed October 24, 2011.

82 *State by Mississippi Ethics Comm'n v. Aseme*, 583 So. 2d 955 (Miss. 1991).

83 *Stern v. Lucy Webb Hayes Nat'l Training School*, 381 F. Supp. 1003 (D. D.C. 1974).

84 *O'Reilly v. Transworld Healthcare, Inc.*, 745 A.2d 902 (Del. Ch. Ct. 1999).

85 *United States v. Thompson*, 366 F.2d 167 (6th Cir.), cert. denied, 385 U.S. 973 (1966).

86 E.g., F. McMorris, Ex-chairman of Health Management is convicted of directing fraud scheme, WALL ST. J., May 11, 1998, B4 [misstatements in financial results for two years].

87 Hospital board member could face fine, jail time, HOUSTON CHRONICLE, Apr. 11, 2003, A36; Hospital board member gets probation open meeting violation, AP, Sept. 27, 2003.

88 *United States v. Thompson*, 366 F.2d 167 (6th Cir.), cert. denied, 385 U.S. 973 (1966); accord, *Beard v. Ackenbach Mem. Hosp. Ass'n*, 170 F.2d 859 (10th Cir. 1948).

89 *Hunt v. Rabon*, 275 S.C. 475, 272 S.E.2d 643 (1980).

90 *Vuitch v. Furr*, 482 A.2d 811 (D.C. 1984).

91 42 U.S.C. §§ 9601(20)(a), 9607(a); *Sidney S. Arst Co. v. Pipefitters Welfare Educ. Fund*, 25 F.3d 417 (7th Cir. 1994).

92 E.g., *Herman v. Health Care Delivery Servs., Inc.*, No. 98-CV-06460 (C.D. Cal. filed Aug. 7, 1998), as discussed in 7 H.L.R. 1324 (1998) [Labor Dept. suit against healthcare organization, eight board members for allegedly transferring pension funds to business].

93 *Oran v. Stafford*, 226 F. 3d 275 (3d Cir. 2000) [failure to show violation by directors].

94 ILL. REV. STAT. ch. 32, § 108.70(a).

95 *Shapiro v. American Home Assur. Co.*, 584 F. Supp. 1245 (D. Mass. 1984); but see *Shapiro v. American Home Assur. Co.*, 616 F. Supp. 900 (D. Mass. 1984) [due to severability provision in policy, Securities Act policy must provide coverage despite fraud of insureds].

96 *Chamison v. Healthust, Inc.*, 735 A.2d 912 (Del. Ch. 1999), aff'd, 748 A.2d 407 (Del. 2000).

97 E.g., *State ex rel. Board of Trustees of City of North Kansas City Mem. Hosp. v. Russell*, 843 S.W.2d 353 (Mo. 1992) [board members selected by mayor with approval of city council, could be removed by city government].

98 *Bedford County Hosp. v. County of Bedford*, 42 Tenn. App. 569, 304 S.W.2d 697 (1957). http://www.ghanaweb.com/GhanaHomePage/NewsArchive/artikel.php?ID=219357.

99 Court rules for board in Health Rite fight, N.Y. TIMES, Dec. 27, 1997, B14.

100 W. VA. CODE § 16-5B-6a; *Christie v. Elkins Area Med. Ctr., Inc.*, 179 W. Va. 247, 366 S.E.2d 755 (1988).

101 *American Hosp. Ass'n v. Hansbarger*, 594 F. Supp. 483 (N.D. W. Va. 1984), aff'd, 783 F.2d 1184 (4th Cir. 1986), cert. denied, 479 U.S. 820 (1986); see also *Blue Cross v. Foudree*, 606 F. Supp. 1574 (S.D. Iowa 1985) [upholding required subscriber majority on board].

102 See Activists named to board at Hardin County Hospital; Facility's ties to OhioHealth are still a concern for some, COLUMBUS DISPATCH [Ohio], Dec. 7, 2002, 3B [two members of community group threatening to sue hospital were appointed to board]; Detroit Medical Center restructures board, AP, June 24, 2003 [part of effort to seek financial support from city, county, and state]; K. Norris, Six named to Detroit Medical Center funding panel, DETROIT FREE PRESS, Aug. 21, 2003 [governor appointed an oversight committee to watch over public funding given to hospitals].

103 *Rhode Island v. Lifespan*, No. 89-2801 (R.I. Super. Ct. settlement Jan. 5, 1999), as discussed in 8 H.L.R. 157 (1999).

104 HCA to overhaul corporate governance; Hospital chain agrees to changes under proposed settlement with state pension funds, L.A. TIMES, Feb. 5, 2003, pt. 3, 13.

105 *State* ex rel. *Welch v. Passaic Hosp. Ass'n*, 59 N.J.L. 142, 36 A. 702 (1897).

106 *Coldiron v. Board of Comm'rs*, 39 Or. App. 495, 592 P.2d 1053 (1979).

107 J. Behrman, Hospital board member under fire, SAN DIEGO UNION-TRIBUNE, July 1, 2001, N1; J. Behrman, Three sworn in as Tri-City Healthcare District board directors, SAN DIEGO UNION-TRIBUNE, Dec. 4, 2002, NC-2.

108 See J. Garofoli, Hospital board ousts duo for missed meetings, SAN FRANCISCO CHRONICLE, Aug. 16, 2000, A21.

109 E.g., Doctors vote against hospital's president, board chairman, AP, Oct. 17, 2002 [Owensboro, Ky.]; Hospital chairman resigns, AP, Oct. 30, 2002 [Owensboro]; S. Vied, CEO of Owensboro, Ky., health system to resign in May 2004, MESSENGER-INQUIRER, Oct. 31, 2003 [public board dissolved, new fourteen-member private board].

110 Queen of Angels board removes dissident physicians after suit, 6 H.L.R. 1817 (1997).

111 HealthPartners vows to fight Hatch on board seats, AP, Jan. 27, 2003; Hatch, HealthPartners reach settlement on Glen Taylor's role, AP, June 11, 2003.

112 For a settlement, see C. Brown, Hospital agreement reached, ATLANTA JOURNAL-CONSTITUTION, Apr. 25, 2002, 3c [settlement of suit over control of hospital, board restructured].

113 Judge says 7 who refused to quit are health care group's board, AP, Feb. 1, 2002; Judge returns West Alabama Health Services control to board, AP, Apr. 27, 2002 [court ends overseer].

114 *Singh v. Bruswick Hosp.*, 2 A.D.3d 433, 767 N.Y.S.2d 839 (2d Dept. 2003) [aff'g appointment of receiver]; B.J. Durkin, Court enters hospital struggle, NEWSDAY (New York, N.Y.), Dec. 8, 2001, A14 [appointment of receiver].

115 But see A. Raghavan, More CEOs say "no thanks" to board seats, WALL ST. J, Jan. 28, 2005, B1.

116 *Exxel/Atmos, Inc. v. NLRB* 307 U.S. App. D.C. 376, 28 F.3d 1243 (1994).

117 See Community hospital's questionable ethics, and Barkholz, Maryland system's board refutes allegations, promises improvements, MOD. HEALTHCARE, June 7, 1985, 5, 44 [hospital operated eighteen months without CEO].

118 See Droste, Temporary CEOs take up the slack in hospitals, 63 HOSPS., Sept. 20, 1989, 104.

119 *Lamm v. Board of Comm'rs*, 378 So. 2d 919 (La. 1979).

120 *State* ex rel. *Stubbin v. Board of County Comm'rs*, 273 Minn. 361, 141 N.W.2d 499 (1966); accord *Heath v. Rosebud Hosp. Dist.*, 620 F.2d 207 (9th Cir. 1980) [CEO not entitled to hearing before termination].

121 See *Heath v. Rosebud Hosp. Dist.*, 620 F.2d 207 (9th Cir. 1980) [42 U.S.C. § 1983 suit dismissed, due process was provided].

122 E.g., *Browning v. Salem Mem. Dist. Hosp.*, 808 S.W.2d 943 (Mo. Ct. App. 1991).

123 E.g., *American Medical Int'l, Inc. v. Giurintano*, 821 S.W.2d 331 (Tex. Ct. App. 1991) [hospital, assistant administrator and individual physicians liable to prospective hospital administrator for intentional infliction of emotional distress for spreading rumors, other actions to prevent appointment].

124 E.g., A. Goldstein, Judge denies severance to former hospital chief, WASHINGTON POST, May 10, 2002, B3; R. Winslow, Regulators stop Oxford ex-chairman's severance, WALL ST. J., Apr. 3, 1998, B5.

125 *Harlem Hosp. Ctr. Med. Bd. v. Hoffman*, 84 A.D.2d 272, 445 N.Y.S.2d 981 (1st Dept. 1982).

126 M. Marizco, Board fires top hospital execs in Winslow, Ariz., ARIZONA DAILY SUN (Flagstaff, Ariz.), Dec. 28, 2002.

127 E.g., *Goldsmith v. DeBuono*, 245 A.D.2d 627, 665 N.Y.S.2d 727 (3rd Dept. 1997).

128 E.g., Former hospital official pleads guilty to manipulating its finances, AP, July 11, 2000 [Lee County Community Hosp., Virginia]; Three convicted of bribery, extortion from medical center, AP, Sept. 7, 2000 [LaFollett Med. Ctr., Tenn.].

129 *Bronstein v. State*, 355 So. 2d 817 (Fla. 3d DCA 1978); see *Touche Ross & Co. v. SunBank*, 366 So. 2d 465 (Fla. 3d DCA), cert. denied, 378 So. 2d 350 (Fla. 1979) [effort by hospital to recover losses due to CEO's crimes]; see also Former Hermann Hospital exec released from prison, MOD. HEALTHCARE, Dec. 18, 1987, 21.

130 18 U.S.C. § 666.

131 *United States v. Stout*, Crim. 1990 U.S. Dist. LEXIS 12343 (E.D. Pa.), post-conviction proceeding, 1994 U.S. Dist. LEXIS 3182 (E.D. Pa.), aff'd without op., 39 F.3d 1173, 1994 U.S. App. LEXIS 31128 (3d Cir. 1994); see also *United States v. Sadlier*,

649 F. Supp. 1560 (D. Mass. 1986) [denying dismissal of charges against respiratory therapist].

132 *United States v. Morrison*, 2002 U.S. App. LEXIS 1948 (4th Cir.).

133 *Roberto v. Brown County Gen. Hosp.*, 59 Ohio App. 3d 84, 571 N.E.2d 467 (1989).

134 *State v. Serebin*, 119 Wis. 2d 837, 350 N.W.2d 65 (1984).

135 E.g., *State v. Boone Retirement Ctr., Inc.*, 26 S.W.3d 265 (Mo. App. 2000); *State v. Cunningham*, 493 N.W.2d 884 (Iowa Ct. App. 1992); *State v. Springer*, 585 N.E.2d 27 (Ind. Ct. App. 1992); Annotation, Criminal liability under statutes penalizing abuse or neglect of the institutionalized infirm, 60 A.L.R. 4TH 1153.

136 E.g., *Portlock v. Perry*, 852 S.W.2d 578 (Tex. Ct. App. 1993) [investor/president of diagnostic radiology center not liable for death of child after technicians gave too much choral hydrate for sedation; claimed failure to have adequate policies and procedures not sufficient to impose personal liability].

137 *Reserve Life Ins. Co. v. Salter*, 152 F. Supp. 868, 870 (S.D. Miss. 1957).

138 *Golding v. Salter*, 234 Miss. 567, 107 So. 2d 348 (1958).

139 *Fegley v. Higgins*, 19 F.3d 1126 (6th Cir.), cert. denied, 513 U.S. 875 (1994).

140 *Dirschel v. Speck*, 1994 U.S. Dist. LEXIS 9257 (S.D.N.Y.).

141 *UHS-Qualicare, Inc. v. Gulf Coast Comm. Hosp.*, 525 So. 2d 746 (Miss. 1987), pet. reh'g withdrawn, 525 So. 2d 758 (Miss. 1988) [settlement].

142 Rev. Proc. 93-17, 93-19; IRS issued proposed regulations on private activity bond restrictions, 59 FED. REG. 67658 (Dec. 30, 1994) [to replace Rev. Proc. 93-17, 93-19].

143 Ex parte *Health Care Management Group*, 522 So. 2d 280 (Ala. 1988).

144 42 U.S.C. § 1395x(e) [hospitals]; 42 C.F.R. pt. 482 [hospitals]; 42 C.F.R. §§ 483.400-483.480 [ICF/MR]; 42 C.F.R. pt. 483 [HHA]; 42 C.F.R. §§ 485.50-485.74 [CORF]; 42 C.F.R. §§ 485.301-485.308 [organ procurement]; 42 C.F.R. §§ 485.601-485.645 [rural primary care hospitals]; 42 C.F.R. §§ 485.701-485.729 [physical therapy, speech pathology]; 42 C.F.R. §§ 483.1-483.75 [long-term care facilities]. In 2005, HCFA proposed changes to the hospital conditions of participation, 70 FED. REG. 15266 (Mar. 25, 2005).

145 42 U.S.C. §§ 1395aa(c), 1395bb; 70 FED. REG. 15331 (Mar. 25, 2005) [JCAHO]; 70 FED. REG. 15333 (Mar. 25, 2005) [AOA]; see also *Cospito v. Heckler*, 742 F.2d 72 (3d Cir. 1984), cert. denied, 471 U.S. 1131 (1985) [not a constitutional violation for patients at psychiatric hospital to lose Medicare, Medicaid benefits when hospital lost JCAHO accreditation].

146 E.g., *Mediplex of Mass., Inc. v. Shalala*, 39 F. Supp. 2d 88 (D. Mass. 1999) [continued Medicare payments ordered for nursing home cited for public health deficiencies until showing of immediate harm to residents]; *Northern Health Facilities, Inc. v. United States*, 39 F. Supp. 2d 563 (D. Md. 1998) [denied injunction of HCFA termination of nursing home from Medicare/Medicaid, despite no immediate jeopardy violations, pact with DOJ to improve conditions; court noted this was

"inequitable result"]; *Ponce de Leon Healthcare Inc. v. Agency for Health Care Administration*, 1997 U.S. Dist. LEXIS 10690 (S.D. Fla.) [nursing home cannot seek injunction of termination of Medicare and Medicaid provider agreements due to deficiencies found in survey until it exhausts administrative remedies].

147 E.g., Burda, Abortion a business hurdle for nation's Catholic hospitals, MOD. HEALTHCARE, Aug. 25, 1989, 40.

148 E.g., *Florida Health Care Ass'n v. Agency for Health Care Admin.*, 1998 Fla. App. LEXIS 14400 (1st DCA) [quashing emergency nursing home rule].

149 *Department of Health & Rehabilitative Servs. v. Delray Hosp. Corp.*, 373 So. 2d 75 (Fla. 1st DCA 1979).

150 *Hospital Ass'n of Pa. v. MacLeod*, 487 Pa. 516, 410 A.2d 731 (1980).

151 *Ortiz v. Dep't of Health*, 882 So. 2d 402 (Fla. 4th DCA 2004).

152 E.g., *Hospital Ass'n of N.Y.S. v. Axelrod*, 164 A.D.2d 518, 565 N.Y.S.2d 243 (3d Dept. 1990); *Village of Herkimer v. Axelrod*, 88 A.D.2d 704, 451 N.Y.S.2d 303 (3d Dept. 1982), aff'd, 58 N.Y.2d 1069, 462 N.Y.S.2d 633, 449 N.E.2d 413 (1983).

153 *Koelbl v. Whalen*, 63 A.D.2d 408, 406 N.Y.S.2d 621 (3d Dept. 1978).

154 *Eden Park Health Servs., Inc. v. Whalen*, 73 A.D.2d 993, 424 N.Y.S.2d 33 (3d Dept. 1980).

155 *Watkins v. Restorative Care Ctr., Inc.*, 66 Wash. App. 178, 831 P.2d 1085 (1992).

156 *Grimes v. Department of Social Servs.*, 70 Cal. App. 4th 1065, 83 Cal. Rptr. 2d 203 (2d Dist. 1999).

157 *Hummel-Jones v. Strope*, 25 F.3d 647 (8th Cir. 1994).

158 E.g., *Stone v. North Carolina Dep't of Labor*, 347 N.C. 473, 495 S.E.2d 711 (1998) [under public duty doctrine, workers injured in fire could not sue state agency for failure to inspect plant].

159 *Woodiwiss v. Jacobs*, 125 Misc. 584, 211 N.Y.S.2d 217 (Sup. Ct. 1961). For a similar result concerning a nursing home, see *Bethune Plaza, Inc. v. Lumpkin*, 863 F.2d 525 (7th Cir. 1988) [issuing conditional license without prior hearing violates due process when no emergency].

160 *Harrison Clinic Hosp. v. Texas State Bd. of Health*, 400 S.W.2d 840 (Tex. Civ. App.), aff'd, 410 S.W.2d 181 (Tex. 1966) [multiple violations of fire, safety rules, multiple citations for poor sanitation justified license revocation].

161 E.g., *Mullen v. Axelrod*, 74 N.Y.2d 580, 549 N.Y.S.2d 953, 549 N.E.2d 144 (1989).

162 *Sherwin Manor Nursing Ctr., Inc. v. McAuliffe*, 37 F.3d 1216 (7th Cir. 1994); Illinois settles with nursing home, WIS. ST. J., Oct. 18, 1997, 8A [$250,000 settlement with state].

163 *Brownsville Golden Age Nursing Home, Inc. v. Wells*, 839 F.2d 155 (3d Cir. 1988).

164 *U.S. Nursing Corp. v. Saint Joseph Med. Ctr.*, 39 F.3d 790 (7th Cir. 1994).

165 E.g., Unions search for regulatory violations to pressure firms and win new members, WALL ST. J., Feb. 28, 1992, B1.

166 E.g., King/Drew gets reprieve, AM. MED. NEWS, Mar. 7, 2005, 14.

167 Joint Commission on Accreditation of Healthcare Organizations, COMPREHENSIVE ACCREDITATION MANUAL FOR HOSPITALS (2005 ed.) [hereinafter 2005 JCAHO CAMH].

168 E.g., Troubled Los Angeles hospital loses accreditation from national commission, AP, Feb. 2, 2005.

169 See http://www.jcaho.org/accredited+organizations/svnp/svnp+qa_tracer+methodology.htm [accessed June 9, 2005].

170 See Status of state legislation regulating acquisition of nonprofit hospitals by nonprofit companies, 6 H.L.R. 1166 (1997); California attorney general approves first nonprofit to for-profit conversion under new conversion law, 25 HEALTH L. DIG. (June 1997), at 93 [Riverside Comm. Hosp.]; Hospital conversions spur states to examine community benefit issues, 7 H.L.R. 653 (1998); State Attorney General disapproves R.I.-Massachusetts hospital group merger, 7 H.L.R. 1436 (1998).

171 Conversion foundation assets grow, prompt controversy over use of funds, 7 H.L.R. 235 (1998).

172 E.g., *Attorney General v. Hahnemann Hosp.*, 397 Mass. 820, 494 N.E.2d 1011 (1986) [conversion to grant-making organization permitted where articles of incorporation permitted this activity].

173 *Kansas East Conf. of United Methodist Church v. Bethany Med. Ctr.*, 266 Kan. 366, 969 P.2d 859 (1998) [corporate law governs the transaction, trust law not applicable]; but see *Greil Mem. Hosp. v. First Ala. Bank of Montgomery*, 387 So. 2d 778 (Ala. 1980) [charitable bequest lapsed when corporation created to treat tuberculosis converted to grant-making foundation].

174 E.g., *ABC for Health, Inc. v. Commissioner of Ins.*, 250 Wis. 2d 56, 640 N.W.2d 510 (App. 2001).

175 Blue Cross & Blue Shield v. Praeger, 276 Kan. 232, 75 P.3d 226 (2003); J. Hanna, Blue Cross won't seek new deal after court ruling, AP, Aug. 7, 2003; see also T. Stuckey, Insurance commissioner rejects CareFirst sale, AP, Mar. 6, 2003 [Md.]; G. Johnson, Premera appeals insurance commissioner's decision, AP, Aug. 14, 2004 [disapproval by Wash. insurance commissioner].

176 *National Med. Enters., Inc. v. Sandrock*, 72 N.C. App. 245, 324 S.E.2d 268 (1985).

177 *University Med. Affiliates, P.C. v. Wayne County Executive*, 142 Mich. App. 135, 369 N.W.2d 277 (1985). Leases have also been upheld in *Kromko v. Arizona Bd. of Regents*, 149 Ariz. 319, 718 P.2d 478 (1986) and *Local Union No. 2490 v. Waukesha County*, 143 Wis. 2d 438, 422 N.W.2d 117 (Ct. App. 1988).

178 *Ullrich v. Board of County Comm'rs*, 234 Kan. 782, 676 P.2d 127 (1984).

179 *Petition of University Hospitals Authority*, 953 P.2d 314 (Okla. 1997); Okla. teaching hospitals transferred to Columbia/HCA, AM. MED. NEWS, Mar. 2, 1998, 10.

180 *Richmond County Hosp. Auth. v. Richmond County*, 255 Ga. 183, 336 S.E.2d 562 (1985).

181 E.g., *Kelo v. City of New London*, 125 S. Ct. 2655 (U.S. 2005) [integrated development plan is permitted public use]; *Long Island Lighting Co. v. Cuomo*, 666 F. Supp. 370 (N.D.N.Y. 1987) [upholding state law authorizing eminent domain to take over power company], vacated, 888 F.2d 230 (2d Cir. 1989) [moot due to settlement]. Mandating hospital governing board composition is not considered a taking of the hospital. See *American Hosp. Ass'n v. Hansbarger*, 600 F. Supp. 465 (N.D. W. Va. 1984), aff'd, 783 F.2d 1184 (4th Cir. 1986), cert. denied, 479 U.S. 820 (1986).

182 *Poletown Neighborhood Council v. City of Detroit*, 410 Mich. 616, 304 N.W.2d 455 (1981); City to settle lawsuit for $68 million, UPI, Apr. 13, 1993 [settlement with hospital owners twelve years later].

183 Punch, Faced with takeover, Charter officials will sell St. Louis hospital for $15 million, MOD. HEALTHCARE, July 19, 1985, 24; New corporation purchases Charter hospital in St. Louis, MOD. HEALTHCARE, Nov. 8, 1985, 11.

184 Dade may force hospital to sell to ease crowding at Jackson, MIAMI HERALD [FL], Mar. 4, 1991, 1B [proposal to take Cedars Medical Center]; Cedars to fight bid to take over hospital, MIAMI HERALD [FL], Mar. 23, 1991, 4B.

185 G.V. Moser & T.L. Driscoll, Going public, THE RECORDER [San Francisco, CA], Jan. 1, 2003, 4.

186 *City of Smithville v. St. Luke's Northland Hosp. Corp.*, 972 S.W.2d 416 (Mo. Ct. App. 1998).

187 E.g., COLO. REV. STAT. 23-21-501 et seq.; WIS. STAT. ch. 233.

188 E.g., Methodist ministers reviewing proposed sale of Wesley to HCA, MOD. HEALTHCARE, Jan. 18, 1985, 9; Wesley trustees, church approve sale, MOD. HEALTHCARE, Feb. 15, 1985, 35 [358 to 252 vote by United Methodist Church; church to get payments from part of interest income on proceeds and get some control over foundation]; J. Moore, Church, hospital clash, MOD. HEALTHCARE, Oct. 6, 1997, 1 [Bethany Med. Ctr.]; *Kansas East Conf. of United Methodist Church v. Bethany Med. Ctr.*, No. 97-C-308 (Kan. Dist. Ct. Sept. 26, 1997), as discussed in 6 H.L.R. 1517 (1997) [hospital allowed to sell assets].

189 M.C. Jaklevic, Market forces hospital to lose Catholic status, MOD. HEALTHCARE, Mar. 6, 1995, 40 [abandoning religious status so it can be sold to non-Catholic system].

190 As health mergers rise, standards of Catholics face a new challenge, N.Y. TIMES, Mar. 8, 1995, A11.

191 E.g., Catholic hospital finalizes sale to for-profit chain, AM. MED. NEWS, Apr. 13, 1998, 34 [St. Louis Univ. Hosp.]; M. Moran, Catholic leaders protest teaching hospital's sale to for-profit, AM. MED. NEWS, Jan. 26, 1998, 4 [St. Louis Univ. Hospital]; V. Foubister, L.A. hospital deal OK'd after endowment fund established, AM. MED. NEWS, June 8, 1998, 14 [Queen of Angels Hosp.]; Attorney General approves Queen of Angels sale to Tenet, 7 H.L.R. 823 (1998); Queen of Angels board amends bylaws to eliminate need for bishop's approval, 7 H.L.R. 493 (1998); Queen of Angels dispute centers around religious law, 7 H.L.R. 367 (1998); Los Angeles Archbishop formally opposes sale of hospital to Tenet, 7 H.L.R. 322 (1998) [Queen of Angels].

192 E. Fein, Catholic hospitals in nonsectarian merger deals set off abortion concerns, N.Y. TIMES, Oct. 14, 1997, A17; L. Kertesz, Community voices concern over hospital's Catholic affiliation, MOD. HEALTHCARE, Feb. 13, 1995, 40; ACLU may sue over dropped services, MOD. HEALTHCARE, Feb. 13, 1995, 41 [elimination of contraceptive services after merger with Catholic hospital].

193 E.g., Larkin, Financial woes force L.A. hospitals to merge, 63 HOSPS. (July 5, 1989), 28.

194 E.g., Hospital corp. completes sale of 104 hospitals, WALL ST. J., Sept. 18, 1987, 20 [sale of 104 hospitals by Hospital Corporation of America to Heathtrust, Inc.].

195 But see *United States v. Vernon Home Health, Inc.*, 21 F.3d 693 (5th Cir.), cert. denied, 513 U.S. 1015 (1994) [asset purchaser liable to U.S. for Medicare overpayments to prior owner, state law preempted].

196 E.g., Golden Valley hospital has Medicare reinstated, AP, May 22, 2002.

197 See Greene, Administrators, attorneys have different approaches to mergers, MOD. HEALTHCARE, July 21, 1989, 38.

198 E.g., D. Burda, Iowa merger off as boards disagree, MOD. HEALTHCARE, Feb. 20, 1995, 8.

199 E.g., *Asseo v. Hospital San Francisco, Inc.*, 1988 U.S. Dist. LEXIS 11873 (D. P.R.) [acquiring hospital found to be successor corporation and obligated to bargain with nurses' union].

200 E.g., 15 U.S.C. § 291i; *United States v. St. John's Gen. Hosp.*, 875 F.2d 1064 (3d Cir. 1989); *United States v. Coweta County Hosp. Auth.*, 603 F. Supp. 111 (N.D. Ga. 1984), aff'd, 777 F.2d 667 (11th Cir. 1985); see also *National Med. Enters., Inc. v. United States*, 28 Fed. Cl. 540 (1993), appeal dismissed, 14 F.3d 612 (Fed. Cir. 1993) [20-year lease is a transfer of hospital triggering Hill-Burton recovery].

201 E.g., IRS PLR No. 9427025 (Apr. 11, 1994); Hospital sale to for-profit firm requires bond redemption in 90 days, 3 H.L.R. 971 (1994).

202 E.g., *Sandpoint Convalescent Servs., Inc. v. Idaho Dep't of Health & Welfare*, 114 Idaho 281, 756 P.2d 398 (1988) [recapture of Medicaid depreciation payments not unconstitutional].

203 E.g., *Creighton Omaha Reg. Health Care Corp. v. Sullivan*, 950 F.2d 563 (8th Cir. 1991) [recapture of Medicare depreciation]; *Bethesda Found. v. Nebraska Dep't of Social Servs.*, 498 N.W.2d 86 (Neb. 1993) [state recapture of Medicaid depreciation on sale to for-profit organization].

204 *Taylor v. Baldwin*, 362 Mo. 1224, 247 S.W.2d 741 (1952).

205 *McDaniel v. Frisco Employees' Hosp. Ass'n*, 510 S.W.2d 752 (Mo. Ct. App. 1974).

206 E.g., WIS. STAT. § 180.1430.

207 E.g., J. Greene, Are foundations bearing fruit? MOD. HEALTHCARE, Mar. 20, 1995, 53; Coady, Not-for-profits, beware – Foundation formed by sale could be short-lived, MOD. HEALTHCARE, Mar. 29, 1985, 138; Carland, Computer model used to evaluate foundation had flawed assumptions, MOD. HEALTHCARE, June 7, 1985), 177; D.W. Coyne & K.R. Kas, The not-for-profit

hospital as a charitable trust: To whom does its value belong? 24 J. HEALTH & HOSP. L. 48 (1991); see also Big charities born of nonprofit-to-profit shifts, WALL ST. J., Apr. 4, 1995, B1 [conversions of Blue Cross and other nonprofit health plans].

208 E.g., *Mussington v. St. Luke's-Roosevelt Hosp. Ctr.*, 18 F.3d 1033 (2d Cir. 1994), aff'g, 824 F. Supp. 427 (S.D.N.Y. 1993) [individuals, three churches sued to stop transfer of hospital services from minority low income neighborhood, but all claims barred by laches or statute of limitations]; *Greenpoint Hosp. Comm. Bd. v. New York City Health & Hosps. Corp.*, 114 A.D.2d 1028, 495 N.Y.S.2d 467 (2d Dept. 1985) [hospital found in contempt of court for violating order on consultations with community board].

209 42 U.S.C. § 1320a-1, which was announced not to be enforced, 53 FED. REG. 10,431 (Mar. 31, 1988).

210 42 U.S.C. §§ 2000d-2000d-6.

211 29 U.S.C. § 794.

212 42 U.S.C. § 4332.

213 *NAACP v. Wilmington Med. Ctr., Inc.*, 426 F. Supp. 919 (D. Del. 1977).

214 *NAACP v. Wilmington Med. Ctr., Inc.*, 436 F. Supp. 1194 (D. Del. 1977), aff'd, 584 F.2d 619 (3d Cir. 1978).

215 *NAACP v. Wilmington Med. Ctr., Inc.*, 453 F. Supp. 330 (D. Del. 1978).

216 *Wilmington United Neighborhoods v. United States, Dep't of HEW*, 458 F. Supp. 628 (D. Del. 1978), aff'd, 615 F.2d 112 (3d Cir.), cert. denied, 449 U.S. 827 (1980).

217 *NAACP v. Medical Ctr., Inc.*, 599 F.2d 1247 (3d Cir. 1979), rev'g, 453 F. Supp. 289 (D. Del. 1978).

218 *NAACP v. Wilmington Med. Ctr., Inc.*, 491 F. Supp. 290 (D. Del. 1980), aff'd, 657 F.2d 1322 (3d Cir. 1981).

219 *Lincoln CERCPAC v. Health & Hosps. Corp.*, 147 F.3d 165 (2d Cir. 1998).

220 *Chavous v. District of Columbia Fin. Responsibility & Mgmt. Assistance Auth.*, 154 F. Supp. 2d 40 (D. D.C. 2001).

221 E.g., *Citizens for State Hosp. v. Commonwealth*, 123 Pa. Commw. 150, 553 A.2d 496 (1989), cert. denied, 494 U.S. 1017 (1990) [citizens]; *Punikaia v. Clark*, 720 F.2d 564 (9th Cir. 1983), cert. denied, 469 U.S. 816 (1984) [patient residents of leprosarium had no property interest in continued operation of facility, so not entitled to hearing before closure].

222 *Greenpoint Hosp. Comm. Bd. v. N.Y.C. Health and Hosps. Corp.*, 114 A.D.2d 1028, 495 N.Y.S.2d 467 (2d Dept. 1985).

223 *City of Paterson v. Paterson Gen. Hosp.*, 97 N.J. Super. 514, 235 A.2d 487 (Ch. Div. 1967).

224 Edgewater hospital closes, AP, Dec. 7, 2001.

225 *Jackson County Hosp. Dist. v. Jackson County Citizens for Continued Hosp. Care*, 669 S.W.2d 147 (Tex. Ct. App. 1984).

226 *Rodde v. Bonta*, 357 F.3d 988 (9th Cir. 2004); *Harris v. Board of Supervisors*, 366 F.3d 754 (9th Cir. 2004).

227 *Lonoke Nursing Home, Inc. v. Wayne & Neil Bennett Family P'ship*, 12 Ark. App. 282, 676 S.W.2d 461, adhered to (en banc), 12 Ark. App. 286, 679 S.W.2d 823 (1984).

228 29 U.S.C. §§ 2101-2109; but see *Jurcev v. Central Comm. Hosp.*, 7 F.3d 618 (7th Cir. 1993), cert. denied, 511 U.S. 1081 (1994) [hospital closure with two weeks notice did not violate WARN because closure due to unforeseeable business circumstance of foundation decision to stop payments to hospital].

229 E.g., *Brindle v. West Allegheny Hosp.*, 406 Pa. Super. 572, 594 A.2d 766 (1991) [dismissed claim by six nurses of fraud in closure of hospital].

230 *Mary Thompson Hosp. v. NLRB*, 943 F.2d 741 (7th Cir. 1991).

231 *City of Destin v. Columbia/HCA Healthcare Corp.*, No. 94-17015-CA (Fla. Cir. Ct. Okaloosa County filed June 15, 1994) [city suit]; *Agency for Health Care Admin. v. Fort Walton Beach Med. Ctr.*, HQA No. 01-094-005-HOSP (complaint filed Aug. 22, 1994 & settled Aug. 30, 1994) [license revocation proceeding], as discussed in 3 H.L.R 877, 1207 & 1280 (1994).

232 E.g., Hospital bankruptcy crisis examined, 7 H.L.R. 905 (1998) [American Hosp. Ass'n analysis being examined by congressional committee]. For an example of multihospital system in bankruptcy, see In re *Allegheny Health, Education & Research Found.*, No. 98-25773 to 98-25777 (Bankr. W.D. Pa. filed July 21, 1998).

233 11 U.S.C. § 101(31).

234 11 U.S.C. § 109; e.g., In re *Estate of Medcare HMO*, 998 F.2d 436 (7th Cir. 1993) [HMO not subject to bankruptcy]; In re *Mich. Master Health Plan, Inc.*, 90 Bankr. 274 (E.D. Mich. 1985) [HMO subject to bankruptcy because not insurance company under state law]; In re *Florida Brethren Homes*, 88 Bankr. 445 (Bankr. S.D. Fla. 1988) [life care facility subject to bankruptcy because not insurance company under state law].

235 E.g., V. Foubister, State declares HIP of New Jersey insolvent, AM. MED. NEWS, Nov. 23/30, 1998, 11.

236 11 U.S.C. § 362.

237 E.g., In re *Grau*, 172 Bankr. 686 (Bkrtcy. S.D. Fla. 1994) [not violation of automatic stay for malpractice creditor to have communication with state licensing board concerning failure of debtor doctor to pay judgment where first report filed prepetition].

238 11 U.S.C. § 362(c), (d); e.g., In re *Corporacion de Servicos*, 60 Bankr. 920 (D. P.R. 1986), aff'd, 805 F.2d 440 (1st Cir. 1986) [exemption from automatic stay for state regulatory actions does not apply when effort to revoke hospital license is subterfuge to force termination of management contract]; In re *Bel Air Chateau Hosp., Inc.*, 611 F.2d 1248 (9th Cir. 1979) [NLRB proceedings not subject to automatic stay, but can be stayed if assets threatened].

239 In re *Lavigne*, 114 F.3d 379 (2d Cir. 1997).

240 11 U.S.C. § 365; e.g., In re *Corporacion de Servicios Medicos Hospitalarios de Fajardo*, 60 Bankr. 920 (D. P.R. 1986), aff'd, 805 F.2d 440 (1st Cir. 1986) [assumption of hospital management contract]; In re *Reph Acquisition Co.*, 134 Bankr. 194 (N.D. Tex. 1991) [debtor's interest in hospital lease deemed rejected when failed to assume lease within allotted time].

241 11 U.S.C. § 1113; e.g., In re *Sierra Steel Corp.*, 88 Bankr. 337 (Bankr. D. Colo. 1988) [approval of modifications in collective bargaining agreement].

242 11 U.S.C. § 1114.

243 E.g., 11 U.S.C. §§ 544, 547, 548, 553; In re *Sheppard's Dental Centers, Inc.*, 65 Bankr. 274 (Bankr. S.D. Fla. 1986) [transfer of management agreement can be voidable transfer].

244 E.g., *St. Francis Physician Network, Inc. v. Rush Prudential HMO Inc.*, 213 Bankr. 710 (N.D. Ill. Bankr. 1997) [bankruptcy law limits HMO's right to deduct from capitation payments to physician networks for sums owed network].

245 11 U.S.C. § 106, as amended by Pub. L. No. 103-394, § 113, 108 Stat. 4117 (1994); *Hoffman v. Connecticut Dep't of Income Maint.*, 492 U.S. 96 (1989). For an example of waiver by filing a claim, see *St. Joseph Hosp. v. Dep't. of Pub. Welfare*, 103 Bankr. 643 (Bankr. E.D. Pa. 1989).

246 *United States v. Consumer Health Servs.*, 323 U.S. App. D.C. 336, 108 F.3d 390 (1997).

247 E.g., In re *Ludlow Hosp. Soc'y*, 124 F.3d 22 (1st Cir. 1997) [bankruptcy court cannot extend time to sell capital assets subject to depreciation credits after terminating Medicare participation].

248 E.g., AMH seeks court approval for sale of Calif. facility, MOD. HEALTHCARE, Oct. 14, 1988, 8.

249 E.g., Care creditors ask court to remove chain's owners, MOD. HEALTHCARE, June 2, 1989, 7.

250 E.g., Bankruptcy judge OKs hospital reorganization plan, AP, Aug. 5, 2003 [Crouse Hosp., Syracuse, N.Y.]; In re *Community Hosp. of the Valleys*, 51 Bankr. 231 (Bankr. 9th Cir. 1985), aff'd, 820 F.2d 1097 (9th Cir. 1987) [confirmation of reorganization plan]; In re *Medical Equities, Inc.*, 39 Bankr. 795 (Bankr. S.D. Ohio 1984) [denial of confirmation]; Judge says plan to reopen hospital is unworkable, MOD. HEALTHCARE, Sept. 2, 1988, 14 [bankruptcy court rejected community group reorganization plan].

251 E.g., 11 U.S.C. §§ 523, 524, 727, 1141(d).

252 *Kawaauhau v. Geiger*, 523 U.S. 57 (1998).

253 Bankruptcy Abuse Prevention and Consumer Protection Act of 2005, Pub. L. No. 109-8 [most changes were effective in October 2005]; S. Block, Filing Chapter 7 bankruptcy will get tougher soon, USA TODAY, Apr. 21, 2005, 4B.

254 In re *Transworld Airlines, Inc.*, 18 F.3d 208 (3d Cir. 2003).

255 A. Goldstein, Judge to allow auction of hospital in SE, WASHINGTON POST, Nov. 23, 2003, B6; B. Brubaker, Tuft's group wins auction for hospitals, WASHINGTON POST, Dec. 18, 2003, E1.

256 *Renger Mem. Hosp. v. State*, 674 S.W.2d 828 (Tex. Ct. App. 1984).

Chapter 3

Regulation of Healthcare Facilities, Equipment, Devices, and Drugs

John E. Steiner, Jr., Esq

Key Learning Objectives

By the end of the chapter, the reader will be able to:

- Understand the legal and regulatory requirements to establish, construct, modify, and operate healthcare facilities.

- Understand the role of the Food and Drug Administration (FDA).

- Appreciate the scope of other federal and state laws applicable to use of medical equipment, devices, drugs, and biologics in healthcare facilities.

This chapter provides an overview of the legal aspects of the creation and maintenance of physical resources necessary to deliver healthcare services including land and buildings, equipment, medical devices, drugs, supplies, biologics, blood, and tissues. The reader will learn how the government regulates these physical resources.

Proper delivery of healthcare services requires significant investment in physical resources. The phrase "property, plant, and equipment" (PPE) is often used in the industry. Hospitals, skilled nursing facilities, physician offices, and many other providers require land and buildings. Some services, such as home health services, might not require land and buildings. Virtually all healthcare services require equipment, other devices, drugs, and supplies. Some healthcare services require blood, biologics, and tissues. This chapter surveys the types of regulations concerning the creation and maintenance of these physical resources.

Related topics are addressed in other chapters, including the relocation and closure of facilities. The decision to create or maintain a specific physical resource is often determined by the availability of financing. Those issues are discussed in this book in the chapters dealing with healthcare financing and payment programs, including the taxability of property, which can also be a factor.

Chapter Outline

Introduction

There are several types of regulations that apply to most healthcare facilities, including:

1. Zoning requirements (3-1.1) specify where facilities can be built.

2. Building codes (3-1.2) specify how most healthcare facilities must be designed.

3. Building permits (3-1.3) are required to build or make major modifications to existing buildings.

4. In some states, a certificate-of-need permit (3-1.4) must be obtained from the state before some facilities can be built or large capital expenditures are made.

The stated basis for zoning requirements and building permits is usually public health and safety. In most cases, that is the focal point of the issuing governmental authority. However, sometimes local governments withhold their approval until the healthcare entity agrees to financial or operational demands related to the project or building.

When zoning authorities impose too many restrictions, healthcare facility operators often look for other locations. For example, in 2002, a Wisconsin hospital had to look for a different clinic site when zoning authorities placed severe size and operating hour restrictions on any clinic on the hospital's land.[2]

Local governments can be required to permit certain exceptions to their zoning requirements when necessary; for example, to avoid discrimination against the disabled. In 2004, a federal court in Wisconsin ordered the City of Milwaukee to issue a special use permit to a community service program that provided services to persons with mental impairments. The court found that the Americans with Disabilities Act required the city to issue this permit as a reasonable and necessary accommodation.[3]

3-1 Land Use, Construction, and Regulations Related to Facility Use for Healthcare Delivery

3-1.1 Zoning Requirements

Zoning ordinances are laws adopted by local governments that specify permitted uses of certain types of land for specific purposes (e.g., commercial, industrial, residential, etc.). Zoning laws are an important part of governmental efforts to assure orderly land development and compatibility of uses in a specific location. That element of predictability usually encourages investment in homes, businesses, and other uses. Zoning ordinances can also limit the height, size, and design of buildings. Zoning laws generally protect hospitals from new uses of nearby land that might be incompatible with a hospital use. But zoning laws also can be a barrier to opening a new healthcare facility or making substantial changes to existing healthcare services provided in a facility. Approvals for a healthcare-related use often are granted without difficulty[1] though zoning laws may restrict expansion or require time-consuming efforts to obtain waivers, variances, or amendments to zoning laws in order for a building project to proceed. Local ordinances usually

are not permitted to exclude hospitals or other healthcare uses, but they can require hospitals to be located in specified areas.

Zoning authorities sometimes issue rulings that create problems after projects are started. In 1988, a Florida hospital obtained a building permit for an office tower and diagnostic clinic. The tower was designed to provide offices for the medical staff. After construction started, the city attorney issued an opinion on the definition of the term "staff offices" in the zoning ordinance. The attorney stated that the ordinance permitted offices only for physicians employed full-time by the hospital. Because most of the medical staff members were not full-time employees, this ruling made it impossible to obtain permanent construction funding or to lease the office space. In 1989, a federal court issued a preliminary injunction preventing enforcement of the city attorney's interpretation. The court found that it was likely the hospital could show due process violations.[4] The hospital and city settled, with the city dropping its interpretation and the hospital agreeing to pay property taxes on the building. In addition, the physicians with offices in the building were subject to an annual city, occupational license fee.[5]

When zoning laws are changed, usually existing uses are permitted to continue as "nonconforming uses" either indefinitely or for a specified period of time. Generally, there are limits on the improvements that can be made to nonconforming uses. For example, a Pennsylvania court found that a hospital demonstrated sufficient use of its helipad to establish it as a nonconforming use. Thus, the hospital did not have to obtain a special exception required for new helipads. The court also ruled that the addition of paving and lighting to the pad did not exceed permitted improvements.[6]

3-1.2 Building Codes

Healthcare facilities are subject to building and fire safety codes. The most widely applicable code is the Life Safety Code®[7] that is intended to protect building occupants from fires. Other building codes address other issues ranging from elevators[8] to earthquakes.[9] These codes authorize inspections of hospitals and other facilities by building inspectors and fire marshals. Those officials can take action through their own agencies or refer the matter to a licensing agency to initiate action. Building and fire safety codes are often enforced through institutional licensing laws.

> Among the list of NFPA codes are: Standard for Integrated Testing of Fire Protection Systems, Standard for Portable Fire Extinguishers, Standard for the Installation of Sprinkler Systems, Standard for Bulk Oxygen Systems at Consumer Sites, Standard for Fire Doors and Other Opening Protections, Hazardous Materials Code.

Compliance with the Life Safety Code is also required for institutional participation in Medicare and for accreditation by accrediting organizations, such as The Joint Commission (TJC).[10] There are several levels of Life Safety Code standards. The most expensive standards apply to space that is used for care of inpatients. There is an intermediate standard that applies to ambulatory care facilities, such as surgical centers. There is a third standard that applies to general business uses where the users typically are able to look out for their own safety (in short, they do not spend most of their time in patient care areas).

The Life Safety Code changes from time to time. Facilities usually try to meet the code applicable at the time the facility is approved for construction. Areas that are subject to major renovation, on the other hand, typically must meet code standards applicable at the time the renovation is approved.

Generally, local government authorities must issue a permit, often called a certificate of occupancy (CO), before a new building can be used. The local authorities require a hospital building also to pass an inspection by the hospital licensing agency before granting a CO.[11]

3-1.3 Building Permits

⚑ Most entities, including healthcare entities, must obtain a building permit to construct new facilities or make major changes to existing facilities. Some governmental hospitals are exempt from building permit requirements.

> One of the strangest zoning battles concerning a building permit occurred in New York. A hospital obtained a building permit and built a new emergency department, which opened in 2001. Neighbors challenged the permit and in 2002, a trial court ruled that the permit was not valid because a state environmental impact assessment requirement had not been satisfied. The court ordered the closure of the emergency department until the permit process was repeated with the required assessment. The court postponed the effect of the closure order until appeals were completed. An appellate court upheld the closure order in 2003, and in 2004 the highest court refused to review the decision. The trial court extended the postponement while the hospital and city sought to fulfill the requirements.[12]

In some areas, hospital-related facilities are entitled to building permits in situations where other uses could not get permits. For example, in 2004, a New York court upheld a building permit for a cancer research laboratory issued to a cancer hospital in New York City, finding that the laboratory was hospital-related.[13]

3-1.4 Certificate-of-Need Laws

Some states require certain healthcare providers to obtain a Certificate of Need (CON) permit from a state agency before expenditures, above a certain level, can be made for certain new buildings, equipment, or services.

In the 1970s, all states had CON laws. The National Health Planning and Resources Development Act of 1974[14] required states to have a CON law to qualify for certain federal health funds. The state CON programs were tied into a national health planning system. When the federal requirement was repealed,[15] many states repealed their CON laws, while others changed the scope of projects subject to the requirement.[16]

> The types of projects requiring a CON vary from state to state. Among the projects requiring a CON permit are: establishment of a new facility/provider (which may include hospital, ambulatory surgery center, freestanding rehabilitation agency, home health agency, kidney dialysis center); relocation of a facility or provider (including those listed above); addition or reduction in the number of beds (some states allow a limited change in bed count and only require a written notification of such a change); establishment of a new service or discontinuation of an existing service (e.g., radiation therapy, cardiac catheterization, open heart surgery, solid organ transplant, specific types of inpatient beds); construction or renovation in excess of a specific capital expenditure (the threshold varies from state to state); acquisition of new or replacement equipment in excess of a specific capital expenditure (the threshold varies from state to state); and change in ownership.

In states that still have CON laws, healthcare organizations that plan capital expenditures or program changes must comply with state CON requirements. These requirements define (1) which expenditures are subject to review, (2) the criteria for evaluating need, and (3) the review procedures. In addition, parties other than the CON applicant often will participate in public hearings to either contest or support the applicant. States vary as to how they permit organizations providing the same service as a CON applicant to challenge the determination of the need for additional facilities, services, or equipment. For example, in 1998, the Mississippi Supreme Court permitted competing hospitals to challenge a primary care center.[17] In 2004, a New York court ruled that a competitor did not have standing to challenge approval of a new dialysis center.[18] When a state permits such involvement, opposition by a competitor is generally not considered illegal antitrust activity.[19]

Some of the categories of expenditures for which review can be required include those that (1) exceed a specified capital threshold, (2) are for starting a new institution, (3) change bed capacity more than a specified amount, or (4) are for starting new services that will involve ongoing annual operational costs that exceed a defined threshold. Some states also require an approved CON permit before an organization can close certain services.[20]

The review criteria vary among the states, but they generally focus on the relationship to the existing healthcare system and to the "need" determined by health planning agencies for facilities, beds, major medical equipment, and services. Some criteria are numerical, such as bed need formulas based on population, while others are more subjective.

> The type of information required in the application for a CON varies from state to state. Some types of information include: ownership; if a current organization, recent volume, financial, and licensure information; consistency of the project with the state health plan; community needs addressed through the project; details on the equipment to be purchased and architectural floor plans for facility renovation or new construction; capital budget and project timeframe; alternatives considered; forecast volume and financial proformas; forecast payer mix (including charity and Medicaid patients to be served); geographic area to be served; source of volume; charity care policy; and impact on other area providers.

Some states favor institutions that treat Medicaid and indigent patients,[21] but at least one state favored a private nursing home over a facility that projected 65 percent Medicaid utilization because the state had insufficient Medicaid funds.[22]

CON procedures also vary, but they generally involve an application, public notice, a hearing with the right to present evidence, a timely decision, and an opportunity to appeal. Most states require technical compliance with the CON application requirements before an application can be processed.[23] In some states, if the agency does not act on the application within a specified time, the CON is automatically approved.[24]

CONs generally specify the timetable for completing the approved project and the maximum amount of authorized capital expenditures. If a good faith effort is not made to meet the timetable, the CON can be withdrawn. If the actual expenditures are expected to exceed the maximum, the project can be subject to further review. The withdrawal of a CON after a project starts could create negative impressions about the hospital. Therefore, a realistic timetable and budget are essential for a well-prepared CON application.

Some states impose limits on total capital expenditures in the state for health care. Other states impose moratoria on approvals of all capital expenditures of certain types, such as expenditures for hospitals[25] or nursing homes.[26] These moratoria and limits have been successfully challenged only when not authorized by state statute.[27] When there is a moratorium on new CONs, changes can occur only through transfers of existing CONs.[28]

Hospitals that are granted CONs generally can be ordered to comply with them.

> For example, an Alabama hospital obtained a CON to operate a long-term facility but operated it with an average length of stay of only 6.6 days. A court ordered that the hospital meet an average length of stay of thirty days or more.[29]

Hospitals that make particular promises in the course of obtaining a CON are generally required to honor those commitments. To settle a CON challenge, a Florida hospital agreed to provide a certain amount of indigent care or to pay a local governmental hospital any shortfall. When the care was not provided, the hospital was ordered to make the payment.[30] Failure to have a CON for a service is generally not a defense to a collection action against a patient for that service. A federal appellate court ruled in favor of the hospital in its suit to collect for a transplant procedure, even though the hospital did not have a CON for the service.[31]

3-2 What Are the Licensure Requirements for Healthcare Facilities?

Some regulatory or accrediting agencies focus on entire institutions. Other agencies focus on individual services or activities, such as pharmacies, laboratories, radiology, or elevators. Some agencies can focus on the institution or on individual activities depending on the circumstances. For example, in a few states, the CON agency must give its permission before certain types of new facilities or new services can be started. Numerous other regulations apply to other aspects of healthcare organizations, such as financing, taxation, waste disposal, communications, transportation, and labor relations.

This section reviews a few of the regulations applying to individual services. Pharmacy regulation is discussed in section 3-3.

CLINICAL LABORATORIES IMPROVEMENT ACT (CLIA). Hospitals and other providers, including physician offices, must meet federal standards for most clinical laboratory services and obtain a federal CLIA certificate to operate those services.[32] The Department of Health and Human Services has broad powers to revoke certificates for noncompliance.[33]

MAMMOGRAPHY QUALITY STANDARDS ACT. Hospitals and other providers, including physician offices, must meet federal standards for mammography and obtain a federal certificate to provide mammography services.[34]

RADIOACTIVE MATERIAL. Hospitals and other providers must obtain a permit to possess and use radioactive material. The Nuclear Regulatory Commission (NRC) administers this requirement at the federal level. Administrative responsibility has been delegated to the state level in states that meet certain standards. The NRC refers to delegated states as Agreement States.[35]

ELEVATORS. Most states require permits for and periodic inspections of elevators.[36]

3-3 What Are the Regulations?

The use of drugs and medical devices is heavily regulated. State laws regulate pharmacies. Federal laws regulate the production, distribution, and use of drugs and medical devices, especially drugs and medical devices involved in interstate commerce. State laws usually regulate intrastate commerce involving drugs that are not regulated by federal laws.[37] TJC standards and the Medicare conditions of participation also address hospital pharmacies. For example, the Medicare conditions of participation require that hospital pharmaceutical services be under the direction of a qualified pharmacist.[38]

This focus is understandable in light of the estimated 40 percent of Americans who take at least one prescription drug and 17 percent who take more than two.[39]

This section discusses:

- State regulation of pharmacies (3-3.1)
- Formulary systems (3-3.2)

- Controlled Substances Act (3-3.3)
- Regulation of drugs and devices by the U.S. Food and Drug Administration (3-3.4)
- Laws related to marketing drugs and devices (3-3.5)

3-3.1 State Regulation of Pharmacies

All states regulate pharmacies. Retail pharmacies are required to have pharmacy licenses. Some states require hospitals to obtain a separate pharmacy license for the hospital pharmacy. Notably, some states regulate hospital pharmacies through the hospital licensing system, exempting hospital pharmacies from the state pharmacy licensing system.[40] Some exemptions only apply to dispensing inpatient drugs and take-home drugs in conjunction with a hospital visit. There are limitations to pharmacy licensing exemptions, which need to be understood and verified by appropriate hospital persons.

For example, states that license hospital pharmacies require a separate community pharmacy license before the pharmacy can fill prescriptions for staff or others for use outside the hospital. Pharmacies in nonprofit hospitals that fill such prescriptions also need to comply with legal limitations on the use of drugs acquired at special prices for the hospital's own use.

Pharmacy licensing laws and regulations usually include staffing requirements. The scope of permitted uses of unlicensed, pharmacy technical staff varies from state to state.

3-3.2 Formulary Systems

Hospitals generally promote rational and cost-effective drug use through a hospital formulary system, which is designed for selection and stocking of drugs primarily for patient care. When a medical staff committee determines that two or more drugs are equivalent, only one is primarily stocked. Hospital formulary drugs are selected by negotiation with or bidding from competing suppliers. When a physician prescribes a drug and an equivalent is stocked by the hospital, the equivalent drug is dispensed. However, if the physician specifies on the prescription form or orders that no substitutions are permitted, then the equivalent drug is not dispensed. Hospital or medical staff rules determine when such a specification will result in obtaining the specified drug and when it will result in an educational effort or other response. Formulary systems are required by Medicare Conditions of Participation.[41] TJC requires a procedure for selecting medications available in the hospital.[42]

There have been legal challenges to hospital formulary systems on the basis of state anti-substitution or generic substitution laws, federal and state drug laws, and trademark laws. These challenges have not been successful when there is agreement between the prescriber and dispenser that an equivalent drug can be dispensed. The equivalent drug is what is actually prescribed, based on the prescription symbols. Usually, the agreement referred to above is in the medical staff bylaws or regulations, which each medical staff member agrees to follow as a condition of medical staff membership.

Managed care organizations typically have formularies for the drugs that they will cover for enrollees and their dependents.[43] Some states have sought to limit the use of managed care formularies.[44]

State Medicaid programs also use formularies to control drug utilization and costs.[45] These formularies have been challenged in court and have generally been upheld as valid.[46] Sometimes, there are intense efforts to influence administrative decisions concerning these lists.[47]

In the absence of an express or implied agreement, substitution of drugs is generally unlawful.[48]

3-3.3 Controlled Substances Act

The Comprehensive Drug Abuse Prevention and Control Act of 1970,[49] commonly known as the Controlled Substances Act, regulates distribution systems and also deals with rehabilitation programs, research in and treatment of drug abuse, and importation and exportation of controlled substances. The Act should be reviewed when hospitals create or revise procedures for handling and administering controlled substances.

Hospitals are defined as "institutional practitioners"[50] and must register under the Act.[51] Each registrant must take a physical inventory of its controlled substances every two years.[52] A separate inventory is required for each registered location and for each independent activity registered. Each registrant must maintain records of receipt and disposal of controlled substances it handles. [53]

Controlled substances are classified into lists, called schedules, based on the level of controls over each class.[54] The Drug Enforcement Administration (DEA) of the Department of Justice decides which substances are placed into each schedule.[55] Schedule I has the tightest controls. Controlled substances in Schedules I through IV can be dispensed only upon the lawful order of a practitioner.

For outpatients, the order must be a prescription that complies with legal requirements.[56] For inpatients, a chart order satisfies the requirement.[57] The practitioner who signs the order must be registered with the DEA or exempt from registration.[58] State law determines which professionals can be practitioners.[59] Persons who are registered with the DEA are issued a DEA number. Compliance issues often arise when private entities use DEA numbers for other purposes.[60]

> The regulation provides for five schedules of controlled substances. The five schedules of drugs vary by potential for abuse, acceptance as a medical use for treatment in the United States, and severity of potential psychological or physical dependence. Examples include: Schedule I: China white, Ecstasy, Schedule II: Cocaine, Codeine; Schedule III: Anabolic steroids (bodybuilding drugs), Vicodin, Norco; Schedule IV: Valium, Xanax; and Schedule V: Lomotil, Lyrica.

Institutions and individual registrants must provide controls and procedures to guard against theft and diversion of controlled substances. Only authorized personnel should have access to the central storage area and to other areas where drugs are kept in the hospital. Controlled substances stored at nursing units should be securely locked.

Federal criminal penalties, including fines and imprisonment, may be imposed for violating the Act.[61] In addition, violators can lose the authority to possess, prescribe, and dispense controlled substances. Most states have controlled substances acts that parallel the federal law, so state sanctions are also possible.[62]

The DEA takes the position that marijuana is a Schedule 1 Controlled Substance (21 USC Section 801, et seq.).[65] The DEA bases its position on what it considers to be the clear weight of the evidence to support its position. That evidence, according to the DEA, includes a high potential for abuse when marijuana is smoked.

Nonetheless, some states continue to pass laws that legalize the medical use of marijuana. Oregon, for example, passed the Oregon Medical Marijuana Act (ORS 475.300 to ORS 475.346). Partly in response to this state legislative activity, the Department of Justice issued a memorandum on October 19, 2009, that provides guidance to federal prosecutors in those states with medical marijuana use laws. In general, prosecutors are discouraged from focusing on individuals who are "in clear and unambiguous compliance with existing state laws providing for the medical use of marijuana."*

Courts have generally ruled that neither the federal nor state constitution grants a right, even to the terminally ill, to use any substance banned by the government.[66] In 1999, a patient with multiple sclerosis was prosecuted in the District of Columbia for medicinal use of marijuana.[67] In 2001, the U.S. Supreme Court ruled that there was no medical necessity defense to federal prosecution for marijuana possession.[68] In 2002, the California Supreme Court interpreted the state law that provided a defense to state prosecution for marijuana use and possession.[69] In 2005, the U.S. Supreme Court ruled that state law provided no protection from federal prosecution for medicinal use of marijuana.[70]

At one time there was concern that even discussing marijuana with a patient could subject a physician to federal penalties. In 2002, a federal appellate court affirmed a permanent injunction keeping the federal government from revoking a physician's license based solely on the physician's professional recommendation of the use of medical marijuana.[71]

3-3.4 Regulation of Drugs and Devices by the U.S. Food and Drug Administration

The FDA enforces a complex system of federal controls over testing, manufacturing, labeling, and distribution of drugs, cosmetics, and devices.[72] These controls appear in the Federal Food, Drug, and Cosmetic Act, which includes the Medical Device Amendments of 1976, and in FDA regulations.[73]

DEFINITION OF DRUGS AND DEVICES. Drugs and devices are broadly defined in statutes and regulations.

> One area of tension concerning the Controlled Substances Act has been the federal prohibition of the medicinal use of marijuana for pain control. In some parts of the country, marijuana has been permitted for medicinal use, while other states follow the federal position.[63] In 1998, voters in five states passed referenda legalizing medicinal marijuana, but these actions remain preempted by federal law.[64]

---

* http://blogs.usdoj.gove/blog/archives/192

The FDA website indicates its responsibilities are: protecting the public health by assuring that foods are safe, wholesome, sanitary, and properly labeled; human and veterinary drugs, and vaccines and other biological products and medical devices intended for human use are safe and effective; protecting the public from electronic product radiation; assuring cosmetics and dietary supplements are safe and properly labeled; regulating tobacco products; advancing the public health by helping to speed product innovations; and helping the public get the accurate science-based information they need to use medicines, devices, and foods to improve their health.

For example, human blood is considered a drug. Virtually all equipment and supplies used in patient care are regulated as devices. In addition to obvious devices such as hip prostheses, pacemakers, and artificial hearts, the term includes common equipment and supplies; including catheters, hospital beds, specimen containers,[74] support stockings, scissors, adhesive tape, elastic bandages, tongue depressors, and sutures. In 1992, a federal appellate court upheld an FDA rule defining replacement heart valve allographs as medical devices.[75] A heart valve allograph is a human heart valve that has been processed and preserved so that it can be stored until needed for implantation.

FDA ENFORCEMENT DISCRETION. The FDA has broad discretion to decide whether to use its powers to investigate or penalize specific activities. When the FDA declined to investigate drugs used to execute condemned criminals, the U.S. Supreme Court was asked to order an FDA investigation. The Court ruled that the FDA and other federal agencies have prosecutorial discretion to decide whether to exercise their discretionary powers in individual cases, so courts cannot review such decisions in most situations.[76]

TIMELINESS OF FDA APPROVAL. The FDA has been attacked for the time it takes to approve new drugs and devices and for the cost of compliance with its requirements, among other factors.[77] On the other hand, the FDA often is recognized and supported for its contribution to protecting public safety. In the mid-1990s, the FDA implemented some reforms to speed review, including exempting many low risk devices from review.[78] In 1997, the FDA law was amended to further expedite review and make other changes.[79] The FDA has subsequently been criticized when approved drugs were later demonstrated to have harmful and even lethal side effects.[80] It is clear that there are competing public interests that cannot all be satisfied. The balance between cost, safety, access, and other factors changes from time to time.

Thalidomide is an example of a drug that illustrates the difficulty in striking the appropriate balance. In the 1950s, thalidomide was used in Europe to treat pregnant women and resulted in the birth of children with missing limbs and other birth defects. The FDA had not approved thalidomide for use in the United States, but a few handicapped children were born to American women after they obtained the drug from Europe. In reaction to thalidomide, the FDA law was amended to significantly increase the powers of the FDA to control the introduction of new drugs. It was later discovered that thalidomide was an effective drug to treat leprosy. In light of the risks associated with use of thalidomide and its high profile role in the history of FDA's control of new drugs, there was reluctance to lift the ban on its use. In 1997, an FDA panel recommended that use of thalidomide be permitted.[81] In 1998, the FDA approved use within strict limits that required registry of patients and special training of prescribing physicians and dispensing pharmacists.[82]

OTHER FDA FUNCTIONS. The FDA performs other important health functions. For example, it has mandated that foods be fortified with various substances that are essential to good health. In 1924, iodizing of salt was required. In 1943, the addition of vitamins and iron to certain foods was required. In 1996, folic acid was ordered to be added to grain foods to cut down on birth defects.[83] The FDA implemented the Food Safety Modernization Act (FSMA) in 2011, with the most comprehensive changes in 70 years. The Act enables the FDA to focus more on prevention than reaction to food borne illness. As an example, the FDA is required under this Act to establish minimum standards for the safe harvesting and production of produce.[†] In 2011, the FDA announced new requirements to take effect in the summer of 2012 for nonprescription sunscreen products in an effort to keep pace with current safety and effectiveness standards.[‡] The FDA also holds educational forums to improve safety and effectiveness. In 2010, the FDA sent a letter to manufacturers of radiation therapy equipment, encouraging their attendance at a public workshop to address problems with under-doses, over-doses, and misaligned radiation exposures.

[†] http://www.fda.gov/downloads/Food/FoodSafety/FSMA/UCM265430.pdf
[‡] http://www.fda.gov/Drugs/ResourcesForYou/Consumers/BuyingUsingMedicineSafely/UnderstandingOver-the-Counter Medicines/ucm258468.htm

INVESTIGATIONAL DRUGS AND DEVICES. Before new drugs and devices can enter general use, an elaborate procedure must be followed to establish their safety and effectiveness. The investigational new drug (IND) and investigational device exemption (IDE) requirements must be met to legally use investigational drugs and devices. With few exceptions, these drugs and devices can be used only in research projects approved by an Institutional Review Board, conducted by a qualified investigator, and sponsored by an appropriate company or institution.[84] Sale or use of unlicensed drugs and devices outside the permitted processes can result in substantial penalties.[85] There is no constitutional right to use unapproved drugs; they can be used only as permitted by law.[86]

Record-keeping. Investigators must maintain complete and accurate records, and the manufacturer must make full disclosure of the results to the FDA. The FDA can use criminal sanctions to enforce its record-keeping and reporting requirements. A Minnesota investigator was convicted of mail fraud and making false statements to the government for submitting false information concerning a study.[87] Officials of manufacturers have been convicted for submitting false information or failing to submit information that should have been submitted.[88] The FDA has taken steps to enhance data integrity with the regulations adopted in 2011, 21 CFR part 11 which establishes criteria for electronic records and electronic signatures to improve the reliability of the data.[§]

Testing Phases. New drugs generally have three testing phases.[89]

- Phase 1 focuses on determining the pharmacologic action of the drug, side effects, and maximum tolerated dose. Phase 1 studies can involve normal volunteers.

- Phase 2 consists of small, controlled clinical studies on patients to evaluate effectiveness for particular indications and side effects.

- Phase 3 consists of expanded, controlled and uncontrolled studies to gather additional information on effectiveness and safety, evaluate the risk-benefit relationship, and provide an adequate basis for labeling. Some drugs that appeared promising in earlier phases have failed in Phase 3.[90] In some circumstances, there are Phase 4 post-marketing studies.[91]

Research on special populations. In order to protect children from risks, research on children was discouraged. However, over time it was recognized that children did not have access to important drugs because there were insufficient data on the effects of those drugs on children. In 1998, the FDA mandated pediatric studies on drugs.[92] In 2002, a federal court struck down the pediatric study mandate as being beyond the authority of the FDA.[93] Congress amended the law to give HHS authority concerning pediatric studies and to reward drug companies with a patent extension for some of the pediatric studies.[94]

In 1998, the FDA also mandated that studies include other important demographic subgroups, including groups based on gender and race.[95]

Treatment uses prior to full approval. The FDA can approve treatment with an investigational new drug outside of clinical trials when the drug is for a serious or immediately life-threatening disease and there is no satisfactory alternative therapy available. This approval is often called a treatment IND.[96] There is also a procedure for approval of emergency shipments prior to IND approval.[97] There are rules permitting humanitarian uses of investigational devices.[98]

Subjects in clinical studies generally do not have a legal right to continued access to investigational drugs after they cease to be subjects.[99] However, consent documents can create a contract to continue to supply the drug.[100]

Payment for use. One controversial aspect of the use of investigational drugs and devices is that some third-party payers refuse to pay for their use. This has led to suits as discussed in Chapter 10 "Healthcare Business Processes."

In 1994, the Office of Inspector General of the Department of Health and Human Services issued a subpoena seeking the records of all uses of investigational devices at many hospitals.[101] The scope of the subpoena eventually focused on certain cardiac devices. There was concern in the hospital industry that HHS was taking an aggressive position regarding the use of investigational devices. That position appeared to be that when an investigational device was used during a hospitalization that the entire hospitalization was not eligible for Medicare or Medicaid payment, In addition, the industry was concerned that even submitting a bill for the hospital stay might be treated as a federal "false claim." This led some hospitals to either stop enrolling Medicare and Medicaid patients in clinical device trials or halting all uses of investigational devices until the legal status of the devices was clarified.[102] Hospitals

---

§ http://www.accessdata.fda.gov/scripts/cdrh/cfdocs/cfcfr/ CFRSearch.cfm?CFRPart=11&showFR=1

sued to challenge the federal enforcement effort. The steps described below followed the filing of that federal lawsuit and illustrate how the FDA, Medicare, and administrative laws interacted to address this serious issue.

In 1996, a federal court invalidated a 1986 instruction issued by the Health Care Financing Administration (HCFA), now known as the Centers for Medicare and Medicaid Services (CMS). The effect of that instruction was to deny payment for services using medical devices under an IDE. The court decided the case based on the fact that it was a new HCFA rule that was not properly promulgated with a notice and comment period.[103] HCFA adopted rules in 1995 that specified the process to determine coverage for investigational devices and related services.[104] In 1997, the FDA adopted rules concerning treatment uses of investigational devices.[105] In 2000, Medicare issued a national coverage decision to pay for routine costs of patients during clinic trials.[106] A few, minor changes were made to the policy in 2007. This 2007 national coverage decision can be found at https://www.cms.gov/medicare-coverage-database/details/lcd-details.

> Some states mandate that private insurers pay for patient participation in some clinical trials of investigational drugs and devices.[107]

APPROVED DRUGS AND DEVICES. When the FDA is convinced that a new drug or device is safe and effective for certain uses, it approves the drug for marketing and general sale. The approval can permit either over-the-counter sales or sales by order of a practitioner. Approval of drugs or devices can include additional restrictions on use.[108]

There often are disputes over whether prescriptions should be required. Granting over-the-counter status makes the items more accessible, removes the protection of practitioner oversight, and usually removes health care insurance coverage for the item.[109]

Labeling. The FDA approval specifies which uses of the drug or device should be included in labeling. In the past, only uses that were proven in controlled studies could be on labels. Special studies on children were required before any uses for children could be on the label, so there was limited label information about uses for children. In 1995, the FDA began permitting more label information about uses for children.[110] In 1998, the FDA amended its regulations concerning disclosure of information about uses of approved drugs and devices that vary from the approved uses.[111] However, a

> A *New England Journal of Medicine* article cites a number of drugs that have shifted from requiring a prescription to being "over the counter," including: nonsteroidal anti-inflammatory drugs; antifungal drugs; smoking cessation aids; anti-diarrheal drugs; decongestants; and hair-growth stimulants.

few months later, a federal court ruled that the FDA could not enforce its restrictions on dissemination of this information, finding the restrictions violated the First Amendment rights applicable to commercial speech.[112] Note that the First Amendment protects only truthful commercial speech, so the FDA still has the authority to address labeling that is not considered to be accurate.

> In 2004, the California Supreme Court ruled that FDA warning label requirements for nicotine patches preempt stricter state-mandated labeling.[113]

Off-label uses. The practice of medicine usually changes more rapidly than FDA approvals, so drug or device use is often different from the approved uses listed on labels.[114] Such uses are often referred to as off-label uses. Drugs are often given for other conditions or in different dosages not specified on the label. It is not a violation of federal law for physicians to order such unapproved uses or for pharmacists to dispense drugs pursuant to such orders. However, unapproved uses that result in injuries to patients can result in liability. Some courts consider FDA-approved labeling to be sufficient evidence of proper use so that no further expert testimony is required.[115] However, when defendants introduce evidence that FDA-approved uses lag behind current medical practice, deviations from FDA-approved uses alone do not conclusively prove negligence. Juries are permitted to consider the FDA position along with other testimony concerning accepted practice in deciding whether an off-label use of a drug was negligent.[116] There is no requirement to obtain informed consent for off-label drug use. However, when a particular use is not widely adopted, it is prudent for the physician to explain the reasons and methods for the unapproved use to the patient. Likewise, it is prudent for the practitioner to obtain the patient's informed consent.

Some payers refuse to pay for some or all off-label uses of approved drugs,[117] even though such uses may be considered the standard of care. In 1998, a federal circuit court ruled that a health plan that limited drug coverage to FDA-approved uses did not unambiguously prohibit coverage for prescribed off-label uses. In that case, the health plan was required to pay for the prescribed, off-label use.[118] Some states require health plans to cover certain off-label uses of approved drugs.[119]

FDA IMMUNITY. The FDA is generally immune from liability for its decisions to approve drugs and devices.[120]

PRESCRIPTIONS. When prescriptions are required, they must be properly documented. Written prescriptions or orders in the medical record satisfy the documentation requirement. The FDA Act requires oral prescriptions to dispense drugs to be "reduced promptly to writing and filed by the pharmacist."[121] This is generally interpreted not to preclude registered nurses and other appropriate personnel to transcribe oral orders to administer drugs in institutional settings. Hospitals should review these requirements and other state requirements, such as hospital licensing regulations, to assure that telephone orders are accepted by proper personnel.

Electronic prescriptions. In 1998, a Wisconsin court ruled that a community pharmacy could accept an e-mail prescription in the same circumstances that it could accept a telephone order, overruling the pharmacy licensing board ruling that an e-mail order violated the requirement of a written signature.[122] Physicians who prescribe electronically should apply the same standards that apply to telephone prescriptions and should be personally familiar with the patient. A Wisconsin physician prescribed Viagra, an erectile dysfunction drug, from a website to persons he had never seen. He was investigated in 1998 by the state medical licensing board and was permitted to keep his license when he agreed to stop the practice.[123]

CMS adopted standards for e-prescribing in a rule published in the Federal Register on April 7, 2008.[124] In an effort to reduce errors, CMS is now encouraging e-prescribing. Section 132 of the Medicare Improvements for Patients and Providers Act of 2008 (MIPPA) authorizes a new and separate incentive program for eligible providers who are successful e-prescribers.[125]

Scope of pharmacist duties. While a pharmacist has a duty to question a prescription that is suspicious on its face, a pharmacist generally does not have a duty to question every prescription. This issue was analyzed in detail by the Utah Supreme Court in a case in which a pharmacist attempted to defend his customer relations problems on the grounds that he had a duty to challenge prescriptions.[126]

DEVICE TRACKING. Manufacturers have a duty to put in place a method for tracking certain devices, including permanently implantable devices, life-support devices for use outside of a hospital, and other devices designated by rule.[127] Hospitals and other distributors are required to provide the necessary information to the manufacturer, unless an exemption is obtained.[128]

MANUFACTURING. Every person who owns or operates any establishment engaged in interstate or intrastate "manufacture, preparation, propagation, compounding or processing" of drugs must register each such establishment.[129] The terms manufacture, preparation, propagation, compounding, and processing include prepackaging or otherwise changing the container, wrapper, or labeling of drugs for distribution to others who will make the final sale or distribution to the ultimate consumer. The Food, Drug, and Cosmetics Act also requires manufacturers to maintain certain records; file specified reports; be periodically inspected; and satisfy other requirements.[130] Manufacturers must file a list of all drugs they manufacture. The FDA exempts most hospitals from these requirements if the hospitals are "in conformance with any applicable local laws."[131] However, if the hospital pharmacy supplies compounded or repackaged drugs to other institutions or pharmacies under circumstances other than emergencies, it can be considered a manufacturer.

The Prescription Drug Marketing Act of 1988[132] places additional restrictions on transfers of drugs to persons other than patients. Drugs can be resold or returned to manufacturers and distributors only if proper procedures are followed.[133]

Hospital blood banks must register and comply with regulations concerning good manufacturing practices for blood and blood components.[134]

BAR CODING. In 2004, the FDA adopted a rule that requires bar coding of drugs and biologic products. The 2004 final rule changes the electronic scanning of bar codes on drugs (blood products) from a permissible activity to a required activity.[135] Newly approved drugs must comply within sixty days of their approval.[136]

The FDA cites that bar coding will reduce the number of medicine and transfusion errors by 502,000 and $93 billion dollars over twenty years.

IMPORTS. Canada has negotiated much lower drug prices than are generally available in the United States. Periodically, there is intense discussion and political advocacy in the United States to permit reimportation of drugs into the United States from Canada at the prices available in Canada. In 2000, Congress authorized HHS to promulgate rules to permit this practice.[137] As of mid-2011, HHS had not yet promulgated such rules.

More recently, Congress rejected the Pharmaceutical Market Access and Drug Safety Act of 2009, which would have allowed Americans to buy FDA-approved prescription drugs from overseas.[138] The Pharmaceutical Market Access and Drug Safety Act of 2011, which also seeks to permit the importation of FDA-approved prescription drugs, was introduced for consideration by Congress.[139] Several states and local governments tried to adopt governmental programs to facilitate importation of prescription drugs. Vermont failed to defend its drug importation program in a suit against HHS because the program would, among other things, violate federal importation laws.[140] Rhode Island enacted regulations permitting Canadian pharmacies to sell drugs to residents and, despite a subsequent letter from FDA prohibiting such conduct, continues to post those regulations.[141]

POISON PREVENTION PACKAGING ACT. The Poison Prevention Packaging Act[142] requires most drugs to be dispensed in containers designed to be difficult for children to open. Exceptions are permitted when authorized by the prescribing physician.

3-3.5 Laws Related to Marketing Drugs and Devices

There are three main sources of regulation of the marketing of drugs and devices: the FDA, Federal Trade Commission (FTC), and Centers for Medicare and Medicaid Services (CMS). Other regulatory agencies, state laws and private lawsuits also constrain marketing activities.

FDA. The FDA regulates the labeling of drugs and devices and seeks to regulate advertising of drugs and devices.

The First Amendment restricts the ability to regulate advertising. In 2002, the U.S. Supreme Court struck down an FDA prohibition of advertising compound drugs, finding it an unconstitutional restriction on commercial speech.[143] A total prohibition on truthful advertising is generally not permitted. Regulation to prohibit false or misleading advertising is permissible. Labeling requirements of the FDA are generally upheld. The FDA frequently directs changes in labeling, both as to content and format.[144] The FDA also challenges advertising or promotions that it considers to be misleading.[145]

There frequently is debate and litigation over the extent to which the FDA can regulate the promotion of off-label uses. In 1999, a federal district court found that the FDA's regulatory efforts under the Food and Drug Administration Modernization Act of 1997 (FDAMA) violated the First Amendment and issued an injunction against the FDA. The FDA appealed and stated during the appeal that FDAMA did not provide it with independent authority to proscribe speech. Based on this concession, the appellate court vacated the district court injunction. The FDA maintained that it still could prosecute any promotion of off-label uses outside the scope authorized by FDAMA. Nonetheless, the challengers decided that they did not want to pursue the case any further and withdrew the lawsuit.[146]

FEDERAL TRADE COMMISSION. The FTC actively regulates advertising, pursuing claims that are false, misleading, or unproven.[147] The Federal Trade Commission Act provides that "unfair or deceptive acts or practices in or affecting commerce are declared unlawful."[148]

"Unfair" practices are defined to mean those that "cause or [are] likely to cause substantial injury to consumers which is not reasonably avoidable by consumers themselves and not outweighed by countervailing benefits to consumers or to competition."[149]

In 2000, a drug company was accused of making unproven claims in its advertising. In a settlement with the FTC, the company entered a consent decree that included a national consumer education campaign.[150]

Private suits can be brought under some of the laws administered by the FTC. Companies sometimes use these laws to challenge claims made by their competitors.[151]

CENTERS FOR MEDICARE & MEDICAID SERVICES (CMS). Medicare and Medicaid laws prohibit inducements to providers to order or purchase, or arrange for the ordering or purchasing of products and services. This prohibition has a substantial impact on marketing activities. In 2003, the Inspector General of the Department of

Health and Human Services issued marketing guidance for pharmaceutical manufacturers.[152]

In 2001, a federal district court ruled that a False Claims Act suit could be brought against a drug manufacturer for promoting off-label use.[153] In September 2009, Pfizer, a drug manufacturer, agreed to a $2.3 billion dollar settlement, the largest healthcare fraud settlement in the history of the Department of Justice. The settlement resolved civil claims and criminal charges from alleged illegal marketing of multiple drugs for uses that were not considered medically accepted indications and allegedly caused false claims to be submitted to governmental healthcare programs. The cases were brought forward by "whistleblowers," and as such the settlement funds were shared between the whistleblowers and Medicare and Medicaid. The settlement agreement includes a comprehensive corporate integrity agreement, requiring procedures be implemented to limit the risk of inappropriate conduct.[154]

In 2003, another drug company agreed to pay $622 million to settle claims regarding marketing of feeding liquids. The company gave free tubes and pumps to providers who were suspected to have billed Medicare and Medicaid for the tubes and pumps.[155]

STATE LAWS ON PRICE ADVERTISING. In the past, many states had laws limiting prescription price advertising. In 1976, the Supreme Court declared unconstitutional all laws that prohibit or unnecessarily restrict advertising of prescription price information. The Court left room for states to control some aspects of advertising, including restrictions on time, place, manner, and false or deceptive practices.[156] Some states now require the posting of prices in pharmacies.

SUNSHINE LAWS. Some states require a report on the number of gifts made to individual physicians from drug companies,[157] consistent with industry guidance admonishing inappropriate marketing activities.[158] Beginning March 31, 2013, federal law will impose a similar requirement on all drug and device manufacturers; among other things, manufacturers must annually report to HHS any payments to physicians and teaching hospitals, such as cash, gifts, entertainment, food, and travel.[159]

Conclusion

Healthcare facilities are highly regulated. In addition to regulations that apply to all buildings in general (e.g., local fire and safety codes and zoning ordinances), healthcare facilities have specific requirements which govern construction, modernization, and operations. These regulations are promulgated at the federal as well as the state level. Most facilities require a variety of permits and certifications, many of which must be updated on a regular basis. Hospitals generally have a license from the state to operate the facility as well as permits for particular hospital functions, including a clinical laboratory, mammography, and possession and use of radioactive material. Pharmaceuticals and medical devices are also heavily regulated by CMS, FDA, DEA, and state laws.

Chapter Summary

This chapter covered a wide range of federal and state laws that regulate the creation of healthcare facilities, and how those facilities are equipped, supplied, and operated. In addition, this chapter provided numerous examples of the types of legal actions brought by government agencies and private parties that are engaged in planning, constructing, and operating healthcare facilities. This chapter also included extensive coverage of regulatory authority and actions taken by the Food and Drug Administration, as well as other enforcement agencies against providers, including hospitals and physicians.

Key Terms and Definitions

Zoning Ordinances - Laws adopted by local governments that specify permitted uses of certain types of land for specific purposes.

Life Safety Code® (LSC) - Standards published by the National Fire Protection Association and intended to supplement building and fire prevention codes. The LSC is not law, but providers and suppliers participating in Medicare and Medicaid programs are required to comply with the LSC. Compliance with the LSC is also required by accrediting organizations, such as The Joint Commission.

The Joint Commission (TJC) - The organization that certifies and accredits healthcare organizations and programs.

Certificate of Need permit (CON) - A formal document issued to a healthcare institution or provider giving permission for construction and modification of health agencies, major equipment expenditures, or new health services.

Clinical Laboratories Improvement Act (CLIA) - A federal law passed in 1988 that regulates every medical test in every laboratory in the nation, including those conducted in physicians' offices. Even those tests that may be purchased over-the-counter at a neighborhood pharmacy require at least federal governmental permission in order to perform the test.

The Comprehensive Drug Abuse Prevention and Control Act of 1970 (or "Controlled Substances Act") - A federal law that regulates the prescribing and dispensing of certain restricted drugs. These restricted drugs are "scheduled" into five categories, with Schedule I drugs considered the most dangerous and to possess the most danger for abuse (no prescriptions may be written) and Schedule V drugs considered to possess the lowest potential for abuse and dependence in the schedules.

Investigational Device Exemption (IDE) - Exceptions that allow certain medical devices to be used in research projects approved by an Institutional Review Board, conducted by a qualified investigator, and sponsored by an appropriate company or institution.

Treatment IND - FDA-approved treatment with an investigational new drug outside of clinical trials, used when the drug is for a serious or immediately life-threatening disease and there is no satisfactory alternative therapy available.

Off-Label Use - When drugs are given or prescribed for other conditions or in different dosages not specified on the drug label.

The Poison Prevention Packaging Act - A federal law that requires most drugs to be dispensed in containers designed to be difficult for children to open.

Instructor-Led Questions

1. Discuss the legal constraints on construction of healthcare facilities. How do zoning requirements, building codes, building permit requirements, and certificate of need laws regulate the creation of healthcare buildings?

2. What are the limits on government use of these regulations to bar healthcare buildings?

3. What are some of the healthcare services that are not authorized by a general institutional license and require special additional licenses?

4. Discuss the legal issues involved in implementing formulary systems.

5. Discuss how the federal Controlled Substances Act regulates the use of controlled substances in health care.

6. Discuss federal Food and Drug Administration (FDA) regulation of new drugs.

7. Discuss off-label uses of drugs.

8. Discuss FDA regulation of new devices.

9. Discuss what constitutes a valid prescription for a drug.

10. Discuss FDA regulation of the importation of low cost drugs from other countries.

11. Discuss the scope of governmental authority to regulate labeling and advertising of drugs and devices.

Endnotes

1 E.g., Commission OKs rezoning for hospital parking lot, TAMPA TRIBUNE, Aug. 19, 2000, 2.

2 Council decision prompts hospital to look for new site, MILWAUKEE JOURNAL SENTINEL, July 19, 2002, 5B.

3 *Wisconsin Cmty. Serv. v. City of Milwaukee*, 309 F. Supp. 2d 1096 (E.D. Wis. 2004).

4 *Mount Sinai Med. Ctr. v. City of Miami Beach*, 706 F. Supp. 1525 (S.D. Fla. 1989).

5 Miami Beach settles with Mount Sinai, FLA. MED. BUS. (S. Fla. ed.), Feb. 28, 1989, 16. For another zoning settlement, see MOD. HEALTHCARE, May 5, 1997, 52 [settlement between Alta Bates hospital, city over whether construction was contrary to zoning, permitting laws].

6 Appeal of Suburban Gen. Hosp., 48 Pa. Commw. 273, 410 A.2d 85 (1980).

7 Life Safety Code® is a registered trademark of the National Fire Protection Association, Quincy, MA.

8 Board grants four variances, CAL-OSHA RPTR., Mar. 5, 2004 [variance granted for oversized platform for wheelchair lift].

9 E.g., CAL. HEALTH & SAFETY CODE § 130000 et seq.; T. Pristin, Decade after big quake, a hospital building boom, N.Y. TIMES, Nov. 24, 2004, C6.

10 Joint Commission on Accreditation of Healthcare Organizations, 2005 COMPREHENSIVE ACCREDITATION MANUAL FOR HOSPITALS, EC.5.20 [hereinafter the manual is referred to as 2005 JCAHO CAMH].

11 E.g., *Miami Heart Inst. v. Heery Architects & Eng'rs, Inc.*, 765 F. Supp. 1083 (S.D. Fla. 1991), aff'd without op., 44 F.3d 1007 (11th Cir. 1994) [alleged breach of contract from failure to draw plans, specifications for hospital in accordance with relevant codes; hospital failed inspections by state hospital licensing agency, City of Miami Beach delaying certificate of occupancy for nearly a year].

12 *Coppola v. Good Samaritan Hosp. Med. Ctr.*, N.Y.L.J., Nov. 2, 2002, 25 [text of trial court order]; E. Holm, Planning board turns back the clock; Court-ordered review of already-built wing at hospital begins, NEWSDAY (New York), Apr. 20, 2003, G23; *Coppola v. Good Samaritan Hosp. Med. Ctr.*, 309 A.D.2d 862, 765 N.Y.S.2d 888 (2d Dept. 2003), app. denied, 1 N.Y.3d 506 (2004); A. Guardino, Zoning and land use; Proceeding with caution after negative declaration, N.Y.L.J., Feb. 17, 2004, 16; L. Jones, Legal limbo; four-year battle over emergency room reaches new stage, N.Y.L.J., Mar. 2, 2004, 16; Court stays enforcement of injunction against emergency room's continued operation, N.Y.L.J., Mar. 3, 2004, 21.

13 *Abady v. Board of Standards & Appeals*, N.Y.L.J., Apr. 14, 2004, 18.

14 Pub. L. No. 93-641, 88 Stat. 2225, § 1523(a)(1)(4) (1975) (codified at 42 U.S.C. § 300m-2(a)(1)(4)). For a short history of the law of health planning, see R. Miller, PROBLEMS IN HOSPITAL LAW, 95-108 (5th ed.).

15 Pub. L. No. 99-660, 100 Stat. 3799 (1986).

16 J. Preston, States ease restrictions on hospitals, N.Y. TIMES, July 27, 1998, C18 [end of requirement of certificate of need for many services]; Lapse of law could mean increase in nursing homes, AP, Jan. 1, 2003 [Missouri]; see also Hospitals lobby to keep planning and review board, AP, Mar. 18, 2003 [N.H.].

17 *St. Dominic-Jackson Mem. Hosp. v. Mississippi State Dep't of Health*, 728 So.2d 81 (Miss. 1998) [successful challenge to primary care center by competing hospitals]; see also *Methodist Healthcare-Jackson Hosp. v. Jackson-Madison County Gen. Hosp. Dist.*, 2003 Tenn. App. LEXIS 369.

18 Matter of MGNH, Inc. & HCA Genesis, N.Y.L.J., May 24, 2004, 22.

19 *Armstrong Surgical Ctr., Inc. v. Armstrong County Mem. Hosp.*, 185 F.3d 154 (3rd Cir. 1999), cert. denied, 530 U.S. 1261 (2000).

20 FLA. STAT. § 395.0146 [CON required to close emergency room].

21 E.g., In re *Hazlet Manor Ass'n*, No. A-1431095T3F (N.J. Super. Ct. App. Div. Jan. 17, 1997), as discussed in 25 HEALTH L. DIG. (Feb. 1997), at 35 [affirming rejection of CON for long-term care facility that refused to commit to 55% Medicaid occupancy].

22 *National Health Corp. v. South Carolina Dep't of Health & Environ. Control*, 298 S.C. 373, 380 S.E.2d 841 (Ct. App. 1989).

23 E.g., In re *Nashua Brookside Hosp.*, 636 A.2d 57 (N.H. 1993) [error of law to review application to convert substance abuse beds to psychiatric beds without required letters from state mental health agency].

24 E.g., In re *VHA Diagnostic Servs., Inc.*, 65 Ohio St. 3d 210, 602 N.E.2d 647 (1992).

25 E.g., J. Piazza, Officials: moratorium on Maine's hospitals will cause drop in issuance, BOND BUYER, July 9, 2003, 3.

26 E.g., *Sheffield Towers Rehab. & Health Care Ctr. v. Novello*, 293 A.D.2d 182, 741 N.Y.S.2d 103 (2d Dept. 2002) [moratorium on nursing homes affirmed].

27   E.g., *Balsam v. Dep't of Health & Rehabilitative Servs.*, 452 So.2d 976 (Fla. 1st DCA 1984); *Arkansas Dep't of Human Servs. v. Greene Acres Nursing Homes, Inc.*, 296 Ark. 475, 757 S.W.2d 563 (1988).

28   For an example of the complications involved in transfers, see *Paragon Health Network, Inc. v. Thompson*, 251 F.3d 1141 (7th Cir. 2001).

29   *Hospital Corp. of Am. v. Springhill Hosps., Inc.*, 472 So.2d 1059 (Ala. Civ. App. 1985).

30   *South Broward Hosp. Dist. v. Nu-Med Penbroke*, 603 So.2d 11 (Fla. 4th DCA 1992).

31   *Rush-Presbyterian-St. Luke's Med. Ctr. v. Hellenic Republic*, 980 F.2d 449 (7th Cir. 1992).

32   42 U.S.C. § 263a; 42 C.F.R. pt. 493; *Consumer Federation of Am. v. U.S. Dep't of H.H.S.*, 317 U.S. App. D.C. 449, 83 F.3d 1497 (1996) [in challenge to CLIA rules, agency ordered to provide rationale or pursue further changes].

33   See *Elsenety v. H.C.F.A.*, 85 Fed. Appx. 405 (6th Cir. 2003) [affirming revocation of CLIA certificates]; *Oakland Med. Group, P.C. v. Sec'y of Health & Human Servs.*, 298 F.3d 507 (6th Cir. 2002) [no right to pretermination hearing].

34   42 U.S.C. § 263b; 21 C.F.R. pt. 900; Newark hospital cited for violation in mammogram unit, AP, Dec. 28, 2001 [federal citation]; Chicago mammography facility fined $30,000, suspended for five years, BREAST IMPLANT LITIGATION RPTR., Aug. 25, 1998, 13; J. Peres, Panel says medical facilities that hold breast cancer screenings must do better, CHICAGO TRIB., May 24, 2005 [Institute of Medicine report].

35   See http://www.nrc.gov/materials/medical.html [accessed Sept. 11, 2004]; NRC imposes fine against hospital, AP, June 18, 2002 [fine for dose of radioactive pharmaceutical to student not approved by a physician]; for other examples of enforcement efforts, see http://www.nrc.gov and enter: Healthcare regulatory enforcement actions in the search box.

36   E.g., Cal. Lab. Code §§ 7300.1 et seq.; Board grants four variances, CAL-OSHA RPTR., Mar. 5, 2004 [CA hospital granted variance to permit platform size wheelchair lift].

37   E.g., Florida allows 2 firms to market interferon under law on cancer, WALL ST. J., Nov. 4, 1983, 46.

38   2005 JCAHO CAMH, MM.1.10 - 8.10; 42 C.F.R. § 482.25.

39   R. Pear, Americans relying more on prescription drugs, report says, N.Y. TIMES, Dec. 3, 2004, A16 [based on National Center for Health Statistics report].

40   E.g., *Missouri Hosp. Ass'n v. Missouri Dep't of Consumer Affairs*, 731 S.W.2d 262 (Mo. Ct. App. 1987).

41   42 C.F.R. § 482.25(b)(9).

42   2005 JCAHO CAMH, MM.2.10.

43   M. Freudenheim, Not quite what doctor ordered, N.Y. TIMES, Oct. 8, 1996, C1.

44   E.g., Governor signs bill to allow patient access to drugs not listed on plan formularies, 7 H.L.R. 1058 (1998) [Cal. Senate Bill 625].

45   42 U.S.C. § 1396r-8(d)(4) [outpatient formularies]; G Aston, Medicaid short list, AM. MED. NEWS, May 3, 2004, 5 [some physicians see preferred-drug lists as barriers to care].

46   E.g., *Karen L. v. Health Net*, 78 Fed. Appx. 772 (2d Cir. 2003) [unpub] [affirm denial of injunction of deletions from Conn. Medicaid formulary]; see also *Pharmaceutical Research & Mfrs. of Am. v. Walsh*, 538 U.S. 644 (2003) [affirming denial of preliminary injunction of Maine program requiring prior authorization for drugs from manufacturers that did agree to rebates]; *Pharmaceutical Research & Mfrs. of Am. v. Thompson*, 360 U.S. App. D.C. 375, 362 F.3d 817 (2004) [approving Michigan program requiring prior authorization for drugs of manufacturers who do not sign rebate agreements].

47   See G. Harris, States try to limit drugs in Medicaid, but makers resist, N.Y. TIMES, Dec. 18, 2003, A1 [describing lobbying against removal of drugs from Medicaid lists].

48   See Pharmacy closed as "danger" to public health, AP, Aug. 27, 2004 [Vir. pharmacy closed for unauthorized substitutions]; L.A. Johnson, Medco settles accusations by 20 states, AP, Apr. 26, 2004 [alleged pressure on physicians to substitute medications that were more profitable to the prescription benefits manager; agreed to payment, practice changes without admitting wrongdoing].

49   Pub. L. No. 90-513, 84 Stat. 1236 (codified as amended in scattered sections of 18, 21, 26, 31, 42, 46, and 49 U.S.C.).

50   21 C.F.R. § 1306.02(c).

51   21 U.S.C. § 822.

52   21 U.S.C. § 827.

53   Id.; Harvard settles suit over pharmacy's laxness, N.Y. TIMES, Oct. 1, 1996, A10 [$775,000 payment for lax security, faulty record-keeping at University pharmacy].

54   21 U.S.C. § 812.

55   E.g., *Alliance for Cannabis Therapeutics v. D.E.A.*, 15 F.3d 1131 (D.C. Cir. 1994) [upholding DEA order refusing to change classification of marijuana to Schedule II].

56   21 C.F.R. pt. 1306.

57   21 C.F.R. §§ 1306.02(f), 1306.11(c), 1306.21(c), 1306.31(c).

58   21 C.F.R. § 1301.24 [exempting medical residents, some agents].

59   21 C.F.R. § 1306.2(b).

60   V. Foubister, Demands for DEA numbers become hassle, AM. MED. NEWS, July 13, 1998, 7.

61   E.g., *United States v. Steele*, 147 F.3d 1316 (11th Cir. 1998) (en banc) [conviction of pharmacist for unlawful dispensing].

62   E.g., *Schmidt v. Iowa State Bd. of Dental Examiners*, 423 N.W.2d 19 (Iowa 1988) [dental license suspended for 30 days for diversions of drugs due to ineffective office controls]; *Schmidt v. Iowa State Bd. of Dental Examiners*, 872 F.2d 243 (8th Cir. 1989) [suspension not a denial of due process].

63   E.g., Florida cabinet opposes legalizing medical marijuana, AM. MED. NEWS, Apr. 13, 1998, 35.

64 L. Page, Five states approve medical marijuana, AM. MED. NEWS, Nov. 23/30, 1998, 5.

65 http://www.justice.gov/dea/marijuana_position.pdf [Dated: January 2011].

66 E.g., *Seeley v. Washington State*, 132 Wash. 2d 776, 940 P.2d 604 (Wash. 1997) [terminally ill bone cancer patient has no state constitutional right to medicinal marijuana].

67 C. Strong, MS patient goes on trial for smoking joint, WIS. ST. J., Feb. 10, 1999, 5A.

68 *United States v. Oakland Cannabis Buyers' Coop.*, 532 U.S. 483 (2001).

69 *People v. Mower*, 28 Cal. 4th 457, 49 P.3d 1067, 122 Cal. Rptr. 2d 326 (2002) [state law does not confer complete immunity for cultivation, use of marijuana; confers limited immunity that permits defense at trial, but defendant need only raise a reasonable doubt].

70 *Gonzales v. Raich*, 125 S. Ct. 2195 (U.S. 2005).

71 *Conant v. Walters*, 309 F.3d 629 (9th Cir. 2002), cert. denied, 540 U.S. 946 (2003).

72 See, e.g., D.A. Kessler, S.M. Pape & D. Sudwall, The Federal regulation of medical devices, 317 NEW ENG. J. MED. 357 (1987).

73 Title 21 of the United States Code and Title 21 of the Code of Federal Regulations; see also T.K. Gilman & B.R. McCormick, Federal Food and Drug Act violations, 38 AM. CRIM. L. REV. 819 (2001) [reviewing criminal penalties for violations].

74 E.g., *United States v. Undetermined Number of Unlabeled Cases*, 21 F.3d 1026 (10th Cir. 1994) [specimen containers for testing for HIV are devices].

75 *Alabama Tissue Ctr. v. Sullivan*, 975 F.2d 373 (7th Cir. 1992); Annotation, What is a "drug," a "device," and a "new drug" within the definitions of these terms in sec.201(g)(1), (h), and (p) of the Federal Food, Drug, and Cosmetic Act as amended, 3 A.L.R. FED. 843; but see *Northwest Tissue Ctr. v. Shalala*, 1 F.3d 522 (7th Cir. 1993) [permitting challenge to the applying of regulations].

76 *Heckler v. Chaney*, 470 U.S. 821 (1985).

77 E.g., P. Huber, FDA caution can be deadly, too, WALL. ST. J., July 24, 1998, A14 [Thalidomide]; F.D.A. becomes target of empowered groups, N.Y. TIMES, Feb. 12, 1995, 12; FDA moves too slowly in approving medical devices, industry critics say, 3 H.L.R. 884 (1994).

78 Administration announces more reforms to speed drug, medical device reviews, 4 H.L.R. 562 (1995); P. Hilts, With record speed, F.D.A. approves a new AIDS drug. N.Y. TIMES, Mar. 15, 1996, A9; FDA cleared 139 products in 1996, a record increase, WALL. ST. J., Jan. 16, 1997, B10.

79 FDA Modernization and Accountability Act of 1997, Pub. L. No. 105-115 (1997).

80 C.L. Bennett, et al., The research on adverse drug events and reports (RADAR) project, J.A.M.A., May 4, 2005, 2131 [proposals regarding postmarketing surveillance]; G. Harris, F.D.A. to create advisory board on drug safety, N.Y. TIMES, Feb. 16, 2005, A1; S. Stapleton, Drug recalls raise questions about FDA drug approvals, AM. MED. NEWS, Aug. 17, 1998, 28; D. Grady, F.D.A. accused of hasty drug approval, N.Y. TIMES, Dec. 3, 1998, A24.

81 S. Stolberg, Thalidomide, long banned, wins support, N.Y. TIMES, Sept. 6, 1997, 11; A. Womack, Panel recommends thalidomide's use in leprosy cases, WALL ST. J., Sept. 8, 1997, B10.

82 S. Stolberg, Thalidomide gets U.S. approval to aid lepers and maybe others, N.Y. TIMES, July 17, 1998, A1.

83 G. Kolata, Vitamin to protect fetuses will be required in foods, N.Y. TIMES, Mar. 1, 1996, A8.

84 21 C.F.R. pts. 50, 56, 312, 812, 813. For a summary of FDA actions for scientific misconduct from 1975 through 1983, see M.F. Shapiro & R.P. Charrow, Scientific misconduct in investigational drug trials, 312 NEW ENG. J. MED. 731 (1985).

85 E.g., *United States ex rel. Zissler v. Regents of Univ. of Minn.*, No. 3-95-168 (D. Minn. settlement Nov. 17, 1998), as discussed in 7 H.L.R. 1897 (1998) [sale of unlicensed drugs].

86 E.g., *Cowan v. United States*, 5 F. Supp. 2d 1235 (D. Okla. 1998) [denial of injunction of FDA to permit AIDS patient to use unapproved drug].

87 *United States v. Garfinkel*, 29 F.3d 1253 (8th Cir. 1994).

88 E.g., *United States v. Chatterji*, 46 F.3d 1336 (4th Cir. 1995) [founder, part owner convicted of fraud for falsifying batches of drug].

89 21 C.F.R. § 312.21.

90 E.g., The tale of a dream, a drug and data dredging, WALL. ST. J., Feb. 7, 1995, B1 [drug designed to heal wounds did well in all tests until it failed to outperform a placebo in its Phase 3 clinical trial].

91 21 C.F.R. § 312.85.

92 63 FED. REG. 66,631 (Dec. 2, 1998).

93 *Ass'n of Am. Physicians & Surgeons, Inc. v. U.S. F.D.A.*, 226 F. Supp. 2d 204 (D. D.C. 2002).

94 21 U.S.C. §§ 355a, 355c.

95 63 FED. REG. 6854 (Feb. 11, 1998).

96 21 C.F.R. § 312.34.

97 21 C.F.R. § 312.36.

98 63 FED. REG. 19,185 (Apr. 17, 1998).

99 E.g., *Kraemer-Katz v. United States Public Health Service*, 872 F. Supp. 1235 (S.D.N.Y. 1994); A. Pollack, Judge rejects patients' suit to get test drug, N.Y. TIMES, June. 8, 2005, C8; but see *Wagner v. Janssen*, N.Y. Sup. Ct., N.Y.L.J., Jan. 2, 2001, 25 [manufacturer ordered to distribute withdrawn drug to individual].

100 E.g., *Dahl v. HEM Pharmaceuticals Corp.*, 7 F.3d 1399 (9th Cir. 1993).

101 IG nationwide hospital investigation seeks data on non-FDA approved devices, 3 H.L.R. 836 (1994).

102 E.g., L. Scott, Hospitals try to devise solutions in device debate, MOD. HEALTHCARE, Feb. 20, 1995, 34.

103 Cedars-Sinai Med. Ctr. v. Shalala, 939 F. Supp. 1457 (C.D. Cal. 1996); on appeal, it was ruled that (1) the district court should consider the HHS motion to dismiss on statute of limitations grounds and (2) a person who brought a qui tam action concerning the same issue could not intervene, *Cedars-Sinai Med. Ctr. v. Shalala*, 125 F.3d 765 (9th Cir. 1997).

104 60 FED. REG. 48,417 (Sept. 19, 1995); see also FDA, Office of Device Evaluation, Implementation of FDA/HCFA interagency agreement regarding reimbursement categorization of investigational devices (Sept. 15, 1995).

105 62 FED. REG. 48,940 (Sept. 18, 1997).

106 Sec. 30-1, Medicare Coverage Issues Manual (Sept. 19, 2000).

107 E.g., Governor signs off on grievance rules, clinical trial coverage, other bills, 7 H.L.R. 743 (1998) [Md.].

108 E.g., S. Stolberg, Thalidomide gets U.S. approval to aid lepers and maybe others, N.Y. TIMES, July 17, 1998, A1.

109 See R. Cohen, The ethicist: Drug providers, N.Y. TIMES MAG., Dec. 7, 2003, 32 [responding to patient requests to shift to prescription drugs covered by insurance]; G. Kolata, There's a blurry line between Rx and O.T.C., N.Y. TIMES, Dec. 21, 2003, 3WK.

110 21 C.F.R. § 201.57(9).

111 63 FED. REG. 31,143 (June 8, 1998).

112 *Washington Legal Found. v. Friedman*, 13 F. Supp. 2d 51 (D. D.C. 1998); FDA motion seeks clarification of order in decision voiding "off-label" policies, 7 H.L.R. 1356 (1998); *Washington Legal Found. v. Friedman*, No. 94-1306(RCL) (D. D.C. Feb. 16, 1999) [upholding 1998 ruling finding some FDA restrictions on off-label information unconstitutional].

113 *Dowhal v. SmithKline Beecham Consumer Healthcare*, 32 Cal. 4th 910, 12 Cal. Rptr. 3d 262 (2004).

114 E.g., T.A. Ratko, Recommendations for off-label use of intravenously administered immunoglobulin preparations, 273 J.A.M.A. 1865 (1995).

115 E.g., *DePaolo v. State*, 99 A.D.2d 762, 472 N.Y.S.2d 10 (2d Dept. 1984).

116 E.g., *Morlino v. Medical Ctr. of Ocean City*, 152 N.J. 563, 706 A.2d 721 (1998) [Physicians' Desk Reference drug warnings do not constitute standard of care; physician failure to follow drug use warnings is not by itself negligence]; *Young v. Cerniak*, 126 Ill. App. 3d 952, 467 N.E.2d 1045 (1st Dist. 1984).

117 See "Off-label" drug use raises a cost flag for managed-care companies, WALL ST. J., Mar. 12, 1998, A1.

118 *I.V. Servs. of Am., Inc. v. Trustees of Am. Consulting Eng'rs Council of Ins. Trust Fund*, 136 F.3d 114 (2d Cir. 1998).

119 E.g., New law requires health plans to pay for "off-label" cancer drugs, 7 H.L.R. 596 (1998) [Minn.].

120 E.g., In re Orthopedic Bone Screw Products Liab. Litig., MCL Docket No. 1014 (E.D. Pa. Nov. 12, 1998), as discussed in 7 H.L.R. 2025 (1998).

121 21 U.S.C. § 353(b).

122 *Walgreen Co. v. Wisconsin Pharmacy Examining Board*, 217 Wis. 2d 290, 577 N.W.2d 387 (1998) Wisc. App. LEXIS 201 (unpub).

123 Doctor who sold Viagra from Web site keeps license, AM. MED. NEWS, May 25, 1998, 6; see also G. Baldwin, Web Rx, AM. MED. NEWS, Aug. 3, 1998, 22.

124 https://www.cms.gov/EPrescribing/

125 https://www.cms.gov/ERXincentive

126 Ryan v. Dan's Food Stores, 972 P.2d 395 (Utah 1999).

127 21 U.S.C. § 360i(e); 21 C.F.R. pt. 821.

128 21 C.F.R. § 821.30; FDA, Guidance on medical device tracking, 7 H.L.R. 400 (1998); the FDA reporting rule was revised, 63 FED. REG. 26,069 (May 12, 1998).

129 21 U.S.C. § 360.

130 See M. Petersen, Drug maker to pay $500 million fine for factory lapses, N.Y. TIMES, May 18, 2002, A1; F.D.A. approves Schering-Plough plan on factories, N.Y. TIMES, June 4, 2003, C4.

131 21 C.F.R. § 207.10(b).

132 Pub. L. No. 100-293, 102 Stat. 95 (codified at 21 U.S.C. §§ 331(t), 333(b), 353(c)(3), 353(d), 353(e)).

133 D. Holthaus, Network of laws governs resale of products, 62 HOSPS. (Sept. 20, 1988), at 54.

134 21 C.F.R. pt. 607 [registration]; 21 C.F.R. pt. 606 [manufacturing practices].

135 69 FED. REG. 9199 (Feb. 26, 2004); M. Kaufman, Bar codes favored to cut hospitals' drug errors; health chief maps rules to encourage their use, WASH. POST, Feb. 26, 2004, A3.

136 http://www.fda.gov/BiologicsBloodVaccines/NewsEvents/WorkshopsMeetingsConferences/ucm113381.htm [accessed February 5, 2012].

137 21 U.S.C. § 384.

138 Bill Summary & Status of Pharmaceutical Market Access and Drug Safety Act of 2009 (S.Amdt.2791). *Available at*: http://thomas.loc.gov/cgi-bin/bdquery/z?d111:SP2793: [accessed August 22, 2011, displaying bill status as withdrawn in the Senate on 12/15/2009 after not having achieved 60 votes].

139 Bill Summary & Status of Pharmaceutical Market Access and Drug Safety Act of 2011 (S.319). Available at: http://thomas.loc.gov/cgi-bin/bdquery/z?d112:SN00319:@@@L&summ2=m& [accessed August 22, 2011, displaying status as being read twice and referred to the Committee on Health, Education, Labor, and Pensions].

140 *Vermont v. Leavitt*, 405 F.Supp.2d 466 (D. Vt. 2005); K. Zezima, New England: Vermont: Lawsuit On Canadian Drugs Is Dismissed, N.Y. TIMES, Sept. 22, 2005, *available at*: http://query.nytimes.com/gst/fullpage.html?res=9804E6DA1730F931A1575AC0A9639C8B63 [accessed August 22, 2011].

141 See, e.g., State of Rhode Island Department of Health, Rules and Regulations Pertaining to Pharmacists, Pharmacies and Manufacturers, Wholesalers and Distributors, R5-19.1-PHAR, § 18.9. *Available at*: http://sos.ri.gov/documents/archives/regdocs/released/pdf/DOH/5891.pdf [accessed August 22, 2011, discussing requirements for Canadian pharmacies that seek licensure in Rhode Island]; FDA Letter to Patrick C. Lynch, Attorney General of Rhode Island, Jan. 28, 2005, *available at*: http://www.fda.gov/drugs/drugsafety/ucm179416.htm [accessed August 22, 2011].

142 Pub. L. No. 91-601, 84 Stat. 1670 (codified as amended in scattered sections of 7,15, 21 U.S.C.).

143 *Thompson v. Western States Med. Ctrs.*, 535 U.S. 357 (2002).

144 E.g., S. Elliott, The F.D.A. may ask drug advertisers to make information on side effects more prominent, N.Y. TIMES, Feb. 5, 2004, C5 [proposed rules].

145 E.g., G. Harris, Federal drug agency calls ads for the cholesterol pill Crestor "false and misleading," N.Y. TIMES, Dec. 23, 2004, A16; Genetech warned by F.D.A., N.Y. TIMES, Aug. 28, 2003, C11 [warned to stop misleading promotions of growth hormone]; E. Douglass, Gilead ordered to stop misstatements, L.A. TIMES, Aug. 8, 2003, pt. 3, 2; J. Bennett, FDA tells Allergan that Botox ads violate federal law, AP, June 24, 2003.

146 *Washington Legal Found. v. Henney*, 56 F. Supp. 2d 81, 87 (D. D.C. 1999) [injunction], vacated, 340 U.S. App. D.C. 108, 202 F.3d 331, 335 (D.C. Cir. 2000), on remand, 128 F. Supp. 2d 11 (D. D.C. 2000); D. Mack, Appeal dismissed in off-label use case; A constitutional question disappears, CORP. LEGAL TIMES, May 2000, 80.

147 http://www.ftc.gov/ [accessed September 18, 2004].

148 15 U.S.C. § 45(a)(1).

149 15 U.S.C. § 45(n).

150 Bayer settles FTC charges of unproven claims in aspirin ads, PHARMACEUTICAL LITIGATION RPTR., Feb. 2000, 6 [*United States v. Bayer Corp.*, No. 00-132 (D NJ, consent decree submitted for court approval Jan. 11, 2000)]; http://www.ftc.gov/os/2000/01/sterlingdecree.htm [accessed September 18, 2004].

151 See H.P. Weinberger & J.M. Wagner, On the false advertising battlefront; fiercest Lanham Act conflicts waged by large pharmaceutical companies over reps' oral claims, N.Y.L.J., July 24, 2000, S3.

152 68 FED. REG. 23,731 (May 5, 2003).

153 *United States ex rel. Franklin v. Parke-Davis*, 147 F. Supp. 2d 39 (D. Mass. 2001).

154 http://www.hhs.gov/news/press/2009pres/09/20090902a.html [accessed February 5, 2012].

155 G. Harris, Abbott to pay $622 million to end inquiry into marketing, N.Y. TIMES, June 27, 2003, C1.

156 *Virginia State Bd. of Pharmacy v. Virginia Citizens Consumer Council*, 425 U.S. 748 (1976).

157 M. Gever, Vermont to Doctors: No More Free Restaurant Lunches, NCSL STATE HEALTH NOTES, Vol. 30, Issue 541, June 22, 2009, *available at*: http://www.ncsl.org/default.aspx?tabid=17760 [accessed August 22, 2011].

158 AvaMed, Code of Ethics on Interactions with Health Care Professionals, Jan. 1, 2009, *available at*: http://www.advamed.org/NR/rdonlyres/61D30455-F7E9-4081-B219-12D6CE347585/0/AdvaMedCodeofEthicsRevisedandRestatedEffective20090701.pdf [accessed August 22, 2011]; Pharmaceutical Research and Manufacturers of America (PhRMA), Code on Interactions with Healthcare Professionals, effective July 1, 2009, *available at:* http://www.phrma.org/sites/default/files/108/phrma_marketing_code_2008.pdf [accessed August 22, 2011].

159 42 U.S.C. § 1320a-7h [as added by Patient Protection and Affordable Care Act, Pub. L. No. 111-148, 124 Stat. 119, § 6002]; *see also* A. E. Lewis, D. I. Sclar, Complying with Federal and State "Sunshine Laws": How Manufacturers Can Avoid Getting Burned, *ABA Health eSource*, Aug. 2010 PPACA Special Ed., *available at*: http://www.americanbar.org/newsletter/publications/aba_health_esource_home/lewis.html [accessed August 22, 2011].

Additional Resources

http://www.justice.gov/dea/marijuana_position.pdf [Dated January 2011].

Chapter 4

Individual Providers and Caregivers

John E. Steiner, Jr., Esq, Erin Dougherty Foley, Esq, Isabel Lazar, Esq

Key Learning Objectives

By the end of this chapter, the reader will be able to:

- Provide an overview of the legal aspects of the relationship of individual health care providers and caregivers in the healthcare delivery system.

- Explain the relationship of licensure to healthcare professionals.

- Explain the relationship of private certification to other professionals.

- Explain the relationship of the healthcare delivery system to employment, independent contractor, volunteer, or student status.

- Describe several areas of federal and state law oversight of employer and employee relationships.

Most of the principles, doctrines, and fundamental legal decisions in this area are fairly straightforward. As a result, there are not frequent, major changes in the general area of licensure laws. More commonly, there are interesting variations and challenges in how those laws are applied. Thus, many of the earlier references in this chapter and endnotes have been retained in this edition.

Most of the principles, federal and state laws, and common law doctrines applied by courts and administrative agencies to the topics covered in this area are fairly well settled. For example, there are not major changes to the generally accepted principles behind licensure laws. More commonly, there are interesting variations and challenges in how those laws are applied. Thus, many of the earlier references in this chapter and endnotes have been retained in this edition. Of course, both federal and state laws change overtime to adapt to changing circumstances. Therefore, this chapter focuses primarily on many of the "building blocks" that support the key learning objectives stated above.

Chapter Outline

 Individual Licensing

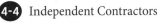 Private Certification of Individuals

4-3 Employment Relationship

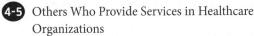 Independent Contractors

4-5 Others Who Provide Services in Healthcare Organizations

Introduction

Healthcare delivery is both an individual and a team effort. There are few situations where an individual can provide health care, beyond first aid, without the support of others. For example, there is an old expression that surgeons cannot do surgery without anesthesiologists. Most healthcare providers are licensed or authorized to practice by a governmental authority. Section 4-1 addresses individual licensing.

Section 4-2 addresses private certification of individuals. In some cases, private certification is required by government authorities in order to qualify for certain positions, status, or payment. The appendix to this chapter is an example of a spreadsheet actively maintained by a healthcare system. That spreadsheet helps the system stay current on licensure, certification, and related requirements for its healthcare personnel.

Individual providers usually have one of four relationships with healthcare organizations:

- Employee
- Independent contractor
- Owners (e.g., partner or shareholder)
- Granted privileges to practice

Individuals may have more than one status with the same healthcare entity. For example, physicians with hospital privileges may also be employees or independent contractors of the hospital. By comparison, physicians may be partners in their medical practice and their only relationship with a hospital is through medical privileges.

Section 4-3 discusses the employment relationship. Section 4-4 discusses independent contractors.

The relationship of partners and shareholders is discussed in Chapter 2 "Organization of the Healthcare Delivery System."

Section 4-5 discusses others who provide services in healthcare organizations, such as volunteers and students.

The organized medical staff and practice privileges are discussed in the next chapter. The chapter on patients, providers, and duties of care expands on the duties of licensed practitioners to their patients, and a later chapter discusses how patients' choices (and those of their legal representatives) interplay with duties and responsibilities of healthcare personnel.

4-1 Individual Licensing

Licensure laws are intended to assure that only properly qualified persons are engaged in healthcare practice. Licensure laws exist to protect the public health by requiring a certain level of education and professional proficiency. These laws also grant specific authority to the licensing entity to suspend, revoke, terminate, and otherwise sanction noncompliant licensees. Concerns about the proficiency of licensed individuals also are addressed by:

- Private certification and review by accrediting bodies (4-2)
- Employers (4-3)
- Institutional providers and provider networks through medical staff processes (5)
- Managed care plans (10-2)
- Malpractice claims (11)
- Criminal prosecutions (12-4.2)

In general, licensing activities provide a foundation for basic quality standards. Periodically, licensing standards are criticized or challenged as barriers to those who desire to enter practice; thus the requirements may be viewed as a restriction on competition.

This section addresses the following questions:

- 4-1.1. When is a license required?
- 4-1.2. What are licensure requirements?
- 4-1.3. What is the scope of practice permitted by a license?
- 4-1.4. What is the scope of the rule-making authority of licensing boards?
- 4-1.5. What is the scope of the disciplinary power of licensing boards?
- 4-1.6. What is the impact of licensing on competition and availability of services?

4-1.1 When Is a License Required?

MANDATORY VERSUS PERMISSIVE LICENSING. Public licensing can be either mandatory or permissive. Mandatory licensing laws require individuals to obtain licenses before practicing, unless the individual is exempted. Permissive licensing laws typically regulate use of titles; an individual cannot use the title without a license, but can perform the functions. In the past, some licensing laws, both mandatory and permissive, provided for registration with no required special qualifications. Today, registration laws are rare. Nearly all licensing laws include educational and examination requirements.

SELECTION OF PROFESSIONS TO LICENSE. States have discretion to determine which professions to license. In 1889, the U.S. Supreme Court upheld mandatory licensing of physicians.[1] This scope of discretion is illustrated by a 1966 Supreme Court decision permitting states not to recognize naturopathy as a discipline distinct from orthodox medical practice.[2] Thus, naturopaths may be required to qualify for a full medical license; states are not required to offer them a separate license, but may do so.[3]

Attempts have been made, unsuccessfully, to use other rights as a basis for requiring separate licensing. For example, a federal appellate court upheld New York's midwife licensing law in 1997. The court did not agree that the right of privacy includes the right of an individual to use a midwife.[4] States are not required to provide a religious exemption to licensing laws. In 1996, a Pennsylvania court upheld fining a member of a religious community who performed dentistry on other members of the community without a license.[5]

Physicians, dentists, registered nurses, and pharmacists are subject to mandatory, state licensing laws. Other professionals, including physical therapists, psychologists, speech pathologists, audiologists, occupational therapists, and podiatrists, are licensed in most states. Some states license technical personnel such as emergency medical technicians and radiology technologists. In addition, some localities have licensing requirements.[6]

The federal government also licenses some individual healthcare providers. For example, professionals who manufacture, prescribe, distribute, or dispense controlled substances must be registered with the Drug Enforcement Administration.[7]

On rare occasions, states suspend specific licensing requirements, especially when they become a threat to patient care. For example, in 2001, Colorado suspended the requirement for licenses for nursing aides because the exam backlog created a shortage that threatened the well-being of nursing home residents.[8]

LICENSE RENEWAL. Failure to timely renew licenses violates licensing laws and may increase liability exposure. The Virginia Supreme Court ruled that the state statutory cap on malpractice damages did not apply to services provided by a physician whose license had expired.[9] Billing for services rendered by an unlicensed professional can be serious and, in some cases, may constitute fraud, leading to prosecution and/or required refunds. A Pennsylvania pharmacist was required to reimburse the state for all prescriptions billed to the state during the period his license had lapsed.[10]

INSTITUTIONAL REVIEW. Healthcare providers maintain formal systems and processes to confirm that staff members have appropriate qualifications and licenses. 🏴 In some states, if a patient is harmed by a staff member who is practicing illegally, the hospital may be liable for the patient's harm.[11] However, in liability cases involving unlicensed staff, most states focus on whether the employee was competent, rather than on lack of a license.[12] Hospitals can be subject to administrative and criminal penalties for using unlicensed staff. For example, a New Jersey hospital was ordered to pay an administrative fine for aiding and abetting the illegal practice of medicine because it employed an unlicensed physician in its emergency room.[13]

In some states, hospitals and other healthcare organizations have the responsibility to determine whether or not certain professional and technical personnel meet government-imposed qualifications.[14] In those states, the organization, instead of a governmental agency, is authorized to evaluate the individual's qualifications.

Usually, courts understand that hospitals must take action against employees who fail to maintain necessary licenses and other requirements. For example, a Pennsylvania court ruled that a nurse who was terminated for failure to renew her license was not entitled to unemployment compensation.[15] The failure was considered "willful misconduct."

OUT-OF-STATE ACTIVITIES. Each state has its own licensing law and professionals generally must obtain a license in each state in which they practice. Some states have exceptions to this general rule. Those states permit persons licensed in another state to provide some services in consultation with a professional licensed in the state, or some emergency services. The scope of this exception varies by state. Professionals who provide services outside their state of primary licensing need to limit their services to those that do not require a license, or they must obtain a license. This is an issue not only when a professional crosses the border, but also can apply when services are provided by Internet to an out-of-state patient.[16]

4-1.2 What Are Licensure Requirements?

States have discretion to determine licensure requirements. Most licensing laws require specified training and tests. Some states impose additional requirements, beyond education and testing.[17] For example, some states require physicians to participate in Medicare and accept its payment as payment in full.[18] In 1998, a federal appellate court upheld the right of states to require physicians to contribute to a malpractice liability fund in order to be licensed.[19] The Illinois Supreme Court ruled that the state can require good moral character and place the burden on the applicant to prove it.[20] Unless the licensing statute authorizes waiver of requirements, generally the licensing agency does not have the discretion to waive requirements that are set by statute.[21]

The Americans with Disabilities Act (ADA) is a federal statute that prevents discrimination on the basis of an individual's real or perceived disability. Among other things, the ADA limits inquiries into physical and mental health and, in appropriate circumstances, requires some accommodations of disabilities.[22] For example, the ADA regulations allow for extra time to be provided to test takers who may need accommodations on timed examinations in some circumstances.[23] In 1999, a federal appellate court ruled that it was not discriminatory to disclose which tests results involved such accommodations.[24]

4-1.3 What Is the Scope of Practice Permitted by a License?

🏴 Mandatory licensing laws establish "scope of practice" parameters for licensees. Scope of practice issues generally fall into two categories:

1. Who makes the judgments that certain procedures will be performed?
2. Who is allowed to perform the procedures?

Although courts typically uphold restrictions on scope of practice adopted under the state police power, occasionally courts find that some laws have gone too far. In 1992, the Georgia Supreme Court declared a statute unconstitutional that permitted only physicians, dentists, podiatrists, and veterinarians to perform any surgery, operation, or invasive procedure in which human or animal tissue was cut, pierced, or altered.[25] The court concluded that there was no rational basis for this statute, which did not permit nurses to give injections or diabetics to inject themselves with insulin.

In general, medical diagnosing and ordering certain diagnostic and therapeutic procedures are activities reserved for physicians. Podiatrists and dentists usually are permitted to diagnose and treat parts of the body related to their practice. Yet, there continues to be disputes over the boundaries.[26] Other professionals are increasingly being permitted to make some diagnoses and order some treatments.[27] In 2004, two states allowed psychologists to prescribe some

drugs, and six states allowed pharmacists to dispense some drugs without a prescription.[28] States vary concerning which procedures may be ordered by physicians' assistants and nurse practitioners and under what circumstances.[29]

Nursing diagnosis is generally viewed differently than physician diagnosis. Generally, nurses determine what nursing care is needed, or when it is insufficient, so that medical attention or instructions must be sought. In some states, nurses are permitted to make some judgments traditionally reserved for physicians when acting pursuant to standing orders or established protocols.[30] Many states license nurse practitioners to independently make some judgments traditionally reserved for physicians, including prescribing many drugs.[31]

There is considerable controversy over the degree of supervision required for nurse anesthetists. Medicare requires physician supervision, unless the state has elected to opt out of the physician supervision requirement, which some states have elected to do.[32]

Most medical procedures, when first introduced, are restricted to physicians. As experience with certain procedures increases, nurses and other allied health practitioners may be permitted to perform the procedures. This evolution varies from state to state and has been recognized in several ways—licensing statute amendments, state attorney general opinions, medical and/or nursing licensing board rules or statements,[33] joint statements of private professional organizations, and judicial decisions.

Sometimes, established practices are overturned by subsequent rulings. For example, the Iowa Supreme Court affirmed an injunction prohibiting a chiropractor from performing acupuncture, drawing blood specimens, and giving advice on diet and nutrition. In that case, the Board of Chiropractic Examiners had issued a declaratory ruling that those practices were permitted.[34] In 1996, an Arizona appellate court upheld rules of the chiropractic board permitting chiropractic assistants to administer physical therapy.[35] Many sources may need to be examined to determine the scope of practice in a particular state.

DELEGATION. Some states give physicians broad authority to delegate functions to nurses and others.[36] For example, Michigan permits physicians to delegate functions to others under proper supervision, if permitted by standards of acceptable and prevailing practice.[37] The Michigan attorney general interpreted this to permit physicians to delegate to nurses the prescribing authority for any drugs, except controlled substances, if the prescription identified the supervising physician.[38]

Other states give licensing boards broad authority to expand nursing functions. For example, Iowa grants authority to the Board of Nursing to expand nursing roles by rule when the expanded roles are recognized by the medical and nursing professions.[39] Oregon goes one step farther and permits nurse practitioners to be selected as the "attending physician" of an injured worker under the workers' compensation law.[40]

⚑ Delegation should be limited to the permitted scope. A physician's assistant was convicted for prescribing a controlled substance without statutory authority when he authorized refilling a prescription for Tylenol with codeine in accordance with written instructions from the supervising physician. The physician and the physician's assistant were excluded from participation in Medicare for five years as a result of the conviction.[41] In 1999, an Illinois physician's license was suspended for permitting a pharmacist assistant to diagnosis and treat patients, including writing prescriptions, giving injections, and removing stitches.[42] In 2002, an Iowa physician was fined for permitting an unlicensed Emergency Medical Technician student to treat a patient.[43]

When acts can be delegated, there usually are supervision requirements. In 2002, a California physician lost his license for permitting medical assistants to perform tests without supervision, among other reasons.[44]

4-1.4 What Is the Scope of the Rule-Making Authority of Licensing Boards?

Licensing boards generally have broad authority. Some rules promulgated by licensing boards are challenged as being beyond the boards' authority.

A New Jersey appellate court upheld a rule requiring licensed radiologists, who provided diagnostic services for other physicians, to provide services for licensed chiropractors.[45] Although this type of service was inconsistent with the practice of many radiologists, the court ruled that it was reasonable, within the board's authority, and promulgated using proper procedures. The Ohio Supreme Court upheld a rule prohibiting the prescription of anabolic steroids for the enhancement of athletic ability.[46] In 1990, the New Jersey Supreme Court upheld a Board of Physical Therapy rule that reduced physician supervision and permitted therapists to modify the prescribed treatment.[47] In 2000, a Florida appellate court upheld an emergency moratorium on all complex, physician office surgery.[48] In 2004,

a federal appellate court ruled that it was not a violation of the First Amendment to limit advertising of medical specialty certification to recognized certifying boards.[49]

Occasionally, specific controversial rules are determined to exceed the board's authority. A Florida appellate court ruled that the licensing board did not have authority to prohibit chelation therapy for arteriosclerosis, unless the board found the therapy was harmful or hazardous to patients.[50] The prohibition was not justified by the lack of proof of effectiveness or the limited number of physicians who used it. An Illinois appellate court invalidated a rule that excluded from the dental licensing examination all persons who were not graduates of schools approved by the American Dental Association or schools with a curriculum equivalent to that of the University of Illinois College of Dentistry.[51] The statute limited the examination to graduates of "reputable" schools. The board could not arbitrarily determine that a school was not reputable; it had to evaluate the school. A Florida appellate court ruled that a Board of Optometry rule authorizing optometrists to use certain drugs was beyond the authority of the board.[52] A Pennsylvania court invalidated a rule requiring physicians to obtain permission from the board on a patient-by-patient basis before prescribing amphetamines.[53] In 2004, a Florida appellate court invalidated a rule that required anesthesia for outpatient surgery to be supervised by an anesthesiologist; a statute specifically limited the board's authority on this issue.[54]

Decisions in one state are of limited help in addressing these issues in other states, but these examples show that it is possible to challenge some rulings of licensing boards.

4-1.5 What Is the Scope of the Disciplinary Power of Licensing Boards?

Licensing boards have broad authority to discipline licensed professionals when they violate professional standards specified in licensing laws or board rules. The discipline can be a reprimand, revocation,[55] suspension, fine,[56] or probationary period during which certain conditions must be met.[57] Most licensing boards have authority to impose conditions, including prohibiting types of practice[58] or requiring substance abuse rehabilitation efforts; practice monitoring; record review; consultation or supervision of specified procedures;

> The range of disciplinary measures available to licensing boards include: reprimand, probation, suspension, fine, and revocation.

completion of education programs; and increased malpractice insurance.[59] Before imposing disciplinary sanctions, licensing boards must provide due process to licensed professionals, including notice of the wrongful conduct and an opportunity to present information.[60]

Many states impose stricter requirements that must be followed for the board's action to be valid. For example, the Colorado Supreme Court ordered reinstatement of a nurse's license because, in part, the statute required the full licensing board to attend the revocation hearing and the full board had not done so.[61] Most licensing laws do not require the presence of the full board, but if this is required, the law must be followed. In some states, the licensing board cannot attend the evidentiary hearing.[62]

▶ NOTICE. To provide due process, licensed professionals must have two types of notices. They must receive individualized notice of the specific, questioned acts and/or omissions that are the basis for discipline.[63] In addition, the statute and regulations must provide general, advance notice that certain types of conduct may lead to discipline. Courts usually rule that prohibition of "unprofessional conduct" gives adequate notice that a wide range of inappropriate behavior is prohibited. "Unprofessional conduct" is not considered too vague when it is applied to conduct widely recognized as unprofessional.

In 1997, the Montana Supreme Court held that conviction for Medicare false claims was unprofessional conduct justifying license revocation.[64] In 1996, a Missouri appellate court held that pushing a nurse in the operating room was unprofessional conduct, justifying suspension of the surgeon's license for one day.[65] The Oregon Supreme Court upheld the revocation of a nurse's license for "conduct derogatory to the standards of professional nursing."[66] She had instructed, recommended, and permitted her daughter to serve as a registered nurse, knowing that her daughter had no nursing license. However, "unprofessional conduct" is not adequate notice for all possible violations. The Idaho Supreme Court ordered reinstatement of a nursing license that was suspended for six months for unprofessional conduct.[67] The Board of Nursing found that the nurse discussed laetrile treatment with a hospitalized leukemia patient without physician approval. That action interfered with the physician–patient relationship. The board considered this to be unprofessional conduct. The court ruled that the board could have prohibited this conduct by rule, but that a prohibition of unprofessional conduct did not give nurses adequate warning that this conduct was prohibited.

GROUNDS FOR DISCIPLINE. Some licensing boards specify by rule more detailed grounds for discipline, but some courts have considered the statutory criteria to be sufficiently clear so that no rules are needed.[68]

With or without rules, licensing boards have sought to impose discipline in several areas.

States have adopted different positions on whether medical directors of managed care organizations can be disciplined for their coverage decisions. For example, in 2001, the Missouri Supreme Court approved review of such coverage decisions.[69] On the other hand, in 1997 a District of Columbia court reached a decision that apparently precludes licensing board review of such decisions in that jurisdiction. The court ruled that a health plan medical director was not practicing medicine, so no license was required.[70]

Boards in some jurisdictions have explored applying discipline for actions taken during litigation. In 1998, a Pennsylvania court upheld the authority of the medical licensing board to discipline a physician for disclosing confidential patient records in the course of business litigation that did not involve the patient.[71] The court ruled that judicial immunity did not provide protection from licensing board discipline. In 1997, the Washington Supreme Court agreed, finding that there could be professional discipline for testimony as an expert witness in a child custody case.[72] In 2000, an Ohio appellate court upheld revocation of a podiatrist's license for perjury during a deposition.[73] In 2003, North Carolina suspended the license of a physician for the content of expert testimony.[74] Absolute immunity for witnesses protects from civil liability but not from discipline.

Some commentators evaluate the licensing process by the number of disciplinary actions that are taken, criticizing jurisdictions that take fewer actions. In reaction, more physicians are being disciplined.[75]

Another interesting development in licensing is the effort by some patients to pressure licensing boards to discipline individual providers.[76]

APPEALS. When licensed professionals prevail in challenges to board actions, they usually cannot get payment from the state or the board members.[77] They are limited to reversal of improper discipline and invalidation of improper rules. In most states, licensing board members have broad immunity from monetary liability.[78]

4-1.6 What Is the Impact of Licensing on Competition and Availability of Services?

States have broad authority to determine which professions to license.[79] ▶ The state is confronted with a difficult analysis whenever it is requested to license a health discipline.

Many professional and technical disciplines seek to be licensed. They claim that licensing is necessary to protect the public from unqualified practitioners. Licensing is also sought because it provides status and often is accompanied by expansion of the scope of practice into areas previously reserved for other licensed professionals. Licensing can be an economic benefit to those licensed because licensure reduces the number of people permitted to perform specific tasks. The educational and testing requirements designed to protect the public increase the time and expense of becoming qualified and thus reduce the number of people available to provide the service. This can have a detrimental effect on the public if the subsequent increase in costs charged by the licensed professionals is too great. It can have a catastrophic effect if too few people meet the requirements for licensure and certain members of the public remain underserved.

Licensing can be a barrier to innovation because of the difficulty in changing statutes and rules that define the licensees' scope of practices. Barriers to entry imposed by licensing are widely accepted for some health professions, especially for professionals who often function independently, such as physicians, dentists, and nurses. The appropriateness of state licensing of some allied health practitioners, who function under the supervision of other licensed practitioners, has been questioned. Some commentators believe that the public health could be adequately protected by placing responsibility on the institution and supervising independent health professionals instead of the system of state licensure. In addition, they say the public interest in innovative, cost-effective health services could be advanced by more flexibility in the use of allied health practitioners. However, the trend appears to continue toward licensing of more health disciplines.

In many cases, the focus is not on the barriers to enter a particular profession, such as the educational requirements to become a physician or a nurse. Instead, sometimes a profession seeks to perform functions that are restricted to another profession. Chiropractors have sought to be permitted to perform functions restricted to physicians.

Nurse practitioners, especially nurse anesthetists and nurse midwives, have sought to practice without a supervising or collaborating physician. Lay midwives have sought to practice without nursing or medical training.

Usually, these questions are decided by the legislature or by regulators. As discussed in 4-1.1, courts will generally defer to legislative judgments about licensure and to regulatory actions taken within the scope of those laws. In one unusual case in 1996, the Kansas Supreme Court addressed permissibility of unlicensed lay midwifery by a creative interpretation of the state licensing laws. The court concluded that lay midwifery was not a healing art and did not fall within the definition of medical or nursing practice, so no license was required.[80]

In summary, licensure rules have been challenged as barriers to competition and to consumer access. The rules have been defended on the basis that they maintain quality by requiring additional training for those who perform specific functions. Evaluating the quality of health delivery and determining the appropriate levels of cost and availability are difficult public policy decisions.

4-2 Private Certification of Individuals

In addition to individual licensing by government agencies, there are many private methods of credentialing, including accreditation of educational programs, certification of individuals, and credentialing by institutions. Credentialing by institutions is addressed in 4-3 and 4-4.

ACCREDITATION OF EDUCATIONAL PROGRAMS. Private professional organizations establish criteria to evaluate educational programs. Periodically, an individual or a team investigates programs that seek accreditation. Although accreditation is voluntary, most educational programs strive to obtain and retain accreditation from established accrediting bodies because students tend to choose accredited programs. Graduates of accredited programs often find it easier to obtain permission to take licensing examinations or to be admitted for advanced study because their degrees are generally accepted without additional proof of their education. Graduates of accredited programs often find it easier to convince employers that they are prepared for employment in the discipline. Others may have to provide more information concerning their training programs to demonstrate the adequacy of their training.

Not all accrediting bodies command the same level of acceptance as longer-standing bodies that accredit medicine and nursing programs. Healthcare organizations should not automatically assume that accreditation assures high standards. If a healthcare organization is not familiar with an accrediting body, it should make inquiries before relying on the accrediting body.

Denials of accreditation have been legally challenged. However, most courts defer to the accrediting bodies. A Pennsylvania hospital that lost accreditation of a general surgery residency program challenged the action in state and federal court. The challenge started with a petition to the state medical licensing board to review the accrediting body's action. The licensing board denied the review request. A lower state court ordered the board to review the action. But, the Pennsylvania Supreme Court reversed, finding that the board did not have authority to review individual residency accreditation decisions.[81] A lower federal court granted an injunction of withdrawal of accreditation of a residency program, which the federal appellate court vacated, finding that the accreditation decision was not state action.[82] When a Maryland Roman Catholic hospital lost accreditation of its obstetrics-gynecology residency program because it failed to prove training in family planning, a federal court found that the loss of accreditation did not violate any constitutional or statutory rights of the hospital.[83]

CERTIFICATION OF INDIVIDUALS. Private, professional organizations sponsor programs to certify that individuals meet certain criteria and are considered prepared to practice in the discipline. Individual certification is generally related to performance and usually requires passing a test. Some certifications, especially certifications by medical specialty boards, have become so widely accepted that it can be difficult to practice without them. However, Medicare participating hospitals cannot adopt an absolute requirement of board certification for specialty clinical privileges.[84] Instead, hospitals can avail themselves of the value of certification, while avoiding the absolute requirement, by requiring "board certification or equivalent training and experience."

Some managed care plans will pay physicians only when they have board certification.[85]

Certifying bodies have proliferated, resulting in a certifying body for virtually every professional and technical healthcare discipline.[86] Not all of these bodies have earned the same acceptance as the longer-standing certification bodies. There is also variation in the acceptance of medical specialties. In 2005, the American Board of Medical Specialties recognized 24 medical specialty boards, while over 180 others existed that have not been recognized.[87] Healthcare organizations should be familiar with a certifying body before giving it substantial weight in evaluating applications. One advantage of the private certification system is that the organization generally has the discretion to use its own evaluation system.

States can require private certification as a condition of state licensing.[88]

Table 4-1

The 24 American Board of Medical Specialties Member Boards
Allergy and Immunology
Anesthesiology
Colon and Rectal Surgery
Dermatology
Emergency Medicine
Family Medicine
Internal Medicine
Medical Genetics
Neurological Surgery
Nuclear Medicine
Obstetrics and Gynecology
Ophthalmology
Orthopaedic Surgery
Otolaryngology
Pathology
Pediatrics
Physical Medicine and Rehabilitation
Plastic Surgery
Preventive Medicine
Psychiatry and Neurology
Radiology
Surgery
Thoracic Surgery
Urology

Individuals who challenge denial of certification are generally unsuccessful.[89] Courts will generally enforce the releases that boards require as part of the application process, except as to antitrust claims.[90] Unsuccessful applicants have generally been unable to state antitrust claims.[91]

In 2004, a federal appellate court upheld a California requirement that physicians could advertise board certification only when the state recognized the board. It was found not to be a violation of the First Amendment to bar advertising certification by an unrecognized board.[92]

4-3 Employment Relationship

Healthcare organizations provide patient care primarily through their employees. The quality and performance of the employed staff and the relationship between the organization and its employees determine whether satisfactory, compassionate care can be provided to patients. Healthcare organizations should carefully select, train, supervise, and discipline employees. Many aspects of employee relations are now subject to detailed state and federal regulation, including equal employment opportunities, compensation and benefits, occupational safety, labor-management relations, and other matters.

⚑ This section discusses some general concerns regarding employee relations and then reviews the pertinent federal laws. Some state laws are mentioned, but a detailed state-by-state analysis is not attempted.

This section is divided into:

- General employee relations issues (4-3.1)
- Equal opportunity employment laws (4-3.2)
- Compensation and benefits (4-3.3)
- Occupational safety and health (4-3.4)
- Labor-management relations (4-3.5)
- State laws (4-3.6)

4-3.1 General Employee Relations Issues

SELECTION. Healthcare organizations must exercise care in selecting their employees. The organization should verify any required licenses and should check references and other information provided by the applicant to confirm that it is reasonable to believe the applicant is qualified.[93] The Immigration Reform and Control Act of 1986 requires all employers to verify the identity and work authorization of each employee.[94] Selection should comply with applicable equal employment opportunity laws that are discussed later in this chapter.

In 1990, a federal appellate court ruled that an employer does not have a duty to the prospective employee to determine whether he is qualified before planning to hire him, so the hospital employer was not liable to a prospective physician when he was not permitted to start the job because he did not have the qualifications.[95] Employers should use caution in their hiring practices to avoid making promises that could be construed as binding or that could form the basis of an employment contact. Some courts will impose liability for breaches of such promises or determine that a contract was made and then breached.[96] One controversial area is the extent to which an employer should or may make inquiries concerning the criminal record of applicants and use the information in employment decisions.[97] The Equal Employment Opportunity Commission has broadly stated that screening applicants for criminal records could have an adverse impact on minority candidates because, the theory goes, such candidates are more likely to have criminal records and then are more likely to be screened out. Similarly, some states, including Wisconsin, Pennsylvania, Massachusetts, Hawaii, and California, do not permit collection or use of such information and all employers who plan to make such inquiries should ensure that they are in compliance with the Fair Credit Reporting Act. In 2003, the Pennsylvania Supreme Court ruled that a criminal background check requirement was an infringement on the individual's rights under the state constitution to pursue an occupation.[98] Some states require collection and use of criminal background information for some healthcare workers.[99] In states where it is permitted, employers have been liable for crimes by employees when no background check was made,[100] and employees have been discharged for failing to disclose their criminal record on an employment application form.[101] In 2002, the Iowa Supreme Court ruled that an arbitrator could not order the reinstatement of an employee who was discovered to have a criminal background through such checks.[102]

HEALTH SCREENING. Employers should screen employees to identify conditions, such as contagious diseases, that can constitute a risk to patients. Likewise, employers should take appropriate steps to assure that persons who may present risks do not have contact with patients or objects that could transmit their condition.* However, employers should be prepared to defend their policies, especially when national guidelines have been adopted, such as the guidelines for AIDS.[103]

---

* Certain religious groups raise concerns with such mandatory testing. However, public health issues typically outweigh such challenges.

The Americans with Disabilities Act requires health screening of applicants to be postponed until after a contingent offer of employment has been made and requires that any screening be for all applicants for covered positions.[104]

Consent of the applicant or employee should be obtained for any type of post-offer testing. Additionally, employers may not knowingly attempt to collect genetic information from employees. Indeed, Title II of the Genetic Information Nondiscrimination Act of 2008 proscribes employers from using prospective and current employees' genetic information in making employment decisions. In particular, it restricts employers and other entities covered by the statute from "requesting, requiring or purchasing genetic information, and strictly limits the disclosure of genetic information. Similarly, in 1998, a federal appellate court found that an employer violated employee rights by testing for genetic disorders, venereal disease, or pregnancy without consent."[105]

TRAINING AND SUPERVISION. Employers can be liable for injuries caused by negligent or intentional acts of their employees in the course of employment. To optimize patient care and minimize liability exposure, health care providers arrange for their employees to have the necessary training and supervision and to participate in continuing education so they maintain and improve their skills.

Regular performance appraisals are important. The Joint Commission requires performance evaluations for hospital employees at least every three years.[106] When human resources personnel learn of employee problems that pose a risk to patients, they need to initiate appropriate action. Failing to do so may expose the employer to heightened liability as well as negligent retention claims. In 1998, the Idaho Supreme Court ruled that a hospital could be sued for the sexual relationship a fired respiratory therapist developed with a former patient, who was a minor, whom he had met while the minor was a patient. The therapist told an Employee Assistance Program counselor that he was terminated from a prior job for sexually molesting a patient.[107]

STAFFING. As healthcare organizations respond to pressures to reduce costs and to shortages of nurses and other professional and technical staff, new ways of structuring care are being developed, and staffing patterns are changing.[108] In most areas, there is some latitude to make changes, but appropriate levels must be maintained.[109] Legally mandated staffing ratios have been proposed, but these efforts have generally been unsuccessful,

except for the California experiment described in the following paragraph. In 2005, New Jersey mandated public disclosure of staffing levels.[110] Some courts have protected individual employees who objected to staffing decisions.[111]

In 1999, California adopted a statute that mandated nurse-to-patient staffing ratios that were phased in starting on January 1, 2004. On July 1, 2003, the ratios were published. It was estimated that the ratios would cost California hospitals over $400 million in 2004, escalating to nearly one billion dollars in 2008. The state interpreted the rule to apply even during short breaks. The hospital association sued to challenge this interpretation. In 2004, a California trial court upheld the interpretation. Surveys indicated that in early 2004 many hospitals were not in compliance. Los Angeles County Hospital sought relief in early 2004. One hospital that closed in early 2004 announced that one reason was the staffing requirements.

Some nurses and their membership organizations sought to reduce or eliminate mandatory overtime. Many healthcare organizations, through policies or collective bargaining agreements, sought to minimize mandatory overtime. However, the unpredictability of hospital workloads in many hospitals and the unpredictability of staff time off for illness, family medical leave, and other purposes make it virtually impossible to avoid situations where patient safety requires mandatory overtime. Several states have considered such laws. By mid-2004, at least seven states passed laws restricting mandatory overtime.[113] The application of these laws differ, as well as the application of their exceptions.

SEARCHING THE WORKPLACE. Public employers need to limit searches of employee workplaces to appropriate purposes and means. In 1987, the U.S. Supreme Court ruled that public employees have a reasonable expectation

> Amendment IV: The right of the people to be secure in their persons, houses, papers, and effects, against unreasonable searches and seizures, shall not be violated, and no warrants shall issue, but upon probable cause, supported by oath or affirmation, and particularly describing the place to be searched, and the persons or things to be seized.[†]

[†] "The Constitution of the United States," Amendment 5.

of privacy in their desks and file cabinets that is protected by the Fourth Amendment prohibition against unreasonable searches and seizures.

However, a search warrant is not required for noninvestigatory, work-related purposes or for work-related misconduct, provided the search is reasonable under all the circumstances in both its inception and scope.[114] The case arose out of a state hospital's search of the office of a psychiatrist, who was chief of professional education. There were concerns about the management of the psychiatry residency program. While the employee was on administrative leave, the hospital inventoried the property in his office and seized personal items. The court remanded the case for a determination of the reasonableness of the search. The first trial resulted in a verdict for the hospital employees who directed and conducted the search. This verdict was overturned on evidentiary grounds.[115] The second trial resulted in a verdict for the searched employee, which was upheld on appeal.[116]

Lower federal court decisions hold that this reasonable expectation of privacy generally does not apply to open, accessible areas, but does apply to enclosed areas provided for an employee's exclusive use.[117] Where there would otherwise be a reasonable expectation of privacy, the expectation can also be overcome by regulations that expressly authorize random searches in some circumstances.[118] Likewise, unionized employers should take extra precaution as the National Labor Relations Board (NLRB) has held that such employers act unlawfully when they create an impression that their employees' union activities have been placed under surveillance or are otherwise being monitored.[119]

The ability to "search" other employer equipment, including computers, email accounts, phone records, and other physical spaces continues to be debated in the Courts. In 2010, the Supreme Court ruled in *City of Ontario v. Quon et al.*, that the employer engaged in an appropriate review of an employee's personal text messages that were made on a work-issued phone because the employer reviewed the text messages to determine whether they were work-related for the legitimate purpose of determining the efficacy of existing character limits to ensure that officers were not paying hidden work-related costs.[120] The Supreme Court determined that the city had not violated the Fourth Amendment in conducting this limited search.

Nonpublic employers are encouraged strongly to articulate a policy that employees in those organizations should not have an expectation of privacy in such employer provided resources.

DISCIPLINE AND DISMISSAL. Healthcare providers should take appropriate steps to enforce institutional policies

to maintain appropriate patient care and institutional integrity. Proper procedures should be followed, and actions should be based on legally permissible grounds.

Generally, employees are considered to be employees at will unless they have contracts for a specified time period. Employers may terminate employees at will at any time without cause so long as the termination does not violate any anti-discrimination laws, and[121] unless (1) the employer is bound by contract or statute to follow certain procedures or standards in terminations or (2) the termination violates public policy.

Many courts view some personnel policy manuals and other procedures for discipline or dismissal to be contracts with the employees that the employer must follow.[122] However, some courts disagree on what constitutes an enforceable policy or procedure.[123] The Delaware Supreme Court ruled that statements in employee handbooks do not change an employee's at-will status, unless they specify a definite term of employment.[124] Some courts have found a healthcare organization's employee manual to be a contract without this specificity.[125] Several courts have ruled that handbooks or manuals are not contracts when they contain disclaimers or other clear indications they are not intended to be contracts.[126]

Some public healthcare employees are covered by civil service laws that require certain procedures be used in issuing discipline or discharging an employee. Absent statutory or contractual requirements, public employees are generally not entitled to a formal hearing prior to termination. For example, in 1985, the U.S. Supreme Court ruled that public employees must be given oral or written notice of the charges, an explanation of the employer's evidence, and a pretermination opportunity to present their side of the story, but a formal hearing was not required.[127]

Employees do not have a constitutional right to due process concerning termination by private employers.[128]

When staff members are covered by individual employment contracts or collective bargaining agreements, procedures specified in the contract or agreement should be followed.[129] Usually, employees will be required to exhaust contractual remedies before being allowed to bring litigation against a former employer.[130] Such contracts do not have to be in writing to be enforceable. A Louisiana court found a hospital liable for breaching an oral promise to five certified registered nurse anesthetists that they would be given a six-month notice of termination.[131] However, if the oral contract is for a specified period of more than one year, instead of at will, it will not be enforceable in most states because the legal theory referred to as the "Statute of Frauds" requires that such contracts be in writing to be enforceable.[132]

As the Louisiana case illustrates, courts generally will not order employees reinstated unless authorized by statute; instead, former employees who are wrongfully discharged are awarded payment of lost wages and other damages. Usually, courts award front pay damages in lieu of reinstatement, when returning to work is not feasible. Some statutes authorize reinstatement.[133]

Employees have protection from retaliatory discharge in some situations. ⚑ In 1998, the U.S. Supreme Court ruled that at-will employees have a constitutionally protected interest in continued employment in certain settings. In that case, an at-will former employee of a home health agency could use the federal civil rights statutes to challenge firing. The former employee alleged retaliation for participating in criminal prosecution of the employer for Medicare fraud.[134]

⚑ Some statutes forbid retaliatory discharge for making certain reports to governmental agencies,[135] and some courts have extended such protection to employees who make other reports,[136] who refuse to testify untruthfully in malpractice cases,[137] who refuse to handle radioactive materials in violation of federal regulations,[138] who refuse to prepare or file false claims with the government,[139] who participate in abuse investigations,[140] or who refuse to work with inadequate staffing.[141] Not all statements are protected.[142] Moreover, courts generally scrutinize claims that discipline is for legally required behavior.[143] In 1998, the Utah Supreme Court rejected a pharmacist's challenge to termination for rude behavior to customers. He claimed that he was fulfilling his legal duty to question the validity of prescriptions. The court gave a detailed analysis of the scope of the pharmacist's legal duties and found that the objectionable behavior was not legally mandated.[144]

Employees of public institutions who are discharged for exercising their rights of free speech have some protection under the First Amendment.[145] Employee grievances that are not matters of public concern are not protected.[146] Employees engaging in protected speech are not protected from being discharged for reasons independent of their speech.[147] The First Amendment does not apply to employment actions by private employers.[148] For example, an Illinois appellate court ruled that even if a nurse had been terminated solely in retaliation for reporting incidents to a newspaper, she would

not be entitled to any more protection than other at-will employees of private employers.[149]

An employer generally does not have a legal duty to inform an employee that it is conducting an investigation of the employee's conduct.[150] However, when an employer conducts an investigatory interview of an employee that might result in discipline and the employee is part of a unit represented by a union, the employee has a right to have a representative present during the interview if the employee so requests.[151] The employer does not have to advise the employee of that right, and the employer may decide not to conduct the interview if the right is invoked. In a collective bargaining agreement, a union can waive the right to representation in such interviews.[152] Nonunion employees generally do not have a right to representatives.[153]

Some provisions of the National Labor Relations Act (NLRA) also apply when employees are not represented by a union. For example, employees who are not otherwise represented by a union remain protected by the NLRA and cannot be discouraged or prevented from discussing the terms and conditions of their employment with their coworkers. This protection applies equally to employee discussions at work as well as in social media forums (i.e., Facebook, MySpace, etc.) provided such discussions relate to the employees' "terms and conditions" of their employment.

The equal employment opportunity laws apply to all aspects of employment, including discipline and dismissal, so the provisions of these laws also must be considered. Employers should also be aware of what grounds for dismissal will be considered "just cause" by the unemployment compensation agency in their state. Various jurisdictions define "misconduct" differently and may allow claims for unemployment benefits to go forward even if the employee violated an employer's policy. With an understanding of how "misconduct" is defined, employers will know whether they will be required to pay unemployment compensation to a dismissed staff member.

Supervision and discipline must be handled in a civilized manner. The Alabama Supreme Court upheld an award to a nurse from a physician who struck her and yelled at her to turn on a suction machine.[154]

Some employee terminations and other discipline must be reported to state agencies.

DRUG TESTING. In a 1989 U.S. Supreme Court case, Customs Service workers challenged a requirement that employees applying for promotion to positions involving interdicting drugs or carrying firearms submit to drug analysis of urine specimens. Because the employer was the government, the Fourth Amendment protected the employees from unreasonable searches.[155] The Court concluded that the urine-testing requirement was a reasonable search, even without suspicion of wrongful conduct by the individual. The Court reasoned that persons in these sensitive positions should be tested and noted that the procedures for collection and analysis minimized intrusion on privacy interests. The government interest in the integrity and capacity of persons in these positions outweighed the employees' privacy rights.

In a companion case, the Court ruled that Fourth Amendment protections also applied to a private employer's testing that was mandated or authorized by governmental regulations.[156] The regulations required tests of railway employees after certain train accidents and authorized tests after violations of certain safety rules. The Court concluded that the tests were reasonable without individualized suspicion of impairment because of the government's interest in the safety of the traveling public. The Court did not address whether the government could require testing of healthcare employees. But, the factors that the Court viewed as important to justify testing (such as the need for unimpaired employees to assure public safety and the highly regulated nature of the industry) appear to apply in the healthcare context.[157]

When an employer wants to begin a drug-testing program, where there is no governmental mandate for the program, generally the employer can do so if there is no collective bargaining agreement and no state or other law forbidding the program. In 1989, the NLRB ruled that drug tests of union workers are a mandatory subject of bargaining, so employers without a governmental mandate cannot, without union concurrence or a legal mandate, start testing union workers.[158]

On the same day of the NLRB ruling, the Supreme Court ruled that when an existing collective bargaining agreement can be construed to permit drug testing, the employer is not obligated in some situations to bargain with the union before starting the program. Nonetheless, the union can challenge the contract interpretation through the grievance and/or arbitration provisions of the contract after the program is initiated.[159] Also, while the NLRB ruled that a program to test job applicants is not a mandatory subject of bargaining, unions are entitled to information concerning the program to monitor employer practices.[160] If there is no collective bargaining agreement, a private employer can start a program within any limitations imposed by state and local laws.[161] A governmental employer must also consider the limits of the Fourth Amendment, discussed in the previous paragraph, which can restrict the ability to extend the program beyond those employees with patient contact or in other safety sensitive positions.

State and local laws vary.[162] For example, in 1997, the California Supreme Court upheld drug testing of all applicants, but not of all current employees.[163] Likewise, Minnesota enacted the Drug and Alcohol Testing in the Workplace Act, which mandates specific employer conduct before an employee can be terminated for violations of an employer's drug testing policy.

OTHER BEHAVIORAL SCREENING. Some employers screen applicants and/or employees for unhealthy behaviors. For example, some employers have excluded smokers from their workforce, even when the smoking only occurs off-the employer's premises.[164] Although this is a controversial practice, courts have generally upheld these policies.[165] Some states have passed laws barring employment decisions based on the use of legal products off the employer's premises during nonworking hours.[166]

POLYGRAPH TESTS. The Employee Polygraph Protection Act of 1988[167] prohibits most uses of polygraph tests on employees. There are some limited exemptions where such tests can still be used, but most employers avoid using the exemptions because (1) the situations that justify a polygraph test generally will justify adverse action against the employee and (2) tested employees can bring federal lawsuits in which the employer must prove the exemption applied.

COMMUNICATIONS ABOUT FORMER STAFF. Employers have been sued for libel or slander by former staff members based on unfavorable evaluations, termination notices, and responses to inquiries from prospective employers.[168] Some supervisory personnel have been reluctant to communicate deficiencies accurately because of liability concerns. In general, communicating the truth cannot result in liability for libel or slander.[169] However, because absolute truth is often difficult to prove, certain communications have a qualified privilege. This means there is liability only if the communication was made with malice. Indeed, courts have recognized that statements made in the context of employee reviews are subject to a qualified privilege and are not actionable unless made with malice.[170] For example, in *Heying v. Simonaitis*,[171] the Illinois Appellate Court rejected claims made by a nurse for defamation and intentional interference with prospective economic advantage against certain doctors arising out of statements they had made during review of her performance. The Illinois Appellate Court held that the doctors' statements were protected by the qualified privilege because the doctors had an interest and a duty in the efficient running of the unit and their statements were limited to a proper forum for addressing the nurse's performance. In *Mittleman,* however, the Illinois Supreme Court allowed a defamation claim by an associate attorney to proceed. There, the supervising partner, Witous, had blamed the associate, Mittleman, for improperly handling two cases after the firm had criticized Witous for his handling of the two cases which had been dismissed because the statute of limitations had runout, costing the firm a large amount of money. In allowing the associate to proceed with his complaint, the Illinois Supreme Court specifically noted that the supervising attorney "had a personal stake in the matter—preservation of his own reputation—which may very well have conflicted with the best interests of the firm."[172]

The qualified privilege applies to communications to persons who have a legitimate interest in the information. However, such communications must be limited in scope and commensurate with that interest. The communications also must be made in a proper manner, so that others do not inappropriately learn about the content of the communications. Courts recognize that an employer or prospective employer has a legitimate interest in employment-related information.[173] The best way to avoid exceeding the qualified privilege is to limit the communication to factual statements and avoid statements concerning personality or personal spite. Usually, neutral factual statements can communicate the deficiencies that need to be communicated without creating the appearance of malice. Knowing communication of false information can be construed to indicate malice and can lead to liability.[174]

Most former employers require a written authorization from the former employee before releasing employment information. This authorization provides some additional protection,[175] but care must still be taken in the wording of any information released.[176]

If a former employee has filed a discrimination complaint, some negative job references can be viewed as retaliation for the complaint, permitting a federal civil rights suit. In 1997, the U.S. Supreme Court decided that a former employee could also sue under Title VII for post-termination retaliation, such as negative job references.[177]

EMPLOYEE LIABILITY. Employees can be liable criminally and civilly for their conduct. For example, a 1988 federal appellate court decision addressed an employee who had arranged for his employer to purchase laser paper at $14.25 per thousand sheets and for the vendor to pay him a kickback of $2.00 per thousand sheets. The court upheld the conviction of the employee for engaging in a conspiracy to defraud.[178]

4-3.2 Equal Opportunity Employment Laws

The federal government enacted several laws to expand equal employment opportunities by prohibiting discrimination on various grounds. These laws include Title VII of the Civil Rights Act of 1964; the Equal Pay Act of 1963; the Age Discrimination in Employment Act; Sections 503 and 504 of the Rehabilitation Act of 1973; and the Americans with Disabilities Act. In addition, numerous state laws address equal employment opportunities.

The older Civil Rights Acts from the 1860s and 1870s provide remedies for a broad range of discrimination, which includes employment discrimination. These older actsare applied in several other contexts involving healthcare organizations, including some medical staff cases.

42 U.S.C. § 1981. Section 16 of the Civil Rights Act of 1870[179] guarantees individuals equal rights under the law, including the right to make and enforce contracts. Because employment is based on contract, this law provides a remedy for some kinds of employment discrimination. This act is codified as 42 U.S.C. § 1981, as amended, so it is usually referred to as § 1981.

Section 1981 has generally been interpreted to apply only to discrimination that is based on race, although some courts have also applied it to alienage (citizenship or immigration status).[180] In 1988, a federal appellate court upheld a judgment under § 1981 against a hospital for discharging an African-American employee due substantially to racial motivation, even though there were nondiscriminatory reasons for the discharge. The employee had been a security guard. He failed three polygraph tests concerning thefts. However, Caucasian guards who had also failed had not been fired.[181]

Due to the impossibility of developing a satisfactory definition of race, the U.S. Supreme Court in 1987 decided that § 1981 protects against discrimination based on being a member of an ethnically or physiognomically distinctive subgroup of a population, but also decided that distinctive physiognomy is not essential.[182] Section 1981 does not apply to discrimination based on such factors as age, gender, and religion.

In 1989, the Court narrowly interpreted making and enforcing contracts so that § 1981 did not apply, for example, to discriminatory conditions of continuing employment.[183] In the same year, the Court also decided another case limiting the reach of § 1981.[184] In an effort to reverse these decisions and to make certain other traditional interpretations were expressed as part of the statute, the Civil Rights Act of 1991 was passed.[185] It amended § 1981 to (a) expand the definition of "make and enforce contracts" to include the enjoyment of the benefits of the contractual relationship and (b) extend express protection from nongovernmental discrimination.

42 U.S.C. § 1983. Section 1 of the Civil Rights Act of 1871[186] addresses deprivation under color of state law of rights, privileges, or immunities secured by the Constitution or laws. Thus, a plaintiff must show (a) the existence of some right secured by the Constitution or law, (b) deprivation of that right, and (c) that the deprivation is under color of state law. Purely private action cannot be remedied under this Act.[187] This Act is codified as 42 U.S.C. § 1983, as amended, so it is usually referred to as § 1983.

Actions of public healthcare entities are generally under color of state law. For example, a discharged quality assurance director was able to sue a county hospital under § 1983 due to the alleged (a) lack of pretermination notice of charges and opportunity to respond and (b) arbitrary, capricious, and improperly motivated basis for her discharge.[188]

Private healthcare providers are generally considered not to act under color of state law; receiving Medicare and Medicaid funds is not sufficient.[189] Being designated by the state as the emergency receiving facility for the mentally ill was held not to be sufficient in one 1994 case.[190] When a nurse sued to challenge her termination, a federal appellate court ruled that the lease of a public hospital to a private corporation did not make the actions of that corporation under color of state law.[191]

Private individuals and entities can act under color of state law when they act in concert with governmental officials. Thus, private hospital paramedics were found to be acting under color of state law when they acted in concert with police to detain a person under the emergency detention state statute.[192]

42 U.S.C. § 1985. The Civil Rights Act of 1861[193] forbids conspiracies to interfere with civil rights, including deprivation of equal protection of the laws or equal privileges and immunities under the laws. This Act is codified as 42 U.S.C. § 1985, as amended, so it is usually referred to as § 1985.

A conspiracy needs to be shown, which means that two or more entities must be acting together. Some courts recognize an intracorporate conspiracy exception so that all of the employees and agents of a corporation generally are treated as one entity,[194] similar to the exception recognized for antitrust.

The conspiracy does not have to involve state action or be under color of state law to violate § 1985.[195] However, when the conspiracy is aimed at interfering with a right that protects only against state interference, the conspiracy must involve state action in order to state a claim under § 1985. For example, the Fourteenth Amendment creates the right to be free from state action that interferes with equal protection or due process. Therefore, a purely private conspiracy would not interfere with Fourteenth Amendment rights. State action would have to be shown to state a claim under § 1985 for a conspiracy to interfere with Fourteenth Amendment rights. A federal appellate court applied this rule to conclude that a physician had failed to state a claim under § 1985 for the termination of his clinical privileges by a private hospital. There was no state involvement, and he based his claim on the Fourteenth Amendment.[196] On the other hand, some federal laws create rights to be free from private action, so no state action would need to be shown.

There generally must be a racial or other class-based, invidiously discriminatory animus behind the conspiracy.[197]

TITLE VII OF THE CIVIL RIGHTS ACT OF 1964. Title VII[198] prohibits discriminatory employment actions based on race, color, religion, sex, national origin, or pregnancy. Harassment (sexual, racial, gender) is also considered a form of discrimination. Title VII applies to hiring, dismissal, promotion, discipline, terms and conditions of employment,[199] and job advertising. It also prohibits an employer from retaliating against an employee who engages in activity protected under Title VII, such as complaining about discrimination (discussed in detail below). It applies to nearly all employers; governmental agencies were included by the 1972 amendments.

The primary enforcement agency of Title VII is the Equal Employment Opportunity Commission (EEOC). In some situations, the EEOC can defer to enforcement by local or state agencies or through individual suits. Generally, employees must exhaust the administrative remedies from the EEOC before they can sue under Title VII. False claims can result in criminal penalties.[200]

🚩 Three legal theories are used as the basis for finding employment discrimination.

1. First, violations can be found on the basis of disparate treatment when work rules or employment practices are not applied in a consistent fashion due to a discriminatory motive. Consistent treatment of all employees can avoid, or at least mitigate, liability for disparate treatment.[201]

2. Second, violations can be found on the basis of disparate impact when an employment practice, such as a written employment test, has an adverse impact on members of a certain protected characteristic, such as African-American individuals, or women, and cannot be justified as job related. In 1988, the U.S. Supreme Court ruled that an employee had to present more than statistics to establish a disparate impact case.[202] The employee must prove specific employment practices that caused the disparate impact. If such practices are proved, then the employer has the burden of presenting legitimate nondiscriminatory reasons for the practices, but need not present formal studies validating the practices. The burden then returns to the employee to prove that the reasons are just a pretext for discrimination.

3. Third, carryover from past discrimination can constitute a violation when minorities are in a disadvantageous position because of prior discriminatory practices.

Prior to 1991, there was no liability under Title VII in mixed motive cases where both prohibited (e.g., race) and nonprohibited factors (e.g., job performance) motivated the employer's action. Title VII was amended by the Civil Rights Act of 1991, so that other factors, if proven, do not eliminate liability but restrict the available remedies.[203]

> Employees can waive Title VII rights in private settlements, but the release must be knowingly and voluntarily entered.[204] Employees cannot be required to waive the ability to bring charges of discrimination with the EEOC, but they can waive their right to obtain monetary (as compared to programmatic) relief as a result of such a settlement agreement.

Employees can agree to arbitration of Title VII claims.[205] In 2001, the U.S. Supreme Court ruled that the Federal Arbitration Act applies to employment claims, so state barriers to arbitration do not apply to contracts that are in interstate commerce.[206] In 2011, the Supreme Court decided *AT&T Mobility LLC v. Concepcion*,[207] which upheld the enforceability of arbitration agreements in legal contracts. The Court held that the FAA was designed to promote arbitration over more costly and lengthy litigation. However, courts continue to disagree on whether to enforce arbitration requirements in employment manuals.[208] In 2012, the NLRB held in *D.R. Horton*, that employers cannot require employees waive their rights to bring class action claims by entering into arbitration agreements, because doing so would bar employees from exercising their rights under the NLRA.

In some jurisdictions, in particular California, certain provisions in arbitration agreements can render them unenforceable. For example, agreements that give the employer discretion to insist on arbitration are generally viewed as one-sided and may be unenforceable.[209] Agreements that do not provide for neutral arbitrators may be unenforceable, and typically the employer cannot insist that the arbitrator be picked from a list that it generates.[210] Agreements that are viewed as placing too much of the costs of the arbitration on the employee may not be enforceable.[211]

Title VII overlaps with the older civil rights acts. Thus, for example, most claims of ethnic-based discrimination in employment can be made under either § 1981 or Title VII. Frequently, claims are made under both statutes. Some courts have considered the elements of the claims to be identical. There are procedural differences; a plaintiff does not have to exhaust administrative remedies by first filing a charge of discrimination with the EEOC before filing a § 1981 suit with the federal court. There are some differences in the remedies granted. Some claims can only be brought under Title VII. For example, a religious discrimination claim against a private hospital that could be brought under Title VII probably could not be brought under the older Civil Rights Acts.

Who Is an Employee? Courts apply several different tests to determine whether a person is an employee and, thus, entitled to the protection of these employment nondiscrimination laws, or an "independent contractor" with whom the company contracts services. Clearly, if the employer withholds employment taxes from the person's income, the person is an employee. In less clear cases, the courts apply one or both of the common law control tests and the economic realities tests. Under the control test, persons are generally considered employees if the company controls the details and means by which the work is

> An employee is an individual who works in the service of another, either under an express or implied contract of hire, under which the employer has the right to control the details of the work performance.[‡] For employees, this means that employers have the advantage of controlling and directing the individual's work during working hours, training the individual, and requiring that the individual work exclusively for the employer. Employers have few restrictions or limitations on what they can assign to the employee or their ability to terminate the employee without paying out a contract. However, true employees have laws and regulations to protect them. Both the federal government and states closely regulate the payment of employee wages or salaries, overtime, and many other employment rules. Employers are subject to payroll tax requirements (including FICA), unemployment insurance, and worker's compensation insurance for employees.[§]

performed. Under the economic realities test, persons are generally considered employees if they are dependent on the business to which they render service.[212] Some courts use a hybrid test that combines elements of both tests.[213] In 1998, one federal court ruled that remuneration was required to make a person an employee, so it rejected the claim by an unpaid volunteer without looking at the other tests.[214] Typically, though the obligations imposed by Title VII an employer can apply to individuals working at the employer, whether an employee, volunteer, or independent contractor. In other words, if an employer receives a complaint that might be in violation of Title VII, an employer is well served to investigate and take remedial action where appropriate.

Generally, nonemployee physicians have been unable to use Title VII to challenge medical staff decisions because they are not employees.[215] However, Title VII also applies to interference with employment opportunities. Thus, in some circumstances, physicians who have been denied or lost medical staff membership have been able to use Title VII to sue hospitals, even when they are clearly not employees of the hospital.[216]

Who Is an Employer? In most cases, the answer to this question is clear. Small employers of less than fifteen

employees are exempt under Title VII.[**] In 1997, the U.S. Supreme Court ruled on how employees would be counted to determine the fifteen-employee threshold.[217]

Supervisors and managers are not "employers" under Title VII and cannot be held personally liable for violation of Title VII. However, conduct by a supervisor or manager can impose liability on an employer in certain circumstances.[218] Coworkers are not employers; they are not personally liable for violations of Title VII, but their actions may impose liability on the employer if the employer did not take prompt remedial action upon learning of a possible violation of Title VII.[219] Generally, a parent company of the employer is not liable as an employer under Title VII.[220]

Race and National Origin. Title VII and Section 1981 prohibit the discrimination of any individual regardless of their race or national origin.[221] In addition, reverse discrimination suits have been brought by Caucasians.[222]

Employers have an obligation to investigate and remediate complaints of discrimination, harassment or retaliation.[223] When complaints of discrimination are promptly corrected, liability can often be avoided, or at least mitigated. In 1996, a federal appellate court found no violation of Title VII because mistaken payment of higher wages to later hired Caucasian unit secretaries had been promptly reduced, with retroactive payment to African-American unit secretaries of the differential for the period of higher wages. The court found that there was no evidence of racial bias by those involved in the salary decision and bias by others was not relevant.[224]

Employers can require experience as a qualification when it is needed,[225] but a neutral requirement of experience for promotion can become discriminatory when the employer discriminates in the opportunities to gain the experience.[226] The Immigration Reform and Control Act[227] also bars some employment discrimination based on national origin or citizenship status, but citizens can be preferred over equally qualified aliens.

Request of the patient for discrimination is no excuse. Employers cannot accede to patient racial preferences concerning their providers. In 2003, a Pennsylvania hospital complied with a man's demand that no African-American staff members assist in the delivery of his child. Although

---

[‡] Garner, B. A., & Black, H. C. (2004). Black's law dictionary. (8th ed.). West Group. http://www.blackslawdictionary.com.

[§] Murray, J. (2011). About.com. Retrieved from Publication 15 (2012) (Circular E, Employer's Tax Guide) at http://www.irs.gov/pub/irs-pdf/p15.pdf. Accessed April 6, 2012.

[**] State Fair Employment Practices statutes, however, may apply to employers with only one employee.

no reported suit resulted, the action was widely criticized in the media, and the hospital publicly apologized.[228]

RELIGION. Employers must make reasonable accommodations for employee religious observances, short of incurring undue hardship.[229] This includes accommodating religious practices that preclude working on certain days. The offering of a reasonable accommodation satisfies the requirement even if it is not the accommodation the employee prefers.[230] Not everything that is claimed to be a religious observance is given this protection.[231] A federal district court rejected a woman's claim that her belief in adultery was religious, so it ruled that her discharge was not religious discrimination.[232]

Not all religious practices have to be accommodated. For example, an employee who professed a religion that promoted body art and piercings claimed that an employer's application of its dress code discriminated against her on the basis of religion. The First Circuit Court of Appeals upheld the employer's decision to terminate the employee when she refused to cover her various facial piercings. The Court determined that the employer required all employees to comply with its dress code and that enforcing the dress code against this particular employee was not discrimination on the basis of her religion. Furthermore, allowing the employee a complete exemption from the dress code policy would have been an undue hardship on the employer, thereby making the employee's requested accommodation unreasonable.[233]

Similarly, a federal appellate court upheld the termination of a Veterans Administration psychiatric hospital chaplain.[234] The court accepted the hospital's explanation that the chaplain's evangelical approach was not appropriate in the hospital and antithetical to its philosophy of care. In 1999, a federal appellate court ruled that a person could be refused employment based on a religious refusal to provide a Social Security number.[235]

Religious employers are exempt from the federal religious discrimination laws.[236] In 2012, the U.S. Supreme Court in *Hosannah Tabor v. EEOC*[237] unanimously ruled that churches enjoy broad, barely defined exemptions from civil rights laws in hiring and firing employees they classify as ministerial. The case stemmed from the firing of a Michigan teacher who had been employed by a school run by the Hosanna-Tabor Evangelical Lutheran Church. In 2004, the teacher went on disability leave after she became ill with narcolepsy. Because school officials were concerned that she would not return to her position for several months,

they asked her to resign. In exchange, the congregation offered to pay a portion of her health insurance premiums. The teacher rejected the offer and returned to work at the expiration of her leave. Upon her return, however, she was told that she must leave and that, if she did not, her employment would likely be terminated.

After being terminated, the teacher contacted the EEOC, which filed suit on her behalf arguing the teacher's termination was in violation of the Americans with Disabilities Act. The Supreme Court disagreed and held that the Religion Clauses of the First Amendment—which states that "Congress shall make no law respecting an establishment of religion, or prohibiting the free exercise thereof"— precludes the government from interfering with the decision of a religious group to terminate the employment of one of its ministers.

Similarly, in 1987, the U.S. Supreme Court ruled that Title VII's religious exemption was constitutional, including its application to secular nonprofit activities, such as hospitals.[238] In 1988, a federal court ruled that a religious hospital does not forfeit its exemption from the religious discrimination statutes by accepting Medicare payments.[239]

Discrimination in favor of a religion can also violate Title VII. A supervisor's preferential promotion of persons of the same religion can be a violation without showing that a specific religion was the target of the discrimination.[240]

Sex. In addition to prohibiting discriminatory employment actions against an employee on the basis of his or her sex, Title VII and corresponding state laws proscribe harassment of employees because of his or her sex. The two forms of sexual harassment are described as "quid pro quo" or "hostile work environment." Quid pro quo means "this for that"— or situations where an employee believes that his or her job benefits hinge on engaging in sexual conduct with a manager or supervisor. Hostile work environment refers to conduct in the workplace that is sexual in nature when the conduct is unwelcome to at least one person and is sufficiently severe or pervasive so as to alter the conditions of employment and create an abusive working environment. Employers are generally liable for any quid pro quo sexual harassment by supervisors.[241] In some situations, employers may be liable for harassment of employees by third parties such as patients and suppliers.[242] In some circumstances, harassment by medical staff members can lead to hospital liability.[243]

In 1986, the U.S. Supreme Court held that sexual harassment that created a hostile or offensive working environment could violate Title VII.[244] It is not necessary to show that the sexual harassment is tied to the granting or denial of an economic benefit. Employers are not strictly liable for hostile environment sexual harassment by their supervisors, but employers are not always shielded from suit by lack of knowledge of the behavior. If the employer has a policy against sexual harassment and has implemented a reasonable procedure to resolve harassment claims, the employer will usually be shielded from liability, absent actual knowledge of misconduct. The procedure should not require that the first step be a complaint to the supervisor who is the source of the harassment.

In 1993, the U.S. Supreme Court made it easier to prove sexual harassment by determining that it was not necessary to prove injury or a serious effect on the employee's psychological well-being.[245]

Federal appellate courts have generally ruled behavior that is merely offensive or boorish is generally not a violation of Title VII.[246] The behavior must be so severe or pervasive as to alter the conditions of employment. However, in some cases, a single egregious incident can be sufficient.[247]

Employees may also bring sex discrimination claims under a gender stereotyping theory. In 1989, the U.S. Supreme Court held in *Price Waterhouse v. Hopkins*[248] that Title VII prohibits employers from penalizing employees for failing to conform to the gender stereotypes associated with their sex.

Although most claims are by females, males may also bring sexual discrimination and sexual harassment claims.[249]

Most courts have held that preferential treatment of an employee on the basis of a consensual romantic relationship between a supervisor and employee is not sexual discrimination.[250]

Some groups have sought to convince courts that Title VII requires adoption of a comparable worth doctrine. This doctrine would require employers to revise wage scales so that pay is based on a comparison of the work done by persons in different job classifications without regard to the labor market. This doctrine goes beyond the Equal Pay Act (discussed in the following section) that requires equal pay for essentially identical work. Courts generally have ruled that Title VII does not require wage scales based on comparable worth.[251]

Pregnancy. In 1978, Title VII was amended to prohibit discriminatory treatment of pregnant women for all employment-related purposes. Employers are not required to provide special considerations.[252] However, for example, if leaves are offered for disability, similar leaves must be offered for disabling maternity. Mandatory maternity leaves not based on inability to work violate Title VII.[253] Pregnancy itself is not considered a disability, but if a pregnant worker becomes unable to work, then disability benefits must be offered the pregnant worker. Some states require employers to offer a leave of absence for pregnancy.

At least one federal court has found that discriminating against an employee based on her intended pregnancy was covered by the Pregnancy Discrimination Act ("PDA"), that her infertility was a medical condition related to pregnancy for purposes of the PDA and that the employee had stated a claim for discrimination under the Americans With Disabilities Act when she was terminated for being absent in order to undergo infertility treatments.[254]

In 1991, the U.S. Supreme Court ruled that Title VII was violated by fetal protection programs that prohibit female employees capable of childbearing from some jobs, such as those with exposure to toxic chemicals or high blood lead levels.[255] In 1994, a federal appellate court ruled that a pregnant home health nurse could be terminated for refusal to treat an AIDS patient.[256]

Employer health plans that cover employee's spouses must cover pregnancy-related disabilities of spouses.[257]

In 1997, a federal appellate court ruled that the pregnancy discrimination law does not apply after birth, so it does not apply to a woman's decisions concerning care for the child after birth.[258]

Bona Fide Occupational Qualifications. In some circumstances, sex or features related to religion or national origin can be bona fide occupational qualifications (BFOQ) reasonably necessary to the normal operation of a particular business. When employers can demonstrate this necessity, the use of the qualification is not a violation of the law. For example, a federal district court ruled that it was not illegal sex discrimination for a hospital to employ only female nurses in its obstetrics-gynecology department.[259] The court noted that the policy was based on the privacy rights of the patients, not just patient preference. An appellate court vacated the decision because the case became moot when the male nurse voluntarily quit his job.[260]

A federal appellate court ruled that it was not illegal discrimination based on national origin for a hospital to require all employees to have some facility in communication in the English language.[261] The court recognized that ability to communicate in English was a BFOQ for virtually every position in a sophisticated medical center. However, requiring employees to speak only English on the job can be national origin discrimination unless the employer can demonstrate business necessity.[262]

Retaliation. Employers are prohibited from retaliating against employees who oppose discrimination by engaging in or opposing activities protected under the various anti-discrimination statutes.[263] A federal appellate court found that a hospital had violated Title VII's anti-retaliation provision when it fired an African-American registered nurse who had complained about African-American patient care.[264] However, filing a discrimination complaint does not shield an employee from all adverse actions. Employees can be disciplined or discharged, even after a complaint has been filed, if the company has a legitimate and nonretaliatory reason to terminate the individual's employment, and the employee cannot show that those articulated reasons are a pretext for retaliation.[265] In 1997, the U.S. Supreme Court decided that a former employee could also sue under Title VII for post-termination retaliation, such as negative job references.[266]

Firing Discriminating Employees. Since employers can sometimes be found liable for discriminatory acts of employees, it is fortunate that most courts recognize such discriminatory acts to be grounds for discipline and even termination of the offending employees.[267] For example, a federal district court ruled that an employer's reasonable belief that a male employee was making unwelcome sexual overtures to female employees was a legitimate, nondiscriminatory reason to terminate the offending employee, and the employee could not show that that reason was a pretext for race discrimination.[268] However, some courts have ruled that discrimination is not good cause for termination of a physician's contract, so there may be liability for breach of contract, in situations where a collective bargaining agreement or an employment agreement allows for terminations only for just cause.[269] In those jurisdictions, contracts can be written to expressly permit appropriate action to deal with discrimination.

State Law. Title VII does not preempt the entire field of equal employment opportunity. While state law cannot permit something prohibited by Title VII, state law can provide additional protection. Thus, many state laws that limit the types of work women may perform are superseded, but state laws requiring employers to offer pregnancy leaves are not suspended.[270] Some state and local laws protect from discrimination employer's decisions based on sexual orientation.[271]

EQUAL PAY ACT OF 1963. This Act[272] is designed to prohibit discriminatory compensation policies based on sex. It requires equal pay for equal work. Equal work is defined as work requiring equal skill, equal effort, and equal responsibility that is performed under similar working conditions. A federal district court in Georgia upheld paying physician's assistants more than nurse practitioners because of the greater training and skills required, even though they provided substantially similar services.[273] The payment of higher wages to male orderlies than to female aides has been challenged in several cases.[274] In general, courts require equal pay, except when the hospital demonstrates actual differences in the work performed during a substantial portion of work time.

AGE DISCRIMINATION IN EMPLOYMENT ACT. This Act (ADEA)[275] prohibits discriminatory treatment of persons forty years of age and older for all employment-related purposes.[276] Mandatory retirement is prohibited except for certain exempted executives. The law applies to employers of twenty or more persons. There are exceptions for BFOQs,[277] bona fide seniority systems, and reasonable factors other than age, such as physical fitness. In 1984, a federal appellate court found a hospital liable for age discrimination because its medical director had fired a 56-year-old secretary and replaced her with a 34-year-old individual.[278] The replacement testified that the medical director told her she was selected for her appearance. Violations can also be found for discriminating in favor of those who are older. An Oregon appellate court found a retirement home liable for age discrimination under a state nondiscrimination law because it had refused to hire a beautician, saying she was too young for its residents.[279]

An employer will not be found liable for termination of an employee who is over the age of 40 if the employer presents valid reasons, such as reduction in force or inability to do the job, that are not pretext for age discrimination.[280]

Employers must be careful not to give the impression of age discrimination. After a 62-year-old day-shift nurse supervisor resigned, she sued the hospital for age discrimination.[281] The federal appellate court ruled that a jury should decide whether the CEO's statements concerning the need for "new blood" and her "advanced age" created intolerable working conditions in violation of the ADEA that forced her to resign.

In 1996, a federal appellate court upheld a jury award in favor of a fired director of a hospital radiology department. The court concluded that the hospital personnel manager had adversely altered the evaluation notes of the employee by his supervisor, so the jury was entitled to conclude that the reasons the employer gave for the firing were a pretext.[282]

Some employers have tried to settle age discrimination suits and have obtained from the employee a signed waiver of the right to sue for damages. Such waivers are not effective under the Older Workers Benefits Protection Act, which is an amendment to the ADEA. Valid waivers must satisfy statutory standards, including that they must be written in a manner that is clearly understood such that waivers are knowing and voluntary, and the waiver must advise the employee to consult an attorney before accepting the agreement, the employee must be given at least 21 days to consider the offer, and seven days to revoke his or her signature.[283] Thus, prior approval from the enforcement agency or a court may be necessary to make such waivers binding.

In 2004, the Supreme Court ruled that younger workers cannot use the ADEA to challenge better benefit packages that are given to older workers.[284]

AMERICANS WITH DISABILITIES ACT. In 1990, Congress passed the Americans with Disabilities Act ("ADA") ushering in a new era of protection for individuals with disabilities. The ADA prohibits discrimination against persons with disability employment, government programs and services, public accommodations and services, and telecommunications. Over the past twenty years, however, many disability rights advocates have contended that the ADA did not fulfill the statute's purpose of creating a more inclusive workplace for people with disabilities. Much of the concern raised by these disability advocacy groups revolved around a series of the U.S. Supreme Court decisions that limited the universe of individuals who qualified as people with disabilities under the ADA. In 2008, Congress responded to these concerns by passing the Americans with Disabilities Act Amendments Act of 2008 (ADAAA), which went into effect on January 1, 2009. Civil Rights activists lobbied Congress to reverse the Supreme Court rulings, which it viewed to narrowly define the concept of disability under the ADA. Employers, recognizing the strong bipartisan support in Congress for amending the ADA, worked to negotiate compromise language. The resulting legislation significantly expands the universe of employees entitled the protection from workplace discrimination due to a disability. The ADAAA's expanded scope will result in many healthcare workers being covered as individuals with disabilities who were not covered under prior law.

An employer may prohibit the use of alcohol and illegal drugs in the workplace; may prohibit employees from being under the influence of illegal drugs in the workplace; and may require compliance with the Drug-Free Workplace Act of 1988.[285]

Essential Functions. A key element of the analysis of whether an individual is qualified includes a determination of the essential functions of the position.[286] That determination also is a key part of assessing whether any proposed "accommodation" is sufficient to enable the person to perform the essential functions of the position. This issue is discussed in the section on Reasonable Accommodations.

Safety Issues/Direct Threat. An individual who poses a direct threat to the health or safety of others is not qualified.[287] The employer generally has the burden of proof on this issue because it is viewed as a defense against an ADA claim. However, in 1997, a federal appellate court recognized that safety issues are not limited to the context of a direct threat defense. The court ruled that when essential job functions involve the safety of others, then safety issues are included in the plaintiff's burden to prove ability to perform the essential job functions in order to be qualified. Thus, a former behavioral therapist, who earlier had attempted suicide with drugs, was required to prove that she qualified to safely perform a job that required her to handle medications for patients.[288] Other conditions have been found to raise direct threat or other safety issues.[289] For example, courts have determined that HIV-positive persons in some hospital positions are a direct threat to the health and safety of others or are otherwise not qualified.[290]

In 2002, the U.S. Supreme Court upheld an EEOC regulation permitting employers to refuse to hire a person when the job poses a direct threat to the person's health.[291]

Hiring Process/Other Inquiries. The law imposes numerous restrictions on the hiring process. While inquiries can be made about the ability to perform job-related functions, no inquiry can be made about whether the applicant has a disability or has any history of workers' compensation. Job criteria and employment tests are scrutinized to determine that they are job related and consistent with business necessity. In addition, tests that screen out disabled people are not permitted when alternate tests are available that disabled people can pass.

A federal appellate court applied the EEOC's Enforcement Guidance which prohibits certain pre-employment medical tests under the ADA. Those tests include pre-employment psychological test designed to identify a mental disorder or impairment. In contrast to that proscription, tests that measure personality traits such as honesty, preferences and habits are permissible.[292] The Minnesota Multiphasic Personality Inventory ("MMPI") test at issue in *Karraker* asked employees questions such as whether they "see things . . . that others do not see" or "have a habit of counting things that are not important." The court found that the MMPI "is designed, at least in part, to reveal mental illness and has the effect of hurting the employment prospects of one with a mental disability." Accordingly, the Court found the test to be a "medical examination" the preoffer use of which violated the ADA. The court specifically did not address whether the test was justifiable as "job-related and consistent with business necessity," noting that the employer offered no such defense.[293] "By prevailing on the latter, defendants could claim that the test is permissible during employment, even if impermissible preoffer. By not arguing that the test is "job-related and consistent with business necessity," [the employer] seeks a clear finding that the MMPI is not a medical examination and thus not regulated at all by the ADA."[294]

After a job offer has been made, medical examinations must be required for all entering employees for the job position, regardless of disability. Also, access to and use of the medical exam information must be limited.

The law has been interpreted to put other restrictions on employer inquiries of employees. In 1997, a federal appellate court ruled that an employer cannot require disclosure or restrict use of prescription drugs by employees.[295] In 1998, another federal appellate court ruled that in some limited circumstances a medical examination can be required of an existing employee.[296]

Job applicants may volunteer information.[297] Employers must be careful in how they use volunteered information.

Reasonable Accommodations. As part of nondiscrimination, covered employers must provide reasonable accommodations that do not involve undue hardship on the employer to individuals who are disabled under the ADA. In 1999, the EEOC published enforcement guidelines concerning reasonable accommodations.[298] The employer and employee must engage in an interactive process to determine what, if any, accommodation is available to assist the employee in performing the essential functions of his or her job. In 1999, a federal appellate court ruled that the ADA does not apply to an employee who effectively resigns before requesting an accommodation.[299]

Notably, the employer need not provide the requested accommodation; the employer is required only to provide a reasonable accommodation. Nor is an employer required to exempt the employee from the essential functions of the job.

Generally, employers can implement temporary accommodations without compromising their position that the accommodation is not required under the ADA. Most courts encourage such temporary accommodations. This approach allows the employer to investigate the circumstances while barring use of a temporary accommodation as proof that such an accommodation can be continued indefinitely. Courts recognize that temporary accommodations would be discouraged if they had to be continued indefinitely. In 1999, a federal appellate court found that an employer who had granted unpaid leave was not required to continue the leave.[300] In 1998, another federal court ruled that the temporary assignment of a nurse to a days-only schedule did not compromise the hospital's position that rotating shifts were an essential function of the job.[301]

Here are some examples where accommodations were not required. Employees have sought to change their work schedules. While in some positions this can be done without undue hardship, there are many positions in healthcare settings where the schedule is an essential part of the job. In 1998, a federal appellate court ruled that a nurse with fatigue-related seizures was not entitled to an accommodation of a days-only shift schedule because rotating shifts were an essential function for her maternity unit job.[302] In 1999, a federal appellate court ruled that working more than forty hours per week was an essential function of the job of director of human resources, so the employee was not entitled to have the job restructured to a forty-hour per week job.[303]

Employees have sought exemption from physical aspects of their jobs. In 1998, a federal appellate court found that a practical nurse with joint disease and arthritis could not perform the essential functions of the job, even with an accommodation, so no accommodation was required.[304] In 1993, a federal appellate court ruled that requiring firefighters to be clean shaven did not violate ADA rights of persons with a skin condition that precluded shaving. There was a business necessity in order to use safely respirators and no showing that a reasonable accommodation was available.[305] Employers are not required to exempt employees from the physically demanding parts of essential training for their positions.[306] Employers are not required to hire assistants to perform part of the essential functions of the job.[307]

Some employees have sought to use the ADA to change their supervisors. Courts have generally rejected that this accommodation as not being reasonable.[308]

Reasonable accommodations may include reassignment to open existing positions for which the employee is qualified.[309] Reassignments sometimes trigger seniority rights. In 2002, the U.S. Supreme Court decided that when a requested accommodation conflicts with a seniority rule, it generally will not be considered a reasonable accommodation.[310] Thus, in most circumstances, the ADA does not require violation of seniority rules.

Generally, when the condition of the employee results in frequent absences without warning, most courts recognize that no reasonable accommodation can be made without undue hardship.[311] However, in some circumstances, paid or unpaid leave can be a reasonable accommodation.[312] The EEOC recognizes that some positions cannot be held open without undue hardship. The EEOC takes the position that if the employer has another equivalent or lower level vacant position for which the employee is qualified, then the employee should be reassigned to that position for the remainder of the leave. However, if no such position exists, the leave may be terminated when the position can no longer be left open.[313] It is generally recognized that an indefinite leave is not a reasonable accommodation.[314]

Employers need to be aware that the EEOC has begun aggressively litigating against employers with maximum leave policies, asserting that they violate the ADA. In September 2009, the EEOC reached a $6.2 million settlement against Sears, Roebuck & Co.[315] In the *Sears* case, the EEOC claimed the retailer's policy of terminating employees on leave due to workers' compensation injuries in excess of the company's one-year maximum leave period violated the ADA. In 2011, a $3.2 million consent decree was reached in *EEOC v. Supervalu, Inc.*, No. 09-5637 (N.D. Ill.), a case where the EEOC again challenged the employer's one-year maximum leave policy. While EEOC regulations make it clear that there is a duty to "modify workplace policies" as a reasonable accommodation, there is disparate guidance as to exactly what this means or requires.

Insurance Benefits. In 1999, a federal appellate court ruled that caps on employee health benefits coverage for HIV did not violate the ADA.[316]

Former employees have sought to use the ADA to challenge disability coverage. Federal courts have disagreed whether a totally disabled former employee is still an employee covered by Title I employment provisions of the ADA.[317] Those courts that do not apply Title I have examined whether the Title III public accommodations provisions apply. Courts have generally limited public accommodations to places, so Title III does not apply to the terms of insurance policies.[318]

REHABILITATION ACT OF 1973. This Act[319] prohibits discrimination on the basis of handicap. Section 503 prohibits discrimination by government contractors, while Section 504 prohibits discrimination by entities that receive federal financial assistance.[320] This law overlaps with the ADA but does not extend to private employers that do not receive federal funding. Because of the overlap in terminology, however, courts often apply the same analysis in deciding Rehabilitation Acts cases, as used in ADA cases, but the detailed requirements are different. Hospitals are generally subject to both laws and need to comply with both.

In 1984, the U.S. Supreme Court ruled that any entity receiving federal financial assistance cannot discriminate in either services or employment.[321] In 1990, the law was amended to prohibit the entire healthcare facility from discriminating, not just the program receiving federal financial assistance.[322] Medicare and Medicaid reimbursement have been interpreted to be federal financial assistance.[323]

When the Rehabilitation Act applies, the institution is prohibited from discriminating against any qualified handicapped person who, with reasonable accommodation, can perform the essential functions of the job in question.[323] Preemployment inquiries about handicaps are prohibited, except that applicants can be asked if they are able to perform the job. Preemployment physical examinations may be required, but only if all applicants for similar positions undergo the same examination.

In 1994, a federal appellate court ruled against a blood bank administrator who was terminated after she asserted that she was unable to work because the ventilation system aggravated her asthma. The court determined she was not handicapped because she was not substantially limited in any major life activity and because her condition was exacerbated only in this one setting.[324]

In 1987, the U.S. Supreme Court ruled that a discharged teacher with a history of tuberculosis was otherwise qualified to teach and therefore must be reasonably accommodated.[325] Persons with HIV infections have been determined to be handicapped and protected.[326] In 1995, a federal appellate court decided that the FBI violated the Act. In that case, the FBI asked a physician under contract to examine an FBI agent to determine whether the agent had AIDS and then terminated his contract based on reports he had AIDS. The court ruled that the contract could not be terminated for his evasiveness about AIDS. In 1996, the U.S. Supreme Court vacated the decision and directed the appellate court to review the case. The appellate court then ruled in favor of the defendants based on sovereign immunity.[327] Numerous other conditions have been ruled to be protected handicaps.[328]

When a handicap precludes a function, the courts look closely to determine whether that function is needed for the job. Thus, a federal appellate court questioned whether heavy lifting was really necessary for a postal job for a person with a back injury.[329] Generally, standards do not have to be lowered, and the nature of the job does not have to be changed. For example, the Federal Register was not required to lower its accuracy standards to accommodate an editor with cerebral palsy.[330] The FBI was not required to change the role of special agents to accommodate an insulin-dependent diabetic.[331]

An employer may refuse to hire or retain a person on the basis of behavioral manifestations of the handicap, such as sleeping on the job by a diabetic[332] or excessive absenteeism.[333] Employers may also refuse to hire or retain persons whose current use of alcohol or drugs prevents them from performing job duties or constitutes a direct threat to property or the safety of others. Employers may strictly enforce rules prohibiting possession or use of alcohol or drugs in the workplace.

In 1985, the U.S. Supreme Court ruled that state agencies could not be sued for violating Section 504 because of their Eleventh Amendment sovereign immunity from being sued.[334] However, the law was amended and subsequently federal appellate courts have permitted suits against state agencies.[335]

4-3.3 Compensation and Benefits

Compensation and benefits of employees are regulated by several federal laws, including the Fair Labor Standards Act, Federal Wage Garnishment Law, Employee Retirement Income Security Act of 1974, Health Insurance Portability and Accountability Act of 1996, Family and Medical Leave Act of 1993, and Internal Revenue Code. In addition, numerous state laws address these issues.

Courts have generally upheld reasonable efforts by employers to monitor benefits use. In 1995, a federal appellate court held that a self-insured employer may monitor employee pharmaceutical use under its health insurance plan, provided the information is used only for monitoring the plan by those with a need to know.[336] The employer had discovered that an employee had AIDS from the drugs he was using, but there was no evidence of any discrimination against the employee.

FAIR LABOR STANDARDS ACT. This Act (FLSA)[337] establishes minimum wages, overtime pay requirements, and maximum hours of employment. Employees of all nonprofit and for-profit hospitals are covered by the FLSA. Bona fide executive, administrative, and professional employees are exempt from the wage and hour overtime provisions when they are paid on a salary basis.[338] While physicians and administrators are clearly exempt, Department of Labor regulations must be consulted to determine the status of other employee classifications.[339] In 2003, the rules defining the scope of the exempt categories were significantly changed, by modifying the income tests and the analysis of duties.[340]

The 1974 amendments to the FLSA extended minimum wage and overtime coverage to almost all employees of state and local governments. The coverage of governmental employees was declared constitutional by the U.S. Supreme Court in 1985.[341] However, in 1999, the Supreme Court decided that states retain their Eleventh Amendment immunity from most private suits.[342]

Most employers are required to pay overtime rates for nonexempt employees who work more than forty hours in seven days. However, hospitals may enter agreements with employees to establish an alternative work period of fourteen consecutive days. If this option is chosen, the hospital pays the overtime rate for hours worked in excess of eighty hours during the fourteen-day period. Even with this option, the hospital must pay overtime rates for hours worked in excess of eight in any one day.

There is still some disagreement among the courts over when persons in on-call status may not have to be paid or may be paid at a different rate. A federal district court ruled that security staff members in one hospital were not entitled to compensation for lunch breaks.[343] The possibility of being called to duty did not make the time compensable. However, another federal district ruled that hospital employees should be paid for their lunch breaks if they were still on call.[344] One federal appellate court ruled that a hospital could pay "on-premises-on-call" operating room technicians and nurses at one and one-half times minimum wage for periods in which they did no work, instead of at one and one-half times their regular hourly wage.[345]

The FLSA also addresses child labor by regulating the hours and conditions of employment of children. The FLSA does not preempt more protective state or local laws that establish a higher minimum wage,[346] a shorter minimum workweek, or more protection for children. There are other federal rules that regulate hours and conditions of employment for specific jobs. For example, the Federal Aviation Administration requires flight crew members, including crews of emergency medical helicopters, to have eight consecutive hours of rest every twenty-four hours.[347]

FEDERAL WAGE GARNISHMENT LAW. One way to enforce a court judgment against another person is to impose garnishment of the debtor's wages. Garnishment is a court order to an employer to pay a portion of the debtor's paycheck to the creditor until the debt is paid. The Federal Wage Garnishment Law[348] and various state laws restrict how much of a paycheck can be garnished. When there are multiple garnishments, proper priorities must be observed not to exceed the limit on aggregate garnishments. Federal law prohibits employers from discharging employees because of garnishment for one debt. The limits on garnishment do not apply to certain bankruptcy court orders or debts due for state or federal taxes.

EMPLOYEE RETIREMENT INCOME SECURITY ACT OF 1974. This Act (ERISA)[349] regulates nearly all pension and benefit plans for employees, including pension, profit-sharing, bonus, medical or hospital benefit, disability, death benefit, unemployment, and other plans. ERISA applies to all plans except for governmental plans, some plans of churches, and some § 401(k) retirement plans. The law regulates many features of these plans, including nondiscrimination, benefit accrual, vesting of benefits, coverage, responsibilities of plan managers, termination of plans, descriptions of plans, and required reports. ERISA requirements should be considered before changing any pension or benefit plan that is not exempt.

Some health benefit plans have attempted to use ERISA to attack state laws that mandate certain benefits. In 1985, the U.S. Supreme Court ruled that neither ERISA nor the National Labor Relations Act preempts state laws that mandate that insured plans provide certain benefits, such as mental illness coverage.[350] However, states cannot require self-insured or uninsured health plans to provide the specific benefits because such plans are not covered by the savings clause in ERISA that allows state regulation of insurance.[351]

Furnishing false information to a health or welfare fund subject to ERISA is a federal crime. The administrator of a provider of outpatient services was convicted of this crime because he did not report actual costs in a utilization report to a fund, but instead reported the estimated value of the services based on charges.[352]

ERISA forbids retaliation against employees for exercising their rights under a benefit plan. Thus, it is a violation of ERISA to discharge an employee to prevent coverage under a medical benefits plan.[353] A federal appellate court held it a violation to fire an employee who refused to become an independent contractor where more than an incidental reason for the change was to eliminate health coverage.[354] However, it is not a violation of ERISA for the employer to change a welfare benefit plan to the extent permitted by the plan. A discriminatory change that reduces benefits for one disease, such as AIDS, does not violate ERISA[355] but generally violates the ADA.

HEALTH INSURANCE PORTABILITY AND ACCOUNTABILITY ACT OF 1996. One focus of this Act (HIPAA)[356] is on making health insurance coverage "portable" and continuous for workers. Employees who change or lose jobs and who meet eligibility conditions have to be accepted into either a group plan or be offered an individual policy.

FAMILY AND MEDICAL LEAVE ACT OF 1993. This Act (FMLA) requires that eligible employees be provided twelve workweeks of leave during any twelve-month period to provide care for a serious health condition of the employee, spouse, child, or parent, or for a birth or adoption. The leave need not be compensated, but health care benefits must be continued during the leave.[357] There are also provisions in the FMLA which allow leave for military personnel and their family to deal with exigencies associated with deployment, military leaves of absence and injuries sustained during combat.

The statute defines a serious medical condition as "any physical or mental condition that involves inpatient care or continuing treatment by a health care provider."[358] Continuing treatment has been further defined by regulations and court decisions.[359] Courts generally require some degree of incapacity.[360] An employer may require that the requested leave "be supported by a certification issued by the health care provider of the eligible employee." An employer generally can rely on an employee's physician's certification that the employee qualifies for FMLA leave.[361] However, the employer may require a second opinion, and disagreements are resolved by a binding third opinion.[362] An employer can require an employee on leave to obtain subsequent recertifications "on a reasonable basis." Although, when an employee has a chronic serious health condition, the employer usually must wait at least thirty days between requests for recertification.[363]

The employee is not required to mention the FMLA to request unpaid leave.[364] The employee need only provide the employer with enough information to put the employer on notice that FMLA-qualifying leave is needed.[365] Advance notice can be required in some circumstances; prompt notice after the fact is permitted in some circumstances.[366]

In 2003, the U.S. Supreme Court ruled that FMLA applies to state employees and that private suits can be brought against states to enforce the part of FMLA related to the care of close family members.[367] It remains an open issue whether private suits can be used to enforce other parts of FMLA against states. One federal appellate court ruled that states are immune from private suits concerning other parts of FMLA.[368]

INTERNAL REVENUE CODE. The Internal Revenue Code requires employee benefit plans to meet certain standards to qualify as deductible business expenses.[369]

The Internal Revenue Service (IRS) is more closely scrutinizing the classification of workers as employees or independent contractors in an effort to require employers to pay employment taxes on more workers.

The IRS continues to scrutinize pension plans, deferred compensation, and other benefits.

4-3.4 Occupational Safety and Health

OCCUPATIONAL SAFETY AND HEALTH ACT OF 1970. Congress enacted this Act (OSHA)[370] to establish standards for occupational health and safety and to enforce the standards. Standards developed for various industries are mandatory for all covered employers. When no federal standard has been established, state safety rules remain in effect. OSHA does not apply to employees of states and their political subdivisions, but many states enforce most OSHA standards through state enforcement agencies.[371]

The Act requires each state to enact legislation to implement the standards and procedures promulgated by the Department of Labor. Litigation has arisen over the issue of inspections used by federal and state officials to enforce OSHA standards. Courts have ruled that an employer can refuse an inspection unless the inspector obtains consent from an authorized agent of the employer or the inspector has a valid search warrant. The U.S. Supreme Court ruled unconstitutional an OSHA provision that permitted spot checks by OSHA inspectors without a warrant.[372]

OSHA regulations prohibit employers from discriminating against employees who refuse to expose themselves to conditions presenting a real danger of death or serious injury in urgent situations where there is insufficient time to pursue correction through OSHA.[373] This regulation was upheld by the U.S. Supreme Court in 1980.[374] However, an Indiana appellate court ruled that a lab technician could be terminated for refusing to test vials of bodily fluids with AIDS warnings because the lab had provided appropriate safety manuals and precautions, so there was insufficient danger to justify the refusal.[375]

Where OSHA applies, OSHA preempts all state occupational safety and health regulations. In 1992, the U.S. Supreme Court decided that states must obtain the approval of the Secretary of Labor for any such state regulations. There is no public safety exception. A nonoccupational impact is not sufficient to defeat preemption.[376]

OSHA adopted rules to protect healthcare employees from blood-borne diseases.[377] A federal appellate court upheld the blood-borne disease regulations, except as to sites not controlled by the employer or another entity subject to the employer's rules.[378] Thus, the regulations could not be applied to home care by home health workers. In 1998, a federal appellate court ruled that employees who refuse to wear protective clothing required by OSHA can be terminated.[379]

OSHA has focused on other areas that have special impact on healthcare areas including latex allergies, needle stick injuries, tuberculosis, and waste anesthetic gasses. Other OSHA initiatives that will impact health care but are not primarily aimed at the healthcare environment, include workplace violence and ergonomics.[380]

There is a general duty clause in OSHA. Under it, hospitals have been cited for, among other things, not protecting workers from tuberculosis,[381] not protecting workers from patient violence,[382] and not vaccinating employees.[383]

Employers cannot retaliate against employees who make OSHA complaints.[384]

STATE OCCUPATIONAL SAFETY LAWS. Employers have a statutory duty in some states to furnish employees with a safe place to work.[385] Even in states that do not have such statutes, employers are liable for most injuries suffered by employees as a result of employment unless the employer is protected by governmental immunity. In most situations, employees can pursue compensation only through the workers' compensation system, not through courts.

Other state statutes require that specific facilities be provided to employees. These facilities, such as lavatories, must be provided for the convenience and safety of employees. Local governmental ordinances and laws also can include requirements, such as sanitary and health codes, to promote and safeguard the health and safety of employees and others. In most states, state institutions are exempt from local regulation unless state laws grant local governments the authority to encompass state institutions.

4-3.5 Labor-Management Relations

Unions are a significant factor in the employee relations of healthcare providers in some parts of the United States. Various labor organizations are recognized as collective bargaining representatives for groups of healthcare employees. There are craft unions that devote their primary organizing efforts to skilled employees, such as carpenters and electricians; industrial unions and governmental employee unions that seek to represent large groups of relatively unskilled or semiskilled employees; and professional and occupational associations and societies, such as state nurses associations, that represent their members and sometimes others.

LABOR-MANAGEMENT RELATIONS ACT. This Act[386] regulates many aspects of the relationship between employers and employees. It prohibits unfair labor practices by employers and unions. It provides hearings for complaints that such practices have occurred. The Act consists of the National Labor Relations Act of 1935 (NLRA),[387] the Taft-Hartley amendments of 1947,[388] and numerous other amendments, including the Labor-Management Reporting and Disclosure Act of 1959.[389] The Act is administered by the National Labor Relations Board (NLRB). The NLRB (1) investigates and adjudicates complaints of unfair labor practices and (2) conducts secret ballot elections among employees to determine whether they wish to be represented by a labor organization and, if so, to determine which organization.

Government hospitals are exempt from the NLRA. This exemption has been interpreted by the NLRB to apply only to hospitals that are owned and operated by governmental entities.[390] For example, a municipal hospital operated under contract can be considered a private entity subject to the NLRB if a private contractor exercises overall daily control. Exempt governmental hospitals are usually subject to state labor laws.

Nonprofit hospitals were exempt until the amendments of 1974 eliminated the exemption.[391] The 1974 amendments attempted to deal with some of the unique aspects of health care by providing legislative direction about collective bargaining, mediation, conciliation, and strikes.

Some religious hospitals have challenged these laws. Federal appellate courts have found that it is not a violation of First Amendment religious freedoms to apply these laws to hospitals owned and operated by religious entities.[392]

The law directs the NLRB to give hospitals some special consideration because of their sensitive mission. Nonetheless, individual NLRB rulings will continue to be made on the basis of many factors, in addition to the uniqueness of health care.

EXEMPT STAFF. Several groups of staff members are excluded from the NLRB's jurisdiction, including independent contractors, supervisors, managerial employees, confidential employees, and some students. Each of these groups has been defined by numerous NLRB and court decisions, so familiarity with those decisions is necessary to determine whether a particular staff member is exempt.

Supervisors. The NLRA imposes a three-part test for determining which employees are supervisors. Employees are statutory supervisors if (1) they hold the authority to engage in any one of the twelve listed supervisory functions; (2) their "exercise of such authority is not of a merely routine or clerical nature, but requires the use of independent judgment"; and (3) their authority is held "in the interest of the employer."[393]

> The NLRA lists these three characteristics of a "supervisor": i. authorized to perform any 1 of 12 supervisory functions; ii. the authority requires the use of independent judgment; and iii. the authority is used in the interest of the employer.

The NLRB interpreted the second test to require that the independent judgment pertains to the other employee's job status or pay. In 1994, the U.S. Supreme Court rejected this interpretation and decided that nurses who direct other employees' treatment of patients can be supervisors without any involvement in determining job status.[394] The NLRB then interpreted there not to be exercise of independent judgment when the employee only applied "ordinary professional or technical judgment in directing less-skilled employees to deliver services in accordance with employer-specified standards." In 2001, the Court ruled that the NLRB could not exclude this type of judgment from the scope of judgment that could satisfy the second test and found that registered nurses in a residential mental health center could be supervisors.[395] The Court also ruled that the employer must prove supervisory status. However, the NLRB continues to find registered nurses in nursing homes not to be supervisors in many cases.[396]

The federal appellate courts have split on whether licensed practical nurses who serve as charge nurses in nursing homes can be supervisors.[397] The NLRB generally finds that they are not supervisors.[398]

UNFAIR LABOR PRACTICES. Section 7 of the National Labor Relations Act establishes four fundamental rights of employees: (1) the right to self-organize; (2) the right to engage in concerted activities for the purpose of collective bargaining or other mutual aid or protection; (3) the right to engage in collective bargaining; and (4) the right to refrain from union activities.

Employer Unfair Labor Practices. An employer commits an unfair labor practice through:

1. interference with any of the four rights recognized in section 7;

2. domination of a labor organization;

3. discouragement or encouragement of union activity;

4. discrimination against employees who file charges or testify in an NLRB proceeding; or

5. violation of the other obligations, including good faith bargaining, specified in section 8(a) of the NLRA.

The NLRA also applies to employers that do not have employees represented by a labor organization. The employee's right to engage in concerted activities for the purposes of mutual aid or protection can apply to isolated incidents, so employers should obtain legal advice before disciplining employees who might be engaged in protected activities. For example, the NLRB ruled that a small group of unorganized staff was protected by the NLRA when members of the group left their workstations to complain to hospital officials concerning work conditions.[399] Not all employee actions are protected. The NLRB upheld the dismissal of two hospital employees for continual criticism of the program director.[400] The NLRB found this activity unprotected because it was aimed at influencing administration of the program, rather than at working conditions. With the advent of social media (Facebook, Twitter, etc.) the NLRB has also begun to investigate and issue unfair labor practices against employers who discipline or terminate employees who exercise their rights to complain about the terms and conditions of their workplace via social media. Such cases involved employee complaints regarding wages, a coworker's erratic attendance and the impact it was having on morale in the department, and an employee's outspoken criticism of hospital policies both on social media and traditional print media. In each case, the NLRB sided with the employee that their rights under the NLRA had been infringed. See NLRB Memorandum OM 11-74 (published August 18, 2011), and NLRB Memorandum OM 12-31 (published January 24, 2012). http://www.nlrb. gov/publications/policies#comments.

A federal appellate court found that an employer had violated the NLRA by discharging a supervisor in retaliation for refusing to engage in unfair labor practice.[401]

Permanent replacement workers have been a contentious issue. A federal appellate court found that a hospital had committed an unfair labor practice by refusing to reinstate striking nurses to prestrike positions and giving those positions to nonstriking nurses. During the strike, the hospital had closed until it was compelled by community needs to open two units and later to open the whole hospital with supervisory personnel, new hires, and striking nurses who crossed picket lines. The hospital had guaranteed returning nurses they could keep their new positions. The court ruled that those who had actually worked in the new positions could have permanent replacement status but that others were nonpermanent and not entitled to keep positions they were promised.[402] In another case, after finding unfair labor practices by the employer, a nursing home was ordered to reinstate former strikers who had been permanently replaced.[403]

There frequently is litigation about what information the union is entitled to receive. For example, a federal appellate court ruled on the scope of information about nonunit employees that the union could access.[404] The NLRB ruled that a hospital had committed an unfair labor practice by not giving information on its benefit plans.[405] A federal appellate court ruled that the union was not entitled to the home addresses of strike replacement workers.[406]

A federal appellate court refused to enforce a nationwide NLRB cease and desist order directed at a nursing home chain. The court ruled that the order had to be directed at specific facilities that had engaged in unfair labor practices, since there was no showing of unlawful acts at a substantial number of facilities.[407] Another federal appellate court upheld a nationwide NLRB order based on a finding of a geographically broad history of widespread unfair labor practices.[408]

Employers should also obtain legal advice before working with employee advisory committees. If their role is not appropriately limited, such committees can be considered labor organizations, and many of the employer's interactions with them could be interpreted as unfair labor practices. For example, the NLRB ruled that a hospital had engaged in the unfair labor practice of management domination of a labor organization because the hospital ran the election for an employee committee and wrote its bylaws.[409] A federal appellate court found that an employer-formed forum for nurses to discuss and consider professional nursing practice issues was not a "labor organization" because it did not deal with the employer on matters affecting employment. There was no pattern or practice of making proposals to which the hospital responded, and isolated instances did not constitute "dealing."[410]

Employers cannot make unilateral decisions to mandatory subjects of bargaining, which generally include anything related to the terms and conditions of the employees' employment, unless the union has clearly and unmistakably waived its right to so bargain under the collective bargaining agreement A federal appellate court ruled that a hospital had committed an unfair labor practice by unilaterally deciding to stop supplying surgical garbs without bargaining with the union, but that the hospital's decision to reduce the number of teams receiving eighty hours pay for seventy hours work to zero was within its authority under the collective bargaining agreement.[411]

Employees do not have the right to falsely and publicly disparage their employer or its products or services. A federal appellate court decided that it was not an unfair labor practice to fire a nurse who had appeared on a local news broadcast and accused her employer hospital of "jeopardizing the health of mothers and babies" by altering the shift assignments and responsibilities of labor and delivery registered nurse first assistants.[412]

Labor Organization Unfair Labor Practices. A labor organization commits an unfair labor practice through:

1. restraining or coercing interference with the exercise of the four rights recognized in Section 7 or interfering in management's selection of its representative;

2. attempting to cause the employer to discriminate to encourage or discourage membership in a labor organization;

3. failing to bargain in good faith;

4. engaging in prohibited secondary boycotts;

5. charging excessive union initiation fees;

6. causing employers to pay for services not performed; or

7. picketing solely to compel an employer to recognize a union (recognitional picketing) or to persuade employees to join the union (organizational picketing) without filing a petition for an election within the appropriate time limit.

The U.S. Supreme Court ruled that a union committed an unfair labor practice by prohibiting members from resigning from the union during a strike or when a strike was imminent.[413]

A federal appellate court affirmed an order that a union not picket a nursing home for one year following its defeat in a decertification election.[414]

A labor organization cannot be liable for the misconduct of its members unless the organization actually participated, gave prior authorization, or ratified such acts after actual knowledge of their perpetration.[415] Applying this rule, an Ohio appellate court ruled that the union could not be liable for the misconduct of its members at a hospital construction site because the required participation, authorization, or ratification had not been shown.[416]

EMPLOYEE REPRESENTATION. A labor organization seeking representation rights for employees may petition the NLRB for a secret ballot election. The petition must make a "showing of interest" supporting the petition. At least 30 percent of the workers who will ultimately make up the bargaining unit must support it and show their interest by signing union authorization cards.

Bargaining Unit Designation. The employer can take the position that certain persons (supervisors, confidential employees, temporary employees) should be excluded from the unit as inappropriate because of the institutional organization. The NLRB will then conduct a representation hearing to determine the appropriate bargaining unit. The NLRB must implement the congressional intent in the 1974 amendments to avoid "proliferation of bargaining units" in the healthcare industry.[417] In addition, Section 9 of the NLRA forbids including professional employees in bargaining units with nonprofessionals unless a majority of the included professionals vote in favor of inclusion.[418]

Until 1984, the NLRB determined whether the proposed unit was appropriate by applying a "community of interest" test. That is, a proposed unit was appropriate if its members had a community of interest. This resulted in the recognition of five basic units in healthcare institutions, as follows:

1. clerical;

2. service and maintenance;

3. technical;

4. professional; and registered nurses.

Traditionally, the NLRB has applied a "community of interest" standard in fulfilling its duty to determine whether a proposed bargaining unit is appropriate, where it has balanced different factors such as the similarity of pay, methods of computing pay, employee benefits, vacation schedules, hours of work, kinds of work performed, qualifications, skills, and training; the physical proximity of employees and frequency of contact and transfers; the functional integration of the firm; its supervisory and organizational structure, especially as it relates to setting and applying labor relations policies; any bargaining history; employee desires; and the extent of union organization within the firm.

In *Specialty Healthcare and Rehabilitation Center of Mobile* ("*Specialty Healthcare*"), 357 NLRB No. 83 (2011), however, the NLRB dramatically changed course by creating a new standard under which a unit of "all employees performing the same job at a single facility" is presumptively appropriate as a general matter in all industries. The NLRB further gave great weight to the unit sought by a union:

[W]e reiterate and clarify that, in cases in which a party contends that a petitioned-for unit containing employees readily identifiable as a group who share a community of interest is nevertheless inappropriate because it does not contain additional employees, the burden is on the party so contending to demonstrate that the excluded employees share an *overwhelming community of interest* with the included employees.

Because there are inevitable distinctions among separate groups of employees, this decision encourages the proliferation of bargaining units at any workplace – each unit sought by a union is likely to share a community of interest bearing some distinction from workers performing a different (but related) job.

Geographic scope of units can also be an issue. In some circumstances, the NLRB applies a single facility presumption. However, the NLRB found the presumption to be overcome by a showing of function integration as to services and employees, so it rejected an attempt to create a unit of the employees of one clinic, insisting that the employees in the entire network of clinics be included in one unit.[423] In another case, the union agreed to a multifacility unit of the employees in the main campus, but the NLRB ruled that employees in off-campus facilities and outlying clinics needed to be included.[424] The single facility presumption was ruled not to apply to a multifacility unit.

Solicitation and Distribution. Most healthcare organizations have rules concerning solicitation of employees and distribution of materials in the facility to avoid interference with patient care. These rules become especially important during campaigns to organize employees, so they should be written to be enforceable under the NLRA. Each policy is examined on a case-by-case basis by the NLRB.[425] Some general guidelines can be derived from past decisions. Nonemployees are generally prohibited access to the facility for solicitation or distribution, except for areas such as the cafeteria, if the hospital allows other groups access to solicit and distribute. Employees can be prohibited from these activities during work time. Work time does not include mealtimes or work breaks.[426] Solicitation or distribution can be limited to nonpatient care areas at all times. The U.S. Supreme Court ruled that solicitation and distribution could be prohibited in areas devoted to patient care.[427] Areas to which visitors have general access, such as cafeterias and lounges, usually cannot be prohibited where a genuine likelihood of patient disturbance cannot be shown.[428] Solicitation at entrances is generally permitted.[429] Another important factor in the exclusion of certain areas is whether reasonable alternative space is designated. A federal appellate court decided that a hospital could enforce its nonsolicitation rule in a cafeteria because no nonemployees had been permitted to solicit there and the presumption of access to the union's message elsewhere had not been rebutted.[430]

However, selective enforcement of such rules will generally preclude enforcement against unions.[431]

ELECTION. A labor organization can become the exclusive bargaining agent for a bargaining unit by winning a secret ballot election conducted by the NLRB. After an election, the employer or the labor organization can challenge the outcome by filing an objection.[432] If misconduct is found, the election can be set aside with a new election ordered.[433]

A labor organization can also be decertified as the collective bargaining agent by an election of its members.[434]

Recognition without an Election. An employer can voluntarily recognize a labor organization as the exclusive bargaining agent without an election.[435] Some employer actions, such as checking union authorization cards or polling employees, can sometimes constitute recognition of a labor organization. Recognition without an election can be challenged as a possible unfair labor practice in some circumstances, especially when other labor organizations are also seeking to represent the employees. Most employers avoid all actions that could be interpreted as voluntary recognition. A second way that a labor organization can be recognized without an election is by NLRB order. When the NLRB finds serious unfair labor practices, it can order the extraordinary remedy of recognition. A third way is accretion.[436] If a labor organization has negotiated a contract with an employer that later acquires a new facility, under some circumstances the new facility is considered to be accreted to the existing one, and new unit employees are automatically covered by the preexisting contract. However, where there is a history of separate bargaining at the two sites, they can sometimes remain separate.[437] A fourth way is that a successor corporation can be required to continue to recognize a union in some circumstances.[438]

COLLECTIVE BARGAINING AND MEDIATION. After a labor organization has been recognized as the exclusive bargaining agent, the employer and labor organization have a duty to negotiate in good faith.[439] They must bargain concerning mandatory subjects, including wages, hours, and other terms and conditions of employment. They may bargain concerning other permissive subjects but are not legally obligated to do so. It is unlawful to bring negotiations to an impasse, strike, or lock out employees over permissive subjects.

Several special notice, mediation, and conciliation safeguards were built into the law to help the healthcare industry avoid strikes when possible. For example, ninety days' notice is required if a party intends to terminate or modify a bargaining agreement, and the Federal Mediation and Conciliation Service (FMCS) must be given sixty days' notice.[440] When notified, the FMCS attempts to bring about an agreement, and all parties must participate fully and promptly in meetings called by the FMCS to pursue a settlement. If a strike is threatened, the FMCS can, under certain conditions, establish an impartial board of inquiry to investigate issues and provide a cooling-off period of up to thirty days.[441]

Another special provision for healthcare institutions is a ten-day advance notice of intention to engage in concerted economic activities, including strikes, picketing, or any other concerted refusal to work.[442] This provision is designed to allow a hospital to make plans for continuity of patient care. Hospitals that use this opportunity to take "extraordinary steps" to stock up on ordinary supplies for an unduly extended period of time may, however, be engaging in an unfair labor practice that would permit the union to strike without notice or during the ten-day period. A Minnesota court ruled that nurses were entitled to unemployment compensation during a layoff where the hospital had laid them off when union gave the ten-day notice of intent to strike.[443] A federal appellate court decided that there was no duty to rehire workers who strike without giving the required notice.[444] In 2005, a federal appellate court upheld an NLRB ruling that when the notice is given that any strike must occur at the designated time or a new notice must be given. The union started the strike four hours after the time stated in its notice pursuant to a prearranged plan that was not disclosed to the clinic employer. Twenty-two striking nurses lost their status as protected employees, so their healthcare employer did not violate the Act by terminating them.[445]

Some courts have ruled that individual unorganized employees do not have to give a ten-day notice of work stoppage. In 1980, a federal appellate court ruled that two physicians who walked out of the hospital and joined the picket line of a lawful strike by other employees did not have to give the notice.[446] The court noted that the action of the physicians was inconsiderate and ethically suspect, but protected.

In some circumstances, the ally doctrine allows a union to strike against a secondary employer not involved in the original dispute. The strike is permitted when the secondary employer loses its neutrality by performing work during the course of the labor dispute that would have been performed by striking employees of the primary employer. The legislative history of the 1974 amendments modifies the ally doctrine by permitting a hospital to accept the critically ill patients of a struck hospital without losing its status as a neutral employer. In an advice memorandum issued by the NLRB in September 1977, a union was said to violate the Act when it threatened to picket two neutral hospitals because they received critically ill patients and forty-six pregnant women transferred from the struck hospital.[447]

When a valid impasse is reached in negotiations, the employer may unilaterally implement its final offer.[448]

ADMINISTERING THE CONTRACT. After negotiating a labor agreement, the employer and labor organization should spend no less care on its administration. Managerial rights that have been established at the bargaining table, sometimes at a high price, can be eroded or entirely lost through inattention. The entire managerial team, especially supervisors, should know the aspects of the contract applicable to their responsibilities. Managers should be trained to ensure that discipline is administered for proper reasons and by appropriate procedures under the contract.

Frequently, collective bargaining agreements provide for arbitration of grievances. When a grievance involves the interpretation of the collective bargaining agreement, the NLRB will generally defer the matter to arbitration. Likewise, courts grant great deference to challenged arbitration decisions unless they violate public policy, but courts seldom find superseding public policies. For example, a federal appellate court upheld an arbitrator decision reinstating an employee caught with marijuana with presumed intent to sell, finding no superseding public policy.[449] Two federal district courts refused to overturn arbitration decisions ordering reinstatement of (1) a nursing attendant who changed an intravenous bag in violation of the state nursing practice act and (2) a nurse who failed to notify a physician of a sudden change in a patient's blood pressure and who committed other violations of proper nursing practices.[450] The Illinois Supreme Court confirmed an arbitration award reinstating two mental health workers whose patient had died while they were on an unauthorized errand.[451] The U.S. Supreme Court upheld an arbitrator's reinstatement of an employee who had been found with traces of marijuana in his automobile.[452] This did not violate public policy because there was insufficient connection with use of the drug.

However, sometimes a superseding public policy is found. A New York court reversed an arbitrator's reinstatement of a respiratory therapist who, after being warned, continued to engage in the life-threatening practice of reusing a syringe to draw blood from multiple patients.[453] The Ohio Supreme Court reversed an arbitrator's reinstatement of an aide terminated for abuse of a mentally retarded patient.[454] A federal district court vacated an arbitration decision ordering reinstatement of a nurse discharged for negligent medication administration because reinstatement would violate state "public policy in favor of providing safe and competent nursing care."[455] A Minnesota court ruled that an arbitrator had improperly reinstated a paramedic. Where all of the paramedic's functions were under the medical director's license and he was responsible for quality of care, the decision concerning competence was for the medical director.[456]

There are frequently disputes over the scope of arbitration.[457] At least one court has ruled that the duty to arbitrate can continue beyond the end of the collective bargaining agreement.[458]

REPORTING AND DISCLOSURE. The Labor-Management Reporting and Disclosure Act of 1959 places some controls on labor unions and their relationship with their members. It also requires employers to report payments and loans made to representatives of labor organizations. Payments to employees for the purpose of persuading them or causing them to persuade other employees to exercise or not to exercise their rights to organize and bargain collectively must also be reported. Many of these payments are illegal, and the reporting requirement does not make them legal. Reports must also be made of (1) expenditures to interfere with employee rights to organize and bargain collectively and (2) certain agreements with labor relations consultants. Reports are made public. Failure to report and false reports can lead to substantial penalties. Governmental hospitals are not subject to these provisions. The Office of Labor-Management Standards in the Department of Labor ("Department" or "DOL") has proposed revisions to two Labor-Management Reporting and Disclosure Act ("LMRDA") reporting forms: (i) Form LM-10 (Employer Report) and (ii) Form LM-20 (Agreements and Activities Report – filed by persuaders). See 76 Fed. Reg. 36178 (June 21, 2011). The LM-10 and LM-20 cover agreements or arrangements between employers and labor relations consultants whereby the consultant undertakes activities to persuade employees concerning their rights to organize and bargain collectively. Included within the proposed changes is a revision to the department's longstanding interpretation of the "advice" exemption to reportable persuader activity under the LMRDA. The proposed reinterpretation would expand the circumstances under which reporting is required by employers as well as by consultants or contractors deemed to be engaged in persuader activity. This narrowing of the advice exemption would have particularly severe consequences for employers and their attorneys who together have traditionally relied upon the advice exemption to seek and provide counsel regarding labor relations matters and issues. The changes, however, have not yet been accepted.

4-3.6 State Laws

While federal laws have preempted many state labor laws,[460] state laws still apply in at least two situations. First, when federal law does not cover an activity, states may regulate it. Second, when courts rule that state law does not conflict with federal law, the state law will be enforceable. Despite the broad scope of federal preemption, states may regulate labor relations activity that also falls within the NLRB jurisdiction when the regulated conduct touches interests deeply rooted in local feeling and responsibility. Thus, violence, threats of violence, mass picketing, and obstructing streets may be regulated by states.

In some states, there are no labor relation statutes, but in others, two types directly affect the rights of employees to organize and bargain collectively: (1) anti-injunction acts and (2) laws regulating union security agreements. Other state labor laws deal with equal employment opportunity, child labor, safety, workers' compensation, and unemployment compensation. Many states have laws concerning the relationship between public employees and governmental employers that apply to governmental hospitals.

ANTI-INJUNCTION ACTS. The federal government and many states have enacted anti-injunction acts that narrowly define the circumstances in which courts may enjoin strikes, picketing, and related activities in labor disputes. The federal statute is the Norris-LaGuardia Act.[461] Some aspects of state anti-injunction statutes can be preempted. Anti-injunction acts generally apply to healthcare providers.[462] Occasionally, judges find the standards to have been met and issue injunctions related to labor activities. For example, in 2004, a California judge ordered nurses at a county hospital to end their sickout.[463]

UNION SECURITY CONTRACTS AND RIGHT-TO-WORK LAWS. Some labor organizations seek union security contracts with employers in the form of either (1) the closed shop contract, which provides that only members of a particular union can be hired, or (2) the union shop contract, which makes continued employment dependent on union membership but does not require the employee to become a member until after being hired. Many states have constitutional provisions or statutes, generally called right-to-work laws, making such contracts unlawful.[464] Other states have statutes or decisions that restrict such contracts or specify procedures that must be followed before such agreements may be made. Some states require an employee election. Some states permit a union shop agreement, but not a closed shop. State right-to-work laws are not preempted by the NLRA because Section 14(b) of the NLRA explicitly authorizes them.[465] In states where such agreements are illegal, any request for such a contract must be refused, and the employer can obtain an injunction to stop a strike or picketing designed to induce such agreements. In states that permit such agreements, there is no legal obligation to agree. It is one of the matters on which there can be bargaining. When these provisions are accepted, employers can be forced to fire noncompliant employees.[466]

WORKERS' COMPENSATION. Every state has workers' compensation legislation to compensate employees for accidental on-the-job injuries. These acts replace the employee's common law remedy of suing the employer for negligence, which was usually an unsuccessful process. Most employers are subject to these acts. Many employers purchase workers' compensation insurance, although self-insurance is usually an option. An employee generally must give written notice of injury to the employer. In cases not routinely paid, the matter will be heard by a state commission to determine liability. State statutes define "employee," "injury," and other terms and have schedules of payment amounts for types of injuries. When the workers' compensation law applies, the employee is barred from suing the employer for the injury.[467] Courts become involved only when there is an appeal concerning a decision of the state commission.

Several issues are frequently litigated. One question is whether the injury arose out of and occurred in the course of employment.[468] A related issue is whether the injury was caused by an accident. Numerous exclusions are usually stated for preexisting or congenital physical conditions and for injuries caused by horseplay or other nonemployment causes.

Workers' compensation laws generally do not bar suits against persons who are not employers. A nurse anesthetist was permitted to sue a psychiatrist for injuries she received while administering electroconvulsive therapy because he was not the employer or a fellow employee.[469] States vary on when fellow employees may be sued.

The California Supreme Court held that a child could sue for in utero injuries that occurred when the mother was injured during her employment. Because there was injury to the child separate from the injury to the mother and the child was not an employee, the court ruled that under California law the workers' compensation law did not bar the suit.[470]

Workers' compensation acts and other benefit programs under which injured workers may seek compensation are often complex. Familiarity with applicable state law is necessary to appropriately address employee injuries.

The U.S. Supreme Court ruled that workers are not entitled to notice and an opportunity to be heard before their workers' compensation benefits are suspended during utilization review.[471]

UNEMPLOYMENT COMPENSATION. State law generally provides for payment of unemployment compensation to many unemployed individuals. Generally, persons who have been discharged for misconduct forfeit all or part of the compensation they would have otherwise received. There is considerable litigation concerning what constitutes misconduct. For example, the Pennsylvania Supreme Court found a nursing assistant guilty of misconduct for smoking in a patient's room contrary to hospital rules, so she was denied compensation.[472] The Vermont Supreme Court ruled that a nurse who had been discharged for giving a patient medication by intravenous (IV) push instead of IV drip was entitled to unemployment compensation because her error had been in good faith.[473] The Nebraska Supreme Court ruled that a change of hours from the 3:00 p.m. to 11:00 p.m. shift to the 11:00 p.m. to 7:00 a.m. shift was not good cause for a licensed practical nurse to resign, so she was not entitled to compensation.[474] The Florida unemployment agency ruled that a hospital laboratory technologist who resigned due to fear of AIDS was not entitled to compensation.[475] A Pennsylvania court decided that it was willful misconduct for a phlebotomist to mislabel a blood sample after three prior reprimands for mislabeling, so compensation was denied.[476] A North Carolina court ruled that a hospital employee was disqualified from compensation for violating the hospital policy against fighting with coworkers.[477]

However, due to the peculiar features of the unemployment compensation process in some states, strange outcomes do occur. The Michigan Supreme Court ruled that under Michigan law a nurse who failed the state licensing exam and, thus, could not legally function as a nurse was entitled to unemployment compensation because the court viewed that she had not lost her job voluntarily.[478] The Nevada Supreme Court ruled that an employee who failed to report to work due to incarceration was entitled to unemployment compensation.[479]

OTHER STATE AND LOCAL LAWS. Some state and local governments regulate the employment relationship in other ways. Here are examples.

Some state and local governments have enacted minimum wage laws that require higher wages than federal law.[480] At least two states have restricted such local laws.[481]

Some states and localities prohibit discrimination based on sexual orientation.[482] Some localities require domestic partner benefits.[483]

Some states extend protection from disability discrimination to conditions that do not qualify as disabilities under federal law.[484]

PUBLIC EMPLOYEES. Because the NLRA does not apply to employees of state and local governmental agencies, the relations between these public employees and their governmental employers are controlled by state law. Some states prohibit collective bargaining by public employees, so employee rights are determined by state civil service laws and individual agency policies. Many states authorize representation by a labor organization and collective bargaining. A state agency similar to the NLRB is usually established to administer the law. State laws frequently limit the subjects that can be determined by collective bargaining, and they are different from the NLRA in other ways. Many states prohibit strikes by all or some public employees and require that bargaining impasses be resolved by arbitration.

4-4 Independent Contractors

Healthcare providers frequently retain independent contractors to provide services. The relationship between an organization and an independent contractor is very different from the relationship with an employee.

The primary distinguishing feature of an independent contractor is that the contractor exercises control over the manner in which the work is completed.[485] This control test is not the only test that is used; other factors are considered in various contexts.[486] In some contexts, withholding taxes or providing some employment benefits is considered determinative, and the control test is not even addressed.

It is important to structure the relationship with independent contractors so that they are consistently treated as independent contractors. When they are treated like employees in one aspect, there is an increased risk that they will considered to be employees for other purposes.

California employers should take extra precaution in classifying employees in light of recent enhanced penalties. On October 9, 2011, Governor Jerry Brown signed California Senate Bill 459 ("SB 459"), which adds sections 226.8 and 2753 to the California Labor Code. SB 459, effective January 1, 2012, imposes steep penalties on employers who willfully misclassify employees. This legislation is but one example of a growing effort at both the federal and state level to identify, reclassify, and prevent misclassification of employees as independent contractors, deterring companies from doing so with significant penalties. Given the hospitality industry's widespread utilization of independent contractor services, hospitality employers should reevaluate their independent contractor agreements and take precautionary measures to ensure compliance with this new legislation.

TAXES. Income taxes are not withheld from independent contractors. The contractor is responsible for making estimated tax payments. The employer does not pay employment taxes on independent contractors; only the contractor pays. Independent contractors can deduct business expenses that employees are not permitted to deduct.[487] Retroactive finding of that the incorrect status was used can lead to tax liability for the business and/or the contractor.

BENEFITS. Employment benefit plans do not apply to independent contractors. Independent contractors must make their own insurance arrangements. Nonemployees sometimes seek retroactive employment status and benefits.[488]

Independent contractors are generally not covered by workers' compensation or unemployment compensation.[489]

DISCRIMINATION. Employment discrimination laws generally apply only to employees, so they generally do not apply to independent contractors.[490] Independent contractors are protected by some discrimination laws that apply to discrimination in contracting.[491]

LABOR LAW. Independent contractors cannot organize for collective bargaining under the NLRA. However, the NLRB has considerable discretion in determining whether particular workers are employees or independent contractors.[492]

WHISTLEBLOWERS. Most of the laws that protect whistleblowers apply only to employees so that independent contractors do not have this protection.[493]

CONFIDENTIALITY OF MEDICAL RECORDS. Independent contractors who need to have access to protected health information can satisfy the requirements of the Health Insurance Portability and Accountability Act (HIPAA) privacy regulations in one of two ways. They can be treated as part of the workforce and receive the training that is mandated for the workforce. Alternatively, they can sign a business associate agreement. (See "Healthcare Information" in Chapter 8 for more details on HIPAA.)

LIABILITY. Employers are liable for most of the acts of their employee in the course of employment under the doctrine of respondeat superior. Businesses are usually not liable for the acts of independent contractors except in unusual circumstances, such as where the contractor is acting as an agent or apparent agent.[494] Businesses can also be liable when their own negligence contributes to the injury. A New Mexico court found a hospital liable for negligent selection of a contract therapist.[495]

4-5 Others Who Provide Services in Healthcare Organizations

In addition to employee and independent contractors, there are several other categories of persons who provide services in healthcare organizations. Three of these categories are nonemployee medical staff, volunteers, and students. Medical staff members are addressed in Chapter 5 "Medical Staff."

VOLUNTEERS. Volunteers present some of the same issues as independent contractors. Volunteers are not protected by most of the employment discrimination laws.[496] When healthcare providers give volunteers employment benefits, there is a risk the volunteers will be considered employees for other purposes. Sometimes former volunteers seek to be retroactively characterized as employees to gain payment or other benefits. These efforts have generally been unsuccessful.[497]

Issues have also been raised about institutional liability for acts of volunteers. Some states have granted volunteers immunity for liability under some circumstances.[498] When immunity does not apply, courts have reached different results concerning institutional liability and insurance coverage.[499]

States vary on the extent of workers' compensation coverage for volunteers. In some states, volunteers are covered only if institutions elect to include them.[500]

States sometimes regulate the use of volunteers. For example, New York limited the use of volunteers in proprietary nursing homes.[501]

STUDENTS. Some students are employees. Some students are volunteers. Some students are simply in training programs sponsored by the institution or an affiliated institution and are neither employees nor volunteers.

All students are subject to academic supervision, evaluation, and consequences that are different from nonstudents. Courts generally show great deference to bona fide academic judgments concerning academic performance.[502]

Otherwise students who are employees are subject to most of the same rules as other employees discussed in section 4-3. In some states, students who are employees are subject to somewhat different rules than other employees.[503]

For nonacademic matters, students who are not employees are generally subject to the same principles as volunteers.[504]

There is one significant difference from volunteers. Generally, formal education programs are considered a service program, so some of the discrimination laws concerning programs and services can apply to decisions regarding nonemployee students. Thus, a federal appellate court concluded that a medical school could be sued for violating the ADA but the school was not required to accommodate a disability when it would alter the service. Requiring the school to permit continued studies after the National Board exam was failed would alter the school's service of educating physicians.[505] In addition, some training programs are educational programs that are subject to Title IX.[506]

In 2003, some students filed an antitrust challenge to the graduate medical education matching program through which students completing medical school are matched with first-year house staff positions. In early 2004, the federal court dismissed the case as to some defendants but permitted the case to proceed against the remaining defendants. Congress passed a law prohibiting antitrust attacks against the matching program. The federal court then dismissed the suit.[507]

In 1999, the NLRB ruled that house staff in institutions subject to the NLRB could organize into unions.[508] The status of house staff in other institutions varies based on state law.

Most training programs are subject to accreditation standards that regulate aspects of the programs. For example, the accrediting body for medical residency programs has limited the number of hours that house staff in accredited programs may be on duty.[509] It has taken steps to actively enforce this requirement.[510] At least one state, New York, also has laws regulating house staff hours.[511] The restrictions had unintended consequences that interfered with teaching, so a few exceptions were introduced.[512]

Chapter Summary

There are some general legal aspects between individual healthcare providers and caregivers in the healthcare delivery system. Healthcare delivery is both an individual and a team effort. To ensure quality in healthcare delivery, most healthcare providers are licensed or authorized to practice by a governmental authority. Licensure laws are intended to assure that only properly qualified persons are engaged in healthcare practice. Licensing laws apply to physicians, dentists, registered nurses, pharmacists, and many other healthcare providers. Each state has its own licensing laws.

States have discretion to determine licensure requirements, and the individual licensing boards have broad authority to enforce licensing laws and rules. Licensing boards may discipline licensed professionals who violate licensing laws or board rules. Before imposing disciplinary sanctions, licensing boards must provide due process to licensed professionals. Due process includes notice of the wrongful conduct and an opportunity to present information.

Besides licensure, there exists private certification—or credentialing—of healthcare professionals. There are many private methods of credentialing. Credentialing includes accreditation of educational programs, certification of individuals, and credentialing by institutions. Private, professional organizations establish criteria to evaluate and accredit educational programs. Private, professional organizations sponsor programs to certify that individuals meet certain criteria and are considered prepared to practice in a particular discipline. Individual certification is generally related to performance, such as passing a test. Medical specialties are an example of individual certification.

There are varying restrictions on the healthcare delivery system, including state and federal laws pertaining to employment and privacy. These restrictions apply to the various types of people involved in the healthcare delivery system. Many healthcare organizations retain employees, nonemployee medical staff, independent contractors, volunteers, and students to provide services. The relationship differs between the healthcare organization and each type of service provider. For example, the relationship between an organization and an independent contractor or student is very different from the relationship with an employee.

Key Terms and Definitions

Licensure - Most healthcare providers are licensed, or authorized to practice, by a governmental authority. Licensure refers to the granting of a license to practice.

Due Process - Licensing boards must provide due process to licensed professionals. Due process includes providing notice of any wrongful conduct and an opportunity to present information before sanctioning the licensed professional.

Certification - In some cases, private certification is required by government authorities in order to qualify for certain positions, status, or payment. Individual certification is generally related to performance, usually including passing a test. Individual certification includes medical board specialties.

Accreditation - Private, professional organizations establish criteria to evaluate educational programs. Accreditation is the process in which certification of competency, authority, or credibility is presented to these educational programs. Accreditation is voluntary, but most educational programs strive to obtain and retain accreditation from established accrediting bodies.

Just Cause - A legally sufficient reason for the termination of an employee that would justify terminating the employee without reasonable notice or payment.

National Labor Relations Board (NLRB) - Independent agency of the U.S. government, the NLRB investigates and remedies unfair labor practices.

Fair Labor Standards Act (FLSA) - Establishes minimum wages, overtime pay requirements, and maximum hours of employment. Employees of all nonprofit and for-profit hospitals are covered by the FLSA.

Employee Retirement Income Security Act (ERISA) - Regulates nearly all pension and benefit plans for employees, including pension, profit-sharing, bonus, medical or hospital benefit, disability, death benefit, unemployment, and other plans. ERISA applies to all plans except for governmental plans, some plans of churches, and some § 401(k) retirement plans.

Family and Medical Leave Act (FMLA) - Requires that eligible employees be provided twelve workweeks of leave during any twelve-month period to provide care for a serious health condition of the employee, spouse, child, or parent, or for a birth or adoption. The leave need not be compensated, but healthcare benefits must be continued during the leave.

Health Insurance Portability and Accountability Act of 1996 (HIPAA) - A federal law that protects health insurance coverage for employees and their families when employees change or lose their jobs, provides provisions for establishing national standards for electronic healthcare transactions and national identifiers for providers, health insurance plans, and employers. Additionally addresses the security and privacy of health data.

Occupational Safety and Health Act (OSHA) - A federal law to establish and enforce standards for occupational health and safety. Standards developed for various industries are mandatory for all covered employers.

Instructor-Led Questions

1. What are the goals of individual licensing? How well does it accomplish these goals? What other effects does individual licensing have?

2. Discuss the selection of roles to license.

3. What are the consequences for the individual and the institution where he or she works when the individual does not have the required license?

4. What limits are there on the legislatures or regulators who define the scope of licensed practice? What are the abilities of these entities to otherwise limit the actions of licensed persons by regulation?

5. When can licensed persons delegate licensed functions to others who are not licensed?

6. What steps must licensing boards follow in disciplining licensed persons?

7. What is the difference between accrediting educational programs and certifying individuals?

8. What are the responsibilities of employers in hiring new healthcare employees? What should be checked?

9. Discuss the effect of mandated staffing levels and restrictions on mandatory overtime.

10. What are the restrictions on discipline and dismissal of staff members?

11. Under what circumstances can employees be tested for drugs?

12. What characteristics of a person trigger the protection of equal employment opportunity laws? When may these characteristics be taken into account in employment decisions?

13. What characteristics must a person have to qualify for protection under the Americans with Disabilities Act? What accommodations are considered reasonable and, thus, required for the employer to undertake?

14. What impact does the Fair Labor Standards Act have on employee compensation?

15. What impact does the Employee Retirement Income Security Act have on employee benefits?

16. Under what circumstances must an employee be given a leave of absence according to the requirements of the Family and Medical Leave Act?

17. What major areas of healthcare employment practice are regulated by the Occupational Safety and Health Act?

18. Describe the framework of federal labor-management relations legislation.

19. Which employees are exempt from National Labor Relations Board jurisdiction?

20. What are unfair labor practices?

21. Discuss the evolution of the bargaining units in health care.

22. How is a labor organization certified as the bargaining agent? How is a labor organization decertified?

23. What is the effect of a union security contract and right-to-work law?

24. What is the function of workers' compensation and unemployment compensation laws?

25. What factors make a person an independent contractor? How does the law treat independent contractors differently from employees?

26. What is the relationship between healthcare organizations and volunteers or students?

Endnotes

1   *Dent v. West Virginia,* 129 U.S. 114 (1889); *St. George's School of Med. v. Dep't of Registration and Educ.,* 640 F. Supp. 208 (N.D. Ill. 1986) [authority to license physicians belongs to state].

2   *Beck v. McLeod,* 240 F. Supp. 708 (D. S.C. 1965), aff'd, 382 U.S. 454 (1966); see also *Peckmann v. Thompson,* 745 F. Supp. 1388 (C.D. Ill. 1990) [state has broad police power to regulate healing arts; no constitutional right to have midwives recognized or licensed].

3   E.g., Judge: Natural health practitioner can keep doors open, AP, Mar. 30, 2002 [natural health practice may continue but practitioner cannot advertise as doctor of naturopathy in S. Dak.].

4   *Lange-Kessler v. Dep't of Educ.,* 1997 U.S. App. LEXIS 15275.

5   *Zook v. State Board of Dentistry,* 683 A.2d 713 (Pa. Commw. Ct. 1996).

6   E.g., P. Sutin, Council is unswayed by patient's opposition to requirement for stretcher van technicians, St. Louis Post-Dispatch, Dec. 3, 2001, 1 [county license].

7   21 U.S.C. § 823; *Pearce v. United States Dep't of Justice,* DEA, 867 F.2d 253 (6th Cir. 1988) [example of revocation of DEA license].

8   A. Imse, Licensing rule suspended for nurse's aides, Rocky Mountain News [Denver, Colo.], June 28, 2001, 16A.

9   *Taylor v. Mobil Oil Corp.,* 248 Va. 101, 444 S.E.2d 705 (1994).

10 *Calabro v. Dep't of Aging,* 689 A.2d 347 (Pa. Commw. Ct. 1997) [PA pharmacist required to refund for prescriptions billed while unlicensed]; Optometrist operating without a license indicted for Medicare fraud, reports U.S. attorney, PR Newswire, Apr. 23, 2002.

11 E.g., *Central Anesthesia Assocs., P.C. v. Worthy,* 173 Ga. App. 150, 325 S.E.2d 819 (1984), aff'd, 254 Ga. 728, 333 S.E.2d 829 (1985) [hospital liable for injuries caused by student nurse anesthetist under supervision of physician's assistant when law required physician supervision].

12 E.g., *Turek v. St. Elizabeth Comm. Health Ctr.,* 241 Neb. 467, 488 N.W.2d 567 (1992); *Leahy v. Kenosha Mem. Hosp.,* 118 Wis. 2d 441, 348 N.W.2d 607 (Ct. App. 1984); see also *Lingle v. Dion,* 776 So. 2d 1073 (Fla. 4th DCA 2001) [failure to comply with office surgery rule not negligence per se].

13 *State Bd. of Med. Exam'rs v. Warren Hosp.,* 102 N.J. Super. 407, 246 A.2d 78 (Dist. Ct. 1968), aff'd, 104 N.J. Super. 409, 250 A.2d 158 (App. Div. 1969).

14 E.g., *Roach v. Kelly Health Care, Inc.,* 87 Or. App. 495, 742 P.2d 1190 (1987) [home health agency violated regulations by using certified nursing assistant who had not received required additional sixty hours of training on home care].

15 *Adams v. Commonwealth, Unemployment Comp. Bd. of Review,* 86 Pa. Commw. 238, 484 A.2d 232 (1984).

16 E.g., California fines six out-of-state doctors, AP, Feb. 11, 2003.

17 E.g., *Dittman v. State,* 191 F.3d 1020 (9th Cir. 1999) [state may require disclosure of social security number in license application].

18 E.g., *Massachusetts Med. Soc'y v. Dukakis,* 637 F. Supp. 684 (D. Mass. 1986), aff'd, 815 F.2d 790 (1st Cir.), cert. denied, 484 U.S. 896 (1987); McGinn, R.I. mandates Medicare assignment for all claims, Am. Med. News, Sept. 22/29, 1989, 3; but see *Hennessey v. Berger,* 403 Mass. 648, 531 N.E.2d 1268 (1988) [nonparticipating physician may refuse to treat Medicaid recipient].

19 *Hayes v. Ridge,* 168 F.3d 478, 1998 U.S. App. LEXIS 29684 (3d Cir. Oct. 27, 1998) (unpub.), earlier decision, 946 F. Supp. 354 (D. Pa. 1996) [denying injunction]; see also *Ubel v. State,* 547 N.W.2d 366 (Minn. 1996), cert. denied, 519 U.S. 1057 (1997) [upholding medical license surcharge].

20 *Abrahamson v. Illinois Dep't of Prof. Reg.,* 153 Ill. 2d 76, 606 N.E.2d 1111 (1992).

21 E.g., *Dep't of Prof. Reg. v. Florida Dental Hygienist Ass'n, Inc.,* 612 So. 2d 646 (Fla. 1st DCA 1993) [agency exceeded delegated authority by permitting hygienists graduated from programs with lower standards than legislative requirement]; but see *Abramson v. Florida Psychological Ass'n,* 634 So. 2d 610 (Fla. 1994) [state must honor settlement with psychology applicants that granted license to person not meeting statutory requirements].

22 E.g., *Hason v. Medical Bd.,* 279 F.3d 1167 (9th Cir. 2002), cert. dismissed, 538 U.S. 958 (2003) [MD may challenge license denial based on mental illness]; *Medical Soc'y of N.J. v. Jacobs,* 1994 U.S. Dist. LEXIS 15261 (D. N.J.) [settlement of ADA challenge to license questions on mental illness, substance abuse, agreed to drop questions, pay legal fees]; but see *Kotz v. State,* 33 F. Supp. 2d 1019 (M.D. Fla. 1998) [federal court will not intervene to stop state licensing board from collecting information about alleged disabilities]; *Colorado State Bd. of Med. Exam'rs v. Davis,* 893 P.2d 1365 (Colo. Ct. App. 1995) [ADA does not bar medical license revocation for recent history of illegal prescription drug use]; *Ramachandar v. Sobol,* 838 F. Supp. 100 (S.D. N.Y. 1993) [Rehabilitation Act does not preclude medical license revocation for mental illness]; see also *Medical Soc'y of N.J. v. Doe,* 191 F. Supp. 2d 574 (D. N.J. 2002) [dismiss challenge to policy of making agreements concerning past substance abuse public records].

23 29 C.F.R. § 1630.2(j)(3)(i); compare *Rush v. National Bd. Med. Exam'rs,* 268 F. Supp. 2d 673 (N.D. Tex. 2003) [ADA testing accommodation ordered] with *Powell v. National Bd. of Med. Exam'rs,* 364 F.3d 79 (2d Cir. 2004) [affirming denial of ADA testing accommodation].

24 *Doe v. National Bd. of Med. Exam'rs,* 199 F.3d 146 (3d Cir. 1999).

25 *Miller v. Medical Ass'n of Ga.,* 262 Ga. 605, 423 S.E.2d 664 (1992).

26 E.g., J. Spencer, Decision lets Texas podiatrists continue treating the ankle, Cox New Service, July 1, 2002 [county judge refused to throw out settlement between state, podiatrists]; Camarillo men fined in cosmetic surgeries, L.A. Times, Feb. 5, 2004, B3 [Calif. dentists performed cosmetic surgery].

27 M. Croasdale, Empowered by insurers and states, nonphysicians push practice limits, Am. Med. News, Feb. 9, 2004, 1; M. Croasdale, Nonphysicians eager to pick up prescription pad, Am. Med. News, Feb. 7, 2005, 1.

28 J. Spencer, Getting drugs without the doctor, Wis. St. J., June 1, 2004, D1 [extension of prescription-writing powers to others; six states allow pharmacists to give out morning-after pill; two states allow psychologists to prescribe some drugs – La. & N. Mex.].

29 E.g., *Rockefeller v. Kaiser Found. Health Plan of Ga.,* 554 S.E.2d 623 (Ga. App. 2001) [violation for PA to provide treatment without supervision by approved physician].

30 E.g., *Sermchief v. Gonzales,* 600 S.W.2d 683 (Mo. 1983).

31 E.g., Wis. Stat., § 441.16.

32 66 Fed. Reg. 56762 (Nov. 13, 2001) [CMS rule granting option]; State Board of Medicine and Surgery supports removing physician supervision for Nebraska's nurse anesthetists, U.S. Newswire, Feb. 25, 2002 [2d state to opt out of MD supervision]; see also Hospital says nurses gave anesthetic without doctor's order, AP, Oct. 4, 2003 [14 nurses fired, 9 disciplined].

33 E.g., *State ex rel. Lakeland Anesthesia Group, Inc. v. Ohio State Med. Bd.,* 74 Ohio App. 3d 643, 600 N.E.2d 270 (1991).

34 *State ex rel. Iowa Dep't of Health v. Van Wyk,* 320 N.W.2d 599 (Iowa 1982).

35 *State Farm Mutual Auto. Ins. Co. v. Arizona Bd. of Chiropractic Exam'rs,* 931 P.2d 426 (Ariz. App. Ct. 1996).

36 E.g., Wis. Stat. § 448.03(2)(e).

37 Mich. Comp. Laws § 333.16215(1).

38 Opinion No. 5630 (Jan. 22, 1980).

39 Iowa Code Ann. § 152.1(6)(d).

40 *Cook v. Workers' Compensation Dep't,* 306 Or. 134, 758 P.2d 854 (1988).

41 *Mullen v. Inspector General,* HHS D.A.B., Civil remedies Div. No. C-94-299, Dec. No. CR227 (Oct. 5, 1994), as reprinted in Medicare & Medicaid Guide (CCH) ¶43,008.

42 *Siddiqui v. Illinois Dep't of Prof. Reg.,* 307 Ill. App. 3d 753, 718 N.E.2d 217 (4th Dist. 1999).

43 Doctor fined for allowing unlicensed student to treat woman, AP, Oct. 2, 2002.

44 Medical board accusation leads to surrender of Burbank physician's medical license, Business Wire, June 27, 2002 [pulmonary function tests, ultrasound tests]; see also M. Lasalandra, State warns heart doctors; Too many complex tasks performed by assistants, Boston Herald, July 17, 2000, 1 [alleged PAs performing invasive heart procedures]; M. Crane, Board revokes doctor's license, Columbus [Ohio] Dispatch, July 13, 2000, 1C [left patients in care of unsupervised assistant].

45 *Brodie v. State Bd. of Med. Exam'rs,* 177 N.J. Super. 523, 427 A.2d 104 (App. Div. 1981).

46 *State Med. Bd. v. Murray,* 66 Ohio St. 3d 527, 613 N.E.2d 636 (1993).

47 *Medical Soc'y of N.J. v. New Jersey Dep't of Law & Pub. Safety,* 120 N.J. 18, 575 A.2d 1348 (1990).

48 *Florida Med. Ass'n v. State,* 766 So. 2d 406 (Fla. 1st DCA 2000); see also Board places 90-day ban on in-office cosmetic procedure, AP, Feb. 7, 2004 [Fla. ninety-day moratorium on office combined tummy tuck, liposuction procedures in MD offices after several deaths].

49 *American Academy of Pain Management v. Joseph,* 353 F.3d 1099 (9th Cir. 2004).

50 *Rogers v. State Bd. of Med. Exam'rs,* 371 So. 2d 1037 (Fla. 1st DCA 1979), aff'd, 387 So. 2d 937 (Fla. 1980); see also P. Simms, Board allows chelation therapy, Wis. St. J., Nov. 25, 2003, C1.

51 *Garces v. Dep't of Registration & Educ.,* 118 Ill. App. 2d 206, 254 N.E.2d 622 (1st Dist. 1969).

52 *Board of Optometry v. Florida Med. Ass'n, Inc.,* 463 So. 2d 1213 (Fla. 1st DCA 1985).

53 *Pennsylvania Med. Soc'y v. Commonwealth, State Bd. of Med.,* 118 Pa. Commw. 635, 546 A.2d 720 (1988).

54 *Ortiz v. Dep't of Health,* 882 So. 2d 402 (Fla. 4th DCA 2004).

55 E.g., Doctor's license revoked for wrong-finger surgery, AP, June 25, 2002 [NY].

56 E.g., Boca doctor fined for surgery mistake, Palm Beach [FL] Post, Feb. 14, 1995, 1B [neurosurgeon fined $5,000 for operating on wrong side of skull].

57 E.g., *Kite v. DeBuono,* 233 A.D.2d 783, 650 N.Y.S.2d 384 (3d Dept. 1996) [medical license revoked for violating probation by disregarding supervisor]; *Birchard v. Louisiana State Bd. of Med. Exam'rs,* 609 So. 2d 980 (La. Ct. App. 1992) [physician on probation with condition he obtain board approval for changes of employment not entitled to hearing on denial of approval].

58 E.g., *Sternberg v. Administrative Rev. Bd. for Prof. Med. Conduct,* 235 A.D.2d 945, 652 N.Y.S.2d 855 (3d Dep't 1997) [barring private practice, limiting to institutional practice]; Doctor disciplined for death of patient after surgery, AP, Apr. 8, 2004 [emergency order restricted Fla. physician license after death during office breast augmentation, cannot perform procedures with general anesthesia].

59 E.g., *Caselnova v. New York State Dep't of Health,* 91 N.Y.2d 441, 672 N.Y.S.2d 79, 694 N.E.2d 1320 (1998) [medical licensing board may condition probation on monitoring, record review, increased malpractice insurance].

60 Annotation, Rights as to notice and hearing in proceeding to revoke or suspend license to practice medicine, 10 A.L.R. 5th 1; *Fleury v. Clayton,* 847 F.2d 1229 (7th Cir. 1988) [right to notice, hearing applies when only sanction is censure]; *Jensen v. California Bd. of Psychology* No. B091019 (Calif. Ct. App. 2d Dist. May 14, 1996), cert. denied, 519 U.S. 1058 (1997), as discussed in 6 Health Law Rptr. [BNA] 72 (1997) [notice sent by certified mail to last address provided to board was sufficient] [hereinafter Health Law Rptr. will be cited as H.L.R.].

61 *Colorado State Bd. of Nursing v. Hohu,* 129 Colo. 195, 268 P.2d 401 (1954); see also In re *Grimm,* 138 N.H. 42, 635 A.2d 456 (1993) [violation of due process for some members of hearing panel, acting in fact-finding capacity, to fail to attend all testimony, especially cross-examination of respondent]; *Pet v. Dep't of Health Servs.,* 228 Conn. 651, 638 A.2d 6 (1994) [remand where no board member attended all hearings, record did not indicate whether voting members had read entire record].

62 E.g., *Virginia Bd. of Med. v. Fetta,* 244 Va. 276, 421 S.E.2d 410 (1992) [proceedings against chiropractor dismissed because board violated law when four of sixteen members sat with hearing officer at evidentiary hearing].

63 E.g., *Devous v. Wyoming State Bd. of Med. Exam'rs,* 845 P.2d 408 (Wyo. 1993) [violation of due process not to notify physician of facts, nature of charges against him].

64 *Erickson v. State* ex rel. *Bd. of Med. Exam'rs,* 282 Mont. 367, 938 P.2d 625 (1997); accord, *Teruel v. DeBuono,* 244 A.D. 2d 710, 664 N.Y.S.2d 381 (3d Dept. 1997) [Medicaid fraud conviction justified revocation of medical license].

65 *Hoffman v. State Board of Registration for the Healing Arts,* 936 S.W.2d 182 (Mo. App. Ct. 1996).

66 *Ward v. Oregon State Bd. of Nursing,* 226 Or. 128, 510 P.2d 554 (1973).

67 *Tuma v. Board of Nursing,* 100 Idaho 74, 593 P.2d 711 (1979).

68 E.g., *Kibler v. State,* 718 P.2d 531 (Colo. 1986).

69 *State Bd. of Reg. for the Healing Arts v. Fallon,* 41 S.W.3d 474 (Mo. 2001), accord, *Murphy v. Arizona Bd. of Med. Examiner,* 190 Ariz. 441, 949 P.2d 530 (Ct. App. 1997); see also D. Gianelli, HMO directors must stand behind their decisions, Am. Med. News, June 21, 1999, 9 [AMA ethics council report].

70 *Morris v. District of Columbia Bd. of Med.,* 701 A.2d 364 (D.C. 1997).

71 *Huhta v. Pennsylvania Bd. of Med.,* 706 A.2d 364 (Pa. Commw. Ct. 1998).

72 *Deatherage v. State Examining Bd. of Psychology,* 134 Wash. 2d 131, 948 P.2d 828 (1997).

73 *Hayes v. State Med. Bd. of Ohio,* 138 Ohio App. 3d 762, 742 N.E.2d 238 (2000).

74 N.C. board suspends license for neurosurgeon's expert testimony, AP, Nov. 22, 2003.

75 A. Goldstein, D.C. is ranked last on punishment of doctor misconduct; nonprofit also faults process in Md., Va., Wash. Post, Sept. 5, 2002, B5; D. Adams, Medical board discipline up; lawmakers demand even more, Am. Med. News, May 9, 2005.

76 See Fremont woman wants licenses revoked for two nurses in Javed clinic, AP, Nov. 25, 2003 [NE]; S. Allen, House approves patients' rights bill: "Taylor's law" allows testimony before disciplinary board, Boston Globe, Feb. 26, 2004, B3 [Mass.].

77 But see *Burns v. Board of Psychologist Examiners,* 116 Or. App. 422, 841 P.2d 680 (1992) [licensing board not liable for tort damages for testing irregularities, but authorized ancillary relief could include repayment for direct losses]; Medical board must pay Raleigh doctor, AP, Dec. 22, 2001 [federal court ordered W. Va. medical bd. to pay $277K in fees, costs].

78 E.g., *Berthiaume v. Caron,* 142 F.3d 12 (1st Cir. 1998) [qualified immunity for nursing board in challenge to making sexual arousal test a condition of license renewal]; *Watts v. Burkhart,* 978 F.2d 269 (6th Cir. 1992) [quasi-judicial immunity for licensing board members in suspension of physician's license]; *Horowitz v. State Bd. of Med. Examiners,* 822 F.2d 1508 (10th Cir.), cert. denied, 484 U.S. 964 (1987) [absolute immunity from civil rights liability]; *Duncan v. Mississippi Bd. of Nursing,* 982 F. Supp. 425 (D. Miss. 1997); but see *Rindley v. Gallagher,* 890 F. Supp. 1540 (D. Fla. 1995) [immunity lost due to allegations of public boasting of illegal input into adjudicative process].

79 E.g., *Sutker v. Illinois State Dental Soc'y,* 808 F.2d 632 (7th Cir. 1986) [state need not offer separate license to denturists].

80 *State Board v. Reubke,* 259 Kan. 599, 913 P.2d 142 (1996); contra, *People v. Odam,* 69 Cal. App. 4th 1192, 82 Cal. Rptr. 2d 184 (4th Dist. 1999) (unpub), app. dismissed, 33 P.3d 450, 113 Cal. Rptr. 2d 26 (2001) [conviction of midwife for practicing medicine without a license].

81 *McKeesport Hosp. v. Pennsylvania State Bd. of Med.,* 539 Pa. 384, 652 A.2d 827 (1995), rev'g, 156 Pa. Commw. 480, 628 A.2d 476 (1993).

82 *McKeesport Hosp. v. A.C.G.M.E.,* 24 F.3d 519 (3d Cir. 1994).

83 *St. Agnes Hosp. v. Ruddick,* 748 F. Supp. 319 (D. Md. 1990).

84 42 C.F.R. § 482.12(a)(7).

85 H. Larkin, All aboard? Am. Med. News, Mar. 13, 1995, 11 [options for those without board certification to deal with managed care, since 35 to 40 percent of physicians are not board certified].

86 E.g., J.L. Fickeissen, 56 ways to get certified, Am. J. Nursing, Mar. 1990, 50.

87 See www.abms.org (accessed Sept. 3, 2005); R. Abelson, New board for surgeons denied again, N.Y. Times, Mar. 18, 2005, C4 [vascular surgeons].

88 *Gilliam v. National Com'n for Certification of Physician's Assistants,* 727 F. Supp. 1512 (E.D. Pa. 1989), aff'd, 898 F.2d 140 (3d Cir.), cert. denied, 495 U.S. 920 (1990).

89 E.g., *Poindexter v. American Bd. of Surgery,* 911 F. Supp. 1510 (D. Ga. 1994); *Patel v. American Bd. of Psychiatry & Neurology, Inc.,* 975 F.2d 1312 (7th Cir. 1992); *Goussis v. Kimball,* 813 F. Supp. 352 (E.D. Pa. 1993); *Sammons v. National Com'n on Certif. of Physician's Assistants,* 104 F. Supp. 2d 1379 (N.D. Ga. 2000); *Gilliam v. National Com'n for Certification of Physician's Assistants, Inc.,* 727 F. Supp. 1512 (E.D. Pa. 1989), aff'd, 898 F.2d 140 (3rd Cir.), cert. denied, 495 U.S. 920 (1990) [not a state actor so not subject to constitutional or § 1983 claims].

90 E.g., *Sanjuan v. American Bd. of Psychiatry and Neurology, Inc.,* 40 F.3d 247 (7th Cir. 1994), amended, reh'g denied (en banc), 1995 U.S. App. LEXIS 565 (7th Cir.).

91 E.g., id.; *Marrese v. American Acad. of Orthopaedic Surgeons,* 977 F.2d 585 (without op.), 1992 U.S. App. LEXIS 25530 (7th Cir.).

92 *American Academy of Pain Management v. Joseph,* 353 F.3d 1099 (9th Cir. 2004).

93 As value of diplomas grows, more people buy bogus credentials, Wall St. J., Apr. 2, 1987, 1.

94 8 U.S.C. § 1324a; see Calif. hospital assessed largest immigration fine, Mod. Healthcare, June 23, 1989, 12 [$183,200 fine for 259 violations].

95 *Carlson v. Arnot-Ogden Mem. Hosp.,* 918 F.2d 411 (3d Cir. 1990).

96 Employers face new liability: Truth in hiring, Wall. St. J., July 9, 1993, B1. *Treadwill v. John Hancock Mut. Life Ins.,* 666 F. Supp. 278 (D. Mass. 1987); *Jula v. J.K. Schofield & Co., Inc.,* 668 F. Supp. 126 (N.D. Ill. 1987).

97 See G. Fields, Security vetting of employees is highly prized, Wall St. J., Feb. 24, 2004, B1 [twelve-month backlog for swamped government background checking staff].

98 *Nixon v. Commonwealth,* 576 Pa. 385, 839 A.2d 277 (2003).

99 E.g., Wis. Stat. §§ 48.685, 50.065; Wis. Admin. Code HFS 12; *Miller v. DeBuono,* 90 N.Y.2d 783, 666 N.Y.S.2d 548, 689 N.E.2d 518 (1997) [state may bar future nursing home employment by aide on abuse registry].

100 *Tallahassee Furniture v. Harrison,* 583 So. 2d 744 (Fla. 1st DCA 1991).

101 E.g., *Curry v. Almance Health Servs.,* No. 2:92CV00351 (M.D. Ga. April 1, 1994), as discussed in 3 Health L. Rptr. [BNA] 519 (1994).

102 *State v. AFSCME Iowa Council* 61, 648 N.W.2d 119 (Iowa 2002).

103 E.g., *Leckelt v. Board of Comm'rs,* 909 F.2d 820 (5th Cir. 1990), aff'g, 714 F. Supp. 1377 (E.D. La. 1989) [not violation of Rehabilitation Act to discharge LPN who refused to disclose her HIV test results]; *Bradley v. University of Tex. M.D. Anderson Cancer Ctr.,* 3 F.3d 922 (5th Cir. 1993), cert. denied, 510 U.S. 1119 (1994) [hospital properly reassigned surgical technician with HIV to purchasing department]; see also *Fedro v. Reno,* 21 F.3d 1391 (7th Cir. 1994) [need not create new position for employee with hepatitis B].

104 42 U.S.C. §§ 12101-12117; 29 C.F.R. pt. 1630.

105 *Norman-Bloodsaw v. Lawrence Berkeley Laboratory,* 135 F.3d 1260 (9th Cir. 1998); Blood tests of workers restricted by court, N.Y. Times, Feb. 5, 1998, A19. http://www.eeoc.gov/laws/types/genetic.cfm.

106 Joint Commission on Accreditation of Healthcare Organizations, Comprehensive Accreditation Manual For Hospitals (2005 ed.), Elements of Performance #1 for HR.3.20.

107 *Doe v. Garcia,* 131 Idaho 578, 961 P.2d 1181 (1998).

108 E.g., L. Tarkan, Nursing shortage forces hospitals to cope creatively, N.Y. Times, Jan. 6, 2004, D5.

109 E.g., Health department cites hospital for violations of patient care laws, 7 H.L.R. 1219 (1998) [nurse staffing].

110 N.J. Stat. § 26:2H-5g (eff. July 23, 2005); Hospitals, nursing homes in New Jersey must post data on nurse staffing levels, H.L.R., Jan. 27, 2005, 131.

111 E.g., *Dabbs v. Cardiopulmonary Management Servs.,* 188 Cal. App. 3d 1437, 234 Cal. Rptr. 129 (4th Dist. 1987) [respiratory therapist could not be discharged for refusing to work night shift as only experienced therapist].

112 J. Coleman, Health regulators unveil nurse-to-patient ratios, AP, July 1, 2003; S. Fox, Hospitals may fail to meet nurse-staffing standard, L.A. Times, Nov. 14, 2003, pt. 2, 4; *California Healthcare Assn. v. California Dep't of Health Servs.,* No. 03-CS-01814 (Cal. Super. Ct. May 26, 2004); D. Vrana, Hospital staffing law is upheld, L.A. Times, May 27, 2004, C2; L.A. hospital closes acute care operations, claims new staffing requirements to blame, H.L.R., Jan. 15, 2004, 90; Staffing has improved, but many hospitals not complying with ratios, surveys say, H.L.R., Feb. 12, 2004, 230; D. Thompson, Schwarzenegger to appeal final ruling on nurse-patient ratio, AP, June 7, 2005.

113 26 Maine R. S. § 603; Md. Labor & Emp. Code Ann. § 3-421; Minn. Stat. §181.275; N.J. STAT. §§ 34:11-56a33-34:11-56a37; Ore. R.S. § 441.160-§ 441.170; Rev. Code Wash. §§ 49.28.130-49.28.140; W. Va. Code §§ 21-5F-1-21-5F-5.

114 *O'Connor v. Ortega*, 480 U.S. 1492 (1987).

115 *Ortega v. O'Connor*, 50 F.3d 778 (9th Cir. 1995).

116 *Ortega v. O'Connor*, 146 F.3d 1149 (9th Cir. 1998).

117 E.g., *Vega-Rodriguez v. Puerto Ricoo Telephone Co.*, 110 F.3d 174 (1st Cir. 1997) [no reasonable expectation of privacy against video surveillance to monitor open work area]; *Shepard v. Beerman*, 18 F.3d 147 (2d Cir. 1994) [no reasonable expectation of privacy in open work areas]; *United States v. Taketa*, 923 F.2d 665 (9th Cir. 1991) [reasonable expectation of privacy against video surveillance of office reserved for exclusive use]; *Gossmeyer v. McDonald*, 128 F.3d 481 (7th Cir. 1997) [state worker had no reasonable expectation of privacy in her locked desk, part of "workplace," not part of "personal domain"].

118 E.g., *American Postal Workers Union v. United States Postal Serv.*, 871 F.2d 556 (9th Cir. 1989); *DeMaine v. Samuels*, 2000 U.S. Dist. LEXIS 16277 (D. Conn.); *United States v. Thorn*, 2004 U.S. App. LEXIS 14295 (8th Cir.) [no reasonable expectation of privacy in office computer contents, employer policy on computer use].

119 See e.g., *PartyLite Worldwide, Inc.*, 344 NLRB 1342 (2005).

120 End Note 131 S. Ct. 2619 (2010).

121 E.g., *Burrell v. Carraway Methodist Hosp.*, 607 So. 2d 193 (Ala. 1993); *Lampe v. Presbyterian Med. Ctr.*, 590 P.2d 513 (Colo. Ct. App. 1978).

122 E.g., *Jones v. Central Peninsula Gen. Hosp.*, 779 P.2d 783 (Alaska 1989); *Duldulao v. St. Mary of Nazareth Hosp. Ctr.*, 115 Ill. 2d 482, 505 N.E.2d 314 (1987); Annotation, Right to discharge allegedly "at-will" employee as affected by employer's promulgation of employment policies as to discharge, 33 A.L.R. 4th 120.

123 E.g., *Hunsucker v. Josephine Sunset Home*, 89 Wash. App. 1041 (1998) [employee manual specifying termination procedures not implied employment contract].

124 *Heideck v. Kent Gen. Hosp.*, 446 A.2d 1095 (Del. 1982); see also *Mursch v. Van Dorn Co.*, 851 F.2d 990 (7th Cir. 1988) [guidelines in employee handbook not a contract].

125 E.g., *Carlson v. Lake Chelan Comm. Hosp.*, 66 P.2d 1080 (Wash. App. 2003); *Watson v. Idaho Falls Cons. Hosps.*, 111 Idaho 44, 720 P.2d 632 (1986); *Jewell v. North Big Horn Hosp. Dist.*, 935 P.2d 135 (1998).

126 E.g., *Bowe v. Charleston Area Med. Ctr.*, 428 S.E.2d 773 (W. Va. 1993); *Lee v. Sperry Corp.*, 678 F. Supp. 1415 (D. Minn. 1987); See annotation, effectiveness of employer's disclaimer of representations in personnel manual or employee handbook altering at-will employment relationship, 17 A.L.R. 5th 1; but see *Doyle v. Holy Cross Hosp.*, 186 Ill. 2d 104; 708 N.E.2d 1140 (1999) [old handbook may create contract despite disclaimer in current handbook]; accord, *Robinson v. Ada S. McKinley Community Servs., Inc.*, 19 F.3d 359 (7th Cir. 1994).

127 *Cleveland Bd. of Educ. v. Loudermill*, 470 U.S. 532 (1985); see also cases finding adequate due process, *Bradley v. Colonial Mental Health & Retardation Servs. Bd.*, 856 F.2d 703 (4th Cir. 1988); *Phares v. Gustafsson*, 856 F.2d 1003 (7th Cir. 1988).

128 E.g., *Simpkins v. Sandwich Comm. Hosp.*, 854 F.2d 215 (7th Cir. 1988).

129 E.g., *Musgrave v. HCA Mideast, Inc.*, 856 F.2d 690 (4th Cir. 1988); *Jackam v. Hospital Corp. of Am. Mideast, Inc.*, 800 F.2d 1577 (11th Cir. 1986).

130 E.g., *Dearden v. Liberty Med. Ctr.*, 75 Md. App. 528, 542 A.2d 383 (1988).

131 *Hebert v. Woman's Hosp. Found.*, 377 So. 2d 1340 (La. Ct. App. 1979).

132 72 Am. Jur. 2d Statute of frauds (1974); e.g., *Santa Monica Hosp. v. Superior Court*, 173 Cal. App. 3d 239, 218 Cal. Rptr. 543 (1985).

133 E.g., 29 U.S.C. § 626(b) [age discrimination].

134 *Haddle v. Garrison*, 525 U.S. 121 (1998).

135 E.g., Fla. Stat. § 440.205 [no retaliation for workers' compensation claims]; but see *Allan v. SWF Gulf Coast, Inc.*, 535 So. 2d 638 (Fla. 1st DCA 1988) [employee may be terminated for other reasons even after claim].

136 E.g., *Shores v. Senior Manor Nursing Ctr.*, 164 Ill. App. 3d 503, 518 N.E.2d 471 (5th Dist. 1988) [patient abuse]; *Palmer v. Brown*, 242 Kan. 893, 752 P.2d 685 (1988) [fraudulent Medicaid billing]; *Kelsay v. Motorola, Inc.*, 74 Ill. 2d 172, 384 N.E.2d 353 (1979) [workers' compensation claim]; contra *Washington v. Union Carbide Corp.*, 870 F.2d 957 (4th Cir. 1989) [no recovery in West Virginia for discharge for reporting safety violations].

137 E.g., *Sides v. Duke Hosp.*, 72 N.C. App. 331, 328 S.E.2d 818 (1985).

138 E.g., *Wheeler v. Caterpillar Tractor Co.*, 108 Ill. 2d 502, 485 N.E.2d 372 (1985).

139 E.g., *Jones v. Lake Park Care Center Inc.*, 569 N.W.2d 369 (Iowa 1997); *Webb v. HCA Health Services of Midwest*, 300 Ark. 613, 780 S.W.2d 571 (1989).

140 E.g., *Fisher v. Lexington Health Care*, 301 Ill. App. 3d 547, 703 N.E.2d 988 (2d Dist. 1998).

141 See supra note 111; but see *Fineman v. New Jersey Dep't of Human Servs.*, 272 N.J. Super. 606, 640 A.2d 1161 (App. Div. 1994) [physician may be terminated for refusing to provide temporary medical care to 300 nursing home patients].

142 E.g., *Goodman v. Wesley Med. Ctr.*, 2003 Kan. LEXIS 591.

143 E.g., *Parent v. Mount Clemens Gen. Hosp.*, 2003 Mich. App. LEXIS 1862 [affirmed at-will lab tech firing for insubordination, refused to use "tray method," not within public policy exception].

144 *Ryan v. Dan's Food Stores*, 972 P.2d 395 (Utah 1999).

145 E.g., *Waters v. Churchill*, 511 U.S. 661 (1994); *Rodgers v. Banks*, 344 F.3d 587 (6th Cir. 2003); *Paradis v. Montrose Mem. Hosp.*, 157 F.3d 815 (10th Cir. 1998); Annotation, First Amendment protection for public hospital or health employees subjected to discharge, transfer, or discipline because of speech, 107 A.L.R. Fed. 21.67.

146 E.g., *Rahn v. Drake Ctr.*, 31 F.3d 407 (6th Cir. 1994), cert. denied, 515 U.S. 1142 (1995); *Havekost v. United States Dep't of Navy*, 925 F.2d 316 (9th Cir. 1991) [mere workplace grievance about dress code, staffing policies not protected]; *Ganthier v. North Shore-Long Island Jewish Health Sys.*, 298 F. Supp. 2d 342 (E.D. N.Y. 2004).

147 E.g., *Pilarowski v. Macomb County Health Dep't*, 841 F.2d 1281 (6th Cir.), cert. denied, 488 U.S. 850 (1988) [layoffs for budget cuts were permitted]; *Black v. City of Wentzville*, 686 F. Supp. 241 (E.D. Mo. 1988) [documented poor work performance].

148 E.g., *Wright v. Shriners Hosp. for Crippled Children*, 412 Mass. 469, 598 N.E.2d 1241 (1992) [reversing award to nurse for dismissal after critical remarks to internal survey team, termination did not violate public policy]; *Willis v. University Health Servs.*, 993 F.2d 837 (11th Cir.), cert. denied, 510 U.S. 976 (1993) [private entity managing county hospital that fired nurse allegedly for free speech was not a public employer].

149 *Rozier v. St. Mary's Hosp.*, 88 Ill. App. 3d 994, 411 N.E.2d 50 (5th Dist. 1980); see also *Maus v. National Living Ctrs.*, 633 S.W.2d 674 (Tex. Ct. App. 1982) [nurse's aide discharged for complaints to superiors concerning patient care].

150 E.g., *Dobinsky v. Rand*, 248 A.D.2d 903, 670 N.Y.S.2d 606 (3d Dept. 1998) [not intentional infliction of emotional distress for hospital to investigate death allegedly implicating plaintiffs, not keeping them abreast of investigation].

151 *NLRB v. J. Weingarten, Inc.*, 420 U.S. 251 (1975).

152 Prudential Ins. Co., 275 NLRB 30 (1985).

153 E.g., IBM Corp., 341 NLRB No. 148 (2004) [no right], rev'g, Epilepsy Found. of Northeastern Ohio, 331 NLRB 676 (2000) [right], rev'g, E.I. DuPont, 289 NLRB 627 (1988) [no right]; *Slaughter v. NLRB*, 876 F.2d 11 (3d Cir. 1989) [upholding NLRB position of no right]; *Epilepsy Found. of Northeastern Ohio v. NLRB*, 268 F.3d 1095 (D.C. Cir. 2001), cert. denied, 536 U.S. 904 (2002) [upholding NLRB position of right].

154 *Peete v. Blackwell*, 504 So. 2d 222 (Ala. 1986).

155 *National Treasury Employees Union v. Von Raab*, 489 U.S. 656 (1989).

156 *Skinner v. Railway Labor Executives' Ass'n*, 489 U.S. 602 (1989).

157 See *Kemp v. Caliborne County Hosp.*, 763 F. Supp. 1362 (S.D. Miss. 1991) [applying Von Raab and Skinner to uphold a hospital screening program].

158 Johnson-Bateman Co., 295 NLRB No. 26 (June 19, 1989); see also, e.g., *Utility Workers v. Southern Cal. Edison Co.*, 852 F.2d 1083 (9th Cir. 1988), cert. denied, 489 U.S. 1078 (1989).

159 *Conrail v. Railway Labor Executives' Ass'n*, 491 U.S. 299 (1989); see also, e.g., *Laws v. Calmat*, 852 F.2d 430 (9th Cir. 1988); *Utility Workers v. Southern Cal. Edison Co.*, 852 F.2d 1083 (9th Cir. 1988), cert. denied, 489 U.S. 1078 (1989).

160 Cowles Media Co., Star Tribune Div., 295 NLRB No. 63 (1989).

161 E.g., *Greco v. Halliburton Co.*, 674 F. Supp. 1447 (D. Wyo. 1987); *Stevenson v. Panhandle E. Pipe Line Co.*, 680 F. Supp. 859 (S.D. Tex. 1987); but see Conn. Gen. Stat. Ann. § 31-51x [prohibition of employee drug testing without showing good cause for suspected drug use].

162 E.g., *Wilcher v. City of Wilmington*, 139 F.3d 366 (3d Cir. 1998) [required direct observation of urine collection does not violate federal rights, remand to reconsider state law invasion of privacy claim].

163 *Loder v. City of Glendale*, 14 Cal. 4th 846, 59 Cal. Rptr. 2d 696, 927 P.2d 1200 (1997).

164 See B. Wysocki, Companies get tough with smokers, obese to trim costs, Wall St. J, Oct. 12, 2004, B1; K. Maher, Companies are closing doors on job applicants who smoke, Wall St. J, Dec. 21, 2004, B6.

165 E.g., *Grusendorf v. City of Oklahoma City*, 816 F.2d 539 (10th Cir. 1987); *City of North Miami v. Kurtz*, 653 So. 2d 1025, 1028 (Fla. 1995), cert denied, 516 U.S. 1043 (1996).

166 E.g., Wis. Stat., § 111.321; Colo. Rev. Stat. § 24-34-402.5.

167 29 U.S.C. §§ 2001-2009; but see *Hossaini v. Western Mo. Med. Ctr.*, 140 F.3d 1140 (8th Cir. 1998) [county hospital is political subdivision, not subject to Act]; *Theisen v. Covenant Medical Center Inc.*, 636 N.W.2d 74 (Iowa 2001) [required voice print analysis not violation of lie detector prohibition].

168 K.B. Stickler & M.D. Nelson, Defamation in the workplace: Employer rights, risks, and responsibilities, 21 J.Health & Hosp.L. 97 (1988).

169 E.g., *McCullough v. Visiting Nurse Serv.*, 691 A.2d 1201 (Me. 1997) [statement that nurse had been terminated for "several" incidents when she had been terminated for two incidents was substantially true, so not defamatory]; *Mayer v. Morgan Stanley & Co.*, 703 F. Supp. 249 (S.D. N.Y. 1988).

170 *Mittleman v. Witous*, 135 Ill.2d 220, 226, 552 N.E.2d 973, 981 (1990).

171 126 Ill.App.3d 157, 466 N.E.2d 1137 (1st Dist. 1984).

172 135 Ill.2d at 250, 552 N.E.2d at 987.

173 E.g., *Gengler v. Phelps*, 92 N.M. 465, 589 P.2d 1056 (Ct. App. 1978), cert. denied, 92 N.M. 353, 588 P.2d 554 (1979) [communication concerning nurse anesthetist].

174 E.g., *Burger v. McGilley Mem. Chapels, Inc.*, 856 F.2d 1046 (8th Cir. 1988); see also Annotation, Defamation: loss of employer's qualified privilege to publish employee's work record or qualification, 24 A.L.R. 4th 144.

175 E.g., *Eitler v. St. Joseph Reg. Med. Ctr.*, 789 N.E.2d 497 (Ind. App. 2003) [release form barred defamation claim].

176 E.g., *Kellums v. Freight Sales Ctrs.*, 467 So. 2d 816 (Fla. 5th DCA 1985) [release form did not preclude liability for deliberate falsehood].

177 *Robinson v. Shell Oil Co.*, 519 U.S. 337 (1997) [former employee can sue under Title VII for posttermination retaliation, including negative job references].

178 *United States v. Kibby*, 848 F.2d 920 (8th Cir. 1988).

179 Act of May 31, 1879, c.114, § 16, 16 Stat. 144.

180 E.g., *Anderson v. Conboy*, 156 F.3d 167 (2d Cir. 1998).

181 *Edwards v. Jewish Hosp.*, 855 F.2d 1345 (8th Cir. 1988); see also *Roberts v. Gadsden Mem. Hosp.*, 835 F.2d 793 (11th Cir. 1988), amended on reh'g, 850 F.2d 1549 (11th Cir. 1988) [violation not to give promoted African-American employees same raise as whites who were promoted]; but see *Armstrong v. Turnage*, 690 F. Supp. 839 (E.D. Mo. 1988), aff'd without op., 873 F.2d 1448 (8th Cir. 1989) [disparate treatment of African-American,

Caucasian hospital pharmacists after errors insufficient to prove motive where rules consistently applied].

182 *St. Francis College v. Al-Khazraji,* 481 U.S. 604 (1987).

183 *Patterson v. McClean Credit Union,* 491 U.S. 164 (1989).

184 *Wards Cove Packing Co. v. Atonio,* 490 U.S. 642 (1989).

185 Pub. L. No. 102-166, 105 Stat. 1071 (1991); *Andrews v. Lakeshore Rehabilitation Hosp.,* 140 F.3d 1405 (11th Cir. May 15, 1998) [former hospital employee claiming retaliatory discharge for filing race discrimination claim with EEOC permitted to sue under 1991 amendments].

186 Act Apr. 20, 1871, c. 22, § 1, 17 Stat. 13.

187 E.g., *Hamm v. Lakeview Commun. Hosp.,* 950 F. Supp. 330 (D. Ala. 1996) [dismissal of former emergency room nurse, claim under § 1983 against physician for alleged harassment when physician not employed by state or not acting under color of state law; physician was employed by private company under contract with community hospital].

188 *Anglemyer v. Hamilton County Hosp.,* 848 F. Supp. 938 (D. Kan. 1994), aff'd, 58 F.3d 533 (10th Cir. 1995).

189 E.g., *Wheat v. Mass,* 994 F.2d 273 (5th Cir. 1993).

190 *Trimble v. Androscoggin Valley Hosp.,* 847 F. Supp. 226 (D. N.H. 1994); but see *Snyder v. Albany Med. Ctr. Hosp.,* 206 A.D.2d 816, 615 N.Y.S.2d 139 (3d Dep't 1994) [holding involuntarily committed patient at private hospital was under color of state law].

191 *Willis v. University Health Servs.,* 993 F.2d 837 (11th Cir.), cert. denied, 510 U.S. 976 (1993).

192 *Moore v. Wyoming Med. Ctr.,* 825 F. Supp. 1531 (D. Wyo. 1993).

193 Acts July 31, 1861, ch. 33, 12 Stat. 284; Acts Apr. 20, 1871, ch. 22, § 2, 17 Stat. 13.

194 E.g., *Travis v. Gary Community Mental Health Ctr.,* 921 F.2d 108 (7th Cir. 1990), cert. denied, 502 U.S. 812 (1991); but see *Fobbs v. Holy Cross Health Sys. Corp.,* 29 F.3d 1439 (9th Cir. 1994), cert. denied, 513 U.S. 1127 (1995) [claim stated against hospital, 27 individual staff physicians]; *Saville v. Houston County Healthcare Auth.,* 852 F. Supp. 1512 (M.D. Ala. 1994) [intracorporate conspiracy exception not available in Eleventh Circuit in § 1985(3) suit].

195 *Griffin v. Breckenridge,* 403 U.S. 88 (1971).

196 *Wong v. Stripling,* 881 F.2d 200 (5th Cir. 1989).

197 E.g., *United Brotherhood v. Scott,* 463 U.S. 825 (1983).

198 42 U.S.C. §§ 2000e-2000e-17.

199 E.g., *Judie v. Hamilton,* 872 F.2d 919 (9th Cir. 1989) [restrictions on supervisory responsibilities of African-American hospital food manager could be violation].

200 E.g., False EEO claims earn former DOE worker heavy sentence, Federal EEO Advisor, June 6, 2003.

201 E.g., *Fitten v. Chattanooga-Hamilton County Hosp.,* 75 Fed. Appx. 384, 2003 U.S. App. LEXIS 18818 (6th Cir.) [affirming dismissal of racial discrimination employment claim, failure to identify comparable nonprotected person who was treated better]; *Beene v. St. Vincent Mercy Med. Ctr.,* 111 F. Supp. 2d 931 (D. Ohio 2000) [terminated African-American registered nurse did not show white nurses treated more favorably for mixing up telemetry strips].

202 *Watson v. Ft. Worth Bank & Trust,* 487 U.S. 977 (1988).

203 42 U.S.C. §§ 2000e-2(m), 2000e-5(g)(2)(B); *Desert Palace, Inc. v. Costa,* 539 U.S. 90 (2003) [direct evidence of discrimination not required to submit mixed motive issue to jury].

204 E.g., *Vital v. Interfaith Med. Ctr.,* 168 F.3d 615 (2d Cir. 1999) [error to dismiss employee claim; employer must show knowing, voluntary release of right to bring Title VII action]; *Beadle v. City of Tampa,* 42 F.3d 633 (11th Cir.), cert. denied, 515 U.S. 1152 (1994).

205 E.g., *Metz v. Merrill Lynch, Pierce, Fenner & Smith,* 39 F.3d 1482 (10th Cir. 1994); see also *Norton v. AMISUB St. Joseph Hosp.,* 155 F.3d 1040 (8th Cir. 1998) [participation in arbitration of Title VII claim without objection or timely motion to vacate award waived right to object to arbitration].

206 9 U.S.C. §§ 1 et seq.; Circuit City Stores, Inc. v. Adams, 532 U.S. 105 (2001) [FAA exemption for some employment contracts applies only to transportation workers], on remand, 279 F.3d 889 (9th Cir. 2002) [arbitration agreement not enforceable because contract unconscionable since not equally binding on both sides].

207 Endnote 131 S.Ct. 1740 (2011).

208 *EEOC v. River Oaks Imaging & Diagnostic,* 1995 U.S. Dist. LEXIS 6140 (S.D. Tex.) [preliminary injunction of employer's alternative dispute resolution policy, retaliation against employees who refused to sign agreement].

209 E.g., *Patterson v. Tenet Healthcare Inc.,* 113 F.3d 832 (8th Cir. 1997) [arbitration procedure in employee handbook binding for Title VII claim, even when handbook not contract under state law]; *Gibson v. Neighborhood Health Clinics, Inc.,* 121 F.3d 1126 (7th Cir. 1997) [refusal to enforce agreement to arbitrate job bias claims for lack of consideration]; Ex parte Beasley, 712 So. 2d 338 (Ala. 1998) [employee handbook that is not binding on employer cannot be basis for mandatory arbitration].

210 *Circuit City Stores, Inc. v. Adams,* 279 F.3d 889 (9th Cir. 2002), on remand from, 532 U.S. 105 (2001).

211 E.g., *Murray v. United Food & Commercial Workers Internat'l Union,* 289 F.3d 297 (4th Cir. 2002).

212 E.g., *McGaskill v. SCI Mgmt. Corp.,* 285 F.3d 623 (7th Cir. 2002) [limits on prevailing employee recovery of attorney fees rendered arbitration unenforceable under Title VII]; see also *Bond v. Twin Cities Carpenters' Pension Fund,* 307 F.3d 704 (8th Cir. 2002) [required split of arbitration cost violated ERISA].

213 E.g., *Diggs v. Harris Hosp.-Methodist, Inc.,* 847 F.2d 270 (5th Cir.), cert. denied, 488 U.S. 956 (1988); *Amiable v. Long & Scott Farms,* 20 F.3d 434 (11th Cir.), cert. denied, 513 U.S. 943 (U.S. 1994).

214 E.g., *Deal v. State Farm County Mut. Ins. Co.,* 5 F.3d 117 (5th Cir. 1993).

215 *O'Connor v. Davis,* 126 F.3d 112 (2d Cir. 1997), cert. denied, 522 U.S. 1114 (1998) [unpaid hospital volunteer (student intern) could not bring sexual harassment claim against hospital for

acts of staff physician because volunteer was not paid and, thus, not an employee].

216 E.g., *Cilecek v. Inova Health Sys. Servs., Inc.*, 115 F.3d 256 (4th Cir. 1997), cert. denied, 522 U.S. 1049 (1998) [independent contractor ER physician could not make Title VII employment discrimination charges].

217 E.g., *Pardazi v. Cullman Med. Ctr.*, 838 F.2d 1155 (11th Cir. 1988) [Title VII claim stated when denial of medical staff membership led to loss of employment opportunity with medical group]; Doe on behalf of *Doe v. St. Joseph's Hosp.*, 788 F.2d 411 (7th Cir. 1986), on remand, 113 F.R.D. 677 (N.D. Ind. 1987) [physicians terminated from medical staff may sue under Title VII if they show interference with employment by others]; *Gomez v. Alexian Bros. Hosp.*, 698 F.2d 1019 (9th Cir. 1983) [rejection of contract proposal by emergency medical professional corporation can violate Title VII as to Hispanic physician employee of corporation]; *Sibley Mem. Hosp. v. Wilson*, 160 U.S. App. D.C. 14, 488 F.2d 1338 (1973) [hospital can violate Title VII by interfering with private duty nurse's employment opportunities]; Annotation, Who is "employee" as defined in sec. 701(f) of the Civil Rights Act of 1964, 72 A.L.R. Fed. 522; but see *Diggs v. Harris Hosp.-Methodist, Inc.*, 847 F.2d 270 (5th Cir. 1988) [physician's "employment" relationship with patients not sufficient to permit Title VII action against hospital]; Mitchel v. Frank R. Howard Mem. Hosp., 853 F.2d 762 (9th Cir. 1988) [relationship with patients and with wholly-owned professional corporation insufficient]; *Shrock v. Altru Nurses Registry*, 810 F.2d 658 (7th Cir. 1987) [nurse referral agency not employer, not liable under Title VII].

218 See e.g., *Faragher v. City of Boca Raton*, 524 U.S. 775 (1998) and *Ellerth v. Burlington Northern*, 524 U.S. 775 (1998).

219 *Walters v. Metropolitan Educ. Enters. Inc.*, 519 U.S. 202 (1997) [payroll method adopted for determining 15-employee threshold].

220 E.g., *Smith v. St. Bernards Reg. Med. Ctr.*, 19 F.3d 1254 (8th Cir. 1994).

221 E.g., *Garcia v. Elf Atochem N. Am.*, 28 F.3d 446 (5th Cir. 1994).

222 E.g., *St. Francis College v. Al-Knazraji*, 481 U.S. 604 (1987) [Arabs are a race for purposes of 42 U.S.C. § 1981 suits; "distinctive physiognomy is not essential"]; *Jatoi v. Hurst-Euless Bedford Hosp. Auth.*, 807 F.2d 1213 (5th Cir.), as modified, 819 F.2d 545 (5th Cir. 1987) [East Indians]; Doe on behalf of *Doe v. St. Joseph's Hosp.*, 788 F.2d 411 (7th Cir. 1986), on remand, 113 F.R.D. 677 (N.D. Ind. 1987) [Asians]; *MacDissi v. Valmont Indust., Inc.*, 856 F.2d 1054 (8th Cir. 1988) [Lebanese]; *Janko v. Illinois State Toll Highway Auth.*, 704 F. Supp. 1531 (N.D. Ill. 1989) [Gypsies].

223 See e.g., *Faragher v. City of Boca Raton*, 524 U.S. 775 (1998) and *Ellerth v. Burlington Northern*, 524 U.S. 775 (1998).

224 E.g., *Adarand Constructors, Inc. v. Pena*, 515 U.S. 200 (1995); *Lawrence v. University of Tex. Med. Branch*, 163 F.3d 309 (5th Cir. 1999) [Caucasian nurse challenged selection of African-American nurse as nursing supervisor as reverse discrimination; defendants prevailed because reason for selection – best qualified candidate – was not pretext]; *Harding v. Gray*, 9 F.3d 150 (D.C. Cir. 1993) [hospital shop foreman; allegations of superior qualifications, if supported by facts, can constitute

sufficient background circumstances to establish prima facie case]; *McNabola v. Chicago Transit Auth.*, 10 F.3d 501 (7th Cir. 1993) [affirming reverse discrimination judgment for Caucasian physician terminated as per diem medical examiner].

225 *Trotter v. Board of Trustees of Univ. of Ala.*, 91 F.3d 1449 (11th Cir. 1996).

226 E.g., *Mosley v. Clarksville Mem. Hosp.*, 574 F. Supp. 224 (M.D. Tenn. 1983); *Dotson v. Blood Ctr.*, 988 F. Supp. 1216 (E.D. Wis. 1998). [African-American medical technologist who had applied for five openings, but had not been hired, failed to state racial discrimination claim where he did not allege he was qualified or that positions remained open after he was not selected].

227 E.g., *Walker v. Jefferson County Home*, 726 F.2d 1554 (11th Cir. 1984).

228 8 U.S.C. § 1324b.

229 Hospital apologizes for keeping black workers from patient's room, AP, Oct. 3, 2003; see also R. Cohen, The ethicist: Dying wish, N.Y. Times Mag., May 11, 2003, 22 [family of African-American patient requested African-American nursing assistant rather than planned Latino]; E. Kane, Hospital case shows danger of power, bias, Milwaukee J. Sentinel, Dec. 14, 2000, 1B [Tenn. surgeon asked black staff to leave room at patient request].

230 *Trans World Airlines, Inc. v. Hardison*, 432 U.S. 63 (1977); *Shelton v. University of Med. & Dentistry*, 223 F.3d 220 (3d Cir. 2000) [offer of lateral transfer accommodated nurses religious belief against abortions]; *Bruff v. North Mississippi Health Services, Inc.*, 244 F.3d 495 (5th Cir. 2001) [EAP counselor may be terminated for religious refusal to counsel on homosexual and extramarital relationship issues, would be undue burden to accommodate].

231 E.g., *Brener v. Diagnostic Ctr. Hosp.*, 671 F.2d 141 (5th Cir. 1982); *Mathewson v. Florida Game & Fresh Water Fish Comm'n*, 693 F. Supp. 1044 (M.D. Fla. 1988), aff'd without op., 871 F.2d 123 (11th Cir. 1989); *Murphy v. Edge Mem. Hosp.*, 550 F. Supp. 1185 (M.D. Ala. 1982).

232 E.g., *Tribulak v. Minirth-Meier-Rice Clinic*, 113 F.3d 135 (without op.), 1997 U.S. App. LEXIS 6932 (8th Cir.) [religious counseling clinic employee resigned after being told to include more prayer; failed to establish bona fide belief his religion would be violated by compliance with employer requirements].

233 *Cloutier v. Costco Wholesale Corporation*, 390 F.3d 126 (1st Cir. 2004).

234 *McCrory v. Rapides Reg. Med. Ctr.*, 635 F. Supp. 975 (W.D. La.), aff'd without op., 801 F.2d 396 (5th Cir. 1986).

235 *Baz v. Walters*, 782 F.2d 701 (7th Cir. 1986); accord, *Grant v. Fairview Hosp*, 2004 U.S. Dist. LEXIS 2653 (D. Minn.) [prohibiting antiabortion proselytizing on the job not religious discrimination, adequate accommodation to permit employee to leave room].

236 *Sutton v. Providence St. Joseph Medical Center*, 192 F.3d 826 (9th Cir. 1999); see also *EEOC v. Allendale Nursing Ctr.*, 996 F. Supp. 712 (W.D. Mich. 1998) [may terminate for religious refusal to obtain Social Security number].

237 132 S.Ct. 694 (2012).

238 42 U.S.C. § 2000e-1; see also *McKeon v. Mercy Healthcare Sacramento,* 19 Cal. 4th 321, 965 P.2d 1189, 79 Cal. Rptr. 2d 319 (1998) [Catholic hospital exempt from nurse's state claims of race, gender bias]; *Tacoma v. Franciscan Found,* 94 Wash. App. 663, 972 P.2d 566 (1999) [state law exempting religious nonprofit organizations from job bias suits preempts application of city discrimination ordinance to religious hospital].

239 *Corporation of Presiding Bishop v. Amos,* 483 U.S. 327 (1987).

240 *Young v. Shawnee Mission Med. Ctr.,* No. 88-2321-S (D. Kan. Oct. 21, 1988), as discussed in 22 J. Health & Hosp. L. 160 (1989).

241 E.g., *Mandell v. County of Suffolk,* 316 F.3d 368 (2d Cir. 2003).

242 E.g., *Steele v. Offshore Shipbuilding, Inc.,* 867 F.2d 1311 (11th Cir.), reh'g denied (en banc), 874 F.2d 821 (11th Cir. 1989); *Sparks v. Pilot Freight Carriers, Inc.,* 830 F.2d 1554 (11th Cir. 1987).

243 E.g., *Turnbull v. Topeka State Hosp.,* 255 F.3d 1238 (10th Cir. 2001) [employer may be liable for sexual harassment of psychologist by patient]; Cal. Gov. Code § 12940(j)(1); *Salazar v. Diversified Paratransit, Inc.,* 117 Cal. App. 4th 318, 11 Cal. Rptr. 3d 630 (2d Dist. 2004) [employers may be sued by employees under state law for some harassment by clients].

244 E.g., *Kopp v. Samaritan Health Sys., Inc.,* 13 F.3d 264 (8th Cir. 1993) [hospital could be liable for hostile environment sexual harassment based on conduct of cardiologist, hospital's response]; but see *Sparks v. Regional Med. Ctr. Bd.,* 792 F. Supp. 735 (N.D. Ala. 1992 [hospital's prompt response to sexual harassment by pathologist prevented hospital liability for physician conduct].

245 *Meritor Sav. Bank v. Vinson,* 477 U.S. 57 (1986), on remand, 25 U.S. App. D.C. 397, 801 F.2d 1436 (1986). For EEOC regulations, see 29 C.F.R. § 1604.11. For examples, see *Ross v. Twenty Four Collection, Inc.,* 681 F. Supp. 1547 (S.D. Fla. 1988), aff'd without op., 875 F.2d 873 (11th Cir. 1989) [liability for sexual harassment]; *Dockter v. Rudolf Wolff Futures, Inc.,* 684 F. Supp. 532 (N.D. Ill. 1988), aff'd, 913 F.2d 456 (7th Cir. 1990) [hostile working environment not shown]; see also *Scott v. Western State Hosp.,* 658 F. Supp. 593 (W.D. Va. 1987) [duty to investigate racial harassment charges, take steps].

246 *Harris v. Forklift Sys., Inc.,* 510 U.S. 17 (1993).

247 E.g., *Patt v. Family Health Systems, Inc.,* 280 F.3d 749 (7th Cir. 2002); *Duncan v. General Motors Corp.,* 300 F.3d 928 (8th Cir. 2002); *Ocheltree v. Scollon Productions,* 308 F.3d 351 (4th Cir. 2002).

248 49 U.S. 228 (1989).

249 E.g., *Little v. Windermere Relocation, Inc.,* 301 F.3d 958 (9th Cir. 2002).

250 E.g., *Carey v. Mt. Desert Island Hosp.,* 156 F.3d 31 (1st Cir. 1998) [affirming award to male executive claiming discharge due to sex discrimination]; *Lynn v. Deaconess Med. Ctr.,* 160 F.3d 484 (8th Cir. 1998) [terminated male nurse may bring sex discrimination claim]; see also *Rene v. MGM Grand Hotel, Inc.,* 305 F.3d 1061 (9th Cir. 2002) [same sex harassment included].

251 E.g., *DeCintio v. Westchester County Med. Ctr.,* 807 F.2d 304 (2d Cir. 1986), cert. denied, 484 U.S. 965 (1987) [writing job description to favor girlfriend not sex discrimination];

Autry v. North Carolina Dep't of Human Resources, 820 F.2d 1384 (4th Cir. 1987); contra *King v. Palmer,* 598 F. Supp. 65 (D. D.C. 1984), rev'd on other grounds, 250 U.S. App. D.C. 257, 778 F.2d 878 (1985).

252 E.g., *Lemons v. City of Denver,* 620 F.2d 228 (10th Cir.), cert. denied, 449 U.S. 888 (1980); *Briggs v. City of Madison,* 536 F. Supp. 435 (W.D. Wis. 1982); *American Nurses Ass'n v. Illinois,* 783 F.2d 716 (7th Cir. 1986) [case settled in 1989, Mod. Healthcare, Mar. 10, 1989, 14]; *AFSCME v. Washington,* 770 F.2d 1401 (9th Cir. 1985), reh'g denied (en banc), 813 F.2d 1034 (9th Cir. 1987) [case settled in 1985, N.Y. Times, Jan. 2, 1986, 7].

253 E.g., *Garcia v. Woman's Hosp. of Tex.,* 143 F.3d 227 (5th Cir. 1998) [not pregnancy discrimination to require all employees to be able to lift 150 pounds]; *Spivey v. Beverly Enterprises, Inc.,* 196 F.3d 1309 (11th Cir. 1999) [pregnant employee has no right to light duty work]; *Stout v. Baxter Healthcare Corp.,* 282 F.3d 856 (5th Cir. 2002) [pregnant employees may be discharged for absenteeism unless absences of nonpregnant employees overlooked].

254 E.g., *Floca v. Homecare Health Servs.,* 845 F.2d 108 (5th Cir. 1988) [violation to terminate pregnant director of nursing]; *Carney v. Martin Luther Home, Inc.,* 824 F.2d 643 (8th Cir. 1987) [violation to force unpaid medical leave while still able to work]; but see *McKnight v. North Charles Gen. Hosp.,* 652 F. Supp. 880 (D. Md. 1986) [hospital hired replacement head nurse for CCU when return from pregnancy delayed; not discrimination to place returning nurse in staff position in same unit].

255 *Pacourek v. Inland Steel Co.,* 858 F. Supp. 1393 (N.D. Ill. 1994); but see, *Tyndall v. National Educ. Ctrs.,* 31 F.3d 209 (4th Cir. 1994) [discharge for health-related absences not protected by ADA]; *Zatarain v. WDSU-Television, Inc.,* 881 F. Supp. 240 (E.D. La. 1995) [employer not required by ADA to accommodate employee's infertility treatment].

256 *International Union United Auto Workers v. Johnson Controls, Inc.,* 499 U.S. 187 (1991).

257 *Armstrong v. Flowers Hosp.,* 33 F.3d 1308 (11th Cir. 1994).

258 *Newport News Shipbuilding & Dry Dock Co. v. EEOC,* 462 U.S. 669 (1983).

259 E.g., *Piantanida v. Wyman Ctr., Inc.,* 116 F.3d 340 (8th Cir. 1997).

260 *Backus v. Baptist Med. Ctr.,* 510 F. Supp. 1191 (E.D. Ark. 1981); accord *Jones v. Hinds Gen. Hosp.,* 666 F. Supp. 933 (S.D. Miss. 1987); Hospitals can ban male nurses from delivery room, Am. Med. News, Oct. 3, 1994, 19 [Cal. Fair Employment and Housing Comm'n]; see also *Jennings v. N.Y. State Office of Mental Health,* 977 F.2d 731 (2d Cir. 1992) [state mental health facility could require at least one security treatment assistant assigned to each ward to be of same gender as patients]; see also *EEOC v. Columbia Lakeland Med. Ctr.,* 1999 U.S. Dist. LEXIS 663 (E.D. La.) [deny hospital its attorney fees against EEOC for defense of suit seeking to force hiring male nurse for maternity ward]; but see *Little Forest Med. Ctr. v. Ohio Civil Rights Comm'n,* 61 Ohio St. 3d 607, 575 N.E.2d 1164 (1991), cert. denied, 503 U.S. 906 (1992) [gender not BFOQ for nurse's aide]; *Slivka v. Camden-Clark Mem. Hosp.,* 594 S.E.2d 616 (W.Va. 2004) [under state law, insufficient evidence presented to dismiss male nurse challenge to denial of obstetrics job, sent back to trial court for further review].

261 *Backus v. Baptist Med. Ctr.,* 671 F.2d 1100 (8th Cir. 1982).

262 *Garcia v. Rush-Presbyterian-St. Luke's Med. Ctr.,* 660 F.2d 1217 (7th Cir. 1981); see also *Velasquez v. Goldwater Mem. Hosp.,* 88 F. Supp. 2d 257 (S.D. N.Y. 2000) [dismiss challenge to firing for violating hospital English-only policy]; *Tran v. Standard Motor Products, Inc.,* 1998 WL 293244 (D. Kan. 1998) [English-only policy during work and meeting did not create a hostile environment in violation of § 1981 or Title VII]; E. Fein, Lack of a common language can hinder care at hospitals, N.Y. Times, Nov. 23, 1997, 1; English-only, a touchy work issue, touches more legal nerves, Wall St. J., Mar. 10, 1998, A1.

263 29 C.F.R. § 1606.7; *Dimaranan v. Pomona Valley Hosp. Med. Ctr.,* 775 F. Supp. 338 (C.D. Cal. 1991) [hospital rule restricting use of Tagalog language by Filipino nurses was not prohibited English-only rule in violation of Title VII where shift-specific directive addressed conflicts among identified nurses]; *McNeil v. Aguilos,* 831 F. Supp. 1079 (S.D. N.Y. 1993) [non-Filipino nurse did not state claim for hospital policy of allowing nurses to communicate in workplace in Tagalog]; *Reed v. Driftwood Convalescent Hosp.,* EEOC Charge No. 377-93-0509 (July 13, 1994) [Calif. Dep't of Health Services policy; employees may speak other languages away from patients, but not to patients]; *EEOC v. Premier Operator Servs.,* 113 F. Supp. 2d 1066 (N.D. Tex. 2000) [business necessity for English-only rule not shown in nonhealth care case]; see also *Yniguez v. Arizonans for Official English,* 69 F.3d 920 (9th Cir. 1995) (en banc) [amendment to state constitution making English the official language of state violates U.S. constitution].

264 42 U.S.C. § 2000e-3; but see *Lewis v. Holsum of Fort Wayne, Inc.,* 278 F.3d 706 (7th Cir. 2002) [no inference of retaliation solely from timing of firing three months after EEOC charge filed].

265 *Wrighten v. Metropolitan Hosp.,* 726 F.2d 1346 (9th Cir. 1984); see also *Sparrow v. Piedmont Health Sys. Agency,* 593 F. Supp. 1107 (M.D. N.C. 1984) [refusal to give reference letter was prohibited retaliation].

266 E.g., *Whittlington v. Dep't of Veterans Affairs,* 132 F.3d 54 (without op.), 1997 U.S. App. LEXIS 34353 (Fed. Cir.) [upheld discharge of nurse for patient abuse, rejecting claim of retaliation]; *Stevens v. St. Louis Univ. Med. Ctr.,* 97 F.3d 268 (8th Cir. 1996) [hospital proved nondiscriminatory reason for terminating nurse who had filed sexual discrimination claim, sufficient evidence of misconduct, job performance issues]; *Vislisel v. Turanage,* 930 F.2d 9 (8th Cir. 1991) [VA did not retaliate for discrimination complaint by requesting physical, mental exam after peculiar behavior]; *Davis v. State Univ. of N.Y.,* 802 F.2d 638 (2d Cir. 1986) [low productivity, inability to accept supervision, angry response to conflict were sufficient nonpretextual reasons]; *Klein v. Trustees of Ind. Univ.,* 766 F.2d 275 (7th Cir. 1985) [refusal to reschedule private practice hours to accommodate student health service hours was nonpretextual reason for discharge].

267 *Robinson v. Shell Oil Co.,* 519 U.S. 337 (1997).

268 E.g., *O'Sullivan v. Cook County Bd. of Comm'rs,* 239 Ill. App. 3d 1, 687 N.E.2d 1103 (1st Dist. 1997) [upholding dismissal of chief engineer for violating policy on sexual harassment, abusive behavior; reversing lower court order to demote without back pay, benefits].

269 *Baker v. McDonald's Corp.,* 686 F. Supp. 1474 (S.D. Fla. 1987), aff'd without op., 865 F.2d 1272 (11th Cir. 1988), cert. denied, 493 U.S. 812 (1989); accord *Stroehmann Bakeries Inc. v. Local 776,* 969 F.2d 1436 (3d Cir. 1992), cert. denied, 506 U.S. 1022 (1992) [public policy violated by arbitrator order reinstating accused sexual harasser]; *Anderson v. Hewlett-Packard Corp.,* 694 F. Supp. 1294 (N.D. Ohio 1988) [personnel manager's constant sexual remarks, innuendos, suggestions to female subordinates created hostile or offensive work environment justifying termination]; see also *Davis v. Monsanto Chem. Corp.,* 858 F.2d 345, 350 (6th Cir. 1988), cert. denied, 490 U.S. 1110 ["In essence, while Title VII does not require an employer to fire any 'Archie Bunkers' in its employ, the law does require that an employer take prompt action to prevent such bigots from expressing their opinions in a way that abuses or offends their coworkers."]; *Stockley v. AT&T Information Sys., Inc.,* 687 F. Supp. 764 (E.D. N.Y. 1988) [since employer obligated to investigate sexual harassment claims, report of investigation protected by qualified privilege in defamation action].

270 *Flanagan v. Aaron E. Henry Comm. Health Servs. Ctr.,* 876 F.2d 1231 (5th Cir. 1987) [termination of Caucasian physician for race discrimination was not good cause under employment contract]; *Szczerbaniuk v. Memorial Hosp. of McHenry County,* 180 Ill. App. 3d 706, 536 N.E.2d 138 (2d Dist. 1989) [action by radiologist for termination of three-year exclusive contract by CEO after allegations of sexual harassment by hospital employees]; *Charter Southland Hosp., Inc. v. Eades,* 521 So. 2d 981 (Ala. 1988) [psychologist independent contractor made sexual advances to hospital employees; termination of contract not justified because contract permitted termination for only death, disability, or conviction for felony].

271 E.g., *California Fed. Sav. & Loan Ass'n v. Guerra,* 479 U.S. 272 (1987) [state statute requiring pregnancy leave, reinstatement not preempted by Title VII].

272 E.g., *Walsh v. Carney Hosp. Corp.,* No. CA-94-2583 (Mass. Super. Ct. jury verdict Dec. 30, 1996), as discussed in 6 H.L.R. 107 (1997) [housekeeping manager at Roman Catholic hospital fired because he was believed to be homosexual awarded $1.275 million by jury for violation of state law against discrimination based on sexual orientation].

273 29 U.S.C. § 206(d); see *Lambert v. Genesee Hosp.,* 10 F.3d 46 (2d Cir. 1993), cert. denied, 511 U.S. 1052 (1994) [female employee in duplicating services department failed to establish Equal Pay Act claim]; *Jones v. Westside-Urban Health Ctr.,* 760 F. Supp. 1575 (S.D. Ga. 1991) [employed male physician stated prima facie case under Equal Pay Act].

274 *Beall v. Curtis,* 603 F. Supp. 1563 (M.D. Ga. 1985).

275 E.g., *Marshall v. St. John Valley Security Home,* 560 F.2d 12 (1st Cir. 1977) [no violation]; *Brennan v. Prince Williams Hosp.,* 501 F.2d 282 (4th Cir. 1974), cert. denied, 420 U.S. 972 (1975) [violation]; *EEOC v. Harper Grace Hosps.,* 689 F. Supp. 708 (E.D. Mich. 1988) [violation].

276 29 U.S.C. §§ 621-634, 663(a).

277 E.g., *Stamey v. Southern Bell Tel. & Tel. Co.,* 859 F.2d 855 (11th Cir.), reh'g denied (en banc), 867 F.2d 1431 (11th Cir.), cert. denied, 490 U.S. 1116 (1989).

278 E.g., *Trans World Airlines, Inc. v. Thurston,* 469 U.S. 111 (1985) [age of less than 60 years not a bona fide occupational qualification for flying engineers].

279 *O'Donnell v. Georgia Osteopathic Hosp., Inc.,* 748 F.2d 1543 (11th Cir. 1984).

280 *Ogden v. Bureau of Labor,* 680 Or. App. 235, 682 P.2d 802 (1984), aff'd in part/rev'd in part, 299 Or. 98, 699 P.2d 189 (1985).

281 E.g., *Stafford v. Radford Comm. Hosp.,* 120 F.3d 262 (without op.), 1997 U.S. App. LEXIS 19741 (4th Cir.) [50-year-old nurse could not show she was performing job at employer's legitimate expectations]; *Vaughan v. MetraHealth Cos.,* 145 F.3d 197 (4th Cir. 1998) [57-year-old woman fired during downsizing; no ADEA claim stated, no age motivation shown]; *Lesch v. Crown Cork & Seal Co.,* 282 F.3d 467 (7th Cir. 2002) [overqualification for position is nonpretextual reason for selecting another person for retention in reduction in force]; *Gehring v. Case Corp.,* 43 F.3d 340 (7th Cir. 1994), cert. denied, 515 U.S. 1159 (1995) [theory of disparate impact of reduction in force not an ADEA theory.]; *Rhodes v. Guiberson Oil Tools,* 39 F.3d 537 (5th Cir. 1994) [reduction in force nonpretexual; to show pretext must show reason false, discrimination was real reason]; *Anderson v. Baxter Healthcare Corp.,* 13 F.3d 1120 (7th Cir. 1994) [goal of reducing salary costs is not age discrimination]; *Grohs v. Gold Bond Bldg. Prods.,* 859 F.2d 1283 (7th Cir. 1988), cert. denied, 490 U.S. 1036 (1989) [difficulty getting along with peers was nonpretextual].

282 *Buckley v. Hospital Corp. of Am.,* 758 F.2d 1525 (11th Cir. 1985).

283 *Shaw v. HCA Health Servs.,* 79 F.3d 99 (8th Cir. 1996).

284 29 U.S.C. § 626(f), as amended by Pub. L. No. 101-433, § 201, 104 Stat. 983 (1990).

285 42 U.S.C. § 12114(c); 29 C.F.R. § 1630.16(b).

286 E.g., *Stafne v. Unicare Homes,* 266 F.3d 771 (8th Cir. 2001) [RN had no ADA claim where rheumatoid arthritis made it impossible for her to perform essential functions of job with accommodation].

287 42 U.S.C. §§ 12111(3), 12113.

288 *EEOC v. Amego Inc.,* 110 F.3d 135 (1st Cir. 1997).

289 E.g., *Hutton v. Elf Atochem North America, Inc.,* 273 F.3d 884 (9th Cir. 2001) [diabetic worker posed direct threat].

290 E.g., *Estate of Mauro v. Burgess Med. Ctr.,* 137 F.3d 398 (6th Cir. 1998), cert. denied, 525 U.S. 815 (1998) [HIV-positive surgical technician posed a direct threat to health and safety of others]; *Bradley v. University of Tex. M.D. Anderson Cancer Ctr.,* 3 F.3d 922 (5th Cir. 1993), cert. denied, 510 U.S. 1119 (1994) [reassignment of an HIV-positive surgical technician to be a procurement technician did not violate the ADA]; *Waddell v. Valley Forge Dental Assocs.,* 276 F.3d 1275 (11th Cir. 2001) [dental hygienist posed direct threat].

291 *Chevron U.S.A. v. Echazabal,* 536 U.S. 73 (2002) [upholding EEOC regulation permitting refusal to hire person when job poses direct threat to person's health].

292 *Karraker v. Rent-A-Car Center,* 411 F.3d 481 (7th Cir. 2005).

293 *Karraker,* 411 F.3d at 835.

294 *Id.*

295 *Roe v. Cheyenne Mountain Conference Resort, Inc.,* 124 F.3d 1221 (10th Cir. 1997); but see *Doe v. Southeastern Pa. Transp.*

Auth., 72 F.3d 1133 (3d Cir. 1995) [use of prescription benefit may be monitored].

296 E.g., *EEOC v. Prevo's Family Market, Inc.,* 135 F.3d 1089 (6th Cir. 1998).

297 See J.S. Lublin, Should job hunters reveal chronic illnesses? The pros and cons, Wall St. J., Jan. 13, 2004, B1.

298 Equal Employment Opportunity Comm'n, Enforcement guidance: Reasonable accommodation and undue hardship under the Americans with Disabilities Act (Mar. 2, 1999) [http://www .access.gpo.gov/eeoc/docs/accommodation.html] [hereinafter cited as EEOC 1999 Guidance].

299 *Hammon v. DHL Airways, Inc.,* 165 F.3d 441 (6th Cir. 1999); accord *Taylor v. Prenapal Financial Group. Inc.,* 93 F.3d 155 (5th Cir. 1996) [employee must request reasonable accommodations].

300 *Walton v. Mental Health Ass'n,* 168 F.3d 661 (3d Cir. 1999).

301 *Laurin v. Providence Hosp.,* 150 F.3d 52 (1st Cir. 1998).

302 *Id.*

303 *Tardie v. Rehabilitation Hosp. of R.I.,* 168 F.3d 538 (1st Cir. 1999).

304 *Jones v. Kerrville State Hosp.,* 142 F.3d 263 (5th Cir. 1998).

305 *Fitzpatrick v. City of Atlanta,* 2 F.3d 1112 (11th Cir. 1993).

306 E.g., *Jones v. Kerrville State Hosp.,* 142 F.3d 263 (5th Cir. 1998) [licensed vocational nurse not otherwise qualified under ADA, not reasonable accommodation to exempt from physical portion of training in managing aggressive behavior of mental patients].

307 E.g., *Reigel v. Kaiser Found. Health Plan,* 859 F. Supp. 963 (E.D. N.C. 1994) [HMO did not violate ADA by firing internist with shoulder injury precluding performance of duties; not required to create position with just supervision, administration, or to hire assistant to perform physical tasks of job].

308 E.g., *Mancini v. General Electric Co.,* 820 F. Supp. 141 (D. Conn. 1993) [employer fired employee with emotional impairment after fight with supervisor; ability to follow orders an essential function of job so not qualified; transfer away from supervisor not a reasonable accommodation]; *Ceazan v. Saint John's Hosp. & Health Ctr.,* 2004 Cal. App. Unpub. LEXIS 3601 (2d Dist.) [not required to give depressed employee a new supervisor].

309 *Aka v. Washington Hosp. Ctr.,* 332 U.S. App. D.C. 256, 156 F.3d 1284 (D.C. Cir. 1998) (en banc); accord, *Gale v. United Airlines,* 95 F.3d 492 (7th Cir. 1996); *Community Hosp. v. Fall,* 969 P.2d 667 (Colo. 1998) [if no positions available at existing pay rate, may be position at reduced pay]; see also *Webster v. Methodist Occupational Health Ctrs., Inc.,* 141 F.3d 1236 (7th Cir. 1998) [not violation to terminate nurse who could not work independently after stroke and refused nonnursing job].

310 *US Airways, Inc. v. Barnett,* 535 U.S. 391 (2002).

311 E.g., *Carr v. Reno,* 306 U.S. App. D.C. 217, 23 F.3d 525 (1994); *Tyndall v. National Educ. Ctrs.,* 31 F.3d 209 (4th Cir. 1994); see also *Earl v. Mervyns, Inc.,* 207 F.3d 1361 (11th Cir. 2000 [not required to permit tardiness as accommodation for obsessive-compulsive disorder].

312 E.g., *Chers v. Northeast Ohio Alzheimer's Research Ctr.,* 155 F.3d 775 (6th Cir. 1998).

313 EEOC 1999 Guidance, question 18.

314 E.g., *Walsh v. United Parcel Service,* 201 F.3d 718 (6th Cir. 2000).

315 *EEOC v. Sears Roebuck & Co.,* No. 04 C 7282 (N.D. Ill.).

316 *Doe v. Mutual of Omaha,* 179 F.3d 557 (7th Cir. 1999), cert. denied, 528 U.S. 1106 (2000).

317 E.g., *Parker v. Metropolitan Life Ins. Co.,* 121 F.3d 1006 (6th Cir. 1997) (en banc); *Ford v. Schering-Plough Corp.,* 145 F.3d 601 (3d Cir. 1998); *Weyer v. Twentieth Century Fox Film Corp.,* 198 F.3d 1104 (9th Cir. 2000).

318 29 U.S.C. §§ 701-794.

319 29 U.S.C. § 793 [section 503]; 29 U.S.C. § 794 [section 504].

320 *Conrail v. Darrone,* 465 U.S. 624 (1984).

321 Pub. L. No. 100-259, § 4, 102 Stat. 29 (1988).

322 *United States v. Baylor Univ. Med. Ctr.,* 736 F.2d 1039 (5th Cir. 1984), cert. denied, 469 U.S. 1189 (1985).

323 E.g., *Tuck v. HCA Health Servs.,* 7 F.3d 465 (6th Cir. 1993) [hospital violated Act by terminating nurse].

324 *Heilweil v. Mount Sinai Hosp.,* 32 F.3d 718 (2d Cir. 1994), cert. denied, 513 U.S. 1147 (1995).

325 E.g., *School Bd. of Nassau County v. Arline,* 480 U.S. 273 (1987), after remand, 692 F. Supp. 1286 (M.D. Fla. 1988) [discharged teacher with history of tuberculosis otherwise qualified, entitled to reinstatement, back pay].

326 *Bragdon v. Abbott,* 524 U.S. 624 (1998).

327 *Doe v. Attorney General,* 95 F.3d 29 (9th Cir. 1996), after remand, *Reno v. Doe,* 518 U.S. 1014 (1996), vacating, Doe by *Laverty v. Attorney General,* 1995 U.S. App. LEXIS 16264 (9th Cir.).

328 E.g., *Carter v. Casa Cent.,* 849 F.2d 1048 (7th Cir. 1988) [director of nursing at nursing home with multiple sclerosis handicapped, otherwise qualified]; *Chalk v. United States Dist. Court,* 840 F.2d 701 (9th Cir. 1988) [teacher with AIDS was handicapped, otherwise qualified to teach; discrimination to assign to administrative job]; *Harrison v. Marsh,* 691 F. Supp. 1223 (W.D. Mo. 1988) [surgical removal of part of muscle of arm made typist handicapped; inadequate efforts to accommodate handicap]; *Hall v. Veterans Admin.,* 693 F. Supp. 546 (E.D. Mich. 1988), aff'd, 1991 U.S. App. LEXIS 26,046 (6th Cir.) [denial of dismissal of suit seeking a smoke-free environment as accommodation of obstructive lung disease]; *Wallace v. Veterans Admin.,* 683 F. Supp. 758 (D. Kan. 1988) [recovering addict could not be denied nursing position because authority to administer narcotics had been restricted; otherwise qualified].

329 E.g., *Hall v. U.S. Postal Serv.,* 857 F.2d 1073 (6th Cir. 1988) [on-the-job back injury precluded heavy lifting; lower court should decide whether lifting requirement essential, whether employee could perform function, if essential, whether reasonable accommodation possible, if not essential].

330 *Bruegging v. Burke,* 696 F. Supp. 674 (D. D.C. 1987) [Federal Register not required to lower standards of accuracy to accommodate editor with cerebral palsy], aff'd without op.,

298 U.S. App. D.C. 97, 976 F.2d 95 (1988), cert. denied, 488 U.S. 1009 (1989).

331 *Davis v. Meese,* 692 F. Supp. 505 (E.D. Pa. 1988), aff'd, 865 F.2d 592 (3d Cir. 1989) [insulin-dependent diabetic applicant for FBI special agent position not otherwise qualified; employer not required to make fundamental alteration in nature of job as accommodation]; accord *Serrapica v. City of New York,* 708 F. Supp. 64 (S.D. N.Y.), aff'd without op., 888 F.2d 126 (2d Cir. 1989) [diabetic not otherwise qualified for sanitation worker job because of heavy vehicles]; see also *Matzo v. Postmaster Gen.,* 685 F. Supp. 260 (D. D.C. 1987), aff'd without op., 274 U.S. App. D.C. 95, 861 F.2d 1290 (1988) [discharged postal service legal secretary manic-depressive, not otherwise qualified because disruptive and had poor attendance, good faith efforts had been made to accommodate her handicap]; *Bailey v. Tisch,* 683 F. Supp. 652 (S.D. Ohio 1988) [postal service applicant not otherwise qualified where heart condition never diagnosed as stable, exercise-related extra heartbeats made him unsuitable].

332 E.g., *Reese v. U.S. Gypsum Co.,* 705 F. Supp. 1387 (D. Minn. 1989) [state Human Rights Act not violated by discharge of diabetic who slept on job].

333 E.g., *Jackson v. Veterans Admin.,* 22 F.3d 277 (11th Cir.), reh'g denied (en banc), 30 F.3d 1500 (11th Cir. 1994) [housekeeping aide not otherwise qualified because did not satisfy presence requirement for job, no duty to accommodate unpredictable absences]; *Lemere v. Burnley,* 683 F. Supp. 275 (D. D.C. 1988) [alcoholic employee lost status as qualified handicapped employee by pattern of unscheduled absences].

334 *Atascadero State Hosp. v. Scanlon,* 473 U.S. 234 (1985).

335 42 U.S.C. § 2000d-7(a)(1); e.g., *Stanley v. Litscher,* 213 F.3d 340 (7th Cir. 2000).

336 *Doe v. Southeastern Pa. Transp. Auth.,* 72 F.3d 1133 (3d Cir. 1995); but see *Roe v. Cheyenne Mountain Conf. Resort, Inc.,* 124 F.3d 1221 (10th Cir. 1997) [ADA bars employer requirement of disclosure of employee prescription drug use, unless business necessity].

337 29 U.S.C. §§ 201-219.

338 See *Auer v. Robbins,* 519 U.S. 452 (1997) [upholding Department of Labor interpretation that a "salary basis" requires that "compensation . . . not [be] subject to reduction because of variations in the quality or quantity of the work performed."]; *de Jesus-Rentas v. Baxter Pharmacy Servs. Corp.,* 400 F.3d 72 (1st Cir. 2005) [pharmacists are professionals]; *Graziano v. Society of N.Y. Hosp.,* 1997 U.S. Dist. LEXIS 15926 (S.D. N.Y.) [salaried professional nurses not eligible for overtime compensation despite employee accrual of leave to cover partial day absences].

339 E.g., *Klein v. Rush-Presbyterian-St. Luke's Med. Ctr.,* 990 F.2d 279 (7th Cir. 1993) [hospital staff nurse not exempt as professional from FLSA, so entitled to overtime]; but see *Reich v. Newspapers of New England, Inc.,* 44 F.3d 1060 (1st Cir. 1995) [listing nursing as example of exempt professional].

340 69 Fed. Reg. 22122 (Apr. 23, 2004); D.K. Haase, Final overtime rules, National L.J., May 24, 2004, 14; D. Rogers, House defeats bid to overturn rules limiting overtime, Wall St. J., July 11, 2003, A2.

341 *Garcia v. San Antonio Metro. Transit Auth.,* 469 U.S. 528 (1985), rev'g, *National League of Cities v. Usery,* 426 U.S. 833 (1976).

342 *Alden v. Maine,* 527 U.S. 706 (1999).

343 *Kaczmerak v. Mount Sinai Med. Ctr.,* 1988 U.S. Dist. LEXIS 18680 (E.D. Wis.).

344 *Hoffman v. St. Joseph's Hosp.,* 1998 U.S. Dist. LEXIS 7911 (N.D. Ga.).

345 *Townsend v. Mercy Hosp.,* 862 F.2d 1009 (3d Cir. 1988), aff'g 689 F. Supp. 503 (W.D. Pa. 1988).

346 See L. Uchitelle, Some cities pressuring employers to pay a higher minimum wage, N.Y. Times, Apr. 9, 1996, A1.

347 E.g., *United States v. Rocky Mountain Helicopters,* 704 F. Supp. 1046 (D. Utah 1989).

348 15 U.S.C. §§ 1671-1677.

349 Pub. L. No.93-406, 88 Stat. 829 (1974) (codified as amended in scattered sections of 5, 18, 26, 29, 31, and 42 U.S.C.); 29 C.F.R. pts. 2509-2677.

350 *Metropolitan Life Ins. Co. v. Massachusetts,* 471 U.S. 724 (1985); see also *Washington Physicians' Service Ass'n v. Washington,* 147 F.3d 1039 (9th Cir. 998), cert. denied, 525 U.S. 1141 (1999) [state law requiring HMOs and health care service contractors to offer alternate medical services not preempted by ERISA].

351 See also *American Med. Security v. Bartlett,* 111 F.3d 358 (4th Cir. 1997), cert. denied, 524 U.S. 936 (1998) [ERISA preempts state regulation of stop-loss coverage levels of self-insured employee benefit plans].

352 *United States v. Martorano,* 767 F.2d 63 (3d Cir.), cert. denied, 474 U.S. 949 (1985).

353 E.g., *Kross v. Western Electric Co.,* 701 F.2d 1238 (7th Cir. 1983).

354 *Seaman v. Arvida Realty Sales,* 985 F.2d 543 (11th Cir.), reh'g denied (en banc), 993 F.2d 1556 (11th Cir.), cert. denied, 510 U.S. 916 (1993).

355 *McGann v. H.& H. Music Co.,* 742 F. Supp. 362 (S.D. Tex. 1990), aff'd, 946 F.2d 401 (5th Cir. 1991), cert. denied, 506 U.S. 981 (1992).

356 Pub. L. No. 104-191.

357 Pub. L. No. 103-3, 107 Stat. 6 (1993) [codified as amended at 29 U.S.C. §§ 2611-2619 and in scattered sections of 2, 5, and 29 U.S.C.]; 60 Fed. Reg. 2180 (Jan. 6, 1995) [final regulations].

358 29 U.S.C. § 2611(11).

359 29 C.F.R. § 825.114; *Thorson v. Gemini, Inc.,* 123 F.3d 1140 (8th Cir. 1997) [combination of conditions that would not each be sufficient can together meet requirement]; *Victorelli v. Shadyside Hosp.,* 128 F.3d 184 (3d Cir. 1997) [ongoing treatable medical condition (peptic ulcer) requiring occasional sick leave can be sufficient].

360 E.g., *Martyszenko v. Safeway, Inc.,* 120 F.3d 120 (8th Cir. 1997).

361 *Stoops v. One Call Communications, Inc.,* 141 F.3d 309 (7th Cir. 1998).

362 29 U.S.C. § 2613.

363 29 U.S.C. § 2613(e); 29 C.F.R. § 825.308(a).

364 29 C.F.R. § 825.303(b).

365 E.g., *Price v. City of Ft. Wayne,* 117 F.3d 1022 (7th Cir. 1997).

366 29 C.F.R. § 825.303; *Holmes v. Boeing Company,* 166 F.3d 1221 (without op.), 1999 U.S. App. LEXIS 377 (10th Cir. 1999) [employer may require notice of absences in nonemergency situations; *Hopson v. Quitman County Hosp. and Nursing Home,* 119 F.3d 363 (5th Cir. 1997) [reduction of thirty-day notice for planned surgeries under FMLA not limited to medical emergencies, can be justified by deadline for insurance coverage].

367 *Nevada Dep't of Human Res. v. Hibbs,* 538 U.S. 721 (2003).

368 *Brockman v. Wyoming Dep't of Family Services,* 342 F.3d 1159 (10th Cir. 2003).

369 E.g., 26 U.S.C. §§ 401-425.

370 Pub. L. No. 91-596, 84 Stat. 1590 (1970) (codified as amended at 29 U.S.C. §§ 651-678 and in scattered sections of 5, 15, 29, 42, and 49 U.S.C.).

371 29 U.S.C. § 652(4); 29 C.F.R. § 1975.5.

372 *Marshall v. Barlow's Inc.,* 436 U.S. 307 (1978).

373 29 C.F.R. § 1977.12(b)(2).

374 *Whirlpool Corp. v. Marshall,* 445 U.S. 1 (1980).

375 *Stepp v. Review Bd.,* 521 N.E.2d 350 (Ind. Ct. App. 1988).

376 *Gade v. National Solid Waste Mgmt. Ass'n,* 505 U.S. 88 (1992).

377 26 C.F.R. § 1910.1030, as amended 61 Fed. Reg. 5507 (Feb. 13, 1996).

378 *American Dental Ass'n v. Secretary of Labor,* 984 F.2d 823 (7th Cir. 1993) [dissent questioned OSHA's involvement in an area already addressed by CDC and its competence to do so], cert. denied, 510 U.S. 859 (1993).

379 *Taylor v. St. Vincent's Med. Ctr.,* 145 F.3d 1333 (without op.), 1998 U.S. App. LEXIS 7991 (6th Cir.).

380 For a NIOSH summary of initiatives in the area listed in this paragraph, see pages on each topic at http://www.osha.gov/SLTC/.

381 E.g., TB control plans focus of settlements between OSHA, two Wisconsin hospitals, 2 H.L.R. 1342 (1993) [hospitals cited under general duty clause for not protecting workers from hazard of TB infection through contact with patients at high risk for TB; failure to record on occupational illness and injury logs workers who tested positive for TB; allowed unapproved respirators and allowed facial hair, skull cap with respirators]; see also 59 Fed. Reg. 54242 (Oct. 28, 1994) [CDC guidelines on TB].

382 Psychiatric hospital in Chicago cited by OSHA for workplace violence, 2 H.L.R. 1479 (1993) [cited for failure to protect workers from patient violence; abatement program worked out].

383 E.g., *Secretary of Labor v. Froedtert Mem. Lutheran Hosp.,* No. 97-1839 (OSHA Rev. Comm. Jan. 16, 2004), as discussed in H.L.R., Jan. 29, 2004, 161 [hepatitis B vaccines and blood-borne pathogen training for temporary housekeeping staff].

384 E.g., *Labor Secretary v. Skyline Terrace Inc.,* No. 95-C-676-K (N.D. Okla. May 22, 1997), as discussed in 6 H.L.R. 912 (1997)

[punitive damages awarded against nursing home for firing nurse in retaliation for filing OSHA complaint about lack of gloves].

385 E.g., Wis. Stat. § 101.11.

386 29 U.S.C. §§ 141-187.

387 Act of July 5, 1935, ch. 372, 49 Stat. 449.

388 Act of June 23, 1947, ch. 120, 61 Stat. 136.

389 Pub. L. No. 86-257, 73 Stat. 519.

390 E.g., *Pikeville United Methodist Hosp. v. United Steelworkers of Am.*, 109 F.3d 1146 (6th Cir. 1997) [active municipal oversight of private hospital not sufficient to make it governmental].

391 29 U.S.C. §§152(2), 158.

392 *St. Elizabeth Comm. Hosp. v. NLRB*, 708 F.2d 1436 (9th Cir. 1983); *St. Elizabeth Hosp. v. NLRB*, 715 F.2d 1193 (7th Cir. 1983).

393 29 U.S.C. § 152(11); *NLRB v. Health Care & Retirement Corp. of Am.*, 511 U.S. 571 (1994).

394 *NLRB v. Health Care & Retirement Corp. of Am.*, 511 U.S. 571 (1994).

395 *NLRB v. Kentucky River Community Care, Inc.*, 532 U.S. 706 (2001).

396 E.g., Madison Ctr. Genesis Eldercare, Inc., Case No. 22-RC-11729 (NLRB Reg. Dir. Jan. 31, 2002).

397 E.g., *Beverly Enterprises v. NLRB*, 165 F.3d 307 (4th Cir. 1999) (en banc) [supervisors]; contra, *NLRB v. GranCare, Inc.*, 170 F.3d 662 (7th Cir. 1998) [not supervisors].

398 E.g., *Beverly Enterprises v. SEIU*, 1-RC-21704 (NLRB Reg. Dir. Feb. 4, 2004); *Integrated Health Servs., Inc. v. District* 1199P, Case No. 6-UC-445 (NLRB Reg. Dir. Dec. 19, 2002).

399 Mercy Hosp. Ass'n, Inc., 235 NLRB 6781 (1978).

400 Good Samaritan Hosp. & Richey, 265 NLRB 618 (1982); see also *Bob Evans Farms, Inc. v. NLRB*, 163 F.3d 1012 (7th Cir. 1998) [workers who walked out to protest firing of popular supervisor not protected].

401 *Marshall Durbin Poultry Co. v. NLRB*, 39 F.3d 1312 (5th Cir. 1994).

402 *Waterbury Hosp. v. NLRB*, 950 F.2d 849 (2d Cir. 1991).

403 *Kobell v. Beverly Health & Rehab. Servs.*, 987 F. Supp. 409 (W.D. Pa. 1997) [order to reinstate former strikers who had been permanently replaced due to ULPs], aff'd, 142 F.3d 428 (3d Cir. 1998), cert. denied, 525 U.S. 1121 (1999).

404 *East Tenn. Baptist Hosp. v. NLRB*, 6 F.3d 1139 (6th Cir. 1993).

405 Swedish Hosp. Med. Ctr., NLRA Cases 19-CA-22412, 22823 (Oct. 14, 1993), as discussed in 2 H.L.R. 1419 (1993).

406 *Chicago Tribune Co. v. NLRB*, 79 F.3d 604 (7th Cir. 1996).

407 *Torrington Extend-A-Care Employee Ass'n v. NLRB*, 17 F.3d 580 (2d Cir. 1994).

408 *Beverly Health & Rehab. Servs., Inc. v. NLRB*, 354 U.S. App. D.C. 414, 317 F.3d 316 (2003).

409 Rideout Mem. Hosp., 227 NLRB 1338 (1977).

410 *NLRB v. Peninsula Gen. Hosp. Med. Ctr.*, 36 F.3d 1262 (4th Cir. 1994).

411 *Gratiot Comm. Hosp. v. NLRB*, 51 F.3d 1255 (6th Cir. 1995).

412 *St. Luke's Episcopal-Presbyterian Hosps., Inc. v. NLRB*, 268 F.3d 575 (8th Cir. 2001).

413 *Pattern Maker's League v. NLRB*, 473 U.S. 95 (1985).

414 *NLRB v. 1115 Nursing Home & Serv. Employees Union*, 44 F.3d 136 (2d Cir. 1995).

415 29 U.S.C. § 106.

416 *Callen v. Internat'l Brotherhood of Teamsters*, 144 Ohio App. 3d 575, 761 N.E.2d 51 (2001).

417 S. Rep. No. 93-766, 93d Cong., 2d Sess. 5, reprinted in 1974 U.S. Code Cong. & Admin. News 3,946, 3,950.

418 29 U.S.C. § 159(b)(1); *Leedom v. Kyne*, 358 U.S. 184 (1958); Pontiac Osteopathic Hospital, 327 NLRB No. 194 (March 31, 1999).

419 St. Francis Hosp. & Int'l Brotherhood of Elec. Workers, 271 NLRB 948 (1984); Health-Care Enters., 275 NLRB No. 194 (1985).

420 29 C.F.R. § 103.30.

421 *American Hosp. Ass'n v. NLRB*, 499 U.S. 606 (1991).

422 Kaiser Found. Hosps., 312 NLRB No. 139 (1993).

423 St. Luke's Health Sys., Inc., 340 NLRB No. 139 (2003).

424 Stormont-Vail HealthCare, Inc., 340 NLRB No. 143 (2003).

425 E.g., *Manchester Health Ctr. v. NLRB*, 861 F.2d 50 (2d Cir. 1988) [rule upheld]; for an example of the analysis, see The Cooper Health System, 327 NLRB No. 189 (1999) [nonsolicitation policy too broad].

426 E.g., *Cooper Tire & Rubber Co. v. NLRB*, 957 F.2d 1245 (5th Cir. 1992); see also One Way, Inc., 268 NLRB 394 (1983) [policy can refer to "work time," but not to "work hours"].

427 *NLRB v. Baptist Hosp.*, 442 U.S. 773 (1979).

428 E.g., *Stanford Hosp. & Clinics v. NLRB*, 325 F.3d 334 (D.C. Cir. 2003).

429 E.g., *Brockton Hosp. v. NLRB*, 352 U.S. App. D.C. 302, 294 F.3d 100 (2002).

430 *Oakwood Hosp. v. NLRB*, 983 F.2d 698 (6th Cir. 1993).

431 E.g., *Fairfax Hosp. v. NLRB*, 14 F.3d 594 (without op.), 1993 U.S. App. LEXIS 31,936 (4th Cir. 1993), cert. denied, 512 U.S. 1205 (1994); *Mt. Clemens Gen. Hosp. v. NLRB*, 328 F.3d 837 (6th Cir. 2003).

432 E.g., *Dacas Nursing Support Sys. v. NLRB*, 7 F.3d 511 (6th Cir. 1993); *Indiana Hosp. v. NLRB*, 10 F.3d 151 (3d Cir. 1993).

433 E.g., Lasalle Ambulance, Inc., d/b/a Rural/Metro Medical Services, 327 NLRB No. 18 (Oct. 30, 1998); *Evergreen Healthcare, Inc. v. NLRB*, 104 F.3d 867 (6th Cir. 1997); see also *Beverly Enterprises Inc. v. NLRB*, 139 F.3d 135 (2d Cir. 1998).

434 E.g., *Americare Pine Lodge Nursing & Rehab. Ctr. v. NLRB*, 164 F.3d 867 (4th Cir. 1999).

435 E.g., *Exxel/Atmos, Inc. v. NLRB,* 307 U.S. App. D.C. 376, 28 F.3d 1243 [new president committed unfair labor practice by refusal to bargain with union that predecessor had voluntarily recognized within prior year], reh'g denied (en banc), 308 U.S. App. D.C. 411, 37 F.3d 1538 (1994).

436 E.g., *Local 144 v. NLRB,* 9 F.3d 218 (2d Cir. 1993).

437 E.g., *Staten Island Univ. Hosp. v. NLRB,* 24 F.3d 450 (2d Cir. 1994).

438 E.g., *NLRB v. Hospital San Rafael, Inc.,* 42 F.3d 45 (1st Cir. 1994); Midwest Precision Heating & Cooling, Inc., 341 NLRB No. 52 (2004) [successor liability for successor company found to be alter ego of prior employer]; *United Steelworkers v. St. Gabriel's Hosp.,* 871 F. Supp. 335 (D. Minn. 1994) [state law requiring business purchaser to honor existing labor contract until expiration conflicts with federal labor law, so preempted; successor liability under federal law only if continuity of workforce].

439 E.g., *Marion Hosp. Corp. v. NLRB,* 355 U.S. App. D.C. 233, 321 F.3d 1178 (2003).

440 29 U.S.C. § 158(d).

441 29 U.S.C. § 183; 29 C.F.R. pt. 1420.

442 29 U.S.C. § 158(g); see also *NLRB v. Stationary Eng'rs,* 746 F.2d 530 (9th Cir. 1984) [notice must specify date].

443 *Metropolitan Med. Ctr. v. Richardville,* 354 N.W. 2d 867 (Minn. Ct. App. 1984).

444 *Beverly Health & Rehab. Servs., Inc. v. NLRB,* 354 U.S. App. D.C. 414, 317 F.3d 316 (2003); see also Alexandria Clinic, P.A., 339 NLRB No. 162 (2003) [may discharge employees who begin strike after originally set tie without giving new ten-day notice].

445 *Minnesota Licensed Practical Nurses Ass'n v. NLRB,* 406 F.3d 1020 (8th Cir. 2005).

446 *Montefiore Hosp. v. NLRB,* 621 F.2d 510 (2d Cir. 1980); see also, e.g., *East Chicago Rehab. Ctr. v. NLRB,* 710 F.2d 397 (7th Cir. 1983), cert. denied, 465 U.S. 1065 (1984) [wildcat strike by seventeen nurse's aides].

447 Memorandum from Dietz, Associate General Counsel, NLRB, to Siegel, Director, Region 31 (Sept. 2, 1977) [concerning cases No. 31-CC-820, 821, 31-CG-7, 8].

448 E.g., *Pleasantview Nursing Home, Inc. v. NLRB,* 351 F.3d 747 (6th Cir. 2003).

449 *Saint Mary Home Inc. v. SEIU,* Dist. 1199, 116 F.3d 41 (2d Cir. 1997).

450 *Flushing Hosp. v. Local 1199,* 685 F. Supp. 55 (S.D. N.Y. 1988) [nursing attendant]; *Brigham & Women's Hosp. v. Massachusetts Nurses Ass'n,* 684 F. Supp. 1120 (D. Mass. 1988) [nurse].

451 *AFSCME v. Illinois,* 124 Ill. 2d 246, 529 N.E.2d 534 (1988).

452 *United Paperworkers v. Misco, Inc.,* 484 U.S. 29 (1987).

453 *State Univ. of N.Y. v. Young,* 170 A.D.2d 510, 566 N.Y.S.2d 79 (2d Dept. 1991), appeal denied, 80 N.Y.2d 753, 587 N.Y.S.2d 905, 600 N.E.2d 632, cert. denied, 506 U.S. 1035 (1992).

454 *Ohio Office of Collective Bargaining v. Ohio Civil Serv. Employees Ass'n,* 59 Ohio St. 3d 177, 572 N.E.2d 71 (1991).

455 *Russell Mem. Hosp. Ass'n v. United Steelworkers,* 720 F. Supp. 583 (E.D. Mich. 1989); accord, *Boston Med. Ctr. v. Service Employees Internat'l Union,* 113 F. Supp. 2d 169 (D. Mass. 2000) [against public policy to reinstate nurse after substandard practice led to preventable death of infant].

456 *County of Hennepin v. Hennepin County Ass'n of Paramedics & Emergency Med. Technicians,* 464 N.W.2d 578 (Minn. Ct. App. 1990).

457 E.g., *Fairview Southdale Hosp. v. Minnesota Nurses Ass'n,* 943 F.2d 809 (8th Cir. 1991) [arbitrator did not exceed his authority in determining hospital could not terminate free parking without bargaining about termination despite contract silence on parking]; *Trustees of Columbia Univ. v. Local 1199,* 805 F. Supp. 216 (S.D. N.Y. 1992) [suit claiming breach of no-strike clause was dismissed, referred to arbitration under broad arbitration clause in contract, despite employer claim arbitration clause intended to apply only to employee grievances]; *Clark County Pub. Employees Ass'n v. Pearson,* 106 Nev. 587, 798 P.2d 136 (1990) [elimination of nursing clinical ladder program subject to binding arbitration].

458 *Luden's Inc. v. Local Union No. 6,* 28 F.3d 347 (3d Cir. 1994).

459 29 U.S.C. §§ 401-531; see *International Union v. Dole,* 276 U.S. App. D.C. 178, 869 F.2d 616 (1989) [scope of reportable activities defined].

460 E.g., *United Steelworkers v. St. Gabriel's Hosp.,* 871 F. Supp. 335 (D. Minn. 1994) [state law requiring business purchaser to honor existing labor contract until expiration conflicts with federal labor law, so preempted].

461 29 U.S.C. §§ 101-111; see, e.g., *Modeste v. Local 1199,* 38 F.3d 626 (2d Cir. 1994) [dismissal of suit against union for alleged intentional torts during strike; Norris-LaGuardia Act does not preempt state law requirement of showing liability of each member of union in order to hold union liable].

462 E.g., *District 1199E v. Johns Hopkins Hosp.,* 293 Md. 343, 444 A.2d 448 (1982).

463 M. Landsberg, Judge tells County-USC nurses to end sickouts, L.A. Times, July 6, 2004, B3.

464 E.g., Fla. Const. art. 1, § 6.

465 29 U.S.C. § 164(b).

466 St. John's Mercy Med. Ctr., 344 NLRB No. 44 (Mar. 31, 2005) [hospital ordered to terminate fourteen nurses who did not pay union dues].

467 E.g., *Chambers v. Hermann Hosp. Estate,* 961 S.W.2d 177 (Tex. Ct. App. 1996).

468 E.g., *Herman v. Sherwood Indus., Inc.,* 244 Conn. 502 701 A.2d 1338 (1998) [workers' compensation covers injury to terminated employee while retrieving personal items].

469 *Salih v. Lane,* 244 Va. 436, 423 S.E.2d 192 (1992).

470 *Snyder v. Michael's Stores, Inc.,* 16 Cal. 4th 991, 68 Cal. Rptr. 2d 476, 945 P.2d 781 (1997).

471 *American Manufacturers Mutual Ins. Co. v. Sullivan,* 526 U.S. 40 (1999).

472 *Selan v. Unemployment Comp. Bd.,* 495 Pa. 338, 433 A.2d 1337 (1981).

473 *Porter v. Dep't of Employment Sec.,* 139 Vt. 405, 430 A.2d 450 (1981).

474 *Montclair Nursing Ctr. v. Wills,* 220 Neb. 547, 371 N.W.2d 121 (1985); accord *Baptist Med. Ctr. v. Stolte,* 475 So. 2d 959 (Fla. 1st DCA 1985), rev. denied, 486 So. 2d 598 (Fla. 1986) [nurse who refuses to accept offered 3-11 position is not "unavailable for work" and, thus, ineligible for unemployment compensation].

475 *Vinokurov v. Mt. Sinai Hosp.,* No. 88-3158U (Fla. Dep't of Labor & Employment Sec. Apr. 1, 1988); see also R.D. Gagliano, When health care workers refuse to treat AIDS patients, 21 J. Health & Hosp. L. 255 (1988).

476 *Holly v. Unemployment Compensation Bd. of Review,* 151 Pa. Commw. 450, 617 A.2d 80 (1992), appeal denied, 534 Pa. 643, 626 A.2d 1160 (1993).

477 *Fair v. St. Joseph's Hosp.,* 113 N.C. App. 159, 437 S.E.2d 875 (1993).

478 *Clarke v. North Detroit Gen. Hosp.,* 437 Mich. 280, 470 N.W.2d 393 (1991).

479 *State Emp. Sec. Dep't v. Evans,* 901 P.2d 156 (Nev. 1995); contra, *Fennel v. Board of Rev.,* 297 N.J. Super. 319, 688 A.2d 113 (App. Div. 1997) [hospital housekeeper who failed to report to work due to incarceration not entitled to unemployment compensation].

480 E.g., N.Y. Labor §§ 650-665; 19 Del. C. §§ 901 - 914; Mayor of Baltimore signs groundbreaking "living wage" bill into law, U.S. Newswire, Dec. 14, 1994; Mayor signs living wage bill, AP, Nov. 27, 2002 [New York City]; Z. Zhao, New minimum wage for health care workers, N.Y. Times, Dec. 1, 2002, 5WC [Westchester County, N.Y.]; Court upholds Santa Fe wage ordinance; landmark ruling confirms power of cities to raise pay for low-wage residents, U.S. Newswire, June 24, 2004.

481 E.g., *New Orleans Campaign for a Living Wage v. City of New Orleans,* 825 So. 2d 1098 (La. 2002) [state ban on local minimum wage law is constitutional (La. R.S. 23:642); New Orleans ordinance invalid]; Wis. Stat., § 104.001, added by 2005 Wis. Act 12; see also D. Lieb, Supreme Court dismisses appeal in living wage case, AP, Sept. 5, 2002 [lower court overturned both Missouri state law banning local ordinances and St. Louis ordinance]; Granholm vetoes bill that would have kept locals from setting minimum wage, AP, May 7, 2004 [Mich.].

482 E.g., Wis. Stat. §§ 111.321, 111.36; *Hyman v. City of Louisville,* 53 Fed. Appx. 740 (6th Cir. 2002) [lacked standing to challenge local ordinance banning employment discrimination based on sexual orientation].

483 E.g., *Catholic Charities of Maine v. City of Portland,* 304 F. Supp. 2d 77 (D. Me. 2004) [city may require domestic partnership benefits for all benefits not subject to ERISA preemption]; but see *Phillips v. Wisconsin Personnel Comm'n,* 167 Wis. 2d 205, 482 N.W.2d 121 (Ct. App. 1992) [Wis. Stat. § 111.321 does not require family benefits for domestic partners].

484 E.g., *Colmenares v. Braemar Country Club, Inc.,* 29 Cal. 4th 1019, 63 P.3d 220, 130 Cal. Rptr. 2d 662 (2003).

485 See *Clackmas Gastroenterology Assocs., P.C. v. Wells,* 538 U.S. 440 (2003).

486 E.g., *Nationwide Mutual Ins. Co. v. Darden,* 503 U.S. 318 (1992) [ERISA term "employee" incorporates traditional agency-law criteria].

487 See *Weber v. C.I.R.,* 103 T.C. 378 (1994) [since not independent contractor, individual must pay tax deficiencies for deductions].

488 E.g., *Hensley v. Northwest Permanente P.C. Retirement Plan & Trust,* 258 F.3d 986 (9th Cir. 2001) [not arbitrary and capricious for ERISA plan administrator to interpret "employee" to mean only persons for whom taxes were withheld; nurse practitioners, physician's assistants not entitled to pension benefits]; *Vizcaino v. Microsoft,* 97 F.3d 1187 (9th Cir. 1996) aff'd on reh'g, 120 F.3d 1006 (9th Cir. 1997), cert. denied, 522 U.S.1098 (1998) [suit seeking inclusion in 401(k) after settlement of employment status of temporary workers with IRS].

489 E.g., *Health Care Associates, Inc. v. Oklahoma Employment Security Comm'n,* 26 P.3d 112 (Okla. 2001) [nurses were independent contractors, not eligible for unemployment compensation].

490 E.g., *Alberty-Velez v. Corporacion de Puerto Rico para la Difusion Publica,* 361 F.3d 1 (1st Cir. 2004) [not covered by Title VII]; *Weary v. Cochran,* 2004 U.S. App. LEXIS 15589 (6th Cir) [insurance agent is independent contractor; not covered by ADEA]; *Lerohl v. Friends of Minn. Sinfonic,* 322 F.3d 486 (8th Cir. 2003) [musicians are independent contractors despite control over rehearsals, performances; not covered by ADA, Title VII].

491 E.g., 42 U.S.C. § 1981; *Gomez v. Alexian Bros. Hosp.,* 698 F.2d 1019 (9th Cir. 1983) [rejection of contract proposal by emergency medical professional corporation can violate Title VII as to Hispanic physician employee of corporation]; see also *O'Hare Truck Serv., Inc. v. City of Northlake,* 518 U.S. 712 (1996) [independent contractor protected by First Amendment form retaliation by city for political association or expression]; *Board of Comm'rs, Wabaunsee Cty. v. Umbehr,* 518 U.S. 668 (1996) [local officials may not terminate an independent contractor for criticizing government policy].

492 See *NLRB v. United Ins. Co.,* 390 U.S. 254 (1968); *Time Auto Transportation, Inc. v. NLRB,* 2004 U.S. App. LEXIS 15270 (6th Cir).

493 E.g., *Bedrossian v. Northwestern Mem. Hosp.,* 2004 U.S. Dist. LEXIS 5542 (N.D. Ill.) [dismiss whistleblower protection claim under False Claims Act against hospital, hospital not employer].

494 E.g., *United States v. Thomas,* 2004 U.S. App. LEXIS 15542 (2d Cir.) [contractor can be agent for crime].

495 *Eckhardt v. Charter Hosp. of Albuquerque, Inc.,* 953 P.2d 722 (N.M. Ct. App. 1997).

496 E.g., *York v. Association of Bar of City of N.Y.,* 2001 U.S. Dist. LEXIS 9457 (S.D. N.Y.) [volunteer not protected by Title VII]; *O'Connor v. Davis,* 126 F.3d 112 (2d Cir. 1997) [student volunteering at hospital to fulfill degree requirements of college is not an employee or student of the hospital, so neither Title VII nor Title IX applies to harassment by supervising physician].

497 E.g., *Silbar v. Office of Personnel Management,* 89 Fed. Appx. 692 (Fed. Cir. 2003) [VA employee not entitled to service credit for time spent volunteering]; *Rodriguez v. Township of Holiday Lakes,* 866 F. Supp. 1012 (S.D. Tex. 1994) [volunteer police chief found to be employee for FLSA, but exempt from FLSA under another section]; but see *Lance v. United States,* 70 F.3d 1093 (9th Cir. 1995) [volunteers at VA hospitals are employees for purposes of the Federal Employees Compensation Act]; *McNichols v. United States,* 226 F. Supp. 965 (N.D. Ill. 1964) [VA hospital volunteer is an employee for purposes of the Federal Tort Claims Act].

498 E.g., Wis. Stat. § 181.0670(2).

499 E.g., *Maynard v. Ferno-Washington, Inc.,* 22 F. Supp. 2d 1171 (E.D. Wash. 1998) [jury question whether sufficient control exercised to make hospital liable for acts of volunteer EMT].

500 E.g., Wis. Stat. §§ 102.07(11), (11m).

501 *Greater N.Y. Health Facilities Ass'n v. Axelrod,* 770 F. Supp. 183 (S.D. N.Y. 1991) [rejecting challenge to state policy memo limiting activities of volunteers].

502 E.g., *McGuinness v. University of N.M. School of Med.,* 170 F.3d 974 (10th Cir. 1998), cert. denied, 526 U.S. 1051 (1999).

503 E.g., Wis. Stat. § 40.22(2)(g) [exclusion from state retirement system].

504 E.g., *O'Connor v. Davis,* 126 F.3d 112 (2d Cir. 1997) [student volunteering at hospital to fulfill degree requirements of college is not an employee or student of the hospital, so neither Title VII nor Title IX applies to harassment by supervising physician]; but see *Silbar v. Office of Personnel Management,* 89 Fed. Appx. 692 (Fed. Cir. 2003) [approved VA hospital practice of granting service credit to formal students, but not to other volunteers].

505 *Powell v. National Board of Medical Ex'ers,* 364 F.3d 79 (2d Cir. 2004).

506 E.g., *Gossett v. Oklahoma,* 243 F.3d 1172 (10th Cir. 2001) [nursing school could be sued under Title XI for alleged discrimination against male students].

507 *Jung v. Association of Am. Med. Colleges,* 300 F. Supp. 2d 119 (D. D.C. 2004), 339 F. Supp. 2d 26 (D. D.C. 2004), 226 F.R.D. 7 (D.D.C. 2005); 15 U.S.C. § 37b.

508 Boston Med. Ctr. Corp., 330 NLRB No. 30 (1999), overruling Cedars-Sinai Med. Ctr., 223 NLRB 251 (1976).

509 L.K. Altman & D. Grady, Hospital accreditor will strictly limit hours of residents, N.Y. Times, June 13, 2002, A1.

510 E.g., A. Barnard, Surgery residents' long hours draw warning for Yale, Boston Globe, May 20, 2002, A1; M. Croasdale, Johns Hopkins penalized for resident hour violations, Am. Med. News, Sept. 15, 2003, 10.

511 See T. Kelley, State says many hospitals violate laws on work hours, N.Y. Times, June 27, 2002, B6.

512 M. Croasdale, Beat the clock, Am. Med. News, Mar. 8, 2004, 9 [barrier to learning]; M. Croasdale, Some work-hour limits could change, Am. Med. News, Apr. 12, 2004, 13 [ACGME considers longer hours for some specialists]; Residencies pinpoint work-hour hurdles, Am. Med. News, Apr. 19, 2004, 12 [AAMC survey – decrease in patient contact, more handoffs, lack of continuity of care, increased faculty hours, and reduced morale].

Appendix 4-1: Scope of Practice Grid

	Practitioner Type	Credentials	Educational Background	Certification	Licensed Y or N	Licensure Renewal Requirements	Approving Organization	CEU and Recertification Requirements
1	Medical Doctor	MD	Doctor of Medicine	Exam thru ECFMG (Educational Commission for Foreign Medical Graduates), USMLE (United States Medical Licensing Examination)	Y	Every 3 years	Illinois Department of Financial and Professional Regulations	150 hours of CME approved by Accreditation Council for Continuing Medical Education (ACME) over 3 years; 60 of 150 must be Category I hours;
2	Doctor of Osteopathy	DO	Doctor of Osteopathic Medicine	Exam thru NBOME (National Board of Osteopathic Medical Examiners)	Y	Every 3 years	Illinois Department of Financial and Professional Regulations	150 hours of CME
3	Advanced Practice Nurse	ANP	Masters or Post-Masters Certificate (those who were grandfathered in)	Exam thru a national certifying organization such as AANP (American Academy of Nurse Practitioners) or ANCC (American Nurses Credentialing Center)	Y (RN & CRNP)	Maintain current RN & CRNP license (renew every two years)	Illinois Department of Financial and Professional Regulations	50 CEU's every 2 years
4	Certified Registered Nurse Anesthetist	CRNA	Masters or Post-Masters	Exam thru CCNA (The Council on Certification of Nurse Anesthetists)	Y (RN)	Maintain current RN licensure (renew every two years, CRNA cert. must be renewed bi-annually)	Illinois Department of Financial and Professional Regulations	50 CEU's within 24 months

(continues)

Appendix 4-1: Scope of Practice Grid (Continued)

	Practitioner Type	Credentials	Educational Background	Certification	Licensed Y or N	Licensure Renewal Requirements	Approving Organization	CEU and Recertification Requirements
5	Physician Assistant	PA-C	Bachelors or Masters plus graduate from accredited PA program	Exam thru NCCPA National Commission on Certification of Physician Assistants	Y	March 1 of even-numbered years	IDFPR – Illinois Department for Professional Regulations	6 year certification (100 hours CEU's every 2 years)
6	Clinical Psychologist/ Psychologist	PhD and/or CP	Doctorate	EPPP (exam for professional practice in psychology) thru ASPPB or Board certified by ABPP (American Board of Professional Psychology)	Y	September 30 of each even numbered year	IDFPR – Illinois Department for Professional Regulations	18 CEU/3 years thru American Psychological Association, AMA, American Psychiatric Association, National Association of Social Workers, etc.
7	Genetic Counselor	CGC Certified Genetic Counselor (optional)	Masters degree or PhD (usually in genetic counseling) 225ILCS 135/1	Exam thru ABGC or ABMG. ABMG only for PhD (American Board of Genetic Counseling or American Board of Medical Genetics) (cite 225 ILCS 135/1)	Y	January 31 of odd numbered years	IDFPR – Illinois Department for Professional Regulations	Recertification by ABGC (American Board of Genetic Counseling) – 30 CEU (250 contact hours over 10 year period. Recertification by exam or CE pathways.
8	Massage Therapist	LMT	Certificate of completion of at least 500 hrs of training of an accredited Massage Therapy School. Licensed by the State of Illinois		Y	Every 2 years	State of IL - IDPR.	IL requires 12 hrs biennially

138

#	Profession	Credential	Education Requirement	Exam		Renewal	Agency	Continuing Education
9	Licensed Clinical Social Worker	LCSW	Bachelors/Masters degree in social work from an educational institution approved by the board	Exam thru Association of Social Work Boards	Y	November 30 of each odd numbered year	IDPR	30 hours of continuing education. At least 3 of the 30 hours must include content related to the ethical practice of social work
10	Speech/Language Pathologist	CCC-SLP	a. master's degree in speech-language pathology from an approved program; b. completion of national exam by National Examination in Speech-Language Pathology and Audiology (PRAXIS) in the form of original grade results from PRAXIS; or submit a copy of certification from the American Speech-Language Hearing Association;	must acquire a current temporary license or pass the State Licensure examination.	Y	Every 2 years	IDPR	20 hrs 2 yrs

(continues)

Appendix 4-1: Scope of Practice Grid (Continued)

	Practitioner Type	Credentials	Educational Background	Certification	Licensed Y or N	Licensure Renewal Requirements	Approving Organization	CEU and Recertification Requirements
			c. nine (9) months of full time supervised professional experience.					
11	Nutritionist	RD	a. bachelor's degree program in human nutrition, foods and nutrition, dietetics, food systems mgt, or nutrition education; b. 900 hours of supervised experience, or current registration with the Commission on Dietetic Registration	Exam thru Commission on Dietetic Registration	Y	2 years	IDFPR	75 hrs every 5 yrs for CDR, 30 hrs every 2yrs for IDPR
12	Physical Therapist	PT, LPT	Bachelors, Masters or PhD in Physical Therapy, Graduate of a physical therapy program approved by the Illinois Department of Professional Regulation (IDPR).	Exam thru NPTE	Y (L.P.T.)	Exp Sept 30th of even number years	IDFPR	No requirement by the State of IL. 30 hours as condition of renewal every 2 years

#							
13	Physical Therapist Assistant	PTA	Graduate of a two (2) year college level physical therapist assistant program approved by the Illinois Department of Professional Regulation (DPR).	Physical Therapist Assistant Exam	Y	Exp Sept 30th of even number years	IDFPR	No requirements by the State of IL
14	Pharmacist	PharmD, RPh	Doctorate in Pharmacy	Must pass NAPLEX (North American Pharmacist Licensure Exam) and MPJE (Multi-state Pharmacy Jurisprudence Exam)	Y	Annually	IDPR	30 hrs every year Determined by IDPR
15	Research Nurse	RN, BSN	BSN	National Council Licensure Examination for Registered Nurse	Y (RN)	Exp May 31 of even number years	IDFPR	20 CEUs every 2 years
16	PCT/CNA	CNA	Professional certification. Applicants must be a graduate of a healthcare training program.	IDPH (IL dept of public health)	N	N/A	IDPH	None required at this time by IL

(continues)

Appendix 4-1: Scope of Practice Grid (Continued)

	Practitioner Type	Credentials	Educational Background	Certification	Licensed Y or N	Licensure Renewal Requirements	Approving Organization	CEU and Recertification Requirements
	Practitioner Type	Credentials	Educational Background	Certification	Licensed Y or N	Licensure Renewal Requirements	Approving Organization	CEU and Recertification Requirements
17								
18	Respiratory Therapist	CRT or RRT	Associates degree from a respiratory therapy education program supported by the Committee on Accreditation for Respiratory Care (CoARC), or its predecessor the Joint Review Committee for Respiratory Therapy Education (JRCRTE), or accredited by the Commission on Accreditation of Allied Health Education Programs (CAAHEP).	Exam thru NBRC (National Board for Respiratory Care)	Y	Every 2 years		24 hours of approved continuing education every renewal period
19	Radiation Therapist	RTT	Associates or Bachelors degree Temporary accreditation requires completion of	Certification thru ARRT (American Registry of Radiologic Technologist), Licensed w/IDFPR	Y	IDFPR - Every 2 years	American Registry of Radiologic Technologists.	Yes, 12 contact hours per year

#	Title	Credential	Education	Certification	Licensure	Renewal	Organization	CE
			an approved educational program. Active accreditation requires passing an approved exam.					
20	Radiologic, Radiology, X-Ray Technologist, Technician or Radiographer	RT or RT(R), IEMA	Graduate of an approved school of Radiologic Technology Licensed in the State of Illinois	Certification thru **ARRT** preferred (American Registry of Radiologic Technologist)	Y	IEMA - 2 years	ARRT (American Registry of Radiologic Technologists) IEMA - IDPR	24 hours every 2 years
21	Interventional Technologist	ARRT, IEMA	Graduate of an approved school of Radiologic Technology	Certification thru **ARRT** (American Registry of Radiologic Technologist)	Y	**RT** - annually IEMA - 2yrs	**RT** - ARRT (American Registry of Radiologic Technologists) IEMA - IDPR (IL Dept of Prof. Regulation)	24 hours every 2 years
22	Computed Tomography Technologist	ARRT(CT), IEMA	Graduate of an approved school of Radiologic Technology	Certification thru **ARRT** (American Registry of Radiologic Technologist)	Y	RT - annually IEMA - 2 yrs	ARRT (American Registry of Radiologic Technologists), IEMA - IDPR	24 hours every 2 years
23	Magnetic Resonance Technologist	ARRT(MR)	Graduate of an approved school of Radiologic Technology + on the job training. (Degree not mandatory)	Certification thru **ARRT** (American Registry of Radiologic Technologist)	Y	RT - annually IEMA - 2 years	ARRT (American Registry of Radiologic Technologists), IEMA - IDPR	24 hours every 2 years
24	Mammographer	ARRT, IEMA	Graduate of an approved school of Radiologic Technology + on the job training.	Certification thru **ARRT** (American Registry of Radiologic Technologist)	Y	RT - annually IEMA - 2 years	ARRT (American Registry of Radiologic Technologists), IEMA - IDPR	24 hours every 2 years

(continues)

Appendix 4-1: Scope of Practice Grid (Continued)

	Practitioner Type	Credentials	Educational Background	Certification	Licensed Y or N	Licensure Renewal Requirements	Approving Organization	CEU and Recertification Requirements
25	Nuclear Medicine Technologist	ARRT or NMTCB, IEMA	Graduate of an approved school of Radiologic Technology	Certification thru **ARRT** (American Registry of Radiologic Technologist)	Y	**RT** - annually IEMA - 2 yrs **NMTCB** - annually	**RT** - ARRT(American Registry of Radiologic Technologists) IEMA - IDPR **NMTCB** - annually	24 hours every 2 years
26	Sonographer or Ultra-sonographer, Vascular Technologist	RDMS, RVT	Graduate of an approved school of medical sonography. Credentials in ultrasound (such as ARDMS-American Registry of Diagnostic Medical Sonographers)	Certification exam administered by ARDMS (American Registry for Diagnostic Medical Sonographer)	N	ARDMS - annually	ARDMS (American Registry for Diagnostic Sonographers)	30 hrs every 3 years
27	Medical Laboratory Technician	MLT(AMT)	Associate degree	Exam thru AMT (American Medical Technologist) Board of Registry Exam through ASCP (American Society for Clinical Pathology)	N	N/A	AMT(American Medical Technologists)	Initial certification after 1/1/06 - 45 points every 3 yrs., initial certification before 1/1/06 - no CEU required
		MLT(ASCP)	Associate degree		N	N/A	ASCP (American Society for Clinical Pathology)	Initial certification beginning 1/1/ 04 - 36

#								credits every 3 years, initial certification before 1/1/04 – no CEU required
28	Phlebotomy Technician	Not required	Phlebotomy certification from a recognized program preferred	Not required	N	Certification does not expire	NA	NA
29	Medical Technologist	MT	Minimum of three years of college plus internship as a Medical Technologist with Bachelor's degree in Medical Technology and certification as an MT or a combination of college credits and a year of full time experience necessary to qualify for certification as a Medical Technologist.	NA	N	NA	NA	NA
30	Acupuncturist	L.Ac	Graduated from the equivalent of a four year bachelors program Graduated from an accredited acupuncture program in the United States	Exam through NCCAOM for national certification; NCCAOM Diplomate status (every 4 years)	Y	Biennial	State of IL	NCCAOM 60 Credits for 4 year renewal; IL 30 hrs 2 years

(continues)

Appendix 4-1: Scope of Practice Grid (Continued)

	Practitioner Type	Credentials	Educational Background	Certification	Licensed Y or N	Licensure Renewal Requirements	Approving Organization	CEU and Recertification Requirements
31	Mind Body Therapist	LCSW	Master's degree in social work or another comparable area of counseling	Licensed or license eligible Association of the Social Work Boards (ASWB)	Y	Two years (All licenses expire on November 30 of each odd numbered year.)	IDFPR	30 hours of continuing education required during pre-renewal period - effective November 1993.
32	Doctor of Naturopathic Medicine	ND	Doctor of Naturopathic Medicine	Exam thru NABNE (North American Board of Naturopathic Examiners); NPLEX Exam (Naturopathic Physicians Licensing Examination)	Y	Based on the licensing state where the ND holds license	Vermont Office of the Secretary of State Washington State Department of Health Naturopathy Program State of Arizona Naturopathic Physician Medical Board Maine Board of Complementary Health Care Providers	Vermont: 30 credits Washington: 20 credits Arizona: 30 credits Maine: 37 credits
33	Dentist	DMD	Doctor of Dentistry		Y	Every 3 years	Illinois Department of Financial and Professional Regulations	32 hours CME

Chapter 5

Medical Staff

Paul J. Voss

Key Learning Objectives

By the end of this chapter, the reader will be able to:

- Describe the organization of the typical hospital and the respective roles of the medical staff and the hospital board.

- Discuss the role of the hospital's governing board and its interaction with the medical staff and the organization of the medical staff.

- Understand the elements of and describe the legal issues associated with the appointment process, delineation of clinical privileges, review and reappointment, modification and termination of clinical privileges.

- Delineate concerns and legal protections available with regard to the procedures for adverse actions against members.

- Understand the scope of liability exposure of participants in the various processes.

Chapter Outline

Introduction

This chapter provides an overview of the legal aspects of the relationship between a hospital and its medical staff, and the relationship of the medical staff with those who seek to be part of it and to exercise clinical privileges needed to practice within the hospital. The legal issues associated with empaneling and maintaining the medical staff are the focus of the chapter. Legal cases and statutes are discussed to illustrate the basic principles, trends, and the types of exceptions that help define and shape the area of "medical staff law." Remember that there are frequent developments in statutory, regulatory, and common law (case law) that alter the positions of courts and enforcement agencies on the legal issues discussed in this chapter.

This chapter addresses the following topics:

- The Organization of the Hospital and Role of the Hospital Board and Medical Staff (5-1)
- Appointment to the Medical Staff (5-2)
- Delineation of Clinical Privileges (5-3)
- Periodic Review and Reappointment (5-4)
- Modification and Termination of Clinical Privileges (5-5)
- Review Procedures for Adverse Actions (5-6)
- Potential Liability of Those Involved in the Process of Making Medical Staff Appointment and Clinical Privilege Decisions (5-7)

5-1 The Organization of the Hospital and Role of the Hospital Board and Medical Staff

As **Figure 5-1** illustrates, nearly one-third of annual healthcare expenditures in the United States is spent on hospital care, making it the largest individual sector of healthcare spending. Tens of millions of patients receive treatment each year in hospitals.

Ensuring that proper structures are in place to ensure the availability and monitor the quality of care is thus a critical function of hospitals. This function, along with the overall operation of hospitals, is administered by management and overseen by hospital governance as well as multiple external regulators. See **Figure 5-2**.

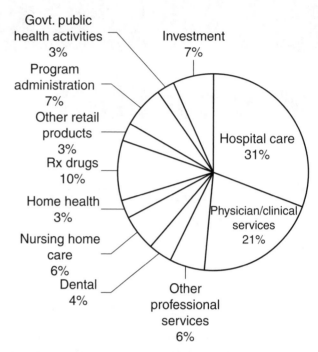

Figure 5-1 National Health Expenditures, 2010

Reproduced from: Martin A.B., et al., (2012). "Growth In U.S. Health Spending Remained Slow in 2010; Health Share of Gross Domestic Product Was Unchanged from 2009," *Health Affairs*, 31(1), 208-219.

Hospital facilities are typically under the authority of a governing board whose roles include oversight and management of the hospital facility. The Joint Commission (TJC), which accredits a large majority of U.S. hospitals, publishes and surveys hospitals for compliance with many "governance" and other standards related to this responsibility as part of its hospital accreditation survey process. Accreditation is discussed in greater detail elsewhere in this text. Like case and statutory law, TJC standards change from time to time and are discussed here for illustrative purposes.

The board has ultimate authority over the hospital; this authority must be exercised consistent with satisfactory patient care. Since typically hospital boards are composed primarily of businesspeople from the community rather than physicians on the staff, a hospital board looks to the medical staff to monitor quality of care and provide expert advice on appointment and clinical privilege decisions. Through the hospital bylaws, the board delegates to the medical staff the authority and duty to carry out medical

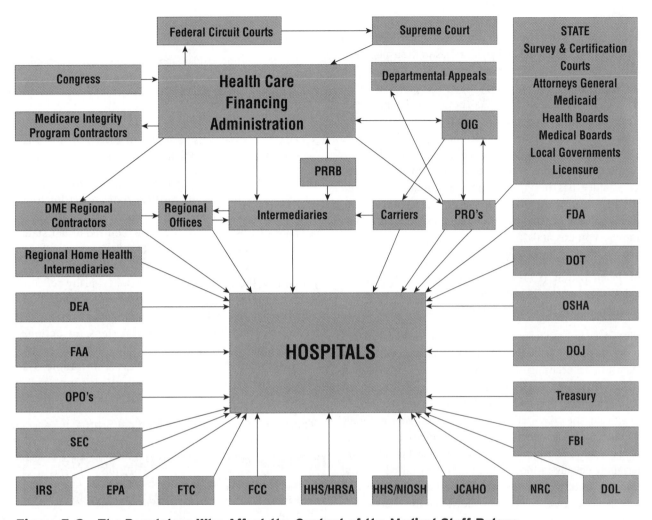

Figure 5-2 The Regulators Who Affect the Content of the Medical Staff Bylaws

Adapted from *Patients or Paperwork* by permission, Copyright 2001, American Hospital Association.

aspects of patient care. The board retains authority and responsibility to approve appointments to the medical staff, grant or decrease clinical privileges, and assure that there is an appropriate procedure for monitoring quality of care, consistent with the standard of care for hospital facilities.

The board's duty to maintain appropriate procedures and to see that they are properly implemented to assure quality care is recognized by some courts as a "nondelegable duty." That means that, although the board can look to the medical staff for expertise in judging qualifications of applicants for medical staff membership and privileges and evaluating the quality of care provided by members,

the board cannot delegate ultimate responsibility for those tasks to the medical staff or any other body. In a representative case, the Wisconsin Supreme Court found a hospital liable for injuries to a patient by a physician because the hospital should never have appointed him to the medical staff.[1] The hospital had not checked his professional credentials and references, a duty that the hospital itself must perform. A check would have uncovered discrepancies and misrepresentations that would have most certainly led to denial of appointment. Similarly, an Arizona court found a hospital liable for failing to curtail the clinical privileges of a physician who had several bad results with a given procedure, resulting in multiple malpractice suits.[2] The absence of a medical staff recommendation to curtail privileges was not an effective excuse. Most states find liability if a hospital fails to act when it has actual knowledge of or reason to suspect serious problems. The Minnesota Supreme Court noted in a related case that some thirty states recognize so-called "negligent credentialing" or "corporate negligence" by a hospital board as an actionable tort theory while only two courts had rejected the theories outright.[3] The Nevada Supreme Court refused to attach a nondelegable duty to a hospital for the care in its emergency room stating, "The Legislature has heavily regulated hospitals and would have codified a nondelegable duty to emergency room patients if the Legislature had intended such a duty to be imposed on hospitals."[4]

TJC accreditation standards, Medicare Conditions of Participation (COPs), and most hospital licensing rules also require board involvement in granting and monitoring the privileges of staff members.[5]

Physicians in hospitals are organized into a medical staff in order to comply with TJC standards, Medicare COPs, and state hospital licensing rules. Other healthcare organizations, such as skilled nursing facilities, can also have a medical staff so that membership and clinical privileges are required to practice in the organization.[6] Those organizations generally do not have as elaborate structures as hospitals do, but many of the legal concerns and principles discussed in this chapter apply equally in those settings.[7] The organized medical staff has collective accountability to the governing board for the quality of care delivered by individual members of the medical staff.

The medical staff organization is required to be "self-governing" under TJC standard LD 01.05.01 and includes officers and an executive committee to act in matters that do not require approval of the entire staff. The staff generally carries out its clinical functions through other committees to address specific issues, such as infection control, pharmaceutical utilization, and credentials review. In smaller hospitals, these functions can be performed by the entire medical staff. In larger hospitals, several specialty departments with their own organizations are often coordinated by the overall medical staff organization. TJC requires clinical department heads to be certified by the appropriate specialty board or to have "affirmatively established comparable competence through the credentialing process."[8]

Functions of the organized hospital medical staff include:

- facilitating communication among the medical staff members and with the hospital;

- implementing hospital and medical staff policies and procedures;

- recommending initial appointments and reappointments to the medical staff and scope of clinical privileges to be granted;

- providing continuing medical education; and

- taking other actions necessary to govern the medical staff and to relate to the hospital board.

MEDICAL STAFF BYLAWS. The organization, rights, and responsibilities of the medical staff are set forth in medical staff bylaws that are approved by the medical staff and the hospital. Hospitals are required under state hospital licensing statutes, TJC Hospital Accreditation Standards, and Medicare COPs to have medical staff bylaws, and the content of the bylaws typically reflects these and other statutory, regulatory, and accreditation requirements. See **Table 5-1**. Components of the medical staff bylaws, such as procedural steps for actions affecting medical staff members, also are shaped by state peer review protections and case law. **Table 5-2** illustrates the key players in the credentialing process.

Table 5-1 The Five R's of Medical Staff Membership

Medical Staff Bylaws typically describe "the Five Rs" of Medical Staff Membership:
The _role_ of the medical staff
Its _relationship_ with the hospital and individual members
The _rights_ of its members
The _responsibilities_ of its members
The _resolution_ of disputes in the various relationships

In some states, medical staff bylaws are considered a contract between the medical staff and the hospital, or, if not a contract per se, a document with which courts will require substantial compliance by the staff and hospital. In other states, the bylaws are not considered a contract or to have the same, binding effect as a contract. Since 1985, TJC has required that medical staff bylaws be adopted and changed only with the mutual consent of the medical staff and hospital.[9] Before 1985, some courts recognized the legal right and even the duty of the hospital board to change the medical staff bylaws unilaterally, when necessary.[10] Hospitals generally seek mutually acceptable changes even when this

Table 5-2 The Credentialing Process

WHO IS INVOLVED IN THE CREDENTIALING PROCESS?
APPLICANT
MEDICAL STAFF OFFICE
OUTSIDE SOURCES OF INFORMATION ABOUT APPLICANT
CREDENTIALS VERIFICATION ORGANIZATION
DEPARTMENT CHAIR
CREDENTIALS COMMITTEE, IF APPLICABLE
MEDICAL EXECUTIVE COMMITTEE
(OUTSIDE REVIEWERS?)
GOVERNING BODY
(THE COURTS?)

Based on a chart in The Joint Commission's "Medical Staff Handbook – A Guide to Joint Commission Standards." [1999]

requires prolonged negotiations. The resulting changes are more likely to be implemented fully when there is mutual agreement. Unilateral changes typically are considered a last resort, adopted only to deal with circumstances such as when impasses in mutual adoption efforts may cause the hospital to be out of compliance with its accreditation or legal obligations.

One of the limits of the contract approach to bylaws is illustrated by a 2003 Illinois appellate court case.[11] According to the court decision, when the hospital found that it had a higher mortality rate for cardiac surgery, it retained an outside peer review group who concluded that some of the problems were due to the care provided by the head of the Department of Surgery. The head initially agreed to have some surgeries supervised. When he later withdrew this agreement and refused supervision, the hospital consulted with medical staff leadership who are alleged to have refused to get involved. Based on imminent danger to patients and the noncooperation of the medical staff leadership, the hospital imposed summary suspension. A trial court issued a temporary restraining order based on its interpretation that the bylaws required all summary suspensions to be initiated by the medical staff. The appellate court reversed the restraining order. The appellate court ruled that under state law, the ultimate responsibility rested with the hospital, so the bylaws could not bar action by the hospital. Any bylaw provision that barred appropriate hospital action would be unenforceable because it would be against public policy. However, the court

interpreted the bylaws to permit the action the hospital had taken. Thus, even in states where bylaws are contracts, there are limits as to what can be put in bylaws and still be enforceable. Medical staff bylaws in "contract states" are, as this case illustrates, subject to the general contract law principles including those that provide that contracts that are against public policy are unenforceable. Litigation resulting from an alleged breach of the "bylaws contract" (especially when staff membership and privileges are adversely affected) is common in a number of states and is discussed further below.

Medical staff bylaws typically define the rights and responsibilities of the medical staff in detail. Those details include procedures that must be followed when determining who may practice in the hospital. Staff members and hospitals have learned (often through litigation) that thoroughly following the procedures outlined in medical staff bylaws can help avoid claims of inappropriate or inadequate credentialing by both excluded practitioners and injured patients.

TJC encountered some of the strongest reaction it had ever dealt with from the hospital industry and hospital and medical staff organizations alike when it proposed a 2007 medical staff accreditation standard, "MS1.20," which required that certain procedures such as the medical staff fair hearing and appeal process (and the related "procedural details") appear in the medical staff document. Many hospitals were concerned because they employed separate manuals, outside of the bylaws, in which fair hearings and other lengthy processes mentioned in MS1.20 (such as credentialing) were described. Such manuals frequently provided that they could be amended by the Medical Executive Committee (the medical staff's internal governance or "MEC") alone, without the consent of the entire medical staff that is required for changes to the bylaws document. Hospital advocates stressed the importance of amending these procedures quickly when deficiencies in them (including those identified by TJC) were identified. Part of TJC's articulated rationale behind MS1.20, however, was to ensure that both the hospital and medical staff have appropriate input on the content and any changes to these important processes.

Based largely upon this critical reaction, TJC suspended implementation of MS1.20 and appointed an eighteen-member task force of industry representatives to consider and address industry concerns in a way that would still achieve the goal of appropriate cooperative hospital/medical staff input on these important medical staff policies. The new standard, MS01.01.01, reflected such a compromise. MS01.01.01 still requires that certain procedures (described in the Elements of Performance that TJC uses to judge a hospital's compliance with a given standard) be included in the medical staff bylaws, but provides that their "associated details" may be placed in any of the medical staff bylaws, rules and regulations, or policies. The standard also permits the medical staff to determine what the "associated details" are, where they will be located, and whether their adoption will be delegated to the MEC acting alone. TJC indicated that the revised standard is "designed to support a well-functioning, positive relationship between a hospital's medical staff and governing body, which is critical to the safety and quality of care provided to patients."[12]

COOPERATION AND CONFLICT. Just as hospitals depend on the medical staff for both providing quality professional care and evaluating those who may do so, medical staff members depend on the hospital for providing the equipment, personnel, and other resources they need. This mutual dependence underscores why it is important that medical staff bylaws include a framework for cooperation and cooperative decision making between the medical staff and board. Mechanisms to assure fair and equal treatment of medical staff members also facilitate this cooperation between the hospital and the medical staff.

Hospital and organized medical staff efforts generally should not be focused on defining ultimate legal rights; they should be focused on minimizing misunderstandings and conflicts, seeking mutually acceptable solutions, and resolving impasses without resorting to the judicial process.

The hospital and medical staff must work together to take appropriate steps to maintain consistent, appropriate standards within the hospital. In some cases, however, this collegial approach breaks down.[13]

For example, medical staff members have become competitors of the hospital and sought to retain their hospital privileges to support their competing businesses. When hospitals have sought to restrict this outside practice by their staff, it has been labeled "economic credentialing," which has been alleged by some medical staffs to be an antitrust violation,[14] challenged by others as violating the fraud and abuse laws, and has been the subject of other litigation. "Economic credentialing," defined by organizations such as the American Medical Association, is "the use of criteria unrelated to professional competence or quality in the granting of medical staff privileges," and is discussed further later in this chapter. Unilateral amendment of medical staff bylaws, briefly discussed above, is another area of hospital-medical staff disputes.

Medical staff have also objected when the hospital appoints officers or rejects the officers nominated by the medical staff. A California court approved a hospital board's rejection of the medical staff's choice for president because the bylaws reserved this authority to the board. The board later settled the suit and accepted the elected president,[15] perhaps to avoid the upheaval in the hospital-medical staff relationship. A Florida appellate court refused to order a hospital to hold a medical staff election.[16] The hospital had appointed temporary officers due to disruption of operations. However, the court indicated that if the medical staff held its own election, a court could then decide which set of officers should preside.

In 1994, a Wisconsin court refused to reinstate a chief of staff who had been removed by a hospital.[17] This type of removal from a medical staff usually is rare, but does occur. Such hospital actions can be disruptive to the relationship between the hospital and other medical staff embers.

In most hospitals, the medical staff is divided into departments along specialty lines. There is generally discretion to reorganize departments, but disputes can arise from such changes.[18] The selection and removal of department heads have likewise led to disputes. Generally, courts will not order the reinstatement of removed officers or department heads,[19] but there have been exceptions.[20]

Some medical staff members have filed complaints with regulatory agencies related to governance disputes with the hospital.[21] There also are cases where medical staffs have sought to remove the hospital CEO and even board members.[22]

Some medical staffs have sought to be recognized as a separate legal entity. A few states have permitted this, with one result being that the medical staff then had standing to sue the hospital, and the hospital could sue the medical staff.[23] Other states have rejected this concept, finding the medical staff to be part of the hospital. One benefit of being recognized as a part of the hospital is that in most jurisdictions, the hospital and medical staff cannot be found to be engaged in a conspiracy, for purposes of antitrust law challenges. In short, the "intra-corporate conspiracy doctrine" states that an entity cannot conspire with itself because there is only one entity, not two or more required for a conspiracy. It has been held that the medical executive committee is not a separate legal entity, thus, it generally does not have standing to bring suit.[24]

Unfortunately, some hospital medical staffs or parts of medical staffs have also responded to disputes by choosing to boycott hospitals.[25] Some hospitals have been reluctant to use the antitrust laws to challenge such boycotts, but some hospitals, other effected entities, and government agencies have initiated action. Most of these enforcement actions have been settled with the boycotting physicians agreeing not to engage in boycotts.[26]

The degree to which medical staffs resort to litigation and the type of issues involved vary from state to state. One source has stated that "reportedly, Los Angeles has two branches of its trial courts which are dedicated to exclusively deal with hospital/medical staff matters."[27] Avoiding all such hospital-medical staff conflicts can help ensure that the vital functions that the medical staff serves both to the hospital and its patients go on unimpeded by what would otherwise mean the direction of time, money, other resources, and attention to litigation instead of toward patient care.

5-2 Appointment to the Medical Staff

Identified, competent practitioners must be responsible for the care of each patient to satisfy most payers' definitions of a "hospital" and of a "medically necessary admission." Failure to satisfy these definitions can mean an institution does not qualify as a "participating hospital" to Medicare or other programs or for payment for its services, respectively.

Medical staffs are primarily composed of physicians, that is, medical doctors and doctors of osteopathy. In its early years, it was alleged that the Joint Commission on Accreditation of Hospitals (which later changed its name to the Joint Commission on Healthcare Organizations [JCAHO] and is now called The Joint Commission [TJC] and organized medicine sought to keep osteopathic physicians off the medical staff.[28] During the 1960s, largely because of lobbying and litigation, most of the barriers were removed.[29] This has not been a significant issue for many years, though it has surfaced from time to time.

Podiatrists and dentists are generally permitted to be members of the medical staff with some states requiring this.[30] Prior to 2004, TJC required podiatrists and dentists to have a physician involved in the care of patients they admit to the hospital. In 2004, TJC deleted this requirement, leaving the determination of the scope of podiatry and dental privileges to state law and hospital policy.[31]

Some hospitals permit psychologists to be members of the medical staff and some states require that hospitals do this as well.[32] When psychologists are permitted to admit patients, they are also generally required to have a physician involved in the care of admitted patients.[33]

Hospitals are generally not required to permit other disciplines to be members of the medical staff,[34] but some have permitted chiropractors,[35] midwives,[36] and persons from other disciplines to be members.

TJC and other accrediting bodies have increased their attention on nurse practitioners and physician's assistants as use of such individuals to save physician time and patient dollars has increased. As they must have for independent licensed physicians and medical staff members, accredited hospitals are required to have a system for reviewing their credentials and determining the scope of what they are permitted to do,[37] but in most states, hospitals are not required to make them members of the medical staff.[38] These individuals have traditionally been credentialed through processes of the medical staff to meet accreditation requirements.

Changes to COPs for hospitals effective July 2012 permit hospitals to grant privileges to both physicians and nonphysicians to practice within their State. The State permitted scope of practice provided that "the medical staff must examine the credentials of all eligible candidates (as defined by the governing body) and then make recommendations for privileges and medical staff membership to the governing body."

Further, the Center for Medicare and Medicaid Services noted that technically, despite apparent confusion on the issue, its current regulations already allow hospitals to appoint nonphysician practitioners as members of their medical staffs, as long as the state law in which the hospital operates permits it. The changes were proposed to "modernize hospitals' medical staffing policies" in order "to provide hospitals the clarity and flexibility they need under federal law to maximize their staffing opportunities for all practitioners . . . particularly for nonphysician practitioners, under their individual states' laws." CMS indicated this could reduce the effect of physician shortages and patient wait times (which may also reduce costs and promote more efficient care).[39]

> Changes to the Medicare COPs for hospitals reflect the industry's movement toward integration and the use of nonphysician treatment where appropriate that are both thought to be essential in containing healthcare costs and providing more efficient care.

A medical license does not give a physician the right to practice in a particular hospital. Hospitals must screen physicians before appointment to the medical staff and each physician, even if employed by the hospital, must apply for medical staff appointment and prove that he or she satisfies the appointment criteria. The burden of proof is on the applying physician, especially if the medical staff bylaws so provide, as many do. Many court cases have involved medical staff credentialing disputes. Most of the cases have alleged that either the criteria were not fairly applied or that such criteria used are not permitted either under the bylaws themselves or otherwise under the law. Procedural issues that have also been litigated are discussed later in the chapter. The following section reviews some common criteria for initial appointment.

PERMITTED CRITERIA. In addition to the obvious "threshold criteria" of licensure, education, training, and experience, some of the criteria that hospitals typically use (and courts have permitted) for review of applicants include:

- a complete and accurate application;
- verification of credentials;
- references;
- a demonstrated ability to work with others;
- board certification or equivalent training and experience;
- payment of dues and assessments;
- geographic proximity to the hospital;
- agreement to provide indigent care;
- malpractice insurance;
- the need for additional staff in the specialty;
- certain economic criteria, such as utilization, especially if related to quality;
- health status; and
- background check.

Some of these criteria, as discussed in the following, are subject to limitations and are not permitted in all states.

Generally, the same standards and criteria should apply to all applicants.[40] Application of uniform criteria to all applicants helps avoid allegations of bias or unfairness in the credentialing process.

Application. Hospitals require a complete and accurate application form, including an agreement to abide by hospital and medical staff rules.[41] Courts have upheld denial of appointment or termination based on

incomplete or falsified applications.[42] Many cases of alleged negligence by a hospital in its credentialing process have pointed to a hospital credentialing an individual despite an incomplete application. Physicians should be required, along with providing other information, to (1) present evidence of medical education, training, recent experience, current competence, current licensure, and health status and (2) disclose professional liability actions and pending and completed governmental, institutional, and professional disciplinary actions against them. In some cases, the health status information may need to be collected later in the process, as discussed later in this section. Some states will suspend or revoke a physician's medical license for false answers on an application for hospital clinical privileges.[43] Refusal to release information concerning discipline at other hospitals may be grounds for denial of an application.[44]

Some states, such as Illinois, specifically permit a hospital to utilize a "preapplication process" to require an applicant to submit proof of meeting certain objective, threshold criteria such as licensure and education before he or she is given a full application. If the applicant fails to provide the required proof in a timely manner, the hospital is not required to give the applicant an application or the greater procedural rights that a full-applicant has under the state's licensing act. Advocates of prescreening processes also suggest that they may lead to less litigation against a hospital because denial of appointment for failure to provide complete information for a prescreening application (or inability to provide evidence of meeting objective threshold criteria) may not be a "quality issue" that is reportable to the National Practitioner Data Bank (NPDB), and discussed in the following.

Without this accompanying "black mark" against the unqualified applicant he may be less likely to fight his denial of an application than he would be if a NPDB report would also result. Hospitals generally do not have to process incomplete applications or applications from persons who made previous commitments not to reapply.[45]

A history of malpractice complaints or judgments does not necessarily disqualify a physician from membership of privileges.[46] Malpractice histories should be examined on a case-by-case basis.

References. Satisfactory references may be required of initial applicants,[47] but some cases suggest, not from the present medical staff whose competence and character have already been established by practice in the hospital.[48]

Ability to Work with Others. Courts in many states have accepted a requirement that applicants and members demonstrate ability to work harmoniously with other physicians and hospital staff.[49] Most states have not limited the degree of inability to work with others that justifies denial, but a few states have placed limits. A New Jersey court accepted that "prospective disharmony" was a reasonable basis for denial if "valid and constructive criticism of hospital practice" is not equated with disharmony.[50] The court noted that "a person has a right to disagree with the policy or practice, but he does not have a right to be disagreeable in doing so." Free speech issues are discussed later in this chapter. The California Supreme Court accepted inability to work with others as a basis for denial when it presents "a real and substantial danger that patients treated by him might receive other than a 'high quality of medical care' at the facility."[51] A hospital that can show that a practitioner's inappropriate or disruptive conduct adversely affects the quality of care provided by others in the hospital will often fair better in litigation involving removal of such member.[52] Disruptive behavior, including related TJC standards, is discussed further below.

Board Certification. Many hospitals require that physicians be board eligible or board certified before being granted specialty privileges. Some hospitals require board certification to be obtained within a specified time.

Most courts have upheld hospital requirements of board certification or completion of an approved residency before specialty clinical privileges are granted.[53] A California appellate court upheld a hospital requirement that dilation and curettage privileges be granted only to physicians who had completed a residency in obstetrics and gynecology.[54] A few courts have invalidated board certification requirements of public hospitals.[55]

One way to avoid controversy is to require board certification or equivalent training and experience.[56] This requirement permits the hospital to avail itself of the strengths of the private certification system while leaving open a channel to deal with individual applicants on a case-by-case basis. Such a case-by-case basis may, however, open up risks of alleged bias since different individuals may be treated differently.

A workable exceptions process also avoids facing a risk of failure to meet Medicare COPs, which specifically forbid basing clinical privilege decisions solely on board status.[57] It is not clear whether individual physicians can use this as a basis for judicial relief from such requirements.[58] It is

probable that only the federal government can enforce the Medicare rules, and its ultimate sanction is to terminate Medicare participation, which is unlikely, especially before a hospital would first have a chance to correct the violation.

TJC states that heads of departments should be board certified in the specialty or prove comparable competence.[59]

Some managed care entities also require board certification for participation.[60]

Dues. Physicians may be required to pay dues, fees, and assessments to apply for and retain medical staff membership.[61] For example, a Michigan appellate court upheld the suspension of a physician who refused to pay a $100 assessment levied by the medical staff executive committee to furnish a medical library.[62]

Geographic Proximity. Some courts have upheld geographic criteria that require an applicant to live or practice within a certain distance of the hospital, stated in terms of miles, travel time, or location close enough that the applicant is reasonably able to provide continuity of care.[63] These rules are intended to assure response to patient needs, especially during emergencies. Hospitals that fail to have appropriate coverage after-hours may risk Emergency Medical Treatment and Active Labor Act ("EMTALA") and Medicare COP violations. In the past, TJC expressly recognized geographic location as an appropriate criterion, but now does not address the issue.[64] Geographic limits based on political boundaries are less likely to be enforceable.[65]

Because the goal of geographic criteria is to assure timely coverage of patient needs, some hospitals accept coverage arrangements as an alternative means of compliance. For example, coverage may include (1) a nearby individual or group that agrees to provide coverage for a more distant applicant or (2) a group of more distant applicants may agree to have one person on duty at the hospital or on call nearby at all times.

Indigent Care. Physicians can be required to provide uncompensated care to those who are unable to pay.[66] Since nearly all hospitals are required to provide some emergency services to those who are unable to pay and many hospitals are required to provide other services to these patients, arrangements must be made for medical coverage. Although some of these services are provided by employed physicians or physicians with special contracts, many of the services are provided by nonemployed members of the medical staff (typically, the vast majority of the medical staff) without a separate contract.

Malpractice Insurance. Since 1975, appellate courts have consistently upheld reasonable requirements of malpractice insurance as a condition of medical staff membership.[67] In a malpractice suit, both the hospital and the physicians are generally sued. If one defendant is not adequately insured, the burden of any payment will fall disproportionately on the others. Thus, there is a legitimate business interest in assuring adequate malpractice protection. In the past, TJC recognized adequate professional liability insurance as an appropriate criterion but is now silent on the issue.[68] Some courts have required flexibility in enforcing such rules because they can become unreasonable when, for example, no malpractice insurance is available.[69] Some states have imposed statutory requirements for coverage,[70] but generally hospitals are still free to impose more strict requirements. Though finding staff bylaws to be contractually binding, an Illinois appellate court allowed a hospital to raise unilaterally (without staff approval) malpractice insurance limits higher than the medical staff bylaws provided.[71] In a few states, hospitals can be liable to malpractice claimants when they fail to check on the physician's insurance status.[72]

Staff Size Limitations. Hospitals may limit the size of the medical staff in some circumstances. Out of concern for antitrust and related reasons, the limits should be adopted unilaterally by the board with documentation of the reasons, which may include quality reasons determined with limited, appropriate quality-related input from the medical staff. Courts are concerned that these limits not be used to protect the economic interests of present medical staff members. Limitations on the number of staff members in certain specialties have been upheld in several court decisions.[73] However, a New Jersey court invalidated a moratorium on new staff appointments because inadequate evidence had been presented that the moratorium was needed to assure appropriate patient care.[74] The New Jersey Supreme Court disapproved closed staff arrangements that permitted only new physicians who associated with current members[75] or who had not practiced in the area for the past two years.[76] A North Carolina appellate court ruled that a hospital could close a part of its medical staff if the moratorium was reasonable for the hospital and community and was fairly administered but that the challenging podiatrist was entitled to a trial in which he could attempt to show the moratorium was unreasonable.[77] In the past, TJC recognized the appropriateness of criteria related to the ability of the hospital to provide facilities and support services but is now silent on the issue.[78]

When a hospital enters into an exclusive contract with one physician or group for a specialty or procedure, others are not eligible to be granted privileges for that specialty or procedure. Courts generally permit hospitals to start a new exclusive contract and terminate the privileges of other physicians to perform the specialty or procedure.[79] In 1994, Illinois passed a law that requires notice and a hearing before privileges of others are terminated due to an exclusive contract.[80] Exclusive contracts are discussed in greater detail below.

One of the factors that the IRS uses for determining whether a hospital qualifies for tax exemption is whether it has an open medical staff.[81] Such factors are not enforceable by private parties, such as other applying physicians. However, the IRS could potentially use the absence of this factor as the basis for considering revocation of the hospital tax exemption or at least as a significant factor among others. The minimum characteristics necessary to assure tax exemption remain unclear (see discussion elsewhere in this text). The purpose behind the open staff requirement was to demonstrate that the hospital "operated to serve a public rather than a private interest." The focus appears to have been on assuring that the general public could gain access to the hospital, not to assure that physicians could use the hospital for their private practices. There was also a concern that a closed staff could result in insider benefit to the physicians on the staff.[82] Again, the focus appears to be on avoiding benefit to insiders, not on providing benefit to other physicians. Thus, it is possible that the IRS would accept a closed staff if there were contractual commitments and hospital policies that assured public access and effective nonphysician control of the benefits received by those on the closed staff. Such an arrangement could provide the public with better access and more reliable, predictable quality coverage than an open staff. Tax exemption has been approved for entities that include closed departments in other contexts without addressing the impact on hospital tax exemption.[83]

Sometimes states attempt to challenge closed staffs in other ways. In 2002, Maine threatened a hospital with loss of a certificate of need for heart surgery unless it opened its staff.[84]

Economic Credentialing in General. As the above discussion reveals, most of the criteria that have been the traditional concern of hospitals and other healthcare entities have been criteria to assure that competent practitioners will provide quality patient care. Some criteria, however, used in determining whether or not a practitioner may obtain and/or maintain medical staff membership and privileges to perform procedures are said to be "unrelated to professional competence or quality of a practitioner's care." Such criteria have been labeled "economic credentialing" criteria. Several different criteria are lumped together under the label of economic credentialing. Three of these criteria are (1) promoting efficient practice, (2) requiring participation in hospital managed care and related arrangements, and (3) avoiding economic competition with the hospital. Some persons also apply the economic credentialing label to exclusive contracts. Exclusive contracts are addressed separately in this chapter. Although still controversial, many of these criteria have been upheld by courts.

Hospitals have generally not required participation in managed care plans as a condition of medical staff membership, except in hospital-based specialties, since these specialties often have exclusive rights, by contract, to provide their services in the hospital and their nonparticipation would mean managed care patients would no receive such services. The requirement for hospital-based specialists to participate is usually found in a contract between the physician and hospital, rather than in the medical staff requirements.

Efficient practice issues usually arise in the context of review of performance, and economic competition issues usually arise in the context of nonrenewal or termination of clinical privileges. These issues will be discussed in those sections of this chapter dealing with economic credentialing of active medical staff members. One case of economic competition did arise in the application context. In 1992, a Florida court upheld denial of surgical privileges to an applicant who was the head of the open heart surgery program at the competing hospital.[85] The South Dakota Supreme Court permitted a private hospital to close its medical staff for some procedures and to deny applications of physicians with an ownership in a competing facility based in part on the duty of the hospital board to ensure the continuing viability of the hospital, akin to the notion of "fiduciary credentialing" discussed below.[86]

Health Status. TJC requires that health status be used as a criterion to the extent permitted by the Americans with Disabilities Act (ADA).[87] The ADA regulates when inquiries can be made concerning health status in situations related to employment. Even though most physicians are not employees, the ADA restrictions may apply to some

medical staff applicants due to the impact of the medical staff membership decision on their other employment relationships.[88] If a hospital determines that the ADA applies, it should limit application inquiries concerning health status to questions permitted by the ADA. Any offer of membership can then be contingent on ascertainment of health status. The ADA permits consistently applied inquiries and examinations after the employment-related decision has otherwise been made.

Background Check. Some states require a criminal background check for all persons who have direct patient contact, including medical staff members, and bar persons with certain convictions from any direct patient contact. Even when it is not required, some health care providers require a background check.[89]

UNACCEPTABLE CRITERIA. Many practitioners who were denied medical staff membership have challenged the criteria that were applied in making such a determination. Some courts have found certain criteria to be unacceptable, including (1) criteria that violate nondiscrimination laws, (2) citizenship requirement, (3) required kickbacks and other illegal contracts, (4) mandatory medical society membership, and (5) nonstandardized tests. Whether or not criteria are permissible (other than those that involve clear violations of federal civil rights and other laws) is often a matter of the given state's case law.

Violation of Nondiscrimination Laws. Hospitals cannot base their refusal to appoint a physician on the applicant's race, creed, color, sex, national origin, or handicap. Alleged violations are often addressed under the antidiscrimination laws discussed elsewhere in this text.[90] These laws generally apply to all institutions receiving federal funds, whether the institutions are public or private. Some of these laws also apply to certain entities that do not receive federal funding.

Some of the nondiscrimination laws apply only to employees; they generally do not apply to nonemployee medical staff members.[91] However, it is advisable to avoid discrimination based on the grounds encompassed in these employment laws because in some circumstances nonemployment nondiscrimination laws may apply.[92]

Citizenship. Citizenship can probably not be used as a criterion.[93] Thus, legal aliens with appropriate licenses and an immigration status permitting medical practice probably cannot be excluded on the basis of lack of citizenship. Exclusion of undocumented aliens has been permitted and in some circumstances required.[94]

Illegal Contracts. In most states, there are limits on the contracts that facilities can require physicians to enter. In 1986, a New York appellate court questioned a nursing home that had required a physician to enter a fee-splitting arrangement before allowing practice in the facility.[95]

Medical Society Membership. Hospitals generally cannot require membership in a medical society.[96] Courts have viewed such requirements as an abdication of the hospital's responsibility to screen applications and have been concerned that medical society membership could be denied for discriminatory reasons. A few older court decisions accepted this criterion for private hospitals,[97] but it is doubtful that courts would permit this criterion today except in states that do not review any private hospital criteria.

Nonstandardized Tests. A California public hospital adopted a requirement that applicants be given "such tests, oral and written, as the credentials committee shall in its discretion determine." A California appellate court invalidated the requirement because it was vague and ambiguous and provided no standards for what the examinations would be.[98] The Alaska Supreme Court also found an oral examination to be prohibited where there was no disclosure of the standards or what was inadequate in the answers.[99] Courts would probably uphold a reasonable, relevant examination uniformly given to all applicants for certain clinical privileges.

WAITING PERIOD. Hospitals generally may impose a reasonable waiting period before accepting another application from a person who has lost membership or privileges or had a prior application denied. In 1989, a federal appellate court upheld a hospital rule that a physician must wait one year after a summary suspension before reapplying for staff membership.[100] An Oklahoma court ruled that a public hospital could refuse to consider the application of a physician previously removed for good cause until he offered evidence that the past problems no longer existed.[101] In 2005, a federal appellate court upheld the refusal of a hospital to accept an application from a physician who had permanently resigned from the staff as part of a prior settlement.[102]

COLLECTION AND VERIFICATION OF INFORMATION. In order to collect and verify information about applicants' qualifications, many hospitals employ a medical staff office to undertake this largely administrative process. Hospitals need to carefully check information supplied by applicants. TJC requires "primary source verification" of many items, that is, confirmation from the entity itself that issued the credential (diploma, license, etc.) or from any other hospitals where the applicant practiced that information he has submitted is accurate, rather than simply accepting the word or copy provided by the applicant.[103] In 2004, TJC added a requirement that the identity of the applicant be verified.[104] Hospitals can be liable for injuries to patients by physicians who would have been denied membership if application information had been properly checked.[105] Generally, hospitals are liable for failing to check applications only when a reasonable check would have led to rejection of the applicant.[106]

Hospitals that have taken adverse action against an individual are often reluctant to release negative information related to such action to other hospitals where the individual later applies. Fear that litigation may result if such information is shared with these other hospitals can negatively affect a requesting hospital's ability to obtain full, accurate information on an applicant.[107] For this reason, many hospitals require that those who request an application and seek medical staff membership and privileges sign a release permitting entities with relevant information to provide it to the hospital at which the applicant is applying, with the applicant's agreement not to sue either hospital related to the release and use of the information. In a case that drew national attention, a federal appeals court held that under Louisiana law a hospital that gave neutral information about a former medical staff member to a second hospital, even though he had left the first hospital after being fired by his group for an alleged drug problem, had no affirmative duty to disclose this information to the second hospital absent a fiduciary relationship between the institutions (such as exists between member hospitals in the same hospital system). The court indicated that there was, however, a duty not to provide affirmative misrepresentations in such circumstances.[108] See **Table 5-3**.

Table 5-3 Claims Sometimes Litigated in Hospital Privilege Denial Cases

Breach of (Bylaws) Contract Claims;
Constitutional (Substantive and Procedural Due Process and–Equal– Protection) Claims;
Libel and Defamation Claims;
Tortious Interference Claims;
Intentional Infliction of Emotional Distress;
Antitrust Group Boycott and Tying Claims;
Title VII Civil Rights and ADA-Discrimination Claims; and
RICO (Racketeering Influenced Corrupt Organization) Claims.

The advent of teleradiology and other telemedicine has made the matter of inquiry and verification of credentials with the other hospitals at which an applicant has privileges much more complicated. Full-time "teleradiologists," for example, who read images remotely for patients in other hospitals and even other states, may be privileged to do so for hundreds of hospitals. Although the TJC had briefly instituted accreditation standards that permitted hospitals to "credential by proxy" (that is, basically adopt the credentialing decision and verification of the TJC accredited teleradiology facility if a teleradiologist were part of such a facility), CMS took a different position on the matter, and resolution of the conflicting positions had to be undertaken by CMS and TJC, a process still in flux in late 2011.[109]

Hospitals must also make an inquiry to the National Practitioner Data Bank (NPDB) concerning each applicant and, at least every two years, concerning each member in order to qualify for the antitrust immunity discussed later in this chapter.[110] Failure to make such inquiry can lead to even greater liability because hospitals are presumed to know information they would have obtained by making such inquiries.[111]

To assist in the process of gathering and verifying the relevant information on multiple applicants, some hospitals utilize the services of "CVOs" or "credentials verification organizations." TJC has stated with regard to such entities, that "[a]lthough healthcare organizations can use the services of a CVO for primary source verification, the healthcare organization cannot delegate the evaluation of that information."[112,113]

After information is gathered by the medical staff office, most bylaws require its review at multiple levels of the medical staff organization, starting typically with the department in which the applicant would practice to a general credentials committee, the Medical Executive Committee, and finally, the hospital board for an independent decision based on the medical staff recommendations. Multiple tiers of reviewers and an independent decision by the board are intended in part to make sure that gaps in the application are not missed (multiple eyes) and to help ensure that bias at any level (competitive or otherwise) will be filtered out so that claims of a tainted credentialing process are less likely to occur and to prevail.

One court discussing the role of the hospital in the credentialing process staked out the position echoed by later courts: "The hospital will be charged with gaining and evaluating the knowledge that would have been acquired had it exercised ordinary care in investigating its medical staff applicants and the hospital's failure to exercise that degree of care, skill and judgment that is exercised by the average hospital in approving an applicant's request for privileges is negligence. This is not to say that hospitals are insurers of the competence of their medical staff, for a hospital will not be negligent if it exercises the noted standard of care in selecting its staff."[114]

Because so many hospitals are TJC accredited, several courts have found that meeting TJC's credentialing requirements constitutes evidence of the hospital meeting the applicable standard of care for credentialing.

5-3 Delineation of Clinical Privileges

Hospitals must also determine the scope of practice for each physician on the medical staff. A licensed physician can act within the entire scope of medical practice without violating the medical licensing laws of some states. However, no physician is actually competent to perform all medical procedures. The hospital protects patients and physicians by examining physician credentials and training and granting clinical privileges limited to a defined scope of clinical practice. The board usually looks to the organized medical staff for expert advice in delineating clinical privileges.

A physician who acts outside the granted scope, except in an emergency, is subject to medical staff discipline, including termination of medical staff membership. However, the lack of clinical privileges is generally not negligence per se in malpractice cases. The lack of privileges may be evidence of negligence, but this determination is not automatic.[115] In several cases, physicians who held themselves out as being able to perform specialized procedures were held to the standard of other specialists.[116]

In addition to evolving issues related to individual practitioners (such as teleradiologists mentioned above) providing care in multiple locations, issues continue to evolve as hospitals themselves evolve from single-site facilities to multi-site hospital systems. Asked if streamlining the credentialing process and setting up the hierarchy needed to perform the process, the same individuals who make up the governing body and/or the same individuals who make up the medical staff can be responsible for more than one hospital, TJC answered: "Yes, as long as the responsibilities for each hospital's governing body and medical staff are performed independent of carrying out responsibilities for another hospital, and there is evidence of such. For example, the same set of individuals may function as the governing body or medical staff for more than one hospital, but they must convene themselves separately as each hospital's governing body or medical staff in order to carry out their responsibilities for each separately certified hospital. . . . Further, with respect to the medical staff, there needs to be a separate privileging process for each hospital, even though the same physicians may practice at both hospitals."[117]

Again, this position underscores the notion of the non-delegable duty of each hospital in credentialing. It does not suggest, however, that certain credentials verification and related duties cannot possibly be shared to achieve efficiencies. Issues such as coverage responsibilities of staff members at the multiple institutions at which the staff practices need to be contemplated and dealt with in the bylaws when such shared staffs occur.

INITIAL APPOINTMENT AND PRIVILEGES. The initial appointment period for most medical staffs is provisional. TJC authorizes, but no longer requires, a provisional period for the initial appointment.[118] During this period, the practice of the new medical staff member is observed to determine whether the member has been granted appropriate "privileges," which refers to those procedures the member has been determined to be capable of performing.[119] A federal appellate court ruled that a holder of provisional privileges in an army hospital did not have a property interest in obtaining full privileges.[120] A federal district court decided that a terminated physician's initial provisional appointment did not create a property interest in the appointment.[121]

There are many ways to delineate clinical privileges. The key element is that they be well defined. Some hospitals grant clinical privileges for individual procedures. Some hospitals group broad categories of patient conditions and procedures into levels, and physicians are granted clinical privileges to perform everything in the appropriate group. Other hospitals grant clinical privileges by specialty, defining what each specialty is permitted to do (sometimes called "core-privileging"). Potential risks are present if a hospital grants a practitioner privileges based on specialty, even though the particular practitioner may not have demonstrated the requisite training and skills in a given procedure. Combinations of these approaches are also used.

Some hospitals require documentation of prior performance of a specified number of certain procedures before privileges are granted for those procedures. Such requirements are generally acceptable if the numbers are reasonably attainable. In 1992, New York adopted official guidelines requiring surgeons to perform at least fifteen laparoscopies under supervision before hospitals could credential them to perform the operation independently.[122] Proctoring of medical staff members is discussed further below.

Hospitals should also require appropriate licensure for the privileges sought. For example, one court determined that it was appropriate for a hospital to require dentists to have a medical license before permitting them to provide anesthesia services for nondental patients.[123]

Hospitals may condition clinical privileges for certain procedures on requirements such as having (1) a consultation, (2) assistants, or (3) supervision. Physicians may be disciplined for violating these conditions. When establishing a consultation requirement, hospitals should consider that at least one court has ruled that a hospital with a consultation requirement must assist physicians in obtaining consultations.[124] Supervision requirements often require that a "proctor" on the medical staff monitor a certain number of cases performed during a prospective member's probationary, "proctoring period." Proctors are sometimes reluctant to provide such services out of fear of litigation from either a harmed patient or a physician whose care is evaluated by the proctor to be substandard. A California court examining the issues in a case brought by a patient ruled that a proctor who did not intervene when he allegedly saw the surgeon he was proctoring commit malpractice did not breach a duty to the patients since, among other reasons, there was no physician-patient relationship between the proctor and patient.[125]

To the extent a proctor's duties are conducted within the scope of the peer review requirements in the given jurisdiction, certain protections of the proctor from suits brought by the proctored doctor should exist.

5-4 Periodic Review and Reappointment

After physicians are appointed to the medical staff and granted final clinical privileges, their performance should be reviewed periodically as part of the process to assure their ongoing quality and to determine whether to grant reappointment. Both TJC and Medicare COPs require review and reappointment assessment.[126]

PERIODIC REVIEW. After the provisional period, hospitals and their medical staffs use several different methods to review performance of individual medical staff members. Ongoing review is conducted by medical staff committees or by an administrative process established to replace or assist with the efforts of the committees.

TJC requires hospitals to have an approach to improving organizational performance,[127] sometimes called a "performance improvement program" and to perform a "periodic performance review," or "PPR." TJC requires that relevant findings of the assessment process be considered in peer review and periodic evaluations of licensed independent practitioners.[128] An additional incentive for conducting a vigorous PPR is that TJC-approved "Plans of Action" to correct deficiencies the hospital itself uncovers between TJC surveys cannot be challenged by TJC during the subsequent survey.[129]

If problems are discovered through this formalized review or through day-to-day interaction, hospitals have a responsibility both to determine what action is appropriate and to initiate that action. Educational efforts directed toward problem member staff members will often be adequate, but sometimes steps such as suspension or termination of all or some clinical privileges may be necessary. Out of concerns raised by hospitals regarding the differences from state to state in peer review privilege laws and possible discoverability of information regarding concerns identified during such reviews, TJC permits hospitals multiple options to perform and document PPR results.

Periodic individual review is also necessary to determine whether each medical staff member is still fulfilling the responsibilities of membership and any clinical privileges granted. Medical staff appointments are for a limited time period, usually one or two years.[130] Before expiration of his or her appointment, each member is reviewed. The review includes clinical performance, judgment, and skills; licensure; health status; compliance with hospital and medical staff policies; and fulfillment of other medical staff responsibilities, such as active involvement in assigned committees.[131] An Ohio appellate court confirmed that review and denial of reappointment can be based on factors other than patient care, such as disruptive behavior and conflicting business interests[132] (both discussed elsewhere in this chapter). A federal appellate court confirmed a trial court's findings that a review did not have to be limited to the period after the previous

"Economic credentialing" has been defined as "the use of criteria unrelated to quality or professional competence in deciding whether or not to grant membership and/or clinical privileges to an individual" (see AMA Policy H-230.975). Promoting efficient practice and minimizing overutilization of care are among the aims of "accountable care organizations," or "ACOs," described in the Patient Protection and Affordable Care Act. Some express concerns that ACO may lead to greater use of inappropriate economic credentialing, while others feel that they are. ("A Prescription to Secure Shared Savings under Accountable Care." Compare S. Black MD, FAAN ACOs – ECONOMIC CREDENTIALING – BUNDLING OF PAYMENTS http://www.americanheadachesociety.org/assets/1/7/ACOs2.pdf with K. Wright and Gregory Drutchas, Economic Credentialing: A Prescription to Secure Shared Savings Under Accountable Care, AHLA Connections, February, 2011.)

review and that denial of reappointment could be based on prior misconduct.[133] Based on this review, a decision is made by the hospital board whether to reappoint the person to the medical staff and whether to maintain present clinical privileges or to modify them.

ECONOMIC CREDENTIALING BASED ON UTILIZATION. The aspect of economic credentialing that is most likely to arise in the periodic review context is the promotion of efficient practice.

Most hospitals attempt to promote cost-effective practices by physicians. One California hospital tried financial incentives in 1985,[134] but the reaction that followed contributed to the impetus toward a federal law that forbids the use of financial incentives to control services to Medicare or Medicaid patients.[135]

Some hospitals use efficiency criteria in clinical privilege decisions. Courts have generally upheld these criteria if they are properly developed and fairly applied.[136] Courts are also more likely to give greater deference to such criteria and their use when their link to quality care can be demonstrated.

Some hospitals require medical staff members to meet minimum utilization requirements in order to be reappointed.[137] Commentators have expressed a concern that this could be construed as a referral requirement in violation of Medicare antikickback provisions.[138] Others have pointed out that unless there is a baseline of clinical activity at the hospital, it is impossible to conduct a meaningful review of the physician's continuing performance. Thus, there are quality-related reasons for requiring minimum utilization. Some hospitals have adopted an activity requirement that can be satisfied by either clinical utilization or other in-house activities, such as consultations, committee work, and teaching and clinical procedures performed in other hospitals. In 1998, the U.S. Supreme Court denied review of a federal appeals court decision that upheld judgment for a hospital in an antitrust suit brought by physicians whose surgical privileges were terminated because they failed to meet surgery volume requirements.[139] Economic credentialing in reappointment is discussed further in this text.

ABUSIVE BEHAVIOR. Some physicians are occasionally physically or verbally abusive to staff, patients, or hospital visitors.[140] In some circumstances, hospitals can be liable for harassment of hospital staff by medical staff members.[141] Hospitals need to investigate promptly all reports of such abusive conduct and take appropriate action when the reports are substantiated. Sometimes peer counseling of the abusive physician is effective. In other cases, however, it is necessary to terminate membership on the medical staff. Recognizing that such behaviors can "undermine a culture of safety," effective January 1, 2009, TJC instituted a new leadership standard (LD.03.01.01) for hospital and all other accreditation programs.[142] The standard addresses disruptive and inappropriate behaviors in two of its "Elements of Performance" by requiring that a hospital have a code of conduct that defines acceptable and disruptive and inappropriate behaviors. It also requires that leaders create and implement a process for managing disruptive and inappropriate behaviors. In addition, TJC's Medical Staff Accreditation Standards for hospitals are organized to follow and review six "core competencies" of medical staff members that include interpersonal skills and professionalism.

DECLINING CAPABILITY. Difficult situations sometimes arise when a physician does not recognize his or her declining capabilities. Frequently, physicians will recognize such changes when they are approached tactfully and will agree to adjust their scope of practice to fit their capabilities. Often this can be done at the time of reappointment if there is not an immediate risk to patient well-being by waiting until that time. Some hospitals have an emeritus staff category for members whose practice is reduced for these or other reasons. If the physician will not agree to needed adjustments, the hospital and medical staff have the duty to protect patients by reducing the physician's clinical privileges to the appropriate scope. Criteria based on capability of a member rather than the member's age are less likely to be deemed discriminatory.

Failure to review performance and take appropriate action can result in hospital liability. For example, a California appellate court ruled that a hospital could be liable for failing to review periodically the performance of those persons granted clinical privileges.[143] However, at least one state passed a statute that bars hospital liability for professional services of professionals who are not employees or agents, so there is no hospital liability in that state for negligent review of independent contractors.[144] "Corporate" or "institutional" liability based in many cases on a hospital's nondelegable duty with regard to evaluating the competence and skills of its medical staff is a common outcome in such cases, however.

In an unusual case in 2003, a Michigan hospital pled guilty to a federal criminal charge of fraud for failing to take credentialing actions against a physician who was performing many unnecessary procedures.[145]

5-5 Modification and Termination of Privileges

Clinical privileges must sometimes be modified or terminated because of changes in the physician's capabilities, violation of hospital or medical staff policies, changes in hospital standards, or for other reasons. When physicians challenge modification or termination of privileges, they typically challenge the adequacy of procedures followed and the reasons given for the action. Procedural issues are discussed in the due process section of this chapter. Actions denying or revoking medical staff membership or privileges are generally referred to as "adverse actions."

Evidence of poor performance or violation of policies should be carefully reviewed and documented before deciding to take adverse action. The hospital should be prepared to justify the action in court.

MEDICAL RECORDS. Clinical privileges are frequently temporarily suspended when physicians fail to complete medical records properly within time limits established by hospital policy.[146] Suspension of admitting privileges usually continues until overdue records are completed. Courts have generally upheld disciplinary actions for failure to complete records.[147] In 1998, a federal appellate court upheld suspending privileges of a physician who had removed a portion of the medical record of her own care until she returned the records.[148]

STANDARDS. Some physicians have challenged adverse actions by claiming that the standards by which they were judged were too vague. Vague standards can violate any applicable due process by failing to give notice of what conduct is expected or prohibited. Courts generally, however, have upheld actions taken on the basis of subjective standards when the standards are applied in a reasonable way.[149] For example, the Nevada Supreme Court upheld a clinical privilege termination based on the general standard of "unprofessional conduct."[150] The court recognized that it was not feasible to specify the variety of unprofessional conduct. The physician had not used gloves when touching a spinal needle before using it and had appeared for surgery in no condition to perform, requiring cancellation of the surgery. The court found that the standard was properly applied. A New Jersey appellate court affirmed a physician's suspension based on a bylaws provision that permitted suspension "for cause."[151] The physician had negligently treated a patient. The court found there was sufficient evidence of cause to terminate the physician, so the term "for cause" was not too vague. The situation leading to suspension in this case demonstrated that all grounds for suspension could not be specified in advance.

Relying on clear, well-documented standards is less likely to lead to protracted litigation and liability in these types of cases.

MODIFYING STANDARDS. When hospitals modify standards, clinical privileges of some physicians may be reduced. Hospitals may change their requirements so that all physicians must begin to meet new conditions. Generally, such universal changes have not been viewed by courts as a reduction in clinical privileges, so no right to hearing or report to a data bank would be triggered. However, in the past, some courts have viewed such changes as a clinical privilege reduction, requiring that each affected staff member be given the same opportunity for a hearing as offered for other reductions.[152] Reasonable changes will generally be upheld. The Ohio Supreme Court upheld a hospital's new requirement that a physician be board certified, be board eligible, be a fellow in the American College of Surgeons, or have ten years' experience to qualify for major

surgical privileges.[153] An Illinois appellate court refused to enjoin a hospital's new requirement that surgeons with general surgery clinical privileges consult with a gynecologist before doing major gynecological surgery. The court ruled that the physician was entitled to a hearing concerning the reasonableness of the rule.[154] Some courts have permitted suits concerning the application of new rules.[155]

When a New Mexico hospital adopted a new rule forbidding all hip-pinning procedures because it lacked the proper equipment, the New Mexico Supreme Court ruled against a physician who lost his hip-pinning privileges.[156]

To the extent such changes are in furtherance of quality care and/or are not inconsistent with existing standards of the hospital and medical staff, including those in the bylaws, they are more likely to withstand judicial scrutiny.

CHANGING TO A FULL-TIME OR EXCLUSIVE STAFFING ARRANGEMENT. Courts have typically been supportive of hospitals that change staffing arrangements. The overall validity of such contracts under the antitrust laws, based in part on the pro-competitive benefits they can bring to healthcare consumers, has been upheld by courts including the U.S. Supreme Court. When a full-time staffing approach is adopted, generally the privileges of those who choose not to be full-time can be terminated.[157] When an exclusive contract approach is adopted, courts in general have held that the privileges of those who do not get the full-time contract can also be terminated, especially if they had a fair opportunity to get the exclusive contract. The Maine Supreme Court upheld a hospital decision that terminated an emergency medicine contract with a group, offered the physicians individual direct contracts, and terminated those who chose not to sign.[158] As noted above, Illinois requires that those who lose their privileges as a result of an exclusive contract be given certain process beforehand.

There are exceptional cases where substantial amounts have been awarded to physicians who are excluded by these arrangements,[159] but generally those involved extenuating circumstances of misconduct beyond the termination of privileges.[160] These changes in staffing arrangements need to be carefully planned and any pro-quality reasons and the unilateral nature of the decision by the hospital board (rather than as the product of two parties conspiring) thoroughly documented to minimize the risk of successful legal challenge.

ECONOMIC CREDENTIALING BASED ON OUTSIDE ACTIVITIES. Some hospitals try to remove physicians who are competing economically with the hospital.[161] Examples of such competition include investing in a competing specialty hospital or ambulatory surgery center. There have been a few cases where trial courts have enjoined removal during litigation, but generally the right of the hospital to exclude competing physicians has been upheld.[162]

In one of the few cases where physicians obtained a temporary injunction, an Arkansas hospital had adopted a policy not to grant privileges to physicians who had an ownership interest in a competing hospital. Cardiologists who had an ownership interest in a competing heart hospital were denied renewal of their privileges. They first sued in federal court, but the court found it had no jurisdiction and dismissed the case. A similar case was then filed in state court. The trial judge issued a temporary injunction, based in part on a determination that the policy was violative of the federal anti-kickback statute and the hospital could not enforce its policy against the suing doctors. On appeal the Arkansas Supreme Court reversed, finding the trial court had erred on the anti-kickback determination and had not adequately evaluated the likelihood of the physicians succeeding on the merits, which is one of the criteria for a temporary injunction. However, the court left the injunction in place while the trial court performed the required evaluation.[163]

In 2002, at the request of the AMA for guidance regarding the legality of economic credentialing practices under the federal anti-kickback statute, the Office of the Inspector General ("OIG") of the Department of Health and Human Services ("HHS") examined the application of the statute to situations where hospitals were refusing to grant staff privileges to physicians who (1) own or have other financial interests in, or leadership positions with, competing healthcare entities, (2) refer to competing healthcare entities, or (3) fail to admit some specified percentage of their patients to the hospital. The OIG also sought public comment on the issues.[164]

The following year, an Ohio health system published a white paper contending that the AMA's definition of economic credentialing may be too broad and in conflict with certain state statutes which permit or require the boards of nonprofit hospitals, on the basis of their fiduciary duty to protect the best interests of the hospitals, to make decisions whether or not to credential medical staff members on criteria such as competition with the hospital[165]

Hospitals have taken action against physicians on the medical staff for economic issues other than competition. In one case, a federal court rejected an antitrust challenge to remove a physician from the emergency on-call schedule allegedly for charging excessive fees.[166]

HUMAN IMMUNODEFICIENCY VIRUS (HIV) AND ACQUIRED IMMUNE DEFICIENCY SYNDROME (AIDS). Hospital actions in restricting privileges of surgeons who test positive for HIV have generally been upheld.[167] The Pennsylvania Supreme Court permitted a hospital to inform patients they may have been exposed to the virus in surgery by an HIV-positive surgeon.[168]

SUBSTANCE ABUSE. Substance abuse by medical staff members has become easier to address with the increased availability of state or medical society programs for rehabilitation[169] and the growing consensus that the first approach to the problem should be to promote rehabilitation. Most physicians are willing to cooperate with these efforts, including temporary reductions in clinical privileges as necessary, to protect patients and avoid revocation of privileges. Unfortunately, it is sometimes extremely difficult for an impaired physician to remain rehabilitated, and the hospital must decide how many rehabilitation opportunities to give. If rehabilitation fails, permanent action must eventually be taken to preserve acceptable standards of patient care.

When a physician's physical or mental health or impairment potentially places patients at risk or when his or her health status interferes with the ability to practice, appropriate action by the hospital needs to occur. There is still some disagreement on the extent to which the ADA applies to nonemployee medical staff members.[170] However, even where the ADA applies, suspension or termination of physicians has been upheld for resulting behaviors that threaten patient care or institutional operations.[171] In 1998, a federal appellate court ruled that it was not an ADA violation to fire a physician with attention deficit disorder. His short-term memory problems led to problems in patient records, and he could not perform the administrative task of his job.[172] Another federal appellate court upheld denial of reinstatement of the terminated clinical privileges of an internist who had been stealing and tampering with internal mail in other physicians' mailboxes.[173] His diagnosis was bipolar disorder, and his physician stated that his conduct was a symptom of his disorder. The intolerable conduct and continuing concerns with his behavior and honesty justified the denial of reinstatement.

In 2008, a federal trial court concluded that, while Title I of the ADA applies only to employed physicians, Title III of the ADA and Section 5.04 of the Rehabilitation Act apply to both independent contractors and employees alike. Though this meant that an orthopedic surgeon with bipolar disorder was entitled to reasonable accommodation based on his disability, the court also held that the proctoring requirement placed on the physician for each surgery by the hospital was part of a reasonable accommodation.[174]

The ADA may apply in some cases to limit otherwise permissible actions.[175] Thus, it is prudent to consider reasonable accommodations even where they may not be legally required and to determine whether the ADA applies and, if so what it requires whenever adverse action is taken in such circumstances.

FREE SPEECH IN PUBLIC HOSPITALS. Public hospitals usually cannot terminate clinical privileges because of a physician's public criticism of the quality of care. Federal courts have found such criticism to be protected by the First Amendment right of free speech.[176] However, physicians cannot insulate themselves from adverse action by public criticism. In 1986, a federal appellate court upheld the dismissal of a physician who had criticized the hospital.[177] The hospital convinced the court the dismissal was due to patient care concerns, not the public criticism.

Public criticism can also exceed the bounds of protected speech. In 1989, a federal appellate court ruled that a physician's caustic personal attacks were disruptive and unprotected, so termination was justified.[178] Termination for disruptive conduct was discussed previously.

In a 1992 hospital case, a federal appellate court applied the general rule that public speech is protected only when it addresses a matter of public concern.[179] Other differences in the legal treatment of public and private hospitals are discussed below.

REPORTING REQUIREMENTS. The Health Care Quality Improvement Act of 1986 (HCQIA) requires all hospitals that want the benefit of HCQIA's liability limitation provisions (discussed below) report certain adverse medical staff actions to the National Practitioner Data Bank (NPDB).[180]

The first physician challenge to the NPBD was dismissed in 1994.[181] A federal appellate court reversed an injunction against reporting a medical staff action.[182]

When a report is challenged, the U.S. Department of Health and Human Services must review the appropriateness of

> The . . . data bank was established by the federal Health Care Quality and Improvement Act of 1986 and generally requires hospitals to report doctors whose privileges have been restricted or revoked for more than 30 days based on competence issues or professional misconduct [the idea being, in part, that other hospitals can learn of such restrictions if the doctor applies there]. . . . But the complexities of the peer review process continue to create uncertainty as to when competence or conduct issues are reportable. . . . As of 2007, nearly half of U.S. hospitals had not filed a report with the National Practitioner Data Bank. (A.L. Sorrel, "When is Conduct Reportable? National Practitioner Data Bank Takes Complaints From Hospitals About Physicians," *American Medical News* (Sept. 21, 2009).)

maintaining a report in the NPDB and its content. The NPDB has been ordered to remove at least one report.[183] In 2004, a federal district court ruled that the federal Privacy Act applied when the NPDB reviewed a challenge to the content of a report.[184]

States have separate reporting requirements that are sometimes different from HCQIA requirements.[185]

In 1985, a federal court of appeals ruled that a hospital could not be sued for defamation for filing a required report of suspension of a medical staff member.[186] The hospital was found immune because the report was mandated. In 1994, another federal appellate court decided that a hospital could be liable for defamation for submitting a report that it knew to be false. In that case, a medical chart had been submitted as evidence of a patient incident with knowledge that the reported physician had not been involved in the care of the patient. The court found that bad faith destroyed the qualified immunity.[187] Similarly, in 1996, a federal appellate court found that a hospital and its staff were not entitled to HCQIA immunity when a physician's privileges were revoked based on a review of the medical records of only two patients, and an incorrect report, based on that review, was submitted to the NPDB.[188]

Almost any voluntary or involuntary adverse action that is taken while a physician is under investigation, other than exoneration, must be reported. This has resulted in physicians challenging the determination that they were under investigation. Courts have generally rejected such challenges and found that reports were properly made.[189] However, in one case a federal judge found that a physician had not been under the investigation at the time of the reported event and that the Department of Health and Human Services should not have accepted the report.[190] The judge ordered the report to be removed from the NPDB. Clearly, defined investigations procedures within the medical staff bylaws can help avoid such claims.

At the point when a hospital's review of a member's care or conduct falls within the circumstances that must be reported to the NPDB, the hospital may no longer consider the option of entering into an agreement that the physician will resign in exchange for the hospital not disclosing the circumstances of the resignation. The enforceability of such agreements may be questionable anyway. In 1989, a federal appellate court ruled that a hospital was not liable for disclosure to another hospital of the circumstances of a physician's resignation because the nondisclosure agreement between the physician and hospital was against public policy.[191] In 1993, the West Virginia Supreme Court ruled that a physician could sue a hospital for reporting to another hospital that his privileges had been summarily suspended, even though they had, in fact, been summarily suspended.[192] The physician claimed that he had voluntarily resigned after the suspension pursuant to a promise that his privileges would be reinstated, the suspension would be expunged, and no reports would be made to anyone. The court ruled (1) the agreement would not be against public policy if it were in recognition that the initial suspension was improper and (2) the physician should have an opportunity to prove that was the basis for the agreement.

It is not uncommon to consult with the physician concerning the content of the NPDB report.[193] This is generally acceptable as long as the final report is accurate and contains the required information.

There is a procedure for updating and correcting NPDB reports. In some jurisdictions, there may be liability to the physician for failure to submit timely updates and corrections.[194]

5-6 Review Procedures for Adverse Actions

Lawsuits arising out of board decisions concerning appointments and clinical privileges of physicians commonly focus on (1) the right of the board to impose the rules applied or (2) the procedures followed in reaching the decision. In most states, public hospital boards have less discretion than private hospital boards.

Public hospitals are subject to some constitutional constraints and may have governmental immunities that do not apply to private hospitals.

Due Process. Public hospitals must satisfy the Fourteenth Amendment to the U.S. Constitution, which says that no state shall "deprive any person of life, liberty, or property, without due process of law." An action by a public hospital is considered a state action. The interest of a physician in practicing in a hospital can be regarded by a court as a liberty or property interest, entitling the physician to "due process of law" when a public hospital makes a decision concerning medical staff appointment or clinical privileges. However, a physician does not have a constitutional right to practice in any public hospital.[195] Physicians must demonstrate that they satisfy valid hospital rules before they may practice in the hospital.

Some federal courts have ruled that an applicant does not have a property or liberty interest in being appointed or being granted privileges.[196] Usually, the property right is in continuation of membership or privileges that have already been granted.[197]

To provide physicians with due process, hospital rules must be reasonable and adequately express the intent of the hospital. Rules that are too arbitrary or vague may be unenforceable. Generally, physicians at public hospitals must be offered fair procedures when they are being deprived of a liberty or property interest. Application of a consistent process, well documented as applicable to all staff members, can also help satisfy notions of due process and equal protection, discussed below. In some circumstances, however, for example where patients are in jeopardy, courts have agreed that summary action may be taken immediately with the due process provided later.[198]

In some states, it may be possible to structure clinical privileges in a public hospital so that no property interest is created, if there is no understanding created that the practitioner is entitled to due process before the hospital can revoke the privileges.[199]

Equal Protection. The Fourteenth Amendment also says that no state shall "deny to any person within its jurisdiction the equal protection of the laws." Equal protection means that like persons must be dealt with in like fashion. The equal protection clause is concerned with whether or not classifications used to distinguish persons for various legal purposes are justifiable. Determining whether a particular difference between persons justifies a particular difference in rules or procedures can be difficult. Courts generally apply a standard that requires public entities to show reasonable bases for such differences in treatment. The major exception to this standard is the strict scrutiny courts apply to distinctions based on suspect classifications, such as race, and the intermediate level of scrutiny applied to sex-based classifications. Noting that "the central purpose of the Equal Protection Clause of the Fourteenth Amendment is the prevention of official conduct discriminating on the basis of Race," a court of appeals refused to dismiss an Equal Protection claim brought by three cardiologists of Indian descent who alleged that the Texas public hospital at which they practiced discriminated against them on the basis of their race when it closed the exercise of privileges in the cardiology department to only the hospital's other cardiologists who had a contract with hospital.[200]

Because of comprehensive legislation prohibiting discrimination based on many characteristics, most challenges to alleged discriminatory actions are based on legislation, rather than on constitutional principles. Nondiscrimination legislation is discussed elsewhere in this text.

Many states have also limited the discretion of private hospitals with regard to criteria they may use and have also required hospitals to provide certain procedural rights for applicants and existing staff members under statutes such as their hospital licensing acts and under their case law. Private hospitals must also meet certain procedural and substantive hearing related requirements that are imposed by TJC and other accrediting organizations, as discussed below.

EXCEPTIONS TO FULL REVIEW PROCEDURES. In some circumstances, full review of adverse actions with regard to medical staff membership or privileges is not required.

Applicants. In many jurisdictions, applicants are not entitled to the same review procedures as medical staff members. Some courts find (and some statutes provide) that the physician's rights are derived from medical staff membership. Because an applicant is not yet a member, the applicant does not have a legal right to make claims on the organization. In these jurisdictions, only actions during the appointment period are viewed as interfering with the rights of physicians and triggering a right to internal procedural review. So-called "preapplicants," discussed above, are generally entitled to even less process, perhaps only notice of their failure to meet threshold requirements for obtaining an application.

The rights of individuals applying for reappointment also vary, with some jurisdictions treating such individuals the same as they treat applicants for initial appointment and some recognizing their entitlement to some review, but not to the full procedures available to physicians disciplined during an appointment period. The scope of rights often depends on whether the hospital has created an entitlement to reappointment, typically in the language of its medical staff bylaws. Some jurisdictions will find that some acts of the hospital have (often inadvertently) created an entitlement to reappointment, so that there is a right to a review process when reappointment is denied. Absent such an entitlement, in some jurisdictions, hospitals may not be as vulnerable to challenges when they deny reappointment as they are when they modify or terminate privileges during an appointment term.[201] In those jurisdictions, hospitals may wait until the reappointment process to address problems with physicians that do not involve immediate risks to patients.

TJC requires a fair hearing for applicants and members, but does not require the procedures to be identical.[202]

Some medical staff bylaws specify that applicants do not have procedural rights. Unless a hospital is in a state that recognizes this difference and the difference is specified in the bylaws, it is prudent to follow the same procedures for both applicants and members.

Substantial Compliance. Most courts do not require technical compliance with every detail of the bylaws procedure. Substantial compliance is usually sufficient.[203] However, given the contractual nature of bylaws in the eyes of many courts and the significance of their place in the relationship between the medical staff and hospital, it is best practice to seek to achieve technical compliance with the bylaws to reduce the number of issues that need to be addressed when adverse actions are challenged.

Informal Reviews. Most courts recognize that medical staff members do not have procedural rights during the informal reviews of potential problems with the member's care that precede the hospital's decision of whether or not to initiate formal proceedings.[204] Although seeking information from the affected physician early in the review is almost always helpful, the physician does not have a legal right to notice and an opportunity to present information until formal action is initiated.

It is best not to call these preliminary reviews "investigations" because this can create confusion concerning whether the physician is "under investigation" for purposes of NPDB reporting requirements described above.

Sometimes the board employs outside experts to assist in medical care review. Usually, this is done with the advice and concurrence of the medical staff. Outside experts often review specialists' care when other staff members do not feel they have the expertise to review the care or when those who are able to conduct the review might appear to be biased. Such review can occur both at the time of a contemplated adverse action and at the time of normal credentialing to avoid alleged bias. Some specialty societies have established programs to provide this consultation. One example of such external review is the 2003 Illinois case discussed earlier in this section.

Seriousness of Actions. The full scope of review procedures is often used only for actions that directly affect the physician's ability to practice, such as decisions concerning the scope of clinical privileges. A New York court ruled that removal from an administrative position and termination of block operating room time did not entitle the physician to review.[205] A federal district court held that a change in an anesthesiologist's case assignments did not trigger a right to review.[206] However, in some states, less serious actions may trigger review rights. For example, a California court ruled that being on the call roster was a clinical privilege, so that removal entitled the physician to a hearing.[207]

Censure usually does not entitle the physician to a hearing.[208]

Waiver by Contract. Even in public hospitals, procedural rights can be waived by contract. Thus, exclusive and other contracts can provide for an enforceable termination of privileges without a hearing when the contract terminates or other specified events occur.[209]

An alternative to formal hearings that some physicians and hospitals may consider in the case of nonquality, contract-related disputes is arbitration.[210] HCQIA authorizes the alternative of using an arbitrator.[211] Some state laws limit the use of arbitration. The Federal Arbitration Act preempts these state laws when the contract affects interstate commerce. Some courts have found that some contracts with physicians affect interstate commerce and have applied federal law to enforce arbitration agreements.[212]

HEALTH CARE QUALITY IMPROVEMENT ACT. As described above, the Health Care Quality Improvement Act, or HCQIA,[213] is a federal statute that describes procedures for investigations prior to adverse actions and hearings that follow such actions. Hospitals are not required to follow HCQIA procedures, but if the procedures described as a "safe harbor" are followed, HCQIA provides protection from monetary damages in private

suits, except under civil rights laws. There is no protection from suits seeking injunctions or from civil rights suits or from suits brought by a state or federal attorney general. However, most suits concerning medical staff matters are private suits, so this protection can be significant. HCQIA states that the "immunity" applies only when the peer review action was taken "in the reasonable belief that the action was in furtherance of quality health care" (which would seem to create an additional incentive against purely economic decisions) and "after a reasonable effort to obtain the facts of the matter." There is a statutory presumption that this standard is met.[214] Further, most courts apply an objective standard to determine whether the reasonableness standards have been met. This means that allegations of bias or bad faith of a peer reviewer or committee have generally not been enough on their own to defeat HCQIA immunity if, objectively, the action against the member could conceivably result in furtherance of quality care.[215] It is thus not easy for a physician to defeat HCQIA immunity.[216,217]

In 1996, a federal appellate court held that HCQIA procedures were needed only for "professional review actions" that affect clinical privileges in order to qualify for HCQIA immunity; "professional review activities," such as fact-finding or decisions to monitor, did not have to follow the HCQIA procedures.[218] What constitutes a professional review action is defined in the statute.

> The Health Care Quality Improvement Act (HCQIA) is a federal statute that offers peer reviewers protection from money damages in lawsuits challenging "professional review actions" in which the peer reviewer participated. In order for immunity to apply under the HCQIA, the statute provides that the professional review action must be taken: (1) in the reasonable belief that the action was in furtherance of quality health care, (2) after a reasonable effort to obtain the facts of the matter, (3) after adequate notice and hearing procedures are afforded to the physician involved or after such other procedures as are fair to the physician under the circumstances, and (4) in the reasonable belief that the action was warranted by the facts known after such reasonable effort to obtain facts and after meeting the requirement of paragraph (3) above. See 42 U.S.C. § 11112(a). The investigation, hearing, and appeal procedures in medical staff bylaws should reflect the substantive and procedural elements described by HCQIA to meet its "safe-harbor."

In 2003, a District of Columbia court ruled that if HCQIA procedures were followed when conditions were imposed that it was not necessary to follow them again when automatically terminating the physician for violating the conditions.[219]

As noted above, HCQIA protects hospitals from monetary liability, not from suit. Thus, a refusal by a trial judge to dismiss such a suit on HCQIA grounds cannot be immediately appealed. The hospital must, in those cases, wait until after there is a final judgment against the hospital to obtain appellate review.[220]

Many hospitals have availed themselves of the protection of HCQIA. In 1988, an Indiana court authorized a hospital to substitute HCQIA procedures for the procedures in its bylaws without first amending the bylaws.[221] It is not clear whether other courts will allow this substitution. However, hospitals and affected physicians can agree to change procedures, and some physicians may agree to HCQIA procedures. Refusal to agree may be a waiver by the physician in some contexts. Because of the strong protections spelled out by HCQIA and recognized by courts hearing challenges to HCQIA's immunity, medical staff bylaws often track in checklist detail the requirements of HCQIA for investigative and hearing procedures to help assure that their procedures satisfy the HCQIA safe harbor.

SUMMARY ACTION. Many state courts and state statutes permit restrictions on clinical privileges to be imposed without prior due process procedures when there is reliable information concerning a potential immediate risk to patient well-being.[222] Although review procedures must usually be followed before adverse action is taken, courts recognize that nonreviewed summary action can sometimes be necessary and appropriate. For example, the Alaska Supreme Court ruled that the fair hearing could be conducted within a reasonable time after the summary suspension of clinical privileges when there was immediate risk to patients.[223]

Courts have issued injunctions prohibiting summary suspension when the risk is not sufficiently immediate.[224] Courts will reconsider an injunction if the physician's conduct during the injunction indicates that summary suspension is needed.[225]

Summary suspension without a hearing is also likely to be deemed appropriate when a physician ceases to be licensed to practice medicine, ceases to have a valid Drug Enforcement Agency ("DEA") registration to prescribe controlled substances, or ceases to meet other objective prerequisites to the appointment.[226] Medical staff bylaws should list the kinds of criteria that can trigger a summary suspension and the procedures required before and after its suspension, which are often dictated by state law.

THE REGULAR REVIEW PROCESS. This section discusses the elements that should be considered when defining the bylaw procedure for conducting a hearing for a medical staff member. Not all of these elements are required in every jurisdiction or for every type of facility. It is prudent to consider these elements and either include them or understand why they are not being included. At a minimum, factors required for the "safe harbor" under HCQIA should be included in the process along with any state required elements.

"Various courts hearing HCQIA cases have overwhelmingly decided in favor of the defendants. Thus, HCQIA has become an effective shield against peer review claims. . . . However, HCQIA only provides immunity if the peer review decision is taken: (1) in the reasonable belief that the action was in the furtherance of quality health care; (2) after a reasonable effort to obtain the facts of the matter; (3) after adequate notice and hearing procedures are afforded to the physician involved. . . ; and (4) in the reasonable belief that the action was warranted by the facts known after such reasonable effort to obtain [relevant] facts." Howard Feller, Peer Review And Hospital Staff Privileges, American Bar Association Health Law Section of Antitrust Law, American Health Lawyers Association "Antitrust in Healthcare Conference," May 15-16, 2003.

Important elements of the hearing process include (1) reasonable notice, (2) hearing, (3) physician presence, (4) legal counsel, (5) composition of the hearing body, (6) discovery, (7) opportunity to present information, (8) opportunity to cross-examine witnesses, (9) record, (10) report, (11) internal review process, and (12) final institutional decision.

Reasonable Notice. Following an appropriate investigation, the first step of any adverse action is to give reasonable written notice of the reasons for the proposed action and of the time and place where the physician may present information in response. Typically, to be deemed reasonable, notice must include sufficient information to permit preparation of a response,[227] but a detailed and exhaustive list of each perceived deficiency is not required in most states.[228] In 1999, a federal appellate court ruled that it was not necessary to identify records with specific complaints when the proposed action was based on a statistical overview of cases.[229] The case involved proposed limitations on performing coronary artery bypass surgery based on a statistically high mortality rate.

The hospital does not have to cater to the idiosyncrasies of the physician in giving notice.[230] Standard methods such as personal delivery or registered mail are appropriate and a consistently applied process may in fact diminish the likelihood of a complaint of inappropriate treatment of a particular physician or failure to follow required procedures.

Hearing. The second step is to provide the physician with an opportunity to present information. Often the physician will have had one or more opportunities to present information during the informal and investigative steps that precede the hearing. However, a formal opportunity to present information is usually required after the recommendation of adverse action. Courts vary on the degree of the formality that they require. It is generally agreed that the physician is entitled to only one hearing unless the bylaws specify otherwise.[231]

An opportunity to have a hearing is all that is required. Health care entities may and usually do require physicians to request a hearing within a specified time. Failure to make such a request waives the right to a hearing and generally waives objections to the process. In 1996, a federal appellate court ruled that a physician could not deprive a hospital of HCQIA immunity by failing to request or participate in the hearing required by HCQIA.[232]

Physician Presence. Hospitals may require that the physician attend the hearing. Unexcused failure to appear can waive the right to the hearing and the right to object to other defects in the proceedings.[233]

Legal Counsel. There is disagreement in the courts on whether the physician should be permitted to be represented by legal counsel at the hearing. While attorneys can assist in assuring that information is provided in an orderly fashion and can help the physician understand the outcomes of the hearing that can be reasonably expected to be disruptive, for example, by attempting to apply formal court rules. As a result, some hospitals do not permit attorneys to be involved; others encourage their involvement.

Courts have disagreed on whether there is a legal right to legal representation and the scope of the attorney's participation. New Jersey requires hospitals to permit representation by an attorney.[234] A federal court ruled that in army hospital proceedings the attorney can be limited to providing advice to the physician and not questioning witnesses or providing argument.[235] California hospitals do not have to permit representation by an attorney, especially when the hospital is not represented by an attorney.[236] Hospitals will have a difficult time convincing any court of the fairness of their procedures if only one side is permitted to have legal representation.

The safe harbor for HCQIA immunity specifies that the physician be given an opportunity to be represented by a lawyer or other person of the physician's choice.[237] This does not create a legal right to an attorney, but denial of an attorney may make it more difficult to maintain HCQIA immunity.

In 2004, the Wisconsin Supreme Court ruled that only attorneys who were admitted to practice in Wisconsin could represent physicians at medical staff hearings, so an out-of-state attorney was not permitted to participate.[238]

Composition of the Hearing Body. The committee or individual conducting the hearing should not be biased against the physician. The South Carolina Supreme Court found that a physician's due process rights were violated when three of the original accusing physicians were members of the joint conference committee that made the final recommendation to the governing board.[239] A California appellate court ruled that a physician had been denied due process because the committee that recommended his suspension was not impartial.[240] Two committee members depended on the obstetrical expertise of the physician who brought the charges. The HCQIA safe harbor requires that the hearing committee not include physicians who are direct economic competitors of the physician involved.[241] State law may specify composition. An Indiana court ruled that under state law only physicians could serve on a hearing committee.[242]

Courts have recognized the virtual impossibility of complete impartiality because all physicians in a hospital have a collaborative relationship. Some courts require a demonstration of actual bias before a due process violation can be found.[243] A California appellate court ruled that the physician should be given an opportunity to examine committee members for possible bias before the hearing.[244] A New Jersey appellate court overturned a lower court ruling that had found that all internal bodies were disqualified and had ordered the county medical society (a private unrelated corporation) to make the final decision on renewal of clinical privileges.[245] The appellate court ruled that participation in prior investigations and preliminary decisions did not disqualify the internal bodies; the institution could combine investigative, charging, and adjudicative functions in the same body. Some courts find that review and approval by an unbiased appeal committee can correct earlier bias,[246] while other courts find no corrective effect.[247]

One federal appellate court ruled that when the applicant falsified his application any bias in the review process was irrelevant because this applicant would have been denied privileges anyway.[248]

Case law is clear that persons with known biases should be excluded from the hearing body. Persons in the same specialty should generally also be excluded because they may appear to be motivated to remove a competitor. Physicians do not have a right to have persons in the same specialty on a hearing body.[249] To the extent feasible, it is helpful to also exclude those who were involved in earlier stages of the investigation and review process because they may be predisposed to find against the physician, but this is not essential in all jurisdictions. These steps will assure fairness and likely minimize the risk of successful challenge to a hospital's final decision.

Discovery. Full discovery of the sort permitted in a court proceeding is generally not required in a hospital hearing. Courts have disagreed on which hospital records of patient care and peer review the physician may obtain to prepare the presentation.[250] The Missouri Supreme Court permitted broad discovery with only redaction of identifying characteristics of patients who were not patients of the physician challenging his loss of staff privileges.[251]

In 1998, a California appellate court ruled that a peer review committee's policy of not disclosing the sources that had triggered the review did not deprive a physician of fair procedure.[252] No formal right of discovery is required under HCQIA.

Opportunity to Present Information. The purpose of the hearing is to give the physician an opportunity to present information on his or her own behalf. One issue is whether the physician is entitled to an opportunity to present witnesses. Some courts have ruled that the bylaws can require all submissions to the hearing body to be in writing.[253] The HCQIA safe harbor includes an opportunity to present witnesses.[254]

Opportunity to Cross-Examine Witnesses. Courts have recognized that hospitals do not have the power to compel witnesses to attend hearings. Due process usually does not require an opportunity to cross-examine all those who have complained about the physician's conduct.[255] However, a few courts have found a right to cross-examine some witnesses.[256] Many hospitals permit cross-examination of witnesses who actually provide information at the hearing. The HCQIA safe harbor includes an opportunity to cross-examine the witnesses who testify.[257]

Record. It is prudent to make a record of hearing proceedings. If the final decision is appealed to the courts, a record will be necessary to prove fairness of the proceedings and evidence of the basis for the decision. A court reporter's transcript of the proceedings is expensive and may not be necessary. However, if the physician requests a court reporter and is willing to share the cost appropriately, a court reporter should be considered. Sometimes a tape recording or, in some situations, detailed notes will be sufficient. In some states, permission of all participants may be required for a tape recording. In 1998, the highest court of Massachusetts held that a hospital had violated the state wiretap law by tape-recording a meeting.[258] The HCQIA safe harbor includes a record of the hearing, but the physician can be required to pay reasonable charges to obtain a copy.[259]

Report. The hearing committee should make a substantive report of its findings, especially when such a report is required by the bylaws. A District of Columbia court ruled that a physician who was denied privileges could base a suit on the lack of an adequate hearing report.[260] The bylaws required the medical executive committee to consider a fact-finding report from the hearing committee. Without an adequate report, it could not do so, so the bylaws were violated. The HCQIA safe harbor includes a written recommendation by the hearing entity and a written decision by the hospital, with each to include a statement of the basis for the recommendation or decision.[261]

Internal Review Process. TJC requires a process of internal review of the hearing committee's decision.[262] Some hospitals seek to comply with this requirement by permitting the practitioner to make a written and/or oral presentation to the board or a board committee after an adverse medical executive committee recommendation, but before the board's decision. This first approach can provide the board with useful information. Other hospitals interpret appellate review to require that an appellate process occur after the board makes an adverse decision. Because the board has the acknowledged authority to make the final decision, such internal appellate review is in essence reconsideration by the board. It is not clear what useful function this second approach performs that justifies the burden on the board.

One physician sought to disqualify the board from acting as its own appellate tribunal. A Colorado court rejected the challenge.[263]

Final Institutional Decision. The final decision in medical staff disciplinary matters is made by the board of directors of the institution after consideration of the findings and recommendations that have been generated by the internal review process. A 2005 decision by the Alabama Supreme Court held that the corporation was not required to adopt the hearing panel's recommendation.[264] Though the board can rely on the expertise of the medical staff in reaching a well-reasoned decision, an independent decision of the board, documented as such, is important in preserving the unilateral nature of the decision to minimize allegations of conspiracy between the medical staff and the hospital when adverse actions are taken.

JUDICIAL APPEAL. Because of the value of medical staff membership and privileges and the lingering taint that can follow physicians if an adverse action against them is then reported to the NPDB, many adversely affected individuals have sought judicial relief. Courts have permitted only the affected physician to seek judicial review of adverse decisions. Courts have not permitted other medical staff members,[265] patients,[266] or families of patients to challenge decisions to grant or deny medical staff membership or clinical privileges. The spouse of the physician also lacks standing, even when the family has to move, causing the spouse to lose his job.[267]

Courts generally require the physician to "exhaust their nonjudicial remedies" by pursuing all procedures available within the hospital before allowing appeal to the courts. If a physician refuses to participate in the hospital hearing, courts will usually not allow an appeal based on denial of procedural due process.[268] However, hospital procedures did not in some cases have to be exhausted before court review when the hospital procedures clearly did not satisfy applicable due process or fair hearing requirements.[269]

THE RULE OF NONREVIEW. Many state courts have adopted a deference to the decisions that hospitals make with regard to their credentialing and privileging, particularly with regard to initial applicants. An Illinois court described this "rule of nonreview" well: "Under this doctrine, as a matter of public policy, internal staffing decisions of private hospitals are not subject to judicial review. The judicial reluctance to review these internal staff

decisions reflects the unwillingness of courts to substitute their judgment for that of hospital officials with superior qualifications to consider and decide such issues. . . . The doctrine of 'non-review' is grounded on the idea that courts are not well equipped to review the action of hospital authorities in rendering medical staffing decisions because those decisions involve specialized medical and business considerations that are uniquely within the province of the medical community and hospital administrators."[270]

> Under this doctrine, as a matter of public policy, internal staffing decisions of private hospitals are not subject to judicial review. The judicial reluctance to review these internal staff decisions reflects the unwillingness of courts to substitute their judgment for that of hospital officials with superior qualifications to consider and decide such issues. . . . An exception to this rule has developed where a physician's existing staff privileges are revoked, suspended, or reduced. In such circumstances, the court will engage in limited review to determine whether the hospital complied with its bylaws in rendering the decision. *Goldberg v. Rush Univ. Med. Ctr.*, 863 N.E.2d 829;309 Ill. Dec. 197.

This court also noted a common, limited exception to this rule. "An exception to this rule has developed where a physician's existing staff privileges are revoked, suspended, or reduced. In such circumstances, the court will engage in limited review to determine whether the hospital complied with its bylaws in rendering the decision." This is reflective of the tendency of courts to give greater significance to loss of membership and privileges rather than denial of them since some courts (especially in public hospitals, as discussed above) characterize an established right to practice as akin to a property right or expectation of continued practice.

Judicial economy, that is, avoiding tying up the courts whenever appropriate, is another public policy reason cited by courts in favor of this doctrine.

When courts do review a hospital action, they usually show great deference to the judgment of the hospital and its medical staff[271] and limit their review to a determination of whether appropriate procedures were followed[272] or, occasionally, whether the action appears arbitrary or capricious. Again, cases reflect a judicial policy that the hospital and staff are uniquely qualified to make credentialing decisions. If credible evidence supports the action and proper procedures have been followed, the judiciary will almost always approve hospital actions. A few states do not follow this principle. For example, in 2003, Maryland rejected deference to hospitals.[273] Missouri applies deference to private hospitals, but not public hospitals.[274] Florida adopted a statutory prohibition of injunctions or damages against hospitals and those who participate in the disciplinary process unless actual fraud is demonstrated.[275] In states with statutory requirements, courts will review whether there has been compliance with the statutes.[276]

Injunction. Some physicians seek injunctions to require hospitals to keep them on or reinstate them to the medical staff. Generally, any person seeking an injunction must prove at least four elements: (1) substantial likelihood of ultimately winning the lawsuit on the merits, (2) irreparable injury, (3) the threatened injury without the injunction outweighs the injury to the opposing party from an injunction, and (4) the injunction will not be adverse to the public interest.[277] An injury is usually not irreparable if it can be compensated by monetary remedies.[278]

In most states, injunctions are seldom issued concerning medical staff privileges.[279] When they are issued, they are generally overturned on appeal.[280] Often this is because (1) money damages are available or (2) potential injuries to the hospital and patients generally outweigh injuries to the physician.

Occasionally, injunctions have been issued requiring reinstatement until the bylaws procedures can be completed.[281] Some state courts are more prone to issue such injunctions.

In 1989, a physician was assessed over $50,000 in damages by an Illinois court for wrongfully obtaining an injunction to restore clinical privileges.[282]

In one very unusual case in 2004, community citizens obtained a temporary restraining order from a Nebraska trial judge without notice to the hospital. When the hospital became involved, the judge realized that the patients did not have standing to seek such an order and dissolved the order.[283]

Mandamus. In California, a writ of administrative mandamus has been issued by a court to compel a hospital to reinstate a physician to medical staff membership and privileges.[284] California courts generally require physicians to pursue a mandamus proceeding before permitting a tort suit concerning medical staff decisions.[285] In other states, a writ of mandamus[286] is generally not available to private individuals unless they have obligations in the nature of a public or quasi-public duty,[287] nor is it available to enforce private rights or to enforce contractual obligations.[288]

Employment contracts, even with public entities, are generally not enforceable by mandamus unless a statute sets the terms of the employment.[289] In 1994, Wisconsin adopted the contrary position, permitting mandamus to be used in some medical staff matters.[290] A writ of mandamus will generally not be available outside California and Wisconsin in medical staff matters.

5-7 Potential Liability of Those Involved in the Process of Making Medical Staff Appointment and Clinical Privilege Decisions

When physicians challenge adverse hospital actions, they often seek payment of money damages in addition to reversal of the hospital action. They base their claims on several grounds, including breach of contract, interference with business relationships, lost earnings or emotional distress during the proceedings,[291] defamation, antitrust violations, and discrimination, among others. Some legal doctrines and some statutes provide those involved in these determinations with limited immunity from some of these claims.

Refusing to take necessary actions also exposes the medical staff and hospital to liability, so inaction does not avoid liability.

WAIVER. Many hospitals require all applicants to sign a waiver protecting those involved in providing information, reviewing it, and making decisions on the applicant's qualifications based on such information from liability. Through 2003, TJC recognized this common practice by requiring applicants to sign such waivers, but was silent on the issue in later standards.[292] Several courts have upheld these waivers,[293] but some courts have declined to enforce them.[294] Where enforceable, waivers in application request forms, the applications themselves, and in the medical staff bylaws can help assure that the applicant is not granted membership and privileges without the waiver being completed. Multiple waivers can also negate arguments that the applicant was not aware of or did not receive sufficient notice of the waiver executed in the application process.

BREACH OF CONTRACT. When a physician has a contract with the hospital, termination or other breach of the contract can result in an assessment of monetary damages for the breach. Some courts view the bylaws as such a contract, permitting a breach of contract claim for violation of the bylaws.[295] Courts in more than twenty states have recognized bylaws as in the nature of a contract or otherwise enforceable.[296]

A federal court in California, for example, held that a hospital's bylaws create a binding contract and a physician whose privileges were terminated when the hospital entered a new exclusive contract could sue for breach of contract.[297] Florida courts have generally been strong and consistent in their recognition of medical staff bylaws as contractual in nature.[298] The Mississippi Supreme Court rejected breach of contract claims by physicians whose privileges were ended when a hospital signed an exclusive contract.[299] Similarly, a Texas appeals court addressed a physician whose privileges were terminated for failure to enter into the hospital's new exclusive contract and found that he could not sue for breach of contract based on the bylaws.[300]

INTERFERENCE WITH BUSINESS RELATIONSHIPS. Adversely affected physicians often claim that the actions of the hospital or its staff tortiously interfered with their business relationships with patients, other physicians, hospitals, and others. Generally, merely denying or terminating privileges or professional service contracts has not been found to constitute tortious interference. Although tort liability for such action is possible,[301] the greatest exposure of hospitals and their staffs occurs when they take additional steps, such as when they try to deny access to billing information or other records,[302] discriminate in access to equipment or staff necessary to exercise remaining privileges,[303] or create or disseminate false information.[304]

Generally, a claim of tortious interference with a business relationship requires a showing of (1) an existing business relationship under which the plaintiff has legal rights,[305] (2) knowledge of that relationship by defendant, (3) an intentional and unjustified interference with the relationship, and (4) damage to the plaintiff as a result of the breach of the relationship.[306] In some jurisdictions, the business relationship that is interfered with does not need to be contractual so some expectancies are protected if there is an understanding that would have been completed if the interference had not occurred. The Florida Supreme Court, however, ruled that this did not permit a claim based on the "mere hope that some of its past customers may choose to buy again" where there was no ongoing relationship with those customers.[307]

In assessing what interference is legally permissible, some courts recognize a privilege of competition that permits a hospital to use efforts to convince others who are in business relationships with the physician that are terminable at will to shift their business, as long as certain prohibited means are not used.[308]

DEFAMATION. Wrongful injury to another person's reputation is defamation. Defamation is discussed in Chapter 11 "Criminal and Civil Penalties." One defense to a defamation claim is a qualified privilege, which means that there is no liability for certain privileged communications, even if they injure another's reputation, if the communications were not made with malice (a so-called "qualified" rather than "absolute immunity"). Most courts apply a qualified privilege to communications during medical staff peer review activities, including hospital board review and action.[309] In 1982, a Pennsylvania court dismissed the portion of a defamation suit against the hospital because no malice had been shown, but refused to dismiss the portion against the physicians.[310] It was asserted that the physicians had made their statements because they wanted the financial benefit of keeping a competitor from obtaining clinical privileges. If proved at trial, the financial motive could establish malice. The immunity statutes discussed elsewhere in this chapter may provide more protection than the qualified privilege. See **Figure 5-3**.

ANTITRUST. Physicians frequently challenge medical staff actions by claiming the actions are a restraint of trade or an attempt to monopolize medical practice, thus violating federal antitrust laws. Reasons for seeking remedy under

Figure 5-3 Wheel of Peer Review Misfortune

Baker, C.H. (2010). How to Avoid Corporate Negligence and Legal Pitfalls When Performing Peer Review Actions, p. 3. http://www.venable.com/files/Event/d1db3c20-33b0-462f-ab55-973e02e0beb4/Presentation/EventAttachment/24a5c64f-933b-4dd7-9673-c18b830bd186/Baker_How_to_Avoid_Corporate_Negligence_and_Legal_Pitfalls_in_Peer_Review_Actions.pdf. Accessed March 23, 2012.

the federal antitrust statutes include: (1), the availability of treble damages if the physician wins, (2) the cost of litigating federal claims which is thought to make hospitals more willing to compromise, (3) the possible inapplicability of state laws that otherwise may protect otherwise peer review documents from discovery, and (4) the perceived advantage of the federal forum itself.

Prior to 1991, one of the major barriers that protected hospitals from medical staff antitrust suits was the difficulty in proving the impact on interstate commerce necessary for federal antitrust laws to apply. In 1991, the U.S. Supreme Court established a new standard so that impact on interstate commerce is easy to demonstrate in many medical staff cases.[311]

Antitrust cases against hospitals still remain difficult for practitioners to win, however. HCQIA provides immunity from monetary liability based on antitrust claims for most credentialing actions, as discussed previously in this chapter. In the unusual cases where the physician can show failure to make reasonable efforts to comply with HCQIA, antitrust liability is still possible.[312]

There are other barriers to successful antitrust suits. Physicians frequently have difficulty showing market power of the hospital, antitrust standing,[313] antitrust injury,[314] or causation of their alleged injuries.[315] Other antitrust issues are discussed elsewhere in this text.

DISCRIMINATION. For obvious reasons, medical staff decisions should not be based on discriminatory criteria, such as race, creed, color, sex, national origin, and handicap. Sometimes medical staff actions are challenged on the basis that they violate federal and state statutes barring discrimination.[316] For example, an African-American physician in the District of Columbia claimed she had been terminated from her position in a health maintenance organization because of her race, violating the federal Civil Rights Act. A federal court found sufficient evidence that her termination was based on complaints of African-American and Caucasian coworkers and on failure to improve her performance after being warned and not on her race, so no violation was found.[317]

In general, staff privileges alone have not been sufficient to trigger coverage under discrimination laws that focus on employment because granting privileges is not employing.[318] However, some discrimination laws apply to interfering with employment opportunities. Thus, in some circumstances, physicians who have been denied or lost medical staff membership have been able to sue the hospital.[319] Appointments to compensated positions, such as director of a department, may be subject to employment protections.[320] Some discrimination laws are not based on employment. Courts have disagreed on whether laws that address discrimination in public accommodations can be applied to medical staff decisions.[321]

Adversely affected physicians have brought claims under a wide variety of other statutory theories including Racketeering Influenced and Corrupt Organizations Act ("RICO")[322] and other common law theories including intentional infliction of emotional distress.[323]

⚑ IMMUNITY. It has been reported that every state provides persons involved in medical staff review some immunity from liability for their statements or actions in appropriate circumstances.[324]

> Federal, rather than state, privilege law applies to a federal action in federal court. Fed. Rule Civil Pro. 501. Every federal court to consider the issue has declined to recognize a federal peer review privilege. (See, e.g., *Ray v. Pinnacle Health Hospitals, Inc., et al.,* No. 1:07-CV-0715 (M.D. Pa. May 22, 2008). Maria Greco Danaher, "Physician Staffing Issues and Employment-Related Lawsuits: A Litigation Epidemic in the Making?" *National Law Review,* June 7, 2010.)

The common law qualified privilege from liability for defamation previously discussed is an example. Some state statutes provide limited immunity from damages for actions in the peer review process.[325] An Arizona appellate court ruled that the chief of staff and the hospital administrator could not be sued for summarily suspending a surgeon's clinical privileges unless there was a showing that the primary purpose of the action was other than safeguarding patients.[326] Because a patient had died following "serious errors in judgment" by the surgeon and the surgeon had scheduled another patient for the same type of surgery, the court found the primary purpose of the suspension was safeguarding patients.

Some states have enacted statutes that grant broader immunity for peer review participants. For example, Florida enacted a statute providing there is no liability of peer reviewers unless intentional fraud is proved.[327] However, the Florida Supreme Court declared unconstitutional an additional requirement that before suing a physician must post a bond to pay the defendants' defense costs if liability is not found.[328] In Illinois, there is strong statutory immunity.[329] The immunity statutes of Louisiana and California have been interpreted to protect only individuals, not institutions.[330] Tennessee's immunity statute has been interpreted to apply to hospitals, even though the term "hospital" does not appear in the statute.[331]

State statutes that prohibit the discovery and use of certain peer review records as evidence may make it impossible to prove certain claims, effectively granting immunity. For example, the Florida prohibition on introducing testimony and records concerning peer review proceedings effectively bars nearly all defamation claims for statements made in the peer review process.[332] Recognizing the important public policy of encouraging peer review to assure quality medical care for their citizens and the reluctance of potential peer reviewers to participate if they will be sued for their candor, states have adopted peer review statutes to protect and encourage the participation of medical staff members in peer review. At the same time, courts recognize that the peer review protections afforded such as privilege, immunity from suit, and nondiscoverability of peer-review materials limit a plaintiff's fundamental rights to access a court and have all relevant evidence heard, counterbalancing public policy issues. Thus many courts tightly construe peer review statutes and only extend protections to those participants, statements, and documents that are generated as part of the peer review process and clearly fall within the scope of the peer review statute. Activities that lead to formal peer review or are undertaken as a result of it are often not deemed to be protected.[333]

A federal judge summarized this common judicial policy in the following manner: "Because the dividing line between peer review and normal business operations can be unclear, courts generally apply the peer review privilege only when the formalities of a peer review process are clearly apparent. For example, conversations between a department chief and nurses will not be protected from discovery if there were no apparent peer review formalities – even when the department chief views his job as "provid[ing] good quality service . . . and coordinat[ing] services between departments" and characterizes the conversations as "quality control." … Formalities such as designated committees and explicitly labeled peer-review reports act as a signal to medical employees, telling them when their opinions will be protected from discovery.[334]

Conclusion

Hospital care is a critical component of American healthcare delivery. The hospital and its medical staff depend on one another for the equipment, facilities, and medical expertise needed to provide patients with quality care. The hospital board and the medical staff each play important roles in ensuring that individuals who provide care in the hospital-setting are well qualified to do so. Because livelihoods and professional reputations are also at stake in such decisions, adverse decisions can lead to litigation in some circumstances. Assuring that criteria and mechanisms are consistent with applicable legal and accreditation standards and are applied in a consistent manner can help avoid or reduce the risk of liability in such cases. Medical staff bylaws help provide the mechanisms and criteria in a standardized, documented form by enumerating applicable standards in a standard template document. Recognizing the importance of the job that hospitals and medical staffs play in assuring quality, states and the federal government have adopted protections to help them achieve their important goals.

Chapter Summary

This chapter covered a wide range of legal issues that arise in the appointment process, delineation of clinical privileges, review and reappointment, and the modification and termination of the clinical privileges process undertaken by the typical hospital and medical staff. The organization of the typical hospital and the interaction and respective roles of the medical staff and the hospital board were discussed in this context. The scope of liability exposure of participants in the various processes was described. Finally, state and federal peer review and other legal protections available with regard to the procedures for adverse actions against members were discussed.

Key Terms and Definitions

Corporate Negligence - "A [common law (judge-made)] doctrine that hospital and health care centers have a responsibility to patients that extends beyond that of merely furnishing facilites for treatment" (*McGraw-Hill Concise Dictionary of Modern Medicine.* © 2002 by The McGraw-Hill Companies, Inc. as cited by http://medicaldictionary.thefreedictionary.com/corporate+liability) Also known as "institutional negligence" and first described in cases such as *Darling v. Charleston Community Memorial Hospital*, 33 Ill.2d 326, 331, 211 N.E.2d 253 (1965).

Credentialing - A term used to describe the process of determining eligibility for hospital medical staff membership and/or privileges to be granted to physicians and allied health professionals (AHPs) in the light of their academic preparation, licensing, training, and performance. A basic premise of credentialing is that the applicant always has the burden to prove that he or she is qualified and capable of performing the requested privileges according to applicable standards.

Disruptive Behavior - TJC describes "disruptive behavior" as "intimidating . . . and overt actions [by healthcare professionals] such as verbal outbursts and physical threats, as well as passive activities such as refusing to perform assigned tasks or quietly exhibiting uncooperative attitudes during routine activities . . . [among the] healthcare team," that "can foster medical errors, contribute to poor patient satisfaction and to preventable adverse outcomes, increase the cost of care, and cause qualified clinicians, administrators and managers to seek new positions in more professional environments." (Behaviors that undermine a culture of safety. *Joint Commission Sentinel Event Alert*, Issue 40, July 9, 2008.)

Economic Credentialing - A term sometimes used to describe decisions by a hospital about medical staff appointment and/or clinical privileges of a practitioner that take economic factors into account, such as patient lengths of stay, number of tests ordered, costs, or competition with the hospital.

Exclusive Staffing Arrangement - An arrangement pursuant to which a hospital assigns responsibility, by contract or otherwise, for a certain area of patient care (frequently radiology, pathology, emergency, and anesthesiology) to one individual or group of individuals, to the exclusion of others. The U.S. Supreme Court recognized the permissibility of exclusive contracts under the antitrust laws in *Jefferson Parish Hosp. Dist. v. Hyde* – 466 U.S. 2 (1984).

Fiduciary Credentialing - Defined by the American Medical Association as "a special case of economic credentialing [pursuant to which there is] a loss of hospital privileges based on a physician's economic competition with a hospital.

Health Care Quality Improvement Act - A federal statute codified at 42 U.S.C. 11101 which places limitation on damages for professional review actions that are conducted in accordance with the safe harbor requirements of the statute.

The Joint Commission (TJC) - A private organization granted authority by the federal government to survey healthcare organizations in accordance with Joint Commission standards and to deem the organizations compliant with the Medicare Conditions of Participation, permitting them to participate in the Medicare program and receive payment for appropriate services provided to Medicare patients.

Medicare Conditions of Participation - Requirements developed by the Center for Medicare and Medicaid Services (CMS) "that health care organizations must meet in order to begin and continue participating in the Medicare and Medicaid programs. These health and safety standards are the foundation for improving quality and protecting the health and safety of beneficiaries." (CMS.gov)

National Practitioner Data Bank (NPDB) - A clearinghouse for information on disciplinary and malpractice actions against physicians created by the Health Care Quality Improvement Act (HCQIA) of 1986, which went into operation in 1990. The act requires that the following actions must be reported to the data bank (NPDB): (1) an insurance company (or other entity) that makes a payment on a malpractice claim (whether in settlement or pursuant to a court decision), (2) a state board of medical examiners that imposes a sanction on a physician, and (3) a healthcare entity (such as a hospital) that takes a professional review action adversely affecting a physician's privileges for more than thirty days. Eligible parties may then inquire of the NPDB for information about a particular physician; for example, a hospital may inquire prior to granting privileges. If a hospital fails to comply with the reporting requirements, it loses for three years the protection it would otherwise have under the act.

Negligent Credentialing - A "progeny of hospital or institutional negligence," *Frigo v. Silver Cross*, 377 Ill. App.3d 43, 876 N.E.2d 697, 315 Ill.Dec. 385 (Ill. App. 1st, 2007). Based on the notion that "a hospital has a duty to exercise due care in the selection of its medical staff," (*Johnson v. Misericordia Community Hospital*, 99 Wis.2d 708, 301 N.W.2d 156 (1981)). The legal analysis examines whether or not a healthcare entity met the standard of care in the processes it utilized in selecting an individual who was alleged to have injured a patient in the institution. "If the physician is not negligent, there is no negligent credentialing claim against the hospital." *Hiroms v. Scheffey, M.D.*, 76 S.W.3d 486, 489 (Tex. App. 2002).

Nondelegable Duty - A duty that can potentially be shared but cannot be delegated and ultimately remains with the body charged with the duty. Many courts say hospitals have a nondelegable duty to maintain appropriate credentialing procedures and to see that they are properly implemented to assure quality care in the institution.

Periodic Performance Review (PPR) - A compliance assessment tool designed to help organizations with their continuous monitoring of performance and performance improvement activities. (*Facts about the Periodic Performance Review*, The Joint Commission, September, 2010.)

The Rule of Nonreview - A judicial (common-law) doctrine stating that, as a matter of public policy, internal staffing decisions of private hospitals are not subject to judicial review. The doctrine is grounded on the idea that courts are not well equipped to review the action of hospital authorities in rendering medical staffing decisions because those decisions involve specialized medical and business considerations. An exception to this rule has developed where a physician's existing staff privileges are revoked, suspended, or reduced. In such circumstances, some courts court will engage in limited review to determine whether the hospital complied with its bylaws in rendering the decision.

Instructor-Led Questions

1. What are the responsibilities of the board of directors and the medical staff concerning patient care?

2. What are medical staff bylaws, and how are they changed?

3. What is the structure of the medical staff, and how are officers selected and removed?

4. What legal constraints are there on medical staff rules and processes?

5. What criteria may institutions consider in determining medical staff membership? What criteria are prohibited?

6. What are the issues involved in restricting membership by physicians who compete with the institution?

7. How should the institution determine which clinical privileges to grant?

8. What factors can the institution consider in making reappointment decisions?

9. What are the permitted grounds for modifying or terminating clinical privileges?

10. What are the issues involved in establishing closed staffs or exclusive arrangements for certain specialties?

11. When must medical staff actions be reported to the National Practitioner Data Bank?

12. What steps are usually followed in medical staff review of adverse actions committed by medical staff? Which steps are required in order to have immunity under the Health Care Quality Improvement Act?

13. When will courts enjoin medical staff actions?

14. What are the grounds for potential liability for medical staff actions?

Endnotes

1   *Johnson v. Misericordia Comm. Hosp.*, 99 Wis. 2d 708, 301 N.W.2d 156 (1981); see also *Sheffield v. Zilis*, 170 Ga. App. 62, 316 S.E.2d 493 (1984) [hospital not liable because it demonstrated adequate review of physician's credentials]; in 2011, a bill was introduced and passed by the Utah senate in a direct attempt to overrule the Utah Supreme Court's finding that a hospital could be liable for negligent credentialing despite language already in the statute that seemed to say otherwise. *Archuleta v. St. Marks Hospital*, 2010 UT 36, 238 P.2d 1044 Annotation, Hospital's liability for negligence in selection or appointment of staff physician or surgeon, 51 A.L.R. 3D 981.

2   *Purcell v. Zimbelman*, 18 Ariz. App. 75, 500 P.3d 335 (1972); see also *Pedroza v. Bryant*, 101 Wash. 2d 226, 677 P.2d 166 (1984) [hospital can be liable for granting privileges to physician who is not competent, but liability does not extend to treatment provided off hospital premises].

3   *Larson v. Wasemiller*, 738 N.W.2d 300 (Minn., 2007).

4   *Renown Health, Inc. v. Vanderford*, 235 P.3d 614 (Nev. 2010). For a discussion of the case and the multiple elements involved in the analysis of whether a hospital is liable for the negligence of its medical staff members, see S. Tovino, Nevada Supreme Court Refuses to Apply Nondelegable Duty to Reno Hospital, UNLV School of Law's UNLV Law Blog September 20, 2011, http://unlvlawblog.blogspot.com/2011/09/nevada-hospital-does-not-have-non.html. In a similar manner, the Supreme Court of Arkansas refused to expand the statutory definition of "medical injury" under the state's medical practice act to include negligent credentialing because as codified by the legislature such injury must "originate with a doctor's order" rather than with a hospital's action. It also refused to create a common law cause of action for negligent credentialing, expressing concern that to do so could "lead to duplicative litigation and encourage inefficient relitigation of issues better handled in the context of the core cause of action" especially "if there are other sufficient avenues, short of creating a new cause of action, that serve to remedy the situation for a plaintiff" which it felt there were. *Paulino v. QHG of Springdale, Inc.*, No. 11-26 (Ark. Feb. 9, 2012) (Slip opinion).

5   For an interesting twist on the notion of a nondelegable duty in the peer review hearing context in the case of *El Attar, M.D. v. Hollywood Presbyterian Medical Center*, see C.Pellon, *Appeals Court Rules Hospitals Cannot Usurp Medical Staff Peer Review Authority*, CMANet, August 29, 2011, http://www.cmanet.org/news/detail/?article=appeals-court-rules-hospitals-cannot-usurp

6   E.g., *Rotwein v. Sunharbor Manor Res. Health Care Facility*, 181 Misc. 2d 847, 695 N.Y.S.2d 477 (Sup. Ct. 1999) [podiatrist lost privileges in nursing home].

7   E.g., WIS. ADMIN. CODE HFS 132.61(1) [organized medical staff optional for nursing home; only medical director required].

8   Joint Commission, 2005 COMPREHENSIVE ACCREDITATION MANUAL FOR HOSPITALS [hereinafter cited as 2005 TJC CAMH], Elements of Performance 8 for MS.1.20.

9   2005 TJC CAMH, MS.1.30.

10   E.g., *Weary v. Baylor Univ. Hosp.*, 360 S.W.2d 895 (Tex. Civ. App. 1962); contra *St. John's Hosp. Med. Staff v. St. John's Reg. Med. Ctr.*, 90 S.D. 674, 245 N.W.2d 472 (1976).

11   *Lo v. Provena Covenant Med. Ctr.*, 342 Ill. App. 3d 975, 796 N.E.2d 607 (4th Dist. 2003), lv. denied, 207 Ill. 2d 605, 807 N.E.2d 976 (2004); T. Albert, Doctors fear precedent in privileges case, AM. MED. NEWS, Nov. 17, 2003, 9 [discussion of *Lo* case from the perspective of organized medicine].

12   "Revisions to Hospital Medical Staff Standard MS.01.01.01 (formerly MS.1.20)," The Joint Commission, April 2010.

13   E.g., D. Adams, Doctors fight for enforcement of staff bylaws, AM. MED. NEWS, Jan. 19, 2004, 9; study finds power shift, AM. MED. NEWS, Apr. 26, 2004, 20; T. Albert, Med staff-hospital fights turn nasty and more litigious, AM. MED. NEWS, Apr. 19, 2004, 1.

14   FTC letter to Georgia Hosp. Ass'n, May 28, 1993, as discussed in 2 H.L.R. 1161 (1993).

15   Eisenhower medical staff to appeal court decision, MOD. HEALTHCARE, Apr. 14, 1989, 24; Staver, Hospital board settles, OKs staff president, AM. MED. NEWS, Nov. 10, 1989, at 6.

16   *Lawnwood Med. Ctr., Inc. v. Cassimally*, 471 So. 2d 1346 (Fla. 4th DCA 1985).

17   E.g., *Keane v. St. Francis Hosp.*, 186 Wis. 2d 637, 522 N.W.2d 517 (Ct. App. 1994) [removal of chief of staff].

18   E.g., *Ann Arundel Gen. Hosp. v. O'Brien*, 49 Md. App. 362, 432 A.2d 483 (1981) [combined radiology and nuclear medicine, entered exclusive contract].

19   E.g., Former CU med chair loses latest try for reinstatement, AP, May 20, 2003 [denial of reinstatement by U.S. magistrate]; *Hrehorovich v. Harbor Hosp. Ctr.*, 93 Md. App. 772, 614 A.2d 1021 (1992).

20   *Shoemaker v. Los Angeles County*, No. BC096101 (Cal. Super. Ct. Jan. 31, 1994), as discussed in 3 H.L.R. 186 (1994) [injunction of county hospital from removing chief of emergency medicine, based on due process, civil service requirements despite threatened loss of accreditation of emergency medicine residency because chief was not board certified]; Agency restores Drew Medical School emergency residency accreditation, 3 H.L.R. 317 (1994) [on Feb. 23, appellate court granted stay of injunction, so board certified interim chair, program director appointed and accreditation was restored the next day]; *Shoemaker v. County of Los Angeles*, 37 Cal. App. 4th 618; 43 Cal. Rptr. 2d 774 (2d Dist. 1995).

21   E.g., J. Olson, Doctors want Alegent bosses out: Bergan Mercy's staff declares "no confidence" in the parent company after decisions they say could jeopardize care, OMAHA WORLD HERALD, Mar. 20, 2003, 1B; N. Aksamit, Alegent criticizes doctors' complaints, OMAHA WORLD HERALD, Sept. 17, 2003, 3B [MDs filing complaints against hospital with state and federal agencies].

22 E.g., Beleaguered hospital exec. resigns, Am. Med. News, Oct. 27, 2003, 10 [Cal.]; Medical staff to consider resolution on hospital CEO, AP, Mar. 31, 2003 [S. Dak.].

23 E.g., D. Kelley, Doctors' lawsuit may go forward; A judge rules that Community Memorial Hospital's medical staff is a legal entity with the right to sue the Ventura facility, L.A. Times, Aug. 8, 2003, pt. 2, 1; D. Kelley, Doctors, hospital settle rights lawsuit; the accord, subject to ratification, is aimed at stopping the flow of disgruntled physicians and their patients from the Ventura facility, L.A. Times, Aug. 18, 2004, B1.

24 E.g., *Board of Surgeon Directors v. Board of Directors* (N.Y. Sup. Ct. June 1999), as reported in N.Y.L.J., June 11, 1999, 25 [no standing to challenge sale of hospital assets, but note the sale was later blocked on petition of the state attorney general - In re *Manhattan Eye, Ear & Throat Hosp*, 186 Misc. 2d 126, 715 N.Y.S.2d 575 (Sup. Ct. 1999)].

25 E.g., *Duson v. Poage*, 318 S.W.2d 89 (Tex. Civ. App. 1958). Often, professional societies submit "friend of the court" briefs in these matters to influence the courts to find in ways that might benefit their membership.

26 E.g., In re *Med. Staff of Good Samaritan Med. Ctr.*, FTC, File No. 901 0032 (settlement Sept. 7, 1994), as discussed in 3 Health L.Rptr. [BNA] 1257 (1994) [agreement of medical staff not to combine to prevent or restrict services of hospital or multi-specialty clinic] [hereinafter Health L.Rptr. cited as H.L.R.]; B. McCormick, Doctors settle FTC boycott case, Am. Med. News, Oct. 3, 1994, at 10 [Good Samaritan]; S. Lutz, Antitrust concerns pit Texas hospital against staff doctors in legal fight, Mod. Healthcare, Mar. 6, 1995, at 18 [hospital accusing eight doctors of conspiring to fix prices, boycott the hospital, pay bribe to CEO]; see also P. Guinta, District sees admissions drop after irking MDs, Fla. Med. Business (S.Fla.Ed.), Mar. 28, 1989, at 6 [drop in admissions at North Broward Hospital District hospitals after privileges granted to Cleveland Clinic physicians]; D.A. Gilmore, The antitrust implications of boycotts by health care professionals: Professional standards, professional ethics and the First Amendment, 14 Law, Med. & Health Care 221 (1988).

27 See "The Joint Commission's New MS 01.01.01 Hospitals and Medical Staffs Can Run But Not Hide From Document Review And Revisions," Dennis J. Purtell, Whyte Hirschboeck Dudek S.C. Special Report October, 2010. Often, professional societies submit "friend of the court" briefs in these matters to influence the courts to find in ways that might benefit their membership.

28 E.g., *Wallington v. Zinn*, 146 W.Va. 147, 118 S.E.2d 526 (1961).

29 See F. Helminski, "That peculiar science: Osteopathic medicine and the law," 12 Law, Med. & Health Care, Feb. 1984, 32.

30 E.g., Fla. Stat. § 395.0191; Cal. Health & Safety Code § 1316; but see *New Hampshire Podiatric Med. Ass'n v. New Hampshire Hosp. Ass'n*, 735 F. Supp. 448 (D. N.H. 1990) [not violation of equal protection to deny podiatrists privileges].

31 2004 TJC CAMH, MS.2.10; 2005 TJC CAMH, MS.2.10.

32 E.g., Fla. Stat. § 395.0191.

33 E.g., Wis. Stat. § 50.36(3g)(c); but see *California Ass'n of Psychology Providers v. California Hosp. Ass'n*, 51 Cal. 3d 1; 793 P.2d 2 (1990) [state could not require physician involvement].

34 E.g., *Petrocco v. Dover Gen. Hosp.*, 273 N.J. Super. 501, 642 A.2d 1016 (App. Div. 1994) [exclusion of chiropractors from hospital privileges upheld]; *Cohn v. Bond*, 953 F.2d 154 (4th Cir. 1991), cert. denied, 505 U.S. 1230 (1992) [no conspiracy in denial to chiropractor because intracorporate immunity applied].

35 E.g., Easing into the medical mainstream: Chiropractors gain acceptance at hospitals, The Herald (Miami, FL), Feb. 18, 1995, 1C [hospital adding a chiropractic department]; D. Fiely, Community hospital extends privileges to chiropractors, Columbus [Ohio] Dispatch, May 17, 1993, 1E.

36 E.g., Midwives allowed to admit, discharge patients at Meriter, AP, Aug. 29, 2003 [WI]; but see, Legislator says hospital breaks law in midwife squabble, AP, Oct. 1, 2003 [IA - midwives permitted to practice under supervision, but not as independent members]; J. Gould, Midwife strife—city hospital bans birthing assistants, N.Y. Post, Nov. 28, 2003, 16 [midwives barred from most deliveries]; *Nurse Midwifery Assocs. v. Hibbett*, 918 F.2d 605 (6th Cir. 1990), op. modified on reh'g, 927 F.2d 904 (6th Cir.), cert. denied, 502 U.S. 952 (1991) [intracorporate conspiracy doctrine protected pediatricians, but not obstetricians, who recommended against nurse's privileges; could find conspiracy between obstetricians, hospital].

37 2005 TJC CAMH, LD.3.70, Element of Performance 2.

38 But see Fla. Stat. § 395.0191(2) [application of advanced registered nurse practitioners must be considered].

39 Federal Register Vol. 76, No. 205/Monday, October 24, 2011.

40 E.g., *Weiss v. York Hosp.*, 745 F.2d 786, 821 (3d Cir. 1984), cert. denied, 470 U.S. 1060 (1985).

41 E.g., *Evers v. Edward Hosp. Ass'n*, 247 Ill. App. 3d 717, 617 N.E.2d 1211 (2d Dist. 1993), app. denied, 153 Ill. 2d 559, 624 N.E.2d 806 (1993) [declined to evaluate application because deemed incomplete]; *Smith v. Cleburne County Hosp.*, 870 F.2d 1375 (8th Cir., cert. denied, 493 U.S. 847) (1989) [failure to submit papers for reappointment was voluntary withdrawal].

42 E.g., *Johnson v. Galen*, 39 S.W.3d 828 (Ky. App. 2001) [misrepresentation on application]; *Pariser v. Christian Health Care Sys., Inc.*, 816 F.2d 1248 (8th Cir. 1987), after remand, 859 F.2d 78 (8th Cir. 1988) [falsely denied prior denial of privileges]; *Lapidot v. Memorial Med. Ctr.*, 144 Ill. App. 3d 141, 494 N.E.2d 838 (4th Dist. 1986) [false denial of prior suspension of privileges]; *Brooks v. Arlington Hosp. Ass'n*. 850 F.2d 191 (4th Cir. 1988) [failure to complete delineation of privileges form]; *Unterthiner v. Desert Hosp. Dist.*, 33 Cal. 3d 285, 188 Cal. Rptr. 590, 656 P.2d 554 (1983); *Yeargin v. Hamilton Mem. Hosp.*, 225 Ga. 661, 171 S.E.2d 136 (1969), cert. denied, 397 U.S. 963 (1970) [exception to agreement to abide by rules]; *Spindle v. Sisters of Providence*, 61 P.2d 431 (Alaska 2002) [reasonable to require applicant to provide discharge diagnoses and summaries on prior cases and to consider application incomplete in absence of this information].

43 E.g., *Abdelmessih v. Board of Regents*, 205 A.D.2d 983, 613 N.Y.S.2d 971 (3d Dep't 1994); *Radnay v. Sobol*, 175 A.D.2d 432, 572 N.Y.S.2d 489 (3d Dep't 1991); contra *Elmariah v. Dep't of Prof. Reg.*, 574 So. 2d 164 (Fla. 1st DCA 1990).

44 E.g., *Scott v. Sisters of St. Francis Health Servs., Inc.*, 645 F. Supp. 1465 (N.D. Ill. 1986), aff'd without op., 822 F.2d 1090 (7th Cir. 1987).

45 E.g., *Khouw v. Methodist Hosp.*, 126 Fed. Appx. 657, 2005 U.S. App. LEXIS 4206 (5th Cir. 2005) (unpub) [resignation agreement effectively barred reapplication].

46 E.g., Dr. allegedly had three prior medmal complaints: *Neff v. Johnson Memorial Hospital*, CONN. L. TRIB., Apr. 26, 2004, 507 [hospital not negligent in credentialing MD with three priors where no expert testimony that it breached standard of care]; but see *Fletcher v. South Peninsula Hosp.*, 71 P.3d 833 (Alaska 2003) [hospital should investigate disclosed prior malpractice claims].

47 E.g., *Truly v. Madison Gen. Hosp.*, 673 F.2d 763 (5th Cir.), cert. denied, 459 U.S. 909 (1982).

48 E.g., *Ascherman v. St. Francis Mem. Hosp.*, 45 Cal. App. 3d 507, 119 Cal. Rptr. 507 (1st Dist. 1975).

49 E.g., *Johnson v. Galen*, 39 S.W.3d 828 (Ky. App. 2001); *Landefeld v. Marion Gen. Hosp, Inc.*, 994 F.2d 1178 (6th Cir. 1993) [stealing internal mail indicated inability to work with others].

50 *Sussman v. Overlook Hosp. Ass'n*, 95 N.J. Super. 418, 231 A.2d 389 (App. Div. 1967).

51 *Miller v. Eisenhower Med. Ctr.*, 27 Cal. 3d 614, 166 Cal. Rptr. 826, 614 P.2d 258 (1980); applied in *Pick v. Santa Ana-Tustin Comm. Hosp.*, 130 Cal. App. 3d 970, 182 Cal. Rptr. 85 (4th Dist. 1982) [sufficient danger shown to justify denial].

52 *Mahmoodian v. United Hospital Center*, 404 SE 2d 750 (W.Va 1991).

53 E.g., *Khan v. Suburban Comm. Hosp.*, 45 Ohio St. 2d 39, 349 N.E.2d 398 (1976).

54 *Hay v. Scripps Mem. Hosp.*, 183 Cal. App. 3d 753, 228 Cal. Rptr. 413 (4th Dist. 1986).

55 E.g., *Armstrong v. Board of Directors*, 553 S.W.2d 77 (Tenn. Ct. App. 1976).

56 E.g., *Sarasota County Pub. Hosp. Bd. v. Shahawy*, 408 So. 2d 644 (Fla. 2d DCA 1981) [public hospital may require board certification or unusual qualifications for cardiac catheterization privileges] [partially superseded by statute, Fla. Stat. § 395.0191(3), that requires acceptance of equivalent osteopathic training].

57 42 C.F.R. § 482.12(a)(7).

58 See, E.g., *Evelyn V. v. Kings County Hosp. Ctr.*, 819 F. Supp. 183 (E.D. N.Y. 1993) [Medicaid Act requirement that state plan provide for maintaining health standards of providers did not authorize suit by recipients against city for deficiencies at municipal hospital]; contra *Fulkerson v. Comm'r*, 802 F. Supp. 529 (D. Me. 1992) [Medicaid recipients may enforce equal access to care provision].

59 2005 TJC CAMH, Elements of Performance 8 for MS.1.20.

60 H. Larkin, All aboard? AM. MED. NEWS, Mar. 13, 1995, 11 [options for those without board certification to deal with managed care, where 35 to 40 percent of physicians are not board certified]; S. McIlrath, Board-certified only need apply, AM. MED. NEWS, Dec. 12. 1994, 1 [medical groups seeking to block requirement of board certification for managed care participation].

61 Rev. Rul. 65-264, 1965-2 C.B. 159 [nondiscriminatory fees do not jeopardize federal tax exemption]; see also Brooks & Morrisey, Credentialing: Say good-bye to the "rubber stamp," 59 HOSPS., June 1, 1985, 50, 52.

62 *Chapman v. Peoples Comm. Hosp. Auth.*, 139 Mich. App. 696, 362 N.W.2d 755 (1984).

63 E.g., *Kennedy v. St. Joseph Mem. Hosp.*, 482 N.E.2d 268 (Ind. Ct. App. 1985) [moved personal residence too far away], disapproved on other grounds, *Pepple v. Parkview Mem. Hosp.*, 536 N.E.2d 274 (Ind. 1989); but see *Quinn v. Kent Gen. Hosp., Inc.*, 617 F. Supp. 1226 (D. Del. 1985) [factual issue of whether fifteen-mile rule was reasonable precluded summary judgment in antitrust case].

64 E.g., 1995 TJC CAMH, at 488.

65 E.g., *Sams v. Ohio Valley Gen. Hosp. Ass'n*, 413 F.2d 826 (4th Cir. 1969) [county boundary not valid geographic limit], disapproved on other grounds, *Modaber v. Culpeper Mem. Hosp.*, 674 F.2d 1023 (4th Cir. 1982); *Berman v. Valley Hosp.*, 103 N.J. 100, 510 A.2d 673 (1986) [geographic limits to control utilization unenforceable under unique New Jersey review of private hospitals as quasi-public entities].

66 *Clair v. Centre Comm. Hosp.*, 317 Pa. Super. 25, 463 A.2d 1065 (1983); accord *Coker v. Hunt Mem. Hosp.*, No. CA-3-86-1200-H (N.D. Tex. July 29, 1986), as discussed in 14 HEALTH L. DIG., Sept. 1986, at 4; *Rooney v. Medical Ctr. Hosp. of Chillicothe*, 1994 U.S. Dist. LEXIS 7420 (S.D. Ohio).

67 E.g., *Backlund v. Board of Comm'rs*, 106 Wash. 2d 632, 724 P.2d 981 (1986), appeal dismissed, 481 U.S. 1034 (1987) [religious objections to insurance do not excuse compliance]; *Scales v. Memorial Med. Ctr.*, 690 F. Supp. 1002 (M.D. Fla. 1988) [insurance with risk retention group not approved by state is not compliance]; *Pollock v. Methodist Hosp.*, 392 F. Supp. 393 (E.D. La 1975); *Wilkinson v. Madera Comm. Hosp.*, 144 Cal. App. 3d 436, 192 Cal. Rptr. 593 (5th Dist. 1983) [hospital can require insurance to be with company approved by the state]; Annotation, Propriety of hospital's conditioning physician's staff privileges on his carrying professional liability or malpractice insurance, 7 A.L.R. 4TH 1238.

68 E.g., 1995 TJC CAMH, at 488.

69 E.g., *Holmes v. Hoemako Hosp.*, 117 Ariz. 403, 573 P.2d 477 (1977).

70 E.g., FLA. STAT. § 458.320.

71 *Fabrizio v. Provena United Samaritans*, 221 Ill.2d 634 (Ill. S.Ct. 2006).

72 E.g., *Megrelishvili v. Our Lady of Mercy Med. Ctr.*, 291 A.D.2d 18, 739 N.Y.S.2d 2 (1st Dep't 2002); *Mercy Hosp. v. Baumgardner*, 2003 Fla. App. LEXIS 19533 (3d Dist.); but see *President v. Jenkins*, 357 N.J. Super. 288, 814 A.2d 1173 (App. Div. 2003) [hospital has no duty to assure MD has insurance, even when bylaws require such insurance].

73 E.g., *Hackett v. Metropolitan Gen. Hosp.*, 465 So. 2d 1246 (Fla. 2d DCA 1985); *Guerrero v. Burlington County Hosp.*, 70 N.J. 344, 360 A.2d 334 (1976); *Davis v. Morristown Mem. Hosp.*, 106 N.J. Super. 33, 254 A.2d 125 (Ch. Div. 1969); see also *Oliver v. Board of Trustees*, 181 Cal. App. 3d 824, 227 Cal. Rptr. 1 (4th Dist. 1986) [requirement of specialty not represented on staff or renowned reputation].

74 *Walsky v. Pascack Valley Hosp.*, 145 N.J. Super. 393, 367 A.2d 1204 (Ch. Div. 1976), aff'd, 156 N.J. Super. 13, 383 A.2d 154 (App. Div. 1978).

75 *Desai v. St. Barnabas Med. Ctr.*, 103 N.J. 79, 510 A.2d 662 (1986).

76 *Berman v. Valley Hosp.*, 103 N.J. 100, 510 A.2d 673 (1986).

77 *Claycomb v. HCA-Raleigh Comm. Hosp.*, 76 N.C. App. 382, 333 S.E.2d 333 (1985), rev. denied, 315 N.C. 586, 341 S.E.2d 23 (1986).

78 E.g., 1995 TJC CAMH, at 480.

79 E.g., *Ann Arundel Gen. Hosp. v. O'Brien*, 49 Md. App. 362, 432 A.2d 483 (1981) [even when the bylaws are viewed as a contract]; *Holt v. Good Samaritan Hosp. & Health Ctr.*, 69 Ohio App. 3d 439, 590 N.E.2d 1318 (1990) [employee of former exclusive provider of emergency medical services not entitled to hearing when clinical privileges lost due to awarding of contract to new group].

80 Governor signs bill that requires fair hearing for excluded providers, 3 H.L.R. 1330 (1994).

81 Rev. Rul. 69-545, 1969-2 C.B. 117.

82 *Sound Health Ass'n v. C.I.R.*, 71 T.C. 158 (1978), acq. 1981-2 C.B.2.

83 E.g., *B.H.W. Anesthesia Found., Inc. v. C.I.R.*, 72 T.C. 681 (1979), nonacq, 1980-2 C.B.2 [closed anesthesia department granted tax exemption]; see also Rev. Rul. 73-417, 1973-2 C.B. 332 [pathologist/hospital laboratory director with apparently exclusive contract was found to be an employee of hospital]; *Kiddie v. C.I.R.*, 69 T.C. 1055 (1978) [pension plan issues concerning pathologist who apparently had exclusive contract with hospital].

84 Concannon warns Central Maine to open doors to outside heart doctors, AP, Apr. 12, 2002.

85 *Rosenblum v. Tallahassee Mem. Reg. Med. Ctr.*, No. 91-589 (Fla. Cir. Ct. June 18, 1992), as discussed in 26 J. Health & Hosp. L. 61 (1993).

86 *Mahan v. Avera St. Luke's*, 621 N.W.2d 150 (S.D. 2001).

87 2005 TJC CAMH, Element of Performance 10 and Note 2, MS.4.20.

88 E.g., *Chadha v. Hardin Mem. Hosp.*, 2000 U.S. App. LEXIS 439 (6th Cir.) [unpub] [Title I of ADA not apply to physician who was not employee]; *Elbrecht v. HCA Health Servs. of Fla., Inc.*, 1994 U.S. Dist. LEXIS 18877 (N.D. Fla.) [neurologist sought exemption from emergency call on disability grounds, but ADA did not apply because hospital was not employer; employment relationship between physician, her patients not sufficient to trigger coverage].

89 E.g., Wis. Stat. § 48.685, 50.065; D. Adams, Criminal checks increasingly a fact of life for physicians, Am. Med. News, Dec. 20, 2004, 1.

90 E.g., *Chowdhury v. Reading Hosp.*, 677 F.2d 317 (3d Cir. 1982), cert. denied, 463 U.S. 1229 (1983).

91 E.g., *Alexander v. Rush North Shore Med. Ctr.*, 101 F.3d 487 (7th Cir. 1996) [no Title VII claim for revocation of privileges, not hospital employee applying common law agency test]; *Shah v. Deaconess Hosp.*, 355 F.3d 496 (6th Cir. 2004) [no ADEA age or Title VII national origin claim for revocation of privileges, not hospital employee].

92 E.g., *Menkowitz v. Pottstown Mem. Med. Ctr.*, 154 F.3d 113 (3d Cir. 1998) [medical staff member can claim disability discrimination under Rehabilitation Act and Title III of ADA]; *Rubin v. Chilton*, 359 N.J. Super. 105, 819 A.2d 22 (App. Div. 2003) [independent contractor pathologists can challenge change in pathology contractors based on age discrimination complaint under state law contract discrimination law, but not under employment law].

93 *Duane v. Government Employees Ins. Co.*, 37 F.3d 1036 (4th Cir. 1994), cert. dismissed, 515 U.S. 1101 (1995) [42 U.S.C. § 1981 prohibits private discrimination against aliens in making contracts]; contra, *Bhandari v. First Nat'l Bank*, 829 F.2d 1343 (5th Cir. 1987) (en banc), vacated, 429 U.S. 901 (1989), reinstated on remand, 887 F.2d 609 (5th Cir. 1989), cert. denied, 494 U.S. 1061 (1990) [with dissent by Justices White, O'Connor], but note Bhandari was decided before 1991 amendment to § 1981; Annotation, Application of 42 USCS § 1981 to private discrimination against aliens, 99 A.L.R. Fed. 835; see also, 8 U.S.C. § 1324b [prohibition of employment discrimination against protected noncitizens]; *Espinoza v. Farah Mfg. Co.*, 414 U.S. 86 (1973) [Title VII does not prohibit discrimination on the basis of citizenship]; accord, *Fortino v. Quasar Co.*, 950 F.2d 389 (7th Cir. 1991).

94 8 U.S.C. § 1324a [prohibition of employment of unauthorized aliens, with subsection (a)(4) including contracts for labor in the definition of employment].

95 *Hauptman v. Grand Manor Health Related Facility, Inc.*, 121 A.D.2d 151, 502 N.Y.S.2d 1012 (1st Dep't 1986).

96 E.g., *Greisman v. Newcomb Hosp.*, 40 N.J. 389, 192 A.2d 817 (1963).

97 E.g., *Natale v. Sisters of Mercy*, 243 Iowa 582, 52 N.W.2d 701 (1952).

98 *Martino v. Concord Comm. Hosp. Dist.*, 233 Cal. App. 2d 51, 43 Cal. Rptr. 255 (1st Dist. 1965).

99   *Kiester v. Humana Hosp. Alaska, Inc.*, 843 P.2d 1219 (Alaska 1992).

100 *Leach v. Jefferson Parish Hosp. Dist.*, 870 F.2d 300 (5th Cir.), cert. denied, 493 U.S. 822 (1989); accord, *Huellmantel v. Greenville Hosp. Sys.*, 303 S.C. 549, 402 S.E.2d 489 (Ct. App. 1991) [one-year wait].

101 *Theissen v. Watonga Mun. Hosp. Bd.*, 550 P.2d 938 (Okla. 1976).

102 *Khouw v. Methodist Hosp.*, 126 Fed. Appx. 657, 2005 U.S. App. LEXIS 4206 (5th Cir. 2005) (unpub).

103 2004 TJC CAMH, MS.4.10.

104 2004 TJC CAMH & 2005 TJC CAMH, MS 4.10, Element of Performance 3.

105 *Rule v. Lutheran Hosps. & Homes Soc'y*, 835 F.2d 1250 (8th Cir. 1987).

106 E.g., *Ferguson v. Gonyaw*, 64 Mich. App. 685, 236 N.W.2d 543 (1975).

107 See P. Davies, "A Doctor's Tale Shows Weaknesses In Medical Vetting," THE WALL STREET JOURNAL, September 21, 2005.

108 *Kadlec Medical Center v. Lakeview Anesthesia Associates*, 527 F.3d 412 (5th Cir. 2008).

109 See Joint Commission Online, December 21, 2011.

110 42 U.S.C. § 1135(a).

111 42 U.S.C. § 1135(b).

112 *The Medical Staff Handbook: A Guide to Joint Commission Standards*, 1st Edition, The Joint Commission. This is consistent with the concept of the "nondelegable duty" of a hospital, mentioned in the text.

113 The practicality of the Joint Commission's advice is illustrated in the case described in the P. Davies article referenced above in note 107.

114 *Johnson vs. Misericordia Community Hospital* (301 N.W.2d 156 (1981).

115 E.g., *Lingle v. Dion*, 776 So. 2d 1073 (Fla. 4th DCA 2001).

116 See S.Y. TAN Which Standard of Care? Internal Medicine News, Digital Edition, February 15, 2010, http://www.internalmedicinenews.com/views/law-medicine-by-dr-s-y-tan/blog/which-standard-of-care/3efc47af59.html discussing *Simpson v. Davis*, 549 P.2d 950 (Kan. 1976). See also *Liguori v. Elmann*, 191 N.J. 527, 924 A.2d 556 (N.J., 2007); *Foster v. Klaumann*, 42 Kan.App. 2d 634, 216 P.3d 671 (Kan.App. 2d, 2009).

117 "Frequently Asked Questions about Accrediting Hospitals in Accordance with their CMS Certification Number (CCN)," The Joint Commission, October 15, 2010. In proposed October, 2011 changes to the "Medical Staff" and "Governing Body" category of the Medicare's Hospital COPs, CMS indicated that because it has always interpreted language in the current COPs as requiring that each hospital facility in a hospital system to have a separate governing body, it was considering language that would instead allow multi-hospital systems to, among other things, "be effectively governed by a single governing body." Comments on the proposed rule suggested at a mixed reaction to the proposed changes by key stakeholders in the credentialing process. See M. Tocknell, *CMS's Proposed Hospital Staffing Revisions Get Cool Reception*, HealthLeaders Media, January 3, 2012. http://www.healthleadersmedia.com/content/QUA-274835/CMSs-Proposed-Hospital-Staffing-Revisions-Get-Cool-Reception.html.

118 2005 TJC CAMH, Element of Performance 11, MS.4.20.

119 One court ruled that a patient cannot sue a monitoring physician who is proctoring surgery during the probationary period, *Clark v. Hoek*, 174 Cal. App. 3d 208, 219 Cal. Rptr. 845 (1st Dist. 1985). For use of unfavorable proctor report, see *Nicholson v. Lucas*, 21 Cal. App. 4th 1657, 26 Cal. Rptr. 2d 778 (5th Dist. 1994); *Payne v. Harris Methodist H-E-B*, 2000 U.S. Dist. LEXIS 21776 (N.D. Tex. magistrate recommendation), adopted 2001 U.S. Dist. LEXIS 815 (N.D. Tex. 2001) [probationary privileges terminated due to observations during proctoring; summary judgment for defendants based on HCQIA immunity from damages and lack of evidence of antitrust conspiracy to support injunction].

120 *Randall v. United States*, 30 F.3d 518 (4th Cir. 1994), cert. denied, 514 U.S. 1007 (1995).

121 *Draghi v. County of Cook*, 991 F. Supp. 1055 (N.D. Ill. 1998).

122 Surgical injuries lead to new rule, NEW YORK TIMES, June 14, 1992, at 1.

123 E.g., *Paravecchio v. Memorial Hosp.*, 742 P.2d 1276 (Wyo. 1987), cert. denied, 485 U.S. 915 (1988).

124 *Johnson v. St. Bernard Hosp.*, 79 Ill. App. 3d 709, 399 N.E.2d 198 (1st Dist. 1979).

125 *Clark v. Hoek* (174 Cal App 3d, 219 Cal Rptr 845 [1st Dist 1985]); see also *Zablocki v. Wilkin, DPM*, 2003 WL 25580058 (Ohio Com.Pl.) (Trial Order).

126 2005 TJC CAMH, Element of Performance 4, MS.4.20; 42 C.F.R. § 482.22(a)(1). Condition Of Participation: Medical Staff, Title 42,Chapter IV, Part 482_ Subpart C, Sec. 482.22(A)(1).

127 2005 TJC CAMH, PI.1.10 - PI.3.20.

128 Id., MS.4.20, 4.40, 4.70.

129 *Facts about the Periodic Performance Review*, The Joint Commission, September, 2010.

130 Id., Element of Performance 4, MS.4.20 [no longer than two years].

131 Id., MS.4.20.

132 *Siegel v. St. Vincent Charity Hosp.*, 35 Ohio App. 3d 143, 520 N.E.2d 249 (1987).

133 *Yashon v. Hunt*, 825 F.2d 1016 (6th Cir. 1987), cert. denied, 486 U.S. 1032 (1988); accord *Bhatnagar v. Mid-Maine Med. Ctr.*, 510 A.2d 233 (Me. 1986).

134 Kickback plan by hospital hit, Am. Med. News, June 28-July 5, 1985, at 1 [Paracelsus Corp. cash reward for minimizing services to Medicare patients]; Investigation into hospital pledged, Am. Med. News, June 28-July 5, 1985, at 34; plan to cut costs by rewarding doctors assailed, New York Times, Sept. 24, 1985, at 12; for-profit chain admits mail fraud, Am. Med. News, Dec. 12, 1986, at 2 [mail fraud plea unrelated to physician bonus, but arose out of IG bonus investigation].

135 42 U.S.C. § 1320a-7a(b).

136 E.g., *Freidman v. Delaware County Mem. Hosp.*, 672 F. Supp. 171 (E.D. Pa. 1987), aff'd without op., 849 F.2d 600, 603 (3d Cir. 1988) [overutilization of bronchoscopies; *Knapp v. Palos Comm. Hosp.*, 125 Ill. App. 3d 244, 465 N.E.2d 554 (1st Dist. 1984) [termination of privileges for overutilization of lung scans, other tests]; J.D. Blum, Evaluation of medical staff using fiscal factors: Economic credentialing, 26 J. Health & Hosp. L. 65 (1993); see also *Hassan v. Independent Practice Assocs., P.C.*, 698 F. Supp. 679 (E.D. Mich. 1988) [upholding decision of IPA to exclude physicians because of indications of unjustified use of tests; cost containment objectives procompetitive].

137 E.g., *Jackaway v. Northern Dutchess Hosp.*, 139 A.D.2d 496, 526 N.Y.S.2d 599 (2d Dep't 1988); see also, *St. Louis v. Baystate Med. Ctr., Inc.*, 30 Mass. App. Ct.393, 568 N.E.2d 1181 (1991) [group lost exclusive contract, terminated for lack of admissions].

138 E.g., J.D. Blum, Evaluation of medical staff using fiscal factors: Economic credentialing, 26 J. Health & Hosp. L. 65, 70 (1993).

139 *Kerth v. Hamot Health Found.*, 989 F. Supp. 691 (W.D. Pa. 1997), aff'g without op. 159 F.3d 1351 (3d Cir. 1998), cert. denied, 525 U.S. 1055 (1998).

140 E.g., *Ross v. Beaumont Hosp.*, 687 F. Supp. 1115 (E.D. Mich. 1988) [verbal abuse by physician]; Nurse gets $65,000 for a pulled ponytail, N.Y. Times, July 24, 1988, 10 [out of court settlement with doctor]; D. Adams, Staff less tolerant of rude doctors, Am. Med. News, Sept. 20, 2004, 1.

141 E.g., *Dunn v. Washington County Hosp.*, 2005 U.S. App. LEXIS 24660 (7th Cir.); K. Hattie, Nurses accuse doc; Eight say he sexually harassed them at B'klyn hospital, Newsday (New York, NY), Aug. 16, 2001, A5 [EEOC filed lawsuit against hospital].

142 For a discussion of the changing attitudes in the hospital setting regarding inappropriate conduct, in part due to The Joint Commission's recent Leadership Standard, see M.A. Pazanowski, "Wyoming High Court Sides With Hospital In Case of Termination of Disruptive Surgeon," BNA's Health Law Reporter, March 3, 2011.

143 *Elam v. College Park Hosp.*, 132 Cal. App. 3d 332, 183 Cal. Rptr. 156 (4th Dist. 1982); see also, Annotation, Hospital liability for negligence in failing to review or supervise treatment given by doctor, or to require consultation, 12 A.L.R. 4th 57.

144 *McVay v. Rich*, 255 Kan. 371, 874 P.2d 641 (1994), aff'g, 18 Kan. App. 2d 746, 859 P. 2d 399 (1993).

145 *U.S. v. United Mem. Hosp.*, No. 1:01-CR-238 (W.D. Mich. pleas entered Jan. 8, 2003).

146 E.g., Hospital suspends 300 Tampa doctors slow on paperwork, Miami Herald, May 18, 1988, 1A.

147 E.g., *Peterson v. Tucson Gen. Hosp.*, 114 Ariz. 66, 559 P.2d 186 (Ct. App. 1976).

148 *Wayne v. Genesis Med. Ctr.*, 140 F.3d 1145 (8th Cir. 1998).

149 E.g., *Jackson v. Fulton-DeKalb Hosp. Auth.*, 423 F. Supp. 1000 (N.D. Ga. 1976), aff'd without op., 559 F.2d 1214 (5th Cir. 1977).

150 *Moore v. Board of Trustees*, 88 Nev. 207, 495 P.2d 605, cert. denied, 409 U.S. 879 (1972).

151 *Pagliaro v. Point Pleasant Hosp.*, No. A-3932-75 (N.J. Super. Ct. App. Div. Jan. 19, 1979), as discussed in 12 Hosp. L., Apr. 1979, at 5; *Sokol v. Akron Gen. Med. Ctr.*, 173 F.3d 1026 (6th Cir. 1999); see also *Yashon v. Hunt*, 825 F.2d 1016 (6th Cir. 1987) [state hospital not limited to previously memorialized standards to review physician].

152 E.g., *Fahey v. Holy Family Hosp.*, 32 Ill. App. 3d 537, 336 N.E.2d 309 (1st Dist. 1975), cert. denied, 426 U.S. 936 (1976).

153 *Khan v. Suburban Comm. Hosp.*, 45 Ohio St. 2d 39, 340 N.E.2d 398 (1976).

154 *Fahey v. Holy Family Hosp.*, 32 Ill. App. 3d 537, 336 N.E.2d. 309 (1975).

155 E.g., *Cooper v. Delaware Valley Med. Ctr* 539 Pa. 620, 654 A.2d 547 (1995).

156 *Clough v. Adventist Health Sys.*, 780 P.2d 627 (N.M. 1989).

157 E.g., *Katz v. Children's Hosp. Corp.*, 33 Mass. Ct. App. 574, 602 N.E.2d 598 (1992).

158 *Bartley v. Eastern Me. Med. Ctr.*, 617 A.2d 1020 (Me. 1992).

159 E.g., B. McCormick, Hospital loses over economic credentialing, Am. Med. News, Mar. 28, 1994, at 4 [radiologist awarded $12.7 million due to exclusive contract].

160 E.g., *American Med. Int'l v. Scheller*, 590 So. 2d 947 (Fla. 4th DCA 1991), rev. denied, 602 So. 2d 533 (Fla. 1992).

161 See R. Abelson, Hospitals battle for-profit groups for patients, New York Times, Oct. 30, 2002, C1 [doctors who invest in other hospitals losing privileges]; Idaho doctors who own specialty facility sue over lost privileges at other hospital, H.L.R., Mar. 11, 2004, 363 [*Biddulph v. HCA Inc.*, No. CV-04-1219 (Idaho Dist Ct. filed Mar. 2004)]; K. Vogt, Doctor-investors could lose Ohio hospital privileges, Am. Med. News, Jan. 12, 2004, 18 [community hospitals terminating privileges for doctors who invested in surgical hospital].

162 *Huhta v. Children's Hosp. of Phila.*, 1994 U.S. Dist. LEXIS 7327 (E.D. Pa.) [dismissal of antitrust suit by former chief of division of pediatric cardiology who had resigned to open a multispecialty group practice at competing hospital after denied access to certain hospital-owned pediatric cardiology equipment, facilities]; *Tarabishi v. McAlester Reg. Hosp.*, 951 F.2d 1558 (10th Cir. 1991), cert. denied, 505 U.S. 1206 (1992) [rejecting antitrust challenge to termination after attempted to open outpatient surgical clinic]; *Katz v. Children's Hosp. Corp.*, 33 Mass. App. Ct.

574, 602 N.E.2d 598 (1992) [hospital may restrict subspecialties to persons who practice full time at hospital]; *Walborn v. UHHS, No. CV-02-479572* (Ohio Com. Pl. June 16, 2003) [court upheld policy forbidding material financial relationship with competing hospital]; *Berasi v. Ohio Health, No. 04CVA-03-2406* (Ohio County Ct. Com. Pl. Mar. 3, 2004) [court denied restraining order to physicians who lost privileges for investing in competing specialty hospital].

163 E.g., Baptist Hospital temporarily enjoined from using economic credentialing policy, H.L.R, Apr. 1, 2004, 455 [*Murphy v. Baptist Health, No. CV2004-2002* (Ark. Cir. Ct. Pulaski County temp. injunction Mar. 22, 2004)]; *Baptist Health v. Murphy*, 2005 Ark. LEXIS 354 (reversing trial court, remanding for further evaluation, but allowing temporary injunction to stay in place).

164 Though it did not indicate that is was specifically responding to this request or the comments it received, the OIG did state in its January 31, 2005 "Supplemental Compliance Program Guidance for Hospitals," that "[c]ertain medical staff credentialing practices may implicate the anti-kickback statute. For example, conditioning privileges on a particular number of referrals or requiring the performance of a particular number of procedures, beyond volumes necessary to ensure clinical proficiency, potentially raise substantial risks under the statute. On the other hand, a credentialing policy that *categorically* refuses privileges to physicians with significant conflicts of interest would not appear to implicate the statute in most situations." Fed. Reg. 4858, 4869 (Jan. 31, 2005).

165 Report of the Council on Medical Service, Subject: Fiduciary Credentialing CMS Report 2-A-06 (June 2006).

166 *Mamakos v. Huntington Hosp.*, 653 F. Supp. 1447 (E.D. N.Y. 1987).

167 E.g., *Estate of Behringer v. Medical Ctr. at Princeton*, 249 N.J. Super. 597, 592 A.2d 1251 (1991) [upholding suspension of surgical privileges of physician with AIDS]; *Scoles v. Mercy Health Corp.*, 887 F. Supp. 765 (E.D. Pa. 1994) [HIV-positive surgeon's practice justifiably restricted]; Court: Hospital may bar HIV-positive doctor from surgery, AM. MED. NEWS, Jan. 16, 1995, at 11 [Scoles may pursue claims of wrongful removal from occupational programs where he did not perform invasive procedures]; *Doe v. University of Md. Med. Sys. Corp.*, 50 F.3d 1261 (4th Cir. 1995) [affirming judgment in favor of hospital on claims under Rehabilitation Act, ADA by resident suspended from surgery when tested HIV positive; was offered nonsurgical residency which he refused; court ruled he posed significant risk to patients that could not be eliminated by reasonable accommodation; hospital may elect to restrict activities of only those known to be HIV positive].

168 In re *Milton S. Hershey Med. Ctr.*, 535 Pa. 9, 634 A.2d 159 (1993); but see *Tolman v. Doe*, 988 F. Supp. 582 (E.D. Va. 1997) [former medical partner liable for defamation for letters sent to patients warning them of HIV status of physician].

169 E.g., FLA. STAT. § 455.261; Goetz v. Noble, 652 So. 2d 1203 (Fla. 4th DCA 1995) [absolute immunity from state law claims, qualified immunity from federal civil rights claims for medical director of program under § 455.261].

170 E.g., *Menkowitz v. Pottstown Mem. Med. Ctr.*, 154 F.3d 113 (3d Cir. 1998) [nonemployee physician permitted to sue under public accommodations provisions of ADA].

171 E.g., *Hong v. Temple University*, 2000 U.S. Dist. LEXIS 7301 (E.D. Pa.) [employer did not violate ADA by terminating anesthesiologist who was unable to concentrate or focus due to pain behind his eye, no reasonable accommodation would allow performing essential functions of job].

172 *Robertson v. Neuromedical Ctr.*, 161 F.3d 292 (5th Cir. 1998), cert. denied, 526 U.S. 1098 (1999); see also *Brohm v. JH Properties, Inc.*, 947 F. Supp. 299 (D. Ky. 1996), aff'd, 149 F.3d 517 (6th Cir. 1998) [no state law disability discrimination claim for physician discharged for sleeping during surgical procedures, notwithstanding claim of sleep apnea].

173 *Landefield v. Marion Gen. Hosp.*, 994 F.2d 1178 (6th Cir. 1993).

174. *Haas v. Wyoming Valley Health Care System,* 553 F. Supp.2d 390 (M.D. Pa. 2008).

175 E.g., *Mark v. Burke Rehab. Hosp.*, 1997 U.S. Dist. LEXIS 5154 (S.D. N.Y. 1997) [deny dismissal of ADA claim that cardiac physician with cancer was fired for refusal to postpone chemotherapy session]; *Hennefent v. Mid Dakota Clinic*. P.C., 164 F.3d 419 (8th Cir. 1998) [dismissal of challenge to termination of employed physician where he refused to report for evaluation of his present disability].

176 E.g., *Ulrich v. San Francisco*, 308 F.3d 968 (9th Cir. 2002) [physician resigned to protest layoffs while under investigation; permitted to challenge denial of request to rescind resignation; possible retaliation for protected speech]; *Malak v. Associated Physicians, Inc.*, 784 F.2d 277 (7th Cir. 1986); *Schwartzman v. Valenzuela*, 846 F.2d 1209 (9th Cir. 1988) [jury questions whether discharge was retaliation]; *Cohen v. County of Cook*, 677 F. Supp. 547 (N.D. Ill. 1988).

177 *Zaky v. Veterans Admin.*, 793 F.2d 832 (7th Cir.), cert. denied, 479 U.S. 937 (1986); accord *Setliff v. Memorial Hosp.*, 850 F.2d 1384 (10th Cir. 1988).

178 *Smith v. Cleburne County Hosp.*, 870 F.2d 1375 (8th Cir.), cert. denied, 493 U.S. 847 (1989).

179 *DeMarco v. Rome Hosp.*, 952 F.2d 661 (2d Cir. 1992).

180 42 U.S.C. § 11133; 45 C.F.R. pt. 60; U.S. Dep't of HHS, National Practitioner Data Bank Guidebook (1990); I.S. Rothschild, Operation of National Practitioner Data Bank, 25 J. Health & Hosp. L. 225 (1992); *American Dental Ass'n v. Shalala,* 303 U.S. App. D.C. 231, 3 F.3d 445 (1993) [HCQIA does not require reports of payments by individual practitioners]; N.J. Schendel, Banking on confidentiality: Should consumers be allowed access to the National Practitioner Data Bank? 27 J. Health & Hosp. L. 289 (1994); OIG Report: Hospital reporting to the National Practitioner Data Bank, Feb. 1995.

181 *Doe v. United States* D.H.H.S., 871 F. Supp. 808 (E.D. Pa. 1994) [no private right of action under HCQIA, no liberty or property interest in having mail fraud conviction excluded from data bank]; see also *Randall v. United States,* 30 F.3d 518 (4th Cir. 1994), cert. denied, 514 U.S. 1107 (1995) [entry in national data base that physician's privileges had been restricted due to incompetence did not deprive of constitutional liberty interest].

182 *Sokol v. Akron Gen. Med. Ctr.*, 173 F.3d 1026 (6th Cir. 1999).

183 *Simkins v. Shalala,* 999 F. Supp. 106 (D. D.C. 1998).

184 *Doe v. Thompson*, 332 F. Supp. 2d 124 (D. D.C. 2004).

185 E.g., Fla. Stat. §§ 395.011(7), 395.0115(4); *Weirton Med. Ctr., Inc. v. West Va. Bd. of Med.*, 450 S.E.2d 661 (W. Va. 1994) [hospital must report disciplinary action against physician within sixty days of completion of formal disciplinary proceedings, again after completion of legal action, if any, but hospital fine of $7,500 reversed due to ambiguity in statute]; *Medical Society of N.J. v. Mottola*, 320 F. Supp. 2d 254 (D. N.J. 2004).

186 *Cuatico v. Idaho Falls Consol. Hosps., Inc.*, 753 F.2d 1081 (9th Cir. 1985) (mem.), as described in 18 Hosp. L., Mar. 1985, at 6; accord *Dorn v. Mendelzon*, 196 Cal. App. 3d 933, 242 Cal. Rptr. 259 (1st Dist. 1987).

187 *Smith v. Cleburne County Hosp.*, 870 F.2d 1375 (8th Cir.), cert. denied, 493 U.S. 847 (1989).

188 *DeMarco v. Rome Hosp.*, 952 F.2d 661 (2d Cir. 1992).

189 42 U.S.C. § 11133; 45 C.F.R. pt. 60; U.S. Dep't of HHS, National Practitioner Data Bank Guidebook (1990); I.S. Rothschild, Operation of National Practitioner Data Bank, 25 J. HEALTH & HOSP. L. 225 (1992); *American Dental Ass'n v. Shalala*, 303 U.S. App. D.C. 231, 3 F.3d 445 (1993) [HCQIA does not require reports of payments by individual practitioners]; N.J. Schendel, Banking on confidentiality: Should consumers be allowed access to the National Practitioner Data Bank? 27 J. HEALTH & HOSP. L. 289 (1994); OIG Report: Hospital reporting to the National Practitioner Data Bank, Feb. 1995.

190 *Doe v. United States D.H.H.S.*, 871 F. Supp. 808 (E.D. Pa. 1994) [no private right of action under HCQIA, no liberty or property interest in having mail fraud conviction excluded from data bank]; see also *Randall v. United States*, 30 F.3d 518 (4th Cir. 1994), cert. denied, 514 U.S. 1107 (1995) [entry in national data base that physician's privileges had been restricted due to incompetence did not deprive of constitutional liberty interest].

191 *Sokol v. Akron Gen. Med. Ctr.*, 173 F.3d 1026 (6th Cir. 1999).

192 *Simkins v. Shalala*, 999 F. Supp. 106 (D. D.C. 1998).

193 *Doe v. Thompson*, 332 F. Supp. 2d 124 (D. D.C. 2004).

194 E.g., Fla. Stat. §§ 395.011(7), 395.0115(4); *Weirton Med. Ctr., Inc. v. West Va. Bd. of Med.*, 450 S.E.2d 661 (W. Va. 1994) [hospital must report disciplinary action against physician within sixty days of completion of formal disciplinary proceedings, again after completion of legal action, if any, but hospital fine of $7,500 reversed due to ambiguity in statute]; *Medical Society of N.J. v. Mottola*, 320 F. Supp. 2d 254 (D. N.J. 2004).

195 *Cuatico v. Idaho Falls Consol. Hosps., Inc.*, 753 F.2d 1081 (9th Cir. 1985) (mem.), as described in 18 Hosp. L., Mar. 1985, at 6; accord *Dorn v. Mendelzon*, 196 Cal. App. 3d 933, 242 Cal. Rptr. 259 (1st Dist. 1987).

196 E.g., *Shahawy v. Harrison*, 778 F.2d 636 (11th Cir. 1985), corrected, 790 F.2d 75 (11th Cir. 1986); see also, *Randall v. United States*, 30 F.3d 518 (4th Cir. 1994), cert. denied, 514 U.S. 1107 (1995) [provisional privileges in army hospital created no property interest in request for full privileges].

197 E.g., *Shahawy v. Harrison*, 875 F.2d 1529 (11th Cir. 1989) [property interest in continuation of privileges].

198 E.g., *Moore v. Middlebrook*, 2004 U.S. App. LEXIS 8558 (10th Cir.) [unpub].

199 See *Lowe v. Scott*, 959 F.2d 323 (1st Cir. 1992).

200 *Gaalla v. Brown*, No. 10-41332 (5th Cir. Jan 13, 2012) citing *Washington v. Davis*, 426 U.S. 229, 239 (1976).

201 E.g., *Jit Kim Lim v. Central DuPage Hosp.*, 871 F.2d 644 (7th Cir. 1989).

202 2005 TJC CAMH, MS.1.20; Element of Performance 1, MS.4.50.

203 E.g., *Houston v. Intermountain Health Care, Inc.*, 933 P.2d 403 (Utah App. 1997); *Owens v. New Britain Gen. Hosp.*, 229 Conn. 592, 643 A.2d 233 (1994); *Everhart v. Jefferson Parish Hosp. Dist.*, 757 F.2d 1567 (5th Cir. 1985); see also *Evans v. Perry*, 944 F. Supp. 2 (D. D.C. 1996) [failure to follow Army regulation, no prejudice to gynecologist whose privileges were restricted at Army community hospital].

204 E.g., *Bryant v. Tenet, Inc.*, 969 S.W.2d 923 (Tenn. App. 1997) [no right to attorney during informal review]; *Setliff v. Memorial Hosp.*, 850 F.2d 1384 (10th Cir. 1988); *Mathews v. Lancaster Gen. Hosp.*, 87 F.3d 624 (3d Cir. 1996) [not necessary to follow HCQIA during informal review to qualify for immunity].

205 *Hanna v. Board of Trustees*, 243 A.D.2d 362, 663 N.Y.S.2d180 (1st Dept. 1997).

206 *Vakharia v. Swedish Covenant Hosp.*, 987 F. Supp. 633 (N.D. Ill. 1997).

207 *Bergeron v. Desert Hosp. Corp.*, 221 Cal. App. 3d 146, 270 Cal. Rptr. 397 (4th Dist. 1990).

208 E.g., *Chaudhry v. Prince George's County*, 626 F. Supp. 448 (D. Md. 1985); *Hoberman v. Lock Haven Hosp.*, 377 F. Supp. 1178 (M.D. Pa. 1974) [hearing not required for censure]; contra *Grodjesk v. Jersey City Med. Ctr.*, 135 N.J. Super. 393, 343 A.2d 489 (Ch. Div. 1975) [censure requires notice, opportunity to respond].

209 E.g., *Bloom v. Hennepin County*, 783 F. Supp. 418 (D. Minn. 1992).

210 E.g., *International Med. Ctrs., Inc. v. Sabates*, 498 So. 2d 1292 (Fla. 3d DCA 1986) [confirming arbitrator award for physician].

211 42 U.S.C. § 11112(a).

212 E.g., *Thornton v. Trident Med. Ctr., L.L.C.*, 357 S.C. 91, 592 S.E.2d 50 (App. 2003).

213 Pub. L. No. 99-660, 100 Stat. 3784 (1986) (codified at 42 U.S.C. §§ 11101-11152).

214 42 U.S.C. § 11112(b)(3)(A)(i).

215 E.g., *Meyers v. Columbia/HCA Healthcare Corp.*, 341 F.3d 461 (6th Cir. 2003); *Mathews v. Lancaster Gen. Hosp.*, 87 F.3d 624 (3d Cir. 1996) [since test is objective, bad faith is immaterial]; *Bryan v. James E. Holmes Reg. Med Ctr.*, 33 F.3d 1318 (11th Cir. 1994), cert. denied, 514 U.S. 1019 (1995) [judge, not jury, determines immunity; jury verdict for physician reversed based on HCQIA immunity].

216 E.g., *Meyers v. Columbia/HCA Healthcare Corp.*, 341 F.3d 461 (6th Cir. 2003); *Brader v. Allegheny Gen. Hosp.*, 167 F.3d 832 (3d Cir. 1999); *Wayne v. Genesis Med. Ctr.*, 140 F.3d 1156 (8th Cir. 1998); *Imperial v. Suburban Hosp. Ass'n, Inc.*, 37 F.3d 1026 (4th Cir. 1994); *Smith v. Ricks*, 31 F.3d 1478 (9th Cir. 1994), cert. denied, 514 U.S. 1035 (1995) [peer review proceedings need not be like trial]; *Meyer v. Sunrise Hosp.*, 22 P.3d 1142 (Nev. 2001).

217 For an analysis critical of this "objective approach" to the application of HCQIA see N. Kadar, M.D., J.D., LL.M., "How Courts Are Protecting Unjustified Peer Review Actions Against Physicians by Hospitals," *Journal of American Physicians and Surgeons*, Vol. 16 No. 1, 2011.

218 *Mathews v. Lancaster Gen. Hosp.*, 87 F.3d 624 (3d Cir. 1996).

219 *Ali v. Medstar Health*, 2003 (D.C. Super. LEXIS 32).

220 E.g., *Decker v. IHC Hosp., Inc.*, 982 F.2d 433 (10th Cir. 1992), cert. denied, 509 U.S. 924 (1993); *Manion v. Evans*, 986 F.2d 1036 (6th Cir. 1993), cert. denied, 510 U.S. 818 (1993).

221 *Van Kirk v. Trustees of White County Mem. Hosp.*, No. 91C01-8809-CP-128 (Ind. Cir. Ct. White County Nov. 9, 1988), as discussed in 16 HEALTH L. DIG., Dec. 1988, at 67.

222 E.g., *Caine v. Hardy*, 943 F.2d 1406 (5th Cir. 1991), cert. denied, 503 U.S. 936 (1992); *Medical Staff of Sharp Mem'l Hosp. v. Superior Court*, 121 Cal. App. 4th 173, 16 Cal. Rptr. 3d 769 (4th Dist. 2004); *Gureasko v. Bethesda Hosp.*, 116 Ohio App. 3d 724, 689 N.E.2d 76 (1996).

223 *Storrs v. Lutheran Hosps. & Homes Soc'y*, 609 P.2d 24 (Alaska 1980), aff'd after remand, 661 P.2d 632 (Alaska 1983); accord *Darlak v. Bobear*, 814 F.2d 1055 (5th Cir. 1987).

224 E.g., *Poe v. Charlotte Mem. Hosp.*, 374 F. Supp. 1302 (W.D. N.C. 1974) [two-year-old incidents were insufficient basis for summary action]; Calif. physicians' summary suspension overturned, Am. Med. News, Feb. 23, 2004, 10 [hospital summarily suspended physician on voluntary leave of absence].

225 E.g., *Conley v. Brownsville Med. Ctr.*, 570 S.W.2d 583 (Tex. Civ. App. 1978) [injunction dissolved after mistreatment of patient].

226 E.g., *Paskon v. Salem Mem. Hosp.*, 806 S.W.2d 417 (Mo. Ct. App.), cert. denied, 502 U.S. 908 (1991).

227 E.g., *Christenson v. Mount Carmel Health*, 112 Ohio App. 3d 161, 678 N.E.2d 255 (1996).

228 E.g., *Woodbury v. McKinnon*, 447 F.2d 839 (5th Cir. 1971).

229 *Sokol v. Akron Gen. Med. Ctr.*, 173 F.3d 1026 (6th Cir. 1999).

230 *Arizona Osteopathic Med. Ass'n v. Fridena*, 105 Ariz. 291, 463 P.2d 825, cert. denied, 399 U.S. 910 (1970).

231 E.g., *Sywak v. O'Connor Hosp.*, 199 Cal. App. 3d 423, 244 Cal. Rptr. 753 (6th Dist. 1988), op. withdrawn, 1988 Cal. LEXIS 177 (May 19, 1988).

232 *Mathews v. Lancaster Gen. Hosp.*, 87 F.3d 624 (3d Cir. 1996).

233 E.g., *Randall v. United States*, 30 F.3d 518 (4th Cir. 1994), cert. denied, 514 U.S. 1107 (1995); in re Corines, 149 A.D.2d 591, 540 N.Y.S.2d 273 (2d Dep't 1989), appeal dismissed, 75 N.Y.2d 850, 522 N.Y.S.2d 923, 552 N.E.2d 171 (1990); *Suckle v. Madison Gen. Hosp.*, 499 F.2d 1364 (7th Cir. 1974).

234 *Garrow v. Elizabeth Gen. Hosp.*, 79 N.J. 549, 401 A.2d 533 (1979).

235 *Randall v. United States*, 30 F.3d 518 (4th Cir. 1994), cert. denied, 514 U.S. 1107 (1995).

236 *Anton v. San Antonio Comm. Hosp.*, 19 Cal. 3d 802, 140 Cal. Rptr. 442, 567 P.2d 1162 (1977); accord *Yashon v. Hunt*, 825 F.2d 1016 (6th Cir. 1987); *Wright v. Southern Mono Hosp. Dist.*, 631 F. Supp. 1294 (E.D. Cal. 1986), aff'd without op., 924 F.2d 1063 (9th Cir. 1991).

237 42 U.S.C. § 11112(b)(3)(C)(i).

238 *Seitzinger v. Community Health Network*, 2004 WI 28, 676 N.W.2d 426.

239 In re Zaman, 285 S.C. 345, 329 S.E.2d 436 (1985).

240 *Applebaum v. Board of Directors*, 104 Cal. App. 3d 648, 163 Cal. Rptr. 831 (3d Dist. 1980).

241 42 U.S.C. § 11112(b)(3)(A).

242 *Mann v. Johnson Mem. Hosp.*, 611 N.E.2d 676 (Ind. Ct. App. 1993).

243 E.g., *Laje v. R.E. Thomason Gen. Hosp.*, 564 F.2d 1159 (5th Cir. 1977).

244 *Lasko v. Valley Presbyterian Hosp.*, 180 Cal. App. 3d 519, 225 Cal. Rptr. 603 (2d Dist. 1986).

245 *Ende v. Cohen*, 296 N.J. Super. 350, 686 A.2d 1239 (App. Div. 1997).

246 E.g., *Ladenheim v. Union County Hosp. Dist.*, 76 Ill. App. 3d 90, 394 N.E.2d 770 (5th Dist. 1979).

247 *Applebaum v. Board of Directors*, 104 Cal. App. 3d 648, 163 Cal. Rptr. 831 (3d Dist. 1980).

248 *Pariser v. Christian Health Care Sys.*, 859 F.2d 78 (8th Cir. 1988).

249 *Ezpeleta v. Sisters of Mercy Health Corp.*, 800 F.2d 119 (7th Cir. 1986).

250 E.g., *Rosenblit v. Superior Court*, 231 Cal. App. 3d 1434, 282 Cal. Rptr. 819 (4th Dist. 1991) [new medical staff hearing ordered for several reasons including failure to give physician copies of thirty charts]. See also *Garrow* mentioned above in endnote 234 [physician is entitled to copies of all relevant materials and reports, including without limitation data referenced in any materials provided to the body that initiates or recommends the action against the physician].

251 State ex rel. *Health Midwest Dev. Group, Inc. v. Daugherty*, 965 S.W.2d 841 (Mo. 1998).

252 *Goodstein v. Cedars-Sinai Med. Ctr.*, 66 Cal. App. 4th 1257, 78 Cal. Rptr. 2d 577 (2d Dist. 1998).

253 E.g., *Ezekiel v. Winkley*, 20 Cal. 3d 267, 142 Cal. Rptr. 418, 572 P.2d 32 (1977).

254 42 U.S.C. § 11112(b)(3)(C)(iii); see also *Poliner v. Texas Health Sys.*, 2003 U.S. Dist. LEXIS 17162 (N.D. Tex.) [no HCQIA immunity when physician not given opportunity to explain].

255 E.g., *Woodbury v. McKinnon*, 447 F.2d 839 (5th Cir. 1971); *Kaplan v. Carney*, 404 F. Supp. 161 (E.D. Mo. 1975).

256 E.g., *Poe v. Charlotte Mem. Hosp.*, 374 F. Supp. 1302 (W.D. N.C. 1974).

257 42 U.S.C. § 11112(b)(3)(C)(iii).

258 *Birbiglia v. St. Vincent Hosp.*, 427 Mass. 80, 692 N.E.2d 9 (1998).

259 42 U.S.C. § 11112(b)(3)(C)(ii).

260 Balkisson v. Capital Hill Hosp., 558 A.2d 304 (D.C. 1989).

261 42 U.S.C. § 11112(b)(3)(D).

262 2005 TJC CAMH, Element of performance 5, MS.4.50.

263 *Leonard v. Board of Directors, Prowers County Hosp. Dist.*, 673 P.2d 1019 (Colo. Ct. App. 1983).

264 *Radiation Therapy Oncology, P.C. v. Providence Hosp.*, 2005 Ala. LEXIS 10 (Jan. 14, 2005).

265 E.g., *Ad Hoc Exec. Comm v. Runyan*, 716 P.2d 465 (Colo. 1986) [committee cannot challenge governing board rejection of suspension it recommended]; *Forster v. Fisherman's Hosp., Inc.*, 363 So. 2d 840 (Fla. 3d DCA 1978) [chief of hospital staff cannot challenge privileges granted after he recommended denial].

266 E.g., *Brindisi v. University Hosp.*, 131 A.D.2d 667, 516 N.Y.S.2d 745 (2d Dep't 1987) [patient cannot challenge denial of privileges to use laser]; *Bello v. South Shore Hosp.*, 384 Mass. 770, 429 N.E.2d 1011 (1981).

267 *Hurst v. Beck*, 771 F. Supp. 118 (E.D. Pa. 1991).

268 E.g., *Yaeger v. Sisters of St. Joseph*, 1988 U.S. Dist. LEXIS 8835 (D. Or.); *Suckle v. Madison Gen. Hosp.*, 499 F.2d 1364 (7th Cir. 1974); but see *Quasem v. Kozarek*, 716 F.2d 1172 (7th Cir. 1983) [failure to pursue hospital procedures does not bar suit seeking only payment of damages by credentials committee member].

269 E.g., *Christhilf v. Annapolis Emergency Hosp. Ass'n, Inc.*, 496 F.2d 174 (4th Cir. 1974).

270 *Goldberg v. Rush Univ. Med. Ctr.*, 863 N.E.2d 829;309 Ill. Dec. 197 (Ill. App. 2007)

271 E.g., *University Health Servs., Inc. v. Long*, 274 Ga. 829, 561 S.E.2d 77 (2002).

272 E.g., *Pepple v. Parkview Mem. Hosp., Inc.*, 511 N.E.2d 467 (Ind. Ct. App. 1987), aff'd, 536 N.E.2d 274 (Ind. 1989).

273 *Sadler v. Dimensions Healthcare Corp.*, 378 Md. 509, 836 A.2d 655 (2003).

274 *Madsen v. Audrian Health Care, Inc.*, 297 F.3d 694 (8th Cir. 2002) [private hospital, applying *Cowan v. Gibson*, 392 S.W.2d 307 (Mo. 1965)]; *Long v. Bates County Mem. Hosp.*, 667 S.W.2d 419 (Mo. Ct. App. 1983) [public hospital].

275 Fla. Stat. § 395.0191(7).

276 E.g., *Medical Ctr. Hosps. v. Terzis*, 235 Va. 443, 367 S.E.2d 728 (1988) [review limited to determination whether written reasons for adverse action are in list of permitted reasons in statute].

277 E.g., *United States v. Jefferson County*, 720 F.2d 1511 (11th Cir. 1983).

278 E.g., *Deerfield Med. Ctr. v. Deerfield Beach*, 661 F.2d 328 (5th Cir. 1981).

279 E.g., *Prakasam v. Popowski*, 566 So. 2d 189 (La. Ct. App.), cert. denied, 569 So. 2d 986 (La. 1990) [error to issue injunction]; *J. Sternberg, S. Schulman & Assocs., M.D., P.A. v. Hospital Corp. of Am.*, 571 So. 2d 1334 (Fla. 4th DCA 1989) [affirming denial of injunction]; *Rdzanek v. Hospital Serv. Dist.*, 2004 U.S. Dist. LEXIS 503 (E.D. La.) [deny injunction of reduction in privileges to consulting privileges].

280 E.g., *University Health Servs., Inc. v. Long*, 274 Ga. 829, 561 S.E.2d 77 (2002).

281 E.g., *Porter Mem. Hosp. v. Malak*, 484 N.E.2d 54 (Ind. Ct. App. 1985); *Lawler v. Eugene Wuesthoff Mem. Hosp. Ass'n*, 497 So. 2d 1261 (Fla. 5th DCA 1986); see also endnotes 191-192, supra.

282 *Knapp v. Palos Comm. Hosp.*, 176 Ill. App. 3d 1012, 531 N.E.2d 989 (1989), cert. denied, 493 U.S. 947 (1989).

283 Citizens obtain restraining order to keep Ord doctor at hospital, AP, Feb. 19, 2004; Judge dissolves restraining order for Ord doctor, AP, Mar. 12, 2004.

284 E.g., *Rosenblit v. Superior Court*, 231 Cal. App. 3d 1434, 262 Cal. Rptr. 819 (4th Dist. 1991) [writ granted], rev. denied, 1991 Cal. LEXIS 4251 (Sept. 19, 1991); *Bollenger v. Doctors Med. Ctr.*, 222 Cal. App. 3d 1115, 272 Cal. Rptr. 273 (5th Dist. 1990) [writ denied for failure to exhaust administrative remedies within hospital]; *Bonner v. Sisters of Providence Corp.*, 194 Cal. App. 3d 437, 239 Cal. Rptr. 530 (1st Dist. 1987) [writ reversed because evidence supported finding that doctor did not meet hospital's reasonable standards]; *Hay v. Scripps Mem. Hosp.*, 183 Cal. App. 3d 753, 228 Cal. Rptr. 413 (4th Dist. 1986) [affirming denial of writ because reasonable to require Ob-Gyn residency for D & C privileges].

285 *Westlake Comm. Hosp. v. Superior Court*, 17 Cal. 3d 465, 131 Cal. Rptr. 90, 551 P.2d 410 (1976) [physician whose privileges are terminated cannot sue hospital or involved individuals in tort without first having hospital action overturned in mandamus proceeding].

286 See also Fed. R. Civ. P. 81(b) [writ of mandamus abolished in federal courts].

287 Am. Jur. 2D, Mandamus § 104.

288 Am. Jur. 2D, Mandamus § 104; *Green v. Board of Directors of Lutheran Med. Ctr.*, 739 P.2d 872 (Colo. Ct. App. 1987) [physician denied privileges not entitled to mandamus relief]; State ex rel. *St. Joseph Hosp. v. Fenner*, 726 S.W.2d 393 (Mo. Ct. App. 1987) [mandamus not appropriate relief for contract dispute between physician and hospital, not appropriate for breach of contract]; *Lawnwood Med. Ctr. v. Cassimally*, 471 So. 2d 1346 (Fla. 4th DCA 1985) [not appropriate to use mandamus to compel election of medical staff officers].

289 Am. Jur. 2D, Mandamus § 69.

290 *Keane v. St. Francis Hosp.*, 522 N.W.2d 517 (Wis. Ct. App. 1994) [mandamus available to reinstate medical staff officer, but denied due to circumstances].

291 E.g., *Laje v. R.E. Thomason Gen. Hosp.*, 665 F.2d 724 (5th Cir. 1982).

292 2003 TJC CAMH, MS.5.10.3.

293 E.g., *Everett v. St. Ansgar Hosp.*, 974 F.2d 77 (8th Cir. 1992); *DeLeon v. St. Joseph Hosp.*, 871 F.2d 1229 (4th Cir.) cert. denied, 493 U.S. 825 (1989) [application release barred defamation claim]; *Stizell v. York Mem. Osteopathic Hosp.*, 768 F. Supp. 129 (M.D. Pa. 1991); *King v. Bartholomew County Hosp.*, 476 N.E.2d 877 (Ind. Ct. App. 1985) [immunity provision on application upheld].

294 E.g., *Westlake Comm. Hosp. v. Superior Court*, 17 Cal. 3d 465, 131 Cal. Rptr. 90, 551 P.2d 410 (1976); *Keskin v. Munster Med. Research Found.*, 580 N.E.2d 354 (Ind. Ct. App. 1991) [release signed as part of application for privileges did not preclude action challenging exclusive anesthesia contract, but hospital found to be within its rights in entering contract]; *Rees v. Intermountain Health Care, Inc.*, 808 P.2d 1069 (Utah 1991) [immunity provisions in bylaws only precluded defamation action, not action for violating bylaws].

295 E.g., *Bass v. Ambrosius*, 185 Wis. 2d 879, 520 N.W.2d 625 (Ct. App. 1994).

296 A. L. Sorrel, *Bulletproof bylaws: Maintaining the right to protect doctors – and patients*, American Medical News, (Feb. 11, 2008). http://www.ama-assn.org/amednews/2008/02/11/prsa0211.htm

297 *Janda v. Madera Comm. Hops.*, 16 F. Supp. 2d 1181 (E.D. Cal. 1998).

298 See *Desai v. Lawnwood Medical Center*, 54 So.3d 1027 (Fla. Dist. Ct. App. 2011).

299 *Sullivan v. Baptist Mem. Hosp.*, 722 So. 2d 675 (Miss. 1998).

300 *East Tex. Med. Ctr. Cancer Inst. v. Anderson*, 1998 Tex. App. LEXIS 6442.

301 See Annotation, Liability in tort for interference with physician's contract or relationship with hospital, 7 A.L.R. 4th 572.

302 E.g., *Scheller v. American Med. Int'l, Inc.*, 502 So. 2d 1268 (Fla. 4th DCA 1987), rev. denied, 513 So. 2d 1068 (Fla.), appeal after remand, 590 So. 2d 947 (Fla. 4th DCA 1991), rev. dismissed, 602 So. 2d 533 (Fla. 1992) [affirming punitive damage award of $19 million]; Doctor, lawyer feud over $15.5 million settlement, Palm Beach Post, June 29, 1992, at 1B [case settled].

303 Id.

304 E.g., *Purgess v. Sharrock*, 33 F.3d 134 (2d Cir. 1994); *Chakrabarti v. Cohen*, 31 F.3d 1 (1st Cir. 1994).

305 E.g., *Scheller v. American Med. Int'l*, 583 So. 2d 1047 (Fla. 4th DCA 1991), rev. denied, 598 So. 2d 78 (Fla. 1992) [no enforceable agreement for perpetual agreement].

306 E.g., id.

307 *Ethan Allen, Inc. v. Georgetown Manor*, 647 So. 2d 812 (Fla. 1994).

308 E.g., *Greenberg v. Mount Sinai Med. Ctr.*, 629 So. 2d 252 (Fla. 3d DCA 1993).

309 E.g., *DeLeon v. St. Joseph Hosp.*, 871 F.2d 1229 (4th Cir.), cert. denied, 493 U.S. 825 (1989); *Sibley v. Lutheran Hosp.*, 709 F. Supp. 657 (D. Md. 1988), aff'd, 871 F.2d 479 (4th Cir. 1989); *Guntheroth v. Rodaway*, 107 Wash. 2d 170, 727 P.2d 982 (1986); *Spencer v. Community Hosp.*, 87 Ill. App. 3d 214, 408 N.E.2d 981 (1980).

310 *Baldwin v. McGrath*, No. 76-5-336 (Pa. C.P. Ct. York County Mar. 18, 1982), as discussed in 10 Health L. Dig., Apr. 1982, at 17.

311 *Summit Health, Ltd. v. Pinhas*, 500 U.S. 322 (1991).

312 E.g., *Brown v. Presbyterian Healthcare Srvcs.*, 101 F.3d 1324 (10th Cir. 1996), cert. denied, 520 U.S. 1181 (1997); see also *Sisters of Providence v. A.A. Pain Clinic, Inc.*, 81 P.3d 989 (Alaska 2003) [upholding antitrust liability under state law].

313 E.g., *Korshin v. Benedictine Hosp.*, 34 F. Supp. 2d 133 (N.D. N.Y. 1999).

314 E.g., *Benjamin v. Aroostock Med. Ctr.*, 113 F.3d 1 (1st Cir. 1997), cert. denied, 522 U.S. 1016 (1997); *Bocobo v. Radiology Consultants*, 305 F. Supp. 2d 422 (D. N.J. 2004); *Angelco v. Lehigh Valley Hosp.*, 984 F. Supp. 306 (E.D. Pa. 1997).

315 E.g., *Read v. Medical X-ray Ctr., P.C.*, 110 F.3d 543 (8th Cir. 1997).

316 E.g., *Fobbs v. Holy Cross Health Sys. Corp.*, 29 F.3d 1439 (9th Cir. 1994), cert. denied, 513 U.S. 1127 (1995) [race]; *Johnson v. Hills & Dales Gen. Hosp.*, 40 F.3d 837 (6th Cir. 1994) cert. denied, 514 U.S. 1066 (1995) [race]; *Gregory v. Georgia Dep't of Human Resources*, 355 F.3d 1277 (11th Cir. 2004) [affirming jury award of $10,000 for race discrimination].

317 *Harris v. Group Health Ass'n, Inc.*, 213 U.S. App. D.C. 313, 662 F.2d 869 (1981).

318 E.g., *Cilecek v. Inova Health Sys. Srvcs., Inc.*, 115 F.3d 256 (4th Cir. 1997), cert. denied, 522 U.S. 1049 (1998); *Alexander v. Rush North Shore Med. Ctr.*, 101 F.3d 487 (7th Cir. 1996), cert denied, 522 U.S. 811 (1997).

319 E.g., *Zaklama v. Mt. Sinai Med. Ctr.*, 842 F.2d 291 (11th Cir. 1988) [resulted in another hospital discharging physician]; *Doe on behalf of Doe v. St. Joseph's Hosp.*, 788 F.2d 411 (7th Cir. 1986) [Title VII claim for interference with employment by others]; but see *Bender v. Suburban Hosp.*, 159 F.2d 186 (4th Cir. 1998) [relationship with patient not employment for Title VII purposes].

320 E.g., *Betkerur v. Aultman Hosp.*, 78 F.3d 1079 (6th Cir. 1996) [reliance on search committee recommendation was nondiscriminatory reason for selection, insufficient showing of pretext].

321 E.g., *Menkowitz v. Pottstown Mem. Med. Ctr.*, 154 F.3d 113 (3d Cir. 1998) [suit permitted under public accommodation provisions of ADA].

322 See *Jackson v. Radcliffe*, 795 F. Supp 197 (S.D. Tx. 1992)

323 See *Murray v. Bridgeport Hosp.*, 480 A.2d 610 (Conn. Super. 1984).

324 A.L. Sorrel Courts examine peer review: Maintaining a proper sense of balance, American Medical News, Sept. 22/29, 2008. http://www.ama-assn.org/amednews/2008/09/22/prsa0922.htm

325 E.g., ARIZ. REV. STAT. ANN. § 36-445.02; *Harris v. Bellin Mem. Hosp.*, 13 F.3d 1082 (7th Cir. 1994).

326 *Scappatura v. Baptist Hosp.*, 120 Ariz. 204, 584 P. 2d 1195 (Ct. App. 1978); accord *Rodriguez-Erdman v. Ravenswood Hosp. Med. Ctr.*, 163 Ill. App. 3d 464, 516 N.E. 2d 731 (1st Dist. 1987).

327 FLA. STAT. §§ 395.011(8), (10), 395.0115(2), (5).

328 *Psychiatric Assocs. v. Siegel*, 610 So. 2d 419 (Fla. 1992).

329 *Cardwell v. Rockford Mem. Hosp. Ass'n*, 136 Ill. 2d 271, 555 N.E.2d 6, cert. denied, 488 U.S. 998 (1990).

330 *Smith v. Our Lady of the Lake Hosp.*, 639 So. 2d 730 (La. 1994); *Axline v. St. John's Hosp. & Health Ctr.*, 63 Cal. App. 4th 907, 74 Cal. Rptr. 2d 385 (2d Dist. 1998).

331 *Eyring v. Fort Sanders Parkwest Med. Ctr.*, 991 S.W.2d 230 (Tenn. 1999).

332 *Holly v. Auld*, 450 S. 2d. 217 (Fla. 1984), Amidst concerns that such strong peer review protection also inappropriately prevented patients from accessing information and, in the words of Florida's 5th circuit, to "foster disclosure of information that will allow patients to better determine from whom they should seek health care, evaluate the quality and fitness of health care providers currently rendering service to them, and allow them access to information gathered through the self-policing processes during the discovery period of litigation filed by injured patients or the estates of deceased patients against their health care providers," on November 2, 2004, voters in Florida "overwhelmingly approved Amendment 7 [to the Florida Constitution]... the 'Patients' Right-to-Know About Adverse Medical Incidents." The amendment, said to "represent one of the most sweeping changes in law and public policy ever adopted in [the] state," is also said to have "lifted the spirits of medical malpractice lawyers in Florida, and the injured patients they represent, by enshrining in the Florida Constitution a virtual patient's Bill of Rights, while 'lift[ing] the shroud of privilege and confidentiality' that has swaddled the health care industry for years." J.B. Harris, "Riding the Red Rocket: Amendment 7 and the End to Discovery Immunity of Adverse Medical Incidents in the State of Florida," *The Florida Bar Journal*, Vol. 83, No. 3, 2009.

333 *Robinson v. Springfield Hospital*, No. 109-CV-75, slip opinion at 2 (D. Vt. Feb. 5, 2010).

334 See, e.g., *Anderson v. Rush-Copley Med. Ctr.*, 385 Ill. App. 3d 167 (2d Dist. 2008).

Additional Resources

The Healthcare Quality Care Improvement Act, 42 U.S.C. 11101. Available at: http://www.ssa.gov/OP_Home/comp2/F099-660.html

National Practitioner Data Bank Healthcare Integrity and Protection Data Bank Fact Sheet for Attorneys. Available at: http://www.peerreview.org/acrobat_files/npdb_fact_sheet-attorneys.pdf

Barbara Blackmond, Hospital Accreditation – Alternatives to The Joint Commission. Available at: http://www.healthlawyers.org/Events/Programs/Materials/Documents/HHS09/blackmond.pdf

Does Your Governing Board Understand Medical Staff Issues - *Help Boards Perform Better Under the Watchful Eye of Regulators. Medical Staff Briefing.* Vol. 20, No. 2, 2010. Available at: http://www.kattenlaw.com/files/Publication/d1f4f7ae-2d6c-46ca-97f3-00c987cb820b/Presentation/PublicationAttachment/50fe84f8-3761-4b51-aecc-0357da812232/CallahanQuote_MSB_Governing_Board.pdf

Michelle Bergholz Frazier, Esquire, Sally A. Ihlenfeld, Esquire, *The Three Cs of Medical Staff Document Review*. American Health Lawyers Association, 2009. Available at: http://www.vonbriesen.com/resourcelibrary/fetcharticle.aspx?id=372

Amy Lynn Sorrel, When is conduct reportable? National Practitioner Data Bank Takes Complaints From Hospitals About Physicians, *American Medical News* (Sept. 21, 2009). http://www.ama-assn.org/amednews/2009/09/21/prsa0921.htm

Michael R. Callahan. *Negligent Credentialing Developments: Impact of Recent Cases and New Joint Commission Medical Staff Standards Illinois Association of Medical Staff Services Webinar Presentation*: Wednesday, April 16, 2008. Available at: http://www.kattenlaw.com/files/Publication/1f4bfe2c-e691-42fb-b894-6aa6e6722bd2/Presentation/PublicationAttachment/f1db5333-28f1-4eb7-9259-6bbe8701cb2d/Negligent%20Credentialing%20Presentation%20Materials.pdf

Chapter 6

Patients, Providers, and Duties of Care

Michelle Garvey, Esq

Key Learning Objectives

By the end of this chapter, the reader will be able to:

- Define the patient-physician relationship.

- Define the patient-hospital relationship.

- Distinguish the patient-physician and the patient-hospital relationship.

- Determine how the patient-provider relationship begins and ends.

- Explain the effect of federal and state emergency exceptions on traditional hospital admission procedures.

- Apply legal reasoning to determine whether a hypothetical patient-provider relationship has started or ended.

- Apply legal reasoning to determine whether a hospital should discharge a patient in a hypothetical situation.

- Describe the liability risks of patient abandonment.

- Explain how antidiscrimination laws affect the formation of patient-provider relationships.

Chapter Outline

Introduction

Although many patients continue to identify with individual physicians, referring to "my cardiologist" or "my obstetrician," health care often is provided through a network of providers. Because most healthcare services are provided by individual physicians with the collaboration and support of a team of providers, most patients establish relationships with individual physicians and a supporting provider network. Traditional notions of how a relationship with a physician begins and ends have altered in light of this gradual change in the delivery of health care. This chapter addresses the current state of the patient-provider relationship and guides the reader in understanding laws that govern that relationship. The chapter also addresses the laws and regulations governing emergency medical situations and best practices for termination of patient-provider relationships.

6-1 Defining the Traditional Patient-Physician Relationship

The patient-physician relationship is contractual, meaning that the physician and the patient mutually agree that the physician will provide medical services to the patient. The physician need not abide by the authority and discretion of the patient in performance of professional duties and, therefore, is not an "employee" of the patient.[1] Rather, the relationship is consensual; the patient knowingly seeks the assistance of the physician and the physician knowingly accepts the individual as a patient.[2] In general, because the relationship is consensual, a physician can refuse to treat a patient, even if the situation is an emergency and no other physician is available.[3] The patient-physician relationship exists between the physician and the individual patient, regardless of who pays for the patient's care. Therefore, physicians who offer services gratuitously owe nonpaying patients the same duties of care, skill, and diligence as they would any paying patient.

6-1.1 Express Contractual Relationship

A contractual relationship can be either "express" or "implied." In an express contractual relationship, the physician generally limits the scope of a contract with a patient and does not assume responsibility for all of a patient's medical needs. For example, specialists frequently limit their services to those that arise in their area of practice; a contract with an internist does not require the internist to perform surgery.[4] Physicians can also limit their services according to their personal beliefs or philosophy of practice. Gynecologists can refuse to perform abortions, and obstetricians can decline home deliveries.[5] In addition, physicians can narrow the geographic scope of their practice and need not travel outside of a geographic area to treat patients.[6] Similarly, a consulting physician who assists a patient's primary care physician can limit involvement with a patient only to the consultation. Limits on the scope of the express contract are discussed further in Section 6-7 on Patient Abandonment.

Physicians may also enter into express contracts to care for members of a certain population. Pathologists, radiologists, anesthesiologists, and emergency physicians frequently contract with hospitals to provide their services to hospital patients. These contracts generally do not permit physicians to refuse to care for hospital patients requiring their services. Physicians may also enter into contracts with nursing homes, athletic teams, schools, and jails to care for members of their specific populations. In limited circumstances, courts have held that patient-physician relationships are not created as a result of some "specific population" contracts. For example, when only examination is provided to determine an individual's fitness for employment or physical activity, a patient-physician relationship is not established. Courts reason that no patient-physician relationship exists because the examination is not provided for the individual or for the purpose of providing treatment.[7] Furthermore, even with a contract to care for a specified population, a physician can decline to accept patients who have unreasonable expectations, refuse to cooperate with treatment, or who threaten the physician.

> Physicians who enter into express contracts to care for members of a certain population should understand that they generally must treat hospital patients who require their services.

6-1.2 Implied Contractual Relationship

In an implied contract, a patient-physician relationship is inferred from physician conduct. Courts generally find a patient-physician relationship where a physician has commenced treatment. Some courts, however, determine that a patient-physician relationship is created even before the start of treatment. For example, the Supreme Court of Iowa found that a patient-physician relationship was created when a physician told a patient that he would perform surgery.[8] Courts differ on whether a phone consultation establishes a relationship with a patient. The New York Supreme Court, Appellate Division, First Department found an implied contract when a physician listened to a patient's symptoms over the phone. Other courts have not found an implied contract during similar phone conversations, determining that "treatment" had not commenced.[9]

	Express Contract	Implied Contract
Description	• Patient-physician relationship created through written or oral contract	• Patient-physician relationship inferred from physician conduct
	• Specialists may limit services to those that arise in their area of practice	
	• Physicians may limit services according to personal beliefs or philosophy of practice	
	• Physicians may enter into contracts to care for a certain population	
Examples	• Internists specifying that they will not perform surgery	• Physician tells patient that he will perform surgery
	• Gynecologists indicating that they will not perform abortions	• Physician listens to patient's symptoms over the phone and offers treatment advice
	• Consulting physicians limiting involvement to consultation only	
	• Pathologists, radiologists, anesthesiologists, and emergency physicians entering into contracts with hospitals to provide services to hospital patients	
	• Physicians entering into contracts with nursing homes, athletic teams, schools, and jails	

Figure 6-1 Comparison of Express and Implied Contracts

6-2 Defining the Patient-Hospital Relationship

Although the patient-physician relationship exists between an individual patient and a physician, the patient-hospital relationship often serves as the context for the provision of medical care. In *nonemergency* situations, an individual generally does *not* have the right to be admitted to a private (nonpublic) hospital. A private hospital can legally refuse to admit any person in a nonemergency situation unless an exception applies.

The cases that have shaped the "no right to admission doctrine" for private hospitals developed at the beginning of the 20th century, and courts apply the same reasoning today.[10]

Other practical reasons for nonadmission include lack of medical necessity or available resources, such as space and staff. If a patient's illness does not necessitate admission to a hospital or if a hospital cannot provide the services that a patient requires, the hospital should not admit the patient. In the latter scenario, if a patient needs emergency care for transfer to an appropriate facility, a hospital must provide stabilizing care to the best of its ability. Under the Emergency Medical Treatment and Labor Act (EMTALA), the scenario is tested by the "capacity and capabilities" of the hospital at the time the individual seeks emergency treatment. Even if space and staff are not available, a hospital must provide emergency care to prepare a patient for transfer. See section 6-4 on the right to emergency treatment.

6-3 Exceptions to the No Right to Admission Doctrine

Exceptions to the no right to admission doctrine are found in common law and contractual and statutory provisions. In common law, an individual generally has a right to be admitted to a hospital when:

1. The hospital is responsible for the original injury;

2. The individual becomes ill or injured in hospital buildings or on hospital grounds, even if the hospital is not responsible for the illness or injury; and

3. If the hospital begins to exercise control of an individual by examining the individual or beginning to provide care.

> Educational Affiliation Agreements between hospitals and universities typically include provisions that require hospitals to treat students who become ill or injured while performing services on hospital grounds during the course of an internship.

As with physicians, once hospitals begin to provide treatment for individuals, they are held to the same standards of care as for any patient.

6-3.1 Contractual Exceptions

Hospitals sometimes enter into contracts to care for a specific population of patients. Hospitals are required to admit patients of these populations when they need care that the hospital is able to provide. For example, hospitals may enter into contracts with employers to provide services to their employees or with health maintenance organizations (HMOs) to accept patients who enroll in HMOs. When executing contracts to care for specific populations, hospitals should ensure that contracts specify that patients will be entitled to admission only when admitted by a physician with clinical privileges at the hospital.

6-3.2 Statutory Exceptions

In the aftermath of World War II, the 1946 Hill-Burton Act gave hospitals, nursing homes, and other health facilities grants and loans for construction and modernization.[11] In return, the facilities agreed to provide a reasonable volume of services to persons unable to pay and to make services available to all individuals residing in a particular geographic area.[12] Although the program stopped providing funds in 1997, roughly 200 healthcare facilities nationwide are still obligated to provide free or reduced-cost care.[13] Specifically, the governing regulations indicate that no person residing in the area serviced by a Hill-Burton funded hospital will be denied admission to any portion of the hospital financed by Hill-Burton funds on any grounds other than the individual's lack of need for services, availability of the needed services, or the individual's ability to pay.[14] Inability to pay cannot itself be grounds for denial if an individual needs emergency services or if the facility has a remaining Hill-Burton uncompensated care obligation under the federal regulations.[15]

> Hill-Burton funded facilities must carefully monitor patient admissions to determine that they are meeting the Hill-Burton community service obligation.

Given this obligation, Hill-Burton funded hospitals cannot require admission only by those physicians with clinical privileges, unless sufficient physicians on staff are willing to admit patients who must be admitted under the community service obligation. If certain staff physicians refuse to admit Medicaid patients, for example, a Hill-Burton hospital must ensure that a sufficient number of the remaining physicians will admit these patients. These hospitals could also condition medical staff privileges on admitting a certain number of Medicaid patients.

In addition to hospitals with Hill-Burton funding, some hospitals are obligated by statute to accept all patients from a certain population, generally a particular geographic area. These hospitals often include county hospitals that may be required to provide care to the residents of a particular county. In some states, hospitals are required to provide free or discounted care for a specified population. In California, for example, the Hospital Fair Pricing Policies Act of 2006 mandates that general acute care hospitals provide free or discounted care to financially qualified patients as a condition of licensure.

According to the Act, financially qualified patients include: (1) uninsured patients whose individual/family income is at or below 350 percent of the Federal Poverty Guidelines and (2) insured patients whose individual/family income is at or below 350 percent of the Federal Poverty Guidelines and whose medical costs exceed 10 percent of the family income from the previous year.[16] The California State Department of Health is responsible for enforcing the Act. Many states including Florida, Iowa, Texas, and Washington have similar free care mandates.

6-4 Federal and State Emergency Exceptions

6-4.1 Federal Emergency Exception

Hospitals once operated like physicians and could refuse to treat patients even in emergency situations. In 1986, Congress passed EMTALA as part of the Consolidated Omnibus Reconciliation Act of 1985 (COBRA) to implement patient "antidumping" provisions into the Social Security Act. EMTALA requires all hospitals participating in the Medicare program to provide services to all patients seeking emergency care regardless of ability to pay.[17] The Act was created to ensure that any individual with an emergency medical condition was not denied lifesaving services due to lack of insurance coverage.

EMTALA essentially imposes a relationship between a patient and a hospital if the patient requires emergency medical treatment. The law applies only to hospitals with emergency departments, not to medical clinics or physicians' offices, and requires only that hospitals provide stabilizing treatment. EMTALA further provides that a hospital failing to fulfill its EMTALA obligations may be subject to termination of its Medicare provider agreement, resulting in loss of all Medicare and Medicaid payments.[18] Likewise, the Act calls for the imposition of civil monetary penalties on a hospital and physician who negligently violate a requirement of EMTALA.[19]

The four main provisions in the EMTALA statute pertain to medical screening, stabilizing treatment, transfers, and enforcement. The following chart outlines these components.

PROVISION	DESCRIPTION	COMMENTS
Medical Screening	If an individual comes to the emergency department of a hospital and a request is made for examination or treatment of a medical condition, the hospital must provide an appropriate medical screening examination to determine whether or not an emergency medical condition exists.[1]	• "Emergency medical condition" is "a medical condition manifesting itself by acute symptoms of sufficient severity (including severe pain) such that the absence of medical attention could result in (1) placing the health of the individual (or unborn child) in serious jeopardy; (2) serious impairment to bodily functions; or (3) serious dysfunction of any bodily organ or part."[2] • Medical screening component does not apply to patients who develop emergency conditions after admission. • The screening requirement does not impose any duty on a hospital requiring that the screening result in the correct diagnosis.[3]

---

[1] 42 U.S.C § 1395dd(a).

[2] 42 U.S.C § 1395dd(e)(1).

[3] *Brooks v. Maryland General Hosp., Inc.*, 996 F.2d 708, 711 (1993).

PROVISION	DESCRIPTION	COMMENTS
Stabilizing Treatment	If any individual comes to a hospital and the hospital determines that the individual has an emergency medical condition, the hospital must provide either (1) further medical examination and such treatment as may be required to stabilize the medical condition, or (2) transfer of the individual to another medical facility.[4]	• Individuals may refuse to consent to treatment.[5] • The hospital's responsibility to provide stabilization services does not apply until the emergency medical condition is determined.[6] • A hospital's duty to stabilize applies only when the hospital "knows" of an emergency medical condition.[7] • EMTALA requirements are satisfied if a patient is stabilized at discharge.
Transfers	A hospital may not transfer an individual with an emergency medical condition that has not been stabilized unless (1) the individual requests the transfer in writing after being informed of the risks; (2) a physician certifies that the medical benefits of the transfer outweigh the risks to the individual; or (3) if a physician is not physically present at the time of transfer, a qualified medical person signs a certification in consultation with the physician.[8]	• An "appropriate transfer" is a transfer in which: ○ **(1) the transferring hospital provides the medical treatment which minimizes risks to an individual's health;** ○ **(2) the receiving facility has available space and personnel and has agreed to accept the transfer;** ○ **(3) the transferring hospital has submitted available medical records to the receiving facility;** ○ **(4) the transfer is effectuated through qualified personnel and equipment; and** ○ **(5) which meets other requirements that the Secretary of the Department of Health and Human Services (HHS) deems appropriate.**

---

[4] 42 U.S.C § 1395dd(b)(1).

[5] 42 U.S.C § 1395dd(b)(2).

[6] *Bryant v. Adventist Health System,* 289 F.3d 1162 (9th Cir. 2002).

[7] See id.

[8] 42 U.S.C § 1395dd(c)(1).

PROVISION	DESCRIPTION	COMMENTS
Enforcement	A Medicare-participating hospital that negligently violates EMTALA is subject to a civil monetary penalty of not more than $50,000 (or $25,000 for a hospital with less than 100 beds). Physicians are subject to a civil monetary penalty of not more than $50,000 for each violation and may be excluded from healthcare programs in light of gross, flagrant, or repeated violations. On-call physicians who fail or refuse to appear may also be subject to penalties.[9]	• There is a two-year statute of limitations for EMTALA claims.[10] • Because EMTALA is not a medical malpractice act, patients may have separate causes of action against hospitals for resulting injuries.

Figure 6-2 EMTALA Provisions

[9] 42 U.S.C § 1395dd(c)(1).

[10] 42 U.S.C § 1395dd(c)(2)(C).

6-4.2 State Emergency Exceptions

Although EMTALA applies only to hospitals that participate in the Medicare program, many states impose liability on hospitals refusing emergency treatment. For example, in *Guerrero v. Copper Queen Hospital*, the Supreme Court of Arizona used a public policy argument to conclude that Arizona hospitals must maintain facilities to provide emergency care.[20] The court leapt from this conclusion to the ultimate holding that hospitals with emergency care capabilities may not deny emergency care to *any* patient without cause.[21] Similarly, in *Stanturf v. Sipes*, the Supreme Court of Missouri determined that the only hospital with an emergency ward in a particular geographic area could not turn away a patient for failure to pay a small admission fee in opposition to traditional hospital policy.[22] Although states are less willing than in the past to impose criminal liability on providers for failing to provide emergency services, civil liability remains a significant deterrent for hospitals considering denial of emergency care.

6-4.3 Continued Care

As noted above, when a hospital provides care under either a federal or a state obligation, there is generally no duty to provide continued care, if arrangements for an appropriate transfer can be made without danger to a patient. Furthermore, if a hospital cannot provide the needed care, it has a duty to attempt a transfer. For example, a California appellate court determined that a hospital and treating physician were liable for negligent care of a patient with severe burns in part because the hospital did not have the facilities to care for severe burns and did not attempt a transfer.[23] However, a New York case held that a hospital is not required to be the best facility for providing needed care. In *Kenigsberg v. Cohn*, the New York Supreme Court, Appellate Division, Second Department determined that a scar resulting from a skin graft conducted at a hospital rather than a burn center did not constitute liability for failure to transfer.[24]

CATEGORIES OF HOSPITAL ADMISSION EXCEPTIONS

COMMON LAW: Causation of injury or exercise of control by the hospital

CONTRACTUAL: Contracts to care for specific populations

STATUTORY: Hill-Burton Act

EMERGENCY: EMTALA, state laws, and regulations

Figure 6-3 Exceptions to No Right to Admission Doctrine

6-5 Terminating the Patient-Physician Relationship

A physician must continue to provide medical care to a patient until termination of the patient-physician relationship. A physician who discontinues care for a patient before the relationship is legally terminated can be liable for abandonment, as addressed in section 6-7 below. However, the patient-physician relationship also can end if:

(1) medical care is no longer needed;

(2) the patient withdraws from the relationship;

(3) care of the patient is transferred to another physician;

(4) adequate notice of withdrawal is given by the physician to the patient; or

(5) the physician is or becomes unable to provide care.

The first scenario above is the most common and presents the lowest risk of liability for the physician.

6-5.1 Patient Withdrawal and Transfer of Care

A patient's passive failure to return for future treatment constitutes withdrawal from the patient-physician relationship and results in termination. When a patient withdraws from the patient-physician relationship (either passively or actively), the physician has a duty to attempt to warn the patient if further care is needed, but the physician need not follow up with the patient afterward. In *East v. U.S.*, a patient fired a physician and a psychiatrist whom the patient held responsible for failure to diagnose a condition. The U.S. District Court of Maryland determined that the treating physicians were not guilty of malpractice for alleged failure to provide adequate follow-up treatment of the patient's condition and resulting depression.[25] The court reasoned that such follow-up would be both "fruitless" and "unethical." However, when a successor physician requests information necessary to continue a patient's treatment, the physician should advise the successor of any information necessary to continue treatment. Physicians may transfer patient care temporarily to attend meetings, outside obligations, and vacations. They may transfer care permanently to retire or to leave a particular community. If a physician transfers a patient's care to another physician, either temporarily

or permanently, the physician meets the duty of care by providing a qualified substitute.[26]

6-5.2 Physician Withdrawal

Physicians may withdraw from the patient-physician relationship without transferring care if the patient has reasonable notice of the withdrawal in writing. If continued care is required, withdrawing physicians must give patients notice with sufficient time for patients to locate substitute physicians. Physicians generally withdraw from the patient-physician relationship when retiring or leaving a practice. In Illinois, retiring physicians can be found liable for patient abandonment if patients do not have reasonable time to find substitute care. In *Magana v. Elie*, an Illinois appellate court determined that physicians have a continuing duty to employ a reasonable amount of care and skill such as that ordinarily possessed by members of the profession.[27] When a physician refuses to treat a patient in need of additional treatment without giving the patient reasonable time to find substitute care, that duty is breached.[28] Although Illinois courts have not found a retiring physician liable for refusal to treat based on improper departing procedures, physicians in Illinois are exposed to risk if they leave a practice without providing adequate notice to patients.

Other states have more delineated requirements. In Iowa, for example, the Administrative Code provides:

Upon a physician's death or retirement, the sale of a medical practice, or a physician's departure from the physician's medical practice:

(1) The physician or the physician's representative must ensure that all medical records are transferred to another physician or entity that is held to the same standards of confidentiality and agrees to act as custodian of the records.

(2) The physician shall notify all active patients that their records will be transferred to another physician or entity that will retain custody of their records and that, at their written request, the records will be sent to the physician or entity of the patient's choice.[29]

Thus, Iowa physicians who withdraw from a patient-physician relationship must ensure proper transfer of medical records and must notify active patients of the record transfer. Furthermore, as in Illinois, Iowa case law dictates that a physician breaches a duty to a patient if the physician leaves a patient in a critical stage of disease without reason or sufficient notice to enable the patient to procure another physician.[30] However, Iowa courts are reluctant to hold physicians liable for patient abandonment without a showing of more than sudden termination of the physician-patient relationship. To prove abandonment, a patient must show not only that the physician terminated the relationship at a critical stage of the patient's treatment, but also that the termination came about without reason or sufficient notice and that the patient was injured as a result.[31] Physicians may choose to withdraw from a patient-physician relationship if a patient is abusive or threatens the physician or other healthcare providers. It is controversial when providers withdraw from patient-physician relationships with patients who have sued other providers. Nonetheless, withdrawal is appropriate when the suit is directed toward the withdrawing physician due to the difficulty of maintaining a professional relationship. However, a pending malpractice suit does not justify withdrawal without adequate notice. In 2003, a Michigan appellate court determined that a surgeon who refused to perform surgery after discovering that the patient had sued his officemate could be sued for abandonment.[32]

6-5.3 Inability to Provide Care

The patient-physician relationship also terminates when the physician becomes unable to provide care. A physician who is physically or mentally ill should attempt to arrange for a substitute. Additionally, because physicians cannot be with two patients simultaneously, physicians may be unable to provide care to a patient. If a physician has a valid excuse for attending to another patient, courts will not impose liability. However, a physician cannot entirely neglect one patient to attend to another. ⚑

6-6 Terminating the Patient-Hospital Relationship

The outpatient-hospital relationship terminates in much the same way as the patient-physician relationship, outlined above. The inpatient relationship, however, usually ends with the discharge of a patient. Because liability can be imposed on a hospital for releasing a patient too soon and for holding a patient too long, hospitals must develop procedures for ending inpatient relationships.

> Hospitals must safeguard against patient stays that end too soon or last too long.

Hospitals should consider the following:

1. The institution's responsibilities in consensual discharge.
2. The institution's obligations in discharging patients who want to leave against medical advice.
3. Appropriate response to patients who refuse to cooperate with the discharge process or refuse to leave.
4. Responsible discharge of patients who need additional inpatient treatment.
5. Permissiveness of temporary releases without discharge.

6-6.1 Consensual Discharge

Medicare participating hospitals must have a discharge planning process and must arrange for the initial implementation of a patient's discharge plan.[33] Hospitals

_____ If patient fails to return for treatment, attempt to warn patient if further care is needed.

_____ Provide qualified substitute if transferring care temporarily (to attend meetings, meet outside obligations, and travel).

_____ If withdrawing permanently, give patients notice with sufficient time for patients to locate substitute physicians.

_____ If withdrawing permanently, ensure proper transfer of medical records and notify active patients of record transfer.

_____ Consider whether permanent withdrawal is best under adversarial circumstances (patient is abusive toward physician or threatens physician with malpractice suit).

Figure 6-4 Termination Checklist for Physicians

typically arrange consensual discharges with a patient and the patient's family, although the family does not have a right to be involved if the patient or the patient's legal guardian wants to exclude the family. After discharge, patients may transfer to home care or a nursing home. Inter-hospital transfer may be appropriate if a patient continues to require specialized care.

Because many hospitals have decentralized hospital services, such as ambulatory procedures, surgery, and imaging, discharge planning has become increasingly complex. When sick patients cannot retain inpatient status and must access additional outside treatment, hospitals are challenged to arrange a discharge that will lead to appropriate care within patients' means. For this reason, nursing homes and hospitals often sign agreements outlining transfer and discharge arrangements. Traditionally, provisions for transfer exist in long-term care facility admission agreements. These provisions inform residents and families about permanent and temporary transfer policies designed to assist patients in moving along a continuum of care.

These agreements describe transfer arrangements and may expose nursing homes and hospitals to liability. For example, in 1996, the Alabama Court of Civil Appeals ruled that a nursing home could be liable to a hospital for violating a transfer agreement when it refused to reaccept a nursing home patient who had been transferred to the hospital for a 23-hour evaluation and had not met hospital admission criteria.[34] Hospitals should exercise care in the consensual discharge of all patients. They should take particular care with the infirm elderly, children, and other patients who are not able to care for themselves. These individuals should be discharged only to an appropriate caretaker.

6-6.2 Discharge Against Medical Advice

In most cases, patients can leave hospitals against medical advice at any time. The healthcare community often uses the acronym "AMA," both verbally and in writing, to refer to a patient who leaves a facility against medical advice. If an adult patient is neither disoriented nor committable, the patient generally has a right to leave a hospital unless a court has ordered treatment. If a hospital interferes with this right, the hospital may face liability, despite the fact that honoring the patient's wishes may put the patient at risk. Hospitals should attempt to advise these patients against the risks of leaving and should encourage patients to reconsider, if further care is needed. In New York, providers have a duty to advise patients not to leave against medical advice. In 2003, an appellate court in the state approved of the revocation of a physician's medical license where the physician had failed to attempt to persuade a patient not to leave a hospital against medical advice.[35]

⚑ Because of the risk of liability, hospitals should document attempts to advise patients not to leave hospitals against medical advice. Hospital staff should ask patients to acknowledge, in writing, that they are leaving against medical advice. If a patient refuses to sign an acknowledgement, the refusal should be documented in the patient's medical record. As expected, hospitals cannot "hold" patients at a hospital until an acknowledgement is signed. Even in the absence of physical restraints or barriers, healthcare institutions can be liable for falsely imprisoning individuals against their will if they require patients to sign acknowledgement forms before leaving.

6-6.3 Exceptions

In spite of the above, hospitals can refuse to discharge patients in certain circumstances. All states and some municipalities have regulations outlining procedures for the commitment of individuals who are seriously mentally ill, are substance abusers, or are dangerous to the public due to contagious disease. For example, the New York City Board of Health requires hospitals and other healthcare providers to consult with the Department of Health and Mental Hygiene at least 72 hours before discharging tuberculosis patients.[36] The providers must obtain the approval of the Board of Health before releasing these individuals.

States also have laws that provide for the holding of minors who are neglected or abused. For example, a Missouri court of appeals ruled that a hospital rightfully retained possession of a newborn baby whose parents were allegedly mentally ill.[37] Furthermore, if parents try to discharge a child when removal presents imminent danger to the child's life or health, most states authorize healthcare providers to retain custody or to obtain court authorization to retain custody. Generally, hospitals can hold minors or individuals who pose threats to others or themselves, if they have reported to authorities and are waiting on a commitment or custody order.

Common Law Duties. When these laws do not apply, hospitals still have a common law duty to protect temporarily disoriented patients. Physicians and hospitals generally have authority under common law to detain and even restrain temporarily disoriented medical patients without court involvement. This authority is inferred from cases in which hospitals have been found liable for injuries to patients who are not restrained during temporary disorientation. However, there is no duty to restrain all disoriented patients; the decision whether to use restraints is a matter of professional judgment. The common law authority to restrain generally does not apply when a patient is being detained for treatment of a mental illness or substance abuse.

Patient Flight. In situations where hospitals have a duty to maintain custody of a patient, hospitals can be sued when patients escape and commit suicide, are injured or killed in accidents, or injure or kill others. In evaluating these cases, courts usually focus on (1) how much those involved in the care of the patient knew or should have known about the dangerousness of the patient to self or others and (2) the appropriateness of the precautions taken to prevent escape in light of that knowledge. Generally, if an injury was not foreseeable, there is little likelihood of liability for failure to take additional precautions. If an injury was foreseeable, courts examine the reasonableness of the precautions, and are more likely to find liability. However, many courts have recognized the therapeutic benefits of less secure patient care units and have found them to be reasonable even for at risk patients. In other cases, the precautions have been found to be inadequate, and courts have imposed liability.

6-6.4 Patients Refusing to Leave

Patients and their representatives do not have the right to insist on unnecessary hospitalization. If patients refuse to leave a hospital or their representatives refuse to remove them after a physician's discharge order, the patients become trespassers, and the hospital can have the patients removed. If the delay in discharge is due to difficulties in arranging subsequent placement (at an assisted living facility, for example), a hospital should take reasonable steps to assist in making arrangements. However, if patients and their representatives do not cooperate, hospitals may use reasonable force to remove patients or may obtain a court order to that effect. In 2002, the Supreme Court, Kings County of New York issued an injunction requiring a patient to leave a hospital even though the patient was dissatisfied with the nursing home that had accepted him.[38] Likewise, when a patient who refuses to leave is mentally ill, the hospital can involuntarily transfer the patient to a mental facility if the patient meets the criteria for involuntary hospitalization. In almost all cases, patients' refusal to cooperate with discharge planning can result in personal liability for the cost of unnecessary hospital care.

6-6.5 Patients Requiring Additional Treatment

Hospitals should generally discharge patients only as a result of (1) a written order of a physician familiar with the patient's condition or (2) the patient's decision to leave against medical advice. Patients need not remain in the hospital until cured and generally can be discharged when the hospital can no longer provide the appropriate level of care. When there are capacity constraints or facilities or service lines close, patients may need to be transferred to the care of other institutions. If insurers and other third parties pressure hospitals to discharge and transfer patients, hospitals should not use these requests as grounds for discharge. Rather, hospital administrators should review each case to minimize legal liability and other adverse effects on the hospital. When an attending physician desires an inappropriate discharge or refuses to cooperate with an appropriate discharge, administrators should consider transferring a patient's case to another physician.

Closing an Institution or a Line of Service. In order to compete in an increasingly competitive healthcare market, hospitals may choose to concentrate on particular service lines such as orthopedic surgery or pediatrics. Concentrating on specialized service lines means that hospitals may close other service lines with lower rates of utilization or profitability. When this is the case, hospitals should assist affected patients with appropriate transfer, even though there is generally no legal duty to arrange for referrals.

Outside Pressure to Discharge. Documenting a treating physician's discharge order is essential when an internal review committee or insurance reviewer suggests that a patient should be discharged, and a patient's treating physician believes that the patient should stay. In order to shield a hospital from liability, the treating physician must determine that discharge is appropriate through exercise of independent judgment. In *Wickline v. California*, for example, a California appellate court determined that a treating physician had the legal responsibility to make a final discharge decision in spite of outside pressure from the state's Medicaid program, which was seeking discharge of the patient.[39]

6-6.6 Temporary Release without Discharge

Children, incompetent adults, cooperative committed patients, or competent adults who need continuing supervision or care may ask to leave the hospital for a short time. This is permissible in many situations and can assist in patient progress. Nevertheless, hospitals should proceed with caution when arranging for patients' temporary release. A written physician authorization should indicate that the temporary release is not medically prohibited. Written authorization from competent adult patients or from the parents or guardians of other patients should acknowledge that the hospital is not responsible for the care of the patient while out of hospital custody. Except for adult patients who are able to take care of themselves and are not a danger to others, patients should be released only to appropriate adults who have been briefed on patient needs during the release (such as use of medications and necessary medical equipment). Proper documentation of temporary releases as well as compliance with established hospital procedures should reduce legal liability risks associated with a temporary absence.

See Figure 6-5 for a list of issues and pertinent questions for providers regarding termination of the patient-hospital relationship.

6-7 Patient Abandonment and Additional Sources of Liability

As suggested in section 6-5.2, a physician can be liable for patient abandonment for unexcused failure to see a patient with whom the physician has a patient-physician relationship. Although the patient-physician relationship is consensual and typically formed through express or implied contracts, physicians cannot assume the patient-physician relationship for only a limited amount of time. Rather, a physician assumes responsibility to offer appropriate treatment to a patient until the relationship is terminated. Failure to meet this responsibility can result in liability for patient abandonment. Likewise, hospitals and other providers can face liability for improperly terminating relationships with patients who require continued medical attention. For example, nurses can be liable for abandonment if they leave assigned shifts without arranging for coverage. In 2000, the New York Supreme Court, Appellate Division, Second Department ruled that a visiting nurse could be liable for the consequences of a fire that took the lives of a seventeen-year-old girl and her stepfather.[40] The fire resulted when the nurse left her site an hour before the end of her shift.[41] Other cases address the responsibility of nurses

when a replacement nurse or nurses fail to arrive at the conclusion of a shift. Although nurses may face personal hardships by staffing a subsequent shift, most states recognize a duty to arrange for coverage and, in some cases, to continue to work into the following shift.

To avoid liability for patient abandonment, physicians in particular should agree to notify patients of their withdrawal from the patient-physician relationship. Hospitals can facilitate the notification process by agreeing with employed physicians on termination procedures. For example, a "Patient Notification and Transition" section of a physician's employment agreement could read:

▶ The departing physician should notify patients in writing thirty to ninety days (depending on specialty) prior to termination/transition of the patient-physician relationship. Each patient should be offered a copy of his or her medical record. Each patient should be notified of his or her right to request the transfer of a copy of his or her medical record to the provider of his or her choice. Although not mandatory, each patient should be provided with the departing physician's contact information. The departing physician should reschedule patient appointments, as necessary. Agreeing on and implementing the above procedure lessens the likelihood that the physician or hospital will be liable for patient abandonment.

Other Forms of Liability. In addition to the risk of patient abandonment, additional liabilities may arise from the patient-provider relationship. In *Herrgesell v. Genesee Hospital*, the New York Supreme Court, Appellate Division, examined whether the physician of a patient with Hepatitis B owed any duty to the patient's daughter. In that case, the daughter lived with and cared for her diseased father and eventually contracted the disease. After she died, the court was asked to determine whether the treating physician had a duty to warn the daughter of the risk of contracting Hepatitis B.[42] The plaintiff argued that the defendant physician and hospital knew or should have known that the deceased daughter was likely to contract the disease and that they failed to warn her to take precautions against infection.[43] Although the court did not rule on whether there was a duty in this specific case, the decision dictates that lower New York courts cannot automatically rule that physicians have no duties beyond those to their patients. Furthermore, the case suggests that physicians may become liable to nonpatients based on failure to act.

Figure 6-5 Terminating the Patient-Hospital Relationship

ISSUE	PERTINENT QUESTIONS FOR HOSPITALS
Consensual Discharge	• Does the facility have a discharge planning process in place? • Has a consensual discharge been arranged with a patient or patient's family? • Is inter-hospital transfer appropriate after this discharge? • Is there an existing agreement that outlines transfer procedures (like a nursing home admission agreement)? • Is this patient a child, infirm senior, or another individual unable to engage in self-care who should be discharged only to an appropriate caretaker?
Discharge Against Medical Advice	• Is this patient an adult patient who is disoriented or committable? • Does this patient have a mental illness, substance abuse issue, or present a danger to the public? • Has hospital staff attempted to advise the patient of the risks associated with leaving? Has the staff encouraged the patient to reconsider, if further care is needed? • Has the hospital documented attempts to advise the patient against premature departure? • Has the hospital asked patients to acknowledge, in writing, awareness of leaving against medical advice? • If applicable, has the hospital documented the patient's refusal to sign in the patient's medical record? • Is the hospital preventing a patient from leaving hospital grounds, suggesting possible liability for false imprisonment?
Patients Refusing to Leave	• Has the patient refused to leave the hospital after a physician's discharge order? • Is the delay in departure due to difficulties in arranging a subsequent placement? • Could the patient incur personal liability for refusing to cooperate with discharge planning in this case?
Patients Requiring Additional Treatment	• Can the hospital no longer provide the appropriate level of care? • Is the hospital facility closing? • Is the hospital discontinuing a particular service line? • Is an internal review committee or an insurer suggesting that a patient be discharged? • Is the treating physician exercising independent judgment in determining whether discharge is appropriate?
Temporary Releases	• Is the temporary release medically prohibited? • Has the hospital obtained written permission from the patient or patient's parent or guardian? • If necessary, has the hospital released the patient to an appropriate adult? • Does the patient pose any danger to him- or herself or others?

6-8 The Impact of Antidiscrimination Laws

Although the patient-provider relationship is a consensual relationship, as outlined in section 6-1 above, providers cannot discriminate against individuals based on race, color, national origin, disability, handicap, or age. These constraints on the consensual nature of the patient-provider relationship ensure that providers receiving federal funding comply with federal laws. The most pertinent antidiscrimination laws include Title VI of the Civil Rights Act of 1964, the Americans with Disabilities Act, and the Age Discrimination Act of 1975.

6-8.1 Title VI

Title VI of the Civil Rights Act of 1964 (Title VI) forbids discrimination on the basis of race, color, or national origin in institutions that receive federal financial assistance.[44] Therefore, hospitals that receive Medicare or Medicaid reimbursement or other federal funds must comply with Title VI and the implementing regulations. Prior to 1988, Title VI applied only to those parts of hospitals supported by federal financial assistance (similar to the Hill-Burton financed facilities, addressed above). After 1988, the law was amended to apply to an entire hospital, if any part of the hospital receives federal financial assistance. The Act has been interpreted to require arrangements for language interpreters and translation of some documents for individuals with limited English proficiency.

6-8.2 The Americans with Disabilities Act

The Americans with Disabilities Act (ADA) prohibits discrimination based on a disability in any privately owned place of public accommodation.[45] A disability is a "physical or mental impairment" that "substantially limits" one or more "major life activities."[46] In *Bragdon v. Abbott*, the U.S. Supreme Court ruled that reproduction is a major life activity that is substantially impaired by being HIV-positive.[47] Therefore, an HIV-positive individual qualifies as disabled, even in the absence of observable symptoms.

Hospitals and physicians' offices fall into the category of covered pubic accommodations (regardless of whether they are privately owned), and individual physicians must comply with the ADA in their individual offices. For example, in *Bragdon*, the Court applied the ADA to a dentist's decision to deny in-office treatment to an HIV-positive patient.[48] The Court determined that the dentist could not deny in-office treatment to the patient based on a good faith belief that the patient posed significant risk to the dentist and other healthcare professionals.[49] The Court reasoned that, although the dentist could refuse to treat a highly risky patient, the grounds for refusal must be based on medical or scientific evidence rather than good faith belief.

The ADA does not guarantee a level of medical care but rather prohibits discrimination in the care that is provided. In 1998, a federal appellate court ruled that the ADA could not supply the basis for challenging the closure of a specialized healthcare facility that treated children with developmental disabilities.[50] Although the ADA covers a large number of qualified individuals, it is properly applied to narrower instances when care is provided or denied.

6-8.3 The Age Discrimination Act of 1975

Lastly, the Age Discrimination Act of 1975 forbids discrimination on the basis of age in federally assisted programs.[51] Like Title VI, the Age Discrimination Act applies to hospitals that receive reimbursement from the Medicare and Medicaid programs. In some circumstances, a recipient of federal funds may engage in action that has a disproportionate effect on persons of different ages.[52] Also, in some circumstances, entities can reasonably make decisions using age as a factor when it is necessary to the normal operation or objective of a program or activity. In spite of the near prohibition of disparate treatment, special benefits to children and elderly persons are permitted under the Act. Although they are not central to discussion of the patient-provider relationship, these antidiscrimination laws create additional parameters to the patient-provider relationship, guiding the relationship from creation to termination.

Chapter Summary

The patient-physician relationship now encompasses more individuals than in the past, including physician networks, hospitals, and patients' family members. Although the scope of the relationship has expanded, the fundamental duties of care, skill, communication, and diligence remain the same. Laws that create exceptions to traditional limitations on inpatient admissions and laws that prohibit discrimination provide additional guidance and liability exposure for physicians and hospitals. Providers must be careful and diligent when forming relationships with patients and must be especially cautious when terminating patient relationships.

Key Terms and Definitions

Common Law – Law developed by judges through court decisions, also known as "case law" or "precedent."

Discharge – The point at which the patient leaves a hospital and either returns home or is transferred to another facility, such as a nursing home or rehabilitation hospital.

Express Contract – A contract in which the agreement of the parties has been expressed in words and in which all elements and terms have been stated.

Implied Contract – A contract in which the agreement arises from conduct or assumed intentions rather than words.

Line of Service – A set of hospital services associated with a particular specialty, such as pediatrics, obstetrics, and orthopedics.

Provider – An individual or institution that provides healthcare services.

Regulation – An action in administrative law designed to carry out and enforce law and policy.

Treatment – The management and care of a patient or the combating of a disease or disorder.

Statute – A written law passed by a legislative body.

Statute of Limitations – A statute prescribing a period of limitation for the bringing of certain kinds of legal action.

Instructor-Led Questions

1. Why is it incorrect to say that a patient "employs" a physician?

2. What is the difference between an express contract and an implied contract?

3. How does a patient-physician relationship begin?

4. Do patients ever have the "right" to be admitted to a hospital?

5. What practical concerns might prevent a hospital from admitting a patient?

6. What is the Hill-Burton Act? What is its legacy in hospitals today?

7. What does EMTALA require hospitals and physicians to provide?

8. What is an "emergency medical condition," according to EMTALA?

9. Under EMTALA, do hospitals have to provide stabilizing treatment to a patient before identifying an emergency medical condition?

10. Under EMTALA, can a hospital transfer a patient who has not been stabilized?

11. What are the five requirements for an "appropriate transfer?"

12. What are the penalties for a hospital and/or physician's failure to comply with EMTALA?

13. Do hospitals have a duty to provide continued care after emergency treatment?

14. When does the patient-physician relationship terminate?

15. What risks arise when physicians withdraw from the patient-physician relationship?

16. When does a patient's relationship with a hospital end?

17. When can hospitals refuse to discharge patients?

18. What is patient abandonment?

19. How can physicians and hospitals prevent patient abandonment?

20. What characteristics cannot be used as the basis for admission decisions as a result of antidiscrimination laws?

Problem 1

The following hypothetical scenario addresses the formation of the patient-physician relationship. Determine whether a patient-physician relationship has been formed and discuss any ambiguities.

You are an orthopedic surgeon, and you own and operate an ambulatory surgery center (ASC) with five other physicians. One day, as you finish surgery, a frantic nurse hands you one of the office phones. She explains that a mother whose son has just been injured at soccer practice is demanding to speak with you. The woman on the phone has refused to speak with the nurse about her son's injuries but mentioned that she is your former high school classmate. You thank the nurse and take the phone. The woman on the other end introduces herself and states that her son has torn his ACL. You confirm that the symptoms she is describing are consistent with such an injury. After suggesting that she make an appointment, you realize that this woman's first name is the same as that of your first high school girlfriend. You recall the relationship ending poorly, and you decide that you do not want to treat her son. Is it too late? Have you formed a patient-physician relationship? If so, what is your responsibility?

Problem 2

The following hypothetical scenario addresses the termination of the patient-physician relationship. Determine whether the relationship has been terminated properly and discuss any ambiguities.

You are a breast cancer survivor who suspects that the cancer may be returning. Although you have been cancer-free for two years, you have not seen your physician in the past eight months, and you fear that your current fatigue is a sign that the disease has returned. You call your physician's office and reach an answering service. You soon discover that your physician has retired in Hawaii after a thirty-year career in oncology. The answering service cannot provide you with your physician's contact information but does inform you that he says "Aloha" and that your medical records have been put in storage. Unfortunately, there is no additional information about where the records are located. Has your physician terminated the patient-physician relationship properly? Does it matter that you have not seen your physician in the past eight months and that you both believed you were cancer-free?

Problem 3

The following hypothetical scenario addresses the termination of the patient-hospital relationship. Determine whether the relationship has been terminated properly and discuss any ambiguities.

You are the Assistant General Counsel of a hospital, and you have just received a call from the supervising nurse in the obstetrics ward. She informed you that a woman who had a baby less than thirty minutes ago is demanding to leave the hospital with her baby daughter. The woman had a natural birth and appears to be in good physical condition. The baby is also doing extremely well, weighing in at a healthy 9 pounds, 5 ounces. The supervising nurse expressed concern that the woman's husband (and child's father) was very emotional after the child's birth and that he quickly left the hospital after the baby was born. The mother is demanding to leave so that she can find him at their home. The supervising nurse feels that it is unsafe for both patients to leave the hospital. What should you advise? Should the mother and her child both be discharged? Can you prevent them from leaving the hospital campus? What obligations does the hospital have to the child?

Problem 4

The following hypothetical scenario addresses antidiscrimination laws in the context of health care. Determine whether the physician is violating the applicable statute and discuss any ambiguities.

You have been living with HIV for the past ten years. Thanks to excellent medical care and positive scientific advances, you have remained relatively symptom-free. You recently moved to Chicago and have been searching for a new orthodontist. You receive a recommendation from a friend and make an appointment with a well-known practitioner. When the orthodontist's assistant calls to confirm your appointment, you mention that you have HIV. The assistant hesitates and asks you to bring documentation of the illness to your upcoming appointment. Your appointment is in two days, and you worry that you will not have time to find your records prior to the appointment, given that most of your things are still boxed up from the move. You explain this to the assistant, but she insists that you must bring the paperwork and informs you that the orthodontist could choose not to treat you, if your case is too severe. Can the orthodontist require this documentation? Is the orthodontist discriminating against you by requiring this paperwork and potentially refusing to treat you?

Endnotes

1   See In re Bridge's Estate, 41 Wash.2d 916, 253 P.2d 394, 39 A.L.R.2d 506 (1953).

2   *Findlay v. Board of Sup'rs of Mohave County*, 72 Ariz. 58, 230 P.2d 526, 24 A.L.R.2d 841 (1951); *Hankerson v. Thomas*, 148 A.2d 583 (Mun. Ct. App. D.C. 1959).

3   See id.

4   E.g., *Skodje v. Hardy*, 47 Wash.2d 557, 288 P.2d 471 (1955).

5   E.g. *Vidrine v. Mayes*, 127 So.2d 809 (La. Ct. App. 1961).

6   *McNamara v. Emmons*, 36 Cal. App. 2d 199, 97 P.2d 503 (4th Dist. 1939).

7   See *Johnston v. Sibley*, 558 S.W.2d 135 (Tex. Civ. App. 1977).

8   *McGulpin v. Bessmer*, 241 Iowa 1119, 43 N.W.2d 121 (1950); see also *Glenn v. Carlstrom*, 556 N.W.2d 800 (1996).

9   See *O'Neill v. Montefiore Hosp.*, 11A.D.2d 132, 202 N.Y.S.2d 436 (1st Dept. 1960); compare *St. John v. Pope*, 901 S.W.2d 420 (Tex. 1995).

10 See *Fabian v. Matzko*, 236 Pa.Super. 267, 344 A.2d 569 (1975).

11 See 42 C.F.R § 124.603.

12 Id.

13 See http://www.hrsa.gov/gethealthcare/affordable/hillburton/.

14 42 C.F.R § 124.603.

15 *See* 42 C.F.R. § 124.503; *Uncompensated services* means:

    (1) For facilities other than those certified under §124.513, §124.514, §124.515, or §124.516, health services that are made available to persons unable to pay for them without charge or at a charge which is less than the allowable credit for those services. The amount of uncompensated services provided in a fiscal year is the total allowable credit for services less the amount charged for the services following an eligibility determination. Excluded are services provided more than 96 hours following notification to the facility by a quality improvement organization that it disapproved the services under section 1155(a)(1) or section 1154(a)(1) of the Social Security Act. 42 C.F.R. § 124.502(m)(1).

16 Cal. Health & Safety Code §§ 127400(c), (f), (g), and 127405(a).

17 42 U.S.C § 1395dd *et seq.*

18 Id.

19 Id.

20 *Guerrero v. Copper Queen Hospital*, 112 Ariz. 104, 106, 537 P.2d 1329, 1331 (1975).

21 Id.

22 *Stanturf v. Sipes*, 447 S.W.2d 558 (1969).

23 *Carrasco v. Bankoff*, 220 Cal. App. 2d 230, 33 Cal. Rptr. 673 (2d. Dist. 1963).

24 *Kenigsberg v. Cohn*, 117 A.D.2d 652, 498 N.Y.S.2d 390 (2d. Dept. 1986).

25 East v. U.S. 745 F.Supp. 1142 (1990).

26 See *Bruse v. Hille*, 1997 S.D. 108, 567 N.W.2d 872 (1972).

27 *Magana v. Elie*, 108 I11.App.3d 1028, 1034, 439 N.E.2d 1319, 1323 (1982).

28 Id.

29 IA ADC 653-13.7(8)(c).

30 *McGulpin v. Bessmer*, 241 Iowa 1119, 1127, 43 N.W.2d 121, 125 (1950). Iowa courts have not issued a ruling on the amount of time required for sufficient notice. See also *Glenn v. Carlstrom*, 556 N.W.2d 800 (1996).

31 *Manno v. McIntosh*, 519 N.W.2d 815, 821 (1994).

32 *Tierney v. University of Mich. Regents*, 257 Mich. App. 681, 669 N.W.2d 575 (2003).

33 42 U.S.C. § 1395x(ee); 42 C.F.R. § 482.43(c).

34 *Haleyville Health Care Ctr. v. Winston Count Hosp. Bd.*, 678 So.2d 789 (Ala. Civ. App. 1996).

35 *Ticzon v. N.Y. State Dept. of Health*, 305 A.D.2d 816, 759 N.Y.S.2d 586 (2d. Dept. 2003).

36 Anemona Hartocollis, *Rules for Monitoring TB are Tightened*, New York Times, June 16, 2010.

37   In re: J.J., 718 S.W.2d 235 (Mo. Ct. App. 1988).

38   In re Wyckoff Heights Med. Ctr., 191 Misc. 2d 207, 741 N.Y.S.2d 400 (Sup. Ct. 2002).

39   *Wickline v. California*, 192 Cal.App.3d 1630, 239 Cal.Rptr. 810 (1987).

40   *Villarin v. Onobanjo*, 276 A.D.2d 479, 714 N.Y.S.2d 90 (2000).

41   Id.

42   *Herrgesell v. Genesee Hospital*, 45 A.D.3d 1488, 846 N.Y.S.2d 523 (2007).

43   Id.

44   42 U.S.C § 2000(d) et seq.

45   42 U.S.C §§ 12181-12189.

46   Id.

47   *Bragdon v. Abbott*, 524 U.S. 624, 118 S.Ct. 2196 (1998).

48   Id.

49   Id. at 626.

50   *Lincoln CERCPAC v. Health & Hops. Corp.*, 147 F.3d 165 (2d. Cir. 1998).

51   42 U.S.C. §§ 6101-6107.

52   45 C.F.R. § 91.14.

Chapter 7

Decision Making Concerning Individuals

Donna Page

Key Learning Objectives

By the end of this chapter, the reader will be able to:

- Identify the appropriate decision maker.

- Determine what information needs to be given to the decision maker.

- Confirm proof of the decision.

- Understand some of the limits on the range of permitted decisions.

- Know when involuntary treatment may be given.

- Identify the consequences of providing services without authorization.

Chapter Outline

Introduction

Who makes the decision about whether a medical examination or procedure will be performed on a patient? The decision is usually made by the provider who is willing to perform the examination or procedure and the patient or the patient's representative who is authorized to make such decisions. Healthcare providers must obtain appropriate authorization before examining a patient or performing diagnostic or therapeutic procedures. Usually, authorization is through the express or implied consent of the patient or the patient's representative. The person giving consent must have sufficient information concerning available choices so that the consent is an informed consent. If the decision is not to consent, usually the examination or procedure cannot be performed. The law overrides some refusals and authorizes involuntary treatment, such as for some mental illness and substance abuse.

Making these decisions about the treatment of individuals presents several recurring problems of healthcare law that will be addressed in this chapter and includes questions such as:

- 7-1. Who is the appropriate decision maker?
- 7-2. What information needs to be given to the decision maker?
- 7-3. Who has the responsibility to provide information?
- 7-4. What should be done to prove the decision?
- 7-5. What constitutes coercion that makes consent involuntary and invalid?
- 7-6. What limits are placed on the permitted range of decisions?
- 7-7. When can the law authorize involuntary treatment?
- 7-8. What are the consequences of stopping treatment or providing unauthorized treatment?

7-1 Who Is the Appropriate Decision Maker?

The general rule is that adults with decision-making capacity make the decisions regarding their own treatment and that decisions continue to be effective after the adult loses capacity. The common law right to refuse or discontinue medical treatment is derived from the long-standing commitment of U.S. law to personal autonomy and self-determination. In 1891, the U.S. Supreme Court said that "no right is held more sacred, or is more carefully guarded by the common law, than the right of every individual to the possession and control of his [or her] own person, free from all restraint or interference of others, unless by clear and unquestionable authority of law."[1]

In 1990, the U.S. Supreme Court, in *Cruzan v. Director, Missouri Department of Health*, reiterated that the right of competent adults to refuse unwanted medical treatment is a liberty interest protected by the Fourteenth Amendment Due Process clause. Some minors with decision-making capacity are treated like adults for some treatments. For all others, someone else must be the decision maker. A major problem for healthcare law is the determination of when the authority of law should be exercised contrary to autonomy for the protection of the patient or others or the accomplishment of other societal priorities.

Healthcare providers have an essential role in the decision-making process. They shape the scope of available options in four ways. First, the healthcare provider is a source of information concerning potential options. However, the provider is not the only source. Many patients gather information independently from other sources, including the Internet. Information gathering is discussed in more detail in section 7-2. Second, the healthcare provider has a professional duty not to provide medically inappropriate services. Third, there are limits on what each healthcare provider has the capability to provide. Thus, the provider can refuse to provide some services that the decision maker wants based on a determination that it is inappropriate or outside the scope of the services provided. The decision maker generally has to choose between (a) accepting the judgment and/or limitations of the provider and (b) seeking another provider. Fourth, in some circumstances providers will not provide services within the scope of their capability based on an unwillingness to establish or continue a relationship with the particular patient, so the decision maker must seek another provider. The relationship with the patient is discussed in more detail later in this text.

In applying the general rule, several problems arise.

- 7-1.1. When does an adult have decision-making capacity?
- 7-1.2. When an adult with decision-making capacity gives directions and later loses capacity, what is the effect of the prior direction?
- 7-1.3. Who makes decisions for adults without decision-making capacity?

- 7-1.4. When can minors make their own decisions?
- 7-1.5. Who makes decisions for minors who cannot decide for themselves?

7-1.1 When Does an Adult Have Decision-Making Capacity?

In the United States, individuals are adults for most purposes on their eighteenth birthday and are able to make their own medical decisions. Adults have decision-making capacity if (1) they have not been declared incompetent by a court and (2) they are generally capable of understanding the consequences of alternatives, weighing the alternatives by the degree to which they promote their desires, and choosing and acting accordingly. The standard is not the degree to which the person's decision agrees with the provider's recommendations. Individuals can refuse even life-saving treatment as long as they understand and accept the consequences. The individual who must live or die with the outcome should usually make the decision.

> Adult Decision-Making Capacity: • Individual not deemed incompetent by Court • Individual capable of understanding consequences of decision.

Virtually all decisions involve external and internal influences, denial of some factors, some misunderstandings, erroneous beliefs, beliefs that are not based on evidence, incomplete information, personal preferences and priorities, concern for the impact on others, and other factors that can be contrary to "ideal" decision making. The determination of capacity is not necessarily the function of psychiatrists. It is usually a practical assessment that should be made by the provider who obtains the consent or accepts the refusal. For most patients, the assessment of capacity is not difficult. Sometimes assessment of capacity is more complex. Patients can have capacity to make some decisions and not have capacity to make other decisions. If there is suspicion of underlying mental retardation, mental illness, or disorders that affect brain functions, consultation with a psychiatrist or appropriate specialist is advisable.

In most states, there is a strong legal presumption of continued capacity. A presumption means that the law assumes that persons have capacity and anyone who disagrees must prove otherwise. For example, a Pennsylvania court found a woman capable of refusing a breast biopsy even though she was committed to a mental institution with a diagnosis of chronic schizophrenia and two of her three reasons for refusal were delusional.[2] She understood the alternatives and consequences and had a no delusional reason for her decision.[3] However, an Illinois court ruled that merely presenting a single nondelusional reason for refusing psychotropic medications did not preclude a finding of incapacity to make reasoned decisions, so that administration of medications could be ordered.[4]

A Florida case involved a patient whose breathing tube had become dislodged and who refused re-intubation for four hours. When she finally consented, she died soon after re-intubation. Her estate and her husband (who had also refused intubation for her) sued claiming she had not been competent to refuse. Their expert pointed out that she was acutely ill, in intensive care, on medication, sleep deprived, and hypoxemic (low oxygen levels in the blood). However, the undisputed evidence was that she was awake, alert, oriented, and asking appropriate questions when she refused. The court ruled that she was competent.[5]

Until recently, only one state, New York, adopted a substantially weaker commitment to autonomy by eliminating the presumption of competency whenever there is medical evidence of mental illness or defect. In 2002, a New York appellate court ruled that when there is such evidence, a presumption against capacity is created, so that the person claiming capacity must prove capacity. In a case involving a patient with Alzheimer's disease, the court ruled that an advance directive was not valid because there was a failure to show that the patient was competent when she signed it.[6] Some patients who are unhappy with cosmetic surgery claim that they lacked capacity to consent because their desire to change their appearance was due to mental illness. The highest court of New York rejected such a challenge in 2001. The court determined that the patient had presented insufficient proof that she had a mental condition that would cause her to lack capacity to consent to elective cosmetic surgery.[7] Many cosmetic surgeons prepare to defend such suits by requiring a psychological evaluation before accepting consent to surgery.[8]

It is generally not the primary responsibility of the hospital to raise the question of incapacity. Illinois courts have ruled that the hospital generally has no duty to inquire into the availability of a surrogate decision maker until the attending physician has determined the patient lacks decisional capacity.[9]

Some states have special rules for determining capacity in certain cases. For example, until 1999, New Jersey required three physicians to determine capacity before a decision to refuse life-sustaining treatment could be honored.

TEMPORARY CAPACITY. Persons who generally lack decision-making capacity might regain capacity for temporary periods. This has long been recognized by courts when they approve wills that are made during lucid intervals by persons who are otherwise generally confused.[10]

TEMPORARY INCAPACITY. Persons who generally have decision-making capacity might have impaired capacity for temporary periods. For example, some drugs can impair capacity, so treatment decisions generally should not be solicited from patients after such drugs have reduced capacity.[11] Not all sedatives render a patient incapacitated.

When a decision must be made in an emergency while a patient is temporarily incapacitated, generally others can make the decisions. In some situations, close family or friends can make the decisions. When time does not permit this consultation, providers can make emergency life-saving decisions that are not contrary to the patient's directions.

In nonemergency situations of temporary incapacity where capacity is likely to be reestablished soon without treatment, consent of others generally should not be relied on. A Utah case involved a patient who was incapacitated temporarily due to preoperative medications. During that temporary incapacity, the physician obtained the wife's consent for surgery. The court ruled that the consent was not valid. The wife could only consent when there was longer incapacity or there was an emergency.[12]

CONSISTENCY. When providers have formally determined that a patient lacks capacity, they should treat the patient consistently as incapacitated until there is a determination that capacity is restored. If a provider intends to rely on a patient making a decision during a lucid interval of capacity after incapacity has been determined, there generally should be a determination with the same degree of formality as the determination of incapacity.

7-1.2 When an Adult with Decision-Making Capacity Gives Directions and Later Loses Capacity, What Is the Effect of the Prior Direction?

Directions that adults give while they have decision-making capacity generally should be followed after they lose capacity. Most persons lose decision-making capacity prior to death. The only way to preserve the right to direct personal treatment is to honor "advance directives" made while the person had decision-making capacity. Most states have

addressed this situation through statutes. In situations in which either there is no applicable statute or the statutory procedures have not been followed, common law and constitutional principles generally require that the patient's directives be followed.

Advance directives can be written or oral. The Federal Patient Self-Determination Act ("PSDA")[13] (enacted in 1990) addresses the right of individuals to articulate their desires regarding their medical treatment in advance – either in a specific document (an advance directive or "AD") or by appointing someone as a healthcare agent to speak for them. This law does not grant new rights; rather, those specific rights are spelled out in state law. However, this federal law does require hospitals and other providers and health plans to maintain written policies and procedures with respect to ADs.[14]

> Right of Self-Determination – Competent Individual (Adult) has the right to determine what happens to his or her own body, including the right to refuse treatment entirely.

WRITTEN DIRECTIVES. The majority of states have statutes that recognize written ADs that are in a certain format. When written ADs are in that format, the directives generally present few legal problems. The primary advantage of directives in the recognized formats is that they usually have the protection of statutory presumptions of validity, so they are somewhat harder to challenge. In the absence of a challenge, there is little or no difference.

States have required several kinds of legal formalities for execution of ADs,[15] including (i) use of standardized statutory forms; (ii) language for authorizing certain wishes; (iii) required witnessing and restrictions on who may be a witness; and (iv) limitations on who may serve as an agent or proxy.

One simple way a written AD can fail to satisfy most statutes is by being unsigned or improperly signed. In a Virginia case, the patient had prepared an AD but before signing it became comatose in an automobile accident. The family initially disagreed on whether tube feeding should be discontinued in accordance with his wishes. On petition of the wife, the trial court authorized that tube feeding be discontinued in accordance with the AD. The other family decided not to contest the decision. The state intervened at the direction of the governor, but the Virginia Supreme Court refused to review the case. So the tube feeding was discontinued.[16]

The need for interpretation is one of the legal problems that can occasionally arise with directives. This can occur whether or not the directive is in the statutory format. Usually, these can be solved without court involvement by careful reading.

Written ADs are rarely challenged as such challenges are largely unsuccessful unless the signature is a forgery or the person lacked decision-making capacity at the time the directive was signed. Providers generally do not have a duty to investigate the circumstances of the signing of a directive, but if they have reasonable suspicions regarding its validity, they should resolve those suspicions before acting on the directive.

At or near the time of admission, patients and families of incapacitated patients should be asked if there is a written directive so it can be documented, discussed, and implemented. Certain provider entities such as hospitals that participate in Medicare are required to make this inquiry.[17] The Joint Commission (TJC) also requires any TJC-accredited facility, including hospitals, outpatient clinics, and nursing homes to make this inquiry.[18]

ORAL DIRECTIVES. Prior to the 1993 Uniform Health Care Decisions Act, no state recognized oral directives. Currently, fourteen states recognize some form of oral directive where a patient's oral "instruction" has been documented in his or her medical record.[19] The difficulty with oral directions is that they can be harder to prove and, thus, easier to contest. When time permits, it is best to write and sign the oral directions. Some persons are willing to discuss their directions but reluctant to write them. When patients do not have written directives, it is helpful for healthcare providers to document discussions with patients about these matters in the medical record. Oral directions given to family and friends can also be strong evidence, but they sometimes can be difficult to assess. Providers can generally rely on reports from family and friends in the absence of conflicting reports or a reasonable basis for suspecting their veracity. If there is no reason to suspect the authenticity of the directive, it should usually be followed. When oral directives are contested, courts place substantial weight on oral directives when they can be proved.

In 1990, the U.S. Supreme Court ruled that states can require that ADs be proved by clear and convincing evidence.[20] This means that there needs to be stronger evidence than is required to meet the usual civil standard of preponderance of the evidence, which only requires proof that it is more likely than not that the directive is what the patient wanted. In states that apply the more restrictive standard, oral directives are sometimes hard to prove when contested. It is preferable to sign a written AD. Oral directives leave open the opportunity for extended family, legal, and political controversies. The extent of the impact of a controversy between family members is best illustrated by the case of Terri Schiavo. On February 25, 1990, Terri Schiavo suffered cardiac arrest and subsequently fell into a persistent vegetative state. In 2001, Florida courts determined after extensive hearings that there was clear and convincing evidence that she had stated a preference for termination of life support, and the court authorized her guardian/husband to end life support. This was reaffirmed in 2003 after a series of legal challenges by her parents. Life support was discontinued in 2004. When her parents continued to object, the Florida legislature quickly passed a special law authorizing the governor to order the tube feeding to be resumed. He issued the order, and the feeding was resumed. A Florida court determined that the special law violated the state constitutional right of privacy of the patient and the separation of powers of the legislature and judiciary. In September 2004, the Florida Supreme Court affirmed the decision, and the U.S. Supreme Court denied review in January 2005. After many additional court proceedings, treatment was discontinued on March 18, 2005. On March 20, Congress enacted a special law permitting federal court review of the case. The reviewing federal courts concluded that the state courts had followed appropriate procedures and refused to intervene. Ms. Schiavo died on March 30, 2005.[21]

INTERPRETING ADVANCE DIRECTIVES. Some ADs direct that certain treatments be provided. Most ADs address refusal of treatments. They specify what treatments are refused and under what circumstances. Many ADs are written in very broad terms so that when a triggering condition occurs a broad range of treatments are refused. Some ADs are complex, specifying different triggering conditions for specified treatments. The more complex directives are sometimes more difficult to interpret and implement, especially when they are written by patients or their attorneys without medical input.

When reviewing written directives, attention should be focused on what condition triggers the refusal of treatment and what treatment is being refused. Some of the triggering conditions that have been used include: (1) terminal illness, (2) imminence of death, (3) loss of capacity to care for self, (4) loss of capacity to make medical decisions, and (5) loss of capacity to recognize or communicate with family. Some of thetreatments refused include: (1) extraordinary procedures, (2) life-prolonging procedures, (3) artificial nutrition and hydration, and (4) all procedures except comfort care.

APPLYING ADVANCE DIRECTIVES WHEN INCAPACITY IS TEMPORARY. When a competent patient still is able to communicate or when there is a reasonable likelihood that the patient will again have decision-making capacity and be able to communicate, reliance usually should not be placed on directives made before the condition was known. The patient should be given an opportunity to recover the ability to communicate and express his or her present directive. The major exception is that providers in most jurisdictions should not wait for recovery before following directives based on religious or other strongly held views that are intended to transcend individual conditions. An example of such a directive is a religious-based refusal of blood transfusions.

When the patient was aware of the current condition when giving the AD, it is generally appropriate to act in accordance with the AD even when there is a possibility of return to capacity. The directive needs to be read carefully. For example, some ADs use irreversible loss of capacity as the triggering condition, so there would be no refusal of treatment during temporary incapacity.

NO FAMILY VETO. Numerous courts have emphasized the concurrence of the family or the absence of family in their decisions.[22] This should not be interpreted to mean that the family could veto the directive of a competent adult. Courts that have addressed actual disagreements have ruled in favor of the patient's directive. For example, in 1981, a federal district court ordered a Veterans Administration hospital to honor a competent adult's directive to discontinue his respirator, despite the opposition of his wife and children.[23] When a competent adult patient consents, the only legally relevant information is the information given to the patient.[24]

7-1.3 Who Makes Decisions for Adults Without Decision-Making Capacity?

When patients have not expressed their directions and are no longer able to do so, some individual or group must be able to make surrogate decisions for them. In most states,

decisions are made by a guardian if one has been appointed by a court. In the absence of a guardian, the healthcare agent designated by the patient makes decisions. In the absence of a designated agent, close family, friends, and others who have assumed supervision of the patient usually make the decisions. The goal of the decision-making process is to make the decision that the patient would make—substitute decision making—and, when it is not possible to determine what the patient would want, to make the decisions that are in the best interests of the patient.

If the incapacity is temporary, the procedure should usually be postponed until the patient regains capacity and can make his or her own decision, unless the postponement presents a substantial risk to the patient's life or health.[25]

EMERGENCIES. In most emergencies, decisions are made by the providers. Consent is presumed to exist in medical emergencies unless the provider has reason to believe that consent would be refused.[26] When treatment has been refused, there can be no implied consent even in life-threatening situations.[27] An immediate threat to life or health is clearly a sufficient emergency. In an Iowa case, implied consent to removal of a limb mangled in a train accident was presumed because amputation was necessary to save the patient's life.[28]

GUARDIAN. In most states, the guardian of the person can make decisions regarding medical care of the patient. Guardianship usually supersedes any AD appointing a healthcare agent. Some court orders appointing guardians limit the authority of the guardian or grant the guardian special powers.

Providers can generally rely on the representations of guardians of the person concerning the scope of their powers, so there is generally no duty to obtain a copy of the guardianship papers, unless there is reason to suspect the information from the guardian. Some providers request copies of guardianship papers and place them in the medical record. When this is done, it is important to review the papers so that limitations or special instructions can be addressed.

A guardian of the estate is granted powers over the person's property and has no authority to make medical decisions. Often a guardian serves as both guardian of the person and guardian of the estate.

A guardian *ad litem* is a person appointed to represent the patient in court proceedings and has no authority to make medical decisions, unless the court has granted this power.

If a guardian *ad litem* asserts decision-making power, it is prudent to obtain a copy of the court order to confirm the power. Generally, the state law or the appointment order grants the guardian *ad litem* access to medical information concerning the patient. However, there can be restrictions on access to some information. Many court decisions concerning terminally ill patients involve guardians because the appointment of a guardian is a procedure courts use to effectuate their judgments. However, generally courts have permitted family members to make these decisions without being legally designated guardians, so it is not necessary to routinely seek guardianship.

In some states, obtaining guardianship can substantially reduce the scope of permitted decisions. For example, in Wisconsin, guardians are not permitted to decide to end life-prolonging treatment unless the patient is in a persistent vegetative state or the decision is pursuant to directions from the patient; the only exception is that guardians can approve do not resuscitate orders.[29]

HEALTHCARE AGENT. In most states, a person can sign an AD designating one or more persons to serve as a healthcare agent to make medical decisions. Often this AD is called a Durable Power of Attorney for Health Care (DPOAHC), but may also be known as a healthcare proxy or surrogate, depending on state law. A power of attorney gives the designated agent the power to make decisions on the behalf of the person giving the power, called the principal. Powers of attorney have long been used to authorize agents to engage in business transactions for the principal. These traditional powers of attorney become invalid when the principal becomes incapacitated. To adapt this to healthcare decision making, special forms authorizing healthcare decisions developed, and they were made durable, which means that they remain valid after the principal loses capacity.

> Healthcare Agent: Individual who helps to make medical decisions on your behalf when you are no longer able/competent to do so.

In most states, the power to act as healthcare agent begins when the AD is activated. Activation occurs when healthcare providers document their determination that the patient lacks decision-making capacity.

PHYSICIANS ORDERS FOR LIFE-SUSTAINING TREATMENT (POLST). First developed in Oregon in the 1990s as a protocol for seriously chronically ill patients, the POLST was intended to bridge the gap between the patient's preferences (AD) and the actual plan of care reflected in the physician's orders. The POLST form (also referred to as a Medical Order for Scope of Treatment or "MOST") covers several decisions common for seriously chronically ill patients, including: CPR, level of medical intervention desired in the event of emergency, use of medications, and the use of artificial nutrition and hydration. A POLST/MOST does not, however, take the place of a living will or a healthcare power of attorney.[30]

> Physicians Orders for Life-Sustaining Treatment (POLST): A standardized medical order form that indicates specific types of life-sustaining treatment a seriously ill patient does not want.

SPOUSE, DOMESTIC PARTNER, CLOSE FAMILY, FRIENDS, AND OTHERS. When decisions concerning treatment cannot be deferred until recovery of capacity, it is common practice to seek a decision from the spouse, domestic partner,[31] other close family members, next of kin, or others who have assumed supervision of the patient.

In most states, laws or court decisions support this practice. The majority of states specify a priority list of who will be decision maker for some decisions.[32] In the absence of state statute or court decision, the most widely accepted order of priority of close family is spouse, domestic partner, adult children, parents, adult siblings, and others. When there is more than one close family member or other person with knowledge of the patient's desires seeking to make decisions, it is common practice to have a family conference to seek consensus. Often consensus can be reached. When consensus among the primary decision makers is not possible, it is sometimes necessary to seek guardianship, so that there can be one decision maker.

In some states, physicians have been given the power to make some medical decisions for incompetents who have no other surrogate decision maker.[33] In 2010, the state of Idaho took an extreme position, whereby healthcare professionals with "sincerely held religious, moral or ethical principles" did not need to provide any health care that violates his or her conscience. Due to public outcry, this law was amended a year later.[34]

SUBSTITUTED JUDGMENT AND BEST INTERESTS. Courts have developed two standards for surrogate decision makers to use. Most courts apply the substituted judgment standard, which requires the decision maker to strive to make the decision the patient would have made if able.[35] When the patient never had decision-making capacity, some courts apply the best interests standard, which focuses not on what the patient would want, but on what is best for the patient in the view of the decision maker.[36]

GIVING WEIGHT TO THE PATIENT'S WISHES. In making a treatment decision, appropriate weight should be given to what is known of the patient's wishes even if the wishes do not qualify as an AD. Patient wishes expressed after loss of capacity should also be considered.

INVOLUNTARY TREATMENT. In several circumstances, the law authorizes treatment without the consent and even over the opposition of the patient or the patient's representative. The authorizing laws specify who may exercise this decision-making power. Involuntary treatment is discussed in section 7-7.

In summary, an "advance directive" is a general term for any document that gives instructions about an individual's ("principle") health care and/or appoints someone ("attorney in fact") to make medical treatment decisions for that individual if he or she cannot make such decisions.

Living wills and Durable Powers of Attorney for Health Care (DPOAHC) are examples of ADs. A living will is a document that states an individual's wishes about life-sustaining medical treatment when the individual is terminally ill, permanently unconscious or in the end-stage of a fatal illness. A DPOAHC (or healthcare proxy) is a document that appoints someone to make medical decisions for an individual (in the way that the individual would want them to be made) in the event that the individual is no longer able to do so. **Table 7-1** offers a side-by-side comparison of the various types of Advance Directives as well as Surrogate Decision Making.

7-1.4 When Can Minors Make Their Own Decisions?

Minors may make their own medical decisions in four circumstances: (1) as permitted by statutes; (2) if emancipated, and then they have the same rights as adults to make medical decisions; (3) if "mature" minors; and (4) if contracting for necessaries. Necessary medical services are usually considered necessaries.

Table 7-1 General Summary/Comparison of Advance Directives (AD) & Surrogate Decision Making[i]

	What It Does	What It Doesn't Do	Who Can/ Must Sign	When It Takes Effect	When It Expires	Who Can Revoke/ Override
Living Will (LW)	AD. Directs that life-sustaining treatment be withdrawn or withheld when (i) incurable or terminal condition or (ii) persistent vegetative state *and* (iii) patient lacks decisional capacity.	Due to limitations, doesn't replace need for additional directives or preferences for care.	Patient (18+ yrs) and 2 witnesses (18+ yrs and not beneficiaries of estate.)	Only when patient has terminal condition and death is imminent.	At death or revocation by patient or patient's POA (if authorized).	Patient, authorized agents. May be challenged in court.
Durable Power of Attorney for Health Care (HCPOA)	AD. Appointed person (agent) to make health-care decisions according to patient's preference. Powers may be very broad or very limited.	Only for health-care decisions, does not grant authority to override patient's preferences, LW, or DNR directive.	Patient (18+ yrs, with decisional capacity) Witnesses requirement varies by state (must be 18+ yrs old) Some states require notarization.	Immediately on signing or once patient incapacitated (temporarily or long term) as determined by physician or court.	At death or revocation by patient, or, if provisional, when patient regains capacity.	Patient, if competent. May be challenged in court. HCPOA agent "trumps" a designated beneficiary or agent.

Do Not Resuscitate (DNR) (also known as CPR directive)	AD. Allows patient to refuse CPR in the event heartbeat and breathing stop. May also authorize limited resuscitative measures in the event a patient's breathing stops but heart is still beating.	Has no effect on any other healthcare interventions in any other circumstances.	Patient or agent *and* in most states, attending physician. Witnesses – requirement varies by state (18+ yrs old)	Upon signature of patient and when very specific conditions are met.	At death or revocation by patient. May be suspended during surgery.	Patient, agent, in some circumstances, if patient authorized anatomical gift, CPR must be provided until conflict resolved.
Health Care Surrogate	Not an AD; state law which allows attending physician to identify an individual (usually a spouse or domestic partner and next-of-kin priority list) to make decisions regarding a patient's health care. State laws vary significantly in the scope of authority and other limitations provided.	Inoperative if there is agent. If no one, a court-appointed guardian may make decisions.	No form, no signatures. Physician documents in medical record that patient lacks decisional capacity. Documentation and witnessing of decision to forego life-sustaining treatment are also, generally, required.	Patient has no AD, lacks decisional capacity, and has a "qualifying" condition, per state law.	At death, or when patient regains decisional capacity or appointment of guardian.	Patient (if competent), any interested party.
Physicians Orders for Life-Sustaining Treatment (POLST) or Medical Orders for Scope of Treatment (MOST)	Not an AD. Protocol for seriously chronically ill patients. End-of-life care decisions incorporated into physicians orders (POLST form). Like a DNR, but not limited to resuscitation, and doesn't presumptively call for withholding medical interventions (permits full range of plans from comfort care only to full treatment).	Replaces an AD.	Patient or agent (18+ yrs old, having decisional capacity) or guardian *and* physician (MD, DO), or in some states where recognized, may be signed by advanced practice nurse (APN) or physician's assistant (PA).	Upon signature of patient or agent. Currently recognized in fifteen states.[ii]	At death of patient, revocation, or replacement.	Patient, agent, or guardian.

Guardianship	Not an AD. Legal process whereby a court appoints a guardian to make decisions for the patient (ward). Powers prescribed by court and generally do not include withholding or withdrawal of life-sustaining procedures unless authorized by court order.	Limited by court orders. Ward may retain certain rights to be consulted on decisions.	Court process.	Per court order.	Death of ward, removal of guardianship by court.	Although subject to challenge, only court can appoint or remove guardian.

[i] See also, the American Bar Association's (ABA) website for an in-depth summary chart, by state, compiled by the ABA's Commission on Law and Aging entitled "Health Care Power of Attorney and combined Advance Directive Legislation" (2009) as well as summary of most recent Health Care Decision Statutes, by state (advance directives, default surrogate laws, POLST, and registries) within the past year.

[ii] The growing list of states recognizing POLST include: OR, CA, WA, ID, NY, PA, UT, MN, CO, WV, NC, TN, HA, WI and IL. See also, AAPR Public Policy Institute "Improving Advance Illness Care: The Evolution of State POLST" (April 2011) at assets.aarp.org/rgcenter/ppi/cons-prot/POLST-Report-04-11.pdf.

STATUTES. Many states have treatment statutes for minors, empowering older minors to consent to medical treatment. The age limits and the scope of the treatments vary from state to state.[47] The legal ability of minors to consent to a range of sensitive healthcare services—including sexual and reproductive health care, mental health services and alcohol and drug abuse treatment—has expanded dramatically in the past thirty years. Most, if not all, states permit minors to obtain contraceptive, prenatal, and sexually transmitted infection (STI) services without parental involvement. Nearly all states permit minor parents to make important decisions on their own regarding their children. In sharp contrast, the majority of states require parental involvement in a minor's abortion.[37]

In most cases, state consent laws apply to all minors age 12 and older. In some cases, however, states allow only certain groups of minors—such as those who are married, pregnant, or already parents—to consent.[38]

EMANCIPATED MINORS. Emancipated minors can consent to their own medical care. Minors are emancipated when they are no longer subject to parental control and are not supported by their parents. The specific factors necessary to establish emancipation vary from state to state.[39] Some states require that the parent and the child agree on the emancipation, so self-emancipation is not possible in those states.

MATURE MINORS. Mature minors may consent to some medical care, based on common law and constitutional principles and under the statutes of some states. In states that do not have an applicable minor consent statute, there still is generally low risk associated with providing necessary treatment to mature minors with only their consent. When the age of adulthood was twenty-one, the English common law used the Rule of Sevens to assess the decision-making capacity of minors. Minors under age seven did not have capacity. From ages seven through thirteen, there was a rebuttable presumption of no capacity. A rebuttable presumption is the default rule that the court follows until it is proven not to apply in the case. Thus, in individual cases, capacity may be proved for this age group. From ages fourteen through twenty, there was a rebuttable presumption of capacity. Unless there are contrary laws or court decisions in the jurisdiction, the Rule of Sevens still provides a good benchmark for evaluating whether a minor is a mature minor. From ages fourteen to twenty, a minor can be assumed to be mature unless it becomes clear during the consent process that the minor cannot understand the consequences of the particular decision that needs to be made. Below age fourteen, maturity cannot be assumed, so it is advisable to require an affirmative demonstration of ability to understand the consequences of the decision to be made.

There are more legal risks associated with permitting mature minors to make decisions that are more elective or higher risk. Thus, for example, it is usually advisable not to perform cosmetic surgery on mature minors who refuse to involve their parents in the decision.

In situations where life-prolonging treatment is refused, the issue is usually not whether the parent or guardian must be involved. In most cases, the parent or guardian is involved, and the issue is whether treatment can be refused when the parent and minor agree. Sometimes the issue is what to do when the parent and mature minor disagree.

Some courts have been reluctant to recognize minors as mature when they are refusing treatment that is likely to restore them to health. In 2000, the Pennsylvania Supreme Court addressed a case where a sixteen-year-old girl had died from untreated diabetes. She and her parents had relied on prayer in accordance with their religious beliefs. Her parents were convicted of involuntary manslaughter and endangering the welfare of a child because they had not sought medical care for her. The court ruled that their daughter's agreement with the approach was not a defense. The court discussed the mature minor doctrine and ruled that it could not be used as a defense by parents who failed to seek medical care.[40] While recognizing the mature minor exception, some courts are reluctant to find maturity in cases where the minor can be restored to health. In cases where the minor is terminally ill or otherwise unlikely to be restored to health by the proposed treatment, courts have generally respected minor refusals, especially when there is concurrence of the parents. For example, after a state agency forcibly removed a fifteen-year-old liver transplant patient from his home and placed him in a hospital to force him to take antirejection drugs, which could cause painful side effects, a Florida trial court authorized the refusal.[41]

The mature minor doctrine has been recognized by the U.S. Supreme Court in cases involving decisions to have an abortion. While states can mandate parental involvement in the decision for minors, states must provide an alternative process to bypass parental involvement in some situations when the minor is mature. Reproductive issues are discussed further later in the text.

NECESSARIES. Under the common law, minors have only limited capacity to enter valid contracts. Most contracts cannot be enforced against minors. Minors can disavow most contracts and get their money back. One of the few exceptions in the common law is that minors can enter binding contracts for necessaries.[42] Necessary medical treatment has long been recognized as a necessary. Necessary medical care is not limited to emergency care; for example, care for extended and chronic conditions can be included. Parents generally have the primary obligation to pay for these necessaries. However, the minor is generally also obligated to pay.[43]

This common law doctrine of necessaries provides precedent to support accepting consent of mature minors in states where courts have not yet expressly addressed consent by mature minors.

URGING PARENTAL INVOLVEMENT. When treating any unemancipated minor, the minor should be urged to involve his or her parents. When a mature minor refuses to permit parental involvement, the provider can provide necessary care without substantial risk unless there is likelihood of harm to the minor or others that requires adult involvement to avoid. When such harm is likely, parents should usually be involved unless state law forbids parental notification or there is reasonable suspicion that the parents can be a source of the risk of harm. When the parents are suspected to be a source of the risk of harm, other adults should be involved, and in many cases, the circumstances can require reporting to child abuse authorities.

7-1.5 Who Makes Decisions for Minors Who Cannot Decide for Themselves?

Consent of the parent or guardian should be obtained before treatment is given to a minor[44] unless it is (1) an emergency, (2) one of the situations in which the consent of the minor is sufficient, or (3) a situation in which a court order or other legal authorization is obtained.

EMERGENCIES. As with adults, consent is implied in medical emergencies when there is an immediate threat to life or health unless the provider has reason to believe that consent would be refused by the parent or guardian. However, when time permits seeking a court order, most providers obtain court authorization when parents refuse necessary treatment. When time does not permit seeking a prior court order, most providers will do that which is necessary to preserve life until a court decision can be obtained. In some states, this is expressly authorized in child abuse statues.

GUARDIAN. When a guardian of the person of the minor has been appointed, the guardian makes medical decisions within the scope of the guardianship. It is not unusual for a guardian to be appointed with the limited authority to consent to only some medical treatments, such as transfusions, leaving all other medical decisions to the parents.

PARENT. When there is no applicable guardianship in effect, either parent can give legally effective consent except when there is legal separation or divorce. When the parents are legally separated or divorced, usually the consent of the custodial parent must be obtained, but sometimes the arrangements can be complex. So it is prudent to ask if the court has specified decision making.[45] If inconsistent or unclear answers are given, it is prudent to obtain a copy of the court's order.

When both parents are available, it is prudent to seek consensus. It is appropriate for one parent to consult with the other. A New York court ruled that it was not neglect for one parent to briefly delay consenting to treatment for child in order to consult with the other parent.[46]

The provider generally has no duty to confirm the identity or parental status of persons who reasonably present themselves as parents. When the circumstances create suspicions, then it is appropriate to confirm identity and status. Persons who misrepresent themselves can be subject to liability, but there is generally no liability for the provider. In some states, there may be a duty to check identification before some procedures. In 2004, Texas adopted a rule that requires identification checks before consent can be obtained for abortions.[47]

ADVANCE DIRECTIVES/AGENTS FOR THE PARENT. It is not uncommon for parents to leave their children in the care of others for hours, days, or weeks. This can include day care, summer camp, visits to grandparents, or living with relatives or others while parents are on active military duty, business trips, vacations, in legal custody, or incapacitated by substance abuse. When the time period becomes too long or the arrangements are not adequate, the parental absence can constitute abandonment under the laws of some states, triggering state intervention to formally modify parental rights and legal custody. In the many situations where these arrangements are acceptable, it is necessary for the persons who are taking care of the child to be able to arrange for necessary medical care. The emergency exception to the consent requirement is not broad enough to address all of the medical needs of children. Two approaches have been used to address parental absence. One approach is for parents to sign forms consenting to medical care. Providers generally prefer to have a decision maker who has the power to make informed decisions concerning specific treatments. Thus, the other approach is for the parents to designate someone as the parent's agent to make decisions for the parents. At least one state has enacted express statutory authority for such a written delegation.[48]

IN LOCO PARENTIS. Some states consider that persons can stand *in loco parentis* (in the place of a parent) to a minor by assuming the status and obligation of a parent without formal adoption or designation by the natural parent. In these states, the term "parent" in some legal contexts is construed to include persons who are *in loco parentis.*[49]

OTHER RELATIVES. Some states recognize that in the absence of a parent or guardian, the closest available relative has authority to consent without an express directive from the parent.[50]

PERSONS WITH CUSTODY. Many minors are in the custody of governmental agencies, public or private facilities, or foster parents designated by governmental agencies. Under the laws of some states, some of these custodians have the statutory power to make some medical decisions. In other states, custodians have no power to make medical decisions, unless a court specifically grants them the power or the parents make the custodian an agent for medical decision making. In those states, the parent or parents generally retain parental rights to make medical decisions.

SUSPECTED CHILD ABUSE CASES. When healthcare providers see minor patients who they suspect have been abused or neglected, there is generally a duty to report this to child abuse authorities.[51] The definition of what constitutes reportable abuse and neglect varies. In some states, child abuse authorities have the power to authorize some treatments.[52] In some states, healthcare providers are authorized to provide some treatments, but curiously most states limit this to diagnostic procedures.[53]

7-2 What Information Needs to Be Given to the Decision Maker?

The general rule is that consent for most treatments must be an informed consent. This means that the treating provider is required to give to the decision maker several elements of information before the consent decision.

⚑ The common law right to refuse or discontinue medical treatment has been recognized for decades, as expressed by Justice Benjamin Cardozo in the 1914 case of *Schloendorff v. N. Y. Hospital*:

"Every human being of adult years and sound mind has a right to determine what shall be done with his own body; and a surgeon who performs an operation without his patient's consent commits an assault."

This right of self-determination was recognized first as the common law offense of battery, which made any offensive, unconsented touching an actionable wrong. When there is no consent or other authorization for a procedure, the physician or other practitioner doing the medical procedure can be liable for battery even if the procedure is properly performed, is beneficial, and has no negative effects.[54]

A shift in the legal application of informed consent occurred in 1960, when the Kansas Supreme Court applied the negligence theory, rather than the battery theory in *Natanson v. Kline*.[55] Today, in most jurisdictions, failure to disclose necessary information does not invalidate consent, so the procedure is not a battery[56] and is typically an issue of negligence in medical malpractice claims, rather than a battery (as further discussed later in the text). Uninformed consent protects from liability for battery, but informed consent is necessary to protect from liability for negligence.

Although some providers view the obtaining of informed consent as simply an administrative burden, providers who actually engage in the intended communication with their patients find that it not only performs its intended function of respecting individual autonomy, but it also can improve compliance, outcomes, and satisfaction.[57]

In applying the general rule, several problems arise.

- 7-2.1. When is informed consent required?
- 7-2.2. What elements of information concerning the treatment should be given?
- 7-2.3. To what extent do alternatives have to be disclosed?
- 7-2.4. What elements of information concerning the provider should be given?
- 7-2.5. What is the effect of information that the decision maker obtains from other sources?
- 7-2.6. What is the effect of barriers to understanding the information?
- 7-2.7 When can information be withheld?

7-2.1 When Is Informed Consent Required?

Most courts apply the informed consent doctrine only to services that are provided. The focus is on whether there was adequate information to obtain consent for the services provided. States vary on which services require consent.

There have been attempts to extend the informed consent doctrine. A person who was involuntarily committed to a Maine facility for mental health treatment claimed that the facility needed her informed consent to wake her in the morning. She wanted to sleep to 11 a.m. In 2001, the Maine Supreme Court ruled that the Commissioner of the Department of Mental Health had properly decided that consent was not required for waking the person since it did not constitute treatment or services, but was instead intended to give her opportunity to participate in treatment, to give clinical staff a chance to observe her, and for smooth hospital operation.[58]

A few courts have extended the informed consent doctrine to require informed refusal. The California Supreme Court ruled that a physician could be liable for a patient's death from cervical cancer because the physician did not inform the patient of the risks of not consenting to a recommended pap smear.[59] The pap smear probably would have discovered her cancer in time to begin life-extending treatment. A New Jersey court ruled that an obstetrician could be sued for failing to advise the patient sufficiently of the hazards of leaving the hospital against medical advice.[60]

There is a trend in some courts to change the focus of the informed consent doctrine in cases involving refusal of transfusions in the emergency context. The trend involves a reversal from a duty of the provider to provide information to a duty of the patient to collect and understand the information. These courts then honor only informed refusals, using the reversal of the informed consent doctrine as the stated rationale for disregarding the patient's directions.

One case involved elective surgery where the patient had expressly conditioned her consent to the surgery on not using transfusions.[61] In another case, the court did not permit the patient to sue a doctor who had unilaterally disregarded the patient's expressed directions without seeking a court order.[62]

In the past, the emergency exception to the consent requirement was limited to cases where the patient's directions were not known. These cases represent a significant retreat from the respect for religious and other beliefs of adults that the law has demonstrated in other jurisdictions. Requiring informed refusal stands the informed consent doctrine on its head. The informed consent doctrine was designed (1) to preserve the individual's right to autonomy and to be left alone by not permitting treatment without informed consent and (2) to promote disclosure of information by physicians to facilitate the exercise of that autonomy. This informed refusal doctrine removes the requirement that providers obtain consent to treatment and permits the courts and doctors to force emergency treatment on a person unless the person can meet a strict standard set by the court.

Most recently, with the emergence of new coordinated-care arrangements, including accountable care organizations (ACOs), there is an increasing push to have physicians employ the concept of "informed refusals" to eliminate unnecessary tests and procedures. However, as the physician will still be held accountable for errors—including over- or underutilization of diagnostic procedures and tests—time will tell whether this practice will result in improved health care eliminating costly and/or unnecessary testing or simply increased malpractice risk for physicians for failure to diagnose or treat properly.

7-2.2 What Elements of Information Concerning the Treatment Should Be Given?

⚑ DISCLOSURE STANDARDS. Courts have developed two standards for determining whether disclosure is adequate: the reasonable physician standard and the reasonable patient standard.[63]

> Informed Consent Standards: • Reasonable Physician Standard — (majority of states) — doctor tells you what he/she thinks you should know • Reasonable Patient Standard — doctor discloses information based upon point of view of patient (what patient would want to know).

Reasonable Physician. The majority of states apply the reasonable physician ("professional") standard of accepted medical practice. In those states, the professional has a duty to make the disclosure that a reasonably prudent physician with the same background, training, experience, and practicing in the same community, would make under the same or similar circumstances.[64] Expert testimony is necessary to prove what disclosure was required.

Reasonable Patient. A significant number of states apply the reasonable patient ("materiality") standard under which the duty to disclose is determined by the patient's informational needs,

not by professional practice.[65] Information that is "material" to the decision must be disclosed. A risk is material "when a reasonable person, in what the physician knows or should know to be the patient's position, would want to know in deciding whether or not to forgo the proposed therapy."[66] No expert testimony is required on the issue of whether specific information should have been disclosed, but expert testimony can sometimes be necessary to prove that a specific risk was present or a specific treatment was actually an alternative.[67]

Consumer Protection Laws. Some aggressive attorneys have tried to convince courts that the scope of disclosure should be subject to consumer protection laws. This has generally been unsuccessful.[68]

⚑ ELEMENTS OF DISCLOSURE. The usual elements to be disclosed under either standard are the patient's medical condition, the nature and purpose of the proposed procedure, its risks and consequences, and the feasible accepted alternatives, including the consequences of no treatment.

> Legal Elements of Informed Consent: • Diagnosis • Nature and Purpose of Procedure • Reasonable Alternatives • Risks and Benefits • Risks and Benefits of Doing Nothing.

Patient's Medical Condition. The decision maker needs to be told about the patient's medical condition, so that the context and purpose of the treatment can be understood.

Nature and Purpose of the Treatment. The decision maker needs to be told what the proposed procedure is and what the purpose of the procedure is. Disclosure should include a realistic discussion of the likelihood of success from the proposed treatment.

Risks and Consequences. Knowledge of risk is an important part of thoughtful decision making.[69] Only risks that are known or should be known by the physician to occur without negligence are required to be disclosed.[70] Nearly all courts recognize that not all risks can be disclosed. Rare risks are generally not considered material and need not be disclosed.[71] However, there is no bright line definition of what percentage constitutes rare. One useful guideline is to disclose the risks of the most severe consequences and the risks that have a substantial probability of occurring.

When risks are disclosed, it is generally not necessary to disclose percentage of risk. However, if statistics are volunteered and significantly wrong, there could be liability for misstating the risks.

Sometimes there are consequences that occur in virtually all cases. These consequences are technically not risks because risk usually implies that there is a chance that the event will not occur. Consequences can include follow-up regimens or changes in bodily functions that will continue for days or weeks or will be permanent. Generally, these consequences should be disclosed.

Alternatives. Known feasible accepted alternatives should be disclosed, including the option of no treatment. This is discussed in section 7-2.3.

Regulatory Status. There are many accepted uses of drugs and devices that are not yet approved by the Food and Drug Administration (FDA). With few exceptions, physicians can use approved drugs for off-label uses. The scope of permitted off-label uses of devices is not as broad. However, many off-label uses do not violate the law. Off-label uses for individual patients outside of research protocols are generally not considered to be research. Some attorneys have tried to establish a duty to disclose such off-label uses. This has generally been rejected by courts. In 1996, an Ohio court ruled that a physician need not disclose that an approved medical device was being used in an off-label manner.[72]

Medicare will not pay for some off-label uses of devices. Medicare law requires patients to be given an advance beneficiary notice (ABN) of these uses for financial reasons so that the patient can decide whether to incur the unreimbursed costs.

RESEARCH. There are federal and state requirements concerning consent for research. Patients ordinarily expect physicians to use the drugs and procedures customarily used for their condition. When experimental methods are used or when established procedures are used for research purposes, the investigator must disclose this to the subject and obtain the consent of the subject or the subject's representative. Governmental regulations specify review procedures for many types of research and specify disclosures that must be made to obtain informed consent to such research.

All research supported by the U.S. Department of Health and Human Services (HHS) must comply with regulations for the protection of human subjects.[73] These regulations require that an institutional review board (IRB) approve the research before HHS can support the research. Each institution must submit an acceptable institutional assurance to HHS that it will fulfill its responsibilities under the regulations before HHS will accept the decisions of its IRB.

The HHS regulations require that consent be sought "only under circumstances that provide the prospective subject or the representative sufficient opportunity to consider whether or not to participate and that minimize the possibility of coercion or undue influence." The information must be in a language understandable to the subject or representative. Exculpatory wording cannot be included in the information given. The federal regulations specify numerous basic elements of information that must be included in the consent form.[74]

Several kinds of studies are exempt from these regulations, such as the "collection or study of existing data, documents, records, pathological specimens, or diagnostic specimens, if these sources are publicly available or if the information is recorded by the investigator in such a manner that subjects cannot be identified. . . ." Expedited review is authorized for categories of research that HHS determines involve no more than minimal risk.[75] Examples of such categories are collection of small amounts of blood by venipuncture from certain adults and moderate exercise by healthy volunteers.

The HHS regulations do not preempt other federal, state, or local laws or regulations. Thus, proposals involving investigational new drugs or devices must also satisfy the regulations of the Food and Drug Administration.[76] State and local law must also be reviewed because several states have enacted laws regulating research with human subjects.[77]

Hospitals should take appropriate steps to review research involving human subjects, regardless of the sponsorship of the research, to protect patients and avoid liability. Some courts have decided that because federal regulations require institutional review of consent for certain research that the reviewing institution can be liable for lack of informed consent for such research.[78]

EFFECT OF PATIENT REQUESTS FOR ADDITIONAL INFORMATION. When a patient indicates a desire for additional information, there is usually a duty to provide it. However, there are limits to the scope of information that must be provided even when requested.

OTHER ISSUES. Some states have passed statutes or created administrative processes that address what disclosure should be made.[79] In one state, the statute requires the physician to ask the patient if a more detailed disclosure is desired. If the physician fails to ask, then the physician has a duty of full disclosure.[80]

There is no constitutional or common law duty to provide such information in the absence of a statutory mandate.[81]

7-2.3 To What Extent Do Alternatives Have to Be Disclosed?

Known, feasible, and accepted alternatives should be disclosed, including the option of no treatment. This is not limited to alternatives that the provider would perform. If the decision maker selects an option that the provider does not perform, the decision maker is declining the services offered by the provider and needs to make arrangements for another provider. Options that are available only in research protocols generally do not have to be disclosed.

The alleged failure to disclose alternatives is often the focus of informed consent cases.[82] This issue is more fully discussed in section 7-6, which discusses limits on treatment that must be offered.

In 2001, the New Jersey Supreme Court ruled that there was no need to discuss a treatment that was not a medically reasonable alternative.[83] Courts have disagreed on whether the availability of additional diagnostic tests should be considered an alternative. In 1999, a New Jersey court decided that an additional diagnostic test was not an alternative.[84] In 1996, a Wisconsin court decided that a jury could find lack of informed consent for failure to disclose availability of diagnostic CT scan.[85]

Some managed care organizations tried to impose "gag" clauses through their contracts, restricting the information physicians could provide to patients. These restrictions were widely attacked, and most were abandoned or modified.[86]

7-2.4 What Elements of Information Concerning the Provider Should Be Given?

It is generally recognized that the identity of the provider should be disclosed. There have been efforts to expand the scope of required information about the individual provider, so additional information is required in some states. When additional information is given, it needs to be accurate.

NAME OF PROVIDER. Patients generally have a right to know the identity of their providers. Undisclosed substitution of surgeons can result in liability.[87] As long as the fact that assistants can be used is disclosed, there is generally no duty to disclose the identity of each assistant.

When residents or students are involved in procedures, it is prudent to disclose that residents or students will be involved.

When a patient directs that a specific physician not perform a procedure and the forbidden physician performs it, both the forbidden physician and those who let that physician perform the procedure can be liable.[88]

CHARACTERISTICS OF PROVIDER. Courts disagree on when physicians are required to disclose certain information about themselves as part of the consent process.

Substance Abuse. There is disagreement over whether substance abuse needs to be disclosed. A Louisiana court found that a surgeon had failed to obtain informed consent when he failed to disclose his chronic alcohol abuse.[89] However, in 1997, a federal court in Hawaii ruled that there was no duty to disclose a past history of substance abuse.[90] In 2000, the Georgia Supreme Court decided that providers have no duty to disclose life factors that might subjectively be considered to adversely affect the performance, absent inquiry from the patient. This included no duty to disclose cocaine use outside of work when not on call.[91] In 2003, an Ohio court ruled that a surgeon did not have to disclose addiction to painkillers where there was no effect on the outcome of the surgery.[92]

Transmissible Disease. Despite the professional debate over the necessity of such disclosures, some courts have ruled that surgeons and some other healthcare professionals should disclose that they are HIV-positive, especially when the patient asks.[93] However, at least one state will permit suits based on nondisclosure only when actual exposure to the disease occurred.[94]

Other Conditions. In 2002, an Iowa court ruled that a surgeon had no duty to disclose the herniated disc in her neck region where it had no impact on her performance of surgery.[95]

Experience. Courts have disagreed on whether a physician must disclose experience or competence with proposed procedures. Most courts have ruled that this is not an informed consent issue. In 1996, the Wisconsin Supreme Court ruled that a physician had a duty to disclose lack of experience in some circumstances.[96] There has been no disagreement concerning the absence of a hospital duty to disclose concerns about competence.[97]

License. An Iowa court ruled that a physician did not have to disclose the probationary status of his license where it was due to the activity of an assistant.[98] However, this may suggest that some restrictions on licenses may need to be disclosed.

Financial Interests. Disclosure of financial interests has been another issue. Generally, courts have not mandated disclosure of financial interests. In 2000, the U.S. Supreme Court ruled that managed care organizations were not required to disclose financial incentives for physicians to control expenditures.[99] One exception is a California Supreme Court ruling that decided a physician could have a fiduciary duty to disclose his economic interest in cells that would be extracted in a procedure, which the physician later developed into a commercially valuable product.[100]

INFORMATION GIVEN SHOULD BE ACCURATE. In 2002, the New Jersey Supreme Court addressed a case in which the physician had misrepresented his credentials. The court ruled that the provider could not be sued for fraud so that extra uninsured punitive damages could not be awarded, but did rule that the provider could be sued for lack of informed consent.[101] However, as previously noted, in 2001, Pennsylvania decided not to permit informed consent claims based on misrepresentation of experience.

7-2.5 What Is the Effect of Information That the Decision Maker Obtains from Other Sources?

When the informed consent doctrine was developed in the 1950s, patients had little access to accurate information about medical knowledge and available treatments. Their primary source of accurate information was their physicians. A few patients in big cities and college campuses did research in medical libraries. Some patients sought second opinions from other physicians. Occasionally, there were articles in newspapers or in television news stories about healthcare topics, especially when a celebrity experienced a particular disease or treatment. Drug companies advertised over-the-counter drugs but limited advertising of prescription drugs to medical journals. Hospitals seldom advertised their services except when they opened a new program or were conducting fundraising.

This has all changed. The amount of healthcare information available has experienced explosive growth, and an ever-growing amount of the information is directly available to the public through the Internet. Data suggests that from 2001–2007 the number of U.S. adults who used the Internet to seek health information nearly doubled and that adults are more likely to seek health information online than from interpersonal sources, such as doctors, friends, family and coworkers.[102] Advertising of healthcare services by providers has also experienced rapid growth. Direct advertising of prescription medicines has exploded "Ask your doctor about . . ." television, newspaper, and other media coverage (including social media) of healthcare topics have increased.

It is not unusual for some patients to arrive at their physician appointments with extensive information about their condition and treatment options.[103] In some cases, they will have information that the physician does not have. Despite the fiction of omniscience that some courts seem to ascribe to physicians, there is a limit to the ability to keep current on all information. Many physicians welcome this active involvement of patients in structuring their own care.

DEALING WITH ERRONEOUS OR MISUNDERSTOOD INFORMATION. The availability of medical information is a mixed blessing. There is evidence that a large percentage of the members of the public have difficulty distinguishing reliable medical information from unreliable and have difficulty understanding reliable medical information.[104] There are also strongly held ethnic and cultural beliefs that predate the Internet. Thus, the provider may have to spend considerable time undoing beliefs that the patient has acquired with great effort or has held for a long time, before being able to convince the patient to accept accurate information.

Generally, the provider does not have a legal duty to undo the patient's mistaken beliefs. The provider's responsibility is to provide accurate information, not to assure that it is believed.

DEALING WITH PATIENT DEMANDS. In some cases, patients arrive demanding particular treatments or drugs. This might be based on advertising, recommendation of a friend, Internet research, or other sources. Providers then have the challenge of staying within professional standards for appropriate use, avoiding unnecessary expense to the patient and the healthcare system, and maintaining a relationship with the patient. As discussed in section 7-6.1, patient demands do not justify inappropriate uses.

IMPACT ON DUTY TO DISCLOSE. Courts are apparently not yet willing to place any responsibility on the patient in this context. In 2003, a New Jersey appellate court addressed a case concerning the adequacy of genetic counseling and found that the patient has no duty to seek information from another source, but acknowledged that when the patient does obtain information from other sources the scope of the physician's duty is reduced to a duty to "fill any informational gaps that preclude a meaningful exercise of the patient's self-determinative right."[105]

7-2.6 What Is the Effect of Barriers to Understanding the Information?

There are several barriers to understanding information presented in the consent process. These barriers can also apply to information that is given concerning the patient and family's role in ongoing care and monitoring.

ILLITERACY. A substantial portion of patients either cannot read or cannot read at the level that most health documents are written. Frequently, patients who cannot read or cannot read technical documents hide this fact from healthcare providers.

Persons are generally presumed to have read and understood documents they have signed. Sometimes courts will not apply this rule when the document is either too technical or in a language foreign to the person. Forms that require too high a level of reading ability have been criticized. It is advisable, when possible, to write forms at an eighth grade or lower reading level as well as to use other means of communication to supplement the forms.[106]

HEALTH ILLITERACY. Sometimes patients can read but cannot understand healthcare information. This is related to the problem of the reading level of the information, but there is a distinct problem with understanding the significance of healthcare information and how it is structured. This is an important issue that is receiving increasing attention.[107]

LANGUAGE AND INTERPRETERS. When the person has difficulty understanding English, the communications need to be in the language of the decision maker. When the provider is not fluently bilingual, an interpreter must be provided for key oral communications related to collecting medical history, making medical decisions, and providing directions related to care. This is required of any healthcare provider that receives federal funds, including reimbursement from Medicare, Medicaid, or other governmental programs.[108] When a patient is incapacitated and another person is acting as decision maker, an interpreter needs to be provided for decision makers who cannot communicate in English.[109] It is no longer adequate

to rely on family or friends of the patient to interpret. National telephone services exist that provide interpretation on demand in virtually any language. This satisfies the requirement. Large providers often hire or contract with interpreters for languages that are frequently encountered. These requirements also apply to providing sign language interpreters for deaf patients.

Translation of forms into other languages is generally not required, with one exception. Providers are expected to have translations of key forms into languages of patient groups who speak a primary language other than English and who constitute a substantial portion of the provider's patients.[110] There is no requirement that all written materials be translated. It is usually sufficient to translate forms and other written materials orally. The involvement of the translator should be documented.

7-2.7 When Can Information Be Withheld?

Courts have recognized several situations in which information may be withheld from patients.

EMERGENCIES. In an emergency, when there is no time to obtain consent, consent is implied.[111] When there is time to obtain some consent but insufficient time for the usual disclosure, an abbreviated disclosure is sufficient.[112]

THERAPEUTIC PRIVILEGE. Most courts recognize a therapeutic privilege not to make disclosures that pose a significant threat of patient detriment.[113] Courts limit the privilege, so it is not applicable when a physician solely fears that the information might lead a patient to forgo needed therapy. Physicians should rely on the privilege only when they can document that a patient's anxiety is significantly above the norm. In some states, when the therapeutic privilege permits nondisclosure, the information must be disclosed to a relative and that relative must concur with the patient's consent before the procedure can be performed.[114] However, at least one court ruled that relatives did not need to be informed of withheld information.[115]

PATIENT WAIVER. A patient can waive the right to be informed.[116] However, courts will be skeptical of waivers initiated by providers, so prudent providers should not suggest waivers but instead should encourage reluctant patients to be informed.

7-3 Who Has the Responsibility to Provide Information?

INDIVIDUAL PROVIDER RESPONSIBILITY. Physicians have the responsibility to provide necessary information and to obtain informed consent; it is generally not a hospital responsibility. Other independent practitioners who order or perform procedures have the same responsibility concerning their procedures.

Physicians who order or perform procedures have the responsibility to obtain consent,[117] generally not the referring physician.[118] However, in some jurisdictions, when the referring physician retains a sufficient degree of participation in the ongoing treatment plan, the referring physician can have a duty to obtain informed consent to services provided by specialists.[119] The duty is discharged if the specialist obtains informed consent; there is no duty to obtain multiple consents.[120]

LIMITED INSTITUTIONAL RESPONSIBILITY. Hospitals are generally not liable for the failure of a physician or other independent practitioner to obtain informed consent unless the professional is the hospital's employee or agent. Both court decisions and state statutes have recognized this principle.[121] Plaintiffs have tried to convince courts to require hospitals to intercede in the professional-patient relationship by imposing institutional liability for inadequate disclosures. These efforts have not been successful except in a few cases.[122] Hospital responsibility for the content of the physician's disclosure would require monitoring that could destroy the physician-patient relationship. The hospital can be liable for failing to intervene when it knows a procedure is being performed without authorization.[123] In 1997, a Wisconsin appellate court ruled that when a nurse found no consent form for a tubal ligation and informed the surgeon of the absence of the form, this was not sufficient to conclude that the procedure was nonconsensual. Based on the surgeon's response, she could reasonably conclude that consent had been obtained and the absence of the form was no more than a clerical error.[124]

TJC provides that accredited hospitals must have policies concerning informed consent but makes it clear that the intent is to establish a "mutual understanding" between the patient and the physician or other licensed independent practitioner.[125]

Research. In addition, some courts have interpreted the federal rules governing research to impose hospital responsibility for informed consent for participation in research projects.[126]

Role of Hospital Staff. The role of nurses and other hospital staff in the consent process varies from hospital to hospital. In some hospitals, hospital staff members are permitted to act as agents of the physician in providing information. In some hospitals, hospital staff members are permitted to obtain signatures on forms after the physician has provided the required information. The other approach is for hospital staff not to be involved in either step. In some states, courts may use the nurses' involvement to shift responsibility for the consent process on the hospital. However, at least one court has ruled that performing the clerical function of obtaining signatures on the forms does not shift responsibility to the hospital.[127] Other courts have recognized that the physician may delegate the providing of information and still remain legally responsible for the informed consent.[128]

Under all these approaches, a hospital employee who becomes aware of a patient's confusion or change of opinion regarding a procedure should notify the responsible physician. If the physician does not respond, appropriate medical staff and hospital officials should be notified so that they can determine whether intervention is necessary.

7-4 What Should Be Done to Prove the Decision?

Most hospitals require the use of a standard form before invasive treatment and procedures. This usually helps to reduce the liability exposure for lack of consent.[129] The battery consent form described in section 7-4.2 is usually used. When the hospital requires consent for a procedure, hospital personnel generally should not participate in the procedure until consent is documented, alternative authorization has been obtained, or there is determination that an exception applies.[130]

This section addresses the following questions:

- 7-4.1. When is express consent required, and when is implied consent sufficient?

- 7-4.2. What information should be in consent forms?

- 7-4.3. For which procedures should a signed consent be obtained?

- 7-4.4. What can be done when a patient with capacity is physically unable to sign?
- 7-4.5. How can the signed consent requirement be met when the decision maker is not present?
- 7-4.6. How long is a consent form valid?
- 7-4.7. What are other ways to document consent?

7-4.1 When Is Express Consent Required, and When Is Implied Consent Sufficient?

Consent may be either express or implied.

> EXPRESS CONSENT—clear communication in verbal or written form; IMPLIED CONSENT — understood from the surrounding circumstances (no verbal or written communication).

EXPRESS CONSENT. Express consent is consent given by direct words, either oral or written. Express consent is generally required whenever consent is not implied and involuntary treatment is not authorized. Written consent is sometimes required. As oral consent is difficult to prove, most prudent providers seek written consent whenever express consent is needed.

IMPLIED CONSENT. Implied consent is (1) inferred from some patient conduct or (2) presumed in most emergencies. Consent is usually implied from voluntary submission to an examination or procedure with apparent knowledge of its nature. Implied consent is why express consent is usually not obtained for physical examinations or minor procedures performed on competent adults.

Consent is presumed to exist in medical emergencies unless the provider has reason to believe that consent would be refused. When treatment has been refused, there can be no implied consent even in life-threatening situations. An immediate threat to life or health is clearly a sufficient emergency. In an Iowa case, implied consent to removal of a limb mangled in a train accident was presumed because amputation was necessary to save the patient's life.[131] Courts have disagreed on whether pain is a sufficient emergency to imply consent.

The existence of an emergency does not overcome the right of a patient with capacity to refuse treatment. When express refusals are ignored in emergencies, it is likely that courts will permit close examination of the circumstances. When unexpected emergency conditions arise during surgery, especially life-threatening conditions, implied consent is sometimes found to extensions or modifications of surgical procedures beyond the scope expressly authorized. Many surgical consent forms include express consent to these extensions or modifications to preserve life or health. However, a federal appellate court ruled that when there is express consent to extensions in the consent form, such extensions should be limited to bona fide emergencies.[132]

7-4.2 What Information Should Be in Consent Forms?

CONSENT FORM TYPES. There are three types of consent forms: (1) blanket consent forms, (2) battery consent forms, and (3) detailed consent forms.

Blanket Consent Forms. Prior to the mid-1960s, many hospitals used blanket consent forms that authorized any procedure the physician wished to perform. Courts have ruled that these forms are not evidence of consent to major procedures because the procedure is not specified on the form.[133] Many attorneys recommend continued use of blanket admission consent forms to cover procedures for which individual special consent is not sought even though implied consent to most of these procedures is inferred from hospital admission and submission to the procedures. Admission forms can serve many other purposes unrelated to consent, such as assigning insurance benefits.[134]

Blanket consent forms are receiving new attention and use for the services of specialized units. Those units use many procedures for which individual consent is often obtained in other settings. In specialized units, however, it would be too burdensome on decision makers and providers to obtain, specific, individual consents due to the volume of consents that would be required.

Battery Consent Forms. Also referred to a general consent form, most hospitals now require this type of consent form, which includes (1) the name and a description of the specific treatment or procedure; (2) statement that the physician has explained to the patient or his or her legal representative the consequences, risks and benefits, and alternatives to such treatment or procedure (including foregoing treatment); (3) statement that all questions have been answered to the person's satisfaction; and (4) that no guarantees have been made. These forms will almost always preclude a successful battery claim if the proper person signs the form and if the described procedure is performed.[135] These forms also bolster the hospital's position that it did not believe that the person who signed was uninformed. The forms also provide some support for the physician's assertion that the patient was informed.[136]

However, courts can still be convinced that the information concerning consequences, risks, benefits, and alternatives was not actually given.[137] Because of this fact, some providers either use more detailed consent forms or supplement the battery consent form with a note in the medical record documenting disclosure of specific risks, benefits, and alternatives, including the use of patient treatment or procedure specific educational and/or handout materials.[138]

Detailed Consent Forms. Some physicians use forms that detail the medical condition, procedure, consequences, risks, benefits, and alternatives. Such forms have been mandated for federally funded sterilizations and research.[139] Plaintiffs can seldom prove that the information included in this form was not disclosed. One difficulty with detailed consent forms is the cost and time to prepare them for each individual procedure and to keep them updated. Some physicians use these forms only for procedures, such as cosmetic surgery, that carry a higher risk of misunderstanding and unacceptable results.

Detailed forms may not provide protection for risks not disclosed on the form.[140] However, detailed forms may make it more difficult for patients who accepted serious consequences to prove that disclosure of additional risks would have made them change their minds.[141]

CONSENT STATUTES. Some states have statutes concerning consent forms.[142] These statutes should be considered when developing consent forms for use in those states. Several states provide that if the consent form contains certain information and is signed by the appropriate person that it is conclusive evidence of informed consent or creates a presumption of informed consent. For example, in Nevada if certain information is on the form, it is conclusive evidence of informed consent.[143] In Iowa, if certain information is on the form, informed consent is presumed.[144] Serious consideration should be given to using forms that qualify, especially when such forms are conclusive evidence.

EXCULPATORY CLAUSES. Exculpatory clauses state that the person signing waives the right to sue for injuries or agrees to limit any claims to not more than a specified amount. Although courts have enforced these clauses in other contexts, courts have not enforced them in suits on behalf of patients against health care providers.

7-4.3 For Which Procedures Should a Signed Consent Be Obtained?

There are several sources of requirements for signed consent. Federal and state statutes require signed consent for some procedures, and these are usually found in institutional and professional licensing requirements or in conditions of participation in payment programs, such as Medicare. Often these sources only require consent and leave the method of documentation to be determined by the provider, but in some cases, signed consent is mandated.

Accreditation bodies are another important source of requirements. While these are not legally mandated, providers who desire accreditation need to meet the standards. TJC accreditation standards provide that informed consent be obtained and documented in accordance with hospital policy.[145] TJC does not specify the procedures or treatments and does not specify how the consent must be documented, except for requiring "written consent" for electroconvulsive therapy.[146]

However, prudent providers generally seek informed consent for all invasive treatments and procedures, including: operative and diagnostic procedures, anesthesiology services, radiotherapy, chemotherapy, dialysis, blood transfusions (including blood products), electroconvulsive therapy, experimental procedures, and procedures that a medical provider believes requires a specific explanation to the patient.

Many institutions exclude certain routine minor procedures from the invasive procedures requiring consent. Examples include venipuncture, peripheral intravenous line placement, insertion of a nasogastric tube, or urinary catheter placement. This position is consistent with TJC's exclusion of these procedures from the scope of its Universal Protocol for Preventing Wrong Side, Wrong Procedure, Wrong Person Surgery.[147]

EXCEPTIONS. The actual process of providing information to the decision maker and of determining that person's decision is more important than the consent form. The form is *evidence* of the consent process, but the informed consent is the actual discussion(s) had between the physician and the patient (or the patient's legal representative) about the treatment or procedure to be performed. Someone should have authority to determine that there is actual informed consent even when the form has been lost or inadvertently not signed prior to patient sedation or when other circumstances make it difficult to obtain the necessary signature.

7-4.4 What Can Be Done When a Patient with Capacity Is Physically Unable to Sign?

It is not necessary that patients be able to sign their normal signatures in order for a consent form, AD, or other document to be valid. When the patient can make a mark, the mark constitutes the signature of the patient. The person witnessing the mark should document the fact that it was made by the patient. When the patient is physically unable to make a mark, the document can be signed by another person at the direction of the patient. In most states, the other person signs the patient's name and then indicates that it is signed at the direction of the patient, signing their own name. Generally, it is advisable for a third party to document witnessing the direction and the signature.

7-4.5 How Can the Signed Consent Requirement Be Met When the Decision maker Is Not Present?

When the decision maker is not physically present and a written consent is required, there are solutions.

The information necessary for an informed consent can usually be provided by telephone. It is prudent to have another staff member listen to the conversation and document the role as witness. The information exchange can be by other means, including e-mail. However, care needs to be taken to assure the security of electronic exchanges.

The documentation of consent can be transmitted by facsimile. Alternatively, telephonic consent should generally be accepted as written consent. The person hearing the consent signs the consent form at the direction of the decision maker, which is the same as the process that is used when the decision maker is physically unable to sign due to physical incapacity. It is prudent to have another staff member listen to the consent and document the role as witness. The actual documentation of the consent can also be done by e-mail, provided that there are systems in place to establish a unique code that qualifies as an electronic signature.[148]

7-4.6 How Long Is a Consent Form Valid?

⚑ There is no limit on the period of validity of consent or the documentation of that consent. However, if the patient's condition or available treatments change significantly, earlier consents are no longer informed, and a new consent should be obtained.[149] Otherwise, the consent is valid until it is withdrawn. A claim that consent was withdrawn becomes more credible as time passes.[150] The guideline some hospitals follow is to recommend a new consent at each admission. Some hospitals use a guideline that consent forms should be signed no more

than thirty days before the procedure. Hospitals are not legally required to have such guidelines, but they generally should follow their own rules. It is helpful for hospital guidelines to state that they are not requirements or that someone has authority to grant exceptions to deal with repetitive treatments for chronic disease, situations in which the person who gave consent now lacks capacity or is unavailable, and other unusual circumstances.

7-4.7 What Are Other Ways to Document Consent?

Some physicians supplement their explanations with other educational materials, such as booklets and videotapes.[151] When these supplements are used, it is helpful to document the name of the educational material in the medical record. Some physicians make audio and visual recordings of the consent process to supplement or substitute for written consent. Some patients are given tests of knowledge or write their own consent forms to document their level of understanding. None of these steps are legally required and may not preclude malpractice suits,[152] but they can be helpful, especially for controversial procedures.

7-5 What Constitutes Coercion That Makes Consent Involuntary and Invalid?

A consent form can be challenged if the signature was not voluntary. The person signing would have to demonstrate that there had been some threat or undue inducement to prove the signature was not voluntary, so this challenge will apply in few hospital situations. However, there are limits to the extent which threats and inducements can be used to obtain consent.

Sometimes the personal circumstances of a patient will create pressure to make a particular decision. Impending loss of insurance coverage may cause patients to elect to undergo procedures they otherwise might delay. Providers are not accountable for these personal circumstances. They do not render the patient's decisions involuntary from a legal perspective.

In 2002, a Minnesota nursing home resident filed suit seeking to return home and claiming that her consent to admission had been coerced by the threat that a court order would compel admission. The suit was dismissed when the patient died, so the court did not rule on the question.[153] However, it is unlikely that the threat of a court order would constitute coercion.

7-6 What Limits Are Placed on the Permitted Range of Decisions?

There are many limits on the permitted range of decisions. This section will first review the differences in the limits on adults, incapacitated adults, and minors. It will then look at the case of withdrawal of consent during a course of treatment. The following questions will be examined:

- 7-6.1. What are the limits on the scope of decision making by adults with decision-making capacity?
- 7-6.2. What are the limits on the scope of decision making for adults without decision-making capacity?
- 7-6.3. What are the limits on the scope of decision making for minors?
- 7-6.4. What limitations are there on withdrawal of consent?

7-6.1. What Are the Limits on the Scope of Decision Making by Adults with Decision-Making Capacity?

In the past, there has been some concern about whether there are limits on the scope of life-sustaining treatment a patient may refuse. Books like this have devoted pages to proving that there is a right to refuse life-sustaining treatment. The right is now clearly established throughout the United States.[154] The remaining issues concerning withholding and withdrawing life-sustaining treatment now center on what others can decide when there are no directions from the patient or the patient's directions are disputed. Refusal by others is discussed in section 7-6.2.

There are some limits on the scope of decision making by adults even when they clearly have decision-making capacity. First, patients cannot select assisted suicide, except in three states. Second, patients cannot select willful injury, such as amputation of a healthy limb. Third, patients cannot select inappropriate or medically unnecessary treatment. Fourth, generally patients do not have to be offered treatment that is unlikely to provide substantial therapeutic benefit and cannot insist that such treatment be provided. Fifth, patients cannot select the use of drugs, devices, or services prohibited by law. Sixth, there is no right to participate in medical experiments. Seventh, as discussed in section 7-7, there are some circumstances where state interests override the patient's rights.

ASSISTED SUICIDE. Providers cannot assist patient with suicide outside the states of Oregon, Washington, and Montana.[155] No constitutional right to assisted suicide has been recognized. The U.S. Supreme Court decided in 1997 that there was no federal constitutional right to physician aid in dying, leaving the issue to individual states.[156] Several state courts have ruled that state constitutions do not afford such a right.[157]

The Oregon law was adopted by a direct vote of the people and has survived numerous court challenges. In 1994, the voters of Oregon approved the Oregon Death with Dignity Act. A federal judge enjoined the law before it could take effect. In 1997, the Oregon voters again approved the law. The U.S. Ninth Circuit Court of Appeals removed the injunction, and the first assisted suicides occurred in 1998. The Oregon law permits actions only with the consent of the patient. In 1999, an Oregon court upheld suspending a physician's license for approving use of an agent to paralyze the patient's muscles resulting in death, where the patient's directions had only permitted discontinuing life support. In 2001, the federal Department of Justice published a ruling that controlled substances could not be dispensed for assisted suicide. In 2002, a federal court granted a permanent injunction against enforcement of this ruling in Oregon.[158]

Since 1994, when Oregon approved assisted suicide by ballot measure, over eighty measures have been introduced in twenty-one states to legalized assisted suicide and/or euthanasia. Nearly all have failed. In 2008, Washington voters approved the Washington death with dignity act.[159] In 2009, in a narrow ruling, the Montana Supreme Court affirmed that "nothing in Montana Supreme Court precedent or Montana statutes indicat[es] that physician aid in dying is against public policy," but declined to rule on the larger question of whether physician-assisted suicide is a right guaranteed under Montana's Constitution.[160]

In 1999, the world's most famous practitioner of physician-assisted suicide, Dr. Jack Kevorkian, was convicted for assisting in the death of a terminally ill patient. Juries had acquitted him in several previous cases, but in 1999, he was convicted of second-degree murder and delivery of a controlled substance.[161]

WILLFUL INJURY/MAYHEM. Intentional maiming or disfiguring of a person without justification is the crime of mayhem, which now is sometimes called willful injury.

Consent or even the request of the victim is not a defense when there is no medical justification.

INAPPROPRIATE OR UNNECESSARY TREATMENT. Physicians have a professional obligation to refuse to provide clearly inappropriate treatment despite patient insistence. Some court decisions in the nineteenth century ruled that patient insistence after being informed of the inappropriateness insulated the physician from liability.[162] Modern cases have consistently ruled that patient consent does not relieve a physician from the obligation to follow the usual standard of care. When patients or their families seek therapies outside the accepted range, the first response is often tactful communications to give them information and support to accept the limitations. In 1997, the U.S. Supreme Court ruled that terminally ill persons have no special right to treatment that the government has declared illegal.[163]

A physician who provides a legal, but inappropriate, treatment can be liable for malpractice, notwithstanding patient consent. When reputable physicians disagree regarding the appropriateness of legal treatment, reasonable efforts should be made to transfer the treatment of the patient to a physician who concurs with the patient. If inappropriate treatment desired by the patient is neither illegal nor dangerous, sometimes it is prudent to acquiesce if the patient is willing to continue other accepted necessary therapy simultaneously.

Under the standards of Medicare and most third-party payers, physicians and hospitals are supposed to provide only medically necessary services. Billing the payer for unnecessary services can be a false claim subject to civil and criminal penalties. Inappropriate treatments can also raise billing issues. A federal appellate court ruled in 1994 that a physician had a duty to disclose the illegality of treatments in his bills to third-party payers, so billing without disclosure was fraud.[164]

These laws generally do not forbid providing additional services, but under Medicare and most managed care contracts, the patient cannot be billed for the additional services unless the patient has been given advance notice that the third-party payer will not pay. In most circumstances, a provider should also have the discretion to decide whether to offer or provide such additional services.

TREATMENT THAT IS UNLIKELY TO PROVIDE SUBSTANTIAL THERAPEUTIC BENEFIT. The more difficult question arises when a treatment could temporarily prolong life but is unlikely to improve the patient's condition. Sometimes this is called futile treatment, although there continues to be debate concerning the use of the term and the practice of not providing futile treatment.[165]

There are indications that physicians forgo futile treatment without involvement of the patient or the patient's representatives in some circumstances. Some institutions have developed policies. In 1999, the AMA Council on Ethics and Judicial Affairs recommended that institutional processes be developed to address these issues.

When courts are confronted with this question, there is still some disagreement. There are two types of cases—those seeking court authorization and those examining decisions that have already been carried out.

Court Cases Seeking Approval. In 1991, Minnesota providers sought court permission to remove the respirator that they believed to be futile for the brain-damaged patient. The family opposed the petition. The court rejected the petition. The patient died a few days later still on the respirator.[166] In 2004, Massachusetts providers sought court permission to remove the ventilator from a patient with Lou Gehrig's disease who had been in the hospital for four years. The daughter (who was the healthcare agent) opposed the petition. The court rejected the petition.[167]

More recently there have been several cases where parents refused to terminate futile treatment for abused children in circumstances where the parents could be charged with murder upon the child's death. Trial courts in some states have authorized the withdrawal of treatment in these circumstances.[168] In other cases, courts have permitted the parent who is not charged to withdraw treatment over the objection of the charged parent.[169] Many of these cases do not result in a court decision because either the provider waits so long before applying to the court that the patient dies before a decision or the family agrees to terminate treatment when they learn that a lawsuit has or will be filed.[170]

Court Cases after Action Taken. In 1995, a Massachusetts jury decided that providers were not liable for discontinuing the respirator for a terminally ill patient after consultation with the hospital Optimal Care Committee, but without patient or family consent, because the treatment was futile.[171] However, in 1998, the Iowa Supreme Court ruled that a physician could be liable for failure to attempt resuscitation, in the absence of either patient or family agreement, even though there was an estimate of only a 10 percent chance of survival.[172]

DRUGS OR DEVICES OR SERVICES PROHIBITED BY LAW. The government has broad power to regulate, license, and prohibit medical services. Some court decisions would appear to permit the prohibition of virtually all healthcare services. In 1889, the U.S. Supreme Court upheld the power of the state to prohibit all physician practice that was not licensed.[173] In 1966, the Supreme Court held that states did not have to create a license for naturopaths but could require them to qualify for a full medical license.[174] In 1997, a federal appellate court decided that there was no right to have midwives recognized or licensed.[175] Most of the uses of this power have been limited and broadly accepted, so there has been little political or judicial exploration of the limits, if any, to this power.

The federal government, through the FDA, has restricted the use of new drugs and devices until their safety and effectiveness are proved. Drugs and devices generally cannot be used legally outside approved testing projects until they are approved by the FDA, even when requested by terminally ill patients who believe they have no alternative.[176]

After drugs are approved for general distribution, many can be distributed only by prescription. A physician or other authorized health professional can write a prescription only for appropriate medical uses. Inappropriate prescriptions can subject the professional to licensing discipline and to criminal prosecution. Consent of the patient to the prescription is not a defense.

The government cannot punish physicians for discussing prohibited drugs. The federal government attempted to bar physicians from discussing the use of marijuana for medicinal purposes. In 2002, a federal appellate court ruled that physicians were protected by the constitutional freedom of speech when they recommended marijuana as medical treatment of their patients, so the federal government could not investigate, threaten, or punish physicians for these recommendations.[177] Since then, sixteen states and the District of Columbia have enacted laws to legalize medical marijuana.[178]

MEDICAL EXPERIMENTS. There is no right to participate in research protocols. Most protocols have inclusion and exclusion criteria as part of the study design and required precautions. Individuals who do not satisfy these criteria cannot be included.

THERE ARE FEW LIMITS ON THE POWER TO REFUSE TREATMENT. In the past, there was some question whether patients could refuse life-prolonging treatment. It is now clear that adults with decision-making capacity can decide to withhold or withdraw virtually any treatment even if it will result in their death. The only exceptions are the situations where involuntary treatment is authorized as discussed in section 7-7.

Constitutional bases of the right to refuse medical treatment have included: (i) First Amendment religious grounds (e.g., Jehovah's Witnesses blood transfusion cases); (ii) right of privacy based primarily on the due process clause of the Fourteenth Amendment and on state constitutions (several state appellate level decisions, including the first well-known "right to die" case of Karen Ann Quinlan in 1976, have upheld decisions to refuse medical treatment on privacy grounds, relying on either or both state and federal constitutions); and (iii) patient's liberty interest, based on the Fourteenth Amendment (Cruzan analysis, though provisional, based on a constitutional "liberty" interest).

> "Right to Die" Cases—Individual has the right to refuse life-sustaining treatment: Karen Quinlan (1975), Nancy Cruzan (1990), and Terri Schiavo (2001).

The right to withdraw treatment includes assistance in the withdrawal. Such assistance in withdrawal is not considered assisting suicide. Individual providers generally may refuse to participate in carrying out these decisions, but this does not permit them to thwart the decision. They must transfer the care to other providers. In most jurisdictions, private institutions can enforce policies that prohibit carrying out some decisions, but this does not permit them to thwart the decision. They must transfer the patient to another institution. In cases where transfer is impossible, some courts will bar the institution from enforcing the policy in the individual case.

The enforcement of such institutional polices can create hardship for patients who live in areas where there are no competing institutions that do not have the restrictive policies. It is an open question whether a state can permit some restrictive policies in the only hospital that the state permits to function in a service area. States might have to permit the creation of competing facilities or mandate that institutions not restrict patient decisions to withhold or withdraw treatment.

Nutrition and Hydration. Withholding and withdrawing artificial nutrition and hydration (tube feeding) continue to receive special attention. There have been several widely publicized controversies over individual cases. Nearly all appellate courts that have addressed the issue have agreed that artificial nutrition and hydration (tube feeding) are medical treatments that can be refused in the same situations in which other medical treatments can be refused.[179]

The Missouri Supreme Court is the only state Supreme Court that has suggested that artificial feeding may be a mandatory procedure that cannot be refused.[180] However, Missouri later permitted withdrawal of artificial nutrition and hydration for the same patient, Nancy Cruzan. In 2003, the legislature and governor in Florida intervened to postpone withdrawal of artificial feeding of Terri Schiavo. In 2005, the U.S. Congress also passed a law intervening in the case. However, after extensive legal proceedings, nutrition and hydration were discontinued, and Ms. Schiavo died. For a detailed discussion of this case, see section 7-1.2.

The American Medical Association has recognized that refusal of artificial nutrition and hydration is appropriate in some cases.[181]

Courts have enforced refusals of this treatment by competent patients[182] and by patient representatives on behalf of patients who are terminally ill[183] or irreversibly unconscious.[184] Courts have had difficulty in defining when substituted decisions to refuse any treatment, including artificial nutrition, should be permitted on behalf of other patients. In 1984, in the only prosecution of physicians for withholding artificial nutrition and hydration from a terminally ill patient, a California appellate court ordered the dismissal of homicide indictments against two physicians.[185] The court ruled that artificial means of feeding are treatment, not natural functions, so there is no duty to continue the treatment when it becomes ineffective. The physicians could not be criminally liable for their professional decision made in concert with the patient's family when the individual was incompetent and terminally ill, with virtually no hope of significant improvement.

7-6.2 What Are the Limits on the Scope of Decision Making for Adults Without Decision-Making Capacity?

Any person acting on behalf of an incapacitated adult or a minor does not have the same latitude for consent as in self-treatment decisions. Decision makers generally cannot authorize two procedures—organ donation and sterilization—for incompetent adults or minors without prior court approval. The issue of sterilization of minors and incompetent adults is discussed in the chapter on reproductive issues. Decision makers do not have the same broad scope to refuse all treatments in the absence of an AD from the patient. The limits on consents by adults for their own treatment discussed earlier in this text also apply to surrogate decisions.

ORGAN DONATION. Courts in a few states will not approve kidney donations by minors and incompetents,[186] but courts in other states have authorized them.[187] Bone marrow donations have been approved.[188] The courts that have approved kidney donations have usually based their approval on the close relationship between the donor and the proposed recipient and on the emotional injury to the donor if the recipient was to die.

SCOPE OF PERMITTED REFUSALS. Nearly all state appellate courts that have addressed treatment refusal have decided that surrogate decision makers may refuse treatment for some incapacitated patients without an AD.[189] At least one state, Missouri, has rejected this position and allows refusals only when there is an AD.[190] New York initially adopted this more restrictive view but has modified its position to permit some surrogate refusals.[191]

The discretion to refuse is generally limited to situations in which the treatment is elective or not likely to be beneficial. Life prolongation is not always viewed as beneficial. States that allow surrogate refusals generally agree that they are permitted when the patient is irreversibly unconscious[192] or terminally ill.[193] Some states are more restrictive. There is no widely accepted definition of terminal illness; it remains a diagnosis based on medical judgment. One element is that no available course of therapy offers a reasonable expectation of remission or cure of the condition. Another element is that death is imminent, but there is no consensus on the time period, largely because it is not possible to predict time of death precisely.[194] Some courts have accepted patients as being terminally ill with predicted lives of one to five years.[195] Thus, the range of medical opinion concerning terminal illness appears to be legally acceptable. It is prudent to avoid establishing a specific time period. Some widely publicized institutional systems for classifying patients have not included a definition of terminal illness, but instead have focused on the appropriate therapeutic effort.[196]

A few courts have addressed refusals on behalf of patients who are incapacitated, conscious, and not terminally ill, but there is no consensus.[197] In 2001, the California Supreme Court decided that nutrition and hydration could be withheld from a patient only when the patient is terminally ill, comatose, or in a persistent vegetative state or has left formal instructions or appointed a healthcare agent.[198] Hospitals should generally take these cases to court unless the issue has been adequately addressed in their state.

7-6.3 What Are the Limits on the Scope of Decision Making for Minors?

All limits on consents by adults for their own treatment and for the treatment of incapacitated adults discussed earlier in this text also apply when parents and guardians make decisions concerning the treatment of minors.

In addition, courts tend to require that decisions on behalf of minors be in their best interests. Because minors have never had decision-making capacity, substituted judgment seldom applies even though courts do often give weight to minors' preferences. In addition to the state interests which the state asserts concerning adults, the state asserts an interest in minors and some incapacitated adults under its *parens patriae* power, the general power as "parent" to protect the welfare of incompetent persons. Parents do still have considerable latitude in decision making concerning their minor children's care.[199]

REFUSALS FOR MINORS. Courts tend to find that because adults with decision-making capacity have the right to refuse treatment that those making decisions on behalf of minors have a right to refuse on their behalf in some situations.[200] However, because the decision makers have an obligation to act in the best interest of the minor, they must provide necessary treatment. Their discretion to decline treatment is generally limited to situations in which the treatment is elective or not likely to be beneficial. The duty to provide necessary treatment to minors is reinforced in all states by legislation concerning abused or neglected minors. This legislation facilitates state intervention to provide needed assistance.

Courts have generally permitted the refusal of treatment for irreversibly comatose minors and some terminally ill minors.[201] For example, in 1982, the highest court of Massachusetts approved a decision not to attempt resuscitative efforts if a terminally ill child less than one year of age experienced cardiac or respiratory arrest.[202] In 1992, a Michigan appellate court authorized parents to terminate the life support of an eleven-year-old in a persistent vegetative state.[203] These decisions are being made on a regular basis without court involvement. Courts have declined to override parental refusals in several situations in which the benefit did not clearly outweigh the risk. Surgery that is not life-saving is frequently not compelled because there is a risk of death from the surgery itself. While parents can decide to take this risk, courts are reluctant to compel it. Risk of death is not the only risk that is considered. Pain and other side effects of the proposed treatment are important, as is the probability of success. In 1991, the Delaware Supreme Court ruled that a three-year-old child with Burkitt's syndrome was not neglected when his Christian Science parents refused to consent to radical chemotherapy that had only a 40 percent chance of success. The court reversed the trial court order that had awarded custody to the state. The Supreme Court applied the "best interests" test and concluded:

"The egregious facts of this case indicate that Colin's proposed medical treatment was highly invasive, painful, involved terrible temporary and potentially permanent side effects, posed an unacceptably low chance of success, and a high risk that the treatment itself would cause death. The State's authority to intervene in this case, therefore, cannot outweigh the Newmark's parental prerogative and Colin's inherent right to enjoy at least a modicum of human dignity in the short time that is left for him."[204]

Some courts do give substantial weight to the integrity of the parent-child relationship. Courts will generally decline to intervene when parents or guardians are following the advice of a licensed physician in good standing even if the advice is unorthodox. In 1998, the Maine Supreme Court affirmed denial of a state application to compel aggressive drug therapy for an HIV-positive four-year-old.[205] The mother had gone through similar treatment with another child who had eventually died, and she had found a licensed physician who supported her approach.

Courts do not have unbridled authority to compel treatment of minors. Courts must follow the proper procedures for their orders to be valid. In 1994, a federal appellate court upheld a $1.95 million award against a physician for the death of a minor after the insertion of a Hickman catheter over the objection of the father.[206] A court order had been obtained but was found to be invalid.[207]

There are practical limits on the ability of the state to intervene. There have been several highly publicized cases in which the state has initiated efforts to compel treatment and has eventually chosen to drop its efforts or compromise with the family. In 2003, Utah obtained a court order placing a twelve-year-old in state custody for chemotherapy when his parents denied that he had cancer and refused the treatment. His parents took him out of state. In the face of strong public reaction and an assessment that it was not feasible to force a twelve-year-old and his parents to submit to eleven months of chemotherapy, authorities dropped the custody and chemotherapy orders. Kidnapping charges were dropped in exchange for a guilty plea to custodial interference. The state later dropped the remaining charges.[208]

Parents who fail to obtain necessary medical care have been convicted of child abuse and even homicide,[209] but criminal liability has generally not been imposed when there are questions concerning (1) the parent's knowledge of the seriousness of the child's condition or (2) the necessity for or net benefit from the proposed services.[210]

INFANTS. The treatment of infants with severe deformities that are inconsistent with prolonged or sapient life has been controversial.[211] It has been accepted practice in many hospitals, upon the concurrence of the parents and the treatment team, to provide only ordinary care to these infants so that their suffering is not prolonged through extraordinary efforts. If parents wish heroic measures, they generally are attempted. If parents refuse treatment when the attending physician believes treatment provides a reasonable likelihood of benefit, child neglect laws are invoked to obtain court authorization for treatment.

Healthcare professionals disagree on whether some conditions are sufficiently severe that treatment offers no reasonable likelihood of benefit. There has been general acceptance of withholding treatment when the condition is anencephaly (the absence of the higher brain) or other conditions that preclude development of sapient life or are inconsistent with prolonged life.[212] In the past, surgical treatment for spina bifida was frequently withheld. With improvements in treatments and outcomes, surgery can now be withheld only in the most severe cases. A New York hospital obtained a court order authorizing surgical repair of a newborn with several of the complications associated with spina bifida.[213]

The HHS began an effort in 1982 to force aggressive treatment of virtually all severely deformed newborns. HHS sent a letter to many hospitals threatening to withhold federal funding from any hospital that permitted medically indicated treatment to be withheld from a handicapped newborn.[214] This letter was a reaction to a widely publicized case in Indiana in which an infant with Down syndrome (which usually results in mental retardation) was permitted to starve to death when relatively minor surgery would have permitted the newborn to live. A court order was sought to authorize the surgery, but the Indiana courts refused to intervene.[215]

In 1983, HHS published rules (1) creating a hotline in Washington, DC, for the reporting of suspected violations and (2) requiring notices to be posted in hospitals announcing the hotline.[216] A federal court enjoined the rules[217] that were widely criticized.[218] HHS published revised rules in 1984 that continued the hotline, required notices to be posted, and recommended the creation of institutional ethics committees.[219] The revised rules were also declared to be beyond the authority of HHS.[220]

In 1983, New York's highest court upheld parental refusal of corrective surgery for a newborn with spina bifida and hydrocephalus.[221] The federal government sought access to the child's medical records, and the parents and the hospital refused to grant access. A federal appellate court refused to order access and ruled that the federal government did not have authority under existing handicapped rights laws to investigate the case.[222] Congress then passed legislation that required states to implement programs within their child abuse prevention and treatment systems to address the withholding of medically indicated treatment from infants with life-threatening conditions.[223] The HHS implementing regulations recommended institutional infant care review committees.[224]

These decisions will continue to be controversial, but the real exposure to potential legal sanctions is minimal if refusals are carefully limited to appropriate cases.[225] When these cases are taken to court, courts approve refusal in appropriate cases. It is important to obtain consultations regarding diagnosis, prognosis, and treatment decisions. Documenting the reasons for the decisions and the decision-making process is essential to ensure that decision makers give principled consideration to all relevant information.

7-6.4 What Limitations Are There on Withdrawal of Consent?

In most circumstances, a patient has the right to withdraw consent to treatment, unless the law authorizes involuntary treatment as discussed in section 7-7. Consent, including signed consent forms, can be challenged by claiming that the consent was withdrawn after it was signed but before the procedure was performed.[226]

Withdrawal of consent in the middle of procedures can be problematic. In 2000, the Kentucky Supreme Court ruled that a patient could revoke her consent to use of an automatic blood pressure cuff during surgery and a jury should decide whether she had done so.[227]

Some courts have indicated that women can withdraw their consent to certain management techniques during labor. In 2002, an Iowa court found that during delivery a woman could withdraw consent to the use of forceps, but in the case, the jury properly found that she had not done so.[228]

At some stages of some procedures, it is not possible to stop without serious injury to the patient. In the past, most of these procedures were performed under general anesthetic, so there was no opportunity to withdraw consent. With the increased use of local anesthetics and conscious sedation, the opportunities have increased. Although there are few cases on the issue, it is likely that when a patient withdraws consent the patient must give the physician an opportunity to sew up the surgical site, withdraw endoscopic instruments, and take other steps to wind up the procedure safely. This should be implicit in the consent to the procedure. This was recognized in a 2004 federal appellate court decision that upheld dismissing a case against an abortion doctor. Complications arose during the procedure. The patient withdrew her consent and demanded transfer to a hospital. The physician restrained her while he took steps to stabilize her and then transferred her to the hospital.[229]

7-7 When Can the Law Authorize Involuntary Treatment?

In some cases, state interests outweigh the right to refuse, so involuntary treatment is authorized.[230] Courts have traditionally used an analysis that focuses on four state interests: (1) preservation of life, (2) prevention of irrational self-destruction, (3) protection of dependent third parties, and (4) protection of the ethical integrity of health professionals. However, in practice, few of these interests ever apply to outweigh the right to refuse. The analysis of the involuntary treatment cases in this section is based on the grounds courts have actually used to justify involuntary treatment. The questions addressed are:

- 7-7.1. When do threats to the community justify involuntary treatment?
- 7-7.2. When does impaired capacity justify involuntary treatment?
- 7-7.3. When do the lives of others justify involuntary treatment?
- 7-7.4. When does criminal law enforcement justify involuntary treatment?

- 7-7.5. When does civil law discovery justify involuntary treatment?
- 7-7.6. When do the needs of the management of governmental institutions justify involuntary treatment?
- 7-7.7. When do the other traditional state interests justify involuntary treatment?

7-7.1 When Do Threats to the Community Justify Involuntary Treatment?

CONTAGIOUS DISEASE. Courts have long recognized the power of the state to require individuals to submit to medical treatment when refusal threatens the community. In 1905, the U.S. Supreme Court upheld the power of the state to require an adult to submit to vaccination to help prevent the spread of disease.[231] In 1973, a federal appellate court upheld a Denver ordinance that required prostitutes to accept treatment for venereal disease.[232] In 1988, a federal district court ruled that a prisoner could not sue for the forcible administration of a diphtheria-tetanus inoculation.[233] In addition to the current laws, many states have utilized the Model State Emergency Health Powers Act to tailor their statutes and regulations to respond to unique or novel situations that may arise in their jurisdiction.[234]

The severe acute respiratory syndrome (SARS) outbreak in 2003 required extensive quarantines in Canada, Hong Kong, and China.[235] Smaller scale quarantines occurred in the United States, focusing new attention in the United States on the containment and treatment of contagious disease. In 2009, extensive quarantines were again required, and the HHS issued a nationwide public health emergency declaration in response to the swine flu (H1N1) pandemic.[236]

DANGEROUSNESS TO OTHERS. Courts have also recognized the power of the state to hospitalize persons who have demonstrated dangerousness to the community due to mental illness or substance abuse.[237]

7-7.2 When Does Impaired Capacity Justify Involuntary Treatment?

When adults have sufficient impairment of their decision-making capacity due to mental illness or substance abuse, the state authorizes involuntary hospitalization and treatment but requires that specific procedures be followed and that the person's condition be proven to a court by clear and convincing evidence. Under the common law, providers may involuntarily treat some temporarily disoriented patients without judicial approval.

INVOLUNTARY HOSPITALIZATION/COMMITMENT. Most states have statutory procedures for involuntarily committing persons to institutions for treatment for mental illness or substance abuse.[238] In 1975, the U.S. Supreme Court ruled that the Constitution permitted involuntary confinement of mentally ill persons, but that they must be treated when their confinement is not based on dangerousness.[239] In 1997, the U.S. Supreme Court clarified that mental illness was not required in all cases.[240] It upheld a statute that permitted commitment of dangerous persons with mental abnormalities. Commitment procedures vary from state to state. For adults, a judicial hearing is generally required, after which the judicial officer decides whether the evidence is sufficient to justify commitment. Many states do not permit involuntary commitment unless the person is found to be dangerous to self or others.

Courts have generally upheld reasonable police procedures, including force, to take such persons into custody.[241] Most states permit adults to be held temporarily on an emergency basis until the judicial officer can act. In 1979, the U.S. Supreme Court ruled that states could permit parents to admit their minor children involuntarily for mental treatment without court authorization if the admission is approved as necessary by a qualified physician after adequate inquiry.[242] However, many states require judicial involvement in the commitment of minors.

Commitment is not the same as a court determination of incompetency. An involuntarily committed person is still competent to be involved in some or all medical decisions unless a court has determined otherwise. Commitment laws usually authorize involuntary treatment that is necessary to preserve the patient's life or to avoid permanent injury to the patient or others. However, there is variation in the extent to which commitment laws authorize the use of antipsychotic drugs or electroconvulsive therapy for purposes of nonemergency treatment of mental illness. Thus, familiarity with local law is important. Most courts have ruled that the constitutional rights to privacy and due process are violated if medication or electroconvulsive therapy is given involuntarily without a judicial finding of incompetency.[243] Some states have resolved this issue by requiring that the judicial officer find the person unable to make treatment decisions as part of the commitment process.[244] In states that authorize involuntary treatment of committed patients without a judicial determination of

inability to make treatment decisions, hospitals should give consideration to this evolving standard in developing their treatment policies.

Some courts have required a judicial determination of the need for antipsychotic medications when a patient who has been adjudicated incompetent refuses the medications in a nonemergency situation.[245]

DISORIENTATION. Disoriented patients are frequently restrained temporarily. Physicians and hospitals have authority under common law to detain and restrain temporarily disoriented medical and surgical patients without court involvement. This authority derives from the hospital's duty to use such reasonable care as the patient's known mental and physical condition requires.[246] Hospitals have been found liable for injuries to patients because they were not restrained during temporary disorientation. This common law authority should not be relied on when a patient is being detained for mental illness or substance abuse. The statutory commitment procedures should be followed for those patients.

7-7.3 When Do the Lives of Others Justify Involuntary Treatment?

Courts ordered treatment for pregnant women to protect the lives of their unborn children but have disagreed on when such orders are permitted. Courts have refused to order persons to donate tissue to save the lives of others. Courts have disagreed on whether the need of dependents for support justifies ordering parents to submit to treatment.

PREGNANCY. Some courts will authorize treatments for pregnant women to preserve the life of the unborn child, especially immediately before and during birth.[247] Other courts have limited their authorizations to transfusions necessary to save the life of the unborn child. In 1981, the Georgia Supreme Court authorized a caesarean operation because it was informed of a near certainty the child would not survive a vaginal delivery.[248] In 1999, a federal court in Florida rejected a challenge to a state court-ordered caesarean operation.[249]

Other courts have refused to authorize treatment for pregnant women even when necessary to preserve the life of the unborn child. In 1993, the Illinois courts ruled that a mentally competent pregnant woman could refuse a caesarian operation even when this might harm her child.[250]

In 1997, the Wisconsin Supreme Court ruled that the child abuse law did not apply prior to birth, so a drug-using woman could not be taken into custody to protect her unborn child.[251] The legislature then enacted a law expressly authorizing custody of a pregnant woman to protect her unborn child.[252]

Some mothers do decide to take significant medical risks for the benefit of their unborn children in situations where courts clearly could not order such behavior. For example, in 1994–1995, a mother delayed chemotherapy for leukemia so that it would not harm her twins. After they were born, it was too late for her to be treated for her leukemia, and she died.[253]

MANDATORY DONATION. Courts have refused to order involuntary donation of tissue to save the life of another.[254] In 1990, the noncustodial father of three-year-old twins sought an order compelling them to submit to a blood test and bone marrow donation for the benefit of his other son, who was their half-brother and had leukemia. The custodial mother of the twins opposed the procedures. The trial court denied the order.[255] The Illinois Supreme Court ordered the trial court to appoint two guardians *ad litem*, one for the twins and one for the other child, and to permit them to present additional evidence.[256] After a hearing, the trial court again denied the order, and the Illinois Supreme Court affirmed.[257]

DEPENDENTS. Some states assert an interest in protecting dependents, especially minor children, from the emotional and financial damage of the patient's death. This interest has been discussed in cases in which Jehovah's Witnesses refuse transfusions. In 1989, the Florida Supreme Court ruled that a lower court had erred in ordering transfusions for a competent adult with minor children when there were other arrangements to care for the child, such as a surviving parent.[258]

In 1992, the Florida Supreme Court reversed a transfusion order directed at a mother where no arrangements had been made for her four other children. The court noted that the children had two living parents and, even though they were separated, the law presumed that as natural guardian the father would assume the responsibilities for the children.[259]

These cases involved patients who could probably be restored to normal functioning by appropriate therapy. It is doubtful whether dependents will be a determinative issue in cases involving the terminally ill or irreversibly comatose because emotional and financial damage will seldom be increased by discontinuing treatment.

7-7.4 When Does Criminal Law Enforcement Justify Involuntary Treatment?

Sometimes the state's interest in gathering evidence for criminal law enforcement justifies involuntary medical procedures. Law enforcement officers frequently call on medical personnel to perform such procedures, including examining suspects, taking blood samples, pumping stomachs, removing bullets, and performing other interventions. Courts have addressed these procedures primarily in two contexts: admissibility of the resulting evidence[260] and liability for performing the procedures.

STOMACH PUMPING. In 1951, the U.S. Supreme Court ruled that police-ordered pumping of a suspect's stomach "shocks the conscience," so the stomach contents were not admissible.[261]

DRAWING BLOOD. In 1957, the U.S. Supreme Court ruled that blood drawn from an unconscious person after a traffic accident was admissible if the blood was drawn after a proper arrest with probable cause to believe the person was intoxicated while driving.[262] In 1966, the U.S. Supreme Court ruled that blood drawn from an objecting defendant without a search warrant is admissible if five conditions are satisfied: (1) the defendant is arrested; (2) the blood is likely to produce evidence for the criminal prosecution; (3) delay would lead to destruction of evidence; (4) the test is reasonable and not medically contraindicated; and (5) the test is performed in a reasonable manner.[263]

If these conditions are present and properly documented, hospital personnel can safely cooperate in drawing blood for law enforcement officers to the extent authorized by state law. Any additional state requirements concerning by whom, how, and when blood may be withdrawn should be observed. In most states, hospitals and health professionals have no legal duty to perform tests requested by law enforcement officers. When providers who perform the tests frequently must testify at criminal trials, some health professionals refuse to perform tests to avoid the disruption of their clinical schedules. When subjects physically resist tests, most professionals refuse to perform the tests to avoid injury to the subject and themselves.

URINE TESTS. In 2001, the U.S. Supreme Court decided that it was a violation of the Fourth Amendment prohibition of unreasonable searches and seizures in a hospital setting. Specifically, a hospital had an arrangement with the local police to routinely perform nonconsensual testing of the urine of pregnant women for cocaine when they were suspected of illegal drug use. The hospital referred these cases to the police when cocaine use was discovered. The Court found that this procedure was unconstitutional.[264]

BULLET REMOVAL. Several cases have involved requests for authorization to remove bullets from suspects. In 1985, the U.S. Supreme Court ruled that the reasonableness and, thus, the constitutionality of court-ordered surgery to remove bullets for evidence is to be decided on a case-by-case basis. Those decisions require balancing the individual's interest in privacy and security against the societal interest in gathering evidence.[265] The Court indicated that the privacy interest was very strong when general anesthesia would be required or other dangers to life and health were present. The Court also indicated that state interests could prevail in few situations. However, when other evidence demonstrates the surgery is likely to produce helpful evidence, that evidence is likely to be sufficient without consideration of the bullet.

WITNESSES. In one case, the state sought involuntary treatment to preserve the life of a witness. In 1985, the Mississippi Supreme Court ruled that the state's interest in prosecuting crimes, even murder, was not sufficient to outweigh the right of an adult Jehovah's Witness to refuse life-saving transfusions even though she was the only eyewitness to a murder.[266]

SMUGGLING DRUGS IN THE BODY. Courts have addressed the steps that can be taken to assure that drugs being smuggled internally are detected and recovered. While suspected carriers intercepted by immigration officials at the borders and other points of entry can be detained, even in a hospital, to be observed until drugs can be expelled, there is disagreement among the courts concerning (1) how soon a court must be involved to authorize continued detention and (2) whether a court order is required before a person can be x-rayed.[267]

7-7.5 When Does Civil Law Discovery Justify Involuntary Treatment?

There are many situations where parties to civil litigation seek medical examination and testing of persons as part of the discovery process. Usually, examination and testing cannot be forced,[268] but a party who refuses to comply with a proper order may have to waive claims or other benefits and may even lose the lawsuit. Thus, most cases focus on what tests can reasonably be demanded as a condition of preserving rights in the suit.

In civil cases where the purpose of the case is to gain medical information, courts will order mandatory tests in some cases. The Wisconsin Supreme Court ruled in 1993 that a trial court could order involuntary HIV testing of a person who bit a social worker and shouted she had AIDS after the biting. The court determined that the victim's need for the information for medical planning could not be satisfied in any other way.[269]

7-7.6 When Do the Needs of the Management of Governmental Institutions Justify Involuntary Treatment?

In unusual individual cases, the state's interest in management of its institutions can justify involuntary treatment. In 1979, the highest court of Massachusetts authorized dialysis for a prisoner because he attempted to manipulate his placement by refusing dialysis until he was moved.[270] Although prisoners ordinarily have the same rights as others to decline treatment, the state's interest in orderly prison administration was found to outweigh those rights.[271] In 1995, a federal appellate court upheld involuntary catheterization of a prisoner to obtain a urine sample for a blood test.[272]

Similarly, in some situations courts have ordered forced feeding of prisoners engaged in hunger strikes but have denied orders in other cases.[273]

Note that generally military requirements have not been considered sufficient to authorize involuntary treatment, but in some circumstances, military personnel can be punished for refusal to submit.[274]

However, it has long been the position of the U.S. military that surgery generally cannot be forced. On December 15, 1917, the U.S. Judge Advocate General of the Army published an official ruling that enlisted men have the right to refuse to undergo a surgical operation unless the attending surgeon certifies that there is no danger to the life of the patient. This was a follow-up to the release of Private Brady E. Cross. Private Cross had been convicted by a court martial and sentenced to two months in prison for refusing to obey orders to undergo surgery necessary to remove a disability that prevented him from performing his duties. The proceedings were declared null and void because there was no certificate of the absence of danger of fatal consequences.[275]

7-7.7 When Do the Other Traditional State Interests Justify Involuntary Treatment?

Several other state and family interests have been asserted, but they generally have not been found to outweigh the right of an adult with decision-making capacity to refuse treatment.

PRESERVATION OF LIFE. The state asserts an interest in the preservation of life. Nearly all courts have ruled that this interest does not outweigh the right of terminally ill patients to refuse treatment. For example, the Quinlan decision[276] ruled that the state's interest in preserving life decreases as the prognosis dims and the degree of bodily invasion of the proposed procedure increases. In the Saikewicz decision,[277] which authorized withholding chemotherapy from a patient with leukemia, the court concluded: "The value of life as so perceived is lessened not by a decision to refuse treatment, but by the failure to allow a competent human being the right of choice." Even when the patient is not terminally ill, courts have generally declined to order life-saving transfusions,[278] amputations of gangrenous limbs,[279] and other procedures.[280] Thus, it is not clear when the state's interest in preservation of life alone could justify involuntary treatment of an adult with decision-making capacity. At least one court has adopted a minority position that this state interest can justify involuntary treatment,[281] but no reported appellate decisions appear to have upheld court-ordered involuntary treatment of an adult with decision-making capacity based on the interest in preservation of life without other state interests being present.

PREVENTION OF IRRATIONAL SELF-DESTRUCTION. The prevention of irrational self-destruction (suicide) is another interest asserted by the state. In 1975, a Pennsylvania trial court authorized transfusions for a bleeding ulcer to prevent self-destruction of a 25-year-old Jehovah's Witness.[282] Other courts have refused to consider refusal of transfusions by adult Jehovah's Witnesses to be irrational self-destruction. Courts have generally recognized that there can be a competent, rational decision to refuse treatment.

Courts generally do not view refusals as suicidal if the patient is not seeking death but is seeking to live without the particular medical treatment. One California appellate court found that the state interest was not sufficient to overcome the refusal of tube feeding by a competent quadriplegic patient who stated that she wanted to die.[283]

Some courts have declined to intervene when terminal patients have taken active steps to hasten death. In 1984, a Florida court addressed the situation of a 55-year-old patient, terminally ill with cancer and in intense pain. After attempting suicide by stabbing herself, she refused surgery for her stab wounds. Even though the wounds were due to a suicide attempt, the court refused to order the surgery.[284]

PROTECTION OF THE ETHICAL INTEGRITY OF HEALTHCARE PROVIDERS. Several courts have discussed whether they should recognize a state interest in maintaining the ethical integrity of the medical profession and allowing hospitals the opportunity to care for patients who have been admitted. The courts have concluded that it is not a countervailing interest. Some courts have found that the right of privacy is superior to these professional and institutional considerations. Other courts have concluded that honoring directives of patients or their representatives is consistent with medical ethics, so there is no conflict. The state interest in preserving the ethical integrity of the medical profession should not be interpreted to permit individual professionals to impose their own standards on patients.[285]

This state interest still affects one aspect of court decisions. Some courts have used this interest as a rationale for not forcing the objecting provider to carry out the directive of the patient or representative, so that the patient must be transferred to another institution or professional.[286] Other courts have refused to require transfers, ordering objecting providers to withhold or withdraw refused treatment,[287] especially when no other institution will accept the transfer[288] or the institution gave no notice of its policies prior to admission.[289]

7-8 What Are the Consequences of Stopping Treatment or Providing Unauthorized Treatment?

There are potential licensing, liability, and criminal consequences for (a) providing treatment without appropriate authorization, (b) withholding or withdrawing life-sustaining treatment in circumstances where this is not permitted, or (c) taking steps other than withholding or withdrawing treatment that cause death.

This section addresses the following questions:

- 7-8.1. What is the civil liability for providing services without consent or other authorization?

- 7-8.2. What is the civil liability for providing services with consent that is not informed consent?

- 7-8.3. What is the civil liability for withholding or withdrawing services?

- 7-8.4. What are the licensing consequences for decisions concerning the treatment of individuals?

- 7-8.5. What are the criminal law consequences of decisions concerning the treatment of individuals?

7-8.1 What Is the Civil Liability for Providing Services Without Consent or Other Authorization?

BATTERY. The common law has long recognized the right of persons to be free from harmful or offensive touching. The intentional harmful or offensive touching of another person without authorization is called battery. When there is no consent or other authorization for a procedure, the physician or other practitioner doing the medical procedure can be liable for battery even if the procedure is properly performed, is beneficial, and has no negative effects. The touching alone leads to liability.

Medical procedures without express or implied consent constitute a battery unless one of the exceptions to the consent requirement applies. Those exceptions to the consent requirement, in which the law authorizes treatment without consent or despite refusal, were discussed earlier in this text. When express consent is given for one procedure and a different procedure is performed, the procedure performed can be a case of battery.[290] When conditions or restrictions are placed on consent, violations can lead to liability. In 1997, the Louisiana Supreme Court decided that a surgeon was liable for failing to use mesh to close a hernia repair when patient had expressly requested mesh and had specified it on the consent form.[291] One court has found that violations of express restrictions can be a breach of contract.[292]

UNWANTED LIFE-SAVING PROCEDURES. Courts have struggled with what to do when unwanted life-saving procedures are provided.

No Liability. In most cases, courts have clearly been troubled with punishing providers for prolonging life and have not imposed liability.[293]

In Ohio, a patient sued a hospital for resuscitation after a no-code order had been written. The court ruled that providers could be sued for battery and negligence, but prolonged life was not a compensable injury as "wrongful living."[294] The Ohio Supreme Court later agreed, but ruled that damages could be awarded only for complications that were caused by the unwanted therapy other than by simply prolonging life. Since the patient had suffered no such damages, the court ruled that the patient could recover no more than nominal damages.[295]

Other illustrative cases include: (i) North Carolina Supreme Court found that there should be no liability for alleged delay in removing a feeding tube until a court order was obtained, notwithstanding an AD.[296] (ii) A Texas appellate court ruled that there should be no liability for the unwanted life-saving treatment in the case due either to statutory immunity or to failure to meet the conditions of the directive.[297] (iii) A Texas jury awarded $42.9 million for resuscitating a severely brain-damaged premature baby against the parents' wishes.[298] The Texas Supreme Court reversed the jury award finding that the parents did not have right to refuse treatment for the infant.[299] (iv) A California appellate court decided that providers had statutory immunity from liability for failure to follow family directions to end life support.[300]

Liability. Some courts have vindicated the right to refuse treatment and have found providers liable, but have often limited the scope of the liability. In one of the first such cases, in 1935, a Canadian appellate court affirmed the liability of a physician for battery for providing life-saving emergency treatment to a competent adult who had refused the treatment.[301]

Other cases include: (i) A federal appellate court affirmed provider tort liability for providing refused care. The physicians involved in implanting a Hickman catheter in a minor pursuant to an ex parte court order could be sued for the death of the minor two weeks later from a massive pulmonary embolus.[302] The implantation was a battery because the court order was not valid because it was not properly obtained. At trial, the father, who had opposed the implantation, was awarded nearly two million dollars, which the appellate court affirmed.[303] (ii) An Illinois appellate court addressed a case in which the hospital and physicians had refused to follow the patient's daughter's direction to discontinue life support pursuant to the patient's AD.[304] The court ruled that a medical battery claim was allowed. In addition, a claim of intentional infliction of emotional distress was stated based on the repeated accusations that the wife and daughter were trying to kill the patient. (iii) A Massachusetts Supreme Court decided that providers could be liable for forcible emergency room care over the patient's objections.[305] The court ruled that the emergency exception to the requirement of consent did not apply when a competent patient refuses. A new trial was ordered because the jury in the first trial had not been properly instructed.

Billing. Even when no liability is imposed, there is a question whether providers can bill for refused treatment. Courts have disagreed. In 1993, the highest court of New York permitted a nursing home to charge for refused services, due to the uncertain state of the law during the period the services were provided.[306] In 2003, a Connecticut court ruled that a hospital could not collect the extra cost of a stay in the intensive care unit from a patient who had refused ICU care.[307]

7-8.2 What Is the Civil Liability for Providing Services with Consent That Is Not Informed Consent?

When consent is given but the person consenting does not have sufficient information for an informed decision, the provider can be liable for violating the duty to disclose such information. In some early cases, courts ruled that providing incorrect or insufficient information invalidated the consent, making the physician liable for battery. Today, in most jurisdictions, failure to disclose necessary information does not invalidate consent, so the procedure is not a battery.[308] There is still a minority position that a medical procedure without informed consent is a battery.[309] The majority rule is that failure to disclose is a separate wrong for which there can be liability based on principles applicable to negligent torts discussed later in the text. Uninformed consent protects from liability for battery, but informed consent is necessary to protect from liability for negligence.

CAUSATION. After it is shown that required information has not been disclosed, causation is the most difficult element to prove in an informed consent case. Since informed consent suits are based on negligence principles, the plaintiff must prove that the deviation from the standard caused the injury. Thus, the plaintiff must prove that consent would not have been given if the risk that occurred had been disclosed.

The two standards of causation are the objective standard and the subjective standard. Some states apply an "objective" standard of what a prudent person in the patient's position would have decided if informed of the risk or alternative.[310] Other courts apply a "subjective" standard, so that it must be proved that the patient would have refused to consent if informed of the risk or alternative.[311]

Either standard provides substantial protection for the conscientious health care professional who discloses major risks and then has a more remote risk occur. A patient who consents to a procedure knowing of the risk of death and paralysis will find it difficult to convince a court that knowledge of a minor risk would have led to refusal. However, courts may be more easily convinced when there are undisclosed alternatives.[312]

A few jurisdictions do not require proof of causation. The Vermont Supreme Court ruled that even though the vasectomy patient could not prove he would have refused if informed of the risk of recanalization, he could still sue for failure to provide accurate information.[313] In 1992, the Pennsylvania Supreme Court ruled that it was not necessary to prove causation in any informed consent case.[314] In Pennsylvania informed consent is required only for operations and surgery.[315] In effect, Pennsylvania considers operations and surgeries without informed consent to be batteries.

FRAUD. Attempts have been made to claim that failure to obtain informed consent is fraud. In 2000, the Georgia Supreme Court rejected an attempt to establish liability for fraud based on a physician's nondisclosure of his personal drug use. Nondisclosure could not be the basis for a fraud claim.[316]

7-8.3 What Is the Civil Liability for Withholding or Withdrawing Services?

Because they fear liability, physicians and hospitals have sometimes been reluctant to follow the directives of patients and their families. While liability is theoretically possible, it is no more likely that physicians and other healthcare providers will be held liable for following treatment refusals than for their many other decisions and actions. Generally, a healthcare provider who makes a good faith healthcare decision based on the provisions of a healthcare directive (or direction of a healthcare agent or surrogate) is immune from criminal and civil liability or professional discipline for carrying out those decisions. Further, a provider is not generally subject to criminal or civil liability or professional discipline for (i) failing to comply with a decision that violates the provider's conscience so long as the provider makes known his or her unwillingness and promptly transfers the responsibility for the patient's care to another provider who is willing to act in accordance with the directive or (ii) relying on a court order concerning the patient.

Civil liability for withholding or withdrawing medical treatment would have to be based on negligent or deliberate failure to act in accordance with some duty to the patient. The duty to the patient is shaped by the patient's directions and condition. There is no duty to provide properly refused treatment or to treat terminally ill or irreversibly unconscious patients as if they are curable. Explicit refusal by an informed patient with decision-making capacity relieves the physician and hospital of further duty to provide the refused treatment unless it is a situation in which involuntary treatment is authorized. If refused treatment is given without legal authorization, liability for battery is possible. The same principles generally apply to proper refusals by an incapacitated patient's representative.

> Individuals have the right to: • Refuse unwanted treatment • Discontinue treatment once started • Forego life sustaining therapies.

A medical decision can be questioned in subsequent litigation and be found to have been negligent. The risk for decisions regarding the treatment of terminally ill and irreversibly unconscious patients is no greater than is the risk for the treatment of other patients. Liability is even possible when physicians act pursuant to a court order if they are negligent in implementing the order. Limited statutory immunity has been granted in some circumstances by living will laws, but those laws have broad exceptions that preserve accountability.

One indication of the limited exposure to civil liability is the small number of civil lawsuits brought against physicians and hospitals for withholding or withdrawing medical treatment from terminally ill patients.[317] One case arose after the physician and the patient's husband decided to discontinue the patient's dialysis at a Minnesota hospital.[318] Six months after the wife's death, the husband died. Three years later, the patient's children sued the physician for her death, but a jury found in favor of the physician. Other courts have found no liability when family members have sued because they had no right to participate in a competent patient's decision.[319]

Liability exposure is possible in cases of misdiagnosis of terminal illness or unjustifiable failure to obtain the concurrence of the patient or, in the case of incapacitated patients, the family.[320]

There is some exposure to civil liability from refusing to honor the directives of the patient and the family.[321] Several suits have been brought against providers who continued treatment for a prolonged period after refusal. Although the exposure to liability still varies between states, liability has been found in some cases.

Several decisions have required providers to pay the attorney's fees of the patient and the family in seeking court orders.[322]

7-8.4 What Are the Licensing Consequences for Decisions Concerning the Treatment of Individuals?

Decisions concerning the treatment of individuals can result in discipline by licensing agencies. Cases involving consent, refusal, and care of persons at the end of life continue to be unusual, but they have occurred.

In one reported case, failure to obtain required consent was the basis for discipline.[323]

Treatment at the end of life has resulted in discipline in a few cases. In some cases, health professionals have surrendered their licenses during criminal investigations as part of defense strategies or bargains with prosecutors.

Licensing boards have imposed discipline that does not appear to be part of a bargain. A few illustrative examples, reported in newspapers or in court decisions, include: (i) A Texas medical licensing board revoked the license of an emergency room physician accused of suffocating a patient who was near death by blocking the breathing tube. The two administrative judges who conducted the hearing for the board found that the physician's actions had not harmed the patient and recommended that she not be disciplined. The board overruled them.[324] (ii) Vermont reprimanded a physician for giving a dying patient a paralyzing drug.[325] (iii) An Iowa nursing home was fined $103,600 by the state because a respiratory therapist allegedly removed two residents from ventilators without a physician's order and one died. The nursing home announced that it was appealing the fine.[326] These cases illustrate that there are potential consequences from these actions. It is prudent to stay within the parameters of accepted practice.

7-8.5 What Are the Criminal Law Consequences of Decisions Concerning the Treatment of Individuals?

In some decisions involving terminally ill patients, courts have discussed the potential criminal liability for withholding or withdrawing medical treatment. In the Quinlan decision, after observing that termination of treatment would accelerate death, the court concluded that "there would be no criminal homicide but rather expiration from existing natural causes." It added as a second reason, "even if it were to be regarded as homicide, it would not be unlawful. . . . The termination of treatment pursuant to the right of privacy is, within the limits of this case, ipso facto lawful." The court discussed the constitutional dimensions:

Furthermore, the exercise of a constitutional right such as we have here found is protected from criminal prosecution. We do not question the State's undoubted power to punish the taking of human life, but that power does not encompass individuals terminating medical treatment pursuant to their right of privacy. The constitutional protection extends to third parties whose action is necessary to effectuate the exercise of that right where the individuals themselves would not be subject to prosecution or the third parties are charged as accessories to an act which could not be a crime.[327]

Thus, there is little risk of criminal liability for these actions.[328] The criminal trials of physicians in the United States for the deaths of unrelated terminally ill patients generally have involved alleged injections of substances to hasten death. In most cases, either the jury has acquitted the physician or an appellate court has reversed the jury conviction. There are a few isolated exceptions. The results of these cases illustrate the difficulty in obtaining convictions when the patient is terminally ill, even in cases alleging active euthanasia. This is one reason prosecutors seldom pursue cases that involve withholding or withdrawing treatment from the terminally ill. The other reason is that it would be difficult to establish a duty to provide the withheld or withdrawn treatment.

There are cases where physicians, nurses, or others have murdered patients. Some of these cases are included in this section to illustrate the range of potential cases. Sometimes law enforcement personnel have had a difficult time distinguishing appropriate medical actions from inappropriate actions. Prudent providers properly document their consultations, decision making, and orders and stay within accepted practice.

This section focuses on deaths of patients. Some of the other consequences of these cases are mentioned, such as loss of license or time in jail or length of time the case was open, to illustrate the impact on the lives of those involved even when no criminal conviction resulted.

PHYSICIANS. Several cases have involved physicians. Some of these cases do not involve consent issues. They are discussed together to facilitate comparisons.

No Charges. Several criminal investigations of physicians for the deaths of their patients have resulted in no charges:

(i) In 1986, the head of cardiovascular surgery at George Washington University Hospital was placed on administrative leave while a hospital and criminal investigation were conducted of the death of a patient. The patient had been declared dead and removed from life support systems with her family's permission, when the physician injected potassium chloride, which stops the heart. At the conclusion of the investigation about one month later, he was reinstated with full privileges.[329] (ii) In 1991, a physician published an article in the *New England Journal of Medicine* reporting that he had assisted in a suicide. Later that year, a New York grand jury refused to indict him.[330]

Charges Dismissed. In several cases, charges were dismissed before trial, for example: (i) In 1981, the parents and physician of newborn conjoined twins were charged with attempted murder for denying the twins food, water, and treatment at the request of the parents. An Illinois judge dismissed the charges finding lack of probable cause. The state's attorney sought an indictment from the grand jury, but it refused to indict the parents or physician. The case was then dropped.[331] (ii) In 1983, two California physicians were charged with murder for terminating all life support, including intravenous feeding, of an irreversibly comatose patient upon the written request of the family. A California appellate court ordered the charges dismissed because the physicians had no legal duty to continue futile treatment and, thus, they did not unlawfully fail to fulfill a legal duty that could be the basis for a murder charge.[332]

Jury Did Not Convict. Juries have acquitted physicians in several cases.[333] In one of the first such cases, in 1915, a Chicago physician was indicted for murder for allowing microcephalic infants to die. A jury acquitted him, but his medical career was ended.[334]

Other cases include: (i) A New Jersey physician was indicted for five murders in the deaths of patients after a *New York Times* reporter wrote about the deaths. The trial judge dismissed two of the indictments. The physician voluntarily surrendered his medical license. In 1978, a jury acquitted the physician for the remaining three murders. In 1982, a court upheld the revocation of his medical license.[335] (ii) A Georgia jury deadlocked seven to five in favor of acquitting a neonatologist accused of killing a premature, terminally ill infant. In 1995, the prosecutor decided to drop the charges. In 1996, the state medical licensing board decided not to impose discipline.[336] (iii) A Florida jury acquitted a physician charged with the death of a terminally ill cancer patient by the administration of morphine and potassium chloride. The jury is reported to have believed the physician administered the drugs to relieve pain and reduce the patient's rapid heart rate.[337]

Convictions Overturned. Convictions of physicians have been overturned in some cases.[338] In 1995, a Kansas physician who was charged with trying to kill an elderly patient surrendered his license. He was convicted of murder, but an appellate court overturned the conviction, finding no medical consensus that the actions were homicidal. His license was reinstated several months later. The state medical society supported the physician, maintaining that the prosecution was deterring physicians from providing needed pain relief to patients.[339]

In 2000, a Utah jury convicted a physician of manslaughter and negligent homicide. The psychiatrist was accused of prescribing fatal amounts of morphine for five elderly patients. The jury verdict was overturned because the prosecutor withheld evidence from the defense. A second jury acquitted the physician.[340]

Convictions Not Overturned. One conviction that was not overturned on appeal was the conviction of the infamous assisted suicide advocate Dr. Kevorkian (nicknamed "Dr. Death") mentioned in section 7-6.1, who himself administered the lethal injection.

There are several cases not involving terminal patients where physicians have been convicted of manslaughter for the deaths of patients after they were prescribed large amounts of drugs.[341]

In 1994, a New York appellate court upheld the conviction of a physician for reckless endangerment for his failure to promptly transfer a patient from a nursing home to a hospital after he mistakenly fed her through a peritoneal dialysis catheter. In 1997, a federal appellate court affirmed a lower federal court's denial of a petition for federal habeas corpus relief. In 1997, the state commuted his sentence to community service.[342]

Guilty Pleas. In 1986, a New Jersey physician pled guilty to killing his aged mother by injecting Demerol into her feeding tube in a nursing home. She had Alzheimer's disease and had lost control of her bodily functions. He was sentenced to two years' probation, a fine, and 400 hours of community service.[343]

In 1989, a Michigan physician pled guilty after being charged with injecting a terminally ill and comatose inpatient with potassium chloride in the presence of other medical staff. He was sentenced to five years of probation and community service.[344]

OTHER HEALTHCARE PROFESSIONALS. Other healthcare professionals have been investigated, charged, tried, and convicted for patient deaths. Some investigations have been dropped.[345]

Charges Dismissed. In 1980, a Nevada nurse was indicted for the death of a terminally ill patient. A judge dismissed the murder charge concluding that there was insufficient evidence. She was reinstated to her job in the ICU.[346]

Jury or Judge Did Not Convict. A few illustrative cases include: (i) A Maryland nurse was accused of disconnecting three patients' respirators and turning down the oxygen flow to a fourth. Tried for one of the disconnection cases, she surrendered her license before the trial. In 1979, the jury deadlocked, and she was not convicted. All charges were then dropped.[347] (ii) A Massachusetts grand jury indicted three nurses for murder for the death of a cancer patient to whom they allegedly gave an overdose of morphine as a pain medication. The trials were separated. In 1981, in the first trial, a licensed practical nurse was acquitted. One of the issues in dispute was whether the physician had given verbal orders for the drug. Charges were then dropped against the other two.[348] (iii) A Massachusetts nurse was charged with attempting to murder a patient with Lou Gehrig's disease by pulling the plug on his respirator. She surrendered her license after she was indicted. He survived and provided videotaped testimony against her at the trial. She was acquitted by the jury.[349] (iv) A nurse in Georgia was accused of injecting six ICU patients with a heart-stopping drug and was found innocent by a jury. She was found guilty but mentally ill of one count of aggravated assault. She was sentenced to seventeen years.[350] (v) A Maryland nurse was charged with giving a lethal drug to an elderly patient in an apparent mercy killing. A judge dismissed the charges, and the case was suspended. She was again charged with three deaths. In January 1988, a court suppressed her confession finding it had been improperly obtained. The federal center for the Centers for Disease Control (CDC) did a statistical analysis of the deaths in the hospital where the nurse worked and found that cardiac arrests in the ICU occurred at a higher rate when she was on duty. In 1988, a judge acquitted her of all charges, finding that the statistical analysis was not sufficient to tie her to the deaths.[351]

Convictions Overturned. Two nurses were accused of poisoning eleven patients at the Ann Arbor Veterans Administration Hospital by injecting a muscle relaxant into their intravenous tubes. The nurses were convicted on several of the counts in 1977, but when the court ordered a new trial, their indictments were dismissed.[352]

Convictions Not Overturned. A few illustrative cases include: (i) A California nurse was charged with killing twelve elderly patients by injecting them with overdoses of lidocaine while working as a temporary overnight nurse in a hospital ICU. In 1984, he was convicted by a judge and sentenced to death. In 1992, the California Supreme Court upheld the murder conviction.[353] (ii) A Texas grand jury investigated a number of suspicious deaths. The CDC conducted an analysis for the grand jury. In 1983, a judge found the University of Texas medical school dean in contempt for withholding documents from the grand jury investigating the case. In 1984, a Texas vocational nurse was convicted of murdering an infant and was sentenced to ninety-nine years. Later the same year, she was convicted of injuring a child and was sentenced to sixty years. During the period between the two trials, the hospital where the death occurred was accused of shredding documents and was enjoined from further document shredding. In 1986, the first conviction was affirmed by the appellate court.[354] (iii) A New York nurse was charged with assault for injecting a patient with a potentially lethal drug. It was reported that he had done this to several patients so that he could play the hero and revive the patients. The hospital where the events occurred was cited by the state for poor record-keeping and inadequate patient monitoring. In 1989, the nurse was convicted of killing four patients and was sentenced to fifty years to life in prison. In 1996, the highest court of New York affirmed the conviction.[355] (iv) An Indiana nurse was found guilty of murdering six patients. The nurse was accused of injecting lethal doses of potassium chloride. He was sentenced to 360 years in prison. In 2002, the Indiana Supreme Court rejected a challenge to the conviction.[356]

Guilty or No Contest Pleas. A few illustrative cases include: (i) A Wisconsin nurse pled no contest to practicing medicine without a license after an elderly comatose patient died when the nurse unhooked the life support system allegedly at the request of the family. The nurse was sentenced to twenty months' probation. In 1985, the nursing license was revoked for one year.[357] (ii) An Ohio nurse's aide pled guilty to killing twenty-four chronically ill patients and was sentenced to multiple life terms. In 1988, the former hospital administrator was sentenced to thirty days in jail after he pled no contest to falsifying the personnel file of the aide in a plea arrangement that resulted in dropping other charges of tampering with evidence.[358] (iii) A California respiratory therapist pled guilty to murdering six elderly patients in a plea agreement to avoid the death penalty. He was accused of injecting the patients with paralyzing drugs. He was sentenced to life without parole. A confession to more than one hundred murders was unsealed at the time of sentencing. In 2003, he settled civil claims with four of the families.[359] (iv) A New Jersey nurse pled guilty to sixteen deaths. In 2003, he had been arrested after disclosing that forty terminally ill patients under his care had died after he had administered fatal drugs. He surrendered his license. Numerous private lawsuits were filed against the institutions where the deaths occurred and where he had worked. Some of these suits were dismissed. New Jersey fined one hospital for violating state standards for handling suspicious deaths. Pennsylvania officials announced that institutions in their state had complied with its laws.[360]

These cases demonstrate the importance of proper documentation of the circumstances under which medical treatment can be withheld or withdrawn so that authorized actions can be distinguished from unauthorized actions. It is prudent for nurses and other hospital personnel to appropriately document the decision making by the physicians and decision makers for the patient before withholding or withdrawing medical treatment in order to minimize the risk of investigation or prosecution in the absence of documented authorization of the actions.

Chapter Summary

This chapter provided an overview of the myriad of federal and state laws that regulate the treatment decision-making process between patient and provider. It also addressed several ethical, legal and regulatory issues raised by the courts that have focused on (i) a physician's responsibility and fiduciary duty and (ii) how such decisions impact the provider-patient decision-making process.

Key Terms and Definitions

Guardian of the Estate - A person who is granted powers over another's property and has no authority to make medical decisions.

Guardian *ad litem* - A person appointed to represent the patient in court proceedings and has no authority to make medical decisions, unless the court has granted this power.

Healthcare Agent - One or more persons designated to serve as a healthcare agent to make medical decisions for another. A power of attorney gives the designated agent the power to make decisions on the behalf of the person giving the power, called the principal.

Physicians Orders for Life-Sustaining Treatment (POLST, also referred to as a Medical order for scope of treatment, or MOST) - Covers several decisions common for seriously chronically ill patients, including: CPR, level of medical intervention desired in the event of emergency, use of medications, and the use of artificial nutrition and hydration. A POLST/MOST does not, however, take the place of a living will or a healthcare power of attorney.

Advance Directive (AD) - A general term for any document that gives instructions about an individual's ("principle") health care and/or appoints someone ("attorney in fact") to make medical treatment decisions for that individual if he or she cannot make such decisions. Living wills and durable powers of attorney for health care are examples of advance directives.

Living Will - A document that states an individual's wishes about life–sustaining medical treatment when the individual is terminally ill, permanently unconscious or in the end-stage of a fatal illness.

Durable Power of Attorney for Health Care (DPO AHC, also called a Healthcare Proxy) - A document that appoints someone to make medical decisions for an individual (in the way that the individual would want them to be made) in the event that the individual is no longer able to do so.

In Loco parentis - A person can stand in place of a parent to a minor by assuming the status and obligation of a parent without formal adoption or designation by the natural parent.

Consent - Can be express (given by direct words, either oral or written) or implied (inferred from some patient conduct or presumed in most emergencies). Consent is usually implied from voluntary submission to an examination or procedure with apparent knowledge of its nature.

General Informed Consent Form - Most hospitals now require this type of consent form, which includes (1) the name and a description of the specific treatment or procedure; (2) statement that the physician has explained to the patient or his or her legal representative the consequences, risks and benefits, and alternatives to such treatment or procedure (including foregoing treatment); (3) statement that all questions have been answered to the person's satisfaction; and (4) that no guarantees have been made. The actual process of providing information to the decision maker and of determining that person's decision is more important than the consent form. The form is evidence of the consent process, but the informed consent is the actual discussion(s) between the physician and the patient (or the patient's legal representative) about the treatment or procedure to be performed.

Exculpatory Clauses - State that the person signing waives the right to sue for injuries or agrees to limit any claims to not more than a specified amount.

Instructor-Led Questions

1. When do adults have decision-making capacity? What is the usual presumption?

2. What is the effect of an advance directive?

3. Who makes decisions for adults who cannot decide for themselves? How do emergencies differ from other situations?

4. What is the difference between a guardian and a healthcare agent?

5. When can minors make their own decisions? What is an emancipated minor? What is a mature minor? What are necessaries?

6. Who makes decisions for minors who cannot decide for themselves? When can persons other than a parent or guardian decide?

7. When is an informed consent required? What information must be provided for an informed consent?

8. What are some of the barriers to patient-physician communication?

9. When may information be withheld from patient? How is this practice distinct from circumstances when it is not feasible to disclose information? Disclosure issues arising from medical errors?

10. Who is responsible for providing the information?

11. What is the difference between express and implied consent? When is implied consent sufficient?

12. When should consent be documented by a signed consent form?

13. When is express consent ineffective?

14. What are the limits on the decisions that adults can make for themselves?

15. What are the limits on the decisions that others can make for adults?

16. What are the limits on the decisions that can be made for minors?

17. When may the law authorize involuntary treatment?

18. What happens when treatment is provided without proper authorization?

19. What are the consequences for unwanted life-saving procedures?

20. What happens when healthcare providers are investigated or charged with murder of patients?

Advance Directives Case Studies

CASE #1: A 37-year-old woman completes an advance directive indicating that she is a Jehovah's Witness and does not want a blood transfusion, even if her life is at risk. She is subsequently admitted three years later, eight months pregnant and gravely ill, requiring a life-saving blood transfusion. Her husband challenges the advance directive, stating that she left the Jehovah's faith when she met him two years ago and her views have changed. Should the advance directive be honored? Was this the intent of the patient?

CASE #2: A 65-year-old man with a malignant brain tumor currently in remission completes an advance directive refusing life-prolonging treatment if the tumor recurs and he loses consciousness. He later suffers a hemorrhagic stroke as a consequence of other treatment and becomes comatose with no prospect of recovery. Should the advance directive be honored? Was this the intent of the patient?

CASE #3: A 27-year-old physically disabled man with learning difficulties is hospitalized after sustaining life-threatening injuries in a car accident. His parents present the hospital with an advance directive refusing all treatment. However, his close friend and partner later informs the hospital that he has heard his family say on numerous occasions that they are fed up having to look after him. He has heard about the advance directive but is aware that his parents took his partner to a lawyer to have it completed. Should the AD be honored? Was this patient competent to make such a decision? Is duress an issue? Should the patient's partner be the decision maker rather than his parents?

Endnotes

1   *Union Pac. Ry. Co. v. Botsford*, 141 U.S. 250 (1891).

2   In re Yetter, 62 D. & C. 2d 619 (Pa. Cm. Pl. Ct. Northampton County 1973).

3   *Lane v. Candura*, 6 Mass. App. Ct. 377, 376 N.E.2d 1232 (1978).

4   In re Jeffers, 239 Ill. App. 3d 29, 606 N.E.2d 727 (4th Dist. 1992), appeal granted, 158 Ill. 2d 552, 643 N.E.2d 839 (1994), adhered to, 272 Ill. App. 3d 44, 650 N.E.2d 242 (4th Dist. 1995).

5   *Rodriguez v. Pino*, 634 So. 2d 681 (Fla. 3d DCA 1994).

6   In re Rose S., 293 A.D.2d 619, 741 N.Y.S.2d 84 (2d Dept. Apr. 15, 2002).

7   *Lynn G v. Hugo*, 96 N.Y.2d 306, 752 N.E.2d 250, 728 N.Y.S.2d 121 (2001).

8   See B. Carey, Obsession with perfection: Some plastic surgeons are conducting psychological tests on patients who fixate on the smallest of flaws, L.A. TIMES, Dec. 17, 2001, S1.

9   *Collins v. Lake Forest Hosp.*, 213 Ill. 2d 234, 821 N.E.2d 316 (2004); *Ficke v. Evangelical Health Sys.*, 285 Ill. App. 3d 886, 674 N.E.2d 888 (1st Dist. 1996).

10 E.g., Estate of Sorensen, 87 Wis. 2d 339, 274 N.W.2d 694 (1979).

11 E.g., *Herrington v. Herrington*, 692 So. 2d 93 (Miss. 1996) [jury questions whether medications rendered patient incapable of consent].

12 *Lounsbury v. Capel*, 836 P.2d 188 (Utah Ct. App. 1992).

13 The Patient Self-Determination Act, Pub. L. No. 101-508, codified at 42 USC §§ 1395cc(f), 1396a(w) (1994), defines an advanced directive as "a written instruction, such as a living will or durable power of attorney for health care, recognized under state law (whether statutory or as recognized by the courts of the State) relating to the provision of health care when the individual is incapacitated."

14 The PSDA requires that these entities meet certain additional requirements in order to be paid under Medicare or Medicaid, specifically: (i) document in the patient's medical record whether or not the patient has a valid AD; (ii) comply with all applicable state laws regarding ADs; (iii) not condition the provision of care or otherwise discriminate against an individual based upon whether or not that individual has an AD; and (iv) inform the individual that complaints concerning implementation of Ads may be files with the state agency that accredits the provider.

15 Summary of "Health Care Power of Attorney and Combined Advance Directive Legislation" – December 2009, American Bar Association Commission on Law and Aging.

16 In re Finn, No. 39711 (Va. Cir. Ct. Aug. 31, 1998); Family will allow a comatose man to die, N.Y. TIMES, Sept. 29, 1998, A21; *Gilmore v. Annaburg Manor Nursing Home*, No. 44386 (Va. Cir. Ct. Chancery Oct. 2, 1998), rev. denied, (Va. Oct. 2, 1998); See *Gilmore v. Finn*, 259 Va. 448, 527 S.E.2d 426 (2000) [denying sanctions].

17 42 C.F.R. 489.102. Other provider entities, such as skilled nursing homes (SNFs), nursing homes, home health care, HMOs, and hospice programs participating in the Medicare or Medicaid programs must comply with this law in order to receive Medicare or Medicaid payment from the federal government.

18 TJC, 2011 COMPREHENSIVE ACCREDITATION MANUAL FOR HOSPITALS (2010): The Official Handbook [cited hereinafter as 2010 TJC CAMH].

19 A few of these fourteen states recognize only oral instructional directives, but not orally designated surrogates.

20 *Cruzan v. Director, Mo. Dept. of Health*, 497 U.S. 261 (1990), aff'g, 760 S.W.2d 408 (Mo. 1988) (en banc).

21 See Calabresi, Steven G., The Terri Schiavo Case: In Defense of the Special Law Enacted by Congress and President Bush, Northwestern University School of Law, Northwestern University Law Review Vol. 100, No. 1 (2006) [review of the moral and legal issues raised]. In all, this matter involved fourteen appeals, numerous motions, petitions and hearings, five suits in federal and district court, and four denials of *certiorari* from the U.S. Supreme Court.

22 E.g., *John F. Kennedy Mem. Hosp. v. Bludworth*, 452 A.2d 921 (Fla. 1984).

23 *Foster v. Tourtellottee*, No. CV-81-5046-RMT (C.D. Cal. Nov. 18, 1981), as discussed in 704 F.2d 1109 (9th Cir. 1983) [denying attorneys' fees]; accord In re Yetter, 62 D. & C. 2d 619 (Pa. Cm Pl. Ct. Northampton County 1973) [disagreement between patient, brother]; *Lane v. Candura*, 6 Mass. App. Ct. 377, 376 N.E.2d 1232 (1978) [disagreement between patient, daughter]; see also *Brooks v. United States*, 837 F.2d 958 (11th Cir. 1988) [no duty to involve relatives].

24 *Dick v. Springhill Hosps.*, 551 So. 2d 1034 (Ala. 1989).

25 E.g., *Eis v. Chesnut*, 96 N.M. 45, 627 P.2d 1244 (App. Ct. 1981).

26 E.g., *Kozup v. Georgetown Univ.*, 271 U.S. App. D.C. 182, 851 F.2d 437 (1988) [jury question whether life-threatening emergency existed to justify transfusions that caused AIDS].

27 E.g., *Rodriguez v. Pino*, 634 So. 2d 681 (Fla. 3d DCA), rev. denied, 645 So. 2d 454 (Fla. 1994); *Mulloy v. Hop Sang* [1935], 1 W.W.R. 714 (Alberta Sup. Ct.).

28 *Jacovach v. Yocum*, 212 Iowa 914, 237 N.W. 444 (1931); accord *Stafford v. Louisiana State Univ.*, 448 So. 2d 852 (La. Ct. App. 1984).

29 *Spahn v. Eisenberg* (In re Edna M.F.), 210 Wis. 2d 558, 563 N.W.2d 485, cert. denied sub nom, *Spahn v. Wittman*, 522 U.S. 951 (1997); WIS. STAT. § 154.225.

30 Currently recognized in thirty-two states which have implemented POLST or are developing similar programs; see the Centers for Ethics in Healthcare, Oregon Health & Science University at http://www.ohsu.edu/polst for more information.

31 June 2, 2010, the U.S. Office of Management Personnel (OPM) issued a memorandum in response to President Barack Obama's June 2009 memorandum regarding same-sex domestic partners, defining "domestic partner," enabling such individuals named in legally valid advance directives and through powers of attorney to have the same rights as immediate family members—paving the way for members of the lesbian, gay, bisexual, and transgender (LGBT) community to have further control over their own medical decisions.

32 E.g., FLA. STAT. § 765.07.

33 E.g., CAL. HEALTH & SAFETY CODE § 1418.8; *Rains v. Belshe*, 32 Cal. App. 4th 157, 38 Cal. Rptr. 2d 185 (1st Dist. 1995) [constitutional to permit doctor to consent to treatment of incompetent in long-term care facility without legal surrogate].

34 See Idaho's Freedom of Conscience for Healthcare Professionals, Idaho Code §18-612. Although this law's primary focus was on contraception, it contained a provision regarding end of life treatment. This law was amended a year later, requiring *physicians* to comply with existing living will law when exercising conscience rights (but *other* healthcare providers not mentioned) and became law on March 31, 2011, without the Governor's signature.

35 E.g., *Superintendent of Belchertown State School v. Saikewicz*, 373 Mass. 728, 370 N.E.2d 417 (1977).

36 E.g., In re Guardianship of Hamlin, 102 Wash. 2d 810, 689 P.2d 1372 (1984).

37 Guttmacher Institute—Overview of Minors' Consent Law (June 1, 2011).

38 Currently six categories of state law that affect a minor's right to consent: (1) contraceptive services; (2) STI services; (3) prenatal care; (4) adoption; (5) medical care for a child of a minor; and (6) abortion. See *Guttmacher Institute—Overview of Minors' Consent Law* (June 1, 2011).

39 E.g., IND. CODE § 16-36-1-3; CAL. FAMILY CODE §§ 7002, 7050.

40 *Comm. v. Nixon*, 563 Pa. 425, 761 A.2d 1151 (2000).

41 Youth who refused a liver transplant drug dies, N.Y. TIMES, Aug. 22, 1994, A7.

42 E.g., *Wiley v. Fuller*, 310 Mass. 597, 39 N.E.2d 418 (1942).

43 E.g., *Wilson v. Knight*, 26 Kan. App. 2d 226, 982 P.2d 400 (1999) [minor is liable for payment for necessaries, including medical treatment].

44 Annotation, Medical practitioner's liability for treatment given child without parent's consent, 67 A.L.R. 4TH 511.

45 But see *Faust v. Johnson*, 223 Wis. 2d 799, 589 N.W.2d 454, 1998 Wisc. App. LEXIS 1436 (unpub.) [joint legal custody after divorce, but sole custody for medical issues to one parent].

46 In re Vulon, 56 Misc. 2d 19, 288 N.Y.S.2d 203 (Fam. Ct. 1968).

47 Texas Board of Health institute's rule requiring proof of identification before getting an abortion, ALL THINGS CONSIDERED (National Public Radio), Mar. 19, 2004.

48 11 PA. STAT. § 2513.

49 E.g., *Gritzner v. Michel R.*, 2000 WI 68, 235 Wis. 2d 781, 611 N.W.2d 906.

50 E.g., *Cobbs v. Grant*, 8 Cal. 3d 229, 502 P.2d 1, 104 Cal. Rptr. 505 (1972).

51 E.g., WIS. STAT. § 48.981.

52 E.g., FLA. STAT. § 39.304.

53 E.g., TENN. CODE ANN. § 37-1-406(f).

54 E.g., *Fox v. Smith*, 594 So. 2d 596 (Miss. 1992) [removal of IUD during laparoscopy could be battery after express directions not to remove]; *Bommareddy v. Superior Court*, 222 Cal. App. 3d 1017, 272 Cal. Rptr. 246 (5th Dist. 1990) [punitive damages allowable for battery, cataract surgery when consent only for tear duct surgery].

55 *Irma Natanson v. John Kline, et al.*, 354 P.2d 670 (1960). This decision had impact on informed consent by establishing that true informed consent required a "thorough going self-determination" rather than the "reasonable physician" standard then in use. It was left to the patient to decide whether or not to undergo a particular procedure.

56 E.g., *Batzell v. Buskirk*, 752 S.W.2d 902 (Mo. Ct. App. 1988); *Kohoutek v. Hafner*, 383 N.W.2d 295 (Minn. 1986); *Moser v. Stallings*, 387 N.W.2d 599 (Iowa 1986).

57 F.J. Skelly, The payoff of informed consent, AM. MED. NEWS, Aug. 1, 1994, at 11.

58 *Green v. Commissioner of Dep't of Mental Health*, 776 A.2d 612 (Me. 2001).

59 *Truman v. Thomas*, 27 Cal. 3d 285, 165 Cal. Rptr. 308, 611 P.2d 902 (1980).

60 *Battenfeld v. Gregory*, 247 N.J. Super. 538, 589 A.2d 1059 (App. Div. 1991).

61 E.g., In re Hughes, 259 N.J. Super. 193, 611 A.2d 1148 (App. Div. 1992).

62 *Werth v. Taylor*, 190 Mich. App. 141, 475 N.W.2d 426 (1991).

63 See Annotation, Modern status of views as to general measure of physician's duty to inform patient of risks of proposed treatment, 88 A.L.R. 3D 1008.

64 E.g., *Gorab v. Zook*, 943 P.2d 423 (Colo. 1997); *Natanson v. Kline*, 186 Kan. 393, 350 P.2d 1093 (1960).

65 E.g., *Korman v. Mallin*, 858 P.2d 1145 (Alaska 1993); *Largey v. Rothman*, 110 N.J. 204, 540 A.2d 504 (1988); *Pauscher v. Iowa Methodist Med. Ctr.*, 408 N.W.2d 355 (Iowa 1987).

66 *Canterbury v. Spence*, 150 D.C. App. 263, 464 F.2d 772, 787, cert. denied, 409 U.S. 1064 (1972).

67 E.g., *Hapchuck v. Pierson*, 495 S.E.2d 854 (W.Va. 1997) [affirming dismissal for absence of expert testimony as to risks, alternatives, and outcome without treatment]; *Moure v. Raeuchle*, 529 Pa. 394, 604 A.2d 1003 (1992).

68　E.g., *Darviris v. Petros*, 442 Mass. 274, 812 N.E.2d 1188 (2004); *Lareau v. Page*, 34 F.3d 384 (1st Cir. 1994); *Foflygen v. Zemel*, 420 Pa. Super. 18, 615 A.2d 1345 (1992); *Benoy v. Simons*, 66 Wash. App. 56, 831 P.2d 167 (1992); but see, *Quimby v. Fine*, 45 Wash. App. 175, 724 P.2d 403 (1986).

69　Communicating risk key step to good care, Am. Med. News, Oct. 20, 2003, 23 [patients cannot make best decisions when they misunderstand risks].

70　E.g., *Tyndall v. Zaboski*, 306 N.J. Super. 423, 703 A.2d 980 (App. Div. 1997) [plaintiff must prove by expert testimony risk was known to practitioners]; *Gilmartin v. Weinreb*, 324. N.J. Super. 367, 735 A.2d 620 (App. Div. 1999) [need not disclose risk of negligence].

71　E.g., *Galvan v. Downey*, 933 S.W.2d 316 (Tex. Ct. App. 1996).

72　*Klein v. Biscup*, 109 Ohio App. 3d 855, 673 N.E.2d 225 (1996).

73　45 C.F.R. pt. 46 [HHS]. The Belmont Report and the Nuremberg Code both address voluntary informed consent as a requirement for the ethical conduct of human subjects research (see http://ohsr.od.nih.gov/guidelines/belmont.html and http://www.cirp.org).

74　The regulations require that the following information must be conveyed to each subject: a statement that the study involves research, an explanation of the purposes of the research and the expected duration of the subject's participation, a description of the procedures to be followed, and identification of any procedures which are experimental; a description of any reasonably foreseeable risks or discomforts to the subject; a description of any benefits to the subject or to others which may reasonably be expected from the research; a disclosure of appropriate alternative procedures or courses of treatment, if any, that might be advantageous to the subject; a statement describing the extent, if any, to which confidentiality of records identifying the subject will be maintained; for research involving more than minimal risk, an explanation as to whether any compensation and an explanation as to whether any medical treatments are available if injury occurs and, if so, what they consist of, or where further information may be obtained; an explanation of whom to contact for answers to pertinent questions about the research and research subjects' rights, and whom to contact in the event of a research-related injury to the subject; and a statement that participation is voluntary, refusal to participate will involve no penalty or loss of benefits to which the subject is otherwise entitled, and the subject may discontinue participation at any time without penalty or loss of benefits to which the subject is otherwise entitled. Additional elements are described at 45 CFR 46.116(b).

75　45 C.F.R. § 46.110; see 46 Fed. Reg. 8,392 (Jan. 26, 1981) [initial approved categories].

76　21 C.F.R. pts. 50, 56, 312, 314, 812.

77　E.g., N.Y. Pub. Health Law §§ 2440-2446.

78　E.g., *Anderson v. George H. Lanier Mem. Hosp.*, 982 F.2d 1513 (11th Cir. 1993) [use of experimental intraocular lens]; *Friter v. IOLAB Corp.*, 414 Pa. Super. 622, 607 A.2d 1111 (1992) [use of experimental intraocular lens]; *Daum v. SpineCare Med. Group*, 52 Cal. App. 4th 1285, 61 Cal. Rptr. 2d 260 (1st Dist. 1997) [spinal fixation device].

79　E.g., *Jones v. Papp*, 782 S.W.2d 236 (Tex. Ct. App. 1989) [form met statutory standard]; *Tajchman v. Giller*, 938 S.W.2d 95 (Tex. Ct. App. 1996) [statute required disclosure of risks, hazards when no state approved consent form; need for cutting vein was step in procedure, not a risk or hazard, so statutory disclosure standard met]; *Eckmann v. Des Rosiers*, 940 S.W.2d 394 (Tex. Civ. App. 1997) [consent form protected by statutory presumption even though medical disclosure panel had not updated requirements].

80　Ore. Rev. Stat. § 677.097(2); *Zacher v. Petty*, 312 Or. 590, 826 P.2d 619 (1992).

81　*Marie v. McGreevey*, 314 F.3d 136 (3d Cir. 2002); D Adams, N.J. OB wins informed consent case, Am. Med. News, Jan. 5, 2004, 11 [N.J. Superior Court ruled in *Acuna v. Turkish* not required to express moral, philosophical or religious judgments in advising about abortion].

82　See Annotation, Medical malpractice: Liability for failure of physician to inform patient of alternative modes of diagnosis and treatment, 38 A.L.R. 4th 900; Wis. Stat. § 448.30 [statutory requirement to disclose alternatives].

83　*Sgro v. Ross*, 166 N.J. 338, 765 A.2d 745 (2001).

84　*Farina v. Kraus*, 333 N.J. Super. 165, 754 A.2d 1215 (App. Div. 1999).

85　*Kuklinski v. Rodriguez*, 203 Wis. 2d 324, 552 N.W.2d 869 (App. 1996).

86　E.g., S. Klein, Texas forces change in Aetna contracts, Am. Med. News, Jan. 19, 1998, at 3 [Aetna agreed to modify provider contract to omit gag clause after challenge by state Dept. of Ins.]; *Weiss v. CIGNA Healthcare Inc.*, 972 F. Supp. 748 (S.D.N.Y. 1997) [plan participant can sue plan for breach of fiduciary duty under ERISA for limiting extent participating physicians may discuss medical treatments with plan members].

87　Annotation, Recovery by patient on whom surgery or other treatment was performed by other than physician who patient believed would perform it, 39 A.L.R. 4th 1034.

88　E.g., *Johnson v. McMurray*, 461 So. 2d 775 (Ala. 1984).

89　*Hidding v. Williams*, 578 So. 2d 1192 (La. Ct. App. 1991).

90　*Domingo v. Doe*, 985 F. Supp. 1241 (D. Hawaii 1997).

91　*Albany Urology Clinic, P.C. v. Cleveland*, 272 Ga. 296, 528 S.E.2d 777 (2000).

92　*Schwaller v. Maguire*, 2003 Ohio 6917, 2003 Ohio App. LEXIS 6227.

93 E.g., *Faya v. Almarz*, 329 Md. 435, 620 A.2d 327 (1993) [HIV-infected surgeon could be liable for failing to inform patients, even when they did not get infected]; *Kerins v. Hartley*, 17 Cal. App. 4th 713, 21 Cal. Rptr. 2d 621 (2d Dist. 1993) [patient asked about surgeon's health and conditioned consent on operation by healthy surgeon, so could sue for battery when HIV-positive status not disclosed], transferred, 28 Cal. Rptr. 2d 151, 868 P.2d 906 (Cal. 1994), on transfer, 27 Cal. App. 4th 1062, 33 Cal. Rptr. 2d 172 (2d Dist, 1994) [statistically insignificant chance of HIV exposure during surgery by infected doctor precluded recovery for emotional distress from fear of AIDS].

94 *Majca v. Beekil*, 183 Ill. 2d 407, 701 N.E.2d 1084 (1998).

95 *Slutzki v. Grabenstetter*, 2002 Iowa App. LEXIS 1028.

96 *Johnson by Adler v. Kokemoor*, 199 Wis. 2d 615, 545 N.W.2d 495 (1996).

97 E.g., *Wachter v. United States*, 877 F.2d 257 (4th Cir. 1989).

98 *Bray v. Hill*, 517 N.W.2d 223 (Iowa Ct. App. 1994).

99 *Pegram v. Herdrich*, 530 U.S. 211 (2000).

100 *Moore v. Regents of Univ. of Cal.*, 51 Cal. 3d 120, 271 Cal. Rptr. 146, 793 P.2d 479 (1990), cert. denied, 499 U.S. 936 (1991).

101 *Howard v. University of Med. & Dentistry*, 172 N.J. 537, 800 A.2d 73 (2002)

102 Elkin N., How America searches: Health and wellness 2008, available at http://icrossing.com/research/how-america-searches-health-and-wellness.php. Additionally, Internet users living with a disability or chronic disease are more likely than other Internet users to be wide-ranging online health research and to report significant impacts from those searched. See "The Engaged E-Patient Population," Pew Internet & American Life Project (2008).

103 See D. Tuller, On rare diseases, parents take hope into their own hands, N.Y. Times, Nov. 17, 2003, 14 [support groups and the Internet]; L. Landro, Internet use for medical data shifts doctor-patient roles, Wall St. J., July 17, 2003, D3; G. Kolata, Web research transforms visit to the doctor, N.Y. Times, Mar. 6, 2000, A1.

104 See A. O'Connor, Finding of fact: Myth about lung cancer can be deadly, N.Y. Times, Oct. 7, 2003, D5 [some Americans refuse life-saving surgery believing that exposing lung cancer tumors spread when exposed to air; survey found 61% of Afro-Americans believed this; 19% cited this as the reason to reject surgery; and 14% said a doctor could not convince them otherwise].

105 *Geler v. Akawie*, 358 N.J. Super. 437, 818 A.2d 402 (App. Div. 2003).

106 See B. Weiss & C. Coyne, Communicating with patients who cannot read, 337 N. Eng. J. Med. 272 (July 24, 1997).

107 See L. Landro, Tips to better understand those doctor's orders, Wall St. J., July 3, 2003, D2 [health literacy program sponsored by Partnership for Clear Health Communication];

S.J. Landers, Low health literacy pervasive, Am. Med. News, Apr. 26, 2004, 23; Agency for Healthcare Research and Quality, Literacy and Health Outcomes (2004); Institute of Medicine, Health literacy: A Prescription to End Confusion.

108 See Executive Order 13166 (August 11, 2000) and DOJ Policy Guidance regarding Limited English Proficient (LEP) individuals (Apr. 12, 2002).

109 E.g., *Aikins v. St. Helena Hosp.*, 843 F. Supp. 1329 (N.D. Cal. 1994).

110 See Note 154, supra; see also *Ramirez v. Plough, Inc.*, 6 Cal. 4th 539, 25 Cal. Rptr. 2d 97, 863 P.2d 167 (1993) [drug manufacturer not liable for labeling nonprescription drug only in English in accordance with FDA regulations].

111 E.g., *Niklaus v. Bellina*, 696 So. 2d 120 (La. Ct. App. 1997) [extension of tumor removal to hysterectomy justified by emergency during surgery].

112 E.g., *Shinn v. St. James Mercy Hosp.*, 675 F. Supp. 94 (W.D. N.Y. 1987), aff'd without op., 847 F.2d 836 (2d Cir. 1988); *Crouch v. Most*, 78 N.M. 406, 432 P.2d 250 (1967).

113 E.g., *Schultz v. Rice*, 809 F.2d 643 (10th Cir. 1986); *Pardy v. United States*, 783 F.2d 710 (7th Cir. 1986).

114 *Lester v. Aetna Casualty & Sur. Co.*, 240 F.2d 676 (5th Cir.), cert. denied, 354 U.S. 923 (1957).

115 *Nishi v. Hartwell*, 52 Haw. 188, 296, 473 P.2d 116 (1970).

116 *Putenson v. Clay Adams, Inc.*, 12 Cal. App. 3d 1062, 91 Cal. Rptr. 319 (1st Dist. 1970).

117 E.g., *Nieves v. Montefiore Med. Ctr.*, 305 A.D.2d 161, 760 N.Y.S.2d 419 (1st Dept. 2003).

118 E.g., *Logan v. Greenwich Hosp. Ass'n*. 191 Conn. 282, 465 A.2d 294 (1983).

119 E.g., *O'Neal v. Hammer*, 87 Haw. 183, 953 P.2d 561 (1998); *Nieves v. Montefiore Med. Ctr.*, 305 A.D.2d 161, 760 N.Y.S.2d 419 (1st Dept. 2003).

120 E.g., *O'Neal v. Hammer*, supra.

121 E.g., *Bryant v. HCA Health Servs.*, 15 S.W.3d 804 (Tenn. 2000); *Espalin v. Children's Med. Ctr. of Dallas*, 27 S.W.3d 675 (Tex. App. 2000); *Pauscher v. Iowa Methodist Med. Ctr.*, 408 N.W.2d 355 (Iowa 1987); *Fiorentino v. Wenger*, 19 N.Y.2d 407, 280 N.Y.S.2d 373, 227 N.E.2d 296 (1967).

122 E.g., *Keel v. St. Elizabeth Med. Ctr.*, 842 S.W.2d 860 (Ky. 1992) [hospital liable for failing to disclose risks of CT scan with contrast since hospital performed procedure]; *Magana v. Elie*, 108 Ill. App. 3d 1028, 439 N.E.2d 1319 (2d Dist. 1982); *Creech v. Roberts*, 908 F.2d 75 (6th Cir. 1990), cert. denied, 499 U.S. 975 (1991) [hospital liable for physician's failure to obtain consent where patient had no prior relationship with physician].

123 E.g., *Urban v. Spohn Hosp.*, 869 S.W.2d 450 (Tex. Ct. App. 1993); *Schloendorff v. Society of N.Y. Hosp.*, 211 N.Y. 125, 105 N.E. 92 (1914).

124 *Mathias v. St. Catherine's Hosp., Inc.*, 212 Wis. 2d 540, 569 N.W.2d 330 (Ct. App. 1997).

125 2010 TJC.

126 E.g., *Anderson v. George H. Lanier Mem. Hosp.*, 982 F.2d 1513 (11th Cir. 1993).

127 *Ritter v. Delaney*, 790 S.W.2d 29 (Tex. Ct. App. 1990).

128 E.g., *Smoger v. Enke*, 874 F.2d 295 (5th Cir. 1989) [cardiologist may delegate disclosure of risks to laboratory technician].

129 E.g., *Graham v. Ryan*, 641 So. 2d 677 (La. Ct. App. 1994) [adult children of deceased surgery patient failed to rebut presumption of informed consent from written consent]; *Jones v. United States*, 720 F. Supp. 355 (S.D. N.Y. 1989) [documentation showed informed consent was obtained]; *Blincoe v. Luessenhop*, 669 F. Supp. 513 (D. D.C. 1987) [required disclosures made, documented in two consent forms].

130 But see *Mathias v. St. Catherine's Hosp., Inc.*, 212 Wis. 2d 540, 569 N.W.2d 330 (Ct. App. 1997) [no duty to intervene in the absence of consent form, surgeon's response that he had obtained consent sufficient].

131 *Jacovach v. Yocum*, 212 Iowa 914, 237 N.W. 444 (1931).

132 *Lipscomb v. Memorial Hosp.*, 733 F.2d 332 (4th Cir. 1984).

133 E.g., *Cross v. Trapp*, 170 W.Va. 459, 294 S.E.2d 446 (1982); *Rogers v. Lumbermen's Mut. Casualty Co.*, 119 So. 2d 649 (La. Ct. App. 1960).

134 E.g., *State Cent. Collection Unit v. Columbia Med. Plan*, 300 Md. 318, 478 A.2d 303 (1984) [valid assignment in registration form].

135 E.g., *Moser v. Stallings*, 387 N.W.2d 599 (Iowa 1986); *Mole v. Jutton*, 846 A. 2d. 1035 (2004).

136 E.g., *Blincoe v. Luessenhop*, 669 F. Supp. 513 (D. D.C. 1987).

137 E.g., *Barner v. Gorman*, 605 So. 2d 805 (Miss. 1992) [signed consent not specific to procedure insufficient to bar action]; *MacDonald v. United States*, 767 F. Supp. 1295 (M.D. Pa. 1991), award of damages, 781 F. Supp. 320, aff'd without op., 983 F.2d 1051 (3d Cir. 1992) [failure to obtain informed consent notwithstanding consent form – no risks or alternatives ever described to patient.

138 "Many sample hospital forms are available on the Internet, see http://www.rush.edu/Rush_Document/General%20Informed-Short_6_09.pdf for illustrative examples of such."

139 42 C.F.R. §§ 441.250–441.259 [sterilization]; 45 C.F.R. pt. 46 [research].

140 E.g., *Bedel v. University OB-GYN Assoc., Inc.*, 76 Ohio App. 3d 742, 603 N.E.2d 342 (1991).

141 See the discussion of the causation requirement in Section 6-8.2.

142 E.g., *Hondroulis v. Schumacher*, 531 So. 2d 450 (La. 1988) [statute establishes rebuttable presumption of consent], on remand, 612 So. 2d 859 (La. Ct. App. 1992) [judgment against physician affirmed].

143 Nev. Rev. Stat. § 41A.110; *Allan v. Levy*, 109 Nev. 46, 846 P.2d 274 (1993) [consent form did not meet requirement of state statute].

144 Iowa Code Ann. § 147.137.

145 2010 TJC, CAMH, Elements of Performance for RI.2.40.

146 2010 TJC CAMH, Elements of Performance for PC.13.50.

147 TJC, See http://www.jointcommission.org.

148 Electronic signatures are acceptable if allowed by state, federal, and reimbursement regulations. In 2000 the U.S. government passed the Electronic Signatures in Global National Commerce Act, which gives electronic signatures the same legality as handwritten signatures for interstate commerce. State regulations and payer policies must be reviewed to ensure acceptability of electronic signatures when developing healthcare organization policies. Electronic signature software binds a signature or other mark to a specific electronic document. It requires user authentication such as a unique code, biometric, or password that verifies the identity of the signer in the system.

149 E.g., *Kratt v. Morrow*, 455 Pa. Super. 140, 687 A.2d 830 (1996) [preoperative fall created jury question whether there were new risks that should have been disclosed for an additional consent].

150 E.g., *Busalacchi v. Vogel*, 429 So. 2d 217 (La. Ct. App. 1983).

151 *Foard v. Jarman*, 326 N.C. 24, 387 S.E.2d 162 (1990) [informed consent claim barred by admission of reading, understanding pamphlet]; see also G. Borzo, CIGNA gives new life to patient empowerment initiative, Am. Med. News, Sept. 19, 1994, 1 [sent outcome-based videotapes to patients to educate about treatment options].

152 E.g., *Hanson v. Parkside Surgery Ctr.*, 872 F.2d 745 (6th Cir.), cert. denied, 493 U.S. 944 (1989) [claim permitted despite videotape, but jury found for defendant physician].

153 W. Wolfe, She fought to return home, and won; Josephine Bronczyk, right, wants a court ruling to protect others from being sent to nursing homes too soon, Star Tribune (Minneapolis, MN), Dec. 9, 2002, 1A ; W. Wolfe, Woman can't replace plaintiff who died, Star Tribune (Minneapolis, MN), Feb. 20, 2003, 3B.

154 E.g., *Cruzan v. Director, Mo. Dep't of Health*, 497 U.S. 261 (1990) [federal constitutional rights]; In re Quinlan, 348 A.2d. 801 (1975), *modified and remanded* 355 A.2d. 647 (1976); In re Shiavo, 780 S.2d. 176, *review denied* 789 So.2d. 348 (Fla 2001); Annotation, Living wills: Validity, construction, and effect, 49 A.L.R. 4th 812 [statutory rights].

155 Although the Supreme Court of Georgia recently struck down a 1994 law which banned people from publicly advertising suicide, holding that such violated free speech rights. *Final Exit Network, Inc., v. State*, Supreme Court of Georgia (decided February 6, 2012). However, the Court found that lawmakers could have imposed a ban on all assisted suicides with no restriction on free speech or sought to prohibit all others to assist in suicides that were followed by the act, but chose not to do either, thus leaving the door open for state lawmakers to explicitly outlaw assisted suicides.

156 *Vacco v. Quill*, 521 U.S. 793 (1997); *Washington v. Glucksberg*, 521 U.S. 702 (1997).

157 E.g., *Krischer v. McIver*, 697 So. 2d 97 (Fla. 1997).

158 Ore. Rev. Stat. §§ 127.800-127.897; *Lee v. State*, 869 F. Supp. 1491 (D. Or. 1994), 891 F Supp. 1429 (D. Or. 1995) [injunction], vacated, 107 F.3d 1382 (9th Cir. 1997), cert. denied subnom, *Lee v. Harcleroad*, 522 U.S. 927 (1997); *Gallant v. Board of Medical Examiners*, 159 Ore. App. 175, 974 P.2d 814 (1999); 66 Fed. Reg. 56607 (2001); *Oregon v. Ashcroft*, 192 F. Supp. 2d 1077 (D. Ore. 2002), aff'd, 368 F.3d 1118 (9th Cir. 2004, cert. granted, 125 S. Ct. 1299 (U.S. 2005).

159 See Chapter 70.245 RCW, which went into effect in March 2009. Allows terminally ill adults (with less than six months to live) seeking to end their life to request lethal doses of medication from physicians; see also Washington State Hospital Association website, http://www.wsha.org.

160 *Baxter v. State of Montana*, 354 Mont. 234 (2009). Although a physician who causes or assists another person's suicide is still subject to civil and criminal liability, the Baxter Court's ruling allows a possible consent defense, dependent upon the unique facts of the particular case. The original lawsuit was brought by four Montana physicians, Compassion & Choices, and a 76-year-old truck driver dying from lymphocytic leukemia. The plaintiffs had asked the court to establish a constitutional right "to receive and provide aid in dying." Montana's 1st Judicial District Court ruled in favor of the plaintiffs (December 5, 2008) finding that "constitutional rights of individual privacy and human dignity, taken together, encompass the right of a competent terminally-ill patient to die with dignity." The Montana Attorney General appealed the case to the state supreme court and oral arguments were heard on September 2, 2009. Amicus briefs filed on behalf of those in support of such a constitutional right included human rights groups, women's rights groups, the American Medical Women's Association, American Medical Students Association, thirty-one Montana state legislators, bioethicists, among others. The Montana Medical Association issued a statement opposing physician-assisted suicide, but refused to file an amicus brief in the appeal.

161 *People v. Kevorkian*, 205 Mich. App. 180, 517 N.W.2d 293 (1994), vacated & remanded, 447 Mich. 436, 527 N.W.2d 714 (1994), cert. denied, 514 U.S. 1083 (1995) [Kevorkian administered the lethal injection to Thomas Youk, 52, and videotaped the death. The video was shown two months later on CBS *60 Minutes*]; see also Schneider, Keith, Dr. Jack Kevorkian Dies at 83; A Doctor Who Helped End Lives, The New York Times (June 3, 2011).

162 E.g., *Gramm v. Boener*, 56 Ind. 497 (1877).

163 *United States v. Rutherford*, 442 U.S. 544 (1979).

164 *Trustees of the Northwest Laundry & Dry Cleaners Health & Welfare Trust Fund v. Burzynski*, 27 F.3d 153 (5th Cir. 1994), cert. denied, 513 U.S. 1155 (1995).

165 E.g., J.R. Curtis, et al., Use of the medical futility rationale in do-not-attempt-resuscitation orders, 273 J.A.M.A. 124 (1995); A. Alpers & B. Lo, When is CPR futile? 273 J.A.M.A. 156 (1995); R.D. Truog et al., The problem with futility, 326 N. Eng. J. Med. 1560 (1992).

166 Judge rejects request by doctors to remove a patient's respirator, N.Y. Times, July 2, 1991, A13 [Helga Wanglie]; Brain-damaged woman at center of lawsuit over life-support dies, N.Y. Times, July 6, 1991, 8; Helga Wanglie's ventilator, Hastings Center Rpt. (July-Aug. 1991), at 23.

167 L. Kowalczyk, Judge rules Mass. General can't end life support for Lou Gehrig's disease patient, Boston Globe, Mar. 24, 2004, C3.

168 E.g., Shaken baby taken off life support, AP, Dec. 12, 2002 [Guardian appointed and Ohio court approved guardian's recommendation]; Abused baby dies after court ends life support, AP Nov. 10, 1998 [Wisconsin]; but see In re Guardianship of Stein, 157 Ohio App. 3d 417, 2004 Ohio 2948, 811 N.E.2d 594 (2004) [upholding decision to appointing guardian with authority to withdraw treatment], stay granted, 102 Ohio St. 3d 1475, 2004 Ohio 2995, 810 N.E.2d 441 (2004), rev'd, 105 Ohio St. 3d 30, 2004 Ohio 7114, 821 N.E.2d 1008 [court must terminate parental rights before it can let guardian withdraw life support].

169 E.g., In re Christopher I., 106 Cal. App. 4th 533, 131 Cal. Rptr. 2d 122 (4th Dist. 2003) [affirming order to withdraw treatment from abused child. Reject appeal of perpetrator father]; see also R. Chase, Woman's agonizing decision leaves baby dead, husband charged with murder, AP, Nov. 15, 2001.

170 E.g., Boy in 2-1/2-year coma dies after respirator stopped, N.Y. Times, June 25, 1990, A11 [parents refused termination in fear mother would face murder charge; when hospital announced plans to sue, father agreed to termination].

171 *Gilgunn v. Massachusetts Gen. Hosp.*, No. 92-4820-H (Mass. Super. Ct. Suffolk County jury decision Apr. 21, 1995), as discussed in 4 H.L.R. 698 (1995).

172 *Wendland v. Sparks*, 574 N.W.2d 327 (Iowa 1998).

173 *Dent v. West Virginia*, 129 U.S. 114 (1889).

174 *Beck v. McLeod*, 382 U.S. 454 (1966).

175 *Lange-Kessler v. Department of Educ. of N.Y.*, 109 F.3d 137 (2d Cir. 1997).

176 E.g., *Rutherford v. American Medical Ass'n*, 379 F.2d 641, 1967 U.S. App. LEXIS 5870 (7th Cir.), cert. denied, 389 U.S. 1043 (1967).

177 *Conant v. Walters*, 309 F.3d 629 (9th Cir. 2002), cert. denied, 540 U.S. 946 (2003).

178 See http://medicalmarijuana.procon.org for further details. States effected: AK, AZ, CA, CO, DC, DE, HI, MA, MI, MT, NE, NJ, NM, OR, RI, VT, WA. States vary widely regarding residency requirements, limitations, and patient registration requirements.

179 E.g., *Brophy v. New Engl. Sinai Hosp., Inc.*, 398 Mass. 417, 497 N.E.2d 626 (1986); In re Tavel, 661 A.2d 1061 (Del. 1995).

180 *Cruzan v. Harmon*, 760 S.W.2d 408 (Mo. 1988) (en banc), aff'd on other grounds, *Cruzan v. Director, Mo. Dep't of Health*, 497 U.S. 261 (1990).

181 American Medical Association, Council on Ethical and Judicial Affairs, Withholding or Withdrawing Life-Prolonging Medical Treatment (Mar. 15, 1986), quoted in *Corbett v. D'Alessandro*, 487 So. 2d 368, 371, n.1 (Fla. 2d DCA 1986).

182   E.g., *Bouvia v. Superior Court*, 179 Cal. App. 3d 1127, 225 Cal. Rptr. 297 (2d Dist. 1986); Application of Plaza Health & Rehab. Ctr. (N.Y. Sup. Ct. Onondaga County Feb. 2, 1984); N.Y. Times (Feb. 3, 1984), at A1 [describing Plaza case]; Williams, Michigan quadriplegic earns right to die, Am. Med. News, Aug. 4, 1989, 3.

183   E.g., In re Guardianship of Grant, 109 Wash. 2d 545, 747 P.2d 445 (1987), corrected, 757 P.2d 534 (Wash. 1988).

184   E.g., *Brophy v. New Engl. Sinai Hosp., Inc.*, 398 Mass. 417, 497 N.E.2d 626 (1986).

185   *Barber v. Superior Court*, 147 Cal. App. 3d 1006, 195 Cal. Rptr. 484 (2d Dist. 1984).

186   E.g., In re Guardianship of Pescinski, 67 Wis. 2d 4, 266 N.W.2d 180 (1975) [incompetent adult]; see Annotation, Propriety of surgically invading incompetent or minor for benefit of third party, 4 A.L.R. 5th 1000.

187   E.g., *Strunk v. Strunk*, 445 S.W.2d 145 (Ky. 1969) [incompetent adult]; *Hart v. Brown*, 29 Conn. Supp. 368, 289 A.2d 386 (Super. Ct. 1972) [minor].

188   E.g., In re Doe, 104 A.D.2d 200, 481 N.Y.S.2d 932 (4th Dept. 1984).

189   E.g., *John F. Kennedy Mem. Hosp. v. Bludworth*, 452 So. 2d 921 (Fla. 1984).

190   E.g., *Cruzan v. Harmon*, 760 S.W.2d 408 (Mo. 1988) (en banc), aff'd, 497 U.S. 261 (1990).

191   In re Storar, 52 N.Y.2d 363, 438 N.Y.S.2d 266, 420 N.E.2d 64, cert. denied, 454 U.S. 858 (1981); *Blouin v. Spitzer*, 213 F. Supp. 2d 184 (N.D. N.Y. 2002) [dismiss suit against NY attorney general for challenging case where court authorized withdrawal of hydration at family direction]; Matter of Christopher, 177 Misc. 2d 352, 675 N.Y.S.2d 807 (Sup. Ct. 1998) [refuse to allow feeding tube over son's objections].

192   E.g., *John F. Kennedy Mem. Hosp. v. Bludworth*, 452 So. 2d 921 (Fla. 1984); In re Quinlan, 70 N.J. 10, 355 A.2d 647 (1976), cert. denied, 429 U.S. 922 (1976).

193   E.g., Fla. Stat. § 765.07.

194   E.g., Survival predictions found imprecise for hospice patients, Am. Med. News, Dec. 9, 1988, 40 [predictions tend to be overly optimistic].

195   E.g., In re Spring, 380 Mass. 629, 405 N.E.2d 115, 118 (1980) [five years].

196   E.g., Wanzer et al., The physician's responsibility toward hopelessly ill patients, 310 N. Eng. J. Med. 955 (1984); Grenvik et al., Cessation of therapy in terminal illness and brain death, 6 Critical Care Med. 284 (1978); Optimal care for hopelessly ill patients, 295 N. Eng. J. Med. 362 (1976).

197   E.g., In re Guardianship of Conroy, 98 N.J. 321, 486 A.2d 1209 (1985); In re Guardianship of Browning, 568 So. 2d 4 (Fla. 1990).

198   Conservatorship of Wendland, 26 Cal. 4th 519, 28 P.3d 151, 110 Cal. Rptr. 2d 412 (2001).

199   E.g., *Grecco v. University of Med. & Dentistry*, 345 N.J. Super. 94, 783 A.2d 741 (App. Div. 2001) [parents have immunity for negligent exercise of parental authority or provision of customary child care unless their behavior is willful and wanton; refusal of a liver transplant was not willful and wanton].

200   E.g., *Ball v. Hamilton County Emergency Med. Servs.*, 1999 Tenn. App. LEXIS 149 [emergency team has no duty to transport to hospital child who appears healthy when mother signs service refusal, so no liability for child's death when breathing problems recurred].

201   E.g., In re L.H.R., 253 Ga. 439, 321 S.E.2d 716 (1984); In re Guardianship of Barry, 445 So. 2d 365 (Fla. 2d DCA 1984), approved, *John F. Kennedy Mem. Hosp. v. Bludworth*, 452 So. 2d 921 (Fla. 1984).

202   Custody of a Minor, 385 Mass. 697, 434 N.E.2d 601 (1982).

203   In re Rosebush, 195 Mich. App. 675, 491 N.W.2d 633 (1992).

204   *Newmark v. Williams/DCPS*, 588 A.2d 1108, 1118 (Del. 1991).

205   In re Nickolas E., 720 A.2d 562, 1998 ME 243; Woman wins the right to deny son AIDS drug, N.Y. Times, Sept. 15, 1998, A20; Mother wins right to stop H.I.V. drugs for her son, 4, N.Y. Times, Sept. 20, 1998, 17.

206   *Bendiburg v. Dempsey*, 19 F.3d 557 (11th Cir. 1994).

207   *Bendiburg v. Dempsey*, 909 F.2d 463 (11th Cir. 1990), cert. denied, 500 U.S. 932 (1991); but see, *Novak v. Cobb County-Kennestone Hosp. Auth.*, 849 F. Supp. 1559 (N.D. Ga. 1994) [Bendiburg does not mean that ex parte orders are invalid in bona fide emergencies].

208   P. Foy, Jensens surrender to state authorities on kidnapping charges, AP, Sept. 10, 2003; P. Foy, Bill would block state from interfering in "competent" parents' medical decisions, AP, Oct. 1, 2003; P. Foy, Parents who fled with son over chemotherapy order face medical neglect trial, AP, Oct. 8, 2003; P. Foy, Utah drops case against parents who refused to give son chemotherapy, AP, Oct. 23, 2003.

209   E.g., K. Auge, Mom sentenced to six years in death of diabetic son, Denver Post, July 17, 1999 B3 [did not provide insulin].

210   E.g., *Martineau v. Angelone*, 25 F.3d 734 (9th Cir. 1994) [in habeas corpus action court found insufficient evidence to support convictions for child abuse for delay in seeking medical attention; state court had affirmed convictions, *King v. State*, 105 Nev. 373, 784 P.2d 942 (1989)].

211   E.g., Lantos et al., Survival after cardiopulmonary resuscitation in babies of very low birth weight. Is CPR futile therapy? 318 N. Eng. J. Med. 91 (1988).

212   E.g., In re Guardianship of Barry, 445 So. 2d 365 (Fla. 2d DCA 1984), approved, *John F. Kennedy Mem. Hosp. v. Bludworth*, 452 So. 2d 921 (Fla. 1984) [approval of termination of ventilator support of infant who had only minimal brain stem function; court review not required when diagnosis confirmed by two physicians]; In re Baby "K," 16 F.3d 590 (4th Cir.), cert. denied, 513 U.S. 825 (1994) [treatment for anencephalic baby after emergency admission required until parents agreed to termination].

213 In re Cicero, 101 Misc. 2d 699, 421 N.Y.S.2d 965 (Sup. Ct. 1979); but see *Johnson v. Thompson*, 971 F.2d 1487 (10th Cir. 1992), cert. denied, 507 U.S. 910 (1993) [no cause of action stated under Rehabilitation Act for treatment of infant with myelomeningocele].

214 HHS letter reprinted in Hastings Center Rpt. (Aug. 1982), at 6.

215 In re Infant Doe, No. GU 8204-00 (Ind. Cir. Ct. Monroe County Apr. 12, 1982), writ of mandamus dismissed sub nom. State ex rel. *Infant Doe v. Baker*, No. 482 S 140 (Ind. May 27, 1982). For a description of the medical status of Infant Doe, see 309 N. Eng. J. Med. 664 (1983). The records of the case are not public records, *Marzen v. Department of HHS*, 825 F.2d 1148 (7th Cir. 1987).

216 48 Fed. Reg. 9630 (Mar. 7, 1983).

217 *American Acad. of Pediatrics v. Heckler*, 561 F. Supp. 395 (D. D.C. 1983).

218 E.g., President's Commission for the Study of Ethical Problems in Medicine and Biomedical and Behavioral Research, Deciding to Forgo Life-Sustaining Treatment 227 (Mar. 1983).

219 49 Fed. Reg. 1622 (Jan. 12, 1984).

220 *Bowen v. American Hosp. Ass'n*, 476 U.S. 610 (1986).

221 *Weber v. Stony Brook Hosp.*, 60 N.Y.2d 208, 469 N.Y.S.2d 63, 456 N.E.2d 1186, cert. denied, 464 U.S. 1026 (1983); parents later authorized limited surgery, N.Y. Times, Apr. 12, 1984, 12.

222 *United States v. University Hosp.*, 729 F.2d 144 (2d Cir. 1984).

223 Child Abuse Amendments of 1984, Pub. L. No. 98-457, 98 Stat. 1753.

224 50 Fed. Reg. 14,878 (Apr. 15, 1985); see Kopelman et al., Neonatologists judge the "Baby Doe" regulations, 318 N. Eng. J. Med. 677 (1988).

225 E.g., *Hillsborough County Hosp. Auth. v. Muller*, No.88-1073 (Fla. Cir. Ct. 13th Cir. Feb. 9, 1988) [ventilator removal authorized for semi-comatose infant]; In re Steinhaus, No.J-8692 (Minn. Dist. Ct. Redwood County Oct. 13, 1986) [treatment removal authorized for comatose infant], as discussed in Am. Med. News, Oct. 24/31, 1986, 1

226 E.g., *Fox v. Smith*, 594 So. 2d 596 (Miss. 1992); *Mullany v. Eiseman*, 125 A.D.2d 457, 509 N.Y.S.2d 387 (2d Dept. 1986); see also *Cook v. Highland Hosp.*, 168 N.C. 250, 84 S.E. 352 (1915) [patient did not waive right to change his mind by signing agreement to abide by hospital rules, so free to leave].

227 *Coulter v. Thomas*, 33 S.W.3d 522 (Ky. 2000).

228 *Even v. Bohle*, 2002 Iowa App. LEXIS 1256.

229 *Roe II v. Aware Woman Ctr.*, 357 F.3d 1226 (11th Cir. 2004).

230 See Annotation, Power of courts or other public agencies, in the absence of statutory authority, to order compulsory medical care for adult, 9 A.L.R. 3d 1391.

231 *Jacobson v. Massachusetts*, 197 U.S. 11 (1905).

232 *Reynolds v. McNichols*, 488 F.2d 1378 (10th Cir. 1973); see also *Love v. Superior Court*, 226 Cal. App. 3d 736, 276 Cal. Rptr. 660 (1st Dist. 1990) [upholding HIV testing of prostitutes]; but see *Hill v. Evans*, 1993 U.S. Dist. LEXIS 19878 (M.D. Ala.)

[state law allowing physician to test patient for AIDS without consent when physician thinks patient at risk violates equal protection, but other exceptions to consent upheld where necessary to protect other health workers or may be necessary to change treatment].

233 *Zaire v. Dalsheim*, 698 F. Supp. 57 (S.D. N.Y. 1988), aff'd without op., 904 F.2d 33 (2d Cir. 1990).

234 See The Model State Emergency Health Powers Act, drafted by The Center for Law and the Public's Health, at http://www .publichealthlaw.net/Resources/Modellaws.htm

235 See D. Beveridge, Hong Kong will move SARS victims from apartment block to quarantine camps; Quarantine set in Beijing areas to fight SARS, N.Y. Times, Apr. 25, 2003, A1; Toronto hospitals hunker down for possible new SARS outbreak, AP Worldstream, May 24, 2003.

236 Shear, Michael D, Stein, Rob "President Obama declares H1N1 flu a national emergency" Washington Post (October 24, 2009).

237 E.g., *Addington v. Texas*, 441 U.S. 418 (1979) [mental illness must be proved by clear, convincing evidence]; *Glass v. Mayas*, 984 F.2d 55 (2d Cir. 1993) [qualified immunity for doctors, nurses in 42 U.S.C.A. § 1983 challenge to involuntary commitment; objectively reasonable belief in dangerousness]; In re Blodgett, 510 N.W.2d 910 (Minn.), cert. denied, 513 U.S. 849 (1994) [state may authorize commitment of persons with "psychopathic personality" even if not medically recognized as "mentally ill"].

238 E.g., *Dudley v. State*, 730 S.W.2d 51 (Tex. Ct. App. 1987) [involuntary alcoholism treatment].

239 *O'Connor v. Donaldson*, 422 U.S. 563 (1975).

240 *Kansas v. Hendricks*, 521 U.S. 346 (1997).

241 E.g., *Estate of Phillips v. Milwaukee*, 123 F.3d 586 (7th Cir. 1997) [affirming summary judgment for defendants, individual died as result of police force used to remove him from hotel room after strange, disorderly behavior, force used was objectively reasonable response to escalating situation]; *S.P. v. City of Takoma Park*, 950 F. Supp. 705 (D. Md. 1997) [police involuntarily transported, detained person for psychiatric evaluation; summary judgment for defendant city, "reason to believe" imminent danger sufficient]; see also *McCabe v. Life-Line Ambulance Serv., Inc.*, 77 F.3d 540 (1st Cir. 1996), cert. denied, 519 U.S. 911 (1996) [city policy permitting forcible, warrantless entries into private residences to enforce involuntary civil commitment order does not violate Fourth Amendment].

242 *Parham v. J.L. & J.R.*, 442 U.S. 640 (1979); *Secretary of Public Welfare v. Institutionalized Juveniles*, 442 U.S. 640 (1979).

243 E.g., In re B., 609 P.2d 747 (Okla. 1980); State ex rel. *Jones v. Gerhardstein*, 141 Wis. 2d 710, 416 N.W.2d 883 (1987).

244 E.g., Iowa Code Ann. § 229.1(2).

245 E.g., *Jarvis v. Levine*, 418 N.W.2d 139 (Minn. 1988); In re Guardianship of Roe, 383 Mass. 415, 421 N.E.2d 40 (1981); *Rogers v. Commissioner of Dep't of Mental Health*, 390 Mass. 489, 458 N.E.2d 308 (1983); contra *United States v. Charters*, 863 F.2d 302 (4th Cir. 1988), cert. denied, 494 U.S. 1016 (1990).

246 E.g., *Boles v. Milwaukee County*, 150 Wis. 2d 801, 443 N.W.2d 679 (1989).

247 See D. Ridley, Treatment refusals by pregnant women, Hosp. L. Newsletter (July 1998), at 1.

248 *Jefferson v. Griffin Spalding County Hosp. Auth.*, 247 Ga. 86, 274 S.E.2d 457 (1981); see also L. J. Nelson & N. Mulliken, Compelled medical treatment of pregnant women: Life, liberty, and law in conflict, 259 J.A.M.A. 1060 (1988).

249 *Pemberton v Tallahassee Mem. Hosp. Med. Ctr.*, 66 F. Supp. 2d 1247 (N.D. Fla. 1999).

250 *Baby Boy Doe v. Mother Doe*, 260 Ill. App. 3d 392, 632 N.E.2d 326 (1st Dist. Dec. 14, 1993 with formal opinion Apr. 5, 1994) [mentally competent pregnant woman has right to refuse cesarean operation even if refusal will harm her child], cert. denied, 510 U.S. 1168 (1994); Illinois is seeking to force woman to have caesarean, N.Y. Times, Dec. 14, 1993, A11; Baby whose mother refused C-section appears healthy, Miami Herald [FL], Dec. 31, 1993, 6A.

251 State ex rel. *Angela M.W. v. Kruzicki*, 209 Wis. 2d 112, 561 N.W.2d 729 (1997); accord, *Winnipeg Child & Family Servs. v. G.(D.F.)*, [1997] 3 S.C.R. 925 [cannot detain mother to prevent harm to unborn child], but see *State v. Whitner*, 328 S.C. 1, 492 S.E.2d 777 (1997) [affirming criminal neglect conviction of mother for causing baby to be born with cocaine metabolites in its system due to her use of crack cocaine during her pregnancy].

252 Wis. Stat. §§ 48.193, 48.203, 48.205, 48.213, 48.345, 48.347; S.B. Lalwani, Pregnant painkiller addict released; She was held under law meant to protect fetus, Milwaukee [Wis.] Journal Sentinel, May 25, 2005, 6.

253 A mother loses life so twins can be born, N.Y. Times, Feb. 13, 1995, A14.

254 See Propriety of surgically invading incompetent or minor for benefit of third party, 4 A.L.R. 5th 1000.

255 *Bosze v. Curran*, No. 87 M1 4599 (Ill. Cir. Ct. Cook County July 18, 1990), as discussed in 23 J. Health & Hosp. L. 282 (1990).

256 *Curran v. Bosze*, No. 70501 (Ill. Aug. 10, 1990), as discussed in 23 J. Health & Hosp. L. 282 (1990).

257 *Curran v. Bosze*, 141 Ill. 2d 473, 566 N.E.2d 1319 (1990); P. Hughes & R. Wood, Comment: *Curran v. Bosze*; Disposing of an incompetent donor consent case: The role of parental autonomy and bodily integrity, 24 J. Health & Hosp. L. 88 (1991).

258 *Public Health Trust v. Wons*, 541 So. 2d 96 (Fla. 1989).

259 In re Dubreuil, 629 So. 2d 819 (Fla. 1993).

260 See Annotation, Admissibility, in criminal case, of physical evidence obtained without consent by surgical removal from person's body, 41 A.L.R. 4th 60.

261 *Rochin v. California*, 342 U.S. 165 (1951).

262 *Breithaupt v. Adams*, 352 U.S. 432 (1957).

263 *Schmerber v. California*, 384 U.S. 757 (1966); *Graham v. Connor*, 490 U.S. 386 (1989) [force seizing person must meet "objectively reasonable" standard]; see also *Hammer v. Gross*, 932 F.2d 842 (9th Cir.), cert. denied, 502 U.S. 980 (1991) [forcible blood sample from suspect in DUI case not objectively reasonable; city liable but individuals escaped liability because standard not clear at time]; *Nelson v. City of Irvine*, 143 F.3d 1196 (9th Cir. 1998) [compelled blood test of suspected drunken driver after consent to breath or urine test violates Fourth Amendment].

264 *Ferguson v. City of Charleston*, 532 U.S. 67 (2001).

265 *Winston v. Lee*, 470 U.S. 753 (1985); see also *People v. Richard*, 145 Misc. 2d 755, 548 N.Y.S.2d 369 (1989) [denial of order to surgically remove bullet].

266 In re Brown, 478 So. 2d 1033 (Miss. 1985).

267 *United States v. Montoya de Hernandez*, 473 U.S. 531 (1985) [particularized, objective basis for suspecting alimentary canal smuggling justifies detention at border for observation]; *Velez v. United States*, 693 F. Supp. 51 (S.D. N.Y. 1988) [X-rays justified, but false imprisonment to delay review by qualified radiologist who would have determined not smuggling].

268 E.g., *C.S. v. Manning*, 713 So. 2d 1026 (Fla. 3d DCA 1998) [taking woman into custody to assure appearance at psychology examination unjustified].

269 *Syring v. Tucker*, 174 Wis. 2d 787, 498 N.W.2d 370 (1993).

270 *Commissioner of Corrections v. Myers*, 379 Mass. 255, 399 N.E.2d 452 (1979).

271 E.g., *Walker v. Shansky*, 28 F.3d 666 (7th Cir. 1994) [cruel, unusual punishment claim stated against officials for forced injections of tranquilizing drugs in prisoners]; but see *Doe v. Dyett*, 1993 U.S. Dist. LEXIS 13,450 (S.D. N.Y.) [not constitutional violation to give involuntary antipsychotic drugs to prisoner in emergency situation where safety of inmate or others threatened].

272 *Sparks v. Stutler*, 71 F.3d 259 (7th Cir. 1995).

273 E.g., *Commonwealth, Dep't of Public Welfare v. Kallinger*, 134 Pa. Commw. 415, 580 A.2d 887 (1990) [forced feeding ordered]; contra, *Thor v. Superior Ct.*, 5 Cal. 4th 725, 21 Cal. Rptr. 2d 357, 855 P.2d 375 (1993) [inmate can refuse life-sustaining treatment; deny application by prison physician to force feed irreversible quadriplegic inmate where no showing it would undermine prison security]; *Zant v. Prevatte*, 248 Ga. 832, 286 S.E.2d 715 (1982); Ethiopian imprisoned in Arizona dies following a hunger strike, N.Y. Times, Jan. 5, 1998, A11 [court had denied order to force feed].

274 E.g., Marine pilot dismissed, jailed for refusing anthrax vaccination, AP, July 8, 2003.

275 Can't compel operation, N.Y. Times, Dec. 16, 1917, 8.

276 In re Quinlan, 70 N.J. 10, 355 A.2d 647 (1976).

277 *Superintendent of Belchertown State School v. Saikewicz*, 373 Mass. 728, 370 N.E.2d 417, 426 (1977).

278 E.g., *Public Health Trust v. Wons*, 541 So. 2d 96 (1989); In re Brooks Estate, 32 Ill. 2d 361, 205 N.E.2d 435 (1965).

279 E.g., *Lane v. Candura*, 6 Mass. App. Ct. 377, 376 N.E.2d 1232 (1978).

280 E.g., In re Farrell, 108 N.J. 335, 529 A.2d 404 (1987) [respirator]; *Bouvia v. Superior Court*, 179 Cal. App. 3d 1127, 225 Cal. Rptr. 297 (2d Dist. 1986) [tube feeding]; see also *Commonwealth v. Konz*, 498 Pa. 639, 450 A.2d 638 (1982) [no duty to intervene when competent diabetic husband discontinued insulin].

281 E.g., *Cruzan v. Harmon*, 760 S.W.2d 408 (Mo. 1988) (en banc), aff'd on other grounds, 497 U.S. 261 (1990).

282 In re Dell, 1 D. & C. 3d 655 (Pa. Cm. Pl. Ct. Allegheny County 1975).

283 *Bouvia v. Superior Court*, 179 Cal. App. 3d 1127, 225 Cal. Rptr. 297 (2d Dist. 1986).

284 N. Laughlin & L. Benet, Dying woman can refuse help, court says, Miami [FL] Herald, Oct. 23, 1984, 1A; Judge rules for woman who attempted suicide, N.Y. Times, Oct. 24, 1984, A16.

285 E.g., *Warthen v. Toms River Comm. Mem. Hosp.*, 199 N.J. Super. 18, 488 A.2d 229 (App. Div. 1985) [upholding termination of nurse who refused to dialyze a seriously ill patient due to moral objections].

286 E.g., *Gray v. Romeo*, 697 F. Supp. 580 (D. R.I. 1988); see also Miles et al., Conflicts between patients' wishes to forgo treatment and the policies of healthcare facilities, 321 N. Eng. J. Med. 48 (1989).

287 E.g., *Bouvia v. Superior Court*, 179 Cal. App. 3d 1127, 225 Cal. Rptr. 297 (2d Dist. 1986).

288 E.g., In re Rodas, No. 86PR139 (Colo. Dist. Ct. Mesa County Jan. 22, 1987), damages denied, *Ross v. Hilltop Rehabilitation Hosp.*, 676 F. Supp. 1528 (D. Colo. 1987).

289 E.g., In re Requena, 213 N.J. Super. 443, 517 A.2d 869 (App. Div. 1986).

290 E.g., *Szkorla v. Vecchione*, 231 Cal. App. 3d 1541, 283 Cal. Rptr. 219 (4th Dist. 1991), rev. dismissed, 13 Cal. Rptr. 2d 53, 838 P.2d 781 (Cal. 1992) [subcutaneous mastectomy performed instead of breast reduction].

291 *Lugenbuhl v. Dowling*, 701 So. 2d 447 (La. 1997).

292 *Dauven v. St. Vincent Hosp. & Med. Center*, 130 Or. App. 584, 883 P.2d 241 (1994).

293 E.g., *Ross v. Hilltop Rehabilitation Hosp.*, 676 F. Supp. 1528 (D. Colo. 1987); *Westhart v. Mule*, 213 Cal. App. 3d 542, 261 Cal. Rptr. 640 (4th Dist. 1989), rev. denied & op. withdrawn, 1989 Cal. LEXIS 4990 (Nov. 22, 1989) [not citable in Cal.] [dismissal of suit arising from insertion of feeding tube contrary to wife's directions; she never asked to have tube removed]; *Bartling v. Glendale Adventist Med. Ctr.*, 184 Cal. App. 3d 961, 229 Cal. Rptr. 360 (2d Dist. 1986) [refusal to find intentional infliction of emotional injuries]; see also *Benoy v. Simons*, 66 Wash. App. 56, 831 P.2d 167, rev. denied,

120 Wash. 2d 1014, 844 P.2d 435 (1992) [family challenged putting child on respirator without consent, but did not claim refusal; refusal to recognize wrongful prolongation of life as cause of action; refusal to find intentional infliction of emotional injuries].

294 *Anderson v. Saint Francis-Saint George Hosp.*, 83 Ohio App. 3d 221, 614 N.E.2d 841 (1992), rev. denied, 66 Ohio St. 3d 1459, 610 N.E.2d 423.

295 *Anderson v. Saint Francis-Saint George Hosp.*, 77 Ohio St. 3d 82, 671 N.E.2d 225 (1996), rev'g, 1995 Ohio App. LEXIS 911.

296 *First HealthCare Corp. v. Rettinger*, 342 N.C. 886, 467 S.E.2d 243 (1996), rev'g, 118 N.C. App. 600, 456 S.E.2d 347 (1995).

297 *Stolle v. Baylor College of Med.*, 981 S.W.2d 709 (Tex. Ct. App. 1998).

298 *Miller v. Woman's Hosp. of Tex.*, No. 92-07830 (Tex. Dist. Ct. Jan. 14, 1998), as discussed in 7 H.L.R. 183 (1998).

299 *Miller v. HCA. Inc.*, 118 S.W.3d 758 (Tex. 2003).

300 *Duarte v. Chino Comm. Hosp.*, 72 Cal. App. 4th 849, 85 Cal. Rptr. 2d 521 (4th Dist. 1999).

301 *Mulloy v. Hop Sang*, [1935] 1 W.W.R. 714 (Alta. C.A.).

302 *Bendiburg v. Dempsey*, 909 F.2d 463 (11th Cir. 1990), cert. denied, 500 U.S. 932 (1991).

303 *Bendiburg v. Dempsey*, 19 F.3d 557 (11th Cir. 1994).

304 *Gragg v. Calandra*, 297 Ill. App. 3d 639, 696 N.E.2d 1282 (2d Dist. 1998), app. denied, 181 Ill. 2d 570, 706 N.E.2d 496 (1998).

305 *Shine v. Vega*, 429 Mass. 456, 709 N.E.2d 58 (1999).

306 *Grace Plaza v. Elbaum*, 82 N.Y.2d 10, 603 N.Y.S.2d 386, 623 N.E.2d 513 (1993); G.J. Annas, Adding injustice to injury: Compulsory payment for unwanted treatment, 327 N. Eng. J. Med. 1885 (1992).

307 *Rockville Gen. Hosp. v. Wirzulis*, 2003 Conn. Super. LEXIS 567.

308 E.g., *Batzell v. Buskirk*, 752 S.W.2d 902 (Mo. Ct. App. 1988); *Kohoutek v. Hafner*, 383 N.W.2d 295 (Minn. 1986); *Moser v. Stallings*, 387 N.W.2d 599 (Iowa 1986).

309 E.g., *Fox v. Smith*, 594 So. 2d 596 (Miss. 1992); *Marino v. Ballestas*, 749 F.2d 162 (3d Cir. 1984) [battery action permitted]; *Hales v. Pittman*, 118 Ariz. 305, 576 P.2d 493 (1978) [battery action permitted]; Ariz. Rev. Stat. Ann. § 12-562(B) (1982) [battery action eliminated by statute]; *Rubino v. DeFretias*, 638 F. Supp. 182 (D. Ariz. 1986) [Arizona statute unconstitutional].

310 E.g., *Caputa v. Antiles*, 686 A.2d 356 (N.J. Ct. App. 1996); *Boyd v. Louisiana Med. Mut. Ins. Co.*, 593 So. 2d 427 (La. Ct. App. 1991); *McKinley v. Stripling*, 763 S.W.2d 407 (Tex. 1989); *Latham v. Hayes*, 495 So. 2d 453 (Miss. 1986); *Pardy v. United States*, 783 F.2d 710 (7th Cir. 1986); *Canterbury v. Spence*, 150 U.S. App. D.C. 263, 464 F.2d 772, cert. denied, 409 U.S. 1064 (1972).

311 E.g., *Arena v. Gingrich*, 305 Or. 1, 748 P.2d 547 (1988); *Wilkinson v. Vesey*, 110 R.I. 606, 295 A.2d 676 (1972).

312 E.g., *Caputa v. Antiles*, 296 N.J. Super. 123, 686 A.2d 356 (App. Div. 1996).

313 *Begin v. Richmond*, 555 A.2d 363 (Vt. 1988).

314 *Gouse v. Cassel*, 532 Pa. 197, 615 A.2d 331 (1992).

315 See *Wu v. Spence*, 413 Pa. Super. 352, 605 A.2d 395 (1992) [informed consent not required for drug administration]; accord *Boyer v. Smith*, 345 Pa. Super. 66, 497 A.2d 646 (1985), but see *Jones v. Philadelphia College of Osteopathic Med.*, 813 F. Supp. 1125 (E.D. Pa. 1993) [transfusion part of surgery, informed consent must be obtained].

316 *Albany Urology Clinic, P.C. v. Cleveland*, 272 Ga. 296, 528 S.E.2d 777 (2000); see also *Saylor v. Providence Hosp.*, 680 N.E.2d 193 (Ohio App. 1996) [failure to state fraud claim against hospital concerning surgical implantation of plate, screws, where no specific allegations of misrepresentations], but see *Luciano v. Levine*, 232 A.D.2d 378, 648 N.Y.S.2d 149 (2d Dept. 1996) [only negligence action allowed; no fraud claim allowed for surgeon's assurances of safety of liquid silicone injection where injuries were the same as injuries from alleged malpractice].

317 E.g, *Payne v. Marion Gen. Hosp.*, 549 N.E.2d 1043 (Ind. Ct. App. 1990) [patient died after no resuscitation pursuant to DNR order entered at sister's request; in suit by estate, sufficient evidence patient still awake, alert, capable of communicating to require remand to determine whether incapacitated]; *Evans v. Salem Hosp.*, 83 Or. App. 23, 730 P.2d 562 (1986), rev. denied, 303 Or. 331, 736 P.2d 565 (1987) [dismissal on procedural grounds of intentional infliction of emotional distress claim for not resuscitating patient where no patient or family approval not to resuscitate].

318 See S. Neu and C.M. Kjellstrand, Stopping long-term dialysis, 314 N. Eng. J. Med. 14, 17 (1986).

319 E.g., *Brooks v. United States*, 837 F.2d 958 (11th Cir. 1988).

320 E.g., *Hartsell v. Fort Sanders Reg. Med. Ctr.*, 905 S.W.2d 944 (Tenn. Ct. App. 1995) [dismissal of outrageous conduct suit against obstetrician, hospital for disconnecting newborn's life support after premature birth; child eventually survived with no evidence of mental injury].

321 Annotation, Tortious maintenance or removal of life supports, 58 A.L.R. 4th 222.

322 E.g., *Hoffmeister v. Coler*, 544 So. 2d 1067 (Fla. 4th DCA 1989); *Gray v. Romeo*, 709 F. Supp. 325 (D. R.I. 1989); *McMahon v. Lopez*, 199 Cal. App. 3d 829, 245 Cal. Rptr. 172 (2d Dist. 1988); *Bartling v. Glendale Adventist Med. Ctr.*, 184 Cal. App. 3d 97, 228 Cal. Rptr. 847 (2d Dist. 1986); see also *Ross v. Hilltop Rehabilitation Hosp.*, 124 F.R.D. 660 (D. Colo. 1988) [after unsuccessfully seeking damages for continuation of unwanted treatment, plaintiff required to pay costs of hospital, physician].

323 E.g., *Colorado State Bd. of Dental Exam'rs v. Micheli*, 928 P.2d 839 (Colo. App. 1996).

324 Doctor loses license over suffocation, AP, Oct. 11, 2003.

325 Case of disciplined doctor sparks life and death debate, AP, July 4, 2003.

326 Nursing home fined after patient dies, AP, April 4, 2003.

327 In re Quinlan, 70 N.J. 10, 355 A.2d 647, 669–670 (1976).

328 See Annotation, Homicide: physician's withdrawal of life supports from comatose patient, 47 A.L.R. 4th 18.

329 D.C. heart surgeon suspended, Miami Herald [FL], May 10, 1986, 3A; Doctor reinstated, N.Y. Times, May 6, 1986, 10.

330 W. Kates, Grand jury: No charges against doctor in suicide case, AP, July 26, 1991.

331 R.L. Zimmer, Judge dismisses charges against doctor, parents of deformed twins, AP, July 17, 1981; State's attorney won't pursue Siamese twins case, AP, Apr. 16, 1982.

332 *Barber v. Superior Court*, 147 Cal. App. 3d 1006, 195 Cal. Rptr. 484 (2d Dist. 1983).

333 D.M. Gianelli, Test case? Physician acquitted after taking infant son off respirator, Am. Med. News Feb. 20, 1995, 3 [Mich. physician charged with disconnecting his own premature child from respirator].

334 Jury clears, yet condemns Dr. Haiselden, Chicago Daily Trib., Nov. 20, 1915.

335 C. Feldman, AP, Oct. 24, 1978; Jersey examiner's board revokes medical license of Dr. Jascalevich, N.Y. Times, Oct. 9, 1980, B6; In re Jascalevich License Revocation, 182 N.J. Super. 455, 442 A.2d 635 (App. Div. 1982) [upholding license revocation]; see also *Shaw v. Riverdell Hosp.*, 150 N.J. Super. 585, 376 A.2d 228 (1977) [denying stay of civil case during criminal trial].

336 R. Ellis, Infanticide case ends in mistrial, "Impossible" deadlock bound jury, foreman says, Atlanta Journal & Const., Nov. 5, 1994, A1; R. Ellis, Carrizales won't face second trial, Atlanta Journal & Const., Apr. 15, 1995, 1B; R. Ellis, No sanctions against physician tried for death of newborn, Atlanta Journal & Const., Feb. 8, 1996, 1C.

337 *Florida v. Pinzon-Reyes*, No. CF-96-00666A-XX (Fla. Cir. Ct. Highlands County verdict June 26, 1997), as discussed in 6 H.L.R. 1050 (1997).

338 E.g., *United States v. Wood*, 207 F.3d 1222 (10th Cir. 2000); No retrial planned for former VA physician, AP, July 28, 2000.

339 J. Hanna, Court of Appeals panel acquits former osteopath accused of murder, AP, July 24, 1998; Naramore's medical license reinstated, AP, Oct. 19, 1998; Medical Society head says many reluctant to treat pain of terminally ill, AP, Nov. 16, 1998.

340 C.G. Wallace, Doctor convicted in drug deaths, AP Online, July 11, 2000; P. Heintz, Prosecutor's actions against doctors have landmark results, AP, Jan. 24, 2003.

341 E.g., T. Albert, Florida physician guilty of manslaughter in OxyContin case, Am. Med. News, Mar. 11, 2002; *Commonwealth v. Youngkin*, 285 Pa. Super. 417, 427 A.2d 1356 (1981); *People v. Schade*, 30 Cal. App. 4th 1515; 32 Cal. Rptr. 2d 59 (6th Dist. 1994).

342 *People v. Einaugler*, 208 A.D.2d 946, 618 N.Y.S.2d 414 (2d Dept. 1994); *Einaugler v. Supreme Court of State of N.Y.*, 109 F.3d 836 (2d Cir. 1997); E.B. Fein, Doctor in negligence case gets his sentence eased, N.Y. Times, June 28, 1997, 25; see M.B. Kapp, Treating medical charts near the end of life: how legal anxieties inhibit good patient deaths, 28 U. Tol. L. Rev. 521 (1997).

343 A.A. Narvaez, Jersey physician is spared prison sentence for mercy killing, N.Y. Times, Dec. 20, 1986, 10.

344 Juries kind to doctors who assist, Cap. Times (Madison WI), Mar. 17, 1992, 1D.

345 E.g., J.B. Frazier, Grand jury refuses to indict nurse in care center morphine deaths, AP, Sept. 14, 2000 [Oregon]; North Memorial nurse won't be charged with felonies, AP, Dec. 19, 2003 [MN nurse investigated for amount of morphine given to patients].

346 P. Arnold, Indictment dismissed, nurse reinstated, AP, May 31, 1980; P.A. Kalisch, B.J. Kalisch & E. Livesay, The "angel of death," 19 Nursing Forum (No.3) (1980), 212.

347 Wiley, Liability for death: nine nurses' legal ordeals, 11 Nursing 81 (Sept. 1981), at 37 [hereinafter cited as Wiley]; C. Hanson, Jury deadlocked, mistrial ruled in nurse's murder case, Washington Star, Mar. 21, 1979, A-1; Nurse admits plug-pulling but is acquitted of murder, Med. World News, Apr. 30, 1979, 48; AP, July 2, 1979 [licensing board revoked nursing license after rejecting surrender of license].

348 F. Bayles, Grand jury probing mercy killing returns indictments, AP, Aug. 13, 1980; Nurse acquitted of killing cancer patient, UPI, Oct. 24, 1981; AP, Nov. 13, 1981.

349 Patient testifies against his nurse, N.Y. Times, Oct. 7, 1984, 16; Nurse is acquitted in respirator case, N.Y. Times, Oct. 17, 1984, 10.

350 Find nurse innocent in patients' death, AP, Sept. 25, 1986; Sentence nurse in patient injection, AP, Oct. 1, 1986; State releases former nurse tried for killing patients, AP, Apr. 2, 2003.

351 Embattled nurse, N.Y. Times, Nov. 11, 1985, 30Y; M. Miller, Murder, by the numbers, Newsweek, May 30, 1988, 58; Judge acquits a nurse accused in deaths of 3, N.Y. Times, June 23, 1988, 9.

352 *United States v. Narciso*, 446 F. Supp. 252 (E.D. Mich. 1976); Wiley supra note 59, at 34.

353 Nurse convicted of murdering 12, N.Y. Times, Mar. 30, 1984, 9; Nurse sentenced to death for 12 hospital murders, AP, June 15, 1984; *People v. Diaz*, 3 Cal. 4th 495 & 757, 11 Cal. Rptr. 2d 353, 834 P.2d 1171 (1992), cert. denied, 508 U.S. 916 (1993), related proceeding, *Diaz v. Lukash*, 82 N.Y.2d 211, 604 N.Y.S.2d 28, 624 N.E.2d 156 (1993) [convicted nurse permitted to inspect autopsy reports to develop theory that no murder occurred].

354 Nurse gets 99 years in Texas injection death, N.Y. Times, Feb. 17, 1984, 8; Nurse gets 60 years for injuring Texas child, N.Y. Times, Oct. 25, 1984, 10; P. Elkind, Death shift, Texas Monthly (Aug. 1983), 106; CDC investigator finishes gathering infant death data, AP, Apr. 20, 1983; K. Gazlay, Dean held in contempt for failing to turn over documents, AP, Dec. 12, 1983; K. Gazlay, Judge issues injunction barring record shredding, AP, Mar. 19, 1984; *Jones v. State*, 716 S.W.2d 142 (Tex. App. 1986).

355 P. Milton, DA: Nurse admits administering fatal drugs, AP, Nov. 16, 1987; M. Humbert, State cites hospital in "angel of death" case, AP, Dec. 17, 1987; P. Milton, Nurse sentenced to 50 years to life, AP, Jan. 24, 1990; People v. Angelo, 88 N.Y.2d 217, 666 N.E.2d 1333, 644 N.Y.S.2d 460 (1996).

356 L. Renze-Rhodes, Judge closes book on Majors case, Indiana Lawyer, Nov. 24, 1999, 3; *Majors v. State*, 773 N.E.2d 231 (Ind. 2002).

357 A.H. Malcolm, Medical workers face ethical dilemmas in new technology, N.Y. Times, Dec. 17, 1984, 12; Wisconsin board revokes license of nurse in mercy killing of man, N.Y. Times, Mar. 20, 1985, 10.

358 J. Nolan, Former nurse's aide sentenced for mass killings, AP, Aug. 18, 1987; Personnel changes planned in wake of Harvey disclosures, AP, Aug. 25, 1987; M. Embry, Judge doesn't buy "mercy" killing explanation, AP. Nov. 3, 1987; J. Kay, Former hospital administrator sentenced to 30 days, AP, May 13, 1988.

359 E. Werner, Angel of death pleads guilty, AP Online, Mar. 12, 2002; P. Lieberman, Hospital "angel of death" gets life without parole, L.A. Times, Apr. 18, 2002, A1; "Angel of death" settles claims with 4 families, L.A. Times, Dec. 20, 2003.

360 T. Bell, Charges filed against nurse who says he killed dozens of patients, AP, Dec. 16, 2003; T. Bell, Nurse who claims to have killed 40 voluntarily surrenders license, AP, Dec. 17, 2003; D. Caruso, Lawsuits fly over nurse charged with overdosing patients, AP, Jan. 15, 2004; New Jersey fines last hospital of nurse accused of killings, N.Y. Times, Feb. 21, 2004, B5; D.B. Caruso, Officials say medical centers complied with law in case of nurse accused of killing patients, AP, Feb. 21, 2004 [PA]; G. Mulvihill, Former nurse pleads guilty in 13 patient deaths, AP, Apr. 29, 2004 [NJ cases]; J. Fisher, Former nurse pleads guilty in killings of another 3, N.Y. Times, May 20, 2004, B5; W. Parry, Judge dismisses 2 lawsuits in killer nurse cases, AP, Sept. 14, 2004 [institutions not obligated to contact prospective future employers regarding suspicions]; Nurse who pleaded guilty to killing 24 patients meets with New Jersey attorney general, AP, May 20, 2005 [part of plea bargain to avoid death penalty required tips on catching other serial killers].

Chapter 8

Healthcare Information

Joan M. Lebow, JD, Joseph L. Ternullo, JD, MPH, Cavan K. Doyle, JD, LLM, Cheryl A. Miller, JD, and Kelly L. Gawne, JD

Key Learning Objectives

By the end of this chapter, the reader will be able to:

- Understand some of the legal issues related to the collection, use, and disclosure of healthcare information.

- Identify some of the underlying issues concerning healthcare information, ownership of the information, requirements about content, privacy requirements, and uses and disclosure of healthcare information.

- Appreciate a wide range of federal and state laws governing the use and disclosure of healthcare information and the security of such information.

- Understand some of the threats to the security of healthcare information in the context of digital media and the Internet.

Chapter Outline

Introduction

The collection, use, and disclosure of healthcare information have become some of the most heavily regulated areas of health care. Healthcare providers must record, generate, and handle a large amount of information. This includes sensitive information about patients that is necessary to provide treatment. It also includes a wide range of information that is required for business and other internal operations, payment, and regulatory purposes.

Providers and others who obtain healthcare information need to be aware of the applicable requirements when collecting, using, and disclosing healthcare information. The details of these requirements are beyond the scope of this book.

This chapter addresses the following questions:

- 8-1. What are the underlying issues addressed through the laws concerning healthcare information?
- 8-2. Who owns medical records?
- 8-3. What records must be created, and how must they be maintained?
- 8-4. What are the laws concerning privacy of healthcare information?
- 8-5. What are the laws concerning use of healthcare information?
- 8-6. What are the laws concerning disclosure of healthcare information?
- 8-7. What legal issues flow from the use of audio and video transmissions and recordings?
- 8-8. What legal issues flow from the use of computers and the Internet?

8-1 What Are the Underlying Issues Addressed Through the Laws Concerning Healthcare Information?

Laws dealing with the use and disclosure of healthcare information seek to address a wide spectrum of troublesome issues. Such problems include: (1) balancing patient concerns for confidentiality with the need for access to healthcare information and the cost of implementing confidentiality protections; (2) balancing accountability for healthcare services with the cost tosatisfy documentation requirements; (3) addressing government and business desires to access information for a wide variety of purposes ranging from law enforcement to budgeting to marketing; (4) managing the sharing of electronic health information across healthcare provider networks; (5) aggregating health information to facilitate research and improve health outcomes; and (6) implementing sanctions and penalties for unauthorized disclosure of health information.

PROVIDING HEALTHCARE SERVICES. Healthcare providers must access, collect, and use healthcare information to provide healthcare services. Specifically, providers use medical records and other types of health information as communication tools in caring for patients with healthcare problems. Patients are often treated by several different providers in multiple different treatment settings. As such, providers must exchange patient information to provide continuity of care. Electronic health records are becoming increasingly prevalent in response to the demand for instant access to information about patients' past and present health conditions and treatment and incentives provided under federal law—the American Relief and Recovery Act of 2009 (ARRA). It provides billions of dollars for health information technology investments. Most of the money is available to hospitals and physicians who adopt and meaningfully use qualified electronic health records. The vision and objective is that these qualifying electronic health records will enable providers to quickly and easily access patient information across diverse treatment settings, thus improving continuity in patient care.

CONFIDENTIALITY. A physician has a duty to protect the confidential health information of his or her patient. The purpose of the duty of confidentiality is to encourage patients to make a full and frank disclosure of information to the physician. Full disclosure enables the physician to diagnose conditions accurately and to provide appropriate treatment to further protect their privacy, patients may seek to limit who, outside of the doctor-patient relationship, has access to their confidential health information. However, the patient's interest in keeping his medical information private may conflict with other entities' interest in accessing the information. For example, an employer may seek information about a potential employee's tobacco use or other health habits, or an insurance company may require a medical exam and information about preexisting health conditions before issuing a health insurance policy. The conflict between the individual's desire to maintain the confidentiality of his or her health information and society's countervailing desire or ability to discover it is at the heart of many of the current debates in healthcare law.

ACCOUNTABILITY. Documentation of patient care and the medical services provided to patients is critical in maintaining provider accountability. Each step of a patient's encounter with a medical professional is documented, through, for example, notations in the patient's medical record, correspondence between the provider and the insurance company, and entries in a pharmacy's computer system. In the event of an adverse event in the patient's care, debate over payment of a provider's bill, or other problem, the collected documentation serves as the primary source of information in determining accountability. To this end, healthcare information and documentation may be used for internal quality review, medical negligence and malpractice liability lawsuits, and regulatory and accreditation requirements.

USES OF INFORMATION FOR OTHER PURPOSES. Individuals, healthcare providers, private businesses, government agencies, and other entities seek access to identifiable healthcare information for a wide range of purposes, including:

1. Performance improvement (finding ways to improve services);

2. Clinical research (advancing medical knowledge and practice);

3. Public health and safety (e.g., protecting from contagious diseases);

4. Billing and collections (justifying payment);

5. Planning and marketing by healthcare providers;

6. Documenting individuals' conditions (e.g., to be excused from specific duties[1] and to make benefits and other legal claims);

7. Law enforcement (e.g., to investigate and prove crimes);

8. Government planning;

9. Media reporting; and

10. Other business uses (e.g., building databases for marketing and planning).[2]

8-2 Who Owns Medical Records?

The hospital or other healthcare institution owns the medical record, which is its business record. Institutional ownership is explicitly stated in the statutes and regulations of some states, and courts have recognized this ownership.[3] If a physician has separate records, they are the physician's property, but the physician is still responsible for maintaining complete institutional records.

The medical record is an unusual type of property because, physically, it belongs to the institution and the institution must exercise considerable control over access, but the patient and others have an interest in the information in the record. The institution owns the paper or other material on which the information is recorded,[4] but it has responsibilities concerning access to and use and disclosure of the information. The patient and others have a right of access to the information in many circumstances, but they do not have a right to possession of original records.[5] Courts have ruled that patients do not have a right to pathology slides[6] or x-ray negatives.[7] The patient does not purchase a picture; the patient purchases the professional service of interpreting the x-ray. Thus, the patient could not use the physician's retention of the x-ray as a defense to a suit to collect professional fees.

The institutional medical record belongs to the institution. While associated with the institution, physicians and other individual providers have access to the records for patient care, administrative uses, and some legal purposes.[8] After physicians or other providers no longer have association with the institution, they have more limited access but generally can obtain access for legal purposes, for example, defending lawsuits and administrative proceedings or collecting bills. However, individual providers generally are not custodians of the records. Subpoenas and other efforts to discover institutional records should be directed to the institutional custodian, not the individual provider.

Ownership issues sometimes arise between providers, especially when physicians are terminated from employment. The outcomes vary depending on state law and what the employment agreement says.[9]

8-3 What Records Must Be Created, and How Must They Be Maintained?

Healthcare providers are required by both governmental and nongovernmental organizations (NGOs) to have accurate and complete medical records. The licensing laws and regulations of many states include specific requirements with which hospitals and other providers must comply. In addition, nongovernmental agencies, such as The Joint Commission (TJC), establish medical records standards.

The primary purpose of medical records is to facilitate diagnosis, treatment, and patient care. Records provide a communications link among the team members caring for the patient. Records also document what was found and what was done so that patient care can be evaluated, billing and collections can be performed, and other administrative and legal matters can be addressed. Medical records are also valuable in hospital educational and research programs.

This section addresses:

- 8-3.1. What elements must healthcare records contain?
- 8-3.2. Why must medical records be accurate, timely, and legible?
- 8-3.3. How should corrections and alterations in records be handled?
- 8-3.4. How long should records be retained, and how should they be destroyed?

8-3.1 What Elements Must Healthcare Records Contain?

Many statutes and regulations require healthcare providers to maintain medical records. Healthcare providers that participate in Medicare must comply with minimum content requirements.[10] Some local governments require additional information to be kept. Billing requirements of other payers also add requirements.

To be accredited, hospitals must meet the TJC's medical records standards, including a long list of items that must be in the medical record to assure identification of the patient, support for the diagnosis, justification for the treatment, and accurate documentation of results.[11] While some items apply only to inpatients, the general standards apply to all patients.

Individual healthcare providers can lose their licenses for failure to maintain required records.[12]

The medical record consists of three types of data: (1) personal, (2) financial, and (3) medical.

Personal information, usually obtained upon admission, includes name, date of birth, sex, marital status, occupation, other items of identification, and the next of kin or other contact person. The accuracy of this information often depends on the knowledge and honesty of the person providing the information. Providers can generally rely on the information provided unless there is significant reason to doubt it. In 1998, a New York court ruled that a hospital could rely on information provided on a patient's behalf, so it was proper to serve a collection action at the address given by an adult patient's father when she was admitted.[13]

Financial data usually include the patient's employer, health insurance identification, and other information to assist billing.

Medical data forms the clinical record, a continuously maintained history of patient condition and treatment, including physical examinations, medical history, treatment administered, progress reports, physician orders, clinical laboratory reports, radiology reports, consultation reports, anesthesia records, operation records, signed consent forms, nursing notes, and discharge summaries. The medical record should be a complete, current record of the history, condition, and treatment of the patient.

Incomplete hospital recordkeeping can sometimes be used to infer negligence in treatment.[14] One federal court found a hospital negligent for permitting its nurse to chart by exception in postoperative monitoring.[15] Minor variations from hospital standards concerning charting do not automatically prove that an examination or treatment did not meet legal standards. A federal court found that an emergency screening satisfied the law even though the full hospital screening procedure was not followed.[16]

Governmental and private third-party payers and managed care organizations are demanding that an increased amount of information be documented to justify treatment, referral, or payment.[17] This is changing the nature of medical practice and diverting clinical time and institutional resources to comply with these requirements.

CODING. Medicare and most managed care companies require providers to code their services, which means that a number must be assigned to each service from a complex coding system. Generally, provider records must include documentation of the diagnosis and treatment to support the coding.

Due to the complexity and changing nature of the coding systems and the liability for coding errors, most institutional providers have had to hire professional coders to assign the codes on each bill.

8-3.2 Why Must Medical Records Be Accurate, Timely, and Legible?

Accurate and timely completion of medical records is essential to maximizing availability of information for treatment, expediting payment, complying with governmental and accreditation requirements, and minimizing liability exposure.

State licensing statutes and regulations and TJC standards require accurate records.[18] ⚑ An inaccurate record can increase the hospital's exposure to liability by destroying the entire record's credibility. In a 1974 Kansas case, the court found that one discrepancy between the medical record and what actually happened to the patient could justify a jury finding that the record could also be erroneous in other parts and be considered generally invalid.[19]

Complete records include observations that the patient's condition has not changed, as well as observations of change. If there is no notation of an observation, many courts permit juries to infer that no observation was made. In 1974, the Illinois Supreme Court decided a case involving a patient admitted with a broken leg.[20] The leg suffered irreversible ischemia while in traction and required amputation. The physician had ordered the nurse to observe the patient's toes, and the medical record indicated hourly observations during the first day of hospitalization. No observations were documented during the seven hours prior to finding the foot cold and without sensation. Though the nurse might have observed the foot during that period, the jury was permitted to infer from the lack of documentation that no observations were made, indicating a breach of the nurse's duty. The hospital, as the nurse's employer, could be liable for resulting injuries.

Failure to document is often also used as an additional offense when providers are charged with other offenses. In 1997, a New York court upheld revocation of a physician's license for a sexual relationship, improper prescribing, and failure to maintain records.[21]

In 1997, a New Jersey court ruled that when errors in records as to time and cause of injury resulted in a low settlement with the person responsible for the injuries, the physician group responsible for the record errors could be sued.[22]

Complete records can often protect hospital and staff. A Kentucky hospital was found not liable for a patient death approximately thirteen hours after surgery because the medical record included documentation of proper periodic nursing observation, contacts with the physician concerning patient management, and compliance with physician directions.[23] Compliance with physician directions does not provide protection when the directions are clearly improper. When the directions are within the range of acceptable professional practice, properly documented compliance provides substantial liability protection.

Medical record entries should usually be made when treatment is given or observations are made. Entries made several days or weeks later have less credibility than those made during or immediately after the patient's hospitalization. Medicare conditions of participation require completion of hospital records within thirty days following patient discharge.[24] TJC's accreditation standards require medical staff regulations to specify a time limit for completion of the record that cannot exceed thirty days after discharge.[25] Persistent failure to conform to this medical staff rule is a basis for suspension of the staff member.[26]

A West Virginia court ruled in favor of a hospital in a case in which a director of social services ordered social workers to review patient charts and complete missing information in master treatment plans for an upcoming accreditation survey. One social worker refused, claiming that it was illegal and then resigned under pressure. The court ruled that completing the plans based on information in the charts was not unethical altering of records.[27]

Medical records should be legible. This does not mean that the patient or another nonhealthcare professional must be able to read the records, but it does mean that other healthcare professionals should be able to read the entries. Otherwise, there is a risk of communication errors that defeat the purpose of the record. Medicare/Medicaid and TJC have long required legible records.[28] In addition, illegible records will not satisfy the other uses of medical records. In 1996, a federal appellate court remanded a disability case because "nontrivial" parts of the medical record were illegible.[29] In 1997, another federal appellate court reversed a judgment in favor of a life insurance company because the only evidence that might support the company was an illegible page of the medical record.[30] In 1999, a physician and pharmacist were found liable for the death of a patient when an illegible prescription was misread.[31] There has been increased public and regulatory attention on legibility.[32] Florida mandated legibility of prescriptions effective July 1, 2003, without specifying penalties, leaving it to the medical licensing board to enforce.[33] In 2003, an Alabama physician lost his license in part for the inability of others to read his prescriptions.[34]

In some circumstances, it is appropriate to use aliases in the place of the names of patients for security or special privacy reasons. This is generally not considered to make the record inaccurate.[35] For example, hospitals that care for high-profile prisoners sometimes give them other names so that persons who seek to help them escape cannot locate them. This is also sometimes done for patients who are celebrities or are under threat from spouses or others. However, there is generally no right to have an alias used.

8-3.3 How Should Corrections and Alterations in Records Be Handled?

Medical record corrections should be made only by proper methods. Improper alterations reduce record credibility, exposing the hospital to increased liability risk.

Medical record errors can be (1) minor errors in transcription, spelling, and the like or (2) more significant errors involving test data, orders, omitted progress notes, and similar substantive entries. Persons authorized to make record entries may correct minor errors in their own entries soon after the original entry. Hospital policies generally limit who may correct substantive errors and errors discovered at a later date. Those who might have been misled by the error should be notified of changes.

Corrections should be made by placing a single line through the incorrect entry, entering the correct information, initialing or signing the correction, and entering the time and date of the correction. Erasing or obliterating errors can lead jurors to suspect the original entry.

After a claim has been made, changes should not be made without first consulting defense counsel. After several New York physicians won a malpractice suit, it was discovered that a page of the medical record had been replaced before the suit, so the court ordered a new trial.[36] A Maryland court ruled that a malpractice insurer could cancel a physician's coverage for alteration of patient records.[37]

Altering or falsifying a medical record to obtain reimbursement wrongfully is a crime.[38] In some states, a practitioner who improperly alters a medical record is subject to license revocation or other discipline for unprofessional conduct.[39] In some states, improper alteration of a medical record is a crime regardless of the purpose. In 1998, a Virginia appellate court affirmed the conviction of a physician for forging a cardiac stress test record by altering the date. The forgery was used to obtain authorization for coverage of a liver transplant. The physician could be convicted even though the insurer was never billed for the transplant. His medical license was automatically suspended for the conviction, but later reinstated.[40]

Some patients request modification of medical records. Because records are evidence of what occurred and were relied on in making patient care decisions, hospitals should usually not modify records except to update patient name changes. If a patient disagrees with an entry, some hospitals permit amendments in the same manner as corrections of substantive errors if the physician concurs in the amendment. Such an amendment should note the patient's request as a means of explaining the change if it is questioned later. Instead of changing original entries, some hospitals permit patients to add letters to the record. Staff concurrence, if any, can be noted on the letter. Occasionally, courts will order record modifications, especially for records of involuntary evaluation or treatment for mental illness.[41]

8-3.4 How Long Should Records Be Retained, and How Should They Be Destroyed?

RECORD RETENTION. Because healthcare records are maintained primarily for patient care purposes, decisions concerning record retention periods should be based on sound institutional and medical practice, as well as on applicable regulations. Some states specify minimum retention periods for some or all records. Medicare requires records to be kept for at least five years.[42] Medicare providers must include in contracts with subcontractors a provision requiring the subcontractor to retain records for at least four years after services are provided and to permit the Department of Health and Human Services (HHS) to inspect them.[43] Several state regulations provide that records be kept permanently, but some require retention for the period in which suits may be filed. Some states provide that records cannot be destroyed without state agency approval.

Where there are no controlling regulations, any retention beyond the time needed for medical and administrative purposes should be determined by institutional administration with advice of legal counsel. In institutions where extensive medical research is conducted, a longer retention period may be appropriate to facilitate retrospective studies.

The importance of retaining records until the time has passed for lawsuits is illustrated by a 1984 Florida appellate court decision.[44] The anesthesia records concerning a patient were lost, so the proof necessary to sue the physician was not available. The court ruled that the hospital could be sued for negligently maintaining its records and that the hospital could avoid liability only by showing that the treatment recorded in the missing records was performed nonnegligently, which would be difficult to do without the records.

An independent tort of spoliation of evidence has been recognized by some jurisdictions.[45] Some jurisdictions have limited its applicability.[46] Other jurisdictions have rejected the independent tort.[47]

Sometimes records are lost due to catastrophe such as fire. One federal court permitted the use in a trial of noncontemporaneous medical records created long after the contemporaneous Veterans Administration (VA) hospital records were destroyed in a fire.[48]

RECORD DESTRUCTION. The issue of record destruction arises when the retention period has passed or when a patient requests destruction.

Some state hospital licensing regulations specify the methods for destroying records. The method should protect confidentiality by complete destruction. When required, certificates of destruction should be retained permanently as evidence of record disposal. Some states require creation of a permanent abstract prior to destruction.

Some patients request premature destruction. Some states forbid destruction on an individual basis.[49] In states without specific statutes, it is still prudent not to destroy individual records unless ordered to do so by a court. Courts have generally refused to order destruction. For example, in 1978, the highest court of New York ruled that records could be ordered sealed, but not destroyed.[50] One exception is a 1978 case in which the Pennsylvania Supreme Court ordered destruction of records of the illegal hospitalization of a mental patient.[51]

8-4 What Are the Laws Concerning Privacy of Healthcare Information?

On April 14, 2003, the laws concerning privacy of healthcare information in the United States were fundamentally changed when the federal privacy regulations under the Health Insurance Portability and Accountability Act (HIPAA) took effect. Any state laws that provide less protection are superseded. State laws that provided more protection remain in effect. ⚑

This section addresses the following:

- 8-4.1. What are the fundamentals of the HIPAA privacy regulations?

- 8-4.2. What state privacy-related laws remain in effect?

- 8-4.3. What other federal privacy laws are still applicable?

8-4.1 What Are the Fundamentals of the HIPAA Privacy Regulations?

The Health Insurance Portability and Accountability Act mandated that HHS issue regulations for the privacy of individually identifiable health information.[52] The privacy rules were initially published in December 2000[53] and then substantially amended in August 2002.[54] The privacy rules took effect April 14, 2003. Courts have rejected challenges to the initial rules and the amended rules.[55] See Figure 8-1.

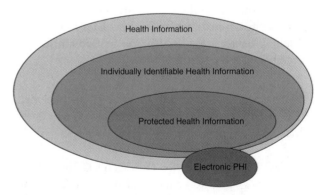

Figure 8-1 Health Information Rings

HIPAA's Privacy Rule provides that a "Covered Entity" may not use or disclose an individual's "Protected Health Information" unless either the disclosure is permitted under the Privacy Rule or the covered entity has obtained the individual's authorization.[56]

COVERED ENTITIES. The HIPAA privacy rules apply to covered entities.[57] Most healthcare providers, health plans, and healthcare clearinghouses are considered covered entities.

Healthcare Providers include: • Physicians • Dentists • Nurses • Clinics • Chiropractors • Nursing Homes Pharmacies; Health Plans include: • Health insurance Companies • HMOs • Company Health Plans • Government Health Programs: Medicare, Medicaid, Tricare, etc. Healthcare Clearinghouses include: Entities that process nonstandard health information they receive from another entity into a standard format.

Healthcare providers for whom no health information is transmitted electronically are excluded, but this exception is illusory because it is virtually impossible to provide treatment or bill without electronic transmission of health information, especially because Medicare requires electronic submission of bills.

Initially, HIPAA required covered entities to enter into Business Associate agreements with Business Associates, requiring them to comply with certain privacy requirements.

In 2009, HIPAA was amended to add that "Business Associates" must comply with the Privacy Rule as covered entities do. Business Associates are persons or organizations that (1) perform functions or activities on behalf of a covered entity or (2) provide services to a covered entity that involve the use or disclosure of individually identifiable health information.[58] The types of business associate services that are covered include: legal, actuarial, accounting, consulting, data aggregation, management, administrative, accreditation, and financial services.[59]

Examples of Business Associate functions include: • Claims Processing • Billing • Utilization Review • Data Analysis

PROTECTED HEALTH INFORMATION. The HIPAA privacy rules apply to confidential patient information, which is called protected health information, or PHI, in the rules.[60] PHI includes virtually all individually identifiable health information, which is defined to include any health information, including demographic information collected from the individual, that:

(1) Is created or received by a healthcare provider, health plan, employer, or healthcare clearinghouse; and

(2) Relates to the past, present, or future physical or mental health or condition of an individual; the provision of health care to an individual; or the past, present, or future payment for the provision of health care to an individual; and

(i) That identifies the individual; or

(ii) With respect to which there is a reasonable basis to believe the information can be used to identify the individual.[60]

When there is no reasonable basis to believe the information can be used to identify the individual, the PHI and the HIPAA rules do not apply. The HIPAA privacy rules apply to PHI in all formats—written, spoken, or electronic.

NOTICE OF PRIVACY PRACTICES. HIPAA requires that upon initial presentation to a healthcare provider, all patients must be given a notice of privacy practices.[61] A record must be kept of giving this notice. Generally, the patient or patient's representative will be asked to sign an acknowledgment.

SAFEGUARDS. HIPAA requires covered entities to take steps to safeguard PHI.[62] They must train their workforces to take common sense steps so that unauthorized persons do not come into contact with PHI. This ranges from not leaving medical records where they can be seen by the public to not talking about patients in cafeterias and elevators, and adopting security standards for providers' computers and handheld devices.

PATIENT AUTHORIZATION. HIPAA permits many internal uses and external disclosures of PHI without patient authorization. In general, uses and disclosures for treatment, payment, or healthcare operations are permitted without authorization.[63] Many disclosures that are required to safeguard the public, such as child abuse reporting, are also permitted.[64] These and other permitted uses and disclosures are discussed in sections 8-5 and 8-6.

Other uses and disclosures generally require authorization from the patient or the patient's representative. There are a few uses, such as listing in a facility directory, where all that is required is that the patient be given an opportunity to object.[65]

It is important for providers to understand which activities can be conducted without patient authorization and which activities require patient authorization.

MINIMUM NECESSARY. Most of the permitted uses and disclosures of PHI are subject to the minimum necessary rule, which requires that uses or disclosures be limited to the minimum necessary information for the permitted purpose.[66]

ALTERNATIVE COMMUNICATIONS. HIPAA requires that patients may request that healthcare providers contact them in a certain way, such as to leave a message on voice mail. Reasonable requests should usually be accommodated.[67]

ACCESS TO RECORDS. HIPAA requires that patients generally may look at their medical and billing records and make copies.[68]

CHANGES TO RECORDS. HIPAA requires that patients may ask for their medical or billing records to be changed, but patients do not have a right to compel changes.[69]

TRACKING OF DISCLOSURES. HIPAA requires that covered entities must maintain a record of some types of disclosures. With a few exceptions, patients have the right to see this list and get a copy of it.[70]

RESTRICTIONS ON USE. HIPAA requires that patients may request restrictions on the use of their patient information, but covered entities are not required to agree to such restrictions.[71] When they do agree, they must comply with their agreements.[72]

ADMINISTRATIVE STEPS. Covered entities are required to have a designated privacy officer, create policies and procedures, train workers, accept privacy complaints, and take corrective steps when there are violations.[73]

MARKETING AND FUNDRAISING. The HIPAA privacy rules generally prohibit using PHI for marketing of healthcare services or fundraising, unless authorization is obtained from the patient or patient's representative.[74]

The HHS Office for Civil Rights (OCR) enforces the privacy rules.

According to the HHS Office for Civil Rights website, the Privacy Rule compliance issues investigated most are: (1) Impermissible uses and disclosures of protected health information; (2) Lack of safeguards of protected health information; (3) Lack of patient access to their protected health information; (4) Uses or disclosures of more than the Minimum Necessary protected health information; and (5) Complaints to the covered entity. The types of covered entities that have most commonly been required to take corrective action to achieve compliance with the Privacy Rule are, in order of frequency: (1) Private Practices; (2) General Hospitals; (3) Outpatient Facilities; (4) Health Plans (group health plans and health insurance issuers); and (5) Pharmacies.

Unlike many other HHS enforcement efforts, the OCR has kept a low profile in its enforcement, focusing its efforts on promoting compliance rather than punishment. Until July 2004, there were no publicized impositions of penalties, although there were reports that unidentified cases had been referred to the Department of Justice for possible prosecution.[76] In August 2004, the first conviction was announced. A Washington healthcare worker pled guilty to having used information from a patient's medical records to obtain credit cards in the patient's name.[77] The facility cooperated in the investigation and was not charged. In June 2005, the U.S. Department of Justice announced that the criminal penalties of HIPAA generally do not apply to individual employees of providers; instead, they apply to insurers, physicians, hospitals, and other providers.[78] In February 2011, the OCR issued the first Civil Monetary Penalty for a violation of the HIPAA privacy rule. Cignet Health of Prince George's County, Maryland ("Cignet"), was fined $4.3 million for denying patients access to their medical records. Specifically, Cignet was fined $1.3 million for failing to give 41 patients access to their medical records between September 2008 and October 2009, and $3 million for failing to cooperate with the OCR investigation.

There is no private cause of action for enforcement of the HIPAA privacy rules.[79] This means that patients and their representatives cannot sue providers seeking payment for violation of HIPAA privacy rules. Patients and their representatives must rely on remedies under other laws. Enforcement of the HIPAA privacy rules is left to the OCR.

8-4.2 What State Privacy-Related Laws Remain in Effect?

HIPAA preempts any state laws that provide less protection, but any state law that provides as great or greater protections than HIPAA remains in effect.[80] Thus, state laws that restrict access to certain information at least as strictly as HIPAA remain in effect.

The general state laws concerning confidentiality of healthcare information also remain important. Because there is no private cause of action under the HIPAA privacy rules, state laws remain as the basis for some private causes of action. States can still enforce individual and institutional licensing rules and criminal laws[81] that generally require confidentiality.

The HIPAA privacy rules permit attorneys to issue subpoenas of PHI without a court order when certain procedural steps are followed. Some states, such as Wisconsin, do not permit this practice, requiring a court order when discovery of PHI is sought without a written authorization of the patient.

The HIPAA privacy rules also recognize the broad authority of courts to order release of PHI. Most states have placed significantly more limitations on the scope of courts to order release of PHI than has the federal government. These state laws continue to be constraints on the judiciary, at least in the cases where state law must be followed. The physician-patient privilege is one of the most important constraints on judicial disclosure of PHI.

MENTAL HEALTH. Many states have statutes that limit access to and disclosure of mental health information. In 1998, an Illinois appellate court ruled that it was a violation of the state confidentiality statute to voluntarily disclose mental health records to a physician appointed by a court to examine a patient for involuntary commitment.[82] In 1996, a federal appellate court applied the state mental health records law to issue a writ of mandamus commanding a lower court not to require a hospital to produce the records of two male patients who had allegedly raped the plaintiff.[83]

HIV/AIDS. Many states have statutes that specify when an HIV test result or a diagnosis of AIDS can be disclosed.[84] These statutes are often strictly interpreted.

A California physician was sued for writing a patient's HIV status in a medical record without the written consent required by state law, even though the patient had given verbal consent. The physician settled the suit.[85] A New York physician was found to have violated the law by disclosing a positive HIV test to an out-of-state workers' compensation board, where the authorization from the patient did not satisfy the statutory requirements.[86] Placing a red sticker on the possessions of a HIV-positive inmate and segregating her improperly disclosed her HIV status to persons who were not authorized to know.[87] In 2004, a District of Columbia court ruled that the law did not prohibit a physician from discussing the case of an HIV-positive patient with another physician in the same office.[88]

However, a Pennsylvania court permitted a hospital to make limited disclosure of a resident physician's HIV-positive status, including disclosure to patients without naming the resident.[89]

A North Carolina court upheld revocation of the clinical privileges of a physician for not complying with a hospital policy that required disclosure to the hospital of any inpatient who was HIV-positive.[90]

In some states, these laws require reporting of HIV/AIDS and disclosure to partners and others.[91]

COMMON LAW. The common law usually does not provide any protection from disclosure in testimonial contexts (e.g., trials, court hearings, subpoenas). Courts generally refuse to impose liability for testimonial disclosures.[92] Physicians and hospitals are usually not obligated to risk contempt of court to protect confidences (except for substance abuse records), although they might choose to do so.

In nontestimonial contexts, courts have found limitations on permissible disclosure based on the implied promise of confidentiality in the physician-patient relationship, violation of the right of privacy, and violation of professional licensing standards.[93] For example, a New York court permanently enjoined a psychoanalyst from circulating a book that included detailed information concerning a patient.[94] The patient was identifiable to close friends despite the psychoanalyst's efforts to disguise her identity. The court ruled that the book violated the implied covenant of confidentiality and the right of privacy. The Oregon Supreme Court held that a physician could be liable for revealing his patient's identity to the patient's natural child, who had been adopted.[95] The court ruled that while it was not a violation of the patient's right of privacy, it was a breach of the physician's professional duty to maintain the patient's confidentiality.

Courts have ruled in favor of healthcare providers in cases where disclosure was intended to prevent the spread of contagious disease or the patient was in a dangerous mental state.[96] As discussed in the section on the common law duty to disclose information, there could be liability in some circumstances for failing to disclose a contagious disease or dangerous mental state. Disclosures to the patient's employer or insurance company have resulted in several lawsuits.[97] The Alabama Supreme Court ruled that disclosures to an employer without authorization violated the implied promise of confidentiality and could result in liability.[98] The employer who induces the disclosure can also be liable.[99] However, a New York court ruled that when a patient authorized incomplete disclosure to his employer that the physician was not liable for giving a complete disclosure.[100] It is questionable whether other courts would rule this way, so the prudent practice is to refuse to release any information when only a misleading partial release is authorized.

Lawsuits for disclosures of confidential informatio have also been based on defamation. In most cases involving physicians, courts have found a qualified privilege to make the specific disclosures.[101] The few cases of liability have involved disclosure of a misdiagnosed embarrassing condition (such as venereal disease) that the patient did not actually have in a manner that demonstrated malice, defeating the qualified privilege.[102]

Misuse of confidential information without disclosure can also lead to sanctions. In 1991, a New York psychiatrist pled guilty to securities fraud for trading in stocks based on inside information received from a patient.[103]

Courts have disagreed on whether claims concerning release of information are subject to state medical malpractice claims procedures.[104]

PHYSICIAN-PATIENT PRIVILEGE. The physician-patient privilege is the rule that a physician is not permitted to testify as a witness concerning certain information gained in the physician-patient relationship. There was no physician-patient privilege from testimonial disclosure under the English common law. Nearly all U.S. courts also have adopted this position, so with few exceptions, the privilege exists only in states that have enacted privilege statutes. One exception is Alaska, which established a common law psychotherapist-patient privilege for criminal cases.[105] Federal courts must apply state privileges in lawsuits concerning state law, but state privileges do not apply in most federal lawsuits concerning federal law.[106]

Approximately two thirds of the states have enacted a statutory physician-patient privilege. Privilege statutes address only situations in which the physician is being compelled to testify, such as in a deposition, administrative hearing, or trial or to release subpoenaed records. There is a widespread misperception that privilege statutes apply to other disclosures, but in most states, this is not true.[107] The duty to maintain confidentiality outside of testimonial contexts is grounded on other statutes and legal principles. Thus, privilege statutes are usually of concern only when providers are responding to legal compulsion.

The privilege applies only when a bona fide physician-patient relationship exists. The privilege usually does not apply to court-ordered examinations or other examinations solely for the benefit of third parties, such as insurance companies.

The scope of the privilege varies. Pennsylvania limits the privilege to communications that tend to blacken the character of the patient,[108] while Kansas extends the privilege to all communications and observations.[109] Michigan limits the privilege to physicians,[110] while New York extends the

privilege to dentists and nurses.[111] When a nurse is present during a confidential communication between a physician and a patient, some states extend the privilege to the nurse, while other states rule that the communication is no longer privileged for the physician. Generally, the privilege extends to otherwise privileged information recorded in the hospital record.[112] However, information that is required to be reported to public authorities has generally been held not to be privileged unless the public authorities are also privileged not to disclose it.

Even when privileges otherwise apply, most state statutes include numerous exemptions from the privilege.[113] They vary between states.

Psychotherapist-Patient Privilege. In many states, a separate statute establishes a psychotherapist-patient privilege. The definition of a psychotherapist varies. The Georgia Supreme Court ruled that the state psychiatrist-patient privilege applied to nonpsychiatrists who devoted a substantial part of their time to mental diseases.[114]

In 1996, the U.S. Supreme Court recognized a federal psychotherapist-patient privilege.[115] The Supreme Court left open the possibility that a dangerous patient exception might develop, but federal appellate courts have refused to create such an exception.[116] In 2000, a federal appellate court ruled that parties waive the privilege when they place their medical condition in issue.[117]

Because most third-party payers require waiver of the privilege before providing payment, some psychotherapists make other arrangements with patients for payment to protect confidentiality.[118]

Waiver. The patient may waive the privilege, permitting the physician to testify. The privilege can be waived by contract. Insurance applications and policies often include waivers. Other actions can constitute implied waiver. Introducing evidence of medical details or failing to object to physician testimony generally waives the privilege.[119] Authorization of disclosure outside the testimonial context usually does not waive the privilege.[120] Thus, the patient generally may authorize other persons to have access to medical records outside of court and still successfully object to having them introduced into evidence unless other actions have waived the privilege. In a few states, authorization of any disclosure to opposing parties waives the privilege.[121] One federal appellate court has ruled that any disclosure to a third party waives the federal psychotherapist-patient privilege.[122]

Making a claim based on emotional distress or other mental condition usually waives the psychotherapist-patient privilege.[123] In some states, if the mental claim is dropped from the suit, the privilege is restored.[124]

Waiver of the privilege usually permits only formal discovery and testimony, not informal interviews. Express patient consent is generally required before informal interviews are permitted.[125] Other courts have permitted informal interviews based on waiver of the privilege.[126] However, in some states, it may be breach of the physician's duty to the patient to engage in informal interviews.[127] Most providers limit disclosures to formal channels unless express patient consent is obtained. One federal trial court has ruled that the HIPAA privacy rules impose this requirement of express consent to informal interviews.[128]

8-4.3 What Other Federal Privacy Laws Are Still Applicable?

The HIPAA privacy rules are not the only federal privacy laws applicable to healthcare information. For example, the federal substance abuse confidentiality rules remain in effect.

SUBSTANCE ABUSE. Special federal rules deal with confidentiality of information concerning patients treated or referred for treatment for alcoholism or drug abuse.[129] The rules apply to any specialized program for substance abuse in any facility receiving federal funds for any purpose, including Medicare or Medicaid reimbursement. Since 1994, the rules have not applied to treatment outside of specialized programs, so they do not apply to most emergency room treatments.[130]

The regulations preempt any state law that purports to authorize disclosures contrary to the regulations, but states are permitted to impose tighter confidentiality requirements. The rules apply to any disclosure, even acknowledgment of the patient's presence in the facility. Information may be released with the patient's consent if the consent is in writing and contains all the elements required by the federal rules.

A court order, including a subpoena, does not permit release of information unless the requirements of the regulations have all been met.[131] ⚑ The regulations require a court hearing and a court finding that the purpose for which the order is sought is more important than the purpose for which Congress mandated confidentiality. The regulations have been interpreted to permit hospitals to tell the court why they cannot comply with the order

until after a hearing. After a hearing, courts have ordered disclosures to assist probation revocation and child abuse proceedings,[132] to assist an Internal Revenue Service investigation of a surgeon,[133] and other situations.[134] Courts have declined to order disclosure when the information was sought to challenge the credibility of witnesses, assist in determining the rehabilitation potential of a convicted person for purposes of sentencing, or assist in a drug possession investigation.[135]

Child abuse reports may be made under state law without patient consent or a court order, but release of records to child abuse agencies requires consent or an order.

Federal courts have ruled that the federal substance abuse rules do not create a private cause of action for violations, so that only the federal government can sue for violations.[136]

FAMILY EDUCATIONAL RIGHTS AND PRIVACY ACT (FERPA). Strict federal rules preclude universities from sharing information about students with their parents or others without the students' consent.[137] This has created controversial situations where schools have not been able to involve parents in dealing with suicidal behaviors.[138] The HIPAA privacy rules do not apply to records that are subject to FERPA.[139]

FAIR AND ACCURATE CREDIT TRANSACTIONS ACT. There are federal restrictions on the use of medical information in credit reports.[140]

PRIVACY ACT. The Privacy Act[141] prohibits disclosures of records contained in a system of records maintained by a federal agency (or its contractors) without the written request or consent of the individual to whom the record pertains, subject to various statutory exceptions.

In some cases, the Privacy Act may prohibit some disclosures permitted by the HIPAA privacy rules. The preamble to the December 2000 HIPAA privacy rules indicates that the HIPAA privacy rules may prohibit some disclosures permitted by the Privacy Act and in those cases the HIPAA privacy rules must be followed.

8-5 What Are the Laws Concerning Use of Healthcare Information?

The HIPAA privacy rules permit broad uses of PHI for treatment, payment, and healthcare operations without patient authorization. This is subject to the requirement that the covered entity has privacy policies, workforce members are trained on the requirements, and contractors who have access to the information have a business associate agreement with the covered entity addressing the requirements.

These uses are generally subject to the minimum necessary standards mentioned in section 8-4.1.

State law has long recognized that providers must be able to use PHI, so the HIPAA privacy rules are consistent with the law of most states.

TREATMENT. Those who are involved in patient care must have timely access to records to fulfill the patient care functions of the records. Records must be readily accessible for present and future patient care. There will always be some risk of occasional unauthorized access by others.

In the past, some courts have tried to draw a distinction between diagnosis and treatment. HIPAA expressly rejects this distinction; treatment is defined to include "the provision, coordination, or management of health care and related services by one or more health care providers" and health care is defined to include diagnosis.[142]

HIPAA includes within the definition of permitted treatment uses the exchange of information among providers for consultation, referrals, and other treatment purposes. It is not unusual for a provider to need to know about the prior or concurrent treatment from other providers.

PAYMENT. Providers must be able to use healthcare information to process claims for payment. Payers have a legitimate need for data to justify their payments, and providers must be able to provide that data. State laws also recognize this.[143] HIPAA broadly defines what is in the scope of payment.[144]

HEALTHCARE OPERATIONS. HIPAA broadly defines the scope of healthcare operations.[145] Medical records are also business records. Many staff members must have access to medical records to operate the healthcare organization. An organization has authority to permit internal access by professional, technical, and administrative personnel who need access.

Under prior law, these administrative uses were so widely understood that they were seldom addressed in reported court decisions. The few cases were decided in favor of administrative access. In 1965, the highest court of New York authorized a trustee to examine medical records of patients involved in a controversial research project.[146] In

> Examples of tasks which may require access to medical records include: • Auditing • Filing • Replying to inquiries • Quality improvement • Risk management • Defending potential litigation

1975, a Missouri court upheld the authority of hospitals to review records for quality assurance purposes.[147] In 1979, a Canadian court ruled that the hospital's insurers and lawyers may have access to prepare to deal with patient claims.[148] However, in 1999, the Ohio Supreme Court ruled that a hospital could not share its records with a law firm that was hired to screen medical records to locate patients who could seek government payments.[149] Other courts have not placed this limit on the ability of hospitals to use agents. Some plaintiffs' attorneys have attempted to bar hospital attorneys from communicating with physicians and hospital employees involved in the case without the presence of the plaintiffs' attorneys. Courts have generally rejected these attempts.[150]

RESEARCH. Prior to the HIPAA privacy rules, healthcare providers generally could use their own records to conduct medical research without patient consent. Federal human subject regulations and many state laws expressly authorized this practice. Federal human subject regulations exempted some research involving only records from review processes or made the research eligible for expedited review.[151] Important medical discoveries have been made through researching medical records.[152]

The HIPAA privacy rules essentially eliminated the exemption from review. An institutional review board or privacy board must review all records research, and patient authorization must be obtained unless an institutional review board or privacy board grants a waiver of authorization.[153]

8-6 What Are the Laws Concerning Disclosure of Healthcare Information?

Courts generally adhere to the doctrine of stare decisis, which is frequently described as "following precedent." This section discusses the circumstances in which healthcare information can or must be disclosed outside of the covered entity and those working for the covered entity.

The following questions are addressed:

- 8-6.1. When can the patient or representative authorize disclosure of PHI?

- 8-6.2. When and how can disclosure be compelled in legal proceedings?

- 8-6.3. When are providers required or authorized to report PHI to legal authorities and others?

- 8-6.4. When may providers disclose PHI in response to inquiries from legal authorities?

- 8-6.5. When may providers disclose PHI in response to inquiries from others?

8-6.1 When Can the Patient or Representative Authorize Disclosure of PHI?

With rare exceptions, the patient (or representative of an incapacitated patient) may authorize release of PHI to themselves or others.

AUTHORIZATION BY PATIENT. Competent patients can generally authorize access to themselves and others. The HIPAA privacy regulations recognize this right, while permitting withholding of information in limited circumstances if specified procedures are followed.[154]

The right of access by the patient has been widely recognized prior to HIPAA either through statutes or court decisions.[155] In 1986, a Pennsylvania court found that denial of access could be intentional infliction of emotional distress.[156] In 1990, the Maryland high court ruled that a hospital could be assessed punitive damages for failing to provide requested medical records within a reasonable time.[157]

In 1994, a Florida appellate court ruled that a healthcare provider could require that the patient's signature on a release form be notarized.[158] This case should not be interpreted to suggest that notarization is necessary. However, it is clear that courts will accept identity checks that are appropriate to the situation.

Providers generally cannot condition release of records on prior arrangements for payment for the documented care. In 1997, a California appellate court ruled that a provider could not require the patient to sign a lien before releasing records.[159]

The right to authorize others to have access has also been widely recognized prior to HIPAA.[160]

HIPAA generally permits disclosures to family members, relatives, and close friends who are involved in the patient's care, unless the patient objects.[161] In essence, there is implied authorization to keep those involved in the patient's care informed, unless the patient objects or other law prohibits the disclosure. The federal substance abuse confidentiality rules discussed in section 8-4.3 restrict disclosures related to substance abuse treatment.

Release of psychiatric information is subject to special restrictions in some states. In 1982, a New York court stated that a spouse should not be given psychiatric information, even when there is no estrangement, unless (1) the patient authorizes disclosure or (2) a danger to the patient, spouse, or another person can be reduced by disclosure.[162] Some states authorize disclosure of psychiatric information to spouses and others in additional circumstances.[163]

Providers can refuse to release records until presented with a release form that complies with their reasonable policies. A Missouri court upheld a hospital's refusal to release records to an attorney who presented a form with an altered date.[164]

When providers agree to release information, they may be liable for failing to do so. In 1999, a federal appellate court ruled that a former patient could sue a psychiatric facility, when a staff member failed to fulfill a promise to inform the patient's employer that the employee was unable to come to work.[165]

EXCEPTIONS. The HIPAA privacy rules recognize that there are some circumstances where release of the information to the patient can endanger the life or physical safety of the patient and permit withholding information in such cases subject to a right to have the decision reviewed.[166] Courts had previously recognized some exceptions to the general rule in favor of access. Courts have generally insisted that medically contraindicated information be made available to the patient's representative, who is frequently an outside professional acting on behalf of the patient. For example, in 1979, a federal appellate court addressed the withholding of information from patients preparing for hearings challenging their transfer to a lower level of care.[167] The court ruled that it was not enough for the state to offer to release information to a representative when the patient did not have a representative. The state was permitted to withhold medically contraindicated information from patients only when they had representatives, provided by the state if necessary.

Mental health information is treated differently in some circumstances. In 1995, the Utah Supreme Court ruled that a mental health clinic could assert a privilege not to disclose its records even after the patient executed a release document.[168] In a 1983 case, a New York mental hospital attempted to enforce its policy of releasing records only to physicians.[169] The court ruled that the records could be protected from disclosure only if the hospital proved release would cause detriment (1) to the patient, (2) to involved third parties, or (3) to an important hospital program. Because none of these was proved, the court ordered disclosure to the persons authorized by the patient. In 1997, a federal court ruled that a Florida statute denying persons with mental conditions access to obtain their medical records after discharge discriminated against persons with mental disabilities, violating the Americans with Disabilities Act.[170]

AUTHORIZATION BY THE PATIENT'S REPRESENTATIVE. When authorization is required and the patient is unable to authorize access because of incapacity, minority, or death, someone other than the patient must authorize access. The HIPAA privacy rules state that a personal representative of the patient has the same rights as the patient and specifies how to determine who may be a personal representative.[171]

Mentally Incapacitated Patients. The HIPAA privacy rules generally look to state law to identify the personal representative. Anyone that state law permits to make medical decisions is a personal representative. Some courts have suppressed family confidences and information that could upset the patient severely.[172] Similarly, the HIPAA privacy rules permit withholding information that is reasonably likely to cause substantial harm.[173]

In 2004, a New York court ruled that under the HIPAA privacy rules an agent under an activated healthcare proxy was entitled to access.[174]

When the mental incapacity is temporary and the release of the information can reasonably wait, it usually is appropriate to wait for the patient's authorization.

MINORS. The HIPAA privacy rules generally look to state law to determine when a parent or other individual who has assumed parental rights, duties, and obligations is the personal representative and may authorize disclosure of PHI.[175] For most minors, state laws provide for the decision whether to release records to be made by a custodial parent. Access rights of noncustodial parents vary from state to state and can depend on the specific wording of the applicable court order assigning custodial rights.[176]

States vary greatly in the extent to which older minors are allowed to control access of parents and guardians to records.[177] Some state statutes specify that information regarding certain types of treatment, such as treatment for venereal disease and substance abuse, cannot be disclosed without the minor's consent. Some statutes specify that parents must be informed before a minor obtains certain kinds of services.[178]

In some states, when minors may legally consent to their own care, parents do not have a right to information concerning the care. If the minor fails to make other arrangements to pay for the care and relies on the parents to pay, the parents can be entitled to more information.

Providers generally can release information concerning immature minors to custodial parents without substantial risk of liability unless state statutes expressly prohibit release. When a mature minor wishes information withheld from parents, the provider must make a professional judgment concerning information release to the parents except in the few circumstances where the law is settled, such as when a constitutional statute requires or forbids notification. Disclosure is generally permitted when there is likelihood of harm (such as contagious disease) to the minor or others and avoidance of that harm requires parental involvement.

STATE STATUTES SHOULD BE FOLLOWED. A Georgia court ruled that a father could sue a psychiatrist for releasing his minor daughter's mental health records to his former wife's attorney for use in custody litigation.[179] The daughter had requested the release and had ratified it after becoming an adult, but the release did not comply with the state statute.

DECEASED PATIENTS. The HIPAA privacy rules apply after the death of the patient.[180] The executor, administrator, or other person authorized to act on behalf of the deceased individual or estate may act as the personal representative.[181] Disclosures can be made without authorization for some law enforcement purposes, disposal of the body, or cadaveric organ donation.[182]

If there is an executor or administrator of the estate, required authorizations should usually be sought from that person.[183] If there is no executor or administrator, in most states authorization should be obtained from the next of kin, such as a surviving spouse[184] or a child.[185] Authorizations signed by the patient before death may still apply.[186]

The Wisconsin Supreme Court ruled that a hospital could insist that the person signing an authorization for release of the records of a deceased person state the authority of the person signing.[187]

8-6.2 When and How Can Disclosure Be Compelled in Legal Proceedings?

Even if the patient or representative opposes information release, healthcare providers can be compelled by law to disclose information in legal proceedings through subpoenas and other procedures to discover evidence.

In lawsuits and administrative proceedings, the parties are authorized by law to demand relevant unprivileged information in the control of others. Lawyers call this the discovery process.

SUBPOENAS AND OTHER DISCOVERY ORDERS. The most frequent discovery demand is called a subpoena. A subpoena is a request for production of documents, or a request for an individual to appear in court or other legal proceeding. In federal courts and in most states, demands to parties are generally called notices of deposition or notices to produce, while actual subpoenas are used only for persons who are not parties to the suit. Notices and subpoenas have essentially the same effect, so what is said about subpoenas in the rest of this chapter also applies to notices. When the demands are ignored, a court can order compliance, and further noncompliance can be punished as contempt of court. Contempt of court is a court order which, in the context of a court trial or hearing, declares a person or organization to have disobeyed or been disrespectful of the court's authority. A judge may hold a litigant "in contempt," and may even impose sanctions, when the judge determines the person has disrupted the court's orderly process.

In some jurisdictions, a subpoena is issued by the court and constitutes a court order. A court order is generally sufficient authorization to release a medical record, unless special protections apply. For example, federal rules require a court order before substance abuse records may be released.

In some jurisdictions where individual attorneys are permitted to issue subpoenas without involvement of a court, noncourt subpoenas are not sufficient authorization to release medical records in some circumstances.[188] In those circumstances, the provider should assert the confidentiality of the records and demand a court order or authorization from the patient or an appropriate representative.[189]

Some states have sought to simplify the discovery process by mandating exchange of records. However, such requirements are not universal. For example, in 1997, the Illinois Supreme Court declared such a law to be an unconstitutional violation of the separation of powers and of privacy rights.[190]

HIPAA REQUIREMENTS. The HIPAA privacy rules permit subpoenas and other court-ordered releases of PHI. However, when a subpoena is issued without a court order, the covered entity must be provided with assurances that there have been reasonable efforts to notify the patient or obtain a protective order.[191]

RESPONSES TO SUBPOENAS AND OTHER DISCOVERY ORDERS. In most situations, the proper response to a valid subpoena or discovery order is compliance. However, prompt legal assistance should be sought because some subpoenas or orders are not valid and others should be resisted.[192] A discovery order should never be ignored. A subpoena is part of a court's legal process and failure to respond is considered contempt of court in most states.

Subpoenas from state courts in other states are usually not valid unless they are given to the person being subpoenaed while that person is in the state of the issuing court. For example, in 1993, a New York appellate court ruled that a New York physician could be sued for releasing information pursuant to a Pennsylvania state subpoena.[193] Courts in some states have authority to issue subpoenas to persons only in a limited area. Most states have a procedure for obtaining a valid subpoena from a local court to require the release of information for a trial in a distant court that does not have the authority to issue a valid subpoena. Some state courts will order a party to sign a document requesting and authorizing release of records, especially out-of-state records, instead of going through the process of obtaining an order where the records are located.[194]

Subpoenas from federal courts in other states are usually valid.

Sometimes challenges to subpoenas are successful. A New Jersey court refused to order a woman or her psychiatrist to answer questions concerning nonfinancial matters in a marriage separation case because the husband had failed to demonstrate relevance or good cause for the order.[195] When judges are not certain whether to order a release, they sometimes will order that the information be presented for court review before ruling.[196]

In some situations, the only way to obtain prompt appellate review of an apparently inappropriate discovery order is to risk being found in contempt of court. In one case a physician challenged a grand jury subpoena of records of sixty-three patients.[197] The trial court found the physician to be in contempt for failing to comply. The Illinois Supreme Court held that he must release the records of the one patient who had waived her physician-patient privilege but reversed the contempt finding on the other sixty-two records. They were protected by the physician-patient privilege in Illinois until a showing of a criminal action relating to the treatment documented in the records was made. In another Illinois case, the appellate court ruled that the trial court had erred in jailing a physician and his attorney for contempt of court concerning a deposition. The applicable statute did not permit more discovery than had been given, and the trial court failed to show any accommodation for the patients scheduled for the physician's care.[198]

Valid subpoenas should never be ignored and should never be challenged except on advice of an attorney, but attorneys should be cautious in giving such advice. A federal court found an attorney to be in contempt and fined the attorney for advising the client to resist a subpoena in a Medicare investigation.[199]

MEDICAL INFORMATION. A subpoena can require that medical records (or copies) be provided to the court or to the other side in the suit. If an individual's physical or mental condition is at issue in the litigation, he or she may also be ordered to submit to a physical or mental examination. During a deposition, a person submits to formal questioning under oath prior to the trial. Deposition testimony may later be used as testimony at trial, if the person questioned is unavailable to testify in person during the trial.

PARTIES. Under the current liberal discovery practices, medical records of parties can nearly always be subpoenaed if the mental or physical condition of the party is relevant. Further, those who provided the health care may be ordered to give depositions.

NONPARTIES. In most circumstances, courts will not permit discovery of information concerning health care of persons who are not parties.[200] Some attorneys have sought such information to establish what happened when similar treatment was given to other patients. Providers have resisted these attempts on the basis that they invade patient privacy, violate the physician-patient privilege discussed in a later section, and are not relevant because of the uniqueness of the condition and reaction of each patient.

The only widely accepted exceptions in which discovery of nonparty records has been permitted have been cases of billing fraud or professional discipline.[201] Some courts have permitted access to medical records of nonparties in malpractice suits but have required all "identifiers" to be deleted.[202] However, other courts have reaffirmed the traditional rule and declined to order access even with identifiers deleted.[203]

PATIENT NAMES. Some attorneys have attempted to bypass the rule against disclosure of nonparty medical records by seeking nonparty patients' names and obtaining their permission to get the records. Providers have resisted these attempts for reasons similar to those for resisting discovery of records. Most courts have not permitted discovery of nonparty patient names. For example, in 2002, the Illinois Supreme Court considered a case where the Department of Professional Regulation subpoenaed the medical records of two individuals who were not parties to the case. The Illinois Supreme Court ruled that merely deleting patient names and other identifying information from patient records before disclosing them violated the physician-patient privilege.[204] In 2004, the Supreme Court of New York held that the discovery of nonparty patient names and addresses violated the physician-patient privilege.[205] Similarly, in 2006, the Superior Court of New Jersey held that information that a patient communicates in confidence to a physician or hospital that is protected from disclosure by the physician-patient privilege includes the patient's name and address.[206]

COMMITTEE REPORTS. Many states have enacted statutes protecting quality improvement and peer review activities and committee reports from discovery or admission into evidence. Peer review is the process by which a committee of physicians examines the work of a peer and determines whether the physician under review has met the accepted standard of medical care. Laws protecting the confidentiality of information discovered during the peer review process are intended to encourage self-regulation by the medical profession through peer review and evaluation. Courts have found these laws constitutional.[207]

Different states have taken different stances with respect to the extent to which the activities and reports of peer review committees should be protected. Some courts have strictly interpreted statutory protections, reducing their effectiveness. For example, in 2009, the Colorado Supreme Court held that Colorado's peer review statute prevented the proceedings of a medical review committee engaged in the process of peer review from being subject to discovery or introduction into evidence in a civil action, but did not bar the disclosure of such information pursuant to the Connecticut Freedom of Information Act.[208] Similarly, a New Jersey court refused to extend the statutory protection for "utilization review committees" to related committees, such as the medical records committee and infection control committee.[209] In 2007, the Florida Supreme Court considered whether Florida's peer review law protected a list generated by a hospital, which included a peer review committee recommendation delineating the privileges given to a member of a hospital staff.[210] The court held that the peer review statute did not exempt the hospital from disclosure of its decision to grant or deny certain practice privileges to a physician.[211] Similarly, the Georgia Supreme Court held that to the extent that there was information in a physician's credentialing files that did not involve a peer review committee's evaluations of his performance of medical procedures, that information was discoverable.[212]

The decision of a West Virginia court is illustrative of the hostility of some courts towards peer review and committee privileges. In that case, the court ruled that judges should not rely on a hospital's assertion of the privilege, but instead should inspect all the documents for which the privilege was claimed and require the hospital to prove that each document was protected by the privilege.[213]

In other jurisdictions, however, courts have interpreted statutory protections more broadly.[214] In 2009, the Alabama Supreme Court, in construing Alabama's peer review statute, stated that the statute protected any document considered by the peer review committee or hospital board in its decision-making process.[215] The Minnesota Supreme Court found that a complications conference report was protected under a statute that protected "the proceedings and records of a review organization."[216] Under some states' laws, the identities of persons involved in peer review are also protected.[217] In 2005, an Ohio appellate court ruled that a hospital did not have to produce a list of peer reviewed documents in order to assert the privilege for them.[218]

Some state laws only protect peer review records from discovery; if they are obtained through other channels they can be used in court.[219] Other laws protect the records from being introduced in lawsuits even if they are obtained outside discovery channels.[220]

Even when the privilege does apply, many state laws permit state licensing agencies to gain access.[221] This can become a significant loophole in the protection of peer review committee information. For example, in 1998, the Kansas Supreme Court permitted private plaintiffs to access and use most of the records the state licensing agency had obtained.[222]

In addition to protections afforded by individual state statutes, federal law also provides some safeguards for information generated in the course of peer review activities. The Health Care Quality Improvement Act (HCQIA) provides immunity from damages to participants in a professional review action if the action meets certain standards

and follows certain procedures.[223] HCQIA provides this immunity as an "incentive and protection for physicians engaging in effective professional peer review."[224] In enacting HCQIA, Congress believed that effective peer review, including mandatory reporting to a nationwide database, could alleviate the national problem of "the increasing occurrence of medical malpractice" by "restricting the ability of incompetent physicians to move from State to State without disclosure or discovery of the physician's previous damaging or incompetent performance."[225] However, HCQIA does not provide unqualified immunity to all peer review decisions. In order to ensure that such review is effective and not abused, HCQIA only provides immunity to "professional review actions" based on a physician's "competence or professional conduct,"[226] and it mandates specific standards and procedures that must be followed.[227]

Nevertheless, because the status of committee reports is still an open question in many states, these reports should be carefully written so that, if they must be released, they will not inappropriately increase liability exposure.

PATIENT SAFETY ORGANIZATIONS. Information pertaining to medical errors may also be protected from discovery in litigation if it is reported to an authorized Patient Safety Organization (PSO). In 1999, the Institutes of Medicine published a report entitled "To Err is Human, Building a Safer Health System," detailing the enormous human, financial, and societal impact of preventable medical errors each year.[228] The report called on Congress to establish a network of independent patient safety organizations nationwide. As a response, the federal Patient Safety and Quality Improvement Act was signed into law in 2005.[229]

The federal Patient Safety and Quality Improvement Act creates PSOs to collect, aggregate, and analyze confidential information reported by healthcare providers.

The federal Agency for Healthcare Research and Quality (AHRQ) is the organization responsible for certifying PSOs, and there are currently approximately 77 federally certified PSOs nationwide.[230] The Act provides federal legal privilege and confidentiality protections to information that is assembled and reported by providers to a PSO or developed by a PSO ("patient safety work product") for the conduct of patient safety activities. Patient safety work product is privileged and not subject to discovery, nor admissible as evidence, in connection with a federal, state, or local civil, criminal, or administrative proceeding, including a proceeding against a medical provider.

8-6.3 When Are Providers Required or Authorized to Report PHI to Legal Authorities and Others?

Federal and state laws compel disclosure of protected health information in many contexts other than discovery or testimony. Reporting laws have been enacted that require such information to be reported to governmental agencies. The most common examples are vital statistics, infectious diseases, child abuse, and wound reporting laws. Familiarity with these and other reporting laws is important to assure compliance and to avoid reporting to the wrong agency. Reports to the wrong agency may not be legally protected, resulting in potential liability for breach of confidentiality.

HIPAA. The HIPAA Privacy Rule permits covered entities to comply with state laws that require reports or other disclosures.[231]

VITAL STATISTICS. All states require the reporting of births and deaths.[232]

PUBLIC HEALTH. Most states require reports of infectious diseases.[233] A California court observed that in addition to criminal penalties for not reporting, civil liability is possible in a suit by persons who contract diseases that might have been avoided by proper reports.[234] Some states require reports of certain poisonings, cancer cases, and other selected noncontagious diseases.

In 1994, a Missouri appellate court barred enforcement of a local court rule requiring correction facilities to disclose the infectious disease reports of inmates before court appearances.[235]

CHILD ABUSE. All states require reports of suspected cases of child abuse or neglect.[236] The HIPAA Privacy Rule expressly permits child abuse reports.[237]

Some professionals, such as physicians and nurses, are mandatory reporters and thus are required to make reports. Anyone who is not a mandatory reporter may make a report as a permissive reporter. In some states, any report arising out of diagnosis or treatment in an institution must be made through the institutional administration. In some states, a professional is a mandatory reporter only when the child has been examined or treated but is a permissive reporter when the abuse is learned from the abuser or another person.[238] In some states, providers are required to report abuse that they learn from others but only if the abuse occurred in the state.[239]

Most child abuse reporting laws extend some degree of immunity from liability for reports made through proper channels.[240] A mandatory reporter who fails to report child abuse is subject to both criminal penalties[241] and civil liability for future injuries to the child that could have been avoided if a report had been made.[242] In 2003, in a prosecution of an emergency nurse, a Missouri trail court decided that the criminal penalties for not reporting were unconstitutional.[243]

There have been disputes in some states over when some activities, such as sexual activity of younger minors, must be reported as child abuse.[244]

ADULT ABUSE/DOMESTIC VIOLENCE. Some states have enacted adult abuse reporting laws that are similar to the child abuse reporting laws.[245] Unlike child abuse laws, these laws are usually more permissive, with no required reporting.[246] The HIPAA Privacy Rule permits required reports; permissive reports are required in some limited circumstances.[247] These laws are controversial.[248]

WOUNDS. Many states require the reporting of certain wounds.[249] Some states specify that all wounds of certain types must be reported. For example, New York requires the reporting of wounds inflicted by sharp instruments that may result in death and all gunshot wounds.[250] Other states limit the reporting requirement to wounds caused under certain circumstances. For example, Iowa requires the reporting of wounds that apparently resulted from criminal acts.[251]

In 2002, a New York district attorney sought to compel New York City hospitals to produce all records pertaining to male Caucasian emergency room patients between the ages of 30 and 45 who sought treatment for knife wounds on two dates. The highest court of New York ruled that the subpoena could not be enforced. The state law that mandated reporting knife wounds was limited to life-threatening stab wounds. Treatment for other stab wounds was privileged.[252]

DRIVERS. A few states require reports to be submitted to state driver licensing agencies of conditions such as seizures that could lead to loss of license. Most states permit such reports but do not require them.[253]

OTHER REPORTING LAWS. Some states require reports of other information, such as industrial accidents and radiation incidents.[254] National reporting laws apply to hospitals that are involved in manufacturing, testing, or using certain substances and devices. For example, fatalities due to blood transfusions must be reported to the Food and Drug Administration (FDA).[255] A sponsor of an investigational medical device must report to the FDA any unanticipated adverse effects from use of the device.[256] There is a duty to report deaths or serious injuries in connection with devices.[257]

Some states require that major adverse incidents be reported to a state agency.[258] The director of nursing at a nursing home was personally fined in New York for failing to make such a report.[259]

In 1977, the U.S. Supreme Court upheld a state law that required reports to a central state registry of all prescriptions of Schedule II controlled substances.[260]

A federal law requires hospitals to notify emergency transport personnel and other individuals who bring emergency patients to the hospital if the patient is diagnosed as having an infectious disease.[261]

COMMON LAW DUTY TO DISCLOSE. In addition to these statutory requirements, the common law has recognized a duty to disclose medical information in several circumstances. Persons who could have avoided injury if information had been disclosed have won civil suits against providers who failed to disclose such information.

INFECTIOUS DISEASES. When an infectious disease is diagnosed, there is a duty to warn third parties at risk of exposure unless forbidden by statute.[262] However, in most states there is no duty to warn all members of the general public. In a California case, the court observed that liability to the general public might result from failure to make a required report to public health authorities.[263] In at least one state, there is a duty to warn a broader range of individuals. In 1986, the South Carolina Supreme Court ruled that a hospital could be sued by the parents of a girl who had died of meningitis. Her friend had been diagnosed and treated at the hospital for meningitis, and the hospital had not notified persons who had prior contact with its patient during the likely period of contagiousness.[264]

THREATS TO OTHERS. Some courts have ruled that there is a duty to warn identified persons that a patient has made a credible threat to kill them. Other courts have expanded the duty. The first decision to impose this duty was *Tarasoff v. Regents of University of California*.[265] When the Tarasoffs sued for the death of their daughter, the California Supreme Court found the employer of a psychiatrist liable for the psychiatrist's failure to warn the daughter that one of his patients had threatened to kill her. The court ruled that he should have either warned the victim or advised others likely to apprise the victim of the danger. In a 1980 case, the same court clarified the scope of this duty by ruling that only threats to readily identified individuals create a duty to warn, so there is no duty to warn a threatened group.[266]

OTHER DUTIES. Courts have recognized other situations that lead to a duty to disclose. One example is the duty of referral specialists to communicate their findings to the referring physician.[267] A competent patient can waive this duty by directing the referral specialist not to communicate with the referring physician.[268]

8-6.4 When May Providers Disclose PHI in Response to Inquiries from Legal Authorities?

The HIPAA Privacy Rule authorizes disclosures of PHI without patient authorization for some public health activities,[269] health oversight activities,[270] administrative proceedings,[271] law enforcement purposes,[272] cadaveric organ, eye, or tissue donation purposes,[273] research purposes,[274] to avert a serious threat to health or safety,[275] and various specialized governmental functions. The HIPAA Privacy Rule defines in detail when disclosures without consent can be made for each of these purposes. This section discusses law enforcement disclosures.

PRESENCE IN FACILITY. Providers may confirm the presence in the facility of a named patient or a patient with a physical description (e.g., height, weight, hair and eye color, race, gender, scars, presence or absence of facial hair, scars, and tattoos), except for patients subject to the substance abuse treatment confidentiality rules.[277]

However, generally providers cannot respond to individual law enforcement requests to report when a patient arrives with a particular medical condition. There are at least three exceptions: (1) when the law requires or permits reports about the medical condition (such as certain wounds) to law enforcement; (2) if the law enforcement officer is trying to locate a suspect, victim, or material witness to a crime, in most states providers may disclose type of injury and date and time of treatment or death; or (3) when a law enforcement officer calls to ask for information and discloses that a person who could become a patient is dangerous, providers can take appropriate steps to protect themselves and others from dangerous persons, which in some cases can involve notifying law enforcement officials to assist in protection.

DISCHARGE OF PRISONERS. When persons in law enforcement custody are discharged from the provider back to a jail or prison, generally medical authorities at the jail or prison can be told the information that is necessary for the ongoing care of the prisoner. Guards who are transporting the prisoner generally cannot be told medical information. However, information that is necessary for a safe transport is permitted, for example, a propensity for violence that is not known by the guards.[278]

POLICE REPORTS. Providers are not permitted to provide PHI to law enforcement officers for the purposes of investigating a crime or completing a police report, unless there is written authorization from the patient or court action (search warrant or court order). This includes requests for the extent of injury, diagnoses, treatment plans, personal impressions (e.g., "Did you smell alcohol on his breath?"), and medications. Law enforcement must obtain a search warrant, court order, or patient authorization before accessing PHI. Failure to do so can bar the admissibility of any information obtained.[279] Generally, if a patient has provided false identification to obtain a prescription or other services, information necessary to investigate this crime on the provider's premises can be disclosed to law enforcement.

COLLECTION AND TESTING OF SAMPLES. It is permissible for providers to draw blood and other forensic samples at the request of law enforcement officers to the extent permitted by state law. The most common example of this is the drawing of a blood sample of someone who is suspected of driving while under the influence of alcohol or drugs. Drawing the sample and delivering it to the law enforcement officer for testing by a forensic laboratory is not a disclosure of PHI.

However, providers must not let law enforcement officers influence their decisions whether to draw blood or collect other samples for clinical purposes and testing by the provider. Clinical sample collection at the direction of law enforcement officers can be a constitutional violation, and the results are generally not admissible in court.[280]

When law enforcement officers seek a sample collected for clinical purposes or the results of testing on the sample, they must obtain a court order or search warrant. Providers must not voluntarily release the samples or results. In most states, voluntarily released samples or results generally are not admissible in court.[281]

REMOVAL OF BULLETS AND OTHER FOREIGN OBJECTS. The law concerning removal of bullets or other foreign objects from patients varies somewhat from state to state. There are constitutional limits on compelling such removal (see section 8-7.4). Assuming the removal is appropriately authorized, there are three approaches to delivering the object to law enforcement. In some circumstances, providers may authorize law enforcement officers to be present during the removal and directly deliver the objects to the witnessing officer without a court order.[282] The circumstances vary from state to state. Wisconsin permits law enforcement officers to be present in the operating room during surgical removal of bags of cocaine if the patient is in law enforcement custody.[283] When law enforcement is not permitted to assume direct custody, the more conservative position is to require a search warrant, court order, or patient consent before releasing objects to law enforcement, but most of the courts that have addressed the question have permitted bullets to be admitted into evidence even when police obtain them without a warrant, order, or consent.[284]

CRIMES ON THE PREMISES. Providers may report crimes that occur on their premises. Usually, disclosure of PHI is not required to make these reports. When PHI is related to the crime, PHI may be disclosed to the extent necessary to provide evidence of the crime. For example, when drugs are stolen, the name and amount of drug may be disclosed, but the diagnosis should generally not be disclosed.

FEDERAL LAW ENFORCEMENT. The HIPAA Privacy Rule permits disclosures for some national security activities and for protective services for the President and others.[285] Disclosures must also be made when necessary for enforcement of the HIPAA Privacy Rules,[286] Medicare, Medicaid, and other governmental payment programs.[287]

8-6.5 When May Providers Disclose PHI in Response to Inquiries from Others?

Some statutes do not mandate reporting but authorize access to medical records, without the patient's permission, on request of certain individuals or organizations or the general public.

WORKERS' COMPENSATION. Some state statutes grant all parties to a workers' compensation claim access to all relevant medical information after a claim has been made.[288] In some states, courts have ruled that filing a workers' compensation claim is a waiver of confidentiality of relevant medical information.[289] However, in at least one state the physician-patient privilege applies in workers' compensation cases.[290] The HIPAA Privacy Rules permits compliance with these workers' compensation laws.[291]

FEDERAL FREEDOM OF INFORMATION ACT. The federal Freedom of Information Act (FOIA) applies only to federal agencies.[292] A provider does not become a federal agency by receiving federal funds, so the FOIA applies to few hospitals outside of the VA and Defense Department hospital systems. FOIA does not apply to medical files; so disclosure of medical information pursuant to a FOIA request would "constitute a clearly unwarranted invasion of personal privacy." Thus, the FOIA provides only limited protection of confidentiality of medical information in the possession of federal agencies. However, the federal Privacy Act may provide some additional protection to such information.[293]

STATE PUBLIC RECORDS LAWS. Many states have public records laws that apply to state agencies that are covered entities, such as public hospitals. Some state statutes explicitly exempt hospital and medical records from disclosure.[294] In a 1974 case, Colorado's law was interpreted not to permit a publisher to obtain all birth and death reports routinely.[295] In 1983, the Iowa Supreme Court addressed the effort of a leukemia patient to force the disclosure of an unrelated potential bone marrow donor whose name was in the records of a public hospital.[296] The court ruled that names of patients could be withheld from disclosure and that although the potential donor had never sought treatment at the hospital, the potential donor was a patient for purposes of the exemption because the medical procedure of tissue typing had been performed. However, in a 1978 Ohio case, the state law was interpreted to require access to the names and the dates of admission and discharge of all persons admitted to a public hospital.[297] In states that follow the Ohio rule, it is especially important to resist discovery of nonparty records because removal of "identifiers" does not offer much protection when dates in the records may make it possible to identify the patient from the admission list.

OTHER ACCESS LAWS. Some federal and state statutes give governmental agencies access to medical records on request or through administrative subpoena.[298] For example, peer review organizations (PROs) have access to all medical records pertinent to their federal review functions on request. Hospital licensing laws often grant inspectors access without subpoena for audit and inspection purposes.

8-7 What Legal Issues Flow from the Use of Audio and Video Transmissions and Recordings?

AUDIO RECORDINGS. Federal law and the law of many states permit recording of conversations by any party to the conversation.[299] In most circumstances, the other states require the consent of all parties to the conversation. In some jurisdictions, these laws apply primarily to recording of telephone and other transmitted conversations; in other jurisdictions, they apply to all conversations but generally do not apply where there is no reasonable expectation of privacy.

VISUAL RECORDINGS. Physicians may take and use photographs of patients for the medical record or for professional educational purposes if the patient expressly consents. The Maine Supreme Court ruled that when a patient had expressly objected to being photographed, there could be liability for photographing the patient even if the photograph was solely for the medical record.[300] Liability for photographs taken without express consent is not likely if the patient does not object and uses are appropriately restricted. A New York appellate court ruled that a physician and nurse could not be sued for allowing a newspaper photographer to photograph a patient in the waiting areas of an infectious disease unit because the individual's presence did not indicate the individual was a patient and the individual was never identified as a patient.[301] Public or commercial showing without consent can lead to liability.[302]

Visual recordings have led to a wide variety of situations that courts have addressed. One group of cases deals with the right to make recordings. In 1985, a New York appellate court ruled that representatives of an incompetent patient do not have a right to photograph the patient in the hospital.[303] The petitioners failed to show a sufficient need to justify a court order that they be permitted to film their comatose daughter in an intensive care unit for eight hours for use in a suit. In an unreported New Jersey appellate court case in 2000, a hospital was ordered to permit videotaping in an intensive care unit.[304]

Other suits have dealt with liability for media recordings.[305] In 1998, the California Supreme Court ruled that an accident victim could sue two television production companies for invasion of privacy for taping the victim's medical helicopter flight to the hospital. The court ruled that some of the recording at the scene of the accident may also have constituted an invasion of privacy.[306]

Other suits have involved the use of recordings.[307] In 2002, a Florida trial court permitted the parents of a comatose woman to televise a videotape of her condition since it had been shown in court.[308] In 2002, a woman used the surgeon's videotape of her surgery to support her suit claiming that he had branded her during the surgery.[309]

TJC requires consent before audio or video recording of patients for any purpose other than identification, diagnosis, or treatment.[310] This means that Joint Commission-accredited hospitals must obtain consent for recordings that are for educational purposes.

8-8 What Legal Issues Flow from the Use of Computers and the Internet?

FEDERAL POLICY. There is an increasing push for use of computerized medical records. In 2004, the President announced an effort to adopt electronic health records by 2014.[311] The Veterans Administration has adopted a computerized medical record.[312] The federal Consolidated Health Informatics Initiative is seeking to establish the framework for sharing health information among federal agencies and is pursuing interoperability standards.[313] An Executive Order in 2004 established a federal Office of Health Information Technology.[314]

The American Relief and Recovery Act of 2009 (ARRA) provides billions of dollars for health information technology investments. Most of the money is available to hospitals and physicians who adopt and meaningfully use qualified electronic health records.

COMPUTERIZED RECORDKEEPING. Computerized records are generally more accessible than paper records for their many functions. Multiple uses can occur concurrently, reducing the need for waiting for others to complete their uses of the paper record. They permit more standardization of datakeeping. They remove some of the problems with legibility of some paper records and assist in reducing some preventable errors. Computer programs can assist physicians in making diagnostic and treatment decisions through clinical decision support. There is an opportunity to build in checking procedures that can call attention to and even bar potentially problematic orders. Computerized records provide an opportunity for more automatic analysis of data.

There are potential disadvantages to computerized systems.[315] Computerized systems are costly.[316] In addition, they can divert professional time from patient care. Data still must be entered by someone. Many approaches require data entry by physicians and other professionals that can divert their time from other functions, reducing the quantity of patient care that can be provided. They create a temptation to require the collection of more data that further diverts resources from patient care. These are not necessarily arguments against computerization. Rather they need to be kept in mind by those structuring the systems.

Another potential disadvantage is the security risk. Unauthorized users can sometimes gain access. Authorized users can access records for unauthorized purposes. However, this is a strong argument against computerized records. Similar risks exist with paper records. In addition, computerized systems are more effective in tracking uses of records than are paper records. Steps are being taken to provide more security for computerized records.

The HIPAA Privacy and Security Rules apply to access to and use of computerized records. The HIPAA Security Rule requires that computerized records and communications meet basic security standards, effective April 21, 2005.

It is cumbersome to structure computerized records so that authorized persons cannot access records beyond those they need for their job because it is usually not possible to determine in advance which records they will need to access. Thus, training, professional standards, and monitoring of lookups are used to deter and detect inappropriate lookups. There have been few legal cases involving inappropriate lookups.[317]

For several years, some healthcare providers have been developing computerized methods for handling some healthcare information. For a time, one legal barrier was the requirement of authentication of physician entries and orders by a physician signature that could only be performed on a hard copy. Electronic signatures are now generally accepted, so this barrier has largely been removed. In 2000, the federal government adopted a law recognizing electronic signatures for most purposes.[318] However, care must still be exercised in the structuring and use of electronic signatures.[319] Some states have had centralized computer records of some healthcare information. In 1977, the U.S. Supreme Court upheld New York's mandatory reporting of prescriptions, discussing how the information was placed into a centralized state computer system.[320]

Another legal barrier was that some jurisdictions would not accept computerized records as official records. Computerized records are now generally accepted as official records for regulatory and evidentiary purposes if they meet basic standards of reliability.[321]

One barrier to the standardization of documentation has been the difficulty in establishing standard terminology. Progress is being made in addressing this issue. On May 6, 2004, the HHS announced that it had licensed the College of American Pathologists Systematized Nomenclature of Medicine Clinical Terms (SNOMED-CT®) for laboratory result contents, nonlaboratory interventions and procedures, anatomy, diagnosis and problems, and nursing and announced that it was making SNOMED-CT available for use in the United States at no charge to users.[322]

E-MAIL. Many providers use e-mail to communicate with patients and other providers.[323] With appropriate attention to confidentiality and the different nature of interaction, this practice appears to offer advantages. In 1998, a Wisconsin appellate court recognized the validity of e-mail prescriptions.[324] One of the impediments to broader adoption of e-mail communications with patients has been the lack of payment for the time spent in this function.[325] Some payers have experimented with payments.[326]

E-mail communications should be treated with the same degree of care and formality as other written communications. They can be discovered and used in criminal investigations and civil lawsuits.[327] Federal courts have generally determined that they are not subject to the same degree of protection as telephone calls, so it may not be a violation of federal wiretap laws to intercept e-mail at several stages in their transmission.[328] Some employers have increased the monitoring of e-mail and other computer use.[329]

E-mail is also sometimes used for threats and harassment.[330]

Care must be taken when sending e-mail in a healthcare environment. There have been a few incidents where medical information was accidentally distributed to the wrong recipients.[331] The HIPAA security rules apply to e-mail and will require encryption and other steps to improve the security of e-mail.

INTERNET. Computerized records have been stolen through the Internet.[332] It is important for those responsible for computers to monitor and implement security precautions.[333]

Computerized records have been accidentally posted on the Internet.[334] It is important to train staff on how to minimize these accidents.

There have been challenges to postings on the Internet. In 1999, a jury awarded $107 million verdict against an antiabortion group who had produced wanted posters of abortion providers and had supplied then to a website.

The trial court enjoined production of the posters and the supplying of them to the website. A federal appellate court upheld the injunction and the verdict against the group but required that the lower court review the amount of the judgment. The appellate court found that there was a sufficient threat of force on the posters to overcome the First Amendment protection for the posters. In 2004, the lower court affirmed the amount of the judgment.[335] In 2001, another antiabortion group created a website that includes photographs and medical records of women who had obtained abortions. A Missouri state lower court enjoined removal of the photographs and records.[336]

In 2002, a Massachusetts court required a patient to remove misleading photos and defamatory statements from a website about a physician.[337] In 2003, a Pennsylvania judge ordered attorneys to close a website for recruiting patients for a class action lawsuit, but it was reopened later after a settlement with the hospital that involved deleting the hospital's name from the website name.[338]

SOCIAL MEDIA. Social media has invaded health care from at least three fronts: innovative startups, patient communities, and medical centers. Patient communities are flourishing in an environment rich with social networks, both through mainline social communities and condition-specific communities. Meanwhile, hospitals and academic medical centers are diving into the social media mix with YouTube channels, Facebook pages, and Twitter accounts.

At the same time, healthcare organizations find challenges in adopting social media. Hospitals and medical practices are risk adverse and generally cautious about new technology trends without clear value. There are questions about whether social media use by hospital employees is a waste of time, or even worse, presents risks of violating HIPAA or leaking proprietary information. Hospital IT departments are concerned about security risks. Individual privacy concerns, particularly the vulnerability of social media accounts, are also cited as a reason to avoid social media in a healthcare setting.

Whether interacting with patients and their healthcare information in person or digitally via the Internet or other social media outlets, providers should always respect patient confidentiality and take care to maintain the security of healthcare information.

Chapter Summary

Medical research increases the body of available clinical data about patients (e.g., genetics data, hormone levels, neurological impairment) while the Internet grows the risk of disclosure of such data exponentially. Access to "private" health information is subject to laws and regulations, which inevitably trail advances in medical research and computing technology. In the United States, efforts to target marketing to individuals utilizing their private health information are pushing the boundaries of applicable law and are past the boundaries applied in the European Union. Debates on the protections that should be applied to private health information are informed by the breadth and scope of law and regulations reviewed in this chapter. The law related to the intersection of private health information with computers, e-mail, social media, and the Internet is still developing. It can be anticipated that new legal issues will continue to flow from this changing area.

Key Terms and Definitions

Healthcare Information - Broadly defined, is aggregate and individually specific patient data including personal information (such as name, date of birth, sex, marital status, occupation, next of kin, etc.), financial information (such as employer, health insurance identification number, and other information to assist in billing), and medical history (such as physical examinations, diagnoses, treatment recommendations and treatment administered, progress reports, physician orders, clinical laboratory results, radiology reports, nursing notes, discharge summaries, etc.).

Medical Records - Created when a person receives treatment from a health professional and includes personal, financial, and medical data.

ARRA - The acronym for the American Recovery and Reinvestment Act of 2009, the economic stimulus package passed by the U.S. Congress and signed into law by President Obama in February 2009. ARRA provided billions of dollars of incentives, in the form of reimbursement, to assist and encourage doctors and hospitals to transition away from the maintenance of paper medical records and adopt electronic health records.

NGO - The abbreviation for nongovernmental organization. NGOs operate independently from federal and state governments. NGOs may receive governmental financial support but maintain their independence by excluding government from NGO membership and management. The Joint Commission is an example of an NGO.

The Joint Commission (TJC) - An independent, not-for-profit organization that accredits and certifies healthcare organizations and programs in the United States.

The Joint Commission accreditation and certification is a recognized symbol of quality that reflects an organization's commitment to certain performance standards. To be accredited, hospitals must meet The Joint Commission medical records standards. To earn and maintain The Joint Commission accreditation submission to periodic on-site survey by a Joint Commission survey team is required.

CMS - The acronym for the Centers for Medicare & Medicaid Services, the branch of the U.S. Department of Health and Human Services that administers Medicare and Medicaid.

Medicare - The U.S. government's national health insurance program for people 65 years or older and under age 65 with certain disabilities.

Medicaid - A jointly funded, federal-state health insurance program for low-income and needy people.

HHS - The acronym for the Department of Health and Human Services, the U.S. government's principal agency for protecting the health of all Americans and providing essential human services.

HIPAA - The acronym for the Health Insurance Portability and Accountability Act of 1996, enacted by the U.S. Congress and signed by President Clinton. Title II of HIPAA directed HHS to draft rules establishing national security and privacy health data standards.

Covered Entities - Healthcare clearinghouses, employer-sponsored health plans, health insurers, and medical service providers to which the HIPAA privacy and security rules regulating protected health information apply.

Business Associates - Independent contractors who engage in business with or otherwise assist covered entities and have access to protected health information.

Protected Health Information - Any information held by a covered entity or its business associates that concerns health status, the provision of health care, or payment for health care and can be linked to an individual.

HHS Office for Civil Rights - Enforces the HIPAA Privacy and Security Rules.

Office of the National Coordinator for Health Information Technology - Organizationally located within HHS and is the principal Federal entity charged with coordinating nationwide efforts to implement and use advanced health information technology and electronic exchange of health information.

HIPAA Privacy Rule - Establishes national standards to protect medical records and other personal health information. It requires covered entities and their business associates to protect the privacy of personal health information and sets limits and conditions on the uses and disclosures that may be made of such information without patient authorization. It also gives patients rights over their health information, including rights to examine and obtain a copy of their health records, and to request corrections.

HIPAA Security Rule - Establishes national standards to protect individuals' electronic personal health information that is created, received, used, or maintained by a covered entity. It requires appropriate administrative, physical and technical safeguards to ensure the confidentiality, integrity, and security of electronic protected health information.

Instructor-Led Questions

1. What are some of the underlying issues that must be balanced in developing laws and policies concerning healthcare information?

2. Who owns the medical record?

3. What information must be collected in a medical record?

4. How should a provider determine how long to keep medical records?

5. What are the basic HIPAA requirements concerning privacy of protected healthcare information?

6. Which state laws are still in effect? What other federal privacy laws remain in effect?

7. When may patients and their representatives authorize disclosure?

8. When may the law compel disclosure?

9. When are reports to legal authorities required?

10. When may providers release information in response to requests from others?

11. Has HIPAA struck the proper balance between privacy and uses of healthcare information?

12. What restrictions are there on audio and video recordings in healthcare settings?

13. What are some of the legal issues related to the use of computers and the Internet in health care?

14. What are some of the advantages and disadvantages of computerized medical records?

Endnotes

1 Inside trader avoids prison, N.Y. Times, Jan. 16, 1999, A16 [convicted lawyer given no prison sentence because his cerebral palsy made him vulnerable to prison hardships].

2 See Massachusetts board probes shared Rx information, Am. Med. News, May 25, 1998, 13 [sharing prescription drug information with marketing company]; *Legal Economic Evaluations v. Metropolitan Life Ins. Co.*, 39 F.3d 951 (9th Cir. 1994), cert. denied, 514 U.S. 1044 (1995) [summary judgment for defendants in suit by consultants who provided services to tort claimants on costs of structured settlements, not antitrust violation for life insurance companies to refuse to provide information other than for defense].

3 E.g., *Pyramid Life Ins. Co. v. Masonic Hosp. Ass'n*, 191 F. Supp. 51 (W.D. Okla. 1961); see also *Archive America, Inc. v. Variety Children's Hosp.*, 873 So. 2d 359 (Fla. 3d Dist. 2004) [warehouseman's lien transferred from stored hospital records to bond].

4 But see *University of Tex. Med. Branch v. York*, 871 S.W.2d 175 (Tex. 1994) [medical record not tangible personal property; information intangible, fact of recordation does not render information tangible].

5 E.g., *Cannell v. Medical & Surg. Clinic*, 21 Ill. App. 3d 383, 315 N.E.2d 278 (3d Dist. 1974).

6   *Cornelio v. Stamford Hosp.*, 246 Conn. 45, 717 A.2d 140 (1998); *Lucarello v. North Shore Univ. Hosp.*, 184 A.D.2d 623, 584 N.Y.S.2d 906 (2d Dept. 1992).

7   E.g., *McGarry v. J. A. Mercier Co.*, 272 Mich. 501, 262 N.W. 296 (1935); *Gerson v. New York Women's Medical*, 249 A.D.2d 265, 671 N.Y.S.2d 104 (2d Dept. 1998) [provider owns mammogram films].

8   E.g., *Caldwell v. Shalala*, 114 F.3d 216 (D.C. Cir.), cert. denied, 522 U.S. 916 (1997) [physician with conditionally reinstated privileges at Army hospital entitled to access medical records].

9   E.g., *Simmons v. Southwest Florida Reg. Med. Ctr.*, No. 98-2046 CA RWP (Fla. Cir. Ct. Lee County Apr. 24, 1998), as discussed in 26 HEALTH L. DIG. (July 1998), 57 [office-generated patient medical records developed by physicians while employed by hospital belong to physicians not hospital that terminated them]; State ex rel. *O'Donnell v. Clifford*, 948 S.W.2d 451 (Mo. Ct. App. 1997) [per written employment agreement, terminated physician entitled to copy medical records of patients he had treated only on request by patient].

10 42 C.F.R. § 482.24(c).

11 Joint Commission, 2011 COMPREHENSIVE ACCREDITATION MANUAL FOR HOSPITALS, Elements of Performance for RC.01.01.01 [hereinafter 2011 JC CAMH].

12 E.g., J. Olson, Pediatrician loses license for failure to keep up records, OMAHA WORLD HERALD, Mar. 18, 2002, 5B.

13 *Nassau County Med. Ctr. v. Zinman* (N.Y. Dist. Ct. Aug. 1998), as discussed in N.Y. L.J, Aug. 3, 1998, 25.

14 E.g., *Valendon Martinez v. Hospital Presbiteriano de la Communidad, Inc.*, 806 F.2d 1128 (1st Cir. 1986).

15 *Lama v. Borras*, 16 F.3d 473 (1st Cir. 1994).

16 *Repp v. Anadarko Municipal Hosp.*, 43 F.3d 519 (10th Cir. 1994).

17 E.g., M. Greenberg, Writer's cramp has reached epidemic levels, AM. MED. NEWS, Aug. 3, 1998, 18 [documentation requirements for referrals]; Budget-killer progress notes tamed, AM. MED. NEWS, Feb.1, 1999, 18.

18 2011 JC CAMH, RC.01.01.01.

19 *Hiatt v. Groce*, 215 Kan. 14, 523 P.2d 320 (1974).

20 *Collins v. Westlake Commun. Hosp.*, 57 Ill. 2d 388, 312 N.E.2d 614 (1974).

21 *Sunnen v. Administrative Review Bd.*, 244 A.D.2d 790, 666 N.Y.S.2d 239 (3d Dept. 1997).

22 *Illiano v. Seaview Orthopedics*, 299 N.J. Super. 99, 690 A.2d 662 (App. Div. 1997).

23 *Engle v. Clarke*, 346 S.W.2d 13 (Ky. 1961); contra *Thome v. Palmer*, 141 Ill. App. 3d 92, 489 N.E.2d 1163 (3d Dist. 1986); *Hurlock v. Park Lane Med. Ctr.*, 709 S.W.2d 872 (Mo. Ct. App. 1985).

24 42 C.F.R. § 482.24(c)(2)(viii).

25 2011 JC CAMH at Elements of Performance RC.01.03.01.

26 E.g., *Board of Trustees v. Pratt*, 72 Wyo. 120, 262 P.2d 682 (1953). Some hospitals use financial incentives, E.g., Incentives spur physicians to complete record-keeping, MOD. HEALTHCARE, Dec. 6, 1985, 64; L. Perry, Emphasis on coordination hastens submission of bills, MOD. HEALTHCARE, July 14, 1989, 39.

27 *Birthisel v. Tri-Cities Health Services Corp.*, 188 W.Va. 371, 424 S.E.2d 606 (1992).

28 42 C.F.R. § 482.24(c)(1); 2011 JC CAMH at Elements of Performance RC.01.04.01 and MS.05.01.03.

29 *Manso-Pizarro v. Secretary of Health & Human Servs.*, 76 F.3d 15 (1st Cir. 1996).

30 *Eldridge v. Metropolitan Life Ins. Co.*, 123 F.3d 456 (7th Cir. 1997).

31 Misread prescription brings $450K award, NATIONAL L. J., Nov. 8, 1999, A4.

32 R.A. Friedman, Do spelling and penmanship count? In medicine, you bet, N.Y. TIMES, Mar. 11, 2003, D5.

33 § 456.42, Fla. Stat.; D. Adams, Florida tells doctors: Print clearly or else, AM. MED. NEWS, Aug. 4, 2003, 1; see also REV. CODE WASH. § 69.41.120 [requiring legible prescriptions].

34 Doctor blames poor penmanship for losing license, AP, Feb. 8, 2003.

35 E.g., *Humphreys v. Drug Enforcement Admin.*, 105 F.3d 112 (3d Cir. 1996) [DEA should not have revoked physician's registration to distribute controlled substances for prescribed drugs for famous patient in another's name to protect patient's privacy].

36 *Kaplan v. Central Med. Group*, 71 A.D.2d 912, 419 N.Y.S.2d 750 (2d Dept. 1979).

37 *Murkin v. Medical Mut. Liability Ins. Society*, 82 Md. App. 540, 572 A.2d 1126 (1990).

38 E.g., *Vest v. United States*, 116 F.3d 1179 (7th Cir. 1997), cert. denied, 522 U.S. 1119 (1998) [affirming physician mail fraud conviction for falsifying medical records, ordering unnecessary procedures]; Dentist pays for altering records, AP, Jan. 7, 2003 [Idaho MD sentenced to 10 months home confinement for altering records to obstruct Medicaid fraud investigation]; Waterbury Hospital fined in audit scandal, AP, Mar. 4, 2003 [Conn. hosp. staff added treatment plans and signatures to records selected by federal auditors].

39 E.g., *Tang v. De Buono*, 235 A.D.2d 745, 652 N.Y.S.2d 408 (3d Dept. 1997) [upholding revoking medical license for falsifying CT scan report for insurance fraud]; *Jimenez v. Department of Professional Reg.*, 556 So. 2d 1219 (Fla. 4th DCA 1990) [one-year suspension of physician's license, $5,000 fine, and two years' probation after suspension for adding false information to records after death of patient]; Doctor fined in teen's death to keep license, PALM BEACH (FLA.) POST, Aug. 6, 1995, 23A [violated state law by ordering partner to falsify medical records; fine, probation, community service].

40 *Stevenson v. Comm.*, 27 Va. Ct. App. 453, 499 S.E.2d 580 (1998), aff'd without op. en banc by equally divided court, 28 Va. Ct. App. 562, 507 S.E.2d 625 (1998).

41 E.g., In re Morris, 482 A.2d 369 (D.C. 1984); see also *Caraballo v. Secretary of HHS*, 670 F. Supp. 1106 (D. P.R. 1987) [judicially altered birth certificate not conclusive evidence of age].

42 42 C.F.R. § 482.24(b)(1).

43 42 U.S.C. § 1395x(v)(1)(I).

44 *Bondu v. Gurvich*, 473 So. 2d 1307 (Fla. 3d DCA 1984); *DeLaughter v. Lawrence County Hosp.*, 601 So. 2d 818 (Miss. 1992) [missing records create rebuttable adverse presumption]; *Phillips v. Covenant Clinic*, 625 N.W.2d 714 (Iowa 2001) [can create inference but not in this case]; Annotation, Medical malpractice: presumption or inference from failure of hospital or doctor to produce relevant medical records, 69 A.L.R. 4TH 906.

45 E.g., *Ortega v. Trevino*, 938 S.W.2d 219 (Tex. Ct. App. 1997); *Holmes v. Amerex Rent-A-Car*, 710 A.2d 846 (D.C. App. 1998).

46 E.g., *Miller v. Gupta*, 174 Ill. 2d 120, 672 N.E.2d 1229 (1996) [lost X-ray; duty to preserve evidence can only arise from agreement, contract, statute, or special circumstance].

47 E.g., *Fletcher v. Dorchester Mut. Ins. Co.*, 437 Mass. 544, 773 N.E.2d 420 (2002); *Temple Comm. Hosp. v. Superior Court*, 20 Cal. 4th 464, 976 P.2d 223, 84 Cal. Rptr. 2d 852 (1999); *Goff v. Harold Ives Trucking Co. Inc.*, 27 S.W.3d 387 (Ark. 2000); *Meyn v. State*, 594 N.W.2d 31 (Iowa 1999); see also *Keene v. Brigham & Women's Hosp.*, 439 Mass. 223, 786 N.E.2d 824 (2003) [trial court cannot bypass rejection of separate spoliation action by imposing a default against hospital].

48 *Elmer v. Tenneco Resins, Inc.*, 698 F. Supp. 535 (D. Del. 1988).

49 E.g., TENN. CODE ANN. § 68-11-305(c).

50 *Palmer v. New York State Dep't of Mental Hygiene*, 44 N.Y.2d 958, 408 N.Y.S.2d 322, 380 N.E.2d 154 (1978).

51 *Wolfe v. Beal*, 477 Pa. 447, 384 A.2d 1187 (1978).

52 PUB. L. 104-191, §§ 264(b), (c)(1) (1996).

53 65 FED. REG. 82,461 (Dec. 28, 2000).

54 67 FED. REG. 53,181 (Aug. 14, 2002), codified as 45 C.F.R. Parts 160, 164, Subparts A, E.

55 *South Carolina Med. Ass'n v. Thompson*, 327 F.3d 346 (4th Cir. 2003), cert. denied, 540 U.S. 981 (2003) [initial rule]; *Association of Am. Physicians & Surgeons v. U.S. D.H.H.S.*, 224 F. Supp .2d 1115 (S.D. Tex. 2002) [initial rule]; *Citizens for Health v. Thompson*, 2004 U.S. Dist. LEXIS 5745 (E.D. Pa.) [amended rule] app'd, 2005 U.S. App. LEXIS 23516 (3d Cir).

56 45 C.F.R. §§ 164.500, et seq.

57 45 C.F.R. §§ 160.102, 160.103.

58 45 C.F.R. §§ 164.500, et seq.

59 Id.

60 45 C.F.R. §§ 164.500(a), 160.103 ["health information"], 164.501 ["individually identifiable health information," "protected health information"].

61 45 C.F.R. § 164.520.

62 45 C.F.R. § 164.530.

63 45 C.F.R. § 164.506.

64 45 C.F.R. § 164.512.

65 45 C.F.R. § 164.510(a).

66 45 C.F.R. § 164.502(b).

67 45 C.F.R. § 164.522(b).

68 45 C.F.R. § 164.524.

69 45 C.F.R. § 164.526.

70 45 C.F.R. § 164.528.

71 45 C.F.R. § 164.522.

72 45 C.F.R. §§ 164.502(e), 164.504(e).

73 45 C.F.R. § 164.530.

74 45 C.F.R. § 164.514(e), (f).

75 http://www.hhs.gov/ocr/privacy/hipaa/enforcement/highlights/index.html

76 Privacy complaints filed with HHS show confusion over rule's scope, requirements, HEALTH LAW RPTR. [BNA], Feb. 26, 2004, 282 [4266 complaints—41% closed]; No prosecutions yet under privacy rule, intent to sell, profit key factors in decision, HEALTH LAW RPTR. [BNA], Mar. 11, 2004, 356.

77 P. Shukovsky, Hospitalized man catches identity thief, ex-lab tech pleads guilty to using private health files, credit cards, SEATTLE POST-INTELLIGENCER, Aug. 20, 2004, B1; First sentence for violating privacy act, N.Y. TIMES, Nov. 7, 2004, 22 [16-month sentence].

78 R. Pear, Ruling limits prosecutions of people who violate law on privacy of medical records, N.Y. TIMES, June 7, 2005, 16. The DOJ memo appears at http://www.justice.gov/olc/hipaa_final .htm [accessed Mar. 4, 2012].

79 E.g, *Univ. of Colo. Hosp. Auth. v. Denver Publ. Co.*, 340 F. Supp. 2d 1142 (D. Colo. 2004).

80 45 C.F.R. §§ 160.201-160.205.

81 E.g., Former Houston hospital worker arrested for stealing, selling patient records, AP, Aug. 28, 2003 [patient care assistant sold records to investigator].

82 *Sassali v. Rockford Mem. Hosp.*, 296 Ill. App. 3d 80, 693 N.E.2d 1287 (2d Dist 1998).

83 *Hahnemann Univ. Hosp. v. Edgar*, 74 F.3d 456 (3d Cir. 1996).

84 E.g., FLA. STAT. § 381.609(2)(f) [AIDS], § 455.2416 [permitting disclosure of AIDS to sexual partner, needle-sharing partner]; *Woods v. White*, 689 F. Supp. 874 (W.D. Wis. 1988), aff'd without op., 899 F.2d 17 (7th Cir. 1990) [prisoner could sue staff for disclosing AIDS test to other prisoners]; Annotation, Validity, construction, and effect of state statutes or regulations expressly governing disclosure of fact that person has tested positive for acquired immunodeficiency syndrome (AIDS), 12 A.L.R. 5th 149.

85 F.W. Hafferty, A new MD "nightmare": HIV status disclosure can mean lawsuits for breach of confidentiality, Am. Med. News, Nov. 4, 1988, 27.

86 *Doe v. Roe*, 155 Misc. 2d 392, 588 N.Y.S.2d 236 (Sup. Ct. 1992), modified & aff'd, 190 A.D.2d 463, 599 N.Y.S.2d 350 (4th Dept. 1993).

87 *Nolley v. County of Erie*, 776 F. Supp. 715 (W.D. N.Y. 1991).

88 *Suesbury v. Caceres*, 840 A.2d 1285 (D.C. App. 2004).

89 In re Milton S. Hershey Med. Ctr., 535 Pa. 9, 634 A.2d 159 (1993).

90 *Weston v. Carolina Medicorp, Inc.*, 102 N.C. App. 370, 402 S.E.2d 653 (1991).

91 E.g., D. Shelton, Naming names, Am. Med. News, Apr. 6, 1998, 11 [Illinois becomes 32nd state to require reporting names of HIV-positive persons]; L. Richardson, New York state sets regulations on H.I.V. reporting and partner notification, N.Y. Times, Mar. 13, 1999, A13; H.I.V. secrecy is proving deadly, N.Y. Times, Nov. 25, 2003, F6 [failure to disclose to partners is factor in spreading HIV].

92 E.g., *Boyd v. Wynn*, 286 Ky. 173, 150 S.W.2d 648 (1941).

93 Annotation, Physician's tort liability for unauthorized disclosure of confidential information about patient, 48 A.L.R. 4th 668.

94 *Doe v. Roe*, 93 Misc. 2d 201, 400 N.Y.S.2d 668 (Sup. Ct. 1977).

95 *Humphers v. First Interstate Bank*, 298 Or. 706, 696 P.2d 527 (1985).

96 E.g., *Simonsen v. Swenson*, 104 Neb. 224, 177 N.W. 831 (1920) [physician]; *Knecht v. Vandalia Med. Ctr., Inc.*, 14 Ohio App. 3d 129, 470 N.E.2d 230 (1984) [receptionist].

97 E.g., *Crippen v. Charter Southland Hosp.*, 534 So. 2d 286 (Ala 1988) [disclosure to employer's psychiatrist]; *Tower v. Hirshhorn*, 397 Mass. 581, 492 N.E.2d 728 (1986) [disclosure to insurer's physician].

98 *Horne v. Patton*, 291 Ala. 701, 287 So. 2d 824 (1973).

99 E.g., *Alberts v. Devine*, 395 Mass. 59, 479 N.E.2d 113, cert. denied, 474 U.S. 1013 (1985).

100 *Clark v. Geraci*, 29 Misc. 2d 791, 208 N.Y.S.2d 564 (Sup. Ct. 1960).

101 E.g., *Thomas v. Hillson*, 184 Ga. App. 302, 361 S.E.2d 278 (1987); see Annotation, Libel and slander: privilege of statements by physician, surgeon, or nurse concerning patient, 73 A.L.R. 2D 325.

102 E.g., *Beatty v. Baston*, 130 Ohio L. Abs. 481 (Ct. App. 1932).

103 *United States v. Willis*, 778 F. Supp. 205 (S.D. N.Y. 1991), 737 F. Supp. 269 (1990); Psychiatrist is sentenced, N.Y. Times, Jan. 8, 1992, C12.

104 E.g., *Brand v. Seider*, 697 A.2d 846 (Me. 1997) [claim against psychiatrist alleging breach of confidentiality subject to state malpractice act]; contra *Champion v. Cox*, 689 So. 2d 365 (Fla. 1st DCA 1997) [defamation action based upon medical disclosure to patient's employer not subject to state malpractice act].

105 *Allred v. State*, 554 P.2d 411 (Alaska 1976).

106 Fed. R. Evid. 501; *United States v. Bercier*, 848 F.2d 917 (8th Cir. 1988) [criminal]; *United States v. Moore*, 970 F.2d 48 (5th Cir. 1992) [IRS summons]; see Annotation, Situations in which federal courts are governed by state law of privilege under Rule 501 of Federal Rules of Evidence, 48 A.L.R. Fed. 259.

107 E.g., *Roosevelt Hotel Ltd. Partnership v. Sweeney*, 394 N.W.2d 353 (Iowa 1986).

108 Pa. Stat. Ann. title. 42, § 5929; In re June 1979 Allegheny County Investigating Grand Jury, 490 Pa. 143, 415 A.2d 73 (1980).

109 Kan. Stat. Ann. § 60-427.

110 Mich. Comp. Laws § 600.2157.

111 N.Y. Civil Practice L. & R. § 4504.

112 E.g., In re *New York City Council v. Goldwater*, 284 N.Y. 296, 31 N.E.2d 31 (1940).

113 E.g., *Edelstein v. Department of Public Health*, 240 Conn. 658, 692 A.2d 803 (1997) [physician-patient privilege not applicable to subpoena by state public health department investigating billing practices].

114 *Wiles v. Wiles*, 264 Ga. 594, 448 S.E.2d 681 (1994).

115 *Jaffee v. Redmund*, 518 U.S. 1 (1996); *Newton v. Kemna*, 354 F.3d 776 (8th Cir. 2004) [denied access to challenge competency of witness); *Oleszko v. State Comp. Ins. Fund*, 243 F.3d 1154 (9th Cir. 2001) [Employee Assistance Program information protected]; *Henry v. Kernan*, 197 F.3d 1021 (9th Cir. 1999) [must have reasonable belief doctor is psychotherapist for privilege to apply]; *United States v. Schwensow*, 151 F.3d 650 (7th Cir. 1998) [communications with the Alcoholics Anonymous telephone hotline volunteers not protected, since not psychotherapists].

116 E.g., *United States v. Chase*, 340 F.3d 978 (9th Cir. 2003) (en banc), cert. denied, 540 U.S. 1220 (2004); *United States v. Hayes*, 227 F.3d 578 (6th Cir 2000); *United States v. Glass*, 133 F.3d 1356 (10th Cir. 1998) [refuse to apply dangerous patient exception to facts of case]: but see also In re Grand Jury Proceedings (Violette), 183 F.3d 71 (1st Cir. 1999) [crime-fraud exception recognized].

117 *Schoffstall v. Henderson*, 223 F.3d 818 (8th Cir. 2000); contra, *Vanderbilt v. Town of Chilmark*, 174 F.R.D. 225, 225-30 (D. Mass. 1997) (declining to find waiver where plaintiff sought emotional distress damages).

118 See Medical records increasingly open, Wis. St. J., May 26, 1997, 3B.

119 E.g., *Inabnit v. Berkson*, 199 Cal. App. 3d 1230, 245 Cal. Rptr. 525 (5th Dist. 1988) [patient's failure to challenge subpoena waived privilege].

120 E.g., *Cartwright v. Maccabees Mut. Life Ins. Co.*, 65 Mich. App. 670, 238 N.W.2d 368 (1975), rev'd on other grounds, 398 Mich. 238, 247 N.W.2d 298 (1976) [when misrepresentations in insurance application, life insurer entitled to verdict when widow invoked privilege].

121 E.g., *Willis v. Order of R.R. Telegraphers,* 139 Neb. 46, 296 N.W. 443 (1941).

122 *United States v. Bishop,* 1998 U.S. App. LEXIS 15147 (6th Cir.) [conviction for murdering fellow VA patient upheld; disclosure to police permitted therapists to testify].

123 E.g., *Maynard v. City of San Jose,* 37 F.3d 1396 (9th Cir. 1994); *Premack v. J.C.J. Ogar, Inc.,* 148 F.R.D. 140 (E.D. Pa. 1993).

124 E.g., *Sykes v. St. Andrews School,* 619 So. 2d 467 (Fla. 4th DCA 1993).

125 E.g., State ex rel. *Kitzmiller v. Henning,* 190 W.Va. 142, 437 S.W.2d 452 (1993); *McClelland v. Ozenberger,* 841 S.W.2d 227 (Mo. Ct. App. 1992); *Loudon v. Mhyre,* 110 Wash. 2d 675, 756 P.2d 138 (1988); *Nelson v. Lewis,* 130 N.H. 106, 534 A.2d 720 (1987).

126 E.g., *Huzjak v. United States,* 118 F.R.D. 61 (N.D. Ohio 1987) [treating physician may voluntarily engage in ex parte contacts, but cannot be compelled to do so]; *Trans-World Invs. v. Drobny,* 554 P.2d 1148 (Alaska 1976); *Gobuty v. Kavanagh,* 795 F. Supp. 281 (D. Minn. 1992) [state law permitted defending physician to informally communicate with plaintiff's treating physician with 15 days' notice].

127 E.g., *Requena v. Franciscan Sisters Health Care Corp.,* 212 Ill. App. 3d 328, 570 N.E.2d 1214 (3d Dist. 1991).

128 *Law v. Zuckerman,* 307 F. Supp. 2d 705 (D. Md. 2004) [HIPAA precludes ex parte contacts with treating MD].

129 42 C.F.R. pt. 2, implementing 42 U.S.C § 290dd-2.

130 *Center for Legal Advocacy v. Earnest,* 320 F.3d 1107 (10th Cir. 2003); 59 Fed. Reg. 42,561 (Aug. 18, 1994).

131 E.g., United States ex rel. *Chandler v. Cook County,* 277 F.3d 969 (7th Cir. 2002) [mandamus striking down discovery order contrary to regulations].

132 E.g., *United States v. Hopper,* 440 F. Supp. 1208 (N.D. Ill. 1977) [probation revocation]; In re Baby X, 97 Mich. App. 111, 293 N.W.2d 736 (1980) [child neglect]; see also *United States v. Corona,* 849 F.2d 562 (11th Cir. 1988), cert. denied, 489 U.S. 1084 (1989) [trial court did not err in permitting use of records of defendant when court could have found criteria for disclosure met].

133 *United States v. Providence Hosp.,* 507 F. Supp. 519 (E.D. Mich. 1981).

134 E.g., In re August, 1993 Regular Grand Jury, 854 F. Supp. 1380 (S.D. Ind. 1994) [grand jury investigation of possible criminal conduct by psychotherapist]; *State Bd. of Medical Examiners v. Fenwick Hall, Inc.,* 308 S.C. 477, 419 S.E.2d 222 (1992) [disclosure to licensing board]; *O'Boyle v. Jensen,* 150 F.R.D. 519 (M.D. Pa. 1993) [civil rights suit for death in police custody].

135 E.g., *United States v. Cresta,* 825 F.2d 538 (1st Cir. 1987), cert. denied, 486 U.S. 1042 (1988) [credibility]; *United States v. Smith,* 789 F.2d 196 (3d Cir. 1986) [credibility]; D. Canedy, Judge upholds privacy for Jeb Bush's daughter, N.Y. Times, Oct. 1, 2002, A22 [drug possession investigation].

136 E.g., *Ellison v. Cocke County, Tenn.,* 63 F.3d 467 (6th Cir. 1995); *Chapa v. Adams,* 168 F.3d 1036 (7th Cir. 1999); *Doe v. Broderick,* 225 F.3d 2000 (4th Cir. 2000).

137 20 U.S.C. § 1232g(d).

138 See S. Tavernise, In college and in despair, with parents in the dark, N.Y. Times, Oct. 26, 2003, 1.

139 45 C.F.R. 164.501 ["protected health information"].

140 15 U.S.C. 1681b(g); D. Paletta, Medical data rules: exceptions proposed, Am. Banker, Apr. 7, 2004, 4; 69 Fed. Reg. 23,380 (Apr. 28, 2004) [proposed rules].

141 5 U.S.C. § 552a.

142 45 C.F.R. §§ 160.103 ["health care"], 164.501 ["treatment"].

143 E.g., *Wilkinson v. Methodist,* Richard Young Hosp., 259 Neb. 745, 612 N.W.2d 213 (2000) [hospital staff may access, use computer information for billing purposes].

144 45 C.F.R. § 164.501 ["payment"].

145 45 C.F.R. § 164.501 ["health care operations"].

146 *Hyman v. Jewish Chronic Disease Hosp.,* 15 N.Y.2d 317, 258 N.Y.S.2d 397, 399, 206 N.E.2d 338 (1965).

147 *Klinge v. Lutheran Med. Ctr.,* 518 S.W.2d 157 (Mo. Ct. App. 1974).

148 In re General Accident Assurance Co. of Canada & Sunnybrook Hosp., 23 O.R.(2d) 513 (Ont. High Ct. of Justice 1979); accord *Rea v. Pardo,* 132 A.D.2d 442, 522 N.Y.S.2d 393 (4th Dept. 1987) [patient request to send record to attorney justified physician sending copy to his insurer]; *Archambault v. Roller,* 254 Va. 210, 491 S.E.2d 729 (1997) [nonparty physician being deposed in malpractice action may disclose patient information to attorney].

149 *Biddle v. Warren Gen. Hosp.,* 86 Ohio St. 3d 395, 715 N.E.2d 518 (1999).

150 E.g., *Lancaster v. Loyola Univ. Med. Ctr.,* 1992 U.S. Dist. LEXIS 15207 (N.D. Ill.) [hospital employees]; *Morgan v. Cook County,* 252 Ill. App. 3d 947, 625 N.E.2d 136 (1st Dist. 1993) [treating physician, when suit seeks to make hospital vicariously liable]; *Alachua Gen. Hosp. v. Stewart,* 649 So. 2d 357 (Fla. 1st DCA 1995) [physician, when suit seeks to make hospital vicariously liable]; but see *Ritter v. Rush-Presbyterian-St. Luke's Med. Ctr.,* 177 Ill. App. 3d 313, 532 N.E.2d 327 (1st Dist. 1988) [hospital not even permitted to interview its codefendant employee treating physicians].

151 45 C.F.R. § 46.101(b)(5); 46 Fed. Reg. 8,392 (1981); see also 56 Fed. Reg. 67,078 (1991) [HCFA allowed release of patient identifiable information from Uniform Clinical Data Set for research purposes].

152 See, E.g., T. Meyer, Chest radiation linked to breast cancer, Wis. St. J., Feb. 13, 1998, 6A [discovery from review of medical records of 3,436 patients]; D. McKenzie, Harvesting data: A little less privacy leads to better care, Am. Med. News, Jan. 26, 1998, 14; Scientists use medical-record data bases to detect adverse side effects of drugs, Wall St. J., Mar. 24, 1988, 33; L. Gordis & E. Gold, Privacy, confidentiality, and the use of medical records in research, 207 Science 153 (1980).

153 45 C.F.R. § 164.512(i).

154 45 C.F.R. §§ 164.524 [self], 164.508 [others].

155 E.g., Fla Stat. § 395.017 [hospitals]; § 455.241 [individual professionals]; Ill. Rev. Stat. ch. 110 §§ 8-2001-8-2004; Annotation, Patient's right to disclosure of his or her own medical records under state freedom of information act, 26 A.L.R. 4th 701; *Wallace v. University Hosps. of Cleveland,* 84 Ohio L. Abs. 224, 170 N.E.2d 261 (Ct. App. 1960).

156 *Pierce v. Penman,* 357 Pa. Super. 225, 515 A.2d 948 (1986).

157 *Franklin Square Hosp. v. Laubach,* 318 Md. 615, 569 A.2d 693 (1990).

158 *Lee County v. State Farm Mutual Auto. Ins. Co.,* 634 So. 2d 250 (Fla. 2d DCA 1994).

159 *Person v. Farmers Ins. Group,* 52 Cal. App. 4th 813, 61 Cal. Rptr. 2d 30 (2d Dist. 1997).

160 E.g., *Pyramid Life Ins. Co. v. Masonic Hosp. Ass'n,* 191 F. Supp. 51 (W.D. Okla. 1961).

161 45 C.F.R. § 164.510(b).

162 *MacDonald v. Clinger,* 84 A.D.2d 482, 446 N.Y.S.2d 801 (4th Dept. 1982).

163 E.g., Iowa Code Ann. § 229.25.

164 *Thurman v. Crawford,* 652 S.W.2d 240 (Mo. Ct. App. 1983).

165 *Byers v. Toyota Motor Manufacturing Ky., Inc.,* 1998 U.S. App. LEXIS 33155 (6th Cir.) (unpub).

166 45 C.F.R. § 164.524(a)(3).

167 *Yaretsky v. Blum,* 592 F.2d 65 (2d Cir. 1979), appeal after remand, 629 F.2d 817 (2d Cir. 1980), rev'd, 457 U.S. 991 (1982) [no right to hearing before transfer].

168 *Salt Lake Child & Family Therapy Clinic, Inc. v. Frederick,* 890 P.2d 1017 (Utah 1995).

169 *Cynthia B. v. New Rochelle Hosp. Med. Ctr.,* 60 N.Y.2d 452, 470 N.Y.S.2d 1221, 458 N.E.2d 363 (1983).

170 *Doe v. Stincer,* 990 F. Supp. 1427 (S.D. Fla. 1997).

171 45 C.F.R. § 164.502(g).

172 E.g., *Gaertner v. State,* 385 Mich. 49, 187 N.W.2d 429 (1971).

173 45 C.F.R. § 164.524(a)(3)(iii).

174 *Mougiannis v. North Shore-Long Island Jewish Health System* (N.Y. Sup Ct. May 2004), as reported in N.Y.L.J., May 19, 2004, 19.

175 45 C.F.R. § 164.502(g)(2),(3).

176 E.g., *Leaf v. Iowa Methodist Med. Ctr.,* 460 N.W.2d 892 (Iowa Ct. App. 1990) [noncustodial parent's access right to minor's medical records].

177 E.g. In the Matter of Marriage of Jones, 983 S.W.2d 377 (Tex. App. 1999) [psychologist must disclose records of treatment of minor to parent]; Attorney ad litem for *D.K. v. Parents of D.K.,* 780 So. 2d 301 (Fla. 4th DCA 2001) [minor may block parent access to mental health records]; *S.C. v. Guardian* ad litem, 845 So. 2d 953 (Fla. 4th DCA 2003) [guardian ad litem cannot have unlimited access to minor's mental health records]; see also T.L. Cheng et al., Confidentiality in health care, 269 J.A.M.A.

1404 (1993) [survey of adolescent attitudes indicated they would not seek health services to avoid disclosure of certain information]; Council on Scientific Affairs, American Med. Ass'n, Confidential health services for adolescents, 269 J.A.M.A. 1420 (1993) [encouraging increased confidentiality].

178 E.g., *H.L. v. Matheson,* 450 U.S. 398 (1981) [Utah parental consent requirement for abortions].

179 *Mrozinski v. Pogue,* 205 Ga. App. 731, 423 S.E.2d 405 (1992).

180 45 C.F.R. § 146.502(f).

181 45 C.F.R. § 146.502(g)(4).

182 45 C.F.R. § 146.512 (f)(4), (g), (h).

183 E.g., *Scott v. Henry Ford Hosp.,* 199 Mich. App. 241, 501 N.W.2d 259 (1993) [only executor may authorize release; wife does not have authority]; In Interest of Roy, 423 Pa. Super. 183, 620 A.2d 1172 (1992) [only executor can authorize release of mental health records]; Annotation, Who may waive privilege of confidential communication to physician by person since deceased, 97 A.L.R. 2d 393.

184 E.g., *Gerkin v. Werner,* 106 Misc. 2d 643, 434 N.Y.S.2d 607 (Sup. Ct. 1980).

185 E.g., *Emmett v. Eastern Dispensary and Casualty Hosp.,* 130 U.S. App. D.C. 50, 396 F.2d 931 (1967).

186 *Metropolitan Life Ins. Co. v. Frenette,* [1992] 1 S.C.R. 647.

187 *Fanshaw v. Medical Protective Ass'n,* 52 Wis. 2d 234, 190 N.W.2d 155 (1971).

188 E.g., In re Grand Jury Subpoena for Medical Records of Curtis Payne, 150 N.H. 436, 839 A.2d 837 (2004); *Rost v. State Bd. of Psychology,* 659 A.2d 626 (Pa. Commw. 1995) [affirming reprimand of psychologist for complying with subpoena by releasing patient records without consent]; *Simms v. Bradach,* No. MON-L-393-01 (N.J. Super Ct. Monmouth County Sept. 13, 2002), as discussed in H. Gottlieb, Judge bars use of subpoenas for medical records patient's authorization is required, N.J.L.J. Nov. 4, 2002.

189 *Washburn v. Rite Aid Corp.,* 695 A.2d 495 (R.I. 1997).

190 *Kunkel v. Walton,* 179 Ill. 2d 519, 689 N.E.2d 1047 (1997).

191 45 C.F.R. § 164.512(e)(1)(ii); E.g., *Hutton v. City of Martinez,* 219 F.R.D. 164 (N.D. Cal. 2003).

192 E.g., *Thomas v. Benedictine Hosp.,* 296 A.D.2d 781, 745 N.Y.S.2d 606 (3d Dept. 2002) [affirming order rejecting plaintiff's effort to depose hospital officials in malpractice lawsuit concerning physician treatment for leg fracture]; *Allen v. Smith,* 179 W.Va. 360, 368 S.E.2d 924 (1988) [if not protected by statute of limitations, psychiatrist could have been sued for complying with insufficient subpoena].

193 *Doe v. Roe,* 190 A.D.2d 463, 599 N.Y.S.2d 350 (4th Dept. 1993).

194 E.g., *Rojas v. Ryder Truck Rental, Inc.,* 641 So. 2d 855 (Fla. 1994); *Doelfel v. Trevisani,* 644 So. 2d 1359 (Fla. 1994).

195 *Ritt v. Ritt,* 52 N.J. 177, 244 A.2d 497 (1968).

196 *Laurent v. Brelji,* 74 Ill. App. 3d 214, 392 N.E.2d 929 (4th Dist. 1979).

197   *People v. Bickham,* 89 Ill. 2d 1, 431 N.E.2d 365 (1982).

198   *Roth v. Saint Elizabeth's Hosp.,* 241 Ill. App. 3d 407, 607 N.E.2d 1356 (5th Dist. appeal denied), 151 Ill. 2d 577, 616 N.E.2d 347 (1993).

199   *United States v. Fesman,* 781 F. Supp. 511 (S.D. Ohio 1991).

200   E.g., *Bristol-Meyers Squibb Co. v. Hancock,* 921 S.W.2d 917 (Tex. Ct. App. 1996) [when surgeon sued breast implant manufacturer for injury to his reputation, income, company denied discovery of medical records of his patients]; *Parkson v. Central Du Page Hosp.,* 105 Ill. App. 3d 850, 435 N.E.2d 140 (1st Dist. 1982).

201   E.g., *St. Lukes Reg. Med. Ctr. v. United States,* 717 F. Supp. 665 (N.D. Iowa 1989) [government entitled to disclosure of physician's medical records by administrative subpoena to investigate Medicaid civil violations]; *Goldberg v. Davis,* 151 Ill. 2d 267, 602 N.E.2d 812 (1992) [professional discipline]; *Dr. K v. State Bd. of Physician Quality Assurance,* 98 Md. App. 103, 632 A.2d 453, cert. denied, 513 U.S. 817 (1994) [professional discipline].

202   E.g., *Amente v. Newman,* 653 So. 2d 1030 (Fla. 1995); *Todd v. South Jersey Hosp. Sys.,* 152 F.R.D. 676 (D. N.J. 1993); *Terre Haute Reg. Hosp. v. Trueblood,* 600 N.E.2d 1358 (Ind. 1992); *Community Hosp. Ass'n v. District Court,* 194 Colo. 98, 570 P.2d 243 (1977); *State ex rel. Lester E. Cox Med. Ctr. v. Keet,* 678 S.W.2d 813 (Mo. 1984) (en banc).

203   E.g., *Buford v. Howe,* 10 F.3d 1184 (5th Cir. 1994); *Glassman v. St. Joseph Hosp.,* 259 Ill. App. 3d 730, 631 N.E.2d 1186 (1st Dist. 1994); *Ekstrom v. Temple,* 197 Ill. App. 3d 120, 553 N.E.2d 424 (2d Dist. 1990).

204   People ex rel. *Dep't of Prof'l Regulation v. Manos,* 202 Ill. 2d 563, 578 (Ill. 2002).

205   *Schechet v. Kesten,* 372 Mich. 346, 126 N.W.2d 718 (1964); *Dorris v. Detroit Osteopathic Hosp. Corp.,* 559 N.W.2d 76 (Mich. Ct. App. 1996) [affirming denial of disclosure of name of nonparty patient who may have witnessed patient's refusal of drug]; accord *Gunn v. Sound Shore Med. Ctr.,* 5 A.D.3d 435, 772 N.Y.S.2d 714 (2d Dept. 2004) [reject release of log of patients in rehab center when accident happened].

206   *Kinsella v. NYT Television,* 382 N.J. Super. 102, 110 (N.J. Super. 2005).

207   E.g., *City of Edmund v. Parr,* 587 P.2d 56 (Okla. 1978); *Jenkins v. Wu,* 102 Ill. 2d 468, 468 N.E.2d 1162 (1984); but see *Southwest Commun. Health Servs. v. Smith,* 107 N.M. 196, 755 P.2d 40 (1988) [law upheld, but court may ignore law when records sufficiently needed in litigation].

208   *Dir. of Health Affairs Policy Planning v. Freedom of Info. Comm'n,* 293 Conn. 164 (Conn. 2009).

209   *Young v. King,* 136 N.J. Super. 127, 344 A.2d 792 (Law Div. 1975).

210   *Brandon Reg'l Hosp. v. Murray,* 957 So. 2d 590, 591 (Fla. 2007).

211   Id.

212   *Hosp. Auth. v. Meeks,* 285 Ga. 521 (Ga. 2009).

213   State ex rel. *Shroades v. Henry,* 187 W.Va. 723, 421 S.E.2d 264 (1992).

214   E.g., *Carr v. Howard,* 426 Mass. 514, 689 N.E.2d 1304 (1998) [reports for peer review committee confidential, cannot be provided to trial judge for in camera review]; Application to Quash a Grand Jury Subpoena, 239 A.D.2d 412, 657 N.Y.S.2d 747 (2d Dept. 1997) [quashing grand jury subpoena of hospital's quality assurance records].

215   Ex parte Fairfield Nursing & Rehab. Ctr., L.L.C., 22 So. 3d 445, 450 (Ala. 2009).

216   *Warrick v. Giron,* 290 N.W.2d 166 (Minn. 1980).

217   E.g., *Cedars-Sinai Med. Ctr. v. Superior Court,* 12 Cal. App. 4th 579, 16 Cal. Rptr. 2d 253 (2d Dist. 1993).

218   *Huntsman v. Aultman Hosp.,* 160 Ohio App. 3d 196, 2005 Ohio 1482, 826 N.E.2d 384.

219   E.g., *Ashokan v. Department of Ins.,* 109 Nev. 662, 856 P.2d 244 (1993).

220   E.g., Fla. Stat. §§ 395.0191–395.0193, 766.101; *Young v. Saldanha,* 189 W.Va. 330, 431 S.E.2d 669 (1993) [physician's use of peer review materials in suit against hospital concerning clinical privileges did not waive evidentiary privilege, so patient could not use materials in malpractice suit against physician].

221   E.g., *St. Elizabeth's Hosp. v. State Bd. of Prof. Med. Conduct,* 174 A.D.2d 225, 579 N.Y.S.2d 457 (3d Dept. 1992).

222   *Adams v. St. Francis Reg. Med. Ctr.,* 264 Kan. 144, 955 P.2d 1169 (1998).

223   42 U.S.C. § 11111(a)(1).

224   Id. at § 11101(5).

225   Id. at § 11101; see also *Moore v. Williamsburg Reg'l Hosp.,* 560 F.3d 166, 171 (4th Cir. S.C. 2009) (discussing the purpose of HCQIA).

226   42 U.S.C. § 11151(9).

227   Id. at § 11112(a).

228   http://www.iom.edu/~/media/Files/Report%20Files/1999/To-Err-is-Human/To%20Err%20is%20Human%201999%20%20report%20brief.pdf

229   http://www.ahrq.gov/qual/psoact.htm

230   http://www.pso.ahrq.gov/listing/alphalist.htm

231   45 C.F.R. §§ 164.512, 164.103 ["required by law"].

232   E.g., Fla. Stat. §§ 382.16, 382.081.

233   E.g., Fla. Stat. § 381.231 [communicable diseases], § 384.25 [venereal diseases].

234   *Derrick v. Ontario Comm. Hosp.,* 47 Cal. App. 3d 145, 120 Cal. Rptr. 566 (4th Dist. 1975).

235   State ex rel. *Callahan v. Kinder,* 879 S.W.2d 677 (Mo. Ct. App. 1994).

236   E.g., Fla. Stat. § 415.504; L.S. Wissow, Current concepts: Child abuse and neglect, 332 N. Eng. J. Med. 1425 (1995).

237   45 C.F.R. § 164.512(b)(1)(ii).

238   E.g., Wis. Stat. § 48.981(2)(a).

239 See A. Goldstein, Hospital for priests not required to report all abuse, WASH. POST, June 30, 2002, C5 [Maryland AG opinion, provider not required to report abuse outside of state].

240 E.g., *O'Heron v. Blaney,* 276 Ga. 871, 583 S.E.2d 834 (2003); *Meyer v. Lashley,* 44 P.2d 553 (Okla. 2002); *Casbohm v. Metrohealth Med. Ctr.,* 746 N.E.2d 661 (Ohio. App. 2000); *Martinez v. Mafchir,* 35 F.3d 1486 (10th Cir. 1994) [social worker protected]; see also *People v. Wood,* 447 Mich. 80, 523 N.W.2d 477 (1994) [social worker could contact police to obtain assistance in investigating possible neglect]; *Bryant-Bruce v. Vanderbilt Univ. Inc.,* 974 F. Supp. 1127. (M.D. Tenn. 1997) [immunity only for report within scope of state duty to report; deny dismissal for other aspects of report]; *Bol v. Cole,* 561 N.W.2d 143 (Minn. 1997) [no immunity for copy of report given to patient's mother; only qualified privilege to release to mother to protect child who cannot otherwise protect self].

241 E.g., *Gladson v. State,* 258 Ga. 885, 376 S.E.2d 362 (1989); Doctor faces penalty for failing to report child abuse, AP, Nov. 8, 2002 [Iowa MD fined $5,000 in settlement with licensing board]; Prosecutors drop charges against doctors accused of failing to report child abuse, AP, Feb. 11, 2004 [Mich.].

242 E.g., IOWA CODE ANN. § 232.75(2); *Stecker v. First Commercial Trust Co.,* 962 S.W.2d 792 (Ark. 1998); *Landeros v. Flood,* 17 Cal. 3d 399, 131 Cal. Rptr. 69, 551 P.2d 389 (1976); contra, *Vance v. T.R.C.,* 229 Ga. App. 608. 494 S.E.2d 714 (1997) [statute requiring child abuse report did not create private cause of action against physician for failure to report]; Annotation, Validity, construction, and application of state statute requiring doctor or other person to report child abuse, 73 A.L.R. 4TH 782; Jury reaches $2 million verdict in injuries to abused infant, AP, Apr. 29, 2002 [Missouri physician, day care center liable]; but see *Cuyler v. United States,* 362 F.3d 949 (7th Cir. 2004) [no implied duty of rescue in Ill. child abuse statute, so no civil liability].

243 Missouri reporting law for healthcare workers is unconstitutional, AP, Sept. 11, 2003; Missouri Supreme Court to hear arguments in nurse appeal, AP, Apr. 30, 2004.

244 E.g., *People v. Stockton Pregnancy Control Med. Clinic,* 203 Cal. App. 3d 225, 249 Cal. Rptr. 762 (3d Dist. 1988) [must report sexual conduct of minors under age 14 if with person of disparate age]; *Planned Parenthood Affiliates v. Van de Camp,* 181 Cal. App. 3d 245, 226 Cal. Rptr. 361 (1st Dist. 1986) [not required to report all sexual activity of minors under age 14]; Doctor seeks special probation, AP, Dec. 12, 2002 [two-year probation for Conn. MD accused of failing to report pregnancy of 10-year-old]; J. Hanna, Kline: Doctors must report youngsters' pregnancies, AP, June 18, 2002 [Kansas AG opinion]; R. Hegeman, Kansas judge says doctors cannot be forced to report underage sex, AP, July 26, 2004; see also WIS. STAT. § 48.981(2m) [providers not required to report some sexual activities of minors].

245 E.g., FLA STAT. § 415.103; M.S. Lachs & K. Pillemer, Current concepts: Abuse and neglect of elderly persons, 332 N. ENG. J. MED. 437 (1995) [42 states required reporting in 1991].

246 E.g., WIS. STAT. § 46.90 [elder abuse].

247 45 C.F.R. § 164.512(c).

248 S. Stapleton, Confidentiality is key in protecting patients, AM. MED. NEWS, July 14, 1997, 3 [Am. Med. Ass'n opposes reporting domestic violence]; A. Hyman et al., Laws mandating reporting of domestic violence: Do they promote patient well-being? 273 J.A.M.A. 1781 (1995) [questioning helpfulness where there are inadequate responses to reports]; see also S. Stapleton, Plans ask doctors to address domestic violence, AM. MED. NEWS, Dec. 21, 1998, 28 [internal reporting within managed care].

249 See D. Hancock, Hospital's inaction delayed arrest, MIAMI (FL) HERALD, Jan. 24, 1996, 6B [no notice to authorities of gunshot victim as required, gave clothing (potential evidence) to family].

250 N.Y. PENAL LAW § 265.25.

251 IOWA CODE ANN. § 147.111.

252 In the Matter of Grand Jury Investigation in New York County, 98 N.Y.2d 525, 779 N.E.2d 173, 749 N.Y.S.2d 462 (2002); but see *State v. Baptist Mem. Hosp.,* 726 So. 2d 554 (Miss. 1998) [state can subpoena records of all patients treated for lacerations during a specified time period as part of a homicide investigation, where the law requires reporting knifings which the court broadly interpreted to include the cases sought by the subpoena].

253 See American Medical Association wants doctors more involved with older drivers, AP Sept. 10, 2003; J.E. Allen, Medicine: Drivers not telling doctors of seizures: Some report concealing episodes because they don't want to lose their licenses, a survey finds, L.A. TIMES, Apr. 7, 2003, 3 [6 states require reports of seizures]; WIS. STAT. § 146.82(3)(a) [permissive]; see also Edina hospital cited for allowing drugged patient drive, AP Aug. 5, 2003 [MN hospital given three citations]; M. Raffaele, Six-pack-a-day drinker loses license, AP, July 13, 2004 [challenge to loss after MD report].

254 E.g., FLA. ADMIN. CODE §§ 10D-91.425, 10D-91.426, 10D-91.428 [radiation incidents].

255 21 C.F.R. § 606.170(b).

256 21 C.F.R. § 812.150(b).

257 21 U.S.C. § 360, 21 C.F.R. § 803.

258 E.g., *Beth Israel Hosp. Ass'n v. Board of Registration in Med.,* 401 Mass. 172, 515 N.E.2d 574 (1987).

259 *Choe v. Axelrod,* 141 A.D.2d 235, 534 N.Y.S.2d 739 (3d Dept. 1988).

260 *Whalen v. Roe,* 429 U.S. 589 (1977).

261 E.g., 42 U.S.C. § 300ff-132.

262 See Annotation, Liability of doctor or other health practitioner to third party contracting contagious disease from doctor's patient, 3 A.L.R. 5TH 370.

263 *Derrick v. Ontario Commun. Hosp.,* 47 Cal. App. 3d 154, 120 Cal Rptr. 566 (4th Dist. 1975).

264 *Phillips v. Oconee Mem. Hosp.,* 290 S.C. 192, 348 S.E.2d 836 (1986).

265 *Tarasoff v. Regents of Univ. of Cal.,* 17 Cal. 3d 425, 131 Cal. Rptr. 14, 551 P.2d 334 (1976).

266 *Thompson v. County of Alameda,* 27 Cal. 3d 741, 167 Cal. Rptr. 70, 614 P.2d 728 (1980).

267 E.g., *Thornburg v. Long,* 178 N.C. 589, 101 S.E. 99 (1919); see also *Gross v. Allen,* 22 Cal. App. 4th 354, 27 Cal. Rptr. 2d 429 (2d Dist. 1994) [original psychiatrists had duty to tell subsequent attending psychiatrist of patient's prior suicide attempts; subsequent psychiatrist called to obtain history].

268 E.g., *Watts v. Cumberland County Hosp. Sys.,* 75 N.C. App. 1, 330 S.E.2d

269 45 C.F.R. § 164.512(b).

270 45 C.F.R. § 164.512(d).

271 45 C.F.R. § 164.512(e).

272 45 C.F.R. § 164.512(f).

273 45 C.F.R. § 164.512(h).

274 45 C.F.R. § 164.512(i).

275 45 C.F.R. § 164.512(j).

276 45 C.F.R. § 164.512(k).

277 45 C.F.R. §§ 164.512(a)(1) [named patient], 164.512(f)(2) [suspect, fugitive, material witness, missing person]; 164.512(f)(3) [victim].

278 See 45 C.F.R. § 512(k)(5); *Johnson v. West Va. Univ. Hosps., Inc.,* 186 W.Va. 648, 413 S.E.2d 889 (1991) [liability for failure to warn hospital security guard of HIV status of patient before asking him to assist in restraint of patient].

279 E.g., M. Stolz, Politician's drug records protected; Judge says police lacked warrant to get evidence from pharmacy, Plain Dealer, Mar. 15, 2002, B3 [Ohio trial court threw out records in prosecution for allegedly lying to obtain pain drugs].

280 E.g., *Ferguson v. City of Charleston,* 532 U.S. 67 (2001) [performing urine tests at request of law enforcement to obtain evidence of cocaine use by maternity patients for law enforcement purposes was unreasonable search violating Fourth Amendment].

281 E.g., *Comm. v. Shaw,* 564 Pa. 617, 770 A.2d 295 (2001) [clinical blood test results obtained by police without warrant not admissible]; *State v. Dyal,* 97 N.J. 229, 478 A.2d 390 (1984) [court-issued subpoena required when police seek to obtain hospital blood test]; contra, *People v. Ernst,* 311 Ill. App. 3d 672, 725 N.E.2d 59 (2d Dist. 2000) [hospital may disclose blood alcohol results to police without court order]; *Hannoy v. State,* 793 N.E.2d 1109 (Ind. App. 2003) [clinical blood alcohol results may be released to police without court order]; but see *State v. Schreiber,* 122 N.J. 579, 585 A.2d 945 (1991) [doctor initiated disclosure of blood test result admissible]; *Tapp v. State,* 108 S.W.3d 459 (Tex. App. 2003) [upholding obtaining clinical blood test results with a grand jury subpoena].

282 E.g., *People v. Gomez,* 147 Misc. 2d 704, 556 N.Y.S.2d 961 (Sup. Ct. 1990) [police witness surgical removal of bags from stomach].

283 *State v. Thompson,* 585 N.W.2d 905 (Wis. App. 1998).

284 E.g., *Comm. v. Johnson,* 556 Pa. 216, 727 A.2d 1089 (1999) [no reasonable expectation of privacy in bullet removed for medical reasons, so no violation to give to police without warrant]; *State v. Cowan,* 46 S.W.2d 227 (Tenn. Crim. App. 2000) [no reasonable expectation of privacy in removed bullet, so admissible even though obtained from hospital without warrant].

285 45 C.F.R. § 164.512(k)(2),(3).

286 45 C.F.R. §§ 164.310(c), 164.502(a)(2)(ii).

287 45 C.F.R. § 164.512(d).

288 E.g., Iowa Code Ann. § 85.27.

289 E.g., *Acosta v. Cary,* 365 So. 2d 4 (La. Ct. App. 1978).

290 *Morris v. Consolidation Coal Co.,* 191 W.Va. 426, 446 S.E.2d 648 (1994).

291 45 C.F.R. § 164.512(l).

292 5 U.S.C. § 552.

293 5 U.S.C. § 552a; *Doe v. Stephens,* 271 U.S. App. D.C. 230, 851 F.2d 1457 (1988) [effect of Privacy Act on grand jury subpoena of VA medical records]; *Williams v. Department of Veterans Affairs,* 879 F. Supp. 578 (E.D. Va. 1995) [Privacy Act is exclusive remedy for wrongful disclosure of medical information by VA].

294 E.g., Iowa Code Ann. § 22.7; *Head v. Colloton,* 331 N.W.2d 870 (Iowa 1983).

295 *Eugene Cervi & Co. v. Russell,* 184 Colo. 282, 519 P.2d 1189 (1974).

296 *Head v. Colloton,* 331 N.W.2d 870 (Iowa 1983).

297 *Wooster Republican Printing Co. v. City of Wooster,* 56 Ohio St. 2d 126, 383 N.E.2d 124 (1978).

298 E.g., *Oklahoma Disability Law Ctr. v. Dillon Family & Youth Servs.,* 879 F. Supp. 1110 (D. Okla. 1995) [plaintiff entitled to discovery of treatment records of its clients, state law authorizing facility to require court order superceded by federal Protection and Advocacy of Mentally Ill Individuals Act].

299 18 U.S.C. § 2511(d).

300 *Estate of Berthiaume v. Pratt,* 365 A.2d 792 (Me. 1976); see Annotation, Taking unauthorized photographs as invasion of privacy, 86 A.L.R. 3d 374.

301 *Anderson v. Strong Mem. Hosp.,* 140 Misc. 2d 770, 531 N.Y.S.2d 735 (Sup. Ct. 1988), aff'd, 151 A.D.2d 1033, 542 N.Y.S.2d 96 (4th Dept. 1989).

302 E.g., *Stubbs v. North Mem. Med. Ctr.,* 448 N.W.2d 78 (Minn. Ct. App. 1989) [publication in promotional, educational materials of before, after photographs of facial cosmetic surgery without patient consent may constitute breach of express warranty of silence arising from physician-patient relationship]; *Feeney v. Young,* 191 A.D. 501, 181 N.Y.S. 481 (1st Dept. 920) [public showing of a film of a caesarean section delivery]; *Vassiliades v. Garfinkels,* 492 A.2d 580 (D.C. 1985) [public use of before, after photos of cosmetic surgery in department store, on television]; see Annotation, Invasion of privacy by use of plaintiff's name or likeness in advertising, 23 A.L.R. 3d 865.

303 In re Simmons, 112 A.D.2d 806, 492 N.Y.S.2d 308 (4th Dept. 1985); but see *North Broward Hosp. Dist. v. ABC,* No. 86-026514 (Fla. Cir. Ct. Broward County Oct. 20, 1986) [hospital cannot prohibit media access to comatose patient when guardian consents].

304 R.J. Peach, Court overrides hospital's ban on photographs in intensive care unit, Legal Intelligencer, Dec. 27, 2000, 6.

305 E.g., Jury acquits reporter of trespassing charge, AP Dec. 23, 2003 [N.C. reporter entered assisted living center with assistance of former staff member and videotaped sleeping residents].

306 *Shulman v. Group W Productions,* 18 Cal. 4th 200, 74 Cal. Rptr. 2d 843, 955 P.2d 469 (1998).

307 E.g., Nurse accused of torturing brain-damaged child, AP Oct. 3, 2003 [use of film from surveillance cameras in WA home installed by grandmother]; Mother accused of contaminating infant daughter's IV, AP, Jan. 15, 2004 [Ind. woman videotaped injecting fecal matter into daughter's IV tube]; *Kinsella v. Welch,* 2003 N.J. Super. LEXIS 253 (App. Div.) [under newsperson privilege media not required to produce video of treatment in hospital, but must produce any portions that will be used at trial].

308 Judge: Media permitted to broadcast video of woman in coma, AP, Oct. 2, 2002.

309 Lawsuit: Woman claims doctor branded her during surgery, AP, Jan. 24, 2003.

310 2011 JC CAMH, RI.01.03.01.

311 Bush promotes technology, UPI, Apr. 26, 2004.

312 See *Schmidt v. U.S. Dep't Of Veterans Affairs,* 218 F.R.D. 619 (E.D. Wis. 2003).

313 Described in http://www.phdsc.org/standards/fse.asp (accessed Mar. 4, 2012).

314 The office website is http://healthit.hhs.gov/portal/server.pt/community/healthit_hhs_gov__home/1204 (accessed Mar. 4, 2012).

315 M. Freudenheim, Many hospitals resist computerized patient care, N.Y. Times, Apr. 6, 2004, C1; R. Koppel et al., Role of computerized physician order entry systems in facilitating medication errors, J.A.M.A., Mar. 9, 2005, 1197.

316 See S. Lohr, Healthcare technology is a promise unfinanced, N.Y. Times, Dec. 3, 2004, C5; J. Morrissey, It's more than just the purchase; make clear the commitments that it will trigger, Mod. Healthcare, July 12, 2004, 30.

317 E.g., *Doe v. Medlantic Health Care Group,* 814 A.2d 939 (D.C. App. 2003) [hospital liable under D.C. law for staff member's dissemination of HIV status after unauthorized lookup]; *Doe v. Dartmouth-Hitchcock Med. Ctr.,* 2001 U.S. Dist. LEXIS 10704 (D.N.H.) [hospital not liable under federal law for MD lookup]; J. Mandak, Researcher sentenced in Wynette case, AP Online, Dec. 1, 2000 [using former physician's password, former research assistant accessed computerized hospital records of late country singer Tammy Wynette and sold them to tabloids; sentenced to six months, fined amount received from tabloids]; *Arbster v. Unemployment Comp. Bd. of Rev.,* 690 A.2d 805 (Pa. Commw. 1997) [nurse fired for lookup of computer records of her family denied unemployment compensation]; see also *Schmidt v. U.S. Dep't of Veterans Affairs,* 218 F.R.D. 619 (E.D. Wis. 2003) [challenge to access to employee social security numbers in VA hospital computerized medical record; description of steps VA had taken to restrict, trace lookups].

318 Electronic Signatures in Global and National Consumer Act, Pub. No. L. 106-229, 114 Stat, 464 (2000), codified in part at 15 U.S. §§ 7001 et seq.

319 E.g., Second doctor sues hospital over Pap smear tests, AP, Jan. 23, 2004 [accusation of misuse of electronic signatures]; Feds find no significant problems with Magee Pap smears, AP, Apr. 13, 2004.

320 *Whalen v. Roe,* 429 U.S. 589 (1977); see also Letcher woman convicted on drug fraud charges, AP, Apr. 4, 2001 [use of KY computerized prescription tracking system to achieve conviction].

321 E.g., 15 U.S.C. § 7001; *United States v. Fujii,* 301 F.3d 535 (7th Cir. 2002) [admissibility of printouts in federal court].

322 See http://www.nlm.nih.gov/research/umls/Snomed/snomed_faq.html (accessed Mar. 4, 2012).

323 See L. Stevens, Virtually there, Am. Med. News, Dec. 21, 1998, 24; B. Kane & D.Z. Sands, Guidelines for the clinical use of electronic mail with patients, 5 J. Am. Med. Informatics Ass'n 104 (1998) [http://jamia.bmj.com/content/5/1/104.full.pdf+html; accessed Mar. 4, 2012]; S.M. Borowitz & J.C. Wyatt, The origin, content, and workload of e-mail consultations, J.A.M.A., Oct. 21, 1998, 1321; A.R. Spielberg, On call and online: Sociohistorical, legal, and ethical implications of e-mail for the patient physician relationship, J.A.M.A., Oct. 21, 1998, 1353; G. Baldwin, Doctor benefits from e-mail efficiency with patients, Am. Med. News, Dec. 21, 1998, 24.

324 *Walgreen Co. v. Wisconsin Pharmacy Examining Bd.,* 217 Wis. 2d 290, 577 N.W.2d 387, 1998 Wisc. App. LEXIS 201 (Unpub).

325 See Online consultations slow to take off, Am. Med. News, Apr. 12, 2004, 21 [consumers say they want e-mail, but unwilling to pay more than $10].

326 E.g., L. Kowalczyk, The doctor will e-you now: Insurers to pay doctors to answer questions over Web, Boston Globe, May 24, 2004, A1.

327 E.g., A. Michaels & D. Wells, HealthSouth investigators reveal damning new e-mail, Financial Times (London), July 11, 2003, 13; J. Sarche, Beware of e-mail, text messages, Wis. St. J., June 7, 2004, A3.

328 E.g., *United States v. Councilman,* 2004 U.S. App. LEXIS 13352 (1st Cir.).

329 E.g., M.A. Nusbaum, New kind of snooping arrives at the office, N.Y. Times, July 13, 2003, 12BU.

330 E.g., Georgia man accused of sending Internet threat to hospital, AP, Mar. 6, 2003.

331 E.g., J. Wells, Wrong MDs got patient records; psychiatric privacy violated, San Francisco Chronicle, Dec. 30, 2000, A13; M.W. Salganik, Health data on 858 patients mistakenly e-mailed to others; medical information was among messages sent out by Kaiser Health Care, Baltimore Sun, Aug. 10, 2000, 1C.

332 E.g., Hacker steals files on patients from UW, Seattle Times, Dec. 9, 2000, B1 [hacker stole files on 4,700 patients].

333 See S. Bakerand & M. Shenk, A patch in time saves nine: Liability risks for unpatched software, Corp. Counsellor, Apr. 5, 2004, 3.

334 E.g., M. Lerner & J. Marcotty, Web posting has health and university officials scrambling; mental health records of children from 20 families were mistakenly put onto the Internet, Star Tribune (Minneapolis, MN), Nov. 8, 2001, 1B; C. Pillar, Web mishap: Kids' psychological files posted, L.A. Times, Nov. 7, 2001, A1.

335 *Planned Parenthood v. American Coalition of Life Activists,*
41 F. Supp. 2d 1130 (D. Or. 1999), rev'd, 244 F.3d 1007 (9th Cir.
2001), rev'd, 290 F.3d 1058 (9th Cir. 2002) (en banc) [reinstating
district court injunction and verdict against defendants], cert.
denied, 123 S. Ct. 2637 (U.S. 2003), on remand, 300 F. Supp. 2d
1055 (D. Ore. 2004) [jury award of punitive damages affirmed].

336 T. Hillig & J. Mannies, Woman sues over posting of abortion
details; her records from Granite City hospital were put on website; hospital, protesters are defendants, St. Louis Post-Dispatch,
July 3, 2001, A1; J. Mannies, Abortion foes are ordered to take
woman's records, photo off Web; patient had complications at
clinic in Granite City, St. Louis Post-Dispatch, July 11, 2001, B1;
Judge keeps woman's records off net, AP Online, Aug. 23, 2001.

337 A. Barnard, Facing criticism cosmetic surgeon sues over postings by a former patient, Boston Globe, Sept. 24, 2002, B1; see
also M. Ko, Judge limits police data online; website operators
must remove officers' Social Security numbers, Seattle Times,
May 11, 2001, B; A. Liptak, Dispute simmers over website posting
personal data on police, N.Y. Times, July 12, 2003, A1.

338 J. Mandak, Judge orders attorneys to shut down hospital lawsuit website, AP, Dec. 23, 2003 [E.D. Pa. judge ordered closing
site recruiting for class action suit against hospital]; Law firms,
hospital agree.

Chapter 9

Healthcare Payment Systems

Ryan Meade

Key Learning Objectives

By the end of this chapter, the reader will be able to:

- Identify the four principal types of healthcare payment systems in the United States.

- Understand the differences between Medicare and Medicaid.

- Explain the four "parts" of Medicare.

- Understand the role of the federal government versus state governments in regulating healthcare payment.

- Discuss the role of contract law in nongovernment healthcare plans.

Chapter Outline

 Nongovernment Health Insurance Programs

 Government-Sponsored Health Insurance

Introduction

The principal objective of this chapter is to provide an overview of the ways healthcare services are reimbursed. This chapter focuses primarily on payment mechanisms and organized programs. You will learn about Medicare, Medicaid, and other major government payer programs, as well as employer-sponsored payment programs and other private payment programs. Healthcare payment is principally provided through health insurance programs that are a mix of government sponsor programs and private sector health insurance plans. This chapter will explore healthcare payments and their legal structures.

The Patient Protection and Affordable Care Act of 2010 (PPACA) is significant legislation that impacts premium levels, how insurance policies can be purchased, prohibits certain denials of issuing coverage, mandates that most individuals have or purchase health insurance coverage, and requires insurance companies to meet certain loss ratio levels. The bulk of the PPACA changes are slated to go into effect by 2014 and require both states and the federal government to adopt extensive regulatory frameworks. At the time this chapter was prepared for publication, much of the regulatory promulgation had not occurred. The PPACA statutes do not significantly affect the legal structure of the reimbursement systems discussed in this chapter. How the anticipated regulations and the patchwork of state insurance exchanges will affect these reimbursement systems will not be known for several years. The impact of those regulations will warrant discussion in later editions of this book.

Payment for healthcare services is one of the most difficult problems of healthcare law and public policy. It is a complex administrative, legal, and political challenge. The U.S. Department of Health and Human Services (HHS) estimates that $2.85 trillion will be spent in the United States on healthcare services in 2011 and that this will increase to $3.9 trillion in a span of five years by 2016.[1] For 2012, the federal government estimates that it will spend $1.05 trillion on health care, while state and local governments will spend an additional $387 billion on their Medicaid contribution as well as other miscellaneous local programs.[2] Expenditures for 2012 are estimated at $585 billion for Medicare to cover almost 50 million people, and $501 billion for Medicaid for 62 million people.[3] The Medicare and Medicaid programs are projected to account for 38 percent of all payments for healthcare services in 2012. When all federal and state health insurance reimbursement is totaled, government health insurance will pay for 50.4 percent of all healthcare expenditures. The same federal projections estimate that individuals will pay $297 billion in cash or out of pocket (10 percent of healthcare expenditures). Private insurance (including employer-based health benefits) or charitable funds will pay for the remaining roughly 40 percent of healthcare expenditures.

There is no one decision maker that addresses which healthcare services are paid for by third parties. The existing healthcare delivery and payment systems exist amid complex interactions based on decisions by governments, payers, providers, and individuals. The full breadth of those interactions is beyond the scope of this chapter. Although payment for healthcare services is a distinct issue from access to healthcare services, the two are interrelated. Simply stated, payment issues weigh heavily on the minds of both provider and patient and often limit access to health care. Nevertheless, this chapter focuses on the current legal structure and payment systems that pertain to health insurance coverage.

The four principal healthcare payment systems can be described as follows:

1. *Employer-sponsored health insurance*: As a benefit of employment, an employer pays, or arranges for the payment of, healthcare services for its employees and their dependents. This may be accomplished by the employer "self-funding" for healthcare service payments. Or, it may be accomplished by an employer arranging for health insurance policies to cover its employees. The employer may require employees to pay a portion of the premium or make some contribution to the health plan. The amounts usually vary by employer, based on the structure of the plan and the benefits offered. The employer-sponsored plan usually includes some level of deductible or co-payments for services. The deductibles or co-payments are the financial responsibility of the insured employee. Employer-sponsored health insurance is regulated by the federal government.

2. *Commercial health insurance*: An individual may purchase a health insurance policy that provides for an agreed upon range of covered services. The coverage may be limited to catastrophic events, such as hospitalization, or it may broadly cover preventive and acute healthcare services. Individuals pay premiums

for this coverage. The insurance arrangement typically has some type of control mechanism in which the individual pays agreed upon "out-of-pocket" amounts (generally, co-payments and deductibles) that vary by the type of plan and amount of premium. Commercial health insurance is regulated principally by state agencies, including the state insurance commission.

3. *Medicare program*: The federal government administers the Medicare program for those who qualify for eligibility. Individuals who enroll in Medicare are called "beneficiaries." For 2012, there is projected to be close to 50 million individuals enrolled in the Medicare program. The number of Medicare enrollees is expected to rise to 62 million by 2019. The Medicare program is a federal health insurance program designed principally to pay for healthcare services for acute and chronic conditions. Medicare was enacted in 1965, and for many decades the program has not focused on "wellness" or preventive care. Over time, a small number of preventive care services have been added to Medicare coverage. Medicare principally covers persons over 65 years of age, individuals with end-stage-renal disease, those considered disabled by the Social Security Administration, and a small number of others with specific medical conditions.

4. *Medicaid program*: States administer the Medicaid program. Medicaid covers individuals with incomes that are within certain levels of the federal poverty guidelines. Those guidelines are updated periodically. Medicaid also covers certain disabled individuals. Medicaid is financed by states and the federal government. The United States provides "matching funds" to each state, based on the poverty level population in the state. Although Medicaid is administered by the state, it is considered a federal healthcare program and is based on a set of federal statutes in the Social Security Act. Each state has discretion to provide more generous coverage than the federally mandated minimums. In 2012, HHS estimates that there will be over 62 million individuals enrolled in the Medicaid program. By 2019, that number is projected to reach 82 million.

This brief outline is the basic framework for our healthcare payment system. Together, these four systems cover roughly 90 percent of U.S. residents with health insurance.[4] There are many other, smaller programs and mechanisms to pay for healthcare services, such as non-Medicare retirement health insurance, healthcare coverage for veterans and active members of the military, and the somewhat recent models

of "concierge plans" administered by individual physicians. A key feature of healthcare payment systems in the United States is the unique legal structure that governs each payment system. Since it is impractical to attempt to cover all of these programs and arrangements in a single chapter, we will focus on the four principal systems summarized above. Near the end of the chapter, a summary of other healthcare payment systems will be discussed.

Each of the four systems addresses payment for healthcare services by a third party—that is, someone other than the patient or provider. Issues related to the medically uninsured population are not addressed in this chapter.

Whether an individual is covered by one or more of these four healthcare payment systems often depends on circumstances that may be beyond the individual's control. However, within some of these systems, individuals do have choices. The Medicare program allows beneficiaries to choose a variety of prescription drug benefit plans for varying premiums levels. Medicare also allows beneficiaries to opt for a "Medicare Advantage" plan that provides an alternative vehicle for paying for a basic package of Medicare covered benefits. Likewise, in the commercial health insurance market, an array of health insurance plans are available to individuals based on varying premiums.

This chapter is structured as follows:

- 9-1. Nongovernment health insurance programs
- 9-2. Government-sponsored health insurance
  - 9-2.1. Medicare
  - 9-2.2. Medicaid
  - 9-2.3. Miscellaneous state programs

9-1 Nongovernment Health Insurance Programs

Private health insurance programs pay for healthcare services in a myriad of ways. At base, all health insurance programs serve as payers on behalf of the individual who receives healthcare services, hence the typical nomenclature of a "third-party payer." Not all pay the healthcare provider directly. Some private payment programs pay the covered person some or all of the charges incurred for healthcare services. In those cases, the provider collects from the patient and the patient collects from the program, with the patient remaining responsible for the difference between the charges and what the program pays. The most common format, however, is for the health insurance program to pay the provider directly and for the patient to pay the uncovered portion. This arrangement is typically agreed upon by all parties in the contractual arrangement between the third-party payer and the individual. In the case of employer-sponsored health insurance, this payment arrangement is stated in the employer's policies or the promises made by the employer to the employee.

Many private payment programs contract directly or indirectly with providers to obtain services at agreed-upon payment rates. What is "covered" by the health insurance plan is typically very different from what is "paid." The payment rate is usually lower than the provider's charges but the patient is not responsible for the difference between the covered amount and the paid amount—though the patient may be responsible for the portion of charges that are not covered. The distinction between "what is covered and what is paid" is fundamental to the four healthcare payment systems discussed in this chapter. It is important to remember that there is more latitude for negotiating payment rates between providers and private health insurers than with government health plans.

In the case of government health insurance programs, the actual amount paid is usually determined by law, so we will see later in the chapter that although Medicare pays

80 percent of charges, the charge is not the provider's "charge" but a government-set "charge." The Medicare fee schedule can be an important marker for negotiating rates with nongovernment health plans because some plans pay based on a percentage of Medicare rates (for example, 140 percent of Medicare) rather than a percentage of the provider's charges.

⚑ The differences between coverage and payment are important. Although professionals deeply involved in payment issues and payment processing systems often use these terms synonymously, in the details of healthcare reimbursement law there can often be highly nuanced differences between "coverage" and "payment." When these terms are used in speech or writing, it is important to understand the audience using them and whether the context is meant to use them synonymously or separately. From a technical perspective, "coverage" has two meanings: (1) that some portion of the item or service is paid for by the health plan and (2) that the full charge for the item or service cannot be billed to the patient. "Payment" means the mechanism and methodology to pay dollars to the provider. For the sake of describing the four principal health payment systems in this chapter, we generally will use the terms "coverage and payment" interchangeably. Finally, it is important to realize that these terms may mean different things to different health insurance programs. It is critical to understand the contract terms and conditions and, as applicable, the regulatory terms used in each of the four payment systems. Within nongovernment health insurance programs, these terms will be heavily negotiated and defined between the provider and the health plan.

With limited exceptions, a provider's direct contract with a payer is only as good as the solvency of the payer. Hospitals can lose substantial revenue (usually as an "account receivable") when payers become insolvent.[5] Insolvency of payers is a problem, whether or not there is a direct contract. But insolvencies become particularly difficult in direct contracting situations. A direct contract usually eliminates or limits a provider's opportunity to pursue collection from the patient. That type of contract also may require the provider to accept additional patients for a period of time after an insolvency case if filed.

Many contracts specify that a provider cannot bill the patient even if the payer fails to pay. The provider can be left with a claim in the bankruptcy or receivership proceedings of a payer. Generally, providers are not given a legal "priority position" in the distribution of assets in such proceedings.[6] To the extent possible, providers need to structure their arrangements to keep their loss exposure

---

Example of Covered Service and Approach to Charges: As an example of how the concept of "covered" interplays with charges, let's look at an example of a hospital that charges $500 for an x-ray. The x-ray is a "covered" service, but the insurer rarely pays the full $500 charge. The insurer may have a negotiated arrangement in which the insurer covers 80 percent of the charge, i.e., $400. Even so, the insurer typically does not pay $400 and instead pays based on a discounted amount of the provider's charges, e.g., 70 percent of charges or $350. The provider is rarely allowed to "balance bill" the patient the $150, i.e., the amount that the insurer did not pay. That balance must be "adjusted" (a generally accepted term that means "written off") to zero. Although the service is "covered," a portion of the charge, in this case 20 percent ($100), remains the patient's responsibility. This co-payment (also called "coinsurance") is paid by the patient. The hospital may start with a charge of $500 for a "covered" service but is paid a total of $450 for the service.

within sustainable limits. Particular attention is needed when drafting contract provisions that describe the "termination or terminating events" that the provider can control and exercise. Insurance companies are not eligible for federal bankruptcy protection. They must go through "receivership" under state law.[7] When health maintenance organizations (HMOs) are treated as insurance companies under state law, they are not eligible for federal bankruptcy protection. However, employers are subject to bankruptcy and a significant quandary exists when an employer with a self-funded health plan declares bankruptcy.

Due to the adverse effect of payer failures, some states have strengthened the financial qualifications required to be an HMO, insurer, or other payer. Many plans have private reinsurance coverage limits that may cover some payments.[8] Some plans are required to contribute to state guaranty funds that pay some of the losses if other health plans become insolvent.

9-1.1 Employer-Sponsored Health Insurance

Private health insurance arranged by employers for their employees is regulated by the federal Employee Retirement Income Security Act of 1974 (ERISA).[9] ERISA established uniform, national standards for employee benefit plans and preempts, in many instances, state laws governing employee health plans.

In an employer-sponsored group health plan, the employer either (a) funds the healthcare payments itself (a "self-insured plan") or (b) purchases policies on behalf of the group of employees. Both of these options are usually referred to as group health plans.

A self-insured plan is a group health plan that must arrange for the payment of healthcare services. A self-insured health plan assumes the risk for paying providers for healthcare services. Frequently, an employer lacks the infrastructure or experience to pay for healthcare services and process claims. In those circumstances, the employer often contracts with a third-party administrator (TPA) to manage the work of running the group health plan. The TPA often is an insurance company that sells and administers commercial health insurance policies. The group health plan may negotiate rates with healthcare providers in the same manner that commercial health insurance companies and managed care organizations negotiate payment rates with providers.

Managed care entities, and other third-party payers, contract directly with employers and other payers to provide care through payer networks that are created by the agreements. To reduce the layers of administration, some hospitals and groups of providers contract directly with employers.

ERISA preemption of state law becomes relevant in day-to-day management of an employer-sponsored group health plan. The preemption doctrine also is relevant when healthcare providers contract with employers. Under ERISA, only contract damages (i.e., the cost of improperly denied treatment) are recoverable as a legal remedy. Consequently, ERISA is often viewed as protection against malpractice actions for managed care organizations that provide care as part of employee benefit plans. In terms of "protection," ERISA limits damage awards for pain and suffering, lost earnings, and costs of future medical care.

An ERISA preemption analysis involves three, separate considerations that are difficult to reconcile. That is one of the reasons for the diverse interpretations of the law by different courts. The three considerations are:

1. State laws that "relate to" any covered employee benefit plan are preempted.[10]

2. An important exception states that state laws that "regulate insurance, banking, or securities" are not preempted.[11]

3. Most employee benefit plans are not considered insurers or banks and are not subject to state insurance or banking laws.[12]

There has been extensive litigation concerning the scope of the ERISA preemption. Many of the decisions are the result of legal actions by plan beneficiaries against managed care organizations for alleged negligence in providing medical care.

The Health Insurance Portability and Accountability Act of 1996 (HIPAA)[13] contains provisions that affect employer-sponsored group health plans, including managed care organizations. Most significantly, HIPAA limits the ability of group health plans to make coverage decisions based on the health condition of the insured.

9-1.2 Private Health Insurance

States regulate private health insurance, which is not provided as part of employer benefits. Private health insurance products often are seen as the face of the health insurance system in the United States. The federal government estimates that individual insurance products cover less than 9 percent of U.S. residents.[14] Nevertheless, the models used for private health insurance are used for employer-based health benefits, especially insurance products purchased by employers for their employees.

Private health insurance products are based on a theory of spreading risk across policyholders. Basically, an insurance company covers a pool of individuals. Policyholders pay premiums for the insurance coverage, and some will have expenditures during a year that add up to less than their premiums, while others will have expenditures more than their premiums. An insurance company's business bet is that in the aggregate their payout is less than the total premiums paid. These insurance concepts apply to virtually all private sector insurance, such as auto or homeowner's insurance. Health insurance is arguably the most complicated of insurance products because the expenditures occur much more frequently and are more varied than other types of insurance such as auto.

When states regulate private insurance products, they tend to set aside special laws and rules for health insurance policies. From a policy perspective, this is presumably to accommodate the close connection that is perceived between having health insurance coverage and seeking healthcare services. There is a public perception that poorly designed private health insurance programs can impact an enrollee's decision to seek basic or emergency care.

Although all states require health insurance products to be registered with the state, the definition of health insurance can vary across the states. Each state adopts its own insurance code, and there are many similarities in each of the codes. Some states adopt their own definition of health insurance.[15]

In most states, what the insurance company pays healthcare providers is a matter of private negotiation between the provider and the insurance company. However, in some states, such as Maryland, rates and payments by insurance companies are highly regulated for most healthcare organizations and allow for very little negotiation.

Health insurance policies serve as a type of contract with the policyholder (the individual). The insurance company will be held to the "rules" it agrees to in the policy as will the individual; though state agencies might void those provisions if a policy conflicts with state law requirements. State laws are subject to intense lobbying efforts by both the health insurance industry and patient advocacy groups. The result is a patchwork of more than 50 individual systems of regulation, appeal, and enforcement among the states and territories.

Along with regulating health insurance products and aspects of the product, such as premiums or how the insurance company may pay the provider, most states allow policyholders to file complaints with the state's insurance commission about any type of registered insurance products. Some states have offices dedicated to focusing on health insurance complaints. For example, in Illinois, the State Attorney General maintains a "Health Care Bureau" where individuals may file healthcare complaints. Those complaints may cover virtually any aspect of healthcare services the individual received, including complaints about insurance coverage and charges.

9-2 Government-Sponsored Health Insurance

There are several federal government programs that provide payment for health care, including Medicare; TRICARE (formerly known as Civilian Health and Medical Program for the Uniformed Services or CHAMPUS);[16] the Federal Employee Health Benefits Program (FEHBP);[17] and the Veterans Administration. There are joint federal-state programs, most importantly Medicaid. There are also various state programs. Finally, there are county (and sometimes city) public health programs that often combine payer and provider. In the Medicare and Medicaid programs, which we will principally discuss, the payer function is separate from the provider function.

Participation by providers in some government programs is limited to those that have a contract with the appropriate government agency. These participants may be referred to as "enrolled" in the program.

It is worth noting at this point in the chapter that health insurance programs do not always use the same terminology and may use the similar terms in entirely different ways. "Enrollment," meaning a provider's participation in a government health insurance program, should not be confused with how individuals may be enrolled in a government healthcare program (i.e., those persons whose health care is "covered" by a government health insurance program). When a person is enrolled in a government health insurance program, he or she is usually referred to as a "beneficiary" and not necessarily an "enrollee." However, private health insurance plans often refer to their covered individuals as "enrollees." Once again we see how important it is to pay attention to the terminology used in health insurance programs.

Because of the ability of federal and state governments to unilaterally change most of government healthcare programs, the right to payment is often determined not by contract, but by statutes and regulations. There are significant exceptions, such as when a government health insurance program allows its beneficiaries to choose to receive their benefits from among competing managed care plans. The managed care plans may negotiate rates with healthcare providers while the plans receive capitated payments from the government program.

9-2.1 Medicare

The 1965 Amendments to the Social Security Act[18] added Title XVIII to the Act. Title XVIII established a two-part program of health insurance for the aged known as Medicare. In 2012, $585 billion is expected to be spent on the Medicare program. Numerous amendments have been made over the decades, but the basic structure remains the same of Medicare being principally designed to cover "items and services" to "diagnose or treat illness or injury." A limited set of preventive care services, such as annual mammograms, have been added on a piecemeal basis.

Persons are eligible to participate in Part A, the hospital insurance program, if they (1) are 65 or older and are receiving retirement benefits under Title II of the Social Security Act or the Railroad Retirement Act, (2) qualify under a special program for persons with end-stage renal (kidney) disease, or (3) have been disabled for at least two years as determined by the Social Security Administration. Anyone age 65 or older who is a U.S. citizen or has been a permanent resident alien for five years may elect to enroll in Part B, a program of supplementary medical insurance. Medicare applies to all qualified people without regard to financial need. It is administered federally, so it is intended to have nationally uniform benefits, but provider relations and payments are administered on a regional basis through contracts with private-sector companies. The statutes allow for some regional variations.[19]

The growth in Medicare spending has weighed on the minds of policymakers for the past few decades. The advent of retirement of the baby boomer generation, rising costs in healthcare services, and the steady advance in cutting edge technologies and therapies make the financing of Medicare a hotly debated question and is relevant in virtually every annual federal budget cycle.

One significant area of healthcare services not addressed by Medicare for many years is outpatient drug costs. Under Parts A and B, drugs are covered only when they are administered to inpatients or when they are *not* self-administered drugs provided in an outpatient setting.[20]

For example, drugs required to be infused or drugs provided with intramuscular injections are covered in the outpatient setting. Meanwhile, drugs in an oral form are not covered in an outpatient setting unless they meet very limited exceptions, such as immunosuppressive drugs after a transplant.[21]

Medicare Part B Coverage of Self-Administered Drugs: Medicare Part B does not cover self-administered drugs that are provided in a hospital outpatient or physician office setting unless the purpose of the drug is among a limited number of exceptions. This is often referred to as the "self-administered drug rule." The exceptions to the self-administered drug rule that allow Medicare coverage involve the following purposes for the drugs:

1. Immunosuppressive drugs

2. Erythropoietin

3. Oral anticancer drugs

4. Antiemetics during chemotherapy

5. Hemophilia clotting factors

For a full discussion of these exceptions and the criteria for meeting an exception, please see the Medicare Benefit Policy Manual, Chapter 15, Section 50.5.

For forty years, Medicare did not pay for most drugs dispensed at a retail pharmacy pursuant to a physician's prescription. There was increasing political attention to the out-of-pocket expenses for outpatient drugs. In 2003, Medicare laws were amended to create a new Part D prescription drug benefit program, which took effect in 2006.[22]

Due to the many out-of-pocket costs associated with Medicare, there is a substantial market for Medigap insurance to cover costs not covered by Medicare. These insurance plans are formally referred to as Medicare Supplement Plans and exist as private products that beneficiaries may purchase. The Medigap plans must follow federal rules.[23]

Between the pressures to expand the program and the pressures to keep the program fiscally sound, it is likely that Medicare coverage and payments will continue to significantly change. The Hospital Insurance Trust Fund Board of Trustees reported in 2011 that the fund is expected to be exhausted in 2024.[24]

The Medicare laws are organized in "parts" of Title XVIII. Those parts have been modified over the years in terms of which healthcare services are addressed by which parts. The current structure sets out the reimbursement portion of the Medicare program in four parts: A, B, C, and D.

PART A. Part A is a program of hospital insurance benefits for the aged and selected others. Part A is financed by a special tax on employers, employees, and the self-employed. The coverage includes a specified number of days of care in a hospital setting or extended care facility, plus post-hospital home care.

Claims must be presented to the Medicare program to trigger reimbursement. Until 1983, reimbursement under Part A was based on certain costs incurred by the facility that provided the care. This was changed by the Social Security Amendments of 1983,[25] so that payment to hospitals for inpatient care is based on a prospectively determined amount per discharge according to the patient's diagnosis and the facility's location. Paying in "lump sums" is known under the Medicare rules as the "prospective payment system." In 2000, home health care and many hospital outpatient procedures were converted to prospective payment systems.[26]

Beneficiaries need to pay certain deductible and coinsurance amounts under Part A. A deductible is the amount of healthcare charges that the patient must incur and pay out-of-pocket (or paid by a Medigap plan) before Medicare pays for any of the remainder. Medicare will pay only a percentage of the remaining covered services. The percentage not paid by Medicare is called a coinsurance payment and is owed by the patient. The federal anti-kickback statute prohibits a provider from routinely waiving patients' coinsurance and deductible obligations, except under very limited circumstances.[27]

PART B. Part B is a program of supplementary medical insurance covering a substantial part of physician and other practitioner services, medical supplies, and x-rays and laboratory tests incident to physician services, as well as other services not covered under Part A, such as ambulance services and prosthetic devices. Hospital outpatient services are covered under Part B because they are seen under the Medicare laws as technical support for specific physician services. In practice, hospital outpatient services are often only loosely connected to a physician service but are nevertheless paid for by Medicare under Part B.

The benefits under Part B are funded from contributions by beneficiaries and the federal government. Beneficiaries must pay a deductible and usually a 20 percent coinsurance amount. Enrollment in Part B is voluntary. Individuals are responsible for their own decision whether to enroll in Part B, though enrollment has been effectively converted to an opt-out approach.

Medicare payments can be made only to the healthcare organization that provides the services or certain entities permitted to bill for the provider. Each physician has a unique national provider identification (NPI) number that must be put on each bill.[28] Another complex matter for Medicare Part B billing is the reality that the physician does not directly provide all the services that may occur in an office or clinic setting. Nevertheless, a mechanism exists for physicians to bill for services, such as x-rays, that are provided by others, such as technicians. The physician may usually only bill for these technical procedures when the services are provided in a way that meets the requirement that the service is "incident to" the physicians' services.[29]

PART C. The Balanced Budget Act of 1997 reorganized Part C of Medicare, establishing the Medicare+Choice program that permitted eligible individuals to elect to receive their Medicare benefits through enrollment in a variety of private health plans.[30] The payment systems for Medicare+Choice were enormously complex and led many private insurance companies either to withdraw from participation in Part C or to reduce their scope of benefits.[31] Reducing the benefits ran counter to the policy goals of establishing Part C. The principal goal of the Medicare+Choice program was to provide a vehicle for Medicare beneficiaries to receive coverage of Part A and Part B benefits either with reduced patient portions or to receive additional benefits not covered by Parts A and B. Effective in 2004, the program was renamed Medicare Advantage and payments were increased and arguably simplified in order to encourage more private sector participation.[32] In 2011, enrollment in some parts of the country, such as California, exceeded 35 percent of the Medicare population.[33]

Each plan must meet detailed requirements to be qualified to participate. There have been attempts by states to regulate Part C plans. One state attempted to require Medicare Part C plans to provide unlimited drug coverage. A federal appellate court declared the state's law to be preempted by federal law.[34]

PART D. The 2003 amendments to the Social Security Act added a prescription drug benefit that became effective in 2006. Part D provides federal payment for part of the costs of outpatient prescription drugs. Rules have been promulgated for creating the drug formularies that will determine which drugs are covered.[35]

MANAGING THE MEDICARE PROGRAM. The Secretary of HHS has the overall responsibility for Medicare. The operation of the program has been assigned to the Centers for Medicare & Medicaid Services (CMS). Congress authorized the delegation of much of the day-to-day administration to state agencies and public and private organizations operating under agreements with the Secretary of HHS.

Most payment claims are processed by private companies that have entered agreements to serve as "intermediaries" for Part A or "carriers" for Part B. This system of "intermediaries" and "carriers" is being transformed into unified contractors for a region and are now known as Medicare Administrative Contractors (MACs).

The MACs make initial determinations about whether services provided to beneficiaries are payable by the program and how much payment is due. Hospitals must be cautious in acting on information provided by MACs. The U.S. Supreme Court ruled in 1984 that the Health Care Financing Administration (the former name of the CMS) could recover Medicare overpayments from a provider despite the fact that the overpayments were due to erroneous information from the intermediary.[36] The Court stated that providers are expected to know the law and cannot rely on information provided by government agents.

On coverage questions that have not been addressed nationally by the CMS, local MACs have the power to adopt local coverage rules (known formally as local coverage determinations (LCDs)). The regional variation in coverage can be confusing for providers, particularly those who operate in multiple jurisdictions.[37] An LCD may also be published by a MAC when a national rule is open to interpretation and the CMS has decided not to weigh in on the question. In 2004, a federal appellate court ruled that local coverage determinations by intermediaries are merely interpretive rules that are not subject to the formal federal rulemaking requirements.[38]

Medicare contractors are subject to many of the same fraud and abuse laws that healthcare providers are subject to when they participate in the Medicare program. Some MACs have been charged with defrauding the government while acting in that capacity.[39] However, federal courts have ruled that since intermediaries and carriers are administering a federal program they are immune when providers sue.[40]

To be a participating provider of services and receive payments from Medicare, a hospital must sign an agreement with HHS and meet the various "conditions of participation" (COP).[41] The participating provider agreement specifies that the hospital will not bill Medicare patients for services except for (1) deductible and coinsurance payments required by law and (2) charges for services that Medicare does not cover. Charges can be made for noncovered services only if the patient has been given adequate notice that they are not covered. A hospital is deemed to meet the COP if it is accredited by The Joint Commission or the American Osteopathic Association unless a Medicare inspection indicates noncompliance.[42] However, mere accreditation does not relieve the hospital of vigilance in complying with the conditions of participation. The CMS has deferred auditing of the COP to state-based agencies and a hospital may be subject to corrective actions and ongoing oversight (or theoretically, exclusion from the Medicare program) if serious noncompliance is identified.

HHS, or its agents, frequently threaten to revoke a provider's participation status (known as exclusion), but most hospitals are able to make changes, undertake corrective actions, and reach settlements that avoid exclusion.[43] Rarely have hospitals had their participation in Medicare revoked. When exclusion occurs, it often causes the provider to go out of business or sell its assets. Obtaining a court ordered injunction in the face of an exclusion while an appeal is heard is generally considered not available.

PROSPECTIVE PAYMENT SYSTEM. Medicare pays the various provider settings differently. The Social Security Amendments of 1983[44] established a Medicare prospective payment system (PPS) based on diagnosis-related groups (DRGs) to pay hospitals for inpatient care. The system has been modified by numerous amendments.[45] The DRG system was subsequently reorganized as the Medical Severity-DRG (MS-DRG). All Medicare acute care inpatients are divided into 745 MS-DRGs based on their discharge diagnoses, complications, comorbidities, and whether certain procedures are performed.[46] Medicare will pay for nearly all of the groups. A small number of groups involve unacceptable diagnoses and invalid data. Each year adjustments are made in the groups and in the assignments to the groups. By statute, no administrative or judicial appeal is permitted for either the MS-DRG groups, assignment to a group, or the weight given to the group.[47]

With a few exceptions, the hospital receives one payment for the entire admission based on the DRG and facility location. The payment also covers some preadmission services.[48] The payment rate varies geographically based on regional wages and other factors.

There is no extra payment for longer stays or additional procedures unless the patient becomes a so-called "outlier."

An outlier is a patient with a high total cost of care. Medicare makes an extra payment for outliers, some bad debts, and some other items.[49] Another exception is that some educational costs and kidney acquisition costs are paid separately from the prospective payment.[50]

An adjustment for indirect medical education costs increases payments to hospitals with medical residency programs.[51] Children's hospitals, long-term care hospitals, psychiatric hospitals, and rehabilitation hospitals were initially exempt from the PPS so they could continue to receive cost-based payment from Medicare.[52] A prospective payment system has been implemented for rehabilitation hospitals,[53] and in 2004, one was implemented for psychiatric hospitals.[54]

A significant exception to PPS is critical access hospitals (CAH) that have twenty-five beds or fewer. CAHs are exempt from PPS and receive cost-based reimbursement. Oftentimes, CAHs are established in rural or underserved areas that do not have the volume to support a large inpatient facility. Without the volume of patients of larger hospitals, a CAH has difficulty purchasing a range of contemporary therapeutic and diagnostic equipment. Likewise, a CAH's size presents challenges for staffing a twenty-four hour emergency room. Consequently, cost-based reimbursement allows CAHs to have access to funds to maintain standard of care therapeutics and diagnostics.

The Prospective Payment System and Hospitals: Despite the terminology, PPS has little to do with paying "prospectively." Payment is made only after services are provided. PPS had a significant impact on provider incentives when it was adopted. This was felt particularly by hospitals. Under the previous cost-based system of Medicare reimbursement, additional hospital days and services meant additional payment. In a cost-based payment system, there was an incentive to give patients all the services that could possibly benefit them. In some situations, unnecessary services were provided, and this was part of the reason Congress began adjusting Medicare payment mechanisms of the PPS. PPS took its concepts from the early ideas of managed care. Under the PPS, hospitals lose money on inpatient stays if the cost of the services during a stay exceeds the MS-DRG payment; however, the hospital keeps the savings when services cost less than the payment.

Other institutional providers are now also paid on a prospective payment basis. For example, skilled nursing facilities are paid on the basis of a resource utilization group (RUG), which is organized around acuity and level of services needed to be provided to the patient. Hospital outpatient services are paid on the basis of the ambulatory payment classification (APC) system, by which outpatient services and procedures are placed in groups that are comparable clinically and in terms of resource use.[55] Home health agencies are paid on the basis of a national, standardized sixty-day episode payment, adjusted for various factors such as a wage index and significant changes in the patient's condition.

MEDICARE AND PHYSICIANS. Physicians who become participating providers are paid directly by Medicare and may charge patients only the Medicare allowed co-payments and deductibles. Although physicians are paid directly by Medicare, the legal structure of Medicare is designed so that the participating physician accepts "assignment" from the patient for the amounts Medicare owes the beneficiary for reimbursement of healthcare services. This is an arcane concept that survives from the origin of Medicare. Nonetheless, it is an important component of how physicians work within the Medicare payment system. When anyone other than the physician receives payment from Medicare, including an employer of the physician, then the physician must "reassign" his or her fees to the employer. The physician must sign a specific statement reassigning the fees.

One important issue for all providers is proper coding of the services provided. The diagnoses and certain other features of the patient's condition or treatment must be coded on the claim. Hospital claims are coded according to the *International Classification of Diseases, Ninth Edition, Clinical Modification* (ICD-9-CM). The ICD-9 system will change to the tenth edition (ICD-10) on October 1, 2014. Physician claims are coded according to the Healthcare Common Procedure Coding System (HCPCS), which includes the physician's Current Procedural Terminology (CPT).[56] The amount of payment is determined by the codes.

Depending on the amount of money in controversy, hospitals may appeal payment decisions that were made under older cost reimbursement systems to the Provider Reimbursement Review Board (PRRB). Larger amounts in controversy are argued before the PRRB while smaller, disputed amounts are pursued through processes followed by MACs. When the issues under appeal apply to several hospitals, group appeals are frequently pursued to reduce the cost to individual hospitals. The Secretary of HHS has the authority to modify the decisions of the PRRB or the MAC. The final decision of HHS concerning a payment issue can sometimes be appealed to the federal courts. However, administrative processes within HHS must be followed before a provider is allowed to appeal a decision to a court.[57] The phrase "exhaustion of administrative remedies" is used to describe this legal requirement, before a matter may be appealed to a court.

The number of issues that can be appealed is limited.[58] In 1993, the U.S. Supreme Court decided that HHS is not required to give providers an opportunity to establish entitlement to payment in excess of limits stated in the regulations.[59] In 1999, the Supreme Court decided that there could be no judicial review of denials of reopening of Medicare cost reports.[60]

Physician challenges to changes in reimbursement policies for individual procedures and specialties have generally been unsuccessful.[61] In 1994, a federal appellate court ruled that a drug manufacturer does not have standing to challenge the Medicare Part B policy of limiting payments for one of its drugs to the amount paid for a competing product.[62]

Sometimes, decisions by the CMS on whether a service is even covered under the Medicare program are challenged. In most cases, courts defer to the CMS and uphold the decisions.[63]

However, occasionally challengers succeed. In 1997, HCFA added a requirement that hospitals must be within a certain distance of a skilled nursing facility in order to be paid for providing respiratory services to the facility. A federal court granted an injunction against this requirement and found it arbitrary because distance was irrelevant and not authorized by statute or regulation.[64]

Patients must follow the administrative appeal procedures established by the CMS.[65] The procedures were adopted after a federal court in Arizona found that the appeal rights, after denials, afforded to Medicare HMO members were inadequate. The court issued an injunction that required the CMS to monitor and enforce denial of care appeals of Medicare patients. In 1998, a federal appellate court upheld the injunction, but in 1999, the U.S. Supreme Court vacated the judgment and sent the case back to the appellate court for reconsideration. The appellate court lifted the injunction.[66] In 2005, the CMS substantially limited the access to personal hearings by reducing the number of hearing sites in the nation from 140 to 4.[67]

9-2.2 Medicaid

Medicaid is a joint federal-state insurance program designed to provide medical assistance to individuals unable to afford health care. Although the Medicaid program is authorized by federal law (Title XIX of the Social Security Act), states are not required to have Medicaid programs. Each state must pass its own law to participate. At the time of this writing, all states participate in Medicaid, including territories.

Under Medicaid, the federal government makes grants to states to enable them to furnish medical insurance to individuals and families with dependent children who fall below certain income and resource levels. The programs also are designed to provide coverage for the aged, blind, or disabled individuals whose income and resources are insufficient to pay for necessary health services. The Secretary of HHS is responsible for administration of federal grants-in-aid to states under Medicaid. The CMS leads the regulation of Medicaid for HHS. Each state assigns a state-based agency to administer the Medicaid program.

Medicaid is different from Medicare in that it provides healthcare insurance for categories of persons in financial need, while Medicare provides healthcare insurance primarily to people 65 years of age or older without regard to financial need. Medicaid varies widely among the states, while Medicare is largely uniform. Medicaid is financed by general federal and state revenues. Medicare is financed by a combination of a special tax on employers and employees for hospital insurance and by contributions by beneficiaries and the federal government for supplementary medical services. Although Medicaid is a health insurance program, it is based in social welfare principles.

MEDICAID SCOPE OF BENEFITS VARIES. Any state adopting a Medicaid plan must provide certain minimum health benefits to the "categorically needy." The categorically needy include individuals receiving financial assistance under the state's approved plan for Supplemental Security Income (Title XVI of the Social Security Act) or for Aid to Families with Dependent Children (Title IV-A of the Social Security Act).

States have the option of including other persons within their plan as medically needy if (1) they would qualify for assistance under one of the preceding programs if their incomes were lower and (2) their incomes would be low enough to qualify for assistance under that program if they were permitted to subtract the healthcare expenses that they have already incurred. This is sometimes called the "spend-down" option because the persons must in effect spend their income down to a threshold level to be eligible for Medicaid.

In 1997, Congress expanded Children Health Insurance Programs (CHIP), Title XXI of the Social Security Act. States were given the option of putting their CHIPs in Medicaid or establishing a non-Medicaid program. However, the CMS favored Medicaid programs.[68]

CHIP was significantly expanded in 2009 as a result of the Children's Health Insurance Reauthorization Act of 2009. CHIP now covers children of legal aliens along with expanded coverage for children of uninsured parents who may not qualify for Medicaid. In 2011, there were 7.7 million children enrolled in CHIP.

Eligible recipients must apply to the designated state agency before Medicaid will pay for the services they receive. State Medicaid plans must meet many conditions before they can be approved, but states are permitted substantial flexibility in the administration of their own programs. States may decide, within federal guidelines, which persons in addition to the categorically needy will be eligible for medical assistance. In determining scope of benefits, states are required to provide at least five basic services to the categorically needy but are free to provide additional services. Although the states are given wide latitude in the administration of their programs, they are sensitive to federal direction because 50 percent or more of the financial support for Medicaid comes from the federal government. Both federal administrative agencies and courts use the threat of withdrawal of federal funds to direct changes in a state's program. For example, when a Florida federal court ruled in 1998 that the state Medicaid program must be expanded to provide prompt institutional care to developmentally disabled persons, there was a threat to enjoin all Medicaid funds to the state if the state did not comply.[69]

PAYMENT BY MEDICAID. Institutional providers of services generally become participants in the Medicaid program by contracting with the state. By doing so, providers agree to provide services to Medicaid recipients in exchange for the payment permitted by the state. Payment cannot be collected from the patient, except to the extent permitted by federal law.[70] Noninstitutional providers generally are not required to enter into any contract with the state. Instead, they participate merely by treating Medicaid recipients and then billing the state. States may directly reimburse physicians who provide covered services to the medically needy, or they may pay the individual beneficiaries, leaving them with the obligation to pay the physician. Payment for physician services can be made only if the physician agrees to accept charges determined by the state as payment in full for the state's portion of the bill.

States have considerable latitude to determine the services to be covered and the amount of payments.[71] States are generally free to establish their own methods of payment for inpatient hospital services as long as the costs do not exceed the Medicare payment for the same services. For several years, the Boren Amendment required the state to find that the rates are "reasonable and adequate to meet the costs which must be incurred by efficiently and economically operated facilities."[72] In 1990, the U.S. Supreme Court ruled that the Boren Amendment created a substantive federal right to adequate reimbursement that could be enforced by healthcare providers.[73] This resulted in many lawsuits challenging the adequacy of Medicaid payment rates. Some decisions required states to reinstate prior payment approaches until proper procedures were followed,[74] while others have upheld the state payment rates.[75] Nevertheless, the Boren Amendment was repealed. This increased the latitude for states to adopt their payment mechanisms. However, the federal Medicaid law still requires state payment rates to be consistent with efficiency, quality of care, and equal access to services.[76] Some federal appellate courts have held that this requires states to follow certain procedures in adopting payment rates, but other courts have disagreed.[77]

States must require that services are provided at the appropriate level of care. However, in 1999, the highest court of Massachusetts, after upholding the state's right to review inpatient services for medical necessity, ruled that the state could not deny all payment for medically necessary services that should have been provided in an outpatient setting. The court required payment at the outpatient rate.[78]

MANAGING MEDICAID WITHIN STATE BUDGETS. In an attempt to manage their budgets, some states have reduced the services covered by their Medicaid programs. When Tennessee reduced the covered days of inpatient care from twenty to fourteen, the reduction was challenged as a violation of the federal laws prohibiting discrimination against the handicapped because they generally need longer stays. The U.S. Supreme Court rejected this challenge, ruling that the handicapped nondiscrimination law does not guarantee equal results from Medicaid services.[79] The Court did not rule on whether the limit was consistent with the Medicaid law. Lower courts have ruled that limits on the number of inpatient days, such as South Carolina's twelve-day limit, are consistent with the Medicaid law.[80] However, the courts will enjoin reductions that fail to preserve mandated services.[81]

Other states place limits on payment to providers. Several states have adopted prospective payment systems for Medicaid similar to the Medicare payment system.[82] Minnesota went one step further in its nursing home payment system. Minnesota pays nursing homes through its Medicaid system only when the nursing home agrees not to charge non-Medicaid patients more than Medicaid pays for comparable care. This system has been upheld by both federal and state courts.[83] In 1985, a Minnesota court ruled that neither the state nor Medicaid patients could stop a nursing home from phasing out participation in Medicaid.[84]

Medicaid plans continue to change and all the detail of their diversity is beyond the scope of this chapter. You should always directly consult the publications of the relevant state Medicaid program. Due to rapidly changing state legislation and budgetary constraints, any comparison charts of a state's Medicaid intricacies could become out of date quickly. Medicaid rules are among the most challenging assemblage of varied regulations that the healthcare industry must monitor.

A driving factor for Medicaid rule changes is the raw reality of limited funds by the federal and state governments. Medicaid generally consumes 20 percent or more of state budgets. Medicaid is one of the fastest growing parts of the budgets of many states. Faced with reluctance to increase tax burdens and the pull of other important state budgetary needs, especially education and law enforcement, most states continue to seek ways to control Medicaid's growth.[85]

Many states have significantly modified their Medicaid programs, usually by adopting managed care approaches, including contracting with private HMOs. Initially the managed care approaches were voluntary.[86] However, the Medicaid laws authorize federal waivers of various requirements, including freedom of choice.[87] Several states have obtained waivers[88] or are requesting waivers.

State governments are confronted with difficult allocation decisions. In ruling that the Medicaid law does not grant an enforceable right to compel expenditure of funds to provide a particular treatment, a federal court in Minnesota stated:

> Unfortunately, funds available for these programs are finite. Ordering the development of the requested facility, at cost far above the currently available funding limits, would rob Peter to pay Paul. Society, through its elected

representatives and appointed agency administrators, has made the difficult decisions regarding the amount and allocation of these funds.[89]

However, other federal courts have mandated expensive modifications to state Medicaid programs expressly rejecting that they should consider the cost as a factor in their decision. For example in 1998, a federal appellate court mandated expanded and timely services to the developmentally disabled, quoting an earlier decision that had stated "inadequate state appropriations do not excuse noncompliance."[90]

In 1994, Tennessee began an ambitious program to expand its Medicaid coverage. The history of this program illustrates the difficulties when open-ended entitlement programs such as Medicaid become difficult for state governments to finance. The program had financial difficulties from its early days. Attempts to control the costs were challenged by advocacy groups. In 2002, a federal court mandated additional services and took over part of the program. As costs escalated in 2004, the legislature adopted an overhaul plan. A federal court again imposed a costly plan on the state. In 2005, the governor announced major cutbacks in TennCare, but the federal judge again blocked the changes. A federal appellate court twice overturned the federal district court. With federal administrative approval, the disenrollment process of downsizing began in August 2005.[91]

9-2.3 Miscellaneous State Programs

Several states have state and local programs that pay for some health care for indigent persons who cannot qualify for Medicaid. These programs vary greatly and often require counties or other units of local government to fund some health care on behalf of their residents who are unable to pay.[92] Frequently, these requirements result in disputes between units or levels of government concerning which is responsible to pay for the care of an individual.[93]

In many states, local governmental units or their police departments are obligated to pay for the care of persons in their custody who are charged with crimes.[94] However, police generally do not assume financial responsibility by bringing to the hospital someone who is not in custody.[95] Some jurisdictions have sought to avoid the cost of caring for prisoners by not charging sick suspects or by releasing sick prisoners.[96] There are frequently disputes over whether an individual was in custody when care was given.[97]

Chapter Summary

The healthcare payment system in the United States is a complex mixture of government and private health insurance programs. Federal, state, and county government health plans pay for over 50 percent of healthcare costs in the United States, while the remainder of healthcare costs are paid by either private sector health plans or out-of-pocket by uninsured individuals. The vast majority of persons insured by nongovernment health plans are covered by employer-sponsored health insurance. A small percentage of individuals purchase commercial health insurance policies on the open market. This chapter

discussed the legal aspects of the four principal types of healthcare payment programs. Two of these programs are government-sponsored (Medicare and Medicaid) and two are private sector arrangements for health insurance (employer-sponsored health insurance and commercial health insurance). The chapter also addressed the ways these four approaches reimburse healthcare organizations for covered items and services, including how contract law influences the private sector health plans and how the nuances of private contractors impact government-sponsored health insurance.

Key Terms and Definitions

Commercial Health Insurance - Health insurance policies that are purchased privately. Commercial health insurance policies are offered for sale by nongovernment organizations (both for-profit and not-for-profit). Commercial health insurance is generally regulated by states. However, the Patient Protection and Affordable Care Act of 2010 allows a variety of federal regulations that will fully come into effect by 2014.

Covered - The items and services that healthcare organizations accept payment for from health plans. A healthcare organization may not bill patients for the full amount of a covered item or service but must accept the payment terms by the health plan. The payment terms for a covered item or service may not necessarily provide specific payment for a covered item or service. Whether the health plan pays for a covered item or service depends on the health plan and the healthcare organization's arrangements with that plan. If allowed by the health plan, the healthcare organization may charge the patient for co-payments for covered items or services or may charge the patient for the covered items and services when the patient has not yet met the annual deductible for the health plan.

Employer-Sponsored Health Insurance - Health insurance that is arranged by employers for employees. Employer-sponsored health insurance involves either a self-funded group health plan in which the employer provides funds to pay for healthcare items and service or the employer purchases fully insured policies for employees. Many self-funded employer-sponsored group health plans

purchase additional stop-loss coverage that limits the company's payment exposure. Employees typically pay a premium amount per month to participate in employer-sponsored health insurance.

ERISA - The Employee Retirement Income Security Act of 1974. ERISA is the principal federal law that regulates employer-sponsored health plans. Under many circumstances, ERISA preempts state regulation of employer-sponsored health insurance.

Medicaid - A federal health insurance program covering the indigent, the disabled, and certain other categories of individuals. The Medicaid plans are administered by the individual states. Medicaid plans are funded by both federal funds as well as state funds.

Medicare Program - A federal health insurance program covering individuals 65 or older, the disabled, persons with end-stage renal disease, and certain other limited categories of individuals. The Medicare program is regulated by the Centers for Medicaid & Medicaid Services, but claims are managed and paid by private "contractors" for Part A and Part B benefits, Medicare Advantage Plans for Part C benefits, and prescription drug plans for Part D benefits.

Third-Party Administrator (TPA) - An organization hired by a self-funded employer-sponsored group health plan to administer the health plan. The third-party administrator processes and pays claims on behalf of the health plan. Third-party administrators are often health insurance companies that have the infrastructure to serve in this role.

Instructor-Led Questions

1. What are the four major healthcare payment systems in the United States?

2. What percentage of the U.S. population is enrolled in government-sponsored health insurance plans versus nongovernment insurance plans?

3. What federal law regulates employer-sponsored health insurance programs?

4. Explain one way in which federal law preempts state law for employer-sponsored health insurance.

5. Describe what types of health insurance programs are regulated by the states versus the federal government.

6. What is the role of contract law in nongovernment health insurance?

7. What are the principal differences between Medicare and Medicaid?

8. Describe the four principal "parts" of the Medicare program.

9. What are the policy goals for establishing the Medicare Part C program (Medicare Advantage)?

10. Describe ways Medicare Part D prescription drug plans can compete with each other.

11. Explain the prospective payment system.

12. Describe the difference between reimbursement rates to providers from government health insurance programs versus nongovernment health insurance programs.

13. Describe at least one way states can differ in designing their Medicaid plans.

14. Are states required to participate in the Medicaid program?

15. What does it mean for an item or service to be "covered"?

Endnotes

1 U.S. Dept. of Health & Human Services, "National Health Expenditure Projections 2009-2019," Table 1 (September 2010).

2 Id., Table 1.

3 Id., Table 3.

4 U.S. Dept. of Health & Human Services, "National Health Expenditure Projections 2009-2019," Table 3 (September 2010).

5 E.g., *McGurl v. Trucking Employees of North Jersey Welfare Fund, Inc.*, 124 F.3d 47 (3d Cir. 1997) [when conflicting, plan of claimant's employer pays]; *Principal Health Care v. Lewer Agency, Inc.*, 38 F.3d 240 (5th Cir. 1994); see also DHHS OIG advisory opinion holds coordination of benefits provision of provider agreement between nursing home and healthcare plan may violate anti-kickback statute, 26 HEALTH L. DIG. (May 1998), at 33 [Advisory Opinion 98-5 (Apr. 24, 1998)].

6 E.g., Blue Cross collapse in West Virginia puts many in dire straits, WALL ST. J., Mar. 8, 1991, 1A [first collapse of a Blue Shield plan, leaving $50 million in unpaid medical bills].

7 E.g., 11 U.S.C. § 109.

8 E.g., In re *International Med. Ctrs., Inc.*, 604 So. 2d 505 (Fla. 1st DCA 1992).

9 42 U.S.C. §§ 1001 et seq.

10 29 U.S.C. § 1144(a).

11 29 U.S.C. § 1144(b)(2)(A).

12 29 U.S.C. § 1144(b)(2)(B).

13 Pub. L. No. 104-191.

14 U.S. Dept. of Health & Human Services, "National Health Expenditure Projections 2009-2019," Table 3 (September 2010).

15 See for example the definitions in Oregon law at ORS 743.960(2) and 750.005(4) contrasted with Illinois law at 215 ILCS 5/370g.

16 10 U.S.C. §§ 1079-1086, 1095; 32 C.F.R. pt. 199.

17 5 U.S.C. §§ 8901-8914; 5 C.F.R. pt. 890; 48 C.F.R. chaps. 1, 16.

18 Pub. L. No. 89-97, 79 Stat. 290 (1965).

19 C. Culhane, Medicare denial rates vary widely: Carriers inconsistent in judging medical necessity, AM. MED. NEWS, Apr. 18, 1994, 3; HCFA defends program appeal process, announces national coverage procedures, 8 H.L.R. 695 (1999) [response to criticism of inconsistency in local determinations].

20 42 U.S.C. 1395y(c).

21 See generally, CMS Pub. 100-04, Section 50, et seq.

22 Pub. No. L. 108-173, Title I, 117 Stat. 2071, codified as 42 U.S.C. § 1395w-101 et seq.

23 42 U.S.C. 1395ss.

24 The Boards of Trustees, Federal Hospital Insurance and Federal Supplementary Medical Insurance Trust Funds, "2011 Annual Report of the Boards of Trustees of the Federal Hospital Insurance and Federal Supplementary Medical Insurance Trust Funds, May 13, 2011, 4.

25 Pub. L. No. 98-21, 97 Stat. 65 (1983), as amended by Pub. L. No. 98-369, 98 Stat. 1073 (1984); 42 C.F.R. §§ 405.470-405.477; J. Tieman, It was 20 years ago today...; some say it's complex and vulnerable to political whims, but Medicare's PPS has helped impose order on hospital finances, MOD. HEALTHCARE, Sept. 29, 2003, 6.

26 V. Galloro, Embracing PPS; Home-care providers see opportunity under new system, MOD. HEALTHCARE, Sept. 25, 2000, 2; V. Galloro, Flipped out over outpatient PPS, MOD. HEALTHCARE, Nov. 20, 2000, 30.

27   42 C.F.R. § 1001.952(k).

28   42 U.S.C. § 1395l(q).

29   42 U.S.C. § 1395x(s)(2)(A).

30   42 U.S.C. §§ 1395w-21 et seq., as added by the Balanced Budget Act of 1997, Pub. L. No. 105-33, § 4001; 42 C.F.R. pt. 422, added by 63 FED. REG. 34,967 (June 26, 1998), amended by 64 FED. REG. 7,967 (Feb. 17, 1999).

31   See L.B. Benko, Hopping mad; Medicare HMOs' restrictions on drug coverage prompt high enrollee turnover, MOD. HEALTHCARE, Apr. 9, 2001, 35.

32   See J. Tieman, Pay increase; increased HMO funding excites many, MOD. HEALTHCARE, Feb. 9, 2004, 17; 70 FED. REG. 4,587 (Jan. 28, 2005).

33   The Henry J. Kaiser Family Foundation, "Medicare Advantage 2010 Data Spotlight: Plan Enrollment, Patterns and Trends," Appendix Table 3.

34   *Massachusetts Ass'n of HMOs v. Ruthardt*, 194 F.3d 176 (1st Cir. 1999).

35   Pub. L. No. 108-173, Title I, 117 Stat. 2071, codified as 42 U.S.C. § 1395w-101 et seq.; R. Pear, U.S. settles on regions for dispensing Medicare drug benefits, N.Y. TIMES, Dec. 17, 2004, A16; R. Pear, New Medicare rules on drugs balance access against costs, N.Y. TIMES, Jan. 22, 2005, A1 [formularies]; 70 FED. REG. 4,193 (Jan. 28, 2005) [formularies]; R. Pear, Defying experts, insurers join Medicare drug plan, N.Y. TIMES, Mar. 6, 2005, 1.

36   *Heckler v. Community Health Servs.*, 467 U.S. 51 (1984).

37   See L. McGinley, Behind Medicare's decisions, an invisible web of gatekeepers, WALL ST. J., Sept. 16, 2003, A1.

38   *Erringer v. Thompson*, 371 F.3d 625 (9th Cir. 2004).

39   E.g., *United States v. Blue Cross & Blue Shield of Mich.*, No. L93-1794 (D. Md. settlement Jan. 10, 1995), complaint reprinted in M.M.G. ¶43,019; Illinois Blues to pay $144 million to settle fraud charges, AM. MED. NEWS, Aug. 3, 1998, 8.

40   E.g., *Midland Psychiatric Assocs., Inc. v. United States*, 145 F.3d 1000 (8th Cir. 1998) [Medicare intermediary immune from tortious interference suit by provider]; *Pani v. Empire Blue Cross & Blue Shield*, 152 F.3d 67 (2d Cir. 1998), cert. denied, 525 U.S. 1103 (1999) [Medicare intermediary immune from tort suits for investigating, reporting possible fraud].

41   42 U.S.C. § 1395x(e); 42 C.F.R. pt. 482. There are also conditions of participation for other providers, e.g., 42 C.F.R. §§ 405.1101-405.1137 [skilled nursing facilities].

42   42 U.S.C.A. §§ 1395aa, 1395bb; *Cospito v. Heckler*, 742 F.2d 72 (3d Cir. 1984), cert. denied, 471 U.S. 1131 (1985) [not improper delegation to Joint Commission because HHS retains ultimate authority].

43   E.g., In re *Westchester County Med. Center*, Docket No. 91-504-2 (H.H.S. Sept. 29, 1992), as discussed in 2 H.L.R. 61 (1993) [revocation of participation of hospital ordered for violation of Rehabilitation Act by restricting HIV-positive worker, but case settled].

44   Pub. L. No. 98-21, 97 Stat. 65 (1983).

45   Pub. L. No. 98-21, 97 Stat. 65 (1983) (codified as amended primarily at 42 U.S.C. § 1395ww); 42 C.F.R. pt. 412.

46   69 FED. REG. 48,916 (Aug. 11, 2004).

47   42 U.S.C. § 1395ww(d)(7); e.g., *Little Co. of Mary Hosp. v. Shalala*, 24 F.3d 984 (7th Cir. 1994) [no right to hearing after hospital failed to correct its own DRG assignment within 60 days].

48   42 C.F.R. § 412.2(c)(5), first printed in 59 FED. REG. 1,654 (Jan. 12, 1994).

49   E.g., 42 U.S.C. § 1395ww(d)(5)(A) [outliers]; 42 C.F.R. §§ 412.80-412.86 [outliers]; 42 C.F.R. §§ 412.115(a), 413.80 [bad debts]; 42 C.F.R. §§ 412.115(c), 466.78 [some copying costs].

50   42 U.S.C. § 1395ww(d)(5)(B); 42 C.F.R. § 413.85 [indirect medical education costs]; 42 C.F.R. § 412.100 [kidney acquisition costs].

51   42 U.S.C. § 1395ww(h); 42 C.F.R. § 412.105.

52   42 U.S.C. § 1395ww(d)(l)(B); 42 C.F.R. § 412.23.

53   42 C.F.R. Part 412, Subpart P, §§ 412.602 et seq.; 70 FED. REG. 30,188 (May 25, 2005).

54   42 C.F.R. Part 412, Subpart N, § 412.400 et seq.; 69 FED. REG. 66,922 (Nov. 15, 2004).

55   42 C.F.R. Part 419, Subpart C, §§ 419.310 et seq.; 65 FED. REG. 18,434 (Apr. 7, 2000).

56   *United States v. Krizek*, 859 F. Supp. 5 (D.D.C. 1994) [although physician barred from participation until he could abide by coding rules, criticism of government for confusing coding requirements]; *Practice Management Information Corp. v. American Med. Ass'n*, 133 F.3d 1140 (9th Cir. 1998), cert. denied, 524 U.S. 952 (1998) [HCFA adoption of CPT code did not cast it into public domain, but terms of AMA exclusive license with agency constituted misuse by specifying agency not to use competitor's products].

57   E.g., *National Kidney Patients Ass'n v. Sullivan*, 958 F.2d 1127 (D.C. Cir. 1992), cert. denied, 506 U.S. 1049 (1993); see also T. Albert, Medicare appeals process too slow, GAO report finds, AM. MED. NEWS, Nov. 17, 2003, 7 [only 43 percent of first-level appeals completed with 30 days required by Medicare, Medicaid, & SCHIP Benefits Improvement Act of 2000 (BIPA)]; see also 69 FED. REG. 35,716 (June 25, 2004) [proposed changes in provider appeal procedures].

58   42 U.S.C. §§ 405(h), 1395ff, 1395ii; *Michigan Ass'n of Independent Clinical Labs. v. Shalala*, 52 F.3d 1340 (6th Cir. 1994).

59   *Good Samaritan Hosp. v. Shalala*, 508 U.S. 402 (1993).

60   *Your Home Visiting Nurse Servs., Inc. v. Shalala*, 525 U.S. 449 (1999).

61   E.g., *Necketopoulos v. Shalala*, 941 F. Supp. 1382 (S.D.N.Y. 1996) [rejecting challenge to abandonment of use of modifier units as basis for Part B payment for anesthesia services]; *American Acad. of Dermatology v. H.H.S.*, 118 F.3d 1495 (11th Cir. 1997) [rejecting challenge to change in payment policy for removal of precancerous skin lesions, failure to exhaust administrative remedies]; *Abbott Radiology Assocs. v. Shalala*, 160 F.3d 137 (2d Cir. 1998).

62 *TAP Pharmaceuticals v. D.H.H.S.*, 163 F.3d 199 (4th Cir. 1998).

63 E.g., *Warder v. Shalala*, 149 F.3d 73 (1st Cir. 1998), cert. denied, 526 U.S. 1064 (1999) [upholding HCFA Ruling 96-1 concerning the scope of coverage for orthotics, reversing a lower court that would have required formal rule-making procedures before the Ruling could take effect].

64 *Vencor, Inc. v. Shalala*, 988 F. Supp. 1467 (N.D. Ga. 1997) [permanent injunction]; see also *Estate of Aitken v. Shalala*, 986 F. Supp. 57 (D. Mass. 1997) [preliminary injunction of implementation of national coverage determination denying payment for electrical stimulation therapy treatments to promote healing of open wounds].

65 62 FED. REG. 25,844 (May 12, 1997); Medicare beneficiaries' appeal rights codified in HCFA final rule, 6 H.L.R. 780 (1997).

66 *Grijalva v. Shalala*, 152 F.3d 1115 (9th Cir. 1998) [decisions by Medicare HMOs are state action entitled to due process, specific procedural protections mandated], judgment vacated, case remanded, 526 U.S. 1096 (1999), remanded to district court, 185 F.3d 1075 (9th Cir. 1999) [injunction dissolved].

67 R. Pear, Medicare change will limit access to claim hearing, N.Y. TIMES, Apr. 24, 2005, 1.

68 Pub. L. No. 105-33, § 4901; 62 FED. REG. 48,098 (Sept. 12, 1997) [guidance to help design plans]; States split evenly between Medicaid, separate programs for kid care effort, 6 H.L.R. 1753 (1997); Non-Medicaid CHIP programs not eligible for federal vaccine funds, HCFA says, 7 H.L.R. 906 (1998); CHIP reporting requirements released: HCFA reminds states about deadlines, 7 H.L.R. 1952 (1998) [non-Medicaid CHIPs must screen for Medicaid eligibility, enroll in Medicaid]; R. Pear, Many states slow to use children's insurance fund, N.Y. TIMES, May 9, 1999, 1.

69 *Doe v. Chiles*, No. 92-0589-CIV-Ferguson (S.D. Fla. bench order Nov. 4, 1998), as discussed in 7 H.L.R. 1856 (1998), implementing, 136 F.3d 709 (11th Cir., 1998).

70 See *Public Health Trust v. Jackson Mem. Hosp.*, 693 So. 2d 562 (Fla. 3d DCA 1996) [Medicaid payment is payment in full, precluding application of third-party recoveries to provider charges in excess of Medicaid rates; contrary state statute preempted].

71 E.g., *Royal Geropsychiatric Servs., Inc. v. Tompkins*, 159 F.3d 238 (6th Cir. 1998) [psychiatrists' challenge to reduced payments for nonhospital treatment of mentally ill rejected].

72 Pub. L. No. 97-35, § 2173 (1981) (codified as amended in 42 U.S.C. § 1395a(a)(13)(A)).

73 *Wilder v. Virginia Hosp. Ass'n*, 496 U.S. 498 (1990).

74 E.g., *Abbeville Gen. Hosp. v. Ramsey*, 3 F.3d 797 (5th Cir. 1993), cert. denied, 511 U.S. 1032 (1994).

75 E.g., *Folden v. Washington State Dep't of Social & Health Serv.*, 981 F.2d 1054 (9th Cir. 1992); *Connecticut Hosp. Ass'n v. O'Neill*, 46 F.3d 211 (2d Cir. 1995).

76 42 U.S.C. § 1396a(a)(30)(A).

77 *Rite Aid of Pa., Inc. v. Houstoun*, 171 F.3d 842 (3d Cir. 1999) [requires certain result, but does not require particular procedures]; contra, *Orthopaedic Hosp. v. Belshe*, 103 F.3d 1491 (9th Cir. 1997) [courts may review payment rates to determine if they bear a reasonable relationship to provider costs]; see also *Minnesota Homecare Ass'n v. Gomez*, 108 F.3d 917 (8th Cir. 1997) [consideration of factors required, but not specific analytical procedure; state methodology met requirements]; Judge orders state to drop budget measure to cut medical payments, AP, Dec. 24, 2003 [federal judge enjoins Calif. Medicaid payment cut for violating quality, access requirements].

78 *Massachusetts Eye & Ear Infirmary v. Division of Med. Assistance*, 428 Mass. 805, 705 N.E.2d 592 (1999).

79 *Alexander v. Choate*, 469 U.S. 287 (1985).

80 *Charleston Mem. Hosp. v. Conrad*, 693 F.2d 324 (4th Cir. 1982).

81 E.g., *Pediatric Specialty Care, Inc. v. Arkansas Dep't of Human Servs.*, 293 F.3d 472 (8th Cir. 2002) [injunction of cutback of services required under Medicaid Act even though budget shortfall].

82 E.g., Michigan, M.M.G. ¶15,600; see also *Presbyterian-Univ. of Pa. Med. Ctr. v. Commonwealth, Dep't of Pub. Welfare*, 553 A.2d 1027 (Pa. Commw. Ct. 1989) [Medicaid DRG payment system upheld].

83 *Minnesota Ass'n of Health Care Facilities, Inc. v. Minnesota Dep't of Pub. Welfare*, 742 F.2d 442 (8th Cir. 1984), cert. denied, 469 U.S. 1215 (1985); *Highland Chateau, Inc. v. Minnesota Dep't of Pub. Welfare*, 356 N.W.2d 804 (Minn. Ct. App. 1984).

84 *LaZalla v. Minnesota*, 366 N.W.2d 395 (Minn. Ct. App. 1985); accord *Catir v. Commissioner of Dep't of Human Servs.*, 543 A.2d 356 (Me. 1988).

85 42 U.S.C. § 1396n(a)(1)(A); see also *Lackner v. Department of Health Services*, 29 Cal. App. 4th 1760, 35 Cal. Rptr. 2d 482 (1st Dist. 1994), rev. denied, 1995 Cal. LEXIS 398 (Jan. 25, 1995) [permissible to enroll persons in managed care if they did not choose an alternative within 30 days of joining].

86 42 U.S.C. § 1396n [§ 1915 of the Social Security Act], which authorizes waivers for two-year periods; 42 U.S.C. § 1315 [§ 1115], which authorizes broader waivers for longer time periods for demonstration projects.

87 E.g., Hawaii Health QUEST, Oregon Reform Demonstration, and TennCare Demonstration Project, M.M.G. ¶¶41580, 41313, & 41908; see also R. Pear, Report criticizes federal oversight of state Medicaid, N.Y. TIMES, July 7, 2003, A1 [GAO study of oversight of waivers].

88 *Jordano v. Steffen*, 787 F. Supp. 886, 891 (D. Minn. 1992).

89 *Doe v. Chiles*, 136 F.3d 709 (11th Cir. 1998).

90 TennCare timeline: From its start in 1994, to its current crisis, AP, May 30, 2005; M. Gouras, Federal government OKs another piece of TennCare reform, AP, June 8, 2005; T. Sharp, Judge orders state to follow new plan for TennCare children, AP, Oct. 26, 2004; 60 FED. REG. 4,418 (Jan. 23, 1995); see http://www.cms.gov/About-CMS/Agency-Information/Emergency/Downloads/ stark1135.pdf (accessed September 13, 2012) for information concerning federal waivers for TennCare; *Rosen v. Tennessee Comm'r of Finance*, 204 F. Supp. 2d 1048 (M.D. Tenn. 2001); 204 F. Supp. 2d 1061 (M.D. Tenn. 2001); 280 F. Supp. 2d 743, (M.D. Tenn., 2002), aff'd in part & vacated in part, 288 F.3d 918 (6th Cir. 2002); 2005 U.S. App. LEXIS 6444 (6th Cir.) (unpub); 2005 U.S. App. LEXIS 9743 (6th Cir.).

91   E.g., *John C. Lincoln Hosp. & Health Corp. v. Maricopa County*, 208 Ariz. 532, 96 P.3d 530 (App. Ct. 2004) [county ordered to pay].

92   E.g., *St. Paul Ramsey County Med. Ctr. v. Pennington County*, 875 F.2d 1185 (8th Cir. 1988) [hospital could not collect from county when it had not filed statement of costs]; *University of Utah Hosp. v. Minidoka County*, 115 Id. 406, 767 P.2d 249 (1989) [claim properly denied because administrative remedies not exhausted]; *Middlesex Mem. Hosp. v. Town of North Haven*, 206 Conn. 1, 535 A.2d 1303 (1988) [hospital must prove eligibility of recipient]; but see *Sioux Valley Hosp. Ass'n v. Yankton Clinic*, 424 N.W.2d 379 (S.D. 1988) [patient's noncooperation in giving information for application did not justify county denial].

93   E.g., *Temple Univ. v. Philadelphia*, 698 A.2d 118 (Pa. Commw. Ct. 1997) [city not responsible for cost of emergency treatment for indigent city residents not eligible for state medical assistance benefits, state's duty to provide medical assistance to poor].

94   E.g., *Emanuel Hosp. v. Umatilla County*, 314 Or. 393, 840 P.2d 56 (1992); *Lutheran Med. Ctr. v. City of Omaha*, 229 Neb. 802, 429 N.W.2d 347 (1988); see also *Borgess Hosp. v. County of Berrien*, 114 Mich. App. 385, 319 N.W.2d 354 (1982) [no obligation to pay for care of former prisoner after discharge from jail]; but see *Northeast Indiana Colon & Rectal Surgeons v. Allen County Comm'rs*, 674 N.E.2d 590 (Ind. Ct. App. 1996) [sheriff not responsible for medical bills for treatment of inmate's preexisting condition after sheriff gave provider notice to directly bill inmate].

95   E.g., *Dade County v. Hospital Affiliates Int'l, Inc.*, 378 So. 2d 43 (Fla. 3d DCA 1979); but see *Susan B. Allen Mem. Hosp. v. Board of County Comm'rs*, 12 Kan. App. 2d 680, 753 P.2d 1302 (1988) [county liable for cost of care of intoxicated person taken into protective custody]; *Albany Gen. Hosp. v. Dalton*, 69 Or. App. 204, 684 P.2d 34 (1984) [county responsible for cost of care of person injured in gunfight with police]; Hospital accuses City of Macon of not paying bills; sues, AP, Nov. 27, 2003 [GA suit seeking payment for persons not under arrest].

96   E.g., More trouble than he's worth, law says, N.Y. TIMES, Nov. 26, 1992, A8 [prosecutor says man accused of theft should be cleared because medical care while in custody is costing county too much]; *Texas Dep't of Corrections v. Sisters of St. Francis of St. Jude Hosp.*, 836 S.W.2d 719 (Tex. Ct. App. 1992) [governor's proclamation granting inmate six-month medical reprieve, provided all financial arrangements for care made by inmate or family did not excuse state from responsibility for medical care; inmate did not sign acceptance until after care rendered; hospital did not know of payment condition before rendering services; unconscionable to require waiver of right to medical care as condition of seeking care away from prison; waiver coerced]; *Meriter Hosp. v. Dane County*, 2004 WI 145, 277 Wis. 2d 1, 689 N.W.2d 627 [county only required to pay while patient was prisoner, even when county changes status after admission].

97   E.g., *Macon-Bibb County Hosp. Auth. v. Reese*, 492 S.E.2d 292 (Ga. Ct. App. 1997) [seeking county payment for detainee care, fact question whether detainee in sheriff's physical custody during medical treatment].

Chapter 10

Healthcare Business Processes

William Hunt, Jon Englander

Key Learning Objectives

By the end of this chapter, the reader will be able to:

- Provide a framework to evaluate all the components of the revenue cycle.

- Understand why providers do things the way they do.

- Understand the incentives that motivate providers.

- Understand why payers (including Medicare, Medicaid, and other government agencies) create programs such as prospective payment, *per diem* rates, bundled charges, and others.

Chapter Outline

Introduction

The largest medical insurer in the United States is the Centers for Medicare and Medicaid Services (CMS). Very often private insurers follow the lead of the CMS. For example, the CMS system for payment of inpatient claims and diagnostic-related groups (DRGs) has been adopted by most payers. This is a prospective payment system (PPS), already in its second major iteration, which statistically groups diagnoses, procedures, and comorbidities into payment categories. This system is independent of the hospital's actual costs or charges. The CMS does not pay claims. There are various contractors, such as insurance companies, which receive and process the claims, and when appropriate, audit them after payment.

Health care in the United States has traditionally defied the core of economics and the law of supply and demand. This has occurred by taking most of the financial part of the purchasing decision away from the user of the services. This chapter will, to some extent, show the impact of that on the revenue cycle.

This chapter will also provide insight as to how all the parts of the revenue cycle fit together. It will show how the revenue cycle "follows the patient" from preadmission to discharge, and how each component is necessary to create a "bill" that is not only accurate in amount, but is also formatted in a way that enables processing by the payer.

10-1 Components of the Revenue Cycle

In order to understand revenue in the healthcare environment, it is important to understand the revenue cycle, and the components of a "fully dressed" bill for healthcare services. The revenue cycle is composed of:

- Appointment scheduling
- Appointment confirmation
- Registration or admittance
- Service performance
- Service documentation and the electronic medical record
- Ordering of ancillary services
- Interface with the chargemaster
- Bill (or other document) creation
- Payment receipt

- Collection
- Payment posting and reconciliation

While not all of these steps occur for every patient, with most occurrences they do. But, they do differ from patient to patient. Patients present themselves for healthcare services in different ways: hospital inpatient, hospital outpatient, inpatient surgery, outpatient surgery, office visit, ancillary service visit, emergency room visit, and so on.

In many cases, the patient is not registered for the healthcare service he or she appears to be. For example, a patient may appear at a physician's office for a simple exam. This would appear to be an office visit, but if the office building is owned by a hospital, it could actually be a hospital outpatient visit. This is referred to as "provider based" or "hospital based" and will be explained later in this chapter.

One way to look at the revenue cycle is performing all the steps necessary to complete the government claim forms for payment and maintaining all the documentation to support every line of the claim. Almost all payers, government and otherwise, use the UB-04 for hospital inpatient and outpatient claims and the CMS1500 for physician claims. Private insurers might require more or less information on these forms than that required by Medicare. Much of the following discussion will address what constitutes a "fully dressed bill," or a bill that when submitted to the payer should be paid properly and in full, or according to an agreement. ◄ A very important part in understanding the revenue cycle is that *very* few payers pay what the provider charges. Almost all payers have contracts with hospitals and physicians, and their payments can be based on groupings of services, per visit, *per diem*, percentage of charges, and others. Therefore, contracting with payers is as much a part of the revenue cycle as any of the other components. Often, these are called "managed care contracts," even though the payer does nothing to manage the care of the patient.

The amount billed by a provider is referred to as "gross revenue." The discount given to payers is the "contractual adjustment." The amount due based on the contract is "net revenue." The following are summaries of topics included in each part of the revenue cycle:

Appointment Scheduling

Scheduling the appointment is one of the most important parts of the revenue cycle. It is at this time that information is taken that identifies the patient's method of payment.

At this point, the provider needs to collect personal information, as well as insurance information.

> Advanced Beneficiary Notice (ABN) Issues (see chapter detail)
>
> Hospital vs. Physician Site of Service
>
> Beginning of Visit Record → Development of Fully Dressed Bill

Appointment Reminder (Confirmation)

> Health Insurance Portability and Accountability Act (HIPAA) Issues
>
> Written/Phone/E-mail
>
> Advise patient what to bring

Registration or Admitting

> HIPAA Issues
>
> Demographics and Insurance Verification
>
> Room and Physician/Caregiver Assignment
>
> Reminder of ABN
>
> Collection of Co-pays, etc.
>
> > Bill Estimator
> >
> > > How collected?
> > >
> > > When calculated?
>
> Population of Patient Visit Record
>
> Patient Status
>
> Hospital based?
>
> Site of Service

Performance of Service

> Supervision of Residents/False Claims
>
> Appropriate Service for the Complaint
>
> Personal Service by Attending Physician after Resident Service
>
> Extenders/Caregivers
>
> Order Entry Systems/EMRs
>
> > Inpatient
> >
> > Outpatient Surgery
> >
> > Hospital Outpatient

Service Documentation and the Electronic Medical Record

> "If it's not documented it's not done."
>
> EMRs
>
> Discoverability

Charge Practices

> CDM Structure
>
> Hospital and Physician Pricing
>
> Order Entry Charging Systems
>
> Explode Charging Mechanisms
>
> Regulatory Resources for Updating Charges
>
> Charging Cycle Overview

Bill (or Other Document) Creation

> Negotiations with Payers
>
> Contract Management Systems
>
> Backend/Pre-submission Editors
>
> Inclusion of All Components (Fully Dressed Bill)
>
> Accounting Interface/Accounts Receivable
>
> Format to 837 File
>
> Bill vs. Claim
>
> Statements
>
> Detail vs. Summary Bill

Payment Receipt

> Internal Controls
>
> Lock Box
>
> Silent PPO
>
> Posting
>
> Overpayments and Credit Balances
>
> Unapplied Cash
>
> Underpayments
>
> > Contract Management System
> >
> > Denials System

Collection

> Internal vs. External
>
> Company-owned Collection Agencies
>
> Federal and State Regulations Regarding Treatment of Debtors
>
> Reporting to Credit Agencies
>
> Uniformity of Collection Efforts (Medicare Bad Debt)

The remainder of this chapter will elaborate on the revenue cycle and the other issues that lead to payment—or nonpayment—of claims for medical services.

10-2 Appointment Scheduling

An appointment can be scheduled in a number of ways. It can be scheduled by the patient, by the physician's staff as a hospital test or admission, by the physician's staff as a referral to another physician, or by the hospital's staff for a follow-up appointment to its own department, another department, or a physician. In any case, the admission or registration staff receiving the appointment should determine if there is already a record on the patient. If so, the appointment should be populated with the demographics from the history and updated at the first contact with the patient. If it is a new patient, and the appointment is not made by the patient, all possible information should be gathered from the person making the appointment. This is quite possibly done by the office staff of a referring physician. By the time the patient begins the appointment all pertinent demographic information required for billing and collection should be obtained and updated. The patient should verify if insurance coverage is current.Then, the insurance coverage should be verified. In most cases, this can be done through third-party services. Most services of this type are electronic, but some services provide this work over the phone. Sometimes the verification provider's records are not current, due to various factors, such as the frequency with which people change jobs, etc. When there is a discrepancy, the patient should be called for verification. Collected information includes name, address, payer, guarantor, and all the other demographic information in the physician billing document Exhibit 1, CMS1500, and the hospital billing document Exhibit 2, UB-04.

When the appointment is scheduled, there needs to be a determination of whether the service is covered. This can vary from payer to payer. Many payers require that the patient be given written notice if the service will not be covered by the payer. This is known as an Advance Beneficiary Notice (ABN). The terminology used by the Centers for Medicare and Medicaid Services (CMS) for uncovered services is "Medically Unnecessary." This is a misnomer, since many uncovered services would be considered medically necessary by most patients and providers; but this term is used by Medicare, Medicaid, and many other payers to define noncovered services. When these services are provided, and the patient is not given the ABN documenting responsibility, the patient will likely *not* be responsible for payment, and the provider will be unreimbursed.

Failure to determine patient coverage decreases likelihood of payment for services. If the patient's bill is denied by insurance due to lapsed coverage or change of jobs, billing of the correct payer might be late, and the coverage by the correct payer might be different. In some cases, the patient cannot be held responsible for payment, and even if he or she is, collection from the patient after completion of treatment ("self-pay" patient) is less probable than collection from a third-party payer.

At the time of appointment, there should be a determination of where the patient is being treated—*the site of service*. Often, hospitals own medical office buildings, and they designate these buildings (or rooms within the buildings) as "hospital" sites of service. In these cases, outpatients will receive a charge from the hospital (facility) *and* a professional fee from the physician. This means that it is likely that the patient will be responsible for two deductibles and two co-insurance payments. Some of these *site of service* issues are obvious and customary: emergency department, radiology, lab, etc. But sometimes what appears to be a physician's office is a hospital site for billing purposes. It should be noted that physicians are paid less by Medicare for work done in a hospital because it is assumed that space and support is provided by the hospital. Since Medicaid is administered by states, reimbursement can vary. Provider contracts for these situations vary widely. Some will refuse payment for the facility fee, except for traditionally hospital-based services. Some will protect the patient by saying the patient is not responsible, and still others will make the patient pay the hospital charge.

It should be obvious here that contract language is vital for payment from the provider or from the patient. The above two points should always be considered in negotiations.

Services provided at sites that appear to be physicians' offices but are defined by the provider as "hospital site of service" have brought a lot of attention to hospitals, mostly larger facilities. In some cities, such as Cleveland, Ohio, the newspapers have made it headline news, as the *Plain Dealer* did with The Cleveland Clinic. Depending on insurance coverage, this practice can have a profound effect on patient liability and may result in patients seeking care elsewhere. (Diane Suchetka, *Plain Dealer,* June 16, 2009)

The appointment scheduling activity is also important because it is the beginning of the record for the patient visit. Determining whether the patient is new is important from a number of standpoints. For example, charges are often higher (and coding is often different) for a "new patient" visit. If the patient is new, a medical record must be assigned. It may be necessary to get medical records from a previous physician, perhaps a referring physician, prior to the visit. Since the appointment is the beginning of the visit record, it should have all of the information necessary to assure that people following up can add all the information to make the record complete for billing, and include all of the information necessary for the staff to prepare for the patient's visit.

The patient should also be aware of when payment will be expected, and to what extent.

10-3 Appointment Reminder

In order to optimize utilization of staff, it is important to minimize missed appointments. For this reason, hospitals and physicians should have a system to remind patients, perhaps a couple of days in advance, that they have an appointment. This serves to remind the patient of the appointment and also gives the patient the opportunity to cancel the appointment if he or she has not already done so.

These reminders can be by phone, mail, or e-mail. Privacy measures should be taken so that the message is directed to the patient and not left with someone else, unless it is specified that it is acceptable to do so. The Health Insurance Portability and Accountability Act of 1996 (HIPAA) requires healthcare providers to protect information and privacy of patients. A reminder that is accessible by people other than the patient, if not carefully worded, can violate that privacy requirement. For example, in most households, multiple people have access to the answering machine or voicemail. The Institution's Privacy Officer, a newly created position responsible for the oversight of HIPAA issues, should be consulted as to the process of reminding patients of appointments.

Presumably, it is best to talk to the patient personally to address any questions there may be. The appointment reminder should advise the patient what to bring to the appointment, for example, insurance cards and lists of medications, allergies, etc. In the case of noninsurance, the patient might be asked to bring financial information, such as tax returns. It is becoming increasingly common for providers, especially physicians, to charge patients for "missed" appointments.

10-4 Registration or Admitting

When the patient begins registration or admitting, it is important to comply with HIPAA guidelines; patients in line should be unable to hear or see the medical situation of the person being served.

At this point, the receptionist should verify insurance, secondary insurance, address, employment, guarantor (the person responsible for payment after insurance), and other pertinent information. The receptionist should request the patient's insurance card for copying (both sides). Insurance forms, waivers, and all appropriate documents should be signed at this time. If an ABN is appropriate, it should be reviewed with the patient at this time, and a signature should be obtained.

It is important to confirm the patient status (inpatient, outpatient, emergency, hospice, etc.) and the site. There may be instances where different rooms in the same building are charged as different sites, for example, hospital versus physician's office.

An evaluation should be made of coverage, including co-payments and deductibles, and based on the policy of the hospital or practice, collections should be made at this time. There should be a process in place to estimate the balance due from the patient, and there should be clear policies as to what should be collected, from whom, and when.

At this point, there should be enough information to determine if the patient has the ability to pay. Providers should realize that not all patients can afford to pay charges. As is explained elsewhere in this chapter, most payers do not pay full charges; however, self-pay patients, who do not have a good stance for negotiating prices, do pay full charges. It is a common practice for providers to offer discounts, up to 100 percent, depending on multiples of the federal poverty guidelines.

Other patients "self-insure" (i.e., they choose not to buy insurance) and assume the risk. In some cases, they participate in tax-deferred accounts, known as health reimbursement arrangements (HRAs), sponsored by themselves or their employers. These are savings accounts, similar to IRAs, designed exclusively for healthcare coverage. Some HRAs are combined with catastrophic insurance coverage, and some provide regular coverage for a period of time, allowing the HRA to grow.

Patients who are self-insured and who cannot qualify through need can be asked for a significant deposit; they also need to be informed of what is expected in terms of payment. In many organizations, their credit history is reviewed, and they should provide a credit card or other evidence of ability to pay.

Providers can offer discounts to patients to help with co-insurance and deductibles, sometimes even waiving them to attract business. Savvy payers will try to identify this and will take money back from the payers. They will claim that the real charges are what they accept and will adjust payment to the provider accordingly.

For example, if a payer pays a hospital 60 percent of charges with a 20 percent co-insurance on a $1,000 bill, the payer will provide $480, with an expectation of $120 from the patient. If the hospital waives the $120, the payer will recalculate its own liability based on 60 percent of $880, or $520 less $104, a net reduction of $64. It should be noted here that the percent co-payment is based on the negotiated payment, not the gross charge. In the past, some payers had the patient or guarantor pay a percent of gross charges, and they would pay the difference. This is no longer a legal practice.

The purpose of co-insurance and deductibles is to have the patient share some risk while discouraging patients from seeking unnecessary care. Because of this payers want to discourage waived charges.

HSAs often have debit cards associated with the account. If there are inadequate resources, and no other coverage, patients should be treated as self-insured.

The record for the visit should be updated to include all the demographic information collected and all financial transactions.

10-5 Performance of Service and Documentation

🚩 "If it's not documented, it wasn't done." This should be at the forefront of the caregiver's mind because if a charge is entered for a service that wasn't documented in the medical record, it can be interpreted as a "false claim." The details of this are discussed elsewhere in this volume, but it is essential to identify in the notes what is done, and by whom.

There are different requirements regarding supervision, and in some cases payment amounts differ depending on who is the actual caregiver. Examples include:

- Residents or fellows
- Nurse practitioners
- Physician assistants
- Certified registered nurse anesthetists (CRNAs)

This becomes a very complex area in performance and charging for services. For example, there are different levels of supervision required for billing, and the required levels of supervision can vary by site of service, state, and even payer. For example, residents and fellows are typically reimbursed as hospital employees. But, they are in training, so their services are supervised. The supervising physician can bill for the services but must review those services with the resident/fellow *and* the patient. If the physician fails to review all services performed by the resident/fellow, and document what was reviewed, there is inadequate support for the charge.

CRNAs have less stringent supervision requirements in some states that have "opted out" of the CMS guidelines. They can also be employed by hospitals, physician groups, or even self employed.

Physician assistants are supervised in most environments. But in certain circumstances, such as critical access areas, physician supervision might not be available.

It is important for revenue cycle staff to understand how to bill for these "physician extender" services, including the expected reimbursement and any special coding. It is also important for the services performed by any caregiver to be appropriate for the patient complaint. For example, physician payment often includes a portion based on the number of body systems reviewed. If the physician codes or charges for more systems reviewed than would be dictated by the symptoms presented by the patient, the claim would be rejected in an audit. Frequent occurrences such as this could result in other penalties. Of course, in order to support the claim, all systems reviewed would have to be documented in the chart.

10-6 Service Documentation and the Electronic Medical Record

The importance of documentation to revenue, and compliance, cannot be overemphasized. All payers, including Medicare, have reviewers who compare the medical record to the claim or bill. Traditionally, a physician or other caregiver performs a service and records it into the medical record. A disconnect occurs if the entry into the billing system does not match the medical record. This will result in denied claims and, in the worst case, accusations of "false claims."

The charge can be generated in a number of ways. In some hospitals, for example, charges can be generated from the order. In such cases, it is important to correct the charge when a procedure is not performed, or if it is determined that a different procedure is more appropriate.

In other cases, charge slips or charge entry occur after the procedure. This can be entered electronically into the billing system (or preliminary system in cases such as laboratory) or manually through a charge slip. Some charge slips are set up to allow stickers to be placed on them when a supply is used on a patient. These stickers have a tendency to go lost, so systems have been developed to charge the patient automatically when supplies are taken from the storage cabinets. This, too, is fraught with opportunities for circumvention.

> The Electronic Medical Record (EMR) can be used as a control to improve the population of services on the bill. As long as the systems are mapped properly to one another, the physician order will remain open until "performed." Therefore, in order to "close" the order, all electronic "paperwork" needs to be completed.

Electronic Medical Records (EMRs) come in many varieties. They offer the opportunity to integrate components of the service and revenue cycle. If an order is placed into the system, it must be "signed off" as completed before charge entry. In addition, the EMR helps guide the caregiver into proper documentation and charging. For example, there are several levels of a regular physician visit. The EMR has the physician "check off" what was performed in the visit and will assign the proper code(s).

The EMR for the visit is set up when the appointment is made (or it can be a visit within an existing record) and is updated throughout the visit. It can be programmed for a reminder, and details are collected during registration. It can integrate directly into the billing system or it can serve as the order entry system, as is discussed in the next section.

10-7 Charge Cycle

Physicians and hospitals have been known for their excellence in medicine and health care; however, very few of them are recognized for their excellence in the business of medicine and health care. Medicare and most other payer[1] insurers reimburse for patient services based on the coding that is submitted pursuant to the clinical care required for the patient. Applying the correct clinical codes is critical in terms of expecting to be fully reimbursed by the insurance company, including Medicare and Medicaid.

Both physicians and hospitals use what is termed as a chargemaster, a uniform structure list for hospitals and physicians to submit standardized charges for any patient with any disease that meets Medicare guidelines. The complexity facing all healthcare providers is that all the adjoining charging systems to the chargemaster must function without flaws along the charging cycle. Consequently, the proper usage of a chargemaster and all associated charging mechanisms is as important as the individual line items and codes contained within the chargemaster.

Many healthcare organizations fail to realize the multimillion-dollar losses associated with erroneous charging practices. A chargemaster that appears to be in good condition may create a false sense of security when viewed as the only charge cycle component.

This chapter will address many of the charging cycle components that are subject to errors. The chargemaster input mechanisms, including order entry systems (OESs) and the provider's ability to identify, summarize, and implement regulatory changes, are crucial to the incessant Medicare changes of codes and regulations. See **Figure 10-1**.

The following areas will be discussed in detail in this section:

- CDM Structure
- Hospital and Physician Pricing
- Order Entry Charging Systems
- Explode Charging Mechanisms
- Regulatory Resources for Updating Charges
- Charging Cycle Overview

10-7.1 Hospital Charging Systems

Hospitals have five basic charging systems that work in conjunction with one another to provide a mechanism to convert the health care for a patient into a numeric digit system to be presented to an insurance payer.

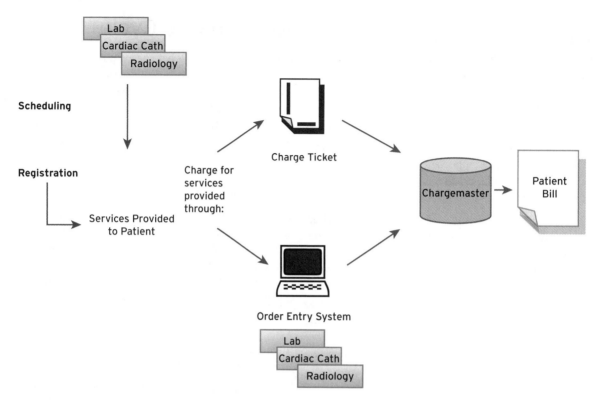

Figure 10-1 Good Charge Practice Cycle

CLINICAL STAFFING. The first charging system is made up of medical and nursing staff, which must be educated continually and remain fluent in the necessary regulations on what and how to charge for patient services. The American Medical Association produces and maintains the copyright to the Current Procedural Terminology codes extensively used by the medical profession for purposes of converting medical care into a numeric description.[2]

ORDER ENTRY SYSTEM. The second charging system is commonly referred to as an order entry system, or OES. The OES is an electronic means of initiating an order for patient services, which then electronically triggers a signal to the chargemaster for billing purposes. There are multiple problems associated with these OES charging mechanisms, ranging from staff's functional knowledge of the software to the intellectual property issues within the systems.

CHARGEMASTER. Thirdly, there comes the most formalized charge structure system that is "fed" by an OES (or charge ticket)—the hospital's chargemaster. A chargemaster is a database or repository of services and supplies that are to be billed to a patient. Each line item listed in a chargemaster is uniformly structured with an item description, a price, a revenue code, and often with a CPT code. Chargemasters can have line item listings from hundreds to tens of thousands of services or supplies. Many chargemasters have a pharmacy section that contains 2,000 to 6,000 drug line items.

MEDICAL RECORDS. Following these three charging systems comes a "quasi-electronic" charge/editing effort from the medical records department, which applies certain codes that have been purposely excluded from the chargemaster. Typically, these codes are surgical and are determined based on the physician's dictation on what was performed on the patient. Furthermore, the chart documentation is examined to assure all "other" supplies and services (such as an implantable device) have been included on the patient's bill.

BACKEND SCRUBBER. Finally, a fifth system called a "scrubber" software product is used that, in an electronic mode, provides a final bill review to ensure that codes and code combinations are valid, modifiers are appropriate, and basic formats have been followed.

There are multiple charging problems with the first and second charge systems, which will be discussed throughout this chapter. Many charging problems are rooted in these first two stages of charging, which create inaccurate or erroneous patient bills.

First, Medicare regulations are complex in terms of the multiple methods of charging. For instance, certain surgical services must be concurrently charged with the corresponding medical device; otherwise, if the device is inadvertently not charged when the service is charged, the payment for the entire procedure and supply may be reimbursed as zero. Secondly, the descriptions, codes, and prices associated with each chargeable item are housed in the chargemaster. If the item being charged via the OES is an MRI of the neck, and the item it is linked to or "mapped" to in the chargemaster is an MRI of the lumbar, this becomes a compliance and reimbursement problem since the chargemaster item has a CPT code imbedded in the line item that will ultimately charge for a lumbar MRI, not a neck MRI as was performed on the patient. The charging staff at the departmental level for the service, however, is not likely to know that the CPT code listed in the chargemaster is incorrect (since the OES is descriptive only), and the charging practice continues through the revenue cycle as incorrect because the OES descriptor is reflective of the patient care; however, it is not the actual charge that will be posted on the bill.

In addition to the quality of staffs' charging knowledge and the quality of the listing of services and coding within the chargemaster, there exists one further complication to the alignment of charging for services and completeness: the hospital's OES. An OES that charges for services is "mapped" or linked to the chargemaster via a common numeric code that provides an electronic connection between the chargemaster and the OES. However, it is the descriptor of the OES and the descriptor of the corresponding line in the chargemaster that must be correctly mapped according to the assigned CPT code. The OESs that actually trigger charges must be in synchronization with the CMS regulatory changes at all times in coordination with the chargemaster. It becomes a potential act of fraud under the False Claims Act when the mapped or linked connection is erroneous. See **Figure 10-2**. For example, the service performed is a CAT scan of the knee but the chargemaster charges for a CAT scan of the brain according to the assigned CPT code. However absurd this may be, it happens every day throughout the business of health care.

10-7.2 Potential Compliance Exposure

Compliance in health care is an absolute standard that must be adhered to at all times, both clinically and administratively. In the business of medicine, when charging for services there are many issues that could

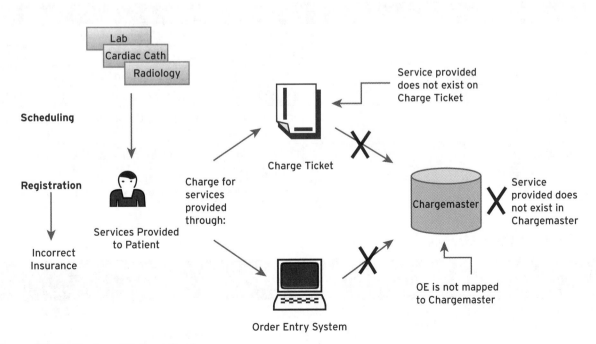

Figure 10-2 Broken Charge Cycle

lead to compliance problems from a charging of services perspective, including:

- Incorrect CPT/HCPCS codes

- Missing a chargeable/billable line wherein the charged item is entered through the OES but fails to trigger a billable item for UB-04 purposes

- Explodes that are improperly structured

- Mismapping of a charged item that incorrectly converts to a billed item

- Incorrect CPT to revenue code mappings

- Volume restriction flags erroneously set

Charge practice errors may be related to hospital personnel—those that are clinically working at the department level, such as laboratory, to initiate the correct charges for the laboratory services provided to the patient. These clinical employees must have a thorough understanding of the following three healthcare components:

1. Expertise in clinical care of medical services.

2. Regulatory understanding of the propagation of Medicare and other payer transmittals, contract stipulations, and medical necessity rules.

3. Comprehensive knowledge of the clinical order entry

charging systems. This includes charge tickets and OESs. Furthermore, regulatory changes that are initiated in the chargemaster must be initiated by these employees for charge ticket and OES modification.

10-7.3 CDM Structure Example

Uniformity of the chargemaster database is essential to the connectivity to all other hospital and physician software billing components. **Table 10-1** shows a skeleton of the chargemaster structure and the essential components that make up the Chargemaster line. Any discrepancy in regulatory terms of how Medicare expects the bills to be submitted may result in possible payment shortfalls or bill rejections.

In the example of a Left Heart Catherization in **Table 10-2**, the procedure code begins with the first three digits 481, which correspond to the department number in the hospital. The AMA's technical (or long) description is published with the appropriate matters pertaining to the service. Correspondingly, the billing description (or short description) should always contain the essential technical elements of the AMA description. For instance, left is essential as there are "right" and "right and left" cardiac catheters that can be performed under differing CPT code numbers.

Table 10-1 CDM Component

Chargemaster Component	Component Definition
Procedure Code	Internally assigned hospital identification number
Billing Description	Short description for item
Technical Description of Service or Supply	Long description for item as defined by the AMA
CPT/HCPCS Code	5-digit billing code to identify the service provided
Modifier	Information to further specify the service, (i.e., right, left, bilateral)
Revenue Code	3-digit code to identify the revenue area of service (i.e., cardiology)
Price	Charge for item established by the hospital or physician

Table 10-2 CDM Line Example

Procedure Code	Billing Description	Technical Description	CPT Code	Modifier	Revenue Code	Price
481-1663	LT HEART CATH	CATH LEFT HEART/ RETROGRD	93452		481	$8,800

CPT CODES. A CPT[3] code is a uniform coding system that contains descriptive terms and identifies the codes that are used to bill for medical services that are performed by physicians and clinical professionals. These CPT codes are used to bill public and private payers. Only the AMA can publish any ongoing additions, deletions, and edits to these codes, as they hold the copyright to the CPT codes. The CPT code is assigned to a procedure, typically by the clinical area of the hospital. This code is instrumental for charging purposes as it must serve as the numeric identifier of the patients' service and will be used for payment purposes by many insurers based on the CPT/HCPCS[4] code submitted. Consequently, if the CPT code by AMA/Medicare definitions is for a CBC lab test, but the description and CPT code erroneously state a mammography, the payer may pay it as a mammography NOT a CBC. Adding to the billing complexity is the fact that nongovernmental payers negotiate or administer CPT differences when compared to the Medicare regulations that require multiple CPT codes for the same service.

CPT CODE NUMERIC CLASSIFICATIONS. The AMA developed CPT codes in a clinical order to numerically classify the services used to attend to patients. The CPT text is subdivided into six general coding categories, as illustrated in **Table 10-3**.

Correctly coding the line with the appropriate CPT code is typically the responsibility of the clinical department, as it has the highest expertise in that clinical area. The revenue code and price are typically assigned by the finance areas.

ICD-9 CODES. International Classification of Diseases, Ninth Revision (ICD-9) is a medical classification published by the World Health Organization (WHO) and used worldwide for morbidity and mortality statistics and reimbursement systems used in the business of medicine. This numeric system of classifying the possible disease or illness of a patient is used to codify the many ailments of a human being. Furthermore it allows the medical problem to be automated into an electronic numeric means for international comparability through the WHO.

MEDICAL NECESSITY. Medicare now uses the ICD-9 in combination with CPT/HCPCS code to prepare a "crosswalk" that identifies allowable or "medically necessary" services. Correspondingly, it identifies which services/supplies are not allowed or denied, which then become the patient's responsibility.

Hospitals are overwhelmed with ever-changing, extremely complex regulations from the largest payer—Medicare. The various regulations and classification systems stem from a myriad of authors, including:

- World Health Organization (WHO)
- International Classification of Diseases (ICD-9)
- American Medical Association (AMA)
- Current Procedural Terminology (CPT)
- Centers for Medicare and Medicaid Services (CMS)
- Health Care Procedure Coding System (HCPCS)

These systems have translated clinical alignments into numeric systems that are efficiently processed electronically. Consequently, the electronic handling of the clinical information permits a multitude of checks and audits to be put into place, such as Medicare's Outpatient Code Editor (OCE). **Table 10-4** gives a basic configuration of how clinical patient information is converted to numerical classifications.

Table 10-3 CPT Ranges

CPT Numeric Ranges	Clinical Area
00000 through 01999	Anesthesia
10000 through 69999	Surgery
70000 through 79999	Radiology
80000 through 89999	Laboratory & Pathology
90000 through 99999	Medicine
99201 through 99499	Evaluation & Management

Table 10-4 Numbers Systems

Typical Diagnostic Terminology	Number System	Example of a Patient Encounter	Examples of How the Data Is Stored in HIS
Disease/Illness	ICD-9 Code	Hypertension-Heart Disease (unspecified)	401.9
Service/Supply	CPT/HCPCS Codes	Cardiac Catheterization	93510
Specificity	Modifiers	Additional or Modified Service	59
Service Area	Revenue Code	Revenue Area	481
Value of Service	Price	Fee for Cardiac Cath	3500.00
Volume of Service	Units	Volume of 1	1
Patient Type	Patient Type Code	Outpatient, Inpatient Emergency Room Skilled Nursing	131,110

HCPCS CODES. The HCPCS (Health Care Procedure Coding System) is divided into two principal subsystems, referred to as Level I and Level II of the HCPCS. Level I of the HCPCS is comprised of CPT codes, a numeric coding system maintained by the AMA. The CPT is a uniform coding system consisting of descriptive terms and identifying codes that are used primarily to identify medical services and procedures furnished by physicians and other healthcare professionals. These healthcare professionals use the CPT to identify services and procedures for which they bill public or private health insurance programs. Decisions regarding the addition, deletion, or revision of CPT codes are published by the AMA and republished annually.

Level II of the HCPCS is a standardized coding system that is used primarily to identify products, supplies, and services not included in the CPT codes, such as ambulance services, durable medical equipment, prosthetics, orthotics, and supplies (DMEPOS) when used outside a physician's office. Because Medicare and other insurers cover a variety of services, supplies, and equipment that are not identified by CPT codes, the Level II HCPCS codes were established for submitting claims for these items. Level II codes are also referred to as alphanumeric codes because they consist of a single alphabetical letter followed by four numeric digits, while CPT codes are identified using five numeric digits.

The 42 CFR Section 414.40 (a) establishes uniform national definitions of services, codes to represent services, and payment modifiers to be used with the codes. There is a special section of Level II HCPCS codes

titled "Pass Through Items" or C codes. The C codes have been in use since 2000 to provide special "pass through" payments in addition to the Outpatient Prospective Payment System (OPPS[5]) for Medicare claims only. An example of a C code would be HCPCS code C2619, pacemaker, dual chamber. See **Table 10-5**.

Level II HCPCS codes can also require additional information by use of a modifier. For instance, A1 is a modifier for a dressing for one wound, and A9 is a modifier for nine or more wounds. These modifiers are either alphanumeric or two letters.

REVENUE CODES. Revenue codes[6] are unique three-digit numbers that are used in hospital billing and are reported to insurance companies on medical claims. Revenue codes tell the insurance company either which department the procedure was performed in or what was used for treatment.

The revenue code is derived according to how it corresponds to the service area, such as laboratory, and/or by the CPT code. There is a regulatory body that assigns the mapping between the revenue code and the CPT codes. It is important that these codes are properly matched in order to receive proper payment. Furthermore, there will be instances where one insurer, such as Medicaid, will require a general 250 revenue code for a drug, while Medicare will require a 636 revenue code for the same drug with the same CPT code.

Revenue codes are used by Medicare to classify the hospital's gross chargeable revenue by clinical area, such as the operating room (revenue code 360) or recover room (revenue code 710). Proper classification is essential when

Table 10-5 "C" Code

Procedure Code	Billing Description	HCPCS Code	Revenue Code	Price
360-1223	Infusion Pump	C1891	278	$9,000

Table 10-6 Modifier Example

Code Type	CPT Code	Description
E/M Code	99282-25	ED Visit, Level II
Procedure Code	93005	Twelve-Lead ECG

filing Medicare's Annual Cost Report due to the effort of matching the hospital's cost to the hospital's revenue by clinical area.

Many payers may specify separate or additional reimbursement for implantable devices. The revenue code typically applied for these items is 278. It is therefore imperative that the correct revenue code is associated with the implantable item. For instance, the revenue code 278 should be associated with an implantable stent.

Payer-specific contract rules should also be followed closely regarding implantable device billing. When the payer agrees to provide separate payment for implantable devices, the additional payment is generally triggered by the submission of a specific revenue code on the UB-04 patient bill. Consequently, when a pacemaker is coded with a general supply revenue code of 270, the payer will not recognize it as an implantable device and therefore will not provide any separate payment.

DESCRIPTORS. AMA Formal Descriptors. The AMA has a formal long, medium, and short description for each CPT-coded item. The same holds true for the HCPCS codes vis-à-vis the CMS. These formal descriptors should always be translated as closely as possible to the chargemaster and other charging systems.

Hospital and Physician Informal Descriptors. The description of a chargemaster line item is crucial in several senses:

1. It is the regulatory description of the service or supply being provided to a patient.
2. When the line item is coded with a CPT/HCPCS code it should be described in a fashion closely aligned with the AMA/CMS description.
3. Abbreviations used within the chargemaster should contain the essential wording to clearly state what is being provided to the patient.

4. A corresponding descriptor is usually required in one of two possible places:
   a. To match the charge ticket check-off sheet description to the line item listed in the x
   b. To match the OES description to the line item listed in the chargemaster[7]

MODIFIERS. A modifier is two- or four-digit code that contains letters and/or numbers that very specifically describe the circumstances under which the service was provided. Modifiers are valid only for usage with CPT/HCPCS codes. Certain modifiers are hardcoded into the chargemaster as static modifiers, while dynamic modifiers must be applied to the UB-04 by medical records based on medical circumstances. Communication and documentation between the ancillary department and the medical records department are crucial to appending the correct modifier.

Static modifiers are hardcoded in the chargemaster for services that are constant, such as left, right, or bilateral. Dynamic modifiers are applied to the patient bill based on the medical circumstances during the patient's care. For instance, a dynamic modifier occurs if a patient requires a second x-ray according to a physician's order, in which case the 59 modifier may be applied as an extension of the CPT code. This indicates to Medicare that it was medically necessary to perform additional x-rays.

MODIFIER EXAMPLE. Modifier 25 should be appended to an emergency room evaluation and management visit (E/M) CPT code to indicate that the patient's condition required a significant, separately identifiable procedure on the same day the E/M service was provided. For example, a patient is seen in the emergency department with the complaint of a rapid heartbeat. During the encounter, a 12-lead electrocardiogram is performed. In this case, CPT codes with the appropriate twenty-five modifier would be reported. See **Table 10-6**.

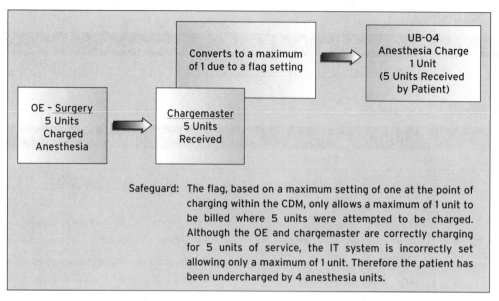

Figure 10-3 System Flag Override Risk

If modifier 25 is not appended to the E/M code 99282, payment for the ECG, in all likelihood, could be $0.00 or the entire charge could be rejected. The interpretation by the payer is conditioned to the terms of the contract or federal regulations.

SYSTEM FLAGS. Flags are most commonly a toggle type of on/off or yes/no switch. Many of the effects of these flags remain unknown or go undetected until the UB-04 or 1500 bills are generated and the explanation of benefits (EOB) indicates errors. This means that the multiplicity of electronic checks and balances are bypassed, as the viewable effects of an erroneous flag will not appear until the bill is produced, thereby creating a necessity to audit the bill to detect any flag faults.

There are many issues that can go wrong due to improper set up or ongoing maintenance, such as the hospital system flag problem illustrated in **Figure 10-3** for a patient receiving anesthesia services.

System flags are used by all hospitals and have tremendous applications for a multitude of issues, such as the following:

- Billable versus nonbillable flag
- Orderable versus nonorderable flag
- Statistical only flag
- Suppress from bill flag
- Volume greater than one flag
- Charge on order flag
- Inpatient only flag

System flags typically are programmed within a software system to allow or disallow a certain function regarding recognizing or charging for patient services. Knowledge of if and where these flags exist is crucial to the charge cycle maintenance components.

Order Entry System Flags.

1. Orderable versus nonorderable: This toggle is set for services that may be ordered for patient care.

2. Volume flag: This setting is used to limit the number of units permitted to be charged. For example, a knee replacement implant charge is limited to a maximum of one for an admission.

3. Charge on order: This triggers a charge when ordered, not when completed.

4. Charge on completion: This triggers a charge when the test is completed or resulted, not when it was ordered.

10-7.4 Hospital and Physician Pricing

First and foremost, pricing of healthcare services in the United States is governed under the uniformity of pricing regulation,[8] where the same price must be charged to all patients regardless of the insurance provider they have, if any. This is extremely important. For instance, if two patients come in for a CAT scan of the knee (assume the hospital charges $2,168.00) and the payment for the Blue Cross-insured patient is based on negotiated fee schedule amount of $1,200.00, and the payment for the Aetna patient is based on a 90 percent of the hospital charge or $1,951.20; the price as published by the hospital in its chargemaster must be the same regardless of the payment differences.

Pricing of hospital services is commonly a dichotomy. There may be reason to increase a price of a common service, (such as an x-ray) in one clinical area and decrease the price of the same service in a different clinical area due to the mix of patients' insurances methodologies. Furthermore, payments for the same service or supply may be completely different dependent on the patient's insurance coverage, whereas the price charged to both insurers must be the same amount under the uniformity of charges provision.

Hospital pricing should address the following issues:

1. Uniformly charge all patients the same dollar amount regardless of their ability to pay and regardless of the insurance coverage.

2. The charge should be related consistently to the cost of the service or supply.

3. For contractual reasons the charge should be higher than each associated fee schedule, as many insurers will negotiate a distinct payment amount per each CPT code for outpatient services.

Over the years hospitals have had great latitude in determining the amount to charge patients for services provided. Many hospitals have taken a conservative approach to pricing of room and board rates, time-based charges, supplies, and procedures. There has been a great change in the effect pricing has on reimbursement in the hospital and physician businesses. In the past, hospitals were able to increase net revenue by increasing prices for the services; however, due to the massive conversion by payer to switch from a percent of charge reimbursement to a fee schedule reimbursement, pricing has minimal effect on overall payments.

Transparency and defensible price settings may be a larger matter in today's healthcare market. Regardless of the charging mechanism, the chargemaster remains the essential repository for pricing of each service.

When healthcare providers apply strategic or across-the-board price increases, they are exposed to defensibility standards as more patients, payers, and even Congress invoke price transparency expectations. Unlike years gone by, in today's market it is unlikely that a hospital can increase overall prices 12 percent, 14 percent, or 16 percent. Furthermore, pricing transparency in the chargemaster structure has become more highly scrutinized, and a chest x-ray provided in the emergency room should be priced equally with one provided in the operating room. Moreover, there should be a direct price relationship between related services that have differing resource utilization. For example, an MRI with contrast should not be priced lower than an MRI without contrast.

The majority of today's reimbursement methodology falls into one of three methods:

- "Percentage of charges" is the method by which the payer reimburses the hospital a negotiated percentage of the hospital charge. This method can be used for both inpatient and outpatient services. For example:

  Hospital Charge for a Cardiac Catheterization

Hospital Price	$8,500.00
Reimbursement %	70 percent
Reimbursement	$5,950.00
Less Patient Co-Pay	600.00
Payer Payment	$5,350.00

- "Fee schedule comparison" is an outpatient payment method by which the payer and provider have negotiated a flat fee payment amount for each CPT code. For example:

  Hospital Charge for Outpatient Cardiac Catheterization
  Payer Fee Schedule Payment $2,500.00

- "Diagnostic-related groups (DRGs)" is an inpatient payment method by which a software product or "grouper" takes into account the inpatient illness as designated by the ICD-9 code. Based upon multiple algorithms the grouper produces the inpatient illness, co-morbidities, and procedures, and, based upon multiple algorithms, assigns a code (the DRG). Each DRG is assigned a payment amount based on predetermined resource utilization factors.

In accordance with Medicare's Uniformity of Billing clause, all patients must be charged the same price regardless of their insurance benefit or payment methodology. This provision of allowing hospitals to be reimbursed under different methodologies by each payer while having to charge the same unit price to all payers leads to great difficulty when determining what price to charge for a service.

DEFENSIBLE PRICING. Medicare expects the price of the service or supply to be related to the cost of the supply. Each hospital information system may have a number of methods to hold pricing structures. **Table 10-7** gives two examples of methods used to handle the pricing. Hospitals may use these fields in one of two ways.

Table 10-7 Price Fields

	Price Field 1	**Price Field 2**	**Price Field 3**
Method 1	Current Price	Prior Price	Future Price
Method 2	Inpatient Price	Outpatient Price	ER Price

Note: Method 1 also utilizes a date field, which is associated with the effective date for each price. This historic information can be valuable as a reference. Method 2 segregates each price and requires more maintenance when updating prices.

Method 1 provides a convenient method of maintaining the current price, prior (historical) price, and future price, and Price Field 1 is the only price available for charging purposes. This places the hospital in a more defensible position rather than allowing inpatient versus outpatient prices or ER prices to stand as described by Method 2. By utilizing only one price for each line in the chargemaster, Method 1 provides the highest flexibility in usage and the lowest maintenance in updating prices. In contrast, Method 2 can create up to three times the amount of effort when updating prices. Furthermore, auditing transparency issues in Method 2 have a compound effect where there exists cross-price transparency liability among inpatient, outpatient, and ER prices.

CONSUMERISM. As insurance carriers continue to transfer a larger percentage of the burden of payment to their subscribers (patients) through increased co-payments, the price that the consumer is willing to pay for services has become more market driven than ever. The public outcry of perceived abuse over exorbitant pricing for healthcare services and supplies has escalated the process reviewing pricing methodologies to involve transparency audits.

While leading the way and raising competition, laboratory services provided by both hospitals and freestanding labs increase price competition. A freestanding laboratory can price a CBC (Complete Blood Count) (for outpatient services) at $10.00, while a hospital CBC may be priced at $58.00. In both cases, Medicare reimbursement is approximately $9.00. Consequently patients and physicians have begun to "shop around" for the lowest price and many times elect not to use the hospital's laboratory. This is further underscored through endorsements by the insurance carrier (payer) to the patient vis-à-vis patient co-pays.

Naturally, not all of the services provided by hospitals are also provided by freestanding units. However, national and global competition to provide services such as open heart surgery in Dubai or London, or even plastic surgery in the physician's freestanding facility is growing at a rapid pace. Global advertisements are now seen by such providers as The Cleveland Clinic and Mayo Clinic. However, more commonly seen is the decrease in hospital outpatient volumes in areas such as radiology services, pharmacy supplies, or rehabilitation services as they migrate to either physician offices or freestanding facilities. It has become critical when pricing the hospital's services that the pricing methodology can simultaneously accommodate not only a competitive structure but also one that optimizes full reimbursement.

Using market comparative data is one method of determining whether the chargemaster prices are publicly acceptable when compared to other hospitals, physician offices, or freestanding labs. It is also feasible to strategically price services utilizing two different market-based comparisons. First, when the hospital has the opportunity to price services upward to match the market, then the increase in gross revenue can be portrayed in a net revenue extraction. Second, when the hospital prices are at the "market ceiling," there may be further pricing opportunity to price services to address any further net revenue improvement without jeopardizing the allowable consumer price index increase per year.

10-7.5 Order Entry Charging Systems

The healthcare industry is comprised of numerous, fragmented software charging systems, or OESs, which must integrate with the legacy IT system of the provider. Most hospitals have a financial system that integrates with the chargemaster to accommodate the production of a UB-04 claim for patient services. The separate clinically based charging software, however, is specific to the clinical area, such as the emergency room or cardiology, and may not be well integrated with the whole-hospital financial software system.

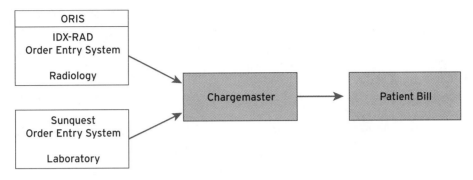

Figure 10-4 OES

Table 10-8 Mismapped Electronic Connectivity

CPT Code	CPT Descriptor	OES Descriptor
70450	CT Brain without Contrast Media	MRI Brain without Contrast

The OES must be "connected" or "mapped" to the chargemaster using a common alphanumeric scheme. The commonality of the numbering scheme is highly dependent upon two factors:

1. The descriptor used to identify the OES item as it relates to the chargemaster; and

2. The chargemaster CPT code description used to relate to the AMA[9] published descriptor.

OVERVIEW OF CHARGING FROM OES. **Figure 10-4** describes the lifecycle of a patient charge request generated by the clinical staff through the OES, which is mapped to the chargemaster and ultimately billed to the patient.

An order entry must be mapped to the hospital's or physician's chargemaster and be an exclusive, one-to-one, line item basis, even when there may be a "many-to-one" mapping, such as multiple size catheters in order entry going only to one line item in the chargemaster. Typically, a departmental staff person is responsible for setting up and maintaining not only the line items within the OES but also the mapping to the chargemaster. Due to the frequency of code changes, this can become a daily effort as the accountability for instituting the change is shouldered by both the Information System staff and the departmental staff. When this occurs it becomes incumbent on both the order entry and chargemaster maintenance staff to insure that the system flags are set to accurately reflect chargeable volumes.

When the mapping from the OES to the chargemaster is not coordinated there exists the strong likelihood of charging and billing errors. The following circumstances can occur due to mismapping:

- Order entry is mapped to incorrect chargemaster line
- Order entry is not mapped to any chargemaster line
- There is no order entry item to charge

The ever-changing coding environment causes the hospital to perpetually examine and update these mappings.

An example of the OES descriptor *not* matching the CPT descriptor is given in **Table 10-8**.

TIMING OF REGULATORY CHANGES AND OES EDITING. Management of the financial well-being of a hospital is the distinct responsibility of all involved, from the board members to the billing and collections staff. OES and charging tickets define when and what is to be charged. One of the most beneficial changes available vis-à-vis the OES is the control to eliminate a charge that expires due to regulatory or contractual changes.

As an example, if a radiation oncology code such as 77881 for cardiac catheter code 93510 is deleted from service on January 1, the OES can stop all usage for this service by removing this charge from the OES. By doing so, the department is prohibited from charging this after December 31 vis-à-vis the OES. On the chargemaster side, the code can be allowed to remain active for 90 days to process the pending bills through year-end.

The OES can be straightforward in design, or it can have a complex architecture that requires expertise to maintain. A straightforward, elementary OES structure also requires synchronized management timing with the chargemaster coding. Difficulties arise when codes in the chargemaster have a dynamic or definitive change in the CPT code; then the department must "remap" the appropriate line item in the OES to correctly correspond to the new code in the chargemaster.

Typically, this requires an ongoing line of communication within the revenue cycle committee (or parts thereof) to notify the OES staff of impending changes and the timing of the implementation. Communication also should extend to the managed care contracting staff as necessitated by major code modifications.

TIMING OF OES AND CHARGEMASTER UPDATES. OESs must be updated, as should chargemasters, in accordance with the regulatory effective date. The three types of changes (add, edit, and delete) all must have "day-of" implementation (or effective deletion dates) at the OES level. The chargemaster routine for the deletion of a code can have a 90-day waiting period to accommodate any bill processing that may be on hold. The delete action for the OES, however, should take place on the "day of" the effective regulatory change to prevent any further ordering of charges with an old code or service.

The same holds true for edits and additions in the OES. Differing from the chargemaster, which can house outdated codes in order to process pending bills, the control for day-to-day charging of services is housed in the OES. When the OES chargeable service is added at the appropriate time and the corresponding outdated service is simultaneously removed, control is now in place.

Utilizing the OES architecture allows for total charge control while permitting the chargemaster to continue to hold outdated services in order to handle the billing cycles that extend beyond the regulatory service dates. It is important that revenue cycle committees recognize this feature of OES control.

Many chargemaster coordinators and finance staff are insulated from the technical working mechanisms of clinical OESs. A lack of understanding regarding the importance of how the OES contributes to proper charging functionality causes it to play a secondary role to the chargemaster, as a dysfunctional system, when in fact they go hand-in-hand.

It is paramount to recognize any of the following OES problems:

- Missing charge activators
- Inactive charge activators
- Incorrectly mapped order entry charges to chargemaster lines
- Order entry charges mapped to "dead" or inactive chargemaster lines
- Order entry charges mapped to nonexistent chargemaster lines

Many hospital staff fall prey to lack of understanding of the functionality of the OES and its primary contribution to the charging cycle. Hospital staff may not know that the OES may have explode structures. Moreover, if the OES contains explode mechanisms and is not regularly maintained, the result typically involves compliance problems.

ORDER ENTRY DESCRIPTORS. When using an OES for charging (on a charge ticket), the *descriptor* is the means of identification by the clinical staff member charging for the service. Commonly, this descriptor is an "alias" titled in a way that is easily and clearly understood by the charging staff yet may differ from the AMA's CPT code descriptor.

OES service items typically do not have the formalized CPT descriptor, whereas the chargemaster CPT/HCPCS codes should provide distinct identification of the service as dictated by the CMS. Instead, the literal or mnemonic descriptors are the primary key link to clinical usage for charging purposes. It is the descriptor of the service that the staff become most familiar with in charging/ordering for services. The descriptor definition by staff must reflect the CPT code technical description as identified by the chargemaster, taking into account the following functional matters:

- Initial or subsequent procedure (such as infusion)
- Dosage/unit of measure

EXPLODE CHARGE MECHANISMS. Explode charge mechanisms[10] provide a means of minimizing and effecting the complete charging for a distinct set of routinely ordered services provided to a patient. By initiating one charge, several others are contemporaneously charged. Explodes may exist in the chargemaster or in the OES. Many times they exist in both places. Wherever the explodes exist, they must be maintained based on the commonality of the OES regulatory maintenance protocol. Explode codes generally have the structures that are illustrated in **Figures 10-5** and **10-6**.

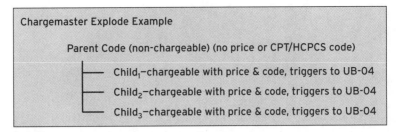

Figure 10-5 CDM Explode

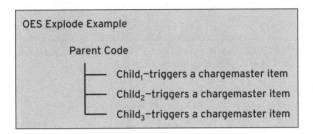

Figure 10-6 OES Explode

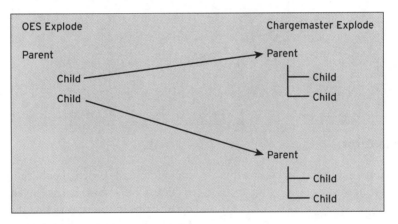

Figure 10-7 Complex Explode

The argument for not using explode codes is that they may be complicated, require expert and careful continuous maintenance, and must be documented. There must be direct coordination to the OES, CDM, and all other connected systems to each explode mechanism. When mishandled, they can cause compliance and payment problems, but the purpose of explode codes is to provide consistency and assurance that the services provided will be accurately charged for patient care.

COMPLEX OES/CHARGEMASTER EXPLODE. Hospitals combine an OES explode with a chargemaster explode as shown in **Figure 10-7**.

This example of an OES explode illustrates how explode mechanisms can be triggered by multiple and simultaneous order entry lines. **Figure 10-8** illustrates how unmaintained mappings from the OES to the CDM can cause compliance problems.

A small misstep in the structure can cause a compliance problem for over-charging, as can be seen in **Figure 10-9**.

Many times there are "unknown" charge elements within the CDM, the order entry/clinical systems, or both. Many hospitals are unaware of these explode structures; consequently, they make chargemaster or OES changes

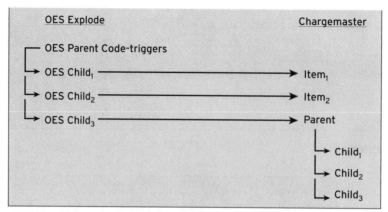

ERROR: OES Child3 should map to a chargemaster single item, not a parent code that causes another explode charge.

Figure 10-8 Explode Error

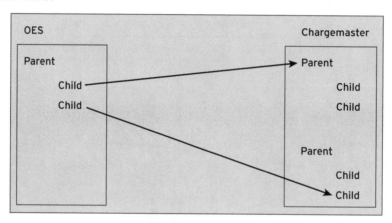

Figure 10-9 Explode Error

without making the corresponding and necessary edits to the existing explode structures.

Furthermore, explode structures may have preassigned volume factors that are greater than one. If this is the case, it becomes even more critical to edit for both the charge combination of services and possible resetting of volume values greater than one.

CHARGEMASTER EXPLODE MECHANISMS. Chargemaster explode structures are similar to OES explodes, with one exception: The chargemaster explode lines will trigger a billable charge to a UB-04. See **Figure 10-10**.

10-7.6 Regulatory Resources for Updating Charges

Monitoring Medicare's daily changes to regulations is essential to properly charging for patient care services. Although the AMA owns the copyright to the CPT codes, it is CMS that can initiate the coding changes through numerous and perpetual publications as illustrated in this section. CMS issues changes on an ongoing basis that can occur daily. It is necessary that the hospital have a means for obtaining these changes as they occur, interpreting them, and implementing the changes as discussed.

REGULATORY CHANGES AND HOSPITAL/ PHYSICIAN RESPONSE. Regulatory changes are typically issued by Local Coverage Determinations and National Coverage Determinations. It is imperative that hospital and physician staff handle the regulatory changes according to the following four points:

1. Interpreting the regulatory publication could affect any or all of the following:

   (a) Descriptors

   (b) CPT and revenue codes

   (c) Volume unit of measures

   (d) Bill type changes

   (e) OES changes

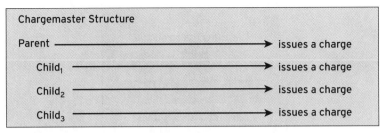

ERROR: Parent should not issue a charge

Figure 10-10 Explode Error

(f) Explode/structure/descriptor changes

(g) Flag settings

(h) Modifiers

(i) ICD-9 coding

(j) NCCI edits

(k) Medical necessity

2. Communication with the clinical staff as the changes are issued by CMS and others is essential as a means to provide education as a basis of support regarding the utilization within the hospital's clinical environment.

3. Provide access to a comprehensive, searchable regulatory library.

4. Audit all changes to insure they are properly structured and coded.

ELECTRONIC REGULATORY LIBRARY. Determining what changes are required for the coding of services should be derived from an electronic source. Attempting to utilize hard-copy regulatory data is cumbersome in two respects:

1. Nearly all regulations are published via the Internet, which would then mandate printing the publication; and

2. Communicating with internal staff utilizing printed media is more lethargic and is typically less effective.

An electronic library can house the actual regulation as well as provide searching capabilities. Many vendors offer an electronic healthcare regulatory library service. Searching the library based on discrete data can be cumbersome when conducted vis-à-vis the Internet. Furthermore, executive summaries of the Medicare publications should provide succinct, immediate insight regarding the incessant regulatory updating from CMS and the A/B MACs (Part A/Part B Medicare Administrative Contractors)[11] relating to all chargemaster and OES and other changes.

The CMS promulgated over 800 regulatory publications through its website during the period of January 1, 2009, to January 31, 2010. An electronic regulatory library should provide the following features and functions:

- Daily download and collection of Medicare regulations

- Storage of CMS publications in electronic media

- Interpretation and summarization of each publication

- A software product that provides searchability of the regulations

- Distribution of the content of the regulation to the clinical department or practice

- Permanent retention of all publications without any expunging

Storage of the various regulations becomes essential for reasons of record retention, but just as important is the connectivity among the various regulatory transmittals, MedLearn Matters, Job Aids, and National Coverage Determinations (NCDs). Local Coverage Determinations (LCDs) are issued by the provider's A/B MAC.

CLASSIFICATION OF AN ELECTRONIC REGULATORY LIBRARY. As with all collections of data, such as Medicare regulations, it is essential to develop an organized, searchable method of retrieval of the regulation. Searching the regulation should be performed in a minimal number of basic modes:

- ICD-9 code (and ranges)

- CPT code (and ranges)

- Modifier

- Text (keyword searches)

- Regulation number

- Release date

- Effective date

- Issue date

There are a number of more advanced modes of regulatory retrieval wherein there exists a connectivity among related

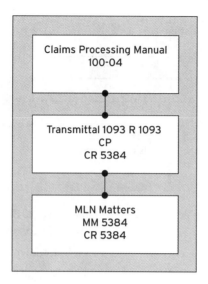

Figure 10-11 Document Flow

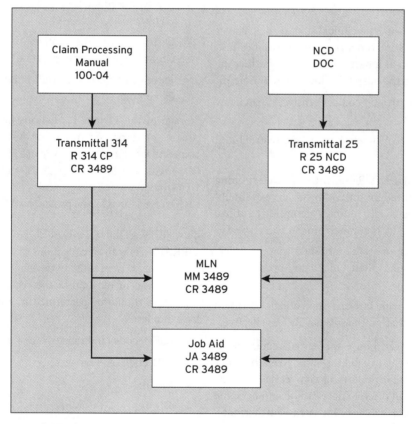

Figure 10-12 Document Flow

documents. For instance, an obvious connection between related documents would be seen in the surgical flowchart in **Figures 10-11** and **10-12**.

In this regulatory publication example, the change request number 3489 is the common element among these transmittals and associated publications.

CMS PUBLICATIONS. Providing new services, removing obsolete services, and changing codes due to regulatory changes demand that hospital and physician chargemasters are perpetually maintained. Any of the payer's actions can trigger the need to update a chargemaster. Staying ahead of the changes is difficult due to large amounts of regulatory information released each month (and sometimes each day) via Internet publications and other electronic means. Interpretation of each regulation is mandatory and, consequently, each transmittal, NCD, or LCD also requires expert scrutiny. Furthermore, there are "grace periods" that need to be observed for nongovernmental payers, which creates a complex implementation schedule of code changes.

Medicare regulations are published electronically and exist on two levels:

> **Level 1:** Federal = CMS (Centers for Medicare and Medicaid Services)
>
> **Level 2:** Local (i.e., Mutual of Omaha, Highmark of Pennsylvania, etc.)

Providers must comply with both federal and fiscal intermediary regulations. Certain regulatory changes will affect the outpatient code editor (OCE), which may then cause denial or bill rejections if the regulatory changes are not implemented properly and on a timely basis.

CMS issues various notices on a very frequent basis:

Program Transmittals

- May be issued daily by CMD and are used to communicate new or changed policies or procedures for all provider types. Changes may include:
  - CPT/HCPCS code changes
  - Fee schedule changes
  - OPPS changes

National Coverage Determination (NCD)

- May be issued on a daily basis by CMS and are used to detail national coverage policies for services

A/B MAC Local Coverage Determination (LCD)

- Are issued on a daily basis by A/B MACs and are used to detail local coverage policies for services

NCCI EDITS. The National Correct Coding Initiative (NCCI) is a table that Medicare developed to provide a comparative list of CPT and HCPCS codes that are not separately payable when billed together except under certain well-defined circumstances. The edits are applied to services billed by the *same provider* for the *same beneficiary* on the *same date* of service. The NCCI includes two types of edits: the bundling, or inclusive, edit and the mutually exclusive edit.

Comprehensive and Component NCCI Edits. Comprehensive codes capture the major procedure or service performed when it is reported with another code. Component codes[12] may not be billed in addition to the comprehensive code, except under special circumstances as denoted by a modifier indicator of "1." The "1" modifier indicator specifies that a modifier is allowed to be reported with this procedure in order to differentiate between the services provided.

Mutually Exclusive NCCI Edits. Mutually exclusive NCCI edits identify procedures that cannot be performed at the same site or at the same time, for example, a specific choice of procedure in lieu of another. These items are identified as code pairs in the Mutually Exclusive edit table. Some of these procedures can be paid if they are performed at different anatomical sites or in separate encounters AND are identified with appropriate modifiers.

Code 1	Code 1 Description	Code 2	Code 2 Description	Modifier
74150	CT Abdomen w/o dye	76380	CT Limited OR Localized Follow-up study	1

Code 1	Code 1 Description	Code 2	Code 2 Description	Modifier
74170	CT Abdomen w/o & w/dye	74150	CT abdomen w/o dye	0

In the above example, the modifier indicator of "0" specifies that there are NO circumstances in which any modifier would be appropriate. The services represented by the code combination will not be paid separately.

10-7.7 Charging Cycle Overview

Many hospitals today are using some sort of software to assist with chargemaster maintenance. Software is an excellent solution to assure the CPT codes are valid. Due to the accuracy of CPT codes as they exist in the charge-masters, many hospitals' management fall into a state of complacency that relieves the scrutiny that continuously should be placed upon the entire "charge cycle." Although the chargemaster is a focal point of all charging, it is not the sole component because the OES is also a component.

EXAMPLE 1. As an example, if a radiology technician does not understand the charging protocol for the third order of interventional coding (and charges for first or second order in addition to third order), the charges (and billing) will be in error, regardless of the perfection of the chargemaster.

EXAMPLE 2. Correspondingly, if a radiology OES is mapped incorrectly from a third order to a first order, the charges (and billing) will be in error, even when the radiology technician and the chargemaster are perfect.

EXAMPLE 3. Many hospital systems have established a corporate chargemaster that can be used by each hospital. The multiplicity of OESs used by each department within each hospital will not be a corporate standard. Therefore, the required attention to the connectivity between each OES and the corporate chargemaster must be handled on an individual basis. As **Figure 10-13** illustrates, OESs and staff knowledge have a predominant presence in whether billed charges go unpaid by insurers due to errors if there is a lack of understanding of the complete charge cycle methodologies.

HOSPITAL CHARGE CYCLE DIAGRAM. To provide an overview of the charge cycle flow of a hospital's steps to correctly provide the issuance of a UB-04 hospital bill, the following **Figure 10-14** illustrates a step-by-step process of establishing the charging cycle of a provider. If any of the transitional six steps fail to occur, the charge cycle is broken (see **Figure 10-15**). Due to the incessant, unpredictable regulatory changes promulgated by Medicare and other payers, the regulatory communication, technical coding modifications, and education must be in daily process to assure that the charging and billing are up to code and practice. Unfortunately, for many providers, there is only sporadic flow (if any at all) of charge upkeep. Step 4, education (staff education) is a major contributor to charging failures when it is not properly performed with the clinical staff at the OES level. Another contributor to charging failures is the lack of proper connectivity maintenance between the OESs and chargemasters, as illustrated in Step 3, charging systems, and as previously discussed.

Charging for services and supplies is a mandatory matter that falls under many regulatory rules and is difficult for the clinical staff to absorb and have the time to absorb. Hospital chargemasters are typically in great shape in terms of the actual codes applied to each service or supply. However, the other components of the chargemaster and charge cycle continue to cause reimbursement shortfalls due to lack of time and expertise to perpetually maintain them. When a chargemaster is found to be in excellent shape, many hospital executives fall into a trap, believing that the entire charge cycle is in the same shape. It is typical for executives to conclude that the charge cycle is *also in great shape*.

As reported in an executive summary to a large hospital system, the following quote was given to the V.P. of Finance stating that the chargemaster is "as clean as a hound's tooth." The use of the chargemaster needed to be revamped. Quoted below is a section of the Executive Summary, as submitted by MedCom Solutions to a large urban hospital, which underscores the need to insure proper usage and expert maintenance of the chargemaster.

"…the Charge Cycle Review ascertained that the charge-master required few coding improvements. Although the validity of the chargemaster codes appears to be fairly up-to-date, the hospital staff's comprehension of charging for services, and the relationship to the intricacies of the chargemaster, were limited and weak. It appears that the staff's knowledge of OPPS fundamentals such as 'N' status codes, usage of Supervision & Interpretation codes, use of the ER modifier – 25 and Pharmacy conversion factors were not well understood. Consequently, revenues are not being accurately charged and billed. Maintenance of

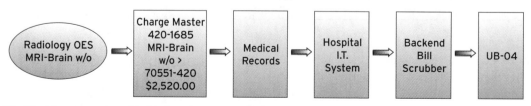

Figure 10-13 Diagram Hospital Charge Entry Cycle

the hospital chargemaster and charging systems requires more healthcare business expertise than what is currently available by clinical and financial staff. Continued and perpetual staff education is crucial when trying to determine the appropriateness of regulatory coding changes, information systems, accounting features, and uniform application of pricing.

Education and availability of regulatory resources would greatly assist the staff in understanding their current limitations, as well as improve their coding and charging knowledge. Providing the departments with the necessary resources is required if they are to be responsible for understanding and maintaining the structure of their chargemaster and associated systems."[13]

Even when a chargemaster is correctly coded, priced, and populated for proper usage, timely updates to not only the chargemaster but to the OES, flag settings, modifiers, and explode codes are key to providing accurate, fully dressed bills to the payers. Many healthcare organizations fail to realize the multimillion dollar loss associated with allowing a ragged charging mechanism to exist. A good chargemaster may create a false sense of security when viewed as the only charge cycle component.

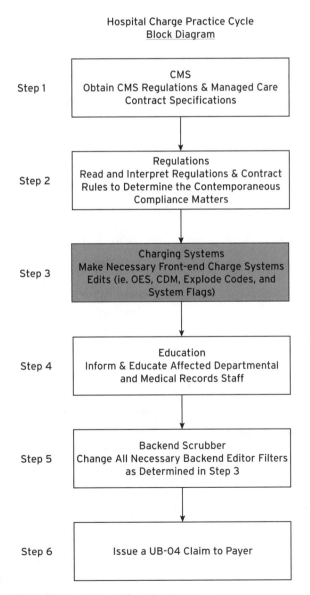

Figure 10-14 Diagram Hospital Charge Practice Cycle

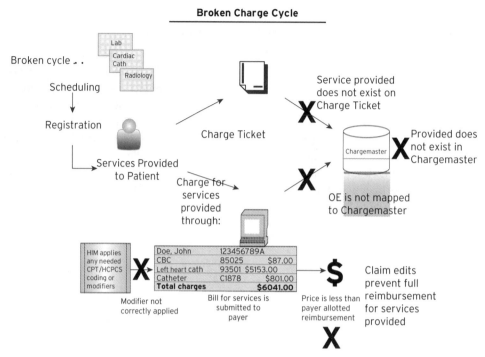

Figure 10-15 Broken Charge Cycle

WHAT HAPPENS WHEN CHARGE CYCLE GOES WRONG. When the charge cycle goes awry an unfortunate sequence of events can begin, resulting in these possibilities:

- Bill denials
- Bill returns to provider
- Reimbursement shortfalls
- Reimbursement overpayments
- Compliance issues
- Payers refuse to pay

More often than not, experience indicates that hospitals understate the patient charges by directly omitting charges or erroneously charging for services with incorrect codes or prices. There are two avenues for this to occur:

First: The chargemaster is not correctly populated, coded, or mapped to the OES or not properly priced.

Second: Use of the chargemaster is poorly understood by any of the following staff members:

- Charge entry staff
- Order entry staff
- Hospital Information System (HIS) staff
- Coding staff
- Chargemaster coordinators

ROUTINE SUPPLY CHARGES. Charging for routine supplies creates problems for the claim submission process because these claims require manual intervention from the payer in order to justify the charges. Reporting routine supplies also has the potential to trigger audits, questions, and complaints from the payers regarding why the charges are being submitted. Alternatively, Medicare typically only recognizes one combined charge per day for routine supplies and services. For example, at a 300-bed hospital, an estimated $1.6 million in routine supply gross dollars is subject to removal; however, the net revenue reduction should be minimal. Typically, if routine supplies are being charged on individual line items, it is advised to consolidate these into one-charge-per-day groupings similar to the standard room and board charge.

CHARGE OMISSIONS. In many hospitals, patient financial services (PFS) reports concerns regarding the high frequency of missed charges.

There are a variety of procedures performed in diagnostic, radiology, interventional, CAT scan, and ultrasound departments that require component charging and coding on charges submitted for payment. When these procedures

Table 10-9 B Status

- CPT 72198 has a status indicator of B and remains eligible for Medicare billing but absent of any payment.
- The OCE editor depicts that the hospital is not reimbursed when this code is submitted.
- The code is a *valid CPT code*, but Medicare has created three more specific HCPCS codes that should be used to report the service and obtain reimbursement.
- When updated CPT codes are not disseminated and users are not educated regarding charging protocol the provider either does not know about the update or does not know how to charge for the items. The bottom line is that the provider will not be paid for the service provided.
- Reimbursement for these codes per Medicare is as follows:

Possible HCPCS Codes	Medicare Payment
C8918	$386.64
C8919	$359.85
C8920	$522.54

are performed there are 70000 series CPT codes that describe the corresponding radiology supervision and interpretation of the service that must be submitted with the procedure CPT. In addition to the 70000 series CPT codes, there are numerous surgical procedures in the CPT range from 10000 through 69999 that may also be charged. For example, when a lumbar myelogram is performed, the staff should charge CPT 72265 for the supervision and interpretation and 62284 for the injection procedure. When either of these codes is missing from the charging practice due to either an omission or lack of charging experience, the hospital is ultimately underpaid for the procedure.

COMPONENT CHARGING. Many cardiac catheterization and electrophysiology charges require an extensive knowledge of component charging and coding. This charging practice is similar to interventional radiology codes. In fact, cardiology uses some of the same codes and methodologies within their chargemaster. Understanding each component of the charge can be difficult.

There are regulations authored by Medicare that compound the coding and charging confusion. Unfortunately, the code that was previously used continues to exist as a status "B" code and may be charged. Medicare may allow the charge to pass without removal but will not reimburse for that "B" status code, as illustrated in **Table 10-9**:

PHARMACY CONVERSION. In order to receive proper reimbursement from the payers, certain drugs that have J codes must be billed with two components: the appropriate HCPCS code and the appropriate number of units administered. With regulations, dosing, and drugs changing rapidly, the pharmacy staff may not completely understand the conversion process. When the conversion factors are not appropriately positioned in the pharmacy's OES it is unlikely that any manual effort is situated to correct the conversion factors prior to dropping to the patient bill. Furthermore, the financial implication for failing to appropriately charge the correct volume is typically very high.

CHARGEMASTER AND ORDER ENTRY UPDATING. One of the most commonly cited problems that occurs within hospitals and physicians' practices is the complaint about the length of time it takes to have an add, edit, or delete implemented into the chargemaster and/or OES. When these time frames exceed five to seven days, many charging staff pass the charge through as a miscellaneous charge. Consequently, this can result in improper coding and pricing.

EXCELLENT CHARGING PRACTICES—RETURN ON INVESTMENT. Lower Compliance Risk. When systems fail to properly engage with one another at the most basic one-to-one mapping arrangements, possible exposure includes the federal False Claims Act (FCA) and its application in health care in the United States. The primary function of the FCA is to prohibit hospitals and physicians from submitting a fraudulent claim for payment from the federal government. Under 31 U.S.C. 3729(a), the liability is for the submission of the claim itself regardless of the dollar amounts. This position dates back to governmental contracts during the Civil War era. It is designed to preclude the actual act of presenting a bill of service that includes fraudulent charges.

It is incumbent upon the management of a hospital to assure that its Medicare charging practices are compliant. This includes all the processes as illustrated in Figure 10-14 of the Charge Cycle. The ongoing cost of remaining compliant is expensive, as it typically includes expertise to conduct reviews and examinations, technology, and staff education and updating under a systematic approach.

One of the criteria of an FCA claim is to determine if the entity submitting the claim is acting with reckless disregard. This includes "acting in deliberate ignorance of the truth…" Consequently, maintenance and auditing of OES to chargemaster mappings and the same efforts toward explode codes signal that the hospital is *not* acting in deliberate ignorance.

Enriched Reimbursement. Although Medicare has established an ongoing predominance of regulations for charging of healthcare services, other payers need to be correctly charged to maintain full reimbursement. Monitoring and systematically, routinely examining the charging practices for accuracy, completeness, and necessity in most cases provides for a positive impact on all payments. For instance, Medicare has a propensity to change the billing rules, such as for infusion charges. An emergency room charge ticket that had not been updated since 2000 (and has provided nearly 9,000 Medicare IV infusions under CPT C8950, which paid approximately $121.00 via the ambulatory payment classification) amounted to a loss in reimbursement of $1,085,000.

10-8 Bill (or Other Document) Creation

Once the visit is over, the goal is to send a bill or claim form out as quickly as possible. It is important that the billing system has a "fully dressed" bill (i.e., one that includes all the elements). These include:

- Demographic information
- Payer (and guarantor—usually the patient)
- Medical record number
- Caregivers
- Site of service
- Type of visit (accident or illness)
- Primary or secondary payer
- Coding

Almost all third-party payers (i.e., insurance companies) utilize the standard CMS claim forms (UB-04 for hospital,

Exhibit 1, and HCFA1500 for physician, Exhibit 2), but some deviate from the CMS standards as to which boxes are filled in and may require different codes. Therefore, it is essential for the billing system to recognize the requirements of each payer.

Medicare is divided into several parts; the best known are Medicare Part A (generally hospital) and Medicare Part B (generally physician and certain other medical services). Private payers generally divide their coverage similarly.

Often, especially with Medicare beneficiaries, there is a second payer that needs to receive a claim. With Medicare, the secondary coverage is sometimes referred to as Medigap, and is provided through private insurance. By law, Medigap is categorized into groups of coverage so beneficiaries can comparison shop. The other type of secondary coverage usually occurs when there are two employers involved in a family. One of these payers will be primary, and the second will pay all or part of the remainder. When a Medicare beneficiary is employed and has employer-sponsored insurance, Medicare will be secondary.

Generally, a claim is a type of bill sent to a third party for payment. A bill is the document sent to the guarantor. A statement is sent to the guarantor to show payments received and amounts due.

There are a number of automated controls to help get the claim billed and paid properly:

- Backend editors identify errors on the bill. They range in level of complexity, but they can only identify errors from items on the claim that do not match. For example, a male with a pregnancy would be rejected. Some of the parameters on these editors are manually set—for example, numbers of a procedure allowed on a particular visit. Care must be taken to set these correctly, or over- and under-payments can occur.

- Contract management systems predict the payment amount from any payer. Well-written contracts with payers are highly predictable, so algorithms can be built to set up the expected receivable. This is valuable in that underpayments do not have to be manually identified, cash flow is more predictable, and the accounting system can reflect the actual accounts receivable.

- Accounting interfaces tie the billing system with the accounting (general ledger) system. These interfaces assure that manual errors do not occur when transferring information. The billing systems are not usually from the same vendor as the general ledger system, although there are some systems that are, especially some designed as integrated practice management systems for physicians' offices.

> Although contract management systems are a valuable tool to identify remittance discrepancies, they are of little value unless great care is taken to develop the algorithms used in calculating every type of payment from every insurer. This requires a great deal of time at the implementation of the contract management system, which must be updated with every payer contract renewal. If the system is used for government payers, it must also be updated for changes in Medicare and Medicaid regulatory publications.

In practice, most claims are not submitted to payers on paper. Hospital and physician claims are usually submitted through the Electronic Data Interchange (EDI), using what is known as the 837 file. Many providers use outside vendors to convert their data into the correct electronic format. Similarly, remittances are often electronic transfers, and electronic remittance advices use an 835 file.

10-9 Payment Receipt

From a business standpoint, prompt receipt of payment is essential. Electronic receipt is ideal because it provides the cash with immediate credit to the provider's account, and because there is an excellent audit trail. All other cash, wherever possible, should be sent to lockboxes, which, to the payer, appear to be post office boxes. Actually, this money is accessed directly by the bank and is credited to the provider's account the day of receipt, and documentation is sent to the provider. Checks, even credit card payments, sent through the mail present greater risk of loss within the provider's environs, are credited more slowly, and are often more difficult to trace to the payer. Of course, there is also greater risk of theft. Employees who receive payments through the mail or through a cashier should *never* have access to patient accounts.

Where possible, the 835 file should be used for electronic posting. This minimizes the likelihood of errors. All other receipts should be posted to patient accounts as soon as possible, since delays could lead to unnecessary bills or statements. Accuracy of posting is essential.

The contract management system will identify variances in expected payments versus posted payments. These differences can be the result of errors by the payer, posting errors, or partial denials, and should be looked into quickly to assure accounts receivable integrity.

> Contract management systems do a great job of identifying payment discrepancies, but providers should make sure that the error is with the payer, not the algorithm set up for the payer.

It is advantageous for providers to identify denials promptly. Some denials are passive; the payer does nothing because the claim requirements allegedly are not met. These will be discovered through an aged accounts receivable. There should be a policy (and process) in place to review all unpaid claims older than a set number of days. Third-party payers should be contacted and asked for causes. Other denials will be in writing from the payers, often with a "denial code." Larger providers utilize automated systems integrated with their billing systems to identify denied claims. All denials should be investigated and corrected. In addition to correcting the individual claims, it is important to identify the cause of the error. This might involve correcting a system error, or possibly educating a staff member or physician.

> Great care should be exercised in identifying denials and appealing or correcting them as quickly as possible. Staff "working" denials should be given adequate training, but of equal importance, tools to appeal or correct the changes easily and quickly. Some providers have systems interfaced with their billing systems to make identification and correction of denials easy.

Overpayments cause "credit balances" in accounts receivable. They are usually caused by posting errors but can also be duplicate payments or overpayments. It is important to identify and correct these quickly because time makes them more difficult to trace. Most states require, after a prescribed period, return of credit balances to the payer or, if the payer cannot be found, to the state. As a result, unresolved credit balances that are posting errors result in lost revenue, since the patient or payer is unlikely to remit a second payment for the same service.

Sound billing and statement practices will help resolve posting error credit balances, since the patient will often bring balance due errors to the attention of the provider.

Sometimes what appear to be underpayments are actually the result of "silent PPOs" (preferred provider organizations). Providers negotiate payer contracts with the understanding that there is some form of steerage to the provider. This could be lower deductibles or some other incentive. If a payer shares (sells) its rates with groups that have no steerage, the insurer of a patient who appears to be a noncontracting (full pay) carrier actually receives what could be a significant discount. It is important for providers to negotiate contracts that prevent this from happening.

Sometimes the provider is unable to identify which patient, or visit within a patient account, should be credited with a payment. When this happens, the patient or payer will continue to be billed for the services. This sometimes results in collection efforts, even to the point of turning the patient's account over to an outside collection firm. For this reason, providers should have a system of filing and tracking these payments and should respond quickly to patient inquiries. Some providers keep databases to sort receipts by date, amount, and other information, such as check numbers, when available.

In most hospitals and physician practices, it is worthwhile to get an independent review of closed accounts that appear to be paid correctly. This can be done through an independent internal group (such as internal auditing) or an external consulting firm. Either way, the reviewers need to have an extensive knowledge of the payment environment, coding, and chart reading. Sometimes underpayments are small enough to fall under the allowance in patient accounting but are part of trends.

Cumulatively, this can amount to significant dollars. In other cases, there can be coding errors and other problems that would not be identified by the contract management software. In smaller hospitals or practices, the absence of contract management software makes this practice even more valuable. Generally, consulting firms in this realm work only on contingency, so there is no cash outlay if everything is correct.

10-10 Collection

When an account is paid slowly, or not at all, it is often necessary to take collection efforts. This usually begins with statements being sent to guarantors reminding them of the debt. Each statement should be a little stronger than the previous one. If the account remains outstanding, calls are made by office or hospital staff, reminding the guarantor of the debt and seeking resolution. Resolution can be immediate payment, a payment plan, or a settlement for less than the amount billed.

If resolution is not reached, accounts are usually referred to an outside agency. Some larger providers will have their employees mask themselves as an outside agency.

Both federal and state laws regulate what collectors can and cannot do. The Fair Debt Collection Practices Act (FDCPA) identifies illegal practices. For example, the Federal Trade Commission's website includes:

"Debt collectors may not harass, oppress, or abuse you or any third parties they contact. For example, they may not:

- use threats of violence or harm;

- publish a list of names of people who refuse to pay their debts (but they can give this information to the credit reporting companies);

- use obscene or profane language; or

- Repeatedly use the phone to annoy someone."[14]

The rules apply regardless of whether collection is conducted internally or externally. Hospitals and physician practices may have more lenient practices than other businesses. Many choose not to report people to credit agencies, and historically most not-for-profit hospitals have elected not to foreclose on homes.

> Controls should be in place to assure that the provider is using effective collection firms, and that the firms are turning all collections over to the provider. Hiring the firm with the lowest contingency rate is not always effective; the firm will put its efforts into those accounts that earn them the best income. Clients who give the firms very old accounts and low commissions should expect the firms to give them a low priority. The best way to evaluate performance is to look at the percentage of funds paid to the healthcare provider net of commission versus net value of accounts given to the firms. Care should be taken to assure the firms compared are given accounts similar in nature.

It is important for hospitals to have a policy on collection of bad debt, because Medicare will reimburse hospitals for its share (or a part of its share) if the hospital has written uniform collection practices for all patients. Each year, hospitals prepare a "cost report" for the CMS. This report gives great detail on where the hospitals incur costs and once were the basis for hospital payments by the CMS. Certain hospitals, such as "Critical Access Hospitals," are still paid based on cost. In addition to that, Medicare bad debt is included on the cost report and is paid to the hospitals according to current regulation.

Sometimes guarantors and patients are not the only collection problems faced by hospitals and physicians. In some cases it is the payers. Most states have "prompt payment" laws that require insurance companies to pay within a stated period of time. However, there are controls that providers must still have in place.

Many of the prompt payment laws relate only to insurance. Therefore, if a payer is a third-party administrator (TPA), the law would not apply. In other cases, the agreement between the hospital and the payer could have priority over the law. In addition, these laws require payment on "clean claims," so insurance companies sometimes delay payment on that basis, often passively.

Therefore, contract language between providers and payers is important. TPAs sell their services to self-insured employers, often based on their discounts. Since there is a contract, payment terms should be negotiated as strongly as other terms.

Chapter Summary

Healthcare law involves many components of the revenue cycle. In order to understand revenue in the healthcare environment, it is important to understand the revenue cycle and the components of a "fully dressed" bill for healthcare services.

The largest medical insurer in the United States is the Center for Medicare and Medicaid Services (CMS). Private insurers usually follow the lead of the CMS. The CMS does not actually pay claims. There are various contractors, usually insurance companies, which receive and process the claims.

When a medical appointment is scheduled, there needs to be a determination if the service is covered. This can vary from payer to payer, and many payers require that the patient be given written notice if the payer will not cover the service.

Documentation of services is very important to the revenue cycle. If a charge is entered for a service that wasn't documented in the medical record, it can be interpreted as a "false claim."

Coding is also crucial to the revenue cycle. Medicare and most other payer insurers reimburse for patient services based on the coding that is submitted pursuant to the clinical care required for the patient. Therefore, applying the correct clinical codes, or CPT codes, is critical in terms of expecting to be fully reimbursed from the insurance company, including Medicare and Medicaid.

Software is an excellent solution to assure the CPT code is valid. Due to the accuracy of CPT codes as they exist in the chargemasters, many hospitals' management fall into a state of complacency that relieves the scrutiny that continuously should be placed upon the entire "charge cycle." Even when a chargemaster is correctly coded, priced, and populated, proper usage and timely updates to not only the chargemaster but to the OES, flag settings, modifiers, and explode codes are key to providing accurate, fully dressed bills to the payers.

Lastly, when it comes time for collection, it is important for hospitals to have a policy on collection of bad debt. Medicare will reimburse hospitals for its share (or a part of its share) if the hospital has written uniform collection practices for all patients.

Key Terms and Definitions

1500 - A *claim* form for professional services, such as those provided by a physician or someone under the supervision of a physician.

Advance Beneficiary Notice - Written advice to a patient that a service being recommended by a *provider* is not a service covered by the patient's insurance,

Medicare, Medicaid, or other payer. Often the term "medically unnecessary" is used, but that is a term of art, not a clinical determination.

Centers for Medicare & Medicaid Services (CMS) - The government agency responsible for setting rules for government patients, including payment methodologies, within the constraints of laws set by the executive and legislative branches.

Charge Cycle - The part of the *revenue cycle* that includes entry of charges and assurance that charge data is configured in a way that the billing system recognizes it, particularly as it interfaces with the *Charge Description Master (Chargemaster)*.

Charge Description Master (CDM) - The part of the billing system that lists the services being performed and the related unit charge (price). Similar to a "price list" in other businesses.

Claim - A request for payment submitted to a third-party payer (i.e., an insurance company, a government agency, or a company providing payment-processing services for a payer other than the insured person).

Codes, Coding - Numbers (or letters) assigned to services, supplies, and diagnoses used for identification and uniformity in billing and payment systems. Payments to *providers* are often determined by these codes. They can be determined by the federal government, state governments, and insurers; they are developed by specialized experts, such as 3M or the American Medical Association, and can be altered to meet the needs of various payers. Examples are DRGs (hospital inpatient codes based on diagnoses and procedures), CPTs (procedure codes), and ICD-9s (diagnoses).

Contractual Adjustment - The accounting adjustment recognizing the difference between charges (provider prices x volume) and expected payment through contractual agreement or government mandate.

Demographics - Nonclinical patient characteristics that allow a *provider* to complete billing information and assure that the correct insurer (or guarantor) is billed. Examples are insurance company, employer, patient address, and many others.

Explode Code - An order entry code that automatically generates more than one code for billing purposes.

Sometimes, a provider performs a service that consists of several pieces, such as certain laboratory tests. If the provider can bill separately for the individual services in the group, the "explode" makes it easier, and assures that all the services in the group are billed.

Gross Charges - Total amount billed.

Managed Care - Formerly, care and incentives intended to optimize the efficiency of patient care, leading to better outcomes and lower costs. In practice, any payment system evolving around negotiated prices between payers and providers.

Net Revenue - That portion of what is billed that can be expected to be converted to cash. Amount billed, less discounts contracted or legislated.

Order Entry System (OES) - Any method of communicating to the billing system that a service is being performed or that a supply is being used. Examples would be laboratory or radiology systems that interface to billing systems but can also include manual or paper-driven entry.

Prospective Reimbursement - Payment for services that is based on an amount that can be determined by diagnosis, as opposed to "fee for service." An example would be DRGs, which are diagnostic groups based on the patient medical problem, not the services and length of time to correct.

Provider - A hospital, physician, nursing home, home health service, or other party delivering care to a patient.

Revenue Cycle - The activity that leads to payment for services. It begins with the first encounter with the patient and includes collection of data, entry of charges, billing, and collection.

Site of Service (or Place of Service) - The location that a service is provided, such as hospital inpatient, hospital outpatient, emergency department, physician office, home, and many others. This is one of the determinants of payment amount and is indicated by a two-digit number on the *claim* form. In some cases, the site of service is defined by the facility, such as a physician's office that is part of a hospital or a hospital-owned property.

UB-04 - A *claim* form for services provided by a hospital or a *provider* acting as a hospital.

Instructor-Led Questions

1. When and from whom should demographic information be collected?

2. Who pays for healthcare services?

3. How is the amount paid for healthcare services determined?

4. What are the advantages of an Electronic Medical Record?

5. What is required for a claim to be paid?

6. What systems can be in place to optimize accurate payment of claims?

7. What is an "explode," and how does it affect the charge?

8. How do different types of caregiver orders get into the billing system?

9. Why is it important for the order entry systems to interface properly with the chargemaster?

10. If Medicare publishes a regulation to delete Cardiac Cath CT code 93510 and replaces it with 93527, what action should take place regarding:

    a. the chargemaster?

    b. the order entry system?

11. What two numbering systems are used to determine medical necessity for a patient?

12. Should a "system flag" be set to a maximum number of units of one when charging for:

    a. initial infusion services?

    b. subsequent infusion services?

    c. a knee implant?

    d. insertion of a pacemaker?

    e. sutures in the hand?

Endnotes

1   The term "payer" is used throughout this chapter to mean one of many types of financially responsible parties to the provider of healthcare services, including the following possible parties: Medicare, Medicaid, Blue Cross, United Healthcare, Aetna, Anthem, Champus, self-pay, or any other private insurer.

2   Current Procedural Terminology® (CPT®) is a 2010 copyright of the American Medical Association. All rights reserved. No fee schedules, basic units, relative values, or related listings are included in CPT. The AMA assumes no liability for the data contained herein. Applicable FARS/DFARS restrictions apply to government use. Federal Acquisition Regulation and Defense Federal Acquisition Regulation is codified in Title 18 of the United States Code of Federal Regulations containing standard contract clauses and solicitation provisions when dealing under a government contract.

3   In 2000, the Department of Health and Human Services designated the CPT code set as the national coding standard for physician and healthcare professional services and procedures under the Health Insurance Portability and Accountability Act (HIPAA), where all healthcare transactions that are sent electronically will use the CPT code set. The Current Procedural Terminology (CPT) first appeared in 1966.

4   The HCPCS, Health Care Procedure Coding System, is a standardized alphanumeric code set used to identify products, supplies, and services not included in the CPT coding, such as durable medical equipment, drugs, prosthetics, dental and orthotics. See C.F.R. 162.10002.

5   The Outpatient Prospective Payment System (OPPS) was initiated by the CMS in 1999.

6   The National Uniform Billing Committee (NUBC) determines the data elements and design of the providers' patient billing formats—the UB-04 (or CMS 1450) and 1500 claim forms. The NUBC membership is comprised by representatives of CMS, Blue Cross/Blue Shield Association, the Health Insurance Association of America (HIAA), the American Hospital Association, the ASC X12N Task Group, the National Uniform Claim Committee, and individual hospitals, to name a few. Each year new billing forms are published on July 1st by the NUBC. The UB-04 claim form is to be submitted electronically using the institutional 837 V5010.

7   For charging purposes it is important to acknowledge the value of matching the descriptor used in the OES to the chargemaster, as this contextual match is essential to assuring that the service being ordered through the OES is the service being charged via the chargemaster. Each year these corresponding descriptors should be run through an audit process to insure they are reflective of one another.

8   See *CMS Provider Reimbursement Manual*, which mandates price uniformity for each service to maintain a consistent cost report factor of cost-to-charge ratio.

9   CPT is a registered trademark of the American Medical Association.

10 There are two schools of thought on the usage of explode codes within the charging system. One school of thought endorses the usage of explode mechanisms, while the other school of thought dismisses such usage. Point in fact is that most hospitals have inherited some form of explode codes used in either the CDM or an OES and are saddled with an obligation to maintain these structures.

11 Part A and Part B Medicare Administrative Contracting authority has 15 jurisdictions for handling claims processing.

12 Component codes are meant as an individual CPT code service such as Pelvic CT Scan.

13 MedCom Solutions consulting review of a Florida hospital's chargemaster in 2005.

14 http://www.ftc.gov/bcp/edu/pubs/consumer/credit/cre18.shtm

Chapter 11

Tort Liability

John E. Steiner, Jr., Esq.

Key Learning Objectives

By the end of this chapter, the reader will be able to:

- Provide an overview of various theories of torts.

- Understand key elements and defenses to tort cases.

- Learn, through numerous cases, how tort theories and defenses are applied by the courts.

- Appreciate attempts to address medical malpractice crises through tort reform proposals and programs.

Chapter Outline

11-1 What Must Be Proved to Establish Liability for Negligence?

11-2 What are Intentional Torts, and How Do They Differ From Negligence?

11-3 What are the Major Defenses to Liability for Suits for Torts?

11-4 What are the Strict Liability Rules for Product Liability?

11-5 Who is Responsible for Paying for Liability?

11-6 What Types of Insurance are Available?

11-7 What are Some of the Tort Reform Proposals to Deal With Periodic Malpractice Crises?

11-8 What are Some Examples of Tort Liability of Healthcare Providers?

Introduction

This chapter provides an overview of legal theories, called "torts," that apply in various healthcare settings. Torts subject people and organizations to civil liability versus criminal liability. A "tort," described in detail below, relates to what someone did not do correctly and, as a result, someone is harmed. So, examining various tort situations is primarily about determining who is at fault. The traditional issues in this area of healthcare law are:

- Liability for negligence
- Liability for intentional torts
- Major defenses to tort claims
- Types of insurance coverage
- Proposals for tort reform

A basic understanding of liability principles can help minimize claims, identify opportunities to improve patient care processes, and improve risk management programs.

Tort liability is imposed by the common law and some statutes for injuries caused by a breach of a duty. Tort liability is not based on contract. One area of torts involves "strict liability," where liability is imposed, regardless of fault.

This section addresses the following:

- 11-1. How Is Liability Established for Negligence?
- 11-2. What Are Intentional Torts, and How Do They Differ from Negligent Torts?
- 11-3. What Are the Major Defenses to Liability Suits for Torts?
- 11-4. What Are the Strict Liability Rules for Product Liability?
- 11-5. Who Is Responsible for Paying for Liability?
- 11-6. What Types of Insurance Are Available?
- 11-7. What Are Some Proposals or Programs to Deal with Periodic Malpractice Crises?
- 11-8. What Are Some Examples of the Tort Liability of Healthcare Providers?

11-1 How Is Liability Established for Negligence?

Negligence is the most common legal theory for imposing liability on healthcare providers. 🏴 Four elements are required to prove negligence:

(1) a duty, that is, what should have been done;

(2) breach of duty, which is a deviation from what should have been done;

(3) injury; and

(4) legal causation, which means that the injury is caused by a breach of a duty owed to the injured party. This also is referred to as "proximate" causation.

There is another aspect of negligence that courts rarely discuss and is worth remembering: Someone must be willing to make a claim. Healthcare providers who establish strong, positive patient relationships are less likely to be sued for negligence. If a healthcare worker observes or thinks that an incident has occurred, the risk manager for the organization should be promptly notified. Then, appropriate steps can be taken to address the incident.

This section discusses the following:

- 11-1.1. When Does a Healthcare Provider Have a Duty to an Individual?
- 11-1.2. What Is the Duty (Standard of Care), and How Is It Proved?
- 11-1.3. What Constitutes a Compensable Injury?
- 11-1.4. How Is Legal Causation Proved?
- 11-1.5. When Does the *Res Ipsa Loquitur* Exception Apply?

11-1.1 When Does a Healthcare Provider Have a Duty to an Individual?

The first element in a negligence suit is proof of a "duty." There are two aspects to consider; (i) a duty owed to the person harmed, and (ii) the scope of the duty, sometimes called the standard of care.

Generally, there is no common law duty for individuals to come to the rescue of others, absent some other responsibility.[1] For example, an individual is not legally obligated to come to the aid of a heart attack victim unless (1) the victim is the person's dependent; (2) the person contributed to the cause of the heart attack; (3) the person owns or operates the premises where the attack occurred; or (4) the person has a contractual obligation to come to the victim's aid, for example, by being on duty as a member of a public emergency care team.

Many of the tort principles presented below are "timeless." That is, the legal theories, legal procedures, and most outcomes of tort cases are well established. This is for a good reason: to ensure that our legal system provides a predictable process for redressing harm caused to individuals due to negligence. Under civil law, the common remedy for negligence is the payment of money by the one at fault to the injured party. Those payments are referred to generally as "damages." In short, the content presented here should be relevant for some time.

DUTIES TO PATIENTS. A duty of care is established when the patient is admitted (in an outpatient setting, the commonly used term is "registered") or when a patient-physician relationship is established. If a person is denied admission (or "registration"), there can be a question as to whether a duty was established. Also, recall that there may be questions as to whether a duty is established based on telephone calls or other interactions, some of which may seem informal. These issues are discussed earlier in this volume in Chapter 6 "Patients, Providers, and Duties of Care."

DUTIES TO NONPATIENTS. A few courts prohibit the imposition of liability on nonpatients for the effects of a patient's diagnosis and treatment plan. For example, the Texas Supreme Court held that a physician did not owe a duty to third parties who were not in a physician-patient relationship, based on alleged failure to properly diagnose and treat a patient.[2]

Injuries by Patients. Several courts have considered whether healthcare providers should be liable to nonpatients injured by a patient.

Plaintiffs injured in car accidents that were caused by patients taking prescription drugs have successfully sued. In 2002, the West Virginia Supreme Court permitted a lawsuit where a patient was negligently prescribed controlled substances and caused a car accident.[3] An Oregon appellate court found liability when a drug, Xanax, was negligently prescribed. The patient was under the influence of the drug when driving and had an accident that killed two children.[4] The Indiana Supreme Court examined a case where a physician failed to monitor a patient's condition. The court found the physician liable for the resulting death of a third person.[5] In that case, the patient had a fatal automobile accident after receiving an immunization and experiencing a fainting spell in his physician's office. By contrast, the Pennsylvania Supreme Court decided that an ophthalmologist could not be held liable for a car accident fatality caused by his patient.[6]

Suits against psychiatrists have been brought by the estates of persons murdered by their patients. Liability has been imposed for failure to warn when a patient makes a credible threat. Liability sometimes is imposed for failure to take steps to detain mental patients. Typically, liability is not imposed for alleged malpractice in managing a patient's treatment plan.[7]

Injuries to Persons Observing Patient Care. There have been suits that seek damages when those observing treatment faint, fall, or are injured in other ways. Courts have uniformly decided that no such duty exists. Courts realize that providers should focus their attention on the patient. Otherwise, liability exposure would force providers to exclude observers.[8] The Illinois Supreme Court held that a hospital had no duty to a nonpatient bystander in the emergency room, unless the person was invited to participate in the treatment.[9] In 2003, the Connecticut Supreme Court agreed, finding no duty to prevent an observer from fainting.[10]

Parents Accused of Abuse. Parents accused of abuse have sued, based on reports provided by healthcare providers. Child abuse reports generally are granted statutory immunity. Most courts find that healthcare providers caring for children owe no duty to their parents. In 2000, the Pennsylvania Supreme Court adopted this rule.[11] However, some states prioritize prevention of child abuse and parental rights differently. In 2004, a Florida court permitted a psychologist to be sued for negligent interference with parental rights.[12]

Spread of Contagious Disease from Patient. Courts have addressed when providers can be liable to persons who receive contagious diseases from patients. Generally, the only duty to the public at large is to make required reports to public health authorities. Sometimes, there is a duty to a nonpatient who has a special relationship to the provider or the patient. Thus, there is generally a duty to advise the immediate caregivers, such as parents of minor patients who live in their home. In some states, this duty is further circumscribed by special confidentiality laws for some diseases, such as HIV/AIDS. In 2003, the highest court of New York applied these principles to conclude that no duty of care was owed to the friend of a patient treated for infectious meningitis; there was no liability when she contracted the disease.[13]

11-1.2 What Is the Duty (Standard of Care), and How Is It Proved?

When a duty is established, the scope of the duty must be determined. This step is sometimes called the obligation to conform to the standard of care. The standard of care for healthcare institutions is usually the degree of reasonable care the patient's known or apparent condition requires. Some states extend the standard to include the reasonable care required for conditions the institution should have discovered through the exercise of reasonable care. The standard for individual healthcare professionals usually is what a reasonably prudent healthcare professional engaged in a similar practice would have done under similar circumstances. A judge or jury will make the determination based on one or more of the following: (1) expert testimony, (2) common sense, or (3) written standards.

Establishing the "standard of care" in a given case helps both parties plan their case and anticipate the likely cost of litigation and/or settlement. Thus, the standard of care is one of the elements that should be carefully examined.

EXPERT TESTIMONY. The technical aspects of care must be proved through expert testimony, usually by other health professionals. When expert testimony is required and the plaintiff has no expert, the case is dismissed.

Qualifications of Experts. As part of tort reform, some states have limited who may qualify to testify as an expert.[14] Expert qualifications usually focus on the credentials of the proposed expert, but may include scrutiny of a person's experience.

Scientific Basis for Testimony. In the 1993 case of *Daubert v. Merrell Dow Pharmaceuticals,* the U.S. Supreme Court established stricter standards concerning expert testimony in federal courts.[15] The Daubert standards focus on the quality of the scientific basis for the expert opinion.

> The Daubert standards apply to expert testimony about standard of care.[16]

Consequences of Testimony. Generally, experts are immune from civil liability for their testimony. However, several courts have ruled that expert witnesses may be sued by the persons who retained them when their performance of litigation services was allegedly deficient. In those states, witness immunity provides protection only from suits by the opposition or third parties.[17]

In addition to the effect on a professional's reputation, there are other potential consequences of questionable testimony. In some jurisdictions, physicians and other licensed professionals may be disciplined under licensing laws for false or misleading testimony.[18] In 2002, the North Carolina Medical Board revoked a surgeon's license based on his expert testimony. A court reinstated the license. On review, the Board suspended the surgeon's license for one year.[19]

Some professional societies also discipline members.[20]

Use of a Provider's Own Testimony. Sometimes, a healthcare provider's out-of-court statements can be used as an admission against the provider. Thus, care must be taken as to what is said or written after an incident.[21] In 2000, the Alaska

Supreme Court permitted the defendant's interrogatory answers to be used to establish the duty.[22]

This legal point can make it difficult for providers to apologize to patients for bad outcomes or to be candid about the cause of the outcome. Some states have laws that bar the use of apologies in malpractice cases. Colorado has a law that extends this protection so that an admission of fault cannot be used against the provider in a malpractice suit.[23]

COMMON SENSE. Nontechnical aspects of care can be proved by laypersons. Some courts permit juries to use their own knowledge and common sense when a duty is considered common knowledge. An Iowa court decided, in 1992, that protecting a disoriented patient from falling was a nontechnical aspect.[24] It is questionable whether this is still supportable in light of legal restrictions on use of restraints and the professional judgment that must be used in choosing between restraints and alternative fall prevention techniques. In 1992, a Texas court ruled that expert testimony was not required to establish negligence. In that case, a nurse was given duty assignments, even though evaluation forms disclosed her unsatisfactory performance, including sleeping on the job.[25] In 2001, a Minnesota court decided that it was common knowledge for a paramedic to know how to locate a home in response to an emergency call.[26]

However, courts are careful when applying this exception to the general reliance on expert testimony in malpractice cases. In 2001, a New Jersey court decided that reading patient slides was not a matter of common knowledge.[27]

WRITTEN STANDARDS. Some courts rely on written standards, such as licensure regulations, institutional rules, and accreditation standards to determine the standard of care. When written standards are permitted as proof, they are used in one of three ways:

(1) evidence the jury can consider in determining the standard of care, without supporting expert testimony;[28]

(2) evidence the jury can consider in determining the standard of care, if there also is expert testimony confirming that the published standard states the actual standard of care;[29] or

(3) presumptively, as the standard of care the jury must accept unless the defendant can prove otherwise.[30]

Statutes and Regulations. Statutes or governmental regulations can be used to establish the standard of care.

When a law requires an action in order to benefit other individuals or forbids an action in order to protect other individuals, a violation is generally considered negligence *per se*. An individual harmed by a violation need only prove that (1) the law is intended to benefit the class of persons of which the individual is a member, (2) the law was violated, (3) the injury is the type that the law was intended to prevent, and (4) the injury was caused by the violation. Some states limit defenses that can be used.[31]

A Maryland court found a hospital liable for injuries resulting from failure to comply with a hospital licensing regulation. The regulation required segregation of sterile and nonsterile needles.[32] A patient had a liver biopsy with a needle that was suspected to be nonsterile, which required immediate treatment to avoid an infection. That treatment step required postponement of other, necessary therapy. This was the type of patient and harm the regulation was designed to address. In 2001, a California court ruled that it was negligence *per se* to violate a state regulation. The regulation required reasonable efforts to assure that infants receive a blood test to detect the presence of neural tube defects.[33]

When a statute or regulation is intended to benefit the general public, a violation is generally not considered negligence *per se*; but the jury may consider the regulation in determining the standard of care. In 2001, a Florida court decided that violation of a statute requiring physicians to have clinical privileges in order to practice in a hospital was not negligence *per se*, because it was for the protection of the general public.[34]

Institutional Rules. Some courts allow institutional rules to be used to establish the standard of care. The highest court of New York ruled in 1975 that a hospital could be liable for injuries due to failure to raise the patient's bed rails. A hospital rule required bed rails to be raised for all patients over the age of fifty.[35] In 2001, a Florida court ruled that internal policies could be introduced into evidence, but were not conclusive on the standard of care.[36]

Some courts that allow policies to be used in this way also permit the defendant to prove unwritten exceptions. In 1994, the New Jersey Supreme Court ruled that the standard of care was established by a hospital policy providing that no patient should be left unattended on an emergency room stretcher with the side rails down. But the court allowed defense experts to explain that the policy would not be violated if the physician was satisfied that the patient was competent and capable of self-care.[37] Other courts do not permit institutional rules to be used for this purpose.

For example, in Wisconsin, internal procedures of private organizations do not set the standard of care for negligence cases. They are relevant only if it is shown that substantially all of the industry has comparable safety regulations.[38] Similarly, in Virginia a person cannot establish the standard of a duty owed by identifying private rules; evidence of internal policies is not admissible in evidence, either for or against a litigant, who is not a party to the rules.[39]

> In states that permit use of institutional rules to establish the standard of care, healthcare personnel need to understand and comply with applicable institutional rules.

Bear in mind that eliminating all institutional rules is not a viable solution. This is because failure to adopt necessary rules can be a violation of the standard of care. In Michigan, a hospital was found liable for an infection transmitted by a transplanted cornea. The hospital did not have a procedure to assure that the relevant medical records of the proposed donor were reviewed prior to the transplant.[40]

Accreditation Standards. Some states permit accreditation standards to be used to establish the standard of care for accredited hospitals. For example, a Texas court decided that standards of The Joint Commission (TJC) concerning anesthesia practice could be considered, but were not determinative.[41] As noted above, regarding institutional rules, some states do not permit privately developed standards to be used to establish the standard of care.

Reference Books. Most courts permit use of certain reference books to establish the standard of care, but only when expert testimony also establishes that material in the book is the standard of care. For example, in 2000, the highest court of New York applied this rule to the *Physicians' Desk Reference* (PDR), which describes uses of drugs.[42] That court's position may not be adopted by all courts. Some states may use the PDR as an independent standard of care and disregard expert evidence of actual practice.

In 2000, the Pennsylvania Supreme Court decided that treatises could be used only to help explain an expert's opinion. They are not an independent source of standards.[43]

Clinical Guidelines. Medical practice guidelines, practice parameters, clinical protocols, and other guidelines for clinical decision making introduce a new dimension to the role of written standards.[44] The goal is to comply with such guidelines and, thereby, preclude suits or show reliance on guidelines in defense of a suit. At least one medical society – sponsored insurer required compliance with guidelines by its insured physicians.[45] Others have developed guidelines for a variety of purposes,[46] including the promotion of more efficient practice.[47]

Physicians are concerned that guidelines are of varying quality and are sometimes contradictory, or may not be sufficiently sophisticated to deal with complex situations. Some studies indicate that guidelines help physicians avoid selecting traditional tests or treatments that are ineffective.[48] Efforts to stop the release of guidelines have generally been unsuccessful.[49]

TWO SCHOOLS OF THOUGHT. Proof of what should have been done in a specific case can become confused if there are two or more professionally accepted approaches. The respected minority or "two schools of thought" rule addresses this situation. If a healthcare professional follows the approach used by a respected minority of the profession, then the duty is to properly follow that approach. Liability cannot be based on a decision not to follow the majority approach.[50] Part of the informed consent process, discussed earlier in this volume in Chapter 7 "Decision Making Concerning Individuals," includes disclosure of alternative treatments. Therefore, a physician should disclose alternative treatment options to the patient, before pursuing a minority approach.

LOCALITY RULE. In the past, some courts limited the standard of care of healthcare institutions and professionals to the practice in the same or similar communities. Under this locality rule, experts testifying on the standard of care had to be from the same or similar communities. The rule was designed to avoid finding rural providers liable for not following the practices of urban medical centers. The rule sometimes made it difficult to obtain expert testimony. Many courts abandoned the rule, permitting any expert to testify when familiar with the relevant standard of care. The jury usually may consider the expert's degree of familiarity with the community in deciding what weight to give the testimony.

Several states, as part of tort reform efforts, enacted statutes that reinstate aspects of the locality rule, restricting which physicians can testify as experts.[51]

LEGALLY IMPOSED STANDARDS. Courts sometimes impose a more stringent legal standard, not previously recognized by the profession, when they find the professional standards to be deficient. For example, in 1974, the Washington Supreme Court established a legal standard that

glaucoma tests must be given to all ophthalmology patients, although the universal practice of ophthalmologists was to administer such tests only to patients over age forty and to patients with possible symptoms of glaucoma.[52] The court disregarded evidence that so few cases would be discovered that expanded testing would not be cost-effective. The court found an ophthalmologist liable for failing to administer the test to a patient under age forty with no symptoms of glaucoma. In the case of *Tarasoff v. Regents of the University of California,* a woman was killed by a psychiatric patient. In that 1976 case, the California Supreme Court found liability for the psychiatrist's failure to warn the woman that his patient had threatened to kill her, even though other psychiatrists would have acted in the same manner.[53]

The national standard of peer review of physicians in hospitals was changed by a 1973 California trial court decision.[54] A hospital was found liable for injuries resulting from treatment provided by an independent staff physician. That hospital did not use available information that would have alerted it to the surgeon's propensity to commit malpractice. The hospital met all of TJC's standards in effect at the time the patient was injured. But the court ruled that the hospital should have had a better system of keeping informed of available information and acting appropriately on that information.

BREACH OF DUTY. After the duty is proved, the second element that must be proved is the breach of a duty – that is, a deviation in some manner from the standard of care. Something was done that should not have been done, or something was not done that should have been done. There is not much law related to this element; it is a matter of proving what happened by following applicable rules of evidence. The legal issues relate to how specific acts or failures to act are assessed or gauged in light of the duty owed to an injured party.

11-1.3 What Constitutes a Compensable Injury?

The third element of the proof of negligence is injury. The person making the claim must demonstrate physical, financial, or emotional injury. In many malpractice cases, the existence of the injury usually is clear by the time of the suit, although there may be disagreement concerning the dollar value of the injury.

It is useful to remember an important concept referred to as "status quo ante." This concept means putting someone back into the situation he or she was before the injury.

In many tort cases, that is not feasible. Thus, money damages are a legal substitute, or surrogate, to help the plaintiff live life as if he or she were placed in the status *quo ante*.

One issue that remains controversial is when to allow claims that result only in negligently inflicted emotional injury.

NEGLIGENTLY INFLICTED EMOTIONAL INJURY. In limited situations, courts may allow suits based solely on negligently inflicted emotional injuries. Such injuries usually only are compensated when they accompany physical injuries. By contrast, *intentional* infliction of emotional injury is generally compensated without proof of physical injury. Also, negligently inflicted emotional injuries sometimes are compensable without accompanying physical injuries. For example, compensation is available in some states when a plaintiff was in the "zone of danger" created by the defendant's negligence – that is, when the plaintiff was actually exposed to risk of injury. A few states also compensate plaintiffs who witness injury to close relatives. A California court permitted a father to sue for his emotional injuries from being present in the delivery room when his wife died and from placing his hands on her body after her death and feeling the unborn child die.[55]

This issue has been presented in cases where persons have had possible exposure to HIV infection or have been erroneously told that they have HIV infection. They claim emotional injury without evidence of actual infection. Courts have reached different conclusions on whether there is a compensable injury.[56]

11-1.4 How Is Legal Causation Proved?

The fourth element is causation, also referred to as "proximate causation." The breach of duty must be proved to have legally caused the injury. For example, when a treatment is negligently administered (which is a breach of duty) a patient may subsequently die (which is an injury), but the person suing must still prove a substantial likelihood that the patient would have lived if the treatment had been administered properly. Causation is often the most difficult element to prove.[57]

An example is a Texas case where a nurse gave a patient solid food immediately after colon surgery (which is a breach of duty). Eight days later the ends of the sutured colon came apart (which is an injury).[58] Because of the time lag, the patient was not able to prove causation.

In 2001, an Illinois court addressed a case where nurses had not notified the surgeon of the patient's symptoms, which

breached their duty. However, the surgeon testified that he was aware of the patient's condition and would not have changed his diagnosis or treatment if contacted with the nurse's information. Thus, the nurse's breach of duty did not cause the patient's injuries.[59]

In many cases, causation can be proved without much difficulty. In an Iowa case a baby was born with Rh blood incompatibility.[60] An outdated reagent was used for blood tests for bilirubin, and the tests erroneously indicated a safe level. When the error was discovered, the high bilirubin level already had caused severe, permanent brain damage. The hospital and pathologists were liable because accurate tests would have led to timely therapy that might have prevented brain damage.

LOSS OF CHANCE. Some courts adopted a standard of causation called the "loss of chance of recovery," which makes it easier for plaintiffs to win suits.[61] Under this standard, the plaintiff shows that the breach of the standard led to a loss of chance of recovery or survival. The plaintiff doesn't have to show that the breach caused the injury. Initially, this standard of causation required a showing of a loss of chance of recovery/survival of greater than 50 percent.[62] However, some courts only require a showing of a loss of chance of recovery of less than 50 percent. The Iowa Supreme Court allowed a claim for loss of chance of survival based on a failure to resuscitate, even when the survival possibility with resuscitation was only 10 percent.[63] Other courts reject this approach, retaining the traditional proximate cause standard.[64] Virginia adopted a hybrid approach under which a showing of loss of a substantial possibility of survival is sufficient to create a jury question, but the jury must be instructed using the traditional proximate cause instruction.[65]

BREAKING THE CHAIN OF CAUSATION. Sometimes, subsequent providers' errors can break the chain of causation.[66] A New York case arose from the suicide of a patient after a transfer.[67] The referring hospital breached its duty by failing to note the patient's suicidal tendencies in the transfer documents sent with the patient. The referring hospital avoided liability because the receiving hospital did not look at the transfer documents until after the patient was discharged. Thus, the transferring hospital's breach had no impact on the outcome.

STANDARDS FOR SCIENTIFIC TESTIMONY ON CAUSATION. As mentioned in Expert Testimony in section 11-1.2, in 1993, the U.S. Supreme Court established a stricter standard for the admissibility of scientific testimony in federal courts.[68] The Daubert standards focus on the quality of the scientific basis for the expert opinion. That case had a major impact on expert testimony concerning causation. So-called "Daubert challenges" of expert witnesses makes it more difficult to pursue product liability suits claiming that products caused adverse consequences.[69]

Generally, the expert must point to reliable scientific evidence to support an opinion of causation. The observation that one event typically follows another is insufficient.[70]

11-1.5 When Does the *Res Ipsa Loquitur* Exception Apply?

One exception to the requirement that the four elements be proved is the doctrine of *res ipsa loquitur*, "the thing speaks for itself." The doctrine was created in an 1863 English case that arose from a barrel flying out of an upper story window and smashing a pedestrian.[71] When the pedestrian tried to sue the building owner, the owner claimed that the four elements had to be proved. The pedestrian could not find out what went wrong in the building, and the case would have been lost. The court ruled that there should be liability when someone has clearly done something wrong, and the court developed the *res ipsa loquitur* doctrine.

The doctrine applies when the following elements can be proved:

1. The accident is of a kind that does not happen without negligence,[72]

2. The apparent cause is in the exclusive control of the defendant,

3. The person suing could not have contributed to the difficulties,[73]

4. Evidence of the true cause is inaccessible to the person suing, and

5. The fact of injury is evident.

Courts applied this rule to two types of malpractice cases: (1) sponges and other foreign objects unintentionally left in the body,[74] and (2) injuries to parts of the body distant from the site of treatment, such as nerve damage to a hand during a hysterectomy.[75] Some courts extend the applicability of the rule to other types of malpractice cases.[76]

Liability is not automatic in these cases. Defendants are permitted to explain why an injury was not the result of negligence.[77] For example, a physician could establish absence of negligence by proving that the sponge was left in the body because the patient had to be closed on an emergency basis to save the patient's life and there was no

time for a sponge count. The evidence necessary to avoid liability varies among states. That is because of variations in how the burden of proof shifts to the defendant in *res ipsa loquitur* cases.

11-2 What Are Intentional Torts, and How Do They Differ from Negligent Torts?

Some actions are considered to be intentional torts. For intentional torts, all that needs to be proven is that the wrongful conduct occurred and that it caused injury. For some intentional torts, at least nominal damages are assumed from the occurrence of the action. There is no requirement that a standard of care be proven. There are privileges and other defenses to some intentional torts, but the burden of proving the applicability of these defenses usually belongs to the defendant. In some states, procedural requirements for malpractice cases do not apply to intentional tort cases.[78]

Intentional torts include assault and battery (11-2.1), defamation (11-2.2), false imprisonment (11-2.3), invasion of privacy (11-2.4), intentional infliction of emotional distress (11-2.5), malicious prosecution (11-2.6), and abuse of process (11-2.7).

11-2.1 Assault and Battery

An assault is an action that puts another person in apprehension of being touched in a manner that is offensive, insulting, provoking, or physically injurious without lawful authority or consent. No actual touching is required; the assault is the credible threat of being touched in this manner.

If actual touching occurs, then the action is called battery. Liability for assault and battery compensates persons for violations of their right to be free from nonconsensual invasions of their person. Assault or battery can occur when medical treatment is attempted or performed without consent or lawful authority.[79] Assault or battery can occur in other circumstances, such as during attempts to restrain patients without lawful authority.

11-2.2 Defamation

Defamation is wrongful injury to a person's reputation. Libel is written defamation, and slander is spoken defamation. The defamatory statement must be communicated to a third person; a statement is not defamatory if made only to the person impugned. A defamation claim can arise from inappropriate release of inaccurate medical information or from untruthful statements about other staff members.

The defenses to a defamation claim include truth and privilege. A true statement is not defamatory, even if it injures another's reputation. Some communications, although otherwise defamatory, are privileged because the law recognizes a higher duty to disclose the particular information to certain persons.

Courts recognize the importance of communications about a staff member's performance to appropriate supervisors and officials. Such communications are protected by a "qualified privilege" when made in good faith to persons who need to know. This protection means that liability will not be imposed for communications later proved to be false, if they were made without malice. Malice is usually found when the communication was made with knowledge of its falsity or with reckless disregard of whether it was false. An example of the qualified privilege is a 1988 New York appellate court decision in which a hospital official's statements to other officials concerning a physician were found to be privileged.[80] Another example is a 1991 Ohio case resulting from a nurse's statements at a nursing technician's predisciplinary hearing.[81] The communication must be made within appropriate channels because discussions with others will not be protected by the qualified privilege. As discussed in Chapter 5 "Medical Staff" earlier in this volume, many states have enacted broader statutory privileges or immunities for participants in some peer review activities. These statutes can provide protection from some defamation claims. Many states prohibit use of some peer review committee proceedings and reports in any civil suit, which in effect may make it impossible to pursue most defamation cases for statements made within the peer review process.[82]

In 2003, a Colorado court addressed a case in which a patient challenged a medical record entry stating that she was experiencing a mental health disorder. The court decided that entries in the medical record could be defamatory, but that there was a qualified privilege for medical record entries.[83]

11-2.3 False Imprisonment

False imprisonment is the unlawful restriction of a person's freedom. Holding persons against their will by physical restraint, barriers, or even threats of harm can constitute false imprisonment, if not legally justified. Claims of false imprisonment can arise from patients

who are being detained inappropriately or from patients who are challenging their commitment for being mentally ill.[84] Healthcare institutions generally have common law authority to detain patients who are disoriented.[85] All states have a legal procedure to obtain authorization to detain some categories of persons who are mentally ill, engage in substance abuse, or are infected with contagious diseases. When relying on these state statutes, care should be taken to follow the specified procedures. An Illinois appeals court ruled that a person could sue for false imprisonment when committed in violation of a time limit in state law.[86] When patients are oriented, competent, and not legally committed, staff should avoid detaining them unless authorized by institutional policy or by an institutional administrator. There are few situations in which institutions are justified in authorizing detention of such patients.

11-2.4 Invasion of Privacy

Claims for invasion of privacy can arise from unauthorized release of information concerning patients. Not all releases of information are intentional torts that violate the right of privacy. For example, in 1982, the Minnesota Supreme Court found that even though the patient had requested that information not be released, it was not an invasion of privacy to disclose orally that the patient had been discharged from the hospital. In addition, the hospital employee disclosed that the patient had given birth in response to a direct inquiry about the patient made about the time of her stay in the hospital.[87] Even when a disclosure is not an intentional tort, the disclosure can violate state or federal laws and regulations; generally providers should attempt to avoid release of discharge and birth information when the patient requests nondisclosure.

Sometimes, information such as a child abuse or contagious disease report is required to be disclosed by law. Such disclosures are not an invasion of privacy or a HIPAA violation because they are required or authorized by law.

11-2.5 Intentional Infliction of Emotional Distress

Intentional infliction of emotional distress is another intentional tort that includes outrageous conduct causing emotional trauma. This tort is easy to avoid by remembering to treat patients and their families in a civilized fashion. The following cases are illustrative.

In a 2001 North Carolina case, the court decided that a physician could be sued for distributing to other local doctors a list with names and addresses of plaintiffs, jurors, and witnesses who found a co-defendant physician liable in a malpractice case.[88] In a Tennessee case, a hospital staff member gave a woman the body of her newborn baby preserved in a jar of formaldehyde.[89] In an Ohio case, a physician sent repeated check-up reminders to a deceased patient's family, who had sued him for malpractice in her death.[90]

In an Illinois case, statements allegedly were made in a public area of a hospital accusing family members of trying to kill a patient when they were seeking to discontinue life support. The court concluded that this provided a basis for a jury to impose liability for intentional infliction of emotional distress.[91]

11-2.6 Malicious Prosecution

Some unjustifiable or harassing litigation constitutes an intentional tort called malicious prosecution.

A plaintiff alleging malicious prosecution must prove that (1) the other person filed a suit against the plaintiff, (2) the suit ended in favor of the plaintiff, (3) there was no probable cause for filing the suit, and (4) the other person filed the suit because of malice. It is rare for healthcare entities to be sued for malicious prosecution. It is unusual for malicious prosecution suits to be successful.[92]

A Michigan trial court permitted a jury to find Blue Cross liable for malicious prosecution of a provider. Blue Cross had reported to law enforcement officials that a dentist had filed claims for which he was not entitled to reimbursement. The dentist was acquitted when prosecuted, and he sued for malicious prosecution, claiming that Blue Cross knew that his billing was permitted. In 1995, an appellate court upheld the liability of Blue Cross, but in 1998, the Michigan Supreme Court reversed, finding that Blue Cross could not be liable.[93] The court found that private entities that had reported possible crimes to law enforcement could not be liable because the prosecution was initiated in the sole discretion of the prosecutor. The state police had conducted an independent investigation supporting probable cause to believe a crime had been committed.

After winning malpractice suits, some physicians sue the patient and/or the patient's attorney for malicious prosecution. Generally, public policy favors giving people an opportunity to present their case to the courts for redress of wrongs; the law protects them when they act in good faith upon reasonable grounds in commencing either a civil or a criminal suit. Few countersuits have been successful.[94]

11-2.7 Abuse of Process

Some other misuses of the legal system constitute intentional torts called abuse of process. A plaintiff alleging abuse of process must prove that (1) a legal process, for example, a notice of suit, subpoena, notice of deposition, or garnishment, was used against the plaintiff; (2) the use was primarily to accomplish a purpose for which it was not designed; and (3) the plaintiff was harmed by this misuse. Suits asserting abuse of process are rarely successful.[95]

11-3 What Are the Major Defenses to Liability Suits for Torts?

There are several possible defenses to liability suits for torts:

1. When a claim has been litigated, a second suit is usually barred by *res judicata* or collateral estoppel.

2. When a claim has been settled, usually a suit is barred by the release obtained in the settlement.

3. There are time limits within which most suits must be brought, and a suit that is too late is barred by the statute of limitations.

4. Some persons are granted immunity from some suits.

5. Persons can sign exculpatory contracts that grant contractual immunity, but usually these are not permitted in healthcare settings.

6. Persons can sign arbitration agreements, so that they cannot sue but use the arbitration process.

7. Conduct of the plaintiff sometimes can bar liability or reduce the amount of liability due to contributory negligence or comparative negligence.

8. In some states, there are damage caps that limit the amount of liability.

RES JUDICATA AND *COLLATERAL ESTOPPEL.* As discussed earlier in this volume in Chapter 1 "Introduction to the American Legal System," sometimes lawsuits are barred by the fact that they deal with matters that have been litigated before. For example, a Maryland court ruled that a physician's unsuccessful defamation suit against a hospital barred a new suit against nurses for the same conduct.[96]

RELEASE. Another defense is release. When a claim is settled, the claimant usually signs a release. When a release is signed, it usually bars a future suit based on the same incident. Sometimes, release of one defendant will release other defendants. A Maryland court ruled that releasing a pathologist released the hospital.[97] However, the North Dakota Supreme Court held that releasing a physician's employer from liability in a medical malpractice action did not also release the physician.[98]

Releases on behalf of minors are often later attacked by the minors.[99] Special attention needs to be focused on complying with state requirements to make such releases binding. In some states, it may be necessary to obtain court approval of a settlement on behalf of a minor.[100]

STATUTE OF LIMITATIONS. All states have laws, generally called statutes of limitations, which limit the time in which suits may be filed. Suits are barred after the time has expired. The time limit varies depending on the nature of the suit and applicable state law. States have different definitions of when the time starts, including (1) the time the incident occurs,[101] (2) the time the injury is discovered,[102] (3) the time the cause of the injury is or should have been discovered, and (4) the time the patient ceases receiving care from the negligent provider.[103]

The rules are complicated in many states. For example, in Florida, medical malpractice cases must be filed within two years from when the incident should have been discovered, but no more than four years after the incident. If there is fraudulent concealment or intentional misrepresentation by the provider that prevents discovery of the incident within the four years, the time is extended. The extension is two years from when the incident should have been discovered, but no more than seven years after the incident.[104] Other states extend the time if there is fraudulent concealment or intentional misrepresentation.[105]

The time limit can be quite long, especially for injuries to children. In many states, the time period for suits by minors does not start until they become adults.[106] Thus, suits arising out of care of newborns may be filed eighteen or more years later. Some states have special rules for minors that do not extend the period to adulthood but give minors more time than adults.[107]

IMMUNITY. Sovereign immunity, charitable immunity, and various statutory immunities are available in some situations.

Governmental hospitals are generally protected by sovereign immunity and cannot be sued unless the immunity is waived. Some state courts have ruled that only governmental functions, not proprietary functions, are protected by sovereign immunity. Most courts have ruled that governmental hospitals are governmental functions.[108]

There are federal and state laws, usually called tort claims acts, that partially waive sovereign immunity and permit claims against governmental entities, but only if certain procedures are followed. These laws typically place limits on the scope of liability.[109] If a governmental hospital purchases liability insurance or establishes a liability trust fund, some courts find that sovereign immunity is waived to the extent of the insurance or trust fund.[110] In some states, sovereign immunity also protects employees.[111]

As discussed in Chapter 1 "Introduction to the American Legal System," the common law doctrine of charitable immunity has been overruled by nearly all courts. However, a few states re-established some charitable immunity by statute.[112] Charitable immunity is generally waived to the extent of any liability insurance purchased by the hospital.[113]

Some states extend statutory immunity to other activities. Good Samaritan laws that protect some emergency services are an example. In a few states, these laws also protect physicians who provide some emergency care in hospitals.[114] Some courts are hostile to these immunities and interpret them very narrowly, even when applied to emergency medical service personnel.[115]

EXCULPATORY CONTRACT. An exculpatory contract is an agreement not to sue or an agreement to limit the amount of the suit. This is different from a release because it is signed before the care is provided. While some courts will enforce these agreements in other contexts,[116] they have consistently refused to enforce these contracts concerning healthcare services on the grounds that they are against public policy.[117] In 2000, the Wyoming Supreme Court enforced an exculpatory agreement concerning a sports medicine clinic. Recreational sports activities have been the area where most courts have enforced such agreements. Even though the plaintiff in that case joined the clinic on doctor's orders, the court saw it more as a recreational activity than as a healthcare service.[118]

ARBITRATION AGREEMENT. When there is a binding agreement to arbitrate a claim, the claim cannot be taken to court unless the right to arbitration is waived. The arbitration process specified in the agreement must be followed. Usually the dispute is submitted to one or more arbitrators who decide whether any payment should be made and, if so, how much. A valid arbitration decision has the same effect as a court judgment and can be enforced using the same procedures. Courts generally refuse to accept the case except for limited review of the completed arbitration process. Generally, courts can set aside arbitration decisions only for limited reasons, such as failure to follow proper procedures or bias of the arbitrator.[119]

Under the common law, agreements to arbitrate are not valid unless signed after the dispute arises; statutes were necessary to validate agreements to arbitrate future disputes. Several states enacted statutes authorizing binding agreements to arbitrate future malpractice disputes.[120] The laws differ on which healthcare providers are eligible to enter arbitration agreements. When the arbitration agreement does not satisfy the statutory requirements, it is not enforceable.[121]

There is a Federal Arbitration Act (FAA) that authorizes agreements to arbitrate future disputes concerning transactions that affect interstate commerce.[122] When the FAA applies it preempts state law so that arbitration agreements can be enforced, notwithstanding state common law or statutory restrictions. Courts have found exceptions to FAA preemption for some claims and some remedies.[123]

Some courts find healthcare arbitration agreements enforceable under the FAA. For example, the Alabama Supreme Court found that receipt of Medicare funds constituted interstate commerce so that an arbitration agreement in a nursing home admission agreement could be enforced.[124]

Some cases address who must sign the arbitration agreement. In 1985, a California appellate court ruled that an arbitration agreement in a group medical contract also applied to the spouse, children, and heirs of the employee.[125] In 2003, a Florida court enforced a nursing home arbitration agreement signed by a person with a power of attorney.[126]

In 1997, the California Supreme Court ruled that the party seeking arbitration in a medical malpractice case can waive the right to arbitration by undue delay in selection of arbitrators or by fraudulent conduct.[127]

Generally, arbitration only binds the parties to the arbitration and those who make claims through the parties. A California appellate court ruled that after a hospital successfully opposed being included in arbitration that the resolution of the arbitration involving the physician did not bar a separate suit against the hospital.[128]

Arbitration is favored by some healthcare providers and patients because it is faster and less costly than litigation. It is also less formal than litigation and avoids adverse publicity. Some oppose arbitration because they prefer to have their disputes decided by a jury and to follow formal, legal procedures. Some providers believe that arbitration improves their chances of avoiding any payment, whereas some patients believe they will receive larger payment awards from a jury. Nonetheless, arbitration can result in substantial payments by providers.[129]

CONTRIBUTORY NEGLIGENCE. Consider this question: To what extent should patients be accountable for their own conduct? Patients may express their desire to exercise autonomy by claiming a right to decide what risks they will take. When those risks materialize, they frequently seek to escape the consequences and place responsibility for resulting injuries and costs on someone else. In the past, courts tended to hold patients more accountable for their conduct. To some extent, courts have diluted patient accountability without also empowering providers to control patient behavior. The appropriate balance between patient and provider accountability remains in flux.

For years, in most states, if a patient did something wrong that contributed to his or her injury and did so to such a degree that the healthcare provider was not fully responsible for the damage, the patient was said to be contributorily negligent. This was a complete defense to a malpractice action. Examples of contributory negligence included the following:

1. The patient fails to follow clear orders and does not return for follow-up care,[130]

2. The patient fails to seek follow-up care when the patient knows of or suspects a problem,[131]

3. The patient walks on a broken leg,[132]

4. The patient gets out of bed and falls,[133]

5. The patient lights a cigarette in bed when unattended,[134]

6. The patient deliberately gives false information that leads to the wrong antidote being given for a drug overdose,[135] and

7. The patient refuses to take antibiotics during the hospital admission.[136]

The success of this defense depended on the patient's intelligence and degree of orientation. A patient who did not appear able to follow orders could not be relied on to do so, thus contributory negligence was not a successful defense against a claim by such a patient.[137]

Contributory negligence is a complete defense in a few states. However, in most states, it has been replaced with comparative negligence, discussed below, or is no longer a complete defense to a malpractice case. Instead, it only reduces the damages that can be awarded. The defendant is not responsible for the portion of the damages that result from the contributory negligence.[138]

COMPARATIVE NEGLIGENCE.

A majority of states abandoned the all-or-nothing contributory negligence rule. Instead, they apply comparative negligence, which means that the percentage of cause due to the patient's conduct is determined and the patient does not collect that percentage of the total amount of the injury award.[139]

Some states with comparative negligence retain a feature of the contributory negligence rule. That is, the patient cannot collect anything if the patient is determined to be responsible for 50 percent or more of the cause.[140]

Patients with mental illnesses may seek to be absolved from accountability. However, courts generally look at the nature of the mental illness and hold individuals accountable to the extent of their capacity.[141]

Other categories of patients may seek to avoid accountability. Most courts examine the extent of their capacity. However, a few courts have absolved some categories of patients from all responsibility, regardless of actual capacity. In 1994, the New Jersey Supreme Court ruled that aged and infirm patients cannot be allocated any responsibility for injuries that result from self-damaging conduct in healthcare institutions.[142]

Failure to follow instructions and failure to return for follow-up examinations are still frequently bases for assigning some of the fault to the patient.[143]

Most courts rule that a patient's actions prior to a provider's malpractice are not to be considered in apportioning responsibility.[144]

DAMAGE CAPS. Some states place statutory limits on the amount that can be awarded in all malpractice suits. Courts have disagreed on the constitutionality of such limits. In 1976, the Illinois Supreme Court declared damage caps to be a violation of the constitutional requirement of equal protection because it could find no rational justification for treating those injured by medical malpractice differently from those injured by other means.[145] In 1980, the Indiana Supreme Court declared damage caps to be constitutional because the need for a risk-spreading mechanism to assure the continued availability of health services provided a rational justification.[146] Generally, when there is a valid state cap on damages, it applies to most federal suits, including EMTALA suits[147] and federal Tort Claims Act suits.[148]

Many states have damage caps that only apply to governmental providers. Those caps are based on sovereign immunity or public policy concerning preservation of public funds. Such caps generally are found to be constitutional.[149]

11-4 What Are the Strict Liability Rules for Product Liability?

The major exception to the requirement that liability be based on fault occurs when liability is based on breach of implied warranties or on strict liability in tort. In this area of the law, liability based on contract and liability based on tort overlap. The implied warranties of merchantability and fitness for a particular use are based in contract theory. These warranties form the basis for finding liability without fault for many of the injuries caused by the use of goods and products. Normally, the seller is liable for the breach of the warranties, but in some situations persons who lease products to others have also been found liable.

Strict liability applies to injuries caused by the use of a product that is unreasonably dangerous to a consumer or user and that reaches the user without substantial change from the condition in which it was sold. Usually the manufacturer or seller of the product is liable. Strict liability in tort does not require a contractual relationship between the seller and the person injured to establish the liability of the seller. Some courts have extended strict liability to persons who furnish goods or products without a sale. Healthcare providers are generally considered to be providing services, not selling or furnishing products; healthcare providers have seldom been found liable for breach of warranties or strict liability. However, plaintiffs have made numerous efforts to convince courts to apply these principles to make it easier to establish liability. These efforts have arisen out of services involving blood transfusions (11-4.1), drugs (11-4.2), radiation (11-4.3), and medical devices (11-4.4).

11-4.1 Blood Transfusions

One known risk of a blood transfusion is the transmission of diseases such as serum hepatitis. In 1954, a New York court ruled that blood transfusions were a service, not a sale, so that hospital liability for diseases conveyed by blood could not be based on breach of warranties or strict liability.[150] However, courts in several other states began applying the product liability principles to blood transfusions.[151] Legislatures in many states enacted statutes intended to reverse these court decisions.[152] Some of the statutes provide that providing blood is a service, not a sale. Other statutes expressly forbid liability based on implied warranty or strict liability. These immunity statutes have been found constitutional.[153] Healthcare providers can still be liable for negligence in administering blood transfusions. Immunity statutes in some states also apply to some other services, such as tissue transplantation.

11-4.2 Drugs

Efforts to use implied warranties or strict liability to impose liability on hospitals for the administration of drugs usually are unsuccessful. For example, a Texas appellate court refused to apply product liability principles to the administration of a contaminated drug.[154] A Pennsylvania court ruled that a hospital was not a merchant when it dispensed a drug incidental to the service of healing, and it was not liable under implied warranties for an allergic reaction.[155]

11-4.3 Radiation

In 1980, the Illinois Supreme Court reversed a lower court's application of strict liability principles to x-ray treatment.[156] The court ruled that the issue in the case was the decision to use a certain dosage. The x-rays themselves were not a defective product; so strict liability in tort was not applicable.

11-4.4 Medical Devices

Most courts have not applied implied warranties or strict liability to hospitals for injuries due to medical devices.[157] For example, a California court ruled that the hospital was the user, not the supplier, of a surgical needle that broke during an operation.[158] Similarly, an Indiana court ruled that products liability law does not apply to a hospital where a pacemaker is implanted.[159] In 1998, a Washington court held that a hospital that furnished a spinal implant cannot be held liable for selling a defective product, concluding that the transaction was a provision of services, not a sale of goods.[160]

However, this position is not unanimous. In 1984, the Alabama Supreme Court ruled that a hospital was liable based on the implied warranty of fitness for intended use when a suturing needle broke and remained in a patient's body.[161] The court viewed the hospital as a merchant, not a user. Even when the healthcare provider is viewed as only a user, the provider still may be liable based on negligence, and the manufacturer of the equipment may be liable based on implied warranties or strict liability.

Some courts may not view certain items supplied by healthcare providers as integral to the provider's service. In 1981, a Texas court found that a hospital could be strictly liable for supplying a hospital gown that was not flame-retardant because it was not integrally related to supplying services.[162]

Some implied warranty and strict liability claims concerning medical devices are preempted by the federal medical device laws.[163] In 1996, the U.S. Supreme Court ruled that some claims were not preempted.[164] The exact contours of which claims are preempted are not entirely resolved.[165]

11-5 Who Is Responsible for Paying for Liability?

Liability can be divided into personal liability, liability for employees and agents, and institutional liability. Individual staff members are personally liable for consequences of their own acts. Employers can be liable for the consequences of the job-related acts of their employees or agents, even when the employer is not individually at fault. Institutions can be liable for consequences of breaches of their duties owed directly to patients and others. Those duties include the proper maintenance of buildings, grounds, and equipment, as well as proper selection and supervision of employees and medical staff.

This section addresses the following questions:

- 11-5.1. When Is an Employer Liable for the Acts of an Employee?

- 11-5.2. When Are Individuals Liable for Their Own Acts?

- 11-5.3. When Is There Liability for the Acts of an Agent?

- 11-5.4. When Is There Institutional Liability Independent of the Acts of Individuals?

- 11-5.5. When Is a Managed Care Organization Liable for the Acts of Providers?

When a judgment is entered, whoever is responsible for payment should either arrange to pay the award or take steps to prohibit collection of the award during any appeals. Otherwise, traditional means of collecting debts may be used. In 1989, an attorney who had won a $1.7 million malpractice award against a hospital, which had not been paid, arranged for police to seize computers, desks, and other hospital property not involved in direct patient care. After the property was loaded on trucks, the hospital promptly paid.[166]

11-5.1 When Is an Employer Liable for the Acts of an Employee?

RESPONDEAT SUPERIOR. Employers are liable for the consequences of their employees' activities within the course of employment for which the employees are responsible. This legal doctrine is called *respondeat superior*, which means "let the master answer." The employer need not have done anything wrong. For example, if a nurse employed by a hospital injures a patient by giving the wrong medication, the hospital can be liable, even if the nurse was properly selected, properly trained, and properly assigned the responsibility.

SCOPE OF EMPLOYMENT. Employers are liable under *respondeat superior* only for employees' actions taken within the scope of their employment. Courts differ on what acts are within the scope of employment. Many courts follow the rule that intentional torts are not within *respondeat superior*, unless an employee is acting in furtherance of the employer's business, no matter how misguided the employee's actions.[167] In 1993, a Georgia court ruled that a hospital was not liable for the lethal injection of five patients by a nurse employee because the nurse was pursuing her own interests.[168] In 1994, a federal court ruled that a physician employer was not liable for the disclosure of confidential medical information by a nurse and her daughter nurse assistant where they were not authorized to make the disclosure and did not make it on work time or space.[169] Courts disagree on when an employer is liable for sexual misconduct by employees.[170]

BORROWED SERVANT AND DUAL SERVANT. In some situations, healthcare providers may not be liable for the consequences of the negligent acts of nurses and other employees because of the borrowed servant doctrine. In some states, when an employer delegates its right to direct and control the activities of an employee to an independent staff physician who assumes responsibility, the employee becomes a borrowed servant. The physician, rather than the employer, is then liable under respondeat superior for the acts of the "borrowed servant" employee.[171] Courts in many states do not apply the doctrine when an employee continues to receive substantial direction from the hospital through its policies and rules. Thus, the trend appears to be toward abandoning the borrowed servant doctrine[172] or replacing it with a dual servant doctrine under which both the physician and the hospital are liable under *respondeat superior* for the acts of the employee.[173]

PHYSICIAN EMPLOYEES. Usually, hospitals and other healthcare institutions are not liable for the negligent acts of independent staff physicians.[174] When a physician is an employee of the hospital, the hospital can be liable under *respondeat superior* for the physician's acts.

Some courts consider an independent physician to be an employee. The criteria for finding an employment relationship focus on whether the hospital has a right to control the time, manner, and method of the physician's work.[175] Some courts require significant control in order to find an employment relationship. For example, a Georgia appellate court declined to conclude that an emergency room physician was a hospital employee despite scheduling, billing, and other control features of the agreement between the physician and the hospital.[176] The court focused on the contract provision that the hospital would exercise no control over the physician's methods of running the emergency room.

Other courts are more liberal in applying the criteria. For example, an Arizona court found a hospital to be the employer of a nonsalaried radiologist. The relevant facts in that case included the hospital's legal right to control the professional performance of medical staff members, exclusiveness of the contract, hospital's role as billing agent, and patient's lack of choice in selecting a radiologist.[177] The court declined to be bound by a statement in the hospital admission form, signed by the patient, acknowledging that the radiologist was an independent contractor and not a hospital employee.

11-5.2 When Are Individuals Liable for Their Own Acts?

Individual staff members are personally liable for consequences of their own acts. Individual liability is nearly always based on the principle of fault. To be liable, the person must have done something wrong or must have failed to do something he or she should have done.

The supervisor is not the employer. *Respondeat superior* does not impose liability on managers and supervisors.[178] Supervisors are liable only for the consequences of their own acts or omissions. The employer also can be liable for acts or omissions of supervisors under *respondeat superior*.

Employer liability is for the benefit of the injured person, not for the benefit of the employee. The employer does not have to provide the employee with liability protection. *Respondeat superior* permits the plaintiff to sue the employer, the employee, or both. If the employee is individually sued and found liable, the employee must pay. If, as often occurs, the employee is not individually sued, then the employer must pay. The employer may sue the employee to get the money back.[179] The repayment is called indemnification. As part of settlements, hospitals sometimes assign their right of indemnity against physicians or others to the plaintiff.[180] However, indemnification is seldom sought except from employees with substantial insurance.

11-5.3 When Is There Liability for the Acts of an Agent?

AGENCY. Hospitals and other healthcare institutions can be held liable for the consequences of their agents' acts in a fashion similar to their being held liable for their employees' acts. For example, a federal district court found a hospital liable for a radiologist's negligence in not promptly relaying to the treating physician the results of an x-ray examination.[181] The court ruled that prompt reporting was an administrative responsibility and that the physician was functioning as an agent of the hospital when relaying the report.

PARTNERSHIP/JOINT VENTURE. Partners are considered agents of each other, and partners are liable for the torts committed by other partners in carrying out partnership activities. A joint venture is a kind of partnership. Healthcare institutions are liable for actions of physicians within the scope of partnerships or joint ventures with those physicians. In 1987, a Florida appellate court expanded the definition of joint venture to include a hospital contract with an anesthesiologist, imposing liability on the hospital for the anesthesiologist's malpractice.[182]

Some healthcare providers refer to themselves as partners in advertising when they are not really partners. Some lawyers advise against this terminology in order to remove this as a basis for courts to misinterpret the relationship. When this was litigated in Connecticut, in 2001, an appellate court ruled that use of the term partner in advertising did not create a partnership.[183]

APPARENT OR OSTENSIBLE AGENCY. Some courts refuse to examine the details of the hospital-physician relationship. Instead, they consider how the relationship appears to patients. If the hospital appears to be offering physician services, the physician is considered a hospital agent under the doctrine of apparent or ostensible agency. For example, the Michigan Supreme Court found a physician to be the hospital's ostensible agent because the patient did not have a patient-physician relationship with the physician independent of the hospital setting.[184] The physician, who was a member of the medical staff, assisted in the patient's treatment. The court ruled that there was sufficient evidence that the hospital appeared to provide the physician for the patient. The court noted there was no evidence the patient received any notice that the physician was an independent contractor. Thus, hospitals may find it helpful to give patients notice.[185] However, even signed acknowledgments may not be sufficient in some states.[186]

Some states limit the scope of the doctrine by requiring that the plaintiff prove actual reliance on the apparent agency, before imposing liability on the institution. In 2000, an Illinois court ruled there was no reliance when the patient went to the hospital on his private physician's orders.[187]

Some hospitals address their liability exposure for physicians' actions by including in physician contracts indemnity or "hold harmless" clauses in which the physician agrees to indemnify the hospital for such losses. These clauses do not bar patients from collecting from the hospital, but they provide a basis for seeking reimbursement from physicians and their insurers.

A few hospitals have statutory immunity from liability for the acts of physicians, and liability based on apparent agency cannot be imposed.[188]

11-5.4 When Is There Institutional Liability Independent of the Acts of Individuals?

Institutions can be liable for the consequences of breaches of duties owed directly to the patient.[189] Two examples of these duties – the maintenance of buildings and grounds and the selection and maintenance of equipment – are discussed below. Proper selection and supervision of employees is a third duty, discussed in Chapter 4 "Individual Providers and Caregivers" earlier in this volume. Proper selection and monitoring of medical staff are increasingly being recognized as institutional duties and are discussed in Chapter 5 "Medical Staff."

In 1978, a Washington appellate court imposed institutional liability on a hospital for treatment provided in an emergency room by an independent professional corporation. The court determined that the emergency services were an inherent function of the hospital's overall enterprise. As such, the hospital had some responsibility.[190] Similarly, in 2000, the South Carolina Supreme Court held that a hospital has a nondelegable duty to provide competent emergency room services and may be liable for negligent actions of emergency room physicians. This was the court's view, even though the admissions form stated that emergency room physicians were independent contractors, not employees.[191] In 2003, Alaska refused to extend the scope of nondelegable duties to the operating room.[192] In 2003, an Ohio appellate court refused to apply corporate liability for having a medical residency training program.[193]

OFF-PREMISES LIABILITY. Some patients seek to hold hospitals liable for the actions of medical staff members in their private practice off hospital premises. Nearly all courts have rejected these attempts.[194] One exception is a 1988 Massachusetts decision that allowed a hospital employee to sue the hospital for a rape by a medical staff member during a house call in his private practice.[195] The hospital was aware of prior complaints about the physician's sexual conduct, had given him a verbal warning, and had required a chaperon to be present when he visited female patients in the hospital. Apparently, the hospital's liability was based on the court's belief that it should have terminated the physician's privileges or taken other disciplinary measures that would have come to the employee's attention.

11-5.5 When Is a Managed Care Organization Liable for the Acts of Providers?

Courts are still struggling with the extent to which managed care entities should be liable for the consequences of errors of participating providers, for their selection of participating providers, and for their decisions not to authorize hospitalization or other treatment. Some employer-sponsored plans have sought to avoid all such liability by asserting ERISA preemption. Managed care entities have sought to avoid all responsibility for errors by participating providers who are not employees or apparent agents of the managed care entity.

11-6 What Types of Insurance Are Available?

OCCURRENCE/CLAIMS-MADE. In the past, most professional liability insurance was on an occurrence basis, which means that a policy purchased for a specific year covered all future claims arising out of incidents during the policy period. Since the 1970s, many professional liability insurance policies have been written on a claims-made basis, which means that a policy purchased for a specific year covers only the claims that are made during that year

that arise from incidents after a retroactive date specified in the policy. Thus, to have coverage for future claims, an additional policy needs to be purchased. This can be a renewal policy with a retroactive date covering incidents in the prior period, or it can be a reporting endorsement, often called a "tail" policy, which covers future claims arising from incidents during the period covered by the prior policy without covering any new incidents.

When providers elect not to buy tail coverage, before expiration of the old policy, they send the insurer a list of potential claims of which they are aware so that a "claim" will be made during the policy period. In 1992, the New Hampshire Supreme Court ruled that these were valid claims triggering coverage.[196] It was not necessary for the claims to come from the patient.

INSTITUTIONAL COVERAGE. Hospitals and other employers frequently provide insurance coverage for their employees. Usually this coverage does not apply to activities outside the scope of employment. Sometimes this coverage is required by statute. Sometimes it is the result of collective bargaining or individual contracts with employees. Sometimes it is a voluntary benefit provided by the employer.

Hospitals may offer malpractice coverage for nonemployee physicians. There have been questions about whether this is permitted by federal law. In some contexts, it is possible that providing free coverage might violate either the Stark Law or the Medicare Anti-Kickback Statute. An Advisory Opinion issued by the HHS Inspector General in 2004 approved a proposal to subsidize the malpractice insurance for four community obstetricians.[197] The analysis concluded that, if the necessary "intent" to induce referrals were present, the arrangement would potentially violate the Anti-Kickback Law. However, the Office of Inspector General did issue a favorable Advisory Opinion, based on the facts presented. The analysis depended in large part on the fact that the proposal almost fit into the safe harbor for subsidies of obstetrical malpractice coverage for those providing primary care in health professional shortage areas.[198]

JOINT UNDERWRITING ASSOCIATIONS. Some states have created agencies, sometimes called joint underwriting associations, which sell insurance coverage to providers, particularly when the commercial market does not offer coverage.

PUNITIVE DAMAGES. States disagree on whether punitive damages may be covered by insurance. Some states permit coverage, while others forbid coverage.[199] Some states permit coverage for some types of punitive damages, but not others. For example, in 2001, an Ohio appellate court ruled that insurance could not cover punitive damages that were awarded upon a finding of malicious, willful, or intentional conduct. But the insurance company had to pay statutory punitive damages for conduct not based on proof of those categories of conduct.[200]

11-7 What Are Some Proposals or Programs to Deal with Periodic Malpractice Crises?

The combined effect of numerous malpractice cases and associated costs of litigation has increased the cost of malpractice insurance and, in some areas, decreased the availability of malpractice insurance at any price. When malpractice protection is unavailable or too expensive, access to needed medical services is compromised.[201] Even when health care continues to be available, costs of our tort system often are passed on to patients and third-party payers. This is illustrated by a threat in 2004 by some Connecticut obstetricians to impose a $500 surcharge on all obstetrical cases. They did not implement the surcharge because payers increased their reimbursement rates.[202]

Periodic malpractice insurance crises led nearly every state to review and revise laws related to tort suits and/or malpractice coverage. States are confronted with difficult questions of what standard of health care is realistic and can be delivered, which events should be compensable, and how injury awards should be determined. Underlying these issues are many questions, including: How to deal with the understandable emotions of patients and families due to poor medical outcomes, regardless of cause? How to deal with continuing medical costs of persons who cannot regain access to the employment-based healthcare insurance system? How to maintain broad based access to healthcare services? How to make healthcare professions attractive career options? How to promote improvement in healthcare outcomes? Thus, the issues go beyond the direct insurance and cost issues.

Some changes have had an effect on the availability of insurance and its cost. However, in many states it is not clear whether those changes provide viable, long-term solutions. Sometimes, aggregate payments have dropped, but the payments remain substantial. The cause of the drops is difficult to assess. There is still substantial dispute concerning the indirect effect of tort liability on the cost of health care through defensive medicine and other practices.[203]

Tort reform efforts include:

(1) Changes in the standard of care (11-7.1);

(2) Changes in dispute resolution mechanisms (11-7.2);

(3) Changes in the amount of the award and how it is paid (11-7.3);

(4) Changes in the statute of limitations that sets the time in which the suit must be brought (11-7.4); and

(5) Other tort reform changes (11-7.5).

These reforms receive a mixed reception in the courts. Courts disagree on whether these reforms violate various state and federal constitutional provisions. When reforms are enacted to apply only to healthcare providers, often there is litigation over whether a particular type of provider is protected by the law.[204]

Some states attempt to address the issue through malpractice coverage reform (11-7.6). This includes state-sponsored coverage, facilitation of development of new private coverage, and mandated coverage as a condition of licensure.

Another fundamental problem of healthcare law is the degree to which the malpractice system disrupts the provision of health care and traumatizes healthcare providers. The discovery process in litigation can be extremely burdensome. It consumes a great deal of provider time in preparation and participation in depositions and other discovery, reducing time available to care for other patients and administer the institution. Courts seldom exercise any effective control over this process; court intervention is available to stop only the most abusive misuse of legal processes. Some plaintiffs' attorneys expressly threaten burdensome discovery in an effort to induce settlement.

The trauma experienced by healthcare providers is another significant issue. While some plaintiffs' attorneys are very professional in their approach, others seek to demonize defendants. In some cases, this may be in response to the demands and expectations of angry clients, but it also appears to be rewarded through large judgments. This is one of the reasons that some providers interested in exploring alternate systems that reduce the trauma experienced by providers.[205] Some observers argue that providers should experience such pressures in return for the trauma experienced by the patient.

11-7.1 Standard of Care

As discussed in section 11-1.2, the standard of care for healthcare institutions is usually the degree of reasonable care the patient's known or apparent condition requires. Some states extend the standard to include the reasonable care required for conditions the institution should have discovered through exercise of reasonable care. Usually, the standard for individual healthcare professionals is what a reasonably prudent healthcare professional engaged in a similar practice would have done under similar circumstances.

Most tort reforms focus on elements of the malpractice process, other than the standard of care. This is understandable because of the difficulty in articulating a different workable standard. However, part of the underlying problem with the tort system is the use of a standard of care that is ultimately unachievable and/or is a "moving target."

The ultimate risk of adopting an unachievable standard for purposes of tort law is that no one will be able to afford to provide the service, except for those who have immunity from liability. This is a theoretical risk for most areas of health care, but is a reality for obstetrical care in some regions.

There is potential for improving the quality of outcomes of healthcare services, but the malpractice system does not appear to be the best way to pursue it. Most providers are committed to processes for reducing errors. Unfortunately, the tort system usually impedes this process, rather than support it. It diverts time, resources, and attention from process improvement. It discourages open information flow that can identify and resolve issues, because that information flow may be used as a basis for imposing liability.[206]

How does the existing system work?

> In most cases, there are competing expert opinions concerning the standard of care, and the jury or judge attempts to evaluate the opinions and select among them.

The process allows a judge or jury to select as the applicable standard what a qualified expert is willing to testify is the standard. ⬛ If there is such testimony on the record, there is often little that appellate courts can do about aberrant findings, except to find a basis to disqualify the expert or find a procedural error that permits the ordering of a new trial. Legislatures and courts have tried to contain the misuse of the process by controlling who can testify and permitting professional licensing boards to discipline professionals whose testimony is aberrant.

Standards of care should recognize human limitations and reflect time pressures and communication issues associated with quality patient care. Standards also need to take into account the uncertainty of medical practice, which is an "art" not a "science," as the saying goes. Notwithstanding efforts to promote evidence-based medicine, the evidence does not exist for a large part of medical practice. Much of medicine is still based on experience and professional judgment. Complex and comprehensive medical literature reviews sometimes are relied on to establish the standard of care for a malpractice case. Those reviews draw upon a range of information that no individual can realistically be expected to master.

There are several ways that the applicable "standard of care" is addressed, directly or indirectly, by courts or legislators.

DESCRIPTION OF STANDARD. At least one court states that an error of judgment can be within the standard of practice and does not automatically constitute negligence.[207]

The two schools of thought doctrine discussed in section 11-1.2 can limit the jury's ability to select a standard stated by one expert when another expert says that what was done was within the standard.

LEVEL OF PROOF. One state requires the standard of care to be proven by clear and convincing evidence in some cases, rather than the preponderance of the evidence standard usually used in civil cases.[208] The practical effect of this difference is that it permits the trial judge or the appellate court more latitude to find that there was not sufficient evidence to support the jury's decision.

11-7.2 Dispute Resolution Mechanisms

Most malpractice claims are either settled or dropped. Litigation is very expensive, disruptive, and uncertain. However, even when cases are settled or dropped, the cost of the litigation to get the case to that point can be burdensome and traumatic.

In an effort to reduce the burden of litigation, alternate dispute resolution mechanisms have been adopted in some states. Screening panels have been adopted with limited success. Arbitration has been pursued.

SCREENING PANELS. Some states enacted laws that require all malpractice claims to be screened by a panel before a suit can be filed.[209] These screening panels were designed to promote settlement of meritorious claims and abandonment of frivolous claims. Some states have abandoned the use of screening panels.[210]

A few courts found the panels unconstitutional as an infringement of state constitutional rights to access to the courts.[211] The Florida Supreme Court declared the state's medical mediation requirement unconstitutional on the ground that it violated due process by being arbitrary and capricious in operation because of its ten-month limitation on the mediation process with no procedure to extend the limit.[212] Most courts upheld the required use of screening panels since plaintiffs still have the right to sue after the screening process is completed.[213]

Federal courts require plaintiffs to complete any state-required screening process before pursuing a state malpractice claim in federal court.[214]

ARBITRATION. Some states passed laws to facilitate arbitration as an alternative to litigation. Arbitration is used extensively in some areas. Arbitration is discussed in section 11-3.

ADMINISTRATIVE SYSTEMS. There are proposals to replace court and arbitration and create an administrative system to determine whether there should be payment and, if so, the amount in all malpractice cases.[215] Appeals to the courts would be allowed only in limited circumstances. No state has enacted such a system. Courts in many states would probably view such a system as a violation of the right under the state constitution to access to the courts. In those states, an amendment to the state constitution may be necessary before such a law would be possible.

The definition of the grounds for entitlement to payment under any administrative system would need to be carefully written. Under the law applicable to Veterans Affairs (VA) hospitals, veterans can claim disability through an administrative process. In 1994, the U.S. Supreme Court ruled that a claim for disability benefits from the VA does not require any fault of the VA hospital.[216]

A few states offer administrative systems that are nonbinding on the claimant for some types of claims. The Florida Birth-Related Neurological Injury Compensation Act provides for an administrative law judge to determine whether a claim is compensable and the amount of the compensation. In order to obtain payment from the fund, the award must be accepted. However, the claimant is free to litigate if dissatisfied with the outcome.[217] This system has been criticized by providers.[218]

11-7.3 Amount and Payment of Award

The amount and payment of damage awards are modified by (1) imposing ceilings on the award, (2) abolishing the collateral source rule, (3) authorizing periodic payments, and (4) modifying joint and several liability.

In 2005, the Supreme Court ruled that a plaintiff must pay income taxes on the entire amount of any award, including the portion paid to the attorney. The payment to the attorney is not deductible, except when a special law applies that permits deduction of attorney's fees in some employment discrimination cases. Thus, plaintiffs keep a smaller portion of the amount awarded, which places upward pressure on the amount of the award.[219]

CEILINGS ON AWARDS. Limitations on the amount that can be awarded in a malpractice suit have been one of the most controversial approaches to tort reform. Several states have enacted limits.[220]

A 1993 study by the Congressional Office of Technology Assessment reported that damage caps were one of the most effective means of reducing malpractice costs.[221] A 2004 study by the Rand Corporation concluded that the California damage cap had cut payouts by 30 percent and that this comprised a 15 percent reduction in payments to patients and a 60 percent reduction in payments to the patients' attorneys.[222]

In 1978, the Supreme Court ruled that Congress could place caps on damages.[223] The case involved liability for nuclear reactors. Although Congress has considered proposals to cap liability in malpractice cases, it has not enacted such a cap, leaving the matter to the states.

State courts disagree on the constitutionality of such limits, under state constitutions.[224] For example, in 1976, the Illinois Supreme Court declared ceilings to be an unconstitutional violation of equal protection because it could find no rational justification for treating those injured by medical malpractice differently from those injured by other means.[225] By contrast, in 1980, the Indiana Supreme Court declared ceilings to be constitutional because it found a rational justification in the need for a risk-spreading mechanism for malpractice liability at a reasonable cost to assure the continued availability of health services.[226] In 2003, the highest court of Massachusetts upheld applying the state's cap on liability of charitable corporations to a charitable hospital.[227] Also in 2003, the Nebraska Supreme Court upheld a malpractice damage cap.[228]

In at least one state, the constitutional objection was addressed by an amendment to the constitution. In 2003, Texas voters approved a constitutional amendment permitting caps in suits against healthcare providers.[229]

One difficulty with state caps is that they sometimes can be bypassed by bringing suit in another state. When a provider does business in another state and the malpractice claim arises out of that business, it is subject to the law of the state where the malpractice occurred. In 1979, the Supreme Court ruled that even a state cap on the liability of the state did not have to be recognized by other states in which the state engaged in business.[230] Sometimes, patients from other states try to bring suit in their home state against out-of-state providers for services provided in the other state. It is usually difficult to obtain jurisdiction over the out-of-state provider, and the suit gets dismissed.[231] However, occasionally the provider has engaged in enough business in the state where the suit is brought to permit obtaining jurisdiction. Then the court must decide which state's law governs. In most cases, the law of the state where the services were provided is applied.[232] However, in some cases, the law of the state where the suit is brought is applied so that the provider loses the benefit of its state cap.

COLLATERAL SOURCE RULE. Under the common law the defendant must pay for the entire cost of the plaintiff's injuries even if the plaintiff has already received some compensation from other sources, such as insurance. This is called the collateral source rule. Several states abolished the collateral source rule, and the amount of compensation the plaintiff receives from other sources is deducted from the amount the defendant owes. This process has been declared constitutional by several courts,[233] but a few courts have disagreed.[234]

When the collateral source rule applies, it often inflates the amount awarded in unexpected ways. For example, in 2001, the Wisconsin Supreme Court ruled that an injured person could recover the full charges for the medical services received even though his healthcare insurer had actually paid much less for the services.[235] The court viewed the medical expenses as a measure of damages rather than as an expense to be reimbursed through the tort system. In 2003, a Florida appellate court ruled that a medical expense award was properly reduced to the amount actually paid for the services.[236]

PERIODIC PAYMENT. Under the common law, the plaintiff is entitled to payment of court judgments in a single lump sum. One advantage of settling cases involving large liabilities is that the parties can agree to periodic payments that are easier for the defendant to pay. Some states have passed laws authorizing courts to direct that large judgments be paid by periodic payments. The courts have not agreed on whether these laws are constitutional.[237]

Some courts may have inherent authority to structure payout of awards to the beneficiary provided the full amount has been paid by the person found liable. Thus, a federal appellate court ruled that there was inherent authority to place an award for a child in a reversionary trust over the objections of the parents who had a conflict of interest.[238]

JOINT AND SEVERAL LIABILITY. Under the common law, when several defendants are found liable, each is liable for the entire amount. The plaintiff can select from whom to try to collect. Thus, for example, when a rider was injured on a ride at Walt Disney World and the jury allocated 14 percent responsibility to the rider, 85 percent to his accompanying fiancé, and 1 percent to Walt Disney World, the rider was permitted to collect 86 percent from Walt Disney World.[239] Under contributory negligence principles, he was not permitted to collect the remaining 14 percent due to his personal fault.

Moreover, under the common law the defendant who pays is not permitted in most cases to recover reimbursement from the other defendants even if they have greater responsibility.[240] Some states have modified these harsh rules by statute.[241]

11-7.4 Statute of Limitations

The statute of limitations specifies the time in which suits must be filed or forever barred. Some states have shortened this time. Prior to the malpractice crisis amendments of the 1980s, nearly all states permitted minors to wait to file suit until they became adults. Some tort reform acts limit minors to a specific number of years after the right to sue accrues. While some courts have upheld these laws, other courts have found them to violate state constitutions.[242]

Some states redefined when the time begins as another way to shorten the time. In most states, the time begins when the patient discovers an injury that may be due to someone else's negligence.[243] Courts disagree on whether limits that start on the date of the incident are enforceable.[244]

Such limits can bar the suit before the patient knows there is a basis to sue. In some cases, such as unwanted births after negligent sterilizations, the injury may not occur until many years after the incident.

11-7.5 Other Tort Reform Measures

Other tort reform measures:

1. Limit the grounds for suits based on lack of informed consent,[245]

2. Restrict contingency fees for lawyers or give courts the authority to modify them,[246]

3. Prohibit asking for a specific amount of money in the suit,[247]

4. Prohibit punitive damages[248] or require part of punitive damage awards to be paid to the state,[249]

5. Require notices of intent to sue,[250] and

6. Require an affidavit of merit from a expert to be attached to the suit.[251]

11-7.6 Malpractice Coverage Reform

Some states tried to address the cost or unavailability of malpractice insurance coverage by facilitating the development of new insurers, developing state-run systems, and subsidizing the cost of insurance directly or indirectly.

NEW INSURERS. In some states, Joint Underwriting Authorities provide insurance to some providers who cannot obtain insurance in the private market.

Some states established other malpractice insurance plans.[252]

GOVERNMENTAL PAYMENT SYSTEMS. Some states have insurance systems that pay part of any malpractice award. These laws have generally been upheld, including the requirement that all healthcare providers contribute to the fund[253] and the requirement that the administrative procedure associated with the system be followed.[254]

The federal government established the National Childhood Vaccine Injury Act to pay for injuries caused by certain vaccination programs.[255]

SUBSIDIES. Some states have provided subsidies directly. For example, Nevada used state funds to start a malpractice plan.[256]

11-8 What Are Some Examples of the Tort Liability of Healthcare Providers?

This section reviews the specific situations where suits are brought against hospitals and healthcare professionals, illustrating the scope of the duty of hospitals and their staff members to patients and others.

HOSPITALS. Hospital liability can be based on (1) a violation by an employee of the employee's duties, or (2) a violation of the hospital's duties. Hospital liability for injuries caused by an employee's violation of the employee's duties is based on the doctrine of *respondeat superior* discussed above.

Whenever individual healthcare professionals function as hospital employees or agents, their liability exposure also constitutes hospital liability exposure. Many hospital duties are not based on *respondeat superior*. To prove liability for injuries caused by breaches of these duties, it is sufficient to show a breach of the hospital's duty. Areas in which hospitals have an independent duty include: (1) maintenance of the physical condition of the buildings and grounds, (2) selection and maintenance of equipment, and (3) selection and supervision of staff.

Physical Condition of the Buildings and Grounds. The hospital must exercise reasonable care in maintaining its buildings and grounds in a reasonably safe condition. An accident alone is not enough to establish liability. State or local regulations may establish standards, and injuries resulting from violations of those standards can lead to liability. If regulatory standards are not violated, hospitals generally are liable only when a plaintiff proves that the hospital's employees or agents created a condition likely to cause injury; or that they knew or should have known of a condition likely to cause injury and failed to take action to provide warning or correct the condition. For example, in 2002, a New York court held that a hospital was not liable to a visitor who slipped and fell on a French fry on the floor of the hospital cafeteria. There was no evidence that the French fry had been there long enough for the hospital to have constructive notice of its presence so that it could correct the condition.[257]

The hospital must exercise the same reasonable care as any other business that regularly invites the public onto its grounds and into its buildings. Hospital buildings and grounds should also be designed and maintained to meet the special needs of the infirm and disabled persons using hospital facilities. The hospital is generally not liable for injuries caused by a dangerous condition when the injured person was aware of the condition, was able to avoid the risk of injury, and, nevertheless, chose to ignore the risk. In a Texas case, the antenna wire for a television in a patient's room was in a place where it could be tripped over. The patient had been aware of the wire and had walked around the set to avoid the wire several times during her stay. On the day of her discharge, she chose to step over the wire and tripped. The hospital won the suit because the danger was open and obvious and the patient had the ability to avoid it.[258] However, the North Carolina Supreme Court ruled that a hospital visitor was not responsible for watching for a three-inch rise in the sidewalk when there were diversions such as low-hanging tree branches and uneven illumination.[259] Suits have arisen out of accidents involving, for example, elevators,[260] broken steps,[261] slippery materials on the floors,[262] defective carpet,[263] automobiles in the parking lot,[264] and malfunction of automatic gates and doors.[265]

Courts disagree on the extent to which a hospital must protect persons on hospital premises from crimes by persons unassociated with the hospital. The California Supreme Court ruled that a hospital had a duty to protect persons in its parking lot in a high crime area, and it could be liable to a physician shot by a robber.[266] A Georgia court ruled that injuries to a hospital employee who was attacked in the hospital parking lot arose out of her employment, so she could only pursue a claim under the workers' compensation law.[267] The Louisiana Supreme Court ruled that a nurse's employer was not liable for her injuries from being stabbed by an unknown person as she exited a hospital elevator where there were no prior similar accidents and nothing could have prevented the assault.[268]

Numerous cases arise out of sexual assaults on patients and others. Courts disagree on the standard for determining when a hospital should be liable. The Alabama Supreme Court ruled that hospitals were responsible for protecting anesthetized patients from sexual assault, even by trespassers.[269] A California court ruled that a hospital could be liable for the sexual assault of a disabled patient if it was shown to have provided inadequate supervision and security.[270] The Oregon Supreme Court ruled that a hospital could be liable for the sexual assault of a patient by an employee only if negligent retention or supervision of the employee was shown. The hospital did not have an independent direct duty to the patient in Oregon, and the act was outside the scope of employment under state law.[271]

Selection and Maintenance of Equipment. Hospitals have an obligation to furnish reasonably adequate equipment for use in the diagnosis and treatment of patients. Problems can arise when hospitals do not have needed equipment, when needed equipment is not available, or when equipment has not been properly inspected and maintained. When a hospital does not have the equipment reasonably necessary for the treatment of certain conditions, patients with these conditions should be advised of the hospital's limitations. In addition, arrangements should be made for the patient's transfer to another hospital with the necessary equipment, unless the patient or the patient's representative makes an informed decision to decline the transfer.

A woman delivered a stillborn baby when the fourteen-bed obstetrical clinic she entered for delivery did not have the facilities for a Caesarean delivery.[272] The court found the clinic liable because it admitted the woman without having the necessary facilities or warning her of the limited nature of the facilities. In a California case, a hospital was found liable for injuries to a patient with third-degree burns who was kept for nearly two months in a hospital that did not have equipment to care for the patient's burns.[273] The court ruled that the hospital had a duty to transfer the patient to another hospital with the necessary equipment. When a patient is reluctant to accept transfer, the most prudent practice is still to encourage transfer, rather than relying on refusal. A federal appellate court ruled that a VA hospital was not negligent for failing to have a lung scan machine and that timely arrangements had been made for transfer to a hospital that had the machine; the United States was not liable for the patient's death.[274]

Hospitals usually are not required to provide the latest equipment. For example, in a Louisiana case, a hospital was found not liable for having older equipment to cut sections of tissue for diagnosis instead of having more modern equipment that could cut thinner sections for a more accurate diagnosis.[275] Several experts testified that the older equipment was widely accepted and produced satisfactory results. A woman whose breast was removed due to misdiagnosis of malignancy was not awarded compensation.

Sometimes equipment might not be available for use due to system design problems or hospital staff failure to plan to have the proper equipment in the area. In a North Carolina case, a hospital was found liable for the death of a patient due to delay in re-intubation because the emergency cart was not stocked with the needed laryngoscope blade.[276] The Georgia Supreme Court decided that a hospital could be liable when its employees supplied incorrect parts for cataract equipment that caused a malfunction that injured the eye.[277] In a Texas case, the hospital was found liable for a patient's death because oxygen was unavailable after she was transferred to a private room.[278] A wall plug in the room supplied oxygen, but the equipment accompanying the patient required a wall plug of a different shape. The design problem was the lack of standardization of wall plugs. Portable oxygen equipment could have supplied the necessary oxygen, but none had accompanied the patient. In 2000, an Illinois court found a hospital liable for not having infant blood pressure equipment available.[279]

A hospital must also exercise reasonable care in inspecting and maintaining equipment. Equipment should be periodically inspected, and discovered defects should be remedied. However, the hospital does not guarantee that the equipment will function properly during customary use. Liability for injuries due to defects in equipment generally depends on whether the defect is latent (hidden) or patent (visible). The user of equipment is generally liable for injuries due to use of equipment with patent defects. The owner of the equipment is generally liable for injuries due to use of equipment with latent defects detectable through reasonable inspections that were not performed. The manufacturer or seller of the equipment is generally liable when the equipment has a latent defect, such as a flaw in the metal, which the owner could not detect through reasonable inspections.

An Ohio case concerned a surgeon who examined a cauterizing machine and then left the operating room.[280] While he was gone, a hospital employee substituted another machine that appeared so similar that the surgeon did not notice the switch. The patient was burned during the surgery due to a defect in the machine. The surgeon was found not to be liable.

When the hospital or physician knows that the equipment is defective, it is easier to establish liability because the defect is clearly patent. In an Oklahoma case, the employer was found liable for an employee's use of equipment that was clearly malfunctioning.[281] The employee knew the electrotherapy machine was malfunctioning, but instead of turning off the machine and seeking assistance, she continued to use the machine until the patient was burned. In an Iowa case, a surgeon was found liable for a patient's infection resulting from contaminated sutures because he knew they were contaminated when he used them.[282] An earlier patient had become infected through use of sutures from the same supply.

Selection and Supervision of Staff. A hospital can be liable for failing to exercise reasonable care in selecting and supervising its staff and in setting staffing levels.[283] This liability applies to both professional and nonprofessional staff. Hospitals have a responsibility to evaluate the credentials of applicants for jobs. When a state license is required, the hospital should determine that the applicant has the license, but checking the license alone is usually not a sufficient check of the applicant's background and qualifications. The hospital should also provide appropriate training, supervision, and evaluation. A Texas appeals court found a hospital liable for the negligence of unsupervised certified registered nurse anesthetists.[284] When evaluations indicate problems, appropriate action should be taken. A Texas court ruled that expert testimony was not required to establish negligence in the supervising and assigning of a nurse, where the employee evaluation forms indicated an unsatisfactory rating over three months before the incident.[285] These issues are discussed in more detail earlier in this volume in Chapter 4 "Individual Providers and Caregivers."

The hospital also has a responsibility to exercise reasonable care in credentialing and monitoring members of the medical staff, as discussed in Chapter 5 "Medical Staff." The potential for hospital liability for acts of physicians was discussed earlier in this chapter.

GOVERNING BODY AND ADMINISTRATOR. Members of the governing body have seldom been found personally liable for the activities of the hospital or for their own activities related to the hospital. Administrators have been found liable for negligently supervising their subordinates, for entering contracts outside their authority, and for breaching duties imposed by statute.

MANAGERS AND SUPERVISORS. Managers and supervisors are not the employers of staff they supervise. Thus, *respondeat superior* does not impose liability on supervisors for the acts or omissions of staff they supervise. Managers and supervisors are liable only for the consequences of their own acts or omissions. The manager or supervisor is usually a hospital employee, and the hospital can be liable under *respondeat superior* for the acts or omissions of supervisors.

The liability of a supervising nurse for the actions of supervised nurses was discussed in a California case involving a needle left in a patient's abdomen during surgery.[286] The patient sued the physicians, hospital, and supervising nurse. The court dismissed the suit against the supervising nurse because she had done nothing wrong. She had assigned two competent nurses to assist with the surgery, and she had not been present. Therefore, she had no opportunity to intervene. The court ruled that *respondeat superior* did not apply to the nursing supervisor because she was not the employer.

The actions that can lead to liability of supervising healthcare professionals are discussed in more detail in a New Jersey court decision.[287] The case involved a surgeon who had ordered a resident physician to remove a tube being used to extract the patient's gastric contents. The patient's esophagus was perforated during the removal. The court ruled that the supervising surgeon was not liable for the resident's acts. The court said that the supervising surgeon could be liable only if (1) it was not accepted medical or hospital practice to delegate the particular function to someone with the resident's level of training, (2) he knew or should have known the individual resident was not qualified to perform the task with the degree of supervision provided, (3) he had been present and able to avoid the injury, or (4) he had a special contract with the patient that he did not fulfill. Since none of these circumstances was present, the supervising surgeon was not liable. In some states, the courts apply a different legal doctrine to supervising physicians. The borrowed servant and dual servant doctrines were discussed earlier in this chapter.

In summary, a supervisor can be liable if:

1. The supervisor assigns a subordinate to do something the supervisor knows or should know the subordinate is unable to do;

2. The supervisor does not supervise a subordinate to the degree the supervisor knows or should know the subordinate needs;

3. The supervisor is present and fails to take action when possible to avoid the injury; or

4. The supervisor does not properly allocate the time of available staff.

NURSES. A professional nurse is usually held to the standard of care generally observed by other competent nurses under similar circumstances.[288] States vary on the standard of care expected of nurses in specialties that overlap with the scope of practice of physicians. In some states, such nurses are held to the standard of physicians. For example, a Louisiana decision ruled that when a person assisting a physician performs a task deemed to be medical in nature, such as removal of a cast with a saw, the person is held to the standard of care applicable to a physician.[289] Other states have recognized a distinct standard of care for such nurses. For example, a Texas ruling held nurse specialists to the standard of care observed by those in the same specialty under similar circumstances.[290] In 1985, the California Supreme Court ruled that nurse practitioners should not be held to the standard of care of a physician even when performing functions that overlap with the physician's scope of practice.[291] In 2004, the Illinois Supreme Court ruled that in most cases the standard of care for nurses had to be established by testimony of other nurses; testimony by physicians did not establish the standard of care.[292]

Duty to Interpret and Carry Out Orders. Nurses have a duty to interpret and carry out orders properly. Nurses are expected to know basic information concerning the proper use of drugs and procedures they are likely to be ordered to use. When an order is ambiguous or apparently erroneous, the nurse has a responsibility to seek clarification from the ordering physician. This will almost always result in correction or explanation of the order. In the unusual situation in which the explanation does not clarify the appropriateness of the order, the nurse has a responsibility to inform nursing, hospital, or medical staff officials designated by hospital policy who can initiate review of the order and, if necessary, other appropriate action. Pending review, if the drug or procedure appears dangerous to the patient, the nurse should decline to carry out the order, but should immediately notify the ordering physician. Hospitals should have established procedures for nurses to follow when they are not satisfied with the appropriateness of an order. Frequently, this procedure will involve notification of a nursing supervisor who will then contact appropriate medical staff officials. Hospital administration may occasionally need to become involved to resolve individual issues.

A North Dakota case arose when a child was born with severe brain damage after a nurse's alleged failure to place the mother on a fetal heart monitor in accordance with her physician's instructions.[293] In a 1973 California case, a hospital was found liable for the death of a patient because a nurse had failed to follow the physician's order to check the patient's vital signs every thirty minutes and had failed to notify the physician when the patient's condition became life threatening.[294] In a New York case, a nurse and a hospital were held liable for the scalding of a young tonsillectomy patient by water that was served as part of his meal by a nurse, contrary to the dietary instructions ordered by the attending physician.[295] A hospital was sued in a New York case for the blindness of an infant caused by too much oxygen when a nurse gave six liters per minute instead of the four liters per minute ordered by the physician.[296] The hospital presented evidence that six liters per minute was within the range of permissible dosages. The court found this evidence irrelevant because the nurse had not been given authority to deviate from the physician's order and, thus, had breached her duty to the patient. The court ordered a lower court to reconsider the case to determine whether the blindness had been caused by breach of duty.

A physician must, however, make the order known to the nurse by putting it in the medical records or informing the nurse directly. There can be no liability for not following orders given privately to the patient.[297]

Nurses are sometimes given authority to adjust, within guidelines, the amounts of some drugs or other substances being given to patients. The nurse then has the added responsibility to exercise appropriate judgment in making those adjustments. In many states, there are legal limits on the discretion that can be delegated concerning some drugs and substances. As with all delegations, the physician should provide appropriate guidance and delegate this responsibility only to nurses who are able to make the required judgments. In 1979, a California court recognized the appropriateness of delegating to a nurse the decision concerning when a prescribed pain medication was needed.[298] The patient suffered cardiopulmonary arrest and died soon after pain medication was given. The court ruled that it was appropriate for the trial court to give the jury two special instructions usually used only for physicians, because the case involved a nurse who was exercising delegated independent judgment. One instruction emphasized that perfection was not required; therefore, liability could not be based on a mere error in judgment by a nurse who possessed the necessary learning and skill and who exercised the care ordinarily exercised by reputable nurses under similar circumstances. The standard applied was the conduct of nurses, not physicians. The other instruction emphasized that when there is more than one recognized method of treatment, it is not negligent to select one of the approved methods that later turns out to be wrong or not to be favored by certain other practitioners. The court upheld the jury verdict in favor of the nurse and the hospital.

Nurses cannot assume that orders have remained unchanged from previous shifts. They have a duty to check for changes in orders. A Delaware case addressed a female patient who was receiving a drug by injection.[299] The physician wrote an order changing the mode of administration from injection to oral. When a nurse prepared to give an injection, the patient objected and referred the nurse to the physician's new order. The nurse told the patient that the patient was mistaken and gave the medication by injection. The nurse's conduct was held to be negligent. The court permitted the jury to find the nurse negligent by applying ordinary common sense, and expert testimony was not necessary to prove the standard of care.

A Louisiana case focused on the nurse's responsibility to obtain clarification of an apparently erroneous physician order.[300] The order was incomplete and subject to misinterpretation. Believing the dosage to be incorrect, the nurse asked two other physicians whether the medication should be given as ordered. The physicians did not interpret the order as the nurse did, and they said the order did not

appear out of line. The nurse did not contact the attending physician and administered the misinterpreted dosage, resulting in the patient's death. The nurse was found liable for failing to contact the attending physician before giving the medication. The physician who wrote the ambiguous order was also found liable.

Duty to Monitor Patients and Communicate Significant Changes. Nurses have a duty to monitor patients. Nurses are expected to distinguish abnormalities in the patient's condition and determine whether nursing care is a sufficient response or whether a physician or others may be required. The nurse has a responsibility to inform the physician promptly of abnormalities that may require physician attention.[301] In a Kansas case, a nurse and a hospital were sued because a woman was injured during delivery of a baby without physician attendance.[302] The nurse had refused to call the physician despite clear signs of imminent delivery. In that case, the nurse and the hospital were found liable. In a West Virginia case, the court ruled that the hospital could be found liable for the death of a patient when the nurse failed to notify the physician of the patient's symptoms of heart failure for six hours.[303] In 1992, a New Mexico court affirmed a jury verdict against a hospital based on a finding that the negligence of the nurses in determining whether a woman was in labor influenced the physician's decision to deliver a baby prematurely.[304]

Observations should be properly documented. In an Illinois case, the hospital was sued for the loss of a patient's leg.[305] The patient had been admitted for treatment for a broken leg. The admitting physician wrote an order to "watch condition of toes" and testified at trial that routine nursing care required frequent monitoring of a seriously injured patient's circulation even in the absence of a physician order. The patient developed irreversible ischemia in his leg, requiring its amputation. The nursing notes for the seven-hour period prior to discovery of the irreversibility of the ischemia did not reflect any observations of circulation. The jury was permitted to conclude that absence of entries indicated absence of observations. Thus, the nurse and the hospital could be liable even if the nurse had actually made the observations.

It is as important to document no change as it is to document changes. A hospital and a physician were sued in a 1963 California case for damage to a patient's leg from infiltration of intravenous fluid into tissue.[306] The nurse observed increasing swelling and redness around the intravenous tube that indicated infiltration. She notified the physician several times of the swelling, but he ordered continuation of the intravenous infusions. There was conflicting testimony at the trial concerning (1) whether the nurse had communicated the seriousness of the swelling when it became markedly worse and (2) whether the nurse had authority to discontinue an intravenous infusion without a physician order. The court overturned the trial court decision in favor of the hospital and the physician and ordered a new trial so that a jury could determine these issues. This case illustrates the importance of clearly communicating changes in the patient's condition and clearly defining the authority of nurses to discontinue harmful therapy.

If the physician fails to respond appropriately when notified that a patient is in a dangerous situation, then the nurse is confronted with the same situation as when the physician has not adequately explained an apparently erroneous order. The nurse has a responsibility to inform nursing, hospital, or medical staff officials designated by hospital policy who can initiate review of the situation and, if necessary, take other appropriate action. This is the way a nurse confronted with the situation in the 1963 California case should respond today if the nurse believes the seriousness of the swelling has been communicated, if the physician neither examines the patient nor orders discontinuance of the procedure, and if the nurse does not have clear authority to discontinue the procedure without an order.

▶ In *Darling v. Charleston Community Memorial Hospital*,[307] one reason for the hospital's liability for amputation of the patient's leg was the nurses' failure to inform hospital administration of the progressive gangrenous condition of the patient's leg and the inappropriate efforts of the attending physician to address the condition. No effective, alternative channel had been established for direct nursing notification of the medical staff and for appropriate medical staff intervention. The court found that hospital administration should have been notified so that it could obtain appropriate medical staff intervention. In most hospitals, direct communication channels have been established between nursing administration and medical staff leadership so that direct hospital administration involvement is less frequent. These channels must be used when necessary. The fact that the nurse believes the physician will not respond does not justify failure to notify the physician and to take other action if the physician does not respond. A California court ruled that two nurses and a hospital could be sued for the death of a woman from severe bleeding from an incision made to assist her in giving birth.[308] Although the nurses believed the patient was bleeding heavily, the physician was not notified until nearly three hours later when the patient went into shock. One nurse explained that she did not call the physician because she did not believe he would respond. The court concluded that she should have notified the attending physician and then notified her superiors if the attending physician did not respond.

As with other negligence cases, in order for there to be liability the deviation from the standard of care must be demonstrated to have caused the injury. In 2001, an Illinois appellate court upheld reversing a jury verdict against the hospital employer of a nurse. The nurse did not communicate patient changes to the physician because the physician testified that the information would not have changed the care of the patient. The failure to report did not cause the subsequent injuries.[309]

Duty to Supervise Patients. When nurses determine that a patient requires supervision, they have a duty to exercise appropriate judgment and provide appropriate supervision within the constraints of proper physician orders and available resources. In 1992, an Oklahoma court decided that a nurse and hospital could be liable for a patient's slip and fall in the shower while unsupervised, after a nurse administered a drug known to cause drowsiness.[310] An Iowa case illustrates that hospitals may have a direct duty to supervise patients in some situations.[311] A patient with a history of fainting spells had a seizure and fell during a shower, breaking her jaw and losing several teeth. An aide was outside the shower room but allowed the patient to enter the shower alone. The court ruled that decisions concerning supervision of patient showers are a matter of routine care, not professional care, so no expert testimony is necessary to establish the standard of care. The jury can apply common sense to determine the reasonable care the patient's known condition requires. The court noted that absence of physician orders requiring close supervision does not insulate the hospital from liability. If subsequent circumstances show a need for change or action, the hospital should make the changes permitted without a physician order and, if further changes are necessary, seek appropriate orders.

Special Duty Nurses. Special duty nurses are held to the same standard of care as other nurses. Because they are not employees of the hospital, the hospital is usually not liable for their actions.[312] Even when hospital rules require special duty nurses they do not become hospital employees. In some situations, nurses who are called special duty nurses may be considered agents or employees of the hospital, so that the hospital can be liable under *respondeat superior*.[313] Agency or employment is likely to be found when special duty nurses are selected by the hospital, not by the patient or the patient's representatives. Collection of the nurse's bills by the hospital has also been interpreted by some courts to indicate agency.

PHARMACISTS. Pharmacies are highly regulated, and standards of practice are frequently found in federal or state statutes, agency regulations, and municipal or county ordinances. These generally require pharmaceutical services to be provided by or under the direction of a licensed pharmacist. Some states require hospitals to have at least one pharmacist with a special pharmacist license.[314] The Joint Commission (TJC) and other accreditation standards also establish duties.[315] The hospital may be liable for drug-related injuries if it fails to employ a licensed and competent pharmacist.[316]

Court decisions concerning pharmacists also help to define their standard of care. Dispensing the wrong drug clearly can lead to liability. In a 1971 Michigan case, a tranquilizer was dispensed instead of the prescribed oral contraceptive.[317] The patient became pregnant, delivered a child, and sued the pharmacist for damages. Damages were awarded, including child support until the child reached the age of majority.

A hospital must take reasonable steps to assure that drugs are available when they are needed. In a 1969 New York case, the hospital was found liable for the suicide of a patient who exhausted his supply of an investigational psychotropic drug.[318] The drug was not available during a long holiday weekend because it was stored in the research department, which was closed. The drug should have been stored in the pharmacy, which was open during the weekend. Some investigational drugs are not available outside of approved research projects, and subjects can no longer receive the drug after they complete their involvement in the study. In 1989, a federal district court applied this principle to dismiss a challenge by an AIDS patient to loss of access to a drug when a study was terminated.[319] Another federal court reached the same conclusion in 2005 concerning access to an investigational drug for Parkinson's disease.[320] This limited availability should be disclosed to the subject before the subject enters the study. In this case, the patient was still in the study. At times, certain noninvestigational drugs are not available because of manufacturing, transport, or stocking problems. The hospital is not an insurer that drugs will continue to be available, but it should take reasonable steps to anticipate needs to minimize nonavailability.

Drugs should be properly stored to avoid deterioration and contamination. The skill with which this is ordinarily done is illustrated by the lack of reported cases that allege a breach of this duty.

Pharmacists sometimes assume responsibility to maintain profiles of drugs administered to patients, advise physicians concerning drug selection, and review appropriateness of drug orders. Until 1995, TJC stated that the pharmaceutical department should provide drug monitoring services, which could include a drug profile for each patient and review of each patient's drug regimen for interactions, consonant with available resources.[321] In 1995, TJC replaced its pharmacy requirements with medication requirements that do not require pharmacists to perform any functions, except reviewing prescriptions and orders and performing other duties required by law.[322] The 2005 standards require that the hospital have a mechanism to capture, use, and communicate important patient medication information, including a medication history, and monitor medication effects, but there is no requirement that this be done by the pharmacy.[323]

Although pharmacists have avoided liability in some cases arising out of these new responsibilities,[324] pharmacists can be liable for failing to fulfill the professional standard of care associated with the responsibilities assumed.[325] While physicians will remain primarily liable for injuries due to negligent prescriptions, pharmacists can be codefendants when they assume the responsibility of review and carry it out negligently.

PHYSICAL THERAPISTS. Most professional liability cases involving physical therapists have dealt with breaches of the duties (1) to follow the physician's instructions, (2) not to subject the patient to excessive therapy, and (3) to supervise the patient properly.

A physical therapist must follow the prescribing physician's instructions, unless they are apparently erroneous and dangerous to the patient. In a Florida case, a hospital was found liable for the injuries to a patient who fell while undergoing physical therapy.[326] The physician had ordered that the patient be attended at all times. The therapist left the patient alone in a standing position while getting her a robe. A fall during that short time resulted in a fractured hip. No expert testimony was required to establish the duty to follow the physician's instructions. In 2001, a Louisiana court upheld finding a physical therapist liable for providing postoperative exercises beyond the scope of the prescription and other deviations from the standard of care. The patient's suture line separated requiring a second surgery.[327]

Physical therapists are expected to be familiar with the appropriate use of the procedures they use. If a physician's order is apparently erroneous, the therapist has a duty to seek modification or clarification from the prescribing physician. In most states, the therapist should not unilaterally initiate different treatment. If the orders are still apparently erroneous after discussion with the prescribing physician and if the ordered therapy is dangerous to the patient, the therapist should decline to provide the prescribed therapy and notify the prescribing physician and the appropriate supervisors, medical staff, or administrative officials in accordance with hospital policy.

Physician's orders often give the physical therapist latitude concerning the therapy to be provided. The physical therapist then is held to the duty of acting as other physical therapists in good standing would act under the circumstances. In 1976, a Pennsylvania hospital was sued by a patient who fell in the physical therapy room and fractured her leg and arm.[328] The patient was receiving gait training after multiple hip surgeries and was instructed to walk between parallel bars. The patient fell either while between the parallel bars or while using her cane to take a few steps away from the parallel bars. The court ruled that the duty of the physical therapist must be established by expert testimony and that only ordinary care and skill were required, and the physical therapist was not liable for a mere mistake in judgment. The court affirmed a verdict for the hospital.

Physical therapists have been found liable for subjecting patients to excessive therapy. The Kentucky Supreme Court applied *res ipsa loquitur* when a femur was fractured during therapy to prepare the stump of a leg for an artificial leg.[329] The court did not believe bones would fracture while a leg was being lifted and lowered unless someone was negligent. Thus, it did not require expert testimony. The court ruled that the physician could also be liable for failing to provide an adequate explanation of the procedure to the therapist.

Falls are a frequent cause of injuries involving patients receiving physical therapy. Some courts tend to apply *res ipsa loquitur* to cases involving falls, as illustrated by the Kentucky case, while other courts analyze the appropriateness of the attendance given from a professional perspective, as illustrated by the Pennsylvania case. Another example of a professional standard involved an Oregon patient undergoing therapy after hip surgery who became dizzy and fainted just after returning to a tilt table after walking between parallel bars.[330] His total hip replacement became dislocated when he fell. The patient's expert witness testified that he should have been given support, including

being strapped to the tilt table, as soon as he became dizzy. The court found the hospital liable for the physical therapist's failure to fulfill this duty.

LABORATORIES AND PATHOLOGY. Liability can arise from injuries due to negligent acts associated with laboratory tests and other pathology services. The error can be committed by a laboratory technician, a pathologist, or other staff members. The hospital can become liable under *respondeat superior* when the person who made the error is the hospital's employee or agent. As discussed in the *Respondeat Superior* (11-5.1) and Agency (11-5.3) sections of this chapter, some courts hold hospitals responsible for the acts of physicians, particularly radiologists, pathologists, and emergency room physicians, by considering the physician to be the agent or apparent agent for the hospital.

Liability has arisen from mishandling specimens.[331] In a Texas case, the hospital was found liable for a patient's mental anguish when an eyeball that had been removed because of a tumor was lost by a technician.[332] The technician was washing the eyeball and dropped it into the sink. The eyeball went down the drain and could not be removed; the pathologist could not diagnose whether the tumor was malignant. In a Florida case, the patient was awarded $100,000 from the hospital and a surgeon because the identities of two specimens were confused, resulting in the unnecessary removal of one of the patient's breasts.[333] The surgeon had removed a biopsy specimen from each breast, and the two specimens were put in the same container without labels telling which breast each came from. The pathologist did not attempt to distinguish the two specimens. One specimen was malignant, and the other was not. Because it was impossible to determine which breast had the malignancy, both breasts were removed. The surgeon was liable for failing to instruct the nurses to label the specimens. The hospital was liable for the nurses' failure to label the specimens and for the failure of its pathologist employee to segregate the specimens.

Misreading a specimen can lead to liability. An Ohio hospital was found liable because its pathologist-employee misdiagnosed a frozen section as indicating cervical cancer.[334] After a total hysterectomy (removal of the uterus and cervix) was performed, it was discovered that the patient did not have cancer. Misdiagnosis alone is not enough to establish breach of duty. A diagnosing physician is not expected always to be correct. Most diagnoses are professional judgments. Thus, for there to be liability, the misdiagnosis must be one that a physician in good standing in the same specialty would not have made in the same circumstances.

Using improper techniques or reagents to conduct a test can be a breach of duty. A federal appellate court found a hospital liable because a technician used sodium hydroxide instead of sodium chloride to perform a gastric cytology test.[335] In an Iowa case, a hospital was found liable for using a reagent that was too old.[336] The pediatrician ordered appropriate blood tests for a baby with symptoms of Rh incompatibility, but the old reagent caused the test results to indicate normal blood levels of bilirubin rather than the baby's actual high levels. When the high levels were discovered, it was too late to avoid permanent severe brain damage that probably could have been avoided had therapy been initiated after the initial blood tests.

Errors in testing can also result in liability. A 1992 case involved a military member who had been told that he was HIV-positive as a result of a false-positive test. A federal appellate court ruled that the government could be sued for the failure of the military to inform him after discharge of its discovery of the error.[337] Courts disagree on whether there can be liability for a false-positive HIV test in the absence of receiving unnecessary and harmful treatment in the mistaken belief of having the virus.

Autopsies and other aspects of handling dead bodies are another area of potential liability arising from pathology services.

RADIOLOGY. Three common problem areas of radiology include radiation injuries, falls and other problems with patient positioning, and errors or delays in diagnosis. There can also be liability for performing radiologic procedures of no beneficial value.[338]

Radiation injuries from excessive radiation or radiation to the wrong body part have resulted in several suits. The application and effect of radiation are not within the knowledge of laypersons, and courts generally require expert proof of how the radiation should have been administered. If the injury is to a body part that was not intended to receive radiation, most courts will apply *res ipsa loquitur*. However, some courts apply *res ipsa loquitur* in all cases involving severe radiation injuries. These courts require the defendant to show the patient was hypersensitive or otherwise explain injuries to avoid liability.

Several cases have addressed the duty to disclose the risk of radiation injuries from therapeutic radiologic procedures. One of the earliest court decisions to apply the requirement of informed consent ruled that a Kansas physician had a duty to inform the patient of the probable consequences of the radioactive cobalt he administered for breast cancer.[339]

A federal appellate court ruled that the physician had to disclose the probable consequences and the experimental nature of the therapy he proposed when he planned to give extremely large doses that exceeded the accepted range and were justified only by research papers read at conferences.[340] When radiologic technologists fail to check patient status adequately, sometimes necessary precautions are not taken for patient protection. When injuries result, liability is likely. In a Louisiana case, the court ruled the hospital could be liable for a patient's broken ankle that was discovered after the patient slumped on an x-ray table.[341] The radiologic technologist had not noticed that the patient was sedated, and the x-ray requisition had not included the brief history required by hospital policy. The technologist had not strapped the patient to the table before raising it. The technologist had a duty to strap the sedated patient. A federal appellate court ruled that the hospital could be sued for the way a radiologic technologist handled a patient.[342] Although the patient was to be x-rayed for suspected neck and spinal injuries from an automobile accident, the radiologic technologist told the patient to scoot onto the table and then twisted the patient's neck to position her, resulting in permanent spinal cord damage. Experts testified the neck should have been immobilized before the patient was moved to the table, and after she was on the table, the machine, not the patient's head, should have been moved to achieve the desired angles.

Misdiagnosis by the physician reading x-ray film or another radiologic test has also led to suits. The radiologist is held to the standard of other physicians. Thus, the misdiagnosis must be more than a mere judgmental error to establish breach of duty. The misdiagnosis must be outside the accepted range of determinations by qualified radiologists under similar circumstances. Even when there is misdiagnosis, liability may be avoided if the misdiagnosis did not cause the injury. In an Iowa case, the court ruled in favor of the radiologists in a suit arising from the loss of a patient's eyesight.[343] The radiologist had not detected a piece of steel in the patient's eye. A second set of x-rays led to the discovery of the piece. The patient was unable to prove that delay in diagnosis had caused the eyesight loss.

Delay in reporting a proper diagnosis can also result in liability. A federal district court decided that an Indiana hospital was liable for the death of a patient due to delay in forwarding a radiologist's report.[344] The patient who had head injuries from a fight was examined by a physician in a hospital emergency room and released. Four skull x-rays were taken. After the release, a radiologist read the x-rays and found a skull fracture. He did not call the physician who had ordered the x-rays. He dictated his report, which was transcribed two days later. The patient was found unconscious after the x-rays had been read. The patient was taken to a hospital where emergency surgery was performed, but he died. The court ruled that the forwarding of reports was the hospital's administrative responsibility and that the physician was a hospital agent when performing that function. Hospitals need a system for promptly reading emergency x-rays and reporting critical x-ray findings.

Radiologists may also be liable for not informing the treating physician that the x-rays ordered are too limited in scope, so that the diagnosis cannot be relied on.[345]

INFECTION CONTROL. Hospitals can be liable for some infections acquired in the hospital.[346] This liability has been based on the hospital's independent duty concerning the physical condition of buildings and grounds and the selection and maintenance of equipment, as well as the hospital's liability under *respondeat superior* for acts of its employees and agents.

In the past, courts found liability for infections when the patient proved the existence of unsanitary conditions in the hospital. Even with improvements in infection control and in determination of infection sources, courts recognize that hospitals cannot guarantee absence of infection and that infections do occur in hospitals for many reasons other than negligence. Thus, most courts require proof of a causal relationship between the alleged injury and a deviation from proper practices.[347] An Ohio court ruled that *res ipsa loquitur* did not apply to a staph infection after a surgical procedure and no break in sterile technique had been identified, and there could be no liability for the infection.[348]

Some hospital licensing rules specify infection control steps that must be taken, particularly isolation and sterilization procedures. These rules can be used to prove the standard of care. In a Maryland case, a hospital was found liable when it failed to comply with a regulation requiring segregation of sterile and nonsterile needles.[349] A hospital may be held to a higher standard of care than is specified in regulations if other hospitals follow a higher standard.

When hospital employees fail to sterilize equipment properly, the hospital can be liable. In a California case, a hospital was found liable for a nurse's failure to sterilize a needle before using it to give a patient an injection.[350] The use of presterilized supplies has reduced both the risk to the patient and the hospital's liability exposure in these situations. If a patient is infected by a presterilized item, the manufacturer will usually be liable unless the item was contaminated by negligent conduct of hospital staff or there was a pattern of infection that should have led the hospital to discontinue the supplies. The Iowa case discussed in the Selection and Maintenance of Equipment section (11-8) of this chapter is an example of a pattern of infection from presterilized supplies.

Another aspect of infection control is preemployment and periodic screening of hospital personnel. The Americans with Disabilities Act (ADA), discussed in Chapter 4 "Individual Providers and Caregivers," limits when preemployment examinations may be given, but examinations are permitted. The ADA does not provide an excuse for not performing necessary examinations. A federal district court found liability for failing to give an employee a preemployment examination before she was assigned to a newborn nursery.[351] The employee had a staphylococcus infection of the same type that was transmitted to a baby. If the hospital becomes aware that a staff member may be infected, it must remove the person from direct and indirect patient contact until the condition is diagnosed and, if the condition is infectious, until the condition is no longer infectious or until appropriate procedures are implemented to preclude infecting others.

Some states require special training for hospital employees concerning HIV and other transmissible diseases.[352] The Occupational Safety and Health Administration (OSHA) requires employers to follow certain precautions concerning blood-borne pathogens, and the Centers for Disease Control (CDC) have provided considerable guidance for handling various diseases.

Hospitals are expected to have a system to monitor their facilities, discover infections, and take appropriate remedial action. TJC standards require such a system.[353] Failure to have an appropriate system could result in liability if a patient's infection could have been prevented by the type of system other hospitals have.

EMERGENCY SERVICES. Emergency services are a source of substantial liability exposure for hospitals and their staff members. The possible bases of liability of the hospital for acts of a physician in the emergency room are discussed earlier in this chapter. This section focuses on issues concerning the examination of the patient.

The responsibility for diagnosis rests with the physician or other independent practitioner. Severely injured patients should generally not be diagnosed over the telephone because of the risk of communication errors. It is best for patients with severe injuries to come to the emergency room. They then need to be given an appropriate medical screening examination that satisfies the EMTALA requirements, unless they refuse the screening.

A Maryland case illustrates the problem.[354] A person who had been drinking was hit by a car and was thrown through the air. He was brought to an emergency room, and the on-call surgeon was telephoned. The surgeon told the nurse to admit the patient and x-ray him in the morning. Since the hospital was full, the patient was placed in the hall outside the nursing station. His condition deteriorated, and he died within three hours of entering the hospital. The autopsy found a lacerated liver and a badly fractured leg and pelvic area, with bone fragments penetrating the peritoneal cavity. The physician and nurses contradicted each other concerning the information exchanged over the telephone. The physician was found liable because he failed to examine the patient personally, and the hospital was found liable because the nurses failed to notify the physician of the deterioration of the patient's condition.

Emergencies are not always apparent. All patients should be treated as having emergencies until they are determined not to have emergency problems. The most obvious aspect of the patient's condition frequently is not the most critical. Several cases have arisen from emergency personnel assuming that drunkenness is the only problem and overlooking more serious problems. In a Florida case, a young man was brought unconscious to an emergency room.[355] A superficial examination indicated he was drunk, and he was turned over to police. He was later found dead in his cell with broken ribs piercing his thoracic cavity. The court ruled that a jury could find responsibility to make a thorough examination of an unconscious patient and to take a history from those accompanying the patient. A history would have uncovered the fact that the patient was found lying on a lawn after a suspected fall from twenty-three feet.

Existing records should be examined when time permits. In a 1974 Louisiana case, a man had chest pains and called his physician, who advised him to go to the emergency room.[356] The physician alerted the emergency room, ordered an electrocardiogram (EKG), and told the emergency room staff to advise him of the outcome. The emergency room physician was not notified of the call; he ordered an EKG and, without comparing it to prior EKGs, decided there was no heart attack. He sent the patient home with medication and instructions to call if he got worse. The personal physician was not called. The patient got worse and was later admitted for cardiac care. The court said the emergency room physician could be sued for his misdiagnosis due to failure to compare the EKG to prior EKGs. This case also illustrates the importance of involving a physician, when available, who knows the patient. Another reason to examine prior records is that distraught patients may forget information, such as allergies. However, reliance can generally be placed on a history from a competent patient. This is illustrated by a Michigan case in which the patient had a fatal allergic reaction to morphine.[357] He had denied allergies to any painkilling drugs. Although records of a prior unrelated stay noted the allergy, the court found the hospital not liable. When laboratory and radiologic diagnostic tests are performed on emergency patients, the patients should be advised not to leave until the tests are completed.

GENETIC SCREENING AND TESTING. The increasing ability to identify genes that cause or increase the likelihood of disease has raised many legal issues and created a growing area of potential liability for healthcare providers.

Both parents and children have sued when negligently conducted tests have led parents to conceive or deliver children with genetic defects.

The duty of a physician to warn relatives of patients found to have genetically transmissible diseases has been the subject of several cases. In a 1995 case, the Florida Supreme Court held that a physician who did not warn a patient that her condition was genetically transferable may be liable to the patient's daughter, who later learned that she had the disease.[358] The court also concluded that the duty to warn of genetically transferable disease may be satisfied by warning the patient. However, in a 1996 case, a New Jersey appeals court held that a physician's duty to warn of genetic disease may extend beyond the patient to immediate family members.[359]

Knowledge of the genetic basis of disease is increasing rapidly, mainly due to the Human Genome project, a government-sponsored program designed to map and sequence the human gene, which completed the first complete sequencing of a human genome in 2003.[360] As more individuals (and their physicians) become aware that they carry genes associated with disease, it is almost certain that litigation related to genetic screening and testing will increase.

Chapter Summary

This chapter covered the basics of negligence, intentional torts, and tort reform proposals and programs. It also illustrated how much of the chapter content is applied by the courts. Most of the legal theory and application of legal principles in negligence and intentional torts have remained constant over the decades. While there are periodic variations in the legal procedures and defenses to these cases, for the most part, tort liability principles are firmly established. Some changes are achieved through tort reform measures; in particular, specific dollar limits on medical malpractice cases have been enacted in several states. The reader will benefit from a careful read of the numerous examples of the application of tort theories in the case summaries presented throughout this chapter.

Key Terms and Definitions

Arbitration Agreement – An alternative to bringing a lawsuit to court. The arbitration process specified in an agreement must be followed. A valid arbitration decision has the same effect as a court judgment.

Borrowed Servant Doctrine – When an employer delegates its right to direct and control the activities of an employee to another, independent party who assumes responsibility, the employee becomes a borrowed servant.

Comparative Negligence – In a negligence lawsuit, comparative negligence means that the percentage of cause due to the patient's conduct is determined and the patient does not collect that percentage of the total amount of the injury award.

Daubert Standards – A 1993 Supreme Court case, *Daubert v. Merrell Dow Pharmaceuticals,* established stricter standards for allowing expert testimony in federal courts. The Daubert Standards focus on the quality of the scientific basis for expert opinion testimony about the standard of care.

Defamation – An intentional tort that causes wrongful injury to a person's reputation. Libel is written defamation, and slander is spoken defamation. The defamatory statement must be communicated to a third person.

Exculpatory Contract – An agreement not to sue or an agreement to limit the amount of the suit.

Negligence – Civil wrong causing injury or harm to another person or to property as the result of doing something or failing to provide a proper or reasonable level of care. These four elements are required to prove negligence: (1) A duty, that is, what should have been done; (2) breach of duty, which is a deviation from what should have been done; (3) Injury; and (4) Legal causation, which means that the injury is caused by a breach of a duty owed to the injured party.

Release – A written document, signed by a claimant, that bars a future lawsuit based on the same incident.

Res Ipsa Loquitor – A Latin term meaning "the thing speaks for itself." A rule of evidence that allows that mere proof that an injury occurred establishes a presumption of negligence on the part of the defendant.

Respondeat Superior – A phrase that means "let the master answer." In law, employers are liable for the consequences of their employees' activities within the course of employment for which the employees are responsible.

Statute of Limitations – A state law that limits the time in which a lawsuit may be filed.

Strict Liability – A legal liability theory that applies to injuries caused by the use of a product that is unreasonably dangerous to a consumer or user and reaches the user without substantial change from the condition in which it was sold. The manufacturer or seller of the product usually is liable.

Instructor-Led Questions

1. What are the four elements of a negligent tort?

2. When does a healthcare provider have a duty to an individual?

3. How is the scope of the duty proven?

4. How is legal causation proven?

5. What are intentional torts?

6. What are the major defenses to liability suits?

7. Discuss the use of arbitration as an alternative to litigation.

8. When does strict liability apply in healthcare settings?

9. When there is liability, who is responsible for making the payment?

10. Discuss *respondeat superior*.

11. When can an institution be held directly liable?

12. What is the difference between occurrence and claims-made insurance?

13. Discuss the periodic malpractice crisis and attempted solutions – changes in the standard of care, changes in dispute resolution mechanisms, changes in the amount of the award and how it is paid, changes in the time in which suits must be filed, malpractice insurance coverage reform, and other changes.

14. What nursing actions are most likely to lead to liability?

Endnotes

1 Annotation, Duty of one other than carrier or employer to render assistance to one for whose initial injury he is not liable, 33 A.L.R. 3d 301.

2 *Van Horn v. Chambers, Tex.*, 970 S.W.2d 542 (Tex. 1998).

3 *Osborne v. U.S.*, 211 W. Va. 667, 567 S.E.2d 677 (2002).

4 *Zavalas v. State, Dep't of Corrections*, 861 P.2d 1026 (Ore. Ct. App. 1993), rev. denied, 319 Or. 150, 877 P.2d 86 (1994).

5 *Cram v. Howell*, 680 N.E.2d 1096 (Ind. 1997).

6 *Estate of Witthoeft v. Kiskaddon*, 557 Pa. 340, 733 A.2d 623 (1999).

7 Judge drops psychiatrist from lawsuit over 1996 Penn State University killing, AP, Aug. 9, 2003.

8 See *Fitzgerald v. Porter Mem. Hosp.*, 523 F.2d 716 (7th Cir. 1975) [husband may be excluded from delivery room].

9 *O'Hara v. Holy Cross Hosp.*, 137 Ill. 2d 332, 561 N.E.2d 18 (1990); see Annotation, Liability of hospital for injury to person invited or permitted to accompany patient during emergency room treatment, 90 A.L.R. 4th 478.

10 *Murillo v. Seymour Ambulance Assoc.*, 264 Conn. 474, 823 A.2d 1202 (2003).

11 Althaus by *Althaus v. Cohen*, 562 Pa. 547, 756 A.2d 1166 (2000).

12 *Welker v. Southern Baptist Hosp.*, 864 So. 2d 1178 (Fla. 1st DCA 2004).

13 *McNulty v. City of New York*, 100 N.Y.2d 227, 792 N.E.2d 162, 762 N.Y.S.2d 12 (2003).

14 E.g., FLA. STAT. § 766.102(2)(c); *Payne v. Caldwell*, 796 S.W.2d 142 (Tenn. 1990) [upheld requirement that an expert be licensed in the state or contiguous state for full previous year].

15 *Daubert v. Merrell Dow Pharmaceuticals, Inc.*, 509 U.S. 579 (1993); *Kumho Tire Co. v. Carmichael*, 524 U.S. 936 (1999) [Daubert also applies to nonscientific experts].

16 E.g., *Schneider v. Fried*, 320 F.3d 396 (3d Cir. 2003).

17 *Marrogi v. Howard*, 805 So. 2d 1118 (La. 2002); M. Hoenig, Suing unreliable experts, N.Y. L. J., Mar. 11, 2002, 3.

18 *Deatherage v. Washington State Examining Bd. of Psychology*, 134 Wash. 2d 131, 948 P.2d 828 (1997) [expert witness does not have absolute immunity from professional discipline]; D. Gianelli, Nonexpert witnesses raise delegates' ire, AM. MED. NEWS, Jan. 4, 1999, at 7 [AMA seeking disciplinary actions against doctors who provide fraudulent testimony].

19 N.C. board suspends license for neurosurgeon's expert testimony, AP, Nov. 22, 2003.

20 E.g., L. Page, Expert witness watchdog; Amid complaints, AANS defenders say the program is necessary, fair, MODERN PHYSICIAN, Aug. 1, 2003, 26.

21 E.g., *Brookover v. Mary Hitchcock Mem. Hosp.*, 893 F.2d 411 (1st Cir. 1990) [father could testify that nurse said after fall of son that son should have been restrained; admissible as a vicarious admission].

22 *D.P. v. Wrangell Gen. Hosp.*, 5 P.3d 225 (Alaska 2000).

23 COLO. REV. STAT. § 13-25-135 (2004); Hospitals with unexpected outcomes explore alternatives to "deny and defend," H.L.R., Feb. 3, 2005, 143.

24 E.g., *Cockerton v. Mercy Hosp. Med. Ctr.*, 490 N.W.2d 856 (Iowa Ct. App. 1992) [fall during x-ray exam; failure to use restraint straps is routine nonmedical care]; see also *Dimora v. Cleveland Clinic Found.*, 683 N.E.2d 1175 (Ohio Ct. App. 1996).

25 *St. Paul Med. Ctr. v. Cecil*, 842 S.W.2d 808 (Tex. Ct. App. 1992).

26 *Blatz v. Allina Health Sys.*, 622 N.W.2d 376 (Minn. App. 2001).

27 *Lucia v. Monmouth Med. Ctr.*, 341 N.J. Super. 95, 775 A.2d 97 (App. Div. 2001).

28 E.g., *Peacock v. Samaritan Health Servs.*, 159 Ariz. 123, 765 P.2d 525 (Ct. App. 1988) [internal hospital protocol for safeguarding psychiatric patients].

29 E.g., *Van Iperen v. Van Bramer*, 392 N.W.2d 480 (Iowa 1986) [JCAHO drug monitoring standard]; *Gallagher v. Detroit McComb Hosp. Ass'n*, 171 Mich. App. 761, 431 N.W.2d 90 (1988) [internal hospital rules].

30 E.g., *Hastings v. Baton Rouge Gen. Hosp.*, 498 So. 2d 713 (La. 1986).

31 57A Am. Jur.2d Negligence §§ 716-803.

32 *Suburban Hosp. Ass'n v. Hadary*, 22 Md. App. 186, 322 A.2d 258 (1974).

33 *Galvez v. Frields*, 88 Cal. App. 4th 1410, 107 Cal. Rptr. 2d 50 (2d Dist. 2001).

34 *Lingle v. Dion*, 776 So. 2d 1073 (Fla. 4th DCA 2001).

35 *Haber v. Cross County Hosp.*, 37 N.Y.2d 888, 378 N.Y.S.2d 369, 340 N.E.2d 734 (1975).

36 *Moyer v. Reynolds*, 780 So. 2d 205 (Fla. 5th DCA 2001).

37 *Tobia v. Cooper Hosp. Univ. Med. Ctr.*, 136 N.J. 335, 643 A.2d 1 (1994).

38 *Johnson v. Misercordia Community Hosp.*, 97 Wis. 2d 521, 294 N.W.2d 501 (Ct. App. 1980); *Cooper v. Eagle River Mem. Hosp.*, 270 F.3d 456 (7th Cir. 2001).

39 *Pullen v. Nickens*, 310 S.E.2d 452, 456 (Va. 1983); Klein v. Boyle, 1993 U.S. App. LEXIS 27628 (4th Cir. 1993).

40 *Ravenis v. Detroit Gen. Hosp.*, 63 Mich. App. 79, 234 N.W.2d 411 (1975).

41 *Denton Reg. Med. Ctr. v. LaCroix*, 947 S.W.2d 941 (Tex. Ct. App. 1997).

42 *Spensieri v. Lasky*, 94 N.Y.2d 231, 723 N.E.2d 544, 701 N.Y.S.2d 689 (1999); accord, *Bissett v. Renna*, 142 N.H. 788, 710 A.2d 404 (1998); *Morlino v. Medical Ctr. of Ocean Cty.*, 152 N.J. 563, 706 A.2d 721 (1998); contra, *Fournet v. Roule-Graham*, 783 So. 2d 439 (La. App. 2001) [liability can be based on PDR even when only expert testimony is that PDR does not reflect practice].

43 *Aldridge v. Edmunds*, 561 Pa. 323, 750 A.2d 292 (2000).

44 M. W. Salganik, Medical mistakes: Finding the cure, Baltimore Sun, May 1, 2005, 1D [care guidelines reduce obstetrics suits]; National Health Lawyers Ass'n, Colloquium Report on Legal Issues Related to Clinical Practice Guidelines (1995); J.C. West, The legal implications of medical practice guidelines, 27 J.Health & Hosp.L. 97 (1994); E.B. Hirshfield, Practice parameters and the malpractice liability of physicians, 263 J.A.M.A. 1556 (1990); FDA, Guidance on the recognition and use of consensus standards, 7 Health L. Rptr. [BNA] 353 (1998) [http://www.fda.gov/cdrh] [hereinafter Health L. Rptr. is cited as H.L.R]; see also S.B. Ransom et al., Reduced medicolegal risk by compliance with obstetrical pathways: A case-control study, 101 Obstetrics & Gynecology 751 (2003).

45 L. Oberman, Risk management strategy: Liability insurers stress practice guidelines, Am. Med. News, Sept. 5, 1994, 1 [Colorado].

46 E.g., Internists call clinical practice guidelines effective, 3 H.L.R. 781 (1994).

47 E.g., Half of unstable angina cases could be treated outside hospital, AHCPR says, 3 H.L.R. 339 (1994) [practice guidelines released Mar. 15, 1994].

48 E.g., I.G. Steill et al., Implementation of the Ottawa ankle rules, 271 J.A.M.A. 827 (1994) [reduced use of ankle radiography].

49 E.g., *Sofamor Danek Group, Inc. v. Clinton*, 870 F. Supp. 379 (D. D.C. 1994) [deny injunction of AHCPR release of clinical practice guidelines for lower back pain].

50 *Furey v. Thomas Jefferson Univ. Hosp.*, 325 Pa. Super. 212, 472 A.2d 1083 (1984); *Fraijo v. Hartland Hosp.*, 99 Cal. App. 3d 331, 160 Cal. Rptr. 246 (2d Dist. 1979) [applied to nursing decision].

51 E.g., Fla. Stat. §766.102(2)(c).

52 *Helling v. Carey*, 83 Wash. 2d 514, 519 P.2d 981 (1974).

53 *Tarasoff v. Regents of Univ. of Cal.*, 17 Cal. 3d 425, 131 Cal. Rptr. 14, 551 P.2d 334 (1976).

54 *Gonzales v. Nork*, No. 228566 (Cal. Super. Ct. Nov. 19, 1973), rev'd on other grounds, 20 Cal. 3d 500, 573 P.2d 458 (1978).

55 *Austin v. Regents of Univ. of Cal.*, 89 Cal. App. 3d 354, 152 Cal. Rptr. 420 (4th Dist. 1979).

56 E.g., *Majca v. Beekil*, 183 Ill. 2d 407, 701 N.E.2d 1084 (1998) [proof of actual exposure to HIV required to claim fear of contracting AIDS]; *Natale v. Gottlieb Mem. Hosp.*, 314 Ill. App. 3d 885, 733 N.E.2d 380 (1st Dist. 2000) [failure to prove actual exposure from use of nonsterile endoscope]; *R.J. v. Humana of Fla., Inc.*, 652 So. 2d 360 (Fla. 1995) [impact rule applies to damages claim for negligent HIV diagnosis claim, so must show emotional distress flows from physical injury of impact; when misdiagnosis results in harmful treatment, treatment may provide impact]; *Lubowitz v. Albert Einstein Med. Ctr.*, 424 Pa. Super. 468, 623 A.2d 3 (1993) [no claim for fear of AIDS due to mistakenly being told exposed to HIV]; *Carroll v. Sisters of St. Francis Health Servs.*, 868 S.W.2d 585 (Tenn. 1993) [no recovery for negligent infliction of emotional distress based on fear of AIDS without showing exposure to HIV virus]; *Herbert v. Regents of Univ. of Cal.*, 26 Cal. App. 4th 782, 31 Cal. Rptr. 2d 709 (2d Dist. 1994) [no claim for emotional distress for HIV fear from needle scratch where HIV chance minimal]; *Marchica v. Long Island R. Co.*, 31 F.3d 1197 (2d Cir. 1994), aff'g, 810 F. Supp. 445 (E.D. N.Y.), cert. denied, 513 U.S. 1079 (1995) [affirming jury verdict for employee for fear of AIDS after puncture wound].

57 E.g., *Smith v. Sofamor*, S.N.C., 21 F. Supp. 2d 918 (W.D. Wis. 1998) [insufficient testimony surgical device caused injury]; *Hodges v. Secretary of DHHS*, 9 F.3d 958 (Fed. Cir. 1993) [failure to prove causation of death of infant after DPT vaccination]; *Campos v. Ysleta Gen. Hosp., Inc.*, 836 S.W.2d 791 (Tex. Ct. App. 1992) [failure to prove causation of child's death].

58 *Lenger v. Physician's Gen. Hosp.*, 455 S.W.2d 703 (Tex. 1970).

59 *Snelson v. Kamm*, 319 Ill. App. 3d 116, 745 N.E.2d 128 (4th Dist. 2001), aff'd in relevant part, 204 Ill. 2d 1, 787 N.E.2d 796 (2003).

60 *Schnebly v. Baker*, 217 N.W.2d 708 (Iowa 1974).

61 E.g., *Lord v. Lovett*, 770 A.2d 1103 (N.H. 2001); *Delany v. Cade*, 255 Kan. 199, 873 P.2d 175 (1994) [may make claim for loss of chance of better recovery, not just loss of chance of survival]; Annotation, Medical malpractice: "loss of chance" causality, 54 A.L.R. 4TH 10.

62 E.g., *Wallace v. St. Francis Hosp. & Med. Ctr.*, 44 Conn. App. 257, 688 A.2d 352 (1997).

63 *Wendland v. Sparks*, 574 N.W.2d 327 (Iowa 1998).

64 E.g., *McKain v. Bisson*, 12 F.3d 692 (7th Cir. 1993) [applying Indiana law]; *Kilpatrick v. Bryant*, 868 S.W.2d 594 (Tenn. 1993).

65 *Blondel v. Hays*, 241 Va. 467, 403 S.E.2d 340 (1991).

66 E.g., *Dillon v. Medical Ctr. Hosp.*, 98 Ohio App. 3d 510, 648 N.E.2d 1375 (1993), appeal dismissed, 72 Ohio St. 3d 1201, 647 N.E.2d 166 (1995) [hospital not liable, despite negligence of nurses, because causation broken by acts of independent physicians].

67 *Rivera v. New York City Health & Hosps. Corp.*, 72 N.Y.2d 1021, 531 N.E.2d 644, 534 N.Y.S.2d 923 (1988).

68 *Daubert v. Merrell Dow Pharmaceuticals, Inc.*, 509 U.S. 579 (1993); *Kumho Tire Co. v. Carmichael*, 524 U.S. 936 (1999 [Daubert applies to nonscientific experts].

69 E.g., *Daubert v. Merrell Dow Pharmaceuticals, Inc.*, 43 F.3d 1311 (9th Cir. 1995), upon remand from, 509 U.S. 579 (1993) [expert scientific testimony not admissible to prove Bendectin caused plaintiff's birth defects]; *Sorensen v. Shaklee Corp.*, 31 F.3d 638 (8th Cir. 1994) [affirming summary judgment for manufacturer in suit claiming mental retardation due to alfalfa tablets; proposed expert testimony did not have sufficient scientific validity in light of Daubert].

70 E.g., *Washburn v. Merck & Co.*, 2000 U.S. App. LEXIS 8601 (2d Cir. 2000).

71 *Byrne v. Boadle*, 2 H. & C. 722 (Exch. 1863).

72 E.g., Robb ex rel. *Robb v. Anderton*, 864 P.2d 1322 (Utah Ct. App. 1993) [not res ipsa loquitur, no showing cardiac arrest during surgery would not occur without negligence]; *Chism v. Campbell*, 553 N.W.2d 741 (Neb. 1996) [not res ipsa loquitur, tooth damage during surgery was known inherent risk of general anesthesia]; *Leone v. United Health Servs.*, 282 A.D.2d 860, 723 N.Y.S.2d 260 (3d Dept. 2001). [not res ipsa loquitur, only expert could say whether nerve injury during vasectomy could only occur with negligence]; see also *States v. Lourdes Hosp.*, 100 N.Y.2d 208, 792 N.E.2d 151 (2003) [expert testimony can be used to establish that damage would not occur without negligence].

73 E.g., *Posta v. Chung-Loy*, 306 N.J. Super. 182, 703 A.2d 368 (App. Div. 1997) [res ipsa loquitur not applicable to hernia one year after surgery, no evidence showing patient's own actions did not cause or contribute].

74 E.g., *Leonard v. Watsonville Commun. Hosp.*, 47 Cal. 2d 509, 305 P.2d 36 (1956).

75 E.g., *Parks v. Perry*, 68 N.C. App. 202, 314 S.E.2d 287 (1984); *Wick v. Henderson*, 485 N.W.2d 645 (Iowa 1992) [damage to ulnar nerve during gallbladder surgery]; *Baczuk v. Salt Lake Reg. Med. Ctr.*, 8 P.3d 1037 (Utah App. 2000) [pressure injury to site distant from surgery].

76 E.g., *Sanchez v. Bay Gen. Hosp.*, 116 Cal. App. 3d 678, 172 Cal. Rptr. 342 (4th Dist. 1981); *Reilly v. Straub*, 282 N.W.2d 688 (Iowa 1979).

77 E.g., *Mulkey v. Tubb*, 535 So. 2d 1294 (La. Ct. App. 1988) [adequate explanation of damage to site distant from surgery].

78 E.g., *Darwin v. Gooberman*, 339 N.J. Super. 467, 772 A.2d 399 (App. Div. 2001) [affidavit of merit not required for battery claim]; but see *Williams v. Boyle*, 72 P.3d 392 (Colo. App. 2003) [certificate of review required for defamation claim for medical record entry where privilege may apply].

79 E.g., *Bommareddy v. Superior Court*, 222 Cal. App. 3d 1017, 272 Cal. Rptr. 246 (5th Dist. 1990), rev. denied, 1990 Cal. LEXIS 4989 (Oct. 30, 1990), disapproved on other grounds, *Central Pathology Serv. Med. Clinic v. Superior Court*, 3 Cal. 4th 181, 10 Cal. Rptr. 2d 208, 832 P.2d 924 (1992).

80 *Murphy v. Herfort*, 140 A.D.2d 415, 528 N.Y.S.2d 117 (2d Dept. 1988); see also, e.g., *Malone v. Longo*, 463 F. Supp. 139 (E.D. N.Y. 1979) [nurse report to supervisor about physician order protected]; *Kletschka v. Abbott-Northwestern Hosp., Inc.*, 417 N.W.2d 752 (Minn. Ct. App. 1988) [performance evaluation protected].

81 *Bartlett v. Daniel Drake Mem. Hosp.*, 75 Ohio App. 3d 334, 599 N.E.2d 403 (1991).

82 E.g., *Feldman v. Glucoft*, 522 So. 2d 798 (Fla. 1988), appeal after remand, 580 So. 2d 866 (Fla. 3d DCA) [no evidence extrinsic to proceedings alleged, judgment for defendants affirmed], rev. denied, 591 So. 2d 181 (Fla. 1991), cert. denied, 503 U.S. 960 (1992).

83 *Williams v. Boyle*, 72 P.3d 392 (Colo. App. 2003).

84 E.g., *Skobin v. County of Los Angeles*, 2004 Cal. App. Unpub. LEXIS 7617 (2d Dist.).

85 E.g., *Boles v. Milwaukee County*, 150 Wis. 2d 801, 443 N.W.2d 679 (App. 1989).

86 *Arthur v. Lutheran Gen. Hosp., Inc.*, 295 Ill. App. 3d 818, 692 N.E.2d 1238 (1st Dist. 1998).

87 *Koudski v. Hennepin County Med. Ctr.*, 317 N.W.2d 705 (Minn. 1982).

88 *Burgess v. Busby*, 544 S.E.2d 4 (N.C. Ct. App. 2001).

89 *Johnson v. Woman's Hosp.*, 527 S.W.2d 133 (Tenn. Ct. App. 1975).

90 *McCormick v. Haley*, 37 Ohio App. 2d 73, 307 N.E.2d 34 (1973).

91 *Gragg v. Calandra*, 297 Ill. App. 3d 639, 696 N.E.2d 1282 (2d Dist. 1998).

92 E.g., *Nicholson v. Lucas*, 26 Cal. Rptr. 4th 778, 26 Cal. Rptr. 2d 778 (5th Dist. 1994) [dismissal of dentist's claim that initiation of medical staff proceedings was malicious prosecution].

93 *Matthews v. Blue Cross & Blue Shield*, 456 Mich. 365, 572 N.W.2d 603 (1998).

94 *Dutt v. Kremp*, 894 P.2d 354 (Nev. 1995); *Spencer v. Burglass*, 288 So. 2d 68 (La. Ct. App. 1974); but see *Bull v. McCluskey*, 96 Nev. 706, 615 P.2d 957 (1980); *Miller v. Rosenberg*, 196 Ill. 2d 50, 749 N.E.2d 946 [law making malicious prosecution suits easier is constitutional]; Doctor sued for malpractice fights back with suit of his own, AP, June 7, 2000 [Ky. jury award doctor $72,000].

95 E.g., *Garrett v. Fisher Titus Hosp.*, 318 F. Supp. 2d 562 (N.D. Ohio 2004); *Hanson v. Hancock County Mem. Hosp.*, 938 F. Supp. 1419 (N.D. Iowa 1996).

96 *Deleon v. Slear*, 328 Md. 569, 616 A.2d 380 (1992).

97 *Anne Arundel Med. Ctr., Inc. v. Condon*, 102 Md. App. 408, 649 A.2d 1189 (1994); contra, *JFK Med. Ctr., Inc. v. Price*, 647 So. 2d 833 (Fla. 1994) [continuation of wrongful death malpractice suit against passive tortfeasor after settlement with active tortfeasor not barred].

98 *Keator v. Gale*, 1997 N.D. 46, 561 N.W.2d 286 (1997).

99 E.g., *Mitchell v. Mitchell*, 963 S.W.2d 222 (Ky. Ct. App. 1998) [release to settle personal injury claim of emancipated and married 17-year-old was void due to incapacity]; but see *Zivich v. Mentor Soccer Club, Inc.*, 82 Ohio St. 3d 367, 696 N.E.2d 201 (1998) [exculpatory agreement in favor of volunteers and sponsors of nonprofit sports activity signed by mother of 7-year-old was enforceable against both parents and child].

100 E.g., *Bowden v. Hutzel Hosp.*, 252 Mich. App. 566, 652 N.W.2d 529 (2002) [settlement remanded to trial court to hold hearing on the minor's best interests before approval]; *Ott v. Little Co. of Mary Hosp.*, 273 Ill. App. 3d 563, 652 N.E.2d 1051 (1st Dist. 1995) [trial judge did not abuse discretion in approving $2 million settlement for minor over objections of parents].

101 E.g., *Nelson v. American Red Cross*, 307 U.S. App. D.C. 52, 26 F.3d 193 (1994) [suit for death from HIV barred by statute of limitations, which started when blood given not when AIDS appeared]; *Weiss v. Rojanasathit*, 975 S.W.2d 113 (Mo. 1998) [rejecting theory of continuing tort; holding statute of limitations period begins to run from date of occurrence of alleged negligent act]; *Charter Peachford Behavioral Health Sys., Inc. v. Kohout*, 233 Ga. App. 452, 504 S.E.2d 514 (1998) [statute of limitations in claim of misdiagnosis of mental illness began to run when misdiagnosis occurred, not when misdiagnosis recognized].

102 E.g., *Katz v. Children's Hosp.*, 28 F.3d 1520 (9th Cir. 1994) [under California law, time period started when harm experienced].

103 See *Tullock v. Eck*, 311 Ark. 564, 845 S.W.2d 517 (1993) [limiting continuous treatment doctrine]; *Anderson v. George*, 717 A.2d 876 (D.C. App. 1998) [continuous treatment doctrine applies to medical malpractice cases in District of Columbia].

104 FLA. STAT. § 95.11(4)(b).

105 E.g., *Roberts v. Francis*, 128 F.3d 647 (8th Cir. 1997) [physician's nondisclosure of removal of ovary was fraudulent concealment extending time]; *McDonald v. United States*, 843 F.2d 247 (6th Cir. 1988) [reassurances of complete recovery can extend time]; *Muller v. Thaut*, 230 Neb. 244, 430 N.W.2d 884 (1988) [fraudulent concealment].

106 E.g., IOWA CODE § 614.8; Annotation, Medical malpractice statutes of limitation minority provisions, 62 A.L.R. 4TH 758; see also *Barnes v. Sabatino*, 205 Ga. App. 773, 423 S.E.2d 686 (1992) [17-year-old not covered by special rule for minors which applied only to persons under age 5]; contra, FLA. STAT. § 95.11(4)(b) [minors subject to same time limit as adults]; *Plummer v. Gillieson*, 44 Mass. App. Ct. 578, 692 N.E.2d 528 (1998) [minors subject to same time limit as adults].

107 E.g., WIS. STAT. § 893.56; *Partin v. St. Francis Hosp.*, 296 Ill. App. 3d 220, 694 N.E.2d 574 (1st Dist. 1998) [statute of limitations baring claims of minors after eight years constitutional].

108 E.g., *Hyde v. University of Mich. Bd. of Regents*, 426 Mich. 223, 393 N.W.2d 847 (1986) [public general hospital is governmental function]. Public hospitals were later removed by statute in Michigan. *McCummings v. Hurley Med. Ctr.*, 433 Mich. 404, 446 N.W.2d 114, 117 n. 3 (1989).

109 E.g., *Allen v. State*, 535 So. 2d 903 (La. Ct. App. 1988) [$500,000 cap on damages applied]; *Eldred v. North Broward Hosp. Dist.*, 498 So. 2d 911 (Fla. 1986) [$50,000 cap on damages applied]; but see *Condemarin v. University Hosp.*, 775 P.2d 348 (Utah 1989) [$100,000 cap on governmental hospital liability unconstitutional].

110 E.g., *Fields v. Curator of Univ. of Mo.*, 848 S.W.2d 589 (Mo. Ct. App. 1993) [sovereign immunity waived by purchase of liability insurance]; *Green River Dist. Health Dep't v. Wigginton*, 764 S.W.2d 475 (Ky. 1989) [sovereign immunity waived to extent of liability insurance]; but see *Hillsborough County Hosp. v. Taylor*, 546 So. 2d 1055 (Fla. 1989) [malpractice trust fund does not waive sovereign immunity]; contra, *Lawrence v. Virginia Ins. Reciprocal*, 979 F.2d 1053 (5th Cir. 1992) [community hospital sovereign immunity protected from punitive damages even when insurance covered such damages]; *Sambs v. City of Brookfield*, 66 Wis. 2d 296, 224 N.W.2d 582 (1975) [insurance waives caps only when insurance policy precludes the insurer from asserting the cap].

111 E.g., *Higgins v. Medical Univ. of S.C.*, 486 S.E.2d 269 (S.C. Ct. App. 1997) [physicians protected by sovereign immunity]; *Joplin v. University of Mich. Bd. of Regents*, 173 Mich. App. 149, 433 N.W.2d 830 (1988), aff'd on remand, 184 Mich. App. 497, 459 N.W.2d 70 (1990) [physicians protected by sovereign immunity]; *Jaar v. University of Miami*, 474 So. 2d 239 (Fla. 3d DCA 1985) [physicians protected]; *DeRosa v. Shands Teaching Hosp.*, 504 So. 2d 1313 (Fla. 1st DCA 1987) [resident physicians protected]; *Canon v. Thumudo*, 430 Mich. 326, 422 N.W.2d 688 (1988) [nurses protected]; see also D. Holthaus, County agrees to shield ob/gyns from liability, 62 HOSPS. (July 20, 1988), at 42 [physicians made county agents so protected by $500,000 liability limitation]; but see *Cooper v. Bowers*, 706 S.W.2d 542 (Mo. Ct. App. 1986) [physician not protected]; *Keenan v. Plouffe*, 482 S.E.2d 253 (Ga. 1997).

112 E.g., *Lazerson v. Hilton Head Hosp.*, 312 S.C. 211, 439 S.E.2d 836 (1994) [statutory $200,000 limit on liability of charitable organizations is constitutional]; *Endres v. Greenville Hosp. System*, 312 S.C. 64, 439 S.E.2d 261 (1993) [after settlement with child at maximum under charitable immunity law, affirmed summary judgment barring parent from collecting derivative maximum again]; *Marsella v. Monmouth Med. Center*, 224 N.J. Super. 336, 540 A.2d 865 (App. Div. 1988) [$10,000 cap on damages against nonprofit hospitals]; *English v. New England Med. Ctr.*, 405 Mass. 423, 541 N.E.2d 329 (1989), cert. denied, 493 U.S. 1056 (1990) [statutory $20,000 cap on liability of nonprofit institutions upheld]; but see *Chandler v. Hospital Auth.*, 500 So. 2d 1012 (Ala. 1986) [charitable immunity statute violated state constitution because it applied to too few hospitals].

113 E.g., *Johnese v. Jefferson Davis Mem. Hosp.*, 637 F. Supp. 1198 (S.D. Miss. 1986) [charitable immunity waived by insurance]; but see *Ponder v. Fulton-DeKalb Hosp. Auth.*, 256 Ga. 833, 353 S.E.2d 515, cert. denied, 484 U.S. 863 (1987) [self-insurance plan did not waive charitable immunity].

114 E.g., *McIntyre v. Ramirez*, 109 S.W.3d 741 (Tex. 2003) [physicians can be protected in hospital in some circumstances]; *Hirpa v. IHC Hosps., Inc.*, 948 P.2d 785 (Utah 1997) [Good Samaritan law applies to hospital-employed physicians who respond to in-hospital immunity without preexisting duty]; *Johnson v. Matviuw*, 176 Ill. App. 3d 907, 531 N.E.2d 970 (1st Dist. 1988) [applied to gratuitous hospital emergency care with no preexisting duty]; *Kearns v. Superior Ct.*, 204 Cal. App. 3d 1325, 252 Cal. Rptr. 4 (2d Dist. 1988) [applied to emergency assistance in surgery]; Annotation, Construction and application of "Good Samaritan" statute, 68 A.L.R. 4th 294; but see *Velazquez v. Jiminez*, 172 N.J. 240, 798 A.2d 51 (2002) [hospital emergency department physicians not protected]; *Deal v. Kearney*, 851 P.2d 1353 (Alaska 1993) [Good Samaritan immunity does not apply when there is preexisting duty to provide aid].

115 E.g., *De Tarquino v. Jersey City*, 352 N.J. Super. 450, 800 A.2d 255 (App. Div. 2002) [EMT has no immunity for failure to document vomiting since documentation is not part of treatment in N.J.]; *Morrell v. Aetna Ambulance Service, Inc.*, 2002 Conn. Super. LEXIS 3252 (unreported) [EMT has no immunity for feeding turkey sandwich to patient because feeding is not part of emergency services in Connecticut].

116 E.g., *Deboer v. Florida Offroaders Driver's Ass'n*, 622 So. 2d 1134 (Fla. 5th DCA 1993) [exculpatory contract protected sponsor of racing event from liability to spectator hit by car while crossing track].

117 E.g., *Cudnik v. William Beaumont Hosp.*, 207 Mich. App. 378, 525 N.W.2d 891 (1994) [exculpatory contract unenforceable]; *Tatham v. Hoke*, 469 F. Supp. 914 (W.D. N.C. 1979), aff'd without op., 622 F.2d 584, 587 (4th Cir. 1980) [agreement to limit all claims to $15,000 unenforceable]; Annotation, Validity and construction of contract exempting hospital or doctor from liability for negligence to patient, 6 A.L.R. 3d 704. For a discussion of the difference between exculpatory, indemnity, hold harmless, and related clauses under Pennsylvania law, see *Vahal Corp. v. Sullivan Assocs., Inc.*, 44 F.3d 195 (3d Cir. 1995), reh'g denied (en banc), 48 F.3d 760 (3d Cir. 1995).

118 *Massengill v. S.M.A.R.T. Sports Med. Clinic, P.C.*, 996 P.2d 1132 (Wyo. 2000).

119 E.g., *Neaman v. Kaiser Found. Hospital*, 9 Cal. App. 4th 1170, 11 Cal. Rptr. 2d 879 (2d Dist. 1992), modified, 10 Cal. App. 4th 293 (1992) [award in favor of hospital vacated and remanded for new panel of arbitrators because "neutral" third arbitrator failed to disclose prior substantial business relationship with hospital].

120 Annotation, Arbitration of medical malpractice claims, 24 A.L.R. 5th 1; *Morris v. Metriyakool*, 418 Mich. 423, 344 N.W.2d 736 (1984) [state arbitration act constitutional].

121 E.g., *Colorado Permanente Med. Group v. Evans*, 926 P.2d 1218 (Colo. 1996).

122 9 U.S.C. §§ 1 - 16.

123 E.g., *Cruz v. Pacificare Health Sys.*, 30 Cal. 4th 303, 66 P.3d 1157, 133 Cal. Rptr. 2d 58 (2003) [some public injunctions not subject to arbitration, exception to FAA preemption]; *Broughton v. CIGNA Healthplans*, 21 Cal. 4th 1066, 988 P.2d 67, 90 Cal. Rptr. 2d 334 (1999) [injunctive relief portion of a deceptive advertising claim under state Consumers Legal Remedies Act (CLRA) is inarbitrable, but action for damages under CLRA is fully arbitrable; exception to FAA preemption]; *Zolezzi v. Pacificare*, 105 Cal. App. 4th 573, 129 Cal. Rptr. 2d 526 (4th Dist. 2003) [McCarran-Ferguson Act blocks FAA preemption of state law health plan arbitration requirements, Medicare law does not preempt for Medicare+Choice plans]; *Allen v. Pacheco*, 71 P.3d 375 (Colo. 2003) [McCarren Ferguson blocks FAA preemption of state law on arbitration of health plan claims].

124 *McGuffey Health & Rehab. Ctr. v. Gibson*, 864 So. 2d 1061 (Ala. 2003); but see *St. Jude Hosp. v. Associated Claims Management*, 2002 Cal. App. Unpub. LEXIS 11201 (4th Dist.) [failure to prove interstate commerce affect].

125 *Herbert v. Superior Court*, 169 Cal. App. 3d 718, 215 Cal. Rptr. 477 (2d Dist. 1985); accord, *Ling Wo. Leong v. Kaiser Found. Hosp.*, 71 Haw. 240, 788 P.2d 164 (1990) [newborn covered by arbitration agreement in father's health plan].

126 *Gainesville Health Care Ctr., Inc. v. Weston*, 857 So. 2d 278 (Fla. 1st DCA 2003).

127 *Engalla v. Permanente Medical Group*, 15 Cal. 4th 951, 938 P.2d 903, 64 Cal. Rptr. 2d 843 (1997); L. Prager, Kaiser will turn over arbitration to neutral party, Am. Med. News, Feb. 2, 1998, 3; J. Appleby, Los Angeles law firm to oversee arbitration for Kaiser Permanente, Contra Costa Times [CA], Nov. 11, 1998; *Saint Agnes Med. Ctr. v Pacificare*, 31 Cal. 4th 1187, 82 P.3d 727, 8 Cal. Rptr. 3d 517 (2003) [discussion of what constitutes waiver of arbitration, no waiver found].

128 *Orrick v. San Joaquin Community Hosp.*, 62 Cal. App. 4th 1466, 73 Cal. Rptr. 2d 757 (5th Dist. 1998).

129 D.E. Beeman, Kaiser loses ruling in newborn's death, Press Enterprise (Riverside CA), Dec. 28, 2002, B1 [arbitrator awards $1 million, reduced to $250,000 under MICRA; Kaiser lost 84 of 228 arbitration cases from 1999 through 2001, with awards ranging from $2,500 to $5.6 million and averaging $207,571].

130 E.g., *McGill v. French*, 333 N.C. 209, 424 S.E.2d 108 (1993); *Gruidl v. Schell*, 166 Ill. App. 3d 276, 519 N.E.2d 963 (1st Dist. 1988); *Roberts v. Wood*, 206 F. Supp. 579 (S.D. Ala. 1962); Annotation, Medical malpractice: patient's failure to return, as directed, for examination or treatment as contributory negligence, 100 A.L.R. 3d 723; *Wilmot v. Howard*, 39 Vt. 447 (1867) [neglect, refusal to obey instructions, follow the treatment prescribed].

131 E.g., *Chudson v. Ratra*, 76 Md. App. 753, 548 A.2d 172 (1988).

132 E.g., *Shurey v. Schlemmer*, 140 Ind. App. 606, 223 N.E.2d 759, rev'd, 249 Ind. 1, 230 N.E.2d 534 (1967) [jury must determine whether contributory negligence].

133 E.g., *Jenkins v. Bogalusa Commun. Med. Ctr.*, 340 So. 2d 1065 (La. Ct. App. 1976).

134 E.g., *Seymour v. Victory Mem. Hosp.*, 60 Ill. App. 3d 366, 376 N.E.2d 754 (2d Dist. 1978).

135 E.g., *Rochester v. Katalan*, 320 A.2d 704 (Del. 1974).

136 *Elbaor v. Smith*, 845 S.W.2d 240 (Tex. 1992).

137 E.g., *Cowan v. Doering*, 111 N.J. 451, 545 A.2d 159 (1988).

138 E.g., *McDonnell v. McPartlin*, 92 Ill. 2d 505, 736 N.E.2d 1074 (2000); *Love v. Park Lane Med. Ctr.*, 737 S.W.2d 720 (Mo. 1987).

139 E.g., *Isern v. Watson*, 942 S.W.2d 186 (Tex. Civ. App. 1997) [jury found patient 35 percent responsible for leg amputation, did not return to emergency room or seek medical care for two days].

140 E.g., *Jensen v. Intermountain Health Care, Inc.*, 679 P.2d 903 (Utah 1984); contra, *Hoffman v. Jones*, 280 So. 2d 431 (Fla. 1973).

141 E.g., *Jankee v. Clark County*, 2000 WI 64, 235 Wis. 2d 700, 612 N.W.2d 297 [mental hospital patient held to standard of sane person when he could control his conduct through medication]; *Sheron v. Lutheran Med. Ctr.*, 18 P.3d 796 (Colo. App. 2000) [suicidal person can be negligent].

142 *Tobia v. Cooper Hosp. Univ. Med. Ctr.*, 136 N.J. 335, 643 A.2d 1 (1994).

143 E.g., *Faulk v. Northwest Radiologists, P.C.*, 751 N.E.2d 233 (Ind. App. 2001).

144 E.g., *Mercer v. Vanderbilt Univ.*, 134 S.W.3d 121 (Tenn. 2004); *Estate of Shinholster v. Annapolis Hosp.*, 255 Mich. App. 339, 660 N.W.2d 361 (2003).

145 *Wright v. Central DuPage Hosp. Assn.*, 63 Ill. 2d 313, 347 N.E.2d 736 (1976). The Illinois Supreme Court again struck down damage caps in 1997. *Best v. Taylor Machine Works Co.*, 179 Ill. 2d 367, 689 N.E.2d 1057 (Ill. 1997); accord, *Morris v. Savoy*, 61 Ohio St. 3d 684, 576 N.E.2d 765 (1991).

146 *Johnson v. St. Vincent Hosp.*, 273 Ind. 374, 404 N.E.2d 585 (1980); accord, *Duke Power Co. v. Carolina Environmental Study Group, Inc.*, 438 U.S. 59 (1978) [Congress may cap damages for nuclear reactor incidents]; *Pulliam v. Coastal Emergency Servs.*, 257 Va. 1, 509 S.E.2d 307 (1999) [cap on malpractice awards constitutional]; *Scholtz v. Metropolitan Pathologists, P.C.*, 851 P.2d 901 (Colo. 1993).

147 E.g., *Power v. Arlington Hosp. Ass'n*, 42 F.3d 851 (4th Cir. 1994).

148 E.g., *Lozada v. United States*, 974 F.2d 986 (8th Cir. 1992).

149 E.g., Wis. Stat. §§ 893.80 & 893.82; *Anderson v. City of Milwaukee*, 208 Wis. 2d 18, 559 N.W.2d 563 (1997).

150 *Perlmutter v. Beth David Hosp.*, 308 N.Y. 100, 123 N.E.2d 792 (1954).

151 E.g., *Shortess v. Touro Infirmary*, 508 So. 2d 938 (La. 1988) [hospital strictly liable for blood with undetectable form of hepatitis]; *Cunningham v. MacNeal Mem. Hosp.*, 47 Ill. 2d 443, 266 N.E.2d 897 (1970).

152 E.g., *Weishorn v. Miles-Cutter*, 721 A.2d 811 (Pa. Super. Ct. 1998), aff'd, 560 Pa. 557, 746 A.2d 1117 (2000) [state blood shield law also protects commercial suppliers from strict liability, breach of warranty].

153 E.g., *Samson v. Greenville Hosp. Sys.*, 295 S.C. 359, 368 S.E.2d 665 (1988); *McDaniel v. Baptist Mem. Hosp.*, 469 F.2d 230 (6th Cir. 1972).

154 *Shivers v. Good Shepard Hosp.*, 427 S.W.2d 104 (Tex. Civ. App. 1968).

155 *Stephenson v. Greenberg*, 421 Pa. Super. 1, 617 A.2d 364 (1992).

156 *Dubin v. Michael Reese Hosp.*, 83 Ill. 2d 277, 415 N.E.2d 350 (1980), rev'g, 74 Ill. App. 3d 932, 393 N.E.2d 588 (1st Dist. 1979); see also *Nevauex v. Park Place Hosp.*, 656 S.W.2d 923 (Tex. Ct. App. 1983) [no strict liability for burns from cobalt radiation therapy].

157 E.g., *Brandt v. Boston Scientific Corp*, 204 Ill. 2d 640, 792 N.E.2d 296 (2003) [implantation of device is service, not sale]; *Royer v. Catholic Med. Ctr.*, 144 N.H. 330, 741 A.2d 74 (1999) [implantation of prosthetic knee is service, not sale]; In re Breast Implant Product Liability Litigation, 331 S.C. 540, 503 S.E.2d 445 (1998); *Rolon-Alvarado v. San Juan*, 1 F.3d 74 (1st Cir. 1993) [provider not strictly liable for latent defect in endotracheal tube manufactured by third party]; *Hoff v. Zimmer, Inc.*, 746 F. Supp. 872 (W.D. Wis. 1990); *North Miami Gen. Hosp. v. Goldberg*, 520 So. 2d 650 (Fla. 3d DCA 1988) [hospital not strictly liable for burn from grounding pad]; *Hector v. Cedars-Sinai Med. Ctr.*, 180 Cal. App. 3d 493, 225 Cal. Rptr. 595 (2d Dist. 1986) [hospital not strictly liable for pacemaker]; Annotation, Liability of hospital or medical practitioner under doctrine of strict liability in tort, or breach of warranty, for harm caused by drug, medical instrument, or similar device used in treating patient, 65 A.L.R. 5th 357; see also *Parker v. St. Vincent Hosp.*, 1996 NMCA 70, 919 P.2d 1104, 1107, 122 N.M. 39 [rejecting products/services distinction, but declining to extend strict liability on policy grounds].

158 *Silverhart v. Mount Zion Hosp.*, 20 Cal. App. 3d 1022, 98 Cal. Rptr. 187 (1st Dist. 1971).

159 *St. Mary's Med. Ctr., Inc. v. Casko*, 639 N.E.2d 312 (Ind. Ct. App. 1994).

160 *McKenna v. Harrison Mem. Hosp.*, 92 Wash. App. 119, 960 P.2d 486 (1998).

161 *Skelton v. Druid City Hosp. Bd.*, 459 So. 2d 818 (Ala. 1984).

162 *Thomas v. St. Joseph Hosp.*, 618 S.W.2d 791 (Tex. Civ. App. 1981).

163 21 U.S.C. § 360c.

164 *Medtronic, Inc. v. Lohr*, 518 U.S. 470 (1996) [for device "substantially equivalent" to devices that preexisted MDA and exempt from the rigorous premarketing approval review, MDA does not preempt the plaintiff's state common law claims for defective design, defective manufacture, failure-to-warn, and failure to comply with FDA standards; MDA may preempt state law tort claim, claim based on state statute, regulation, but federal, state requirements must specifically apply to particular medical device, state requirement must add to or be different from federal requirement]; *Buckman Co. v. Plaintiffs' Legal Comm.*, 531 U.S. 341 (2001) [common law claims of fraud on FDA preempted by MDA, tort claims alleging violations of FDCA preempted].

165 E.g., *Horn v. Thoratec Corp.*, 376 F.3d 163 (3d Cir. 2004) [state defective design claims preempted]; *Brooks v. Howmedica, Inc.*, 273 F.3d 785 (8th Cir. 2001) (en banc) [failure to warn claim preempted]; *Martin v. Medtronic, Inc.*, 254 F.3d 573 (5th Cir. 2001), cert. denied, 534 U.S. 1078 (2002) [state product liability claims are preempted by MDA]; *Whitson v. Safeskin Corp., Inc.*, 313 F. Supp. 2d 473 (M.D. Pa. 2004) [implied warranty claims related to latex gloves preempted]; In re St. Jude Medical, Inc. Silzone Heart Valves Products Liability Litigation. 2004 U.S. Dist. LEXIS 148 (D. Minn.) [failure to warn claims not preempted].

166 Lawyer hauls off hospital assets in dispute over malpractice award, Mod. Healthcare, July 28, 1989, 69.

167 E.g., *Rice v. Nova Biomedical Corp.*, 38 F.3d 909 (7th Cir. 1994), cert. denied, 514 U.S. 1111 (1995).

168 *Lucas v. Hospital Auth. of Dougherty County*, 193 Ga. App. 595, 388 S.E.2d 871 (1989).

169 *Jones v. Baisch*, 40 F.3d 252 (8th Cir. 1994).

170 *Thompson v. Everett Clinic*, 71 Wash. App. 548, 860 P.2d 1054 (1993) [clinic not liable for sexual misconduct by employee physician with male patient during examination]; *P.S. v. Psychiatric Coverage, Ltd.*, 887 S.W.2d 622 (Mo. Ct. App. 1994) [sexual relations with patient not within scope of employment, clinic not liable]; contra, *Morin v. Henry Mayo Newhall Mem. Hosp.*, 29 Cal. App. 4th 473, 34 Cal. Rptr. 2d 535 (2d Dist. 1994) [hospital liable under respondeat superior for sexual misconduct of ultrasound technician]; *Samuels v. Southern Baptist Hosp.*, 594 So. 2d 571 (La. Ct. App. 1992), cert. denied, 599 So. 2d 316 (La. 1992) [hospital liable for sexual assault by employee nursing assistant during working hours on premises because reasonably incidental to employee's performance of his duty]; Annotation, Liability of hospital or clinic for sexual relationships with patients by staff physicians, psychologists, and other healers, 45 A.L.R. 4th 289.

171 E.g., *Krane v. St. Anthony Hosp. Sys.*, 738 P.2d 75 (Colo. Ct. App. 1987).

172 E.g., *Lewis v Physicians Ins. Co.*, 2001 WI 60, 243 Wis. 2d 648, 627 N.W.2d 484; *Holger v. Irish*, 316 Or. 402, 851 P.2d 1122 (1993).

173 E.g., *Somerset v. Hart*, 549 S.W.2d 814 (Ky. 1977) [surgeon, hospital both liable for nurse's instrument count].

174 E.g., *Menzie v. Windham Commun. Mem. Hosp.*, 774 F. Supp. 91 (D. Conn. 1991); *Reed v. Good Samaritan Hosp. Ass'n*, 453 So. 2d 229 (Fla. 4th DCA 1984).

175 E.g., *Linkous v. United States*, 142 F.3d 271 (5th Cir. 1998) [dismissal of claim against U.S. because physician in Army hospital was independent contractor, not government employee, insufficient control].

176 *Overstreet v. Doctor's Hosp.*, 142 Ga. App. 895, 227 S.E.2d 213 (1977).

177 *Beeck v. Tucson Gen. Hosp.*, 18 Ariz. App. 165, 500 P.2d 1153 (1972).

178 *Maldonado v. Frio Hosp. Ass'n*, 25 S.W.2d 274 (Tex. App. 2000) [management company is not employer of hospital employees].

179 E.g., *St. John's Reg. Health Ctr. v. American Cas. Co.*, 980 F.2d 1222 (8th Cir. 1992) [indemnity from nurse's liability insurer].

180 E.g., *Deal v. Kearney*, 851 P.2d 1353 (Alaska 1993).

181 *Keene v. Methodist Hosp.*, 324 F. Supp. 233 (N.D. Ind. 1971).

182 *Arango v. Reykal*, 507 So. 2d 1211 (Fla. 4th DCA 1987); contra, *Underwood v. Holy Name of Jesus Hosp.*, 289 Ala. 216, 266 So. 2d 773 (1972); see R. Miller, Joint venture: another theory of hospital liability for physicians, 5 Hosp. L. Newsletter (Sept. 1988), at 5; see also, *Suarez Matos v. Ashford Presbyterian Comm. Hosp.*, 4 F.3d 47 (1st Cir. 1993) [granting staff privileges along with sharing profits was joint enterprise under Puerto Rican law which could make hospital liable for pathologist's reporting of tumor as benign although he knew it was not].

183 *Davies v. General Tours, Inc.*, 63 Conn. App. 17, 774 A.2d 1063 (2001).

184 *Greve v. Mt. Clemens Gen. Hosp.*, 404 Mich. 240, 273 N.W.2d 429 (1978); accord, *Creech v. Roberts*, 908 F.2d 75 (6th Cir. 1990), cert. denied, 499 U.S. 975 (1991); *Gilbert v. Sycamore Mun. Hosp.*, 156 Ill. 2d 511, 622 N.E.2d 788 (1993) [hospital liable for acts of physician at hospital regardless of status as independent contractor unless patient knew or should have known he was independent contractor]; *Clark v. Southview Hosp. & Family Health Ctr.*, 68 Ohio St. 3d 435, 628 N.E.2d 46 (1994) [same]; see also, *Pamperin v. Trinity Mem. Hosp.*, 144 Wis. 2d 188, 423 N.W.2d 848 (1988); *Boyd v. Albert Einstein Med. Ctr.*, 377 Pa. Super. 609, 547 A.2d 1229 (1988) [HMO may be liable for ostensible agent].

185 E.g., *Baptist Mem. Hosp. Sys. v. Sampson*, 969 S.W.2d 945 (Tex. 1998) [hospital not liable for emergency room physician's negligence, no affirmative act to create appearance of agency, reasonable efforts to inform patients by posting signs, patients signed consent form disclosing status]; *James v. Ingalls Mem. Hosp.*, 299 Ill. App. 3d 627, 701 N.E.2d 207 (1st Dist. 1998) [disclaimer in treatment form signed by patient disclosing independent contractor status precludes hospital liability for doctor]; *Holmes v. University Health Serv., Inc.*, 205 Ga. App. 602, 423 S.E.2d 281 (1992) [residents provided by medical college not apparent agents of hospital, especially where decedent had signed document acknowledging that physician was not employee or agent of hospital].

186 E.g., *Beeck v. Tucson Gen. Hosp.*, 18 Ariz. App. 165, 500 P.2d 1153 (1972).

187 *Butkiewicz v. Loyola Univ. Med. Ctr.*, 311 Ill. App. 3d 508, 724 N.E.2d 1037 (1st Dist. 2000).

188 E.g., Wis. Stat. § 233.17.

189 E.g., *Thompson v. Nason Hosp.*, 527 Pa. 330, 591 A.2d 703 (1991).

190 *Adamski v. Tacoma Gen. Hosp.*, 20 Wash. App. 98, 579 P.2d 970 (1978); accord *Griffin v. Matthews*, 36 Ohio App. 3d 228, 522 N.E.2d 110 (1987).

191 *Simmons v. Tuomey Reg. Med. Ctr.*, 341 S.C. 32, 533 S.E.2d 312 (2000); contra, *Baptist Mem. Hosp. Sys. v. Sampson*, 969 S.W.2d 945 (Tex. 1998) [no nondelegable duty for emergency room].

192 *Fletcher v. South Peninsula Hosp.*, 71 P.3d 833 (Alaska 2003).

193 *Sullins v. University Hosps.*, 2003 Ohio 398 (App Ct.)

194 E.g., *Pedroza v. Bryant*, 101 Wash. 2d 226, 677 P.2d 166 (1984).

195 *Copithorne v. Framingham Union Hosp.*, 401 Mass. 860, 520 N.E.2d 139 (1988).

196 *Concord Hosp. v. New Hampshire Med. Malpractice J. U. A.*, 63 A.2d 1384 (N.H. 1993).

197 HHS OIG, Advisory Opinion 04-11 (Sept. 9, 2004) [http://oig.hhs.gov/fraud/docs/advisory opinions/ 2004/ao0411.pdf.

198 42 C.F.R. § 1001.952(o).

199 E.g., *Johnson & Johnson v. Aetna Cas. & Sur. Co.*, 285 N.J. Super. 575, 667 A.2d 1087 (App. Div. 1995).

200 E.g., *The Corinthian v. Hartford Fire Ins. Co.*, 143 Ohio App. 3d 392, 758 N.E.2d 218 (2001).

201 See D.P. Kessler, W.M. Sage & D.J. Becker, Impact of malpractice reforms on the supply of physician services, J.A.M.A., June 1, 2005, 2618.

202 Ob/Gyns say they'll surcharge deliveries to make up insurance costs, AP, May, 18, 2004; Doctors opt out of surcharge plan, AP, Sept. 14, 2004.

203 See D.M. Studdert et al., Defensive medicine among high-risk specialist physicians in a volatile malpractice environment, J.A.M.A., June 1, 2006, 2609.

204 See Annotation, Medical malpractice: who are "health providers," or the like, whose actions fall within statutes specifically governing actions and damages for medical malpractice, 12 A.L.R. 5th 1 (1993); *Weinstock v. Groth*, 629 So. 2d 835 (Fla. 1993) [psychologist not healthcare provider under Florida tort reform law]; *Perez v. Bay State Ambulance & Hosp. Rental Service, Inc.*, 413 Mass. 670, 602 N.E.2d 570 (1992) [ambulance company not healthcare provider so not subject to panel review].

205 D. Shapiro, Beyond the blame: A no-fault approach to malpractice, N.Y. Times, Sept. 23, 2003, D6 [the trauma of malpractice suits].

206 See also A. Robeznieks, JCAHO: liability crisis is a barrier to patient safety, Am. Med. News, Feb. 28, 2005, 13.

207 *Ezell v. Hutson*, 105 Wash. App. 485, 20 P.3d 975 (2001); contra, *Shumaker v. Johnson*, 571 So. 2d 991 (Ala. 1990) [rejecting good faith error of judgment defense].

208 *Harvest v. Craig*, 202 Ariz. 529, 48 P.3d 479 (App. Ct. 2002) [upholding statute that requires clear and convincing evidence in some malpractice cases arising out of births – Ariz. Rev. Stat. § 32-1473].

209 See Annotation, Validity and construction of state statutory provisions relating to limitations on amount of recovery in medical malpractice claim and submission of such claims to pretrial panel, 80 A.L.R. 3d 583.

210 See *Eby v. Kozarek*, 153 Wis. 2d 75, 450 N.W.2d 249 (1990).

211 E.g., *Hoehm v. State*, 756 P.2d 780 (Wyo. 1988); *Bernier v. Burris*, 113 Ill. 2d 219, 497 N.E.2d 763 (1986); State ex rel. *Cardinal Glennon Mem. Hosp. v. Gaertner*, 583 S.W.2d 107 (Mo. 1979).

212 *Aldana v. Holub*, 381 So. 2d 231 (Fla. 1980).

213 E.g., *Keyes v. Humana Hosp. Alaska, Inc.*, 750 P.2d 343 (Alaska 1988); Paro v. Longwood Hosp., 373 Mass. 645, 369 N.E.2d 985 (1977); *Johnson v. St. Vincent Hosp., Inc.*, 273 Ind. 374, 404 N.E.2d 585 (1980); *Cha v. Warnick*, 476 N.E.2d 109 (Ind. 1985), cert. denied, 474 U.S. 920 (1985).

214 E.g., *Daigle v. Maine Med. Ctr., Inc.*, 14 F.3d 684 (1st Cir. 1994) [affirming judgment for hospital after findings of prelitigation hearing panel used in accordance with Maine law].

215 E.g., P.R. McGinn, Vermont MDs push tort system revamp: medical negligence bill calls for administrative system, Am.Med. New, April 28, 1989, pg 3.

216 E.g., E.K. Solender, New Zealand's no-fault accident compensation scheme has some unintended consequences: a caution to U.S. reformers, 27 Int'l Law. 91 (1993).

217 Fla. Stat. § 766.304.

218 E.g., S. Martin, NICA - Florida Birth-Related Neurological Injury Compensation Act: four reasons why this malpractice reform must be eliminated, 26 Nova L. Rev. 609 (2002).

219 *C.I.R. v. Banks*, 125 S. Ct. 826 (U.S. 2005).

220 See Annotation, Validity and construction of state statutory provisions relating to limitations on amount of recovery in medical malpractice claim and submission of such claims to pretrial panel, 80 A.L.R.3d 583; R. Zimmerman & J.T. Hallinan, As malpractice caps spread, lawyers turn away some cases, Wall St. J., Oct. 8, 2004, A1.

221 OTA, Impact of Legal Reforms on Medical Malpractice Costs (Oct. 27, 1993).

222 R.L. Rundle, Malpractice cap helps out doctors, Wall St. J., July 13, 2004, D4; see also Study says caps lower premiums, Am. Med. News, Feb. 9, 2004, 16 [Health Affairs].

223 *Duke Power Co. v. Carolina Environmental Study Group, Inc.*, 438 U.S. 59 (1978).

224 See K.A. Olson, Survey of constitutional arguments in medical malpractice award limit cases, 23 J. Health & Hosp. L. 328 (1990).

225 *Wright v. Central DuPage Hosp. Ass'n*, 63 Ill. 2d 313, 347 N.E.2d 736 (1976); accord, *Morris v. Savoy*, 61 Ohio St. 3d 684, 576 N.E.2d 765 (1991) [statutory damage cap unconstitutional]; *Sofie v. Fibreboard Corp.*, 112 Wn. 2d 636, 771 P.2d 711 (1989); *Reynolds v. Porter*, 760 P.2d 816 (Okla. 1988); *Smith v. Department of Ins.*, 507 So. 2d 1080 (Fla. 1987) [unconstitutional].

226 *Johnson v. St. Vincent Hosp., Inc.*, 273 Ind. 374, 404 N.E.2d 585 (1980); accord, *Scholtz v. Metropolitan Pathologists*, 851 P.2d 901 (Colo. 1993) [cap on noneconomic damages constitutional]; *Adams v. Children's Mercy Hosps.*, 832 S.W.2d 898 (Mo. 1992) [cap on damages constitutional]; *Butler v. Flint Goodrich Hosp.*, 607 So. 2d 517 (La. 1992) [cap on medical malpractice judgments not violation of equal protection]; *Samsel v. Wheeler Transp. Servs., Inc.*, 244 Kan. 726, 771 P.2d 71 (1989); *Boyd v. Bulala*, 877 F.2d 1191 (4th Cir. 1989) [Virginia cap on damages upheld]; *Etheridge v. Medical Center Hosps., Inc.*, 237 Va. 626, 376 S.E.2d 525 (1989) [cap on total damages upheld]; *Franklin v. Mazda Motor Corp.*, 704 F. Supp. 1325 (D. Md. 1989) [cap on noneconomic damages upheld]; *Williams v. Kushner*, 524 So. 2d 191 (La. Ct. App. 4th Cir. 1988) [cap upheld]; *Fein v. Permanente Medical Group*, 38 Cal. 3d 137, 695 P.2d 665, 211 Cal. Rptr. 368 (1985), appeal dismissed, 474 U.S. 892 (1985) [cap on noneconomic damages upheld].

227 *Conners v. Northeast Hosp. Corp.*, 439 Mass. 469, 789 N.E.2d 129 (2003).

228 *Gourley v. Nebraska Methodist Health Sys., Inc.*, 265 Neb. 918, 663 N.W.2d 43 (2003).

229 R. Blumenthal, Cap on suits vs. doctors is approved in Texas vote, N.Y. Times, Sept. 15, 2003, A12.

230 *Nevada v. Hall*, 440 U.S. 410 (1979).

231 E.g., *O'Brien v. Hackensack Univ. Med. Ctr.*, 305 A.D.2d 199, 760 N.Y.S.2d 425 (1st Dept. 2003) [no NY jurisdiction over NJ hospital]; *Townsend v. University Hospital - University of Colorado*, 83 S.W.3d 913 (Tex. App. 2002) [Internet communications, acceptance of referrals not sufficient business for jurisdiction]; *Smith v. Gottlieb*, 2002 U.S. Dist. LEXIS 15343 (N.D. Ill) [no jurisdiction over University of Wisconsin Hospitals and Clinics Authority].

232 E.g., *Bledsoe v. Friedman*, 270 U.S. App. D.C. 308, 849 F.2d 639 (1988) [requiring D.C. resident suing Md. provider for care in Md. to follow Md. law].

233 E.g., *Bernier v. Burris*, 113 Ill. 2d 219, 497 N.E.2d 763 (1986); *Rudolph v. Iowa Methodist Medical Center*, 293 N.W.2d 550 (Iowa 1980).

234 E.g., *Coburn v. Augustin*, 627 F. Supp. 983 (D. Kan. 1985).

235 *Koffman v. Leichtfuss*, 2001 WI 111, 246 Wis. 2d 31, 630 N.W.2d 201; accord, *Rose v. Via Christi Health Sys., Inc.*, 276 Kan. 539, 78 P.3d 798 (2003) [recovery of full charges even where Medicare paid lower rate].

236 *Goble v. Frohman*, 848 So. 2d 406 (Fla.2d DCA 2003).

237 E.g., *Desiderio v. Ochs*, 100 N.Y.2d 159, 791 N.E.2d 941, 761 N.Y.S.2d 576 (2003) [uphold applying structured settlement law even when it might exceed jury award]; *Bernier v. Burris*, 113 Ill. 2d 219, 497 N.E.2d 763 (1986) [constitutional]; *American Bank & Trust Co. v. Community Hosp.*, 36 Cal. 3d 359, 683 P.2d 670, 204 Cal. Rptr. 671 (1984) [constitutional]; contra, *Smith v. Myers*, 181 Ariz. 11, 887 P.2d 541 (1994) [periodic payment statute unconstitutional limit on remedies]; *Kansas Malpractice Victims Coalition v. Bell*, 243 Kan. 333, 757 P.2d 251 (1988).

238 *Hull v. U.S.*, 971 F.2d 1499 (10th Cir. 1992).

239 *Walt Disney World v. Wood*, 515 So. 2d 198 (Fla. 1987).

240 E.g., *Florida Patient's Compensation Fund v. St. Paul Fire & Marine Ins. Co.*, 535 So. 2d 335 (Fla. 4th DCA 1988).

241 Fla. Stat. §768.81 [joint and several liability modified], §768.31 [contribution permitted]; see also *Smith v. Dep't of Ins.*, 507 So. 2d 1080 (Fla. 1987) [§768.81 constitutional]; *Fabre v. Marin*, 623 So. 2d 1182 (Fla. 1993) [§768.81(3) not ambiguous; entry of judgment on basis of percentage fault means judgment must be based on percentage of total fault regardless of whether others responsible could have been joined as defendants]; *Freyer v. Albin*, 5 P.3d 329 (Colo. App. 1999) [physician not liable for acts of another physician unless employee, partner, joint venturer, or acting in concert].

242 E.g., *Baird v. Loeffler*, 69 Ohio St. 2d 533, 434 N.E.2d 194 (1982) [one-year limit upheld]; *Douglas v. Hugh A. Stallings, M.D., Inc.*, 870 F.2d 1242 (7th Cir. 1989) [upheld requirement that minors injured when less than six years old sue by age eight]; contra, *Stahler v. St. Luke's Hosp.*, 706 S.W.2d 7 (Mo. 1986) (en banc) [minors have right to wait until becoming adults to sue]; *Barrio v. San Manuel Div. Hosp.*, 143 Ariz. 101, 692 P.2d 280 (1984) [unconstitutional to require minors injured when less than seven years old to sue by age ten].

243 E.g., *Hershberger v. Akron City Hosp.*, 34 Ohio St. 3d 1, 516 N.E.2d 204 (1987).

244 E.g., *Carr v. Broward County*, 541 So. 2d 92 (Fla. 1989) [suit can be barred before discovery possible]; *McDonald v. Haynes Medical Laboratory, Inc.*, 192 Conn. 327, 471 A.2d 646 (1984) [suit can be barred before injury occurs]; contra, *Hardy v. VerMeulen*, 32 Ohio St. 3d 45, 512 N.E.2d 626 (1987) [suit cannot be barred before discovery]; *Shessel v. Stroup*, 253 Ga. 56, 316 S.E.2d 155 (1984) [suit cannot be barred before injury occurs].

245 E.g., Fla. Stat. § 768.46.

246 E.g., Iowa Code §147.138; *Newton v. Cox*, 878 S.W.2d 105 (Tenn. 1994) [upholding cap on contingent fees in medical malpractice cases]; see also *Walters v. National Ass'n of Radiation Survivors*, 473 U.S. 305 (1985); *National Ass'n of Radiation Survivors v. Derwinski*, 994 F.2d 583 (9th Cir. 1992), cert. denied, 510 U.S. 1023 (1993) [upholding $10 limit on fees veteran can pay attorney for assistance in VA claim, but note Congress removed the $10 limit in 1988 in Pub. L. No. 100-687, 102 Stat. 4105, for later claims]; *Beck v. Secretary of HHS*, 924 F.2d 1029 (D.C. Cir. 1991) [attorney in successful Vaccine Act claim limited to fees provided in Act].

247 E.g., Iowa Code § 619.18; contra, *White v. Fisher*, 689 P.2d 102 (Wyo. 1984) [unconstitutional]; but see *Boothe v. Lawrence Hosp.*, 188 A.D.2d 435, 591 N.Y.S.2d 412 (1st Dept. 1992) [only sanction for violation was striking offensive reference].

248 E.g., *Williams v. Chicago Osteopathic Med. Ctr.*, 173 Ill. App. 3d 125, 527 N.E.2d 409 (1st Dist. 1988); *Shackleford v. State*, 534 So. 2d 38 (La. Ct. App. 1988).

249 E.g., Fla. Stat. § 768.73; Punitive damages tax falls short as New York state revenue source, Wall St. J., Nov. 13, 1992, B10.

250 E.g., *Hardy v. New York City Health & Hosps. Corp.*, 164 F.3d 789 (2d Cir. 1999) [EMTALA suit must comply with state notice of claim requirement]; *Patry v. Capps*, 633 So. 2d 9 (Fla. 1994) [acknowledged receipt of hand-delivered notice is sufficient despite statutory requirement of certified mail]; *Boyd v. Becker*, 627 So. 2d 481 (Fla. 1993) [90-day presuit period began on mailing not receipt, so suit untimely].

251 E.g., *Horizons/CMS Healthcare Corp., Inc. v. Fischer*, 111 S.W. 3d 67 (Tex. 2003) [nurse's expert report did not satisfy requirement, so case properly dismissed]; *Mosberg v. Elahi*, 80 N.Y.2d 941, 605 N.E.2d 353, 590 N.Y.S.2d 866 (1992) [dismissal mandated where affidavit of merit not filed]; *Williams v. Boyle*, 72 P.3d 392 (Colo. App. 2003) [dismissal for failure to attach certificate of review]; *Estate of Cassara by Cassara v. State*, 853 F. Supp. 273 (N.D. Ill. 1994) [dismissal for failure to comply with state law requirement of attached affidavit of professional attesting to reasonable and meritorious case]; see also *Witte v. Azarian*, 369 Md. 518, 801 A.2d 160 (2000) [interpreting statute that bars professional witnesses who spend more than 20 percent of their time directly involved in testimony in personal injury claims].

252 E.g., Insurers see Nevada malpractice agency as temporary fix, AP, Mar. 15, 2002 [state run malpractice insurance agency].

253 E.g., *King v. Virginia Birth-Related Neurological Injury Compensation Program*, 410 S.E.2d 656 (Va. 1991) [constitutional to require physicians to contribute to fund]; *McGibony v. Florida Birth-Related Neurological Injury Comp. Plan*, 564 So. 2d 177 (Fla. 1st DCA 1990) [no fault compensation plan not violation of due process or equal protection rights of physicians who were required to contribute; lawful to delegate to Department of Insurance power to increase assessments on actuarial sound standard]; *Johnson v. St. Vincent Hosp., Inc.*, 273 Ind. 374, 404 N.E.2d 585 (1980); *Meier v. Anderson*, 692 F. Supp. 546 (E.D. Pa. 1988).

254 E.g., *Turner v. Hubrich*, 656 So. 2d 970 (Fla. 5th DCA 1995) [Birth-Related Neurological Injury Compensation Act, Fla. Stat. §§ 766.301-766.316, provides exclusive administrative remedy against participating providers if they give notice of their participation to patients prior to services; claimant allowed to amend to claim lack of notice].

255 See *Schindler v. Secretary of DHHS*, 29 F.3d 607 (Fed. Cir. 1994); *Patton v. Secretary of DHHS*, 25 F.3d 1021 (Fed. Cir. 1994); *Weddel v. Secretary of DHHS*, 23 F.3d 388 (Fed. Cir. 1994); Whitecotton by *Whitecotton v. Secretary of HHS*, 17 F.3d 374 (Fed. Cir. 1994).

256 See supra, note 298.

257 *Mulvihill v. Good Samaritan Hospital* (N.Y. Sup. Ct. 2002), N.Y.L.J., April 16, 2002, 20.

258 *Charrin v. Methodist Hosp.*, 432 S.W.2d 572 (Tex. Civ. App. 1968); accord, *Collum v. Jackson Hosp. & Clinic, Inc.*, 374 So. 2d 314 (Ala. 1979); *Spann v. Hosp. Auth. of Calhoun County*, 208 Ga. App. 494, 430 S.E.2d 828 (1993) [nurse's aid].

259 *Pulley v. Rex Hosp.*, 326 N.C. 701, 392 S.E.2d 380 (1990).

260 E.g., *Shoemaker v. Rush-Presbyterian-St. Luke's Med. Ctr.*, 187 Ill. App. 3d 1040, 543 N.E.2d 1014 (1st Dist. 1989); J.A. Lozano, Family of doctor killed in elevator accident at Houston hospital files wrongful death lawsuit, AP, Aug. 29, 2003 [portion of head of resident physician cut off when elevator doors closed].

261 E.g., *DeKalb County Hosp. Auth. v. Theofanidis*, 157 Ga. App. 811, 278 S.E.2d 712 (1981); see Annotation, Hospital's liability to visitor injured as result of condition of exterior walks, steps, or grounds, 71 A.L.R. 2D 427.

262 E.g., *Calvache v. Jackson Mem. Hosp.*, 588 So. 2d 28 (Fla. 3d DCA 1991); *Burwell v. Easton Mem. Hosp.*, 83 Md. App. 684, 577 A.2d 394 (1990); *Gales v. United States*, 617 F. Supp. 42 (W.D. Pa. 1985); see Annotation, Hospital's liability to visitor injured by slippery, obstructed, or defective interior floors or steps, 71 A.L.R. 2D 436.

263 *Pierson v. Sharp Mem. Hosp., Inc.*, 216 Cal. App. 3d 340, 264 Cal. Rptr. 673 (4th Dist. 1989).

264 E.g., *Lovell v. St. Paul Fire & Marine Ins. Co.*, 310 Ark. 791, 839 S.W.2d 222 (1992); *Chernov v. St. Luke's Hosp. Med. Ctr.*, 123 Ariz. 521, 601 P.2d 284 (1979); see Annotation, Liability of owner or operator of parking lot for personal injuries caused by movement of vehicles, 38 A.L.R. 3D 138.

265 E.g., *McHenry v. Utah Valley Hosp.*, 724 F. Supp. 835 (D. Utah 1989), aff'd, 927 F.2d 1125 (10th Cir.), cert. denied, 502 U.S. 894 (1991) [gate]; *McDonald v. Aliquippa Hosp.*, 414 Pa. Super. 317, 606 A.2d 1218 (1992) [doors]; see Annotation, Liability of owner or operator of business premises for injuries from electronically operated door, 99 A.L.R. 2D 725.

266 *Isaacs v. Huntington Mem. Hosp.*, 38 Cal. 3d 112, 211 Cal. Rptr. 356, 695 P.2d 653 (1985); see Annotation, Parking facility proprietor's liability for criminal attack on patron, 49 A.L.R. 4TH 1257.

267 *Maxwell v. Hospital Auth.*, 202 Ga. App. 92, 413 S.E.2d 205 (1991); see Annotation, Workers' compensation law as precluding employee's suit against employer for third person's criminal attack, 49 A.L.R. 4TH 926.

268 *Mundy v. Dep't of Health & Human Resources*, 620 So. 2d 811 (La. 1993).

269 *Young v. Huntsville Hosp.*, 595 So. 2d 1386 (Ala. 1992); accord, *K.M.H. v. Lutheran Gen. Hosp.*, 230 Neb. 269, 431 N.W.2d 606 (1988) [direct hospital duty independent of respondeat superior].

270 *Andrea N. v. Laurelwood Convalescent Hosp.*, 13 Cal. App. 4th 1992, 16 Cal. Rptr. 2d 894 (2d Dist. 1993) [not citable in Cal.]; accord, Gregory by *Gregory v. State*, 195 A.D.2d 1030, 601 N.Y.S.2d 720 (4th Dept. 1993) [supervision adequate].

271 *G.L. v. Kaiser Found. Hosps., Inc.*, 306 Or. 54, 757 P.2d 1347 (1988).

272 *Hernandez v. Smith*, 552 F.2d 142 (5th Cir. 1977); see Annotation, Hospital's liability to patient for injury allegedly sustained from absence of particular equipment intended for use in diagnosis or treatment of patient, 50 A.L.R. 3D 1141.

273 *Carrasco v. Bankoff*, 220 Cal. App. 2d 230, 33 Cal. Rptr. 673 (2d Dist. 1963).

274 *Ducharme v. United States*, 850 F.2d 27 (1st Cir. 1988).

275 *Lauro v. Travelers Ins. Co.*, 261 So. 2d 261 (La. Ct. App.).

276 *Dixon v. Taylor*, 111 N.C. App. 97, 431 S.E.2d 778 (1993).

277 *Lamb v. Chandler Gen. Hosp., Inc.*, 262 Ga. 70, 413 S.E.2d 720 (1992).

278 *Bellaire Gen. Hosp. v. Campbell*, 510 S.W.2d 94 (Tex. Civ. App. 1974).

279 *Suttle v. Lake Forest Hosp.*, 315 Ill. App. 3d 96, 733 N.E.2d 726 (1st Dist. 2000).

280 *Clary v. Christiansen*, 54 Ohio Abs. 254, 83 N.E.2d 644 (Ct. App. 1948); see Annotation, Malpractice: attending physician's liability for injury caused by equipment furnished by hospital, 35 A.L.R. 3D 1068.

281 *Orthopedic Clinic v. Hanson*, 415 P.2d 991 (Okla. 1966).

282 *Shepard v. McGinnis*, 251 Iowa 35, 131 N.W.2d 475 (1964).

283 See Annotation, Medical malpractice: hospital's liability for injury allegedly caused by failure to have properly qualified staff, 62 A.L.R. 4TH 692; Annotation, Hospital's liability for injury resulting from failure to have sufficient number of nurses on duty, 2 A.L.R. 5TH 286.

284 *Denton Reg. Med. Ctr. v. LaCroix*, 947 S.W.2d 941 (Tex. Ct. App. 1997).

285 *St. Paul Med. Ctr. v. Cecil*, 842 S.W.2d 808 (Tex. Ct. App. 1992).

286 *Bowers v. Olch*, 120 Cal. App. 2d 108, 260 P.2d 997 (2d Dist. 1953).

287 *Stumper v. Kimel*, 108 N.J. Super. 209, 260 A.2d 526 (App. Div. 1970); see Annotation, Liability of one physician or surgeon for malpractice of another, 85 A.L.R. 2D 889.

288 E.g., *Deese v. Carroll City County Hosp.*, 203 Ga. App. 148, 416 S.E.2d 127 (1992); *Cox v. Board of Hosp. Managers*, 467 Mich. 1, 651 N.W.2d 356 (2002) ["the skill and care ordinarily possessed and exercised by practitioners of the profession in the same or similar localities"]; see Annotation, Nurse's liability for her own negligence or malpractice, 51 A.L.R. 2D 970.

289 *Thompson v. Brent*, 245 So. 2d 751 (La. Ct. App. 1971).

290 *Webb v. Jorns*, 473 S.W.2d 328 (Tex. Civ. App. 1971), rev'd on other grounds, 488 S.W.2d 407 (Tex. 1972).

291 *Fein v. Permanente Med. Group*, 38 Cal. 3d 137, 211 Cal. Rptr. 368, 695 P.2d 665, appeal dismissed, 474 U.S. 842 (1985).

292 *Sullivan v. Edward Hosp.*, 209 Ill. 2d 100, 806 N.E.2d 645 (2004).

293 *Nelson v. Trinity Med. Ctr.*, 419 N.W.2d 886 (N.D. 1988).

294 *Cline v. Lund*, 31 Cal. App. 3d 755, 107 Cal. Rptr. 629 (1st Dist. 1973).

295 *Striano v. Deepdale Gen. Hosp.*, 54 A.D.2d 730, 387 N.Y.S.2d 678 (2d Dept. 1976).

296 *Toth v. Community Hosp.*, 22 N.Y.2d 255, 292 N.Y.S.2d 440, 239 N.E.2d 368 (1968).

297 E.g., *Hering v. McShane*, 145 A.D.2d 683, 535 N.Y.S.2d 227 (3d Dept. 1988).

298 *Fraijo v. Hartland Hosp.*, 99 Cal. App. 3d 331, 160 Cal. Rptr. 246 (2d Dist. 1979).

299 *Larrimore v. Homeopathic Hosp. Ass'n*, 54 Del. 449, 181 A.2d 573 (1962).

300 *Norton v. Argonaut Ins. Co.*, 144 So. 2d 249 (La. Ct. App. 1962).

301 E.g., Rampe by *Rampe v. Commun. Gen. Hosp.*, 241 A.D.2d 817, 660 N.Y.S.2d 206 (3d Dept. 1997) [nurse breached duty to notify physician of decelerations in heart rate, but no proof this caused injuries]; *Gill v. Foster*, 157 Ill. 2d 304, 626 N.E.2d 190 (1993) [nurse breached duty by failing to tell doctor of patient's complaints of pain at discharge, but not cause of injury because doctor already knew of pain]; *McMillan v. Durant*, 439 S.E.2d 829 (S.C. 1993).

302 *Hiatt v. Groce*, 215 Kan. 14, 523 P.2d 320 (1974).

303 *Duling v. Bluefield Sanitarium, Inc.*, 149 W.Va. 567, 142 S.E.2d 754 (1965).

304 *Lopez v. Southwest Comm. Health Servs.*, 114 N.M. 2, 833 P.2d 1183 (Ct. App. 1992).

305 *Collins v. Westlake Commun. Hosp.*, 57 Ill. 2d 388, 312 N.E.2d 614 (1974).

306 *Mundt v. Alta Bates Hosp.*, 223 Cal. App. 2d 413, 35 Cal. Rptr. 848 (1st Dist. 1963).

307 *Darling v. Charleston Commun. Mem. Hosp.*, 33 Ill. 2d 326, 211 N.E.2d 253 (1965), cert. denied, 383 U.S. 496 (1966).

308 *Goff v. Doctors Gen. Hosp.*, 166 Cal. App. 2d 314, 333 P.2d 29 (3d Dist. 1958).

309 *Snelson v. Kamm*, 319 Ill. App. 3d 116, 745 N.E.2d 128 (4th Dist. 2001), aff'd in pertinent part by, 204 Ill. 2d 1, 787 N.E.2d 796 (2003).

310 *Pierce v. Mercy Health Ctr., Inc.*, 847 P.2d 822 (Okla. Ct. App. 1992).

311 *Kastler v. Iowa Methodist Hosp.*, 193 N.W.2d 98 (Iowa 1971).

312 See also Robinson by *Bugera v. Faine*, 525 So. 2d 903 (Fla. 3d DCA 1987) [agency not liable for private duty nurse's negligence where she was independent contractor].

313 *Emory Univ. v. Shadburn*, 180 Ga. 595, 180 S.E. 137 (1935).

314 E.g., FLA. STAT. § 465.019(5) [consultant pharmacist license].

315 Joint Commission on Accreditation of Healthcare Organizations, 2005 COMPREHENSIVE ACCREDITATION MANUAL FOR HOSPITALS, MM.4.10, 4.50 [hereinafter cited as 2005 JCAHO CAMH].

316 *Sullivan v. Sisters of St. Francis*, 374 S.W.2d 294 (Tex. Civ. App. 1963).

317 *Troppi v. Scarf*, 31 Mich. App. 240, 187 N.W.2d 511 (1971); see Annotation, Druggist's civil liability for injuries sustained as a result of negligence in incorrectly filling drug prescription, 3 A.L.R. 4TH 270.

318 *McCord v. State*, Nos. 43405, 43406, and 43407 (N.Y. Ct. Cl. 1969).

319 *DeVito v. HEM, Inc.*, 705 F. Supp. 1076 (M.D. Pa. 1989).

320 *Suthers v. Amgen Inc.*, 2005 U.S. Dist. LEXIS 11119 (S.D. N.Y.).

321 Joint Commission on Accreditation of Healthcare Organizations, 1994 ACCREDITATION MANUAL FOR HOSPITALS, 162.

322 Joint Commission on Accreditation of Healthcare Organizations, 1995 COMPREHENSIVE ACCREDITATION MANUAL FOR HOSPITALS, 139-50.

323 2005 JCAHO CAMH, MM.1.10, MM.6.10.

324 E.g., *Morgan v. Wal-Mart Stores, Inc.*, 30 S.W.3d 455 (Tex. Ct. App. 2000) [no generalized duty to warn patients of potential adverse reactions to prescription drugs]; *Mielke v. Condell Mem. Hosp.*, 124 Ill. App. 3d 42, 463 N.E.2d 216 (2d Dist. 1984) [no liability for not notifying physician of drug interaction discovered by monitoring systems]; *Walker v. Jack Eckerd Corp.*, 209 Ga. App. 517, 434 S.E.2d 63 (1993) [pharmacist has no duty to warn customer or notify physician that drug is being prescribed in dangerous amounts].

325 E.g., *Happel v. Wal-Mart Stores, Inc.*, 199 Ill. 2d 179, 766 N.E.2d 1118 (2002) [pharmacist duty to warn in some circumstances]; *Cottam v. CVS Pharmacy*, 436 Mass. 316, 764 N.E.2d 814 (2002); *Hooks SuperX, Inc. v. McLaughlin*, 642 N.E.2d 514 (Ind. 1994) [pharmacist has duty to cease filling refills when they are being sought at an unreasonably faster rate than prescribed].

326 *South Miami Hosp. v. Sanchez*, 386 So. 2d 39 (Fla. 3d DCA 1980); see Annotation, Liability for injuries or death resulting from physical therapy, 53 A.L.R. 3d 1250.

327 *Pontiff v. Pecot & Assocs. Rehab & Physical Therapy Servs. Inc.*, 780 So. 2d 478 (La. Ct. App. 2001).

328 *McAvenue v. Bryn Mawr Hosp.*, 245 Pa. Super. 507, 369 A.2d 743 (1976).

329 *Meiman v. Rehabilitation Ctr., Inc.*, 444 S.W.2d 78 (Ky. 1969).

330 *Forsyth v. Sisters of Charity*, 39 Or. App. 851, 593 P.2d 1270 (1979); accord, *Hodo v. General Hosps.*, 211 Ga. App. 6, 438 S.E.2d 378 (1993); but see *Gilles v. Rehabilitation Inst.*, 262 Or. 472, 498 P.2d 777 (1972) [no liability because of patient's efforts to thwart therapist from preventing fall].

331 But see, *Holdren v. Legursky*, 16 F.3d 57 (4th Cir.), cert. denied, 513 U.S. 831 (1994) [handling of blood sample at hospital that precluded DNA test did not violate due process].

332 *Mokry v. University of Tex. Health Science Ctr.*, 529 S.W.2d 802 (Tex. Civ. App. 1975).

333 *Variety Children's Hosp. v. Osle*, 292 So. 2d 382 (Fla. 3d DCA 1974).

334 *Lundberg v. Bay View Hosp.*, 175 Ohio St. 133, 191 N.E.2d 821 (1963); see Annotation, Malpractice in connection with diagnosis of cancer, 79 A.L.R. 3D 915.

335 *Insurance Co. of N. Am. v. Prieto*, 442 F.2d 1033 (6th Cir. 1971), cert. denied, 404 U.S. 856 (1971).

336 *Schnebly v. Baker*, 217 N.W.2d 708 (Iowa 1974), overruled in part on other grounds, *Franke v. Junko*, 366 N.W.2d 536 (Iowa 1985).

337 *M.M.H. v. United States*, 966 F.2d 285 (7th Cir. 1992).

338 E.g., *Riser v. American Med. Int'l*, 620 So. 2d 372 (La. Ct. App. 1993).

339 *Natanson v. Kline*, 187 Kan. 186, 354 P.2d 670 (1960).

340 *Ahern v. Veterans Admin.*, 537 F.2d 1098 (10th Cir. 1976).

341 *Albritton v. Bossier City Hosp. Comm'n*, 271 So. 2d 353 (La. Ct. App. 1972).

342 *Modave v. Long Island Jewish Med. Ctr.*, 501 F.2d 1065 (2d Cir. 1974).

343 *Barnes v. Bovenmeyer*, 255 Iowa 220, 122 N.W.2d 312 (1963).

344 *Keene v. Methodist Hosp.*, 324 F. Supp. 233 (N.D. Ind. 1971); see also *Davidson v. Mobile Infirmary*, 456 So. 2d 14 (Ala. 1984) [failure to inform treating physician of x-rays showing large number of pills in stomach].

345 E.g., *Shuffler v. Blue Ridge Radiology Assocs.*, 73 N.C .App. 232, 326 S.E.2d 96 (1985).

346 Annotation, Hospital's liability for exposing patient to extraneous infection or contagion, 96 A.L.R. 2D 1205.

347 *Helman v. Sacred Heart Hosp.*, 62 Wash. 2d 136, 381 P.2d 605 (1963) [hospital liable for staphylococcus infection where nurses failed to take necessary precautions, such as handwashing, to avoid cross-infection from other patient in room who was infected with the same staphylococcus organism]; *Wilson v. Stilwill*, 411 Mich. 587, 309 N.W.2d 898 (1981) [res ipsa loquitur not applicable to hospital infection]; *Vogt v. Katz*, 745 S.W.2d 221 (Mo. Ct. App. 1987) [failure to clean injection site established claim for infection].

348 *Mahan v. Bethesda Hosp., Inc.*, 84 Ohio App. 3d 520, 617 N.E.2d 774 (1992).

349 *Suburban Hosp. Ass'n v. Hadary*, 22 Md. App. 186, 322 A.2d 258 (1974).

350 *Kalmus v. Cedars of Lebanon Hosp.*, 132 Cal. App. 2d 243, 281 P.2d 872 (2d Dist. 1955).

351 *Kapuschinsky v. United States*, 248 F. Supp. 732 (D. S.C. 1966).

352 E.g., FLA. STAT. § 381.0035.

353 2005 Joint Commission CAMH, IC.1.10 – IC.6.30.

354 *Thomas v. Corsco*, 265 Md. 84, 288 A.2d 379 (1972).

355 *Bourgeois v. Dade County*, 99 So. 2d 575 (Fla. 1957).

356 *Fox v. Argonaut Sw. Ins. Co.*, 288 So. 2d 102 (La. Ct. App. 1974).

357 *Howell v. Outer Drive Hosp.*, 66 Mich. App. 142, 238 N.W.2d 553 (1975).

358 *Pate v. Threlkel*, 661 So. 2d 278 (Fla. 1995).

359 *Safer v. Pack*, 291 N.J. Super. 619, 677 A.2d 1188 (App. Div. 1996).

360 Researchers complete sequencing of human genetic code, opening way for new medicine, AP, Apr. 14, 2003.

Chapter 12

Criminal and Civil Penalties

Lawrence Vernaglia, Lisa Noller, Joseph Van Leer, Katie Miller

Key Learning Objectives

By the end of this chapter, the reader will be able to:

- Provide an overview of criminal liability and civil penalties.

- Understand enforcement agencies; the differences between criminal and civil penalties; criminal law; suspension, recoupment, and exclusion from federal programs; civil money penalties; and methods of mitigating potential liability.

- Explain the three primary civil statutes that expose providers to liability: the False Claims Act (FCA), the Anti-Kickback Statute (AKS), and the Ethics in Patient Referrals Act (Stark Law).

- Understand the changes to each of these laws as a result of recent congressional healthcare reform set forth in the Patient Protection and Affordable Care Act (PPACA).

Chapter Outline

Introduction

Since the early 1990s, there has been an explosive growth in applying criminal law and civil penalties to healthcare providers who have violated the law. For the foreseeable future, anyone in the healthcare field would do well to recognize that there is a risk that they and their organizations are being or will be subjected to criminal or civil investigation.

This chapter reviews some of these criminal laws and civil penalties and how they have been applied to healthcare providers. The sections address enforcement agencies (12-1); the differences between criminal and civil penalties (12-2); criminal law (12-3); suspension, recoupment, and exclusion from federal programs (12-4); civil money penalties (12-5); and mitigating liability (12-6).

12-1 Enforcement Agencies

Enforcement efforts typically are initiated by three primary sources—federal and state administrative agencies, federal and state prosecutors, and private individuals and organizations. The focus here will be on two federal enforcement agencies—the Office of the Inspector General (OIG) of the U.S. Department of Health and Human Services (HHS) and the U.S. Department of Justice (DOJ). State agencies also actively pursue providers, often working together with federal law enforcement. Actions by private individuals will be discussed later in the chapter.

12-1.1 Office of the Inspector General

The administrative agency that has been most widely publicized and active in penalizing healthcare providers is arguably the OIG. The OIG has taken a lead in civil enforcement of Medicare, Medicaid, and other civilian healthcare programs of the federal government. The Department of Defense and Veterans Administration healthcare systems also employ separate law enforcement agents (who often work together with OIG).

One manner in which OIG enforces applicable laws is by implementing national enforcement plans. For example, Operation Restore Trust started in 1995, and the Comprehensive Plan for Program Integrity started in 1999. In addition, the OIG publishes an annual work plan identifying the issues on which it is focusing. This is supplemented by periodic fraud alerts detailing other areas of focus. For example, in 1999, the OIG issued a Special Fraud Alert that detailed the liability of physicians when they falsely certify the need for medical equipment or home health services, and in

2003, it issued an alert concerning contractual joint ventures.[1] The purpose of the alerts is to put providers on notice, which in some instances can also increase their level of knowledge, and thus their level of culpability.

In 1998, the Health Care Financing Administration (HCFA, now known as the Centers for Medicare & Medicaid Services (CMS)) supplemented the OIG's efforts with two new programs. CMS began using private subcontractors to help with its enforcement efforts. In addition, as authorized by the Health Insurance Portability and Accountability Act (HIPAA), CMS began a controversial program of training beneficiaries to act as spies and report suspected violations.[2] Providers have expressed concerns about the effects of this program on the relationship of trust necessary for patient care.

Although the OIG does not have authority to enforce the criminal provisions of the Anti-Kickback Statute (AKS) or the False Claims Act (FCA), it works closely with the DOJ and FBI and also may suspend or exclude providers participating in federal healthcare programs (e.g., Medicare) based on violations of those laws. There are mandatory and permissive exclusions, based on different factors enumerated by statute. The OIG must exclude a provider if it falls under mandatory exclusion criteria, such as a felony healthcare fraud conviction. By contrast, the OIG may, but is not required to, exclude a provider for permissive criteria, such as misdemeanor healthcare fraud violations.

Note that healthcare reform via the Patient Protection and Affordable Care Act (PPACA) expanded the list of permissive criteria that may be considered by the OIG in excluding providers. The expanded list provides the OIG additional opportunity to exclude providers it believes are causing harm to the program. OIG has steadily increased the number of permissive exclusions since 1998.

12-1.2 Department of Justice

The DOJ is comprised of a central office in Washington, DC, and the U.S. Attorney's offices in each federal judicial district, which function with great autonomy. When the OIG determines that criminal prosecutions should be considered, the case is referred to the DOJ. The DOJ can also initiate prosecutions on its own, and teams with the OIG and FBI agents to investigate providers.

Most prosecutions are local and focused on individual providers based on a case-by-case assessment. These prosecutions have in most cases targeted serious violators, for example, those who have been billing for services not provided. This is an essential role in the enforcement of appropriate standards.

12-1.3 Conflicts Created by Multiple Enforcement Agencies

The existence of multiple independent enforcers makes enforcement more complex for the enforcers and makes resolving an issue with any one enforcement agency more complex for providers. Agents must consider potential actions by other agencies. Each enforcer can make a commitment concerning only its own enforcement activities. However, any nonconfidential or non-grand jury evidence gathered by one agency can be shared with others; a deal struck with one agency generally creates the possibility of prosecution or penalties by other agencies. This has also complicated responses to efforts by many enforcement agencies to encourage self-reporting of detected violations.[3]

Some enforcement agencies have developed cooperative agreements concerning some aspects of their operations.[4] In some cases, they have worked with providers to resolve cases with multiple agencies at the same time.

12-2 Differences Between Criminal and Civil Penalties

There is a fundamental difference between criminal penalties and civil penalties. See **Table 12-1**. Criminal penalties can only be imposed by courts. Civil penalties may be imposed directly by administrative agencies or by courts, but generally they must follow specified administrative procedures. The government does not have to follow criminal law procedures before it can impose civil penalties.

There is also a fundamental difference in the burden of proof the government must meet before imposing penalties. For a criminal conviction, the government must prove its case beyond a reasonable doubt. Certainty is not required, but any reasonable doubt must be resolved against the government. For crimes where the maximum prison term is in excess of six months, the accused also has a right to have a jury make the determination of guilt or innocence.[5] To impose a civil penalty, the government need only prove its case by a preponderance of the evidence (i.e., the government need only show that it is more likely than not that the violation occurred). In civil penalty cases, there is no right to a jury trial. However, there is generally a right to judicial review after the administrative process is completed. Civil penalties cannot include imprisonment, but they can include large civil money penalties and exclusion from participation in government programs, such as Medicare and Medicaid.

A third fundamental difference is that criminal health-care statutes require the government to prove a provider violated the law "knowingly" (i.e., he purposely intended to violate the applicable statute). However, for a provider to be civilly liable, the government need only prove he acted in reckless disregard of a statute or should have known his actions would violate the law. There is also a concurrent knowledge issue, in that when a provider acts "knowingly," the government may elect to pursue either civil penalties or criminal penalties against him.

There is one aspect of proof that surprisingly may be easier in criminal cases than in some civil cases. Most states require expert medical testimony to establish proper medical practice before the imposition of civil tort liability. In criminal cases, that depends on whether proper medical practice was followed, and some courts have not required expert medical testimony.[6]

The Double Jeopardy Clause of the U.S. Constitution bars a second criminal prosecution for the same offense. Although "same offense" has a technical definition that leaves open the possibility of a second prosecution in some circumstances,[7] the Double Jeopardy Clause does provide

Table 12-1 Criminal and Civil Law Differences

Civil Law	Criminal Law
Proof Required: Preponderance of the Evidence	Proof Required: Beyond a Reasonable Doubt
Right to Jury Trial: Sometimes	Right to Jury Trial: Yes
Penalties: Money Penalties and/or Exclusion from Medicare or Medicaid	Penalties: Prison, Money Penalties, and/or Exclusion from Medicare or Medicaid
Standard: Knowing Action or Reckless Disregard	Standard: Knowing Action

substantial protection. However, in 1997, the U.S. Supreme Court ruled that a prior civil administrative proceeding that imposed severe monetary penalties and occupational disbarment did not bar a subsequent criminal prosecution.[8]

12-3 Criminal Law

This section is divided into five subsections. First, it discusses some aspects of criminal investigations (12-3.1). Then, it addresses criminal penalties for three areas—healthcare decisions (12-3.2), failure to meet billing requirements (12-3.3), and business arrangements that violate Medicare and Medicaid fraud and abuse laws (12-3.4). The final subsection reviews other criminal laws often used against healthcare providers (12-3.5), but it does not discuss many other actions, such as theft, trespass, sexual contact, or disorderly conduct, that are not unique to healthcare settings.

12-3.1 Criminal Investigations

In most circumstances, individuals have a right not to answer questions from criminal investigators. This is part of the right against self-incrimination guaranteed by the Fifth Amendment to the U.S. Constitution. Thus, in most circumstances, persons whose statements are being requested or compelled by subpoena have an opportunity to seek legal counsel before answering questions. Fifth Amendment protections do not apply to corporations, and prosecutors may compel disclosure of corporate records.

When individuals elect to answer questions from criminal investigators, they must answer truthfully, since it is a separate crime to make a false report to the government.[9] In 1998, the U.S. Supreme Court ruled that even a false denial of guilt was a crime.[10] One federal court has interpreted medical records to be statements to federal officials whenever those records are required by federal law.[11] Thus, knowingly making false statements in medical records presented to the government or supporting a claim for government reimbursement can also be federal crimes.

Healthcare organizations may advise staff of the criminal risks of responding and of their right to seek counsel before responding, ask staff to advise them when contacted by investigators, and offer to provide counsel. However, they cannot tell their staff not to respond or threaten adverse employment consequences for responding or not reporting contacts. If they do, such directions may be viewed by the government as obstructing their investigation, which is another separate crime.

Investigators have broad powers to use undercover means, including wiretapping and recording of meetings and conversations, provided certain statutory requirements are met.[12] Furthermore, prosecutors have broad powers to seize or freeze assets prior to conviction.[13] This is permitted even when the seizure does not leave assets for a legal defense.[14]

12-3.2 Criminal Penalties for Healthcare Decisions

Criminal law addresses healthcare decisions in at least three ways. Some cases focus on all healthcare decisions regardless of outcome. Other cases focus on deaths or significant injuries that result from healthcare decisions. The third type of case is the rare challenge to intentional end-of-life decisions.

PROSECUTIONS WITHOUT REGARD TO HEALTHCARE OUTCOME. The Medicare rules are just one example of the government's use of criminal penalties to punish healthcare decisions without regard to healthcare outcome. Medicare requires that services be medically necessary, meet professionally recognized standards of care, and be supported by evidence in the required form and fashion.[15]

The government takes the position that any Medicare bill is a certification of compliance with these and other Medicare requirements. Thus, it asserts that any bill for a service that does not meet the necessity, quality, and documentation requirements may be fraudulent. At least one federal appellate court has decided in the civil penalties context that even decisions not to provide elements of care can violate the requirement of meeting professionally recognized standards of care.[16]

Cases selected for criminal prosecution so far have generally been egregious deviations from acceptable practice. However, in jurisdictions where the courts do not limit the use of the FCA, prosecutorial discretion is the only limit that keeps this law from creating a federal criminal law of medical malpractice.

The government also has adopted the position that submission of a bill to Medicare is an implied certification of the provider's compliance with several other regulatory requirements. This theoretically enables the use of the False Claims Act, as discussed below, to punish violations of other requirements. Some courts have permitted this approach.[17]

PROSECUTIONS FOR BAD HEALTHCARE OUTCOMES. The law of medical malpractice and professional licensing was developed in early America as an alternative to criminal prosecution. In earlier days, criminal cases were brought as the primary means of legal regulation of medical practice. Many prosecutors still exercise their discretion not to apply criminal law,[18] but it may be difficult to make such a decision when elected prosecutors are pressured by the media and the families of those injured. There are several examples, in the healthcare system, where criminal laws are used to redress actions within the scope of medical practice.[19]

For example, in 2011, authorities in California prosecuted and convicted a physician for the death of Michael Jackson. In 2009, Michael Jackson died from an overdose of a powerful anesthetic, propofol.[20] The defendant, Conrad Murray, did not use several of the safeguards necessary to ensure that a patient does not overdose. Furthermore, the government proved propofol was not an appropriate treatment for insomnia, and the defendant did not properly monitor Jackson. Also, the government proved the defendant failed to retrieve necessary medical records prior to treatment.

In 1996, a California physician saw an eleven-month-old child with diarrhea and vomiting at a small hospital's emergency room. The physician concluded that he could not provide the care the child required; he then had the parents drive the child to a tertiary care facility over one hour away because of delays in availability of ambulance service. The baby died. Both a civil liability case and licensing review were initiated. However, in addition, the prosecutor brought criminal charges against the physician, obtaining a grand jury indictment of second-degree murder, involuntary manslaughter, and child endangerment. The trial court permitted the prosecutor to present the case, but at the conclusion of the prosecutor's case, the court dismissed the case and acquitted the physician because there was insufficient evidence.[21]

There also are cases of prosecution of physicians for prescribing pain medications.[22] For example, in 1999, a California physician was charged with murder, prescription violations, and fraudulent medical claims after five patients he was treating with painkillers died. During the trial, the prosecutor withdrew the murder charges. In 2004, a jury acquitted him of the remaining charges.[23] In some cases, the physician's "care" was clearly outside the scope of accepted practice. In other cases, it was not clearly articulated how those cases selected for prosecution differed from physicians who regularly dealt with patients with severe chronic pain. Thus, in some cases, there has been fear that cautious physicians will reduce their prescription of needed pain medications. Attempts have been made to promulgate guidelines of practices that will not be prosecuted. However, the tension between pain control and drug enforcement practices is likely to continue.

Physicians and nurses have been prosecuted for theft of drugs, and [24] nursing home officials have been prosecuted for the death of residents. For example, in 2000, a Missouri appellate court upheld the conviction of a nursing home administrator for felony neglect after the death of two residents.[25]

12-3.3 Criminal Penalties for Billing

MEDICARE FRAUD AND ABUSE. In health care, many civil and criminal liability claims arise from fraud and abuse in the industry. Through statutes, cases, and advisory opinion processes, the government gives healthcare providers an idea of the types of actions that may constitute "fraud" or "abuse."[26] These actions include, but are not limited to:

A. Billing under the provider number of another provider[27]

B. Billing for services when the provider is not present

  i. Example: In Washington, a physician was sentenced to five years of probation, 1,000 hours of community service, and $100,000 in restitution for noting on a chart that he was present during dialysis when he was not.[28]

C. Billing for unnecessary services or for services not rendered

  i. Example: A physician in Detroit, Michigan, was sentenced to 72 months in prison for participating in a conspiracy to defraud the Medicare program. Among other things, the physician prescribed medications for patients at a clinic he owned that the patients did not need, and in many cases were never provided to them at all.

D. Payments made to induce referrals (Anti-Kickback Statute (AKS), discussed below)

E. Payments if a provider has a "financial relationship" with the entity to whom the referral is made and the relationship does not fit within an exception (the "Stark Law")

F. Upcoding

    i.   Improper coding of bills (in any way) may make a claim "false." Through enforcement efforts, the government focuses on certain codes where there are significant differences in payment based on similar codes.

G. In pneumonia cases, diagnosis related groups (DRGs), the manner by which providers are paid based on diagnosis rather than per service, are a frequent target of Medicare fraud. Physicians and hospitals will bill under DRG 79 (respiratory infections and inflammations) when they should bill under DRG 80 (pneumonia without complications) or DRG 89 (pneumonia with complications). DRG 79 pays twice as much as DRG 80.[29]

FALSE CLAIMS ACT. The FCA carries both civil and criminal penalties for anyone who knowingly presents, or causes to be presented, to the U.S. government a false or fictitious claim for payment.[30] The FCA's authority encompasses more than just healthcare claims; it applies equally to all others who make claims for payment from government funds to the government. Penalties for a violation of the FCA are three times the damages suffered by the government plus a penalty of $5,000 to $10,000 per false claim.[31]

> Example Case: In March 2010, a physician clinic owner was convicted of thirteen counts of Medicare fraud for his role in an $18.3 million fraud scheme. A month later, he was sentenced to fourteen years in prison and ordered to pay $9.4 million in restitution. The physician conspired in the fraud by creating falsified therapy files for services not rendered, bribing physical and occupational therapists to sign the fictitious therapy files, signing prescriptions and certifying the need for therapy services without patient evaluation, paying cash kickbacks to Medicare beneficiaries in exchange for their Medicare numbers and signatures on documents falsely indicating they received services, and profiting from home visits that did not actually occur.

Federal courts generally require that FCA cases identify *specific claims*. Broad claims of bad practices are generally insufficient to state a claim upon which relief may be granted.[32] Thus, many FCA cases are brought by whistle-blowers, or corporate insiders, instead of directly by the government.

FCA—*Qui Tam* Actions. Whistleblower suits under the FCA are known as *qui tam*[33] actions. Through *qui tam* actions, individuals bring lawsuits in the name of the United States as "private attorneys general."[34] The individual filing the suit is known as the relator. The relator must be the "original source" of the information that forms the basis of the action. A *qui tam* suit cannot be based on publicly available information. Thus, a healthcare facility can block *qui tam* actions by disclosing improper or illegal actions. There are specific procedures that a relator or whistle-blower must follow in these cases. The federal government has the opportunity to intervene and take over control of the case. For his or her part in bringing the action, the relator is awarded part of any recovery, including settlement amounts, in the suit.[35]

> Example Case: In March 2010, a whistle-blower received $2.64 million of a $12 million settlement between the United States and a cancer center for allegations that the cancer center violated the FCA by submitting false claims to Medicare and the military's healthcare program. The whistle-blower brought this case to the United States' attention when he noticed that the cancer center was inflating claims through various schemes such as upcoding, billing for unnecessary services, and billing for duplicate services.

FCA—Healthcare Reform. As part of healthcare reform, the passage of the Fraud Enforcement and Recovery Act (FERA) enhanced the strength of the FCA.[36] The FERA clarifies that a failure to repay any known overpayment constitutes a false claim.[37] Thus, any improper billing by a healthcare provider may now trigger FCA sanctions. The FERA also expanded whistle-blower protection, which the government hopes will further foster the disclosure of fraud and abuse by providers.[38]

▶ 12-3.4 Criminal Penalties for Business Arrangements

MEDICARE AND MEDICAID FRAUD AND ABUSE (ANTI-KICKBACK STATUTE). The AKS prohibits the knowing solicitation, receipt, offer, or payment of remuneration (anything of value) in exchange for or to induce the arranging or provision of items or services that are reimbursable under Medicare, Medicaid, or other government healthcare programs.[39] Prohibited remuneration may be direct or indirect, overt or covert, and made in cash or in kind. Since the AKS uses the term "knowing," AKS is an intent-based criminal statute.

AKS Elements: 1. Knowingly 2. Solicits or receives 3. Remuneration 4. In return for referral 5. Payment made in whole or part by Medicare and Medicaid • If each prong is met, then some exceptions (called "safe harbors") apply, and you should try to fit the arrangement into a safe harbor.

Both paying and receiving inducements are possible offenses. Additionally, solicitations and offers of inducements are offenses. There are two statutory exceptions to the AKS:[40]

1. Properly disclosed discounts or reduction in price obtained by providers; and

2. Bona fide compensation paid by an employer to an employee.

The AKS also provides regulatory exceptions, called regulatory "safe harbors." Each safe harbor has several elements that must be met to ensure that the arrangement qualifies for an exception (i.e., a "safe harbor").[41] See **Figure 12-1**.

Examples of safe harbors: • Investment Interests (Large and Small Entities) • Space Rental • Equipment Rental • Personal Services and Management Contracts • Sale of Practice (Practitioner to Practitioner) • Referral Services • Warranties • Discounts • Waiver of Beneficiary Coinsurance and Deductible Amount • Electronic Health Records

One Example of a Safe Harbor is the "Space Rental Safe Harbor." Elements include: Remuneration does not include any payment made by a lessee to a lessor for the use of premises as long as the following standards are met: • Set out in writing • Specifies the premises covered • Specifies the exact schedule of intervals when the space will be used • Term is not less than one year • The aggregate rental charge is set in advance • The rental charge is consistent with fair market value and does not take into consideration the volume or value of referrals • The aggregate space rented does not exceed what is reasonably necessary.

Unlike the exceptions to the Stark Law, which this chapter discusses *below*, if a healthcare provider does not meet all the elements of a particular safe harbor, it does not

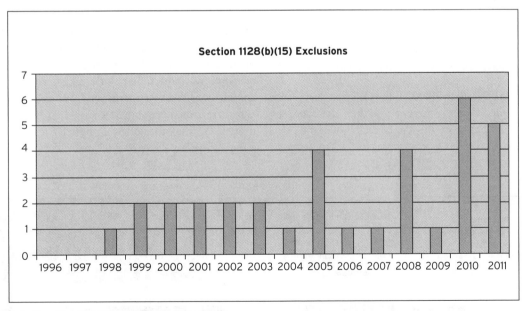

Figure 12-1 Section 1128(b)(15) Exclusions

necessarily mean the entity is automatically in violation of the AKS. Rather, the AKS is judged on the "facts and circumstances" of the arrangement and the parties' intent in entering into the business arrangement. The amount of risk a particular provider is willing to take is roughly analogous to its point on a sliding scale, which ranges from meeting all elements of the relevant safe harbor(s), or fitting into a statutory exception (definitely safe), to missing a nonessential element of a safe harbor for a good reason (probably safe), to entering into an arrangement that does not fit into a safe harbor and on its face is entered into for the purpose of soliciting or receiving referrals (prohibited). **Figure 12-2** illustrates this point.

- Because most arrangements will fall short of fitting into a safe harbor or statutory exception, it is important to understand where on the sliding scale a given arrangement fits, and how much risk the provider is willing to take. See **Table 12-2**.

AKS—Penalties. Violation of the AKS can result in both criminal and civil liability, is a felony, and can result in up to five years of imprisonment, fines up to $25,000, and/or Civil Monetary Penalties (CMPs).[42] In addition, a provider that violates the AKS risks exclusion from participation in the Medicare, Medicaid, or other government healthcare program. Exclusion from government programs is not a minor penalty.

AKS—Healthcare Reform. The passage of the PPACA established a requirement that there be a direct connection between violation of the AKS and a subsequent submission of a false claim.[43] Thus, any violation of the AKS is subject to penalties under the FCA. Additionally, the intent requirement changed as a result of the PPACA.

Intent Required. Before the PPACA, the OIG had historically relied on *United States v. Greber* regarding the scope of the AKS.[44] In that case, the court established the "one purpose" test. Under the "one purpose" test, if one purpose

of a payment was to induce future referrals, or pay for past referrals, the AKS has been violated. Later, the Ninth Circuit Court of Appeals interpreted the AKS to require "specific intent."[45] Thus, the offender had to (i) have knowledge of the specific referral prohibitions contained in the AKS and (ii) violate the law with specific intent to do so. The PPACA significantly diminished this intent requirement.[46] The new section now states that a person need not have actual knowledge of the AKS or specific intent to violate it; he must merely "knowingly" violate the law. The amendment thus lessens the burden on the government to demonstrate a violation of the AKS, and subsequently to establish a false claim.

AKS—Other Administrative Guidance. OIG has issued several fraud alerts stating that certain conduct is prohibited or suspicious. The fraud alerts address: (1) joint venture arrangements; (2) waiver of co-payments and deductibles; (3) hospital incentives to physicians; (4) prescription drug marketing; (5) clinical laboratory arrangements; (5) offering of gifts and other inducements to Medicare and Medicaid beneficiaries; and (6) other areas.[47]

Federal courts have been reluctant to provide authoritative guidance as to what conduct is permitted. For example, at various times, federal courts have been reluctant to decide whether it would be a violation for a physician who admitted patients to a hospital also to own part of the hospital.[48]

AKS—State Law. Some states also have laws that forbid kickbacks for referrals[49] or splitting of fees.[50]

STARK LAW (ETHICS IN PATIENT REFERRALS ACT). Overutilization of healthcare services is a problem that has long affected the healthcare industry. This is largely because of a fee-for-service reimbursement system in which physicians receive more money for a higher volume, or higher complexity, of services performed. For example, if a physician performs more shoulder surgeries, he receives more money. Or, the more often a physician recommends that a patient get an X-ray or a CT scan, the more money the

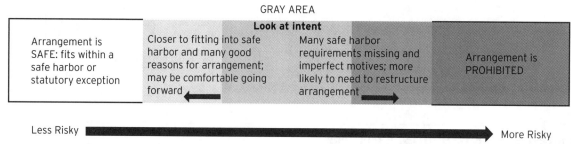

Figure 12-2 Safe Harbor Spectrum

Table 12-2 Three Examples to Illustrate the Safe Harbor Concept

Example 1:

Dr. Thompson, a neurologist, enters into a space rental agreement with St. Vincent Hospital, which owns an office building. The agreement is in writing and signed by both parties, sets a rental rate of $5,000/month, and specifies that Dr. Thompson will use the space full time. The leased space is outlined in the contract as a waiting area and two exam rooms, just enough space for Dr. Thompson to conduct his practice. Further, it has already been determined that the rental rate is consistent with fair market value. Dr. Thompson is a high source of referrals for St. Vincent. Will the hospital be subject to sanctions under the AKS for this lease agreement?

ANSWER: No. The agreement fits into a safe harbor.

Example 2:

Suppose Dr. Thompson enters into the same agreement as in Example 1, except it appears the fair market value rental rate for the space is really $6,000/month, instead of the charged $5,000/month. In a recent St. Vincent board meeting, the minutes reflect a discussion between the CEO of the hospital and the board members that Dr. Thompson is a very valuable practitioner to have affiliated with the hospital. They note that while he is a referral source, his lower rate is mainly intended to keep him in the geographic area in order to increase the prestige of the hospital as a whole. Because of this, they decide that decreasing his rental rate is the best way to ensure he continues to have a good relationship with the hospital. How is this arrangement analyzed under the AKS?

ANSWER: This arrangement falls somewhere in the middle of the sliding scale. Because the rental rate is not set at fair market value, it does not fit safely into a safe harbor. Next, the intent of the hospital in entering into this agreement with a referral source must be analyzed. It appears the hospital wants to please Dr. Thompson so that he stays in the area and continues to serve as a referral source. The CEO also states that he believes the presence of Dr. Thompson will increase the hospital's prestige and reputation. If the motivating factor for the lower rental rate is, in fact, to increase the prestige of the hospital through Dr. Thompson's affiliation, the arrangement is likely to be safe. However, if it is really a disguise to reward Dr. Thompson for the volume or value of referrals he sends to the hospital, then the arrangement will not be safe.

Example 3:

Now suppose Dr. Thompson rents the same space as above for the lower rental rate. This time, the board meeting minutes reflect that the hospital has attempted to find a tenant at the rate of $5,000/month but has been unsuccessful. Thus, they agree to decrease the rental rate in order to obtain a tenant, Dr. Thompson. Is this agreement compliant with AKS?

ANSWER: Again, this agreement does not fit into a safe harbor because the rental rate is not at fair market value. However, because the reason for lowering the rental rate is that a tenant cannot be found who will pay the higher amount, and without the reduction the space would continue to be unoccupied, it is more likely that this arrangement will be safe from AKS scrutiny, as opposed to Example 2.

physician receives if he owns the equipment. This type of problem prompted passage of the "Stark Law," named after its key sponsor, Congressman Pete Stark.

In 1989, the OIG issued a special report with empirical evidence that suggested physicians were abusing the referral process to financially enrich themselves.[51] The study found that much of physician ownership was concentrated in the area of independent clinical laboratories (ICL) and independent physiological laboratories (IPL). In fact, it found that nearly 25 percent of these laboratories were owned by referring physicians. What was startling about the study was not physician ownership in these entities, but rather the utilization rates at these sites. The OIG found that patients of physicians who own or invest in ICLs or IPLs received 45 percent and 13 percent more services, respectively, than average Medicare patients. This resulted in increased costs—approximately $28 million in clinical labs alone.[52]

The report made several recommendations, including, among others, the prohibition of physician referrals to certain or all entities with which they have a financial interest and requiring physicians to disclose these interests.[53] Eventually, Congress included a provision in the Omnibus Budget Reconciliation Act of 1989, which placed certain limitations on physician referrals to clinical laboratories. This is now commonly known as Stark I.

Later, more evidence of overutilization of services surfaced in many other service areas, including, in particular, diagnostic imaging.[54] In response, Representative Stark introduced H.R. 345, which expanded the limitations on referrals to a list of "Designated Health Services," including physical therapy services, occupational therapy services, radiology services (including magnetic resonance imaging (MRI), computerized axial tomography, and ultrasound services), the furnishing of durable medical equipment, the furnishing of parenteral and enteral nutrition equipment and supplies, the furnishing of outpatient prescription drugs, ambulance services, home infusion therapy, and inpatient and outpatient hospital services (including rehabilitation and psychiatric hospital services).[55]

H.R. 345 did not pass, but much of the language was included in Section 13562 of the Omnibus Budget Reconciliation Act of 1993 (OBRA 93).[56] This bill created what is commonly referred to as Stark II. Five years later, the CMS issued a proposed rule, known as Stark II–Phase I, which defined many of the terms in regulations (e.g., referral, financial interest, etc.). Then Stark II–Phase II[57] created many of the exceptions to the law, including the bona fide employment and personal services exception. The CMS has also made many changes to the law through other rulemaking procedures, including changes to the Medicare Physician Fee Schedule rules.[58]

Stark Law—Relationships Governed. At its most basic level, the Stark Law prohibits a physician from referring Medicare patients for certain types of services to an entity with which the physician (or an immediate family member) has a financial relationship, unless an exception applies. The law not only bars physicians from making such a referral, but also bars the entity that has received the referral from billing Medicare or Medicaid. The Stark Law is a strict liability statute, meaning that intent to violate the statute is immaterial.

For a violation of the Stark Law to occur, the following elements must all be present:

1. A *referral*
2. By a *physician*
3. of a *Medicare or Medicaid patient*
4. For *designated health services*
5. To an *entity*
6. With which the physician has a *financial relationship*
7. Unless an *exception* applies

Stark Law—Penalties. Claims submitted in violation of the Stark Law prohibition may trigger the following sanctions:

- denial of payment;[59]
- requiring amounts received to be refunded;[60]
- civil monetary penalties of $15,000 per service where the violation is knowing;[61] and
- exclusion from the Medicare and Medicaid programs where a physician or entity has knowingly entered into an improper cross-referral arrangement or scheme designed to circumvent the self-referral prohibition.[62]

Stark Law—Exceptions. There are thirty-five exceptions under the Stark Law. All organizations should carefully review their financial relationships with physicians to ensure that they remain in compliance with these regulations. See **Table 12-3**.

Stark Law—Healthcare Reform. The PPACA, as of 2012, restricts physician ownership in hospitals to which they refer. If physicians do have an ownership interest, the hospital must submit a report to CMS containing a description of the ownership interests.[63] Each physician-owner is also required to disclose his or her ownership or investment interest in the hospital to patients whom the physician refers

Frequently used exceptions include the following: • Personal Services Exception • Bona Fide Employment Exception • Leasing of Equipment and Space Exceptions • Electronic Health Record System Exception • Isolated Transaction Exception • Fair Market Value Exception • Indirect Compensation Exception • In-Office Ancillary Services Exception

Table 12-3 Examples of Elements of an Exception

The Personal Services Exception
The Personal Services Exception is widely used for numerous contracts with physicians when they are not employed by the entity. Typical agreements covered by the Personal Services Exception include, among others, physician contracts to provide medical services at a facility or facilities, medical director agreements, and even management contracts. In order to meet the Personal Services Exception, the agreement must comply with the following criteria: • Arrangement is set out in writing, is signed by the parties, and specifies the services covered by the arrangement; • Arrangement is for at least one year, but not more than three years; • Compensation is set in advance; • Aggregate services contracted for do not exceed those reasonable and necessary for legitimate business purposes; • Compensation does not exceed fair market value (as determined by a third party appraiser) and is not determined in a manner that takes into account the volume or value of any referrals by a referring physician; • Services furnished under the arrangement do not involve the counseling or promotion of a business arrangement or other activity that violates state or federal law.
Many providers hope to tie compensation to certain performance benchmarks, such as productivity and quality of care. This compensation is then contingent upon obtaining these benchmarks, so the total actual compensation is theoretically not set in advance. However, compensation is considered "set in advance" if the aggregate compensation, a time-based or per-unit-of-service-based (whether per-use or per-service) amount, or a specific formula for calculating the compensation is set in an agreement between the parties before the furnishing of the items or services for which the compensation is to be paid. The formula for determining the compensation must be set forth in sufficient detail so that it can be objectively verified, and the formula may not be changed or modified during the course of the agreement in any manner that takes into account the volume or value of referrals or other business generated by the referring physician.

Example Case: *Kosenske v. Carlisle HMA, Inc.* Hospital (CHHS) contracted with a group of anesthesiologists (BMMA) to provide exclusive anesthesia services at the hospital. The CHHS agreed to provide, at no charge, equipment, space, supplies, and certain staff support necessary for anesthesia services. Years later, the hospital built a surgery center and pain clinic (Clinic), and BMMA began providing services at the Clinic under the same contract. A former BMMA physician filed a *qui tam* suit (whistle-blower suit) alleging violation of the Anti-Kickback Statute and the Stark Law.

The appellate court found that providing equipment, space, supplies, and certain staff support at no charge constituted "remuneration" between CHHS and BMMA. Thus, the arrangement must satisfy a Stark Law exception. The court found that the agreement between CHHS and BMMA for services at the hospital satisfied the Personal Services Exception because it did not apply to the Clinic. The first prong of the Personal Services Exception requires that the arrangement is set forth in writing, is signed by the parties, and specifies the services covered by the arrangement. Although the contract contemplated services that BMMA might provide in the future, the court found that the written contract could not apply to services provided at a facility that did not exist at the time the parties signed the contract.

to the hospital. If a physician does not, as of March 23, 2010, have an ownership interest in a particular hospital, they are restricted from obtaining a new interest or a greater interest moving forward. See **Table 12-4**.

12-3.5 Other Criminal Laws

Prosecutors have included claims of bribery, mail or wire fraud, money laundering,[64] filing false tax returns,[65] obstructing justice,[66] witness tampering,[67] embezzlement from an entity providing Medicare/Medicaid services,[68] and other criminal laws in cases against healthcare providers.[69]

ANTI-BRIBERY ACT. The federal Anti-Bribery Act makes it a federal crime to engage in fraud or bribery involving an organization that receives federal funds.[70] In 2000, the U.S. Supreme Court decided that receipt of Medicare funds is sufficient to trigger applicability of this law.[71]

MAIL FRAUD AND WIRE FRAUD. False claims and other false statements sent through the mail can be punished under the mail fraud law.[72] If statements are sent by wire (for example, by facsimile or e-mail), the provider may be punished under the wire fraud law.[73] Generally, the government must prove the victim (which can be Medicare, Medicaid, or a private payer) has suffered some tangible harm to obtain a conviction under these laws; however, it is not necessary that the victim have suffered an actual

Table 12-4 Three Problems

Problem 1 – Determining Whether a Financial Relationship Exists

Dr. Thompson is a neurologist who provides care in Mainstreet, Indiana. She owns her own practice, but costs to maintain her MRI equipment are increasing. She is considering using space at St. Vincent Hospital and sending patients that require MRI or other imaging procedures to St. Vincent's radiology department. Her longtime friend, whom she met in medical school, is the CEO of St. Vincent's and told her she can use the space for free for a while until her practice recovers.

- Does Dr. Thompson have a financial relationship with St. Vincent Hospital?

ANSWER: Yes. Although there is no actual money changing hands here, St. Vincent's is giving, and Dr. Thompson is receiving, something of value (i.e., free rent). This creates a direct financial relationship.

- Does Dr. Thompson refer patients to St. Vincent Hospital?

ANSWER: Yes.

- What if Dr. Thompson does not see Medicare or Medicaid patients?

ANSWER: This could reduce the chance that Dr. Thompson will violate the Stark Law. However, the issue is not whether Dr. Thompson sees Medicare or Medicaid patients, but that she refers those patients to an entity with which she has a financial relationship. If she truly turns Medicare and Medicaid patients away prior to treating them, and does not refer them to St. Vincent's, then she may be in compliance. Note that it is not advisable to rely on not treating Medicare or Medicaid patients because it is possible to have a claim slip through.

- Do you think Dr. Thompson has violated the Stark Law? Why?
- How would you fix this?

Problem 2 – Determining Whether a Lease is Compliant [continued facts from above]

On advice of counsel, Dr. Thompson decided to sign a lease with St. Vincent's Hospital while she uses their space. The agreement is in writing and signed by Dr. Thompson and St. Vincent's CEO. The term of the agreement is for one year and three months. Dr. Thompson and her friend, the CEO, agree that the lease price will be $5,000 for the first month but that they will renegotiate the price each month. Additionally, the space used by Dr. Thompson has much more space than she needs, but the CEO wants to make her feel comfortable.

- Does this lease agreement comply with the Rental of Office Space Exception?

ANSWER: No. Charges are not set in advance and the amount of space exceeds what is reasonable and necessary for Dr. Thompson.

- How would you modify the agreement?

ANSWER:

Problem 3 – Determining Whether a Physician Services Arrangement is Compliant [facts continued]

After working with counsel to modify Dr. Thompson's lease, St. Vincent's CEO suddenly needs a neurologist to practice at one of St. Vincent's off-campus departments. The CEO only needs someone three days per week, and Dr. Thompson needs to pay off her medical school debt, so she agrees to fill the position. The CEO agrees to pay Dr. Thompson $37 ($39 per patient is the average in the area) for each patient she sees. The term is one year and six months and only applicable to services performed at the off-campus location. Dr. Thompson and the CEO ask counsel to write the contract, and then they both sign a written copy.

- Does the agreement comply with the Stark Law?

ANSWER: Yes. EXPLAIN (discuss assumption of some facts).

- If so, under what exception? What if the only evidence of an agreement was Dr. Thompson and the CEO's handshake?

ANSWER:

loss of money or property, just that the defendant intended such loss to occur.[74] Physicians have been convicted of mail fraud for submitting false bills to private insurers.[75]

In 2003, in one of the first criminal prosecutions of a hospital corporation, the government charged a Michigan hospital with mail and wire fraud for the submission of bills for medically unnecessary procedures. The case was resolved by the hospital pleading guilty and being placed in federal pretrial diversion with a compliance agreement for three years, the hospital paying a $1 million fine and full restitution to Medicare and private insurers, and some individual defendants pleading guilty to state misdemeanor charges, paying fines and restitution, providing community service, and being placed in federal pretrial diversion.[76]

12-4 Suspension, Recoupment, and Exclusion from Federal Programs

The federal government, including CMS, has broad powers to suspend and recoup payment from healthcare providers who violate the law. Courts will not review such suspensions.[77] When CMS chooses not to suspend payments, it also has the power to recoup disputed past payments from current payments.[78] Courts typically do not intervene in this exercise of agency discretion, even in bankruptcy cases. There is one unusual case in which CMS's predecessor entity (HCFA) agreed in a settlement to stop recoupment and to refund recouped funds until the matter could be heard in court.[79]

Additionally, the government is able, in certain circumstances, to exclude a provider from federal healthcare programs. Exclusion from federal healthcare programs is a drastic penalty and, for most providers, means the provider can no longer operate because it cannot submit claims for reimbursement. The Department of Health and Human Services (HHS) has broad powers to exclude any providers who violate false claims, anti-kickback, self-referral, medical necessity, or medical quality requirements from participation in Medicare, Medicaid, and other federal programs. In some cases exclusion is mandated, and in other cases it is permissive.[80] See **Table 12-5**. When exclusions are permissive, HHS may offer corrective action plans in lieu of exclusion and generally does so. Providers who desire to continue in business generally cooperate in developing such plans because failure to do so can result in exclusion.[81] Exclusions generally remain in effect during appeals.[82]

Medicare and Medicaid providers are not permitted to employ or contract with persons or entities that have been excluded. To assist in enforcing this requirement, the OIG maintains a website with a list of all who have been excluded.[83] These actions are collected in the Healthcare Integrity and Protection Data Bank.[84]

HHS sometimes reinstates institutional providers after a change in ownership or management.[85]

12-5 Civil Money Penalties

HHS has the authority to impose significant civil money penalties for violations of the Medicare and Medicaid fraud and abuse requirements.[86] This includes misrepresentations in claims and reports, kickbacks, and other violations.

False claims can now result in civil money penalties of $5,500 to $11,500 per item or service and, in addition, assessments of up to $25,000 per item or service, plus three times the amount claimed.[87]

Another reason providers need to be careful about fraud and abuse issues is that even when the government chooses not to challenge the arrangement, one of the parties can try to use a violation as a basis for avoiding its responsibilities in a business arrangement. Illegality of a contract can be a reason to declare a contract void and unenforceable. One Texas court declared a physician recruitment contract void as an illegal inducement of referrals; when the physician violated the contract by refusing to make required repayments, the hospital could not recover the money it

Table 12-5 Exclusions

Mandatory Exclusions	• Federal healthcare-program-related offenses • Patient abuse or neglect • Felony healthcare fraud offenses • Felony controlled substance violation offenses
Permissive Exclusions	15 bases, including: • Misdemeanor fraud conviction • Obstruction conviction • Misdemeanor controlled substances violation • License revocation or suspension • Entity controlled by excluded individual (and vice versa)

had advanced.[88] A California court ruled that a hospital's free rent office arrangement with a physician was an illegal inducement for referrals, and the hospital could get out of the lease.[89] A federal court in Illinois found that a laboratory management agreement was unenforceable because it was an illegal inducement for referrals. Although the court questioned whether there was sufficient proof of willfulness for any crime to have occurred yet, the court ruled that future performance would be willful after the decision in the case was issued.[90] These attacks do not always succeed. A California jury rejected a radiologist's challenge to a marketing agreement with a hospital and required him to pay the fee under the contract.[91]

12-6 Mitigating Liability

Many times, a healthcare provider does not know if a given arrangement will subject it to civil liability. In that case, before it enters into an agreement, it may seek an advisory opinion. At the other end of the transaction, a provider may discover that an arrangement that is in force is noncompliant. At that point, the provider must determine how it will move forward. These decisions, involving the avoidance of liability or mitigating liability, are usually the product of collaboration between compliance specialists, attorneys, and the provider and have a great impact on the profitability and reputation of a medical practice.

12-6.1 Advisory Opinions

Federal administrative agencies have been reluctant to give authoritative guidance concerning what is permitted under the AKS. When the federal government approves certain conduct, it is not permitted to prosecute that conduct as fraud and abuse.[92] In 1997, HHS began providing advisory opinions.[93] While relevant opinions should be examined when structuring arrangements because they give some guidance, they are generally worded to minimize the extent to which they provide providers with any legal protection because they explicitly only apply to specific facts and parties that submitted the request for guidance. Additionally, the advisory opinion process is expensive.[94] Further, many providers rely on opinions from their counsel regarding their arrangements, rather than wait for release of an OIG advisory opinion, which can take many months.

CMS also issues certain advisory opinions that provide guidance on whether a proposed arrangement complies with the Stark Law.

12-6.2 Self-Referral Disclosure Protocol

The PPACA made available a Self-Referral Disclosure Protocol,[95] which provides for entities and individuals who have violated the Stark Law to, in good faith, explain what they did and seek leniency in exchange for bringing the matter to the government's attention. While CMS will review the circumstances surrounding the disclosed matter, it is not bound by any conclusions made by the disclosing party or obligated to resolve the matter in any particular manner. Disclosures can have several advantages. As discussed above, public disclosure can block *qui tam* actions. Additionally, disclosure may afford the provider leniency if the government views the disclosure as cooperation on the part of the provider. However, many providers are wary of disclosure because the government is not required to grant any leniency or reduce penalties in any way if a provider voluntarily discloses noncompliance, and telling the government about wrongdoing may alert it when it otherwise is not aware of any violation.

CMS posts protocol settlements on its website.[96] As of February 2012, the website contained brief summaries of four settlements and the amounts for each, ranging from $4,500 to $579,000. However, CMS has not disclosed the full scope of the government's investigations in these matters, nor the possible potential penalties the government could have sought if it had pursued the matter on its own. Thus, it is difficult to ascertain whether the protocol saved the providers money.

12-6.3 Compliance Programs

While it may be difficult for healthcare providers to prevent violations of the AKS, CMP, and Stark Laws altogether, they can take measures to reduce their exposure to liability by implementing comprehensive compliance programs. Moreover, federal prosecutors must evaluate an organization's compliance program in determining whether to charge the company. A meaningful, effective compliance program may save the entity from prosecution. First, providers should routinely assess risk areas by reviewing the typical internal arrangements and transactions.[97] Second, providers should establish an internal audit system to monitor compliance. The intensity of any audit system will largely depend on the size and compliance history of the organization. To administer an effective compliance program and ensure organization-wide compliance, providers should educate staff on compliance matters such as proper coding, billing, and broader regulatory proscriptions. To be truly successful, the organization must foster a culture of compliance. While implementation of a compliance program may be difficult, the use of outside counsel can assist in this task.

12-6.4 Settlements

Because the potential penalties under AKS and Stark can be so large, many cases are settled before a trial on the merits of the claim. Additionally, as trials and the events leading up to trials take a lot of time and resources, these costs must also be considered when a provider is deciding whether to settle. However, the fear of large verdicts against a provider, and large legal fees, also creates an incentive to settle even in cases where the provider has not done anything wrong.

Example Case: In December 2009, a health system agreed to pay the United States almost $700,000 to settle claims alleging it violated the FCA. If the system had not settled, it would have faced substantially larger penalties, plus any legal fees it would incur. As with many settlements, and a benefit of such, the health system was not required to admit liability.

Many times, settlements are also accompanied by a requirement that the provider institute an ongoing corporate compliance agreement or corporate integrity agreement.[98]

Chapter Summary

Healthcare providers operate under the constant pressure to comply with various laws regulating billing, financial relationships, and licensure, to name a few. Since the early 1990s, and with an added focus in recent years with healthcare reform, the federal government has increasingly begun to apply both criminal and civil laws to providers of healthcare services. The aim of these enforcement efforts has been to combat alleged fraud and abuse in the industry and thereby protect the patients who are receiving healthcare services. Many providers, however, believe that these enforcement efforts are merely a way to drive an increase in revenue to the federal government. Regardless of the reason for the increased enforcement, anyone who is involved with healthcare organizations must be aware of the severe penalties that can be assessed on a healthcare provider for various actions and relationships.

This text has covered both criminal and civil penalties that may be imposed on a healthcare entity. The text began by introducing you to the various enforcement agencies. This text then explored the federal Anti-Kickback Statute and Stark Law in depth, as well as provided a brief overview of various other laws. Additionally, the text provided realistic ways in which a healthcare provider can seek to limit its liability in the current legal landscape.

Key Terms and Definitions

Anti-Kickback Statute (AKS) - A federal law that prohibits the knowing solicitation, receipt, offer, or payment of remuneration (anything of value) in exchange for, or to induce the arranging or provision of, items or services that are reimbursable under Medicare, Medicaid, or other government healthcare programs.

Ethics in Patient Referrals Act ("Stark Law") - A federal law named after its key sponsor, Congressman Pete Stark, that prohibits a physician from referring Medicare patients for certain types of services to an entity with which the physician (or an immediate family member) has a financial relationship, unless one of thirty-five exceptions applies.

False Claims Act (FCA) - Federal act passed under the administration of President Abraham Lincoln, which carries both civil and criminal penalties for anyone who knowingly presents, or causes to be presented, to the U.S. government a false or fictitious claim for payment. The FCA's authority encompasses more than just healthcare claims; it applies equally to all others who make claims for payment from government funds to the government.

Fraud Enforcement and Recovery Act (FERA)- Federal act passed as a part of healthcare reform. Enhanced the strength of the FCA and clarified that a failure to repay any known overpayment constitutes a false claim.

Office of the Inspector General (OIG) - Administrative agency of the U.S. Department of Health and Human Services that actively conducts criminal, civil, and administrative investigations of fraud and misconduct related to Medicare, Medicaid, and other federal healthcare programs.

Patient Protection and Affordable Care Act (PPACA)- Principal federal law of current healthcare reform. This statute is expansive and includes the following provisions: expands the list of permissive criteria that may be considered by the OIG in excluding providers; establishes a requirement that there be a direct connection between violation of the AKS and a subsequent submission of a false claim; diminishes the intent requirement of the AKS; and restricts physician ownership in hospitals to which they refer.

U.S. Department of Justice (DOJ) - The primary federal criminal investigation and enforcement agency. When the Office of the Inspector General determines that criminal prosecutions regarding healthcare providers should be considered, the case is referred to the DOJ. The DOJ can also initiate prosecutions on its own, and teams with the OIG and FBI agents to investigate providers.

Instructor-Led Questions

1. Discuss compliance programs and corporate integrity agreements.

2. Discuss the agencies that enforce criminal law and civil penalties.

3. What are the differences between criminal penalties and civil money penalties?

4. What are the consequences of various approaches to respond to criminal investigations?

5. What are the criminal penalties imposed for healthcare decisions?

6. What are the criminal penalties imposed for billing issues?

7. What are criminal penalties imposed for business arrangements?

8. Discuss the range of safe harbors and exclusions from the Anti-Kickback Statute and Stark Law.

9. Discuss the power of the Centers for Medicare & Medicaid Services to suspend or recoup provider payments and to exclude providers from Medicare participation.

10. Discuss the scope of civil money penalties that the Department of Health and Human Services can impose.

11. Discuss private *qui tam* suits to enforce the False Claims Act. Who may bring such suits?

Endnotes

1   OIG documents can be found at http://oig.hhs.gov/.

2   42 U.S.C. § 1395b-5(b); 42 C.F.R. §§ 420.400, 420.405; 63 FED. REG. 31,123 (June 8, 1998); HCFA to pay seniors for tipping off government to Medicare fraud, 2 H.C.F.R. 442 (1998); G. Weinreich, Medicare incentive program: A new fix or another problem? 2 H.C.F.R. 484 (1998).

3   63 FED. REG. 58,399 (Oct. 30, 1998); J. Meyer, The self-disclosure protocol: treading warily under the HHS IG's eye, 3 H.C.F.R. 304 (1999); for an OIG assessment of self-disclosure, see http://oig.hhs.gov/fraud/cia/docs/assessment.htm (accessed Sept. 4, 2004); for an example of self-disclosure, see Community Health Systems, Inc. agreement with OIG finalized; Voluntary disclosure and self-audit yields release of liability and $31 million repayment to government, PR Newswire, Mar. 3, 2000.

4   E.g., DHHS & DOJ, Fraud and Abuse Control Program as Mandated by the Health Insurance Portability and Accountability Act of 1996 (Jan. 24, 1997).

5   *Duncan v. Louisiana*, 391 U. S. 145 (1968) [right to jury trial for serious offenses, not petty offenses]; *Blanton v. North Las Vegas*, 489 U. S. 538 (1989) [offense with maximum sentence of up to six months presumed petty, unless severe additional statutory penalties indicating legislature considered offense serious]; *Lewis v. United States*, 518 U.S. 322 (1996) [no right to trial by jury when prosecuted for multiple petty offenses even when maximum aggregate sentence exceeds six months].

6   E.g., *Einaugler v. Supreme Court*, 109 F.3d 836 (2d Cir. 1997), application for stay of mandate denied, 520 U.S. 1238 (1997) [denial of habeas corpus for absence of expert testimony where physician convicted of reckless endangerment for not transferring nursing home patient to hospital more quickly after treatment error]; but see *United States v. Wood*, 207 F.3d 1222 (10th Cir. 2000) [reversing conviction of physician for death of patient, ordering new trial, degree of deviation from standard of care a central issue].

7   *Blockburger v. United States*, 284 U.S. 299 (1932); *United States v. Dixon*, 509 U.S. 688 (1993) [two criminal laws provisions not "same offense" if each contains element not included in other].

8   *Hudson v. United States*, 522 U.S. 93 (1997) [disavowing *United States v. Halper*, 490 U.S. 435 (1989)]; *United States v. Lippert*, 148 F.3d 974 (8th Cir. 1998) [double jeopardy does not bar fine after conviction, applying Hudson]; see also *Smith v. Doe*, 538 U.S. 84 (2003) [retroactive application of sex offender registration law not violation of ex post facto prohibition since not punitive].

9   18 U.S.C. § 1001; *United States v. Brown*, 151 F.3d 476 (6th Cir. 1998) [affirming conviction for false statements to federal agency as to one defendant, reversing as to other]; M. Morris, Pharmacist's wife gets one day of probation for making false statement to FBI, KANSAS CITY STAR, Feb. 8, 2003; see also Editorial, Martha Stewart misgivings, WALL ST. J., Mar. 8, 2004, A16 [this discourages persons from talking to governmental agents].

10 *Brogan v. United States*, 522 U.S. 398 (1998) [no exception to 18 U.S.C. § 1001 for exculpatory "no"]; L. Greenhouse, Court backs prosecution for false denial of guilt, N.Y. TIMES, Jan. 27, 1998, A12.

11 *United States v. Rutgard*, 116 F.3d 1270 (9th Cir. 1997) [false statements in physician's files can be statements to federal agency in violation of § 1001 when required by Medicare as documentation of medical necessity].

12 E.g., P. Callahan & T.M. Burton, U.S. Abbott probe involves sting, undercover tapes, WALL ST. J., July 18, 2003, A3.

13 HIPAA's emphasis on parallel proceedings prompts increased use of mail fraud statute, 1 H.C.F.R. 757 (1997) [power of government to seize assets, destroy business before day in court]; *United States v. Oncology Associates*, 198 F.3d 489 (4th Cir. 1999); *United States v. Sriram*, 147 F. Supp. 2d 914 (N.D. Ill. 2001); L. Browning, $500 million frozen in I.R.S. crackdown in doctors' tax case, N.Y. TIMES, Nov. 5, 2004, A1; T. Zeller, U.S. seizes assets of operator of online drug business, N.Y. TIMES, May 23, 2005, C2; but see *S.E.C. v. HealthSouth Corp.*, 261 F. Supp. 2d 1298 (N.D. Ala. 2003) [dissolving freeze].

14 See *United States v. Kirschenbaum*, 156 F.3d 784, 1998 U.S. App. LEXIS 24431 (7th Cir.).

15 42 U.S.C. § 1320c-5(a).

16 *Corkill v. Shalala*, 109 F.3d 1348 (9th Cir. 1996).

17 E.g., *United States ex rel. Augustine v. Century Health Servs.*, 289 F.3d 409 (6th Cir. 2002); *United States ex rel. Barrett v. Columbia/HCA Healthcare Corp.*, 251 F.3d 28 (D. D.C. 2003) [applying implied certification theory]; see also *Shaw v. AAA Engineering & Drafting, Inc.*, 213 F.3d 519 (10th Cir. 2000) [implied certification permitted in non-Medicare case]; *Mikes v. Straus*, 274 F.3d 687 (2d Cir. 2001) ["implied false certification is appropriately applied only when the underlying statute or regulation. . . expressly states the provider must comply in order to be paid"]; *contra U.S. ex rel. Willard v. Humana Health Plan of Tex.*, 336 F.3d 375 (5th Cir. 2003)

18 E.g., Prosecutor decides against charging doctor, AP, Nov. 5, 2001 [18-year-old patient died two days after liposuction]; see also S.K. Dewan, When is an accident a crime, N.Y. TIMES, Feb. 1, 2003, 12WK [discussion of analogous problem of deciding when to prosecute police for shooting civilian].

19 E.g., Alan Duke, *Conrad Murray Found Guilty in Michael Jackson Trial*, CNN.com (Nov. 7, 2011), http://articles.cnn.com/2011-11-07/justice/justice_california-conrad-murray-trial_1_surgical-anesthetic-propofol-defense-attorney-ed-chernoff-conrad-murray?_s=PM:JUSTICE; *United States v. Wood*, 207 F.3d 1222 (10th Cir. 2000) [reversing conviction of physician for death of patient, ordering new trial, degree of deviation from standard of care a central issue; discusses

cases where physicians have been prosecuted for the outcome of patient care]; J.A. Filkins, 'With no evil intent:' the criminal prosecution of physicians for medical negligence, 22 J. LEGAL MED. 467 (2001); see also Nurse pleads guilty to neglect in death of patient, AP, Jan. 7, 2003 [Fla. nurse anesthetist failed to monitor vital signs during surgery]; Caregiver sentenced to 90 days in jail for death of patient, AP, Jan. 23, 2002 [Wis. assisted living facility caregiver left mentally retarded resident in bathtub, drowned].

20 Jim Avila, Kaitlyn Folmer, & Jessica Hoppper, ABCNews.com (Oct. 13, 2011), http://abcnews.go.com/US/michael-jackson-death-trial-conrad-murray-prosecutors-call/story?id=14731374#.Tzp4i07y_To.

21 *People v. Schug*, No. CR 4514 (Cal. Super. Ct. Lake County Feb. 20, 1998), as discussed in 7 H.L.R. 470 (1998); L. Prager, Keeping clinical errors out of criminal courts, AM. MED. NEWS, Mar. 16, 1998; see also Doctor faces 2nd-degree murder charge in baby's death, AM. MED. NEWS, Sept. 21, 1998, 9 [Dr. Turner; Washington]; Murder charge dropped in case against doctor, N.Y. TIMES, Feb. 2, 1999, A15 [Dr. Turner].

22 See *DEA v. Doctors*, AM. MED. NEWS, Dec. 1, 2003, 14 [441 actions by DEA in first three quarters of 2003]; A. Barton, Psychiatrist pleads in drug death, Palm Beach Post [Fla.], Dec. 7, 2002, 1C.

23 R. Vartabedian, Jury finds doctor not guilty, L.A. TIMES, May 20, 2004, B6.

24 E.g., Nurse accused of drug tampering sentenced to nine years, AP, Sept. 13, 2003 [Idaho nurse accused of stealing lifesaving medication from hospitalized seizure patient].

25 *State v. Boone Retirement Ctr., Inc.*, 26 S.W.3d 265 (Mo. App. 2000).

26 Fraud is defined as "wrongful or criminal deception intended to result in financial or personal gain." Abuse is defined as "improper use of something; unjust or corrupt practice." Merriam-Webster Dictionary, 2010.

27 E.g., *United States v. Mitrione*, 357 F.3d 712 (7th Cir. 2004).

28 Doctor Sentenced for Health-care Billing Fraud, AP, Sept, 26, 2003.

29 Kristen Harrington *et. al.*, *Restraining Medicare Abuse: The Case of Upcoding*, Research in Healthcare Financial Management, Jan 1, 2007.

30 31 U.S.C. § 3729-3731 (2010).

31 31 U.S.C. § 3729(a).

32 *United States ex rel. Karnelas v. Melrose-Wakefield Hosp.*, 360 F.3d 220 (1st Cir. 2004).

33 *Qui tam pro domino rege quam pro se ipso in hac parte sequitur*-"who pursues this action on our Lord the King's behalf as well as his own." *Vermont Agency of Natural Resources v. U.S. ex. Rel. Stevens*, 120 S.Ct. 1858 (2009).

34 31 U.S.C. § 3730(b) (2010).

35 A relator who challenged a lease arrangement between a medical group and a hospital was awarded 24 percent of a $6,525,000 settlement, *United States ex rel. Johnson-Pochardt v. Rapid City Reg. Hosp.*, 252 F. Supp. 2d 892 (D. S.D. 2003).

36 The Fraud Enforcement and Recovery Act, Pub. L. No. 111-121, 123 Stat. 1617 (2009).

37 31 U.S.C. § 3729(b)(1)-(3).

38 31 U.S.C. § 3730(h).

39 42 U.S.C. § 1320a-7b.

40 42 U.S.C. § 1320a-7b(b)(3).

41 42 C.F.R. pt. 411.

42 42 U.S.C. § 1320a-7b(a).

43 Patient Protection and Affordable Care Act, Pub. L. No. 111-148, 124 Stat. 119, § 6402(f)(1) (2010).

44 *U.S. v. Greber*, 760 F.2d 68 (3rd Cir. 1985), cert denied, 474 U.S. 988 (1985).

45 *Hanlester Network v. Shalala*, 51 F.3d 1390 (9th Cir. 1995).

46 Patient Protection and Affordable Care Act, Pub. L. No. 111-148, 124 Stat. 119 (2010) § 6402(f)(2).

47 59 Fed. Reg. 65,372 (Dec. 19, 1994); 67 Fed. Reg. 55,855 (Aug. 30, 2002).

48 *Bakersfield Commun. Hosp. v. Sullivan*, No. 89-1056-TPJ (D. D.C. Aug. 8, 1989), as discussed in 17 Health L. Dig. (Sept. 1989), at 15; D. Burda, Judge refuses to rule on hospital sale, Mod. Healthcare, Sept. 1, 1989, 7.

49 E.g., Fla. Stat. §§ 395.0185, 455.237; see also *Schmidt v. Foundation Health*, 35 Cal. App. 4th 1702, 42 Cal. Rptr. 2d 172 (3d Dist. 1995) [illegal kickback for health insurance broker to rebate commission to subscribers].

50 E.g., Fla. Stat. § 458.331(1)(i).

51 U.S. Dep't of Health & Human Servs., Office of Inspector General, *Financial Arrangements Between Physicians and Health Care Businesses*, (1989) [hereinafter *Financial Arrangements*].

52 See *Financial Arrangements*, supra note __, at iii.

53 See *Financial Arrangements*, supra note __, at iii.

54 See, e.g., Bruce J. Hillman et al., *Frequency and Costs of Diagnostic Imaging in Office Practice - A Comparison of Self-Referring and Radiologist-Referring Physicians*, 322 New Engl. J. Med., 1604, 1604 (1990); Jean M. Mitchell & Elton Scott, *Physician Ownership of Physical Therapy Services: Effects on Charges, Utilization, Profits, and Service Characteristics*, 268 JAMA 2055, 2055 (1992).

55 H.R. 345, 103rd Cong. (1993).

56 Morey J. Kolber, *Stark Regulation: A Historical and Current Review of the Self-Referral Laws*, 18 HEC Forum 61, 63-64 (2006).

57 Physicians' Referrals to Health Care Entities with Which They Have Financial Relationships (Phase II), 69 Fed. Reg. 16,054, 16,054 (Mar. 26, 2004) [hereinafter Physicians' Referrals (Phase II)] (to be codified at 42 C.F.R. pts. 411 and 424).

58 Changes to the Hospital Inpatient Prospective Payment Systems and Fiscal Year 2009 Rates, 73 Fed. Reg. 48,434, 48,688 (Aug. 19, 2008) (to be codified at 42 C.F.R. 411-413, 422, and 489).

59 42 U.S.C. § 1395nn(g)(1) (2010).

60 42 U.S.C. § 1395nn(g)(2).

61 42 U.S.C. § 1395nn(g)(3).

62 42 U.S.C. § 1395nn(g)(4).

63 42 U.S.C. § 411.362(a).

64 18 U.S.C. § 1957; *United States v. Rutgard*, 116 F.3d 1270 (9th Cir. 1997) [proof of violation of § 1957 requires proof of transfer of particular criminal proceeds].

65 26 U.S.C. § 7206.

66 18 U.S.C. § 1503; *United States v. Vaghela*, 169 F.3d 729 (11th Cir. 1999) [reversing conviction obstructing justice, affirming other convictions; agreed acts did not meet nexus requirement–the act must have relationship in time, causation, or logic with the judicial proceedings–applying *United States v. Aguilar*, 515 U.S. 593 (1995)].

67 18 U.S.C. § 1512; *United States v. Mills*, 138 F.3d 928 (11th Cir. 1998), cert. denied, 525 U.S. 1003 (1998) [affirming conviction of officers of home health company for witness tampering].

68 18 U.S.C. § 669, added by HIPAA (Pub. L. No. 104-191); *United States v. Rector*, No. 3:98-CR39WN (S. D. Miss. May 1, 1998) [guilty plea resulted in first conviction under law].

69 E.g., 18 U.S.C. § 286 [conspiracy to defraud the government with respect to a claim]; 18 U.S.C. § 287 [fictitious or fraudulent claims]; 18 U.S.C. § 371 [conspiracy to commit offense or defraud]; 18 U.S.C. § 494 [contractors, bonds, bids, and public accords]; 18 U.S.C. § 495 [contracts, deeds, and powers of attorney]; 18 U.S.C. § 1001 [statements or entries generally]; 18 U.S.C. § 1002 [possession of false papers to defraud U.S.], see *United States v. Radetsky*, 535 F.2d 556 (10th Cir. 1976), cert. denied, 429 U.S. 820 (1976) [conviction for false Medicare billing under 18 U.S.C. §§ 1001, 1002], overruled in part on other grounds, *United States v. Dailey*, 921 F.2d 994 (10th Cir. 1990), cert. denied, 502 U.S. 952 (1991); 18 U.S.C. §§ 1961-1963 [racketeer influenced, corrupted organizations (RICO)]; 18 U.S.C.§ 1018 [official certificates, writings]; 18 U.S.C. § 1505 [obstruction of proceedings before departments, agencies, committees]; 31 U.S.C. § 231 [liability of persons making false claims].

70 18 U.S.C. § 666.

71 *Fischer v. United States*, 529 U.S. 667 (2000).

72 18 U.S.C. § 1341; *United States v. Woodely*, 9 F.3d 74 (9th Cir. 1993) [mail fraud conviction for Medicare claims by nursing home]; *United States v. Migliaccio*, 34 F.3d 1517 (10th Cir. 1994) [conviction of doctors for mail fraud for sending false CHAMPUS claims reversed and new trial ordered, alleged misrepresentation of surgical procedures performed, inadequate jury instructions]; *United States v. Vest*, 116 F.3d 1179 (7th Cir. 1997), cert. denied, 522 U.S. 1119 (1998) [mail fraud conviction of physician].

73 18 U.S.C. § 1343.

74 See *United States v. Jain*, 93 F.3d 436 (8th Cir. 1996), cert. denied, 520 U.S. 1273 (1997) [mail fraud conviction reversed, no evidence any patient experienced tangible harm].

75 E.g., *United States v. Hooshmand*, 931 F.2d 725 (11th Cir. 1991).

76 Cases in court, Health Care Fraud & Abuse, Feb. 13, 2003, 7; G. Martin & B.C. Tanase, The first criminal prosecution of a hospital: lessons from the United Memorial Hospital case, presented at the Am. Health Lawyers Ass'n 2003 Annual Meeting in San Antonio, Tex.

77 E.g., *Clarinda Home Health v. Shalala*, 100 F.3d 526 (8th Cir. 1996) [no jurisdiction to review suspension of Medicare payments during investigation]; sees also Feds cite mistakes at State Hospital prior to suicide, AP, Sept. 27, 2003 [Vt. state hospital participation terminated].

78 See HCFA changes instructions for suspending payments and recouping overpayments, 2 H.C.F.R. 407 (1998) [Intermediary Manual Transmittal No. 1745; Carriers Manual Transmittal No. 1604].

79 *Fendell v. Shalala*, No. 4:97-CV-118-MP (N.D. Fla. settlement agreement June 19, 1997) [HCFA agreed not to recoup from current claims for prior disputed payments]; settlement on Aug. 26, 1998, in which HCFA refunded $2.2 million until hearing, 2 H.C.F.R. 743 (1998).

80 42 C.F.R. pts. 1001 (Medicare), 1002 (Medicaid); 62 Fed. Reg. 67,392 (Dec. 24, 1997) [permissive exclusion guidelines]; 63 Fed. Reg. 46,676 (Sept. 2, 1998) [IG exclusion rules]; R. Roth & T. Hoffman, HHS IG makes power play in finding exclusion authority over indirect providers, 2 H.C.F.R. 797 (1998); 63 Fed. Reg. 57,918 (Oct. 29, 1998) [modifying IG exclusion rules]; 63 Fed. Reg. 68,687 (Dec. 14, 1998) [final rule on procedures to impose civil money penalties, assessments, exclusions].

81 E.g., *Corkill v. Shalala*, 109 F.3d 1348 (9th Cir. 1996) [affirming three-year exclusion of physician for violating medical necessity, quality requirements; refused to enter corrective action plan].

82 E.g., *Erickson v. United States ex rel. D.H.H.S.*, 67 F.3d 858 (9th Cir. 1995) [reversing injunction of exclusion pending appeal].

83 See http://exclusions.oig.hhs.gov.

84 64 Fed. Reg. 57,740 (Oct. 26, 1999), codified in 45 C.F.R. pt. 61.

85 E.g., Golden Valley hospital has Medicare reinstated, AP, May 22, 2002.

86 42 U.S.C. § 1320a-7b; 42 C.F.R. pts. 402, 1003 [civil money penalties, assessments]; 42 C.F.R. pts. 400, 1005 [procedures]; 63 Fed. Reg. 68,687 (Dec. 14, 1998); 65 Fed. Reg. 24,400 (Apr. 26, 2000); 67 Fed. Reg. 11,928 (Mar. 18, 2002).

87 42 U.S.C. § 1320a-7a; 42 C.F.R. pts. 402, 1003.

88 *Polk County v. Peters*, 800 F. Supp. 1451 (E.D. Tex. 1992).

89 *Vana v. Vista Hosp. Sys., Inc.*, No. 233623, 1993 WL 597402 (Cal. Super. Ct. Riverside County Oct. 25, 1993). The case settled in 1994, 3 H.L.R. 180 (1994).

90 *Modern Med. Labs., Inc. v. Smith-Kline Beecham Clinical Labs., Inc.*, No. 92 C 5302 (N.D. Ill. Aug. 16, 1994), reprinted in Medicare & Medicaid Guide [CCH] ¶42754.

91 *Klaczak v. Consolidated Med. Transport, Inc.*, 2002 U.S. Dist. LEXIS 16824 (N.D. Ill.) [denying dismissal of *qui tam* action brought by former employees of transport company alleging ambulance services were provided that were medically unnecessary, kickbacks were paid for referrals]; *Anaheim General Hosp. v. Pacific Coast Radiology Med. Group*, No. 660926 (Cal. Super. Ct. Oct. 11, 1994); B. McCormick, Antikickback law no defense for not paying fee, Am. Med. News, Nov. 14, 1994, at 8.

92 42 C.F.R. pt 1008.

93 42 C.F.R. pt 1008.

94 The cost of an advisory opinion is $86/hr. Advisory opinions can take several months to be completed.

95 Patient Protection and Affordable Care Act, Pub. L. No. 111-148, 124 Stat. 119 (2010) § 1128J(d)(2).

96 http://www.cms.gov/PhysicianSelfReferral/DPS/list.asp#TopOfPage

97 Office of the Inspector Gen., Health & Human Servs., *Compliance Program Guidance for Hospitals*, 63 Fed. Reg. 8989 (Feb. 23, 1998).

98 See Office of Inspector General, Corporate Integrity Agreements, available at http://oig.hhs.gov/fraud/cias.asp.

Chapter 13

Reproductive Issues

Nicole Huberfeld

Key Learning Objectives

By the end of this chapter, you will be able to:

- Understand key legal concepts surrounding the modern complexities of human reproduction.

- Explain what kinds of decisions or acts may be protected from government intervention.

- Differentiate between different methods of intervention that can facilitate or prevent reproduction.

Chapter Outline

Introduction

State law and federal law often overlap in the area of human reproduction, and a handful of Supreme Court decisions set the floor for the degree and kind of regulation that can limit or expand the possibilities for reproductive health. This chapter will help you understand the federal and state law pertaining to some of the more major reproductive health issues, such as access to contraception, sterilization, assisted reproduction, abortion, negligent sterilizations, and failure to inform of genetic risks.

13-1 Contraception

Numerous contraceptive drugs and devices are available to reduce the probability of pregnancy, and they are widely used. The Centers for Disease Control (CDC) National Center for Health Statistics reported that from 2006–2008 approximately 99 percent of women ages fifteen to forty-four who had ever had sex with a male had used at least one contraceptive method. In that same time frame, about 93 percent of sexually active women had a partner use a male condom; 82 percent of women used oral contraceptive pills; and about 20 percent relied on female sterilization, while approximately 13 percent relied on male sterilization.[1]

This section will discuss the constitutional basis for the right to access and use contraceptives as well as differences that may exist between adults and minors in accessing contraception.

13-1.1 Adults

The ability to purchase and use contraceptives is deemed a fundamental right and categorized as a privacy right protected by the Fifth and the Fourteenth Amendments to the U.S. Constitution. This means that states cannot prohibit the purchase or use of contraceptives by adults without a compelling reason to limit such access, and any such law must be narrowly tailored to the stated compelling governmental interest. This protection dates to 1965, when the Supreme Court in *Griswold v. Connecticut* declared a law forbidding the use of contraceptives by married persons to be an unconstitutional violation of the right to privacy.[2] In 1972, the Court expanded the protection when it declared a law forbidding unmarried persons to buy or use contraceptives to be unconstitutional in *Eisenstadt v. Baird*.[3] The Court in *Eisenstadt* held that states could not legitimately differentiate between married and unmarried adults regarding access to contraceptives.

> Individuals have a constitutionally protected privacy right to access and use contraceptives, regardless of marital status.

Despite the constitutional protection for use of contraception, states try to regulate sales of contraceptives in the name of protecting the public health. The Supreme Court limited the permissible scope of such regulations in the 1977 decision *Carey v. Population Services International*.[4] In that case, a New York statute prohibited distribution of nonprescription contraceptives to persons over the age of sixteen by anyone other than licensed pharmacists; the Court held that this law constituted an undue burden on an individual's right to decide whether to bear a child, which is subsumed within the right to privacy. The Court also invalidated the state's prohibition on advertising and display of both prescription and nonprescription contraceptives by persons licensed to sell such products as interfering with the right to procreate (or refrain from procreating).

Some contraceptives require a prescription, or a fitting, and must be obtained through a qualified person, generally a physician or a nurse practitioner. Other contraceptives may be purchased without medical professional intervention. Though it would seem that this is a clear dividing line, disputes can still arise. For example, when emergency contraception, sometimes called the morning-after-pill, became available in 2003, a Food and Drug Administration (FDA) expert advisory panel recommended over-the-counter (OTC) status so that a prescription would not be required, but the FDA rejected the recommendation and required a prescription. A back-and-forth ensued, and the end result was that emergency contraception was available OTC for women seventeen years of age and older but that girls younger than seventeen must obtain a prescription. Interestingly, about ten states mandate that healthcare providers offer emergency contraception to rape victims who want it, and offering emergency contraception to rape victims appears to have become the standard of care in some jurisdictions, including states with no legislative mandate.

13-1.2 Minors

In some states, minors face obstacles to obtaining contraceptives, though their ability to access and use contraception is protected to some degree. In the 1977 decision of *Belotti v. Baird*,[5] the Supreme Court struck down part of a New York law that prohibited the sale or distribution of nonprescription contraceptives to minors under sixteen years of age. The Supreme Court has not ruled directly on this issue again, but a pattern can be seen in the various lower court decisions relating to minors' access to contraception.

For example, in 1980, a federal appellate court ruled that minors have a right to obtain contraceptive devices from a county-run family planning center without parental notification or consent.[6] A 1981 federal law required that federally funded family planning projects "encourage family participation" in counseling and decisions about services.[7] The Department of Health and Human Services (HHS) proposed rules that would have required parental notification after services were initially provided to any minor under eighteen in most circumstances as well as compliance with state laws demanding parental notification or consent.[8] The proposed rules were blocked by a federal court, which ruled that Congress intended to encourage but not require parental involvement.[9] In 1983, a federal district court declared a Utah law unconstitutional because it required parental notification before furnishing contraceptives to minors.[10] In 1988, a federal district court ruled that a Roman Catholic foster child care agency engaged in unconstitutional state action when it confiscated contraceptive devices and prescriptions from minors placed in its care by the state.[11]

The cases show a pattern of protecting minors' access to contraception, so while it is prudent to encourage minors to involve their parents, many minors cannot or will not accept parental involvement and cannot be forced to include adult guidance. Healthcare providers must then decide whether to prescribe contraceptives in the absence of parental involvement. Several states explicitly authorize minors to consent to these services.[12] But even in states without a minor consent statute, the legal risk seems to be small, especially if the minor is mature.

Emergency contraception serves as another example. Minors under seventeen need a prescription for the drug, but those over the age of seventeen do not. A recent report by the CDC stated that almost half of all teenagers in high school are sexually active.[13] Access to contraception is an important public health question, both in terms of preventing disease and in terms of preventing teen pregnancy, which results in unhealthy outcomes for both the young parents and their children. Nevertheless, states often push the boundaries of denying access to contraception in efforts to encourage teenage abstinence. The hard question is how healthcare providers should respond to such state restrictions.

13-1.3 Pharmacist Refusals

Some pharmacists have sought to establish a right to refuse to supply prescription contraceptives when they have personal moral objections. Such refusals can effectively foreclose the purpose of and access to not only everyday contraception but also emergency contraception, as there is a short time period in which it must be taken. Some states have disciplined pharmacists and pharmacies that have refused to provide such services. On the other hand, a number of states have passed or proposed legislation permitting pharmacists to refuse to participate in the supply of contraceptives through laws that are often referred to as "conscience clause laws."

The conflict could be eliminated in part if emergency contraceptives were granted a status that does not require dispensing by a pharmacist. But federal laws also complicate the situation by specifically allowing healthcare providers to refuse to participate in abortion, sterilization, and contraception without fear of discrimination or repurcussion.[14]

13-2 Sterilization

Sterilization involves a permanent end to the ability to produce children. Sterilization may be the desired result of a surgical operation or the incidental consequence of an operation to remove a diseased reproductive organ or to cure a malfunction of such an organ. When the reproductive organs are not diseased, most sterilizations are effected by vasectomy for males and tubal ligation ("tube tying") for females. Generally sterilization must be voluntary, but in limited circumstances it may be performed even when involuntary.

13-2.1 Voluntary Sterilization

Sterilization is set against the background of a 1927 case called *Buck v. Bell*, in which the Supreme Court allowed Virginia to forcibly sterilize a young woman because she was an "imbecile" who had gotten pregnant.[15] This case resulted in part from the eugenics movement, which furthered the idea that some traits such as "pauperism" and "criminality" were hereditary and undesirable (the eugenics movement fed into Nazism and ended with the rise of

Nazi Germany). Though *Buck v. Bell* was not formally over-ruled, it was practically overturned when the Court decided that a fundamental right to procreate is protected by the Constitution in the 1942 decision *Skinner v. Oklahoma*.[16]

> *Skinner v. Oklahoma* protects the right to procreate, making involuntary sterilization almost always impermissible.

Since then, sterilization has existed in a delicate balance. On the one hand, voluntary consensual sterilization has been permitted for competent adults regardless of the purpose for undergoing the surgery.[17] On the other hand, governments have been careful to ensure that sterilization is never forced except in certain extraordinary circumstances. By example, if Medicaid, the public healthcare program for poor Americans, pays for a sterilization, then federal regulations require the signing of a special consent form at least thirty days prior to the procedure to ensure that the sterilization is not being improperly imposed on vulnerable populations (exceptions exist for some therapeutic procedures).[18] Also, some states impose special requirements on all sterilizations performed in the state to protect vulnerable populations and to ensure no coercion occurs.[19]

Sterilization is a tricky subject, and careful consent should be obtained before any operation that may result in sterilization is performed. Absent consent, sterilization almost always constitutes a battery, even if the operation is medically necessary. When it can be predicted that an operation poses the risk of sterilization, this consequence should be clearly brought to the patient's attention. Courts are much less likely to find implied consent to sterilization than to other extensions of surgical procedures.

In the case of operations intended to sterilize, a consent form should include not only information about the consequences of sterilization, but also disclose the risk that the sterilization may not be successful. Failure to inform of the risk of future reproductive ability can expose healthcare providers to liability for wrongful conception or wrongful birth.

The patient's consent alone is sufficient authorization for a legal operation. Some hospitals and physicians have a policy of also requiring spousal consent for sterilization of married patients, but they may not be permitted to enforce such policies. At least one court has found such public hospital policies to be an unconstitutional violation of the right to privacy.[20] One federal appellate court ruled that a governmental hospital could not impose greater restrictions on sterilization procedures than on other procedures that are medically indistinguishable in the risk to the patient or the demand on staff or facilities.[21] A federal court declared state laws requiring spousal consent to sterilizations to be unconstitutional.[22] Federally assisted family planning projects must follow all state requirements for consent to sterilization, except spousal consent requirements.[23] However, private hospitals may forbid contraceptive sterilizations or require spousal consent.[24] Performing a sterilization procedure without spousal consent presents little legal risk. For example, when a husband sued an Oklahoma physician for sterilizing his spouse without his consent, the court dismissed the suit because his marital rights did not include a childbearing wife, so he had not been legally harmed.[25]

Voluntary contraceptive sterilization of minor patients presents special problems; local laws concerning minor consent should be carefully reviewed. In some circumstances, minors may be permitted to consent, but some state statutes authorize such sterilizations only if the parent or guardian also consents.[26] Other state statutes forbid sterilization of an unmarried minor.[27] As is discussed in the following section, parents or guardians alone cannot authorize sterilizations. Patient consent is essential unless court authorization is obtained. Unless there is a medical reason for sterilization and the consents of the minor and the parent are clearly voluntary, informed, and unequivocal, prudent healthcare providers should be reluctant to sterilize a minor without a court order. Federal funds pay for sterilizations only if the person is competent and at least twenty-one years old.[28]

Some states have enacted legislation that hospitals are not required to provide sterilization procedures and healthcare providers cannot be required to participate in such procedures or be discriminated against for refusal to participate.[29] Federal laws reinforce such protections for healthcare providers, thus making it harder to obtain sterilization, especially for impoverished people.[30]

13-2.2 Involuntary Sterilization

Statutes and courts in some states have authorized involuntary sterilization of severely retarded people who are sexually active, unable to use other forms of contraception, and unable to care for offspring. The primary focus of these laws is the best interests of the individual and potential future offspring. These laws have been upheld consistently. For example, North Carolina's statute[31] was upheld by the North Carolina Supreme Court and by a federal district court.[32] The key elements of a constitutional statute appear to be (1) identification of an appropriate class of persons subject to the statute without discrimination or arbitrary bias and (2) guarantees of procedural due process, including notice, hearing, right to appeal, and assurance that decisions will be supported by qualified medical opinion. Notably, parents or guardians do not have the authority to consent to sterilization of mentally retarded children without a valid court authorization.[33]

Courts have considered applications for orders authorizing involuntary sterilizations in states that do not have statutes specifically giving the court authority to issue such orders. Prior to 1978, most ruled that they did not have the authority and refused to issue orders authorizing sterilization.[34] In 1978, the U.S. Supreme Court held that a court of broad general jurisdiction has the authority to consider a petition for sterilization of a minor unless statutes or case law in the state circumscribe the jurisdiction to foreclose consideration of such petitions.[35]

Since 1978, several state courts have ruled that they have authority to authorize involuntary sterilization of incompetents.[36] The decisions have set forth processes and criteria that are generally similar to those specified in modern statutes.[37] However, not all courts are willing to exercise this authority; for instance, the Alabama Supreme Court ruled that its state courts do not have such authority.[38] In 1981, the Wisconsin Supreme Court adopted the unusual position that it had the authority but would not exercise it.[39]

In 1985, the California Supreme Court declared that a law that prohibited sterilizations of incompetents violated the federal and state constitutions.[40] The court found that the developmentally disabled have a constitutional right to procreative choice and that the state had not demonstrated a compelling state interest to overcome that right. However, the court declined to authorize sterilization in the particular case because there was no evidence of contraceptive necessity or of the lack of alternative, less intrusive means.

Hospitals, physicians, and other healthcare providers should participate in involuntary sterilizations only when court authorization has been obtained following process and criteria established by statute or by case law.[41] The procedures should include notice, a hearing, and an opportunity to appeal.

13-3 Abortion

Medically, an abortion is defined as the premature expulsion of the products of conception from the uterus. An abortion can be classified as spontaneous or induced; spontaneous abortion is commonly called "miscarriage." An induced abortion may occur to save the life or health of the mother or terminate the pregnancy to preclude birth. Much of the debate in the law has focused on induced abortions that are intended to terminate pregnancy regardless of the life or health of the mother.

Historically, the law did not prohibit induced abortion prior to the first fetal movements, called quickening, and abortion was legal at the time the Constitution was ratified. During the Victorian era, many states made induced abortion a crime, whether before or after quickening, unless performed to preserve the life of the mother. These laws were intended to protect physicians, who were eager to exclude nurse midwives from participating in childbirth; to encourage childbirth by "desirable" families (meaning white, wealthy families); and to protect women from unsafe procedures, as sterile surgery and antibiotics did not exist at the time. Some of these laws were amended in the 1960s and early 1970s to permit induced abortions when there were threats to the physical or mental health of the mother, when the child was at risk of severe congenital defects, or when the pregnancy resulted from rape or incest. A few states, such as New York, permitted induced abortion up to a designated point in pregnancy so long as it was performed by a licensed physician in a licensed hospital. However, many states outlawed abortion until 1973.

13-3.1 Protected Decision to Terminate Pregnancy

Women's access to abortion has coincided with the protections afforded or limited by the Supreme Court. In 1973, the Supreme Court decided in *Roe v. Wade* that a Texas criminal law prohibiting all abortions not necessary to save the life of the mother violated privacy rights protected by the Due Process Clause of the Fourteenth Amendment.[42] The Court wrote that the right to privacy includes the decision as to whether to terminate pregnancy. The analysis was physician-oriented and described the importance of doctors being able to protect their patients in some detail.

Roe v. Wade protects a woman's right to access abortion at all points of pregnancy, but as pregnancy progresses that right may be balanced against the state's interest in the potential life of the fetus and in regulating medical care for public safety purposes.

The decision also balanced the woman's fundamental right to access abortion as part of the right to procreate against the state's interest in protecting the woman's health and its interest in the potential life of the fetus, but the Court weighed in favor of the woman's rights. The Court adopted a three-part breakdown to describe this balance: (1) during the first trimester of pregnancy, the right to privacy of the woman and her physician precluded most state regulation of abortions performed by licensed physicians; (2) from the end of the first trimester until viability, states could regulate to protect maternal health; and (3) after viability, states had a compelling interest in the life of the unborn child, so that abortions could be prohibited except when necessary to preserve the life or health of the mother. After *Roe*, many laws were modified or enacted to regulate and limit abortions.

Despite finding a fundamental right to access abortion, which meant that states could not outlaw abortion, the Court subsequently permitted a number of other restrictions on abortion. They have included: (1) restrictions on the use of public funds for abortions;[43] (2) informed consent requirements that include specific statements delivered by particular healthcare professionals (usually physicians);[44] (3) requirements of parental consent for minors if a timely alternative procedure was available for mature minors and other minors whose best interests indicated that their parents should not be involved;[45] and (4) recordkeeping and reporting requirements if confidentiality was maintained.[46]

Since *Roe*, the law regarding abortion has narrowed the woman's liberty interest and expanded the state's interest in the potential life of the fetus. This trend started in earnest in 1989 when the Supreme Court upheld a state law that prohibited use of public employees and facilities to perform abortions and that created a presumption of viability at twenty weeks' gestation, which a physician could overcome by medical tests.[47] In 1991, the Court upheld a rule that prohibited federally funded family planning clinics from giving abortion advice.[48]

In 1992, the Supreme Court reaffirmed constitutional protection for a woman's right to choose an abortion before fetal viability but abandoned the trimester framework in ▶ *Planned Parenthood of Southeastern Pennsylvania v. Casey*.[49] The Court in *Casey* adopted an "undue burden" test to evaluate abortion restrictions before viability, which allows for recognizing the state's interest in potential life more than *Roe* had done.

The Court explained that the government imposes an undue burden if it acts with the purpose or effect of discouraging abortion, but the Court also stated that government can act with the purpose and effect of encouraging childbirth over abortion. The Court upheld several state restrictions on abortion, such as a twenty-four hour waiting period after consent, and a requirement that a physician provide certain information before the procedure, as not constituting undue burdens. One requirement, spousal notification, was struck down as creating an unconstitutional undue burden.

> *Casey* upheld *Roe v. Wade* but created a new standard, the "undue burden" test, to determine when governments may regulate access to abortion.

13-3.2 State and Federal Abortion Bans

In recent years, a number of states have enacted legislation banning so-called "partial-birth abortions," a term that is not found in medical literature but that has become prevalent in legislation. In 2000, the Supreme Court held that a Nebraska partial-birth abortion ban was unconstitutional in *Stenberg v. Carhart* because it was so vague as to ban not only very late-term abortion methods but also abortions commonly used before viability.[50] The law also did not contain an exception for women's health, which had been required by the *Casey* decision. This decision marked the first time the Court applied *Casey*, and in so doing it reiterated the core holding of *Roe* as well as the decision in *Casey*.

In 2007, the Court was asked to consider the federal Partial-Birth Abortion Ban Act of 2003, which was substantially similar to the ban that had been declared unconstitutional in *Stenberg v. Carhart*.[51] In writing the legislation, Congress made findings that an intact dilation and extraction (what Congress was calling the "partial-birth abortion") is never medically necessary, and therefore Congress banned the procedure except to save the life of the mother. Despite the lack of a health exception for the pregnant woman, and despite the fact that intact D & E is a common and medically appropriate second trimester abortion method, the Supreme Court upheld this federal law in ▶ *Gonzales v. Carhart*. The Court assumed that *Casey* and *Roe* are still good law and reasoned that Congress made rational findings that the ban was a necessary way to "express respect for the dignity of human life."[52] This decision appears to have lowered the bar for governments interested in placing limits on abortion procedures by applying a more deferential level of scrutiny to the law in question. Many states now have partial-birth abortion bans in place, some of which contain no exceptions for either the life or health of the pregnant woman.[53]

13-3.3 Other State-Based Issues

In addition to the federal constitutional considerations in this area, states have expanded or contracted the right based upon interpretations of state constitutions. For example, in 2000, the Tennessee Supreme Court ruled that the state constitution barred a state statute that imposed requirements concerning informed consent, a mandatory waiting period, second trimester procedures only in hospitals, and all abortions only by physicians.[54]

In 1989, the Florida Supreme Court ruled that the state constitutional right of privacy protected the abortion decision prior to viability and struck down the state requirement of parental consent for abortions for unmarried minors.[55] The Oklahoma Supreme Court has upheld the constitutionality of state statutes that restrict the performance of abortions after the first trimester to general hospitals, reasoning that such location restrictions do not place an undue burden on a woman's right to an abortion.[56]

At least one state has ruled that some hospitals must permit their facilities to be available for abortions.[57] In 1997, the Alaska Supreme Court ruled that the only hospital located in a rural area of the state cannot prohibit or place restrictions on the performance of lawful abortions at the hospital.[58] The Court ruled that the hospital was a quasi-public institution because government funds constituted a significant portion of its operating funds.

Funding can also be an issue at the state level. On the one hand, the Arkansas Supreme Court upheld a state law enjoining public hospitals from performing abortions unless paid for in advance by the patient or payment is guaranteed by a third party.[59] On the other hand, several state courts have ruled that the state constitution prohibits some limits on state funding of abortions.[60]

13-3.4 Minors

Parental approval or notification is not required for abortions for minors unless the state has enacted such a requirement, which is constitutional under the holding in *Casey*. However, it is prudent to encourage minors to involve their parents or other adult relatives in these decisions. Most states that require parental involvement have a procedure for minors to obtain judicial approval without parental involvement, often called a "judicial bypass." Prudent healthcare providers should insist that a court order be obtained in each case where the woman is unable or unwilling to consent.

13-3.5 Conscience Laws

As has been mentioned, states have enacted conscience laws that prohibit discrimination against physicians and other hospital personnel who refuse to participate in abortions. These laws have been found to be constitutional.[61] In 1980, a New Jersey court ruled that it was not discrimination to transfer a refusing nurse from the maternity to the medical-surgical nursing staff with no change in seniority, pay, or shift.[62] Thus, in some jurisdictions, staff may be transferred to areas where they are not involved with the procedure without violating their right to refuse. The current debate is whether it is appropriate for healthcare providers who know they would refuse to place themselves in positions where they would obstruct a woman obtaining a safe abortion. While federal and state law often make such behavior legal, arguably this blocks medical care and may not be ethical.

13-4 Wrongful Conception, Wrongful Birth, and Wrongful Life Claims

Parents have sued physicians and hospitals for wrongful conception when sterilization fails, resulting in children they did not want, or for wrongful birth when they give birth to children with genetic or congenital conditions they would have aborted had they known of the condition. Children with genetic or congenital conditions have sued for their alleged wrongful life, claiming they were injured by being born. Courts have struggled with these suits to determine when there should be liability and what the basis for calculating the payment by the defendants should be.

13-4.1 Wrongful Conception and Wrongful Birth

The term wrongful conception is used, whether or not birth results, when (1) an unwanted pregnancy results from medical negligence or (2) a fetus with a genetic condition is conceived after the parents were not informed or were misinformed of the risk of the genetic condition. The term wrongful birth is used when (1) a birth results from a wrongful conception or (2) a birth follows medical negligence after conception that denies the mother the opportunity to make a timely informed decision about whether to have an abortion. Parents have made six basic types of wrongful conception or wrongful birth claims. Three types concern unsuccessful sterilization and abortion procedures, and the other three types concern genetic counseling and testing. Notably, some states have barred wrongful birth claims by statute or by court decision. These statutes have consistently been upheld.[63]

UNSUCCESSFUL STERILIZATION OR ABORTION. The three claims that arise from unsuccessful sterilization and abortion procedures include: (1) claims that parents were not informed of risks that the procedure might be unsuccessful; (2) claims that the parents were promised a successful procedure; or (3) claims that the procedure was performed negligently. The first type is based on lack of informed consent, the second on breach of contract, and the third on medical malpractice.

Pregnancy is a known risk of properly performed sterilization and abortion procedures, so the occurrence of pregnancy alone does not establish negligence. Because it is usually difficult to establish negligence (malpractice), claims tend to be of the first two types. A well-written consent form can make the first two types of claims difficult to pursue. For example, in 1975, a Colorado court affirmed the dismissal of a parental suit because the consent form included a statement that no guarantee had been made concerning treatment results.[64]

GENETIC OR CONGENITAL CONDITION. The other three types of claims arise when a child is born with a genetic or congenital condition who would have been aborted if the parents had known of the condition. The parental claims parallel the claims that arise from negligent sterilizations. The parents claim that (1) they were not advised of the possibility of the condition and the availability of tests; (2) they were told there was no risk of the particular condition; or (3) the tests were performed negligently, and the condition was not discovered. Thus, when a reason exists to suspect that a problematic condition is present, parents should be advised and offered available tests.

In 1987, the Minnesota Supreme Court ruled that a genetic counselor could not be liable for nondisclosure of risks that proper procedures did not reveal.[65] In 1998, the California Supreme Court ruled that a state law, under which the state health department is required to test newborn infants for certain genetic and congenital conditions, does not impose a duty on the state to conduct accurate tests and report their results, but rather gave the state discretion in formulating and reporting testing standards.[66] In the case, an infant with ambiguous test results was reported to have tested negative for hypothyroidism; later she was found to have no thyroid gland. In 2003, a New Jersey appellate court ruled that even

where initial genetic counseling and offering of testing had occurred, there could be liability for not following up to determine if testing occurred.[67]

This set of claims is particularly tricky because of the underlying issue of abortion. The parents are claiming they would have ended the pregnancy if they had been given correct information. Some state courts have been squeamish about allowing this cause of action for fear that it would encourage abortion. On the other hand, many courts have treated wrongful birth as a basic malpractice claim.

Courts have generally awarded parents some payment when they are able to prove one or more of the six claims. There is some disagreement on the calculation of the payment, especially whether defendants must pay the cost of raising the child to adulthood. A few courts have permitted parents to collect the entire cost of child-rearing.[68] At least one court allowed parents to recover the special costs of raising a disabled child and for emotional distress.[69] Several courts have permitted parents to collect the cost of child-rearing, reduced by the amount the jury believes the parents benefit from the joy and other advantages of parenthood.[70] Most courts have refused to permit parents to collect the cost of child-rearing, especially for healthy children.[71] Courts have based their refusal on public policy considerations. They have been reluctant to label as an injury the presence of an additional child in a family. They have been concerned about the implications of the general rule that those who are injured must take steps to reduce their injuries, which could mean parents would be required to seek an abortion or put the child up for adoption to reduce their injuries. In 1998, a federal district court in New Jersey ruled that under wrongful birth claims, plaintiffs need not prove that they would have aborted the fetus if given accurate information and held that a parent's decision to continue a pregnancy would not bar a malpractice claim.[72] Several courts that generally do not award the costs of child-rearing do allow the special additional expenses of raising a disabled child to adulthood.[73]

13-4.2 Wrongful Life

Some children with genetic or congenital conditions have sued physicians and hospitals for wrongful life, claiming they were injured by being born. They have based their suits on the same claims that their parents have made. Most courts have refused to allow suits by these children. In one of the earliest cases addressing this issue, the New Jersey Supreme Court observed that compensation is ordinarily computed by "comparing the condition plaintiff would have been in, had the defendants not been negligent, with plaintiff's impaired condition as a result of the negligence."[74] The court wrote that it could not affix a price tag on nonlife, and it would be impossible to compute an amount to award.

In 1982, the California Supreme Court adopted the unusual position of permitting a child to collect for the extraordinary expenses of living with deafness due to a genetic defect, even though there was no way the child could have been born without the deafness.[75] From the perspective of the defendant's actual liability, the decision does not appear unusual. The court permitted the child to collect the same amount the parents could have collected in several other states if the suit had been in their names. A few other states have adopted this position.[76]

13-5 Assisted Reproduction

When individuals who desire children cannot achieve pregnancy, they often seek medical assistance or intervention. A recent estimate by the CDC was that about 12 percent of women in the United States had used assisted reproductive technologies, and that did not include less technological forms of assistance.[77] A number of techniques have become common, such as assisted insemination, surrogacy, and in vitro fertilization, and each raises legal issues such as parentage, property, and termination of pregnancy.

> More than 1 in 10 Americans engages in assisted reproductive technologies, but assisted reproduction is largely unregulated and has led to complex legal and ethical questions.

13-5.1 Assisted Insemination

Assisted insemination, sometimes referred to as artificial insemination, is arguably the oldest form of assisted reproduction, as it requires very little to no technology. Assisted insemination may be used when a male reproductive partner has a low sperm count or sperm with low motility, or if a woman desires to become pregnant without a male partner. Depending on the male partner's fertility, either the partner's semen will be used or donor semen may be used. In 2004, the FDA published safety rules that require the screening of donors and testing of donated tissues, including ova, sperm, and embryos.[78]

Assisted insemination with donor semen presents more legal issues than insemination with spousal semen. Several states have passed statutes concerning assisted insemination. Typical statutes specify that (1) the child is "legitimate" when the husband consents to insemination (meaning the child is considered to be the offspring of the legally married parents) and (2) the donor is not responsible for child support.[79] In states without statutes, some courts have ruled that the child is legitimate and the consenting husband is responsible for child support.[80] However, some courts have ruled that the child may not be legitimate under the common law.[81] At least one court has permitted a sperm donor to obtain a paternity order.[82] In some cases, the donor may be found responsible for child support. In most states, the mother cannot waive the child's support claims. Some states have specific procedures that can be followed that will protect the donor. When those procedures are not followed, some courts have held the sperm donor to be the father.[83] Attempts to hold the clinic or physicians responsible for child support have been unsuccessful.

Most state statutes require the procedure to be performed by a licensed physician.[84] Assisted insemination may involve varying degrees of invasiveness, and although physically the procedure can be performed by untrained persons,[85] the most prudent practice is to have trained healthcare providers perform the procedure.

Many sperm donors seek to maintain their anonymity.[86] In some cases, it may be possible to breach anonymity, especially if a serious health problem arises. For example, a California appellate court permitted the parents of a child with kidney disease, allegedly from the sperm donor, to discover information about the donor in their suit against the sperm bank.[87]

Some men have their semen frozen as part of other assisted conception procedures or as a precaution in case they are no longer able to produce semen.[88] Generally, this semen may be used, even after the man's death, as long as the use is clearly authorized by the man. However, when the semen is used after the man's death, there can be questions concerning rights of the child related to the father. For example, in 2004, a federal appellate court ruled that twins conceived from frozen semen after their father's death were eligible for Social Security benefits.[89]

13-5.2 Surrogacy

When a woman cannot conceive or conception would pose serious health risks to the woman, some couples seek a surrogate mother to bear a child after assisted insemination with the male's semen, though in some instances donor semen may be used as well. In addition, some persons seek to have a surrogate bear a child for them.[90] If an egg donor, sperm donor, and intended parental couple are involved, then at least four adults have participated in the birth of one child. The more people that are involved in the birth of a child, the more complex the legal issues become.

CUSTODY. The artificial insemination or implantation of the embryo is legal in most states, but any pre-birth agreement by the surrogate mother to relinquish custody of the child is generally not enforceable, as it may be deemed "baby selling," which is illegal. In most states, the woman who delivers the child is legally the mother, and any transfer of custody of the child must occur after the child is born, as with adoption.[91] The New Jersey Supreme Court ruled against enforceability of pre-birth agreements to transfer custody of the child in the first opinion to address surrogacy.[92] In 1998, the Massachusetts Supreme Court ruled that a surrogacy agreement providing that a surrogate mother would receive payment of thousands of dollars in excess of her pregnancy expenses for bearing a child and giving up custody of the child to the biological father is unenforceable under state law.[93] Some states have passed statutes that regulate the use of surrogate mothers, and these laws generally permit contracts for surrogacy that include payments for expenses only.[94] In 2000, a California appellate court ruled that in some circumstances a woman who violated a surrogacy contract could be liable for monetary damages.[95]

BIRTH CERTIFICATES. Several cases have addressed the names that should be placed on the birth certificate as parents without addressing custody issues. In most states, the gestational mother is automatically listed as the mother on the birth certificate unless there are proceedings after the birth to change the certificate. For example, in 2000, a New Jersey court refused to issue a pre-birth order but authorized a post-birth change prior to filing with the state.[96] However, in 2001, the highest court of Massachusetts authorized uncontested pre-birth orders to place the biological parents' names on the birth certificate when the gestational mother supports the petition.[97]

OTHER DISPUTES. Surrogacy arrangements lead to complex disputes.[98] Some fertility centers seek to avoid involvement in these disputes by limiting their role to providing medical procedures. For example, in 2000, New York courts addressed a complex case where the wrong embryo was mistakenly implanted in a woman. The gestational mother voluntarily transferred custody to the biological parents four months after the birth, and the parties signed a visitation agreement. When the gestational mother sought to enforce visitation rights, the court denied her such

visitation rights under New York law due to her knowledge of the mistake soon after the implantation.[99]

13-5.3 In Vitro Fertilization

Some couples produce viable reproductive cells, but conception is not possible naturally or through assisted insemination. In vitro fertilization (IVF) and other assisted reproductive technologies (ART) are available for some of these couples.[100] In IVF, the reproductive cells (egg and sperm) are combined outside the woman's body, allowed to begin growing, and are implanted in a woman's uterus when there is a chance of successful implantation. With appropriate screening, consent, and technical procedures, IVF is legally performed in most jurisdictions. Complex legal issues related to frozen embryos, status of children, insurance coverage, and other matters can arise. In 2002, 391 ART clinics reported to the CDC that they had performed 115,392 ART cycles. These procedures resulted in 45,751 babies from 33,141 live births.[101] By 2008, 436 fertility clinics reported that 148,055 IVF-related procedures were performed that resulted in 46,326 live births and 61,426 infants.[102] IVF has grown in popularity, despite the fact that most health insurance does not cover the very expensive services provided.

FROZEN EMBRYOS. Frozen embryos can be stored for later implantation, which can lead to complex legal questions. Several cases have arisen where the couple that created the embryo later becomes estranged or divorced. The general rule is that embryos cannot be implanted if either the man or the woman does not consent.[103] For example, when a couple in Tennessee disputed ownership of frozen embryos in their divorce proceedings, the Tennessee Supreme Court ruled that if the parties did not agree otherwise the embryos should be destroyed. The embryos were ultimately destroyed.[104] In 2000, a New Jersey appellate court ordered the destruction of frozen embryos after a divorce where the couple could not agree on their use.[105] In 2004, a Massachusetts jury found a fertility clinic liable to a man for implanting a frozen embryo in his estranged wife without his consent in 1995. He had provided the semen for consensual IVF and a child had resulted in 1994. The clinic agreement provided for the remaining excess embryos to be discarded or donated to another couple. The clinic used one of the embryos for the unauthorized 1995 implantation.[106]

Frozen embryos may be donated to another person for implantation or may be donated for use in research, but the initial consent forms should carefully document the couple's choices. For example, in 1998, a New York appellate court rejected a woman's request for sole custody of frozen embryos and ruled that the IVF informed consent document and a subsequent uncontested divorce instrument, which provided for the use of remaining embryos for research if one prospective parent withdrew from the IVF program, governed the disposition of the embryos.[107]

Care must be taken when reproductive cells and embryos are destroyed. In one lawsuit arising from IVF, a university, a hospital, and a physician were found liable by a federal jury in New York for the emotional distress of a couple following intentional destruction of a cell culture containing their reproductive cells.[108] This case illustrates the need for procedures and timelines that are understood by all involved.[109]

STATUS OF CHILDREN. In 1997, a child was born in California as the result of IVF techniques using donor eggs, donor sperm, and a surrogate mother (who was not the egg donor). Before the child was born, the couple who entered into the IVF agreement separated, and the husband claimed there were no children of the marriage in divorce proceedings after the child was born. A California appellate court concluded that the persons who entered into the IVF arrangement were the legal parents of the child, reversing the trial court, which had ruled the child was legally parentless.[110] In 2002, a California appellate court addressed a case where a couple suspected that their genetic material had been misappropriated by a clinic, resulting in twins who had been born to another couple using the clinic. The court ruled that they could not sue to assert parental rights over the twins even if they were the biological parents. The interests of the children in stability prevailed, and the court did not permit testing.[111]

REGULATION. Fertility clinics are not well regulated. The Fertility Clinic Success Rate and Certification Act of 1992 is a federal law that has two regulatory aspects. First, it requires fertility clinics to report pregnancy success rates to the CDC, which publishes the results. Second, the law provided a model program for states to certify embryo laboratories, but adoption of the scheme is voluntary.[112] Occasional news items about extreme multiple births increase talk of federal regulation of fertility clinics, but the only federal regulation adopted after 1992 is an FDA rule mentioned earlier that requires the screening and testing of donated tissues to ensure their health.[113]

States regulate assisted reproductive technologies in different ways. For example, California requires written informed consent of the donors of sperm, ova, or embryos before implanting such materials into a woman's uterus (other than re-implantation into the donor or the donor's spouse).[114] A few states have passed other laws that regulate the participants in and providers of IVF. None of the laws are comprehensive, but it is important to check the status of IVF in any state in which the procedure is being performed.

INSURANCE COVERAGE. The scope of insurance coverage for IVF has caused tense debates. Some plans expressly exclude or limit coverage for fertility treatments. Some plans have sought to exclude IVF under their general exclusion of experimental procedures, but courts have found that many IVF procedures are no longer considered experimental.[115] Some states have required coverage by statute. In 1998, the U.S. Supreme Court ruled that reproduction is a "major life activity," so that conditions that significantly impair reproduction can be disabilities under the Americans with Disabilities Act. This may have implications for efforts to obtain assistance in conception.[116]

Chapter Summary

U.S. Supreme Court decisions determine the acceptable boundaries of government intervention or regulation of aspects of reproductive medicine. This chapter introduced the relevant cases so you understand the federal and state law pertaining to the more prevalent issues arising in health policy related to human reproduction. The rights protected in this area of the law are often subject to new challenges, and those who work in this area should proceed with caution.

Key Terms and Definitions

Assisted Insemination - A form of assisted reproduction that is sometimes called artificial insemination and that facilitates delivery of donor semen into the uterus by a process that is not sexual intercourse.

Conscience Laws - Federal or state laws that protect healthcare providers who for religious or moral reasons refuse to participate in procedures related to reproduction such as sterilization, abortion, and assisted reproduction.

Contraception - Prevents fertilization of an ovum ("egg"), during or immediately after sexual intercourse; contraceptive methods take many forms and may be medical in nature ("the pill" or Plan B) or consist of medical devices (such as a diaphragm or a condom).

Fundamental Rights - Constitutionally protected rights that the U.S. Supreme Court has determined will receive special judicial protection from government interference based upon language in the U.S. Constitution, usually the Fourteenth Amendment.

Induced Abortion - A medical or surgical procedure to terminate an existing pregnancy by expelling an embryo or fetus.

In Vitro Fertilization - A method of joining an egg and sperm outside the body of the donors; the resulting embryo is implanted either in the biological mother's uterus or in the uterus of a surrogate.

Sterilization - A surgical procedure that prevents future procreation and can be performed on either a woman (tubal ligation) or a man (vasectomy).

Surrogacy - A method of assisted reproduction that involves a third party female who carries the intended parents' fetus to term; a surrogate may donate only her uterus or her eggs and her uterus to the couple desiring to conceive. After birth, a surrogate mother assigns her parental rights to the biological father and his wife (who may be the biological mother).

Instructor-Led Questions

1. To what extent can government regulate access to contraceptives by adults? How is the answer different for minors?

2. To what extent can government regulate access to sterilization by adults with decision-making capacity? How is the answer different for those with no legal capacity, including minors?

3. To what extent can government regulate access to abortion by adults with decision-making capacity? How is the answer different for minors?

4. What are the legal issues related to assisted insemination?

5. What are the legal issues related to surrogacy?

6. What are the legal issues related to in vitro fertilization (IVF)?

7. When is liability allowed to be imposed for wrongful conception, wrongful birth, or wrongful life?

Endnotes

1   Centers for Disease Control, *Use of contraception in the United States – 1982-2008*, Data from the National Survey of Family Growth, Aug. 2010. Available at: http://www.cdc.gov/nchs/data/series/sr_23/sr23_029.pdf [Accessed April 15, 2011].

2   *Griswold v. Connecticut*, 381 U.S. 479 (1965).

3   *Eisenstadt v. Baird*, 405 U.S. 438 (1972).

4   *Carey v. Population Servs. Int'l*, 431 U.S. 678 (1977).

5   *Belotti v. Baird*, 443 U.S. 622 (1979).

6   *Doe v. Irving*, 615 F.2d 1162 (6th Cir. 1980); see also *Jane Does v. Utah Dep't of Health*, 776 F.2d 253 (10th Cir. 1985).

7   42 U.S.C. § 300(a).

8   48 Fed. Reg. 3,600-3,614 (Jan. 26, 1983).

9   *Planned Parenthood Fed'n v. Schweiker*, 559 F. Supp. 658 (D. D.C. 1983), aff'd, 229 U.S. App. D.C. 336, 712 F.2d 650 (1983); *New York v. Heckler*, 719 F.2d 1191 (2d Cir. 1983).

10 *Planned Parenthood Ass'n v. Matheson*, 582 F. Supp. 1001 (D. Utah 1983).

11 *Arneth v. Gross*, 699 F. Supp. 450 (S.D. N.Y. 1988).

12 E.g., CAL. FAM. CODE § 6925.

13 Centers for Disease Control, Vital Signs, Preventing Teen Pregnancy in the U.S., available at http://www.cdc.gov/vitalsigns/TeenPregnancy/LatestFindings.html [accessed May 2, 2011].

14 See, e.g., the Church Amendment, 42 U.S.C. § 300a-7 (2006) (named after its sponsor, Senator Frank Church of Idaho, this amendment states that federal fund recipients are not required to provide abortion or sterilization and prevents healthcare providers from experiencing discrimination on the basis of their refusal to perform or participate in such healthcare services).

15 *Buck v. Bell*, 275 U.S. 200 (1927).

16 *Skinner v. Oklahoma*, 316 U.S. 535 (1942).

17 See, e.g., In re *Guardianship of B*, 190 Misc. 2d 581, 738 N.Y.S.2d 528 (County Ct. 2002) [moderately retarded woman could consent]; accord, *Avila v. New York City Health & Hosps. Corp.*, 136 Misc. 2d 76, 518 N.Y.S.2d 574 (Sup. Ct. 1987); but see *Vaughn v. Ruoff*, 253 F.3d 1124 (8th Cir. 2001).

18 42 C.F.R. §§ 441.250-441.259.

19 CAL. ADMIN. CODE title 22, §§ 70707.1-70707.8; *California Med. Ass'n v. Lachner*, 124 Cal. App. 3d 28, 177 Cal. Rptr. 188 (3d Dist. 1981) [requirement of written consent constitutional]; *Kaplan v. Blank*, 204 Ga. App. 378, 419 S.E.2d 127 (1992) [oral consent was no consent to tubal ligation under Voluntary Sterilization Act, so battery]; *Chasse v. Mazerolle*, 622 A.2d 1180 (Me. 1993) [nineteen-year-old sterilized in 1973, claimed she was not competent to consent; failure to follow statutory consultation process can be basis for liability].

20 *Sims v. University of Ark. Med. Ctr.*, No. 1R76-C67 (E.D. Ark. Mar. 4, 1977).

21 *Hathaway v. Worcester City Hosp.*, 475 F.2d 701 (1st Cir. 1973).

22 *Coe v. Bolton*, No. C-87-785A (N.D. Ga. Sept. 30, 1976).

23 42 C.F.R. § 50.204(f).

24 *Taylor v. St. Vincent Hosp.*, 523 F.2d 75 (9th Cir. 1975), cert. denied, 424 U.S. 948 (1976).

25 *Murray v. Vandevander*, 522 P.2d 302 (Okla. Ct. App. 1974).

26 E.g., COLO. REV. STAT. ANN. § 25-6-102.

27 E.g., GA. CODE ANN. §31-20-2.

28 42 C.F.R. §§ 50.203, 441.253.

29 E.g., KAN. STAT. ANN. §§ 65-446, 65-447.

30 See the Church Amendment, supra note 14; see also the Danforth Amendment, which prevents governments receiving federal funds from discriminating against healthcare providers that refuse to provide a range of abortion-related services and protects doctors, medical students, and health training programs from losing accreditation. 42 U.S.C. § 238n (2006). The Weldon Amendment allows publicly funded institutions to refuse to provide abortion care and referrals for any reason, it need not be a religious objection. Pub. L. No. 108-447, § 508(d) (2005), 42 C.F.R. § 59.5(a)(5); Pub. L. No. 109-149, § 508(d) (2006).

31 N.C. GEN. STAT. §§ 35-36 – 35-50.

32 In re *Sterilization of Moore*, 289 N.C. 95, 221 S.E.2d 307 (1976); *North Carolina Ass'n of Retarded Children v. North Carolina*, 420 F. Supp. 451 (M.D.N.C. 1976).

33 E.g., In re *Grady*, 85 N.J. 235, 426 A.2d 467 (1981); In re *Mary Moe*, 385 Mass. 555, 432 N.E.2d 712 (1982).

34 *Wade v. Bethesda Hosp.*, 337 F. Supp. 671 (S.D. Ohio 1971); *Wade v. Bethesda Hosp.*, 356 F. Supp. 380 (S.D. Ohio 1973); *Sparkman v. McFarlin*, 552 F.2d 172 (7th Cir. 1977).

35 *Stump v. Sparkman*, 435 U.S. 349 (1978).

36 E.g., In re *Wirsing*, 456 Mich. 467, 573 N.W.2d 51 (1998).

37 E.g., *Lulos v. State*, 548 N.E.2d 173 (Ind. Ct. App. 1990); In re *Hayes*, 93 Wash. 2d 228, 608 P.2d 635 (1980).

38 *Hudson v. Hudson*, 373 So. 2d 310 (Ala. 1979).

39 In re *Guardianship of Eberhardy*, 102 Wis. 2d 539, 307 N.W.2d 881 (1981).

40 *Conservatorship of Valerie N.*, 40 Cal. 3d 143, 707 P.2d 760, 219 Cal. Rptr. 387 (1985).

41 E.g., *Lake v. Arnold*, 112 F.3d 682 (3d Cir. 1997) [mentally retarded protected by 42 U.S.C. § 1985(3), so woman, her husband could sue her parents, hospital, physicians for conspiracy to deprive her of right to procreate].

42 *Roe v. Wade*, 410 U.S. 113 (1973).

43 E.g., *Harris v. McRae*, 448 U.S. 297 (1980); *Williams v. Zbaraz*, 448 U.S. 358 (1980); see also *Britell v. United States*, 372 F.3d 1370 (Fed. Cir. 2004) [CHAMPUS not required to cover abortions].

44 *City of Akron v. Akron Center for Reproductive Health, Inc.*, 462 U.S. 416 (1983); *Planned Parenthood Ass'n v. Fitzpatrick*, 401 F. Supp. 554 (E.D. Pa 1975), aff'd without opinion sub nom. *Franklin v. Fitzpatrick*, 428 U.S. 901 (1976); see also *Summit Med. Ctr. v. Riley*, 274 F. Supp. 2d 1262 (M.D. Ala. 2003) [state may require distribution of educational materials to patients but may not require provider to pay for them].

45 E.g., *Hartigan v. Zbarez*, 484 U.S. 171 (1987), aff'g per curiam by equally divided court, 763 F.2d 1532 (7th Cir. 1985); *H.L. v. Matheson*, 450 U.S. 398 (1981); *Bellotti v. Baird*, 443 U.S. 622 (1979).

46 E.g., *Planned Parenthood Ass'n v. Ashcroft*, 462 U.S. 476 (1983); *Planned Parenthood v. Danforth*, 428 U.S. 52 (1976).

47 *Webster v. Reproductive Health Servs.*, 492 U.S. 490 (1989).

48 *Rust v. Sullivan*, 500 U.S. 173 (1991).

49 *Planned Parenthood v. Casey*, 505 U.S. 833 (1992).

50 *Stenberg v. Carhart*, 530 U.S. 914 (2000).

51 *Gonzales v. Carhart*, 550 U.S. 124 (2007).

52 Id. at 157.

53 K.R.S. 311.765 (1998). The statute simply states: "No physician shall perform a partial-birth abortion."

54 *Planned Parenthood of Middle Tenn. v. Sunquist*, 38 S.W.2d 1 (Tenn. 2000).

55 In re *T.W.*, 551 So. 2d 1186 (Fla 1989).

56 *Davis v. Fieker*, 952 P.2d 505 (Okla. 1997), modified on reh'g, 1998 Okla. LEXIS 7 (Okla. Jan. 1998) (unpublished).

57 *Doe v. Bridgeton Hosp. Ass'n*, 71 N.J. 478, 366 A.2d 641 (1976), cert. denied, 433 U.S. 914 (1977).

58 *Valley Hosp. Ass'n, Inc. v. Mat-Su Coalition for Choice*, 948 P.2d 963 (Alaska 1997).

59 *Unborn Child Amendment Comm. v. Ward*, 328 Ark. 454, 943 S.W.2d 591 (1997).

60 E.g., *Moe v. Secretary of Admin. & Fin.*, 382 Mass. 629, 417 N.E.2d 387 (1981); *State v. Planned Parenthood of Alaska*, 28 P.3d 904 (Alaska 2001) [state ban on payment for medically necessary abortions for low-income women violates equal protection requirement in state constitution].

61 *Doe v. Bolton*, 410 U.S. 179 (1973).

62 *Jeczalik v. Valley Hosp.*, 87 N.J. 344, 434 A.2d 90 (1981).

63 E.g., *Wood v. University of Utah Med. Ctr.*, 67 P.3d 436 (Utah 2002); *Campbell v. United States*, 962 F.2d 1579 (11th Cir. 1992), cert. denied, 507 U.S. 909 (1993).

64 *Herrara v. Roessing*, 533 P.2d 60 (Colo. Ct. App. 1975).

65 *Pratt v. University of Minn. Affiliated Hosps.*, 414 N.W.2d 399 (Minn. 1987).

66 *Creason v. State Dep't of Health Services*, 18 Cal. 4th 623, 76 Cal. Rptr. 2d 489, 957 P.2d 1323 (1998).

67 *Geler v. Akawie*, 358 N.J. Super. 437, 818 A.2d 402 (App. Div. 2003).

68 E.g., *Zehr v. Haugen*, 318 Ore. 647, 871 P.2d 1006 (1994); *Lovelace Med. Ctr. v. Mendez*, 111 N.M. 336, 805 P.2d 603 (1991); *Marciniak v. Lundborg*, 153 Wis. 2d 59, 450 N.W.2d 243 (1990); *Gallagher v. Duke Univ.*, 852 F.2d 773 (4th Cir. 1988).

69 *Emerson v. Magendantz*, 689 A.2d 409 (R.I. 1997).

70 E.g., *Jones v. Malinowski*, 299 Md. 257, 473 A.2d 429 (1984); *Univ. of Arizona Health Sciences Ctr. v. Superior Court*, 136 Ariz. 579, 667 P.2d 1294 (1983); *Ochs v. Borrelli*, 187 Conn. 253, 445 A.2d 883 (1982); *Sherlock v. Stillwater Clinic*, 260 N.W.2d 169 (Minn. 1977).

71 E.g., *Chafee v. Seslar*, 786 N.E.2d 705 (Ind. 2003); *McAllister v. Ha*, 347 N.C. 638, 496 S.E.2d 577 (1998); *Miller v. Johnson*, 231 Va. 177, 343 S.E.2d 301 (1986).

72 *Provenzano v. Integrated Genetics*, 22 F. Supp. 2d 406 (D.N.J. 1998).

73 E.g., *Haymon v. Wilkerson*, 535 A.2d 880 (D.C. 1987); *Smith v. Cote*, 128 N.H. 231, 513 A.2d 341 (1986); *Fassoulas v. Ramey*, 450 So. 2d 822 (Fla. 1984); see Annotation, Recoverability of compensatory damages for mental anguish or emotional distress for tortiously causing another's birth, 74 A.L.R. 4TH 798.

74 *Gleitman v. Cosgrove*, 49 N.J. 22, 227 A.2d 689, 692 (1967); accord, *Willis v. Wu*, 362 S.C. 146, 607 S.E.2d 63 (2004); *Liniger v. Eisenbaum*, 764 P.2d 1202 (Colo. 1988); *Goldberg v. Ruskin*, 113 Ill. 2d 482, 499 N.E.2d 406 (1986).

75 *Turpin v. Sortini*, 31 Cal. 3d 220, 643 P.2d 954 (1982); *Gami v. Mullikan Med. Ctr.*, 18 Cal. App. 4th 870, 22 Cal. Rptr. 2d 819 (2d Dist. 1993).

76 E.g., *Walker v. Rinck*, 604 N.E.2d 591 (Ind. 1992); *Procanik v. Cillo*, 97 N.J. 339, 478 A.2d 755 (1984).

77 CDC, Assisted Reproductive Technology Success Rates for 2008 (2008), at http://www.cdc.gov/art/ART2008/PDF/ART_2008_Full.pdf.

78 69 Fed. Reg. 29786 (May 25, 2004).

79 E.g., OKLA. STAT. tit. 10, §§ 551–553; FLA. STAT. §742.11; see also *Michael H. v. Gerald D.*, 491 U.S. 110 (1989) [general statutory presumption of husband's paternity does not violate due process rights of man alleging paternity].

80 E.g., *People v. Sorenson*, 68 Cal. 2d 280, 437 P.2d 495 (1968); *Estate of Gordon*, 131 Misc. 2d 823, 501 N.Y.S.2d 969 (Sur. Ct. 1986); see also In re *Proceeding under Article 3A*, 127 Misc. 2d 14, 484 N.Y.S.2d 780 (Fam. Ct. 1985) [female declared to have paternal support responsibility because, while living as husband, consented to artificial insemination of partner].

81 E.g., *Gursky v. Gursky*, 39 Misc. 2d 1083, 242 N.Y.S.2d 406 (Sup. Ct. 1963).

82 *Thomas S. v. Robin J.*, 209 A.D.2d 298, 618 N.Y.S.2d 356 (1st Dept. 1994); see also *Matter of William "TT" v. Siobhan "TT"* (N.Y. Fam. Ct), N.Y.L.J., Oct. 2, 2000, 21 [sperm donor father given more visitation rights than in agreement with mother].

83 E.g., *Jhordan C. v. Mary K.*, 179 Cal. App. 3d 386, 224 Cal. Rptr. 530 (1st Dist. 1986) [man used as sperm donor by two women who wish to raise a child together without assistance of physician is legal, natural father of child conceived through this artificial insemination].

84 E.g., Or. Rev. Stat. §§ 109.239 – 109.247.

85 E.g., *C.M. v. C.C.*, 152 N.J. Super. 160, 377 A.2d 821 (Juv. & Dom. Rel. Ct. 1977); D.J. Robb, Mom gets 3 years for pregnancy plot, Plain Dealer (Ohio), May 8, 2002, B1 [mother artificially inseminated daughter with her stepfather's sperm]; C.J. Johnson, Court: unexpectant father can sue for distress, but she didn't steal sperm, AP, Feb. 24, 2005 [Illinois appellate court allows man to sue woman for allegedly using his sperm to impregnate herself, but still required to pay child support as father].

86 *See*, J. Spano, Sperm bank wins right to withhold identity of donor, L.A. Times, Oct. 16, 1987, pt. 2, 1.

87 *Johnson v. Superior Court*, 80 Cal. App. 4th 1050, 95 Cal. Rptr. 2d 864 (2d Dist. 2000).

88 *See*, Soldiers freeze sperm before heading to gulf, Capital Times [Madison, Wis.], Feb. 7, 2003, 5C.

89 *Gillett-Netting v. Barnhart*, 371 F.3d 593 (9th Cir. 2004); accord Tot conceived after dad died can get his benefits, Palm Beach [Fla.] Post, May 31, 1995, at 2A. [decision by ALJ].

90 See, Woman gives birth to her own grandchildren, Wis. St. J., Oct. 16, 2002, A3 [S. Dak.].

91 E.g., *Weaver v. Guinn*, 176 Ore. App. 383, 31 P.3d 1119 (2001) [affirming award of custody to mother, refusing to enforce surrogacy agreement granting custody to father]; Judge allows surrogate mother to be legal parent of triplets, AP, Apr. 11, 2004 [but she must work out visitation, other rights with biological father]; *Arredondo v. Nodelman*, 163 Misc. 2d 757, 622 N.Y.S.2d 181 (Sup. Ct. 1994) [granting uncontested postbirth petition by genetic parents to declare genetic mother the legal mother, to order issuance of new birth records].

92 In re *Baby M*, 109 N.J. 396, 537 A.2d 1227 (1988); accord, *Doe v. Kelly*, 6 Fam. L. Rptr. 3011 (Mich. Cir. Ct. Jan. 28, 1980), aff'd sub nom. *Doe v. Attorney Gen.*, 160 Mich. App. 168, 307 N.W.2d 438 (1981), leave to appeal denied, 414 Mich. 875 (1982), cert. denied, 459 U.S. 1183 (1983), but see *Syrkowski v. Appleyard*, 420 Mich. 367, 362 N.W.2d 211 (1985) [court has jurisdiction over biological father's request for order declaring him father of child born pursuant to surrogate parenting agreement].

93 *R.R. v. M.H.*, 426 Mass. 501, 689 N.E.2d 790 (1998).

94 See J. Graham, State sets standards on surrogate birth, Chicago Trib., Jan. 2, 2005, § 1, 1 [Ill.].

95 *Dunkin v. Boskey*, 82 Cal. App. 4th 171, 98 Cal. Rptr. 2d 44 (1st Dist. 2000).

96 *A.H.W. v. G.H.B.*, 339 N.J. Super. 495, 772 A.2d 948 (Ch. Div. 2000).

97 *Culliton v. Beth Israel Deaconess Med. Ctr.*, 435 Mass. 285, 756 N.E.2d 1133 (2001).

98 E.g., *Stiver v. Parker*, 975 F.2d 261 (11th Cir. 1992) [surrogate mother impregnated by husband rather than donor; her child contracted cytomegalovirus from untested donor semen]; *Adoption of Matthew B.*, 232 Cal. App. 3d 1239, 284 Cal. Rptr. 18 (1st Dist. 1991), cert. denied, 503 U.S. 991 (1992) [surrogate mother denied custody rights without ruling on validity of surrogate contract]; *Soos v. Superior Court*, 897 P.2d 1356 (Ariz. Ct. App. 1994) [statute that allows biological father to prove paternity and grants surrogate mother status of legal mother, violates equal protection by failing to give egg donor means to prove paternity]; *Belsito v. Clark*, 67 Ohio Misc. 54, 644 N.E.2d 760 (Cm. Pl. 1994) [when child delivered by gestational surrogate who was impregnated by IVF, natural parents shall be identified as persons who provided genetic imprint, genetic parents have legal status of natural parents unless relinquished or waived, so adoption required, hospital delivering child improperly told genetic mother that surrogate would be listed as mother on birth certificate].

99 *Perry-Rogers v. Fasano*, 276 A.D.2d 67, 715 N.Y.S.2d 19 (1st Dept. 2000); see also *Perry-Rogers v. Obasaju*, 282 A.D.2d 231, 723 N.Y.S.2d 28 (1st Dept. 2001) [related malpractice case for implantation of embryo in another woman]; *Fasano v. Nash*, 282 A.D.2d 277, 723 N.Y.S.2d 181 (1st Dept. 2001) [malpractice case for implantation of wrong embryo in plaintiff]; S. Maull, Black N.J. couple settles suit against doctor who gave their embryo to white Staten Island woman, AP, Sept. 13, 2004.

100 For a layman's description of ART procedures, see Am. Society for Reproductive Med., Assisted Reproductive Technologies: A Guide for Patients (2003), http://www.asrm.org/Patients/patientbooklets/ART.pdf [accessed June 11, 2005].

101 CDC, 2002 Assisted Reproductive Technology Success Rates, http://www.cdc.gov/reproductivehealth/ART02/PDF/ART2002.pdf [accessed June 11, 2005].

102 CDC, Assisted Reproductive Technology Success Rates for 2008, 13 (2008), at http://www.cdc.gov/art/ART2008/PDF/ART_2008_Full.pdf.

103 E.g., S.S. Luh, Embryos to stay frozen until 2050, Chicago Sun-Times, Mar. 26, 2000, 26 [settlement of Illinois divorce dispute over embryos].

104 *Davis v. Davis*, 842 S.W.2d 588 (Tenn. 1992), cert. denied, 507 U.S. 911 (1993).

105 *J.B. v. M.B.*, 331 N.J. Super. 223, 751 A.2d 613 (App. Div. 2000); see also *A.Z. vs. B.Z.*, 431 Mass. 150, 725 N.E.2d 1051 (2000) [in divorce, wife enjoined from using frozen embryo].

106 J. Lindsay, Jury awards $108,000 to man who said wife wrongly impregnated, AP, Jan. 30, 2004.

107 *Kass v. Kass*, 235 A.D.2d 150, 663 N.Y.S.2d 581 (2d Dept. 1997), aff'd, 91 N.Y.2d 554, 673 N.Y.S.2d 530, 696 N.E.2d 174 (1998).

108 *Del Zio v. Presbyterian Hosp.*, 1978 U.S. Dist. LEXIS 14450 (S.D.N.Y.).

109 See *York v. Jones*, 717 F. Supp. 421 (E.D. Va. 1989) [suit seeking transfer of cryo-preserved human pre-zygote].

110 In re *Buzzanca*, 61 Cal. App. 4th 1410, 72 Cal. Rptr. 2d 280 (4th Dist. 1998).

111 *Prato-Morrison v. Doe*, 103 Cal. App. 4th 222, 126 Cal. Rptr. 2d 509 (2d Dist. 2002).

112 Fertility Clinic Success Rate and Certification Act of 1992, Pub. L. No. 102-493, 106 Stat. 3146 (1992) [codified in 42 U.S.C.A. §§ 263a-1-263a-7]; 42 C.F.R. pt. 493.

113 69 Fed. Reg. 29,786 (May 25, 2004).

114 Cal. A.B. No. 2513 (New Laws 1996) [codified at Cal. Bus. & Prof. Code § 2260] and Cal. S.B. 1555 (New Laws 1996) [codified at Cal. Penal Code § 367g].

115 E.g., *Reilly v. Blue Cross & Blue Shield*, 846 F.2d 416 (7th Cir.), cert. denied, 488 U.S. 856 (1988); but see *Northwestern Farm Bureau Ins. Co. v. Althauser*, 90 Or. App. 13, 750 P.2d 1166 (1988) [IVF not covered because not medically necessary].

116 *Bragdon v. Abbott*, 524 U.S. 624 (1998).

Chapter 14

Antitrust

John E. Steiner, Jr., Esq.

Key Learning Objectives

By the end of this chapter, you will be able to:

- Provide an overview of the antitrust laws with a focus on how those laws apply in healthcare settings.

- Explain key antitrust laws (Sherman Antitrust Act, Clayton Act, and Federal Trade Commission Act); some exemptions from liability; and how the laws are enforced.

- Understand the specific situations in healthcare business arrangements, contracting, and managed care organization activities that involve the antitrust laws.

- Explain some of the exceptions to the application of the antitrust laws, both in general and in specific healthcare situations.

Chapter Outline

Introduction

Antitrust laws apply to most hospitals and other healthcare organizations.[1] Federal and state antitrust laws are designed to preserve the private competitive market system by prohibiting various anticompetitive activities. Antitrust suits can be brought both by private parties and government agencies. Antitrust challenges often arise in mergers, exclusive contracts, medical staff privilege denials and terminations, exchanges of price information, and other actions of healthcare organizations. 🚩 Most antitrust lawsuits are highly fact dependent, complex, expensive to litigate, and often involve opinions of economic experts. Organizations need to be aware of potential antitrust problems so that questionable conduct either can be avoided or structured to provide the strongest possible defense.

PRIMARY ANTITRUST LAWS

The primary federal antitrust laws are the:

- Sherman Antitrust Act[2]
- Clayton Act[3]
- Federal Trade Commission Act[4]
- Robinson-Patman Act[5]

Some of these laws are aimed at relationships among competitors, called "horizontal" relationships. Other laws are aimed at relationships among different levels of production and distribution, called "vertical" relationships. Most states have parallel antitrust laws that apply to intrastate activities.

Federal antitrust laws apply only to actions affecting interstate and foreign commerce. Interstate commerce has been broadly defined by the U.S. Supreme Court to include intrastate or local activities that have a substantial economic effect on interstate commerce. For example, in 1976, the U.S. Supreme Court ruled that Mary Elizabeth Hospital, a forty-nine-bed proprietary hospital operated by Hospital Building Company, was involved in interstate commerce. The hospital purchased $100,000 worth of medicines and supplies from out-of-state vendors and received considerable revenues from out-of-state insurance companies and federal payers.[6]

The court considered that activity sufficient to affect interstate commerce. Hospital Building Company had sued a competing hospital, Rex Hospital, which had opposed expansion of Mary Elizabeth Hospital. The Court ruling allowed the trustees of Rex Hospital to be sued under the antitrust laws for an alleged conspiracy to restrain trade by blocking the expansion. However, Rex Hospital ultimately won the suit because a jury found that its actions had been reasonable and

Rex Hospital had, in good faith, participated in the health planning process.[7] In 1991, the Court established a standard for determining effect on interstate commerce that means virtually all healthcare cases affect interstate commerce.[8] A plaintiff does not have to allege an actual effect on interstate commerce. The court has to look at the impact on other participants and potential participants in the market, not just the impact on the plaintiff. Thus, the revocation of the clinical privileges of an ophthalmologist at one hospital was found to affect interstate commerce.

🚩 A recent example of the application of the interstate commerce clause is the legal challenge to the constitutionality of the Patient Protection and Affordable Care Act (sometimes referred to as the "Accountable Care Act" or "ACA") (Pub. L. No. 111-148, 124 Stat. 119 (2010). The Attorney General of Virginia challenged the constitutionality of the enforcement provision in ACA.[9] That provision, Section 1501, is known as the "Minimum Essential Coverage Provision." Under that section, individuals who fail to maintain a minimum level of healthcare insurance coverage by the beginning of 2014 are subject to a penalty. The penalty is in the form of a tax, and ACA places the oversight and enforcement authority for the tax with the Internal Revenue Service. The position of the plaintiff (Attorney General of Virginia) is that Section 1501 exceeds the power of Congress under the Interstate Commerce Clause. The Supreme Court allowed the minimal essential coverage requirement to stand as a permitted exercise of Congressional taxing authority. In doing so, the Court essentially avoided squarely addressing whether the individual mandate exceeds the intended scope of the Commerce Clause.

KEY FEDERAL ANTITRUST AGENCIES. One unique aspect of the federal antitrust laws is the existence of two independent federal agencies, the Antitrust Division of the Department of Justice (DOJ) and the Federal Trade Commission (FTC), with overlapping authority to evaluate and prosecute actions as antitrust violations. As more attention has been focused on this anomaly, these two organizations have developed joint guidelines and taken other steps to coordinate their activities.[10] However, these competing agencies retain their independent authority.

Both of these agencies give binding advance rulings approving proposed actions.[11] However, a curious anomaly in the antitrust law and weakness of these agencies is that a ruling from them or a settlement with them does not bar a private action by anyone with standing who is dissatisfied with the ruling or settlement.[12]

This chapter discusses the Sherman Antitrust Act (13-1), the Clayton Act (13-2), the Federal Trade Commission Act (13-3), and some of the exemptions from antitrust laws (13-4).

14-1 Sherman Antitrust Act

The Sherman Antitrust Act ("Sherman Act") is aimed at eliminating both restraints of trade and monopolies. Violations of the Sherman Act are federal crimes. The federal government and private parties can also obtain injunctive relief from violations. Any person who is injured in business or property by a violation can recover three times his or her actual damages in a civil lawsuit. Such damages are referred to as "treble damages."[13] The effect of trebling damages is illustrated by an Ohio case in which 1,800 physicians brought a class action against an HMO. In 1988, a jury found the HMO had engaged in price-fixing and other violations, causing over $34 million in damages. After trebling, the jury award was over $100 million. The parties settled the suit and the HMO paid $37.5 million and agreed not to appeal.[14]

> The Sherman Antitrust Act focuses on "restraints of trade" and "monopolies."

This section discusses Section 1 (13-1.1) and Section 2 (13-1.2) of the Sherman Act. Physicians bring antitrust suits under Sections 1 and/or 2 of the Sherman Act for various reasons. Those reasons include (i) challenges to exclusive hospital contracts with other physicians and (ii) other hospital actions that negatively affect physicians' membership on the medical staff or their clinical privileges in the hospital.

14-1.1 Sherman Antitrust Act Section 1

Section 1 of the Sherman Act forbids "every contract, combination . . . or conspiracy, in restraint of trade" in interstate or foreign commerce.[15]

RULE OF REASON. The U.S. Supreme Court recognizes that a literal reading of this section would forbid virtually all commercial contracts. Therefore, the Court interprets this section to forbid only unreasonable restraints. ⚑ The rule of reason standard looks at challenged agreements on a case-by-case basis to determine whether they promote or suppress competition.[16] Courts examine the structure of the industry, defendant's operation in that industry, history and duration of the restraint, and reasons for its adoption.

RELEVANT GEOGRAPHIC AND PRODUCT MARKET. The plaintiff has the initial burden of presenting evidence to prove the relevant geographic and product markets at issue in the lawsuit. The relevant geographic market in hospital cases generally includes facility locations that might be attractive alternatives to referring physicians and patients. For many healthcare services, this usually includes several adjoining counties.[17] However, the relevant geographic area can be a smaller or larger area, as determined on a case-by-case basis. For example, an international referral center may consider most or all of the United States as the relevant geographic market for specialized surgeries (e.g., heart transplants, specialized cancer care, etc.).

Where a company presently competes does not necessarily determine the relevant market for antitrust purposes.[18] The Department of Justice, Federal Trade Commission, and courts realize that when a company attempts to engage in anticompetitive behavior, such as raising prices too high, consumers usually look for alternatives.[19] Many antitrust cases are dismissed based on the failure to allege a relevant geographic market.[20]

The relevant product market varies depending on the action being challenged.[21] In many hospital merger cases, the relevant product market is acute care hospital services.[22] When individual professionals bring antitrust actions, the services they provide determine the product market. Thus, when an anesthesiologist challenged an exclusive agreement with an anesthesiology group, the patient market for individual anesthesia services constituted the relevant product market.[23] In some cases, a single brand of a product or service can constitute the relevant product market.[24]

MARKET POWER. In addition to proving the relevant market, a plaintiff must prove the defendant has significant market power. In short, that means the ability to harm customers by curtailing output or raising prices, without competitors entering the market. When this is not proven, Section 1 claims fail.[25] There also is a companion concept of economic harm to consumers when a competitor can decrease quality and not lose market share.

ANTITRUST INJURY. In order to have standing to bring an antitrust suit, the plaintiff must also prove an antitrust injury. In 1990, the U.S. Supreme Court ruled that to be an "antitrust injury" the injury must be attributable to an anticompetitive aspect of the practice under scrutiny. Thus, the alleged injury cannot merely be a loss stemming from continued competition.[26] Another way of saying this is that the antitrust law is designed to protect competition in the relevant market, not to protect competitors. Some antitrust cases are rejected because the plaintiff fails to allege or show more than harm to himself as an individual competitor.

> Simply stated, antitrust law is meant to protect competition in the relevant market.

For example, a radiologist challenged exclusion from a hospital staff and an independent practice association providing services to an HMO. An independent practice association is a legal entity that serves as a contracting entity on behalf of numerous physicians, who maintain their individual, private medical practices.

The case was dismissed because there was no antitrust injury, since there was no harm to competition. The court found pro-competitive reasons for the exclusion and, also, that there was no duty to aid the plaintiff who was a competitor.[27]

In a challenge to the termination of a contract with nurse anesthetists, one federal appellate court ruled that the staffing decisions at a single hospital generally do not constitute an antitrust injury.[28] The court listed many of the cases dealing with staffing decisions at a single hospital. Although the court decisions in those cases relied on a variety of different reasons, with only a few exceptions, the cases found no violation of Section 1 of the Sherman Act. The court could find only one case in which a plaintiff successfully established an antitrust liability for the staffing decision at a single hospital. In that case, the court found that the relevant market in a remote area of Montana had only two hospitals.[29]

Similarly, in 2002, a federal district court dismissed a lactation consultant's challenge to exclusion from a hospital. That was because she actually practiced in other area hospitals and could not show antitrust injury.[30]

In 1998, a federal court dismissed an antitrust suit by nurse anesthetists. The nurse anesthetists claimed that outsourcing constituted monopolization of the anesthesia services market. The court ruled that they had failed to show antitrust injury.[31]

In 2004, a federal district court in New York found sufficient antitrust injury to permit an ambulatory surgery center to pursue a challenge to the exclusive contract of a hospital with a managed care organization.[32]

⚑ Challenges to exclusive physician contracts are often barred on the basis of lack of antitrust injury.[33]

EFFICIENT ENFORCER. Courts also ask whether the particular plaintiff is an efficient enforcer,[34] which means that the plaintiff has a strong interest in the antitrust goals of promoting competition. Persons who are not efficient enforcers also lack standing to sue.[35]

PER SE VIOLATIONS. When the relevant market, significant market power, and antitrust injury are shown by an efficient enforcer, then the rule of reason is applied. There is, however, an exception to the foregoing statement.

Some business agreements are considered by the courts as *per se* (i.e., by itself) unreasonable. *Per se* unreasonable agreements are viewed as lacking potentially redeeming competitive benefits. Courts presume that these agreements are unreasonable, and the plaintiff does not have to prove unreasonableness, which shortens and simplifies some trials. *Per se* violations include price-fixing, market division, tie-ins, and boycotts. Losses flowing from *per se* violations are not automatically "antitrust injuries."[36]

> *Per se* violations of antitrust law are serious, primarily because they lack positive, competitive benefits.

PRICE-FIXING. Price-fixing agreements among competitors for the purpose of raising, lowering, or stabilizing prices are *per se* violations. No defense or justification is recognized, except for a governmental mandate. The U.S. Supreme Court ruled that a maximum fee schedule for physicians set by physicians was price-fixing and, thus, a *per se* violation.[37] Most requirements of sellers concerning the price at which their products may be resold are *per se* violations. A seller's nonprice restrictions on resale, such as territorial limits, are generally examined under the rule of reason.[38] One federal court ruled that a discharged anesthesiologist lacked standing to claim that a hospital and an anesthesiology department were engaged in price-fixing. In that case, the only injury claimed from the alleged price-fixing was the inability to participate in the scheme.[39] In 1994, the American Medical Association requested approval from the Federal Trade Commission (FTC) for a proposed program of advisory peer review of physicians' fees. The FTC did not object to some aspects of the proposed program, but rejected some aspects as price-fixing.[40]

In 2003, a federal appellate court ruled that in the circumstances of the particular case, joint efforts by a consortium of physician and consumer groups to negotiate nonprice terms with a health plan did not constitute a conspiracy to fix prices or to boycott.[41]

Attempts by physicians to jointly establish fees to be paid by third-party payers can be price-fixing,[42] unless the group is sufficiently integrated. In general, integration amongst physician practices is assessed based on the degree of clinical, financial, and administrative integration. There has been aggressive enforcement against physician groups that seek to collectively bargain without sufficient integration. This has resulted in numerous consent decrees.[43]

MARKET DIVISION. Any agreement among competitors to divide up the market is a *per se* violation.[44] For example, if two competing hospitals agree that one will provide obstetrical services, while the other will provide open heart surgery services, this would be a *per se* violation. In 2003, the state of Florida entered a consent judgment with two hospitals that had agreed to allocate markets as part of a settlement of certificate of need litigation.[45] The judgment barred the hospitals from honoring or entering any allocation agreements.

TYING ARRANGEMENTS. Under a "tying" arrangement, the seller refuses to sell product A to a customer unless that customer agrees to buy product B from the seller. If three conditions are present, a tying arrangement is generally a *per se* violation: (1) products A and B must be separate, (2) the seller must have sufficient market power to restrain competition in product B, and (3) the arrangement must sufficiently affect commerce.[46] In 1984, the U.S. Supreme Court found an exclusive hospital contract with an anesthesia group not to be a *per se* violation.[47] Similarly, in 1988, a federal appellate court ruled that an exclusive pathology contract was not an unlawful arrangement because pathology services are not a separate product but part of hospital services.[48] However, another federal appellate court in the same year found there was a separate demand for anesthesia services, making them a separate product, so that a nurse anesthetist could successfully challenge an exclusive hospital contract with a group of anesthesiologists.[49] The case was viewed as different from the 1984 U.S. Supreme Court anesthesia case because it involved an alleged conspiracy to eliminate the availability of nurse anesthetist services in the hospital.

Market power in the tying product must be shown to make a claim. In 1998, a federal appellate court ruled that it was not illegal tying for an HMO to require that a pharmacy company use the HMO's subsidiary as the third-party administrator in order to obtain approval of more of its pharmacies as providers for the HMO.[50] The court found that the HMO did not exercise sufficient market power in the tying market and that there was no demonstrated harm to competition in the tied market.

There is no illegal tying as long as the buyer is free to choose to buy the two products separately. Discount packages are permitted as long as the products are offered separately.[51] This is especially true when there is also a market for discount packages in which there is also competition.[52] When dealers of sound systems for cars challenged the inclusion of the sound systems in the price of vehicles, a federal court ruled that there was insufficient market power to trigger the *per se* rule and that the seller could take advantage of market failure due to inadequate consumer information. As long as the seller does nothing to stop comparison shopping, the seller has no duty to promote comparison shopping.[53]

BOYCOTTS. Any agreement among competitors not to deal with anyone outside the group or to deal with them only on certain terms is considered a boycott and a *per se* violation. For example, in a 1942 decision, a federal appellate court found the American Medical Association ethics rules against salaried practice to be a *per se* violation.[54]

Hospitals have been on both sides of boycott claims. Hospitals and others have accused physicians of boycotts of hospitals. An Arizona medical staff settled a claimed boycott of a hospital in 1994 by agreeing not to combine to restrict services to the hospital.[55] In 1994, a federal court ruled that a hospital was not engaged in an illegal boycott where it followed a policy of sending its patients for radiology services only to another Joint Commission accredited facility. In that case, the hospital's former chief of radiology, who brought the lawsuit, operated a freestanding radiology clinic. The court found that he failed to show that the hospital's policy had any anticompetitive effects in a relevant market.[56] The chief's contract with the hospital was terminated when he refused to enter a new agreement limiting his right to compete. In 1993, a federal court ruled that it was not an illegal boycott for an HMO to pay a contracting physician more if he did not work for competing HMOs. In that case, the contract did not mandate an exclusive relationship between the HMO and the physician, and it could be terminated by either party with thirty days advance notice.[57]

In 1997, a federal appellate court refused to apply the *per se* doctrine in a suit involving a retina specialist.

The specialist claimed a referral agreement between a competitor and an ophthalmologic group was a boycott. The court found that there was historical acceptance of eye care networks that affiliated with only one retina group. Moreover, the network controlled only 15 percent of retina referrals, which was not sufficient market power to restrain trade. Thus, the court then applied a rule of reason analysis to affirm rejection of the claim.[58]

JOINT VENTURES. Basically, a joint venture is a business undertaking involving at least two parties who agree to share the risks and rewards of the venture. Usually when two competitors enter a joint venture, the courts will apply a rule of reason analysis. This is because the integration of resources in a joint venture can produce efficiencies and new products. Courts determine whether the restraints on competition resulting from the joint venture are necessary to achieve the permitted purpose. For example, in 1988, a federal district court dismissed a physician's price-fixing antitrust suit against an HMO because (1) the HMO was a legitimate joint venture with a shared risk of loss and (2) the price agreement was necessary to distribute the revenues and control costs to remain competitive.[59] Attention has been focused on the minimum characteristics necessary to demonstrate sufficient integration.[60] The 1996 joint statements of the Department of Justice (DOJ) and FTC on antitrust enforcement discuss hospital joint ventures and physician network joint ventures.

> The basic definition of a "joint venture" is a business undertaking between at least two parties who agree to share the risks and rewards of the venture.

INFORMATION EXCHANGE. Exchange of information, especially price information, among competitors can be a violation. Exchange of past price information is less likely to be a violation. In 1993, the DOJ approved a voluntary salary survey by an independent contractor that only reported aggregated data that was at least three months old.[61] Current and prospective salary information generally cannot be directly exchanged. The DOJ successfully challenged exchange of current and prospective nursing salary information among Utah hospitals. That challenge resulted in a consent decree in 1994 that specified what conduct would be permitted.[62] Nonprice information typically is viewed more leniently, except where it appears to be aimed at suppressing competition. The 1996 joint statements of the DOJ and FTC on antitrust enforcement discuss exchange of information. The FTC and DOJ have issued letters approving additional exchanges of information.[63]

TRADE ASSOCIATIONS. "Self-regulation" by trade associations must be carefully structured. Any suppression or destruction of competition can be a violation. In 1994, an association of Iowa hospitals agreed to a consent decree with the DOJ. That decree ended an agreement that limited competitive advertising by the hospital members.[64]

In 1999, the U.S. Supreme Court vacated and remanded a federal appellate court ruling involving a trade association's advertising policy. The Court focused on whether the trade association's advertising policy was an unreasonable restraint of trade by restricting truthful, nondeceptive advertising.[65] The Court ordered the lower court to more carefully examine the professional context of the advertising. On remand, the federal appellate court found the restrictions to be pro-competitive and ordered the FTC to dismiss the case.[66]

AGREEMENT. Many violations require the showing of an "agreement" among competitors. ⚑ It is not always necessary to show an actual agreement. Courts have stated that "interdependent conscious parallelism" among competitors can provide the basis for inferring an agreement.[67] For example, assume that the dominant health insurer in an area announced that it would not send patients to any hospital that also accepted patients covered by a competing health insurer. Also assume that all the hospitals in the area stopped accepting the competing insurer's patients. In this example, an agreement could be inferred from this parallel behavior that cannot be justified by independent business judgment. It would not be necessary to prove actual communication among the hospitals. However, parallel business behavior is not sufficient when independent business judgment can justify the decisions. For example, if all the hospitals in an area independently decide to stop dealing with a nursing agency that charges more than any other agency, or provides unresponsive service, the parallel business behavior could be justified by independent business judgment.

CONSPIRACY/INTRACORPORATE IMMUNITY. Section 1 of the Sherman Act requires a conspiracy between separate economic entities. An unincorporated association of otherwise competing physicians can constitute a conspiracy.[68] However, a single integrated entity cannot conspire with itself.[69] Usually, a corporation cannot conspire with itself or its employees.[70]

There is disagreement among the federal circuit courts whether a hospital and medical staff are a single entity for antitrust conspiracy purposes; or whether they are multiple entities that can conspire. At least four circuits have ruled that, when engaged in peer review, the hospital and medical staff are a single entity protected by the intracorporate conspiracy doctrine.[71] One of these circuits recognized an exception to intracorporate immunity when a physician acts pursuant to an independent personal stake,[72] while one of the circuits has rejected any such exception.[73] One court indicated that while the hospital could not conspire with its medical staff, the members could conspire among themselves. However, in that case, since the ultimate decision was by the board of directors, any conspiracy among the medical staff could not cause antitrust injury.[74] At least two other circuits ruled that hospitals and their medical staffs are separate entities capable of conspiracy.[75] Other circuits have declined to rule on the issue.[76] To avoid both the "personal stake" exception and the appearance of a conspiracy, hospitals should limit the involvement of physicians in recommendations and decisions concerning those involved in the same or competing specialties. For example, when a medical staff committee is hearing or considering charges against a cardiac surgeon, other competing cardiac surgeons should not serve on the committee.

14-1.2 Section 2

Section 2 of the Sherman Act prohibits monopolizing, attempts to monopolize, and combinations or conspiracies to monopolize any part of interstate or foreign commerce.[77]

Like Section 1, a plaintiff in a Section 2 lawsuit must prove a relevant geographic and product market.

MONOPOLY POWER. Monopoly power is the power to control prices or exclude competition. Courts usually look to market share as a sign of monopoly power. To establish a monopolization claim under Section 2, it must be shown that defendants possess monopoly power in the relevant market.[78] ▶ However, mere possession of monopoly power is not a violation if it is due to a superior product, business acumen, or a historical accident. For example, it is not an illegal monopoly to be the sole community hospital when, by historical accident, only one hospital was ever established in the area. Or, in this example, the only competitors in the area suffered business failures without illegal acts committed by the survivor.

In 2004, a federal court in Ohio found that an anesthesia group had monopoly power in the relevant market for anesthesia services. A hospital declined to enter an exclusive anesthesia agreement with the group. In turn, the group entered into agreements with independent physicians in the area. The agreements required those physicians to use the group's certified registered nurse anesthetists (CRNAs) as their primary source of anesthesia services. Then, the group refused to provide anesthesia services at the hospital for any physician who did not sign an agreement with the group. The hospital challenged the arrangements.[79]

PURPOSEFUL ACT. Monopolizing requires possession of monopoly power in a relevant market, plus a "purposeful act." A purposeful act is the willful acquisition or maintenance of monopoly power.

ELEMENTS OF A CLAIM. In 1993, the U.S. Supreme Court ruled that a plaintiff must prove the following to demonstrate attempted monopolization:

(1) use of unfair or predatory means, such as boycotts or discriminatory pricing, with

(2) specific intent to monopolize, and

(3) a dangerous probability of achieving monopoly power. In determining the third element, courts consider

    a. the relevant markets, both the product and the geographic markets, and

    b. market power, that is, the defendant's ability to lessen or destroy competition in that market.[80]

In 2002, a federal appellate court addressed a case involving an ambulatory surgery center that challenged certain actions by a hospital. Those actions included entering an exclusive contract with a managed care organization that precluded use of the surgery center and refusing to enter a transfer agreement with the surgery center. After a trial without a jury, the federal district court ruled in favor of the hospital. The district court concluded that attempted monopolization was not demonstrated. The surgery center did not prove either predatory conduct by the hospital or a dangerous probability that the hospital would achieve monopoly power in the outpatient surgery market. The district court rejected the conspiracy claim. Moreover, the parties involved were principal and agent. Thus, they were incapable of conspiring with one another. The appellate court affirmed the district court.[81]

14-2 Clayton Act

Four parts of the Clayton Act are discussed in this section: Section 2 (13-2.1); Section 3 (13-2.2); Section 7 (13-2.3); and Section 4 (13-2.4).

14-2.1 Section 2

Section 2 of the Clayton Act, as amended by the Robinson-Patman Act, forbids certain price discrimination.[82]

▶ It is unlawful to discriminate in price between different purchasers when selling commodities of like grade or quality where the effect may be substantially to lessen competition or to injure, destroy, or prevent competition. At least one of the two comparative transactions must cross state lines. The section applies only to commodities, so sales of services and intangibles are not affected, and the section applies only to sales, so leases and consignments are not affected.

Section 2 also prohibits indirect price discrimination through seller-supplied facilities, services, or payments. For example, if the seller provides special promotional advertising for one buyer, this service is indirect price discrimination in favor of that buyer.

The seller is not the only possible violator. A buyer who knowingly induces or receives discriminatory prices also violates Section 2.

EXEMPTIONS. Nonprofit institutions have an exemption for purchases "for their own use."[83] As a result, hospital pharmacies in nonprofit hospitals usually buy drugs from manufacturers at a discount not available to commercial pharmacies. These drugs can be used only "for their own use." ▶ In 1976, the U.S. Supreme Court defined "for their own use" to be limited to the following:

> Nonprofit institutions have an exemption from the Clayton Act for certain purchases; those are called "for their own use" purchases.

(1) Treatment of inpatients at the hospital;

(2) Treatment of admitted emergency patients in the hospital;

(3) Personal use by outpatients on the hospital premises;

(4) Personal use away from the premises by inpatients or emergency patients upon their discharge;

(5) Personal use away from the premises by outpatients;

(6) Personal use by hospital employees, students, and their immediate dependents; and

(7) Personal use by medical staff members and their immediate dependents.[84]

Thus, hospitals must confine their sales of drugs purchased at a discount to these groups to avoid possible civil liability, including treble damages and loss of the valuable discount.

Purchasers who do not qualify include: (1) former patients who wish to renew prescriptions given when they were inpatients, emergency facility patients, or outpatients; (2) physicians who are medical staff members and who intend to dispense the drugs in the course of their private practices away from the hospital; and (3) walk-in customers who are not hospital patients. Hospitals should refuse to sell to these groups or set up a separate purchase order system to fill their requests.

FTC staff members have further interpreted the scope of "own use" in staff advisory letters. For example, one letter concluded that contracted workers who technically were not employees could receive discounted drugs because they were assigned exclusively to the hospital as their regular place of work.[85]

In 1987, a federal court ruled that drug companies and a hospital could be sued for the hospital's alleged transfer of drugs between its in-house pharmacy and its retail pharmacy.[86]

Governmental entities generally are exempt from the price discrimination prohibition. However, in 1983, the U.S. Supreme Court ruled that governmental hospitals must observe the same restrictions on resale of discount drugs that apply to nonprofit hospitals.[87] In 1984, a federal appellate court ruled that resale of drugs by health maintenance organizations to their own members is "for their own use."[88]

There is no exemption for for-profit hospitals; their purchases must be on the same volume discount basis as generally available to other consumers.

In 1989, a federal appellate court upheld the fraud conviction of an operator of a shared services organization. The operator obtained pharmaceuticals at lower prices in excess of the amount needed by qualified member hospitals and sold the surplus to wholesale drug companies.[89]

14-2.2 Section 3

Section 3 of the Clayton Act[90] prohibits sales of commodities that are conditioned on the buyer not dealing with competitors of the seller. Examples include tie-in sales and exclusive dealing arrangements where the effect "may be substantially to lessen competition or tend to create a monopoly" in any line of commerce. Section 1 of the Sherman Act prohibits the same conduct not only for commodities, but also for services, intangibles, and real property. Examples of the prohibited conduct are included in the discussion of that section earlier in this chapter.

14-2.3 Section 7

Section 7 of the Clayton Act[91] prohibits acquisitions or mergers where the effect "may be substantially to lessen competition or tend to create a monopoly in any line of commerce in any section of the country." 🏴 With the rapid growth in some national hospital companies and the consolidation of providers, this section has increasingly been applied to hospitals.

Relevant product and geographic markets must be identified in a manner similar to the analysis under Section 2 of the Sherman Act.

Section 7 is preventive, not merely corrective. A reasonable likelihood of substantially lessening competition is sufficient to establish a violation.

MERGER GUIDELINES. The DOJ and FTC issued merger guidelines in 1992 that are not binding on courts but give some direction.[92] In 1994, the DOJ and the FTC issued further guidelines that created a "safety zone" for mergers with older hospitals with fewer than one hundred beds and an average census of fewer than forty patients.[93] One of the 1996 joint statements from the DOJ and FTC addressed hospital mergers.

HERFINDAHL-HIRSCHMAN INDEX. One of the tools used to measure market concentration is a formula, the Herfindahl-Hirschman Index (HHI). The HHI is calculated by adding the squares of the percentage market shares of the entities in the market. For example, if there were twenty competing hospitals and each had 5 percent of the market, the HHI would be 500 [each of the twenty hospitals contribute 25 (5×5)]. If a merger results in an HHI less than 1,000, the government generally will not challenge the merger, so four of the twenty hospitals in the example could merge into one hospital (HHI = 800). [The merged hospital would have a 20 percent share, contributing 400 (20×20), while the remaining 16 hospitals would each contribute 25 (5×5).]

There are potential significant federal competitive concerns depending on other factors stated in the 1992 guidelines. However, there is no presumption of violation if (a) the resulting HHI is from 1,000 to 1,800 and is more than 100 points above the pre-merger HHI or (b) the resulting HHI is over 1,800 and is 50 to 100 points above the pre-merger HHI. If the resulting HHI is over 1,800 and is more than 100 points above the pre-merger HHI, there is a presumption that the merger will create or enhance market power.[94]

This would occur if the twenty hospitals in the example merged into four hospitals with equal market shares of 25 percent (HHI = 2,500). [Each of the four new hospitals would contribute 625 (25×25).] This presumption can be overcome by showing efficiencies and other factors.

HOSPITAL MERGERS. Section 7 has been used by both the FTC and the DOJ to attack mergers of hospitals. Section 7 clearly applies to for-profit hospital mergers. For example, in 1986, a federal appellate court upheld a FTC order that a for-profit hospital chain divest itself of two of three hospitals that it owned in the Chattanooga, Tennessee area and notify the FTC in advance of any plan to make a similar acquisition.[95] Generally, when large chains combine, the resulting entity finds itself with too many hospitals in one or more local markets, and the entity has to divest itself of one or more hospitals in those areas.[96] Failure to comply with divestiture orders can result in substantial civil money penalties.[97] Challenges to mergers can sometimes result in consent decrees that put conditions on the behavior of the resulting organization. For example, in 2000, a court order was obtained to enforce a 1994 Florida consent decree.[98]

> Section 7 of the Clayton Act has been used to challenge hospital mergers.

There is still a question of whether Section 7 applies to nonprofit hospitals. Section 7 applies to (1) persons who acquire shares of stock or capital and (2) persons subject to the jurisdiction of the FTC. Nonprofit companies do not have shares of stock or capital, and Section 7 applies to nonprofit hospitals only if they are subject to the jurisdiction of the FTC. There is a question whether nonprofit hospitals are subject to the jurisdiction of the FTC within the meaning of Section 7; the FTC takes the position that they are. In 1988, the FTC ordered two nonprofit hospitals in Reading, Pennsylvania to separate.[99] Some courts have agreed. One federal appellate court ruled in 1991 that Section 7 does apply to asset acquisitions by nonprofit hospitals.[100]

The DOJ challenged the proposed merger of two nonprofit hospitals in Rockford, Illinois. In 1989, a federal district court in Illinois enjoined the proposed merger. It found that the merger violated Section 7.[101] The appellate court found Section 7 not applicable to the merger of two non-stock, nonprofit hospitals but upheld barring the merger because it violated Section 1 of the Sherman Antitrust Act.[102]

The appellate court indicated that its decision on Section 7 was limited by the way the parties framed the issues. The court indicated its belief that Section 7 would be applicable if the government presented its case correctly.

One other court has found that Section 7 does not apply. The DOJ challenged the proposed merger of two hospitals in Roanoke, Virginia. A federal district court in Virginia ruled in 1988 that Section 7 did not apply to affiliations of nonprofit entities where there was no exchange of stock or share capital. Then, in 1989, the court ruled that the merger did not violate Section 1 of the Sherman Antitrust Act under the rule of reason.[103] In 1989, a federal appellate court affirmed the decision but did not issue an opinion.[104]

In 1989, the FTC began challenging the acquisition of a small hospital in Ukiah, California by a large hospital chain that owned the other small hospital in the town.[105] The hospitals tried to stop the FTC from proceeding with its complaint on the grounds that the FTC lacked jurisdiction under Section 7, but the federal court refused to rule until after the FTC had made a final ruling on jurisdiction.[106] In 1990, an Administrative Law Judge (ALJ) dismissed the complaint on the grounds of lack of jurisdiction, but the FTC reversed. In 1992, the ALJ again dismissed, but on the basis that the acquisition was not likely to substantially lessen competition when the proper geographic market was considered.[107] In 1994, the FTC affirmed, dismissing the complaint on the basis that there was insufficient evidence to establish the relevant geographic market.[108] Thus, it is unlikely that the jurisdictional issue will protect hospitals from the expense of responding to the FTC.

The FTC continues to challenge acquisitions of nonprofit hospitals.[109] However, it has generally been unsuccessful.[110] In 2002, the FTC Bureau of Competition created a Merger Litigation Task Force to focus on whether consummated mergers had resulted in anticompetitive price increases.[111] In 2004, the FTC launched a challenge to the merger of hospitals in Evanston, Illinois.[112]

In April 2005, the hospitals settled a portion of the case dealing with negotiating fees, but the challenge to the merger continued. In October 2005, a FTC administrative law judge ruled that the hospital merger in Evanston violated Section 7 of the Clayton Act and ordered Evanston Northwestern Healthcare Corporation (ENHC) to sell Highland Park Hospital. ENHC appealed, seeking review by the FTC.[113]

14-2.4 Section 4

Section 4 of the Clayton Act[114] gives any person the right to sue for treble damages when injured by violations of the Sherman Antitrust Act or the Clayton Act. There are no criminal sanctions for violations of the Clayton Act, but violations can be enjoined.

14-3 Federal Trade Commission Act

Section 5(a) of the Federal Trade Commission Act[115] prohibits "unfair methods or competition in or affecting commerce and unfair or deceptive acts or practices in or affecting commerce." The FTC has exclusive authority to enforce this section; private individuals cannot use it as a basis for suits. The FTC can also take action to enforce the Sherman Antitrust Act or the Clayton Act, but its authority is not exclusive. Examples of FTC action are included in the discussion of Section 7 of Clayton Act (13-2.3).

The FTC can (1) issue an order to cease and desist from violating antitrust laws, (2) seek a court-imposed fine for a violation of a cease and desist order, (3) seek injunctions of prohibited conduct, and (4) seek court-ordered restitution to consumers and others from violations.

14-4 Exemptions

The U.S. Supreme Court has made it clear that healthcare providers are treated in the same way as other industries for antitrust purposes. For example, in 1975, the Court ruled that the learned professions, such as law and medicine, were not exempt from the antitrust laws.[116]

> The Supreme Court ruled in 1975 that the legal and medical professions are not exempt from the antitrust laws.

There are several laws and legal principles that do exempt some activities or some actors from antitrust liability. This section discusses six sources of exemptions:

- The Health Care Quality Improvement Act of 1986 (14-4.1);
- State action (14-4.2);
- Petitioning government (14-4.3);
- The business of insurance (14-4.4);

- The medical residency match (14-4.5); and
- Implied exemptions (14-4.6).

This section concludes with a warning that exemption from one law may not be an exemption from another (14-4.7).

14-4.1 Health Care Quality Improvement Act of 1986

The Health Care Quality Improvement Act of 1986 (HCQIA) extends protection from monetary liability in private suits under the antitrust laws for professional review activities that meet its procedural standards.[117] HCQIA does not protect from suit, governmental actions, or injunctions.[118]

14-4.2 State Action

The law has recognized an exemption from antitrust liability for state action. ▶ In 1943, the U.S. Supreme Court ruled that state-compelled activities were immune from antitrust liability to preserve the state's authority to supervise economic activity within the state.[119] The state action doctrine was clarified in 1980 when the Court ruled that state authorization is not enough. The actions must be pursuant to a clearly articulated and affirmatively expressed state policy actively supervised by the state.[120] The doctrine was further defined in 1985 when the Court ruled that the clearly defined state policy did not have to compel the actions to bring them within the state action immunity.[121] Collective rate-making by motor carriers was found to be protected as state action because the states expressly permitted the rate-making and actively supervised it. On the same day, the Court ruled that active state supervision is not a requirement for exemption when the actor is a municipality, rather than a private individual.[122]

One area of dispute has been whether state medical peer review laws provide the requisite state action to protect hospitals from antitrust liability for their peer review activities. Prior to 1988, several courts found various such laws did provide the requisite state action.[123] In 1988, in a medical peer review case, the U.S. Supreme Court tightened the active supervision requirement to require that "state officials have and exercise power to review particular anticompetitive acts of private parties and disapprove those that fail to accord with state policy."[124] The case dealt with an Oregon law that did not include any state administrative review of hospital peer review decisions. The defendants argued that the availability of state judicial review was sufficient active

supervision. Applying the new standard, the Court decided that the judicial review available in Oregon was not sufficient without ruling that state judicial review could never provide sufficient state supervision. The efforts to obtain state action immunity for these activities have been reduced since it has become clearer that the HCQIA provides significant protection from antitrust liability for medical peer review actions.[125]

> The Health Care Quality Improvement Act (HCQIA) provides significant protection from antitrust law for medical peer review activities.

Numerous actions by governmental hospitals have been found to be immune under this standard. Statutory authority to acquire other hospitals is sufficient to immunize acquisitions.[126] Statutory authority to own and operate hospitals immunizes acquisitions of other hospitals.[127] In 1994, a federal appellate court found that state action immunity protected the proposed purchase of Cape Coral Hospital. The purchase was made by a healthcare authority created by Florida as a special purpose unit of local government that already owned another hospital in the county and that had authority to acquire other hospitals.[128] However, authority to do business is not sufficient alone to demonstrate a state intent to displace competition.[129] In 1999, a federal appellate court ruled that authority to contract for health services alone was not sufficient to grant a hospital service district immunity. The allegations against the hospital included exclusive contracting with managed care plans that excluded a competing outpatient surgical center.[130]

Governmental hospitals can also have state action immunity from physician challenges to peer review and staffing decisions.[131]

In 1991, the U.S. Supreme Court ruled that there was no conspiracy exception to the state action immunity.[132]

The Local Government Antitrust Act of 1984[133] extends statutory immunity from antitrust damage claims to local governmental agencies and their employees and agents. This applies to local government hospitals.[134] The law does not provide protection from antitrust suits seeking injunctions, but many of those will be precluded by the state action doctrine.[135]

Several states have passed laws providing a mechanism by which healthcare providers can apply to obtain state approval and, thus, antitrust immunity.[136] Some state approvals have been given under these laws.[137]

14-4.3 Petitioning Government

In two cases, the U.S. Supreme Court ruled that the antitrust laws do not apply to most activities intended to induce governmental action, such as lobbying.[138] This concept is called the Noerr-Pennington doctrine and is based on the right under the First Amendment to petition the government and on a judicial interpretation that lobbying activities are not a restraint of trade. The petitioning must be conducted honestly and for the legitimate purpose of influencing governmental policy. For example, a federal appellate court ruled in 1986 that the Noerr-Pennington doctrine protected a hospital's full use of the administrative process (including delaying tactics and appeals) to challenge a competing hospital's application for a certificate of need for a cardiac surgery program, but the doctrine did not protect misrepresentations to the governmental agency.[139] Efforts that are considered a "mere sham" to suppress competition are not protected. For example, repetitive insubstantial lawsuits might be a mere sham to tie up the competitor so that it cannot make financing or other business arrangements.[140] However, an objectively reasonable effort to litigate is not a sham, regardless of the plaintiff's subjective intent.[141]

14-4.4 Business of Insurance

The McCarran-Ferguson Act created a statutory exemption for the "business of insurance" when it is regulated by state law and does not constitute coercion, boycott, or intimidation.[142] The U.S. Supreme Court has taken a restrictive view of what constitutes the business of insurance entitled to this exemption. For example, in 1979, the Court limited the exemption to the business of insurance, not the business of insurers.[143] It defined the business of insurance as limited to the procedures and activities related to the spreading of risk among policyholders. It held that special reimbursement arrangements between Blue Shield and participating pharmacies were not within the business of insurance, but instead were merely the business of insurers.

14-4.5 The Medical Residency Match

In 2003, students filed an antitrust challenge to the process by which medical students are matched to first-year residency programs. In early 2004, the federal court dismissed the case as to some defendants but permitted the case to proceed against the remaining defendants. In 2004, Congress passed a law prohibiting antitrust attacks against the graduate medical education matching program through which students completing medical school are matched with first-year house staff positions. After the protective law was passed, the federal court dismissed the suit.[144]

14-4.6 Implied Exemptions

In 1981, the U.S. Supreme Court ruled that implied exemptions to antitrust laws are not favored and will be applied only to the limited extent necessary to fulfill the purposes of other laws.[145] The Court ruled that the national health planning law which was then in effect did not provide implied protection for an insurer from antitrust law liability. The case involved the insurer's position that it would not deal with a hospital that did not obtain approval from a planning agency for its new building. State law did not require approval. This principle was applied by a federal appellate court in 1984 when it ruled that a certificate of need does not protect a provider from being charged with monopolization.[146] The provider must still comply with all other laws, including antitrust laws.

14-4.7 Scope of Exemptions

When an exemption from one antitrust law applies, other antitrust laws still must be followed. In 1988, a federal district court ruled that "conduct that is specifically exempted from a particular antitrust law may nonetheless be prohibited by another statute. If that same conduct violates another law, the exemption does not follow."[147]

Chapter Summary

This chapter addresses many of the key principles, landmark cases, and theories supporting our country's antitrust laws. As an essential component of our economy, the healthcare industry is subject to potential antitrust scrutiny on several fronts. As explained in this chapter, there are only a few, statutory sources for the definition and application of our country's antitrust laws. Each of those laws includes broad definitions that have been interpreted by our federal court system over many decades. In addition, each law has limited exceptions and immunities that apply in the healthcare industry. Thus, the challenge for healthcare providers, and their advisers, is to stay current with the application of the laws and exceptions covered in this text.

Key Terms and Definitions

Boycott - To refuse to have dealings with a person or organization or to refuse to buy a product or service as an expression of protest or a means of coercion.

Cease and Desist Order - An order issued by a court or an administrative agency that prohibits a person or entity from continuing a specific course of action or conduct.

Clayton Act of 1914 - This Act is an amendment to the Sherman Antitrust Act (which was enacted in 1890) and prohibits certain acts or practices that unduly restrict trade and commerce. In brief, the Act makes these business practices illegal: (1) price discrimination; (2) tying and exclusive dealing contracts; (3) certain corporate mergers; and (4) interlocking directorates. These practices are illegal when they "substantially lessen competition" or tend to create a monopoly.

Federal Trade Commission Act of 1914 - This Act created the Federal Trade Commission (FTC), a bipartisan body with five members appointed by the President of the United States for seven-year terms. Among its powers under the Act, the FTC has the authority to issue "cease and desist" orders to companies to stop unfair trade practices.

Health Care Quality and Improvement Act of 1986 (HCQIA) - An Act that extends principles of state peer review immunity on a federal level. Thus, under HCQIA, members of a hospital peer review committee are protected from prosecution under various, federal antitrust lawsuits.

Horizontal Integration or Relationship - A type of ownership and control that occurs when a company is taken over by, or merged with, another company in the same industry and in the same line of business. For example, when one car manufacturer merges with another car manufacturer.

Injuction - An order of a court that requires a person or entity to act, or not to act, in a particular situation or manner. An injunction is considered an "extraordinary remedy" and only used when temporary maintenance of the status quo is necessary.

Market Power - Ability of a company to change the market price of a good or service without losing its customers to the competition. In a perfectly competitive market, the companies in a specific market would not have market power.

McCarran-Ferguson Act of 1945 - The Act gives the states the power to regulate the "business of insurance," without interference from federal regulation, unless federal law specifically states otherwise. The Act does not define the phrase "business of insurance." Court cases have established these three key factors to help make that determination: 1. Does the practice have the effect of transferring or spreading the policy-holder's risk? 2. Is the practice an integral part of the policy relationship between the insurer and the insured? 3. Is the practice limited to entities within the insurance industry?

Monopoly Power - Under the Sherman Antitrust Act, monopoly power is the ability of a business to control a price within its relevant product market or its geographic market or to exclude a competitor from doing business in those markets.

Noerr-Pennington Doctrine - Under this doctrine, private entities are immune from antitrust liability for attempts to influence the passage or enforcement of laws, even if those efforts are in support of laws that may have anticompetitive effects.

Per se Violation - A type of violation of the Sherman Antitrust Act, Section 1, which covers agreements, conspiracies, or trusts in restraint of trade. A *per se* violation does not require proof of the actual effect of a certain type of practice on the market or the intent of the parties engaged in the conduct. Examples include price-fixing among direct competitors (i.e., horizontal price-fixing) and division of markets amongst direct competitors (i.e., horizontal market division).

Price Discrimination - The sale of the same product to similarily situated buyers at different prices.

Price-Fixing - An agreement between parties, on the same side in a market, to sell or buy a product, service, or commodity at a fixed price, or to maintain prices at a specified level by controlling supply and demand.

Rule of Reason Analysis - Under the Sherman Antitrust Act, Section 1, this test considers the totality of the circumstances. The key question is whether the challenged conduct promotes or discourages market competition. The intent and motive of the parties alleged to be involved in the questionable conduct are relevant considerations.

Sherman Antitrust Act of 1890 - The first federal statute to limit cartels and monopolies. The Act is one of the most important laws used by the federal government to bring antitrust cases. "Antitrust" law is sometimes referred to as "competition" law because the main purpose of the Act is to promote and protect the concept of competitive markets. When the Act was passed, "trusts" were commonly used legal entities used to hold business interests.

Tying and Exclusive Dealing Contracts - The sale of products on the condition that the buyer not deal, or stop dealing, with the seller's competitors.

Vertical Integration or Relationship - The merging of companies that are within a chain of companies handling a single item (e.g., from the raw material, through production and to sale).

Instructor-Led Questions

1. Discuss liability under the Sherman Antitrust Act.

2. Discuss the rule of reason.

3. Discuss antitrust injury.

4. Discuss *per se* violations of the Sherman Antitrust Act.

5. Discuss intracorporate immunity.

6. Discuss monopoly power.

7. Discuss liability under the Clayton Act.

8. Discuss the scope of the "own use" exemption from price fixing restrictions for drug purchases by nonprofit institutions.

9. Discuss the federal efforts to challenge hospital mergers.

10. Discuss the Federal Trade Commission Act.

11. Discuss the scope of healthcare exemptions from antitrust laws.

12. Discuss the significance of the Health Care Quality and Improvement Act (HCQIA).

Endnotes

1   FTC & DOJ, Improving Health Care: A Dose of Competition (July 2004), http://www.usdoj.gov/atr/public/health_care/204694.htm.7

2   15 U.S.C. §§ 1-7.

3   15 U.S.C. §§ 12-27, 44.

4   15 U.S.C. §§ 41-58.

5   15 U.S.C. § 13c.

6   *Hospital Bldg. Co. v. Trustees of Rex Hosp.*, 425 U.S. 738 (1976).

7   *Hospital Bldg. Co. v. Trustees of Rex Hosp.*, No. 4048 (E.D.N.C. Dec. 5, 1984), aff'd, 791 F.2d 288 (4th Cir. 1986).

8   *Summit Health, Ltd. v. Pinhas*, 500 U.S. 322 (1991).

9   Commonwealth of Virginia ex rel. Cuccinelli, II vs. Sec. of HHS, (E.D. Va. Dec. 13, 2010).

10 E.g., Department of Justice (DOJ) & FTC, Statement of Antitrust Enforcement Policy Regarding Accountable Care Organizations Participating in the Medicare Shared Savings Program (Oct. 20, 2011); Department of Justice & FTC, Statements of antitrust enforcement policy in health care (Aug. 28, 1996), http://www.usdoj.gov/atr/public/guidelines/1791.htm (accessed Sept. 6, 2004) [hereinafter Statements will be cited "as 1996 DOJ/FTC Statements"]; revised Justice/FTC Enforcement Guidelines for Health Care Industry (Sept. 27, 1994), reprinted in 3 Health L. Rptr. [BNA] 1376 (1994) [hereinafter Health L. Rptr will be cited as H.L.R] [hereinafter the Guidelines will be cited as "1994 DOJ/FTC Guidelines"]; see also Protocol for coordination in merger investigations between the federal enforcement agencies and state attorneys general (Mar. 11, 1998); Federal, state antitrust authorities post joint merger investigation protocol, 7 H.L.R. 445 (1998).

11 http://www.ftc.gov/bc/advisory.htm and http://www.usdoj.gov/atr/public/busreview/letters.htm (accessed Sept. 6, 2004).

12 E.g., Physicians' group clashes with hospital over standing, 3 H.L.R. 1646 (1994) [after hospital settled with federal government, physicians sued Santa Cruz, Calif. hospital that had acquired other hospital in town]; *Santa Cruz Med. Clinic v. Dominican Santa Cruz Hosp.*, No. C93 20613 RMW (N.D. Cal. Mar. 28, 1995), as discussed in 23 Health L. Dig. (May 1995), at 18 [physicians have antitrust standing to sue over hospital acquisition], 1995 U.S. Dist. LEXIS 21032 (N.D. Cal. Sept. 7, 1995) [partial summary judgment granted for defendants on tying, channeling claims, but denied on exclusive dealing claim].

13 15 U.S.C. §§ 1, 2, 4, 15.

14 *Thompson v. Midwest Found. Indep. Physician Ass'n*, No. C-1-86-744 (S.D. Ohio Mar. 14, 1988) [jury verdict]; 124 F.R.D. 154 (S.D. Ohio Dec. 4, 1988) [settlement approved]. Note that not all IPA HMO arrangements are antitrust violations, e.g., *Hassan v. Independent Practice Assocs., P.C.*, 698 F. Supp. 679 (E.D. Mich. 1988).

15 15 U.S.C. § 1.

16 E.g., *Westchester Radiological Assocs., P.C. v. Empire Blue Cross & Blue Shield*, 707 F. Supp. 708 (S.D.N.Y.), aff'd, 884 F.2d 707 (2d Cir. 1989), cert. denied, 493 U.S. 1095 (1990).

17 E.g., *Cogan v. Harford Mem. Hosp.*, 843 F. Supp. 1013, 1019 (D. Md. 1994); *Morgenstern v. Wilson*, 29 F.3d 1291 (8th Cir. 1994), cert. denied, 513 U.S. 1150 (1995); N. Hershey, Geographic market definition critical to monopolization claim, 12 Hosp. L. Newsletter (July 1995), at 5 [discussing *Morgenstern*].

18 E.g., *Morgan, Strand, Wheeler & Biggs v. Radiology, Ltd.*, 924 F.2d 1484 (9th Cir. 1991).

19 E.g., DOJ & FTC 1992 Horizontal Merger Guidelines (Apr. 2, 1992), 57 Fed. Reg. 41,552 (Sept. 10, 1992), reprinted in 4 Trade Reg. Rep. (CCH) ¶13,103 (1992) [hereinafter "1992 DOJ/FTC Guidelines"]; In re *Adventist Health System/West*, FTC Docket No. 9234 (Apr. 1, 1994) [FTC dismissal of complaint due to failure to address sufficiently where services would be sought in the event of anticompetitive behavior].

20 E.g., *Arani v. TriHealth, Inc.*, 77 Fed. Appx. 823, 2003 U.S. App. LEXIS 20231 (6th Cir. 2003) [challenge to exclusion from physician panel who interpreted electrocardiograms and Holter Monitor results]; *Surgical Ctr. of Hammond, L.C. v. Hospital Serv. Dist No. 1*, 309 F.3d 836 (5th Cir. 2002) [exclusion of competing surgical center from managed care contracts].

21 E.g., *Continental Orthopedic Appliances, Inc v. Health Ins. Plan of Greater N.Y.*, 994 F. Supp. 133 (E.D. N.Y.1998) [proper product market in antitrust attack on HMO exclusive contract for orthotics not the provision of orthotic services to the HMO's enrollees, orthotics company given opportunity to replead], 40 F. Supp. 2d 109 (E.D.N.Y. 1999) [deny dismissal of claim based on product market of orthotics services to all HMO patients, although reservations about limiting to HMO patients, permitted to proceed with discovery].

22 E.g., *FTC v. University Health, Inc.*, 938 F.2d 1206 (11th Cir. 1991); see also *Forsyth v. Humana, Inc.*, 827 F. Supp. 1498 (D. Nev. 1993) [rejecting attempt to limit market to large for-profit hospitals].

23 *Oltz v. St. Peter's Commun. Hosp.*, 861 F.2d 1440 (9th Cir. 1988).

24 E.g., *Eastman Kodak Co. v. Image Technical Services, Inc.*, 504 U.S. 451 (1992).

25 E.g., *Minnesota Association of Nurse Anesthetists v. Unity Hospital*, 208 F.3d 655 (8th Cir. 2000) [affirming dismissal of CRNA challenge to exclusive anesthesia contracts with MDs; not boycotts & failure to demonstrate market power]; *Ford v. Stroup*, 113 F.3d 1234 (without op.), 1997 U.S. App. LEXIS 8692 (6th Cir. 1997) [summary judgment for defendants in challenge to exclusive contract for linear accelerator treatment for failure to show market power; market share of 50-55 percent alone not sufficient]; *Flegel v. Christian Hosp., Northeast-Northwest*, 4 F.3d 682 (8th Cir. 1993); *Cogan v. Harford Mem. Hosp.*, 843 F. Supp. 1013 (D. Md. 1994).

26 *Atlantic Richfield Co. v. USA Petroleum Co.*, 495 U.S. 328 (1990).

27 *Williamson v. Sacred Heart Hosp.*, 41 F.3d 667 (without op.), 1994 U.S. App. LEXIS 33199 (11th Cir. 1994); see also *Cogan v. Harford Mem. Hosp.*, 843 F. Supp. 1013 (D. Md. 1994).

28 *BCB Anesthesia Care v. Passavant Mem. Area Hosp. Ass'n*, 36 F.3d 664 (7th Cir. 1994).

29 *Oltz v. Saint Peter's Commun. Hosp.*, 861 F.2d 1440 (9th Cir. 1988).

30 *Volm v. Legacy Health Sys. Inc.*, 237 F. Supp. 2d 1166 (D. Or. 2002); *Volm v. Legacy Health Sys. Inc.*, 91 Fed. Appx. 581 (9th Cir. 2004) [upholding jury verdict for Volm on remaining state law claims].

31 *Minnesota Ass'n of Nurse Anesthetists v. Unity Hosp.*, 5 F. Supp. 2d 694 (D. Minn. 1998), aff'd, 208 F.3d 655 (8th Cir. 2000).

32 *Rome Ambulatory Surgery Ctr. LLC v. Rome Mem. Hosp.*, 349 F.2d 389 (N.D.N.Y. 2004).

33 E.g., *Imaging Ctr. v. Western Md. Health Sys.*, 2004 U.S. Dist. LEXIS 16138 (D. Md.); *Kochert v. Greater Lafayette Health Srvs.*, 2004 U.S. Dist. LEXIS 28059 (N.D. Ind.) [dismissal of antitrust challenge to loss of subcontract to perform anesthesia service in hospital that had exclusive contract with group; no antitrust injury]; *Bobcobo v. Radiology Consultants*, 305 F. Supp. 2d 422 (D.N.J. 2004) [radiologist failed to show antitrust injury when excluded from exclusive contract].

34 E.g., *Todorov v. DCH Healthcare Auth.*, 921 F.2d 1438 (11th Cir. 1991); but see *Ertag v. Naples Commun. Hosp. Inc.*, 121 F.3d 721 (11th Cir. 1997) [neurology group had standing to challenge hospital decision to permit only radiologists to provide official MRI interpretations].

35 E.g., *Korshin v. Benedictine Hosp.*, 34 F. Supp. 2d 133 (N.D.N.Y. 1999) [anesthesiologist not efficient enforcer in challenge to exclusive anesthesia contract]; *Feldman v. Palmetto Gen. Hosp., Inc.*, 980 F. Supp. 467 (S.D. Fla. 1997).

36 *Atlantic Richfield Co. v. USA Petroleum Co.*, 495 U.S. 328 (1990).

37 *Arizona v. Maricopa County Med. Soc'y*, 457 U.S. 332 (1982).

38 *Continental T.V. v. GTE Sylvania, Inc.*, 433 U.S. 36 (1977).

39 *Purgess v. Sharrock*, 806 F. Supp. 1102 (S.D.N.Y. 1992).

40 FTC Advisory Opinion Letter to General Counsel of AMA and the Chicago Medical Society, No. P923506 (Feb. 14, 1994), as discussed in 22 Health L. Dig. (Mar. 1994), at 6; B. McCormick, FTC gives qualified OK to medicine's fee-review plan, Am. Med. News, Mar. 7, 1994, at 3.

41 *International Healthcare Management v. Hawaii Coalition for Health*, 332 F.3d 6000 (9th Cir. 2003).

42 See D. Marx, Messenger models: what can the agencies do to prevent provider networks from violating the antitrust laws? Health Lawyers News, Apr. 2004.

43 E.g., In re *SPA Health Org.* (FTC consent order June 9, 2003) [network of Texas physicians agreed not to negotiate with payers unless certain qualified arrangements were in place]; In re *Carlsbad Physicians Ass'n, Inc.* (FTC consent order May 2, 2003) [agreement to dissolve organization that had been bargaining with health plans on behalf of physicians], http://www.ftc.gov/opa/2003/05/carlsbad.htm (accessed Sept. 6, 2004).

44 E.g., *Palmer v. BRG of Georgia, Inc.*, 498 U.S. 46 (1990).

45 *State v. Hospital Corp. of Am.*, 2003 Trade Cas. (CCH) ¶74,027 (M.D. Fla. Apr. 18, 2003).

46 See *Eastman Kodak Co. v. Image Technical Services, Inc.*, 504 U.S. 451 (1992).

47 *Jefferson Parish Hosp. Dist. v. Hyde*, 466 U.S. 2 (1984).

48 *Collins v. Associated Pathologists, Ltd.*, 844 F.2d 473 (7th Cir.), cert. denied, 488 U.S. 852 (1988).

49 *Oltz v. St. Peter's Commun. Hosp.*, 861 F.2d 1440 (9th Cir. 1988).

50 *Brokerage Concepts, Inc. v. U.S. Healthcare, Inc.*, 140 F.3d 494 (3d Cir. 1998).

51 E.g., *Northern Pacific Ry. Co. v. United States*, 356 U.S. 1 (1958).

52 E.g., *Nobel Scientific Indust., Inc. v. Beckman Instruments, Inc.*, 670 F. Supp. 1313 (D. Md. 1986), aff'd, 831 F.2d 537 (4th Cir. 1987), cert. denied, 487 U.S. 1226 (1988).

53 *Town Sound & Custom Tops, Inc. v. Chrysler Motors Corp.*, 959 F.2d 468 (3d Cir.), cert. denied, 506 U.S. 868 (1992).

54 *American Med. Ass'n v. United States*, 76 U.S. App. D.C. 70, 130 F.2d 233 (1942), aff'd, 317 U.S. 519 (1943).

55 In re *Med. Staff of Good Samaritan Med. Ctr.*, FTC File No. 901 0032 (settlement Sept. 7, 1994), as discussed in 3 H.L.R. 1257 (1994); B. McCormick, Doctors settle FTC boycott case, Am. Med. News, Oct. 3, 1994, 10.

56 *Cogan v. Harford Mem. Hosp.*, 843 F. Supp. 1013 (D. Md. 1994).

57 *U.S. Healthcare, Inc. v. Healthsource, Inc.*, 986 F.2d 589 (1st Cir. 1993).

58 *Retina Associates, P.A. v. Southern Baptist Hosp. of Fla., Inc.*, 105 F.3d 1376 (11th Cir. 1997).

59 *Hassan v. Independent Practice Assocs., P.C.*, 698 F. Supp. 679 (E.D. Mich. 1988).

60 See 1994 DOJ/FTC Guidelines; Capitation seen as brightest line in quest for sufficient integration, 4 H.L.R 269 (1995).

61 Business Review Letter from Assistant Attorney General Anne K. Bingaman to Counsel for the New Jersey Hospital Ass'n, DOJ, Antitrust Div. (Feb. 18, 1994), as discussed in 22 Health L. Dig. (Mar. 1994), at 9; New Jersey hospital salary survey satisfies antitrust enforcement guidelines, 3 H.L.R. 237 (1994).

62 *United States v. Utah Soc'y for Healthcare Human Resources Admin.*, 1994 U.S. Dist. LEXIS 17531 (D. Utah consent decree Mar. 14, 1994).

63 E.g., Washington State Med. Ass'n. (DOJ letter Sept. 23, 2003), http://www.usdoj.gov/atr/public/busreview/200260.htm (accessed Sept. 6, 2004); PriMed Physicians (FTC letter Feb. 6, 2003), http://www.ftc.gov/bc/adops/030206dayton.htm (accessed Sept. 6, 2004).

64 *United States v. Hospital Ass'n of Greater Des Moines*, No. 4-92-70648 (S.D. Iowa settlement Sept. 22, 1992); Hospitals settle suit alleging anticompetitive ad rules, Am. Med. News, Oct. 12, 1992, 12.

65 *California Dental Ass'n v. FTC*, 526 U.S. 756 (1999), rev'g, 128 F.3d 720 (9th Cir. 1997).

66 *California Dental Ass'n v. FTC*, 224 F.3d 942 (9th Cir. 2000).

67 *Interstate Circuit, Inc. v. United States*, 306 U.S. 208 (1939).

68 *Anesthesia Advantage, Inc. v. Metz Group*, 708 F. Supp. 1180 (D. Colo. 1989), rev'd on other grounds, 912 F.2d 397 (10th Cir. 1990).

69 *Copperweld Corp. v. Independence Tube Corp.*, 467 U.S. 752 (1984); e.g., *HealthAmerica Pa., Inc. v. Susquehanna Health Sys.*, 278 F. Supp. 2d 423 (M.D. Tenn. 2003) [summary judgment for defendants functioning as a single entity; defendant's alliance had been formed pursuant to a consent decree with the state attorney general in 1994], but see *New York ex rel. Spitzer v. Saint Francis Hosp.*, 94 F. Supp. 2d 399 (S.D.N.Y. 2000) [hospitals not sufficiently integrated to be single entity].

70 E.g., *Podiatrist Ass'n, Inc. v. La Cruz Azul De Puerto Rico, Inc.*, 332 F.3d 6 (1st Cir. 2003) [dismiss challenge to exclusion of podiatrists from standard benefit packages; intracorporate immunity; input by physicians does not show control]; *Viazis v. American Ass'n of Orthodontists*, 314 F.3d 758 (5th Cir. 2002) [orthodontist suspended from association membership for claims in flyers sent to public promoting his patented orthodontic bracket; dismiss claim of conspiracy to exclude brackets from market; no showing of concerted action].

71 *Oksanen v. Page Mem. Hosp.*, 945 F.2d 696 (4th Cir. 1991) (en banc), cert. denied, 502 U.S. 1074 (1992); *Weiss v. York Hosp.*, 745 F.2d 786 (3d Cir. 1984), cert. denied, 470 U.S. 1060 (1985); *Nanavati v. Burdette Tomlin Mem. Hosp.*, 857 F.2d 96 (3d Cir. 1988), cert. denied, 489 U.S. 1078 (1989); *Potters Med. Ctr. v. City Hosp. Ass'n*, 800 F.2d 568 (6th Cir. 1986); *Nurse Midwifery Assocs. v. Nibbett*, 918 F.2d 605 (6th Cir. 1990), modified on reh'g, 927 F.2d 904 (6th Cir.), cert. denied, 502 U.S. 952 (1991); *Pudlo v. Adamski*, 789 F. Supp. 247 (N.D. Ill. 1992), aff'd without op., 2 F.3d 1153, 1993 U.S. App. LEXIS 20, 442 (7th Cir. 1993), cert. denied, 510 U.S. 1072 (1994).

72 *Oksanen v. Page Mem. Hosp.*, supra, note 70.

73 *Nurse Midwifery Assocs. v. Nibbett*, supra, note 70; see also *Chiropractic Ass'n v. Trigon Healthcare, Inc.*, 367 F.3d 212 (4th Cir. 2004) [in challenge to health plan policies on coverage of chiropractic services, managed care advisory panel and health plan part of single entity, so could not conspire; independent personal stake exception does not apply where no power to bind corporation].

74 *Pudlo v. Adamski*, supra, note 70.

75 *Bolt v. Halifax Hosp. Med. Ctr.*, 851 F.2d 1273 (11th Cir.), vacated, 861 F.2d 1233 (11th Cir. 1989), reinstated in part, 874 F.2d 755 (11th Cir. 1989) (en banc), after remand, 891 F.2d 810 (11th Cir.), cert. denied, 495 U.S. 924 (1990); *Oltz v. St. Peter's Commun. Hosp.*, 861 F.2d 1440 (9th Cir. 1988).

76 E.g., *Willman v. Heartland Hosp.*, 34 F.3d 605 (8th Cir. 1994), cert. denied, 514 U.S. 1018 (1995); *Okusami v. Psychiatric Inst. of Wash., Inc.*, 959 F.2d 1062 (D.C. Cir. 1992).

77 15 U.S.C. § 2.

78 E.g., *United States v. Grinnell Corp.*, 384 U.S. 563 (1966); but see *United States v. Dentsply International, Inc.*, 277 F. Supp. 2d 387 (D. Del. 2003), appeal docketed, No. 03-4097 (3d Cir. 2004) [exclusive distributor contracts by manufacturer of over 75 percent of fabricated teeth not a violation because competitors could sell directly to labs, so contracts did not exclude rivals from market].

79 *Defiance Hosp. v. Fauster-Cameron, Inc.*, 344 F. Supp. 2d 1097 (N.D. Ohio 2004).

80 *Spectrum Sports, Inc. v. McQuillan*, 506 U.S. 447 (1993); *Copperweld Corp. v. Independence Tube Corp.*, 467 U.S. 752 (1984).

81 *Surgical Care Ctr. v. Hospital Service Dist. No. 1*, 309 F.3d 836 (5th Cir. 2002).

82 15 U.S.C. § 13.

83 15 U.S.C. § 13c.

84 *Abbott Labs. v. Portland Retail Druggists Ass'n, Inc.*, 425 U.S. 1 (1976).

85 Valley Baptist Medical Ctr., http://www.ftc.gov/os/2003/03/030313vbmc.htm (accessed Sept. 6, 2004).

86 *Rudner v. Abbott Labs.*, 664 F. Supp. 1100 (N.D. Ohio 1987).

87 *Jefferson County Pharmaceutical Ass'n, Inc. v. Abbott Labs.*, 460 U.S. 150 (1983).

88 *DeModena v. Kaiser Found. Health Plan, Inc.*, 743 F.2d 1388 (9th Cir. 1984), cert. denied, 469 U.S. 1229 (1985).

89 *United States v. Stewart*, 872 F.2d 957 (10th Cir. 1989).

90 15 U.S.C. § 14.

91 15 U.S.C. § 18.

92 1992 DOJ & FTC Guidelines, supra, note 18.

93 1994 DOJ/FTC Guidelines, Statement 1.

94 E.g., *FTC v. University Health, Inc.*, 938 F.2d 1206 (11th Cir. 1991) [HHI would increase by over 630 to 3,200].

95 *Hospital Corp. of Am. v. FTC*, 807 F.2d 1381 (7th Cir. 1986), cert. denied, 481 U.S. 1038 (1987).

96 E.g., Columbia, Health Trust will sell 3 Utah sites amid FTC discussions, Wall St. J., Feb. 17, 1995, B6.

97 E.g., *F.T.C. v. Columbia/HCA Healthcare Corp.*, No. 98 CV 1889 (D.D.C. July 30, 1998), as discussed in 7 H.L.R. 1239 (1998) [$2.5 million civil penalty for late divestiture of hospitals]; L. Legnado, Columbia agrees to pay $2.5 million FTC fine, Wall St. J., July 31, 1998, A3.

98 Florida, U.S. Department of Justice require hospitals to enter into enforcement order in consent decree case, National Ass'n of Attorneys General Antitrust Rept., July/Aug. 2000, 5.

99 McGinn, A first: FTC tells two nonprofit hospitals to separate, Am. Med. News, Oct. 7, 1989, 3.

100 *FTC v. University Health, Inc.*, 938 F.2d 1206 (11th Cir. 1991); see also *California Dental Ass'n v. FTC*, 526 U.S. 756 (1999) [under § 5, FTC has jurisdiction over nonprofit association providing economic benefit to for-profit members].

101 *United States v. Rockford Mem. Corp.*, 717 F. Supp. 1251 (N.D. Ill. 1989).

102 *United States v. Rockford Mem. Corp.*, 898 F.2d 1278 (7th Cir. 1990), cert. denied, 498 U.S. 920 (1990).

103 *United States v. Carilion Health Sys.*, 707 F. Supp. 840 (W.D. Va. 1989).

104 *United States v. Carilion Health Sys.*, 892 F.2d 1042 (without op.), 1989 U.S. App. LEXIS 17,911 (4th Cir.).

105 Burda, FTC files complaint against hospital merger, Mod. Healthcare, Nov. 17, 1989, 4 [challenge to merger in Ukiah, California].

106 *Ukiah Valley Med. Ctr. v. F.T.C.*, 911 F.2d 261 (9th Cir. 1990).

107 In re *Adventist Health Sys./West*, FTC Docket No. 9234 (A.L.J. Dec. 9, 1992).

108 In re *Adventist Health System/West*, FTC Docket No. 9234 (Apr. 1, 1994).

109 E.g., *FTC v. Freeman Hosp.*, 911 F. Supp. 1213 (W.D. Mo. 1995) [injunction of hospital merger denied].

110 See D. Ho, Government looks for ways to break losing streak in challenging hospital mergers, AP, Mar. 28, 2003.

111 http://www.ftc.gov/opa/2002/08/mergerlitigation.htm (accessed Sept. 6, 2004); R. Abelson, Merged hospitals gain both power and critics, N.Y. Times, Sept. 26, 2002, C1; R. Abelson, F.T.C. opens inquiry into hospital merger, N.Y. Times, Nov. 6, 2002, C4 [Poplar Bluff, Mo.].

112   *Evanston Northwest Healthcare Corp*, FTC Docket No. 9315 (2004); B. Japsen, FTC says merger of Chicago hospital operators violated antitrust laws, Chicago Trib., Feb. 11, 2004; B. Wysocki, FTC targets hospital merger in antitrust case, Wall St. J, Jan. 17, 2005, A1 [seeking to undo acquisition of Highland Park Hospital by Evanston Northwestern Healthcare Corp.].

113   Hospital group settles part of FTC complaint, AP, Jan. 19, 2005; Chicago-area doctors settle charges involving collective bargaining of fees, H.L.R., Apr. 7, 2005, 449 [In re *Evanston Northwestern Healthcare Corp.*, FTC Dkt. No. 9315 (Apr. 5, 2005)]; Judge voids suburban hospital merger, AP, Oct. 22, 2005 [In re *Evanston Northwestern Healthcare Corp.*, FTC Dkt. No. 9315 (Oct. 20, 2005)]; for documents in the *Evanston* case, see http://www.ftc.gov/os/adjpro/d9315/index.htm (accessed Nov. 1, 2005).

114   15 U.S.C. § 15.

115   15 U.S.C. § 45.

116   *Goldfarb v. Virginia State Bar Ass'n*, 421 U.S. 773 (1975).

117   42 U.S.C. § 11111(a)(1); Annotation, Construction and application of Health Care Quality Improvement Act of 1986, 121 A.L.R. Fed. 255.

118   Id.

119   *Parker v. Brown*, 317 U.S. 341 (1943).

120   *California Retail Liquor Dealers Ass'n v. Midcal Aluminum, Inc.*, 445 U.S. 97 (1980).

121   *Southern Motor Carriers Rate Conference, Inc. v. United States*, 471 U.S. 48 (1985).

122   *Town of Hallie v. City of Eau Claire*, 471 U.S. 34 (1985).

123   E.g., *Marrese v. Interqual, Inc.*, 748 F.2d 373 (7th Cir. 1984), cert. denied, 472 U.S. 1027 (1985).

124   *Patrick v. Burget*, 486 U.S. 94 (1988); see also *Shahawy v. Harrison*, 875 F.2d 1529 (11th Cir. 1989) [judicial supervision in Florida insufficient to provide state action immunity for medical staff actions]; *FTC v. Ticor Title Ins. Co.*, 504 U.S. 621 (1992) [state regulatory scheme insufficient to provide immunity for setting prices for title insurance].

125   E.g., *Bryan v. James E. Holmes Reg. Med. Ctr.*, 33 F.3d 1318 (11th Cir. 1994), cert. denied, 514 U.S. 1019 (1995).

126   *FTC v. University Health, Inc.*, 938 F.2d 1206 (11th Cir. 1991).

127   *Askew v. DCH Reg. Health Care Auth.*, 995 F.2d 1033 (11th Cir. 1993), cert. denied, 510 U.S. 1012 (1993).

128   *F.T.C. v. Hospital Bd. of Directors*, 38 F.3d 1184 (11th Cir. 1994).

129   E.g., *Lancaster Commun. Hosp. v. Antelope Valley Hosp. Dist.*, 940 F.2d 397 (9th Cir. 1991), cert. denied, 502 U.S. 1094 (1992).

130   *Surgical Care Ctr. of Hammond v. Hospital Serv. Dist No. 1*, 171 F.3d 231 (5th Cir. 1999) (en banc); but see *Jackson v. West Tennessee Healthcare, Inc.*, 2004 U.S. Dist. LEXIS 4571 (W.D. Tenn.) [state action immunity protected exclusive contract that kept competing hospital out of managed care arrangements].

131   E.g., *Cohn v. Bond*, 953 F.2d 154 (4th Cir. 1991), cert. denied, 505 U.S. 1230 (1992); *Todorov v. DCH Healthcare Auth.*, 921 F.2d 1438 (11th Cir. 1991); *Shaw v. Phelps County Reg. Med. Ctr.*, 858 F. Supp. 954 (E.D. Mo. 1994); *Crosby v. Hospital Auth. of Valdosta*, 873 F. Supp. 1568 (M.D. Ga. 1995) [government hospital, its officials protected in medical staff privilege case by state action immunity, Local Government Antitrust Act, and HCQIA].

132   *City of Columbia v. Omni Outdoor Advertising, Inc.*, 499 U.S. 365 (1991); *Bolt v. Halifax Hosp. Med. Ctr.*, 980 F.2d 1381 (11th Cir. 1993).

133   15 U.S.C. §§ 34-36.

134   E.g., *Sandcrest Outpatient Servs., P.A. v. Cumberland County Hosp. Sys., Inc.*, 853 F.2d 1139 (4th Cir. 1988).

135   *Bloom v. Hennepin County*, 783 F. Supp. 418 (D. Minn. 1992) [challenge by physician whose privileges were terminated when he ceased to be employed by group with exclusive contract; Act protected hospital from liability, state action doctrine protected from injunction].

136   E.g., Antitrust Immunity and Competitive Oversight, Substantive Rules and Procedural Rules (Washington Health Services Comm'n Jan. 26, 1995), as discussed in 23 Health L. Dig. (May 1995), at 19; Little activity seen under state laws granting antitrust immunity, 4 H.L.R. 303 (1995) [20 states have such laws, but only Minnesota, Maine had approved applications by Dec. 1994; table of laws at 333]; Health department drafts rules to implement new antitrust immunity, 4 H.L.R. 434 (1995) [Wyo.]; D. Burda, Mont. hospitals asking state for immunity, Mod. Healthcare, Mar. 6, 1995, 36.

137   E.g., AG approves joint venture between benefits, rival surgical center in Great Falls, Mont., 7 H.L.R. 91 (1998); In re *Inland Northwest Health Servs.* (Washington Health Servs. Comm'n Mar. 1995), In re *Inland Northwest Health Servs.* (Wash. Att'y Gen.) (informal op.), as discussed in 23 Health L. Dig. (May 1995), at 20.

138   *Eastern R.R. President's Conference v. Noerr Motor Freight, Inc.*, 365 U.S. 127 (1961); *United Mine Workers v. Pennington*, 381 U.S. 657 (1965); *Boulware v. State*, 960 F.2d 793 (9th Cir. 1992) [opposition to physician construction of MRI facility].

139   *St. Joseph's Hosp. v. Hospital Corp. of Am.*, 795 F.2d 948 (11th Cir. 1986), reh'g denied (en banc), 801 F.2d 404 (11th Cir. 1986); see also *Kottle v. Northwest Kidney Ctrs.*, 146 F.2d 1056 (9th Cir. 1998), cert. denied, 525 U.S. 1140 (1999) [Noerr-Pennington doctrine protects competitor opposition to issuance of CON].

140   *Otter Tail Power Co. v. United States*, 410 U.S. 366 (1973).

141   *Professional Real Estate Inv., Inc. v. Columbia Pictures Indus., Inc.*, 508 U.S. 49 (1993).

142   15 U.S.C. § 1012(b).

143   *Group Life & Health Ins. Co. v. Royal Drug*, 440 U.S. 205 (1979).

144   *Jung v. Association of Am. Med. Colleges*, 300 F. Supp. 2d 119 (D.D.C. 2004), 339 F. Supp. 2d 26 (D.D.C. 2004) [barred by new law], 226 F.R.D. 7 (D.D.C. 2005) [not permitted to amend complaint]; 15 U.S.C. § 37b.

145   *National Gerimedical Hosp. v. Blue Cross*, 452 U.S. 378 (1981).

146   *North Carolina ex rel. Edmisten v. P.I.A. Asheville, Inc.*, 740 F.2d 274 (4th Cir. 1984), cert. denied, 471 U.S. 1003 (1985).

147   *American Academic Suppliers, Inc. v. Beckley-Cardy, Inc.*, 699 F. Supp. 152 (N.D. Ill. 1988).

Chapter 15

What Is Bioethics?

Mary Rose Jeffry

Key Learning Objectives

By the end of this chapter, the reader will be able to:

- Provide a philosophical and historical perspective on the topic of bioethics.

- Explain key terms used in bioethics and their application.

- Describe how bioethical principles are applied in healthcare settings.

- Explain the range of legal processes and documents used to help patients (and their legal representatives) make critical healthcare decisions.

- Understand bioethics in light of rapidly expanding knowledge in the fields of scientific medicine, including biology, genomics, etc., and applied medicine, including surgery, pharmacology, etc.

Chapter Outline

Introduction

Classic medical ethics is part of the Hippocratic tradition, which is understood as the ethics of the physician-patient relationship. Traditionally, medical ethics was viewed from the perspective of an individual doctor's behavior and character. The profession of medicine required a doctor to be both socially responsible and professionally competent. Medical ethics became almost synonymous with the rules for professional cohesion and respectability.

Bioethics emerged as a field during a time of important developments in culture and science. These developments presented a staggering range of difficult and seemingly new moral problems. Advancements in medicine and the life sciences raised questions that went beyond the framework of the Hippocratic tradition. Bioethics went beyond the individualistic ethics of the physician-patient relationship. The field of bioethics grew to involve questions of social nature, such as the ethics of medical research, the power of medicine to greatly prolong life, to transform the essential human experiences of reproduction, to change the very definition of personal identity in genetics, and to raise questions of a theological nature through the techniques of germ line, human genetic engineering.

Society needs a public set of criteria for moral decision making that can be defined and argued rationally. Philosophy provides the form for the rational, argumentative justification of medical decision making. Religious traditions become relevant insofar as they are able to convey theological and moral arguments for medical decision making. Law and public policy provide a body of principles and regulations for medical decision making. Bioethics provides an interdisciplinary argument examining the ethical criteria of human dignity, beneficence, nonmaleficence, autonomy, and justice.

Bioethics is a discipline for addressing society's response to these great changes. It examines ethical issues at the heart and cutting edge of modern medicine, technology, and the life sciences. ⚑ The public character of bioethics generates the need for interdisciplinary analysis. Disciplines that traditionally participate in the interdisciplinary discourse of bioethics include, but are not limited to, theology, philosophy, medicine, law, and biology.

So what exactly is bioethics? The Oxford English dictionary defines it as "the discipline dealing with ethical questions that arise as a result of advances in medicine and biology." In 1977, the philosopher, Samuel Gorovitz defined bioethics as "the critical examination of the moral dimensions of decision making in health-related contexts and in contexts involving the biological sciences."[1]

> A modern philosopher, Samuel Gorovitz defines "bioethics" as the examination of moral dimensions for decision making in the contexts of health and the biological sciences.

Finding the exact foundation of bioethics is difficult. Many disciplines and professions are necessary if one seeks to find a way through the challenges and opportunities of modern medicine. Whatever name we choose to give to the moral reflection needed in this era of health care and modern medicine, such reflection cannot thrive in isolation. Moral life in modern times is multi-dimensional because human relationships are multi-dimensional. A critical question is: What is a good moral decision and is there such a thing as human good? Biomedical, social, and environmental sciences present new choices and new moral dilemmas, forcing us to confront how we view human nature and the value of human life. As Edmond Pelligrino puts it: "There seems little question that the complex nature of the problems associated with the applications of biological knowledge to human affairs will continue to pose ethical questions and that their resolution will require some form of collaborative effort between almost every human discipline."[2]

Chapter Outline

15-1 The Language of Bioethics

Language is used in many different ways to communicate meaning. The meaning is tied to what is happening when the specific language is being used. Just as the disciplines of law, medicine, theology, philosophy, and science have their specific language so does the discipline of bioethics. ⚑ The following section will introduce you to some of the commonly used terms in bioethics so that you may understand the meaning behind the language used.

15-1.1 Justice

In bioethics, there are three distinct types of justice: distributive, communicative, and contributive justice. Distributive justice is the most commonly used term used in bioethical discussions. This poses the question as to what society owes an individual. An individual may be thought of as a single person or as an organization or group. The major dilemma here is who has access to health care and how healthcare resources are to be distributed to individuals in society at large.

The next type of justice is communicative justice. This addresses the questions of the exchange of goods and services between individuals and groups. Questions are asked about the costs of medicines and procedures, the services of healthcare professionals, and the cost and availability of healthcare insurance.

Finally, there is contributive justice. This involves the individual's responsibility to society. What does an individual owe to society? How much tax should be imposed on an individual or group to pay for health care? Do individuals bear any responsibility for their life style decisions such as smoking and risky behaviors as well as their medical conditions such as obesity and AIDS

and the associated costs of treating these conditions? These areas of justice are discussed and analyzed while discussing health care and its costs and availability to the individuals in society.

15-1.2 Beneficence and Nonmaleficence

Beneficence and nonmaleficence are other terms used in bioethics discussions. Nonmaleficence is the technical term used to state that we have an obligation to do no harm to the patient. This is one of the most basic of all medical ethical terms. It is derived from the Hippocratic tradition dating to ancient Greek of "First of all, do no harm." The harm we understand today is both physical and mental harm to the patient through the quality of the medical care provided.

Beneficence is the positive dimension of nonmaleficence. The principle of beneficence involves the duty to regard the welfare of others and to be of assistance to them as they fulfill their potential. In a medical sense, we understand that to mean the provision of necessary and appropriate treatment to achieve a good clinical outcome.

15-1.3 Human Dignity

Human dignity is a term that is used in many different contexts, both in bioethics and society at large. It is a difficult term to succinctly define since it can take on many different meanings depending on the context in which it is used. The Latin root of the word "dignity" is from the words *dignitas* and *dingus,* which mean worth and worthy. Therefore, human dignity may be considered to be the value or worth attributed to human life. Some people attribute human dignity to individuals because they have some value to society. Other people focus on human dignity from the theological perspective in that individuals have an intrinsic dignity by virtue of being created by God.

> There are many contexts in bioethics that involve human dignity.

The concept of human dignity arises in many bioethical contexts. There are the beginning of life concerns of abortion, reproduction technologies, and embryonic stem cell research. Then there are the end-of-life concerns of forgoing and withdrawing treatment, palliative care, euthanasia, and physician-assisted suicide. Even though human dignity is elusive in its exact meaning, it is still a central concept in bioethics with multiple implications.

15-2 Health Insurance Portability and Accountability Act (HIPAA)

Among these implications is respect for the right of patients to maintain the privacy of information about their health, including medical records. In 1996, the Health Insurance Portability and Accountability Act (HIPAA) recognized these rights and Congress directed the Secretary of Health and Human Services to develop regulations to ensure that protected health information, or PHI, would be protected from improper use or disclosure. Since then, regulations known as the HIPAA Privacy Rule and the HIPAA Security Rule have been put in place and govern the use and disclosure of PHI. States also regulate the privacy and security of medical information. In general, if there is a conflict between a federal and state privacy requirement, and the state law is more restrictive, then the more restrictive requirement applies. HIPAA establishes specific rights for patients with regard to their PHI, generally referred to as "medical records." Patients may see and receive copies of their medical records. Patients may request corrections to their medical records. Patients must receive a notice from providers about how their PHI will be used and disclosed. Patients may request to be asked permission before their health information is shared for marketing purposes. Patients may request an accounting of how their PHI has been shared for something other than treatment, healthcare operations, or payment purposes.

Unauthorized use or disclosure of PHI is subject to both civil and criminal sanctions under HIPAA. In addition to HIPAA, the Health Information Technology for Economic and Clinical Health (HITECH) Act, promulgated as part of the American Reinvestment and Recovery Act of 2009, specifically addresses protections to prevent unauthorized access to and use of electronic PHI as part of efforts to increase the use of electronic medical records. It also created a tiered system of penalties for violations of HIPAA and HITECH, based on the level of knowledge and culpability of the actors.

15-3 Genetic Information Nondiscrimination Act

The Genetic Information Nondiscrimination Act of 2008 (GINA) expands HIPAA protections explicitly to genetic information. GINA prohibits health insurers or employers from using such information to discriminate in providing health insurance or employment, subject to various exceptions.

15-4 Principle of Autonomy

In the older tradition of practicing medicine, physicians were the authorities and made the paramount moral value decisions. The physician was charged with the responsibility to do good for their patients. Tradition argues that the physician knows more, has more experience, and that illness clouds the patient's ability to think clearly and rationally.

The principle of autonomy has replaced this traditional thinking in decisions in health care. The primary responsibility for decision making lies with the individual. In their book *Principles of Biomedical Ethics*,[3] Beauchamp and Childress define autonomy as a form of personal liberty or action in which the individual determines his or her course of action in accordance with a plan of his or her own choosing. Autonomy mandates a strong sense of personal responsibility for our own lives. It also requires that we accept the consequences of the decisions we make.

However, in the delivery of health care, there is often a clash between autonomy and beneficence, what is medically considered best for the patient. In cases such as these, autonomy usually wins. The classic medical example is the case of a Jehovah's Witness coming into an emergency ward with a life-threatening injury. A core belief of a Jehovah's Witness is that they are not to receive any blood or blood products other than their own. They often carry a card with them that states this belief. In an emergency situation, the delivery of blood transfusions will often make a difference as to whether an individual will live or die. In this case, the omission of what is considered standard medical treatment is not allowed and the individual dies.

Sometimes the principle of autonomy can be pushed to an unreasonable point. An individual may demand medically inappropriate treatment or engage in behavior that is counter-productive to the treatment being given. The best way to avoid this type of situation is to develop a relationship with the healthcare provider that allows for shared decision making.

The mere fact that an individual exercises his or her right to choose what will be done to his or her own body does not necessarily justify the morality of that choice. It is not sufficient to state that this is what the individual wishes and therefore it is the right and appropriate thing to do.

The true test of what is the right thing to do is whether what is done achieves the good, not whether the individual autonomously chooses it him- or herself.

A major component in autonomy of decision making in health care is the concept of informed consent.

> Informed consent is a process by which a fully informed patient can participate in healthcare choices.

Informed consent is a process by which a fully informed patient can participate in choices about his or her health care. It originates from the legal and ethical right the patient has to direct what happens to his or her body and from the ethical duty of the physician to involve the patient in this process. The physician has an ethical obligation to help the patient make choices from among the therapeutic alternatives, consistent with good medical practice. Informed consent is a basic policy in both ethics and law that physicians must honor, unless the patient requests not to be informed, or is incapable of consenting and harm from failure to treat is imminent. In rare circumstances, it may be appropriate to postpone disclosure of information to the patient.

◣ The consent process typically has three elements: information, comprehension of that information, and voluntariness. In order for an individual's consent to be considered legally valid, he or she must be given the appropriate information to make a decision, and be considered competent to make the decision at hand, and the consent must be voluntary.

It is generally accepted that a complete informed consent includes a discussion of the necessary information needed to make a decision. It should include, but not be limited to, the following:

1. a description in as ordinary language as possible of the nature of the proposed decision and or the description of the procedure;

2. reasonable alternatives to the proposed intervention; and

3. the relevant risks, benefits, and uncertainties related to each alternative.

Even if an individual has the necessary medical information, he or she must nevertheless be considered capable of making a decision.

> "Capacity" to decide, under the law, means an individual's ability to understand the nature and consequences of decisions and to communicate the decisions.

Capacity defined under the law means a person's ability to understand the nature and consequences of decisions and to make and communicate a decision.[4] Capacity includes, in the case of proposed health care, the ability to understand its significant benefits, risks, and alternatives.

The patient's primary treating physician should be the one responsible for determining whether the patient has the capacity to make a healthcare decision. The patient should be able to demonstrate a basic understanding of the treatment information with respect to the proposed treatment. Does the patient understand the nature and seriousness of the underlying illness? Does the patient understand the proposed medical treatment? Does the patient understand the probable degree and duration of any benefits and risks of the proposed medical treatment, the consequences of the lack of treatment, and the nature of risks and benefits of any reasonable alternatives? There are also legal factors that should be considered by the primary care physician. Does the patient respond knowingly and intelligently to questions about the proposed medical treatment? Does the patient participate in the treatment decision by means of a rational thought process?

Finally, once it is determined that the patient has the appropriate information and has demonstrated the capacity to understand that information, the consent must be given voluntarily. There can be no undue pressure from the physician, family, or friends that influences the patient in their medical decision making related to the consent.

15-4.1 Advance Directives

Advance directives (ADs) are the continuation of the principle of patient autonomy. Patients have the ability to predetermine medical decisions regarding their treatment in the event they are unable to make them. This includes decisions not to take action. ADs are also used in conjunction with a Durable Power of Attorney for Health Care.

◣ In 1991, the Federal Patient Self-Determination Act took effect, requiring healthcare institutions to ask all adults, admitted as inpatients to their facilities, whether they have an AD and to inform them of their right to refuse treatments. This law has three primary purposes:

- To educate the public about state laws governing the refusal, withholding, and withdrawal of treatment at the end of life.

- To encourage wider use of ADs to prevent the uncertainty among physicians and other healthcare providers and family members in the treatment of the patient. Unwanted treatment can unnecessarily prolong the dying process. In some cases, misinterpretation of the patient's wishes and perceived standard of care in medicine can lead to lengthy court battles.

- To help contain costs of treatment at the end of life by reducing unwanted and unnecessary intervention and address physicians' perceptions of the need to practice defensive medicine.

15-4.2 Durable Power of Attorney for Health Care

A Durable Power of Attorney for Health Care (DPAHC) is a document in which one person (the patient) names another person (the agent) to make decisions about his or her health care. A DPAHC remains legally effective or becomes effective when the patient becomes incapable of making healthcare decisions. A DPAHC differs from a living will in that it focuses on the decision-making process and not on a specific decision. Accordingly, the power of attorney can cover a broad range of healthcare decisions.

Once in effect, the agent can review medical records, serve as an advocate, discuss care with the medical staff, and decide what the patient would want or what is in the best interest of the patient. The DPAHC may include a living will provision—a description of healthcare preferences—or any other instructions.

15-5 Patient's Bill of Rights and Responsibilities

An important development in the area of bioethics is the patient's rights movement. There are several sources, addressed below, that describe these rights in the context of access, treatment, and payment.

For example, The Patient Protection and Affordable Care Act (sometimes referred to as "PPACA," or as the "Affordable Care Act" ("ACA")) was signed by President Obama on March 23, 2010. The U.S. Supreme Court

decided on June 28, 2012 to uphold the ACA. That health reform legislation includes many provisions that one can consider as a "Patient's Bill of Rights."[5]

The following list briefly describes rights that individuals have under the ACA, especially in terms of coverage, access, and cost;

- Access to coverage for those with pre-existing conditions;

- Young adults (under 26 years) may be covered on their parents' health plan;

- Removes lifetime limits on coverage for most health benefits;

- Removes pre-existing exclusions in certain situations (e.g., children);

- Ends certain insurance coverage withdrawals (also referred to as "recissions");

- Establishes mandatory levels of expenditures for health services by health plans as a percentage of health insurance premiums collected.

In addition to ACA, a Patients' Bill of Rights and Responsibilities was created in 1973 by the American Hospital Association and approved by The Joint Commission in 1991, with amendments in 2005.[6] The preamble to that document states:

"The basic rights of human beings for independence of expression, decision, action and concern for personal dignity and human relationships are always of great importance. During sickness, however, the presence or absence of these rights becomes a vital, deciding factor in survival and recovery. Thus, it becomes a prime responsibility for hospitals to endeavor to assure that these rights are preserved for their patients."

Following this preamble, the document lists both patients' rights and responsibilities.

The patients' rights are to be supported both by medical treatment facility (MTF) and dental treatment facility (DTF) personnel. The list of patients' rights concisely describes the following:

- Right to quality care and treatment consistent with available resources and generally accepted standards. Right to refuse treatment, consistent with legal standards and government.

- Right to privacy and confidentiality concerning medical care.

- Right to respectful treatment.

- Right to know the identities and credentials of the healthcare personnel involved with the patient's care.

- Right to receive information pertaining to the patient's care.

- Right to receive pain assessment and management.

- Right to be involved in decisions about care, treatment, and services provided, and to be properly informed before consenting to treatment.

- Right to receive information about advanced directives.

- Right to care and treatment in a safe environment.

The AHA and TJC document also explains patients' responsibilities, since providing quality health care is a complex task that requires communication, cooperation, and assumption of responsibilities by both sides. Thus, responsibilities of patients include:

- Provide information about his or her health status, medications, past illnesses, etc., to healthcare personnel

- Behave in a respectful and considerate manner when interacting with healthcare personnel, hospital property, and other patients

- Comply with medical and/or dental care

- Participate with healthcare personnel to discuss, plan, and follow a pain management plan, as needed

- Follow the MTF or DTF rules and regulations, including rules regarding smoking

15-6 Beginning-of-Life Issues

15-6.1 Wrongful Birth and Wrongful Life

The development of genetic tests that make it possible to determine, at very early stages of pregnancy, whether a child will be born with a potentially incapacitating genetic disorder also creates a complex and ethically challenging area of litigation: "wrongful birth" and "wrongful life" claims. The discovery of certain genetic disorders such as Down's syndrome and other trisomies, microcephaly, or Tay-Sachs disease or other fetal malformations such as neural tube disorders leads some parents to terminate pregnancies. But because such tests are not error-proof, in certain cases infants are born with severe disabilities that parents may believe to have been ruled out by genetic testing.

Such situations give rise to claims of wrongful birth or wrongful life. In such claims, the plaintiff—the parent in a wrongful birth claim and the child in a wrongful life claim—asserts that the party performing the test made a mistake. The allegation is that the mistake was negligent and that the pregnancy would have been terminated if there had not been a mistake. The allegation continues to assert that costs associated with raising a child with a severe disability could have been avoided. Or, framed more starkly, the child would not have existed, and as such, the plaintiff should be compensated for the costs associated with raising and caring for the child.

Despite their origin in the same negligent act, states treat actions for wrongful births and those for wrongful life differently. Many states recognize wrongful birth as falling within the realm of the traditional tort of negligence. The claim encompasses negligent sterilization claims and negligent genetic counseling. It also includes claims arising out of the failure to detect fetal abnormalities in sufficient time for the parents to determine whether or not to carry the pregnancy to term. In those cases, where courts recognize the cause of action, it is often based on the broader right to choose whether or not to carry a pregnancy to term. In wrongful birth cases, courts award damages to plaintiffs as an incentive to providers (the usual defendants in such cases) to provide quality prenatal care and genetic testing. Wrongful life cases, on the other hand, are perceived as requiring a judgment that the plaintiff would have been better off not existing. Courts have been predictably reluctant to come to this conclusion in wrongful life cases.[7]

"BABY DOE" LAWS AND THE BORN-ALIVE INFANT PROTECTION ACT. In the early 1980s, an Indiana child was born with Down's syndrome and a surgically correctable intestinal malformation common to babies with that condition. The parents elected not to have surgery performed on the child. The mother indicated to the doctors that she did not want this child. For this reason, the parents refused to consent to the surgery to save the child's life. The hospital staff did not seek a court order to override their decision. The child was put in a side room and, after eleven days, died of starvation.[8]

In response to this case, Congress amended the Child Abuse Prevention and Treatment Act (CAPTA).[9] Under CAPTA, states that receive federal child abuse prevention funds must have provisions in place to detect and prevent withholding of life-saving treatment from disabled children. Those provisions must include "authority to initiate legal proceedings. . . as may be necessary to prevent the withholding of medically indicated treatment."[10] The requirement does not apply in certain situations defined in regulation. One of those situations is when an infant is "chronically and irreversibly" comatose. In that situation, the care would merely prolong imminent death or treatment itself would be inhumane.

▶ These laws are significant because they conflict with the widely established principle that parents have broad discretion to make medical decisions for their children.[11] Further, within the medical profession, many have criticized the law's interference with physicians' discretion to determine the best interests of their patients.[12]

BORN-ALIVE INFANT PROTECTION ACT. In addition to the federal Baby Doe laws and state laws and regulations that followed, the Born-Alive Infant Protection Act (BAIPA) was enacted in 2002. BAIPA added a section to federal law clarifying that "person, human being, child, or individual" includes infants born at any stage of development, whether as a result of early labor, caesarian section, or an induced abortion. This definition implicates the medical neglect provision of CAPTA described above because BAIPA broadly defines when a child is "born alive," including whether the child "breathes or has a beating heart, pulsation of the umbilical cord, or definite movement of voluntary muscles."[13] Thus, even a child born without brain activity could be considered a "born-alive" infant subject to the protections of CAPTA.

EMERGENCY MEDICAL TREATMENT AND LABOR ACT (EMTALA). In 2005, the Centers for Medicare and Medicaid Services (CMS) issued a letter to state survey agency directors that noted BAIPA's addition of born-alive infants to the definition of "individual." CMS emphasized that BAIPA brought such infants under the protection of the Emergency Medical Treatment and Labor Act (EMTALA). Concerns have been raised that in certain situations an infant may be born alive within the meaning of the definition added by BAIPA, but that hospitals have failed to comply with the screening and stabilization requirements of EMTALA. In such situations, a request might be made on an infant's behalf for screening for an emergency medical condition. Or, a prudent layperson might conclude, based on the infant's appearance or behavior, that the infant needed examination or treatment for an emergency medical condition. In that case, a request might be made for a screening exam and, if indicated, stabilization care. Further, a hospital or physician may

be liable for violating EMTALA if the required screening examination is not provided.[14] Arguably, an EMTALA whistleblower could initiate investigations of failures to provide care to infants who, as defined in BAIPA, have no chance of survival. As a result of this legal framework, infants may receive futile care and experience suffering while succumbing to an unavoidable death. Even the most medically compromised infants, who experience extreme pain and suffering, can never be denied their dignity and respect by receiving futile treatment.

15-7 End-of-Life Issues

15-7.1 Definition of Death

Through advances in modern technology, public sanitation, clean drinking water, and modern medicine, our generation has the ability to prolong the dying process. A renowned medical economist, Uwe Reinhardt, once lamented in a speech that because of our love of medical technology, the prevailing view in America was that death, which once used to be part of the life process, is now optional in America.[15]

15-7.2 Uniform Determination of Death Act

The Uniform Determination of Death Act is a model law approved in the United States in 1981 by the National Conference of Commissioners on Uniform State Laws, in cooperation with the American Medical Association, the American Bar Association, and the President's Commission for the Study of Ethical Problems in Medicine and Biomedical and Behavioral Research. ▶ The Act has been adopted by most U.S. states and provides a uniform definition of death: "An individual who has sustained either (1) irreversible cessation of circulatory and respiratory function, or (2) irreversible cessation of all function of the entire brain, including the brain stem. A determination of death must be made in accordance with accepted medical standards."[16]

The use of respirators and other life support systems complicates the definition and recognition of death. The use of technology clouds the traditional criteria of death which was the spontaneous cessation of breathing and heartbeat. Is this criterion even relevant now that machines perform those vital bodily functions to sustain life? As the growth of life-sustaining technology continues, it becomes necessary to examine the definition of death as well as the criteria used to make this pronouncement. It is important to give the medical community the responsibility for determining the criteria for death, while at the same time, allowing for criteria to change as knowledge and technology continue to evolve.

15-7.3 Ordinary and Extraordinary Means

The idea of ordinary and extraordinary means originated in the tradition of Roman Catholic moral theology when medical treatments were much simpler. It provided a framework for the acceptance or rejection of proposed medical treatments. The basic principle was that although human life is sacred and valuable, moral ethics does not require a person to use extraordinary measures to preserve it. Therefore, if a patient decided to forgo extraordinary treatment, the physician who adhered to the patient's wishes by either withdrawing or withholding treatment was acting morally, even if death ensued. On the other hand, if the patient's wishes were to forgo what was considered ordinary treatment, it would not be morally justified.

In modern medicine, the question arises as to how do we determine what ordinary treatment is and what is extraordinary?

> With continuous advances in medical science and technology, it is increasingly difficult to describe the difference between "ordinary" and "extraordinary" treatment.

With the advancements in medical technologies there is no longer a way to easily make this distinction. Therefore, the distinction between ordinary and extraordinary must be evaluated through the use of prudent and moral reasoning to determine what achieves the greatest human good. This determination will vary from individual to individual.

15-7.4 Medical Futility

Futile treatment was not considered a problem until recently. If a physician thought that a treatment was futile, then he would not provide it. It is the evolution of patient autonomy, self-determination, and medical information from the Internet that has created this conflict. The solution is to attempt to determine the meaning of futility.

Medical futility refers to interventions that are unlikely to produce significant benefit for the patient. The ethical

authority to render futility judgments rests primarily with the medical profession as a whole, not with individual physicians at the bedside. Thus, futility determinations in specific cases must conform to the general professional standard of care. A patient may decide that a particular outcome is not worth striving for and reject a treatment. This decision may be based solely on personal preferences, not necessarily on futility.

Physicians are not ethically obligated to deliver care that, in their best professional judgment, does not have a reasonable chance of helping their patients. In most cases, the distinction between effective and futile treatment is not so clear. Patients should not be given treatments simply because they demand them. Denial of treatment should be justified by reliance on openly stated ethical principles and acceptable standards of care and not on the concept of "futility," which cannot be meaningfully defined. In March 1999, the American Medical Association's Council on Ethical and Judicial Affairs issued a report that recommended that institutions avoid policies that try and define futility and instead develop a fair and open multi-step process to resolve conflicts about treatments at the end of life.[17]

Conflicts between patients and physicians, as well as between patients and the institution, may arise when trying to determine what futility is in a particular instance. Such conflicts often interrupt satisfactory decision making and adversely affect patient care, family satisfaction, and physician-clinical team functioning. To assist in fair and satisfactory decision making about what constitutes futile intervention, all healthcare institutions should adopt a policy on medical futility that should follow a due process approach.

The AMA policy guidelines for developing a policy on medical futility suggest the following seven steps as a "due process" approach for deciding futility in specific cases:[18]

1. Earnest attempts should be made in advance to deliberate over and negotiate prior understandings between patient, proxy, and physician on what constitutes futile care for the patient and what falls within acceptable limits for the physician, family, and possibly also the institution.

2. Joint decision making should occur between the patient or proxy and physician to the maximum extent possible.

3. Attempts should be made to negotiate disagreements if they arise and to reach resolutions within all parties' acceptable limits, with the assistance of consultants, as appropriate.

4. Involvement of an institutional committee such as a bioethics committee should be requested if disagreements are irresolvable.

5. If the institutional review supports the patient's position and the physician is not persuaded, transfer of care to another physician within the institution may be arranged.

6. If the process supports the physician's position and the patient and or proxy remains not persuaded, transfer to another institution may be sought and, if done, should be supported by the transferring and receiving institution.

7. If transfer is not possible, the intervention treatment may not be offered.

15-8 Other Bioethical Issues

15-8.1 Organ Transplantation

Surgeons have been inserting organs, tissues, and other artificial devices into their patients for several decades. With the advancement of both technology and the development of anti-rejection drugs, the number and types of body parts being transplanted have increased. Organ transplantation directly implicates the need for bioethical discourse, both clinically and institutionally. The need for organs far exceeds the availability of viable organs for transplantation. According to the national Organ Procurement and Transplantation Network (OPTN), as of September 24, 2010, there were 108,725 people in the United States awaiting an organ transplant. Through mid-September of this year, 14,140 people had received needed donations from 7,136 donors.[19] On a federal level, the National Organ Transplant Act established the OPTN, which maintains a national registry of people awaiting transplants, determines medical criteria for determining the relative medical need of patients for transplants, helps to coordinate donations between states, and forbids commercial transactions in organs.[20] In addition, the Organ Donation Recovery and Improvement Act of 2004, which was passed but has not been funded, sought to publicize the need for organ donations and encourage individuals to donate.[21]

15-8.2 Clinical Research

Research involving both animals and humans is an important part of modern medicine. New techniques, technologies, and new drugs are routinely tested on humans and evaluated before a physician is able to use them in a normal clinical practice. Bioethics has the duty to ask whether the actual or potential harms caused by this research are reasonable and consistent with the good of the patient.

There are two different kinds of research conducted on patients. The first is nontherapeutic research. In this research the subjects are not ill, or if they are sick, there is no real expectation of any benefit to them from the research. The second is therapeutic research where the subjects are sick and the hope is that the research will benefit them and also provide knowledge of this benefit for others.

Current bioethical awareness of clinical research on human subjects and associated laws and regulations regarding this activity evolved in response to many abuses of human subjects who participate in clinical research projects. There is much to be learned from remembering how medical research became unethical. A fundamental reason is the desire to achieve scientific knowledge and medical progress at the expense of the moral dignity and well-being of the patients involved.

One of the most notorious examples of questionable ethics in research is the Tuskegee Syphilis Study, which was conducted from 1932–1972. The U.S. Public Health Service wanted to find out how lethal syphilis could be if not treated. The study included African American men with syphilis and compared the health and longevity of people infected with the disease and those not infected, but the government denied the men treatment long after an effective cure became available. In 1972 when the details of this studied became public it sparked tremendous shock and outrage.[22] In response, Congress passed the National Research Act,[23] creating the National Commission for the Protection of Human Subjects of Biomedical and Behavioral Research. The commission drafted a document that laid out the fundamental framework for research involving human subjects in the United States known as the Belmont Report.

Nonetheless, ethical controversies involving human subjects continue to arise. In the mid-1990s the Kennedy-Krieger Institute and Johns Hopkins University conducted a study of lead paint abatement methods that led to a lawsuit against the institution that alleged ethical violations.[24]

Currently, the Department of Health and Human Service's Office of Human Subjects Research oversees the issuance of federal-wide assurances (FWAs) of adherence to human subjects' research protection policies.[25]

Any research conducted by a federal agency or with federal support must adhere to the federal regulations governing the ethical conduct of research.

The basic tenets of these regulations are the individuals participating in the study must give their informed consent to participate. In addition, the study must be reviewed for ethical compliance by an Institutional Review Board (IRB). The regulations provide additional protection for institutionalized subjects, including prisoners, mental health patients, pregnant women, fetuses, newborns, and children. In its role as an institutional watchdog, the IRB serves a critical function in ensuring that research involving human subjects continues in an ethical manner.

Despite this, errors in research will occur. Even though the IRB does its best to protect research subjects, it is the responsibility of any person participating in a clinical trial to be proactive in protecting their own health. Participants should keep notes on their current health and any changes they notice in their health status. Additionally, participants should not be afraid to speak up and ask questions about the study and how it affects them. Finally, participants should realize that they can withdraw from the study at any time.

15-8.3 Genetic Medicine

Medical genetics is the aspect of human genetics that is concerned with the relationship between heredity and disease.[26] Some of the more common areas of medical genetics study are diagnosis of genetic diseases (e.g., prenatal screening), elimination of disease-related traits, gene therapy, and stem cell research. Medical genetics is often associated with biotechnology in the fields of embryonic stem cell research and human cloning.

Biotechnology pursuits and genetic information are growing at an exponential rate. These fields of study are continually changing with new information and possible applications surfacing nearly daily. One hardly has time to analyze the newest discovery before another one is announced.

With the rapid growth in these areas of research and its potential impact on human society, a number of important questions need to be addressed:

- How will we protect the confidentiality of a person's genetic information?
- Should we apply new technology involved in gene therapy to enhancing ourselves?
- Who owns the rights to the genes and their sequences once they are discovered?
- Who will have fair access to the new biotechnologies once they are developed?
- Will we discriminate on the basis of genetic makeup?[27]

We have become a country of high-tech, high-cost "rescue" medicine that contributes to escalating costs, and the emphasis is largely focused on the cure rather than prevention. It makes for much better press to talk about the latest breakthrough in genetic research rather than exercise and healthy eating. But the fact remains that curing is an attempt to reverse the harm done by the disease, a process much more complex than attempts to prevent the disease initially. Perhaps the ethical focus should not be on the development of genetic medicine but on the high-tech, high-cost, defensive medicine that is practiced today. Poverty and lack of health care are major contributors to diseases. Maybe it is time to focus on prevention of disease and access to health care. Genetic and biotechnology research will continue to bring benefits to many. However, there will be members of society who will not share in these benefits without access to health care.

15-9 The Bioethics Committee

The typical bioethics committee includes physicians on the medical staff along with nurses and others on the healthcare delivery team, including nurses and case managers, and there should be at least one community member, preferably with a background in theology, philosophy, or a related discipline. Other members may include hospital administration and compliance, legal, and risk management staff.

The function of the bioethics committee is to provide advice and guidance on institutional bioethics and situational bioethics. Institutional bioethics involves the development and application of ethical principles in the medical facility. The bioethics committee provides education to the medical staff and members of the healthcare team, patients, and employees. Requests for consultation may come from the physician, the patient or a member of their family, or an employee of the facility. The consultation initially may be handled by a clinical ethicist. As necessary, a subcommittee of the bioethics committee may be specially convened. This step may be needed for consultation on a particular case where it is necessary to distinguish medical decisions from legal decisions. The bioethics committee sometimes makes recommendations regarding guidelines and policy and suggests methods to implement regulatory requirements.

⚑ Situational bioethics involves a consultation process to aid in the resolution of ethical conflicts in the delivery of care and management of patients. This is the key role for most bioethics committees. As necessary, a subcommittee of the bioethics committee may be specially convened to consult on a particular case. The committee's role is advisory and its recommendations are not binding on the attending physician, the patient, or their representative decision maker. Nevertheless, the bioethics committee can assist in resolving conflicts between treating physicians and patients or their families as well as others on the healthcare team. The bioethics committee can also provide guidance to physicians or others faced with difficult decisions involving complex ethical considerations.

Chapter Summary

This chapter covered the history and evolution of the field and discipline of "bioethics." That evolution continues today and is largely driven by the continuous and rapid changes in societal norms, medical experimentation, and proven advances in medical science. There are also many individual healthcare situations that require careful and thoughtful decisions. Some of the key laws, ethical principles, and options for making those decisions were explored in this chapter. This chapter reinforced the inherent individualistic nature of diseases, illness, and options to treat or withhold treatment and explained the important role of bioethics in institutions and individual patient cases.

Key Terms and Definitions

Advance Directive (AD) - A method to indicate, in advance, treatment preferences and the substitute (or surrogate) who will make decisions if a person becomes incapable of making decisions. There are three general categories of advance directives: living will, durable power of attorney for health care (DPAHC), and healthcare proxy.

Beneficence - Action taken for the benefit of others. Beneficent actions can be taken to help prevent or remove harm or to improve the situation of others.

Bioethics - The discipline dealing with ethical questions that arise as a result of advances in medicine and biology, or the critical examination of moral dimensions of decision making in health-related contexts and in contexts involving the biological sciences.

Capacity - Under the law, capacity is an individual's ability to understand the nature and consequences of decisions and how to communicate the decisions.

Individually Identifiable Health Information - A term used in HIPAA, which means a subset of health information, collected from an individual, created or received by a healthcare provider, health plan, employer, or healthcare clearinghouse. The information relates to the past, present, or future physical or mental health or condition of an individual. It also may relate to the provision of health care or payment for the individual's health care. Finally, the information must identify the individual or provide a basis to reasonably believe that the individual can be identified. This term is used to define "protected health information" under HIPAA.

Informed Consent - A process by which a fully informed patient can participate in healthcare choices. This process has three elements—information, comprehension of that information, and voluntariness.

Medical Futility - Interventions unlikely to produce significant benefit for a patient.

Nonmaleficence - Means to "do no harm." For example, physicians must refrain from providing ineffective treatments. The key ethical issue is whether the benefits outweigh the burdens.

Protected Health Information (PHI) - "Individually identifiable health information" transmitted or maintained electronically or in any other form.

Instructor-Led Questions

1. What type of court battle could occur as a result of a patient not clearly stating his or her intentions in an advance directive?

2. Should patients always be given complete autonomy with regard to their healthcare decisions?

3. Does the definition of futility change with the age of the patient (child, young adult, or senior)?

4. How would you describe the role of a bioethicist to a healthcare provider?

5. How would you describe the role of a bioethicist to a patient?

6. Briefly explain the legislative purposes of the following laws:

   * National Research Act (1974)

   * Born-Alive Infant Protection Act (2002)

7. What are the key provisions in the Patient's Bill of Rights, created in 1973 by the American Hospital Association and approved by The Joint Commission in 1991?

Endnotes

1   Samuel Gorovitz, "Bioethics and Social Responsibility," The Monist 60 (January 1977)3.

2.   Edmund Pellegrino, The Origins and Evolution of Bioethics: Some Personal Reflections. Kennedy Institute of Ethics Journal. [9:1(March 1999)]

3   Principles of Biomedical Ethics, by Beauchamp and Childress

4   Cal. Probate Code section 4631

5   Patient's Bill of Rights http://www.cancer.org/treatment/findingandpayingfortreatment/understandingfinancialand legalmatter/patients-bill-of-rights

6   Patient Protection and Affordable Care Act (PPACA) www .hhs.gov, Search term: The Center for Consumer Information & Insurance Oversight (CCIIO)

7   Brad Doerr, The "Wrongful Life" Debate, http://www.genomicslawreport.com/index.php/2009/09/22/the-wrongful-life-debate.

8   On Moral Medicine Theological Perspectives in Medical Ethics second edition, James M. Gustafson, Mongolism, Prenatal Desires, and the Right to Life, (1998).

9   42 U.S.C. section 5106a(b)(2)(B)

10   42 U.S.C. section 5106a(b)(2)(B)(iii)

11   University of Washington School of Medicine, Ethics in Medicine: Parental Decision-making, http;// depts.washington.edu/bioethx/topics/parent.html

12   American Academy of Pediatrics Committee on Bioethics, Ethics and the Care of Critically Ill Infants and Children, 98(1) Pediatrics 149 (1996); Jason Morrow, Making Mortal Decisions at the Beginning of Life: The Case of Impaired and Imperiled Infants, 284(9) J. Am. Med. Assoc.1146(2000).

13   1 U.S.C.section 8.

14   http://pediatrics.aappublicationos.org/context/116/4/e576 abstract by SA Sayeed 2005.

15   Reinhardt, Uwe: "Access Quality and Capital Costs in the Era of Consumerism" keynote presentation at The California Medical Association Eighth Annual Leadership Academy, La Quinta, California. November 19, 2004.

16   National Conference of Commissioners of Uniform State Laws

17   Ethics in Medicine, Futility, http://depts.washington.edu/bioethx/topics/futil.html.

18   AMA Policy, E-2.037, Medical Futility in End-of-Life Care.

19   OrganDonor.Gov: Access to U.S. Government Information on Organ & Tissue Donation and Transplantation, http://organdonor.gov

20   42 U.S.C. section 273

21   Legislation and Legislative History, http://www.OrganDonor.gov

22   Raymond J. Devette, Practical Decision Making In Health Care Ethic, Cases & Concepts 2nd ed., Georgetown University Press 2000.

23   Pub. L. 93-348 (1974).

24   Grimes v. Kennedy Krieger Inst., 782 A.2d 807 (Md. 2001). See Robert M. Nelson, Nontherapeautic Research, Minimal Risk, and the Kennedy Krieger Lead Abatement Study, 23(6) IRB: Ethics & Human Research 7 (2001).

25   Office of Human Research Protection, http://www.hhs.gov/ohrp/assurances index.html

26   Victor A. McKusick, Human Genetics, 2nd edition (Englewood Cliffs, NJ: Prentice-Hall, 1969) 181.

27   Shannon and Walter, The New Genetic Medicine Theological and Ethical Reflections. Rowan & Littlefield Publishers, Inc.: New York, 2003.

Books Consulted

1   Shannon, Thomas A. and Kockler, Nicholas J. An Introduction to Bioethics fourth edition revised and updated. New York/Mahwah, NJ: Paulist Press, 2009.

2   Devettere, Raymond J. Practical Decision Making In Health Care Ethics second edition. Washington D.C., Georgetown University Press, 2000.

3   On Moral Medicine Theological Perspectives in Medical Ethics second edition. Edited by Stephen E. Lammers and Allen Verhey, Grand Rapids, MI: William B. Eermans Publishing Company, 1998.

4   Shannon, Thomas A. and Walter, James J. The New Genetic Medicine Theological and Ethical Reflections. New York: Rowan & Littlefield Publishers, Inc., 2003.

5   Skloot, Rebecca. The Immortal Life of Henrietta Lacks. Crown Books, 2010.

6   Health and Human Flourishing Religion Medicine and Moral Anthropology. Edited by carol R. Taylor and Roberto Dell'Oro. Washington, D.C.: Georgetown University Press, 2007.

Chapter 16

Clinical Research

Heidi Carroll, Amy Leopard

Key Learning Objectives

By the end of this chapter, the reader will be able to:

- Describe the responsibilities of at least four organizations, including government agencies, to protect human participants in clinical research.

- Identify three key ethical principles that guide the conduct of research for human participants.

- Describe content included in an informed consent document, conditions that may affect an individual's capacity to consent, and exceptions for obtaining informed consent.

- Describe four responsibilities of an Institutional Review Board.

- Identify legal and financial aspects of clinical trial agreements.

Chapter Outline

Introduction

Research is a systematic investigation undertaken to contribute to a body of generalizable knowledge. There are various forms of research, such as basic or laboratory research (sometimes called "bench" research), translational research, and clinical trials. This chapter will focus primarily on principles and laws pertaining to clinical trials and the protection of human participants in those trials.

There are diverse roles and responsibilities associated with clinical trials. Those include the duties owed to trial participants by the clinical trial site, the personal responsibilities and possible liabilities of "principal investigators" (sometimes referred to as "PIs"), and the various financial, legal, and operational roles of the clinical trial site.

Chapter Outline

- 16-1. History of the Development of the Ethical Principles and Regulations That Protect Human Subject Research Participants in Clinical Trials
- 16-2. Overview of the United States Agencies That Regulate Clinical Trials
- 16-3. Key Elements of a Clinical Trial
  - 16-3.1 Principal Investigator Responsibilities
  - 16-3.2 IRB Review and Approval/Informed Consent
  - 16-3.3 Vulnerable Populations
- 16-4. Protecting Participant Health Information and the Health Insurance Portability and Accountability Act (HIPAA) Medical Privacy Rule
- 16-5. Financial Relationships and Conflicts of Interest
- 16-6. Public Health Service (PHS) Conflicts Rules
- 16-7. Research Fraud and Abuse
- 16-8. Federal Healthcare Program Anti-Kickback Statute

16-1 History of the Development of the Ethical Principles and Regulations That Protect Human Subject Research Participants in Clinical Trials

Protection of human subject research participants has evolved over the last century as a result of some of the most horrific abuse to human participants in research. Awareness of abuse to human participants began as a result of the post–World War II Nuremberg Trials. At the Nuremberg Trials, twenty-three Nazi doctors and officials were tried before a military tribunal of the Allies for their use of concentration camp prisoners as human participants in medical or scientific research. In his opening statement, U.S. Brigadier General, Telford Taylor, stated that the German militarists were "utterly ruthless . . . and callous to the sufferings of people whom they regarded as inferior."[1] The German officials were willing to gather whatever scientific data the hideous experiments conducted on the prisoners yielded.[2] The prisoners were forced to endure the following atrocities:[3]

1. High altitude experiments: The Nazi doctors placed prisoners into low-pressure tanks in order to determine how long they could survive with little oxygen. In some instances, the prisoners were in the vacuum chamber until their lungs exploded.

2. Experiments that measured the effects of cold: Naked prisoners were forced outside to endure freezing temperatures for 9 to 14 hours. Others were forced to remain in a vat of freezing water for 3 hours at a time. The Nazi doctors would then attempt to re-warm and resuscitate the dead prisoners, but their attempts often failed.

3. Mustard gas and phosphorous burn experiments: The prisoners were deliberately burned with phosphorous material taken from the Allies' incendiary bombs. Others were forced to inhale mustard gas, or were inflicted by wounds that were further aggravated by mustard gas.

4. Sulfanilamide experiments: Prisoners were severely wounded. In order to mimic battlefield conditions, the wounds were aggravated with glass shards or wood shavings in addition to bacteria or gangrene cultures. Some wounds were then treated with sulfanilamide, while others were not, to measure the effects of sulfanilamide healing.

5. Experiments were conducted on malaria, epidemic jaundice, and typhus: Since these diseases had to be combated by the Germans in occupied territories, the scientists infected the prisoners in order to test vaccines or treatments on them.

6. Poison experiments: The prisoners at Buchenwald, who were shot with poisoned bullets, were not guinea pigs to test an antidote for the poison; their murderers

really wanted to know how quickly the poison would kill. Other prisoners were fed poison.

7. Twin experiments: In order to understand twins, blood was drawn from them so many times that they bled to death.

8. Sterilization experiments: Prisoners were subjected to chemical and x-ray sterilization experiments.

As part of their defense, the lawyers of the accused military Nazi doctors argued that there were no laws or regulations that defined human research, and the experiments conducted on the prisoners were no different than the ones that they had conducted prior to the war. The judges at the Nuremberg Trials then decided that in addition to the sentencing of the Nazi doctors, they needed to develop a formal statement on medical ethics and clinical research. This statement became known as the Nuremberg Code. The Nuremberg Code is comprised of ten standards for experiments on human participants as follows:

1. Voluntary informed consent must be obtained;

2. The experiment should yield results that would benefit society that could not be obtained by other means;

3. The experiment should not cause undue harm or mental suffering;

4. No experiment should be conducted where the anticipated end result is death or disabling injury;

5. The degree of risks should be minimal compared to the humanitarian importance;

6. The experiment should be conducted by scientifically qualified individuals;

7. Proper safeguards should be put in place to prevent even the remote possibility of death or serious injury;

8. The research participants should be able to end their participation at will;

9. The investigator must be able to end the experiment at any time if he or she believes that the experiment would result in injury or death;

10. The experiment should be designed based on knowledge of the disease process and sound scientific research that has been previously conducted on animals.

The Nazi Germans believed in some instances that they were conducting experiments that would ultimately assist the German troops in surviving the harsh conditions of the results of war injuries and/or environmental factors such as freezing temperatures. Although the Nazi Germans believed that they had legitimate reasons to conduct their studies, the means by which they conducted the research on prisoners was the atrocity. As prisoners, the participants did not volunteer to participate in the experiments and were not permitted to withdraw. Furthermore there were no precautions to protect participants from injury, serious bodily harm, disability, or death. Instead, the experiments involved unnecessary extreme pain or torture that often resulted in death, mutilation, or serious bodily injury.

The Nuremberg Code marked the beginning of the development of ethical principles that emphasized the protection of human participants in research. In response to the Nuremberg Code, the World Medical Association (WMA), an international conference for doctors, drafted its own set of ethical principles. The WMA provided an intellectual and international forum for physicians to discuss the matters that related to medical ethics and research, and in 1964, it developed the Declaration of Helsinki as a statement of ethical principles for medical research involving human participants.[4] The Declaration of Helsinki expanded upon the Nuremberg Code and was the first set of research principles to suggest that each research trial should be reviewed by an independent committee to evaluate and monitor the ethical conduct of human participant research. It also expanded the notion of subject participant autonomy by formalizing what is and is not informed consent for persons who are and are not able to give such consent.[5] The WMA took into consideration the necessity to include in research individuals such as children and mentally ill participants that may not have the ability to consent to research. The Declaration of Helsinki included the necessity of having a legal guardian's consent if the individual did not have the capacity to consent. Issues of potential conflicts of interest involving investigators were also introduced.[6] Over the years there have been six revisions to the Declaration of Helsinki, and although it has no legal authority, its principles have been the basis of most subsequent ethical documents and regulations.

Both the Nuremberg Code and the Declaration of Helsinki emphasized informed consent and the need to terminate an experiment if there was a strong likelihood that continuing the study would cause injury. Despite the development of these international ethical principles a very disturbing trial was being conducted in the United States. The experiment known as the Tuskegee Syphilis Study was initiated in 1932 and continued until 1972.

The Tuskegee Syphilis study was designed to document the natural progression and long-term effects of the syphilis disease on African American men, without treatment. The study was conducted by the U.S. Public Health Service in conjunction with the Tuskegee Institute and funded by the U.S. government. The government physicians chose a remote and isolated location in Macon County, Alabama because of the high occurrence of syphilis in the African American population. The African American men were deceived into enrolling in the trial by being made to believe that the U.S. Public Health Service had started a new health program for individuals in Macon County that had "bad blood." All individuals were provided free exams, and those that were selected as subject participants in the trial were then offered continual free exams and alleged treatment. Participants were never told they had syphilis, the course of the disease, or treatment. The treatment was comprised of spinal taps, which were described as "spinal shots."[7] The physicians monitored the participants over the years but did not provide the participants with any actual treatment because they wanted to study the progression of the disease without medical intervention.

This deception was extremely tragic and unethical, because at the time the trial began there was a well-known published standard therapy for syphilis. Furthermore in 1945, penicillin was discovered to be a far more effective treatment.[8] The study prevented almost 400 individuals from being treated for syphilis.[9] The study included a total of 600 participants; approximately 400 were individuals infected with syphilis and 200 were healthy control individuals.[10] It is estimated that at least twenty-eight of the participants, but possibly 100 individuals, died from nontreatment of the disease. The total impact on the population is unknown as many of the untreated men had families and sexual partners. It was the longest nontherapeutic trial in the United States.[11]

The study only ceased when it was leaked to the national press by a whistleblower. The story was published first in the *Washington Star* on July 25, 1972. The next day, the *New York Times* headline read "Syphilis Victims in U.S. Study Went Untreated for 40 Years." The Associated Press stories about the Tuskegee Study caused a public outcry that led the Assistant Secretary for Health and Scientific Affairs to appoint an Ad Hoc Advisory Panel to review the study.[12] The panel had nine members from the fields of medicine, law, religion, labor, education, health administration, and public affairs.[13] The panel re-evaluated the U.S. government research practices.

The 1974 National Research Act mandated the creation of the National Commission for the Protection of Human Subjects of Biomedical and Behavioral Research (The National Commission).[14] The National Commission met at the Belmont Conference Center in Elkridge, Maryland in February 1976 to draft "*Ethical Principles and Guidelines for the Protection of Human Subjects of Research, Report of the National Commission for the Protection of Human Subjects of Biomedical and Behavioral Research*," also known as the Belmont Report.[15] The Belmont Report provides the ethical basis for understanding the U.S. regulations protecting human participants in clinical research and was published by DHHS in the Federal Register to be made readily available to scientists, IRB members, and federal employees as a statement of basic ethical principles.[16]

In the Belmont Report, the National Commission identified three basic ethical principles that should underlie the conduct of research involving human participants—respect for persons (autonomy), beneficence, and justice—and developed guidelines that should be followed to ensure that such research is conducted in accordance with those principles.[17]

The ethical principle of beneficence is the act of providing a benefit to a human participant rather than causing harm, that is, harm to human participants should be minimized and the benefit to participants should be maximized. Consideration of potential harm to human participants involves a careful investigation, anticipation, and weighing of the risks and benefits of the study. A truly ethical study should have benefits that outweigh risks to participants. For example, when an investigator is trying to develop a new diagnostic tool in radiology such as an improved MRI scan, the benefit to the participant should be outweighed by the minimal additional time in the MRI scan needed to obtain the second image.[18]

Respect for persons, also known as autonomy, is the second requirement for ethical research using human participants. This requirement has two components:

1. Respecting the decision-making capacity of persons; and, when appropriate,

2. Protecting individuals with diminished capacity for self-determination.[19]

Individuals who lack the maturity and/or physical, social, or mental capacity to make informed decisions require and deserve special protections to consent to and participate in research studies. Respect for individual autonomy requires the recognition of the individual's considered opinions and choices and restraint from obstructing the individual's actions unless those actions clearly harm others.[14,20] The third requirement is justice—the fair distribution of the burdens and benefits of research across groups of people. Justice refers to the fair treatment of disadvantaged participants or vulnerable populations such as women, children, prisoners, and mentally handicapped individuals; for example it would be unethical to conduct research on whether or not a vaccine works only on prisoners, because they may be coerced into participating in the research without the freedom to choose whether or not to participate in the research project. The use of disadvantaged participants in the study must be justified in order for the research to be ethical. For example, providing a new noninvasive technique to measure tumor growth or shrinkage in cancer patients who are undergoing treatment would be beneficial to all participants including prisoners and children. The researcher would be justified in using all potential populations of participants, because the risks and benefits are the same. To the extent possible, only competent adults should be participants in research with more than minimal risk, and there must be compelling scientific and logical reasons to include less advantaged persons in the research project. The clearest example of injustice is research that uses only disadvantaged persons as research participants and makes the benefits of the research available to only advantaged individuals.[21]

In addition, the National Commission proposed that regulations be created that include the adoption of the ethical principles outlined in the Belmont Report. The National Commission advised the U.S. Department of Health and Human Services (DHHS) to revise and expand its regulations for the protection of human participants. In 1981, DHHS and the FDA revised the regulations that pertain to research involving human participants. The DHHS regulations are codified at Title 45 Part 46 of the Code of Federal Regulations. Those "basic" regulations became final on January 16, 1981, and were revised effective March 4, 1983, and June 18, 1991. The June 18, 1991, revision involved the adoption of the Federal Policy for the Protection of Human Subjects. The Federal Policy (or "Common Rule," as it is sometimes called) was promulgated by the sixteen federal agencies that conduct, support, or otherwise regulate clinical research; the FDA also adopted many of the Common Rule provisions. As is implied by its title, the Federal Policy is designed to make uniform the human participant protections in all relevant federal agencies and departments.[22] The current regulations protect human subject participants and the integrity of the research process by defining the roles and responsibilities of the institutions, sponsors (individuals, government, and public), investigators, and independent review boards that are responsible for the approval of research projects.

16-2 Overview of the United States Agencies That Regulate Clinical Trials

Research is regulated by several of the U.S. federal administrative agencies that generate regulations, policies, and guidelines for protecting clinical trial participants. The DHHS is the federal government's principal agency dedicated to protecting the health of all Americans. Within the DHHS, the U.S. Public Health Service oversees key administrative agencies involved in research such as the National Institutes of Health (NIH) and the Food and Drug Administration (FDA). The NIH is the United State's medical research agency dedicated to advancing discoveries in research. NIH is one of the major funding sources of clinical research. In addition, the FDA is responsible for ensuring all clinical research that involves a drug, biologic, and/or device is conducted properly so that the therapy is proven safe and effective before being placed on the market.

The FDA regulates the distribution and sale of human and veterinary drugs, biological products, medical devices, our nation's food supply, cosmetics, and products that emit radiation. To ensure that the products it regulates are safe the FDA developed regulations compatible with the Common Rule that require IRB review and informed consent. The FDA regulations provide a framework for clinical researchers involved in drug, biologic, and device trials.[23]

The FDA also regulates testing of new drugs and devices to ensure that they are safe and effective prior to their entrance into the market. The requirement for testing drugs and devices was developed as a result of Elixir Sulfanilamide. In 1937, Elixir Sulfanilamide, which contained diethylene glycol, a chemical analogue of antifreeze, was distributed throughout the United States. As a result of taking Elixir Sulfanilamide, more than 100 people died, many of them children.[24]

The FDA ensures oversight of the safety and effectiveness of new drugs and devices through the development and release of regulations, policies, and guidance documents. Sponsors and clinical investigators are required by FDA regulations governing the conduct of clinical studies (21 CFR Part 312 for drugs and biologics and 21 CFR Part 812 for devices) to obtain approval by the Independent Review Committee or IRB before any trial begins.

In furtherance of its commitment to protect the integrity of research, DHHS also created the Office of Research Integrity (ORI) and Office of Human Research Protection (OHRP) to oversee and direct the Public Health Service (PHS) research activities that are conducted primarily by the NIH. The ORI mission is to

1. oversee the institutional handling of research misconduct allegations involving research, research training, and related research activities that PHS supports;

2 provide education in the responsible conduct of research;

3. prevent research misconduct; and

4. promote compliance with the PHS Policies on Research Misconduct ("the PHS regulations").[25]

The OHRP is responsible for interpreting and overseeing implementation of the DHHS regulations regarding the basic protection of human research participants for all research conducted, supported, or subject to regulation by federal agencies, also known as the "Common Rule."[26]

16-3 Key Elements of a Clinical Trial

Clinical trials involve researchers who obtain and analyze data about human participants, either through observation or an intervention (e.g., such as a medication, device, teaching concept, training method, or behavioral change) to answer a scientific or medical question.[27] The Department of Health and Human Services (DHHS) defines the following elements of a clinical trial :

- Research means a systematic investigation, including research development, testing, and evaluation, designed to develop or contribute to generalizable knowledge.

- A human participant is a live person about whom the researcher obtains identifiable private information or information through intervention (e.g., medical procedures or environmental manipulations) or interaction with the individual, directly or indirectly (e.g., through the medical record).[28]

Regardless of the type of clinical trial, each trial is conducted in a systematic manner and includes the following steps:

1. Each research trial begins with a specific question that an investigator wants to answer. A study design concept/scientific question is developed that identifies a potentially better way to prevent, screen for, diagnose, or treat a disease (new device or drug or procedure). Some trials may be designed to compare a new treatment to a known

treatment while others are designed to observe behavior or the response to a change in behavior.

2. Funding is secured (e.g., governmental funding such as grants or private industry funding from drug or device companies).

3. The research question is answered through the use of a protocol (i.e., a study plan describing what will be done and how the study will be conducted). The protocol outlines the benefits and risks to the participants and how those risks will be monitored and reduced.

4. The Independent Review Committee reviews the study protocol to ensure it meets the requirements in the Common Rule before approving the study.

5. The study is conducted.

6. The study is closed and the data is analyzed and interpreted.

7. Study results are communicated through publications, presentations, and various government agencies, etc.[29]

Each clinical trial involves a research team that includes physicians and nurses as well as social workers and other healthcare professionals. During the course of a clinical trial, research participants are followed and closely monitored by the research team to ensure their health and safety. The research team is also responsible for the continuous and ongoing disclosure of any newly discovered risks and benefits, as well as participant education.

16-3.1 Principal Investigator Responsibilities

Each clinical trial has a principal investigator (PI) with overall responsibility who is appointed to ensure that the trial is run properly. It is a key responsibility of the PI to ensure the following:

- The research team is conducting scientifically valid research. The PI must ensure that the study is properly designed and scientifically sound to yield valid results, and that research participants meet the selection (inclusion) criteria.

- The PI is responsible for ensuring that the basic elements of informed consent are met so participants truly understand what their involvement entails, including potential risks and expected benefits (physical, emotional, and financial) associated with the clinical research project.[30]

- The PI monitors the welfare of all participants in the trial, ensuring that IRB approval is obtained, the trial is conducted according to the protocol, adverse events are reported accurately and promptly, and team members are qualified and properly trained for the role they play in the research project.

- The research participants' information is protected as required under state laws and the Health Insurance Portability and Accountability Act of 1996 (HIPAA) Medical Privacy Rule.

16-3.2 IRB Review and Approval/ Informed Consent

Clinical trials involve risks to human participants, and it is therefore important that the risks to participants are evaluated to determine that the benefits to the participants outweigh those risks. As discussed above, the ethical principles, the FDA regulations, and the Common Rule require the Institutional Review Board (IRB) to review, approve, and monitor clinical research trials involving human participants. The IRB ensures research conducted on human participants is scientifically valid, ethical, and in compliance with the regulations. Institutional Review Boards review the protocols and approve them; approve them with conditions; or reject them. A clinical trial involving human participants cannot begin until the IRB has approved the trial and any conditions have been met. The relevant criteria for IRB approval are:

1. The risks to participants are reasonable in relation to the anticipated benefits;
2. The risks to participants are minimized by the use of sound scientific design;
3. Adequate safeguards to protect the privacy of and confidentiality of participants have been established when appropriate;
4. Informed consent is obtained and documented from either the participant or the participant's legally authorized representative; and
5. The research plan makes adequate provisions for ongoing monitoring for participant safety.[31]

Determining if study procedures are ethical or unethical in terms of risks and benefits is rarely straightforward. Generally, risks are evaluated and assigned to one of two categories:

1. minimal risk, and
2. greater than minimal risk.[32]

The Institutional Review Board reviews the protocol to determine if the risks to participants are minimized by using known scientific methods and if applicable, that clinical procedures are those which would otherwise be performed for diagnostic or treatment purposes.[33] The regulations define minimal risks as those that are not greater than the risks a participant would normally encounter in daily life or by routine exams or therapies that the participant would otherwise undergo.[34] For example, a participant may require an MRI scan that includes an injection of a contrast agent as part of the clinical treatment. The protocol may require the participant to stay in the MRI scanner a little longer to take additional images for the testing of a new software program. Because participants already would undergo the contrast agent risk as part of their standard routine care and the additional time in the MRI scanner is all that is required, the additional risks to the participants may be considered minimal.

Risks greater than minimal require special protections and should be balanced by greater benefits. Harm and discomfort can be physical, psychological, or social in nature. Often, the main challenge of the assessment is determining the likelihood and severity of these risks. Examples of risks greater than minimal are spinal taps, experimental medications and procedures, surveys about illegal behaviors, and biopsies. Potential consequences of these research procedures should be adequately anticipated and investigated and likely effective precautions and safeguards instituted.[35] The IRB should determine that the risks to the participants are reasonable in relation to any anticipated benefits and the importance of the knowledge that may reasonably be expected to result from the conduct of the research.[36] Clinical trials can and sometimes should (when risks are greater than minimal) achieve direct benefits. Benefits to society at large would be the acquisition of information useful for developing preventions, therapies, and treatments at some point in the future.

The IRB must review the protocol to ensure that there is equitable selection of participants and that any necessary additional safeguards are put into place to ensure that vulnerable populations such as children, prisoners, pregnant women, mentally disabled persons, or economically or educationally disadvantaged persons are sufficiently protected.[37] Given the risks to some participants the protocol may need to be reviewed to ensure that there is an adequate provision for monitoring the data collected to ensure participant safety.[38]

INFORMED CONSENT. Informed consent of the research participant is an essential component to the ethical conduct of research. Informed consent is the process of conveying accurate and relevant information about a study regarding its purpose, known risks, benefits, and alternatives, and answering all questions related to participation from the potential enrollee. To help someone decide whether or not to participate, the doctors and nurses involved in the trial explain the details of the study. Informed consent is a continual process that occurs throughout the study. Participants must be made aware of any changes in risks or new discoveries as the study progresses. The obtaining of voluntary informed consent is a process that includes both a written document and oral presentation and discussion with the potential research participant. As established in the Belmont Report, the research participant must have:

1. sufficient information;
2. comprehension; and
3. voluntariness.[39]

These elements should be emphasized during the discussion with the participant and in the informed consent document as required by federal regulation 45 C.F.R. § 46.116 and the FDA regulation so that the research participant understands the following:

1. That this is a research study and its purpose. The participant must understand the time commitment and the expected duration of participation and receive an explanation of any procedures considered experimental;
2. Any known foreseeable risks or discomforts to the participant;
3. Any reasonably expected benefits to the participant or to others;
4. Relevant known alternative procedures or courses of treatment that might be advantageous to the participant;
5. How the confidentiality of records identifying the participant will be maintained (if applicable);
6. If the research involves greater than minimal risk, whether any compensation or any medical treatments are available if injury occurs;
7. Participation in the research is voluntary, refusal to participate will involve no penalty, and the participant may discontinue participation at any time without penalty.[40]

In addition to the elements of informed consent listed above, when appropriate, one or more of the following elements of information also must be provided to each participant:

1. A statement that the particular treatment or procedure may involve unforeseeable risks to the participant or, in the event of female participant, the embryo or fetus;

2. Circumstances under which the investigator may terminate the participant's participation without regard to the participant's consent;
3. Any additional costs to the participant that may result from participation in the research;
4. The consequences of a participant's early withdrawal from the research and procedures for orderly termination of participation;
5. A statement that the participant will be informed about significant new findings developed during the course of the research that may influence the participant's willingness to continue participation; and
6. The approximate number of study participants.[41]

Finally, clinical trials regulated by the FDA are required to include a statement that informs the participants that a description of the clinical trial will be made available on the National Institutes of Health/National Library of Medicine website at www.clinicaltrials.gov.[42] The statement must inform the individuals that www.clinicaltrials.gov will not include individually identifiable information.[43]

EXCEPTIONS TO THE REQUIREMENT FOR INFORMED CONSENT. Although the ethical codes all recommend voluntarily informed consent and safeguards for vulnerable populations, there are limited circumstances where informed consent may not be possible. Both the Common Rule and FDA regulations permit the waiver of the requirement for informed consent. An IRB may waive the requirements to obtain informed consent provided the IRB finds and documents that:[44]

1. The research involves no more than minimal risk to participants;
2. The waiver of informed consent will not adversely affect the rights and welfare of the participants;
3. The research could not practicably be carried out without the waiver or alteration; and
4. Whenever appropriate, participants will be provided with additional pertinent information after participation.

The FDA may permit the use of an investigational device or drug without the requirement of informed consent in the event of emergency use situations under 21 CFR §50.24. The research plan must be approved in advance by the FDA and the IRB and publicly disclosed to the community in which the research will be conducted. The FDA has even provided safeguards for such emergency use situations where informed consent cannot be obtained. The investigator is required to obtain informed consent of the participant or the participant's legally authorized representative, or in instances were this is not feasible then the investigator and a physician who is not otherwise participating in the clinical investigation must certify in writing all of the following requirements from 21 C.F.R §50.23(a) are met:

1. The participant is confronted by a life-threatening situation making the use of the test article necessary.

2. It is not possible to communicate with or obtain legally effective informed consent from the participant.

3. There is not sufficient time to obtain consent from the participant's legal representative.

4. No alternative method of approved or generally recognized therapy is available to provide a better likelihood of saving the participant's life.[45]

16-3.3 Vulnerable Populations

As noted in the ethical codes and U.S. federal regulations, certain populations are more vulnerable to injustice. These participants are vulnerable because of their dependent status and their frequently compromised capacity for free consent.[46] Special study protections are warranted to protect these participants from being manipulated as a result of their vulnerability and from the danger of being involved in research solely for administrative convenience.[47] Vulnerable populations are individuals who are relatively or absolutely incapable of protecting their own interests and include:

- Children[48]

- Prisoners (e.g., who believe research participation will impact their sentencing or parole)[49]

- Fetuses and newborns[50]

- Pregnant women[51]

- Terminally ill individuals

- Students/employees

- Individuals with questionable capacity (mentally disabled, neurologic conditions, comatose, substance abuse, psychiatric illnesses, metabolic disorders)

When conducting research on children, special precautions should be taken. Generally, the legal age of consent is 18 years, but exceptions exist depending on the focus of the study relative to appropriate laws. Children can assent or agree to participate, but their legal consent must come in the form of permission from their parents or guardians. When the research involves greater than minimal risk, permission from both parents must be obtained when possible.

In some circumstances, parental consent can be waived for studies. In situations where parental or guardian consent is not likely to be protective (e.g., neglected or abused children), permission can be waived given that an alternative protective mechanism is provided for the child. For example, research on HCV risk among young injection drug users has been permitted to waive parental consent for minors because many have extremely unhealthy relationships with their parents or guardians. In lieu of parental consent, potential participants were given contact information for a service organization that provides support for troubled and homeless youth. They were encouraged to call the organization if they have any questions or concerns about study participation. It is important that the protective mechanism be independent of the research team, institution, and funder and have no conflict of interest with the study.

In addition to the special requirements, the DHHS regulations at 45 CFR part 46, subpart D have provided additional safeguards for vulnerable populations such as children by only permitting IRBs to approve the three following categories of research involving children as participants:

1. Research that involves minimal risk to the children;[52]

2. Research that involves greater than minimal risk but presents the prospect of direct benefit to the individual child participants;[53] and

3. Research involving greater than minimal risk and no prospect of direct benefit to the individual child participants involved in the research, but likely to yield generalizable knowledge about the participant's disorder or condition which is of vital importance for the understanding or amelioration of the disorder or condition.[54]

16-4 Protecting Participant Health Information and the Health Insurance Portability and Accountability Act (HIPAA) Medical Privacy Rule

Both the Common Rule and the FDA regulations for the protection of human subjects require measures to protect personal information gained during the research from inappropriate use or disclosure. It is the Institutional Review Boards, research team and institution's responsibility to ensure that the rights and welfare of each research participant is protected and to establish safeguards to protect participant privacy and maintain the confidentiality of data.[55] Privacy protections for participants extend to the protection of their personal health information. The Health Insurance Portability and Accountability Act of 1996 (HIPAA)[56] protects the use and disclosure of individually identifiable health information (protected health information) by hospitals and healthcare facilities that submit healthcare claims electronically ("covered entities"). Covered entities that participate in research involving protected health information must consider HIPAA when documenting Institutional Review Board oversight of privacy, developing patients' informed consent and authorization forms, and drafting business associate agreements for disclosures of protected health information to subcontractors.

HIPAA regulates health information created or received by healthcare providers relating to the physical or mental health or condition of an individual or the provision of health care to an individual which either identifies the individual or there is a reasonable basis to believe could be used to identify the individual.[57] "De-identified health information" which does not identify the individual and for which there is no reasonable basis to believe the individual can be identified is not regulated by HIPAA.[58] Generally, de-identification can be accomplished under HIPAA by having a statistician verify that the information has been properly de-identified or by removing certain enumerated identifiers about the individual and household members of the individual and having no knowledge that the information remaining could be used to reidentify the individual.[59]

Under HIPAA, if the information cannot be de-identified, the research participant must authorize the use or disclosure of their protected health information or a valid waiver or other HIPAA exception must be met. Research participants can be required to sign a separate HIPAA authorization form or the authorization can be incorporated as part of the informed consent document. In addition, HIPAA contains provisions that allow protected health information to be used for certain research activities. Commonly, the IRB or a privacy board at the institution may determine that written HIPAA authorizations from participants will not be required under a waiver. The research waiver contains procedural and documentation requirements that certain criteria have been met, namely that no more than a minimal risk of privacy exists and that the research could not be conducted without the waiver and without access to and use of the protected health information.[60] Second, the HIPAA research rule allows researchers to use and disclose protected health information when it is considered preparatory to research (necessary and used solely to prepare a research protocol and no protected health information is removed from the covered entity).[61] Third, HIPAA allows research on protected health information of decedents (necessary and used solely for research).[62] In addition, HIPAA allows uses and disclosures of protected health information for research purposes using a limited data set (excluding designated identifiers) under a data use agreement between the covered entity and the researcher that restricts the use of the data, prohibits the researcher from identifying the information or contacting the individual, and requires the researcher to use certain safeguards to protect the information.[63]

In order to protect the personal information of the human participants, healthcare providers that delegate any research activities involving the use of protected health information to subcontractors must enter business associate agreements with those subcontractors, called business associates under HIPAA. Business associate agreements ensure that that the research participant's information continues to be protected because the agreements require business associates to:

- Comply with the HIPAA restrictions on uses and disclosures.
- Notify the covered entity if there is a breach of unsecured protected health information so that the covered entity may notify the individual and DHHS.
- Comply with the administrative, technical, and physical security standards that apply to the covered entity.[64]

Business associates are liable to the covered entity for any violation of the HIPAA business associate agreement. Under the Health Information Technology for Economic and Clinical Health Act (HITECH) enacted in 2009, many of the HIPAA privacy and security requirements applicable to covered entities will apply directly to business associates, and business associates will be subject to the same HIPAA civil and criminal penalties as covered entities.[65] Therefore business associates must document all security and technical measures that they have taken to ensure the personal information is protected.

16-5 Financial Relationships and Conflicts of Interest

Research is not only funded through federal agencies, but also through private industry groups such as drug and device companies.[66] Industry relationships are common in medicine and can create important benefits for patient and public health that would not otherwise be possible. Nonetheless, these financial relationships between healthcare professionals and drug and device manufacturers in industry present the potential for conflicts of interest. The primary concern is the financial relationship itself will compromise the independent professional judgment of the researcher and that as a result, patients and the research's integrity may be harmed. Actual, apparent, or potential conflicts of interest (COIs) create a situation in which financial or other personal considerations have the potential to compromise or bias professional judgment and objectivity. "Such conflicts of interest threaten the integrity of scientific investigations, the objectivity of medical education, and the quality of patient care. . . . They may also jeopardize public trust in medicine."[67]

The public needs to trust that the financial ties do not compromise these judgments. Laws and rules for dealing with conflicts often require disclosure and proper management of conflicts, and in some instances, a wholesale prohibition. There are two essential DHHS conflicts of interest regulations, one under the FDA for studies under its jurisdiction and another under the Public Health Service (PHS) for funding from PHS sources (e.g., NIH and CDC). Section 6002 of the health reform legislation included Sunshine Act provisions designed to further expand on regulation through required disclosures of financial relationships among physicians, teaching hospitals, and industry. Several states have passed legislation regulating financial relationships, most notably Massachusetts. Finally, the federal Anti-kickback statute and the federal False Claims Act serve as tools to impose liability where federal funds are involved.

Under the FDA clinical investigator disclosure rules at 21 C.F.R. 54.1, the FDA states it may consider clinical study data inadequate if the design, conduct, reporting, and analysis of the study fail to minimize bias. FDA concerns regarding bias in clinical studies include any financial interest of the clinical investigator in the outcome of the study owing to the way payment is arranged (e.g., a royalty), or because the investigator has a proprietary interest in the product (e.g., a patent), or because the investigator has an equity interest in the sponsor of the covered study.[68] Under the FDA conflicts rules, applicants must disclose certain financial arrangements between the clinical investigators and study sponsor(s) so that the reliability of the data can be assessed.

In May 2011, the FDA issued a draft Guidance for Clinical Investigators Industry, and FDA Staff: Financial Disclosures by Clinical Investigators for complying with 21 C.F.R. Part 54.

The FDA under the applicable regulations (21 CFR Parts 54, 312, 314, 320, 330, 601, 807, 812, 814, and 860) requires an applicant to submit to the FDA a list of clinical investigators who conducted covered clinical studies and certify and/or disclose certain financial arrangements as follows:

1. Certification that no financial arrangements with an investigator have been made that affect the outcome of the clinical trial; that the investigator has no proprietary interest in the tested product; that the investigator does not have a significant equity interest in the sponsor of the covered study; and that the investigator has not received significant payments of other sorts;[69] and/or

2. Disclosure of specified financial arrangements and any steps taken to minimize the potential for bias.[70]

The FDA defines disclosable financial arrangements as follows:

A. Compensation made to the investigator in which the value of compensation could be affected by study outcome.[71]

B. A proprietary interest in the tested product, including, but not limited to, a patent, trademark, copyright, or licensing agreement.[72]

C. Any equity interest in the sponsor of a covered study, i.e., any ownership interest, stock options, or other financial interest whose value cannot be readily determined through reference to public prices. This requirement applies to all covered studies, whether ongoing or completed.[73]

D. Any equity interest in a publicly held company that exceeds $50,000 in value. The requirement applies to interests held during the time the clinical investigator is carrying out the study and for 1 year following completion of the study.[74]

E. Significant payments of other sorts, which are payments that have a cumulative monetary value of $25,000 or more made by the sponsor of a clinical trial toward the Institution's expenditures of any funds under a PHS-funded research project covered study to the investigator or the investigators' institution to support activities of the investigator exclusive of the costs of conducting the clinical study or other clinical studies (e.g., a grant to fund ongoing research, compensation in the form of equipment or retainers for ongoing consultation, or honoraria), during the time the clinical investigator is carrying out the study and for 1 year following completion of the study.[75]

16-6 Public Health Service (PHS) Conflicts Rules

In 2011, the Department of Health and Human Services amended the PHS regulations "Responsibility of Applicants for Promoting Objectivity in Research for Which Public Health Service Funding Is Sought"[76] and "Responsible Prospective Contractors."[77] The regulations require all institutions receiving funds for research from an office or agency within PHS to maintain a written and enforced set of financial conflict of interest (FCOI) polices to manage, reduce, or eliminate financial conflicts. All financial conflicts of interest must be reviewed prior to institutional expenditures of any funds under a PHS-funded research project. The policies must at a minimum require:

1. A designated official within the institution responsible for the management, reduction, or elimination of the conflict.

2. Investigators to disclose all significant financial interest to their institutions. The investigators are required to disclose all significant financial interests, no later than the date of submission of the institution's proposal for PHS funded research. In addition, the investigator is under a duty to report significant financial interests on an ongoing basis as they arise or are discovered and annually.

3. The institution through an appointed official to determine whether or not the investigator has a significant financial interest that could directly and significantly affect the design, conduct, or report of the PHS-funded research.

4. The development of a management plan that eliminates or reduces the significant financial interest.

5. The institution to report to the PHS funding component all identified conflicts of interest including information such as the name of the investigator, the nature of the financial conflict of interest, the key elements of the institution's management plan and the investigator's agreement to the plan, the rationale for maintaining an investigator with a conflict of interest on the project, and a description of the monitoring the plan.

6. The significant financial interest is to be defined as any interest or payment that is for a minimum of $5,000. The significant financial conflict of interest may be in the form of equity, consulting fees, traveling reimbursement, honoraria, etc.

7. Require all investigators to complete training related to the regulations and their institutions' conflict of interest polices.

8. In the event a significant financial interest was not disclosed to the institution in a timely manner, the institution should have a process to review the financial interest and implement a management plan to manage the FCOI going forward, and develop a plan to retrospectively review the investigator's activities and the PHS-funded research to determine whether any portion of the research during the time of noncompliance was biased in the design, conduct, or reporting of such research.

16-7 Research Fraud and Abuse

Institutions and researchers can be subject to liability for scientific misconduct and research fraud, including false and misleading statements in federal research grant applications or research administration or the submission of false claims to federal agencies for improper reporting of time and effort, improper charge allocations to PHS awards, and reporting of outside financial support.

The Office of Research Integrity (ORI) has published rules that require research organizations receiving PHS funds to maintain policies and procedures for dealing with research misconduct, investigate allegations of research misconduct, and report results of misconduct to ORI.[78] The FDA has issued proposed rules requiring research sponsors to report the falsification or possible falsification of data to the relevant FDA center within 45 days of learning of the falsification of data. Falsification of data includes creating data not obtained, altering data, inaccurately recording or obtaining data, or omitting data.

Criminal prosecutions and civil False Claims Act cases have been brought in the clinical research arena for submitting false statements to the government in a research grant, falsifying or failing to maintain accurate clinical records in an FDA-approved study, and healthcare fraud. The federal civil False Claims Act (FCA) is a mechanism by which the government or private citizens can recover federal funds that have been fraudulently paid by the U.S. government, such as payments made to providers by government-funded healthcare programs. The FCA, like the state false claims laws, imposes liability only for "knowing" misconduct or situations in which someone recklessly disregards or acts with deliberate ignorance concerning the truth or falsity of a claim.[79] Additionally, DHHS may take administrative actions against anyone engaging in research misconduct, including requiring retractions and corrective articles, institutional supervision, and federal debarment. HHS also can impose civil monetary penalties or exclude parties from federal healthcare programs when there is a finding of false claims for payment of government funds. Individuals and entities that submit, cause others to submit, or conspire to submit false or fraudulent claims to the federal government are subject to treble damages and $5,500 to $11,000 for each false or fraudulent claim.

Clinical trials sponsorship by a manufacturer may implicate the FCA. Providers must pay close attention to the requirements governing the Medicare Clinical Trial National Coverage Determination (NCD) and federal grant award regulations governing research due to the potential for false claims liability. Clinical trial agreements that are not structured properly may violate the FCA if the providers bill Medicare for services or items offered as part of the care required under the research protocol. The provider/researcher must not submit claims to the federal government payers or other payers if:

1. The manufacturer agreed to pay for the services as part of the clinical trial agreement; or

2. The services are not covered.

It is improper to double bill both Medicare and a clinical trial sponsor for the same services. In addition, when a clinical trial agreement simply indicates a fixed amount of remuneration per research subject, the FCA may be implicated. Such agreements do not link payments to specific services and therefore it is difficult to discern which services are covered by the sponsor and which are to be billed to a third-party payer.

A good example of research fraud and abuse issues is the self-disclosure and settlement of Tenet Healthcare Corporation and Tenet Health System KNC, Inc., doing business as USC Norris Cancer Hospital ("Tenant USC"). Tenant USC agreed to pay $1.9 million to resolve civil monetary penalty liability for submitting claims to federal healthcare programs for clinical research-related items or services

1. Paid for by clinical research sponsors or grants under which the clinical research was conducted;

2. Identified as free of charge in the research informed consent;

3. For research purposes only and not for the clinical management of the patient; or

4. Otherwise not covered under the CMS Clinical Trial Policy.[80]

This settlement comes on the heels of the settlement of FCA allegations against numerous prestigious institutions, including the Mayo Foundation ($6.5M for allegations that it allocated unrelated research costs to government research grants) and Northwestern University ($5.5M for overstatement of cost and time reporting).[81]

16-8 Federal Healthcare Program Anti-Kickback Statute

Drug and device manufacturers often contract with research institutions to conduct research on their behalf. During the conduct of a clinical research trial, the provider and researcher may make a referral for the use of a device or drug manufactured by the sponsor that is paid for by the federal government or other healthcare plans. Improper payments to a researcher or research institution may pose a danger to patients where the payment interferes with a physician's judgment in determining the most appropriate treatment for a patient.

Clinical trial agreements that do not comply with the federal or state regulations governing referrals potentially jeopardize the financial and operational viability of the clinical research operation and the institution. An agreement that does not comply may result in enormous settlement costs and damages arising from actions under federal and state false claims acts or the federal healthcare program anti-kickback statute, or exclusion from federal healthcare programs.

The federal healthcare program anti-kickback statute, 42 U.S.C. 1320a-7b(b), is a conflict of interest law that prohibits any remuneration intended to induce referrals of patients or services paid for, in whole or in part, by any federal healthcare program, such as Medicare and Medicaid. The statute imposes criminal penalties on any person that knowingly and willfully offers, pays, solicits, or receives anything of value intended to induce referrals for items or services covered by federal health programs, including drugs and devices. When a provider enters into a clinical trial agreement with the manufacturer of a device or drug, the agreement must be structured so that it does not violate the anti-kickback statute.

Areas where the Office of Inspector General (OIG) has identified concerns under the anti-kickback statute include research that is not legitimate or necessary, research initiated by drug and device sales and marketing divisions (as opposed to the research and science divisions), and post-marketing research that is simply a pretext to generate prescriptions. In addition, a clinical trial sponsored by a manufacturer will raise concerns under the anti-kickback statute when:

1. The investigator receives money directly from the company in the form of an inducement or bonus for agreeing to conduct the trial, recruit and enroll participants, or publish the results.

2. The clinical trial agreement contains rates that exceed fair market value. Payments for services and resources provided pursuant to a research agreement must be for fair market value without regard to referrals for items and services covered by federal health programs. The services also must be legitimate, reasonable, and necessary to carry out the research trial. Therefore, all budgets should contain a detailed analysis of the services and items provided, for example physician time and effort, nursing time, overhead costs, IRB application costs, etc.

3. The clinical trial has no scientific value and is really a scheme to compensate for referrals (e.g., the company's substantial payments to physicians for de minimis recordkeeping tasks).[82]

A clinical trial sponsorship arrangement can be structured to fall within the safe harbor for personal services and management contracts if it meets the following standards:[83]

1. There is a signed written agreement;

2. The agreement specifies all services to be provided;

3. Explicit schedules, with the exact charge components and length are provided for part-time or sporadic services;

4. The term of the agreement is at least a one year;

5. The aggregate compensation is set forth in advance and based on fair market value without taking into account the volume or value of referrals or other business generated between the parties for which payment may be made under federal healthcare programs;

6. The contract is for a legitimate purpose and does not involve counseling or promotion of a business arrangement or other activity that violates state or federal law;

7. The aggregate services contracted for are commercially reasonable.

Arrangements that do not meet a safe harbor may still pass muster but should be reviewed to ensure that no part of the compensation is intended to induce referrals.

Conclusion

Clinical research is a highly regulated arena and significant legal, ethical, and regulatory guidance governs protections for human subject research, informed consent, and conflicts of interests. This chapter has provided the ethical principles and guidelines for clinical research found in the Nuremberg Code, the Declaration of Helsinki, and the Belmont Report. The U.S. DHHS has used these ethical principles to develop safeguards requiring IRB review of clinical research, informed consent of the individual research participants (including additional safeguards for vulnerable populations), and privacy and confidentiality regulations governing the uses and disclosures and written authorization for using protected health information for research purposes. Principal investigators take on key responsibilities to monitor and protect the integrity of the research and the welfare of the participants. DHHS has proposed significant regulatory changes for research protections under the Common Rule to extend those protections to all research conducted in the United States.

Clinical research is subject to numerous fraud and abuse laws. Researchers are subject to conflict of interests rules, whether through the FDA for studies under its jurisdiction or through the PHS rules for PHS-funded research projects, as well as the federal anti-kickback statute and the federal health reform sunshine act requiring disclosure of industry relationships with physician and teaching hospitals. Where researchers or institutions bill federal healthcare programs and other payers for care provided pursuant to a research study, they must follow the Medicare NCD for clinical trials. Finally, in this era of government scrutiny, researchers and research institutions should have compliance plans in place to avoid liability for research misconduct, including falsification of data and the underlying reporting of time, charge allocations, and outside financial support.

Chapter Summary

Given the historical atrocities and lack of compassion, respect, and beneficence to fellow human beings, regulations have been developed by multiple government agencies. The Common Rule regulations in the United States protect human research participants by ensuring that research participants are respected and free from coercion, their consent is voluntarily given, risks are minimized, and they understand the risks and benefits associated with their participation. The regulations are consistently changing and developing to continually ensure public safety. As noted, in 2011 new conflict of interest regulations were passed to ensure that research is not biased by investigators that may financially benefit from the outcome of the research.

Currently the Department of Health and Human Services is revising its regulations to further strengthen human participant protection. Since the adoption of the Common Rule, in 1980, there has been a major increase in research, and new technologies have been developed for research—genomics, imaging, informatics—that have altered the methods and aims of research with human participants.

Recently, the federal government proposed numerous changes to the Common Rule to bring the regulations up to date. The changes that DHHS has proposed would provide increased protection by:

1. Reviewing the level of risks to participants;

2. Streamlining the Institutional Review Board review process for research projects conducted at more than one location or institution;

3. Updating the forms and processes used for informed consent;

4. Mandating data security and information protection standards to protect participants' identifiable information;

5. Providing a systematic and uniform approach to the collection and analysis of data on unanticipated problems and adverse events across all trials; and

6. Extending the federal regulatory protections to apply to all research conducted at U.S. institutions receiving funding from the Common Rule agencies.

Instructor-Led Questions

1. Summarize how the Nuremberg Code (if adopted into regulations) would have prevented the Nazi experiments during WWII.

2. List the three ethical principles in the Belmont Report and identify the regulations in the Common Rule that embody the principle.

3. Summarize the governmental offices within the United States that regulate research, and describe their roles and responsibilities.

4. When research patient has to give his or her permission to enter voluntary into a trial, one has to obtain informal consent. Describe the key elements of informed consent process.

5. Summarize and describe some of the additional safeguards that IRBs require when reviewing study protocols for vulnerable populations.

6. Compile a list of examples of criteria that should be considered by an IRB during the course of its review.

7. Conduct a search on the Internet and either find a hypothetical or actual example of a research trial that has a potential or an actual conflict of interest. Be prepared to discuss in the actual example the consequences of the investigator actions or, in the hypothetical question, how the conflict of interest was managed, eliminated, or reduced.

Endnotes

1 Taylor, Telford "Opening Statements," *Trials of War Criminals before the Nuremberg Military Tribunals under Control Council Law No. 10.* Nuremberg, 1946. Washington DC, U.S. G.P.O., 1949.

2 Emanual, Ezrkiel J., et al. *Ethical and Regulatory Aspects of Clinical Research.* Baltimore/London: The Johns Hopkins University Press, 2003.

3 Id.

4 World Medical Association, "WMA Declaration of Helsinki - Ethical Principles for Medical Research Involving Human Subjects," (1964, last revised 2008) available at www.wma.net/en/30 publications/10policies/b3/

5 Id. at Principle 24.

6 Id.

7   Heintzelman, C.A. "The Tuskegee Syphilis Study and Its Implications for the 21st Century," The New Social Worker, Vol. 10, No. 4 (Fall 2003), available online at www.socialworker.com/tuskegee.htm (last accessed Sept. 28, 2012).

8   Centers for Disease Control and Prevention, *"U.S. Public Health Service Syphilis Study at Tuskegee"* available at www.cdc.gov/tuskegee/timeline.htm#%3E (last accessed Sept. 29, 2012).

9   Id.

10 Id.

11 Brandt, Allan M. "The Case of the Tuskegee Syphilis Study." *The Hastings Center Report* 8.6 (1978): 21-29.

12 Centers for Disease Control and Prevention. *U.S. Public Health Service Syphilis Study at Tuskegee.* 19 09 2011, available at http://www.cdc.gov/tuskegee/timeline.htm#.

13 Centers for Disease Control and Prevention. *U.S. Public Health Service Syphilis Study at Tuskegee* (2011), available at www.cdc.gov/tuskegee/timeline.htm.

14 National Research Act (Pub. L. No. 93-348) (1974).

15 The National Commission for the Protection of Human Subjects of Biomedical and Behavioral Research, 44 Fed. Reg. 23192 (April 18, 1979).

16 Id.

17 Id.

18 Bailey, Susan and Handu, Deepa (2012). *Research Ethics.* Epidemiologic Research Methods in Public Health Practice. Jones & Bartlett Learning, Burlington, MA.

19 44 Fed. Reg. at 23193.

20 Id.

21 Bailey, Susan and Handu, Deepa (2012). *Research Ethics.* Epidemiologic Research Methods in Public Health Practice. Jones & Bartlett Learning, Burlington, MA.

22 Robin Levin Penslar, "OHRP IRB Guidebook," First Clinical Research, available at http://firstclinical.com/regdocs/doc/?showpage=7&db=OTH_OHRP_IRB_Guidebook.

23 See 21 CFR Part 50 (Protection of Human Subjects), 21 CFR Part 56 (Institutional Review Boards), 21 CFR Part 21 (Investigational New Drug Applications), and 21 CFR Part 812 (Investigational Device Exemptions).

24 See "Taste of Raspberries, Taste of Death: The 1937 Elixir Sulfanilamide Incident," FDA Consumer Magazine (1981) available at www.fda.gov/AboutFDA/WhatWeDo/History/ProductRegulation/SulfanilamideDisaster/default.htm.

25 HHS Office of Research Integrity Annual Report 2007, available at ori.dhhs.gov/documents/annual.../ori_annual_report_2007.pdf

26 The Common Rule is codified at 45 CFR Part 46 (Protection of Human Subjects).

27 National Institutes of Health, *National Institute of Health, Eunice Kennedy Shriver National Institute of Child Health and Human Development, Clinical Trials and Clinical Research,* available at http://www.nichd.nih.gov/health/clinicalresearch/aboutclinicaltrials.cfm/.

28 See definitions at 45 CFR §46.102.

29 *National Institutes of Health, Eunice Kennedy Shriver National Institute of Child Health and Human Development,* "Steps Involved in Clinical Research Efforts," (2008), available at www.nichd.nigh/gov/health/clinicalresearch/steps.cfm.

30 45 C.F.R. Section 46.116.

31 See 45 C.F.R. §46.111.

32 Bailey, Susan and Handu, Deepa (2012). *Research Ethics.* Epidemiologic Research Methods in Public Health Practice. Jones & Bartlett Learning, Burlington, MA.

33 45 C.F.R. §46.111(a)(1).

34 45 C.F.R. §46.102.

35 See Institutional Review Board Guidebook, Chapter III, "Basic IRB Review," available at www.hhs.gov/ohrp/archive/irb/irb_chapter3.htm#e1.

36 45 C.F.R. §46.111(a)(2).

37 45 C.F.R. §46.111(a)(3), (b).

38 45 C.F.R. §46.111(a)(6).

39 44 Fed. Reg. 23192, at 23195 (April 18, 1979).

40 45 C.F.R. §46.116(a).

41 45 C.F.R. §46.116(b).

42 21 C.F.R. § 50.25(c).

43 21 C.F.R. §50.25 (c).

44 45 C.F.R. §46.11(d).

45 See Emergency Use of an Investigational Drug or Biologic - Information Sheet Guidance for Institutional Review Boards and Clinical Investigators, available at http://www.fda.gov/RegulatoryInformation/Guidances/ucm126491.htm

46 Belmont Report at 23197.

47 Id.

48 45 C.F.R. §46.401.

49 45 C.F.R. §46.301; 45 C.F.R. § 46.302.

50 45 C.F.R. §46.201.

51 45 C.F.R §46.201.

52 45 C.F.R. §46.404.

53 45 C.F.R. §46.405.

54 45 C.F.R. §46.406.

55 45 C.F.R §46.111(a)(7); 21 CFR §56.111(a)(7).

56 Health Insurance Portability and Accountability Act of 1996, Pub. L. No. 104-191, 110 Stat. 1936 (1996).

57 45 C.F.R. §160.103.

58 45 C.F.R. §164.514(a).

59 Id.

60 See waiver criteria at 45 C.F.R. §164.512(i)(2).

61 45 C.F.R. §164.512(i)(1)(ii).

62 45. C.F.R. §164.512(i)(1)(iii).

63 45 C.F.R. §164.514(e).

64 45 C.F.R. §164.514(e).

65 Section 13404 of the HITECH Act, in the American Recovery and Reinvestment Act of 2009, Pub. L. No. 111-5 (2009).

66 (U.S. National Institutes of Health) National Institutes of Health. 009 02 2011. 17 06 2011 http://www.nichd.nih.gov/health/clinicalresearch/aboutclinicaltrials.cfm.

67 Lo, B. & Field, M.J. (Eds). *Conflict of interest in medical research, education, and practice.* Washington, DC: National Academies Press, 2009.

68 21 C.F.R §54.1(b).

69 21 C.F.R §54.4(a).

70 21 C.F.R. §54.4(a), 54.5.

71 21 C.F.R §54.2(a) "Guidance for Industry: Financial Disclosure by Clinical Investigators" at www.fda.gov/RegulatoryInformation/Guidances/ucm126832.htm

72 21 C.F.R. §54.2(c) *"Guidance for Industry: Financial Disclosure by Clinical Investigators."* www.fda.gov/RegulatoryInformation/Guidances/ucm126832.htm

73 21 C.F.R. §54.2(b) *"Guidance for Industry: Financial Disclosure by Clinical Investigators."* www.fda.gov/RegulatoryInformation/Guidances/ucm126832.htm

74 Id.

75 21 C.F.R. §54.2(f) *"Guidance for Industry: Financial Disclosure by Clinical Investigators."* www.fda.gov/RegulatoryInformation/Guidances/ucm126832.htm

76 42 C.F.R. Part 50 subpart F.

77 45 C.F.R. Part 94.

78 42 C.F.R. Part 93.

79 31 U.S.C. 3729-3733.

80 See http://oig.hhs.gov/fraud/enforcement/cmp/false_claims.asp#2010

81 Id.

82 DHHS Office of Inspector General (OIG) Special Fraud Alert, http://oig.hhs.gov/fraud/docs/alertsandbulletins/121994.html

83 42 C.F.R. §1001.952(d).

Chapter 17

Behavioral Health Care

Russell A. Kolsrud, Gregory W. Moore, and Ryan J. Lorenz Clark Hill PLC Health Care Practice Group, and Michael W. Matthews, JD, Vice President, Medical Groups, Holland Hospital[1]

Key Learning Objectives

By the end of this chapter, the reader will be able to:

- Understand the evolution (from institutionalization to community outpatient care) of treating and caring for individuals with mental illness.

- Understand the basic principles and models of care with respect to treating and caring for individuals with mental illness.

- Explain the legal duties, risks, and challenges associated with treating behavioral healthcare consumers in community-based settings.

- Identify the various payer sources for behavioral healthcare services.

- Recognize the role that HIPAA plays with respect to behavioral healthcare providers.

- Recognize the importance of establishing a compliance program even though the Office of Inspector General has not offered specific guidance to behavioral health providers.

- Discuss some of the key provisions affecting behavioral health under health reform (the Patient Protection and Affordable Care Act of 2010).

Chapter Outline

Introduction

- The objective of this chapter is to provide an overview of behavioral health care, how behavioral health services are delivered and funded, as well the basic HIPAA requirements concerning privacy of "consumer"[2] health information and a brief summary of health reform's impact on behavioral health providers.

- Behavioral health care on one hand is simply another type of healthcare service, but on the other hand it is significantly different. Behavioral health care, sometimes referred to as "mental health care," is used in a variety of contexts to capture a wide variety of services from family and marital counseling to treatment for severe mental health conditions such as schizophrenia. In this chapter, we use the term "behavioral health care" in reference to delivery and treatment of mental illness and the term "consumer" as a commonly accepted term for those individuals seeking and receiving behavioral healthcare services.[3]

- Unlike treatment for various physical ailments such as heart disease, cancer, or other so-called traditional medical treatments or "physical medicine," delivery and treatment for mental illness is often misunderstood and carries a significant social stigma. Because of society's negative perception of mental illness, individuals often avoid seeking treatment. For example, an individual obtaining an annual physical rarely has a discussion with his or her physician about emotional or behavioral health issues; therefore, the physical exam is completed without addressing any applicable behavioral health needs. As a result, delivery of behavioral healthcare services remains fragmented and uncoordinated.

17-1 Background

Until the mid-twentieth century, most persons with serious mental illness were institutionalized.[4] The resident population of state and county mental hospitals in the United

States peaked at 560,000 in 1955.[5] The development of affordable, effective antipsychotic medications coupled with the realization by policymakers that persons with mental illness could function in society if community-based support was available resulted in deinstitutionalization.[6] By the 1960s the policy shifted 180 degrees from institutional care to promoting community-based outpatient treatment and integrating persons with mental illness into the community.[7]

Community support programs multiplied in the 1970s. The community-based system advocated a continuous system of care that could serve the comprehensive needs of persons with mental illness. The community-based programs generated a new type of behavioral health worker—the case manager.[8] The role of case managers is to ensure that the behavioral healthcare needs of persons with mental illness (consumers) are met by linking them with appropriate outpatient services.[9] ⚑ An important feature of managing and treating individuals is case management.

Case management, also commonly known as "care coordination," is a process to help ensure an individual's care is coordinated across a continuum of healthcare services. In its purest form, care coordination involves a multi-disciplinary team of professionals (e.g., primary care physicians, psychiatrists, social workers, nurses, nursing assistants, and others) who evaluate and develop an individualized plan of care, addressing and treating not only a consumer's behavioral healthcare needs but also a consumer's physical healthcare needs.

Accompanying the movement to outpatient treatment has been the recognition and strict enforcement of consumers' rights.[10] Most states have enacted community-based behavioral health statutes and regulations to assure that the rights of the consumer are no less than anyone else living in our society.[11]

People who need and use community-based services are guaranteed the right to privacy, to confidentiality, to personal freedom, "to associate with anyone of the client's choosing," to treatment under "conditions that support the client's personal liberty," and to refuse treatment and medication.[12] In publicly funded behavioral health systems, caregivers are required to make services available in the least restrictive settings, to support the patient's personal liberty, to encourage self-determination and freedom of choice, and to maximize patients' integration into the community.[13] In publicly funded behavioral health systems, caregivers are required to make services available in the least restrictive settings, to support the patient's personal liberty, to encourage self-determination and freedom of choice, and to maximize patients' integration into the community.[14]

17-2 Government and Community Roles in Behavioral Health Care

In 1960 the U.S. Supreme Court articulated the constitutional principle that legitimate government objectives may not be pursued in ways that intrude upon fundamental personal liberties when the same objectives can be achieved using less intrusive means.[15]

In 1963, Congress enacted the Community Mental Health Centers Act.[16] It was the federal government's first attempt to address comprehensive mental health needs for individuals with serious mental illness.

Despite great expectations regarding the Community Mental Health Centers Act, by the early 1970s it became clear that the community mental health system under the Mental Health Centers Act, focusing particularly on symptom control and stabilization, could not adequately address the social and more comprehensive needs of persons with serious mental illness.[17]

In the late 1970s a further developed approach advocating "community support systems" was created to help restore the individual's ability to function in the community. Known as psychosocial rehabilitation or the "Rehabilitation Model," this approach involved mental health professionals providing services to support the individual's ability to cope with the environment. These services included medication treatments, psychological counseling and support, social and leisure skills training, independent living skill training, housing, education and vocational training. Through case managers, the focus was on helping individuals develop skills and learn how to utilize resources so they could live in the community. The idea of psychiatric rehabilitation took hold as a systematic effort to help adults with serious mental illness move forward with their lives notwithstanding their mental illness.[18] The strategy is to help persons with mental illness achieve normal roles in society, integrating them into a setting of their choosing by providing behavioral health services necessary for success in those settings.[19]

17-3 The Recovery Model

Even as the Rehabilitation Model took hold, many consumers continued to feel something was missing, that services were being provided to them rather than for them, that a voice in their own treatment reflecting their own needs was lacking.[20] In the 1980s consumers who had recovered in significant respects were "able to write about their experiences of coping with symptoms, getting better and gaining an identity."[21]

These writings helped inspire the Recovery Model, in which "consumers. . . take an active role in their own care and support and in making policy."[22] This model, or movement, has been gaining strength in the United States and worldwide ever since. In the early 1990s, recovery became a concept in the design of behavioral health programs. Even individuals committed to state mental institutions were entitled to be placed in community settings for treatment and recovery.[23]

> The behavioral health system in the United States moved from a medical model focused on treating symptoms to a Rehabilitation Model seeking to maximize functioning to a Recovery Model aimed at achieving a meaningful life, hope, and independence.

⚑ The philosophy of the Recovery Model is about focusing on the process of recovery, not on the illness itself. Recovery refers to the manner in which a person with a mental illness experiences and manages his or her disorder in the process of reclaiming his or her life in the community. Recovery-oriented care is what the treatment and service practitioners offer in support of the person's own recovery efforts.[24] It recognizes the ability of all individuals to achieve a meaningful life.

> Essentially a consumer movement, the Recovery Model in behavioral health became public policy in most states through legislative enactments.[25]

Recovery in the behavioral health context is a process, a way of life, and a way of approaching the daily challenges of persons with mental illness.[26] Recovery is about "gaining a new and valued sense of self and of purpose," about aspiring "to live, work, and love in the community in which one makes a significant contribution."[26] At the heart of recovery is empowerment: "gaining control over one's life in influencing the organizational and societal structures in which one lives." The recovery philosophy makes the consumer rather than the caregiver the center stage.[28] In the context of recovery, the fundamental goal for the person with mental illness is to assume the responsibility for the management of his or her long-term illness and to achieve a self-determined life.[29]

Recovery is not a linear process. Persons with mental illness falter, relapse, regroup, and start again. When this occurs, persons with mental illness frequently come face-to-face with the legal system. Each person disabled by mental illness recovers from their illness by shifting the focus of their attention from their illness to getting on with their lives.[30] However, when the Recovery Model comes face-to-face with the legal system, which is premised on fault and blame, the success of the Recovery Model is jeopardized.

17-4 Delivery of Behavioral Health Services

Behavioral health services are offered in a variety of healthcare provider settings including hospitals, nursing homes, outpatient clinics, rural health clinics, and through community-based behavioral health services programs.

Community-based behavioral health services programs in some states are coordinated through agencies or authorities that are organized pursuant to state statutes. For example, community-based mental health services in Michigan are coordinated and rendered through community mental health services programs organized by one or more counties, and the state of Michigan financially supports such programs.[31] One or more counties may organize a community mental health agency, organization, or authority to render behavioral services.[32]

In general, the purpose of a community mental health services program is to provide a comprehensive range of mental health services for individuals located within a certain geographic service area and usually such services must be offered regardless of an individual's ability to pay. In Michigan, for example, the range of services must include, at a minimum, all of the following:

1. Crisis stabilization and response including a 24-hour, 7-day per week, crisis emergency service that is prepared to respond to persons experiencing acute emotional, behavioral, or social dysfunctions, and the provision of inpatient or other protective environment for treatment;

2. Identification, assessment, and diagnosis to determine the specific needs of the recipient and to develop an individual plan of services;

3. Planning, linking, coordinating, follow-up, and monitoring to assist the recipient in gaining access to services;

4. Specialized mental health recipient training, treatment, and support, including therapeutic clinical interactions, socialization and adaptive skill and coping skill training, health and rehabilitative services, and pre-vocational and vocational services;

5. Recipient rights services;

6. Mental health advocacy;

7. Prevention activities that serve to inform and educate with the intent of reducing the risk of severe recipient dysfunction; and

8. Any other service approved by the department.[33]

In addition to county or state organized community mental health service programs, many community-based outpatient behavioral health services are offered through private entities that are generally organized as state nonprofit corporations and exempt from federal taxation. Often the services provided by such private entities include partial hospitalization programs, assertive community treatment programs, clinical and outpatient services for adults with severe and persistent mental illness (who are at risk of hospitalization and who require ongoing care, medication, and monitoring), case management services, and support for employment services.

Most private behavioral health providers, similar to other institutional healthcare providers (e.g., hospitals and nursing homes), are subject to various state licensing rules and regulations including, without limitation, protection of consumer rights. Additionally, many private behavioral health providers elect to obtain accreditation from The Joint Commission or other applicable accrediting bodies. Like other healthcare providers, behavioral health providers receiving payment from Medicare and Medicaid must comply with the Medicare Conditions of Participation and all Medicaid rules and regulations including, without limitation, the medical necessity of services rendered.

17-5 Treatment: Involuntary and Voluntary

One unique and legally challenging aspect of behavioral health care is the admission process. The law prescribes narrow circumstances where a mentally ill individual may be admitted to a behavioral health treatment program "involuntarily." As discussed below, such involuntary admission implicates an individual's constitutional rights and such rights must be carefully protected and balanced against the individual's need for treatment.

17-5.1 Involuntary Treatment

An involuntary admission for mental health services generally begins with an application by an interested person to have a mentally ill individual admitted to a facility or outpatient treatment program when such mentally ill individual does not have the capacity to seek voluntary admission and/or will not accept treatment on a voluntary basis. Usually involuntary admissions are associated with inpatient hospitalization and not outpatient treatment. Thus, for purposes herein, we focus on inpatient hospitalization with respect to admissions for treatment.

Involuntary admissions require certification by a physician or a clinical psychologist or other professional qualified by state law to certify that an individual is mentally ill and poses a danger to himself or herself or others. Essentially, state statutes prescribe the specific process for involuntary admissions and case law, both state and federal, and define the limitations and basis for involuntary admissions.

A court-ordered treatment for mental health services is deemed involuntary and is called a "commitment" or "civil commitment." The process usually begins after an interested party petitions the court that an individual is mentally ill and is a danger to himself or herself and others. The petition also includes a certification by a physician or licensed psychologist that the individual requires mental health services.

🚩 Keep in mind that a civil commitment (i.e., court-ordered) affects an individual's constitutional rights; therefore, involuntary commitment is an extreme option,

> The U.S. Supreme Court "repeatedly has recognized that civil commitment for any purpose constitutes a significant deprivation of liberty that requires due process protections."[34]

and is recommended by a physician only when no less restrictive treatment setting is appropriate and commitment is truly warranted.

Accordingly, the Court has made clear that a state may exercise its police powers to involuntarily commit only those who are both "mentally ill and dangerous" to themselves or others.[35] Both elements must be proven with clear and convincing evidence.[36]

As mentioned above, a court-ordered commitment for treatment may be through either an inpatient or an outpatient mental health program. The period of commitment varies by state law, usually ninety days, and generally includes an option for the court to either shorten or extend the period of time for treatment through periodic reviews of the individual's status. However, unlike voluntary treatment, discussed below, an individual is not permitted to leave treatment without express permission from the court.

17-5.2 Voluntary Treatment

Voluntary treatment for behavioral health services (i.e., hospitalization) embodies the same legal issues as those covered in the text with respect to patient and provider relationships, decision making by individuals, treatment options, consent and informed consent, and others. Accordingly, unlike involuntary admissions, an individual eighteen years of age or over may choose to be hospitalized for mental health services as a voluntary patient if requested by such individual.[37] State laws normally define the process for voluntary hospitalization and often the request for admission may be either oral or in writing.

In most states, where an individual voluntary admits himself or herself into an inpatient hospitalization program, such individual may also voluntarily leave treatment and terminate his or her hospitalization.[38]

With respect to patient choice, as discussed earlier in the text, a "voluntary admission" for mental health treatment permits patient choice. Accordingly, an individual may choose to continue or discontinue mental health treatment similar to any other type of physical medicine treatment choices (e.g., discontinuing cancer treatment or leaving the hospital before the date of discharge).

Thus, for any type of voluntary treatment, whether behavioral health or physical medicine, the patient has a choice and such choice must be honored by the healthcare provider.

17-6 Behavioral Healthcare Law—Legal Duties

17-6.1 Legal Duty to Protect Others from Injury by Patient

Negligence claims involving third parties suing behavioral healthcare providers for patient-caused injuries are rising dramatically throughout the country. These actions are filed against providers for failing to protect a third party from being harmed by a patient being treated by a service provider.[39] The increasing number of this type of case brought by or on behalf of injured third parties reflects a willingness by our court system to recognize a broad legal duty owed by mental healthcare providers to their patients.

When a patient with mental illness commits a violent act and injures someone, who has potential liability? The patient? The behavioral health provider?

The landmark case defining the legal duty of a behavioral health provider to protect others from harm committed by their patient is *Tarasoff v. Regents of University of California* (1976).[40] The *Tarasoff* court ruled that when a psychiatrist determines, or through use of violence assessment tools should have determined, that a patient presents a serious danger of violence to another, the psychiatrist incurs a duty to use reasonable care to protect the intended victim against the danger. *Tarasoff* created a legal duty, not to the caregiver's patient, but *through* the caregiver's patient to a patient's potential victim. ◗ The duty owed by a caregiver to a potential victim created in *Tarasoff* has been adopted in most states.[41] For example, in *Arizona Hamman v. County of Maricopa* (1989)[42] the court acknowledged that a caregiver's duty *to prevent* a third person from harming another could arise where a "special relationship exists between the [caregiver] and the third person which imposes a duty upon the [caregiver] to control the third party's conduct."[43]

Other states adopt an approach that permits mental healthcare providers to breach a patient's confidentiality and warn potential victims, but refuse to impose a duty to do so, deferring instead to the provider's professional judgment.[44] No state imposes a legal duty to institutionalize a person who might be dangerous. Involuntary commitment, never a duty, is a treatment option requiring the careful exercise of professional judgment to avoid unnecessary harm to the patient, unwarranted deprivation of liberty, and damage to the effectiveness of treatment.[45]

Beyond the potentially indefinite loss of freedom, involuntary commitment subjects the patient to other long-lasting injuries:

> [I]t is indisputable that involuntary commitment to a mental hospital after a finding of probable dangerousness to self or others can engender adverse social consequences to the individual. Whether we label this phenomena "stigma" or choose to call it something else is less important than that we recognize that it can occur and that it can have a very significant impact on the individual.[46]

Where a provider does not believe clear and convincing evidence supports commitment, it is inappropriate for the tort system to impose a duty on him to burden the patient and the court with commitment proceedings.

The *Tarasoff* legacy is not easily implemented. How does a behavioral health caregiver determine that a patient's behavior poses a risk of harm to a readily identifiable person? Typically, the court's answer is that the risk of harm must be "imminent."[47] The term "imminent," however, is not a scientifically grounded, meaningful term. In stark contrast, the legal system, based on the premise of blame and fault, submits the question of "imminent" to the jury to decide. In the context of the *Tarasoff* legacy, it transforms behavioral health providers into victims for not using their talents to predict and prevent violence from occurring.

17-6.2 Assessing the Risk of Violence

There is no reliable, empirical evidence that a behavioral health provider can predict violent behavior over the long term of a patient's life.[48] Although assessment tools are available that help identify populations that are more likely to be violent, there is no evidence that can predict the specific risk of violence for a given individual.[49] Empirical studies reveal that despite best efforts, predictions of future violence are more often than not wrong. One study concluded that "[o]f those predicted to be dangerous, between 54 percent and 99 percent are false positives—people who will not, in fact, commit a violent act."[50] Recent studies confirm that "[l]ittle has transpired in the intervening decades to increase confidence in the ability of mental health professionals, using their unstructured clinical judgment, to accurately assess violence risk."[51]

The behavioral healthcare provider's skill and ability to predict violence is examined under the law's malpractice

criteria of legal duty and conformance to a standard of care. The dilemma created is that the law applies standards to skills that do not exist. In *Tarasoff*, Justice Mosk recognized that application of legal standards in the mental illness arena "will take us from the world of reality into the wonderland of clairvoyance."[52]

17-6.3 Behavioral Health Care and Tort Law Collide

In the legal arena, judges and juries render decisions after a violent act has already occurred, when everybody already knows the outcome. The goal in the legal arena is to assess blame and fault in individual cases. Behavioral health providers in the legal arena are held accountable based upon the perception that the behavioral health provider has the ability to predict violence and prevent it from occurring. Questions of "readily identifiable" victim and "imminent" threat identified in *Tarasoff* are left for the jury to decide.

Given the documented obstacles in predicting violence accurately, it is fundamentally unfair for the legal system's tort law to impose liability on a behavioral health provider who makes a prediction that turns out to be wrong. Judging the question of potential violence after a tragedy occurs ignores the difficulty of the clinical evaluation, undermines the Recovery Model, and introduces heuristic biases into the courtroom.

17-6.4 Hindsight Bias—Strike One

In the context of a lawsuit against behavioral health providers, hindsight bias overwhelms clinical judgments of predicting behavior. Hindsight bias is the tendency for persons (lawyers, judges, juries) with outcome knowledge (injury and death) to exaggerate their ability to predict the inevitability of the tragic event. Hindsight bias is a person's tendency to focus on the death or injury and interpret antecedent behavior or events in a backward processing mode that confirms the outcome. This tendency explains all facts as leading to the known outcome and ignores the reality that, prior to the known event, other outcomes were just as likely.[53]

Participants in our legal system overestimate both the likelihood of the known outcome and the ability to foresee the outcome.[54] One prominent study concluded that the participants exhibited hindsight bias with little awareness of its occurrence because they were unable to consciously avoid the bias when asked to ignore knowledge of the tragic event. Later studies by other psychologists substantiate these findings.[55]

A person's tendency to focus on a given outcome and interpret antecedent behavior or events in a backward processing mode is the same cognitive logic plaintiff lawyers use to analyze potential lawsuits. The plaintiff's lawyer is presented with a tragic event by a plaintiff and then looks for someone to blame. The plaintiff's lawyer falls victim to hindsight bias by focusing on the event (injury and death) and then locating antecedent events to focus the alleged cause of the violent act on the behavioral healthcare provider. The lawyer then presents the hindsight story to the jury with the injury or death as the focal point of the case. During this mental thought process, the fact finder cognitively rewrites the story "so its beginning and middle are causally connected to its end."[56]

If, instead, the lawyer, judge, and jury could set aside the known outcome of the patient's behavior, and, instead, reconstruct the conditions under which the behavioral health provider exercised foresight prior to the incident, the plausibility of alternative outcomes is substantially increased.[57]

17-6.5 The Stigma of Mental Illness—Strike Two

People in our society believe there is a strong correlation between mental illness and violent behavior.[58] Statistically accurate surveys of the population show that the stigma of mental illness is prevalent throughout society.[59] Three quarters of surveyed participants view people with mental illness to be violent toward others.[60] This perception manifests deep-seated stereotypes and prejudices about persons with mental illness: "crazy people are dangerous."[61]

The stigma of mental illness in the context of a negligence case generally exploits society's "mentalism" toward persons with mental illness for the purpose of assessing blame.[62] The belief is that people with mental illness do not recover, will remain a burden on society, and must be taken care of rather than encouraged to become independent, contributing members of our communities.[63] Similar to racism, sexism, and other forms of prejudice and discrimination, mentalism has the effect of confining a segment of the general population to second-class citizenship.[64] When such beliefs are given the judicial stamp of approval, mentalism together with hindsight bias become the basis of judicial decisions rather than relevant facts and applicable legal principles. The defendant behavioral healthcare provider has two strikes against it before the trial starts. At this point, our system of justice loses credibility and slips "into the wonderland of clairvoyance" articulated in *Tarasoff*.

17-6.6 The Recovery Model Is a Policy Decision

Fundamentally, the adoption of the Recovery Model by legislatures and courts is a policy decision by our society that the risk of violent behavior by a person with mental illness is an acceptable risk, given the alternative of locking them up in government operated asylums and drugging them senseless. This policy decision means that behavioral health providers cannot be charged with safeguarding the public against random acts of violence simply because the person committing the violence suffers from mental illness.

The legal system's premise of blame and fault does not acknowledge this policy. Instead, the legal system perceives the behavioral health clinician as the active agent and the person with mental illness as the passive agent. This perception is incongruent with the Recovery Model which empowers the individual, not the clinician.[65]

A risk assessment tool for potential violent behavior that yields accuracy at rates one click above chance may have tremendous value in the scientific community.[66] However, the inaccuracy of these assessment tools metamorphosis into jury questions in the legal system.

17-6.7 Expansion of a Provider's Legal Duty Undermines Effective Psychotherapy Practice

The *Tarasoff* rule is nearly universally accepted by the courts and provides the basis on which mental health professionals are trained. *Tarasoff* and similar decisions strike a balance between the rights of the persons with mental illness to recover and the interests of others in not being physically harmed.

Most trials, however, find it impossible to apply this principle. Hindsight bias, stigma of mental illness, and the legal system's premise of blame and fault necessarily result in behavioral health providers over-diagnosing potential violence.[67] Physicians cannot ignore the personal consequence of malpractice liability resulting in adapting their practice to mitigate the risk of liability. Empirical studies indicate that legal duties imposed on behavioral healthcare providers may influence clinical behavior even where they are not "the law," either because providers do not understand the limitation of common law decisions, or because they fear the rule in one state will soon extend to another.[68]

17-6.8 Non-Tort-Related Legal Duties

MENTAL INCOMPETENCY AND THE LAW. The *Diagnostic and Statistical Manual of Mental Disorders*–IV does not have definitions for competency and incompetency. Incompetency is not a disease. Instead, it is a legal status that signifies that an individual's mental impairment justifies delegating to someone else the power to make decisions related to some aspect of that individual's life.[69]

Incompetency is a factual conclusion found by a court to determine whether a person is mentally able to engage in a privilege, receive a benefit, participate in the judicial process, or consent to treatment. The evidence needed to justify a finding of incompetency varies depending upon the nature of the proceeding. For example, a person may be under a court-ordered guardianship, yet still be competent to make a valid will or enter into a contract. A higher evidence standard arises when the question is whether a patient lacks the competency to make a behavioral health treatment decision.

Competency in the treatment context involves the notion of informed consent, which must be made knowingly and voluntarily. The standard of proof required for the court to order someone to make a treatment decision for a patient depends upon the legal standards in each individual jurisdiction.[70] Within each jurisdiction the finding of incompetency under one standard may have little or no relationship to finding incompetency under another civil standard. For example, a person can be found to meet the criteria for involuntary commitment but that does not mean the patient is also legally incompetent to make a treatment decision.[71] It is also important to recognize that the law presumes persons are competent unless the specific individual has been adjudicated incompetent under a specific statutory scheme.

QUALIFYING FOR ENTITLEMENT PROGRAM BENEFITS. The legal standards for establishing the requisite impairment to qualify for entitlements and benefits fall into two general categories The first category focuses on the impairments that create a substantial limitation on a person's major life activities. The second category is comprised of government-sponsored entitlement and benefits based on the functioning level or employability of the individual.

The Americans with Disability Act (ADA) enacted in 1990 together with many state disability discrimination statutes are premised on the notion that many citizens suffer discrimination in gaining access to services, employment, and other aspects of community life others take for granted. The ADA protects persons from discrimination and relies on the concept of reasonable accommodation to implement remedies to eliminate specific acts of discrimination. This concept creates a legal duty for those covered under the ADA and related state statutes to take reasonable steps to assist persons who have qualifying disabilities to overcome the limitations and obstacles created by their impairment.

The ADA gives substantial deference to the *Diagnostic and Statistical Manual of Mental Disorders,* Fourth Edition ("DSM 4") to define specific qualifying mental impairments. However, expressly excluded from the ADA's umbrella are criminal and sexual conditions such as pedophilia, transsexual disorders, gender disorders, and compulsive gambling.[72] Most state jurisdictions enacted similar statutes within the analytical framework of the ADA. Although there are many different statutory schemes, nearly all require a plaintiff to exhaust administrative remedies before filing a lawsuit.[73]

The second category of impairment creating legal duties arises under the Social Security laws. In contrast to the ADA, which protects people that have the ability to work, the Social Security programs provide financial aid to those whose impairment prevents them from functioning at a level required to earn a living.[74] The legal contours defining a disability for Social Security purposes are contained in the Code of Federal Regulations.[75] As in the ADA, the Social Security benefits are disallowed for persons with a qualifying impairment when the impairment is related to a felony conviction.[76]

In these contexts, legal duties are created and limited by specific statutory and regulatory schemes. These legal duties are policy decisions made by legislative bodies. The participants in the judicial process must first know and understand what legal duty is at issue and then focus on the type of matter pending before a tribunal. For example, in a hearing regarding informed consent to treatment the legal duty is designed to protect the patient from the patient's impairment. When care or treatment is at issue, the person with the mental disability is the plaintiff enforcing a legal duty owed by the behavioral healthcare providers. In cases involving entitlements, the duty owed by the governing body gives rise to the person with the disability pursuing the patient's rights to benefits.

17-7 Funding

17-7.1 Treatment Options for the Uninsured

RELIGION-BASED. An uninsured indigent patient seeking treatment can seek pastoral counseling, pastoral psychotherapy, or clinical chaplain support through a religious organization. Religion-based treatment weaves a religious and spiritual dimension into supportive recovery. These disciplines focus clinical behavioral health practice on culturally and spiritually sensitive counseling. Formal theological training and education for pastoral counseling has been evolving for over eighty years.[77] Pastoral counseling is available in virtually all faiths. Pastoral counseling can be financed or supported by the local, regional, national, or international organization of the particular religion. However, pastoral counselors operating outside the context of the religious institution can also conduct a fee-based practice, eligible for payment from insurance and/or government programs.[78]

LICENSING AND CREDENTIALING OF PASTORAL COUNSELORS. Education and credentialing is available from several private organizations including the National Board for Certified Pastoral Counselors (NBCPA) and the Association of Clinical Pastoral Education, Inc. (ACPE). The College of Pastoral Supervision and Psychotherapy, Inc. offers an accreditation program to institutions offering pastoral counseling courses of study. Ethical standards of practice are promulgated by the American Association of Pastoral Counselors.[79] The ACPE also issues annual standards.

Licensing of pastoral counselors, psychotherapists, and chaplains is a function of state-by-state regulation.[80] In states that do not have specific licensing for pastoral counselors, a general statutory or regulatory scheme for behavioral health providers, social workers, and counselors (general, family, substance abuse, etc.) may apply.[81] However, in some states, the statutes impose licensing requirements on pastoral counselors only if they charge a fee for their services.[82] Regulations impacting the actual practice of pastoral counselors such as confidentiality remain the same. However, additional protection of communication between a person and a pastoral counselor is available as a matter of evidentiary privilege.[83]

SELF-HELP GROUPS. Self-help groups, mutual help, mutual aid, and support groups are groups of people who provide mutual support for each other. In a self-help group, the members share a common problem, often a common disease or addiction.

> Self-help groups are a common referral suggestion for behavioral health patients to save costs of treatment for a hospital, clinic, or other provider.

These groups are usually funded by private donations. Perhaps the most prominent self-help organization, Alcoholics Anonymous (AA), raises virtually all of its capital, for use in its nontreatment activities, from its members and the public at large.[84] Apart from taxation restriction, self-help programs are not required to be licensed, unless a group leader is conducting group therapy.

SELF-PAY. Whenever insurance is used, a patient's diagnosis will likely become known to his or her insurance company and possibly his or her employer.[85] This can be intrusive because a managed care insurer may need personal information about the insured in the course of utilization management or utilization review. The compromise to privacy may have a chilling effect on the otherwise open relationship of a patient with a therapist. Patients can avoid this by declining to use insurance and self-paying for services.

In addition, patients may prefer to select a therapist outside of the network of chosen providers. Treatment can endure as long or short as the patient chooses. Treatment may be as frequent as the patient chooses. Other advantages of self-pay are the ability to make use of treatment for nondiagnostic support, rather than having to be "sick" in order to avail oneself of services. Patient autonomy and self-determination are unrestricted by insurance or managed care models of traditional medicine.[86]

17-7.2 Private Insurance

Historically, mental health treatment was not a covered expense or was only available for acute inpatient hospitalization.[87] Standard indemnity insurance, fee-for-service plans, group health plans, managed care plans, major medical insurance, health maintenance organization plans, preferred provider organization plans, and point-of-service plans are all private health insurance that may provide coverage for mental health treatment. Under the Paul Wellstone Mental Health and Addiction Equity Act of 2007 (MHAEA), an employer-sponsored plan may not impose a lifetime limit on mental health benefits if there is no lifetime limit on medical/surgical benefits.[88]

The challenge of insurance is to balance meeting the patient's needs while simultaneously mitigating costs to the insurer and insured.[89] In the 1980s and early 1990s, mental health and substance abuse costs, as a component part of healthcare expenses, grew exponentially.[90] The last decade's march toward mental health and substance abuse parity has had little if any effect on increasing costs to employers and employees.[91]

Managed care can include an employee assistance program (EAP). A typical EAP involves a dedicated, around-the-clock, toll-free telephone line staffed by masters-level mental health professionals. The intake counselor screens for risk factors, explains the benefits available, makes referrals to appropriate, convenient network providers, and authorizes the initial increment of services—typically ten sessions of outpatient care. If additional or more intensive care is required, a care manager (a licensed clinician) reviews the patient's clinical status and authorizes additional care as needed.[92]

17-7.3 Public Assistance

In fiscal year 2005, state spending on mental health services exceeded $29.4 billion.[93] This equates to $100 per resident in each state. From 2001 through 2005, these expenditures (adjusted for inflation) increased by 8 percent, which is only 1.9 percent per year. From 1981 through 2005, state spending grew from $6.1 billion to $29.4 billion, representing a 6.8 percent increase each year. Adjusted for inflation and population increase, state spending declined by 4.6 percent or an average of 0.2 percent per year.[94]

State spending also saw dramatic shifts from inpatient hospitalization expenditures to community-based treatment. The percentage of total mental health expenditures in fiscal year 1981 was 63 percent for psychiatric hospitalization and 33 percent for community-based treatment. In contrast, in fiscal year 2005, the percentages had completely reversed to 27 percent for psychiatric hospitalization and 70 percent for community-based treatment. During the same timeframe, mental health–related spending by states as a percentage of all state expenditures declined. In 1981, state spending for mental health care was $6.1 billion, 2.09 percent of all state expenditures. By 2005, the percentage was 1.98 percent.[95]

State spending on mental health care and treatment is funded by federal spending, federal grants, and state revenue. In fiscal year 2005, state general and special revenues accounted for $13.9 billion of spending. Additional state funds of $4.8 billion were spent matching Medicaid

benefits. The combined state revenue and Medicaid financed 40 percent of total expenditures. Federal spending financed 31 percent consisting of Medicaid ($7.6 billion), Medicare ($54 million), Community Mental Health Block grants ($40 million), and other federal funding ($498 million). Local governments accounted for $407 million of state spending.[96]

17-7.4 Social Security

DISABILITY STATUS OCCASIONED BY MENTAL ILLNESS. As an insurance program, Social Security offers benefits to persons who are or become disabled. In summary, a person must demonstrate that a medically demonstrable disease or injury is expected to render the person incapable of performing any substantial gainful activity for not less than twelve months.[97] This includes mental disorders. The Social Security Administration has compiled a list of impairments which includes several mental disorders, including organic mental disorders; schizophrenic, paranoid, and other psychotic disorders; affective disorders; mental retardation; anxiety-related disorders; somatoform disorders; personality disorders; substance addiction disorders; and autistic disorder and other pervasive developmental disorders.[98]

Claims for disability caused by mental illness have increased substantially in the last few decades. From 1987 to 2005, the percentage of claims owing to mental illness increased from 24.1 percent to 35.9 percent.[99] According to the World Health Organization, mental illness is the leading cause of disability in industrialized countries.[100] Mental illness presents difficult eligibility questions of disability because the earning capability of mentally ill applicants may not be severely compromised, provided the person complies with a treatment plan, takes his or her medication, and makes a sincere effort to stay involved in substantial gainful activity.[101]

Eligibility determinations for disability benefits may also be complicated by the existence of co-occurring substance abuse. Applicants are ineligible for disability benefits if the disability is caused by substance abuse.[102] If the applicant would be disabled in the absence of substance abuse, he or she can be awarded a benefit.[103]

SSDI AND SSI. The Social Security Administration oversees two separate benefit programs: Social Security Disability Insurance (SSDI) and Supplement Security Income. Eligibility for disability benefits is determined using the same standard for each program.[104] Mental illness accounts for 28 percent of all persons on the SSDI rolls and

35 percent on the SSI rolls.[105] The Social Security benefit is determined based upon threshold contributions to the program by the applicant. It is intended to replace lost income, which not necessarily would be spent for treatment. The recipient can designate a third-party payee to manage the benefit for use for treatment costs.[106]

17-7.5 Medicare

The Medicare Program provides hospital insurance (Part A coverage) and supplementary medical insurance (Part B coverage). Coverage for Part A is automatic for people age sixty-five or older (and for certain disabled persons) who have insured status under Social Security or the Railroad Retirement Act. Coverage for Part A may be purchased by individuals who do not have insured status through the payment of monthly Part A premiums. Coverage for Part B also requires payment of monthly premiums. People with Medicare who have limited income and resources may get help paying for their out-of-pocket medical expenses from their state Medicaid program.[107] Medicare also provides prescription drug benefits and coverage under Part D. Unlike Parts A and B, Part D affords a number of prescription drug plan options.

17-7.6 Medicare Savings Programs

Beneficiaries of Medicare may pay cost-sharing requirements in the form of Part B (and, occasionally, Part A) premiums and deductibles. In addition, Medicare's exclusion of certain services, such as outpatient prescription drugs and nursing home care, may impose an unsustainable burden. The Medicare Savings Programs were enacted to provide low-income beneficiaries with relief from out-of-pocket costs and improve access.

Beneficiaries can qualify for the Medicare Savings Programs under five main categories:

- Qualified Medicare Beneficiary (QMB)
- Specified Low-Income Medicare Beneficiary (SLMB)
- Qualifying Individual-1 (QI-1)
- Qualified Disabled and Working Individual (QDWI)
- Medicaid Only Dual Eligibles

The benefits and eligibility criteria vary for each category. The QMB program was created under the Medicare Catastrophic Coverage Act (MCCA) of 1988, which mandated Medicaid payments toward Medicare cost-sharing requirements (premiums, deductibles, and co-insurance) for Medicare

beneficiaries with incomes up to 100 percent of the federal poverty level (FPL) and resources not in excess of twice the SSI resource limit.

Medicaid pays the Medicare Part B premiums for QMB enrollees, as well as their deductibles and co-insurance. States also have the option of providing full Medicaid benefits to Medicare beneficiaries with incomes up to 100 percent of FPL and resources not in excess of the SSI resource level.

Beginning in 1993, the SLMB program expanded these protections by mandating Medicaid coverage of Part B premiums for Medicare beneficiaries with incomes up to 120 percent of FPL and resources that do not exceed two times the SSI limit. QI-1s have income limits from 120 to 135 percent of FPL. QDWIs are people with incomes up to 200 percent of FPL that have lost their Medicare Part A benefits as a result of returning to work. Beneficiaries in both categories are allowed resources up to two times the SSI limit. Like SLMBs, Medicaid reimburses only the Part B premiums for QI-1s. Medicaid pays the Medicare Part A premiums for QDWIs. Medicaid Only Dual Eligibles are typically individuals that need to "spend down" to qualify for Medicaid or fall into a Medicaid eligibility poverty group with better coverage than the limits of the QMB, SLMB, QI-1, and QDWI programs. These categories of recipients get full Medicaid benefits and coverage of Medicare deductibles. States also have the option of covering their Part B premiums.

Medicaid has historically supplemented Medicare for recipients of SSI by paying Medicare's cost-sharing requirements and for services that are not covered by Medicare. States also have the option of providing full Medicaid coverage for catastrophic medical expenses to medically needy Medicare beneficiaries whose income and assets exceed SSI criteria. All SSI recipients and some needy eligibles are classified as QMBs. Thus, the QMB category includes both dually eligible beneficiaries receiving full Medicaid benefits and those whose coverage is limited to Medicare cost-sharing. The SLMB category may encompass some full-benefit medically needy eligibles, as well as those eligible only for coverage of Part B premiums. These groups are distinguished as "QMB-plus" and "SLMB-plus" (full-benefit dual eligibles) and "QMB-only" and "SLMB-only" (duals eligible for coverage of Medicare cost-sharing only).[108]

17-7.7 Medicaid

The Medicaid program supplements Medicare coverage by providing services and supplies that are available under state Medicaid programs. Services that are covered by both programs will be paid first by Medicare and the difference by Medicaid, up to the state's payment limit. Medicaid also covers additional services (e.g., prescription drugs). Some Medicaid benefits are also available to pay for out-of-pocket costs not fully covered by Medicare. The Medicaid program will assume their Medicare payment liability if they qualify.

Though participation in Medicaid is voluntary, every state now participates.[109] The Centers for Medicare and Medicaid Services (CMS) are authorized to waive the general state program requirements to permit states to provide additional services for chronic mental illness.[110] States have differing eligibility criteria for Medicaid benefits, and some offer benefits only to the "seriously mentally ill" or "seriously emotionally disturbed" (SMI or SED).[111] The scope of services offered also varies. In addition to treating SMI (e.g., schizophrenia, bipolarity), many states also address other areas of neurological afflictions, including children's behavioral disorders, traumatic brain injuries, developmental disabilities, and Alzheimer's disease and dementia.[112] A majority of states offer mental health and substance/alcohol abuse services through the same agency. Greater than half of people receiving state-funded mental health services receive at least some benefit from Medicaid.[113]

The flow of funding down from the federal government to the states is disbursed differently depending upon the organization of the delivery system. The portion of each state's Medicaid program that is paid by the federal government, known as the Federal Medical Assistance Percentage (FMAP), is determined annually by a formula that compares the state's average per capita income level with the national income average.[114] By law, the FMAP cannot be lower than 50 percent nor higher than 83 percent. The wealthier states have a smaller share of their costs reimbursed. For fiscal year 2011 (October 1, 2010 through September 30, 2011), the Department of Health and Human Services published FMAP rates, as shown in **Table 17-1**. Enhanced FMAP rates (eFMAP) are used in the Children's Health Insurance Program under Title XXI (CHIP or State CHIP, known as SCHIP)[115] and in the Medicaid program for certain children for expenditures for medical assistance.[116]

Some states contract through inter-governmental agreements with local government agencies, other states contract with private contractors, and still other states directly provide services through state employees.[117] Thirty-three states use managed care practices for oversight of expenditures.[118]

The Medicaid programs of the states are subject to extensive regulation and oversight. CMS provides regulatory oversight of Medicaid.[119] In addition to promulgated regulations, CMS has also issued a series of manuals to guide Medicaid at the state level as well as for use by individual providers as listed in **Table 17-2** below.

Payments for providers are expected to follow fairly rigid requirements for payment of claims. The manuals and, in particular, the State Medicaid Manual, are to be considered authoritative statements on which the CMS issues mandatory, advisory, and optional Medicaid policies and procedures to the Medicaid state agencies.[120]

17-7.8 Children's Health Insurance Program

The Children's Health Insurance Program (CHIP) was enacted under the Balanced Budget Act of 1997.[121] Title XXI of the Social Security Act anticipated the expenditure of $40 billion over the course of ten years through state-created and state-implemented programs that expanded Medicaid coverage to children.[122] Whether and to what extent CHIP will remain funded as a part of Medicaid, however, remains uncertain.[123]

Under SCHIP or CHIP, states must cover children under age 6 with family income below 133 percent of FPL and children age 6 to 18 with family incomes below 100 percent of FPL.[124] There was not and remains no mental health specific benefit. However, CHIP plans that included an Early and Periodic Screening, Diagnosis and Treatment (EPSDT) benefit encompass mental health treatment.[125]

By 2009, one in four children in the United States were dependent on Medicaid/CHIP for healthcare coverage and one in two among low-income children.[126] In response to high demand, Congress enacted the Children's Health Insurance Program Reauthorization Act of 2009 (CHIPRA) which amended the 2008 Mental Health Parity and Addiction Equity Act of 2008 (MHPAEA) to impose a parity requirement for SCHIP at the state level.

Table 17-1 Federal Medical Assistance Percentages and Enhanced Federal Medical Assistance Percentages Effective October 1, 2012 to September 30, 2013 (Fiscal Year 2013)*

State	Federal Medical Assistance Percentage	Enhanced Federal Medical Assistance Percentage
Alabama	68.53	77.97
Alaska	50.00	65.00
American Samoa	55.00	68.50
Arizona	65.68	75.98
Arkansas	70.17	79.12
California	50.00	65.00
Colorado	50.00	65.00
Connecticut	50.00	65.00
Delaware	55.67	68.97
District of Columbia	70.00	79.00
Florida	58.08	70.66
Georgia	65.56	75.89
Guam	55.00	68.50
Hawaii	51.86	66.30
Idaho	71.00	79.70
Illinois	50.00	65.00
Indiana	67.16	77.01
Iowa	59.59	71.71
Kansas	56.51	69.56
Kentucky	70.55	79.39
Louisiana	61.24	72.87
Maine	62.57	73.80
Maryland	50.00	65.00
Massachusetts	50.00	65.00
Michigan	66.39	76.47
Minnesota	50.00	65.00
Mississippi	73.43	81.40
Missouri	61.37	72.96
Montana	66.00	76.20
Nebraska	55.76	69.03
Nevada	59.74	71.82
New Hampshire	50.00	65.00
New Jersey	50.00	65.00
New Mexico	69.07	78.35
New York	50.00	65.00

North Carolina	65.51	75.86
North Dakota	52.27	66.59
Northern Mariana Islands	55.00	68.50
Ohio	63.58	74.51
Oklahoma	64.00	74.80
Oregon	62.44	73.71
Pennsylvania	54.28	68.00
Puerto Rico	55.00	68.50
Rhode Island	51.26	65.88
South Carolina	70.43	79.30
South Dakota	56.19	69.33
Tennessee	66.13	76.29
Texas	59.30	71.51
Utah	69.61	78.73
Vermont	56.04	69.23
Virgin Islands	55.00	68.50
Virginia	50.00	65.00
Washington	50.00	65.00
West Virginia	72.04	80.43
Wisconsin	59.74	71.82
Wyoming	50.00	65.00

* Federal Register, Vol. 26, No. 23 pp. 74061-74063 (Nov. 30, 2011).

Table 17-2 List of Cms Publications for Medicaid*

CMS Publ. No./ Medium	Title
06 Paper[†]	Coverage Issues Manual
09 Paper	The Outpatient Physical Therapy/CORF Manual
10 Paper	The Hospital Manual
11 Paper	The Home Health Agency Manual
12 Paper	The Skilled Nursing Facility Manual
13 Paper	The Intermediary Manual
14 Paper	The Carriers Manual
15-1 Paper	The Provider Reimbursement Manual - Part 1
15-2 Paper	The Provider Reimbursement Manual - Part 2[‡]
19 Paper	The Peer Review Organization Manual
21 Paper	The Hospice Manual
23 Paper	The Regional Office Manual
27 Paper	The Medicare Rural Health Clinic and Federally Qualified Health Center Manual

29 Paper	The Medicare Renal Dialysis Facility Manual
45 Paper	The State Medicaid Manual
81 Paper	The End-Stage Renal Disease Network Organization Manual
100 Internet-Only (IOM)	Introduction
100-01 IOM	Medicare General Information, Eligibility and Entitlement Manual
100-02 IOM	Medicare Benefit Policy Manual
100-03 IOM	Medicare National Coverage Determinations (NCD) Manual
100-04 IOM	Medicare Claims Processing Manual
100-05 IOM	Medicare Secondary Payer Manual
100-06 IOM	Medicare Financial Management Manual
100-07 IOM	State Operations Manual
100-08 IOM	Medicare Program Integrity Manual
100-09 IOM	Medicare Contractor Beneficiary and Provider Communications Manual
100-10 IOM	Quality Improvement Organization Manual
100-11 IOM	Reserved
100-12 IOM	State Medicaid Manual[§]
100-13 IOM	Medicaid State Children's Health Insurance Program
100-14 IOM	Medicare ESRD Network Organizations Manual
100-15 IOM	State Buy-In Manual
100-16 IOM	Medicare Managed Care Manual
100-17 IOM	CMS/Business Partners Systems Security Manual
100-18 IOM	Medicare Prescription Drug Benefit Manual
100-19 IOM	Demonstrations
100-20 IOM	One-Time Notification
100-21 IOM	Recurring Update Notification

[*] "http://www.cms.gov/Regulations-and-Guidance/Guidance/Manuals/index.html?redirect=/Manuals/

[†] "Paper" manuals may be downloaded from the CMS website.

[‡] Active cost report forms are furnished in two formats for visually impaired and nonimpaired users.

[§] Under development. Publication Number 45 remains effective as of September 5, 2012 as to Publication Number 100-12.

17-7.9 Veterans Health Administration

The Veterans Health Administration (VHA) offers inpatient and outpatient mental health services at its medical centers and outpatient clinics. The VHA also offers readjustment counseling services "Vet Centers." Mental health services are available in specialty clinics, primary care clinics, nursing homes, and residential care facilities as part of a complete continuum of health care. The VHA also offers intensive case management, day centers, work programs, and psychosocial rehabilitation for those with serious mental health problems. The VHA may contract with private providers to deliver these services.[127] Services and programs that are supported by the Office of Mental Health Services include:

- Inpatient care
- Residential care
- Outpatient mental health care
- Homeless programs
- Programs for incarcerated veterans

- Specialized post-traumatic stress syndrome (PTSD) services
- Military sexual trauma
- Psychosocial rehabilitation and recovery services
- Substance use disorders
- Suicide programs
- Geriatrics
- Violence prevention
- Evidence-based psychotherapy programs
- Mental health disaster response/post-deployment activities

Eligibility for services and benefits depends upon the service of the veteran, the discharge status, and familial relationship of dependents.

17-7.10 Community Mental Health Services Block Grants

In 1992, the Department of Health and Human Services, Alcohol, Drug Abuse and Mental Health Administration (ADAMHA) was reorganized as the Substance Abuse and Mental Health Services Administration (SAMHSA).[128] SAMHSA was to include Centers for Mental Health Services (CMHS) for substance abuse prevention and for substance abuse treatment. The CMHS was authorized to make an allotment of funds to each state for issuance of the previously created Community Mental Health Services Block Grants (CMHSBG).[129] State allotments may be reduced based upon annual reporting to Congress.[130]

From 1983 through 2005, CMHSBG spending increased by 74 percent from $230 million to $400 million. In real terms, however, adjusted for inflation, this increase represents a decrease of 46 percent. Over the same timeframe, as a percentage of total state expenditures, CMHSBG expenses went from 10.7 percent to 1.9 percent.[131]

Though the prevalence of block grant funding has diminished, states generally reported that the block grants promote greater flexibility than fee-for-service or capitation financing supplied by Medicare and Medicaid. For example, states have reported making use of block grant funds for supported employment, vocational employment, sheltered employment, supported residence/housing, housing/case management, housing support activities, transitional shelter programs, supervised apartments, supported independent living, assisted living housing, supported housing pilot projects in

urban and rural settings, outpatient psychiatric treatment, therapeutic foster or group homes, assessments, medication management, outpatient counseling, services in nursing homes, in-home, on-site treatment, residential services/support, day treatment, illness (co-mordity) management, therapeutic nursing services, short-term intervention, intake/triage, rehabilitation services, therapeutic rehabilitation, day rehabilitation, community rehabilitation, psychosocial rehabilitation, respite care, aftercare, family support, transportation, peer support, crisis stabilization, mobile crisis, crisis support, crisis/emergency screening, crisis telephone, integrated dual disorders, drop-in/self-help centers, club houses, warm-lines, social clubs, peer case management support, peer-delivered community support, and consumer network and outreach to priority or at-risk populations (e.g., elderly, homeless, incarcerated, disabled, cultural minorities, and veterans). Though block grant funding can only be allocated to a limited quantity of administrative costs, states report beneficial use in building a delivery system and setting up infrastructure. Indeed, since 2006, SAMHSA has asked states to begin reporting in their Mental Health Block Grant Plans (MHBG Plans)[132] about the transformational activities in which they were engaged, to meet the goals of the presidential commission report "Achieving the Promise: Transforming Mental Health Care in America."[133]

17-8 Health Information Laws and Compliance Programs in a Behavioral Health Setting

17-8.1 HIPAA/HITECH

> HIPAA applies to behavioral healthcare providers similar to any other type of healthcare provider.

The year 2010 was a dynamic one for the healthcare industry—across the board. Of significant importance to healthcare compliance was the passage of the American Recovery and Reinvestment Act (ARRA), which contained the Health Information Technology for Economic and Clinical Health Act (HITECH). Additionally, Congress brought us the Fraud Enforcement and Recovery Act of 2009 (FERA) intended to further the Centers for Medicare and Medicaid Services' (CMS) reach in fighting fraud, waste, and abuse claims.

With the passage of each new law, rule, or regulation, behavioral health organizations had to assess whether they were in compliance with the new control, or whether they needed to implement new systems to better monitor their daily operations. Fortunately, because most of the new and revised rules apply equally across all healthcare providers, behavioral health organizations have had the ability to see what other healthcare sectors are doing while they are implementing their own processes.

Although the common elements applicable to all healthcare sectors may be helpful to organizations looking at compliance concerns, no one size fits all. Where the treating environment is one based on the mental health of those individuals that are seeking necessary assistance from a behavioral health provider, broad-based compliance rules intended to apply to most if not all healthcare organizations do not always make sense.

In the past, Congress has recognized certain sensitivities when legislating for behavioral and other mental health providers, in particular when dealing with mental health records. For example, HIPAA provides an exception to the rule regarding certain disclosures of patient protected health information (PHI) existing in the patient's designated record set that may include psychotherapy notes.[134]

HIPAA specifically states that a covered entity must obtain an authorization for any use or disclosure of psychotherapy notes except for those notes that are used to carry out treatment, payment, or healthcare operations.[135] However, authorization is not required for:

"(A) Use by the originator of the psychotherapy notes for treatment;

(B) Use or disclosure by the covered entity for its own training programs in which students, trainees, or practitioners in mental health learn under supervision to practice or improve their skills in group, joint, family or individual counseling; or

(C) Use or disclosure by the covered entity to defend itself in a legal action or other proceeding brought by the individual."[136]

Because of the heightened standard requiring patient authorization for the release of psychotherapy notes, the behavioral health organization does not have to account to the patient for disclosures made pursuant to that authorization.[137]

When Congress eliminated the accounting for disclosures requirement with regard to psychotherapy notes, a number of mental health professionals raised specific concerns about the removal of this requirement believing that "their patients should always have the right to monitor access to their personal information."[138]

In response to the industry's concerns, Congress stated that, "[i]t is because of these concerns that the Rule requires, with limited exceptions, individual authorization for even routine uses and disclosures of psychotherapy notes by anyone other than the originator of the notes."[139] This is an example of where Congress specifically addressed the needs of mental health professionals and patients.

However, the newest wave of HIPAA privacy and security regulations implemented as a result of ARRA and HITECH do not specifically include considerations for behavioral health providers and their patients. In failing to do so, Congress may have acted to the detriment of the consumer.

Consider the following example in relation to the applicability of the new Breach Notification Rule issued on August 24, 2009, as implemented by HITECH, in a scenario involving particular privacy concerns in the behavioral health industry.

A behavioral health provider discovers that one of its laptops containing a collection of physician notes discussing a patient currently under the care of the physician has been lost or stolen. Now consider that the behavioral health provider failed to secure or otherwise encrypt the information that was contained on the laptop. Therefore, anyone could pick up the laptop and access this information.

After discovery of the breach, the provider conducts a risk assessment attempting to identify the potential harm to the patient as a result of the breach. In its risk assessment, the provider properly tells the physician that the physician's psychotherapy notes on the patient have been lost. In response, the physician tells the provider that the patient is not emotionally prepared to learn that his personal information may have been lost. Based on the physician's opinion, the provider properly determines that the patient is at significant risk of reputational harm. Further, the provider determines that, because HITECH requires the provider to notify the patient of a breach where there is the "unauthorized acquisition, access, use or disclosure of protected health information in a manner not permitted under [the Privacy Rule] which compromises the security or privacy of the protected health information,"[140] the provider is going to notify the patient.

Under HIPAA, "a covered entity must. . . treat a personal representative as the individual for purposes of [HIPAA]."[141] The law goes on to state that, "[i]f under applicable law a person has authority to act on behalf of an individual who is an adult or an emancipated minor in making decisions related to health care, a covered entity must treat such person as a personal representative under [HIPAA], with respect to protected health information relevant to such personal representation."[142]

Notification to a personal representative in matters involving the mental condition of the patient is also supported in the preamble to the Breach Notification Rule. There, the Secretary states that, "where the individual affected by a breach is a minor or otherwise lacks legal capacity due to a physical or mental condition, notice to the parent or other person who is the personal representative of the individual will satisfy the requirements of [notification to the Individual]."[143]

If a patient does not currently have a personal representative in place, there may be an opportunity for the provider, physician, and patient to have a dialogue about the benefits of a personal representative. However, even though the Breach Notification Rule requires notification "without unreasonable delay."[144] It could certainly be argued that the process to establish a personal representative for the patient is reasonable where the patient's physician believes that notification to the patient may cause undue harm.

17-8.2 Benefits of an Effective Corporate Compliance Program

Like all other healthcare providers, behavioral healthcare providers will likely benefit from implementing an effective compliance program. The healthcare industry, including behavioral healthcare providers, is one of the most highly regulated industries in the United States.

> The purpose of establishing and maintaining a "compliance program" is to help ensure that the organization, its employees, and its agents comply with all of the applicable laws, regulations, and standards including, without limitation, compliance with Medicare and Medicaid regulations.

In 1991, the Department of Justice first promulgated the U.S. Sentencing Guidelines (USSG) identifying the basic elements of effective compliance programs for organizations. Today, the revised USSG sets forth that an effective compliance program has, at a minimum, the following seven components: 1) compliance standards and procedures, 2) oversight responsibilities, 3) appropriate screening procedures, 4) training and education, 5) auditing and monitoring, 6) enforcement and discipline, and 7) response and prevention.

Beginning in 1997, the Office of the Inspector General (OIG) began its process of supplementing the USSG elements with specific compliance program guidance (CPG) directed at a number of individual healthcare sectors. Interestingly, the OIG stated in its initial plan that, "[a]doption of the clinical laboratory model compliance plan. . . and future model compliance plans for other health care providers, will be voluntary."[145]

To date, the OIG has issued guidance specifically directed at the hospital industry, home health agencies, clinical laboratories, third-party billers, the durable medical equipment industry, hospice providers, Medicare+Choice (Medicare Advantage) organizations, nursing facilities, ambulance suppliers, pharmaceutical manufacturers, and individual and small group physician practices. Beyond the OIG, Congress for the first time issued a statutory mandate for compliance program implementation in health care as part of the Patient Protection and Affordable Care Act of 2010 (P.L. 111-148). Specifically, the Act requires all skilled nursing facilities and nursing facilities to implement compliance and ethics programs for all employees and agents prior to March 23, 2013. While there has been no specific guidance to date directed at the behavioral health sector, the statutory mandate in the Act should be viewed by all segments of the healthcare industry as an example of what may occur if providers ignore the recommendation to voluntarily adopt a compliance program.

Even though the OIG has not offered specific guidance for behavioral health providers, the OIG treats behavioral health providers who have committed any wrongdoing in the same manner that it treats other healthcare providers. For example, when entering into a corporate integrity agreement with a behavioral health provider, the OIG almost always requires that the provider implement a compliance program.

Therefore, behavioral health providers should review the existing guidance offered by the OIG in the various sectors and adopt corporate compliance programs based on common threads between those OIG programs and the original guidance offered by the Department of Justice.

17-9 Healthcare Reform and Behavioral Health

The Act is generally intended to ensure that almost every American will have comprehensive health insurance coverage, including coverage for treatment of mental illness and substance use disorders (SUD). Furthermore, individuals may no longer be excluded due to pre-existing conditions or dropped because of their health status. The Act will likely have far-reaching, primarily positive, effects on behavioral health providers and their patients. Several of the key provisions that will affect behavioral healthcare providers include:

- Parity for mental health and SUD treatment: The Act requires mental health and SUD benefits to be offered at "parity" with other medical and surgical benefits for all insurance plans sold within the health insurance exchanges. The exchanges are designed to be a competitive marketplace for individuals and small employers to shop for health insurance.[146]

- Essential benefits package: The Act includes mental health and SUD treatment in the required essential benefits package offered in the state health insurance exchanges, which are required to be implemented by 2015.[147]

- Support, education, and research for postpartum depression: Provides support services like screening to women suffering from postpartum depression and psychosis and also helps educate mothers and their families about these conditions. The Act also provides support for research into the causes, diagnoses, and treatments of postpartum depression and psychosis.[148]

- Co-locating primary and specialty care in community based mental health settings: The Act authorizes $50 million in grants for coordinated and integrated services through the co-location of primary and specialty care in community-based mental and behavioral health settings.[149]

- Centers of excellence for depression: The Act directs the Administrator of the Substance Abuse and Mental Health Services Administration to award grants to centers of excellence in the treatment of depressive disorders beginning in 2011.[150]

- Medicaid Emergency Psychiatric Demonstration Project: The Act requires the Secretary of Health and Human Services to establish a three-year Medicaid demonstration project in up to eight states. Participating states would be required to reimburse certain institutions for mental disease for services provided to Medicaid beneficiaries between the ages of 21 and 65 who are in need of medical assistance to stabilize an emergency psychiatric condition under EMTALA.[151]

- Community health centers: The Act increases funding for community mental health centers.[152]

- Patient-Centered Medical Home: A Patient-Centered Medical Home (PCMH) is a team-based model of care led by a personal physician who provides continuous and coordinated care throughout a patient's lifetime to maximize health outcomes. The PCMH practice is responsible for providing for all of a patient's healthcare needs or appropriately arranging care with other qualified professionals. This includes the provision of preventive services, treatment of acute and chronic illness, assistance with end-of-life issues, and behavioral health. It is a model of practice in which a team of health professionals, coordinated by a personal physician, works collaboratively to provide high levels of care, access and communication, care coordination and integration, and care quality and safety.[153]

It's clear under the Act that behavioral health providers will likely have access to commercial payer sources which were not otherwise available in the past, and behavioral healthcare providers will have opportunities to seek grants and other funding to expand services and explore opportunities to integrate care with physical medicine providers (e.g., PCMHs and Community Health Centers).

Chapter Summary

Behavioral health care is simply one type of service along the healthcare continuum. Keep in mind that we have broadly used the term "behavioral health care" in this chapter to capture a wide variety of services from family and marital counseling to treatment for severe mental health conditions such as schizophrenia. It's helpful and important to be aware that an individual's behavioral health needs can affect and be related to such individual's physical healthcare needs, and vice versa. Accordingly, coordination of care is key to treating and caring for consumers in community-based settings.

Behavioral healthcare providers are subject to many of the same laws, rules, and regulations that govern other provider types and are also subject to similar legal risks. However, treating individuals in a community-based behavioral health setting creates certain risks (both legal and social) that are unique to the behavioral health industry.

Key Terms and Definitions

Case Management – A collaborative process of assessment, planning, facilitation, care coordination, evaluation, and advocacy for options and services to meet an individual's and family's comprehensive health needs through communication and available resources to promote quality cost-effective outcomes.[154]

Commitment or Civil Commitment – Commonly used terms to described involuntary court-ordered treatment for behavioral healthcare services.

Compliance Program – An internal program established by a healthcare organization to encourage the development and use of internal controls to monitor adherence to applicable statutes, regulations, and program requirements (e.g., compliance with submitting claims and receiving payment from federal healthcare programs such as Medicare or Medicaid). Compliance program guidance has been published by the OIG and is available online at: http://oig.hhs.gov/compliance/compliance-guidance/index.asp

Diagnostic and Statistical Manual of Mental Disorders, 4th Ed. – Commonly known as the "DSM-4," it's a manual published by the American Psychiatric Association and covers all mental health disorders in adults and children.

Health Reform or Health Care Reform – A phrase generally referring to the Patient Protection and Affordable Care Act of 2010 (P.L. 111-148).

Recovery Model – A type of treatment process through which consumers take an active role in their own care and support. The Recovery Model focuses on the process of recovery and not on the illness itself.

Instructor-Led Questions

1. Discuss the Recovery Model. What is the overall purpose of the Recovery Model?

2. How is a behavioral health consumer's treatment different than a typical acute care patient?

3. What is the purpose of case management or care coordination? How does such process assist with caring for consumers?

4. What is the process for an involuntary inpatient admission for psychiatric services?

5. What protections are granted to an individual who is subject to such involuntary admission? What is the court's role?

6. When a patient with a mental illness commits a violent act and injures someone, who has potential liability?

7. What legal duty or duties does a behavioral health provider have to protect others against harm? How does the *Tarasoff* decision balance the interest between a behavioral health consumer's right to recover and potential physical harm to others?

8. How do individuals pay for behavioral health services? What types of payer sources are available for behavioral health services?

9. Why might an individual pay privately for behavioral health services?

10. What role does HIPAA play with respect to behavioral healthcare providers?

11. What is the purpose of a compliance program and why would behavioral healthcare providers implement such a program?

12. The Patient Protection and Affordable Care Act, under health reform, provides access to funding for the co-location of acute primary care services and behavioral health services. What would be the advantage(s) of integrating behavioral healthcare services with physical medicine services? What would be the disadvantage(s)? Would there be cost savings? Would such integration of care help with the social "stigma" of mental health services?

Endnotes

The authors wish to express gratitude to their colleagues, Peter Domas and Neda Ryan, for their work in editing this chapter.

1   The Health Care Practice Group of Clark Hill PLC is co-chaired by Russell A. Kolsrud and Gregory W. Moore. Portions of this chapter have been reprinted from the *2011 Health Law and Compliance Update,* John Steiner, Editor, Wolters Kluwer Law & Business, Aspen Publishers.

2   Individuals seeking behavioral healthcare services are often referred to as "consumers" as opposed to "patients."

3   Note that the term "consumer" and patient may be used interchangeably throughout this chapter.

4   Grob, G., *The Mad among us: A history of the care of America's mentally ill*. Cambridge: Harvard University Press (1995).

5   P. Corrigan, K. Mueser, G. Bond, R. Drake & P. Solomon, *Principles and Practice of Psychiatric Rehabilitation: An Empirical Approach,* Ch. 3 Guilford Publications, Inc. (2008).

6   A. Harris and A.J. Lurigio. *Mental Illness and Violence: A Brief Review of Research and Assessment Strategies.* Aggression and Violent Behavior 12 (2007) 542-551.

7   Id.; Stone, *"The Tarasoff Decisions: Suing Psychotherapists to Safeguard Society,"* 90 HARD. L. REV. 358, 364 (1976); see also 42 U.S.C. § 9401.

8   Id.

9   Id.

10 *Olmstead v. Zimring*, 527 U.S. 581 (1999); *Addington v. Texas*, 441 U.S. 418, 425, 99 S. Ct. 1804, 60 L. Ed. 2d 323 (1979).

11 See Ariz., A.R.S. § 550, et seq.; A.R.S. §§ 36-3403, 36-3407, 36-3408; A.A.C. § R9-21-201 through R9-21-207; see also 42 U.S.C. § 9501; see, e.g., Colo. Rev. Stat. § 13-21-117; Del. Code Ann. Tit. 16, ch. 54, § 5402; Idaho Code § 6-1902; Ind. Code Ann. §§ 34-30-16-1, 34-30-16-2; Ky. Rev. Stat. Ann. § 202A.400; La. Stat. Ann. 9:2800.2; Md. Cts. & Jud. Pro. § 5-609; Mass. Gen. Laws, ch. 123, §36B, ch. 112, § 129A; Mich. Stat. Ann. § 14.800 (1946); Minn. Stat § 148.975; Miss. Code Ann. § 41-21-97 (2006); *Bradley v. Ray*, 904 S.W.2d 302 (Mo. Ct. App. 1995); Mont. Code Ann. § 27-1-1102; Nebr. Rev. Stat. §§ 71-1, 206.30 and 71-1,336; N.H. Rev. Stat. Ann. §§ 329:31, 330-A:35; N.J. Stat. § 2A:62A-16; Ohio Rev. Code Ann. § 2305.51(B); Okla. Stat. 59 §1376; *Emerich v. Philadelphia Ctr. For Human Dev.*, 720 A.2d 1032 (Pa. 1998); *Bishop v. S.C. Dep't of Mental Health*, 502 S.E.2d 78 (S.C. 1998); Tenn. Code Ann. §§ 33-3-206, 33-10-302; Utah Code Ann. §78-14a-101; *Peck v. Counseling Service of Addison County*, 499 A.2d 422 (Vt. 1985); Wash. Rev. Code Ann. § 71.05.120 (West); *Schuster v. Altenberg*, 424 N.W.2d 159 (Wisc. 1988). See *Nasser v. Parker*, 455 S.E.2d 502 (Va. 2005) (under Virginia law, psychiatrist and hospital have no duty to control outpatient or warn potential victim).

12 Id., Ariz. Stat. et al.

13 See e.g. A.A.C. R9-21-201 (Arizona regulation defining rights of persons with serious mental illnesses.)

14 42 U.S.C. § 9501; A.R.S. § 36-550(1); Ariz. Admin. Code R9-21-201 through R9-21-207.

15 *Shelton v. Tucker*, 364 U.S. 479 (1983).

16 Public Law 88-164 (1963); see also Corrigan, Supra note 5.

17 R. Drake, A. Green, K. Mueser, & H. Goldman, The History of Community Mental Health Treatment and Rehabilitation for Persons With Severe Mental Illness. *Community Mental Health Journal*, 39, 427–440 (2003).

18 Corrigan, supra note 5.

19 Id.

20 Id.

21 Id.

22 Id.

23 Id. *Olmstead v. Zimring*, 527 U.S. at 599; R. Drake, A. Green, K. Mueser & H. Goldman, The History of Community Mental Health Treatment and Rehabilitation for Persons with Mental Illness; Community Mental Health Journal, 39, 427–440 (2003).

24 Tondora, J., Davidson, L., Yale University Program for Recovery and Community Health; Practice Guidelines for Recovery-Oriented Behavioral Health Care (2006).

25 Arizona enacted a statutory scheme invoking the Recovery Model. A.R.S. § 36-550 through 550.08 (1980); A.R.S. §§ 36-3401 through 3435 (1986); see also 16 Del. C. § 5402 (2007), N.J. Stat. § 2A:62A-16 (2007), Cal. Civ. Code § 43.92 (2006), Rev. Code Wash. § 71.05.120 (2007), Texas H&S Code 2006, Miss. Code Ann. § 41-21-97 (2006), Fla. Stat. § 491.0147 (2006), and R.I. Gen. Laws § 40.1-5-2 (2007).

26 Report of the Surgeon General on Mental Health at 98 (1999) (Citing, Deegan, P. E., Recovery: The lived experience of rehabilitation. Psychiatric Rehabilitation Journal, II, 11–19. (1988)).

27 Id.

28 Corrigan, supra note 5.

29 Id.

30 Id.

31 MCL § 330.1202.

32 MCL § 330.1204.

33 MCL § 330.1206.

34 *Addington v. Texas*, 441 U.S. 418, 425 (1979).

35 *Jones v. United States*, 463 U.S. 354, 362 (1983)

36 *Addington*, 441 U.S. at 431-32; *Foucha v. Louisiana*, 504 U.S. 71, 75-76 (1992); A.R.S. § 36-540(a).

37 MCL 330.1411.

38 MCL 330.1412.

39 R.I. Simon & R.L. Sadoff, *Psychiatric Malpractice Cases and Comments for Clinicians* 137 American Psychiatric Publishing. (1992).

40 17 Cal.3d 425, 551 P.2d 334, 131 Cal.Rptr. 14.

41 See, e.g., Colo. Rev. Stat. § 13-21-117; Del. Code Ann. Tit. 16, ch. 54, § 5402; Idaho Code § 6-1902; Ind. Code Ann. §§ 34-30-16-1, 34-30-16-2; Ky. Rev. Stat. Ann. § 202A.400; La. Stat. Ann. 9:2800.2; Md. Cts. & Jud. Pro. § 5-609; Mass. Gen. Laws, ch. 123, § 36B, ch. 112, § 129A; Mich. Stat. Ann. § 330.1946; Minn. Stat. § 148.975; *Bradley v. Ray*, 904 S.W.2d 302 (Mo. Ct. App. 1995); Mont. Code Ann. § 27-1-1102; Nebr. Rev. Stat. § 38-2137; N.H. Rev. Stat. Ann. §§ 329:31, 330-A:35; N.J. Stat. § 2A:62A-16; Ohio Rev. Code Ann. § 2305.51(B); Okla. Stat. 59 § 1376; *Emerich v. Phila. Ctr. For Human Dev.*, 720 A.2d 1032 (Pa. 1998); Bishop v. *S.C. Dep't of Mental Health*, 502, S.E.2d 78 (S.C. 1998); Tenn. Code Ann. § 33-3-206; Utah Code Ann. § 78B-3-502; *Peck v. Counseling Serv. of Addison County, Inc.*, 499 A.2d 422 (Vt. 1985); Wash. Rev. Code. Ann. § 71.05.120 (West).

42 161 Ariz. 58, 775 P.2d 1122 (1989).

43 Id. at 62.

44 See Alaska Stat. § 08.86.200(a)(3); Conn. Gen. Stat. §§ 52-146c(c)(3) and 52-146f(2); D.C. Code. Ann. § 7-1203.03; Fla. Stat. § 491.0147(3); Ill. Compl. Stat. Ann. Ch. 740, § 110/11(viii); Miss. Code Ann. § 41-21-97; N.Y. Mental Hygiene Law § 33.13(c)(6) (Consol.); Or. Rev. Stat. § 179.505(12); R.I. Gen. Laws § 5-37.3-4(b)(4); Tex. Health & Safety Code § 611.004(a)(2); W.Va. Code Ann. § 27-3-1(b)(5).

45 Paul B. Herbert and Kathryn A. Young, Tarasoff at Twenty-Five, 30 J. Am. Acad. Psychiatry & L. 275, 275 (2002).

46 *Addington*, 441, U.S. at 425-26; *see also Vitek v. Jones*, 445 U.S. 480, 492 (1980).

47 Ginsberg, B., *Tarasoff at Thirty: Victim's Knowledge Shrinks The Psychotherapist's Duty to Warn and Protect*, Journal of Contemporary Health and Law Policy (Winter 2004), Issue 1; Vol. 21 p.1.

48 Mossman, D., The Imperfection of Protection Through Detection and Intervention, 30 J. Legal Med. 109, 113 (2009).

49 Miller, M.C., *Forensic Psychiatry A Model for the Assessment of Violence*. Harvard Review of Psychiatry, 2000; 7(5): 299-304.

50 Monahan, J., *The Prevention of Violence*, in Community Mental Health and the Criminal Justice System 13, 21 (John Monahan ed., 1976).

51 Monahan, J., *Tarasoff at Thirty: How Developments in Science and Policy Shape the Common Law*, 75 U. Cin. L. Rev. 497, 500 (2006).

52 *Tarasoff v. Regents of Univ. of Cal.*, 551 P.2 334, 354 (1976).

53 Stallard and Worthington, Reducing the Hindsight Bias; *Law and Human Behavior*, Vol. 22, No. 6, 671–683 (1998).

54 Fischhoff, B. (1975). (Hindsight-foresight): *Journal of Experimental Psychology: Human Perception and Performance*, 1, 288-299.

55 Hawkins, S.A., & Hastie, R. (1990). Hindsight: Biased Judgments Of Past Events After The Outcomes Are Known. *Psychological Bulletin*, 107, 311-327.

56 Wasserman, D. (1991). Hindsight and causality: *Personality & Social Psychology Bulletin*, 92, 683-700.

57 Id.

58 Id., Harris, A. and Lurigio, A., at 543-45.

59 Monahan, J., Arnold, J., "Violence By People with Mental Illness: A Consensus Statement by Advocates and Researchers," 19 Psychiatric Rehabilitation J. 67 (1996).

60 Id.

61 Id.

62 Tondora, J., Davidson, L., *supra* note 24.

63 H. Bursztajn, T. Gutheil, A. Brodsky, and E. L. Swagerty, "Magical Thinking," Suicide, and Malpractice Litigation, *Bulletin Am. Acad. Psychiatric Law*, Vol. 16, No. 4, p. 369-377 (1988).

64 Tondora, J., Davidson, L., *supra* note 24.

65 Corrigan, supra note 5.

66 Lake, "Revisiting *Tarasoff*," 58 ALB. L. Rev. 97, 98 (1994); Dvoskin, J. & Heilbrunk, "Risk Assessment and Release Decision-Making: Toward Resolving the Great Debate, 29 J. Am. Acad. Psychiatry & L. 6 (2001).

67 Stone, supra note 7 at 375.

68 *See* Daniel J. Givelber, et al., *Tarasoff, Myth and Reality: An Empirical Study of Private Law in Action*, 1984 Wisc. L. Rev. 443, 468-72 (1984) (within five years of the *Tarasoff* decision, a majority of therapists outside California believed that the law derived from this case governed their conduct; non-California providers gave more warnings to potential victims after *Tarasoff*, believing they had a legal duty to do so even if the warning compromised their clinical judgment. Such a result is also contrary to society's policy decision that the risk of violent behavior by a person with mental illness is an acceptable risk, given the alternative of deprivation of a person's independence and human dignity).

69 T. Sasz, "Medical Incapacity, Legal Incompetency and Psychiatry," 23 Psychiatric Bulletin, 517-9 (1999).

70 P.S. Applebaum & T. Griso, "The MacArthur Treatment Competency Study. I Mental Illness and Competency to consent to treatment," 19 L. & Hum. Behav. 105 (1995).

71 H. Schwartz, Shifting Competency During Hospitalization: A Model for Informed Consent Decision," 37 Hosp. & Community Psychiatry, 1256-60 (1986).

72 42 U.S.C. § 12101-12211.

73 Compare Or. Rev. Stat. § 695.400 (1999) with R.I. Gen. Laws § 28-5-6 (4) (2000); see also Alaska Stat. § 48.80.300 (12) (2000); Neb. Rev. Stat. Ann. § 48-1107.02 (2000); Tex. Law. Code Ann. § 21.002(6) (2000).

74 42 U.S.C. §§ 401-433 (1935).

75 20 C.F.R. §§ 404.1501-1575 (2000).

76 20 C.F.R. § 404.1506(a).

77 Miller, Perry N, Lawrence, Raymond J, and Powell, Robert C; "Discrete Varieties of Care in the Clinical Pastoral Tradition;" Journal of Pastoral Care & Counseling 57(2) at 111-16 (2003).

78   Federal funding for religious organizations may be obtained without regard for religious affiliation in the same fashion as any other nonprofit entity. 42 U.S.C. § 290kk-1.

79   See N.H. Rev. Stat. § 330-A:10(VII).

80   See, Ky. Rev. Stat. § 335.600 et seq.; 32 Maine Rev. Stat. § 13851 et seq.; Mont. Code Annot. § 37-17-104; N.H. Rev. Stat. § 168-B:18; N.C. Gen. Stat. § 90-380 et seq.; Tenn. Code. Annot. § 63-22-201 et seq.

81   But see, 59 Okla. Stat. § 1932(A)(4) and 63 Penn. Stat. § 1203(3) (exempting pastoral counselors from behavioral practitioner licensing requirements).

82   See, e.g., Ky. Rev. Stat. § 335.600 et seq.

83   *Cox v. Miller*, 296 F.3d 89, 102 (2d Cir. 2002); R. Michael Cassidy, Sharing Sacred Secrets: Is it (Past) Time for a Dangerous Person Exception to the Clergy-Penitent Privilege?, 44 Wm. & Mary L. Rev. 1627, 1645 (2003).

84   According to GuideStar USA, Inc., a nonprofit tax return database, the General Service Board of Alcoholics Anonymous, Inc., reported $10.2 million in gifts, grants, and contributions for 2008. None of these dollars were reported as government grants.

85   See, e.g., N.J. Rev. Stat. § 45:14B-2 (diagnostic information, status/severity of condition, prognosis including minimum time of continued treatment).

86   See generally, Miller, Ivan; "The Death of Independent Practice Has Been Greatly Exaggerated and How Guilds Can Help"; 20 Independent Practitioner at 180-181 (2000).

87   Frank, R. G., McGuire, T. G., & Goldman, H. Buying in the public interest. Washington, DC: Bazelon Center (1996).

88   29 U.S.C. § 1185a(a)(1)(A). See 110 P.L. 343; 122 Stat. 3765. See also, 42 U.S.C. § 300gg-26.

89   Frank, R. G., Goldman, H. H., & McGuire, T. G. "A model mental health benefit in private health insurance"; 11(3) Health Affairs at 98-117 (1992).

90   Goldman, W., McCulloch J., Cuffel, B., & Kozma, D. "More Evidence of the Insurability of Managed Behavioral Health Care." 18(5) Health Affairs at 172-81 (1999).

91   U.S. Department of Health and Human Services. *Mental Health: A Report of the Surgeon General – Executive Summary*. Rockville, MD: U.S. Department of Health and Human Services, Substance Abuse and Mental Health Services Administration, Center for Mental Health Services, National Institutes of Health, National Institute of Mental Health, Ch. 6. 1999.

92   Id.

93   These figures do not account for a federal match of funding for Medicaid nor mental health benefits funded directly by the federal government to beneficiaries. However, because public funding of mental health treatment falls broadly on the shoulders of the Medicaid program, figures provided in this paragraph are gross state spending, regardless of the revenue source for that expenditure. It should be noted that gross federal spending increased dramatically as a result of the American Recovery and Reinvestment Act of 2009, under which Congress and the president authorized the expenditure of an estimated $149 billion in health spending of which $87 billion is for a temporary increase in the federal share of Medicaid costs. Kaiser Commission on Medicaid and the Uninsured. "American Recovery and Reinvestment Act: Medicaid and Health Care Provisions." Medicaid Facts, Publication #7872 (2009).

94   Lutterman, T., Berhane, A., Phelan, B., Shaw, R., & Rana, V. Funding and characteristics of state mental health agencies, 2007. HHS Pub. No. (SMA) 09-4424. Rockville, MD: U.S. Department of Health and Human Services, Substance Abuse and Mental Health Services Administration, Center for Mental Health Services, at 87-95 (2009).

95   Id.

96   Id. at 95-98.

97   42 U.S.C. §§ 423, 1382.

98   Social Security Administration, Bluebook (SSA Pub. No. 64-039, ICN 468600), September 2008 (http://ssa.gov/disability/professionals/bluebook/general-info.htm).

99   Social Security Administration, Annual Statistical Report on the Social Security Disability Insurance Program, 2007, 2008.

100 As of 2000, mental illnesses accounted for 24 percent of disabilities. This figure excludes substance and alcohol abuse and degenerative mental problems normally associated with old age such as Alzheimer's disease and dementia. World Health Organization. *The World Health Report 2001 - Mental Health: New Understanding, New Hope*. Geneva: World Health Organization (2001).

101 Danziger, S., Frank, R., and Meara, E. "Mental illness, work, and income support programs." 166(4) Am. J. Psychiatry, 398, 399 (2009).

102 42 U.S.C. § 423(d)(2)(C); *Vester v. Barnhart*, 416 F.3d 886, 888 (8th Cir. 2005).

103 20 C.F.R. § 404.1535(b)(1); *Brueggemann v. Barnhart*, 348 F.3d 689, 694-95 (8th Cir. 2003); Bustamante v. Massanari, 262 F.3d 949, 955 (9th Cir. 2001); Drapeau v. Massanari, 255 F.3d 1211, 1214 (10th Cir. 2001).

104 42 U.S.C. §§ 423(c) and 1382c(a)

105 President's New Freedom Commission on Mental Health. Achieving the Promise: Transforming Mental Health Care in America, at 29 (2003).

106 42 U.S.C. § 405(j).

107 42 U.S.C. §§ 1395c, 1395j.

108 Haber, S., et al. Evaluation of Qualified Medicare Beneficiary (QMB) and Specified Low-Income Medicare Beneficiary (SLMB) Programs. Research Triangle Institute: Waltham, MA (2003).

109 In 1988, Arizona became the fiftieth state to enact a program, the Arizona Health Care Cost Containment System, to participate in Medicaid. Ariz. Rev. Stat. § 36-2901 et seq.

110 42 U.S.C. § 1396n(c) and (i); Social Security Act § 1915(c) and (i).

111 Lutterman et al., supra, at 21-22.

112 Id. at 2.

113 Id. at 31-32.

114 42 U.S.C. § 1396(b).

115 The column for "Enhanced FMAP" (eFMAP) is equal to the federal medical assistance percentage (as defined in the first sentence of 42 U.S.C. § 1396b(b)) increased by a number of percentage points equal to 30 percent of the number of percentage points by which (1) such federal medical assistance percentage for the state, is less than (2) 100 percent; but in no case shall the enhanced FMAP for a state exceed 85 percent. Example: Alaska's FMAP is 50 percent. Its FMAP is 50 less than 100 percent. Thirty percent (0.3) of that amount is 15, which is added to its FMAP, for an eFMAP of 65 percent. eFMAP rates are for use in computing certain child benefits under 42 U.S.C. § 1396b(u)(2) and (3). 42 U.S.C. § 1397ee(a)(1).

116 74 Fed. Reg. 63,315 (Nov. 27, 2009). FMAP rates are for benefits. The federal government matches fifty percent of administrative costs for most functions "across-the-board" for every state.

117 Id. at 35.

118 Id. at 37-38.

119 43 C.F.R. 430 et seq.

120 42 C.F.R. § 433.123.

121 42 U.S.C. § 1397aa et seq.; 105 Pub. Law 33; 111 Stat. 251 (1997).

122 Committee on Child Health Financing. "Implementation Principles and Strategies for Title XXI (State Children's Health Insurance Program)." 101(5) Pediatrics at 944 et seq. (1998).

123 V. Smith, S. Rosenstein, & R. Rudowitz, "Medicaid's Continuing Crunch in a Recession: A Mid-Year Update for State FY 2010 and Preview for FY 2011," Kaiser Commission on Medicaid and the Uninsured (February 2010).

124 42 U.S.C. § 1397cc.

125 Parisi, L. & Bruno, R. "Dental and Mental Health: Benefit Improvements in CHIPRA." Families USA, (http://www.familiesusa.org/issues/childrens-health/chipra-implementation-series.html) (January 2010).

126 C. Hoffman, et al., "The Uninsured: A Primer," Kaiser Commission on Medicaid and the Uninsured (October 2009); Kaiser Commission on Medicaid and the Uninsured. "Medicaid Enrollment: June 2009 Data Snapshot," (February 2010).

127 38 U.S.C. § 1712A.

128 102 Pub. Law 321; 106 Stat. 323 (1992)

129 42 U.S.C. §§ 300x and 300x-7.

130 42 U.S.C. § 300x(d)(2)(B).

131 National Association of State Mental Health Program Directors (NASMHPD) Research Institute, Inc. "How State Mental Health Agencies Use the Community Mental Health Services Block Grant to Improve Care and Transform Systems: 2007." Rockville, MD (2007).

132 Mental health block grant funds are distributed by CMHS to eligible states. In order to receive mental health block grant funds, a state must complete an application and prepare a comprehensive annual plan for providing community mental health services (i.e., a MHBG Plan). Once the application and MHBG Plan are approved by CMHS, then a state receives funding in accordance with a formula that takes into consideration certain economic and demographic factors.

133 Id.; [29], supra.

134 45 C.F.R. § 164.508 (2009).

135 Id.

136 Id. (authorization is also not required for use and disclosure (i) at the request of the Secretary to determine HIPAA compliance; (ii) as required by law; (iii) for use in oversight activities by the originator of the psychotherapy notes; (iv) by a coroner or medical examiner; or where there may be a serious or imminent threat to the health or safety of a person or the public).

137 45 C.F.R. § 164.528(a)(1)(iv) (2009).

138 Standards for Privacy of Individually Identifiable Health Info., 67 Fed. Reg. 53244 (Aug. 20, 2002).

139 Id.

140 Breach Notification for Unsecured Protected Health Info.; Interim Final Rule, 74 Fed. Reg. 42743 (Aug. 24, 2009).

141 45 C.F.R. § 164.502(g)(1).

142 45 C.F.R. § 164.502(g)(2).

143 Breach Notification for Unsecured Protected Health Info.; Interim Final Rule, 74 Fed. Reg. 42750 (Aug. 24, 2009).

144 74 Fed. Reg. at 42749 (Aug. 24, 2009).

145 62 Fed. Reg 9435 (Mar. 3, 1997).

146 Ibid Section 1311(j) and 1562(c)(4); See also http://archive.constantcontact.com/fs091/1101795608829/archive/1103249925487.html

147 Ibid Section 1302; See also http://archive.constantcontact.com/fs091/1101795608829/archive/1103249925487.html

148 Ibid Section 2952; See also http://archive.constantcontact.com/fs091/1101795608829/archive/1103249925487.html

149 Ibid Section 5604; See also http://archive.constantcontact.com/fs091/1101795608829/archive/1103249925487.html

150 Ibid Section 10410; See also http://archive.constantcontact.com/fs091/1101795608829/archive/1103249925487.html

151 Ibid Section 2707; See also http://archive.constantcontact.com/fs091/1101795608829/archive/1103249925487.html

152 Ibid Section 5207. See also http://archive.constantcontact.com/fs091/1101795608829/archive/1103249925487.html

153 Ibid Section 3502; See also http://www.acponline.org/running_practice/pcmh/understanding/what.htm/

154 The Case Management Society of America, http://www.cmsa.org.

Chapter 18

Intellectual Property Issues in Health Care

Alicia M. Passerin, Ph.D., Esq., Christine W. Trebilcock, Esq.

Key Learning Objectives

By the end of this chapter, the reader will be able to:

- Understand the four types of intellectual property.

- Identify when intellectual property has been created.

- Understand when intellectual property can and should be protected.

- Explain the laws by which intellectual property can be protected.

- Discuss why management of an intellectual property portfolio is important to a healthcare institution.

Chapter Outline

Introduction

Health care as an industry involves creative and driven individuals and includes medical personnel, researchers, professors, and other technical specialists. Healthcare providers, large academic medical centers, and private corporations have realized the economic benefit of protecting intellectual property rights, whether those rights are embodied in a trademark that a well-known medical institution has used for years or in a patent that discloses a new drug therapy discovered through research at an academic institution. This chapter provides an overview of the four types of intellectual property and the laws in place to protect that intellectual property.

18-1 Types of Intellectual Property

Every business, including those in the healthcare sector, owns subject matter that results from creations of the mind known as "intellectual property" and that fosters innovation and profitability, thereby providing that business with certain competitive advantages that lead to the foundation for and maintenance of market dominance. Therefore, it is in every business's best interest to constantly develop, evaluate, and protect its intellectual property portfolio.

The term "intellectual property" reflects that the subject matter is a product of intellectual rather than physical activity and includes such creations as inventions, designs, logos and tag-lines, trade secrets, and original works of authorship. These "creations of the mind" are similar to personal and real property in that they can be protected under the law through various government-recognized entitlements attached to certain forms of ideas, information, and other intangible assets. The owner of these entitlements generally may exercise, or may authorize others to exercise, *exclusive* rights to use or otherwise exploit the subject matter.

There are four distinct fields of intellectual property: patents, trade secrets, trademarks and service marks, and copyrights. In general, patents and trade secrets protect technology and inventions, trademarks and service marks protect the goodwill associated with goods and services, and copyrights protect authored works such as art and literature. A business's ultimate legal protection often derives from a diverse intellectual property portfolio that is comprised of various embodiments of each type of intellectual property.

This chapter begins by providing a basic background and general discussion of each distinct field of intellectual property and provides examples of how a healthcare institution may generate and need to protect such intellectual property. The chapter then discusses the importance of managing an intellectual property portfolio for a healthcare institution.

18-1.1 Patents[1]

The rights of the U.S. government to grant patents derive from the U.S. Constitution.[2] Patent rights are codified in Title 35 of the U.S. Code.

On September 8, 2011, the U.S. Senate passed the Leahy-Smith America Invents Act (AIA), one of the most sweeping patent reforms of the patent laws in the United States since the Patent Act of 1952. See H.R. 1249, 112th Cong. (2011). President Obama signed the AIA into law on September 16, 2011. The scope of the changes to the patent laws is significant. However, Congress did build transition periods into the AIA in order to assist patent applicants, patent holders, and the United States Patent and Trademark Office (USPTO) to adjust to these sweeping changes. Although the default effective date of the AIA is September 16, 2011, many of the provisions have their own effective dates. Perhaps one of the most fundamental changes of the AIA switches the U.S. patent system from a "first-to-invent" system to a "first-inventor-to-file system" in which the right to patent an invention is given to the first inventor to file a patent application. The first-inventor-to-file system goes into effect on March 16, 2013.

A patent is an exclusive right granted by the government upon application by an inventor to exclude others from "making, using, offering for sale, or selling the invention throughout the United States or importing the invention into the United States, and, if the invention is a process, of the right to *exclude* others from using, offering for sale or selling throughout the United States, or importing into the United States, products made by that process."[3]

Examples of technology that may be developed and patentable by healthcare institutions include a new medical device for use in performing knee surgery developed by a physician on staff at a hospital, a new therapeutic drug composition for treating cancer developed by a researcher at a research institution, or an information technology system for managing electronic medical records developed by a product development team at a healthcare institution.

A patent is therefore sometimes described as a "negative right" because it provides the patent owner with the right to exclude others from practicing the patented invention rather than granting the patent owner the right to practice the invention. The right to exclude others from practicing the claimed invention is made in exchange for public disclosure and use after expiration of the exclusive right. The exclusive rights granted in a patent are "for a term beginning on the date on which the patent issues and ending twenty years from the date on which the application for patent was filed. . . ."[4]

Congress has provided for extensions of the patent term for special classes of inventions by passing legislation designed to permit patent term extension for products, such as drugs, which must be approved by the FDA before marketing. In the past, the often time-consuming FDA approval procedure was criticized as a disincentive for the development of new drugs. For example, a new drug might not be approved by the FDA until ten years after a patent for the drug had been obtained, leaving the patentee with a shortened time in which to market the drug exclusively. For many companies, such a short term of effective patent protection would preclude recovery of the investment required to develop the new drug.

Why are patents important to the healthcare sector? Bringing a new product into the marketplace is costly and risky and requires significant investment from the research and development stage up through utilization and commercialization. Patents help organizations to recoup this investment by preventing competitors from copying the invention and competing against them. Examples: • When a physician develops a medical device for use in knee surgery, he spends time and hospital resources in designing, testing, and perfecting the device. Patenting, and then perhaps licensing the technology to a medical device company, helps the hospital that employs that doctor to recoup the investment of physician time and hospital resources. • Drug compositions take years of bench-top research to formulate before going to market. Patenting the composition allows the research institution an exclusive period in which to sell the composition in order to recoup that investment in years of research and development.

The number of patent applications filed by U.S. applicants over the past decade has increased by nearly 47 percent (from 164,795 applicants filed in 2000 to 241,977 applications filed in 2010) and the number of patents issued to U.S. patentees over the past decade has increased by nearly 27 percent (from 85,068 patents issued in 2000 to 107,792 patents issued in 2010).[5]

WHAT IS PROTECTED? A utility patent, as the name implies, is granted exclusively by the federal government through the U.S. Patent and Trademark Office (USPTO) for inventions that perform some function or utility. This is in contrast to those that are merely ornamental and therefore fall within the scope of design patents, or those that involve plants and may be protected by plant patents.

Inventions protectable by utility patents include processes, machines, articles of manufacture, compositions of matter, and improvements on any one of these. The healthcare sector generates numerous inventions that fall into a variety of categories of subject matter, including medical devices, pharmaceutical compositions, therapeutic agents, and business methods. Protecting these inventions against copying by competitors and accelerating their entry into the marketplace is key to a healthcare organization's gaining and maintaining a competitive advantage

The term "process" means not only an actual process, but may also refer to an "art" or "method," or a "new use of a known process, machine, manufacture, composition of matter, or material." 35 U.S.C. § 100 (2006). This includes automated data processing technologies and business methods. Compositions of matter generally refer to new compounds created by man. These include new chemical compounds, mixtures, alloys, and drugs. Improvements on such compositions or composite articles are also subject to patent protection.

STANDARDS FOR PROTECTION. An important principle of patent law relating to patentable subject matter is that abstract ideas or conceptions are not patentable. A patent allows the patentee to exclude others from making, using, offering for sale, selling, or importing an invention. There are specific statutory guidelines that limit patents to those inventions which, upon an in-depth review by an examiner at the USPTO,[6] meet specific statutory requirements.

> After a patent application is filed with the USPTO, an examiner is assigned to review the application for patentability. To be patentable, the invention must be useful, novel (i.e., new), not an obvious combination of existing elements, and adequately described so that others can practice the invention. The U.S. Supreme Court has defined "useful" to include "anything under the sun that is made by man" and to exclude "laws of nature, natural phenomenon, and abstract ideas." *Diamond v. Chakrabarty*, 447 U.S. 303, 309 (1980). If the examiner finds that the statutory requirements are satisfied, then a patent will be issued from the application. Patents have a term of twenty years from the date on which the application was filed. Information on how to file a patent application is available on the USTPO website at http://www.uspto.gov.

THE DECISION TO PATENT — THE MEMORANDUM OF INVENTION. Issues relating to management of an intellectual property portfolio are discussed in section 18-2 of this chapter.

One of the most difficult things for a business to oversee is identification of patentable inventions. This section discusses steps that a business should take in identifying and protecting inventions.

A Memorandum of Invention should be filed on any discovery that is technically new. In case of any doubt, the memorandum should be filed or a member of the patent committee should be consulted.

> A patent committee is a panel that a business establishes to evaluate inventions and to determine how to protect the intellectual property embodied in those inventions. During the course of contact between the inventor and the patent committee, it may become apparent that, while the invention is patentably significant, the value to the company would be greater if the invention were kept secret. See trade secrets discussion in section 18-1.2.

A Memorandum of Invention should be filed when the work has progressed to the point where the utility of the invention is known and some idea of the scope of the invention has been obtained. Even if the invention merely relates to an idea that has not been fully developed, with no actual reduction to practice, it is generally good practice to require employees to file the invention disclosure appraisal form. It is not necessary, nor is it effective to wait for commercial interests to develop.

A sample Memorandum of Invention is provided in Appendix A. Copies of pertinent notebook pages, reports, or drawings should be attached to the completed memorandum because they help to establish the earliest date of invention.

The purpose of the memorandum is to establish the state of the art prior to the invention, what the invention is, how the invention differs from the prior art, the improvements that the invention offers, and the like. Additionally, the memorandum should indicate if the invention has been disclosed, and if so, to whom and on what date. The date of any disclosure is critical for determining if the invention is eligible for patent filing in the United States or abroad.

The Memorandum of Invention should be reviewed and one of the following should happen, as laid out in Appendix A: (a) patent application(s) will be drafted and filed in an appropriate patent office; (b) a patentability study will be conducted to determine if the invention meets the requirements of patentability; (c) further work will be required from research; (d) the disclosure will be inactivated; or (e) the invention will be maintained as a trade secret.

18-1.2 Trade Secrets

PROTECTING TRADE SECRETS. Simply stated, a trade secret is confidential information that has commercial value. A business typically invests significant time, money, and energy into generating information that is core to its position in the marketplace, and access to such information by competitors can impair a business's economic vitality. Trade secret law provides a means by which to protect this confidential information.

Trade secret laws are included under state laws to protect against the misappropriation of certain confidential information that has commercial value. Virtually any type of useful information can qualify as a trade secret so long as the information derives independent economic value from not being generally known or readily ascertainable and the owner of the information has used reasonable efforts to maintain the secrecy of the information. In general, there are two categories of trade secret information: technical information, including formulae, processes, designs, devices, software, and research and development, and business information, including commercially useful information such as business methods, distribution processes, strategic plans, customer lists, pricing information, and marketing and advertising strategies.

> Examples of technology or data that may be held as a trade secret by a healthcare institution include vendor lists, financial information, patient lists, marketing strategies, business plans, processes for evaluating or managing patient data, or pricing or cost data.

🏴 Most states have ratified the Uniform Trade Secrets Act (UTSA),[7] which defines a trade secret as "information, including a formula, pattern, compilation, program, device, method, technique, or process, that: (i) derives independent economic value, actual or potential, from not being generally known to, and not being readily ascertainable by proper means by, other persons who can obtain economic value from its disclosure or use, and (ii) is the subject of efforts that are reasonable under the circumstances to maintain its secrecy."[8] However, the statutory language by which a trade secret is defined and the type of information that is subject to trade secret protection vary by jurisdiction.[9] In general, however, there are three elements common to all trade secret definitions:

i. the information making up the trade secret is information that is not generally known to the public;

ii. the information provides economic value to the owner that derives from the information not being generally known; and

iii. the information making up the trade secret is the subject of reasonable efforts to maintain its secrecy.

Some factors that courts consider in determining if a trade secret exists include:

i. the extent to which the information is known by third parties;

ii. the extent to which the information is known by employees and others involved in the company's business;

iii. the extent of measures taken by the company to guard the secrecy of the information;

iv. the value of the information to the company and to its competitors;

v. the amount of effort or money expended by the company in developing the information; and

vi. the ease or difficulty with which the information could be properly acquired or duplicated by others.[10]

In *Amedisys Holdings, LLC v. Interim Healthcare of Atlanta*, Plaintiff Amedisys claimed that two materials were trade secrets: its "Referral Logs," a resource to track patient referrals, used to target sales efforts to clinicians and facilities likely to refer patients to Amedisys, and its "Workbooks," which contain doctor referral statistics and industry metrics, used to target doctors who frequently refer patients for home health care and hospice services. *Amedisys Holdings, LLC v. Interim Healthcare of Atlanta, Inc.*, No. 11:11-cv-1437, 2011 U.S. Dist. LEXIS 59260, *2-*3 (June 3, 2011). The court found that the Referral Logs and Workbooks were trade secrets because they "contain valuable, proprietary information uniquely known to Amedisys, and which is not publicly available. This information, which Amedisys collects, evaluates, analyzes, and arranges, enables Amedisys employees to make informed, fact-based decisions on where to focus their business solicitation efforts. It is this information that transforms an ordinary list of doctors and healthcare providers to a trade secret." *Amedisys*, 2011 U.S. Dist. LEXIS 59260, at *17-*18.

🏴 Upon public disclosure, the information loses its trade secret status.[11] Thus, the owner of a trade secret must take reasonable affirmative steps to maintain a trade secret.[12] Examples of such steps include:

i. having a written trade-secret policy;

ii. marking trade secret documents as "Proprietary and Confidential";

iii. restricting access to trade secrets to a need-to-know basis;

iv. locking areas that house trade secrets;

v. requiring employees to sign employment agreements with confidentiality provisions; and

vi. requiring third parties who are given access to the trade secret to sign nondisclosure and/or noncompete agreements.

Such protective measures essentially permit a trade secret to be of unlimited duration as long as the information can be and is kept secret and provides a commercial advantage to its owner by virtue of its secrecy.

> An example of a confidentiality provision follows: Confidentiality. Receiving Party may, with respect to Disclosing Party's Confidential Information: (i) only use the Confidential Information for the purposes envisaged under this Agreement; (ii) ensure that only those of its officers and employees who are directly concerned with the carrying out of this Agreement have access to the Confidential Information on a strictly applied "need to know" basis and are informed of the secret and confidential nature of it; (iii) keep the Confidential Information secret and confidential and not directly or indirectly disclose or permit to be disclosed, make available or permit to be made available the same to any third party for any reason without the prior written consent of Disclosing Party; and (iv) not copy, reproduce or otherwise replicate for any purpose or in any manner whatsoever any documents containing the Confidential Information except as necessary to exercise the rights granted it under this Agreement.

MISAPPROPRIATION OF TRADE SECRETS. The misappropriation of trade secrets is actionable if the secrets were acquired improperly, such as through theft, bribery, espionage, or misrepresentation, or if an individual violates a duty to maintain a confidentiality.[13] There are three elements to proving misappropriation of a trade secret. First, the holder of the trade secret must prove that the trade secret is information that provides economic value to the owner and that is not generally known to the public. Second, the holder of the trade secret must prove that the defendant acquired the trade secret information wrongly (i.e., the information was misappropriated). The owner of a trade secret cannot enforce trade secret rights against another who *independently* develops or discovers the same subject matter. Rather, misappropriation of a trade secret requires objective evidence that the trade secret was taken by one who had an obligation to the owner of the trade secret to maintain the secrecy of the trade secret. Third, the holder of the trade secret must prove that affirmative steps were taken to prevent disclosure of the trade secret.

Remedies for misappropriation of trade secrets can include preliminary or permanent injunctions, actual and punitive damages, profits gained by the party who misappropriated the trade secret, and reasonable royalties.[14]

TRADE SECRETS AND DEPARTING EMPLOYEES. One challenge that many businesses face is how to protect trade secrets from misappropriation by departing employees. Some key steps that a business can take to protect its trade secrets from such misappropriation include having clear written policies in place with respect to the confidentiality of trade secrets, and employment and noncompete agreements, where allowed, that set forth an employee's obligations to the employer with respect to confidential and proprietary information.

> In the healthcare industry, one example of a trade secret is a patient list. The issue of misappropriation of the patient list typically arises when a physician leaves a practice and takes a patient list with him. In general, courts balance the right of the employee to pursue his occupation against the right of the employer to be protected against improper use of a trade secret. In re *Phoenix Dental,* 144 B.R. 22, 24 (Bankr., W.D. Pa. 1992).
>
> Where the customer names and information represent a material investment by the employer, the information is a valuable asset of the employer that is not subject to use by a former employee. Id. at 25. Such protection does not extend to information that is widely known or readily ascertainable from an independent source. Id.
>
> Patient lists generally qualify for trade secret protection because the names of the patients are unique and are not available from an outside source, the list is a valuable asset to the practice, and the relationships with the patients resulted from an investment made by the employer. See e.g., id. at 22; see also *Dickinson Med. Grp. v. Foote,* No. 834-K1984 Del. Ch. LEXIS 429 (May 10, 1984).

18-1.3 Trademarks

WHAT IS A TRADEMARK OR SERVICE MARK? A trademark is a word, phrase, logo, or symbol that the producer of a good (or, in the case of a service mark, the provider of a service)[15] uses to distinguish his or her goods (or services) in commerce. Trademark law in the United States is governed by the Lanham Act of 1946, which is codified in Title 15 of the U.S. Code.[16] A trademark is a basic form of intellectual property that is used by a business to identify and distinguish its goods and services from those produced by others. The purpose of a trademark is to prevent confusion among consumers as to the source of the goods offered in connection with the trademark and to prevent fraud and misrepresentation as to their source. A trademark connotes a standard of quality in the goods or services with which it is used. As such, a trademark accrues "goodwill" as consumers associate positive feelings or experiences with the goods and the associated source of the goods.

Examples of marks owned by members of the healthcare sector include service marks owned by a physician practice, hospital, or clinic and used in connection with providing healthcare services.

There are several categories of trademarks: (1) A trademark is a mark that distinguishes one's goods from those of another. A trademark that is not federally registered (discussed below) is designated by the "TM" symbol. A trademark that is federally registered (discussed below) is designated by the "®" symbol. (2) A service mark is a mark that distinguishes one's services from those of another. (3) A trade name is used to identify a business, symbolizes the reputation of the business as a whole, and is protectable under the same general principles as a trademark. See, e.g., *The Value House v. Phillips Mercantile Co.,* 523 F.2d 424 (10th Cir. 1975). (4) Trade dress refers to product packaging, while product configuration refers to a distinctive design or shape of a product. The packaging for a HERSHEY® Bar or the décor of a chain of restaurants are examples of trade dress, while the shape of the Coca-Cola® bottle is an example of product configuration. (5) A certification mark is used to certify that a particular product meets particular product standards, regardless of the specific source of that product. Certification marks are generally used by commercial groups such as trade associations to identify a particular type of good. Certification marks are not limited to use by a single source of the goods, but rather must be available to anyone who meets the standards outlined in the certification. (6) A collective mark is a mark held by a group for use by its member.

A trademark is protectable either as common law or as a registered mark when the mark is used and the public recognizes the mark as identifying the goods with which the mark is used as emanating from a particular source, such that the goods are distinguished from those offered by others. As described in greater detail in the following, marks are categorized based on the degree to which they are distinctive, and thus, their strength. Inherently distinctive marks (those that are

"arbitrary," "fanciful," or "suggestive" are automatically eligible for trademark protection, while those that are "descriptive" are only eligible for protection when they have acquired secondary meaning). "A mark has attained 'secondary meaning' when customers make a mental association between the mark and its unique source (i.e., when the mark and the business become synonymous in the public mind)."[17] Generic terms are never eligible for trademark protection.

Federal registration of a trademark requires use of the mark in interstate commerce, while state registrations are based upon use in intrastate commerce. However, it is not registration of a trademark, but *actual use* of the mark that creates rights in and priority over the rights of others. The senior user is the first to use the mark anywhere in the United States.[18] Rights in a trademark inure to the senior (i.e., first) user of the mark such that the senior user owns the mark and may prevent junior (i.e., subsequent) users from using the same or a similar mark where there is a likelihood that the consuming public will be confused as to the source of the goods.

A trademark is always used as an adjective to describe the goods or services with which it is used. Some examples of proper and improper uses of a trademark follow:

- Never use a trademark as a noun:

    Correct: Kleenex® tissues are soft

    Incorrect: Kleenex® are soft

- Never use a trademark as a verb:

    Correct: I searched for widgets using the Google® search engine

    Incorrect: I Googled® widgets

- Never use in the plural:

    Correct: Nike® shoes are comfortable

    Incorrect: Nikes® are comfortable

- Never use in the possessive form:

    Correct: Kids prefer Nabisco® brand cookies

    Incorrect: Kids prefer Nabisco's® cookies

Using a trademark as something other than an adjective can destroy rights in the trademark by causing the term to become "generic."[19] A mark is generic where the term in the minds of the consuming public is the product or service, not the producer of the product or service.[20] The policy consideration behind prohibiting a generic term from being a trademark is that one business should not be able to deprive competing manufacturers of the product of the right to call an article by its name, placing competitors at a serious competitive disadvantage.[21] Examples of trademarks that have become generic over the years include: thermos, aspirin, and escalator.

Trademarks can be words, names, symbols, colors, scents, or devices. Some examples include:

(1) Word: HIGHMARK[22]

(2) Slogans: HAVE A GREATER HAND IN YOUR HEALTH[23]

(3) Symbols

(4) Colors: Canary Yellow[24]

(5) Sounds: NBC chimes[25]

CHOOSING A TRADEMARK 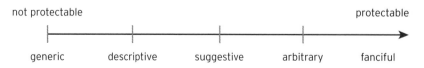. In order to be a trademark, a mark must be distinctive, meaning it must be able to identify the source of a particular good.[26] The distinctiveness, and therefore the protection afforded to a mark under the law, is measured along a continuum from nondistinctive to inherently distinctive, as illustrated below. Courts group marks into four categories based upon the relationship between the mark and the product or service with which it is used: (i) generic, (ii) descriptive, (iii) suggestive, and (iv) arbitrary or fanciful. Generic marks, which are not protectable, are the weakest marks, while arbitrary and fanciful marks are the strongest marks. The legal protection afforded to a mark depends upon in which category the mark falls. As described in greater detail below and as illustrated in **Figure 18-1**.

Generic Marks. A term is generic if it functions as the common descriptive name of a product class and where the term is used in connection with that product.[27] Generic marks are not registerable on either the Principal or Supplemental Registers.[28] A generic term for a product "tell[s] the buyer what it is, not where it came from."[29] For example, the mark "Car" is a generic term for automobiles. Therefore, a manufacturer selling "Car" brand automobiles would have no exclusive rights to use that term in connection with automobiles. "Because a generic term denotes the thing itself, it cannot be appropriated by one party from the public domain; it therefore is not afforded trademark protection even if it becomes associated with only one source."[30] Types of evidence to be considered in determining whether a mark is generic include: dictionary definitions, generic use of the term by competitors and other persons in the trade, plaintiff's own generic use generic use in the media, consumer surveys, and whether there are commonly used alternative means to describe the product or service.[31]

Descriptive Marks. A descriptive mark is any term that describes a trait, function, characteristic, quality, or the like of the goods or services with which it is used. For example, the mark HONEY-BAKED®[32] ham is descriptive because it describes an ingredient or characteristic of the ham. Descriptive marks are not registerable on the Principal Register unless they have acquired secondary meaning, but are registerable on the Supplemental Register without having acquired secondary meaning as long as the mark is actually being used in connection with the goods or services in interstate commerce.

> In order for a descriptive mark to be registerable on the Principal Register, the term must have acquired secondary meaning. "The doctrine of secondary meaning is the law's recognition of the psychological effect of trade symbols upon the buyer's mind." McCarthy, supra n. 162, at § 15.5. Secondary meaning is acquired when the term is used in such a way that its primary significance in the minds of the consuming public is the identification of the product or service with a single source, not the identification of the product itself. In fact, the consuming public does not even need to be able to identify the source, it only needs to recognize that the product comes from a single source. In short, "[s]econdary meaning has been defined as an association, nothing more." Id. (citing *Carter-Wallace, Inc. v. Procter & Gamble Co.,* 434 F.2d 794, 802 (9th Cir. 1980)).

not protectable   protectable

|———————|———————|———————|———————|————→

generic   descriptive   suggestive   arbitrary   fanciful

Figure 18-1 Trademark Classifications

Suggestive Trademarks. A suggestive mark is a term that suggests something about the product with which it is used by indirectly alluding to a quality or characteristic of the product. Suggestive marks differ from descriptive marks because a suggestive mark requires some "imagination" or a "mental leap" in order to come to a conclusion about what the product is. For example, the mark MUSTANG®[33] for automobiles is suggestive because it suggests a quality of the product (i.e., fast) but is not a term that consumers would automatically associate with automobiles.

Arbitrary and Fanciful Marks. An arbitrary mark is a common word that is applied to a product in an uncommon way (i.e., it is used in a way that has no relationship to the product with which it is used). For example, "ivory" is a common word with a specific meaning, but when IVORY®[34] is applied to soap, it is an arbitrary trademark.

A fanciful mark is a term that has no dictionary definition other than its meaning as a trademark. Examples of fanciful marks are KODAK®[35] cameras, NIKE®[36] shoes, and EXXON®[37] gasoline.

Arbitrary and fanciful marks are the strongest categories of marks because such marks bear no relationship at all to the products they describe. The association that consumers make between the mark and the source of the product comes from the *use* of the mark in commerce rather than a natural association in the mind of the consumer between the term and the product with which the term is used. Arbitrary and fanciful marks are inherently distinctive, meaning they are inherently capable of identifying the product with which they are used.

PROTECTING A TRADEMARK.[38] Common Law Versus. Federal Registration. Rights in a trademark belong to the first to actually use the mark in commerce. Where the mark is not registered, protection of the mark arises under the common law (i.e., rights to the mark derive from court precedent rather than statutory laws). A common law mark owner's rights only extend to the geographic areas where the mark is actually used in commerce, such as by sales or advertisements, and to the goods with which the mark is used.[39] In contrast, federal registration of a trademark grants the registrant of the mark the right to use and exclude others from using the mark or a mark confusingly similar to the mark on identical or similar goods throughout the United States.[40] Senior rights arising under the common law are not terminated by another's application for or registration of a federal trademark. Rather, the

common law rights of the senior user continue regardless of the registration of the same or a similar mark. However, courts will limit the rights of the senior user, generally to the same geographic region in which the senior common law rights arose and/or to the goods or services with which the senior user has used the mark under the common law.[41] As such, the senior user is prevented from expanding its use either geographically or to other related goods or services.[42]

The Benefits of Federal Registration. The Federal Lanham Act extends protection to unregistered marks.[43] Therefore, there is no requirement that the owner of a mark federally register that mark. There are, however, many advantages to federally registering a trademark, including that a federally registered mark:

(a) is *prima facie* evidence of validity and ownership of the mark;[44]

(b) provides a presumption of nationwide use of the mark;[45]

(c) provides constructive notice to the public of ownership of the mark;[46]

(d) provides federal court jurisdiction;[47]

(e) provides for the possibility of achieving incontestable status after five years, which enhances rights by eliminating a number of defenses available to an alleged infringer;[48]

(f) provides a basis for foreign registrations;[49]

(g) provides the owner the right to file with U.S. Customs to prevent the importation of goods bearing infringing marks;[50] and

(h) in some instances, may provide statutory damages to the owner of an infringed mark.[51]

State Registration. Registration of a trademark with a particular state only protects the mark in the state in which it is registered. As such, a federal trademark owner may have stronger rights in the mark, except to the extent that the state trademark owner is the senior user of the mark, in which case the state registrant will have the right to use the mark within the state of registry and in conjunction with the goods or services with which the mark has been used.[52]

In general, state trademark applications require the applicant to complete an application which requires a statement that the mark is in use in commerce and that there is no likelihood of confusion of the mark with other marks.[53]

18-1.4 Copyrights

WHAT IS COPYRIGHTABLE? 🏴 A copyright is an intangible right in a work of authorship that must be fixed in a tangible medium to qualify for protection under the Copyright Act. Like patents, the rights of the U.S. government to grant copyrights derive from the U.S. Constitution.[54] Copyright rights are codified in Title 17 of the U.S. Code. The U.S. Copyright Office registers works, but, in contrast to the USPTO, does not examine applications for copyright and does not issue copyrights. The purpose of copyright protection is to promote creativity, but that benefit is balanced against the costs of restricting access and use.[55] As discussed in the following, copyrights give owners the right to prevent unauthorized copying of their works, and the right to prevent others from certain limited uses of those works.[56]

> Examples of copyrightable subject matter that a health-care institution may own include source code or object code for a proprietary software product, databases of patient data, costs and pricing data, clinical trial data, and research data.

Copyrightable Subject Matter. Section 102 of the Copyright Act provides that copyrightable subject matter is: "original works of authorship fixed in any tangible medium of expression. . . ."[57] As we will see from the standards which the courts have developed for "originality," the requirements for copyright are much lower than those for patents (where an invention must be useful, novel, nonobvious, and enabled).

Originality. The term "original" is not defined by the Copyright Act, but the courts have defined an "original work" to be a work that is independently created, or not copied from another. This standard is in contrast to the patent standard for novelty, which requires that the invention not be previously known or practiced.[58] Even where a work is independently created, it must have some "modicum of creativity," or minimal amount of creativity, to qualify as copyrightable subject matter.[59] It is the expression of an idea, not the idea itself, that is copyrightable.[60] Where the number of ways to express an idea is limited, the expression becomes unprotectable.[61] Source code and object code is protectable by copyright as a literary work (discussed below) because there are multiple ways to write code to accomplish the same task.[62]

Under these standards, certain works are excluded from copyright protection because they are not "original." Examples of such works that are not eligible for copyright protection include facts and discoveries such as compilations or historical interpretations of facts (*Feist Publ'ns, Inc. v. Rural Tel. Serv. Co.,* 499 U.S. 304 (1991)), abstract ideas such as themes (*Nichols v. Universal Pictures Corp.,* 45 F.2d 119 (2d Cir. 1930)) or characters (*Metro-Goldwyn-Mayer v. American Honda Motor Corp.,* 900 F. Supp. 1287 (C.D. Cal. 1995)), functional works such as systems or methods (*Baker v. Selden,* 101 U.S. 99 (1879)), words or phrases, and useful articles (*Mazer v. Stein,* 347 U.S. 201 (1954)).

Fixation in a Tangible Medium. The Copyright Act provides that "[a] work is 'fixed' in a tangible medium of expression when its embodiment in a copy or phonorecord, by or under the authority of the author, is sufficiently permanent or stable to permit it to be perceived, reproduced, or otherwise communicated for a period of time of more than transitory duration. A work consisting of sounds, images, or both, that are being transmitted, is 'fixed' for purposes of this title if a fixation of the work is being made simultaneously with its transmission."[63] The "fixation" requirement derives directly from the text of the U.S. Constitution, which provides that copyrights may be extended to "writings" and is satisfied where the work can be perceived, communicated, or reproduced, directly or with the assistance of a machine or device.[64]

Ownership. Initial ownership of a copyright belongs to the one who creates a work at his own expense (i.e., the author).[65] There are various types of "authors" for purposes of the copyright protection. For example, where a work is created by two or more authors, the authors are co-owners of the copyright in the work.[66] An "anonymous work" is one in which "no natural person is identified as author."[67] A collective work occurs where multiple authors contribute to a collective whole such that each author of a copyrightable contribution to the collection of works owns a copyright to that contribution, while the "compiler" of the collective work owns a copyright in the collection as a whole. By default, each author that contributes to a collective work retains ownership of his copyrightable contribution unless there is a contractual arrangement whereby ownership is transferred to another, such as the owner of the collective work.

One typical issue that employees and employers often face is a whether an authored work is a "work made for hire." The Copyright Act defines a "work made for hire" as:

(1) a work prepared by an employee within the scope of his or her employment; or

(2) a work specially ordered or commissioned for use as a contribution to a collective work, as part of a motion picture or other audiovisual work, as a translation, as a supplementary work, as a compilation, as an instructional text, as a test, or as an atlas, if the parties expressly agree in a written instrument signed by both of them that the work shall be considered as a work made for hire.[68]

Thus, there are two ways in which a work made for hire may be created: (1) from works created within the scope of employment and (2) works created by independent contractors where there is an express writing signed by both parties that the work shall be considered a work made for hire. A work made for hire has a term of 95 years from publication, or 120 years from creation, whichever expires first.[69]

The U.S. Supreme Court has held that, for purposes of a work made for hire, an employee is defined under agency law.[70]

Various factors are used to determine whether an individual is an employee under common agency law: (1) Who has control over the work being performed? If the hiring party does, then this points toward the hired party being an employee. (2) What level of skill is required to accomplish the task? If a high level of skill is required, then the hired party is likely an independent contractor. (3) Who provides the instruments and tools to accomplish the task? If the hiring party does, then this points toward the hired party being an employee. (4) Where is the work being performed? If the work is performed at the hiring party's location, then the hired party is likely an employee. (5) What is the duration of the relationship? If the relationship is of a short duration, then the hired party is likely to be an independent contractor. (6) Is there a right to assign additional projects? If so, then the hired party is likely an employee. (7) What type of discretion does the hired party have in performing the work? If he has discretion, then he is likely an independent contractor. (8) What is the payment method? If the hiring party is paid a salary, then he is likely an employee.

(9) What is the hired party's role in hiring and paying assistants? If the hired party has discretion to hire and pay assistants, then he is likely an independent contractor. (10) Is the work part of the regular business of the hiring party? If so, then this suggests that the hired party may be an employee. (11) Does the hired party receive employee benefits or payment of taxes? If so, then this favors finding that the hired party is an employee rather than an independent contractor. *Feist Publ'ns, Inc. v. Rural Tel. Serv. Co.*, 499 U.S. 304 (1991).

The courts will balance these factors to determine if an individual is an employee or an independent contractor.

The courts consider various factors in determining if a work is prepared within the scope of employment, including: (1) Whether the work was of the type the employee was hired to perform; (2) Whether the creation of the work occurred within the "authorized time and space limits" of the employee's job; and (3) Whether the employee was "actuated, at least in part, by a purpose to serve" the employer's purpose. Restatement (Second) of Agency § 228 (1958).

THE RIGHTS OF A COPYRIGHT OWNER. Copyrights give the author the right to prevent unauthorized copying of his works, and the right to prevent certain limited uses. While several categories of protected expression are set forth in the Copyright Act,[71] certain subject matter is also expressly excluded from copyright protection. For example, Section 102(b) provides that "[i]n no case does copyright protection for an original work of authorship extend to any idea, procedure, process, system, method of operation, concept, principle, or discovery, regardless of the form in which it is described, explained, illustrated, or embodied in such work."[72] Thus, the Act extends protection to the *expression* of an idea while expressly excluding factual information from protection.[73]

Section 106 of the Copyright Act grants a copyright owner several exclusive rights that create the boundaries of copyright ownership. Section 106(1) grants to the copyright owner the exclusive right "to reproduce the copyrighted work in copies or phonorecords."[74] This protects the copyright owner against any unauthorized reproductions of the copyrighted work, including private, undistributed reproductions of copyrighted works.

Section 106(2) grants to the copyright owner the exclusive right to prepare derivative works based upon the copyrighted work.[75] A "derivative work" means "a work based upon one or more preexisting works, such as a translation, musical arrangement, dramatization. . . , or any form in which a work may be recast, transformed, or adapted."[76] Any modification of a copyrighted work that results in a derivative work may also constitute copyright infringement if unauthorized. For example, an author who writes a book in English has the exclusive right to translate that book into another language and any translated version made without the copyright holder's permission is an infringement of the right to prepare derivative works.

The copyright owner is also granted the exclusive right to distribute copies or phonorecords of the copyrighted work to the public in Section 106(3).[77] This section implicates the exclusive right to control the transfer of physical copies of the work.

Section 106(5) grants to the copyright holder the exclusive right to publicly display the copyrighted work.[78] Display is defined in § 101 of the Act to mean "to show a copy of it, either directly or by means of a film, slide, television image, or any other device or process or, in the case of a motion picture or other audiovisual work, to show individual images nonsequentially."[79] This right applies to all forms of copyrighted works except for sound recordings and architectural works.

Finally, §§ 106(4) and 106(6) grant to the copyright holder the exclusive right to perform the copyrighted work publicly.[80]

The Copyright Act grants to the copyright holder enumerated exclusive rights. The copyright holder's exclusive rights, however, are subject to the limitations set forth in §§ 107-122 of the Copyright Act. 17 U.S.C. §§ 107–122 (2006). Fair use, set forth in Section 107 of the Copyright Act, is a defense to what would otherwise be copyright infringement by placing limitations on the copyright holder's exclusive rights. Fair use is determined on a case-by-case basis, although Section 107 sets forth four broad factors to be considered in evaluating whether a third party's use of a copyrighted work constitutes fair use. Specifically, Section 107 provides that: ". . . the fair use of a copyrighted work, including such use by reproduction in copies or phonorecords or by any other means specified by that section, for purposes such as criticism, comment, news reporting, teaching (including multiple copies for classroom use), scholarship, or research, is not an infringement of copyright. In determining whether the use made of a work in any particular case is a fair use the factors to be considered shall include: (1) the purpose and character of the use, including whether such use is of a commercial nature or is for nonprofit educational purposes; (2) the nature of the copyrighted work; (3) the amount and substantiality of the portion used in relation to the copyrighted work as a whole; and (4) the effect of the use upon the potential market for or value of the copyrighted work." 17 U.S.C. § 107. Courts will generally balance the "fair use factors," although the case law surrounding fair use is unpredictable at best.

THE BENEFITS OF COPYRIGHT REGISTRATION. Although copyright registration is permissive, without federal registration, a copyright owner cannot exercise his rights that derive from copyright ownership. Thus, copyright registration carries with it many benefits, including:

(1) provides the copyright owner with the right to take legal action against an alleged infringer, and provides access to the federal courts;[81]

(2) a registration certificate is prima facie evidence of the validity of a copyright if the copyright is registered within five years of publication;[82] and

(3) if registered within three months of publication or before an infringement occurs, then a proven infringer may be liable for statutory damages of up to $150,000 plus attorney's fees.[83]

18-2 Managing an Intellectual Property Portfolio

18-2.1 Reasons a Business Should Protect Its Intellectual Property

Nearly every business, including those in the healthcare industry, owns some form of intellectual property and one key to succeeding in the marketplace is proper management of the business's intellectual property portfolio.

As competition increases among healthcare providers, those who have a solid stronghold in the marketplace are the ones who will survive. And one avenue to reaching that stronghold is through the identification, protection, and enforcement of the business's intellectual property.

As discussed in the preceding sections of this chapter, there are four types of intellectual property, each of which provides a unique set of exclusive rights to the owner. Among the strongest and most valuable intellectual property portfolios are those that protect each aspect of a business's intellectual property, from inventions (i.e., patents and trade secrets) to the business's goodwill (trademarks and service marks) to authored works (copyrights). Sometimes there is overlap, such as where a company's logo (protectable as a trademark) is also an authored work (i.e., a design) that is eligible for copyright protection.

🏴 Not only does a solid intellectual portfolio provide a business with a valuable asset, patents and trade secrets and the technology they protect give the business a competitive advantage by placing that business on the leading edge of development in its niche industry. Similarly, trademarks and service marks help businesses to distinguish themselves from competitors. And such a competitive advantage fosters continuing profitability and often creates new jobs and opportunities. Competitive advantages don't come from development of products and services alone. Building a solid business reputation and creating trademarks or service marks that consumers recognize and associate with a business is also key to success. Such goodwill is critical to an industry such as healthcare and for institutions such as these, a solid trademark and service mark portfolio can be an invaluable asset.

🏴 But simply being a leader in innovation may not be enough. Many businesses invest significant resources into research and development of new products or services. That investment alone generally is not enough. Rather, that investment has to be protected, generally by taking affirmative steps to protect the intellectual property that is generated by that research and development. Without such an investment, competitors may be able to copy or reverse engineer products, designs, and the like, or trade on another's good business reputation. The unfortunate result is that the competitor, for no investment in its own research and development, gets the benefit of the first company's investment by copying the end product. At the end of the day, the innovator in this situation may actually lose its footing in the marketplace because its competitor may be able to make the copied product, design, or the like for a lower price because it did not have the expenses of full research and development.

18-2.2 Steps to Take to Protect Intellectual Property

The first step to protecting one's intellectual property is to actually be able to identify when intellectual property is created. Internal management is key to this critical step. And, one way to do so is to have a simple system in place for employees to disclose to management when intellectual property is generated. Management may not choose to take affirmative steps to protect every creation, but full and timely disclosure of creation to management ensures that management can implement a business strategy for obtaining protection that is aligned with the business's overall goals.

Following identification of intellectual property, the next step is to file a patent application or registration application for trademarks and copyrights. Where the invention is to be kept secret, affirmative steps must be taken to maintain the secrecy, as discussed in the preceding sections of this chapter. But even taking steps to receive these exclusive rights is not enough.

In addition, a savvy businessperson will continually monitor the activities of its competitor, including the intellectual property being generated, research and development being conducted, and new products and services being offered. Several questions should be considered on a routine basis: What sort of information does the competitor have on its website? What new products and services is the competitor offering? How is the competitor branding its new products and services? What types of patent, trademark, or copyright applications is the competitor filing? Is the competitor infringing on any exclusive rights?

Where an infringement is suspected, the business may have no choice but to protect its place in the marketplace by enforcing its exclusive intellectual property rights against the competitor. After all, proper management of a business's intellectual property is more than simply creating the intellectual property; it is also protecting and enforcing it. Businesses who are able to achieve a balance between creation, protection, and enforcement of intellectual property are the ones who are leaders in their industry.

Chapter Summary

Members of the healthcare industry, like many other industries, continually create various forms of intellectual property that provide economic benefit and commercial advantage. Recognition of and protection of this intellectual property in an increasingly competitive environment can lead to market dominance. Therefore, healthcare institutions should be dedicated to developing and maintaining diverse intellectual property portfolios.

Key Terms and Definitions

Common Law - A system of law that is derived from court decisions rather than from statutes.

Copyright - A governmental grant that confers upon the creator of an original work of authorship a set of exclusive rights with respect to the original work.

Intellectual Property - Intangible rights protecting a work or invention that is the result of creation of the mind.

Leahy-Smith America Invents Act - H.R. 1249, 112th Congress (2011), signed into law on September 16, 2011, making significant changes to the Patent Act of the United States.

Patent - A governmental grant that confers upon the creator of an invention the exclusive right to make, use, or sell the invention for a limited period of time.

Service Mark - A distinctive logo, symbol, word(s), picture, or design that is used in connection with the sale of services to identify the source of the services and to distinguish the services from those sold by others.

The Copyright Act - The federal copyright statute of the United States, codified at 17 U.S.C. 101 et seq.

The Lanham Act - The federal trademark statute of the United States, codified at 15 U.S.C. 1051 et seq.

The Patent Act - The federal patent statute of the United States, codified at 35 U.S.C. 1 et seq.

The Uniform Trade Secrets Act - A model law drafted by the National Conference of Commissioners on Uniform State Laws to provide uniform standards across all 50 states regarding trade secret protection. The Uniform Trade Secrets Act has been adopted by all 50 states except New York, Texas, and North Carolina.

Trade Secret - Any valuable and secret commercial information that provides the owner of the information with a commercial advantage over those who do not have the information.

Trademark - A distinctive logo, symbol, word(s), picture, or design that is used in connection with the sale of goods to identify the source of the goods and to distinguish the goods from those sold or made by others.

Instructor-Led Questions

1. What are the four types of intellectual property?

2. What is the length of the patent term?

3. Why is a patent described as a "negative" right?

4. What is a Memorandum of Invention?

5. What are the purposes of a confidentiality agreement?

6. How is a trade secrete defined?

7. If a company's trade secret product is reverse engineered by a competitor, what recourse does the owner of the trade secret have against its competitor? How would the outcome change if a former employee of the company disclosed the trade secret to the competitor? If the product is covered by a patent rather than being kept as a trade secret, what recourse would the owner of the patent have?

8. Does a hospital employee who leaves to go work for a competitor have the right to take a customer list with him or her and use it to his or her new employer's advantage?

9. What is misappropriation of a trade secret?

10. What is the difference between a trademark and a service mark?

11. When is it appropriate to use the ® designation?

12. Distinguish between generic, descriptive, suggestive, arbitrary, and fanciful marks.

13. What makes subject matter copyrightable?

14. Define a "work made for hire."

15. What exclusive rights does the owner of a copyright have?

Problem 1

You work on a software development team for a leading healthcare provider. You have been asked to develop a software program that physicians can use to track the time they spend on various tasks throughout the day, including time spent with patients, time spent on administrative matters such as billing and the like, time spent on research activities, and time spent on continuing medical education. You and your team work for several months developing the software while the marketing team comes up with a name and logo for the software and advertises the soon-to-be released software. What type(s) of intellectual property has(ve) been generated by this project? What steps should be taken to protect those rights? Who owns the intellectual property? Why?

Problem 2

Hospital management decides the hospital needs to revamp its image. You form a committee that generates various ideas for presenting the new image. An outside marketing firm is engaged to refine the ideas. It proposes a design for a new logo and creates marketing materials incorporating a "look and feel" for the new image. A software company is also engaged to produce a website embodying the new look and feel of the image, and having improved user functionality. What steps should be taken to ensure the hospital owns all rights to the new logo and collateral for the new image? What steps should be taken to ensure the hospital owns all rights to the design, content, and functionality of the website? What notices should appear on the website to protect the IP? What disclaimers should be posted for users of the website?

Problem 3

Eager to assist patients recovering from major surgery, a young physician prepares a booklet titled "Return to Fitness." The introductory chapter of the booklet includes several photos and an essay written by the young physician detailing his miraculous year-long recovery from a life-threatening climbing accident. Following the introduction are a variety of health, wellness, and physical therapy articles collected and assembled by the young physician along with a day-by-day recovery plan that he wrote. Who has rights to the booklet? What types of IP does it contain? Can they be protected? What clearances are required to publish and distribute the booklet?

Problem 4

A nurse develops a unique walker device. She builds a prototype by modifying an old walker with materials from home and allows several patients to try it out. The walker device first comes to your attention when a patient approaches you to share his confidence found when using the walker. Do you advise management about the situation? If so what do you advise them? If not, why not? In either scenario, is the walker eligible for patent protection? If so, who would have rights to file a patent application? How could you assess the likelihood that a patent would issue? What steps should be taken to preserve the hospital's rights?

Endnotes

1   The discussion provided herein relates to utility patents. There are two other types of patents, namely design patents and plant patents. A design patent protects the ornamental features of an article and provides the patentee with protection against unauthorized copying or imitation. 35 U.S.C. § 171 (2006). A design patent has a term of 14 years from the issue date and does not require the payment of maintenance fees. 35 U.S.C. §§ 173, 41(b) (2006). A plant patent is the right granted to one who invented and asexually reproduced any distinct and new variety of plant. A plant patent must satisfy the requirements set forth in 35 U.S.C. § 161, which provides that "whoever invents or discovers and asexually reproduces any distinct and new variety of plant, including cultivated sports, mutants, hybrids, and newly found seedlings, other than a tuber propagated plant or a plant found in an uncultivated state, may obtain a patent therefor. . . ." 35 U.S.C. § 161 (2006).

2   U.S. Const. art.I, § 8, cl.8.

3   35 U.S.C. § 154 (2006) (emphasis added).

4   35 U.S.C. § 154(a)(2). "The term of a patent that is in force on or that results form an application filed before [June 8, 1995 is] the greater of the 20-year term. . . or 17 years from grant . . ." 35 U.S.C. § 154(c)(1).

5   U.S. Patent Statistics Chart Calendar Years 1963-2011, available at http://www.uspto.gov/web/offices/ac/ido/oeip/taf/us_stat.htm

6   35 U.S.C. § 131 (2006).

7   All 50 states except NY, TX, and NC have adopted a version of the UTSA and in 2011, MA and NJ introduced two bills, respectively, to adopt the UTSA.

8   Unif. Trade Secrets Act, § 1(4) (1985).

9   See, e.g., Cal. Civ. Code § 3426.1(d) (2010), which defines a trade secret as "information, including a formula, pattern, compilation, program, device, method, technique, or process, that: (1) Derives independent economic value, actual or potential, from not being generally known to the public or to other persons who can obtain economic value from its disclosure or use; and (2) Is the subject of efforts that are reasonable under the circumstances to maintain its secrecy." Cf. Pa. Cons. Stat. § 5302 (2010), which defines a trade secret as "information, including a formula, drawing, pattern, compilation, including a customer list, program, device, method, technique or process that: (1) Derives independent economic value, actual or potential, from not being generally known to and not being readily ascertainable by proper means by other persons who can obtain economic value from its disclosure and or use. (2) Is the subject of efforts that are reasonable under the circumstances to maintain its secrecy."

10 See, e.g., *Bimbo Bakeries USA v. Botticella*, 613 F.3d 102, 109 (3d Cir. 2010).

11 See, e.g., Unif. Trade Secrets Act § 1(4) (1985) (defining a trade secret as "information. . . that [is] not generally known to, and not. . . readily ascertainable by proper means by, other persons. . ..").

12 See, e.g., *Amedisys*, 2011 U.S. Dist. LEXIS 59260, at *20 (finding that Plaintiff undertook reasonable efforts to maintain the confidentiality of its Referral Logs and Workbooks, which it found to be trade secrets, by "only transmitting the Referral Logs and Workbooks through its protected computer network and email system. [Plaintiff] made geographically specific Workbooks available only to Account Executives who work in those areas. Finally, [Plaintiff] marked each page with a 'confidential property' designation.").

13 See Unif. Trade Secrets Act § 1(1) (defining "improper means" to include "theft, bribery, misrepresentation, breach or inducement of a breach of a duty to maintain secrecy, or espionage through electronic or other means"); see also Restatement of Torts, § 757 (providing that "[O]ne who discloses or uses another's trade secret, without a privilege to do so, is liable to the other if (a) he discovered the secret by improper means, or (b) his disclosure or use constitutes a breach of confidence reposed in him by the other in disclosing the secret to him. . . ."

14 In determining whether to grant a preliminary injunction, the party seeking the injunction must satisfy four factors: (1) a likelihood of success on the merits; (2) he or she will suffer irreparable harm if the injunction is denied; (3) granting injunctive relief will not result in even greater harm to the nonmoving party; and (4) the public interest favors injunctive relief. See, e.g., *Bimbo Bakeries USA v. Botticella*, 613 F.3d 102, 109 (3d Cir. 2010).

15 In general, the rules that apply to trademarks also apply to service marks and therefore the discussion that follows refers generally to "trademarks" but is meant to include trademarks, service marks, and other types of marks defined in the Lanham Act.

16 15 U.S.C. §§ 1051 (2006) et seq.

17 *Laurel Capital Grp., Inc. v. BT Fin. Corp.*, 45 F. Supp. 2d 469, 481 n.11 (W.D. Pa. 1999) (quoting J. McCarthy on Trademarks § 15.5).

18 930 F.2d at 292 (noting that with respect to ownership of an unregistered mark, the first party to begin making continuous commercial use of a mark may assert ownership rights in the mark).

19 Generic marks are discussed in greater detail in Section IV.B, infra.

20 See *American Online, Inc. v. AT & T Corp.*, 64 F. Supp. 2d 549, 560 (E.D. Va. 1999), aff'd in part, vacated in part, remanded by, 243 F.3d 812 (4th Cir. 2001) ("A mark is generic when it 'identifies a class of product or service, regardless of source.'") (citations omitted).

21 See *Delaware Valley Fin. Grp., Inc. v. Principal Life Ins. Co.*, 640 F. Supp. 2d 603, 618 (E.D. Pa. 2009) ("The Lanham Act protects only some of these categories of terms — it provides no protection for generic terms because a first user of a term cannot deprive competing manufacturers of the product of the right to call an article by its name.") (internal quotation and citations omitted).

22 Registration No. 2,204,203, owned by Highmark Inc., Fifth Avenue Place, 120 Fifth Ave., Pittsburgh, PA 15219-3099.

23 Registration No. 3,217,043, owned by Highmark Inc., Fifth Avenue Place, 120 Fifth Ave., Pittsburgh, PA 15219-3099.

24 Registration No. 2,390,667, owned by 3M Company, 3M Center, 2501 Hudson Rd., St. Paul, MN 55144.

25 Registration No. 916,522, owned by NBC Universal Media, LLC, 30 Rockefeller Plaza, New York, NY 10112.

26 15 U.S.C. § 1052(e) (2006).

27 *Vision Ctr. v. Opticks, Inc.*, 596 F.2d 111, 115 (5th Cir. 1980).

28 The Principal Register is the primary trademark register of the USPTO. Registration of a mark on the Principal Register entitles the mark to protection of all of the rights available under the federal law. The Supplemental Register is a secondary registry of the U.S. Trademark Office that offers trademark owners limited protection of their marks. A chart outlining the differences between trademark protection provided to marks registered on the Principal Register compared to the protection provided to marks registered on the Supplemental Register is provided in Appendix B.

29 2 J. McCarthy, Trademarks and Unfair Competition § 12:1 (4th ed. 2011). See also, *Filipino Yellow Pages, Inc. v. Asian Journal Publ'ns, Inc.*, 198 F.3d 1143, 1147 (9th Cir. 1999) (explaining that "[i]n determining whether a term is generic, we have often relied upon the 'who-are-you/what-are-you' test: A mark answers the buyer's questions 'Who are you?' 'Where do you come from?' 'Who vouches for you?' But the generic name of the product answers the question 'What are you?'").

30 *Blinded Veterans Ass'n. v. Blinded Am. Veterans Found.*, 872 F.2d 1035, 1039 (D.C. Cir. 1989).

31 *Pilates, Inc. v. Current Concepts, Inc.*, 120 F. Supp. 2d 286, 297 (S.D.N.Y. 2000).

32 Registration No. 3,049,064, owned by HBH Limited Partnership.

33 Regulation No. 1,467,208, owned by Ford Motor Company Corp.

34 Regulation No. 54,415, owned by Proctor & Gamble Co.

35 Regulation No. 399,092, owned by Eastman Kodak Co.

36 Regulation No. 978,952, owned by Nike, Inc.

37 Regulation No. 3,736,429, owned by Exxon Mobil Corp.

38 Although this discussion is limited to protection of a trademark within the United States, trademark rights are available on a country-by-country basis, with rights deriving from use of the mark in foreign countries. In addition, an international application that is filed within six months of the filing of a trademark application in the United States may claim priority to the U.S. application such that the date goes back to the filing date of the U.S. application.

39 *Tana v. Dantanna's*, 611 F.3d 767, 780-81 (11th Cir. 2010).

40 15 U.S.C. § 1115 (2006).

41 Tana, 611 F.3d at 780-81.

42 Id.

43 15 U.S.C. § 1125 (2006).

44 15 U.S.C. § 1057(b) (2006).

45 15 U.S.C. § 1057(c).

46 15 U.S.C. § 1057(b).

47 15 U.S.C. § 1121 (2006).

48 15 U.S.C. §§ 1065, 1115(b) (2006).

49 Protocol Relating to the Madrid Agreement Concerning International Registration of Marks, Madrid Union, June 27, 1989 (entered into force Dec. 1, 1995), S. Treaty Doc. No. 106-41 (2000), 1997 U.K.T.S. No. 3 (Cmnd 3).

50 15 U.S.C. § 1124 (2006).

51 15 U.S.C. § 1117(c) (2006).

52 *Malibu, Inc. v. Reasonover*, 246 F. Supp. 2d 1008, 1014 (N.D. Ind. 2003).

53 See, e.g., Pennsylvania Trademark Act, 54 Pa. Cons. Stat. § 1112 (2010), which provides that "any person who has adopted and used a mark in this Commonwealth may file ... an application for registration of that mark, setting forth the following information: (1) The name of the person applying for such registration, the residence, location or place of business of the applicant, and, if a corporation, the jurisdiction of incorporation, or, if a partnership, the state in which the partnership is organized and the names of the general partners. (2) The goods or services on or in connection with which the mark is used. ... (3) The date when the mark was first used anywhere and the date when it was first used in this Commonwealth by the applicant or the predecessor in interest. (4) A statement that the applicant is the owner of the mark, that the mark is in use and that to the knowledge of the person verifying the application [the mark is not] ... to cause confusion or to cause mistake or to deceive.... ."; see also Florida Trademark Act, Fla. Stat. § 495.031 (2010), which provides that "... any person who uses a trademark or service mark in this state may file with the department ... an application for registration of that mark setting forth ... but not limited to, the following information: (a) The name and business address of the person applying for such registration, and, if a business entity, the place of incorporation or organization; (b) The goods or services on or in connection with which the mark is used ... (c) The date the mark was first used anywhere and the date it was first used in this state by the applicant, the applicant's predecessor in interest, or a related company of the applicant; and (d) A statement that the applicant is the owner of the mark, that the mark is in use, and that, to the best of the applicant's knowledge, has registered such mark in this state, or has the right to use such mark in this state, either in the identical form thereof or in such near resemblance thereto as to be likely, when applied to the goods or services of such other person, to cause confusion, to cause mistake, or to deceive."

54 U.S. Const. art.I Section 8, cl.8.

55 See *Sony v. Universal Studios*, 464 U.S. 417 (1984).

56 It should be noted that ownership of a copy is different from ownership of a copyright.

57 17 U.S.C. § 102(a) (2006). Copyright protection also extends to "collective works" and "compilations." The Copyright Act expressly defines a "collective work" as "a work, such as a periodical issue, anthology, or encyclopedia, in which a number of contributions, constituting separate and independent works in themselves, are assembled into a collective whole. 17 U.S.C. § 101 (2006). The Copyright Act defines a "compilation" as a "work formed by the collection and assembling of preexisting materials or of data that are selected, coordinated, or arranged in such a way that the resulting work as a whole constitutes an original work of authorship. The term 'compilation' includes collective works." Id.

58 See Section 11-1.1b, supra.

59 *Feist Publ'ns, Inc. v. Rural Tel. Serv. Co.*, 499 U.S. 304 (1991).

60 Id.; *Baker v. Selden*, 101 U.S. 99 (1879).

61 *Morrissey v. Procter & Gamble*, 379 F.2d 675 (1st Cir. 1967).

62 *Apple Computer, Inc. v. Microsoft Corp.*, 35 F.3d 1435 (9th Cir. 1994).

63 17 U.S.C. § 101 (2006).

64 *Goldstein v. California*, 412 U.S. 546 (1973).

65 17 U.S.C. § 201 (2006).

66 The Copyright Act defines a "joint work" as "a work prepared by two or more authors with the intention that their contributions be merged into inseparable or interdependent parts of a unitary whole." 17 U.S.C. § 101.

67 Id.

68 Id.

69 17 U.S.C. § 302(c) (2006).

70 *Community for Creative Non-Violence v. Reid*, 490 U.S. 730 (1989).

71 17 U.S.C. § 106 (2006).

72 Id.

73 *Feist Publ'ns, Inc. v. Rural Tel. Serv. Co.*, 499 U.S. 304 (1991).

74 17 U.S.C. § 106(1).

75 17 U.S.C. § 106(2).

76 17 U.S.C. § 101 (2006). Derivative works themselves are copyrightable provided the modification is more than trivial. The derivative work copyright extends to original elements added by the derivative work author, not to the underlying work. Therefore, to the extent that a third party has permission to modify a copyrighted work and creative elements are added to that original work, the third party will be the copyright holder of the derivative work.

77 17 U.S.C. § 106(3).

78 17 U.S.C. § 106(5).

79 17 U.S.C. § 101.

80 17 U.S.C. § 106.

81 23 U.S.C. § 1338 (2006).

82 17 U.S.C. § 410 (2006).

83 17 U.S.C. § 504 (2006).

Confidential Memorandum of Invention

A. General

1. List names of Inventor(s):

2. Title of Invention:

3. The invention is a new: Product_Process Apparatus_ Method of Use

   Please check all appropriate categories.

4. State, in general terms, the general purpose of the invention and the objects of the invention.

5. Explain the commercial significance of the invention.

B. Invention History

1. Identify and attach copies of pertinent memos, reports or other written materials.

2. When was the idea conceived?

3. What is date of first written document describing or discussing the invention?

4. Describe the invention.

5. Where was the invention fist successfully operated?

6. Date of successful operation.

7. By whom was first successful operation carried out? Witnessed?

8. Where was first successful operation recorded?

9. To whom was invention first disclosed?

10. Date invention first was disclosed.

C. Background of Invention

1. Describe the old manner(s), if any, of performing the function of the invention.

2. Indicate the disadvantages of the old means and how the invention overcomes these disadvantages.

D. Description of the Invention

1. Product, Process, or Apparatus?

   (1) Describe the construction of your invention, showing the changes, additions, and improvements over that which is old. Point out the features of the invention that are believed to be new. Where applicable, illustrate the invention with sketches, drawings, or photographs, wherein the parts referred to in your description are identified by reference number, or by name.

   (2) Explain the principles involved in the invention.

   (3) Give details of operation, if not already described.

   (4) State the advantages of the invention over what has been done before.

   (5) Indicate any alternative method(s) of construction or operation.

   (6) If there is more than one inventor, indicate what contribution was made by each inventor.

2. If the invention is a software system, please also provide the following:

   (1) Provide detailed schematic diagrams, flow charts, and/or source-code histories that show essentials of processes and/or data structure.

   (a) Describe the invention functionally showing variety of layers, i.e., a high-level diagram and more detailed diagrams to describe the actual invention. Provide:

   i)   Block-structured diagram or program language;

   ii) flow chart diagrams to show software-implemented methods as sequence of steps, and/or;

   iii) state diagrams for more task-related processes.

   (b) List several examples of different schematics of the circuit processes or program.

   (c) List alternative schematics.

   (d) Identify any hardware that is used to perform the illustrated operations; identify hardware on diagrams.

   (e) Identify any pseudocode, i.e., for a well-commented program, delete most of the code except for program headers (data structure/ sharing), procedure calls (program flow), and comments explaining process functions comprising the program.

   (2) Indicate operating parameters or conditions of the process.

   (a) Identify widest operable parameters or conditions that will work.

(b) Identify narrower parameters within these parameters that will provide optimum results.

(c) State disadvantages of using conditions outside the parameters selected.

(3) Identify the minimum program and data structures that are needed to support the invention.

(a) Identify the invention (it may be a relatively small part of the program when dealing with software applications). Parts of the program (such as those that establish the initial conditions or process the output data to produce a useful result) may not need to be described in as much detail as the portion of the program that performs the inventive data processing.

(b) Identify which parts of the software system would be understood readily by a skilled programmer and which would not.

(c) If inventive modules or processes interact with known parts in a new way, describe interaction.

(4) Give specific examples of practice of the invention in various modifications, and with preferred embodiments.

(a) Examples should illustrate diverse conditions under which the invention may be practiced.

(b) Include enough examples of specific combinations to form basis for as broad claims as possible.

(c) Be certain best mode known of practicing the invention is described.

(5) Note any surprising results which would not be forecast by the mythical "expert in the art."

(a) Explain the surprising results, if possible.

(b) Emphasize any results which are contrary to what would have been expected.

(6) Identify any testing of the invention, including good and bad results.

(7) Identify any testing of prior art and comparison with the invention.

(8) Indicate whether any of the source code, or other copyrighted material, is copyrighted.

E. Information Disclosure

1. Prior Patents and Publications

Append bibliography and key prior art descriptions based on search of internal and public literature, including patent literature. Identify bases searched.

2. Commercial Use or Sale

Identify any prototypes, models, samples, or commercial products embodying the invention (that is the product or apparatus of the invention, a product or apparatus containing the invention as a component, or a product or item which has been produced by the inventive process) which:

(1) Have been delivered or exhibited to anyone;

(2) Have been made the subject of a quotation or offer for sale or in some way have been involved in a commercial discussion: and

(3) Have occurred in or were in any way connected with the United States.

3. Publication or Communications Outside the Company

(1) Identify all written material directed to the invention that has been published or communicated outside of the company in the form of a printed publication.

4. Tests

(1) Identify and provide the results of all tests, if any, of the invention.

(2) Identify and provide the results of all tests, if any, of the prior art and an accurate summary of comparisons, if any, with the invention.

F. Witness

Date

Signature of Witness

Signature of Person Submitting Disclosure

Supervisor's recommendation and comments as to importance and plans for future work. Identify critical timing factors.

Supervisor's Signature

Comparison of Provisional Versus Nonprovisional Patent Applications

Provisional Application	Nonprovisional Application
Provides patent pending status	Provides patent pending status
Requires conversion to nonprovisional application within 1 year from filing	
Not examined by USPTO	Examined by USPTO
Requires enabling disclosure	Requires enabling disclosure
Informal drawings are acceptable	Formal drawing requirements
Claims are not required	Requires claim set

Comparison of Principal Versus Supplemental Trademark Registers

Principal Register	Supplemental Register
® symbol may be used upon registration to provide public notice of a federal registration	® symbol may be used upon registration to provide public notice of a federal registration
"Descriptive" marks not permitted for registration	"Descriptive" marks permitted registration if mark is in current interstate commerce use
Considered "constructive notice" or "legal presumption" to the public of the ownership and owner's exclusive rights to the mark and validity of registration	Will not be considered "constructive notice," "legal presumption" or "prima facie" evidence to the public of the ownership and owner's exclusive rights to the mark
Ability to bring an action concerning the mark in a federal court based on ownership and exclusive rights to the mark	Limited rights (nonexclusive) to the mark and therefore limiting rights to bring action concerning the mark in a federal court
Ability to Petition to Cancel potentially conflicting third-party registrations in the U.S. Trademark Trial and Appeal Board	Petitions to Cancel based on Supplemental Registrations are not permitted
Ability to Oppose a potentially conflicting third party pending application in the U.S. Trademark Trial and Appeal Board	Oppositions based on Supplemental Registrations are not permitted
Ability to Petition the Director for Trademarks for an Interference showing extraordinary circumstances between a potentially conflicting third-party mark	Petition of Interference based on Supplemental Registrations are not permitted
Marks are published for 30 days in the *Official Gazette* prior to the allowance for registration to allow third parties to oppose mark prior to registration	Marks are not published in the *Official Gazette* prior to registration
Ability to prevent importation of infringing foreign goods by filing the registration with the U.S. Department of Treasury/Customs Services	Cannot be filed with the U.S. Department of Treasury/Customs Services to prevent (potential infringing) importations
"Constructive use" (priority/effective filing date) of the mark is considered the date of filing an application	The effective filing date of mark is either: 1. The date of application filing, if use of the mark has been more than one year 2. The date the application is amended to the Supplemental Register, if use of the mark has been less than 1 year
Nothing can prevent registration of a mark on the Principal Register if "distinctiveness" is claimed and proven (mark(s) may become distinctive after 5 years of interstate commerce use)	Cannot claim "distinctiveness"
Right to "incontestability" after 5 years of registration (third parties can no longer object (oppose, cancel, etc.) to registration of mark)	Cannot claim "incontestability" after 5 years of registration

Ability to base foreign trademark applications on U.S. registration or claim the U.S. filing date in the foreign trademark application (also known as claiming "priority")	Cannot claim base or claim "priority" to U.S. mark in foreign trademark applications
Ability to file an application based on *bona fide* "intention to use" mark	Mark **must** be in use in interstate commerce in connection with the goods and/or services

Source: 15 U.S.C. 1051, et seq.

Glossary

1500 A *Claim* form for professional services, such as those provided by a physician or someone under the supervision of a physician.   10

Accreditation   Private, professional organizations establish criteria to evaluate educational programs. Accreditation is the process in which certification of competency, authority, or credibility is presented to these educational programs. Accreditation is voluntary, but most educational programs strive to obtain and retain accreditation from established accrediting bodies.   4

Administrative Law The collection of rules, regulations, guidance, and decisions created by administrative agencies of the government.   1

Advance Beneficiary Notice   Written advice to patient that a service being recommended by a *Provider* is not a service covered by the patient's insurance, Medicare, Medicaid, or other payer. Often the term "medically unnecessary" is used, but that is a term of art, not a clinical determination.   10

Advance Directive   A general term for any document that gives instructions about an individual's ("principle") health care and/or appoints someone ("attorney in fact") to make medical treatment decisions for that individual if he or she cannot make such decisions. Living Wills and Durable Powers of Attorney for Health Care are examples of advance directives.   7

Anti-Kickback Statute ("AKS")   A federal law that prohibits the knowing solicitation, receipt, offer, or payment of remuneration (anything of value) in exchange for, or to induce the arranging or provision of, items or services that are reimbursable under Medicare, Medicaid, or other government healthcare programs.   12

Arbitration Agreement   An alternative to bringing a lawsuit to court. The arbitration process specified in an agreement must be followed. A valid arbitration decision has the same effect as a court judgment.   11

ARRA   The acronym for the American Recovery and Reinvestment Act of 2009, the economic stimulus package passed by the U.S. Congress and signed into law by President Obama in February 2009. ARRA provided billions of dollars of incentives, in the form of reimbursement, to assist and encourage doctors and hospitals to transition away from the maintenance of paper medical records and adopt electronic health records.   8

Articles of Incorporation   A document required to be filed with a government agency, usually the Secretary of State, if the owners of a business want it to be recognized as a corporation. The "articles" (sometimes called a Certificate of Incorporation) must contain certain information, as required by state law.   2

Assisted Insemination   A form of assisted reproduction that is sometimes called artificial insemination and that facilitates delivery of donor semen into the uterus by a process that is not sexual intercourse.   13

Bankruptcy   A federally authorized procedure that allows a debtor (e.g., person, corporation, or municipality) to discharge all liability for debts in return for making court-approved arrangements for partial repayment. In general, one is "bankrupt" when one is unable to pay debts as they are due (referred to as "cash flow insolvency") and a court issues a legal order intended to remedy the bankruptcy.   2

Beneficence   Action taken for the benefit of others. Beneficent actions can be taken to help prevent or remove harms or to improve the situation of others.   15

Bioethics   The discipline dealing with ethical questions that arise as a result of advances in medicine and biology, or the critical examination of moral dimensions of decision making in health-related contexts and in contexts involving the biological sciences.   15

Board of Directors   A body of individuals, elected or appointed, who jointly oversee the activities of a company or organization. The board's activities are determined by the powers, duties, and responsibilities typically delegated to the board by the bylaws of the company or organization. In short, the board "governs" the company, but does not "manage" it.   2

Borrowed Servant Doctrine   When an employer delegates its right to direct and control the activities of an employee to another, independent party who assumes responsibility, the employee becomes a borrowed servant.   11

Boycott   To refuse to have dealings with a person or organization or to refuse to buy a product or service as an expression of protest or a means of coercion.   14

Breach   Failure to keep a promise or a violation of a legal obligation, such as a contract of a law.   1

Business Associates   Independent contractors who engage in business with or otherwise assist covered entities and have access to protected health information.   8

Capacity   Under the law, capacity means an individual's ability to understand the nature and consequences of decisions and how to communicate the decisions.   15

Case Management   A collaborative process of assessment, planning, facilitation, care coordination, evaluation, and advocacy for options and services to meet an individual's and family's comprehensive health needs through communication and available resources to promote quality cost-effective outcomes.   17

Cease and Desist Order   An order issued by a court or an administrative agency that prohibits a person or entity from continuing a specific course of action or conduct.   14

Center for Medicare & Medicaid Services (CMS)   The government agency responsible for setting rules for government patients, including payment methodologies, within the constraints of laws set by the executive and legislative branches.   10

Certificate of Need Permit (CON)   A formal document issued to a healthcare institution or provider giving permission for construction and modification of health agencies, major equipment expenditures, or new health services.   3

Certification   In some cases, private certification is required by government authorities in order to qualify for certain positions, status, or payment. Individual certification is generally related to performance, usually including passing a test. Individual certification includes medical board specialties.   4

Charge Cycle   The part of the *Revenue Cycle* that includes entry of charges, and assurance that charge data is configured in a way that the billing system recognizes it, particularly as it interfaces with the *Chargemaster (CDM)*.   10

Charge Description Master (CDM)   The part of the billing system that lists the services being performed, and the related unit charge (price). Similar to a "price list" in other businesses.   10

Claim   A request for payment submitted to a third-party payer, that is, an insurance company, a government agency, or a company providing payment-processing services for a payer other than the insured person.   10

Clayton Act of 1914   This Act is an amendment to the Sherman Antitrust Act (which was enacted in 1890) and prohibits certain acts or practices that unduly restrict trade and commerce. In brief, the Act makes these business practices illegal: 1. price discrimination; 2. tying and exclusive dealing contracts; 3. certain corporate mergers; and 4. interlocking directorates. These practices are illegal when they "substantially lessen competition" or tend to create a monopoly.   14

Clinical Laboratories Improvement Act (CLIA)   A federal law passed in 1988 that subsequently regulates every medical test in every laboratory in the nation, including those conducted in physicians' offices. Even those tests that may be purchased over-the-counter at a neighborhood pharmacy require at least federal governmental permission in order to perform the test.   3

CMS   The acronym for the Centers for Medicare & Medicaid Services, the branch of the U.S. Department of Health and Human Services that administers Medicare and Medicaid.   8

Codes, Coding   Numbers (or letters) assigned to services, supplies, and diagnoses used for identification and uniformity in billing and payment systems. Payments to *Providers* are often determined by these codes. They can be determined by the federal government, state governments, and insurers; they are developed by specialized experts, such as 3M or the American Medical Association, and can be altered to meet the needs of various payers. Examples are DRGs (hospital inpatient codes based on diagnoses and procedures), CPTs (procedure codes), and ICD-9s (diagnoses).   10

Commerce Clause   One of the "enumerated powers" listed in the U.S. Constitution (Article I, Section 8, Clause 3). The Commerce Clause states that the Congress shall have power "To regulate Commerce with foreign nations and among the several States, and with the Indian Tribes." The clause is one of the most fundamental powers delegated to Congress by the framers of the U.S. Constitution.   1

Commercial Health Insurance   Health insurance policies that are purchased privately. Commercial health insurance policies are offered for sale by non-government organizations (both for-profit and not-for-profit). Commercial health insurance is generally regulated by states. However, the Patient Protection & Affordable Care Act of 2010 allows a variety of federal regulations which will fully come into effect by 2014.   9

Commitment or Civil Commitment   Commonly used terms to described involuntary court ordered treatment for behavioral healthcare services.   17

Common Law   Principles and rules of action, reflected in court decisions, rather than in legislation. The common law applies to the protection of persons and property and is based on community customs and traditions, as interpreted over time by judges.   1

Comparative Negligence   In a negligence lawsuit, comparative negligence means that the percentage of cause due to the patient's conduct is determined and the patient does not collect that percentage of the total amount of the injury award.   11

Compliance Program   An internal program established by a healthcare organization to encourage the development and use of internal controls to monitor adherence to applicable statutes, regulations, and program requirements (e.g., compliance with submitting claims and receiving payment from federal health care programs such as Medicare or Medicaid). Compliance program guidance has been published by the OIG and is available online at: http://oig.hhs.gov/compliance/compliance-guidance/index.asp.   17

Conscience Laws   Federal or state laws that protect healthcare providers who for religious or moral reasons refuse to participate in procedures related to reproduction such as sterilization, abortion, and assisted reproduction.   13

Consent   Can be express (given by direct words, either oral or written) or implied (inferred from some patient conduct or presumed in most emergencies). Consent is usually implied from voluntary submission to an examination or procedure with apparent knowledge of its nature.   7

Contraception   Prevents fertilization of an ovum ("egg"), during or immediately after sexual intercourse; contraceptive methods take many forms and may be medical in nature ("the pill" or Plan B) or medical devices (such as a diaphragm or a condom).   13

Contractual Adjustment   The accounting adjustment recognizing the difference between charges (provider prices × volume) and expected payment through contractual agreement or government mandate.   10

Copyright   A governmental grant that confers upon the creator of an original work of authorship a set of exclusive rights with respect to the original work.   18

Corporate Negligence   "A [common law (judge-made)] doctrine that hospital and healthcare centers have a responsibility to patients that extends beyond that of merely furnishing facilites for treatment" (*McGraw-Hill Concise Dictionary of Modern Medicine.* © 2002 by The McGraw-Hill Companies, Inc. as cited by medical-dictionary.thefreedictionary.com/corporate+liability). Also known as "institutional negligence" and first described in cases such as *Darling v. Charleston Community Memorial Hospital,* 33 Ill.2d 326, 331, 211 N.E.2d 253 (1965).   5

Covered The items and services which healthcare organizations accept payment for from health plans. A healthcare organization may not bill patients for the full amount of a covered item or service but must accept the payment terms by the health plan. The payment terms for a covered item or service may not necessarily provide specific payment for a covered item or service. Whether the health plan pays for a covered item or service depends on the health plan and the healthcare organization's arrangements with that plan. If allowed by the health plan, the healthcare organization may charge the patient for co-payments for covered items or services or may charge the patient for the covered items and services when the patient has not yet met the annual deductible for the health plan.   9

Covered Entities Healthcare clearinghouses, employer-sponsored health plans, health insurers, and medical service providers to which the HIPAA privacy and security rules regulating protected health information apply.   8

Credentialing "Review procedures conducted for the purpose of determining whether a potential or existing provider meets certain standards that are a prerequisite for them to begin or continue participation in [patient care at a hospital or other health care facility or in] a given health care plan." (State Program Integrity Assessment (SPIA) Federal Fiscal Year 2008 GLOSSARY OF TERMS).   5

Daubert Standards A 1993 Supreme Court case, *Daubert v. Merrell Dow Pharmaceuticals,* established stricter standards for allowing expert testimony in federal courts. The Daubert Standards focus on the quality of the scientific basis for expert opinion testimony about the standard of care.   11

Defamation An intentional tort that causes wrongful injury to a person's reputation. Libel is written defamation, and slander is spoken defamation. The defamatory statement must be communicated to a third person.   11

Demographics Nonclinical patient characteristics that allow a *Provider* to complete billing information, and assure that the correct insurer (or guarantor) is billed. Examples are insurance company, employer, patient address, and many others.   10

Diagnostic and Statistical Manual of Mental Disorders, 4th Ed. Commonly known as the "DSM-4," it's a manual published by the American Psychiatric Association and covers all mental health disorders in adults and children.   17

Discharge The point at which the patient leaves a hospital and either returns home or is transferred to another facility, such as a nursing home or rehabilitation hospital.   6

Disruptive Behavior The Joint Commission describes "disruptive behavior" as "intimidating . . . and overt actions [by health care professionals] such as verbal outbursts and physical threats, as well as passive activities such as refusing to perform assigned tasks or quietly exhibiting uncooperative attitudes during routine activities. . . . [among the] health care team," that "can foster medical errors, contribute to poor patient satisfaction and to preventable adverse outcomes, increase the cost of care, and cause qualified clinicians, administrators and managers to seek new positions in more professional environments." (Behaviors that undermine a culture of safety. *Joint Commission Sentinel Event Alert,* Issue 40, July 9, 2008.)   5

Due Process Licensing boards must provide due process to licensed professionals. Due process includes providing notice of any wrongful conduct and an opportunity to present information before sanctioning the licensed professional.   4

Durable Power of Attorney for Health Care (or Health Care Proxy) A document that appoints someone to make medical decisions for an individual (in the way that the individual would want them to be made) in the event that the individual is no longer able to do so.   7

Duty of Care As used in corporate law, this is part of the fiduciary duty owed to a corporation by its directors. It means that a director owes a duty to exercise good business judgment and to use ordinary care and prudence in the operation of the business.   2

Duty of Loyalty As used in corporate law, this duty requires fiduciaries of the company (principally, its Directors) to put the corporation's interests ahead of their own.   2

Economic Credentialing Though defined differently by various interested parties, this is generally defined as the use of criteria unrelated to professional competence or quality in the granting of medical staff privileges.   5

Employee Retirement Income Security Act (ERISA) Regulates nearly all pension and benefit plans for employees, including pension, profit-sharing, bonus, medical or hospital benefit, disability, death benefit, unemployment, and other plans. ERISA applies to all plans except for governmental plans, some plans of churches, and some § 401(k) retirement plans.   4

The Employee Retirement Income Security Act of 1974. ERISA is the principal federal law that regulates employer-sponsored health plans. Under many circumstances, ERISA preempts state regulation of employer-sponsored health insurance.   9

Employer-Sponsored Health Insurance Health insurance which is arranged by employers for employees. Employer-sponsored health insurance involves either a self-funded group health plan in which the employer provides funds to pay for healthcare items and service or the employer purchases fully insured policies for employees. Many self-funded employer-sponsored group health plans purchase additional stoploss coverage which limits the company's payment exposure. Employees typically pay a premium amount per month to participate in employer-sponsored health insurance.   9

Ethics in Patient Referrals Act ("Stark Law") A federal law named after its key sponsor, Congressman Pete Stark, that prohibits a physician from referring Medicare patients for certain types of services to an entity with which the physician (or an immediate family member) has a financial relationship, unless one of 35 exceptions applies.   12

Exclusive Staffing Arrangement An arrangement pursuant to which a hospital assigns responsibility, by contract or otherwise, for a certain area of patient care (frequently radiology, pathology, emergency, and anesthesiology) to one individual or group of individuals, to the exclusion of others. The United States Supreme Court recognized the permissibility of exclusive contracts under the antitrust laws in *Jefferson Parish Hosp. Dist. v. Hyde* - 466 U.S. 2 (1984).   5

Exculpatory Clauses State that the person signing waives the right to sue for injuries or agrees to limit any claims to not more than a specified amount. 7

Exculpatory Contract An agreement not to sue or an agreement to limit the amount of the suit. 11

Exhaustion of Administrative Remedies This principle is important in administrative law. Many disputes are first handled by administrative agencies. The applicable agency typically has primary responsibility for disputes (or cases) that involve the rules or regulations that are administered by the agency. "Exhaustion of administrative remedies" requires a person to first seek a resolution of a matter by following agency hearing and appeals processes. Once those steps are completed, a party who is dissatisfied with the agency decision may file a complaint in court. 1

Explode An order entry code that automatically generates more than one code for billing purposes. Sometimes, a provider performs a service that consists of several pieces, such as certain laboratory tests. If the provider can bill separately for the individual services in the group, the "explode" makes it easier, and assures that all the services in the group are billed. 10

Express Contract A contract in which the agreement of the parties has been expressed in words and in which all elements and terms have been stated. 6

Fair Labor Standards Act (FLSA) Establishes minimum wages, overtime pay requirements, and maximum hours of employment. Employees of all nonprofit and for-profit hospitals are covered by the FLSA. 4

False Claims Act (FCA) Federal act passed under the administration of President Abraham Lincoln, which carries both civil and criminal penalties for anyone who knowingly presents, or causes to be presented, to the United States government a false or fictitious claim for payment. The FCA's authority encompasses more than just healthcare claims; it applies equally to all others who make claims for payment from government funds to the government. 12

Family and Medical Leave Act (FMLA) Requires that eligible employees be provided twelve workweeks of leave during any twelve-month period to provide care for a serious health condition of the employee, spouse, child, or parent, or for a birth or adoption. The leave need not be compensated, but healthcare benefits must be continued during the leave. 4

Federal Trade Commission Act of 1914 This Act created the Federal Trade Commission (FTC), a bipartisan body with five members appointed by the President of the United States for seven-year terms. Among its powers under the Act, the FTC has the authority to issue "cease and desist" orders to companies to stop unfair trade practices. 14

Fiduciary Credentialing Defined by the American Medical Association as "a special case of economic credentialing [pursuant to which there is] a loss of hospital privileges based on a physician's economic competition with a hospital." 5

Fraud Enforcement and Recovery Act (FERA) Federal act passed as a part of healthcare reform. Enhanced the strength of the FCA and clarified that a failure to repay any known overpayment constitutes a false claim. 12

Fundamental Rights Constitutionally protected rights that the United States Supreme Court has determined will receive special judicial protection from government interference based upon language in the United States Constitution, usually the Fourteenth Amendment. 13

General Informed Consent Form Most hospitals now require this type of consent form, which includes (1) the name and a description of the specific treatment or procedure; (2) statement that the physician has explained to the patient or his or her legal representative the consequences, risks and benefits, and alternatives to such treatment or procedure (including foregoing treatment); (3) statement that all questions have been answered to the person's satisfaction; and (4) that no guarantees have been made. The actual process of providing information to the decision maker and of determining that person's decision is more important than the consent form. The form is evidence of the consent process, but the informed consent is the actual discussion(s) had between the physician and the patient (or the patient's legal representative) about the treatment or procedure to be performed. 7

Gross Charges Total amount billed. 10

Guardian Ad Litem A person appointed to represent the patient in court proceedings and has no authority to make medical decisions, unless the court has granted this power. 7

Guardian of the Estate A person who is granted powers over another's property and has no authority to make medical decisions. 7

HealthCare Agent One or more persons designated to serve as a healthcare agent to make medical decisions for another. A power of attorney gives the designated agent the power to make decisions on the behalf of the person giving the power, called the principal. 7

HealthCare Information Broadly defined, is aggregate and individually specific patient data including personal information (such as name, date of birth, sex, marital status, occupation, next of kin, etc.), financial information (such as employer, health insurance identification number, and other information to assist in billing), and medical history (such as physical examinations, diagnoses, treatment recommendations and treatment administered, progress reports, physician orders, clinical laboratory results, radiology reports, nursing notes, discharge summaries, etc.). 8

Health Care Quality and Improvement Act of 1986 (HCQIA) An Act that extends principles of state peer review immunity on a federal level. Thus, under HCQIA, members of a hospital peer review committee are protected from prosecution under various, federal antitrust lawsuits. 14

Health Care Quality Improvement Act A federal statute codified at 42 U.S.C. 11101 which places limitation on damages for professional review actions that are conducted in accordance with the safe harbor requirements of the statute. 5

Health Insurance Portability and Accountability Act of 1996 (HIPAA) A federal law that protects health insurance coverage for employees and their families when employees change or lose their jobs, provides provisions for establishing national standards for electronic healthcare transactions and national identifiers for providers, health insurance plans, and employers. Additionally addresses the security and privacy of health data. 4

Health Reform or Health Care Reform A phrase generally referring to the Patient Protection and Affordable Care Act of 2010 (P.L. 111-148). 17

HHS The acronym for the Department of Health and Human Services, the U.S. government's principal agency for protecting the health of all Americans and providing essential human services. 8

HHS Office of Civil Rights Enforces the HIPAA Privacy and Security Rules. 8

HIPAA The acronym for the Health Insurance Portability and Accountability Act of 1996, enacted by the U.S. Congress and signed by President Clinton. Title II of HIPAA directed HHS to draft rules establishing national security and privacy health data standards. 8

HIPAA Privacy Rule Establishes national standards to protect medical records and other personal health information. It requires covered entities and their business associates to protect the privacy of personal health information and sets limits and conditions on the uses and disclosures that may be made of such information without patient authorization. It also gives patients rights over their health information, including rights to examine and obtain a copy of their health records, and to request corrections. 8

HIPAA Security Rule Establishes national standards to protect individuals' electronic personal health information that is created, received, used, or maintained by a covered entity. It requires appropriate administrative, physical and technical safeguards to ensure the confidentiality, integrity, and security of electronic protected health information. 8

Horizontal Integration or Relationship A type of ownership and control that occurs when a company is taken over by, or merged with, another company in the same industry and in the same line of business. For example, when one car manufacturer merges with another car manufacturer. 14

Implied Contract A contract in which the agreement arises from conduct or assumed intentions rather than words. 6

In Loco Parentis A person can stand in place of a parent to a minor by assuming the status and obligation of a parent without formal adoption or designation by the natural parent. 7

In Vitro Fertilization A method of joining an egg and sperm outside the body of the donors; the resulting embryo is implanted either in the biological mother's uterus or in the uterus of a surrogate. 13

Individually Identifiable Health Information A term used in HIPAA, which means a subset of health information, collected from an individual, and is created or received by a healthcare provider, health plan, employer, or healthcare clearinghouse. The information relates to the past, present, or future physical or mental health of condition of an individual. It also may relate to the provision of health care or payment for the individual's health care. Finally, the information must identify the individual or provide a basis to reasonably believe that the individual can be identified. This term is used to define "protected health information" under HIPAA. 15

Induced Abortion A medical or surgical procedure to terminate an existing pregnancy by expelling an embryo or fetus. 13

Informed Consent A process by which a fully informed patient can participate in healthcare choices. This process has three elements – information, comprehension of that information, and voluntariness. 15

Injuction An order of a court that requires a person or entity to act, or not to act, in a particular situation or manner. An injunction is considered an "extraordinary remedy" and only used when temporary maintenance of the status quo is necessary. 14

Intellectual Property Intangible rights protecting a work or invention that is the result of creation of the mind. 18

Investigational Device Exemption (IDE) Exceptions that allow certain medical devices to be used in research projects approved by an Institutional Review Board, conducted by a qualified investigator, and sponsored by an appropriate company or institution. 3

Joint Commission An independent, not-for-profit organization that accredits and certifies healthcare organizations and programs in the United States. Joint Commission accreditation and certification is a recognized symbol of quality that reflects an organization's commitment to certain performance standards. To be accredited, hospitals must meet Joint Commission medical records standards. To earn and maintain Joint Commission accreditation submission to periodic on-site survey by a Joint Commission survey team is required. 8

The organization that certifies and accredits healthcare organizations and programs. 3

Jurisdiction Authority given by law to a court to determine the outcome of disputes and rule of legal matters in a specific geographic area or over specific types of legal disputes. 1

Just Cause A legally sufficient reason for the termination of an employee that would justify terminating the employee without reasonable notice or payment. 4

Licensure Most healthcare providers are licensed, or authorized to practice, by a governmental authority. Licensure refers to the granting of a license to practice. 4

Life Safety Code® (LSC) Standards published by the National Fire Protection Association and intended to supplement building and fire prevention codes. The LSC is not law, but providers and suppliers participating in Medicare and Medicaid programs are required to comply with the LSC. Compliance with the LSC is also required accreditation by accrediting organizations, such as The Joint Commission. 3

Line of Service A set of hospital services associated with a particular specialty, such as pediatrics, obstetrics, and orthopedics. 6

Living Will A document that states an individual's wishes about life-sustaining medical treatment when the individual is terminally ill, permanently unconscious, or in the end-stage of a fatal illness. 7

Managed Care Formerly, care and incentives intended to optimize the efficiency of patient care, leading to better outcomes and lower costs. In practice, any payment system evolving around negotiated prices between payers and providers. 10

Market Power Ability of a company to change the market price of a good or service without losing its customers to the competition.

In a perfectly competitive market, the companies in a specific market would not have market power, as defined above.   14

McCarran-Ferguson Act of 1945   The Act gives the states the power to regulate the "business of insurance," without interference from federal regulation, unless federal law specifically states otherwise. The Act does not define the phrase "business of insurance." Court cases have established these three key factors to help make that determination: 1. Does the practice have the effect of transferring or spreading the policy-holder's risk? 2. Is the practice an integral part of the policy relationship between the insurer and the insured? 3. Is the practice limited to entities within the insurance industry?   14

Medicaid   A jointly funded, federal-state health insurance program for low-income and needy people.   8

Medical Futility   Interventions unlikely to produce significant benefit for the patient.   15

Medical Records   Created when a person receives treatment from a health professional and includes personal, financial, and medical data.   8

Medicare   The U.S. government's national health insurance program for people 65 years or older and under age 65 with certain disabilities.   8

Medicare Conditions of Participation   Requirements developed by the Center for Medicare and Medicaid Services (CMS) "that health care organizations must meet in order to begin and continue participating in the Medicare and Medicaid programs. These health and safety standards are the foundation for improving quality and protecting the health and safety of beneficiaries" (CMS.gov).   5

Monopoly Power   Under the Sherman Antitrust Act, monopoly power is the ability of a business to control a price within its relevant product market or its geographic market or to exclude a competitor from doing business in those markets.   14

National Labor Relations Board (NLRB)   Independent agency of the United States government, the NLRB investigates and remedies unfair labor practices.   4

National Practitioner Data Bank   "A computerized data bank maintained by the federal government that contains information on physicians who have paid malpractice claims or against whom certain disciplinary actions have been taken" (State Program Integrity Assessment (SPIA) Federal Fiscal Year 2008 GLOSSARY OF TERMS).   5

Negligence   Civil wrong causing injury or harm to another person or to property as the result of doing something or failing to provide a proper or reasonable level of care. These four elements are required to prove negligence: (1) A duty, that is, what should have been done; (2) breach of duty, which is a deviation from what should have been done; (3) Injury; and (4) Legal causation, which means that the injury is caused by a breach of a duty owed to the injured party.   11

Negligent Credentialing   A "progeny of hospital or institutional negligence," (*Frigo v. Silver Cross*, 377 Ill.App.3d 43, 876 N.E.2d 697, 315 Ill.Dec. 385 (Ill. App. 1ˢᵗ, 2007). Based on the notion that "a hospital has a duty to exercise due care in the selection of its

medical staff" (*Johnson v. Misericordia Community Hospital*, 99 Wis.2d 708, 301 N.W.2d 156 (1981)). The legal analysis examines whether or not a healthcare entity met the standard of care in the processes it utilized in selecting an individual who was alleged to have injured a patient in the institution. "If the physician is not negligent, there is no negligent credentialing claim against the hospital." *Hiroms v. Scheffey, M.D.*, 76 S.W.3d 486, 489 (Tex.App.2002).   5

Net Revenue   That portion of what is billed that can be expected to be converted to cash. Amount billed, less discounts contracted or legislated.   10

NGO   The abbreviation for nongovernmental organization. NGOs operate independently from federal and state governments. NGOs may receive governmental financial support but maintain their independence by excluding government from NGO membership and management. The Joint Commission is an example of an NGO.   8

Noerr-Pennington doctrine   Under this doctrine, private entities are immune from antitrust liability for attempts to influence the passage or enforcement of laws, even if those efforts are in support of laws that may have anticompetitive effects.   14

Non-Delegable Duty   A duty that can potentially be shared but cannot be delegated and ultimately remains with the body charged with the duty. Many courts say hospitals have a non-delegable duty to maintain appropriate credentialing procedures and to see that they are properly implemented to assure quality care in the institution.   5

Non-Maleficence   Means to "do no harm." For example, physicians must refrain from providing ineffective treatments. The key ethical issue is whether the benefits outweigh the burdens.   15

Occupational Safety and Health Act (OSHA)   A federal law to establish and enforce standards for occupational health and safety. Standards developed for various industries are mandatory for all covered employers.   4

Off-Label Use   When drugs are given or prescribed for other conditions or in different dosages not specified on the drug label.   3

Office of the Inspector General (OIG)   Administrative agency of the United States Department of Health and Human Services that actively conducts criminal, civil, and administrative investigations of fraud and misconduct related to Medicare, Medicaid, and other federal healthcare programs.   12

Office of the National Coordinator for Health Information Technology   Organizationally located within HHS and is the principal Federal entity charged with coordinating nationwide efforts to implement and use advanced health information technology and electronic exchange of health information.   8

Order Entry System   Any method of communicating to the billing system that a service is being performed or that a supply is being used. Examples would be Laboratory or Radiology systems which interface to billing systems, but can also include manual or paper-driven entry.   10

Patent   A governmental grant that confers upon the creator of an invention the exclusive right to make, use, or sell the invention for a limited period of time.   18

Patient Protection and Affordable Care Act (PPACA)   Principal federal law of current healthcare reform. This statute is expansive and includes the following provisions: expands the list of permissive criteria that may be considered by the OIG in excluding providers; establishes a requirement that there be a direct connection between violation of the AKS and a subsequent submission of a false claim; diminishes the intent requirement of the AKS; and restricts physician ownership in hospitals to which they refer.   12

Per se Violation   A type of violation of the Sherman Antitrust Act, Section 1, which covers agreements, conspiracies, or trusts in restraint of trade. A per se violation does not require proof of the actual effect of a certain type of practice on the market or the intent of the parties engaged in the conduct. Examples include price fixing among direct competitors (i.e., horizontal price fixing) and division of markets among direct competitors (i.e., horizontal market division).   14

Periodic Performance Review (PPR)   A compliance assessment tool designed to help organizations with their continuous monitoring of performance and performance improvement activities. (*Facts about the Periodic Performance Review*, The Joint Commission, September, 2010.)   5

Physicians Orders for Life-Sustaining Treatment (POLST, also referred to as a Medical Order for Scope of Treatment or MOST)   Covers several decisions common for seriously chronically ill patients, including: CPR; level of medical intervention desired in the event of emergency; use of medications and the use of artificial nutrition and hydration. A POLST/MOST does not, however, take the place of a living will or a healthcare power of attorney.   7

Police Power   This is the basic authority of governments to make laws and regulations for the benefit of their communities. The police power is granted to the states through the 10th Amendment to the U.S. Constitution.   2

Price Discrimination   The sale of the same product to similarly situated buyers at different prices.   14

Price Fixing   An agreement between parties, on the same side in a market, to sell or buy a product, service, or commodity at a fixed price; or to maintain prices at a specified level by controlling supply and demand.   14

Prospective Reimbursement   Payment for services that is based on an amount that can be determined by diagnosis, as opposed to "fee for service." An example would be DRGs, which are diagnostic groups based on the patient medical problem, not the services and length of time to correct.   10

Protected Health Information   Any information held by a covered entity or its business associates that concerns health status, the provision of health care, or payment for health care and can be linked to an individual.   8

Provider   A hospital, physician, nursing home, home health service, or other party delivering care to a patient.   10

An individual or institution that provides healthcare services.   6

Recovery Model   Type of treatment process through which consumers take an active role in their own care and support. The Recovery Model focuses on the process of recovery and not on the illness itself.   17

Regulation   An action in administrative law designed to carry out and enforce law and policy.   6

Release   A written document, signed by a claimant, that bars a future lawsuit based on the same incident.   11

Res Ipsa Loquitor   A Latin term meaning "the thing speaks for itself." A rule of evidence that allows that mere proof that an injury occurred establishes a presumption of negligence on the part of the defendant.   11

Res Judicata   In Latin it means "the thing has been judged." In the law, the term refers to a thing or matter decided by the judgment of a court that involves the same parties.   1

Respondeat Superior   A phrase that means "let the master answer." In law, employers are liable for the consequences of their employees' activities within the course of employment for which the employees are responsible.   11

Revenue Cycle   The activity that leads to payment for services. It begins with the first encounter with the patient, and includes collection of data, entry of charges, billing, and collection.   10

Rule of Reason Analysis   Under the Sherman Antitrust Act, Section 1, this test considers the totality of the circumstances. The key question is whether the challenged conduct promotes or discourages market competition. The intent and motive of the parties alleged to be involved in the questionable conduct are relevant considerations.   14

Service Mark   A distinctive logo, symbol, word(s), picture, or design that is used in connection with the sale of services to identify the source of the services and to distinguish the services from those sold by others.   18

Sherman Antitrust Act of 1890   The first federal statute to limit cartels and monopolies. The Act is one of the most important laws used by the federal government to bring antitrust cases. "Antitrust" law is sometimes referred to as "competition" law because the main purpose of the Act is to promote and protect the concept of competitive markets. When the Act was passed, "trusts" were commonly legal entities to hold business interests.   14

Site-of-Service (or, Place of Service)   The location that a service is provided, such as hospital inpatient, hospital outpatient, emergency department, physician office, home, and many others. This is one of the determinants of payment amount and is indicated by a two-digit number on the *Claim* form. In some cases, the site-of-service is defined by the facility, such as a physician's office that is part of a hospital or a hospital-owned property.   10

Standing   The right of a party to file a lawsuit under the circumstances in a particular court or other body with authority to make decisions that bind the party.   1

Statute   A written law passed by a legislative body.   6

Statute of Limitations   A state law that limits the time in which a lawsuit may be filed.   11

Statute of Limitations   A statute prescribing a period of limitation for the bringing of certain kinds of legal action.   6

Sterilization   A surgical procedure that prevents future procreation and can be performed on either women (tubal ligation) or men (vasectomy).   13

Strict Liability   A legal liability theory that applies to injuries caused by the use of a product that is unreasonably dangerous to a consumer or user and reaches the user without substantial change from the condition in which it was sold. The manufacturer or seller of the product usually is liable.   11

Subchapter S   A choice, under the Internal Revenue Code, that allows a small corporation to be treated like a partnership for taxation purposes.   2

Surrogacy   A method of assisted reproduction that involves a third party female who carries the intended parents' fetus to term; a surrogate may donate only her uterus or her eggs and her uterus to the couple desiring to conceive. After birth, a surrogate mother assigns her parental rights to the biological father and his wife (who may be the biological mother).   13

The Comprehensive Drug Abuse Prevention and Control Act of 1970 (or Controlled Substances Act)   A federal law that regulates the prescribing and dispensing of certain restricted drugs. These restricted drugs are "scheduled" into five categories, with Schedule I drugs considered the most dangerous and to possess the most danger for abuse (no prescriptions may be written) and Schedule V drugs considered to possess the lowest potential for abuse and dependence in the schedules.   3

The Poison Prevention Packaging Act   A federal law that requires most drugs to be dispensed in containers designed to be difficult for children to open.   3

The Rule of Non-Review   A judicial (common-law) doctrine stating that, as a matter of public policy, internal staffing decisions of private hospitals are not subject to judicial review. The doctrine is grounded on the idea that courts are not well equipped to review the action of hospital authorities in rendering medical staffing decisions because those decisions involve specialized medical and business considerations. An exception to this rule has developed where a physician's existing staff privileges are revoked, suspended, or reduced. In such circumstances, some courts court will engage in limited review to determine whether the hospital complied with its bylaws in rendering the decision.   5

Third-Party Administrator   An organization hired by a self-funded employer-sponsored group health plan to administer the health plan. The third-party administrator processes and pays claims on behalf of the health plan. Third-party administrators are often health insurance companies that have the infrastructure to serve in this role.   9

Trade Secret   Any valuable and secret commercial information that provides the owner of the information with a commercial advantage over those who do not have the information.   18

Trademark   A distinctive logo, symbol, word(s), picture, or design that is used in connection with the sale of goods to identify the source of the goods and to distinguish the goods from those sold or made by others.   18

Treatment   The management and care of a patient or the combating of a disease or disorder.   6

Treatment IND   FDA-approved treatment with an investigational new drug outside of clinical trials, used when the drug is for a serious or immediately life-threatening disease and there is no satisfactory alternative therapy available.   3

Tying and Exclusive Dealing Contracts   The sale of products on the condition that the buyer not deal, or stop dealing, with the seller's competitors.   14

UB-04   A *Claim* form for services provided by a hospital or a *Provider* acting as a hospital.   10

Ultra Vires Doctrine   In the law of corporations, if a corporation enters into a contract that is beyond the scope of its corporate powers, the contract is illegal.   2

U.S. Department of Justice (DOJ)   The primary federal criminal investigation and enforcement agency. When the Office of the Inspector General determines that criminal prosecutions regarding healthcare providers should be considered, the case is referred to the DOJ. The DOJ can also initiate prosecutions on its own and teams with the OIG and FBI agents to investigate providers.   12

Vertical Integration or Relationship   The merging of companies that are within a chain of companies handling a single item (e.g., from the raw material, through production, and to sale).   14

Zoning Ordinances   Laws adopted by local governments that specify permitted uses of certain types of land for specific purposes.   3

Index

A

ABN	Advance beneficiary notice
ADA	Americans with Disabilities Act
ADEA	Age Discrimination in Employment Act
AID	Artificial insemination with donor semen
AIDS	Acquired Immune Deficiency Syndrome
ALJ	Administrative law judge
AMA	American Medical Association
AOA	American Osteopathic Association
APC	Ambulatory payment classification
ART	Assisted reproductive technology

B

BFOQ	Bona fide occupational qualification

C

CDC	Centers for Disease Control
CEO	Chief Executive Officer
CHAMPUS	Civilian Health and Medical Program for the Uniformed Services
CHIP	Children Health Insurance Programs
CLIA	Clinical Laboratory Improvement Act
CMS	Centers for Medicare & Medicaid Services
CO	Certificate of occupancy
COBRA	Consolidated Omnibus Budget Reconciliation Act
CON	Certificate of need
COPs	Conditions of Participation (in Medicare)
CPT	Physician's Current Procedural Terminology
CRNAs	Certified Registered Nurse Anesthetists
CT	Computerized tomography

D

D&O	Directors and Officers liability insurance
DEA	Drug Enforcement Administration
DNR	Do not resuscitate
DOJ	Department of Justice
DRGs	Diagnosis-related groups

E

EEG	Electroencephalogram
EEOC	Equal Employment Opportunity Commission
EKG	Electrocardiogram
EMTALA	Emergency Medical Treatment and Active Labor Act
ERISA	Employee Retirement Income Security Act
ESOP	Employee Stock Ownership Plan

F

FAA	Federal Arbitration Act
FDA	Food and Drug Administration
FDAMA	Food and Drug Administration Modernization Act
FDCPA	Fair Debt Collection Practices Act
FEHBA	Federal Employee Health Benefit Act
FEHBP	Federal Employee Health Benefits Program
FERPA	Family Educational Privacy and Rights Act
FHA	Federal Housing Administration
FLSA	Fair Labor Standards Act
FMCS	Federal Mediation and Conciliation Service
FMLA	Family and Medical Leave Act
FOIA	Freedom of Information Act
FTC	Federal Trade Commission

G

GAAP	Generally accepted accounting principles

H

HCFA	Health Care Financing Administration (predecessor to CMS)
HCPCS	CMS Common Procedure Coding System (formerly the HCFA Common Procedure Coding System)
HCQIA	Health Care Quality Improvement Act of 1986
HEW	U.S. Department of Health, Education and Welfare (predecessor to HHS)
HHI	Herfindahl-Hirschman Index
HHS	U.S. Department of Health and Human Services
HIPAA	Health Insurance Portability and Accountability Act of 1996
HIV	Human immunodeficiency virus
HMO	Health maintenance organization
HCQIA	Health Care Quality Improvement Act of 1986

I

ICD-9-CM	International Classification of Diseases, Ninth Edition, Clinical Modification
IDE	Investigational device exemption
IND	Investigational new drug
IPA	Independent practice association
IRB	Institutional review board
IRS	Internal Revenue Service
IV	Intravenous
IVF	In vitro fertilization

J
JCAH   Joint Commission on Accreditation of Hospitals
JCAHO   Joint Commission on Accreditation of Healthcare Organizations

L
LLC   Limited liability company
LLP   Limited liability partnership
LUPA   Low utilization payment adjustment

M
MAAC   Maximum allowable actual charge
MCOs   Managed care organizations
MRI   Magnetic resonance imaging

N
NAFTA   North American Free Trade Agreement
NCQA   National Committee for Quality Assurance
NGOs   Nongovernmental organizations
NLRA   National Labor Relations Act
NLRB   National Labor Relations Board
NPDB   National Practitioner Data Bank

O
OCR   Office of Civil Rights
OIG   Office of Inspector General of HHS
OPTN   Organ Procurement and Transplantation Network
OSHA   Occupational Safety and Health Act of 1970
OTC   Over-the-counter

P
PBM   Pharmacy benefit manager
PCP   Primary care physician
PDR   Physician's Desk Reference

PEP   Partial episode payment
PHI   Protected health information
PHO   Physician-hospital organization
PICU   Pediatric intensive care unit
PLR   I.R.S. Private letter ruling
POS   Point-of-service
PPO   Preferred provider organization
PRO   Peer review organization
PPS   Prospective payment system
PRRB   Provider reimbursement review board

Q
QMB   Qualified medical beneficiaries

R
RBRVS   Resource-based relative value scale
RICO   Racketeer Influenced and Corrupt Organizations Act
RUG   Resource utilization group

S
SARS   Severe acute respiratory syndrome
SCIC   Significant change in condition
SNOMED-CT®   Systematized Nomenclature of Medicine Clinical Terms®
SOA   Sarbanes-Oxley Act
SEC   Securities Exchange Commission

U
UAGA   Uniform Anatomical Gift Act
UCC   Uniform Commercial Code
UPIN   Unique physician identification number

V
VA   Veterans Affairs (formerly Veterans Administration)

Introduction to Index of Cases

The numbers and letters after each case name tell where to find the court's decision. For example, look at Ravenis v. Detroit Gen. Hosp., 63 Mich. App. 79, 234 N.W.2d 411 (1975), which is cited on page 784 in footnote 73 of Chapter 15. The numbers 63 and 235 are volume numbers. They are followed by the abbreviations for the reporter systems: "Mich. App." refers to the reports of the Michigan Court of Appeals, which is the intermediate appellate court for the state of Michigan, while "N.W.2d" refers to the Northwest Reporter, Second Series. The final numbers 79 and 411 are the page numbers in the volumes. The number in parenthesis is the year of the decision. When the abbreviation of the reporter system does not disclose the court that rendered the decision, an abbreviation of the court's name will also appear in the parenthesis. An example where the reporter abbreviation does not disclose the name of the court is Corbett v. D'Alessandro, 487 So.2d 368, 371 n.1 (Fla. 2d DCA 1986), which is cited on page 378 in footnote 244 of Chapter 7. Since Southern Reporter, Second Series, abbreviated "So.2d," includes decisions from several states and Florida no longer has a separate reporting system for its courts decisions, if it's necessary to include the abbreviation "Fla. 2d DCA" in parenthesis to indicate that it is a decision of the Second District Court of Appeal of Florida. "371 n.1" is inserted to indicate that the referenced quotation appears in note 1 on page 371 of the opinion.

When there is another set of numbers and letters after the parenthesis, they refer to another court's decision concerning the same case. If the second court is a higher court, it will be preceded by letters such as aff'd, rev'd or cert. denied, which indicate the court affirmed, reversed, or declined to review the lower court decision. (See Chapter 1 for a discussion of cert. denied.) Sometimes the order of references is reversed, so that the higher court decision is listed first. In these situations the abbreviations will be aff'g or rev'g, indicating whether the higher court is affirming or reversing the lower court.

Some cases are not reported in any reporter system. Some of these cases are available in commercial computer databases. An example is United States v. Thorn, 2004 U.S. App. LEXIS 14295 (8th Cir.), which is cited on page 144 in footnote 118 to chapter 4. This is form the LEXIS database. The first number is the year; the abbreviation after the year indicates that it is a decision by a United States Court of Appeals; and next number is the database's sequential page number for cases from that court in that year. Since these symbols do not disclose the specific court, the parenthetical material is added to indicate that it is a decision of the Eighth Circuit Court of Appeals.

When references to commercial databases were not available, the court file number, the name of the court, and date of the ruling are given. For an example, see footnote 347 of chapter 7 on page 396.

Subject Index

Figures and tables are indicated by an italic *f* or *t* respectively.